Handbook of Research on E-Learning Standards and Interoperability:
Frameworks and Issues

Fotis Lazarinis
Teesside University, UK

Steve Green
Teesside University, UK

Elaine Pearson
Teesside University, UK

Information Science REFERENCE

INFORMATION SCIENCE REFERENCE
Hershey · New York

Director of Editorial Content: Kristin Klinger
Director of Book Publications: Julia Mosemann
Acquisitions Editor: Lindsay Johnston
Development Editor: Joel Gamon
Publishing Assistant: Milan Vracarich, Jr.
Typesetter: Keith Glazewski, Deanna Jo Zombro
Production Editor: Jamie Snavely
Cover Design: Lisa Tosheff

Published in the United States of America by
Information Science Reference (an imprint of IGI Global)
701 E. Chocolate Avenue
Hershey PA 17033
Tel: 717-533-8845
Fax: 717-533-8661
E-mail: cust@igi-global.com
Web site: http://www.igi-global.com

Library of Congress Cataloging-in-Publication Data

Handbook of research on e-learning standards and interoperability : frameworks and issues / Fotis Lazarinis, Steve Green, and Elaine Pearson, editors.
p. cm.
Includes bibliographical references and index.
Summary: "This handbook promotes the discussion and solutions for increasing the interoperability of future standalone and Web-based educational tools, specifically focusing on content reusability and interoperability"--Provided by publisher.
ISBN 978-1-61692-789-9 (hardcover) -- ISBN 978-1-61692-790-5 (ebook)
1. Computer-assisted instruction--Standards--Handbooks, manuals, etc. 2. Educational technology--Standards--Handbooks, manuals, etc. 3. Internetworking (Telecommunication)--Handbooks, manuals, etc.
I. Lazarinis, Fotis. II. Green, Steve, 1957- III. Pearson, Elaine, 1957-
LB1028.5.H3165 2011
371.33'4072--dc22

2010010156

British Cataloguing in Publication Data
A Cataloguing in Publication record for this book is available from the British Library.

Editorial Advisory Board

List of Reviewers

List of Contributors

Table of Contents

Section 3
Metadata, Learning Objects, Ontologies and Semantic Web

Section 4
Approaches and Issues in Interoperable Applications

Detailed Table of Contents

Section 1
Interoperable E-Assessment Applications

This section presents five chapters related to interoperable e-assessments. The research studies included in this section discuss the role of e-learning standards such as IMS QTI in encoding testing data. They further present emerging forms of e-assessment and discuss how these can be accommodated by using one specification or a combination of e-learning standards.

The aim of this chapter is to illustrate some affordances of machine-processable competency statements. Such competency statements are supported by ontologies and taxonomies of competency. Machine processing can offer interoperable and reusable resources and applications that are pedagogically effective for e-learning and assessment. A competency statement which can be read, processed, and interpreted by machine contributes to the automatic generation of questions and offers a semantic structure using the Web Ontology Language (OWL) to express competencies for further processing. The generated questions are expressed in the IMS Question and Test Interoperability specification (IMS QTI) to enable interoperability.

This chapter discusses some of the issues involved in developing online testing of learning outcomes. The research is focused on the changes and implementation scenarios of the latest versions of IMS QTI – the major technical specification for testing. Standardization of content and applications used for online testing is partly driven by the paradigm shifts that are taking place in the fields of pedagogy and Web technology. This chapter pays a special attention to the increasing trend of using Web 2.0 technology in education, especially Mash-up Personal Learning Environments and their impact on the architectural decisions while developing the next generation online assessment tools.

This chapter focuses on the reusability and sustainability of electronic tests and presents the IMS QTI specification. The main aim of the chapter is to investigate whether this specification improves the interoperability among testing systems and the shareability of the data. The author claims that the specification has not significantly advanced the main aims of the specific standard.

The chapter first describes how the needs for interoperability in exchanging competency information have been addressed so far and then discusses the issues related to the exchange of competency information across systems. The third part is the core part of this chapter as it describes the 4 levels of the proposed approach: the Conceptual Reference Model (CRM), the Semantic Model, the Information Model and the Data Model. The final section presents the research directions currently envisaged, and the research programme needed to make the proposed approach operational.

Section 2
Personalization, Interoperability and E-Learning Standards

The second section focuses on the personalization and adaptation of learning materials to the needs and special abilities or disabilities of learners. The role of standardised structures in encoding adaptive learning content is discussed and specific proposals are made. The efficiency of the current e-learning specifications for building adaptive tools is researched and methodologies for assessing the quality of standards-based e-learning tools are discussed.

This chapter concentrates on the problem of adaptive sequencing which is about finding the optimum sequence of learning resources with respect to the special characteristics, goals, needs, and background of learners. An appropriate sequencing, adapted to the student, has a positive impact on motivation and learning. However, this is a problem that has not been yet carefully considered in any standard or specification, hindering interoperability among platforms that adapt the sequencing of learning content to their users. This chapter reviews the two specifications most relevant for the standard expression of adapted sequencings: IMS Simple Sequencing and IMS Learning Design. The strong and weak points of each specification are highlighted, showing their implications on adaptive sequencing interoperability.

This chapter introduces a standards-based and adaptive framework whose main objective is to adapt user interfaces, content and learning environment to learners' needs, including their functional diversity issues (i.e. disabilities). The framework is intended to be general (e.g. two different learning management systems and two large pilot sites are being considered) and to that end it is implemented in terms of an open architecture, which aims at providing services for Accessible Lifelong Learning. The chapter focuses on accessibility and adaptation issues, and their interoperability requirements.

tors. For that reason, SCORM is used in learning objects to manage a course in Moodle for the students of English at the University of Alicante. The purpose of the chapter is to give an account of the problems and solutions encountered by using SCORM in Moodle and to explain the guiding aims of a framework for language teaching.

Section 3
Metadata, Learning Objects, Ontologies and Semantic Web

This section contains studies related to the role of metadata schemata and XML structures in enriching educational resources. Learning objects and ontologies of educational material are used in the adjustment of semantic data to achieve specific technical and pedagogical goals. Mappings between different technologies which could eventually lead to the re-use of learning resources are also presented.

This chapter presents the basic characteristics of some educational metadata schemata and application profiles with a focus on IEEE LOM standard. The study shows how the IEEE LOM metadata set can be incorporated in the default DSpace's qualified Dublin Core metadata schema, introducing enhancements to the existing University of Patras live installation. For this reason, the authors document a potential LOM to Dublin Core metadata mapping and reveal potential advantages of such an approach. Further, they propose an ontological model for the repository's metadata, taking into account the educational characteristics of resources.

Educators working with eXtended Markup Language (XML) have a variety of XML based technologies to choose. Another option is to use XML to generate web resources from a relational database, such as MySQL, or with a knowledge database, such as Prolog. This chapter looks at how these technologies can interchange information with the help of new intelligent resources such as the OpenMind project that are beginning to model the world around us. Advances in these areas pave the way for more automatic acquisition of knowledge from existing texts using tools such as MontyLingua to provide a basic semantic understanding of the material and promote interoperability. Examples of the technologies are used to illustrate the benefits of structuring new learning materials, and options for integrating heritage materials are examined.

Section 5
Quality and Pedagogy in Learning Technology

The last section presents research studies related to quality and pedagogy of e-learning applications. These studies relate to the diverse abilities that e-learning tools should have, i.e. affordability, usability and shareability. Therefore it focuses on more general topics which they can increase the acceptance of learning applications by educators. The presented criteria and issues could be utilized by developers of interoperable applications in order to increase the utility of their tools.

This chapter aims at both groups of teachers or instructional developers, by offering a review of the e-learning possibilities and criteria, based on several analyses carried out by the authors on higher educational settings. Based on the learner cantered perspective, this chapter proposes some criteria for assuring the quality in higher education e-learning contexts, mainly based on three categories: psycho-pedagogical utility, usability and accessibility. One of the principal goals is to support -by means of the criteria- the selection of technologies and functionalities (collaborative tools, e-learning 2.0 solutions...), considering, above all, the learning objectives and the specific learning contexts.

The chapter presents the importance of providing high quality e-learning and the need to apply the requirements of the standards from ISO 9000 series for continual improvement of the quality management systems in education. The work applies the main principles for multiple criteria decision making. An approach for satisfaction measurement is developed. It uses weighting coefficients as qualitative valuation of the importance of the quality characteristics and numerical valuation for the level of satisfaction with the quality characteristics. The suggested approach is suitable to apply for different purposes in education in order to achieve high quality e-learning. It is also suitable to apply to different areas within quality management systems.

This chapter will introduce the e-Learning Guidelines for New Zealand and show how organisations have used them. It will present some of the benefits of the guidelines as well as the limitations and dis-

Foreword

Over the last few decades the use of computer technology within education for the support of learning, teaching and training (and their management) has become a major growth area within virtually all areas of human endeavour. Computers are now used extensively in schools, colleges and universities; they are also used in people's homes and work environments in order to support a wide range of learning, skill development and knowledge acquisition processes. As well as their use in formal compulsory and post-compulsory education, various forms of computer technology are also used as agents to facilitate the lifelong learning activities that are now necessitated by ongoing change within a world-wide arena. Nowadays, change is so rapid, I believe that it would be extremely difficult for people and organisations to survive without effective and efficient computer systems to help them learn and develop the skills and knowledge that is needed to face and solve the new problems with which they are continually being confronted.

Bearing in mind what I have said above, it is important to remember that there is now a plethora of hardware, software and supporting technologies available for use in the various learning environments that we create. Of course, it is vital that all of the different hardware, software and interface components work together in a seamless and transparent way. Within this book, the term '*interoperability*' is used to describe this important requirement. Of course, '*transferability*' is also an important goal to achieve. Ideally, a piece of software written to run on one computer should be executable on any other computer that meets that software's resource requirements. A similar argument applies to the various hardware components that are used to build computer systems - for example, a USB memory stick should be usable on any computer that provides an appropriate host port and a suitable software driver.

Naturally, within an educational system there are other important issues to consider in addition to the basic hardware and software standards. Because education is a people-orientated activity, it is also necessary to consider the many human, pedagogic and curricula factors that are likely to influence the interoperability of a computer-based learning environment. For example, the psychological factors that govern the different ways in which people learn and solve problems are also vitally important areas which warrant attention in relation to interoperability. Furthermore, the ability to tailor an educational system to the needs of particular users is also an imperative pre-requisite in order to accommodate differences in each individual's capability and capacity to learn. In my view, the days of 'one size fits all' have long gone.

In order to achieve the goals of interoperability and transferability, a range of different *standards* and *specifications* are needed. A standard is essentially an 'agreed way of doing something' - to which everyone agrees and subscribes. For example, in a keyboard interface, the backspace key is used to delete the character that lies immediately to the left of the current cursor position. This is an example of a very simple standard to which all 'standard keyboards' conform. It is through the use of standards that we can achieve ease of use and the transferability of skills (from one situation to another similar situation) when people use technology (in general) and computer systems (in particular). Of course, as has been suggested above, standards are important because they under-pin the approaches that are used to realise the interoperability of learning system components and the transferability of human skills. Of course, standards themselves need to be defined in terms of clear and precise specifications. Special linguistic tools, such as metanotation (and metadata), are therefore often needed in order to state, in a unique and un-ambiguous way, the nature of the standards that are to be used in order to achieve the goals of interoperability and transferability.

I believe the contributions to this book address many of the important issues that we need to consider in order to achieve, in a successful way, the goals that I have outlined above - within the context of electronic learning (e-learning) systems for use in different educational contexts. Indeed, the twenty-five chapters that make up this volume describe, discuss and debate a broad range of important interoperability issues relating to the creation and sharing of e-learning resources and the assessment of the learning outcomes that are derived from their use. In my opinion, this book offers much useful advice and it documents valuable experience which will be of benefit to all those who are involved in the design, production and use of e-learning applications - be these to support an individual learner or a learning community. Indeed, I am sure that the content of many of the chapters in this book will form sound 'stepping stones' that will 'lead the way' forward for future developments in this vital area of human endeavour.

Philip Barker
Emeritus Professor
School of Computing
Teesside University, UK

***Philip Barker** is a distinguished emeritus professor within the school of computing at Teesside University in the United Kingdom. He is a founder member of and a principal researcher in the interactive systems research group - a multidisciplinary team of computer scientists and psychologists involved in studying various aspects of human-computer interaction and the effects of electronic technology on people's mental and physical behaviour. Professor Barker is a national teaching fellow of the UK's higher education academy and acts as co-editor of the journal 'innovations in education and teaching international'. He has published numerous books and research papers. His latest book entitled 'Electronic Performance Support: Using Digital Technology to Enhance Human Ability' was published in February 2010 by Gower. He is currently working with Springer on a major reference work entitled the 'Encyclopaedia of the Sciences of Learning' for which he is the associate editor for the section that deals with cognitive psychology and cognitive science. Further details are available at http://refworks.springer.com/.*

Preface

Educational technology is a key interdisciplinary area. The main aim of educational technology is the support of teachers and students with computer tools in order to complete their tasks faster, more accurately and more efficiently. Various tools and techniques for supporting teaching and learning have been proposed and implemented over the years and especially with the advancement of Web technologies. The development of applications and tools for e-learning is complicated due to the heterogeneity of the user aims and the development approaches and the dynamic behaviour of users which the tools needs to accommodate. As the e-learning industry continues to expand every day, and the methods and tools necessary to create and maintain content and infrastructure applications become more complicated, there is an inherent need for these applications to interoperate and exchange data in order to better support the needs of learners and educators.

The Advanced Distributed Learning initiative (ADL – www.adlnet.gov) defines a set of abilities for e-learning tools and technologies. These abilities are reusability, accessibility, interoperability, adaptability, durability, and affordability. The IEEE (Institute of Electrical and Electronics Engineers - http://www.ieee.org) defines interoperability as the ability of two or more systems or components to exchange information and to use the information that has been exchanged. In e-learning the ability of tools to interoperate is of crucial importance as it will allow systems of diverse educational aims to work together, re-using the learning data and the accumulated knowledge about learners. This will eventually reduce the maintenance costs and the efforts of the educational content providers and will allow the development of more complete and adaptable interactive learning environments.

To increase the ability of educational hypermedia applications to re-use the learning data, several organizations are working to develop learning standards. CETIS (Centre for Educational Technology Interoperability Standards - http://www.cetis.ac.uk) states that standard ways of describing educational materials are needed so that they can be easily searched for and located (http://www.cetis.ac.uk/static/standards.html). Learning standards refer to the standardization of XML structures which are used to describe various aspects of the learning procedure.

The following organizations and committees have been involved in developing the best known standards:

- ADL - Advanced Distributed Learning Project (http://www.adlnet.gov)
- AICC - Aviation Industry Computer-Based Training Committee (http://www.aicc.org)
- ARIADNE - Alliance of Remote Instructional Authoring and Distribution Networks for Europe (http://www.ariadne-eu.org)
- CEN - European Committee for Standardisation (http://www.cen.eu)

- DCMI - Dublin Core Metadata Initiative (http://dublincore.org)
- IEEE LTSC - Learning Technologies Standards Committee (http://ieeeltsc.org)
- IMS Global Learning Consortium (http://www.imsglobal.org)

These organizations and consortiums have developed, among others, XML standards for e-lessons, user profiles, e-portfolios, testing data and metadata. Standards are generally developed to promote interoperability between otherwise competing implementations.

One of the most well known learning standards for coding learning data is Sharable Content Object Reference Model (SCORM - http://www.adlnet.gov/Technologies/scorm/). SCORM is an XML-based framework used to define and access information about learning objects so they can be easily shared among different learning management systems (LMSs). SCORM was developed in response to a United States Department of Defense (DoD) initiative to promote standardization in e-learning.

The IMS Question and Test Interoperability (IMS QTI - http://www.imsglobal.org/question/) specification describes an XML based technical format for the coding and exchange of assessment content from individual questions through to complete tests. IMS QTI, or simply QTI, structures material into assessments, sections, and items and provides support for adaptive items.

The IEEE's Public and Private Information (IEEE PAPI – http://jtc1sc36.org/doc/36N0186.pdf) for Learners XML standard is a data interchange specification that describes learner information for communication among cooperating systems. The IMS Learner Information Package (IMS LIP - http://www.imsglobal.org/profiles) is based on a data model that describes those characteristics of a learner needed for the general purposes of recording and managing learning-related history, goals, and accomplishments of learners.

IMS Learning Design (IMS LD - http://www.imsglobal.org/learningdesign/) is a specification which enables the modelling of learning processes. The specification can be likened to a stage-play where people act in different roles. These roles work towards specific objectives by performing learning and/or support activities. The activities are conducted within an environment consisting of learning objects and services. This specification is used to model entire educational activities where several people and educational activities are involved.

The Dublin Core (http://dublincore.org/) metadata is a standard for cross-domain information resource description. Dublin Core was standardised by ISO in 2003. The semantics of Dublin Core have been established by an international, cross-disciplinary group of professionals from librarianship, computer science, text encoding, the museum community, and other related fields of scholarship and practice.

IEEE Learning Object Metadata (IEEE LOM - http://www.ieeeltsc.org/standards/1484-12-1-2002) is a data model encoded in XML, used to describe a learning object and similar digital resources used to support learning. The purpose of learning object metadata is to support the reusability of learning objects, to aid discoverability, and to facilitate their interoperability, usually in the context of online learning management systems.

IMS Simple Sequencing (IMS SS - http://www.imsglobal.org/simplesequencing) defines a method for sequencing discrete learning activities in a consistent way. Initially some researchers considered IMS SS as a simple adaptive learning system itself, but currently most of its features have been integrated into other standards such as IMS LD and IMS QTI.

More standards for metadata and for packaging or sharing learning and testing data exist. The development and diffusion of e-learning standards raised new research questions related to how they can be efficiently utilized in order to increase the reusability and syntactic interoperability of learning content. Pedagogy and content quality related issues in interoperable tools are also important.

The present volume aims at promoting the discussion and presenting specific solutions for increasing the interoperability of future standalone and Web based educational hypermedia tools. Further, the role of learning standards and the issues arising from their deployment are investigated. The ultimate goal of the publication is to be a scholarly edition, suitable for practitioners and researchers in the area of educational technology with a focus on content reusability and interoperability.

With respect to our open call for the present handbook, 72 proposals were submitted and after a double blind review process by at least 2 reviewers, 25 articles were selected for inclusion in this volume, based on their relevance, clarity of presentation of the research issues, and diversity of topics. The selected chapters negotiate technical issues related to the efficient deployment of e-learning standards and interoperability and present evaluation studies which critically review the importance of e-learning specifications. Some of the studies deal with metadata or issues such as pedagogy and quality in interoperable systems.

Chapter 1, by Yongwu Miao, Jo Boon, Marcel van der Klink, Peter Sloep and Rob Koper, presents a combined use of IMS QTI and IMS LD. The combined system is able to support interoperability and reusability of emerging forms of assessment, such as self assessment for example.

Next, Chapter 2, written by Onjira Sitthisak and Lester Gilbert, aims at illustrating some affordances of machine-processable competency statements. Such competency statements are supported by ontologies and taxonomies of competency. Machine processing can offer interoperable and reusable resources and applications that are pedagogically effective for e-learning and assessment. The generated questions are expressed in the IMS Question and Test Interoperability specification (IMS QTI) to enable interoperability.

Vladimir Tomberg and Mart Laanpere in Chapter 3, discuss some of the issues involved in developing online testing of learning outcomes. The research is focused on the changes and implementation scenarios of the latest versions of IMS QTI. The chapter pays special attention to the increasing trend of using Web 2.0 technology in education, especially Mash-up Personal Learning Environments and their impact on the architectural.

Chapter 4, by Michael Piotrowski, focuses on the reusability and sustainability of electronic tests and presents the IMS QTI specification. The main aim of the chapter is to investigate whether this specification improves the interoperability among testing systems and the shareability of the data.

Chapter 5 by Bernard Blandin, Geoffrey Frank, Simone Laughton, and Kenji Hirata describes how the needs for interoperability in exchanging competency information have been addressed so far and then discusses the issues related to the exchange of competency information across systems.

Sergio Gutiérrez-Santos in Chapter 6, studies the problem of adaptive sequencing which is about finding the optimum sequence of learning resources with respect to the special characteristics, goals, needs, and background of learners. This chapter reviews the two specifications most relevant for the standard expression of adapted sequencings: IMS Simple Sequencing and IMS Learning Design. The strong and weak points of each specification are highlighted, showing their implications on adaptive sequencing interoperability.

An extended study by O.C. Santos, J.G. Boticario, E. Raffenne, J. Granado, A. Rodriguez-Ascaso and E. Gutierrez y Restrepo is presented in Chapter 7. This chapter introduces a standards-based and adaptive framework whose main objective is to adapt user interfaces, content and learning environment to learners' needs, including potential disabilities. The framework is intended to be general and to that end it is implemented in terms of an open architecture, which aims at providing services for Accessible Lifelong Learning.

Stephen Marshall in Chapter 8, presents the e-learning Maturity Model which provides a standard that guides professionals and organizations in assessing their e-learning capability, but also complements with quality enhancement and feasibility elements that support reflection, prioritization of resources and guide personal and organizational development of e-learning.

The research reported in Chapter 9 by Helen Farley, explores some of the issues associated with using the IMS LD specification for learning designs in virtual worlds such as Second Life and multi-player online role playing games such as World of Warcraft. The main issues relate to the inadequate description of collaborative activities and the inability to alter the design 'on-the-fly' in response to learner inputs. Some possible solutions to these problems are considered.

The following Chapter 10, written by Steve Green, outlines the problems associated with inclusive e-learning and the role that user profiles and an adaptation service can have to support personalization. The chapter introduces the idea of an Adaptable Personal Learning Environment (APLE) and looks at how one component, the Transformation, Augmentation and Substitution Service (TASS), can be formally specified using Prolog. The compliance with standards like IMS ACCLIP and ACCMD is identified. The chapter also considers issues of IMS and SCORM content packaging, learner information profiles and the JISC definitions for a Personal Learning Environment, all within the context of inclusive e-Learning support.

Chapter 11 by Francisco Arcos and Pablo Ortega uses SCORM in learning objects to manage a course in Moodle for the students of English. The purpose of the chapter is to give an account of the problems and solutions encountered by using SCORM in Moodle and to explain the guiding aims of a framework for language teaching.

Chapter 12 by Andreas Alexopoulos, Georgia Solomou, Dimitrios Koutsomitropoulos and Theodore Papatheodorou, presents the basic characteristics of some educational metadata schemata and application profiles with a focus on IEEE LOM standard. The study shows how the IEEE LOM metadata set can be incorporated in the default DSpace's qualified Dublin Core metadata schema. The authors document a potential LOM to Dublin Core metadata mapping and reveal potential advantages of such an approach. Further, they propose an ontological model for the repository's metadata, taking into account the educational characteristics of resources.

Chapter 13 reported by Kate Taylor looks at how XML technologies can interchange information with the help of new intelligent resources such as the OpenMind project that are beginning to model the world around us. Advances in these areas pave the way for more automatic acquisition of knowledge from existing texts using specialized tools to provide a basic semantic understanding of the material and promote interoperability.

Dimitris N. Kanellopoulos in Chapter 14 presents a localisation-aware semantic e-learning approach to integrate multilingual content provision, learning process and learner personality in an integrated semantic e-learning framework. An architecture for supporting localisation of e-learning content is proposed and a basis for further development of automatic localisation services that will be able to reason on top of such an explicit infrastructure is presented.

Chapter 15, by Marta R. Ariza, Antonio Quesada, offers a brief overview of the main ideas underlying the learning object (LO) paradigm, with special emphasis placed on pedagogical aspects. Requirements for the interoperability and reusability of learning objects (LOs) are discussed, with attention drawn to the need of developing new metadata models to fully benefit from this approach.

In Chapter 16 by Barbara Vagiati the efforts to harmonize MPEG-7 and SCORM are discusssed. In particular a model for the interoperability between these standards is developed. The MPEG-7 provides a standardized set of technologies for describing multimedia content, while SCORM is a collection of specifications for developing, organizing and delivering instructional content. The proposed model concerns the semantic mapping between the different elements of these standards.

Ricardo J. Rejas-Muslera, Alvaro J. García-Tejedor, and Olga Peñalba Rodriguez in Chapter 17 present an overview of Open Educational Resources (OER) in e-learning, focusing on technical issues, mainly standards and socio-economic and legal questions. The OER's role in education, especially for e-learning performance is considered.

Chapter 18 by Natalia I. Hughson deals with the fundamental principles of interoperability of complex and dynamic global education systems. The contemporary approaches to systems theory, entropy and autopoetic theory, social system theory, sociocybernetics, the strengths and limitations of these approaches, and their potential applications in education are examined.

M. C. Mora-Aguilar and J. L. Sancho-Brú in Chapter 19 focus on e-assessment tools. In particular, diagnostic and formative e-assessments implemented on a Moodle-based VLE environment has been introduced in different subjects. The benefits and the underlying problems of their approach are described here.

Chapter 20 by Carmen Bao and José María Castresana starts with a brief background to worldwide standardization activities in the field of educational technologies as means of enhancing the accessibility, interoperability, durability, reusability and efficiency of e-learning resources. Then it presents a possible framework, which helps to reconcile different data models, by e-learning systems and learning standards and standardization process.

In Chapter 21, Marta Fuentes Agustí, Margarida Romero Velasco and María José Hernández Serrano, offers a review of the e-learning possibilities and criteria, based on several analyses carried out by on higher educational settings. Based on the learner cantered perspective, this chapter proposes some criteria for assuring the quality in higher education e-learning contexts, mainly based on three categories: psycho-pedagogical utility, usability and accessibility.

Chapter 22 by Lilyana Nacheva-Skopalik presents the importance of providing high quality e-learning and the need to apply the requirements of the standards from ISO 9000 series for continual improvement of the quality management systems in education. The work applies the main principles for multiple criteria decision making. An approach for satisfaction measurement is developed which uses weighting coefficients as qualitative valuation of the importance of the quality characteristics.

John Milne and Gordon Suddaby in Chapter 23 introduce the e-Learning Guidelines for New Zealand and show how organisations have used them. It presents some of the benefits of the guidelines as well as the limitations and discusses how these limitations may be managed. The guidelines allow organisations to share their e-learning knowledge and experiences.

Brian Nolan and Lorraine Leeson in Chapter 24 present the efforts of two institutes who have partnered to create a unique e-learning environment based on MOODLE for teaching Sign Languages to deaf people. The work discusses the aspects of sign languages that can best be supported and assessed online and the decisions regarding annotation and mark-up standards for sign languages. It also presents a corpus utilized within digital learning objects in a MOODLE environment and the architecture of the developed tools.

The final Chapter 25 by Olugbemiga T. Ekundayo and Francis Tuluri focus on learners and learning management describing some of its implications for pedagogy. Their Chapter describes contemporary definitions of LMSs and proposes a comprehensive definition of LMS. Then it classifies various tools according to current applications in the industry and it also describes resource poor environments and discusses some problems in resource poor settings.

The above studies discuss technical issues related to the topic of interoperability and learning standards and more theoretical topics related to the designing and acceptance by educators of interoperable and semantic learning applications. Overall, the handbook attempts to provide alternative views on related subjects and to bring closer technologists and educators.

Fotis Lazarinis
Teeside University, UK

Steve Green
Teeside University, UK

Elaine Pearson
Teeside University, UK

Section 1
Interoperable E-Assessment Applications

Chapter 1
Support Interoperability and Reusability of Emerging Forms of Assessment Using IMS LD and IMS QTI

Yongwu Miao
Open University of the Netherlands, The Netherlands

Jo Boon
Open University of the Netherlands, The Netherlands

Marcel van der Klink
Open University of the Netherlands, The Netherlands

Peter Sloep
Open University of the Netherlands, The Netherlands

Rob Koper
Open University of the Netherlands, The Netherlands

ABSTRACT

Emerging forms of assessment (e.g., self-/peer assessment and 360 degree assessment) involve multiple phases and multiple roles/persons, which are process-oriented assessment. IMS Question and Test Interoperability (QTI) is an open technical specification for task-oriented assessment, which has insufficient expressiveness to specify emerging forms of assessment. Meanwhile, existing software tools supporting emerging forms of assessment lack interoperability and reusability. In this chapter, the authors claim that a combined use of QTI and IMS Learning Design (LD) is able to support interoperability and reusability of emerging forms of assessment. In order to support this claim, they analyze the characteristics of four emerging forms of assessment from the perspective of process technologies and present the method to specify emerging assessment forms using QTI and LD. Furthermore, the authors present the difficulties and problems that they encountered when modeling emerging assessment forms and propose possible solutions to solve the problems.

DOI: 10.4018/978-1-61692-789-9.ch001

INTRODUCTION

Competence is defined as 'effective overall performance within an occupation, which may range from the basic level of proficiency through to the highest level of excellence' (Cheetham & Chivers, 2005). A competence is the ability to handle a complex professional task by integrating the relevant cognitive, psychomotor and affective skills. Information gathering for the assessment of competences is increasingly based on qualitative, descriptive and narrative information, in addition to quantitative, numerical data. Such qualitative information cannot be judged against a simple, pre-defined standard (Vleuten & Schuwirth, 2005). Some emerging forms of assessment have gained in acceptance and popularity in education. Examples of such forms of assessment are self- and peer assessment, accreditation of prior learning, and 360 degree assessment. These forms of assessments address complex traits of students, foster deep learning and the development of competences (Topping, 1998; Boud, Cohen et al., 1999; Gipps, 1999).

Assessment consists of making judgments (task aspect) and carrying out administrative activities (process aspect). In comparison with traditional assessment, both of these aspects of assessment are much more problematic in emerging forms of assessment. In particular, emerging forms of assessment usually involve multiple phases and multiple roles/persons. The difficulties and the potential for errors and omissions increase in a non-linear fashion as the number of candidates and assessors involved grows (Rosbottom, 1994). As Bartram pointed out, 360 degree assessment by its very nature is an administrative nightmare to manage. People involved in the process tend to be geographically dispersed but also need close supervision in order to ensure that the ratings are carried out to schedule and that sufficient raters are obtained for each focus of the assessment (Bartram, 2005).

In order to make emerging forms of assessments work effectively and efficiently, many software tools have been developed and are increasingly being used. For example, MUCH (Rada, Acquah et al., 1993; Rushton, Ramsey et al., 1993), Peers (Ngu, Shepherd et al., 1995), Peer Grader (Gehringer 2001), SPARK (Freeman and McKenzie 2002), and ESpace (Volder et al., 2007) are multi-user tools that support self- or/and peer-assessment. The eSPRAT system (Lockyer, 2003; Davies & Archer, 2005) and Appraisal360 (Appraisal360 home page) are example tools that support 360 degree assessment. In self- and peer assessment, with the help of software tools, the tutor, freed from administrative chores, is able to provide a useful, added-value service to students by acting as a problem solver. Student-assessors can concentrate on the clarity, correctness and completeness of each individual exercise without worrying about the relationship with other exercises (Rosbottom, 1994). Similarly, for supporting 360 degree assessment, the software tools manage the workflow associated with the 360 degree assessment process, from initial set-up and preparation of the people involved, through the management of the rating process (including delivery and scoring of questionnaires), to the production of reports and their delivery to feedback providers (Bartram, 2005).

However, existing software tools supporting emerging forms of assessment are stand-alone and offer limited or no support for interoperability of systems and reusability of assessment resources. They each have their own data representation and their data are not interpretable and operable by other application tools. This prompts the question of whether existing e-learning technical specifications can be used to support emerging forms of assessment. The leading specification for the exchange and interoperability of assessments is IMS Question and Test Interoperability (IMS QTI, 2003). However, the QTI specification addresses the task aspect of assessment. Examples of specified assessment tasks are multiple choices, fill-in-the-blank, and matching items. QTI provides no means to support the design and management of assessment processes. Specifically, it ignores who will be involved and what roles they will play at the process level, what kinds of activities should be performed by whom and in which sequence, what assessment resources will be produced and used in which activities, and what dynamic changes may take place in the assessment process and under which conditions. In short, it provides insufficient support for the representation and execution of an assessment plan (Miao et. al. 2008). Therefore, QTI can not independently support emerging forms of assessment. The limitation of QTI on supporting emerging forms of assessment has been analyzed in depth in (Joosten-ten, et. al. 2007).

In QTI v2, a technical solution to integrate QTI with the integration of QTI and IMS Learning Design (IMS LD, 2003) was specified. LD is an open e-learning technical specification that provides a pedagogy-neutral modeling language. It can be used to specify a teaching/learning process as a formal model, which can then be executed in a specification-complaint run-time environment (Koper & Olivier, 2004). The integration between QTI and LD provides a possibility to technically model an aligned teaching, learning, and assessment process. Furthermore, a solution based on QTI v2 to integrate CopperCore (CopperCore home page), a LD engine, and APIS (APIS home page), a QTI player, has been implemented (Vogten et. al. 2006). Initial work to support formative assessment through a combined use of LD and QTI has been done recently (Koper & Burgos, 2005; Miao et. al, 2007a; Hernandez-Leo, et. al. 2009). Another effort has been made to support the design of LD-compliant adaptive courses through intensive use of standards including IMS QTI, IMS LIP, IMS MD, and IMS CP (Boticario & Santos, 2007). However, only little reported work has been carried out on modeling emerging forms of assessment using LD and QTI. The objective of this chapter is to explore the possibility to support emerging forms of assessment by using existing e-learning technical specifications. Concretely speaking, we investigate the expressiveness of LD and QTI in the representation of emerging forms of assessment by using a case-based analytical method. For each emerging assessment form, we analyze its key features from the perspective of process modeling and identify possible alternative scenarios in practice. We intend to share our experiences with readers in modeling emerging forms of assessment in LD and QTI. In addition, we will identify hurdles which may keep educators and assessment designers from using LD and QTI to specify their assessment. Finally, we propose possible solutions to overcome these difficulties.

BACKGROUND

Most open e-learning technical standards for course development and delivery (e.g., IEEE LOM, IMS CP, IMS SS, ADL SCORM) concern learning content (e.g., the description of content and the organizational structure of the content). Only IMS Simple Sequencing specification (IMS SS, 2001), which is also included in ADL SCORM, provides simple mechanisms to represent the sequence of content. In QTI v2, the integration between QTI and IMS SS has been specified as well. The effort has been made by the ASSIS project (ASSIS homepage) to integrate assessment into adaptive sequences of content. This approach enables a seamless integration between instruction and assessment and supports interoperability and reusability. However, such an approach assumes a learning model in which individual learners consume learning content with certain conditional control. It does not support the integration of learning activities with assessment activities. Instead, it just integrates learning materials with questions/questionnaires. The evaluation results of learners' answers are used to control the sequence of the presentation of the content, not the activity sequence. Therefore, it can not support emerging forms of assessment that involve multiple roles/users and complicated interactions among them.

In the development of e-learning technical standards, the release of LD signals an exciting paradigm shift from a content-centric approach to an activity-centric approach. LD provides a framework to express the pedagogical meaning of instructional content and in doing so reflects in a deeper and more creative way on how to design and structure activities (Koper & Olivier 2004). It can be used to specify a collaborative assessment process in which multiple people with diverse roles (e.g., designer, candidate, assessor, decision-maker, and other stakeholders) perform various activities (e.g., design assignment, create/collect evidence, evaluate evidence, and make decision) in sequence and/or in parallel coordinately at process level. However, LD can not explicitly support various types of assessment tasks. Assessment components within the Educational Modeling Language, the base of LD, were excluded when LD was adopted by IMS, because of the existence of QTI. QTI describes a data model for the representation of assessment item/test and the result report. It defines a set of interaction types which can be used to specify basic question types and complicated question types through combination. Many QTI-compliant application tools have been developed such as e-QTI (Martínez-Ortiz et. al. 2006), AQuRate (AQuRate homepage), and R2Q2 (Wills et. al. 2006; Wills et. al. 2009). The evaluation on the conformance of some QTI-compliant tools has been conducted and reported in (Lazarinis et. al. 2009a; Lazarinis et. al. 2009b). However, as mentioned before, QTI provides no support to model a multi-users/roles-involved and multi-phase assessment at process level. It is obvious that LD and QTI have their respective strengths and weaknesses when it comes to supporting emerging forms of assessment at process and task level. What is interesting is that their strengths and weaknesses are complementary. In the next section, we will examine whether an integration of LD and QTI can indeed support emerging forms of assessment.

A STANDARD-BASED APPROACH TO SUPPORT EMERGING FORMS OF ASSESSMENT

We present a standard-based approach to support four emerging forms of assessment: self assessment, peer assessment, accreditation of prior learning, and 360-degree assessment. The four emerging assessment forms presented in this chapter have in common that they are necessary for effective lifelong learning, whereas traditional forms of assessment are restricted to grades and examinations in the educational area but are of little value after one's graduation. Boud (2000) argues that the era of lifelong learning requires employees having the ability to assess themselves throughout their careers using colleagues, peers and drawing on different sources that are found in the workplace or society in generable. For example, it is essential to develop competences for conducting self-assessment and reflective assessments with peers/colleagues to generate performance-oriented information that increases one's self-awareness and consequently can be used for considering options for further learning and education. If employees do no possess these competences then it is quite difficult to become a successful self-directed employee in the 21st century (see for example, Duffy & Holmboe, 2006). The four forms presented in this chapter roughly cover the entire range of emerging assessment forms that are subject to intense and ongoing debate about the role and function of assessment in professional and vocational education and lifelong learning activities, respectively. Table 1 shows the number of hits in de period 2004-2009 on the internet, using databases from Google Scholar and EBSCO.

Table 1. References to different assessment forms

	Google scholar (*)	EBSCO (**)
Self assessment	2490	65
Peer assessment	534	31
Accreditation of prior learning	18	0
360-degree assessment	27	2

(*) term in title, period 2004-2009,
(**) with option Keywords, January 2004 – June 2009P, peer reviewed articles, linked full texts

Google scholar is chosen because it gives a good reflection of the academic mainstream in topics, EBSCO is chosen because it reflects a more specialized collection, mainly consisting of empirical research articles. The ten articles found first in both databases are used as background for the descriptions of the assessment forms hereafter. Most of these articles offered some examples of assessment forms and these examples served as the input for the descriptions of the four assessment forms in the following sections.

Characterizing Four Assessment Forms from Perspectives of Process Modeling

We first analyze the characteristics of the four forms of assessments from the perspective of process support technologies.

Key Features of Self Assessment

Self assessment (SA) refers to a method where an individual assesses his or her own performance regarding a specific topic. The method is largely used both in work situations as in educational settings to initiate self reflection on issues related to performance. Also in many health related situations self assessment is a relevant method for self diagnosis. In work and educational situations the method is often combined with 360 degree assessment or with peer evaluation; in both cases the self assessment is a first step in the procedure, designed to make comparison with assessment of others and reflection on this comparison richer (Johnston et al. 2004). The function of SA is evaluation or judgment of the worth of one's performance and the identification of one's strengths and weaknesses with the aim to improve one's learning/working/health outcomes. In educational settings SA is considered a method to support learning (Schelfhout et al., 2004; Kirby et al. 2007), for example using SA in portfolios (Dysthe et al, 2004). Methodological issues are inter group differences in self assessment ratings (Backs et al. (2005) and various factors obscuring the validity of self assessment (Williams, 2004) including the reluctance of individuals to assess themselves (Evans et al., 2005). Table 2 lists the key features of SA from the perspectives of process modeling and alternative scenarios.

Key Features of Peer Assessment

Peer assessment (PA) can be characterized as the process in which students collaborate and evaluate their own performance as well as those of fellow-students (Sluijsmans et al. 2004; Gulikers, Sluijsmans, Baartman and Bartolo 2009). Peer assessment is usually applied for formative assessment purposes to provide students feedback on their performance that subsequently enables them to consider points of improvements for future learning experiences. Most implementations of peer assessment are not restricted to evaluating a peer's performance as such. In many educational contexts the basic idea is that it is essential that both actors, the candidate who undergoes the assessment (the assessed student) and the peers who conduct the peer assessment, should benefit from the peer assessment experience. Peer assessment is primarily used in professional and vocational education (see, for example, Danver and Kamvounias, 2005 and Keppel, Ada & Chan, 2006). In some professions there is growing interest in

Table 2. Key features of Self Assessment

Roles	- the individual the representative of the learning or working context; this might be - the teacher - the manager - the peers
Artifacts	- goals, criteria, procedures - scoring list or questionnaire on the relevant topics - evidence on performance using the scoring list or the questionnaire - the answers to the questionnaire or scores
Activities	- define the goal and the rules, criteria of the assessment. - score performance - report assessment result
Interaction	1. Preparation: Representatives of the context together with the individual define the goal and the rules, criteria of the assessment. 2. Assessment The individual scores him/herself on the relevant issues 3. Finalization The individual communicate with others about the scores
Alternative scenarios	- Self assessment can be conducted by every individual without feedback to the organization. It is possible that a SA scenario has no the final phase. - Self assessment is often used as a first step in a process of 360 degree assessment or peer assessment as a part of an overall assessment process.

peer assessment (e.g. teaching profession) as a tool to enhance continuous professional development (Sluijsmans et al. 2004). Table 3 lists the components of a PA, the main procedures of PA, and alternative scenarios.

Key Features of Accreditation of Prior Learning

Accreditation of prior learning (APL) supports lifelong learning by assessing and recognizing someone's competences obtained informally through (paid and unpaid) work experiences (Joosten-ten Brinke, 2008).

APL is mainly used for summative assessments and is usually offered by educational providers who promote APL in order to attract non-traditional student groups (Valk, 2009). It is primarily used as a means to determine the content and size of one's study program prior to study entrance (Duvekot, 2002). However, APL is only beneficial for adults who posses sufficient work experience in the domain they want to be educated for. Outcomes of the APL procedures are utilized by examination boards to determine what needs to be learned by prospective students in order to receive a particular certificate or diploma. In Table 4, we present the key features of APL from the perspectives of process modeling and alternative scenarios.

Key Features of 360 Degree Assessment

360 degree assessment is also known as multi-source performance assessment or 360 degree feedback. The method refers to the process by which performance appraisals are collected from different sources, such as supervisors, peers, subordinates and sometimes also customers - rather than from a single source. A key issue is the comparability of different raters (Craig et al, 2006; van der Heijden, 2004). This should provide the feedback recipient with a unique combination of information which is not otherwise available. It is assumed that the feedback givers chosen are in the

Table 3. Key features of peer assessment

Roles	- teacher - candidate - assessor
Artifacts	- instruction - standards and criteria - evidence - assessment form - feedback - improvement
Activities	- inform students - group students - create evidence - assess evidence - evaluate feedback - compose points of improvement
Interaction	1. Preparation Teacher informs students about goals, procedures, timelines etceteras; Teacher groups students in pairs, trios or larger groups. 2. Creating evidence Candidate uses instruction, the standards and criteria to create the evidence. 3. Assessing evidence Peers use the instruction, the standards and criteria to evaluate candidate's performance; Peers fulfill assessment form and write feedback. 4. Reaction Candidate evaluates the feedback and composes points of improvement;
Alternative scenarios	- Peer assessment often has a reciprocal nature, meaning that after the first round, roles shift, and that the candidates subsequently become peers and vice versa. - Not always there is written evidence to be judged afterwards. In some cases, peers observe the behavior of the candidate, which then is the evidence to be judged (for example student teachers who assess each other during internships in schools) - In many cases peers are required to reflect on their role as peer assessor. - Sometimes the candidate informs his peers about the quality of the received feedback

best position to observe and evaluate certain types of behaviors. The method can be used for assessing performance and designing professionalization or development paths, sometimes the method is used to analyze interpersonal behavior (Whitehouse et al., 2007) or for training evaluation (Jellema et al, 2006). The method is emerging in specific professional contexts for example doctors (Rees, 2005) or nurses (Garbett et al., 2007). It is used sometimes as a decision making tool (for example on career advancements or salary increases). 360 degree assessment is usually used at workplaces, both private and public. It can also be used in a class situation for educational purposes, but this is less likely. Table 5 shows the key features of 360 degree assessment.

Modeling Emerging forms of Assessment Using LD and QTI

QTI v2 specified integration of LD with QTI by coupling an LD property to a QTI outcome variable. The original motivation for integrating LD and QTI stems from use cases involving formative assessment and summative assessment using assessment items with traditional question types. Here we try to extend the application areas of the integration of LD and QTI and to improve the benefit of their combined use. As a consequence, the emerging forms of assessment can be modeled as a unit of assessment, a process-oriented assessment model represented in the form of a specific unit of learning. Thus, such a unit of assessment can be executed in an LD and QTI compliant run-time

Table 4. Key features of procedures for accreditation of prior learning (APL)

Roles	- mentor - assessor - employee's (prior) employer - employee (hereafter candidate) - examination board
Artifacts	- description of set of competencies, including standards and requirements for portfolio - evidence and portfolio - form to check candidate's portfolio - rubrics and scoring forms for assessors - APL certificate - form to notify candidate on study program reduction - form for candidates to appeal against the outcome of their APL procedure
Activities	- discusses - select the competences - collect evidence and store in a portfolio - check portfolio - assessed portfolio using rubrics and scoring forms. - write report (APL certificate) - decide to what extend it is allowed to reduce the candidate's study program.
Interaction	1. Candidate-profiling Candidate discusses with mentor the possibilities for APL; Candidate receives description of set of competencies, including standards and requirements for portfolio. 2. Evidence gathering Candidates collect and classify evidence about their previous experience; Mentor checks the content of candidate's portfolio. 3. Assessment Assessors review the quality of a candidate's evidence using assessment standards and rubrics; Candidate receives a report that describes to what extend the candidate master the competences that are included in the competence profile. 2. Recognition Assessors compose APL certificate and send to candidate; Candidate send APL certificate to examination board; Examination board notify candidate about decision on study program reduction.
Alternative scenarios	- Candidates assess their own prior experience in light of the standard and include the outcomes of this self-assessment in their portfolio; - Besides portfolio assessment one or more additional assessment activities usually will take place, such as a criterion-based interview, demonstration, knowledge test.

environment. Furthermore, a unit of assessment can be instantiated as a complete model many times and can be customized or partially reused by different groups/organizations.

When analyzing the emerging forms of assessment, we have created a table for each form of assessment in the last sub-section. There are five rows in each table: roles, artifacts, activities, interaction, and alternative scenarios. The first three rows are components of a process. The interaction describes how participants with diverse roles perform activities in sequence and/or in parallel and how artifacts are used, produced, and transferred in/between activities. Alternative scenarios describe some variations in assessment practices. In this sub-section, we present how to model them through a combined use of LD and QTI.

Modeling Multiple Roles

As we have seen in each table, multiple roles are involved in each form of assessment. When modelling an emerging form of assessment, it is required to explicitly define multiple roles. The QTI specification is concerned with individual

Table 5. Key features of 360 degree Assessment

Roles	- feedback receiver (or target employee) - responsible for process (RFP), can be a HRM representative - feedback giver: - supervisor - peers/co-worker - subordinate
Artifacts	- form with closed and open questions on issues and criteria to be used as a questionnaire or a guide for an interview - mission statement of organization with competency map - appraisal and feedback - summary and priorities
Activities	- define assessment goals - instruct - formulate appraisal - structure feedback - communicate feedback
Interaction	1. Preparation - HRM representative define assessment goals; - HRM representative instructs all participants on procedure, roles, goals and criteria. 2. Assessment - Downward appraisal from supervisor - Lateral appraisal from peers/co-workers - Upward appraisal from subordinates - Inward appraisal from target employee 3. Finalization - HRM representative summarizes feedback - HRM representative formulates next steps trajectory
Alternative scenarios	- The target employee formulates improvement goals at the beginning of the process and the different feedback givers react on these - The input from each appraisal is discussed consequently with the target employee - The target employee gives feedback on improvement goals to the superior, peer or subordinate - The self assessment is not always part of the procedure. Some authors argue that self assessment optimizes the process (Garbett et al., 2007) - More than one employee from each role-group is appointed (more than 1 supervisor, peer, subordinate) - Feedback can be given during a group session; this could reinforce the effects of reflection (van der Heijden and Nijhof, 2004) - Feedback can be given anonymously or non-anonymously - A group of employees instead of a target employee can be the feedback receiver - A training is given to participants if necessary - Some companies collect feedback from the customer

learners. Although QTI does not prohibit use in contexts involving other actors (e.g., instructors, supervisors, and peers), it does not explicitly support defining other roles or sequencing behaviors that result from participation of other actors. However, LD can support a multi-role/user teaching-learning process. In LD, two primary roles (learner and staff) are pre-defined. Each role can have sub-roles defined by designers to fit the context of the learning design. A role is bound with certain activities as role-parts. At run-time a person with a certain role will have privileges and responsibilities which allow him or her to perform the activities and to access certain learning resources according to the definition of the learning design. With LD, multiple roles as listed in the four tables can be modeled. The hierarchical structure of roles (e.g., in 360 degree assessment the role of feedback giver has three sub-roles: supervisor, peers/co-worker, and subordinate) can be modeled as well. Note that in LD each role can be played by multiple users at run-time. Thus, it can be modeled that more than one employee from each sub-role of feedback giver can be appointed in 360 degree assessment.

Modeling Artifacts

In each emerging form of assessment various types of artifacts are created and/or used in activities. Some are represented in the form of questions (e.g., some assignment forms for creating evidence and some assessment forms with rubrics) and some are documents for different purposes (e.g., assessment goal and feedback). Usually, an artifact in the form of question/questionnaire can be modeled using QTI, which can represent many types of questions such as multiple-choice/response, Likert-scale, open-question, fill-in-blank, hot-spot, matching, ordering, association, slider, drag&drop, and upload-file. QTI also provides sufficient flexibility to grow into the advanced constructed-response items and interactive tasks we envisage as the future of assessment (Almond, Steinberg et al. 2001). Furthermore, it provides mechanisms to design structured assessment and control branches and calculate weighted scores. That is, all standard questions and structured tests/exams that form the core of current practice can be supported by using QTI. In addition, LD can be used to represent non-question artifacts. Although LD has no concept of "artifact" in the specification, it enables to define a property with a data type, such as string, text, Boolean, integer, real, url, time, duration, and file. A kind of artifact can be modeled as a property using an appropriate data type. For example, an assessment goal or a feedback item can be defined as a property with the string or text type. A structured document can be modeled as a file-type property. Note that reusable documents can be put on the web and can be accessed by many assessment processes through using URLs of the web pages.

Modeling Activities

In each emerging form of assessment, various activities are performed by diverse roles. LD provides constructor (i.e. activity and environment) to define an activity with some attributes (i.e., title, description, and completion). Most activities listed in the tables can be easily modeled in LD through specifying the values of attributes. For modeling some assessment activities, the question/questionnaire should be modeled as a QTI document as described above, which has to be referred to by an information item within the activity or in the associated environment. It is important to note that a corresponding LD property should be defined in such a way that its identifier is a combination of the identifier of the QTI document and the identifier of the corresponding outcome variable, such as a score. When a candidate/assessor accesses the activity or the environment at run-time, the question/questionnaire will be presented to the candidate/assessor by the QTI engine. After the candidate/assessor submits the answer(s), the QTI engine will evaluate the response and transfer the result to the LD engine. Then LD engine can then adapt the teaching/learning process to the assessment result. For supporting some online activities, such as interview, monitoring, and group meetings, additional services are needed. Fortunately, LD provides some built-in services such as conference and monitor, which can be used to support online communications and monitoring works of participants with a given role.

Modeling Interaction

As illustrated in the tables, emerging forms of assessment are phase-based processes, in which multiple participants with diverse roles perform various activities in sequence and/or in parallel and artifacts are transferred from one activity/role to another.

QTI allows candidates to answer questions in a pre-defined sequence or in any order to finish an assessment test. However, such control of the sequence of the tasks is restricted within an individual assessment test. LD can support the modeling of a learning flow with complex process controls. Activities can be arranged as a sequence or a selection structure. A set of role-parts can be performed in parallel within an act, and acts within a play will be carried out in sequence. Multiple plays can be executed as concurrent threads. The termination of one activity may trigger the start of another activity. In addition, conditions and notifications provide more powerful mechanisms to control the process. The support provided at LD levels B and C makes it possible to trigger the start and termination of activities in a data-driven manner as well.

Some artifacts such as evidence and feedback are intermediate products, which are transferred from one activity/role to another. Some are predefined and assessable in the assessment process. QTI provides mechanisms for declaring outcomes. The outcome of an item, a section or a test can be processed as the output of an assessment. QTIv2 specifies how an outcome variable of QTI can be coupled to a LD property. With the help of this mechanism, an item response and an assessment score can be transferred to relevant participants. That is, the data produced by a participant (e.g., a candidate) can be presented to another one (e.g., an assessor). Additionally, scores given by all assessors can be processed according pre-defined calculation rules as a final result. This result can be transferred to a candidate or even can be used to control the branching. Furthermore, LD provides rich mechanisms to produce and transfer artifacts that are modeled as properties. For example, set-property, change-property, and view-property are basic mechanisms to create, modify, and retrieve artifacts. The local property and global property allow one to transfer artifacts within a learning design and across learning designs. The monitor service can support to view the artifacts produced by other roles.

In summary, both LD and QTI have certain strengths and weaknesses in their support of emerging forms of assessment, but they cannot model all features of emerging assessment forms independently. However, they complement each other on task and process aspects. Thus a combined use of LD and QTI can model most of the features of emerging assessment forms listed in the tables. In the next sub-section, we will use this standard-based method to model an example of an emerging form of assessment.

An Example

In this sub-section we describe a 360 degree assessment scenario. Then we model it with LD and QTI and present how to execute it.

Description of a 360 Degree Assessment Scenario

Professor Hiks works at department C of a university and he is responsible for the coordination of one of the sections of this department, focusing on the theme of consumer education. He develops research proposals and acquires research funds, supervises young researchers and has contacts with paying clients outside the university who want to have his advice on consumer education. He has three senior researchers who support him in his job.

In the department where he works a competence profile is developed that describes all the competences relevant for different staff members in different jobs. In the beginning of the year, the management team decides that a new round of 360 degree assessments will be organized. The staff member who is responsible for the coordination of sections sends mister Hicks a mail explaining the procedure, and setting a time frame for about when he will have a talk with his manager, in his case the director of the department.

First, professor Hiks uses the competence map to perform a self assessment. Using the map he rates his score on the relevant competences and decides on which topics he would like to have more formal and informal training in the coming year. Second, he invites a coordinator of another section, one of the young researchers he is supervising, as well as one of the clients he worked for during the last months. He asks all three feedback givers to fill in a short questionnaire with questions on his commitment, the quality of his output, the degree to which he keeps his appointments and the quality of his functioning as a team member. The questionnaire leaves room for other remarks on his performance. Three feedback givers send their reactions to the director of the department and send a copy to professor Hiks himself.

At the agreed date, the director of the department receives the self assessment and the information of the three feedback givers and Hiks's report of the 360 degree assessment of last year. He uses all this information to have a discussion with professor Hiks about his performance. In the self assessment Hiks indicates some competences, like supervision and time management that require additional training. It turns out that his colleague coordinator is very positive on all points and only mentions that sticking to appointments is sometimes a problem; professor Hiks often comes late in meetings and has to leave early. The young researcher is also very positive but mentions that she has to wait sometimes for weeks before receiving feedback on research proposals. The client is very satisfied on all the points and mentions that for the next contract he wants professor Hiks to advise him on a specific new topic. During the discussion with the director of the department appointments are made about training in time management, delegation of tasks and setting of priorities. The appointments are formalized in a short report and stored in the personnel portfolio of professor Hiks.

Modeling the 360 Degree Assessment Scenario

We can develop a descriptive model that formally specifies the scenario with LD and QTI. A descriptive model abstractly describes how a process is performed in a particular environment in an inductive manner. In the model, five roles are defined: feedback receiver, manager, and three feedback givers including colleague, subordinate, and client. The competence map is modeled as a QTI test document including a list of Likert-scale questions. Three short questionnaires for feedback givers are modeled as QTI test documents as well. The reports of the 360 degree assessment of last year and this year are modeled as file-type properties. Five activities are defined: one self-assessment, three assessment activities of feedback givers, one discussion. The whole process consists of three phases: self assessment, assessment of feedback givers, and discussion and decision. Self assessment result and all feedbacks created in the first two phases will be used in the discussion. A short report will be produced in the discussion.

Execution of the Model and Reuse of the Model

The model can be published in a LD and QTI compliant run-time environment. If the assessment would be conducted in the computer-supported environment, the process will be carried out as below.

The staff member who is responsible for the coordination of sections, instantiates the model by creating a new run of the model. S/he has to prepare settings for this run through assigning the role of feedback receiver to Hiks and assigning the role of manager to the director of the department. The staff member will arrange a conference service if the discussion is an online activity. Otherwise, a meeting room should be arranged with a scheduled duration for the discussion. After that, the staff member will inform all about the start of the assessment. Professor Hiks can access the first activity in which the instruction about how to carry out the assessment and the competence map are available. The expected output of this activity is the self assessment result. Then, he invites three participants by assigning the role of colleague to the coordinator, the role of subordinate to the young researcher, and the role of client to the person for whom professor Hiks has worked during the last months. The invited feedback givers will be informed and can find an assessment activity in their to-do list. After accessing the activity, s/he can read the instruction and the short questionnaire. After having answered the questionnaire, s/he can simply submit it. All assessment results and the report of 360 degree assessment of the last year can be accessed in the discussion activity. In the time scheduled, Hiks and the director of the department can access the activity work space and discuss results either using the online service or face-to-face. The director writes a short report in the activity work space and delivers this to professor Hiks. This then terminates the execution of the assessment.

It is important to note that this model can be reused for assessing other colleagues of the department. For this purpose, the staff member only needs to create other runs and to assign the role of feedback receiver to other colleagues. The model can also be reused for assessing the performance of professor Hiks in the next year. Finally, it can be customized by other departments through modifying the competence map and questionnaires.

FUTURE RESEARCH DIRECTIONS

When modeling emerging forms of assessment, we encountered some difficulties and problems. Firstly, it is difficult to perform statistical analyses (By statistical analyses we do not refer to the usual analysis of assessment results, but rather data analyses that lead to an adaptation of the assessment process itself), if the number of role members is not fixed in an assessment process. Even if the number of candidates is predictable, the degree of complexity of the model will increase as the number increases. For example, if the number of peers is unpredictable, the score given by each peer can only be modeled as a personal property. However, LD provides no means to express the calculation of the mean of the scores given by all peers. Secondly, the adaptation of an assessment is currently restricted within the definition of the assessment and the assessment can be adapted only to candidates' responses to the questions. It is difficult to adapt assessment to the learners' characteristics and environmental information. For example, the competence map cannot be adapted to the position/function of the feedback receiver. Thirdly, assignments and/or assessment forms, sometimes, have to be developed by the participants at run-time, not by the designer at design-time. It is difficult to include new assessment after a UoL has been published. For example, in accreditation of prior learning (APL) it is unpredictable what additional questions are required to answer. The assessor may need to create a questionnaire for collecting additional evidence at run-time. Fourthly, it is difficult to integrate assessment-specific services in LD. For example, in APL additional assessment activities may be needed in which assessment-specific services such as certain simulators and concept-mapping tools are needed.

In the near future, research should target solving the problems just identified, if we want genuinely to support emerging forms of assessment in an interoperable and reusable manner. Firstly, LD would have to be able better to deal with personal properties (e.g., the sum of scores given by multiple peers when the score is modeled as a personal property); this can be done by extending the specification of the expression element. Secondly, the concept of 'income variable' should be introduced in QTI, so that the information can be transferred from teaching-learning activities to assessment. The adaptation can be defined in such a way that it adapts assessment to the value of income variable. Thirdly, QTI editor had better be specified as a built-in service in LD, so that LD can handle the QTI documents created at the run-time. Fourthly, a more generic solution (like BPEL4WS in business process management) should be developed to integrate third-part services in LD, so that the external services can be specified in the design-time, can be configured at instantiation-time, and then can be invoked at the run-time easily.

Finally, the standard-based approach for modeling emerging forms of assessment described in this chapter suits only technical developers who have a sound knowledge of process modeling and technical specifications. As pointed by Miao and Koper (2007b), it is very difficult if not impossible for practitioners to model a complicated teaching, learning, and assessment process with LD and QTI. In order to support 'ordinary' teachers and assessment designers to specify and customize an assessment plan, a high-level assessment modeling language is needed; this we are currently working on (Miao et al. 2008 and Miao et. al. 2009). For the sake of interoperability and reusability, an assessment plan represented in such a high-level modeling language will be transformed into an executable model represented in LD and QTI. Thus the assessment process can be supported by using existing LD and QTI complaint run-time environment.

CONCLUSION

New forms of assessment are becoming increasingly important in the educational sector. Through an analysis of key features of four emerging assessment forms from the perspective of process technologies, we found that all these forms of assessment (1) involve multiple roles/participants; (2) deal with various artifacts; (3) consist of various activities; and (4) include a complicated control-flow and data-flow. Although many software tools have been developed to support emerging forms of assessments, these software tools are stand-alone and lack interoperability and reusability. QTI, the leading specification for the exchange and interoperability of assessments, supports task-oriented assessment, but cannot support process-oriented assessment. LD, a process-oriented modeling language, can be used to model multi-role/user and multi-phase processes, but lacks facilities to model various assessment tasks. That is, neither of them can fully support emerging forms of assessment.

In this chapter we developed and presented an approach to support interoperability and reusability of emerging forms of assessment. The approach is based on the existing open e-learning standards LD and QTI. Through a combined use of LD and QTI, emerging forms of assessment can be modeled as units of assessment, which then can be executed in any LD and QTI compliant run-time environment. That is, an emerging form of assessment represented as an executable model can be reused and customized by other groups/organizations. Meanwhile, the components of a model can be reused as well. Because the model is represented in LD and QTI, all standard-compliant tools (irrespective of the authoring tool, repository, simulator, or engine) can interoperate on the assessment model.

We also indicated some difficulties we met when modeling emerging forms of assessment with LD and QTI. We proposed solutions to overcome them. As part of that, we are working on a high-level, assessment process modelling language. It is designed for practitioners to allow them to specify or customize emerging forms of assessment. Using this language, the emerging form of assessment can be specified as a high-level assessment process model, which can be automatically transformed into an executable model represented in LD and QTI. Once this goal is achieved, practitioners will be able to reap the benefits from using technical standards without the need to handle technical complexity.

ACKNOWLEDGMENT

This work is supported by the European Commission under the TENCompetence project [project No: IST-2004-02787].

REFERENCES

Almond, R. G. Steinberg, l., et al. (2001). A sample assessment using the four process framework. *CSE Report 543. Center for study of evaluation*. Los Angeles: University of California.

APIS home page, Assessment Provision through Interoperable Segments. (n.d.). Retrieved Oct. 10, 2009, from http://www.jisc.ac.uk/whatwedo/projects/apis.aspx

Appraisal360 home page. (n.d.). Retrieved July 12, 2009, from http://www.appraisal360.co.uk/home

AQuRate homepage. (n.d.). Retrieved Oct. 10, 2009, from http://aqurate.kingston.ac.uk/index-old.htm

ASSIS. home page, (n.d.). Retrieved July 12, 2009, from http://www.hull.ac.uk/esig/assis.html

Backs, R. W., da Silva, S. P., & Han, K. (2005). A comparison of younger and older adults, self-assessment manikin ratings of affective pictures. *Experimental Aging Research*, *31*, 421–440. doi:10.1080/03610730500206808

Bartram, D. (2005). Testing on the Internet: Issues, Challenges and Opportunities in the Field of Occupational Assessment. In Bartram, D., & Hambleton, R. (Eds.), *Computer-Based Testing and the Internet: Issues and Advances*. Chichester, UK: John Wiley and Sons. doi:10.1002/9780470712993.ch1

Boticario, J., & Santos, O. (2007) An open IMS-based user modelling approach for developing adaptive learning management systems. *Journal of Interactive Media in Education*, 2. Retrieved Oct. 10, 2009, from: http://www-jime.open.ac.uk/2007/02/

Boud, D. (2000). Sustainable assessment: rethinking assessment for the learning society. *Studies in Continuing Education*, *22*(2), 151–167. doi:10.1080/713695728

Boud, D., & Cohen, R. (1999). Peer Learning and Assessment. *Assessment & Evaluation in Higher Education*, *24*(4), 413–426. doi:10.1080/0260293990240405

Cheetham, G., & Chivers, G. (2005). *Professions, Competence and Informal Learning*. Cheltenham, UK: Edward Elgar Publishing.

CopperCore, home page. (n.d.). Retrieved Oct. 12, 2009, from http://coppercore.sourceforge.net/

Craigh, S., & Hannum, K. (2006). Research update: 306 degree assessment. *Consulting Psychology Journal: Practice and Research*, *58*(2), 117–122. doi:10.1037/1065-9293.58.2.117

Danver, D., & Kanvounias, P. (2005). Student involvement in assessment: a project designed to assess class participation fairly and reliable. *Assessment & Evaluation in Higher Education*, *30*(4), 445–454. doi:10.1080/02602930500099235

Davies, H., & Archer, J. (2005). Multi-source feedback: development and practical aspects. *The Clinical Teacher*, *2*(2), 77–81. doi:10.1111/j.1743-498X.2005.00064.x

Duffy, F. D., & Holmboe, E. S. (2006). Self-assessment in Lifelong Learning and Improving Performance in Practice. *Journal of the American Medical Association*, *296*(9), 1137–1139. doi:10.1001/jama.296.9.1137

Duvekot, R. (2002). The dynamics of non-formal learning and the opening-up of national learning systems. In D. Collardyn (Ed.), *Lifelong Learning: which ways forward,* 89-104. Utrecht, The Netherlands: Lemma.

Dysthe, O., & Engelsen, K. T. (2004). Portfolios and assessment in teacher education in Norway: a theory based discussion of different models in two sites. *Assessment & Evaluation in Higher Education, 29*(2), 239–257. doi:10.1080/0260293042000188500

Evansa, A. W., & McKennaa, C. (2005). Trainees' perspectives on the assessment and self-assessment of surgical skills. *Assessment & Evaluation in Higher Education, 30*(2), 163–174. doi:10.1080/0260293042000264253

Freeman, M., & McKenzie, J. (2002). Implementing and evaluating SPARK, a confidential web-based template for self and peer assessment of student teamwork: benefits of evaluating across different subjects. *British Journal of Educational Technology, 33*(5), 553–572. doi:10.1111/1467-8535.00291

Garbett, R., Hardy, S., Manley, K., Titchen, A., & McCormack, B. (2007). Developing a qualitative approach to 360-degree feedback to aid understanding and development of clinical expertise. *Journal of Nursing Management, 15*(3), 342–347. doi:10.1111/j.1365-2834.2007.00692.x

Gehringer, E. F. (2001). Electronic peer review and peer grading in computer-science courses. In *Proceedings of the 32nd SIGCSE Technical Symposium on Computer Science Education, Charlotte, North Carolina.*

Gipps, C. (1999). Socio-cultural perspective on assessment. *Review of Research in Education, 24*, 355–392.

Gulikers, J., Sluijsmans, D., Baartman, L., & Bartolo, P. (2009). The power of assessment in teacher education. In Swennen, A., & van der Klink, M. (Eds.), *Becoming a teacher educator. Theory and practice for teacher educators* (pp. 173–188). Dordrecht: Springer.

Hernandez-Leo, D., Moghnieh, A., Navarrete, T., Blat, J., Gilabert, S., Santos, P., & Perez-Sanagustin, M. (2008). From planning learning paths to assessment: Innovations to the practical benefits of Learning Design. In *European LAMS Conference 2008* (pp. 139-140). June, 25-27, 2008, Cádiz, Spain.

IMS LD. (2003). *IMS Learning Design Specification.* Retrieved July 12, 2009, from http://www.imsglobal.org/learningdesign/index.cfm

IMS QTI. (2003). *IMS Question and Test Interoperability Specification.* Retrieved July 12, 2009, from http://www.imsglobal.org/question/index.html

IMS SS. (2003). *IMS Simple Sequencing Specification.* Retrieved July 12, 2009, from http://www.imsglobal.org/simplesequencing/index.html

Jellema, F., Visscher, A., & Scheerens, J. (2006). Measuring change in work behavior by means of multisource feedback. *International Journal of Training and Development, 10*(2), 121–139. doi:10.1111/j.1468-2419.2006.00248.x

Johnston, L., & Miles, L. (2004). Assessing contributions to group assignments. *Assessment & Evaluation in Higher Education, 29*(4), 751–768. doi:10.1080/0260293042000227272

Joosten-ten Brinke, D. (2008). *Assessment of prior learning.* Heerlen, The Netherlands: Open Universiteit Nederland.

Joosten - ten Brinke, D., Van Bruggen, J., Hermans, H., Latour, I., Burgers, J., Giesbers, B., & Koper, R. (2007). Modeling Assessment for Reuse of Traditional and New Types of Assessment. *Computers in Human Behavior, 23*(6), 2721-2741.

Keppel, M., Ada, E. A., & Chan, C. (2006). Peer learning and learning-oriented assessment in technology enhanced environments. *Assessment & Evaluation in Higher Education, 31*(4), 453–464.

Kirby, N. F., & Downs, C. T. (2007). Self-assessment and the disadvantaged student: potential for encouraging self-regulated learning? *Assessment & Evaluation in Higher Education, 32*(4), 475–494. doi:10.1080/02602930600896464

Koper, R., & Burgos, D. (2005). Developing advanced units of learning using IMS Learning Design level B. *International Journal on Advanced Technology for Learning, 2*(4), 252–259.

Koper, R., & Olivier, B. (2004). Representing the Learning Design of Units of Learning. *Journal of Educational Technology & Society, 7*(3), 97–111.

Lazarinis, F., Green, S., & Pearson, E. (2009a). Measuring the conformance of hypermedia assessment tools to QTI. *Int. J. of Innovation and Learning, 6*(2), 127–146. doi:10.1504/IJIL.2009.022809

Lazarinis, F., Green, S., & Pearson, E. (2009b). Engineering an interoperable multimedia assessment authoring and run-time environment conforming to IMS QTI. *International Journal of Advanced Media and Communication, 3*(3), 260–276. doi:10.1504/IJAMC.2009.027012

Lockyer, J. (2003). Multisource feedback in the assessment of physician competencies. *The Journal of Continuing Education in the Health Professions, 23*(1), 4–12. doi:10.1002/chp.1340230103

Martínez-Ortiz, I., Moreno-Ger, P., Sierra, J. L., & Fernández-Manjón, B. (2006). <e-QTI>: a Reusable Assessment Engine. *Proceedings of the 5th International Conference on Web-based Learning*, Penang, Malaysia, (LNCS 4181, pp. 134-145).

Miao, Y., & Koper, R. (2007b). An Efficient and Flexible Technical Approach to Develop and Deliver Online Peer Assessment. In A. Clark Chinn, Erkens, G., Puntambekar, S. (Ed.), *Mice, Minds, and Society, Proceedings of the 7th Computer Supported Collaborative Learning (CSCL 2007) conference*, (pp. 502-511), July 16-21, 2007, New Jersey, USA.

Miao, Y., Sloep, P., & Koper, R. (2008) Modeling Units of Assessment for Sharing Assessment Process Information: towards an Assessment Process Specification. In *Proceedings of the 7th International Conference on Web-based Learning (ICWL 2008)*, (LNCS 5145, pp. 132-144), Jinhua, China. Berlin: Springer.

Miao, Y., van der Klink, M., Boon, J., Sloep, P. B., & Koper, R. (2009). Enabling Teachers to Develop Pedagogically Sound and Technically Executable Learning Designs [special issue: Learning Design]. *Distance Education, 30*(2), 259–276. doi:10.1080/01587910903023223

Miao, Y., Vogten, H., Martens, H., & Koper, R. (2007a). The Complementary Roles of LD and QTI in Supporting Effective Web-based Formative assessment. In V. Uskov (Ed.), *Proceedings of the 10th IASTED International Conference on Advanced Technologies in Education (CATE 2007)*, 212-218. October, 8-10, 2007, Beijing, China.

Ngu, A. H. H., Shepherd, J., & Magin, D. (1995). Engineering Peers: Computer-Assisted Approach to the development of Peer Assessment System. *Research and Development in Higher Education, 18*, 582-587. *Blending Tradition and technologies, HERDSA 95*, Rockhampton, Queensland.

Rada, R., Acquah, S., & Ramsey, R. (1993). Collaborative learning and the MUCH System. *Computers & Education, 20*(3), 225–233. doi:10.1016/0360-1315(93)90022-B

Rees, C., & Shepherd, M. (2005). The acceptability of 360-degree judgements as a method of assessing undergraduate medical students' personal and professional behaviours. *Medical Education, 39*(1), 49–57. doi:10.1111/j.1365-2929.2004.02032.x

Rosbottom, J. (1994, September). *Software Tools for Peer Assessment.* Paper presented at the 2nd All Ireland Conference on the Teaching of Computing, Dublin, Ireland.

Rushton, C., & Ramsey, P. (1993). Peer assessment in a collaborative hypermedia environment: A case-study. *Journal of Computer-Based Instruction, 20*(3), 75–80.

Schelfhout, W., & Dochy, F. (2004). The use of self, peer and teacher assessment as a feedback system in a learning environment aimed at fostering skills of cooperation in an entrepreneurial context. *Assessment & Evaluation in Higher Education, 29*(2), 177–201. doi:10.1080/0260293042000188465

Sluijsmans, D., Brand-Gruwel, S., van Merriënboer, J., & Martens, R. (2004). Training teachers in peer assessment skills: effects on performance and perceptions. *Innovations in Education and Teaching International, 41*(1), 60–79. doi:10.1080/1470329032000172720

Topping, K. J. (1998). Peer assessment between students in colleges and universities. *Review of Educational Research, 68*(3), 249–276.

Valk, A. (2009). Recognition of prior and experiential learning in European universities. *Assessment in education, principles, policies & practice, 16*(1), 83-95.

Van der Heijden, B., & Nijhof, A. (2004). The value of subjectivity: problems and prospects for 360-degree appraisal systems. *International Journal of Human Resource Management, 15*(3), 493–511. doi:10.1080/0958519042000181223

Vleuten, C. P. M. d., & Schuwirth, L. W. T. (2005). Assessing professional competence: from methods to programmes. *Medical Education, 39*(3), 309–317. doi:10.1111/j.1365-2929.2005.02094.x

Vogten, H., Martens, H., Nadolski, R., Tattersall, C., Rosmalen, P., & Koper, R. (2006). CopperCore Service Integration - Integrating IMS Learning Design and IMS Question and Test Interoperability. In *Proceedings of The 6th IEEE International Conference on Advanced Learning Technologies,* (pp. 378-382), Kerkrade, The Netherlands. Washington, DC: IEEE Computer Society.

Volder, M. D., Rutjens, M., Slootmaker, A., Kurvers, H., Bitter, M., Kappe, R., et al. (2007). *Espace: A New Web-Tool for Peer Assessment with In-Built Feedback Quality System.* Paper presented at ABR & TLC Conference, 2007, Hawaii, USA.

Whitehouse, A., Hassel, A., Bullock, A., Wood, L., & Wall, D. (2007). 360 degree assessment (multisource feedback) of UK trainee doctors: Field testing of team assessment of behaviors (TAB). *Medical Teacher, 29,* 171–176. doi:10.1080/01421590701302951

Williams, W. M. (2004). Blissfully incompetent. *Psychological Science in the Public Interest, 5*(3), i–ii. doi:10.1111/j.1529-1006.2004.00017.x

Wills, G., Davis, H., Chennupati, S., Gilbert, L., Howard, Y., Jam, E. R., et al. (2006). R2Q2: Rendering and Reponses Processing for QTIv2 Question Types. In M. Danson (ed.), *Proceedings of the 10th International Computer Assisted Assessment Conference,* (pp. 515-522). Loughborough University, UK.

Wills, G., Davis, H., Gilbert, L., Hare, J., Howard, Y., & Jeyes, S. (2009). Delivery of QTIv2 question types. *Assessment & Evaluation in Higher Education, 34*(3), 353–366. doi:10.1080/02602930802071106

ADDITIONAL READING

Andersson, P., & Harris, J. (Eds.). *Re-theorising the recognition of prior learning.* Leicester: National Institute of Adult Continuing Education. ASDEL home page*: Assessment Delivery Engine for QTIv2 Questions.* Retrieved Oct. 10, 2009, from http://www.asdel.ecs.soton.ac.uk/.

Black, P., Harrison, C., Lee, C., Marshall, B., & Wiliam, D. (2003). *Assessment for learning.* Maidenhead, UK: Open University Press.

Bouzo, J., Batlle, H., & Blat, J. (2007). Enhancing IMS QTI assessment with web maps, *in Proceedings of the TENCompetence Open Workshop on Current Research on IMS Learning Design and Lifelong Competence Development Infrastructures*, 63-74, June 21-22, 2007, Barcelona, Spain.

CEDEFOP. (2009). *European guidelines for validating non-formal and informal learning.* Luxembourg: Office for official publications of the European communities.

Earl, L. M. (2003) *Assessment as learning.* Thousand Oaks, Corwin Press. FREMA home page, Retrieved Oct. 10, 2009, from http://www.frema.ecs.soton.ac.uk/

Garcia-Robles, R., Blat, J., Sayago, S., Griffiths, D., Casado, F., & Martinez, J. (2004). Supporting usability and reusability based on eLearning standards, *in Proceedings of IEEE International Conference on Advanced Learning Technologies (*ICALT), 495–499, 30 August - 1 September 2004, Joensuu, Finland.

Giacomini Pacurar, E., Trigang, P., & Alupoaie, S. (2005). A QTI editor integrated into the netUniversité web portal using IMS LD. *Journal of Interactive Media in Education, 9.* http://jime.open.ac.uk/2005/09/.

Gorissen, P. (2006) Usability Study of QTI (Quickscan QTI), Digitale Universiteit, The Netherlands, Retrieved Oct. 10, 2009, from: http://www.gorissen.info/Pierre/QTI/Quickscan_QTI_2006.pdf.

Koper, E. J. R., & Tattersall, C. (Eds.). (2005). *Learning Design: A Handbook on Modelling and Delivering Networked Education and Training.* Berlin: Springer.

Koper, R. (Ed.). (2009). *Learning Network Services for Professional Developments*, Springer publishers.

Koper, R., & Miao, Y. (2008). Using the IMS LD Standard to Describe Learning Designs. In L. Lockyer, S. Bennet, S. Agostinho and B. Harper (Eds.), *Handbook of Research on Learning Design and Learning Objects: Issues, Applications and Technologies* (pp. 41-86). IDEA group. Retrieved Oct. 10, 2009, from http://hdl.handle.net/1820/927.

Lazarinis, F., Green, S. and Pearson, E. Focusing on content reusability and interoperability in a personalized hypermedia assessment tool, *Multimedia Tools and Applications Journal*, Springer, Retrieved Oct. 10, 2009, from http://www.springerlink.com/content/u34211037737ur42/

Lesage, M., Riopel, M., Raiche, G., & Sodoke, K. (2008). IMS-QTI sub-standards in computerised adaptive testing and interfacing. *International Journal of Advanced Media and Communication, 2*(2), 115–137. doi:10.1504/IJAMC.2008.018503

Lockyer, L., Bennet, S., Agostinho, S., & Harper, B. (Eds.). (2008). *Handbook of Research on Learning Design and Learning Objects: Issues, Applications and Technologies.* IDEA group.

Mason, J., Wendy, P., & Radford, A. (2008). *Processes, systems and tools supporting recognition of prior learning. Final Report.* Brisbane, Flexible Learning Framework QuestionMark home page. Retrieved Oct. 10, 2009, from http://www.questionmark.com/us/index.aspx

Nicol, D. J., & Macfarlane-Dick, D. (2006). Formative assessment and self-regulated learning: a model and seven principles of good feedback practice. *Studies in Higher Education, 31*(2), 199–218. doi:10.1080/03075070600572090

Respondus home page. Retrieved Oct. 10, 2009, from http://www.respondus.com/.

Zualkernan, I. A., Ghanam, Y. A., Shoshaa, M. F., & Kalbasi, A. S. (2007). An architecture for dynamic generation of QTI 2.1 assessments for mobile devices using flash lite, *Proceedings of the 7th IEEE International Conference on Advanced Learning Technologies (ICALT)*, 194–195. July 18-20 2007, Niigata, Japan.

KEY TERMS AND DEFINITIONS

360 Degree Assessment: An assessment method where performance appraisals are collected from different sources.

Accreditation of Prior Learning: The assessment and recognition of one's competences developed through work experiences.

IMS LD: An open e-learning technical specification that provides a pedagogy-neutral modeling language for specifying a teaching/learning process and associated learning resources.

IMS QTI: An open e-learning technical specification that describes a data model for representing assessment as a hierarchical structure and processing responses.

Interoperability: The ability to take instructional components (e.g., an activity or a question) developed in one system and to use them in another system without special effort.

Peer Assessment: The assessment of a student's performance by his/her fellow students.

Reusability: The flexibility to incorporate instructional components (e.g., an activity or a question) in multiple applications and contexts.

Self Assessment: A method where an individual assesses his or her own performance regarding a specific topic.

Chapter 2
Interoperable Assessment Based on Competency Modelling

Onjira Sitthisak
Thaksin University, Thailand

Lester Gilbert
University of Southampton, UK

ABSTRACT

The aim of this chapter is to illustrate some affordances of machine-processable competency statements. Such competency statements are supported by ontologies and taxonomies of competency. Machine processing can offer interoperable and reusable resources and applications that are pedagogically effective for e-learning and assessment. A competency statement which can be read, processed, and interpreted by machine contributes to the automatic generation of questions and offers a semantic structure using the Web Ontology Language (OWL) to express competencies for further processing. The generated questions are expressed in the IMS Question and Test Interoperability specification (IMS QTI) to enable interoperability.

COMPETENCY MODELLING, ONTOLOGIES, AND IMS QTI

The use of competency modelling, ontologies, and IMS QTI overcomes limitations of interoperability, portability, and reusability in assessment. Competency modelling supports consistency checking, assessing differences in knowledge levels, and comparing achievement in related domains, which were essentially impractical previously. Using ontologies and Semantic Web technologies addresses many of the problems of extending and combining structured content in different formats from different schemas. The IMS QTI specification facilitates the sharing of questions and tests, enabling investment in the development of common tools such as Web-based authoring and delivery applications.

A competency model has the great advantage of providing a machine-processable shared understanding of a domain. The model supports consistency checking, assessing differences in knowledge levels, and comparing achievement in related domains, which were essentially imprac-

DOI: 10.4018/978-1-61692-789-9.ch002

tical previously. The issue of how to represent competency as a rich data structure is focused on supporting collaboration between different communities and the tracking of the knowledge state of the learner. The same competencies may appear in more than one place in the competency hierarchy. Thus, it makes sense to capture the data model of those competencies in some reusable form, so they have to be defined only once. It is suggested that information about competencies should form the basis of pedagogically-informed metadata which would be relevant to any description of content or process in a learning and teaching situation.

Ontologies support connecting resources available in a domain and representing knowledge states of students. Ontological metadata expresses terms defined formally and unambiguously. This metadata provides information for e-assessment in supporting the integration and reuse of these data with other systems, and for adaptive assessment systems in supporting the adaptation of their behaviour and structure. Structuring knowledge in a new domain by using ontological conceptualization should allow the faster build of new systems.

The proposed competency model, named COMpetence-Based learner knowledge for personalized Assessment (COMBA), has been developed because of the unsatisfactory results delivered by existing competency standards and desired taxonomies of competence. This model reflects all relevant features of the learner's behaviour and their knowledge, skills, and attitudes that affect their learning and performance. Statements of competency are machine-readable. Machine processing can offer interoperable and reusable resources and applications that are pedagogically effective for e-learning and assessment. A competency statement which can be read, processed, and interpreted by machine contributes to the automatic generation of questions, distractors, feedback, and question sequences, and offers a semantic structure for further processing. The use of a competency model allows the recording of the achieved competencies of learners, and provides an integration of the system proposed here with adaptive assessment.

THE DEVELOPMENT OF COMPETENCY MODELS

A competency may be considered to be based on subject matter knowledge and skill, contextualized with respect to particular situations or scenarios (Harzallah, Berio and Vernadat, 2006). Competencies may be assembled and linked in a rich data structures. A competency may appear in more than one place in a competencies hierarchy. Thus, it makes sense to capture the data model of competencies in some reusable form, so they have to be defined only once.

The possible requirements for describing competencies based on an analysis of the general structure of existing competency standards and competency ontologies (Trichet and Leclère, 2003; Draganidis and Mentzas, 2006; Schmidt and Kunzmann, 2006) are listed below. The list is general and captures the type of information modelled in existing standards, rather than defining a canonical set of properties.

- **Description:** the general description of the competency.
- **Type:** type of trait that represents an aspect of the competency such as knowledge, skill, attitude, and so on.
- **Relationship:** relationship to other competencies such as "part-of", "child competency", and "parent competency".
- **Proficiency level:** a measurement of the degree to which the competency has been achieved.
- **Measurement scale:** a scale that relates to proficiency level and weight.
- **Taxonomy:** a taxonomy reference for structuring competency data.

- **Evidence:** facts or indicators about the achievement of a competency, such as test results and certificates.
- **Tools:** any tool(s) required to support reaching the competency.
- **User area:** Other data, such the description of a job position.

There are currently two international competency standards: the IMS Reusable Definition of Competency or Educational Objective (RDCEO) specification, and the HR-XML Consortium competencies schema. A comparison of these two competency standards according to these requirements is shown in Table 1 (Sitthisak et al., 2007).

First, IMS RDCEO provides a flexible definition of competency using unstructured textual definitions. Often a less precise definition is very useful, especially when dealing with competency data from different communities of practice. However, this leads to shortcomings in domain definition, ontology use, the ability to compare competency data between different communities, the tracking of the knowledge state of the student, and machine processability.

Table 1. A comparison of the capabilities of competency standards

Categories	Sub-categories	IMS RDCEO	HR-XML
Competency description		■	■
Competency type	Knowledge	▣	▣
	Skill	▣	▣
	Attitudes	▣	▣
Competency relationship		▣	□
Proficiency level		▣	■
Measurement scale		▣	■
Taxonomy		▣	■
Evidence		▣	■
Tools		▣	□
User area		▣	■

Support: '■' = full, '▣' = partial, '□' = none

Second, HR-XML addresses some shortcomings of RDCEO while still missing the important categories of 'competency relations' and 'tools', as illustrated in Table 1. Although HR-XML provides for competencies to be composed of other competencies, it does not have an element referring to the competency relation. This may cause selection problems. For example, in a competency hierarchy, it should be possible to specify which elements of the competency hierarchy are mandatory and which are optional.

These existing e-learning competency standards, however, are not able to accommodate complex competencies, link competencies adequately, support comparisons of competency data between different communities, or support tracking of the knowledge state of the student.

The IMS RDCEO specification still has problems with: the level of the competency described separated from its narrative description; the grading scale of a competency; the success threshold of a competency; and the structure of complex competencies (Hersh et al., 2006; Karampiperis, Sampson and Fytros, 2006). One of the problems with the HR-XML competency standard is that, in focusing on helping an organization improve communication across its HR (human resources) activities by enhancing recruiting systems, it does not address improving the use of competency information in education and training (Sitthisak, Gilbert et al., 2007). Solving these problems results in a competency model presented later in this chapter, reflecting all relevant features of the student's behaviour and their knowledge and skills that affect their learning and performance.

Ontologies

At present, representing the meaning of objects on the Web to allow machine-accessibility and processing is the main obstacle to supporting Web users (Antoniou and Harmelen, 2004). A semantic network has been applied to the Web in order to allow any existing knowledge representation system to be exported onto the Web. This is called the Semantic Web.

The power of the Semantic Web is that machines become much better able to process and understand the data that they merely display at present, such as data and rules for reasoning (Berners-Lee, Hendler and Lassila, 2001).

The Semantic Web has the potential to increase the effectiveness of educational functions according to three fundamental affordances which are:

- semantic conceptualisation and ontologies,
- common standardised communication syntax, and
- large-scale service-based integration of educational content and functionality provision and usage (Aroyo and Dicheva, 2004).

Anderson and Whitelock (2004) also support this view that the vision of the educational Semantic Web is based on the capacity for effective information storage and retrieval, the capacity for non-human autonomous agents to augment the learning and information retrieval, and the capacity of the internet to support, extend, and expand communications capabilities of humans.

An ontology is a core component in the Semantic Web, and is an explicit and formal specification describing the main concepts of a domain and providing a shared understanding of a domain. The ontology uses the Web Ontology Language (OWL) to represent the formal common agreement about meaning of data. OWL adds more vocabulary to describe properties and classes than RDF or RDF Schema. In addition, it can describe relations between classes such as disjointness, cardinality, and characteristics of properties. OWL is designed for use by applications that need to process the information contained in documents. OWL has three sublanguages: OWL Lite, OWL DL, and OWL Full. OWL Lite supports a classification hierarchy and simple constraint features such as thesauri and taxonomies. OWL Description Logic (DL) supports the maximum expressiveness with computational completeness. OWL Full is fully compatible with any reasoning software. It supports maximum expressiveness with no computational guarantees.

Kalfoglou (2001) proposed criteria for design ontologies:

- **Clarity:** minimal ontological ambiguity. All definitions should be communicated effectively.
- **Coherence:** the ontology should be internally and logically consistent.
- **Extendibility:** adding new terms in the existing ontology should be flexible without the revision of existing definitions.
- **Encoding bias:** minimised when the representation is made purely for the convenience of notation or implementation.
- **Minimal ontological commitment:** the ontology should allow freedom to specialise and instantiate the ontology as required.

The following discussion focuses on some applications of ontologies in learning technology. Dicheva et al. (2005) considered ontologies as a knowledge base component. Ontologies may also support the presentation and delivery of course material and assisting and assessing students (JISC, 2004).

In the area of learning objects, the content and structure of learning materials may be represented using ontologies and the Semantic Web (Jovanovic, Gasevic and Devedzic, 2006). Learning Web applications may generate content semantically personalised to the student's goals, preferences, and learning styles (Stojanovic, Staab and Studer, 2001). Such applications may provide more comfortable search and navigation through the learning material.

In the area of educational Web portals, Dicheva, Sosnovsky et al. (2005) developed the Ontologies for Education (O4E) Web Portal for publishing the created ontology and serving as a point of access to the relevant online information. 'Onto-portal' was an ontological hypertext framework for building educational Web portals based on a simple domain ontology (Woukeu et al., 2003).

In the area of Web-Based Educational System (WBES), Semantic Web technologies were employed in WBES to enhance adaptation and flexibility (Aroyo and Dicheva, 2004). Topic Maps for Learning (TM4L) (Dicheva, Dichev and Wang, 2005) and AIMS (Aroyo and Dicheva, 2001) involved exploring the domain ontology and searching the repository for information related to a specific task.

IMS QUESTION AND TEST INTEROPERABILITY

Currently, many assessment systems such as Problets (Dancik and Kumar, 2003), ILE (Cristea and Tuduce, 2005), QuizPACK (Brusilovsky and Sosnovsky, 2005), and Jeliot 3 (Myller, 2007) offer remarkable automatic generation of questions and adaptation of questions, but only for specific domains, and they lack integration, interoperability, portability, and reusability with other systems and environments. In addition, such systems are difficult to use in e-Learning systems, particularly in assessment systems. For example, consistency checking, assessing differences in knowledge levels, and comparing achievement in related domains remain essentially impractical.

The IMS QTI specification (IMS QTI, 2006) describes an information model for representing questions, tests, and results. This specification enables the exchange of item; test, and results data between authoring tools, item banks, and test construction tools, as well as learning systems and assessment delivery systems. In addition, this specification has been designed to support both interoperability and innovation (IMS QTI, 2006). It describes the basic structure that is necessary to represent questions (AssessmentItem) and test of evaluations (AssessmentTest). QTI version 2.0 processing is illustrated in Figure 1. Regarding to adaptation issues, metadata associated to IMS QTI items play a very important role for typifying an item (Boticario and Santos, 2007).

When a student accesses a Virtual Learning Environment or Learning Management System (VLE/LMS) to view and respond to a QTI question, the system initially sends a QTI XML file (See Figure 2) to a QTI processing service where a Question renderer renders the question. The rendered question is sent back to the VLE/LMS for display to the student. The student's answer

Figure 1. QTI version 2.0 processing (Wills et al., 2006)

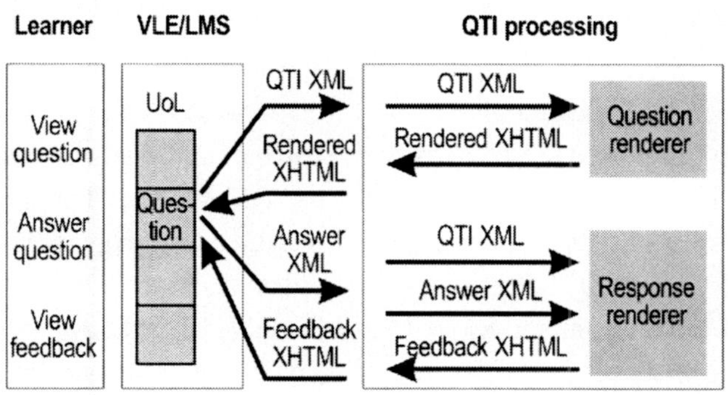

(UoL: Unit of Learning)

Figure 2. Example of QTI question in XML format

```xml
<?xml version="1.0" encoding="UTF-8" ?>
- <assessmentItem
   xsi:schemaLocation="http://www.imsglobal.org/xsd/imsqti_v2p0
   imsqti_v2p0.xsd" title="Question" adaptive="false" timeDependent="false"
   xmlns:xsi="http://www.w3.org/2001/XMLSchema-instance"
   identifier="question20" xmlns="http://www.imsglobal.org/xsd/imsqti_v2p0">
 + <responseDeclaration baseType="identifier" cardinality="single"
     identifier="RESPONSE">
 + <responseDeclaration baseType="integer" cardinality="single"
     identifier="sequencecap">
 + <responseDeclaration baseType="integer" cardinality="single"
     identifier="sequenceSMC">
 + <responseDeclaration baseType="integer" cardinality="single"
     identifier="subSequence">
 + <responseDeclaration baseType="integer" cardinality="single"
     identifier="subSequenceSMC">
 + <outcomeDeclaration baseType="integer" cardinality="single" identifier="SCORE">
   <outcomeDeclaration identifier="FEEDBACK" cardinality="single"
     baseType="identifier" />
 - <itemBody>
     <p />
     <p />
   - <choiceInteraction responseIdentifier="RESPONSE" shuffle="false"
       maxChoices="1">
     - <p>
       - <b>
           <prompt>The formula of the complexity adjustment factor
             may be defined as</prompt>
         </b>
       </p>
       <simpleChoice identifier="Choice2">The aggregate of the ratings of the
         19 influence factors.</simpleChoice>
       <simpleChoice identifier="Choice1">0.65 plus degree of influence
         divided by 200</simpleChoice>
       <simpleChoice
         identifier="Choice3">0.26*tof+0.56*tif+1.66*tea</simpleChoice>
       <simpleChoice identifier="Choice4">200 plus 0.65 divided by degree of
         influence</simpleChoice>
     </choiceInteraction>
   </itemBody>
 + <responseProcessing>
   <modalFeedback outcomeIdentifier="FEEDBACK" identifier="Choice1"
     showHide="show">Yes, that is correct.</modalFeedback>
   <modalFeedback outcomeIdentifier="FEEDBACK" identifier="Choice1"
     showHide="hide">No, the correct answer is "0.65 plus degree of influence
     divided by 200".</modalFeedback>
</assessmentItem>
```

is sent to the QTI Response renderer which marks the answer and provides feedback. The rendered feedback is sent back to the VLE/LMS for display to the student.

There is a gradually growing number of QTI related studies and tools including QTI tool for assessing physics (Bacon, 2003), integration of a QTI editor and player in a web portal (Pacurar, Trigang and Alupoaie, 2005), Assessment Delivery Engine for QTIv2 questions (ASDEL) (Wills, Davis et al., 2006), and aLFanet (Lazarinis, Green and Pearson, 2009). The aims of these tools were to evaluate the potentials of IMS QTI in real assessment and to develop a web application tool to deliver the tests. In this research, ASDEL was deployed as a stand-alone web application to deliver the tests to the learners. ASDEL allows a learner to view a question, to answer it, to receive feedback, and to view the test result.

COMBA SYSTEM

We have developed an improved competency model, named COMpetence-Based learner knowledge for personalized Assessment (COMBA), which uses ontologies. The model has been used to automate question generation in adaptive assessment systems. More generally, it offers interoperable, portable, and reusable resources for e-learning and knowledge management applications that define and update knowledge throughout a student's life.

COMBA is able to accommodate complex and linked competencies, where the resulting competencies structure may be used to support tracking of the knowledge state of students. The system focuses on the identification and integration of appropriate subject matter content (represented by a content taxonomy) and appropriate cognitive ability (represented by a capability taxonomy) into a hierarchy of competencies. The resulting competencies structure has been shown to be able to generate questions and tests for formative and summative assessment. These questions can be expressed as IMS QTI compatible XML files to enable interoperability.

The system was built on an ontological database that describes the resources (subject matter, capability, competency) and the relationships between them. The advantage of ontological schemas over database schemas is that the former define explicit formal specifications and include machine interpretable definitions, to enable sharing common understanding of the structure of information among people or software agents. Thus, the ontological database is flexible and extensible, allowing the resources in the system to be described on the Semantic Web, reasoning about them, and interoperated on different systems.

An assessment for a competency often actually tests component competencies, and is supported by the linked nature of the competencies hierarchy. For example, a statistics course may test knowledge of the confidence interval (Field, 2005) by testing the students' ability to calculate, explain, and define the confidence interval in a variety of situations.

An assessment item can be directly formulated from a competence by using the parameters of that competence: capability, subject matter content, and other contextual elements. For example, the assessment corresponding to the learning outcome, "Students understand the concept of a confidence interval" might be something like "Calculate the confidence interval for the following situation", or "Explain the importance of the confidence interval in the following situation", or "Define standard error".

The Competency Model

COMBA is informed by the results of comparing the competency standards against the desired taxonomy of competence and this point is discussed above. The improved competency model is represented in Figure 3. The heart of this model

Figure 3. Competency model

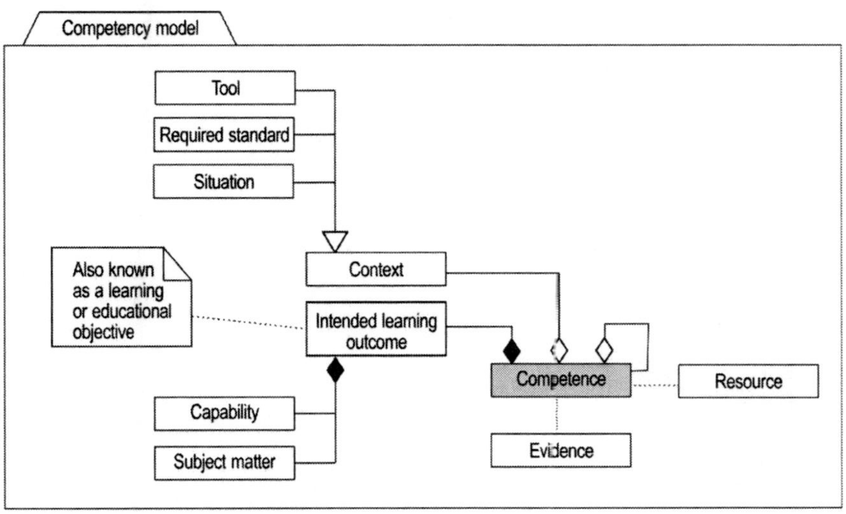

is the treatment of knowledge, not as possession, but as a contextualized multidimensional space of either actual or potential capability.

A competency involves a capability associated with subject matter content and optionally a contextualisation (the situation or scenario, tools, and standard of performance). A competency can be linked to one or more resources, and a student may evidence a competency in one or more ways.

Capability is behaviour that can be observed, based on a domain taxonomy of learning such as Bloom's (Bloom and Krathwohl, 1956), Gagné's Nine Areas of Skill (Gagne, 1970), or Merrill's Cognitive Domain (Merrill, 1999).

Subject matter content is the subject domain of what the student can do by the end of course. The competency *evidence* substantiates the existence, sufficiency, or level of the competency, and might include test results, reports, evaluation, certificates, or licenses. External knowledge resources and *tools* support and promote the problem solving, activity performance or situation handling of the competency. The *situation* identifies the particular circumstances and conditions of the competency, for example, its time limit.

The proposed competency model involves three important principles: an orientation towards, and focus upon, activity-based teaching and learning, the identification and integration of appropriate subject matter content within a broader teaching and learning context, represented by a hierarchy of linked competencies, and the identification of the assessment that would demonstrate successful teaching and learning has been accomplished.

Architecture of COMBA System

The COMBA implementation consists of a number of modules, illustrated in Figure 4. The Competence navigator is responsible for retrieving the requested competence, based on the domain request from the student, and passing the competence to the Subject Matter Content and Capability navigator modules.

In using the model for the automatic generation of questions, the relevant subject matter and capability data, together with the authoring question template files, are assembled to generate questions derived from the matrix of competencies crossed with cognitive abilities. Given a question which is now ready for further use, it is formatted using the QTI specification.

The QTI specification facilitates the sharing of questions and tests, enabling investment in

Figure 4. Architecture of the COMBA system

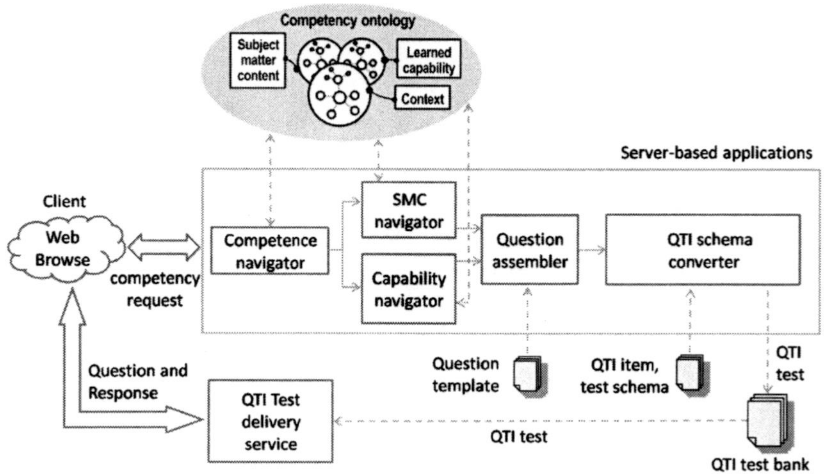

the development of common tools such as Web-based authoring and delivery applications. For an adaptive test, this specification supports the use of pre-conditions and branching, allowing the embedding of sequencing and adaptive logic into a test. Adaptivity is limited to the questions referred to within the test. As a result, if the student answered, it may not be possible to branch in directions not provided in the test. In addition, the inability to import external data may limit adaptivity.

In order to develop a test, the generated questions are linked together for storing in a test bank. For the delivery of the test, the system deploys an assessment delivery service (QTI tools[1]) to allow a student to view a question, to answer it, to receive feedback, and to view the assessment results.

Ontologies for Competency Modelling

The domain subject matter content, capability taxonomy, and competence are based on the Simple Knowledge Organisation System (SKOS) (W3C, 2005). SKOS is used to express the structure of content, capability, and competence. Subject matter content is represented in the form of an ontology, based on the structure of its domain rather than on the structure of its content.

In the COMBA system, the ontology was based on OWL-Lite (W3C, 2004) which was sufficiently expressive to describe the subject matter hierarchy and provides for higher performance reasoning. The ontologies adhere to the criteria of ontology design: clarity, coherence, extendibility, minimal encoding bias, and minimal ontological commitment (Kalfoglou, 2001). Sharing and reuse of information are integral aspects of the Semantic Web.

The framework of the COMBA ontology, shown in Figure 5, is implemented in Protégé 3.3. The Protégé tool supports knowledge acquisition and knowledge base development (Gennari et al., 2003). The definitions of the elements in the competence ontology are shown in Table 2.

IMS QTI with Question Delivery

'QTItools' player was deployed as a stand-alone Web application to deliver the tests to the students. 'QTItools' player allows a student to view a question, to answer it, to receive feedback (shown in Figure 6), and to view the test result (shown in Figure 7).

Figure 5. Ontology of COMBA

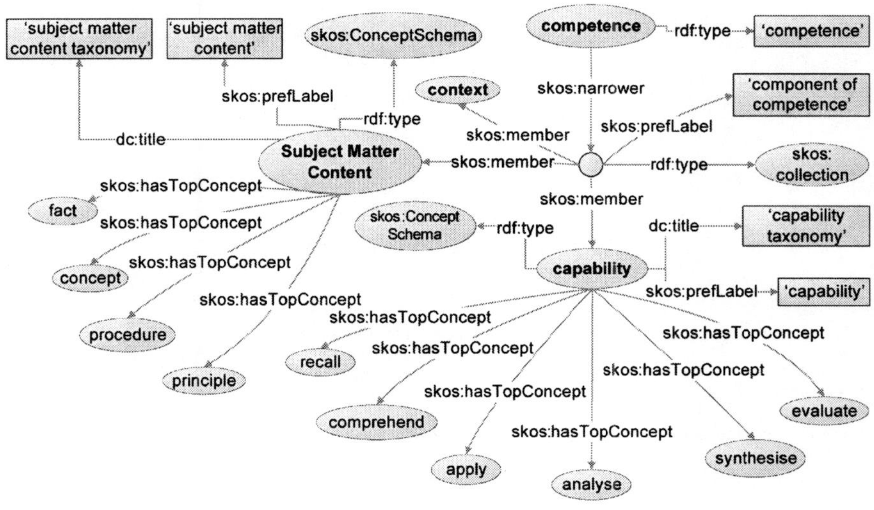

Table 2. The definitions of each element in the competence ontology

Element	Definition
Competence	Defines a capability associated with subject matter content, a proficiency level, evidence, any required tools, and definition of the situation which contextualizes the competency.
SMC	Defines the subject domain of what the student can do by the end of the unit of teaching and learning.
Capability	Defines behaviour that can be observed, based on a taxonomy of learning such as Bloom's, Gagné's nine areas of skill, or Merrill's cognitive domain.
Context	Defines the particular context and conditions of the competency, such as tools and situations.
Fact	Defines statements, or factual information, which consists of an attribute and a value.
Concept	Defines a group of objects or ideas which are designated by a single word or term. A concept has a number of attributes which are used to classify or categorize objects according to their values.
Procedure	Defines a sequential set of steps to accomplish a task or make a decision.
Principle	Defines cause-effect relationships describing the behaviour of a system. It can usually be expressed as some sort of an equation if the system is in the scientific or engineering domain.
Recall, Comprehend, Apply, Analyse, Synthesise, and Evaluate	Cognitive domain capabilities according to Bloom.

Figure 6. 'QTItools' player displaying a question, receiving an answer, and giving feedback

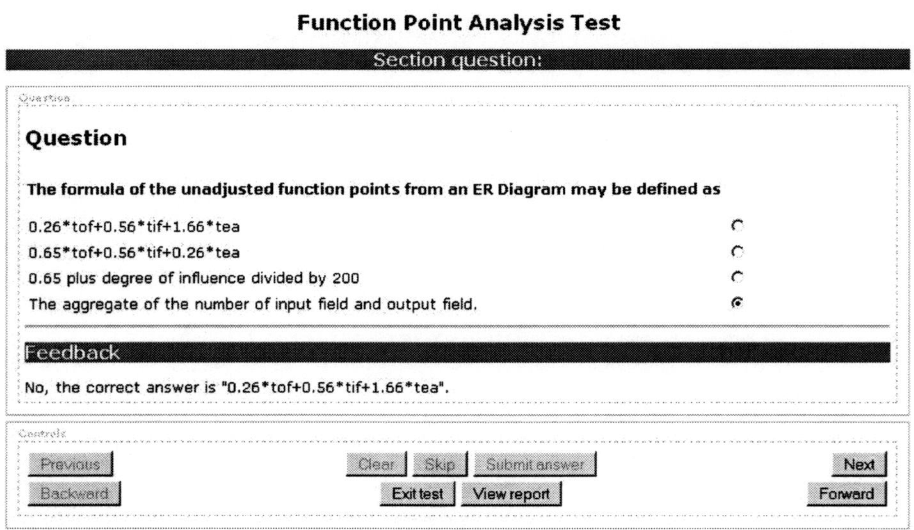

Figure 7. 'QTItools' player showing the test result

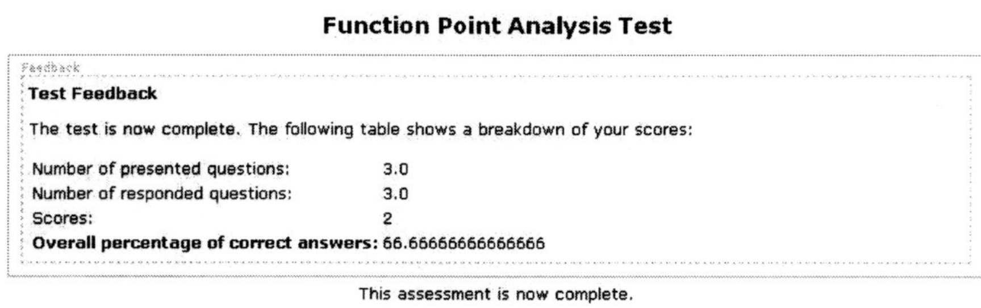

USING COMBA FOR AUTOMATING QUESTION GENERATION

The COMBA model provides a number of affordances for interoperability in e-learning and assessment. In this section, we present the use of the model in automating question generation. Using question templates, the model enables an assessment item to be formulated directly from a competence structure. The templates are designed to have the structure of a well-constructed question, parameterized by the elements of a competency: capability, subject matter content, and other elements such as the situation. This enables the generation of a series of questions from the same template.

Question generation begins from the competency of interest, shown in Table 3, where we illustrate the process using a competency from a course on introductory statistics. Figure 8 represents these competencies graphically. The Competence Navigator module (shown in Figure 4) retrieves subject matter as shown in Table 4 and capability nodes relevant to the competency as shown in Table 5, using the competency ontological database. Figure 9 represents the subject matter for Table 4 graphically. Figure 10 represents the capability for Table 5graphically.

Given the subject matter and capability of the competency, the related topics in the subject matter category tables and the related capabilities in the 'capability ordering' table are retrieved as well. For example, if the requested subject matter is 'confidence intervals', the retrieved related subject matter includes 'critical z score' and 'standard error'. For the 'calculate' capability, 'explain' and 'define' capabilities were retrieved as well.

Table 3. Examples of confidence interval competency

Competence	Subject Matter	Capability	Context	Sub-competence
Students can calculate the confidence interval	Concept: the confidence interval	Apply: Calculate	Nine hundred high school first year students were randomly selected for a national survey. Among survey participants, the mean grade-point average was 2.7, and the population standard deviation was 0.4. Assume a 95% confidence level.	Students can calculate the standard error
Students can calculate the standard error	Concept: the standard error	Apply: Calculate	(same as above)	–

Figure 8. Conceptual model of competency examples

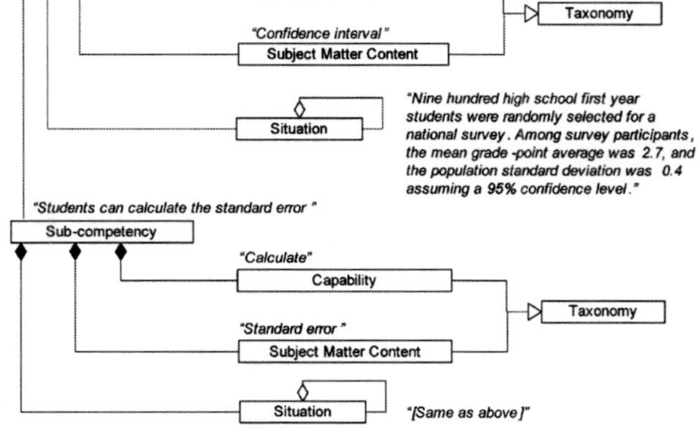

Table 4. Example of subject matter content based on the confidence interval topic

Subject Matter	Related subject matter
Concept: the confidence interval	Concept: the standard error Fact: the alpha value Fact: the critical z score
Concept: the standard error	Fact: the measure of dispersion Fact: the sample size

Table 5. Example of capabilities based on the confidence interval topic

Capability	Supporting capability
Apply: Calculate	Comprehend: Explain
Comprehend: Explain	Know: Define

Figure 9. Related topics of the confidence interval topic mapped to the underlying subject matter content ontology

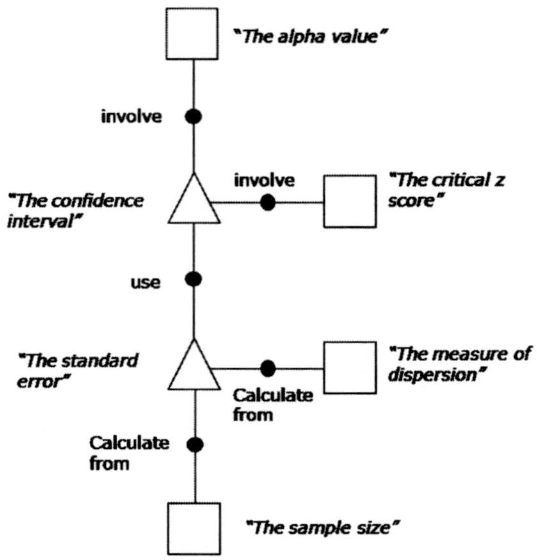

Figure 10. Related capabilities mapped to the capability ontology

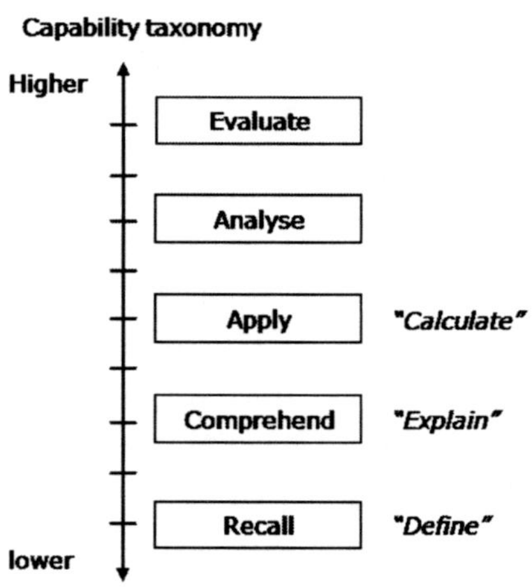

Question templates, illustrated in Table 6 are used to assemble the retrieved subject matter and capability into questions. For example, given the 'confidence interval' competency, the related subject matter and capabilities are inserted into the question templates to yield questions such as 'Explain the importance of the critical z score', as shown in Table 7.

Experimental Validation of Generated Questions

An experiment (Sitthisak, Gilbert and Davis, 2008) was carried out to demonstrate the acceptability of the generated questions from the competency model, exploring the following two questions:

- Were the generated questions semantically intelligible to an expert teacher of the domain?
- How did students rate the generated questions on the criteria of clarity, usefulness, challenge, and match with the learning outcomes?

The results indicate that the generated questions were of acceptable value to the students. The student ratings showed the specific questions were more useful, and the generic questions were more challenging. This finding suggests that the students did not enjoy answering with definitions and explanations, and preferred questions with a variety of specific situations.

The finding that both types of question did not differ significantly on the two other criteria, their clarity and whether they matched the intended learning outcomes, is not unexpected. Interestingly, there was no effect of capability type, and no interaction between capability type (define, explain, and calculate) and question type (specific and generic), indicating that ratings were similar for the three capability types. The diversity of capability type was limited. This point suggests the need to explore creative use of question styles and capability vocabularies in order to examine interaction effects between capability type and question type. Questions such as "what", "who", "when", "where", "why", may provide for new

Table 6. Illustrative question template summaries

Template No.	Question Template
1	[Capability] + [Subject Matter]
2	[Capability] + [Related Subject Matter]
3	[Capability] + [Subject Matter] + [Situation]
4	[Capability] + [Related Subject Matter] + [Situation]

Table 7. Sample generated questions

Competence	Generated question	Question Templates No.
Students can calculate the confidence interval	Calculate the confidence interval Calculate the critical z score Calculate the alpha value	1
	Calculate the standard error Calculate the measure of dispersion Calculate the sample size	2
	Explain the importance of the confidence interval Explain the importance of the critical z score Explain the importance of the alpha value	1
	Explain the importance of the standard error Explain the importance of the measure of dispersion Explain the importance of the sample size	2

question styles which include more challenging capability vocabulary such as 'analyse' and 'synthesis'.

USING COMBA FOR GENERATING ADAPTIVE QUESTION SEQUENCES

In this section, we present the use of the model in automating question sequence generation. A competency hierarchy supports a variety of adaptive rules to adjust questions to the students' capability and to the nature of their knowledge. Many methods of traversing the competency hierarchy may be applied, involving different starting points and algorithms. These methods may lead to interesting issues which should be considered in adapting to the students' particular talents, strengths, weakness, and own learning preferences. Within a test constructed according to the IMS QTI specification, the sequencing and adaptive logic are expressed in branching rules. For example, an adaptive sequence may provide a question at a slightly higher level if a student succeeds or a question at a lower level otherwise.

Figure 11 presents an example QTI question file for adaptive assessment using QTI constructs which may be incorporated into a test. Portions labelled A and C show the student items called "question1" and "question2" respectively. The portion labelled B illustrates a branching rule. If the student succeeds on question1, the test jumps forward to the end of the test (shown as branchRule target= 'EXIT_TEST') or goes to "question2" in the section labelled C otherwise. The 'QTItools' validator graph[2] of this adaptive sequencing is shown in Figure 12.

Experimental Validation of Generated Question Sequences

An experiment was designed to validate a sequence of questions, generated using the COMBA model. The particular sequence experienced by a student was dependent upon the student's answers, and so was adaptive. If the student succeeded on a question, where possible the next question was

Figure 11. Example of QTI branching rules in XML format

```
  <?xml version="1.0" encoding="UTF-8" ?>
- <assessmentTest xmlns="http://www.imsglobal.org/xsd/imsqti_v2p1"
    xmlns:xsi="http://www.w3.org/2001/XMLSchema-instance"
    xsi:schemaLocation="http://www.imsglobal.org/xsd/imsqti_v2p1
    http://www.imsglobal.org/xsd/imsqti_v2p1.xsd" identifier="TEST"
    title="Function Point Analysis Test">
  - <testPart identifier="part1" navigationMode="linear" submissionMode="individual">
      <itemSessionControl showFeedback="true" />
    - <assessmentSection identifier="sectionquestion1" title="Section question:"
        visible="true">
        <assessmentItemRef identifier="question1" href="question1.xml" />
      </assessmentSection>
    - <assessmentSection identifier="sectionRquestion1" title="SectionR question1"
        visible="true">
      - <branchRule target="EXIT_TEST">
        - <equal toleranceMode="exact">
            <variable identifier="question1.SCORE" />
            <baseValue baseType="float">1.0</baseValue>
          </equal>
        </branchRule>
      </assessmentSection>
    - <assessmentSection identifier="sectionquestion2" title="Section question:"
        visible="true">
        <assessmentItemRef identifier="question2" href="question2.xml" />
      </assessmentSection>
    </testPart>
  + <outcomeProcessing>
  + <testFeedback access="atEnd" showHide="hide"
      outcomeIdentifier="outcomeIdentifier" identifier="outcomeValue" title="Test
      Feedback">
  </assessmentTest>
```

Figure 12. Flow of questions in a QTI test

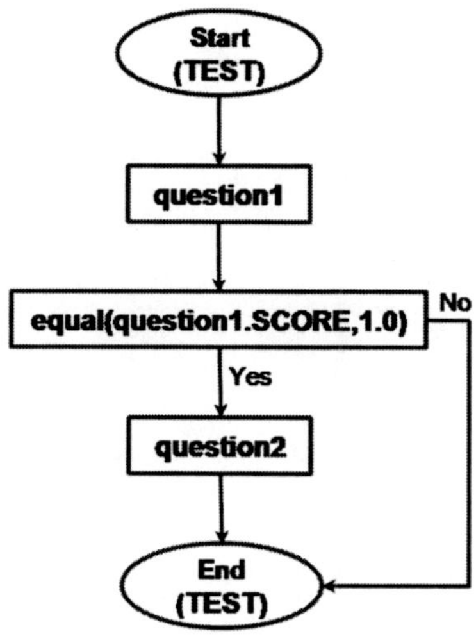

a question at the same capability level and at a higher subject matter level than the previous question. If the student failed the question, the system presented where possible an easier question. This was a question at the same capability level and at the lower subject matter level than the previous question. Questions started from the highest subject matter level and the highest ability level, and the sequence stopped when the student answered a question correctly.

The experiment focused on the opinions of students on the efficiency and effectiveness of the adaptive sequence. The questions explored student ratings of the sequencing, on the criteria of fairly assessing their knowledge (TestAssessKw), helping them to understand how a given learning outcome separated into "learning outcome components" (DecomposeLO), helping them to separate a given learning outcome into "topics" (DecomposeTopic), adapting to their level of knowledge (AdaptQuestion), being useful for self-assessment (UsefulForSelfAssessment), identifying their lack of knowledge (IdentLO), and providing appropriately difficult questions (ShowDifficultQ).

Competencies were collected from the INFO2007 Systems Analysis and Design course at the University of Southampton. The topic of the course instantiated in the model involved function point analysis and associated issues including: adjusted function points, unadjusted function points, complexity adjustment, the formula for complexity adjustment, degrees of influence, the formula for unadjusted function points, and calculating function points from an ER Diagram.

The participants were voluntary 2nd year undergraduate students. Instruction sheets were distributed to all attending students at the end of a lecture, and asked the students to rate the generated questions against the criteria on a 4-point forced-choice Likert scale ('Strongly disagree', 'Disagree', 'Agree', 'Strongly agree', coded as 1, 2, 3, and 4 respectively) that best described their opinion.

Results and Discussion

The study gathered data from 19 students. A one-sample t test was used to test differences between the observed sample means and an expected sample mean of 2.5, being mid-way between agreeing and disagreeing on the measurement scale. As can be seen in Table 8, the mean rating was significantly higher than 2.5 for 9 of the 12 measured variables.

The students did not think that the test particularly assessed their knowledge on average. It is not clear why they thought this; one hypothesis is that the 'stopping rule' (at the first correct answer) did not give them confidence that their knowledge had indeed been thoroughly tested.

Interestingly, the students agreed that the adaptive sequence helped them to understand how a given learning outcome separated into "learning outcome components", but they did not agree that it helped them to separate a given learning outcome into "topics". Whilst a learning outcome component involves capability and subject matter, a topic involves only subject matter. This suggests that the generated questions helped the students to understand the decomposition of capability, but

Table 8. t Test

Measured Variables	Test Value = 2.5			
	t	df	Sig. (2-tailed)	Mean Difference
TestAssessKw	–0.224	18	0.826	–0.026
AdaptQuestion	5.786	18	0.000	0.711
UsefulforSelfAssessment	2.471	18	0.024	0.500
IdentLO	3.269	18	0.004	0.500
DecomposeLO	3.139	18	0.006	0.447
DecomposeTopic	0.907	18	0.376	0.184
ShowDifficultQ	8.367	18	0.000	0.605

were not particularly helpful in understanding the decomposition of topics.

The results of the remaining t-tests were straightforward: the students agreed that their question sequence was well adapted, was useful for self-assessment, helped identify their lack of knowledge, and provided appropriately difficult questions.

Broadly speaking, this experiment and the earlier one (reported in Sitthisak, Gilbert and Davis (2008)) show that the questions and the adaptive test sequences were acceptable to students, and hence that the COMBA model is capable of generating good assessments.

OTHER COMBA AFFORDANCES

Generating Various Methods for Adaptive Question Sequences

A competency hierarchy could support a variety of adaptive rules to adjust questions to the student's capability and to the nature of their knowledge. Many methods of traversing the competency tree could be applied, involving different starting points and algorithms. These methods may lead to interesting issues which should be considered in adapting to the learners' particular talents, strengths, weakness, and own learning preferences.

The key contribution is supporting a variety of ways of developing adaptive sequences. Future work could focus on methods for generating adaptive question sequences and considered their pedagogical value. For example, it is possible that students might have differing abilities in quite similar content areas. In this case, learners may not achieve an appropriate level of their capability and content. New adaptive question sequences could employ different traversal algorithms. If the learner failed a question, the system could present the next question at a lower capability level and at the same subject matter level; or at the same capability level and at the nearest subject matter level to the previous question. The pedagogical value of a particular method would need further investigation for successful learning and teaching, but having such varieties of methods could provide fruitful areas of exploration.

Generating Distracters

One of the main challenges in generating multiple choice questions is the provision of plausible distractors. A competency hierarchy allows the selection of plausible distractors derived from nodes semantically close to the 'correct' node. This would make each distractor 'similar' to the correct answer, as well as consistent with the key concepts of the question. The methodology of selecting distractors can be based on pedagogical methods by adapting the traversal algorithm. For example, distractors can be selected from unfamiliar words in context, requiring students to make inferences.

Each generated distractor may be constructed from nodes of the tree which can represent plausible and common errors that a student might make. When generated from the competency tree that reflects levels of content taxonomy and capability taxonomy, these distractors could enable the development of a rich breadth and depth of multiple choice questions.

Using such questions, teachers can contribute to an analysis of a student's pattern of misunderstanding in the subject area. The competency tree allows the question to have distractors spread across all level of a content taxonomy, thereby helping the teacher identify the student's possible misunderstanding.

Generating Feedback for Formative Assessment

One of main challenges in formative assessment is creating effective feedback. Effective feedback needs to provide information that helps students self-correct and helps clarify what good performance is. A competency hierarchy would allow the generation of feedback derived from nodes semantically close to 'incorrect' nodes in the hierarchy. Feedback could relate to the concepts of the incorrect answer, as well as maintain consistency with the key concept of the question. Generating such feedback could be based on pedagogically-driven processes by adapting the traversal algorithm. For example, feedback could be generated from the closest node to the incorrect node, requiring the student to reflect on their answers.

Future work could focus on automatically generating feedback which reflects levels of content taxonomy and capability taxonomy, encouraging interaction and dialogue around learning, and supporting self-assessment and reflection in learning. This would allow students to take more control of their learning and develop their reflective skills.

CONTRIBUTIONS OF INTEROPERABLE ASSESSMENT

The key contributions of this study are that the use of the competency model, ontologies, and IMS QTI overcomes limitations in interoperability, portability, and reusability. The model supports consistency checking, assessing differences in knowledge levels, and comparing achievement in related domains, which were essentially impractical previously. Using ontologies and Semantic Web technologies addresses many of the problems of extending and combining structured content in different formats from different schemas. The IMS QTI specification facilitates the sharing of questions and tests, enabling investment in the development of common tools such as Web-based authoring and delivery applications.

The model has the great advantage of providing individuals with a more detailed identification of students' performance. The model could be used in conjunction with a development discussion between the student and teacher to provide focus on the key aspects to be developed for each competency. It is suggested that information about competencies should form the basis of pedagogically-informed metadata which would be relevant to any description of content or process in a learning and teaching situation.

The ontology supports connecting resources available in a domain and representing knowledge states of students. Ontological metadata expresses terms defined formally and unambiguously. This metadata provides information for e-assessment in supporting integration and reuse these data with other systems, and for adaptive assessment systems in supporting the adaptation of their behaviour and structure according to the personal needs and ability of each student. Structuring knowledge in a new domain by using ontological conceptualization should allow faster build of new systems.

Automatic generation of questions using parameterised templates could exploit a competency ontology model which provides an alternative to the lengthy and demanding activity of developing effective questions. In assisting developers to produce questions in a fast and expedient manner without compromising quality, the use of automatic generation of questions saves both time and production costs. This methodology is general and can be extended to other fields.

REFERENCES

W3C. (2004). *OWL Web Ontology Language (OWL).* Retrieved October 27, 2007, from http://www.w3.org/TR/owl-ref/

W3C. (2005). *SKOS Core Guide.* Retrieved November 4, 2008, from http://www.w3.org/TR/swbp-skos-core-guide/

Anderson, T., & Whitelock, D. (2004). The Educational Semantic Web: Visioning and Practicing the Future of Education. *Journal of Interactive Media in Education, 1*(9).

Antoniou, G., & Harmelen, F. v. (2004). *A Semantic Web Primer*. Cambridge, MA: The MIT Press.

Aroyo, L., & Dicheva, D. (2001). AIMS: Learning and Teching Support for WWW-based Education. *International Journal of Continuing Engineering Education and Lifelong Learning, 1*(1/2), 152–164. doi:10.1504/IJCEELL.2001.000390

Aroyo, L., & Dicheva, D. (2004). The New Challenges for E-learning: The Educational Semantic Web. *Education Technology and Society, 7*(4), 59–69.

Bacon, R. A. (2003). Assessing the use of a new QTI assessment tool within Physics. In *the 7th CAA Conference,* Loughborough University, Loughborough, UK.

Berners-Lee, T., Hendler, J., & Lassila, O. (2001). The Semantic Web. *Scientific American, 284*, 34–43. doi:10.1038/scientificamerican0501-34

Bloom, B. S., & Krathwohl, D. R. (1956). *Taxonomy of educational objectives: The classification of educational goals by a committee of college and university examiners*. New York: Longman.

Boticario, J. G., & Santos, O. C. (2007). An Open IMS-based user modelling approach for developing adaptive learning management systems. *Journal of Interactive Media in Education*, 2.

Brusilovsky, P., & Sosnovsky, S. (2005). Individualized exercises for self-assessment of programming knowledge: An evaluation of QuizPACK. [JERIC]. *Educational Resources in Computing, 5*(3), 6. doi:10.1145/1163405.1163411

Cristea, P., & Tuduce, R. (2005). Automatic Generation of Exercises for Self-testing in Adaptive E-learning Systems: Exercises on AC Circuits. In *3rd Workshop on Adaptive and Adaptable Educational Hypermedia at the AIED '05 conference, (A3EH).*

Dancik, G., & Kumar, A. (2003). A Tutor for Counter-Controlled Loop Concepts and Its Evaluation. *Frontiers in Education Conference*, USA.

Dicheva, D., Dichev, C., & Wang, D. (2005). Visualizing Topic Maps for e-Learning. In *Proceedings of IEEE International Conference on Advanced Learning Technologies*, Kaohsiung, Taiwan.

Dicheva, D., Sosnovsky, S., Gavrilova, T., & Brusilovsky, P. (2005). Ontological Web Portal for Educational Ontologies. In *Proceedings of Artificial Intelligence in Education*, Amsterdam, Netherlands.

Draganidis, F., & Mentzas, G. (2006). Competency based management: a review of systems and approaches. *Information Management & Computer Security, 14*(1), 51–64. doi:10.1108/09685220610648373

Effective Practice with e-Learning. (2004). JISC. Retrieved June 24, 2009 from www.jisc.ac.uk/elearning

Field, A. (2005). *Discovering Statistics Using SPSS* (p. 779). London: SAGE Publications Ltd.

Gagne, R. (1970). November 4, 2000. "Robert Gagne's Nine Steps of Instruction." Retrieved January 3, 2006, 2006, from http://www.nwlink.com/~donclark/hrd/learning/development.html

Gennari, J. H., Musen, M. A., Fergerson, R. W., Grosso, W. E., Crubézy, M., & Eriksson, H. (2003). The Evolution of Protégé: An Environment for Knowledge-Based Systems Development. *International Journal of Human-Computer Studies*, *58*(1), 89–123. doi:10.1016/S1071-5819(02)00127-1

Harzallah, M., Berio, G. & Vernadat, F. (2006). Analysis and Modeling of Individual Competencies: Toward Better Management of Human Resources. *IEEE Transactions on Systems, Man and Cybernetics: Part A: System and Humans, 36*(1).

Hersh, W. R., Bhupatiraju, R. T., Greene, P. S., Smothers, V., & Cohen, C. (2006). Adopting e-learning standards in health care: competency-based learning in the medical informatics domain. *AMIA... Annual Symposium Proceedings / AMIA Symposium. AMIA Symposium*, *2006*, 334–338.

IMS QTI. (2006). *IMS Question and Test Interoperability Overview*. Retrieved November 4, 2008, from http://www.imsglobal.org/question/qtiv2p1pd2/imsqti_oviewv2p1pd2.html

Jovanovic, J., Gasevic, D., & Devedzic, V. (2006). Ontology-Based Automatic Annotation of Learning Content. *Semantic Web and Information Systems*, *2*(2), 91–119.

Kalfoglou, Y. (2001). *Exploring Ontologies 1: Fundamentals* (pp. 863–887). Washington, DC: World Scientific Publishing.

Karampiperis, P., Sampson, D., & Fytros, D. (2006). Lifelong Competence Development: Towards a Common Metadata Model for Competencies Description - The Case Study of Europass Language Passport. In *Proceedings of the 6th IEEE International Conference on Advanced Learning Technologies*, Kerkrade, The Netherlands.

Lazarinis, F., Green, S., & Pearson, E. (2009). Measuring the conformance of hypermedia assessment tools to QTI. *International Journal of Innovation and Learning*, *6*(2), 127–146. doi:10.1504/IJIL.2009.022809

Merrill, M. D. (1999). *Instructional Transaction Theory (ITT): Instructional Design Based on Knowledge Objects*. Retrieved January 3, 2009, from http://www.indiana.edu/~idtheory/chapter_17_summary.html

Myller, N. (2007). Automatic Generation of Prediction Questions during Program Visualization. [ENTCS]. *Electronic Notes in Theoretical Computer Science*, *178*, 43–49. doi:10.1016/j.entcs.2007.01.034

Pacurar, G., Trigang, P., & Alupoaie, S. (2005). A QTI editor integrated into the netUniversite web portal using IMS LD. *Journal of Interactive Media in Education*, 9.

Schmidt, A., & Kunzmann, C. (2006). []. Berlin: Springer.]. *Lecture Notes in Computer Science*, *4278*, 1078–1087. doi:10.1007/11915072_10

Sitthisak, O., Gilbert, L., & Davis, H. C. (2008). An evaluation of pedagogically informed parameterised questions for self assessment. *Learning, Media and Technology*, *33*(3), 235–248. doi:10.1080/17439880802324210

Sitthisak, O., Gilbert, L., Davis, H. C., & Gobbi, M. (2007). Adapting health care competencies to a formal competency model. In *the ICALT*, Niigata, Japan.

Stojanovic, L., Staab, S., & Studer, R. (2001). eLearning based on the Semantic Web. In *World Conference on the WWW and Internet*, Orlando, Florida, USA, (pp. 23-27).

Trichet, F., & Leclère, M. (2003). *A Framework for Building Competency-Based Systems Dedicated to Human Resource Management (LNCS 2871)*. Berlin: Springer.

Wills, G., Davis, H., Chennupati, S., Gilbert, L., Howard, Y., Jam, E.-R., et al. (2006). R2Q2: Rendering and Reponses Processing for QTIv2 Question Types. In *10th International CAA Conference*, Loughborough University, UK.

Woukeu, A., Wills, G., Conole, G., Carr, L., Kampa, S., & Hall, W. (2003). Ontological Hypermedia in Education: A framework for building web-based educational portals. *World Conference on Educational Multimedia, Hypermedia & Telecommunications*, Honolulu, Hawaii, USA.

KEY TERMS AND DEFINITIONS

A Competency: Involves a capability associated with subject matter content, a proficiency level, evidence, any required tools, and definition of the situation which contextualises the competency.

Attitude: The way in which a learner exhibits their knowledge and skill, perhaps categorised using a version of Krathwohl's taxonomy (Krathwohl and Anderson, 2002).

Capability: Behaviour that can be observed, based on a domain taxonomy of learning such as Bloom's (Bloom and Krathwohl, 1956), Gagné's Nine Areas of Skill (Gagne, 1970), or Merrill's Cognitive Domain (Merrill, 1999).

IMS Question and Test Interoperability (QTI) Specification: A specification to describe a data model for representing question and test data, as well as their corresponding result reports.

Proficiency Level: Indicates the level of proficiency that learners should or do possess of a particular competency.

Subject Matter Content: The subject domain of what the learner can do by the end of course.

The Competency Evidence: Substantiates the existence, sufficiency, or level of the competency, and might include test results, reports, evaluation, certificates, or licenses.

ENDNOTES

1. http://playr.qtitools.org/playr/
2. http://validatr.qtitools.org/

Chapter 3
Implementing Distributed Architecture of Online Assessment Tools Based on IMS QTI ver.2

Vladimir Tomberg
Tallinn University, Estonia

Mart Laanpere
Tallinn University, Estonia

ABSTRACT

This chapter addresses the decade of development and state of the art in the domain of online testing of learning outcomes. The authors focus on the changes and implementation scenarios of the latest versions of IMS QTI – the major technical specification that has became the de facto standard in the domain. Standardization of content and applications used for online testing is partly driven by the paradigm shifts that are taking place in the fields of pedagogy and Web technology. This chapter pays a special attention to the increasing trend of using Web 2.0 technology in education, especially Mash-up Personal Learning Environments and their impact on the architectural decisions while developing the next generation online assessment tools.

INTRODUCTION

The need for reusing computer-based quizzes has been driving the efforts of technical standardization of questions and tests. Although the last decade has seen rapid development in this field, there are no official standards. The closest thing to the standard is IMS QTI, the leading technical specification that defines the meta-language for describing computer-based tests, types and components of test questions, assessment-related roles and workflows etc. The second version of QTI was released in 2006 and it has become a basis for developing modular, distributed online assessment systems. We will provide below two cases that illustrate this approach.

Although Web 2.0 is not a new technology, it has changed the patterns of using the Web. The new situation has been created by the appearance

DOI: 10.4018/978-1-61692-789-9.ch003

of the social software – now anyone is an author, publisher and designer of one's own virtual activity space. It has an impact on online education, where monolithic and highly institutionalized Learning Management Systems are loosing the territory to Mash-up Personal Learning Environments (Wild 2008). Finding the fit between QTI-based online assessment tools and the new landscape of E-learning 2.0 is becoming a challenge that should be addressed by the future research initiatives.

EVOLUTION TOWARDS STANDARDS

During second half of the '90s, Computer Based Training (CBT) systems became the mainstream software applications in the educational domain. These systems had been developed in universities but were very quickly demanded also by business organizations because of their high efficiency. In such systems a process of assessment is often implemented by means of automated testing. There are much of examples of well-known systems, especially in the domain of vocational education. Cisco Networking Academy, Microsoft certification courses, almost any CBT system have included this useful functionality. With the lapse of time this functionality has been distinguished also as independent type of application, and received a name Computer Based Assessment (CBA). CBA functionalities were easily included in CBT systems (and later in Learning Management System, LMS) or to be released as a separate software package. From the beginning of the 21st century teachers widely began to prepare and use online tests for assessments of learning outcomes in universities and schools.

However, first compatibility problems have appeared quite soon. Preparation of test questions is handwork that is difficult to automate. Instructors wanted to have an ability to re-use questions and test repeatedly and transfer them into different software systems. In the middle nineties the two main obstacles have been revealed, those were incompatibilities between different systems at file level and at questions' level. CBT systems of that period of time usually were commercial software with proprietary closed source code. Their architecture was monolithic and tightly coupled (Wills et al., 2009, p. 354). Such system usually saved data in some kind of self-developed database or in own file format. An internal structure of such files was proprietary, closed. Because of that it was impossible to open and use a file with questions from one software application in another.

The paper-and-pencil tests became popular during the twentieth century. A multitude of testing methodologies was developed in different research areas, especially in psychology and sociology. They were used separately without need of any interoperability. Therefore there was not a common point of view for that, which types of questions can be used in computer assessment. The absence of standards in area of testing has leading to appearance a multitude of incompatible systems, each of them with own set of supported question types. Of course there was nothing doing with data interchange; in such circumstances there was logical an appearance in 1999 a technical specification for Question and Test Interoperability (QTI).

The QTI describes a data model for the representation of question and test data and reporting of testing results. The specification enables the exchange of questions, tests, and results data between authoring tools, item banks, test constructional tools, learning systems, and assessment delivery systems (IMS 2006). This standard has been developed by Instructional Management Systems Global Learning Consortium (IMS GLC or IMS).

Main purposes of IMS at that time were (QTI White Paper, 2000):

- *Ensuring reusability, portability, platform independence, and longevity for both consumers and developers*. This means that files with question data can be exchanged between systems, that incompatible in other aspects. Once prepared data can be reused over and over again, from one set of questions can be constructed different tests.

- *Stimulating production of high quality testing content by making it open to big communities of designers*. Openness of learning content always leads to quality's rising, because good content always in demand; bad content disappears under process of natural selection.
- *Simplification of aspects of product analysis and design by using ready-to-use templates in the form of data models implemented in XML*. Specifications not only propose file format, but also give to developers architectural issues. Modularity gives possibilities to reuse not only testing data but also reuse software modules in different LMS suites.
- *Increasing of the overall market size as products specialize, diversify, and find new audiences*. Simplification of producing and subsequent reduction in cost attract to education market more and more players. By using wide choice of open source software even small institution can participate now in mainstream of education processes.

The first version of QTI specification 0.5 was published by IMS consortium in 1999 and then released as version 1.0 in 2000. At first, the specification seemed to be challenging for developers and was subjected to criticism from different sources. Many of researchers have testing of data model at the basis of sporadically developed software that declared their QTI conformance. Main tested feature was possibility of exporting QTI XML by one system and importing received data to another system. E.g. Whittington (2001, p. 15) wrote, 'The transfer process at present is crude and requires a large degree of expert knowledge and intuition to succeed'. That research was done with three very early packages of QTI and showed insufficient results of interoperability. In 2003 Gorissen tested six ready QTI compliant products but got the same, not very optimistic result, 'None of the applications tested in this quickscan have support for all options of the QTI specification'.

IMS continued work on QTI specification by releasing version 1.1, then 1.2., and 1.2.1, where some shortcomings were fixed and some new functionality was added. Version 1.2.1 reached of maximum popularity among developers; almost each new testing system since its appearing has declared a conformance to this version. Unfortunately the QTI compatibility study repeated by Gorissen in 2006 shows that overall picture has been not very changed again for that time.

In spite of unsuccessful attempts of researchers to achieve full interoperability, in beginning of twenty-first century the market of testing software is still valuing the compliance with QTI specification. The use of online testing systems in education has been increasing; the need for interoperability between proprietary testing systems became obvious more than before. The second version of QTI specification was released in 2005. Although the specification is already quite mature and has been available for several years, it has not gained such high popularity among developers of testing systems as version 1.2 had. By 2005, significant share of available online testing systems had already implemented compliance with QTI version 1.2. Switching to the new version of QTI specification would have required investments, but did not promise quick return of the money. Another factor that influenced to slow spreading of IMS QTI version 2.0 was absence of test-level functionality in specification, as only question items were described there. Although in 2006 version 2.1 was released where the test-level standardization was addressed, the new version did not achieve the same level of popularity among developers during its first three years. For example, the widely distributed and popular test authoring tool *Respondus* still supports only old QTI 1.2 version that means it can import and export tests only in IMS QTI 1 compliant XML format.

Nevertheless, support to IMS QTI version 2.1 slowly begins to appear in different software applications. Transition to the second version of the specifications is especially important because it offers not only a new way of coding of testing content but also proposes new approaches to the architecture and implementation of testing systems in general. Below we try to outline briefly the differences of first (1.2) and second (2.1) version of IMS QTI and some problems related to both of them. It is very important because both version have no compatibility between them, have architectural differences and also different levels of interoperability. Designers and developers of LMS should be aware of these differences because they affect the system's performance.

Developers of IMS QTI 1 specification tried to make visualizations of questions as versatile as possible. They have pre-defined a set of all possible types of questions and methods of visualization, allowing to apply any visualization method to any question type. Obviously, their goal was to give freedom to developers of questions and tests. Actually it led only to excessive confusion. The software developers had to keep a track of possible visualization methods for each type of a question. It was not a simple task, because combining all possible types of questions with all possible visualization methods results with 180 probable variations and the majority of these are never used in practice: e.g. a true/false answer rendered as a slider, or a fill-in-the-blanks rendered using a drop-down list (Wilson, 2005). The authors of the second version of QTI have changed their approach. Instead of allowing all possible combinations of question types and visualizations they have suggested to use only widespread accepted 20 basic item types. Visualization methods can be issued in different ways: 9 question types can be handled with pure HTML, 11 question types require extra or embedded interface (Strobbe, 2006).

Each type of interaction assumes now only one native method of visualization that, although, can be extended by certain standardized ways. Big advantage of QTI version 2 is possibility of usage of XHTML syntax inside of XML document, and also possibility of extension of QTI XML by means of other XML syntaxes. Specification QTI 1.2 instead of that allows only using a clean QTI XML syntax; this circumstance imposed limitations to representation of questions for developers. Use of XML extensions allows simplifying tasks related to visualization of complex question types. XHTML allows an embedding tables and structured preformatted texts into body of questions. By means of CSS and images a question now can contain rich formatted content easily. Using of other XML syntaxes allows expanding functionalities of QTI; for example using of MathML XML syntax gives possibility to introduce mathematical formulas in tests.

What are the main issues related to implementation of QTI-conformant systems? In the first place it is compatibility of testing systems with QTI XML syntax. It sounds as unexpected for mentioning systems that specially designed for QTI support, but it is a fact — most of them cannot process QTI XML right. Sometimes systems generate such code that cannot be even validated, in other words — not valid XML code. There is nothing to do further with XML code if it is not valid; software just cannot process it and should return an error. From 2003 (Gorissen, P.) there several studies was conducted by different researchers. The aim of them was a finding out how careful was implemented a functionality of QTI XML importing and exporting to/from testing systems or LMS tools that have declared these features. In most cases the results showed a very low level of compliance. Today we can understand reasons for such poor results; in the first place they were related to above mentioned shortcomings of first generation QTI specifications. Presented in first version a huge amount of combinations of question-types and methods of visualization is very hard to implement in practice. There was not developed any software that can process all imaginable types of QTI 1.2 questions, just because some of these types are absurd. This was a reason for parallel appearance of simplified specification's version — *QTI lite*, a subset of full version, where only some kind of multiple choice question type was used. In second version of specification amount of such problems is considerably decreased. Though, some question-types of second version remain to be complex for implementation in some aspects of visualization today also.

Because of realignment of modern education to online the assessments more frequently are based at web technologies. Most widespread and simple way for supplying a web page with some behavior is *JavaScript*. With help of such language syntax it is possible to program both visual representation of test content and its behavior. Though, some from 11 complex types of QTI 2 interactions such as HotSpot, Slider and Associate it is not very simple to implement in JavaScript. To workaround these shortcomings developers sometimes used such tools as *Flash*.

Another problem of interoperability that mentioned Lazarinis (2009) is an absence of methodic for evaluation of software compatibility to QTI specifications. In consideration of that many testing software only have partial conformance to specifications there is necessity to declare someway this conformance level exist. Especially it is matter for users who need to move their tests from one system to another. Lazarinis suggest a simple scale for grading software by dividing a level of QTI supporting to four parts — *No support*, *Basic support*, *Medium support* and *Advanced support*. For each level the precise criterions are described, what system can, or cannot to do. Using such scale developers can now declare level of QTI conformance more precisely; that in turn should to simplify to users and system integrators a choice of right system for them.

One could claim that the IMS QTI standard already reached its "state of the art", 'The newest version of QTI is rich in options and flexible enough to cover the needs of different test creators' (Lazarinis et al., n.d.). The last Public Draft version 2.1 had no update at current moment three years and recently there were no reasons to assume that it should be changed in close future. On the other hand, this unfinished second version of the specification exists simultaneously with an incompatible version 1.2.1 which has a status of a Final Specification. A paradox consist that two popular versions of one standard intended for interoperability are not compatible one with another; this lead opposite to interoperability decrease. Because of mentioned above difference in methods of visualization and question types it is impossible to create fully compatible questions set for both versions. Only certain types can be converted from one version to another. Thereby, testing systems that used different QTI versions are found in parallel worlds that practically cannot intersect. Only one possibility to repair a situation is transition of all system to most advanced today version 2.1 as soon as possible.

QTI 2.1 AND MODULAR APPROACH

One of the most deserved of attention difference of second version QTI specification is a proposal of modular architecture. The modular approach gives to developers an extraordinary flexibility. Reference to modularization was sounded already as far as first specification was released, 'Interoperability encourages modularization, diversification and specialization among LMS's, and enables them to move beyond cumbersome vertical product designs' ("QTI White Paper, " 2000). However because of novelty of QTI at the time of first version the more attention was paid to XML compatibility level. At the time when second version arrived the attention became to shift more to modularity. To understand what means

Figure 1. Use case of QTI 2 specifications. (© 2006, IMS Global Learning Consortium, Inc.)

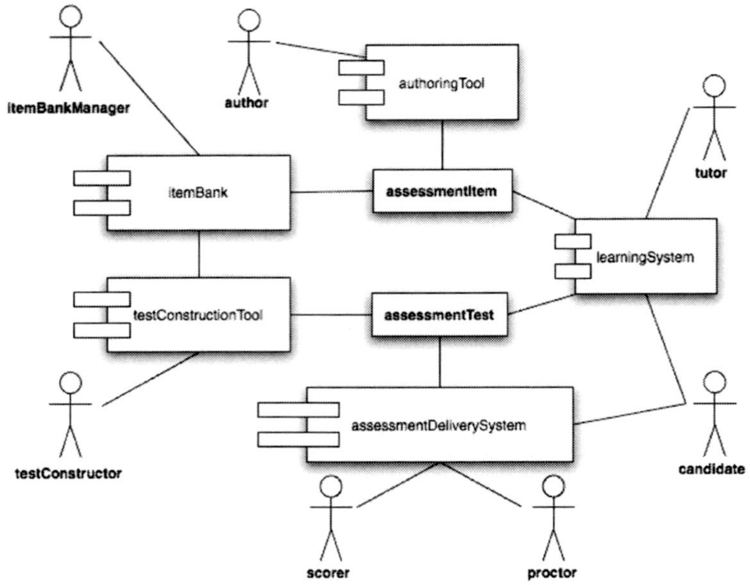

the modular approach for QTI, we need to refer a use case. The following figure 1 represents a use case proposed by QTI 2 specifications.

As illustrated on the Figure 1, the QTI 2.1 as it predecessor proposes a use of QTI XML syntax for description of two main units of information interchange. The first minimal unit of information is the XML element 'Assessment Item' (assessmentItem) that is actually a question. The 'Assessment Test' (assessmentTest) represents a consisting of questions compound test that supplied with certain rules of processing for it. These two basic units serve all information interchanges between independent application modules. Process of test data exchange typically begins from creation of questions. Authors use for this purpose an Authoring Tool module. QTI specification itself not describes in detail a functionality of any module that shown in the figure; an obligatory precondition only is ability of the application to process QTI XML at the input or/and output interface. After creation in the Authoring Tool a question should be saved somewhere. It can be saved sometimes directly to the Authoring Tool, if software provides such functionality. But for purpose of data reusing a separate Item Bank in use case is provided. Item Bank is a repository that provides storage services, indexing and searching facilities and also ensures a direct or network access both to individual questions and compound tests. Next module in given use case is a Test Construction Tool which can have an access to questions from the Item Bank. The Test Constructor (testConstructor) can get questions out from the Item Bank; he chooses the suitable questions, builds a new test (assesmentTest) from them and stores the ready test in the Item Bank. Next the tests can be delivered on demand to the Assessment Delivery System for immediate testing of Candidates. In addition, as figure shows, questions or tests can be exchanged with some Learning System also. Any specific requirements to Learning System are not described in details by QTI: Learning Systems can have different levels of functionality; they can also provide functions of any of above mentioned modules.

The described use case proposes a modular architecture for developers and allows creating efficient solutions on the basis of QTI 2 specifications. Such approach delivers from the difficulty of integrating all functionalities into one uniform LMS system. The software modules in QTI suite can to be exist separately, independently one from another. There are many different scenarios of exchange testing content among independent modules can be used because of possibility of use different forms of relationships — one-to-one, one-to-many and many-to-many. For example, one Authoring System to many Item Banks, or one Item Bank to many Assessment Delivery System and so on. Under certain conditions these modules can be produced by different independent developers too. They only should to pay attention to using of uniform protocols for exchange of QTI XML data. Such flexibility allows an implementing of many complex use cases of interaction between systems from different suppliers.

The Future Perspectives of QTI

Prediction of the future of QTI is a difficult task for current moment, mainly because of ambiguity of IMS's current position about QTI development. From one side many researchers considered already that QTI 2.1 at current time reached its perfection. In March 2009 IMS surprised the QTI community, when removed from their Web site all information about version 2.1 of QTI specification. IMS motivated this activity in such way that they have not received from community enough feedback related to QTI 2.1. That means IMS not sure about usefulness of this version and supposed to stop its wide spreading. Second illustration of unexpected relationship to QTI 2.1 was fact that only version 1.2 was included in Common Cartridge, which was released in 2008. IMS says that they consider version 2.1 as raw and untested. First version QTI according to IMS is operable enough and because of this it still can be recommended for developing. After these actions of IMS the community of developers not stayed to be indifferent to perspectives of QTI 2.1; there was active discussion in QTI mailing list. Both developers and researchers have reacted to IMS because present scope of questions equally important as for market as for educational science. The basic idea that was sounded by community consisted that second version of QTI specifications is so good, so there is not object for criticism at all. On the contrary to IMS claim, the business de-facto actively uses QTI 2 compliant software in practice to satisfy own needs; business sometimes not advertizes this fact by private reasons, so it left be hidden from IMS. A pressure from community to IMS was so high and reasonable that IMS finally was forced to return specifications back to web-site. IMS also has added caution that given version is incomplete and 'This specification will be superseded by an updated release based on the input of the project group participants'. Probably it is clear that in close time can be expected an appearance of version 2.2 or 2.X. It seems this fact will occur after extensive testing of specification, as it was announced by IMS.

As other perspectives of IMS QTI it is possible to expect a progress of integrating into questions external resources from Web 2.0 sources. While integrating of images and audio-video data today is not difficult for implementation, some developers discover new original opportunities. For example Bouzo et al. (2007) propose to use Web maps from Google Maps in QTI assessment. Apparently these steps are first in future activities of mash-ups of new forms of media in QTI tests.

Implementing QTI 2

During 'QTI 1 epoch' majority of QTI-supporting systems were proprietary. Partially it was in this way because an implementing of system with rich functionality and at the same time in conformity with standards was expensive task and possible for the commercial organizations only. A separate module is much easier for implementing than multilevel compound system. Especially this is true for second versions of QTI specifications. Mentioned above issue of simplification of visualization in version 2 together with modularity issue has allowing to developers produce first universal module for test visualization. A word 'universal' means that it is became possible to visualize almost any type of question that was hard to do for first version of QTI because of great number of possible question types. An *R2Q2* project of University of Southampton was first where such functionality was implemented; in framework of R2Q2 was developed standalone module of visualization of QTI 2 questions (http://www.r2q2.ecs.soton.ac.uk/). This software can receive QTI XML code at input, visualize 16 types of questions (actually in QTI 2.1 there are 20 types of questions) and interact with the user by browser interface. After user interaction R2Q2 returns a feedback to user and can send results of test to LMS.

Great importance of R2Q2 was that this software solved most important and difficult task of QTI specification — visualization of questions in web environment. This has giving to many developers chance to implement own system without concern about visualization problems. Thereby development of QTI 2 has become a catalyst for small projects aiming at producing separate testing system modules, which are based on Service-Oriented Architecture and are released under an open-source license. Possibility of using modules made by third party developers simplifies implementation of new software products.

One of the advantages of modular architecture is enhanced interoperability. Separately developed software module can be once validated for conformance to standards and then many times be integrated into different testing suites. Development of such systems should be simplified because there is no necessity for developers to concern about testing their new software for standards' conformance; all necessary testing already has been done before. Such validated and controlled modules can be used by designers of learning software as construction set; a smart manipulating with these modules can propose in future developing appearance of very flexible systems. A higher level of interoperability means that instead of spending resources for testing for QTI XML conformance level, now developers only need to test the applications for possibility to work together with other software.

So far as one program could read QTI XML code generated by other program the process of exchange can be automated. Generally, two alternative methods for this exchange are possible: through file exchange or Web services. The first way more often is used directly by people, for example by Administrators of LMS or Item Bank Managers. Instructors can save their tests into QTI XML format for backup purpose or for manual importing to another system. They export a set of questions from one system, save them to some storage in repository and then load them into another testing system or LMS. For successful communications between multiplatform software in heterogeneous environment like web here is a necessity of common interfaces exist. Wills et al. (2009) says, 'One way to promote QTIv2 is through a reference implementation of the standard written within the service-oriented paradigm'. Network interactions more suits for automated exchange, the machines today use *Web services* as the common interface. Web services are well-known, standardized enterprise set of protocols and languages that can be implemented at any modern software platform. Web services use several industry standards — *WSDL* for description of service, *UDDI* for informing a peer and the process of publication, and *SOAP* for an exchange of messages. Main features of Web services are modularity, interoperability and extensibility. Due *Service Oriented Architecture* (*SOA*) applications can be developed and deployed incrementally; new features can be added to applications after the system is deployed (Wills et al. 2006). Because Web services are based fundamentally on XML, theirs support of QTI XML is native. Today web services more and frequent used for exchange the questions and tests between independent QTI-compatible applications modules.

Above mentioned QTI visualization tool R2Q2 is using Web services as an interface for input and output data. The best known online testing software suite that uses Web services today is *QTItools*; it is developed in School of Electronics and Computer Science, University of Southampton in the framework of Assessment Delivery Engine for QTIv2 Questions Project (*ASDEL*) and funded by Joint Information Systems Committee (*JISC*). QTItools suite consist of certain software modules such as *JQTI* — a core software library for the development of QTI applications, R2Q2 (today R2Q2 already is obsolete, developers recommend to use a its replacement QTIEngine), *playr* — a tool for playing QTI assessments, *validatr* — a tool for validating QTI assessments, *assessr* — a Web application for scheduling assessments and collating results and *constructr* — a web-application for constructing simple assessments from items from an item-bank. All these software modules use Web services for communication process. Indeed these modules can be implemented into new suites separately or together, as it was done with item banking software Minibix (Cambridge) and with item authoring software AQuR@te (Kingston). 'Together the three projects tell an end-to-end story: AQuR@te will allow people to author items, which are stored in MiniBix. A test will incorporate these items and will be played through ASDEL, which we have called the Playr.' (Wills et al., 2009, p. 363) The schema of integration of modules is illustrated at figure 2. As it can be seen, external communications occurs by means of Web services. In spite of that figure clearly outlines only external Web services, internal communications inside of QTITools suite also occurred by means of Web services.

The authors of this chapter contributed to development of another set of open-source QTI tools in the Centre for Educational Technology, Tallinn University. Figure 3 demonstrates a structure of our modular system that has been mapped to IMS QTI use case. QTI ver. 2.1 compliant assessment suite consists of three original open-source software modules that have been developed in Centre for the Educational Technology (CET), with the assistance of the authors of this chapter. These modules are:

- Waramu (see http://trac.htk.tlu.ee/waramu): a QTI-compliant Learning Object Repository or, in QTI terms, an

Figure 2. Integration of the ASDEL, AQuRate Item Authoring (Kingston) and MiniBix, Item Banking (Cambridge).

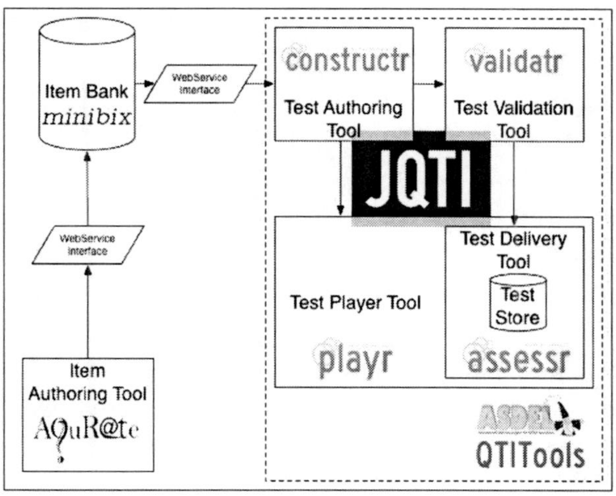

Figure 3. Online assessment tools developed in Tallinn University.

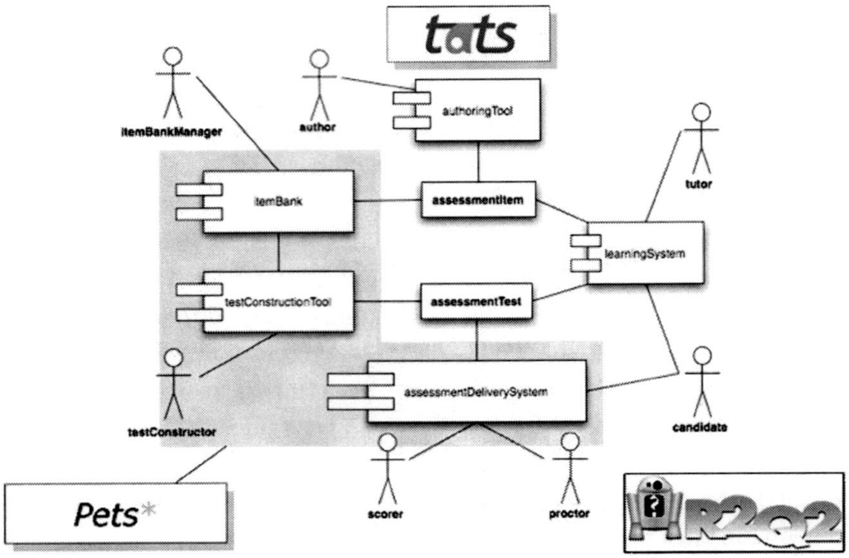

Item Bank that allows storing, annotating, searching and retrieving questions and tests. Waramu can be used for storage of other learning objects like text documents and presentations, it has SQI and FIRE interfaces for communicating with other Web applications and also with the European Federation of Learning Object Repositories (LRE). Waramu is built with Java and it runs on Glassfish server.

- TATS (see http://trac.htk.tlu.ee/modules/wiki/Tats): an authoring tool for creating and sharing questions and tests. Questions developed with TATS can be saved in the local database of TATS or exported to another Web application, e.g. to a Learning Object Repository. TATS has also a "light" test delivery functionality using e-mail invitations with unique URLs for personalized test instances – students do not need user accounts in TATS in order to access and fill in the test. TATS is a Zope product, programmed in Python and using the native database of Zope: ZODB.
- PETS (see http://trac.htk.tlu.ee/modules/wiki/Pets): an assessment delivery system that includes also functions of test construction tool. PETS can import test questions from files or repositories (like Waramu) and compile tests from them. In PETS environment, as in assessment delivery system, groups and users can be registered. Then tests can be assigned both for groups and personal users by several different ways; these ways provide different scenarios both for formative and summative assessments. PETS can be used as secure environment by supporting strong authentication.

Each of described software modules is able to exchange the QTI-compliant content with others using Web services.

Both TATS and PETS are using R2Q2 for rendering the test questions, but some adaptations were made to original R2Q2 code. The visualization clients for three question types (slider, pairs, hotspots) were rewritten in Ajax to replace too "heavy" Java applets. This modification supports additional stability of visualization engine and speeds up the use of the system, because there is no need to download Java code during execution of assessment.

All above mentioned software modules have been released under BSD license; they can be installed and used separately but also can be without problems integrated into one suite.

MASH-UP PERSONAL LEARNING ENVIRONMENTS AND QTI

The use of Web 2.0 technologies enhances and simplifies a resource sharing. Ease of use of mash-up technologies and availability of various free social networking environments has created a boom of Personal Learning Environments (Attwell, 2007). Innovative educators try to adapt to learning process any new feature from Web 2.0 with hope that all of these can be useful. Assessment is important part of learning and teaching process, in turn a testing is one of the important and popular ways to evaluate the competency level of learners. Therefore it is natural that in educational domain interest to implementing of tests in Web 2.0 environment is growing.

Here are some obvious and hidden problems are presented. Some of them have a pedagogical aspect. Attwell (2007) by describing Personal Learning Environments in Web 2.0 says that 'QTI…specification for assessment has inhibited the introduction of peer assessment and focused assessment on what people know, rather than on assessment for learning'. This viewpoint is shared by increasing number of educators today, having a significant impact on further development of online testing. Another problem has more ideological nature: there is a conflict between openness of Web 2.0 and formal nature of assessment. The ideology of Web 2.0 implies use of open resources; certain open services like Flickr or Delicious are proposed for storage of them, authors place their content at Web under Creative Commons license more and more frequent. Elliott (2008) says, 'Openness not only refers to the use of open source software for many Web 2.0 services but also the philosophy of the free sharing of information and resources among users, making it relatively straight-forward to capture and share information or resources'. Openness of Web 2.0 is suitable for not-automated and ill-structured methods of formative assessment, allowing the learner to 'obtain meaningful feedback, and see how well they are progressing in their understanding of the material' (Wills et al., 2009, p. 354). However summative assessment usually requires a special confidentiality and security issues, especially if it should to officially confirm a level of competencies of evaluated person. In this case, openness can have negative impact to learning process. So, what potential solutions exist today for implementation of structured, protected summative assessment in such democratic environment as Web 2.0 on the assumption of security and integrity of assessment process?

Common Cartridge

One answer can be found in latest development of IMS — a specification called *Common Cartridge* (CC), which was released in 2008. Common Cartridge was designed for online support of different forms of teaching and learning. The term Common Cartridge means 'A content packaging profile agreed between content providers and LMS providers, offering a common format for the distribution of both open and access protected content. The profile harnesses Content Packaging, LOM Metadata, and QTI' (IMS CC, 2008). The features of this new specification are very flexible and can satisfy a want of different learning scenarios.

An internal structure of Common Cartridge is outlined at Figure 4. Common Cartridge correspond a package that is packed according to improved version of IMS Content Packaging specification; inside of it the directories and files

Figure 4. Common Cartridge package interchange file. (© 2008, IMS Global Learning Consortium, Inc.)

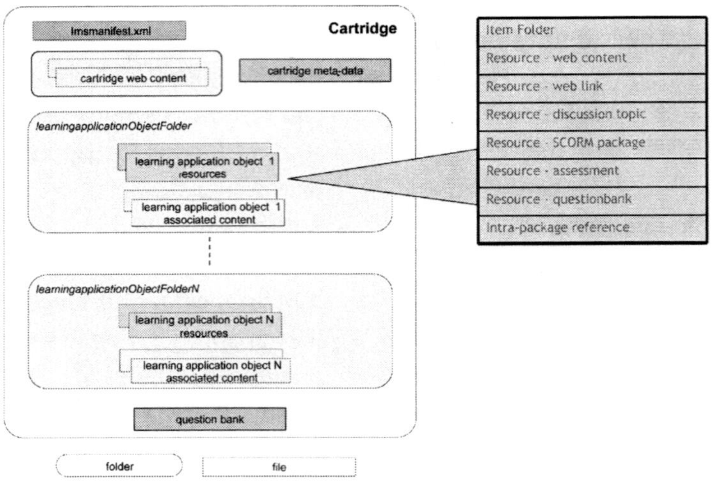

accompanied by metadata are stored. Such package can be imported from course provider into LMS and later executed by learner in the scope of course. Results of the course executing can be stored in the LMS Gradebook.

Content of package is described in manifest file. In each directory the associated files-components are stored; they are described by means of LOM metadata. Each type of static or dynamic learning content like HTML, PDF, pictures or video files and even assessment tests QTI XML files can be a component of Common Cartridge package.

The user's authorization can be applied both to whole cartridge, and also to separate components of cartridge. For example course materials can be accessed by users freely, but for summative assessment users should authorize themselves. Authorization occurs by means of Web services that described in another specification — *IMS Common Cartridge Authorization Web Service*. This specification was released in one time with Common Cartridge as escort specification. Specification recommends implementing of authorization as a SOAP service between the LMS and cartridge publisher. Specification describes a process of authorization by the following, 'When a user attempts to access or import protected cartridge content, the LMS will prompt the user for an access code. The LMS will then use the service to send to the cartridge publisher the access code and some unique identifier for the cartridge being accessed. The cartridge publisher's system will attempt to validate the provided information. If the information is valid the service will respond with a success code and optionally an expiration date after which access by the user should once again require contacting the service. If the information is deemed invalid, an error code is returned along with a human-readable description of why the credentials were rejected' (IMS CC Authorization, 2008).

The fundamental difference Common Cartridge from preceding standards that describe delivery of learning resources to learner is a possibility to serve not only internal data but also links to external resources. This means that inside of Common Cartridge can be not only resource itself, but link to URL that contain necessary resource. It allows a launching and exchanging data with external applications, thereby the same resources can be reused many times in different courses or teaching activities. The resources oneself are distributed and can be placed in any network location; these circumstances are well in line with Web 2.0 concepts; it allows to easily integrate into learning/teaching activity materials from traditional Web 2.0 sources such as Flickr, YouTube, Slideshare etc.. Such issue gives an opportunity to independent update of content with always having most recent version of resource without necessity to edit that inside of cartridge.

Another novel characteristic of Common Cartridge is appearance of dynamic learning objects. Some types of learning objects that require additional processing and interpretation now called in specification *Learning Application Objects*. This name means that in role of resource now can be web content, web link, discussion topic, assessment or intra-package reference. For example it can be IMS QTI assessment or question bank for use in formative assessments. Architecture of Common Cartridge allows execute Learning Application Objects both, as in LMS settings, as independent application by means of special web player or web-widgets. Most interesting at the current moment are example of integration of player in *Facebook* and case of encapsulation of QTI widget in *Blogspot*. These and some more examples of implementing of Common Cartridge can be learned at website of *Icodeon Common Cartridge Platform* Blog from Icodeon Ltd., Cambridge; there many of working examples of different Common Cartridge use are purposed (http://ccplatform.blogspot.com/). Undoubtedly that are just first steps, in close future we can expect from developers wide support of Common Cartridge at other web platforms also.

From point of view of assessment tests' using the Common Cartridge proposes new options for QTI 1.2 integration into education content. By using such established, standardized formats as IMS QTI, IMS Content Package, IMS Authorization Web Service and other, the Common Cartridge allows implementing high level of interoperability between Web applications. In above examined use case the QTI XML has used as standalone package; thus it was a logical assumption that testing process was considered as separate type of activity, because it had no relation with any other activities. By help of Common Cartridge the QTI now can be easily integrated into any logical sequence of activities which can be considered as united instance of learning process.

Shortcomings of Common Cartridge

So what are facilities of Common Cartridge use for LMS that not support specification yet? What scenarios for knowledge building in a distributed and collaborative environment are supported by Common Cartridge?

Essentially Common Cartridge is a kind of a centralized resource. It is obvious that each Common Cartridge profile should be prepared first and only then can be used. Such issue is very suitable for traditional forms of learning, but it is hard to implement it for some scenarios. Today's knowledge building is dynamic process. Referring to Web 2.0 McLoughlin (2007) says that students are able to use collective intelligence to create "the wisdom of crowds", connecting within rich and dynamic social environments, rather than studying in solitude through impersonal learning management systems designed by administrators. In modern education described issue is a main trend driven by constructivism as a theory of teaching. In case of Common Cartridge today we not have dedicated tools for group works, with the exception of integrated discussion forum initiation, which still remains to be complex for applying in practice. A beforehand prepared cartridge after loading it into LMS cannot be dynamically changed, or we have no scenarios and instrumentality for implementation of such changes. Conception about that, how Common Cartridge profile can be used in collaborative knowledge building is not clearly described for now too.

Complexity of practical implementation is another shortcoming of Common Cartridge from the point of Web 2.0 perspective. This technology cannot be realized at empty place, it demands an appropriate infrastructure. Common Cartridge provides examples of integration with 3-rd party platforms, but integration process can be somewhat difficult for small education institution. At the current time members of Common Cartridge Alliance mostly are such large-scale organizations as Microsoft, IBM and so on. It seems too hard to implement such full-scale set of technologies for small universities and educational foundations without well-developed ICT infrastructure. Therefore a wide spreading of issues which based at specification will be estimated only after appearance of sufficient amount of tools for work with Common Cartridge. It is desirable that these tools will be under open source license because this type of licensing always stimulates developers for activities.

From QTI point of view the Common Cartridge is not a step forward because it uses an old version of specification, 1.2.1. In spite of all advantages of second version, IMS has made such decision because version 2.1 still have status Public Draft; it seems that IMS wants to include in Common Cartridge only released versions of specifications. They decided to do that, even in spite of that version 1.2.1 is hard for practical implementation for reasons mentioned above. Compatibility Problems of QTI 1.2.1 that was repeatedly studied and described now become apparent in early demos of Common Cartridge; in most cases there are errors of QTI XML handler and these errors are well predictable. IMS plans a transition of Common Cartridge to second QTI version in close future, but exact date is unknown for time of this writing. It is possible to predict only that it should probably be very close to time of QTI 2.X release.

What possibilities exist if someone wants to implement solution based on QTI 2.1 that means without use of Common Cartridge? In spite of its novelty Common Cartridge is based at many well known and widely adapted standards. For first can be specified IEEE Learning Object Model, ISO 15836:2003 — Dublin Core Metadata Element Set, IEEE 1484.12.1-2002 — Learning Object Metadata, IEEE 1484.12.3-2005—LOM Schema binding (loose binding). In addition specifications IMS Content Packaging v1.2 and IMS Question & Test Interoperability v1.2.1 are supported too. Only one exclusive new standard is used Common Cartridge — IMS Authorization Web Service v1.0. All standards included to Common Cartridge can be coupled together and interact themselves outside of Common Cartridge scope. Thereby there is no a barriers for developers to implement a software compatible with second version of QTI specifications. QTI 2.1 can be temporarily used in conjunction with other standards outside of Common Cartridge, in spite of Draft status of QTI 2.1.

SOLUTIONS AND RECOMMENDATIONS

Let's examine an example of use case, relating to QTI 2.1 standard, which intended for issue of secure summative assessment in Web 2.0 environment. In our case we originate from assumption that LMS is a lightweight system of services which is a broker between browser of learner and learning objects. Each learning object presents some kind of Web 2.0 content, e.g. text file, image, video or some other learning activity. Any traditional Web 2.0 applications like teacher's blog at Wordpress, Flickr, Google maps, YouTube, Delicious and so on, can be a supplier of content. A fundamental task of lightweight LMS is aggregation of learning content according to set of rules that outgoing from certain kind of learning sequence; typically this sequence is a course. The aim is an implementation of learning course that will finish by summative testing assessment. In most case such task can be fulfilled by way of using existing Web services and standards without using of additional package like Common Cartridge. Indeed, a great number of freeware that is being distributed with an open source license allows an implementation in web environment required aggregation of content

Figure 5. Delivery of QTI 2.1 content for summative assessment from WEB 2.0 sources

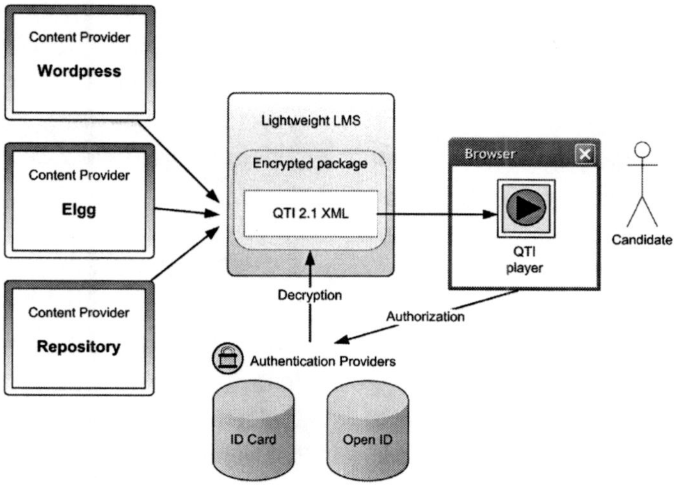

from different Web 2.0 sources. Thanks to big choice of such software this aggregation can take place dynamically; LMS can link together blogs of instructors and portfolios of learners in one environment, allowing collaborative knowledge building. One of that is difficult to implement for current moment is summative assessment. But using a complex tool as Common Cartridge based one only for testing purpose seems unreasonable. Instead of that is possible to use for example QTI 2.1 data with the Common Cartridge Authorization Web Service and Content Packaging technology. A conceptual schema can be viewed at Figure 5.

By the means of Web services, a packaged and for security purpose encrypted QTI content can be on demand transferred from its storage to learner browser for execution. Some kind of web player should be provided for playing QTI content in web-browser. Because Common Cartridge Authorization Web Service not defines exactly encryption methods, it is possible to use different ones, subject to goals of assessment. For less formal authorization that is required only for tracking of learners' results, Open-ID authorization can be used. Such authorization cannot provide highest level of authentication but will allow assessments' results correlating with specific learner ID without expensive cost. In case of more formal assessment, e.g. for vocational attestation, it is possible to use identification of user at a governmental level. It can be varied against country; e.g. it can be authentication by means of ID card that used very defensive encryption algorithms. ID cards already actively used at government level for authentication and authorization, for example in Estonia they used for user access to personal or financial data and also since recently for electronic elections. Authentication authorities propose own services for governmental and business organizations. Such strict level of security allows accurate confirmation of authenticity of users and can be used for confirmation of result of assessment validating hereby user's competencies.

Proposed issue uses QTI version 2.1 compatible tests and can be developed today bypassing a Common Cartridge restrictions to QTI. However when IMS will update QTI an Common Cartridge specifications there will be nothing that can prevent developers from using these solutions together.

While developing new Web applications for online testing purposes, it is highly recommended to use today the most recent version of QTI XML. At first, because of minimizing of potential problems, related to visualization of questions. Second reason for this is a modular architecture and presence of many software implementations under open source license. In case of designing own web-based QTI-compliant solution the Web services also recommended to be accounted as extensible and standard communication issue. Using of Web services allows including modules from different developers into integrated suites, as well as saves time and money on development and testing.

Counter-evidence against second version of QTI is the Public Draft status and today absence of this version in Common Cartridge specification. Though in this paper many reasons are described, temporariness of these limitations is obvious. Using different workarounds today is possible to implement many software solutions compatible with last version of QTI, applications that evidently will be compatible with future developments.

FUTURE RESEARCH DIRECTIONS

Online assessment and especially automated testing is still a lively field of research that will drive the future development of related standards and specifications. We can envisage some new research directions emerging in this field, partly inspired by paradigm shifts in the educational science and computing, partly by appearance of new technological platforms. For instance, increasing interest towards collaborative knowledge building among educational researchers will probably result with the future extensions of the QTI specification so that is can support peer assessment and team-based testing. Recently introduced interactive features of streaming video solutions will open new horizons for simulation-based testing in line with authentic assessment paradigm. Increasing use of mobile devices in education will create the need for researching possibilities of augmented reality in testing. With the simultaneous use of various online and mobile platforms, federated identity management and trust management continue to be in focus of developers of online assessment systems. And finally, advances in speech synthesis allow creating new assessment solutions that will be able to analyze free text and speech. All of that hopefully makes online assessment a dynamic and interesting field for new researchers.

CONCLUSION

This chapter addressed the evolution of standards in the domain of online assessment, with the special focus on the development of modular testing solutions that can be used in distributed learning environments. Although the current version of IMS QTI specification provides some support for building testing systems with Service-Oriented Architecture, the future developments will lead to more flexible and interoperable online assessment tools.

ACKNOWLEDGMENT

This study was funded by ESF grant 7663 and MER targeted research 0130159s08.

REFERENCES

A QTI White Paper from IMS. (2000). IMS Global Learning Consortium, Inc. Retrieved July 4, 2009, from http://www.imsglobal.org/question/whitepaper.pdf

Attwell, G. (2007, January). Personal Learning Environments - the future of eLearning? *eLearning Papers, 2*(1). Retrieved from http://www.elearningpapers.eu/

Bouzo, J., Batlle, H., & Blat, J. (2007) *Enhancing IMS QTI assessment with web maps*, TENCompetence Open Workshop on Current Research on IMS Learning Design and Lifelong Competence Development Infrastructures. Retrieved July 04, 2009, http://dspace.ou.nl/handle/1820/1114

Elliott, B. (2008). *Assessment 2.0: modernising assessment in the age of Web 2.0*. Retrieved July 9, 2009, from http://www.scribd.com/doc/461041/Assessment-20

Gorissen, P. (2003) *Quickscan QTI, Usability study of QTI for De Digitale Universiteit*. De Digitale Universiteit, the Netherlands. Retrieved July, 10, 2008, from http://www.gorissen.info/Pierre/QTI/Quickscan_QTI_UK.pdf [09/24/2005]

Gorissen, P. (2006). *Quickscan QTI 2006*. De Digitale Universiteit, the Netherlands. Retrieved July, 10, 2008, from http://www.gorissen.info/Pierre/QTI/Quickscan_QTI_2006.pdf

IMS Global Learning Consortium. *IMS Common Cartridge Profile Date: 1 October 2008. Version 1.0 Final Specification*. (2008). Retrieved July 10, 2009, from http://www.imsglobal.org/cc/ccv1p0/imscc_profilev1p0.html#0_pgfId-1754146

IMS Global Learning Consortium, Inc. (2006) *IMS Question and Test Interoperability Version 2.1 Public Draft Specification*. Retrieved July 01, 2009, from http://www.imsglobal.org/question/qtiv2p1pd2/imsqti_oviewv2p1pd2.html

Lazarinis, F., Green, S., & Pearson, E. (2009). Measuring the conformance of hypermedia assessment tools to QTI. *International Journal of Innovation and Learning*, *6*(2), 127–146. doi:10.1504/IJIL.2009.022809

Lazarinis, F., Green, S., & Pearson, E. (n.d.). *Engineering an interoperable multimedia assessment authoring and run-time environment conforming to IMS QTI*.

Strobbe, C. (2006). *Accessibility Issues in Two Specifications for E-Learning Tests: IMS QTI 1.2 and IMS QTI 2.0* (. *LNCS*, *4061*, 544.

Whittington, D. (2001). *Testing IMS in real context implementing IMS specifications implications and best practice*. University of Glasgow. Retrieved April 26, 2009, from http://www.gla.ac.uk/rcc/projects/tircs/tircs-full.pdf

Wild, F., Mödritscher, F., & Sigurdarson, S. (2008). Designing for change: Mash-up personal learning environments. *eLearning Papers, 9*. Retrieved July 29, 2009 from http://www.elearningeuropa.info/files/media/media15972.pdf

Wills, G., Davis, H., Chennupati, S., Gilbert, L., Howard, Y., Jam, E. R., et al. (2006). R2Q2: rendering and reponses processing for QTIv2 question types. In *Proceedings of 10th International CAA Conference,* Loughborough University, UK.

Wills, G., Davis, H., Gilbert, L., Hare, J., Howard, Y., Jeyes, S., et al. (2009). Delivery of QTIv2 question types. *Assessment & Evaluation in Higher Education*, *34*(3), 353–366. doi:10.1080/02602930802071106

Wilson, S. (2005, January 21). *In Praise of Simpler Standards?* Scott's Workblog, Retrieved April 22, 2009, from http://zope.cetis.ac.uk/members/scott/entries/20050121223821

ADDITIONAL READING

R2Q2: Rendering and Response processing services for QTIv2 questions. (n.d.). Retrieved July 29, 2009, from http://www.r2q2.ecs.soton.ac.uk/.

ASDEL. *Assessment Delivery Engine for QTIv2 Questions*. (n.d.). Retrieved July 29, 2009, from http://www.asdel.ecs.soton.ac.uk/.

Assessment: JISC. (n.d.). Retrieved July 29, 2009, from http://www.jisc.ac.uk/whatwedo/topics/assessment.aspx.

FREMA. *e-learning framework reference model for assessment.* (n.d.). Retrieved July 29, 2009, from http://www.frema.ecs.soton.ac.uk/.

IMS Global Learning Consortium. *IMS Common Cartridge Specification.* (n.d.). Retrieved July 29, 2009, from http://www.imsglobal.org/cc/index.html.

IMS Global Learning Consortium. *IMS Question & Test Interoperability Specification.* (n.d.).

Retrieved July 29, 2009, from http://www.imsglobal.org/question/.

Interoperability: JISC. (n.d.). Retrieved July 29, 2009, from http://www.jisc.ac.uk/whatwedo/topics/interoperability.aspx.

PmWiki - Main - QTItalk (new version, under development). (n.d.). Retrieved July 29, 2009, from http://qtitalkdev.nbwebsites.com/pmwiki.php?n=Main.HomePage.

QTI related files. (n.d.). Retrieved July 29, 2009, from http://www.gorissen.info/Pierre/QTI/.

QTI Training Guide - CETISwiki. (n.d.). Retrieved July 29, 2009, from http://wiki.cetis.ac.uk/QTI_Training_Guide.

QTItools. (n.d.). Retrieved July 29, 2009, from http://qtitools.org/.

Respondus: Assessment Tools for Learning Systems. (n.d.). Retrieved July 29, 2009, from http://www.respondus.com/.

XQuestion - Surveys. *Assessment, Tests from XML*. (n.d.). Retrieved July 29, 2009, from http://www.xquestion.com/.

Chapter 4
QTI:
A Failed E-Learning Standard?

Michael Piotrowski
ZHAW Zurich University of Applied Sciences, Switzerland

ABSTRACT

The creation of good tests is time-consuming and expensive. Tests should therefore be reusable to ensure sustainability and to preserve investments and intellectual assets. This requires a standard, platform-neutral, vendor-independent interchange file format for tests. IMS Question and Test Interoperability (QTI) aims to be this standard. Almost a decade after the publication of the first version of QTI, even the interchange of simple multiple-choice tests between different systems remains problematic. In this chapter, the author present a critical analysis of QTI. His conclusion is that QTI has failed to provide interoperability of questions and tests due to serious problems in its design.

INTRODUCTION

Assessment has always played an important role in education. Most, if not all, types of formal education use some sort of assessment, typically including a final exam to earn a grade, a degree, a license, or some other form of qualification.

Today, assessment is no longer restricted to grading at the end of a course (*summative assessment*), but it has been recognized that assessment is also useful for continuous monitoring and guiding of the learning progress (*formative assessment*), without being necessarily used for grading purposes (Boud, 2000).

DOI: 10.4018/978-1-61692-789-9.ch004

Formative assessment, including *self-assessment*, can play a vital role in motivating students since it provides them with a way to judge their own competency level and allows them to track their progress. It also enables students to identify areas where more work is required, and to thereby remain motivated to improve further. Of course, this requires that students receive feedback as quickly as possible (Gibbs and Simpson, 2004).

Formative assessment also provides timely feedback for instructors, both with respect to the effectiveness of the course and the performance of the students; it thus helps to identify points that might need clarification.

For both groups, instructors and students, frequent testing is preferable. Case and Swanson (2002) argue that infrequent testing makes each exam a "major event," with students investing much effort into preparation—they may even stop attending class to prepare for the exam. They also note that, with infrequent tests, students may be unable to determine whether they are studying the right material and with sufficient depth. Case and Swanson therefore conclude:

Though it may be more time consuming for faculty, frequent testing reduces the importance of each individual exam and helps students to better gauge their progress. (Case and Swanson, 2002, p. 116)

Assessment is always a time-consuming activity for instructors, especially if large numbers of students are to be assessed or, if assessment is frequent. This has motivated the development of technical devices to support assessment, starting with relatively simple mechanical devices in the 1920s and evolving to today's *computer-aided assessment (CAA)* or *e-assessment*.

E-assessment is one of the fundamental elements of e-learning: Piotrowski (2009, p. 41) defines six activities that characterize e-learning platforms: *Creation*, *organization*, *delivery*, *communication*, *collaboration*, and *assessment*. Furthermore, of these six activities, assessment is the only one that is specifically educational; the other five activities are generic and not specific to e-learning.

The most frequently used form of e-assessment are multiple-choice tests. Multiple-choice tests have a number of practical advantages; in particular, scoring can be automated. This makes them especially attractive in e-learning settings, as it allows to make assessment available "anyplace, anytime."

Creating high-quality multiple-choice tests, however, is challenging, especially if they are to assess higher-order cognitive levels, such as application, analysis, synthesis, and evaluation in the traditional taxonomy of Bloom (1956). Or, as Astin (1991) puts it:

While multiple-choice tests are indeed inexpensive to score, they are extremely expensive to construct: item writing is a highly refined and time-consuming art, especially if one expects to develop good items that are relatively unambiguous. (Astin, 1991, p. 148)

Ensuring the reusability, longevity, and platform independence of tests can mitigate the high costs of creation and can help preserve investments and intellectual assets when hardware and software change, thus ensuring sustainability. This requires a standard, platform-neutral, vendor-independent interchange file format for multiple-choice tests.

A number of standards aiming to promote interoperability and sustainability of e-learning content and e-assessment have emerged over the last decade. *IMS Question and Test Interoperability* (IMS QTI) is the best-known standard for tests. Most e-learning platforms today claim to support "IMS QTI." And this is where the problems start: Which version of IMS QTI is supported? Does "support" refer to authoring or delivery of tests, or to import and export? IMS QTI has become one of the buzzwords in the e-learning community.

In this chapter, we will question this authority. When trying to implement IMS QTI or when trying to use IMS QTI for authoring tests, the user will soon become aware of serious shortcomings, which are a result of fundamental design flaws. Effectively IMS QTI is not able to fulfill the promise of interoperability. We therefore argue that IMS QTI is a failed e-learning standard. Unfortunately, this means that there currently exists no standard for interchanging tests. As a contribution to the development of a practicable future standard, we outline requirements an interchange format has to meet to actually play the role IMS QTI claims to play.

In the rest of this chapter, we will first describe several formats used for authoring tests. We will then outline the requirements for interchange formats before introducing the IMS QTI specification. Based on our experiences with implementing IMS QTI we will describe some exemplary problems and review the standard critically.

BACKGROUND

In this section, we will outline the main principles and terms on which this chapter is based. We will also describe the project in which we used IMS QTI, and from which our experience and critique is derived.

E-Assessment

Besides relieving instructors, e-assessment in particular offers new possibilities and new opportunities. For example, frequent formative tests are only practicable using e-assessment, and e-assessment also makes new or unorthodox assessment methods feasible, such as peer assessment.

Automated assessment started with a basic, now ubiquitous, assessment methodology, namely objective selected-response tests. While there are many possible types of selected-response tests, the best-known type is probably the classic *multiple-choice test*, which is particularly well-suited for automated assessment. We therefore concentrate on multiple-choice tests in this chapter; however, the issues discussed in this chapter also apply to other types of electronic tests. Furthermore we consider only the interchange of test definitions, not the gathering of "secondary metadata" (i.e., the annotation of tests with usage data) or the exchange of test results.

Conceptually, e-assessment involves a number of systems and various actors, i.e., persons. In reality, systems and persons often function in several roles; for example, at universities, instructors also act as test authors, proctors, and scorers. In this chapter we use the term *delivery platform* to refer to a system (or part of a system) which is primarily used for making tests available to candidates and which allows candidates to take the tests, whereas *authoring system* refers to a system (or part of a system) primarily designed for creating tests. The QTI specification (IMS GLC, 2005, Overview, p. 5) contains more detailed model, but we do not need it for the discussion in this chapter.

In the preceding section, we have already mentioned some motivations for an interchange format for tests. Besides the interchange of finished tests, an additional issue is the production, or *authoring*, of tests. File formats are not only necessary for storing quizzes and for interchanging questions and tests between different delivery platforms, but they also provide a way to interface a test delivery platform to a test authoring system. Many e-learning platforms with assessment facilities—such as the commercial systems Blackboard, Clix, and Desire2Learn, or the open-source platforms ILIAS, Moodle, OLAT, and Sakai—provide support for both authoring and delivery of tests. However, the authoring support of such systems is often limited or cumbersome; thus, many test authors either prefer specialized tools, such as Respondus or Questionmark Perception, or text-based formats that allow them to write tests in any text editor. The finished tests are then uploaded to a delivery platform or a repository, a so-called *item bank*. The text-based file formats for tests thus have multiple functions: They serve for authoring, for (local) storage, and for the interchange of tests. We will describe a number of such formats below.[1]

E-Learning Standards

There are a number of standards in the e-learning domain. Since assessment is such a central concept in learning, many of these standards concern, in some way, e-assessment.

The most widely known e-learning standard is probably *SCORM*, the Sharable Content Object Reference Model. SCORM is a specification created and maintained by ADL, the Advanced Distributed Learning Initiative of the U.S. Department of Defense. At the time of this writing, the current version of SCORM is SCORM 2004 4th Edition (ADL, 2009), released in March 2009. SCORM is actually not a single standard but "a collection, integration and harmonization of specifications and standards that have been bundled into a collection of 'technical books'" (ADL, 2009, Overview p. 4); these books cover the primary parts of SCORM: The Content Aggregation Model (CAM), the Run-time Environment (RTE), and Sequencing and Navigation (SN). SCORM primarily draws on standards and specifications by ARIADNE (Alliance of Remote Instructional Authoring & Distribution Networks for Europe)[2], AICC (Aviation Industry CBT Committee)[3], the IEEE Learning Technology Standards Committee (LTSC)[4], and the IMS Global Learning Consortium[5].

The primary goal of SCORM is to enable the creation of e-learning content in the form of so-called "shareable content objects," or SCO, which can be loaded into any conforming Web-based e-learning platform ("learning management system" (LMS) in SCORM terminology). In particular, SCORM defines a run-time environment in which SCOs are executed and a corresponding API (application programming interface), which allows for communication between an SCO and the hosting e-learning platform. For example, an SCO may report the assessment score of a student to the e-learning platform.

One IMS standard used in SCORM—and in other standards—is the *IMS Content Packaging Specification* (IMS CP) (IMS GLC, 2004). IMS CP defines a standardized set of structures for packaging content, so that it can be exchanged between systems. In short, an IMS Content Package is an archive file (such as a ZIP file) containing a so-called *manifest* in the top-level directory. The manifest is an XML file containing information about the files that make up the actual content. IMS CP can be considered a low-level specification on which other e-learning standards can build. SCORM is one example: An SCO is actually an IMS Content Package. Another example is the *IMS Common Cartridge Profile* (IMS CC) (IMS GLC, 2008).

IMS CC is somewhat similar to SCORM in that it aims to provide a standard way to represent learning content, so that it can be used with a wide variety of e-learning platforms. However, whereas SCORM was developed to enable portability of self-paced computer-based training content, IMS CC is intended for instructor-led courses, such as university courses. For the description of quizzes, IMS CC uses a profile of IMS QTI 1.2.1. As IMS QTI is the topic of this chapter, it will be described in more detail below.

eduComponents

The review and discussion of QTI in this chapter is based on the experience with QTI in the development of ECQuiz, the quiz component of the eduComponents. The eduComponents are a component-based e-learning system architecture, realized as software components (so-called *products*) extending a general-purpose content management system—namely the open-source system Plone[6] —with facilities for course management and assessment.

The eduComponents architecture is based on the following ideas. After an analysis of the current state of the art in e-learning platforms, we came to the conclusion that the functionality of conventional e-learning platforms consists of basic content management and communications facilities (such as forums, chats, wikis, etc.) and functionality for assessment (such as quizzes). However, only assessment functionality is actually specific to e-learning. Furthermore, the content management and communication functionality in e-learning platforms (such as Blackboard or Moodle) is typically restricted and often inferior when compared with the more general implementations available in Web content management systems (such as Plone, Apache Lenya, Drupal, or Vignette).

Since content management systems (CMS) offer more general and more robust functions for managing content, we concluded that e-learning platforms should be based on content management systems. Only assessment functions are actually specific to e-learning and need to be added to a CMS; obviously, this requires the architecture of the CMS to be modular.

The eduComponents can be seen as a proof of concept for this approach. The eduComponents have been released as open source[7] and have been in productive use since several semesters at Otto von Guericke University and other institutions worldwide.

ECQuiz is the eduComponents product for multiple-choice tests. It supports single-answer, multiple-answer, scale, and tutor-graded free-text questions. Related questions can be grouped into question groups, which are then treated as a unit. Questions and answers can be displayed in fixed or randomized order. It is also possible to present different randomly selected subsets of questions and answers to each student.

ECQuiz offers different modes of operation for self-assessment tests and exams. Instructors can access detailed reports, providing an overview of the performance of all test takers. The reports can also be exported for further processing in a spreadsheet or statistics program.

QTI conformance was a key requirement in the development of ECQuiz to enable the interchange of tests; both individual questions and complete tests can be imported and exported as files in IMS QTI 2.0 format.

Piotrowski (2009) offers a detailed description of the concepts and the implementation of the eduComponents, including ECQuiz. The implementation of QTI in ECQuiz is discussed below in the section "QTI in ECQuiz."

TEXT-BASED FORMATS FOR TESTS

A straightforward way to store a simple multiple-choice test is in the form of a text file that lists the prompts and the choices, with some marker for the correct choices. A natural extension is then to define further markers to allow for some formatting or highlighting of text, e.g., as bold or italic. Such a format could be called "wiki-like."

Since their invention by Ward Cunningham in 1994 (Leuf and Cunningham, 2001), *wikis* have quickly become a widespread way for creating content on the Internet. One important aspect of wikis is that text is written in a non-WYSIWYG fashion using simple markup languages or "editing conventions." For example, bulleted lists are typically created by starting a line with an asterisk, and emphasized text is marked up by surrounding it with asterisks.

The idea behind wiki markup is that it is easy to learn—since it is based on existing conventions or because the markup alludes to the rendered form—and that it requires no special software for reading and writing it, so that as many people as possible can contribute. And in fact, wiki markup is now being used by large numbers of people, e.g., in Wikipedia[8]. This also shows that, despite the ubiquity of graphical user interfaces and WYSIWYG, users apparently not only accept, but actually prefer, text-based, non-WYSIWYG interfaces for some tasks.

There are a number of formats for describing tests in a wiki-like syntax. Some formats probably predate wikis, nevertheless they are similar to wiki syntaxes—and wiki syntax in turn is also based on earlier conventions from e-mail and Usenet communication. The most widespread wiki-like format is perhaps Moodle's *GIFT* ("General Import Format Technology") format for describing quizzes. For example, a multiple-choice question may be written as:[9]

```
Who's buried in Grant's tomb?{~Grant
~Jefferson =no one}
```

Listing 1. A Multiple-Choice Item in GIFT Format

This format is easy to learn and efficient for simple items. For more complex items, however, the syntax is no longer intuitive but more or less arbitrary:

```
::Jesus' hometown::Jesus Christ was
from {
~Jerusalem#This was an important
city, but the wrong answer.
~%25%Bethlehem#He was born here, but
not raised here.
~%50%Galilee#You need to be more spe-
cific.
=Nazareth#Yes! That's right!
}.
```

Listing 2. A More Complex Item in GIFT Format

```
What is the correct answer to this
question?
A. Is it this one?
B. Maybe this answer?
C. Possibly this one?
D. Must be this one!
ANSWER: D
```

Listing 3. A Quiz Item in Aiken Format

```
# Start of question: Multiple Choice
Question
:TYPE:MC:1:0:C
:TITLE:Multiple Choice Question
:FEEDBACK
Darwin invented the theory of evolu-
tion and created Darwinism.
:QUESTION:H
Where is the Darwin Research Center?
:IMAGE:
:LAYOUT:vertical
:ANSWER1:0:H
Menlo Park, California
:REASON1:H
Sorry!
:ANSWER2:0:H
Vancouver, Canada
:REASON2:H
Sorry!
:ANSWER3:100:H
Galapagos Islands, Ecuador
:REASON3:H
Correct Answer!
:ANSWER4:0:H
London, England
:REASON4:H
Sorry!
:ANSWER5:0:H
Sidney, Australia
:REASON5:H
Sorry!
:CAT:Default
# End of question: Multiple Choice
Question
```

Listing 4. A Quiz Item in WebCT Text Format

```
Title: Speed of Light
3) Who determined the speed of light?
a. Albert Einstein
@ No. Albert Michelson determined the
exact speed of light.
*b. Albert Michelson
@ Yes. Albert Michelson won the Nobel
Prize for Physics for determining the
exact speed of light.
c. Thomas Edison
```

```
@ No. Thomas Edison did not determine
the exact speed of light.
d. Guglielmo Marconi
@ No Guglielmo Marconi did not dis-
cover the exact speed of light, but
he did win the Nobel Prize for Phys-
ics for his work with radio waves.
```

Listing 5. Quiz Item in Respondus Standard Format (example taken from (Respondus, 2008))

Other wiki-like formats for describing tests include the "Aiken" format (apparently also a Moodle design, listing 3), WebCT's text format (listing 4), and Respondus "Standard Format" (listing 5).10

The different formats share many characteristics. For example, most formats are more or less line-oriented and require rigid adherence to the layout: Typically a new item must start on a new line, various parts are identified by specifics characters at the beginning of a line, and in some cases, e.g., the Aiken format, the question must be all on one line.

Furthermore, some information is only given implicitly; in GIFT format, for example, an item containing *only* true answers (marked with "=") is treated as a short answer question.

These properties and the fact that there are no formal definitions for most of these formats (including GIFT) make them unsuitable for use as interchange formats. We consider them also suboptimal for authoring questions, as the syntax for more complex items is hard to remember, and, as the format is hard to parse, it is difficult to give test authors good feedback in case of errors.

REQUIREMENTS FOR INTERCHANGE FORMATS

Before taking a closer look at QTI, we should step back and think about the requirements for interchange formats. Whether or not two systems can directly exchange data depends on the existence of a common data format. In practice, however, this alone is not yet a guarantee for trouble-free interchange. The reliability of the interchange depends almost directly on the specification of the interchange format. If the interchange format is insufficiently specified it is possible—and even likely—that different developers interpret and implement the specification in different ways. This means that data interchange may be impossible even though all variants may in principle conformant with the specification. Furthermore, it can be assumed that the higher the complexity of the specification, the higher the likelihood for errors in the implementation.

If a system reads or writes the interchange format incorrectly, it is consequently probable that the interchange will not work or will not work correctly. The latter case is potentially more dangerous since the interchange may seem to be successful but, in fact, data may have been lost or corrupted. This type of errors can remain undetected for a long time and may, in the case of tests, lead to candidates being assigned an incorrect score.

Formal Definition

These considerations suggest a number of requirements for interchange formats for tests and their specifications. First of all, a standard—or a specification intended as such—should rely as far as possible on existing and proven standards. Many, if not most, specifications for data formats therefore currently are based on XML (World Wide Web Consortium, 2006). This allows keeping the specification of the interchange format concise and enables implementers to make use of available and proven tools.

The use of XML in a specification is, however, only useful if it includes a formal definition in a schema language such as Relax NG (ISO (International Organization for Standardization),

2003) or W3C XML Schema (World Wide Web Consortium, 2004). A specification should make full use of the facilities provided by the schema language so that conformance can be verified as far as possible by an XML parser; natural-language requirements and restrictions are hard to verify automatically and thus error-prone and should thus be avoided as far as possible.

A schema describes the *syntax* of a data format. An implementation that is supposed to read and write the format requires a complete specification of the *semantics*, i.e., the meaning of the individual elements, so that it can interpret and transfer tests in the form intended by the original author.

Separation of Content and Form

There are different scenarios for the interchange of tests. In some cases, tests may be reused in their entirety, whereas in other cases only individual items from a test or a test collection (*item bank*) may be integrated into another test. It is therefore essential to clearly separate the different aspects of tests, especially *content*, *appearance*, and *behavior*.

Size and Scope

An interchange format that is able to describe all of the functionality of *all* systems may seem desirable to enable the interchange of complete tests with all their properties. Looking closer, one can see that this requirement is illusionary: The facilities of test systems are too diverse and too varied and no system supports all test and scoring types.

An interchange format should therefore restrict itself to a relatively small "core set" of test and item types. Further types can be added later on once it has become clear which types are actually required in practice. The specification of optional parts or alternatives should, however, be avoided at all costs, as it has been shown to severely impede the development of interoperable implementations.[11]

Longevity

Finally, an interchange format should ensure longevity, i.e., items and tests described using the format should remain processable for as long as possible. For correcting errors and extending the format new revisions will become necessary from time to time, but it must be avoided that new revisions interfere with the data interchange. This means that different revisions should be compatible with each other as far as possible. Gratuitous incompatibilities must be avoided at all costs; sometimes, however, incompatible changes may be necessary.

To mitigate the potential negative impact of such changes, rigorous revision management is essential, starting with the distinction between major and minor revisions and corresponding numbering schemes. Incompatible changes must then only be introduced in major revisions, after having been announced before. Inside a major revision, say, 1.x, all minor revisions (e.g., 1.1, 1.2, etc.) are all compatible with each other. Revision 2.0 may introduce incompatible changes, but not 2.1. This ensures that implementers and users can easily and reliably decide whether a specific file can be processed or not.

IMS QUESTION AND TEST INTEROPERABILITY

IMS Question & Test Interoperability Specification (QTI) (IMS GLC, 2005) is currently the only public, implementation-independent specification for the description of multiple-choice tests and similar test types. What is more, the IMS consortium can be considered a *de facto* standards body in the e-learning domain.

This section gives a brief overview of QTI and of the implementation of QTI in ECQuiz. Based on our experience with QTI we subsequently present requirements for interchange formats and analyze the suitability of QTI for the purpose of question and test interchange.

A Brief Overview of QTI

The QTI specification describes a data model and a corresponding XML representation for coding assessment items and tests. The declared goal of the specification is to enable the "exchange of this item, assessment and results data between authoring tools, item banks, learning systems and assessment delivery systems" (IMS GLC, 2005, Overview, p. 3). Thus, QTI is intended to be an interchange format.

QTI version 1.0 was published in 2000 and subsequently revised several times in response to issues raised by implementers, ultimately leading to version 1.2.1, released in March 2003. When systems claim "QTI support" (e.g., Respondus, WebCT, or OLAT), this typically refers to a version of QTI 1.x. Smythe and Roberts (2000) offer a brief description of QTI 1.0 by members of the QTI working group.

A number of conceptual problems with QTI 1.x were detected during practical use; García-Robles et al. (2004), for example, discuss problems that constrain the design of assessment scenarios and limit reusability. According to the QTI specification (IMS GLC, 2005, Overview, p. 3), some of the issues could not be dealt with by revising QTI 1.x, "as they required changes to the specification that would not be backwardly compatible or because they uncovered more fundamental issues that would require extensive clarification or significant extension of the specification to resolve." The QTI working group therefore considered a completely new design necessary to resolve these issues.

QTI 2.0, published in 2005, represents this new design. Despite the promises of far-reaching compatibility by IMS—Smythe and Roberts (2000) claimed that "software that is compliant with the V1.0 DTD will be able to import V2.0 Items providing it ignores the optional tags"—QTI 2.0 is based on a fundamentally different model and uses a completely different XML structure and is incompatible with QTI 1.x. Furthermore, QTI 2.0 does not cover all areas covered by QTI 1.x; in particular, QTI 2.0 can only be used to describe individual items but not complete tests.

The facilities missing in 2.0—including the aggregation of items into sections and tests or the reporting of results—were supposed to be specified in version 2.1. The first public draft of QTI 2.1 was released in January 2006, the second public draft in June 2006. An addendum with bug fixes was published in April 2008.

In March 2009, however, IMS withdrew the QTI 2.1 draft specification. Naturally, this raised considerable concerns.[12] In an effort to clarify this decision, Rib Abel, CEO of IMS had the following message[13] posted to the mailing list, in which he explained:

QTI v2.1 was under public review for more than 2 years and did not achieve sufficient implementation and feedback to warrant being voted on as a final specification. Therefore it has been withdrawn for further work by the IMS membership. IMS cannot continue to publish specifications that have not met the rigors of the IMS process.

Abel stated that IMS were "very encouraged and hopeful that a new version will be available in due time, possibly a QTI v2.2," cautioning however that one "cannot assume that it will be a linear evolution from QTI v2.1." He further declared that until that time, "the only version of QTI that is fully endorsed by IMS GLC is v1.2.1." He acknowledged that QTI 2.0 had been released as a final specification, but noted that "it's deficiencies are well known and IMS does not recommend implementation of it." Thus, IMS withdrew not only the QTI 2.1 draft specification, but effectively also QTI 2.0.

Nevertheless, since the QTI implementation in ECQuiz is based on QTI 2.0, and since it is the last "final specification," the references below will be to QTI 2.0.

The QTI specification consists of several parts. The Information Model describes an abstract data model, defining, for example, what a *question* is and what attributes it has. The XML Binding defines a mapping of the abstract model into a concrete XML representation, which is in turn described by a W3C XML Schema and a DTD. Other parts of the specification cover various details and give guidance for implementers and users of QTI.

```
<?xml version="1.0"?>
<!DOCTYPE assessmentItem SYSTEM "im-
sqti_v2p0.dtd">
<assessmentItem identifier="EX1"
title="Formula-1"
adaptive="false"
timeDependent="false">
<responseDeclara-
tion identifier="REX2"
cardinality="multiple">
<correctResponse>
<value>choice1</value>
<value>choice2</value>
</correctResponse>
</responseDeclaration>
<itemBody>
<choiceInteraction
responseIdentifier="REX2"
shuffle="true" maxChoices="0">
<prompt>Indicate the years in which
Michael Schumacher was
Formula 1 racing champion.</prompt>
<simpleChoice
identifier="choice1">1994</sim-
pleChoice>
<simpleChoice
identifier="choice2">2000</sim-
pleChoice>
<simpleChoice
identifier="choice3">2006</sim-
pleChoice>
</choiceInteraction>
</itemBody>
</assessmentItem>
```

Listing 6. Simple Example of a QTI 2.0 File

The basic element of QTI 2.0 is the *item*, i.e., a question and the corresponding answer choices. For the markup of the item content a subset of XHTML (World Wide Web Consortium, 2002) extended with test-specific elements is used.

Listing 6 is an example of a basic item coded in QTI 2.0; it defines a multiple-choice question with multiple selection. The <itemBody> element contains the question (in the <prompt> element) and the answer choices. Since candidates "interact" with the presented choices, QTI refers to this part as *interaction*. The example uses <choiceInteraction>, with the choices contained in <simpleChoice> elements. The correct choices are specified in the <correctResponse> at the top of the file.

QTI in ECQuiz

As mentioned above, we selected QTI as an interchange format for ECQuiz since we considered interchange of tests important, and since QTI was the only standard available, it seemed to be a logical decision.

However, we did not design ECQuiz in terms of QTI because

- QTI 2.0 had not yet been finalized at the time we started development
- QTI is an interchange specification, not a design specification
- Due to the large number of optional items and ambiguities it is not suitable as a design specification.

We therefore first implemented the functionality we needed using a suitable model, and then started to specify a mapping to and from QTI.

The smallest element in the ECQuiz test model is the *question*. Currently ECQuiz supports two basic types of questions: *Multiple-choice questions*, where candidates have to select one or more answers from a choice of answers, and *extended text questions*, where candidates are supposed to write a textual answer. Related questions, e.g., referring to a common passage or text or an image, can be grouped together in a *question group*; common content is stored in the so-called *directions* of the question group. Figure 1 schematically shows an exemplary test structure; Figure 2 shows how question groups are displayed.

For ECQuiz we implemented QTI as far as necessary to enable a *round trip*, i.e., we ensured that data exported by ECQuiz could be imported by ECQuiz without loss of information. While designing the mapping from the ECQuiz test model to QTI we encountered several problems that required ECQuiz-specific extensions.

As mentioned above, unlike QTI 1.x, QTI 2.0 specifies only individual assessment items and does not update those parts of the specification that dealt with the aggregation of items into sections and assessments or the reporting of results.[14] Since ECQuiz handles both complete tests and groups of items, it was clear that we needed a way to describe them in a portable way. The QTI Integration Guide and the QTI Migration Guide briefly mention some pertinent issues, but many questions with regard to a concrete implementation remain open, for example:

As this version of the QTI specification does not define either an information model or a binding for section, assessment and objectbank objects no recommendations on how to interpret collections of packaged version 2 items are made. However, packaged items may be referred to individually in an associated learning design or set of sequencing rules. (IMS GLC, 2005, Integration Guide, p. 4)

The Integration Guide also reveals that the integration of the various IMS specifications is far from optimal:

IMS Learning Design and IMS QTI are natural partners in the learning process. [...] However, the type systems used in IMS LD and IMS QTI differ: [...] A final complicating factor is the presence of multi-valued variables in QTI which have no equivalent in IMS LD. (IMS GLC, 2005, Integration Guide, pp. 7 and 9)

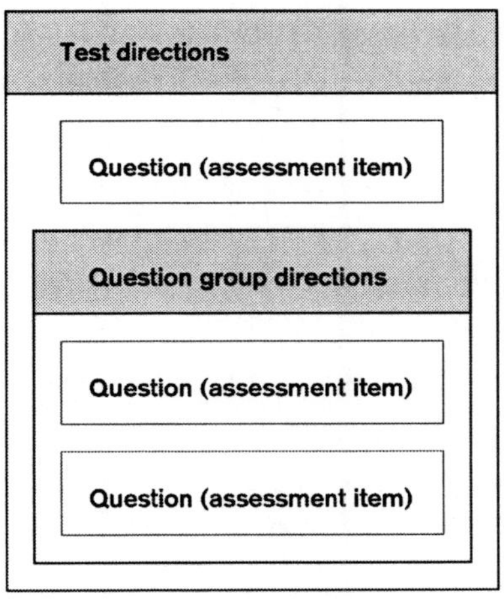

Figure 1. Example test structure in ECQuiz. Questions can be grouped into question groups. Question groups and tests can be preceded by prefatory material called directions

For implementing QTI support in ECQuiz we chose the following approach, which involves three IMS specifications:

1. IMS Question & Test Interoperability Specification (QTI) (IMS GLC, 2005) Each question (with its associated answers) is mapped to an <assessmentItem>, and thus to a separate file. The prefatory material of tests and question groups is treated as an <assessmentItem> without interaction.[15] This approach allows a syntactically valid

Figure 2. Example of a test (in results view) with two question groups (Ê and Ë) and the corresponding directions (Ì and Í)

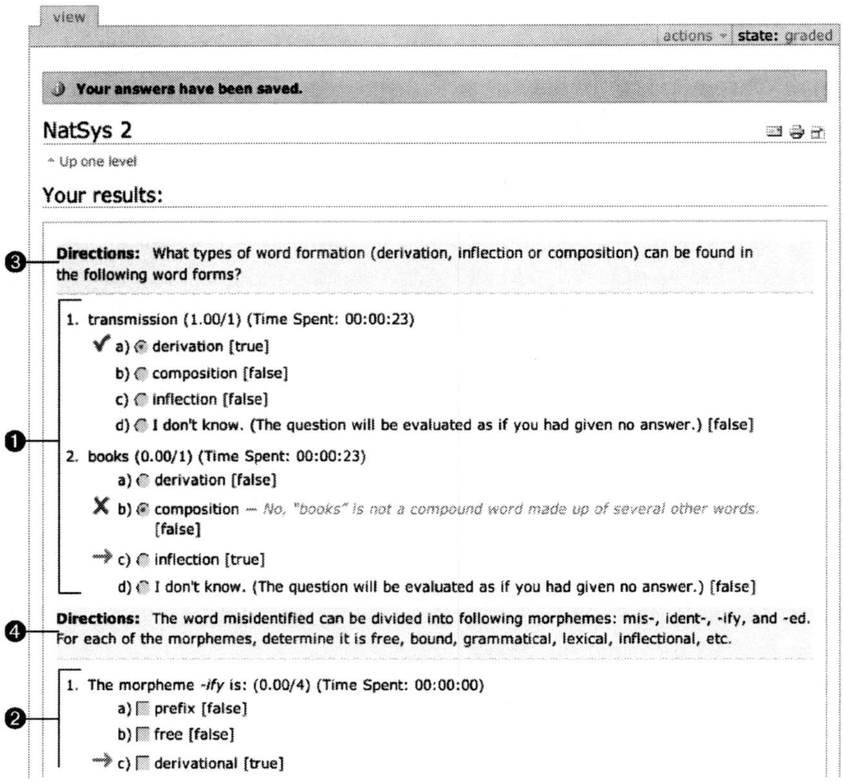

representation of ECQuiz tests; it is not guaranteed, however, that other systems are able to correctly interpret this use of the <assessmentItem> element.

2. IMS Content Packaging Specification (CP) (IMS GLC, 2004) Content Packaging is used to assemble the individual assessment items into a test. *Packaging* basically means that all files, along with a *manifest*, are packaged into a ZIP archive. The manifest is an XML file named imsmanifest.xml in the root directory of the archive listing the resources contained in the package. Also, the manifest can contain a definition[16] of the structure of the packaged learning material in the <organization> element. This provides a way to represent question groups.
3. IMS Simple Sequencing Specification (IMS GLC, 2003) The randomization of answers inside an assessment item is covered by QTI, but ECQuiz also supports the randomization of questions (including the presentation of only a selection of all available questions); this behavior can also be controlled inside question groups. The Simple Sequencing Specification defines elements which can be used to describe the sequential structure of a learning experience. These elements can be used inside the manifest's <organization> elements. In our context, we can use them to specify randomization of questions, number of attempts and availability dates.

In summary, the implementation effort required for QTI support in ECQuiz proved to be very high. Since we wanted to ensure that round trips are possible, we had to implement, besides QTI, parts of IMS CP and IMS Simple Sequencing. During the work it became obvious that the specifications are not aligned. Furthermore, we had to find work-arounds for idiosyncrasies and restrictions imposed by QTI. Consequently, the QTI module accounts for almost 50% of the total code of ECQuiz. To limit the implementation costs and due to a dearth of other QTI 2.0 implementations, the QTI import facility of ECQuiz is primarily designed for the import of ECQuiz-generated items and content packages. Experiments with QTI files and content packages from other sources were unsatisfactory, except for very simple items. For example, QTI 2.0 items and content packages produced by Moodle did not even conform to the specifications, so that import into ECQuiz was not possible.

Due to the numerous problems we encountered during the implementation of QTI import and export in ECQuiz, we will discuss some of them in more detail in the following section.

PROBLEMS WITH QTI

Issues raised by implementers of QTI 1.x was taken into account during the design of QTI 2.0 (IMS GLC, 2005, Overview, p. 3). Nevertheless, we discovered numerous flaws while implementing support for QTI 2.0 in ECQuiz, describe in the preceding section. Most of the problems can be classified into one of three categories: (1) Design problems, (2) formal weaknesses, and (3) technical problems related to the XML mapping.

With respect to the development of the QTI specification it is important to note that QTI 2.0 does *not* codify existing practice, but that it was written "from scratch." In contrast to the IETF standards process for RFCs (Bradner, 1996), for example, IMS does not require two independently developed interoperable implementations either, nor is there a reference implementation for QTI 2.0.

Design Problems

QTI 2.0 is a very large specification with many optional parts. To ensure interoperability between systems that do not implement all parts of the standard, the specification provides for the definition of *profiles*. Profiles provide for a way to describe the subset implemented by a system. Two profiles, *QTI-Lite* and *QTI-All*, are predefined.

Both of the predefined profiles are of little practical use. QTI-Lite defines a minimal subset that is too restricted for even the simplest tests: For example, QTI-Lite-conformant items cannot contain enumerations or tables and may only use JPEG and GIF images, but not the W3C-standard PNG format—restrictions which are hard to justify on technical grounds. QTI-All, on the other hand, requires the implementation of the complete specification. At the time of this writing, we are not aware of any complete implementation of QTI 2.0; considering the size and scope of the specification and the problems discussed below, we doubt that a QTI-All implementation will ever be produced.

The QTI specification tends to be quite liberal in many points; for example, almost arbitrary structures are allowed inside an item. This means that an empty item is fully conformant, as are items without <itemBody> element (and thus without a question text) or items with multiple interactions, e.g., an item that is a multiple-choice and a cloze question at the same time.

The advantage of this approach is that many question types can be modeled in QTI. The disadvantage is, however, that the import of QTI items from unknown sources becomes very complex. Since the specification does not define the *meaning* of, say, an empty item or an item with multiple interactions, it is hard to guarantee that an item is imported and interpreted as originally intended by its author. This, in turn, means that the main purpose of an interchange format is not met.

In addition to the description of assessment items, QTI specifies a programming language for *response processing* (RP), i.e, the processing of candidate responses. Since the description of an item and the scoring of candidate responses to an item are two completely different issues, we would argue that the response processing should have better be described in a separate standard. This would have reduced the size and complexity of the QTI specification and may have allowed for a better design of the RP language.

The separation of content, appearance, and behavior (mentioned above in the requirements for interchange formats) is hardly to be found in the design of QTI. Many element definitions that describe the content of an item, e.g., <feedbackBlock>, <feedbackInline>, or <responseDeclaration>, contain dependencies to the item's behavior, which is defined by the response processing. Even if scoring is not done in terms of QTI response processing (which is legal) specific elements and attributes must always be present for conformance with the specification.

Formal Weaknesses

The QTI specification is often imprecise or ambiguous; many questions remain unanswered and the reader is required to guess. It thus does not fulfill our desideratum of preciseness, and we find it unlikely for two QTI implementations to agree in their interpretation of the specification to the extent that is necessary for interchange.

For example, the XML Binding defines the data type language simply as a "trivial restriction of xsd:string" (IMS GLC, 2005, XML Binding, p. 52). There is no mention of the value range of the data type. The definition of the format of the type identifier, on the other hand, is very verbose, but equally puzzling. Instead of a formal definition in Backus Naur Form (ISO (International Organization for Standardization), 1996) or as a regular expression (Friedl, 2002), the QTI specification gives the following long-winded definition in natural language:

An identifier is a string of characters that must start with a Letter or an underscore ('_') and contain only Letters, underscores, hyphens ('-'), period ('.', a.k.a. full-stop), Digits, CombiningChars and Extenders. Identifiers containing the period character are reserved for future use. The character classes Letter, Digit, CombiningChar and Extender are defined in the Extensible Markup Language (XML) 1.0 (Second Edition) [XML]. Note particularly that identifiers may not contain the colon (':') character. Identifiers should have no more than 32 characters. for [sic] compatibility with version 1 They [sic] are always compared case-sensitively. (IMS GLC, 2005, Information Model, p. 52)

The typos make the reference to "compatibility with version 1" unclear. In contrast to the definition cited above, the XML Schema for QTI 2.0 provided by IMS defines the type identifier as NMTOKEN, which means that the Schema *does* allow periods and colons in identifiers. Consequentially, this means that the application has to implement the restrictions given in the specification even though it would have been trivial to implement them in the XML Schema. The specification also does not define whether identifiers *may* be longer than 32 characters and up to which character they have to be unique; in fact, the specification does not contain *any* statement on the uniqueness of identifiers.

Yet another example can be found in the definition of the element intended for free-text answers, <extendedTextInteraction>. This element has the attributes expectedLines and expectedLength. Both are meant to give candidates some indication of the expected length of their answers (see IMS GLC, 2005, Information Model, p. 29):

Attribute: expectedLines [0..1]: integer The expectedLines attribute provides a hint to the candidate as to the expected number of lines of input required. A Delivery Engine should use the value of this attribute to set the size of the response box, where applicable.

Attribute: expectedLength [0..1]: integer The expectedLength attribute provides a hint to the candidate as to the expected overall length of the desired response. A Delivery Engine should use the value of this attribute to set the size of the response box, where applicable.

It is impossible to determine the difference (if any) between these two attributes from the nearly identical descriptions. No precedence is defined for the case that both are specified. Furthermore, the meaning of the values is not defined: The specification of a number of lines using expectedLines would only make sense if the length of the lines were known; the value of expectedLength may, e.g., refer to the number of words, the number of sentences, or even to the width (in centimeters) of the input form. For an application importing an item from an unknown source it is thus impossible to determine the intended meaning of these attributes.

Technical Problems Related to the XML Mapping

As mentioned above, one part of the QTI specification is the XML Binding, which defines a mapping of the Information Model to a W3C XML Schema. Regrettably, the facilities offered by XML and XML Schema are only utilized to a small extent, so that QTI files can only be partially validated by standard XML tools. Thus, another one of our desiderata is not fulfilled. We will show examples to illustrate some of the issues.

In many cases, QTI uses an attribute containing the identifier of the target element for cross references. Sometimes, however, other mechanisms are used. As can be seen in listing 6, the correct choices for a multiple-choice question are indicated using the <correctResponse> element, which contains one or more <value> elements. The *content* of each <value> element is the identifier of a correct <simpleChoice> element.

The problem here is that, if the capabilities of XML had been fully used, a much more robust and elegant solution would have been possible. For cross referencing of elements XML specifically offers the attribute types ID, IDREF, and IDREFS. When using attributes of these types, an XML parser can ensure that all identifiers of type ID are unique and that all elements referenced by IDREF or IDREFS actually exist. It is likely that these are the semantics intended by the QTI specification; however, the QTI XML Schema does not use *any* of these attribute types *at all.*

The element <rubricBlock> is representative for many other shortcomings in the XML Binding. In the definition of this element the Information Model notes: "Although rubric blocks are defined as simpleBlocks they must not contain interactions." IMS GLC The XML Schema, however, does not enforce this restriction, even though W3C XML Schema provides the necessary facilities to do so.

A CRITICAL REVIEW OF QTI

On the basis of our experience with QTI 2.0 during the implementation of a subset in ECQuiz and through the analysis of the QTI specification, our conclusion is that QTI 2.0 is unsuitable for the exchange of tests. While it does, in principle, allow the description of a large number of item types and scoring methods, a complete implementation would require a prohibitive effort, whereas partial implementations—such as the one in ECQuiz—do not achieve the required level of interoperability.

We are not alone in our criticism of QTI. Gorissen has evaluated the QTI support of a number of systems[17] in 2003 and 2006 (Gorissen, 2003, 2006). His results show that all systems support only very small subsets of QTI. Moreover, in most cases information is lost during import. He also notes that the situation has not improved in 2006.

Strobbe (2006) has examined QTI specifically with regard to accessibility, i.e., support for users with disabilities. He reports that QTI 2.0 solves some of the accessiblity issues of QTI 1.2, but that the ambiguity with regard to the intent of interaction types was not sufficiently addressed. Instead of a learning outcome, only the visual renderings are considered; for example, the names of question types such as <hotspotInteraction> or <drawingInteraction> suggest a specific rendering rather than a learning outcome. This problem is compounded by the general lack of well-defined semantics that also hampers effective interchange.

Sclater (2007, p. 70) agrees that the QTI specification is "unreadable by the vast majority of candidates likely to be undertaking an online assessment and of no concern to those setting the questions."

Lazarinis et al. (2009) have evaluated the QTI support of four systems (OLAT, ECQuiz, Respondus, and QuestionMark Perception) in order to measure the conformance of assessment tools to QTI, considering both version 1.2 and 2.1. Lazarinis et al. defined four levels of compatibility to rate import and export capabilities, ranging from "no support" over "basic support" and "medium support" to "advanced support". Each compatibility level (with the exception of "no support") requires support for specific QTI features: "Basic support" means that a system supports multiple-choice questions, "medium support" means support for complex items such as gap matching, and "advanced support" requires the capability to handle tests with sections. Just as in previous evaluations, the results were disappointing: Of the four systems evaluated, only ECQuiz had "basic support" for creating and importing files that conformed to QTI 2.1.[18] OLAT and Respondus were found to have "basic support" for QTI 1.2, while the files produced by Questionmark Perception did not conform to any version of QTI (even though it claims to support QTI). Lazarinis et al. (2009, p. 138) conclude: "In any case it seems that it is premature to discuss about true interoperability among educational tools."

The criticism of QTI brings up a number of questions. Gorissen (2006) states that there is an "obvious business need for better interoperability." The question is then why we still have the current state of low interoperability. Gorissen's conclusion is that "the market does not yet see the importance of that and their customers fail to explain that need to them." To remedy this situation, he calls for more explicit action from funding bodies, such as requiring the use of tools that support interoperability. Regarding the complexity of QTI, which hinders the development of QTI support, Gorissen suggests the development of an open-source reference implementation by the "educational community," so that the effort for implementing QTI support is reduced.

Sclater (2007) concurs that "IMS QTI is unarguably a complex and difficult specification for vendors to implement," but he argues that this is not the primary reason for the slow adoption of QTI. Like Gorissen, he finds that the market does not demand interoperability, however for different reasons: Universities own the assessment process and thus have no need to exchange assessment data with other institutions, so that interoperability is effectively irrelevant. Furthermore, commercial vendors are largely uninterested in interoperability, since they see no clear business case for it, and even if interoperability is a (nominal) selection criteria, institutions tend to simply believe vendors' claims, so that there is little pressure on vendors to invest in interoperability.

Furthermore, Sclater sees the market as basically split up between "BlackCT"[19] and Moodle, and since the systems take radically different approaches, he considers it unlikely that an institution which has opted for one system will ever move to the other system, though he acknowledges that a growing number of universities are moving from commercial e-learning platforms to Moodle.

His conclusion is that there is currently effectively no *need* for interchange formats and only a market for e-assessment *content* would drive QTI adoption.

Sclater's comments and conclusions should perhaps be seen on the background of an earlier publication, Sclater et al. (2002), a 2002 report of an interoperability evaluation for QTI 1.1 and 1.2.[20] The results of this evaluation were—like those reported by Gorissen (2003)—disappointing: Both LMSs effectively failed to either import or export QTI-encoded tests; the other systems had various problems, including showing the wrong feedback text, even though the two test items used in the evaluation were extremely simple. In the light of these results Sclater et al. thus wondered:

If, despite the programmers' expertise and the relative simplicity of the questions chosen, they are still failing to be rendered correctly does this bode well for interoperability? (Sclater et al., 2002, p. 324)

Practically the same comments were made in 2002 regarding the complexity of QTI 1.x as are now being made with regard to QTI 2.x:

There is no doubt that the QTI specification is highly complex, with some remaining apparent inconsistencies and ambiguity making it difficult to implement. (Sclater et al., 2002, p. 324)

Finally, Sclater et al. also discussed the unattractiveness of interoperability for commercial vendors:

While it is helpful to be able to claim that your product is interoperable it is not necessarily to your advantage as a vendor for it to be so. As well as adding to your system development costs your clients may ultimately decide to move to another system and use your interoperability feature to take their content with them. (Sclater et al., 2002, p. 325)

With the emergence of strong open-source competition (especially from Moodle), the market situation has changed compared to 2002 (see the discussion of universities migrating away from commercial platforms below), but the implementation situation of QTI is effectively unchanged. Sclater's views may thus be interpreted as resignation in the face of the slow progress being made:

If there's nothing to interoperate with and if the content is effectively "future-proofed" by being exportable into XML this begs the question: does it matter at all whether Moodle properly adopts the IMS QTI specification? (Sclater, 2007, p. 73)

Lazarinis et al. (2009, p. 138) consider the "severe changes from one version to the other" to be a likely cause for the slow adoption of and the low level of support for QTI 2.1. They ask that e-learning standards should become easier to use and suggest two ways to achieve this: One way is the availability of what they call "add ons," i.e., software libraries, so that not each application programmer would have to implement support for standard interchange formats from scratch. The other way Lazarinis et al. propose is for e-learning standards to be designed in a modular fashion, so that there are several implementation levels to chose from; the authors suggest that this would allow developers to better specify and reach conformance and users to better determine the actual capabilities of a system.

We agree with Gorissen's analysis, but we do not think that the effort necessary for a reference implementation would be justifiable, since the problems are rooted in the design of QTI; the same basically applies to Lazarinis et al.'s suggestion of "add ons". There are many examples that show that the availability of ready-to-use software libraries drive the adoption of standards and this would certainly also be true for QTI—but it would not fix the problems with QTI.[21] What is more, given the problems with QTI, it may be even counterproductive for the development of open standards, as it would likely freeze further development: If there were a "libqti" software developers could freely use, all applications using this library would probably be able to interchange questions and tests. However, given the complexity of the QTI specification and the fact that there is no such library, it is unlikely that there would be alternative implementations. Thus, since everybody would rely on QTI as implemented by "libqti," the implementation would turn into a *de facto* standard replacing the original standard. Such a situation is contrary to the intentions of an open standard and clearly undesirable. Consequently, we think that a fundamentally different approach would be necessary to create an interchange format that meets the requirements outlined in the section "Requirements for Interchange Formats" above. We agree with Lazarinis et al. suggestion that a standard should be "modular," i.e., allow for clearly defined implementation levels.

We also agree with Sclater's analysis in that institutions may not see a pressing need for interoperability, whether because they do not see a need to exchange tests with others, or whether they do not see themselves moving to a different platform. However, we think that these believes are based on wishful thinking rather than on reality. The fact that, as Sclater mentions, more and more institutions are moving from commercial e-learning platforms to open-source platforms shows that even university-level strategic decisions may be revised, making interoperability suddenly critical. Here are some current examples of universities migrating from Blackboard or WebCT to other e-learning platforms (see also Trotter (2008); universities are obviously not only migrating to Moodle; in fact, Mahlow (2010) shows that Moodle is unsuited for many universities).

- Louisiana State University started migration from Blackboard to Moodle in 2008. The University decided the switch to Moodle was necessary because of financial reasons. (Nagel, 2007; Stuart, 2008)
- Idaho State University (ISU) also decided to adopt Moodle to replace WebCT. The background given for this decision shows that a migration to another platform may not be solely a decision of the university: "In the fall semester of 2005, ISU was informed by WebCT that our current platform – WebCT CE 4.0 – would no longer be supported after July of 2007. The new version (WebCT CE 6.0) was identified as requiring a significant shift in personnel and equipment support and resources. Soon after the version 4.0 "end of life" and support deadline was announced, Blackboard Corporation, which makes a competing LMS product, announced its acquisition of WebCT. This merger was finalized in April of 2006 and created additional concerns for product directions, pricing, and support requirements." (Instructional Technology Resource Center, 2007, p. 10)
- In February 2009, the University of Hamburg decided to migrate from Blackboard to OLAT. The Blackboard license will end in April 2010 and will not be renewed. The University has stated that OLAT is as powerful as Blackboard, and not only less expensive but also more flexible and dynamic (Universität Hamburg, 2009).
- In April 2007, the University of Vienna, started a tendering process for an e-learning platform, since the licensing contract for WebCT would end in February 2009. Even though the University was dissatisfied with both WebCT and the service and support, in particular after Blackboard had acquired WebCT, the public invitation to tender also allowed Blackboard to submit an offer. With 72,000 students and 6,200 faculty members, the University of Vienna is a very large potential customer; however, Blackboard was unable or unwilling to submit a bid that would fulfill the formal

criteria. Eventually the University selected Fronter[22] and has been using it since winter semester 2008. Fronter is a commercial platform, but customers have full access to the source code. (Lorenz, 2009)

- In the beginning of 2007, Brandeis University started a project aiming to replace WebCT—which had been in use at the university since 1997—with Moodle. After a three-year transition to WebCT Vista from the earlier "Campus Edition" version, WebCT proved to be unstable, a problem that was aggravated by a lack of support after the purchase of WebCT by Blackboard Inc. (Hanson et al., 2007)
- In February 2008, the University of Kent started a project to migrate the university's of e-learning platform from WebCT to Moodle, since it was concluded that "future progress will require a move to a more modern and flexible platform."[23]
- In March 2008, the University of Puget Sound decided to adopt Moodle to replace Blackboard, which had been in use since 2003. The university's report (LMIS Committee, 2008) cites "gradual and growing faculty dissatisfaction with Blackboard, its outdated and poor feature set, its general 'buginess,' [*sic*] poor security and lack of integration with official course enrollment data, and low level of support from the vendor" as reasons for the decision to move to the new system.

The above examples show that migration to a new system is often not a deliberate decision, but may be forced by a variety of circumstances, which are hard to foresee. Nevertheless, when running a mission-critical system—such as an e-learning platform of a university—one should have contingency plans; being able to move content from one system to another should be an important part of such a plan.

There are two further issues Sclater fails to mention: First, interoperability is necessary for cooperation among institutions, whether it is voluntary, e.g., for joint projects or degree programs, or required, e.g., as a condition for certain grants. For example, the Swiss Virtual Campus (SVC) program of the Swiss government[24] only accepted project proposals when the project involved partners from at least three universities. Projects had to produce e-learning content cooperatively. Since typically every university uses a different e-learning platform, interoperability of e-learning content is indispensable to effectively create, distribute, and deploy tests and learning material.

Second, interoperability is also an important concern for instructors. When instructors teach at several institutions or move from one institution to another, they need to be able to continue using their educational material, including their tests. Thus, many instructors have a daily need for interoperability.

CONCLUSION

We have shown in this chapter that there are good reasons and very real needs for interoperability of questions and tests. We have described several application-specific formats for multiple-choice tests and presented the IMS QTI specification, which aims to define an interchange format for tests. We have then reported on our experience gained with QTI during the implementation of ECQuiz, which uncovered many shortcomings of the QTI 2.0 specification. An analysis of the specification has shown many more problems with QTI. In addition, many authors have reported serious implementation and interoperability problems, to the effect that a successful interchange of tests is the exception rather than the rule.

What is more, the conduct of IMS is, with respect to QTI, highly dubious. QTI now has a long history of half-baked releases and broken promises of compatibility, leading up to the public drafts for QTI 2.1. This version was supposed to add the facilities for describing complete tests missing in QTI 2.0. However, besides this addition, the draft contained a number of smaller changes which would have caused QTI 2.1 to be not completely backward-compatible with QTI 2.0, meaning that many items conformant with QTI 2.0 would have required changes to be conformant with QTI 2.1. The latest event was, as mentioned above, the withdrawal of the QTI 2.1 draft specification. While we agree that QTI 2.1 has serious problems and that any further development of it would be a waste of resources, the comportment of IMS towards the users of its specifications clearly showed that it is not a partner to rely on. QTI 2.0 was published as a final specification in 2005—four years later, IMS decided to deprecate it without any previous warning, leaving the community with QTI 1.2.1—a specification that, as IMS itself admits, has "fundamental issues that would require extensive clarification or significant extension of the specification to resolve" (IMS GLC, 2005, Overview, p. 3).

At the beginning of this chapter we asked: QTI—a failed e-learning standard? We think that the evidence shown in this chapter has shown that QTI is indeed a failure: It has clearly failed to enable the interchange of questions and tests.

The current, unsatisfactory state shows, in our opinion, three points: First, that the IMS is unable to produce a practicable standard for the interchange of tests. QTI 1.x has fundamental issues and QTI 2.x can be considered a typical case of both "design by committee" and of "second-system effect" (Brooks, 1995): It was clearly not developed on the basis of actual usage or clear requirements, but it is rather a hodgepodge of every imaginable feature.

Second, it is obvious that those who need interoperability are unable to make themselves heard, *not* that there is no need for it. One factor may be that the IMS is dominated by large vendors of systems (such as Blackboard) and e-learning content (such as Pearson), which do not necessarily have the same priorities as educational institutions and individual instructors. It may also be that the majority of instructors are "just users" and lack the technical knowledge to express their needs.

Third, we think that the problems with QTI are also the result of a more general problem in e-learning, namely the failure to abstract. For example, Piotrowski (2009) has shown that both currently available e-learning platforms and architectures proposed in research publications generally fail to abstract the functionality used in e-learning from its domain context. It thus seems to be generally accepted that an e-learning platform needs, for example, its own communication facilities (e-mail, forums, chat, etc.), even though their functionality does not differ from other implementations.

There is a similar problem in the design of QTI: The specification tries to account for all *known* types of tests, but it does not abstract from the concrete instances to provide more general facilities. For example, it does not recognize that a quiz is effectively a program that defines a user interface for the candidate and, given input in the form of the candidate's choices, calculates a resultant test score according to some specification. Thus, a programming language is needed to adequately and uniformly represent tests. Computer science has developed a significant body of knowledge about the design and implementation of programming languages. The realization that a quiz is a program would allow to draw on this knowledge and could help to find new solutions that go beyond the limited line-oriented file formats, such as GIFT, and the failed attempts of QTI.

REFERENCES

ADL. (2009). *Sharable Content Object Reference (SCORM) 2004*. Advanced Distributed Learning, 4th, version 1.0 edition. Retrieved 2009-08-06, from http://adlnet.gov/.

Astin, A. W. (1991). *Assessment For Excellence: The Philosophy And Practice Of Assessment And Evaluation In Higher Education*. American Council on Education Oryx Press Series on Higher Education. Phoenix, AZ: Oryx Press. doi: 10.1336/1573565512.

Bloom, B. S. (Ed.). (1956). *Taxonomy of Educational Objectives, Handbook 1: Cognitive Domain*. White Plains, NY: Longman.

Boud, D. (2000). Sustainable assessment: rethinking assessment for the learning society. *Studies in Continuing Education, 22*(2), 151–167. .doi:10.1080/713695728

Bradner, S. (1996). *The Internet standards process – revision 3. RFC 2026 (BCP 9), Internet Engineering Task Force*. Retrieved 2008-10-17, from http://ietf.org/html/rfc2026.

Brooks, F. P. Jr. (1995). *The Mythical Man-Month* (2nd ed.). Harlow, UK: Addison-Wesley.

Case, S. M., & Swanson, D. B. (2002). *Constructing Written Test Questions For the Basic and Clinical Sciences,* (3rd ed.). National Board of Medical Examiners, Philadelphia, PA. Retrieved 2008-10-17, from http://www.nbme.org/PDF/ItemWriting2003/2003IWGwhole.pdf

Friedl, J. (2002). *Mastering Regular Expressions* (2nd ed.). Sebastopol, CA: O'Reilly.

García-Robles, R., Blat, J., Sayago, S., Griffiths, D., Casado, F., & Martinez, J. (2004). Limitations of some eLearning standards for supporting learning. In M. Auer & U. Auer, (Ed.), *Proceedings of the International Conference of Interactive Computer-Aided Learning, ICL 2004, Villach (Austria)*. In cooperation with ACM-Austrian Chapter, and supported by IEEE Education Society. Retrieved 2008-10-17, from http://www.iua.upf.es/ dgriffit/papers/garcia-griffiths_villach.pdf

Gibbs, G., & Simpson, C. (2004). Conditions under which assessment supports students' learning. *Learning and Teaching in Higher Education, 5*(1), 3–31. Retrieved 2008-10-17, from http://www.glos.ac.uk/shareddata/dms/2B70988BBCD42A03949CB4F3CB78A516.pdf

Gorissen, P. (2003). *Quickscan QTI: Usability study of QTI for De Digitale Universiteit*. Retrieved 2008-10-17, from http://www.gorissen.info/Pierre/qti/Quickscan_QTI_UK.pdf

Gorissen, P. (2006). *Quickscan QTI – 2006: Usability study of QTI for De Digitale Universiteit*. Retrieved 2008-10-17, from http://www.gorissen.info/Pierre/qti/Quickscan_QTI_2006.pdf

Hanson, P., Tomecka, A., & Wawrzaszek, S. (2007). *LTS statement on course management systems at Brandeis University*. Technical report, Brandeis University, Library & Technology Services, Waltham, MA, USA. Retrieved 2007-04-19, from http://latte.brandeis.edu/project/LTS-statement-on-CMS-at-Brandeis.pdf

IMS GLC. (2003). *IMS Simple Sequencing Specification*. IMS Global Learning Consortium. Retrieved 2008-10-17, from http://imsglobal.org/simplesequencing/. Version 1.0

IMS GLC. (2004). *IMS Content Packaging Specification*. IMS Global Learning Consortium. Retrieved 2008-10-17, from http://imsglobal.org/content/packaging/. Version 1.1.4

IMS GLC. (2005). *IMS Question & Test Interoperability Specification*. IMS Global Learning Consortium. Retrieved 2008-10-17, from http://imsglobal.org/question/. Version 2.0 Final Specification.

IMS GLC. (2008). *IMS Common Cartridge Profile*. IMS Global Learning Consortium. Retrieved 2009-08-06, from http://www.imsglobal.org/cc/. Version 1.0 Final Specification.

Instructional Technology Resource Center. (2007). *Final evaluation and recommendation report.* Technical report, Idaho State University, Pocatello, Idaho, USA. Retrieved 2008-12-11, from http://www.isu.edu/itrc/resources/LMS_FINAL_REPORT_MOODLE.pdf.

ISO (International Organization for Standardization). (1986). [E] [. Information processing — Text and office systems — Standard Generalized Markup Language] [SGML]. *ISO*, *8879*, 1986.

ISO (International Organization for Standardization) (1996). ISO/IEC 14977:1996. Information technology – Syntactic metalanguage – Extended BNF.

ISO (International Organization for Standardization) (2003). ISO/IEC 19757-2:2003. *Information technology – Document Schema Definition Language (DSDL) – Part 2: Regular-grammar-based validation – RELAX NG.*

Lazarinis, F., Green, S., & Pearson, E. (2009). Measuring the conformance of hypermedia assessment tools to QTI. *International Journal of Innovation and Learning*, *6*(2), 127–146. .doi:10.1504/IJIL.2009.022809

Leuf, B., & Cunningham, W. (2001). *The Wiki Way: Quick Collaboration on the Web*. Harlow, UK: Addison-Wesley.

LMIS Committee. (2008). *Learning management system recommendation*. Technical report, University of Puget Sound, Tacoma, WA, USA. Retrieved 2008-10-17, from http://projects.ups.edu/rwthornton/LMS_Moodle_finaldraft.pdf

Lorenz, A. (2009). Elchtest in Austria – Umstände eines LMS-Wechsels und seine Folgen – ein Prüfbericht . In Apostolopoulos, N., & Schwill, A. (Eds.), *Lernen im digitalen Zeitalter. GMW09 – 4. Europäische Jahrestagung Gesellschaft für Medien in der Wissenschaft (GMW)*. GMW.

Mahlow, C. (2010). Choosing the appropriate e-learning system for a university . In Kats, Y. (Ed.), *Learning Management Systems Technologies and Software Solutions for Online Teaching: Tools and Applications*. Hershey, PA: IGI Global. doi:10.4018/978-1-61520-853-1.ch004

Nagel, D. (2007). Louisiana State moves to Moodle. *Campus Technology*. Retrieved 2008-10-17, from http://www.campustechnology.com/article.aspx? aid=52667

Piotrowski, M. (2009). *Document-Oriented E-Learning Components*. PhD thesis, Otto-von-Guericke-Universität, Magdeburg, Germany. Retrieved 2009-10-25, from http://edoc.bibliothek.uni-halle.de/servlets/DocumentServlet? id=7205

Respondus (2008). *Respondus User Guide*. Respondus, Inc., Redmond, WA, USA. Retrieved 2008-10-17, from http://www.respondus.com/downloads/Respondus35UserGuidePN.doc

Sclater, N. (2007). The demise of eAssessment interoperability? In Davis, H., Duval, E., Muramatsu, B., White, S., and Van Assche, F., editors, *Proceedings of the Workshop on Exchanging Experiences in Technology Enhanced Learning – What Went Wrong? What Went Right? (WWWrong'07)*, volume 317 of *CEUR Workshop Proceedings*, pages 70–74, Sissi, Greece. CEUR-WS.org. Retrieved 2008-10-17, from http://ceur-ws.org/Vol-317/paper07.pdf

Sclater, N., Low, B., & Barr, N. (2002). Interoperability with CAA: does it work in practice? In M. Danson, (Ed.), *Proceedings of the 6th International Conference on Computer-Assisted Assessment*, (pp. 317–326). Loughborough University. doi: 2134/1890

Smythe, C., & Roberts, P. (2000). An overview of the IMS Question & Test Interoperability specification. In *Proceedings of the 4th CAA Conference*, Loughborough, England. Loughborough University. Retrieved 2008-10-17, from http://hdl.handle.net/2134/1784.

Strobbe, C. (2006). Accessibility issues in two specifications for e-learning tests: IMS QTI 1.2 and IMS QTI 2.0. In *Computers Helping People with Special Needs, 10th International Conference, ICCHP 2006, Linz, Austria, July 11–13, 2006* (LNCS 4061, pp. 544–551). Berlin: Springer. doi: 10.1007/11788713_81.

Stuart, E. (2008). University to implement Moodle by end of year. *Daily Reveille, 112*(127). Retrieved 2008-10-17, from http://www.lsureveille.com/news/1.762154.

Trotter, A. (2008). Blackboard vs. Moodle: Competition in course-management market grows. *Digital Directions, 2*(Spring/Summer), 21. Retrieved 2008-10-17, from http://edweek.org/dd/articles/2008/06/09/01moodle.h02.html

Universität Hamburg. (2009). OLAT – eine neue eLearning-Plattform an der Universität Hamburg. *UHH Newsletter*, (3). Retrieved 2009-08-05, from http://www.uni-hamburg.de/newsletter/OLAT-ndash-eine-neue-eLearning-Plattform-an-der-Universitaet-Hamburg.html

World Wide Web Consortium. (2002). *XHTML 1.0 The Extensible HyperText Markup Language*. Retrieved 2008-10-17, from http://www.w3.org/TR/html

World Wide Web Consortium. (2004). *XML Schema*. Retrieved 2008-10-17, from http://www.w3.org/XML/Schema

World Wide Web Consortium. (2006). *Extensible Markup Language (XML) 1.0*. Retrieved 2008-10-17, from http://www.w3.org/TR/xml.

KEY TERMS AND DEFINITIONS

Authoring System: A system (or part of a system) primarily designed for creating electronic tests.

Computer-Aided Assessment, E-Assessment: Assessment that relies on information technology for the whole assessment activity, from the presentation of tasks, over the recording and evaluation of responses, to the reporting of results.

Delivery Platform: A system (or part of a system) primarily designed for making tests available to candidates and which allows candidates to take the tests.

IMS Content Packaging Specification (IMS CP): A standardized set of structures for packaging content (in particular e-learning content) for exchange between systems.

IMS Question and Test Interoperability (IMS QTI): A set of specifications for the description of electronic tests, intended as an interchange format with the goal of providing interoperability between different test authoring and delivery systems.

Interchange Format: In the narrow sense, a standardized, platform-neutral, vendor-independent file format designed for the interchange of data between different systems. In a wider sense, any format that fulfils this role, including de-facto standards.

XML: Extensible Markup Language, a metalanguage for defining markup languages. For example, XHTML or DocBook are widely used markup languages defined in terms of XML. Since XML allows to create formal specifications and provides tools for validating documents with respect to their conformance to the specification, it is commonly used for the description of interchange formats.

ENDNOTES

1. Web sites for the systems mentioned in this paragraph: Blackboard: http://blackboard.com/, Clix: http://www.im-c.com/, Desire2Learn: http://desire2learn.com/, ILIAS: http://ilias.de/, Moodle: http://moodle.org/, OLAT: http://olat.org/, Sakai: http://

sakaiproject.org/, Respondus: http://respondus.com/, Questionmark Perception: http://questionmark.com/.

2 http://www.ariadne-eu.org/

3 http://www.aicc.org/

4 http://ieeeltsc.org/

5 http://www.imsglobal.org/

6 http://plone.org/

7 See http://wdok.cs.uni-magdeburg.de/ forschung/projekte/ educomponents (accessed 2009-08-06) for download links.

8 http://wikipedia.org/ (accessed 2008-10-17)

9 The following GIFT examples (listings 1 and 2) are taken from the Moodle online help (http://docs.moodle.org/en/GIFT (accessed 2008-12-11)).

10 The examples in listings 3 and 4 are taken from the Moodle documentation (http://docs.moodle.org/en/Aiken (accessed 2008-12-11) and http://docs.moodle.org/en/WebCT_format (accessed 2008-12-11), resp.).

11 The SGML and XML specifications may serve as a good example. The SGML standard (ISO (International Organization for Standardization), 1986) contains numerous optional parts: Despite being published over twenty years ago, there is no parser that implements all parts of the standard. XML is a subset of SGML, which does not contain any optional parts: In a very short period of time, a large number of conforming and interoperable implementations have become available and XML has spread almost universally.

12 See the thread starting March 27, 2009 on the QTI mailing list: http://lists.ucles.org.uk/public/ims-qti/2009-March/001456.html (accessed 2009-08-03),

13 http://lists.ucles.org.uk/public/ims-qti/2009-March/001459.html (accessed 2009-08-03)

14 QTI 2.1, now withdrawn, was supposed to add these specifications.

15 Theoretically, XHTML could be used for these items, but fragments, e.g., just a <p> element, would not be valid, while valid XHTML documents would require further elements (e.g., <head>, <title>, <body>) which are meaningless in this context.

16 Actually, the manifest can contain more than one structure definition.

17 The systems reviewed in 2006 were: Respondus, Questionmark Perception, N@tschool!, Blackboard, Learn eXact (QTI 1.2), and TOIA (QTI 2.1)

18 ECQuiz only claims support for QTI 2.0; however, as long the relevant subset of QTI remained unchanged between versions 2.0 and 2.1, ECQuiz can be said to also support QTI 2.1.

19 That is, Blackboard and WebCT; Blackboard Inc. has acquired WebCT and now offers a single e-learning platform called Blackboard Learn.

20 Systems evaluated were Questionmark Perception, WebCT, Blackboard, Canvas Arena, and CETIS Rendering Tool.

21 For example, in the area of graphics formats, libjpeg from the Independent JPEG Group (http://www.ijg.org/ (accessed 2009-08-06)), LibTIFF (originally by Sam Leffler, http://www.libtiff.org/ (accessed 2009-08-06)), and libpng (http://www.libpng.org/pub/png/libpng.html (accessed 2009-08-06)) allow developers to easily add read and write support for the JPEG, TIFF, and PNG file formats and certainly played a significant role in the widespread acceptance of the corresponding standards.

22 http://com.fronter.info/

23 http://www.kent.ac.uk/ elearning/moodle/announcement.html (accessed 2008-10-17)

24 http://www.virtualcampus.ch/ (accessed 2009-08-05)

Chapter 5
Interoperability Issues for Systems Managing Competency Information: A Preliminary Study

Bernard Blandin
Université Paris Ouest and CESI Group, France

Geoffrey Frank
RTI International, USA

Simone Laughton
University of Toronto Mississauga Library, Canada

Kenji Hirata
Toyo University, Japan

ABSTRACT

This chapter has four sections. The first one describes how the needs for interoperability in exchanging competency information have been addressed so far. The second part adopts a "Digital Services Supply Chain" approach and discusses the issues related to the exchange of competency information across systems regarding this approach. The third part is the core part of this chapter. It describes the 4 levels of the proposed approach: the Conceptual Reference Model (CRM), the Semantic Model, the Information Model and the Data Model. The final section presents the research directions currently envisaged, and the research programme needed to make the proposed approach operational.

INTRODUCTION

We are living in a world of transformative change, where new and emerging technologies are being used increasingly for activities that support learning, education, and training (Thiriet et al., 2002; Schubert & Leimstoll, 2007). Competency frameworks, taxonomies, and Information Technology (IT) systems are being developed and used to support the management and exchange of competency information within and amongst organizations, government departments, and

DOI: 10.4018/978-1-61692-789-9.ch005

educational institutions (CEN, 2005; Thieriet et al., 2002; Lindgren, Henfridsson, & Schultze, 2004; Zouaq, Nkambou, & Frasson, 2007; Government of Alberta, 2005). At both local and international levels, it is essential that IT systems can interface and operate cohesively (Owen, 1999 cited in Fleishmann, 2007). The development of IT standards at an international level can help to ensure consistency and efficiency of these different systems. This chapter will explore interoperability issues for systems managing competency information that are relevant to researchers as well as to practitioners.

HOW THE NEED FOR INTEROPERABILITY ACROSS DIGITAL SERVICES SUPPLY CHAINS HAS BEEN ADDRESSED SO FAR

Competency management has become a core issue in learning, education and training (LET). Research is ongoing within the field of education regarding the structuring and integration of competencies and skills in systems that support learning and education within countries as well as transnationally (Pacquette et al., 2007; Najjar & Klobučar, 2009). In the Human Resources Management (HRM) field during the last quarter of the 20th century we have seen extensive development of the use of IT systems; and, electronic processing of competency information has been progressively incorporated into daily operations within companies' Human Resources (HR) departments. Driven by international organisations like OECD, the shift from "knowledge-oriented" education to "competency-oriented" education has gained prominence in the academic area in the last three decades of the 20th century (Gardiner, 1994 cited in Sauber et al., 2008).

Knowledge sharing, innovative technology transfer, and lifelong learning are viewed as three key strategies that have the potential to enable humankind to successfully meet the challenges that are being encountered and that will be encountered in the years to come (Namara et al., 2007; Sherwood & Covin, 2008; Om, Lee, & Chang, 2007). However, underlying structures and technologies need to be in place in order to support the communication and connections required to work together to develop and apply skills and knowledge in a manner that is ethical and sustainable (Morgan, Raidén, Naylor, G. 2008; Beer & Meethan, 2007; Bernstein & Cashore, 2007). Competency acquisition in the Knowledge society requires adaptive, flexible learning systems that support individual human development across multiple contexts, - education systems, work environments, informal learning opportunities, etc. (Pacquette et al., 2007). Interoperability between IT systems managing competency information in different sectors (companies, schools and universities, employment agencies, etc.) has become a critical issue.

Some Definitions that are Used in this Chapter

Definition of a Digital Services Supply Chain Approach

Configuring a Digital Services Supply Chain (DSSC) for Learning, Education and Training (LET) requires a holistic systems approach that documents the interrelationships and interconnections of constituent parts (Mentzer et al., 2001; Al-Turki, Dufuaa, Ayar, & Demirel, 2008; Beer & Meethan, 2007; Lummus, Krumwiede, & Vokurka, 2001). There are many stakeholders from different social "worlds" who have an interest in competency information, all with different views of the information and different terminologies about competency information. For example: "a learning objective" may be described in a Course Management System, but not in a HRM system. For LET applications, a Digital Services Supply Chain approach is defined as: process of the delivery of digital products and services from point(s) of origin (provider) to destination (stakeholder) to support learning, education and training.

Considering the information systems in each "world" as a DSSC and modelling them using the ISO/IEC Joint Technical Committee 1 Sub-Committee 36 (ISO/IEC JTC1 SC36) Conceptual Reference Model (CRM) for Competencies and Related Objects (ISO/IEC 24763) is a first step towards more effective management and exchange of competency information across sectors, languages, and cultures.

A Definition of Competency

Competency has multiple definitions according to the community in which the term is used. The ISO/IEC JTC1 SC36 definition of competency is:

A *competency* is the observable or measurable ability of an actor to perform necessary action(s) in given context(s) to achieve specific outcome(s).

Existing Approaches

Several organizations have attempted to develop information technology specifications or standards concerning competency information and competency data models in different professional environments:

- IMS Global Learning Consortium Inc., with its Reusable Definition of Competency or Educational Objective (RDCEO),
- IEEE Learning Technology Standards Committee (IEEE LTSC), with its Reusable Competency Definition (RCD)
- The HR-XML Consortium, Inc., with its HR XML Competencies specifications ("Competencies schemas").

The application of these standards in real systems has been studied by Hirata and Brown (2007, 2008) and they report the following problems:

1. HR information cannot be shared with different HR-related platforms,
2. HR information is not used within HRD easily, because it usually does not deal with detailed skill and competency information in HR-related systems,
3. Individual status regarding degree attainment and skill and competency proficiency, for example, is not addressed well within many HR related systems and skills management systems,
4. Individual developmental paths cannot be formulated due to the limitations of many HR-related systems.
5. Individuals and organizations cannot design career strategies and career paths using existing common dimensions that are available within HR-related systems,
6. Skill and competency evidentiary information cannot be easily shared with other systems,
7. Evaluation biases in human assessment are hard to avoid without supporting systems.
8. *Human assessment cannot be reflected by everyday operation and work performance using HR-related systems.*

One approach for capturing competency information is to focus on a specific sector of industry that has a common knowledge domain vocabulary. For example, the *Skills Framework for the Information Age* (SFIA) in the U.K. provides a common reference model that is intended to support the training and development needs of IT professionals (SFIA foundation, 2008). Similarly, the Japanese Embedded Technology Skills Standards (ETSS) focus on unifying the description of competencies and skills across the embedded systems sector, and were initiated and developed jointly by the Japanese Ministry of Economy, Trade and Industry (METI) and the Information technology Promotion Agency (IPA) (Hirata, Seta, Makiuchi, 2007). Such an approach at a national level is interesting, since it allows interoperability between information systems in different areas such as employment (career / job description), HRM (skills description) and education and training (training and development guidelines). These industry sector approaches benefit from a common vocabulary for competencies, but this benefit also imposes a limit on the scope of competency data sharing.

Another approach for making competency information usable within Learning Management Systems is based on creating links between Learning Resources and competency taxonomies through the use of metadata. (Ostyn, 2005; Frank, Gemeinhardt & Ostyn, 2005). A taxonomy typically is a type of controlled vocabulary that has a hierarchical structure. The multiple levels of abstraction in the taxonomies used in this approach allow an organization to adhere to the taxonomy structure at an extended abstract level and to tailor the taxonomy to their specific requirements at the more detailed levels of the taxonomy. This approach has been used by the U.S. Navy, which has converted its high level competencies in the competency model to adhere to the taxonomy underlying O*Net (O*Net, 2009), while tailoring the detailed levels to their competency specialities (Krain & Gabel, 2007). They have benefited from this approach by being able to compare the projected supply and demand for similar military and civilian jobs and to assess qualification standards for comparable jobs. The O*Net taxonomy can be automatically transformed into the IEEE RCD format (Ostyn, 2005), which can be a helpful approach to leverage taxonomic structures. IMS RDCEO, the precursor of the IEEE RCD, provides similar capabilities. Using a national occupation source such as the O*Net initiative (O*Net, 2009), in the USA, it is possible to identify common competency structures that are present in separate occupations, thus identifying fields of work where competencies may be transferable.

At a more formal transnational level, the Europass is an interesting example of an approach that is intended to enhance qualification recognition, comparability, and transparency (Deane, 2005). Several separate documents are linked in the Europass approach including (EC, 2009; Deane, 2005):

- CV – used by an individual to make her/his qualifications and skills visible;
- Language Passport – description of language and related skills crucial for learning and working in Europe;
- Certificate Supplement – detailed information related to vocational education and training (provided by a certifying authority);
- Diploma Supplement – detailed information regarding higher education diplomas and degrees (issued by a higher education institution); and,
- Mobility – record of a recognized period of time of learning or training in another European country.

Taking the example of the Europass Language Passport, there are several telling aspects to the approach that are instructive. The Language Passport defines a competency ontology that includes 3 complex competencies and 5 simple competencies (Deane, 2005; Sampson, Karampiperis & Fytros, 2007).

More generic is the approach proposed by Hirata and Brown (2008) in their Skills-Competency Management Architecture (C-March) proposal, which attempts to solve the problems raised by the use of current standards that they have identified and which are listed above. Their model is based on 7 interlinked entities within the Information System:

- e-profile, containing personal information, including knowledge, skills, abilities…
- competency information, describing competencies taxonomies and structures of competency descriptions (machine readable information),

- competency semantic information, which allow the machine able to understand man-readable information),
- evidence information, related to the processing of competency evidence,
- assessment methods and metrics, describing the assessment methods and the measurement of competencies,
- meta model, which structures and allows for monitoring of the other elements, and describes how to harmonize structures, descriptions, and semantics

The C-March approach provides a detailed and holistic overview that is intended to enhance interoperability for future systems, it is yet to be determined if it will allow existing systems to interoperate. Furthermore, mechanisms used by the meta model entity or by the competency semantic information entity are not widely implemented so far, and the feasibility and optimal use of this approach may require further research.

SHARING COMPETENCY INFORMATION ACROSS DIGITAL SERVICES SUPPLY CHAINS: THE ISSUES

In this section, issues and problems that interoperability of competency information across DSSCs has to address are presented.

General Issues

IT systems managing competency information have to face the following challenges, which are given here unprioritized or unordered in terms of importance:

- There is no single definition of competency that is accepted by all. Instead, there are many definitions, using varied structures and vocabularies, describing different levels of competency. It has even been suggested that competency is an unobservable entity, and therefore that it cannot be traced measured or recorded.
- IT systems may be designed, developed, and implemented with specific labels for competency information in mind: according to the context in which it is used. The term "competency" can be considered in its
  - "*actual*" dimension, and expressed as such;
  - "*desired*" dimension and appear as "training goals", "learning objectives", "educational objectives", "abilities" or "capabilities", etc.;
  - "*required*" dimension, and can be found under the same labels as previously, or as an "aptitude".
- IT systems need to provide cost-effective support for the description of competencies at multiple levels of abstraction and in various formats.
  - The description of a competency depends on the paradigm (the theory) in use or which underlies the IT system. Sometimes, it must include factors such as context, level, or evidence.
  - Competency may improve or deteriorate over the course of time depending on opportunities for practice and application. So, obsolescence factors might be included.
  - An evidence of a competency comes in a very broad variety of forms. Thus, another challenge for competency information standards is related to the provision of methods for accurately associating competency requirements with appropriate evidence.
- IT systems may need to comply with international, national and regional legislative requirements.

- Competency information is data about people that can be used to make decisions related to employment, advancement, admission, accreditation, etc. Where competency information is linked to an identifiable individual, the protection of the privacy of that identifiable individual is essential.

Several key issues have been identified that need to be solved if competency information is to be shared across IT systems. As indicated by Sampson, Karampiperis & Fytros, it is essential that an IT system be able to support representation of competency level, grading scale [or metric method], and threshold (2007). In addition, the IT system needs to be able to support the capability of recombinant competency construction (Sampson, Karampiperis & Fytros, 2007).

Specific Issues Related to the Application of the Digital Services Supply Chain (DSSC) Approach to Learning, Education, and Training

The Digital Services Supply Chain approach can be applied to the field of learning, education, and training; however, there are specific issues that need to be considered and addressed in order for this approach to be successfully implemented. A review of the literature suggests that:

- Service industry supply chains tend to be very short and may involve a service provider who acts as an agent on behalf of customers (Al-Turki, Dufuaa, Ayar & Demirel, 2008);
- Relationships in a service supply chain may be viewed more as a hub indicating that the relationships may be more complex than a simple chain (Al-Turki, Dufuaa, Ayar & Demirel, 2008);
- Representatives of multiple communities are involved with and rely upon Digital Services Supply Chains and bring their own perspectives and terminologies. A digital services supply chain may involve different communities. For example, in one digital services supply chain there could be four different communities involved: industry, academic institutions, faculty and professional consultants, and the learners who want to be workers. Many other combinations of communities are possible as well.
- Each of the entities participating in a DSSC has an interest in protecting its intellectual property. The nature of a supply chain means that each link adds value to a product. This makes it difficult to identify how the value in the end result of the chain should be assigned to the participants in the process.
- Each of the entities participating in a DSSC has an interest in protecting its "brand" or personal identification information and assuring that only the relevant aspects of that information are passed on to other suppliers in the supply chain.
- Also, education and some forms of learning, and even some forms of training (e.g., first aid training) could be categorized as "public goods", which has implications for the application, implementation, and evaluation of a Digital Services Supply Chain approach. A "public good" is a service or a commodity that when supplied to one person can be provided to others at no additional cost (Black, 2003). A pure "public good" is "non-rival in consumption (one person's consumption of the good does not reduce its availability to anyone else), and has the characteristic of non-excludability" (Black, 2003).

Specifications and Standards that Currently Provide Components for a Digital Services Supply Chain Approach for Learning, Education, and Training

Several organisations throughout the world are developing consensus in different areas related to specific processes and components for a Digital Services Supply Chain approach for learning, education, and training. For example, different aspects of a *Digital Services Supply Chain* approach for LET may involve one or a combination of specific fundamental specifications and standards such as:

- IMS LD for instruction design,
- IEEE LOM, which defines learning object metadata requirements,
- The ISO/IEC JTC1 SC36 MLR for the selection of metadata to describe learning objects,
- IMS CP and now IMS CC for learning resources development and delivery,
- IMS LIP Learner Information Package including Accessibility for LIP (ACCLIP),
- IMS Enterprise or the future IMS LIS for learning services management,
- HR-XML to support Human Resource Management business processes,
- IEEE LTSC API or the future IMS LTI for learning services delivery,
- IMS QTI for assessments,
- ETSS & ITSS, to provide a framework, contents, metrics, and a guideline for skill, job, and training
- Dublin Core Education Application Profile (DC-Ed, 2008)

Some of these specifications and standards may be considered as "stand-alone", relating to a particular part of a *Digital Services Supply Chain* approach (e.g. IMS LD), and others can be combined into coherent sets (e.g. IEEE LOM, IMS CP and IEEE LTSC API are parts of the ADL SCORM) and may be used by different parts of a *Digital Services Supply Chain* approach for LET. This type of combination is more frequently required to implement interoperable complex systems supporting an increasing number of processes, and this is the trend in current standards development thinking, as expressed in the recent LETSI Assumptions Document on SCORM 2.0 (LETSI, 2009).

Sometimes, interoperability concerns more than one single Digital Services Supply Chain (*DSSC*), as is the case for standards related to *digital description of competencies*: today, at least, the Digital Services Supply Chain approach for academic organizations, human resources management services, and employment services are required by their stakeholders to become interoperable and to be able to transfer information across different supply chains, using uniquely constructed definitions of the word "*competency*" and different information models, for various purposes, in diverse contexts. This particularly complex situation leads the authors of this paper to work out a specific methodology to address this type of *cross-DSSC interoperability* in the context of ISO/IEC JTC1 SC 36 Information Technology for Learning, Education, and Training (see next section).

Organization and Aggregation of Competency Information

The issue of interoperability between systems managing and exchanging competency information is often hidden or masked behind this issue: "organization and aggregation of competency information".

One of the difficulties arising when addressing the issue of interoperability under this guise comes from the fact that competency information has several meanings.

1. In some systems competency information is used as metadata that distinguishes educational resources from other digital information resources

(Currier et al., 2008). For example, competency information can serve as a link between the content of an educational resource and assessments of how well the learner has absorbed that content. Thus a training course can be configured by using competency information associated with a general knowledge resource to find matching assessment packages.

Competency information serves as an essential description for the purpose of assessments (IMS QTI, 2008), which may be viewed as a particular subclass of educational resources. However, appropriate design and labeling of assessment resources are some of the most controversial aspects of the design and documentation of educational resources. Ensuring that assessments are valid (i.e., that the assessment results are accurate predictors of future competency), reliable (i.e., that the assessment results are consistent across multiple uses), and fair are significant intellectual and ethical challenges. At the same time, assessment can play a high-stakes role in determining the future of the learner and the instructor (U.S. Department of Education, 2004). This combination of intellectual and ethical challenges and the potential impact on the learner ensures a high level of controversy.

2. Competency information can be an educational resource in itself. For example, a job profile can be considered an educational resource. Later in this chapter, we describe ISO/IEC JTC1 SC36 CRM for Competencies and Related Objects (ISO/IEC 24763), which can be used to define queries across multiple databases for different purposes such as the configuration of job profiles.

3. Competency information can be used as a guide for selecting participants to fill roles in collaborative workgroups (ISO/IEC 19778). In this case, the required dimension of competency information associated with the workgroup roles is matched against the actual dimension of competency of the candidate participants to determine which participants may be candidates to fill specific roles.

4. In a more general sense, competency information may be organized or aggregated in some typical ways (Hirata, Seta & Makiuchi, 2007) for example to:

- describe
    - learner profiles,
    - learning records, and
    - learning objectives;
- assess learners' knowledge and skills
    - before and after learning,
    - to measure and document transfer of training;
- express one's ability and experience in
    - a resume,
    - an ePortfolio;
- identify
    - job specifications, and,
    - skill gaps.

Each of these may involve combining different levels of competency information etc. Therefore, in order for these different systems to interoperate competency information may need to be defined in concert with contextual information. Additionally, competency information may need to be aggregated to enable exchange between various systems.

The paper cited above uses the following terms,

- competency organization: structuring information about a way to build or formulate a competency model or a competency structure, which consist of competencies.
- competency composition: information aggregation of a competency or a set of competencies, which consist of competency elements such as title, description, related knowledge, related skill, sub-competencies etc.
- competency package: an aggregated information for a competency or a set of competency to provide information that can be

used in applications or as an application form.

A common paradigm for constructing competency information structures is through the definitions of queries that link data from multiple database tables, etc., possibly across different databases. Exchange of data between multiple databases is facilitated by standards such as XML, Xpath, XQuery, and SRU/SRW (Standards Australia, 2007). Common index terms are needed to link these structures and are necessary for interoperability in this paradigm. One strategy for ensuring common index terms is the use of controlled vocabularies.

A controlled vocabulary is a mechanism that has been used for defining competency. The occupational specialty codes used by the U.S. military are an example of a controlled vocabulary that is used for training and for definition of organizational roles (Frank, Gemeinhardt & Ostyn, 2005). Controlled vocabularies require a simple information model that is easy to maintain. The items in a controlled vocabulary are unique and can be used as index terms for queries. However, the matching has to be exact. Unlike taxonomies, controlled vocabularies do not provide a structure for abstraction or approximate matching, and are therefore unforgiving mechanisms for interoperability. The expense of retrospective indexing of competencies using controlled vocabularies in a dynamic human resource environment is daunting.

Controlled vocabularies have been used successfully in limited ways. For example, both the IEEE LOM (2002) and the Dublin Core Education Application Profile (DC-Ed, 2008) use small vocabularies including terms such as teacher, author, publisher, learner, manager to specify roles such as intended user. However, incompatibilities between these vocabularies prevent completely automatic translations and consequently prevent effective interoperability.

An alternative to the use of controlled vocabularies to define index terms is the use of taxonomies as index terms. Taxonomies allow matches at different levels of abstraction. This approach is particularly useful in collecting summative data from less precise input sources. For example, this approach was used to match driver training methods with accident reports (Frank, Hubal, & O'Bea, 2007). In this example the analysis of training costs and risks required the construction of competency definitions as an ontology that connected established taxonomies reflecting specific domain knowledge. The basic form of the competency may be viewed as a task, condition, and standard triple where the task is defined as "drive a vehicle." In this case, a taxonomy of vehicles developed by the U.S. Federal Highway Administration was used. This taxonomy is widely used for regulatory and driver certification or licensing. The terms in the taxonomy also are used as a controlled vocabulary by the U.S. Army for reporting accidents. However, the precision of the vehicle type identification in the reports varied widely. The same controlled vocabulary was used with much greater precision to report the equipment used for training. Increases in the frequency and severity of driving accidents led the U. S. Army to review its driver training programs. The competency ontology provided a framework for comparing the aggregate costs of upgrading the vehicles used for the training against the risks indicated by the accident data. The taxonomy allowed comparable accident risk and equipment cost data to be aggregated to any desired level of abstraction as a decision aid for training system managers. This example also demonstrates interoperability across two DSSCs: The training DSSC for the U.S. Army and the risk management section of the U. S. Army Personnel Command.

Competency information is most useful when defined in a context. This context includes information about:

- The organizations involved in the development or previous use of the competency information and the roles that they played;

- The environment in which competency either is evaluated or is applied;
- The methods, processes, and criteria used to assess the competency; and,
- The outcomes of the use of the competency and the evidence that demonstrates the competency.

Therefore, information models for competency information should provide ways of including this contextual information.

Issues and Challenges as They are Currently Seen

The controlled vocabularies being developed as part of standards about educational resources are one way of meeting the need for contextual information. Both the IEEE LOM standard (IEEE, 2002) and the Dublin Core Education Application Profile (DC-Ed, 2008) include vocabularies addressing these aspects of competency information. Ongoing work on the ISO/IEC JTC1 SC36 CRM for Competencies and Related Objects is described in detail below and may be used to help capture these contextual relations.

The memo of understanding between the IEEE LTSC and the Dublin Core Metadata Initiative (DCMI, 2007) identifies three goals that apply to competency information standards: extensibility, modularity, and potential for refinement.

An extensible standard should allow new semantic constructs to be added by different communities of interest. These extensions should not compromise cross-domain interoperability. The CRM for Competencies and Related Objects ("Competency CRM") provides guidelines for achieving extensibility by defining a structure of entities and properties linking those entities. The entities are defined in terms of extensible class hierarchies. The effort needed in extending the standard includes refining definitions of the properties associated with new subclasses of entities.

A modular standard should be defined in terms of several independent modules that can be extended or refined by different communities of practice. A modular standard is a method for achieving cross-domain interoperability. Thus competency information is viewed as a modular component of a larger set of metadata standards for learning, education, and training. For example, the IEEE LOM (IEEE, 2002) includes competency information as a component of learning metadata. Similarly, metadata for learning resources should be a modular component of a larger set of metadata standards for digital multimedia materials. So the Dublin Core Education Application Profile (DC-Ed, 2008) is working on standards for learning resources as a modular component of the Dublin Core metadata. The entities of the CRM for Competencies and Related Objects are defined and the properties that describe the relationships between entities are provided in a manner that supports a modular approach that is applicable across different domains. In addition to modularity, standards also should provide a mechanism for refinement. The class hierarchies used in the CRM for Competencies and Related Objects are the primary mechanism for refinement as further described in a section further on regarding the proposed multi-layered approach.

Competency information itself can be defined modularly. For example, some competencies can be defined in terms of knowledge, skills, and attitudes. Frank, Gemeinhardt, and Ostyn (2005) showed how defining a competency using the IEEE RCD as an aggregate of modular knowledge, skills, and attitudes allows specific educational assets to be associated with the knowledge and skills modules.

This allows a database of competency information to interoperate with databases of knowledge assets and separate skills assets.

The memo of understanding between the IEEE LTSC and the Dublin Core Metadata Initiative (DCMI, 2007) identifies eliminating semantic overlap as a method for achieving interoperability

Figure 1. The general framework for DSSC Interoperability

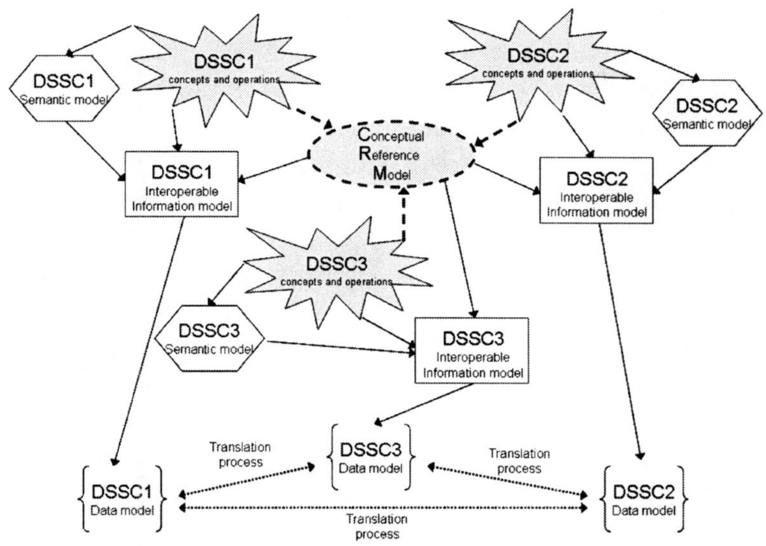

between databases using different standards. The class hierarchies of an ontology like the Competency CRM suggest a strategy for estimating the level of semantic overlap in terms of identifying overlapping areas of the taxonomies.

These are some of the challenges as currently seen by the standardization organizations mentioned in this section. Discussion regarding a possible alternative approach is provided in the next section.

USING A DIGITAL SERVICES SUPPLY CHAIN APPROACH FOR COMPETENCY INFORMATION

In this section, we describe a methodology which is proposed to overcome the difficulties identified in section 1 and to address the issues mentioned in section 2.

For this, we need to introduce a fourth element to the generally accepted 3-layer model for data model interoperability specifications: meta model (1st layer), information model (2nd layer), and data model (3rd layer) (Hirata, Ohara, & Makiuchi, 2007). This 4th element does not correspond to a 4th layer. It is a more conceptual approach, akin to a semantic model, and is referred to as a common "*Conceptual Reference Model (CRM)*" that may be used to describe and compare the internal semantics of disparate Digital Services Supply Chains.

The CRM for Competencies and Related Objects (ISO/IEC 24763) within a general framework for digital services supply chain interoperability is described in Figure 1 below.

This 4th element allows for the description of the processes in each *DSSC,* and handles information about the *commonly-used-across-DSSC* concept of "*competency*", whether as an input to or an output of the processes. No matter how the information is labelled or structured, the *Conceptual Reference Model* provides the means to identify where "*competency information records*" reside in the digital services supporting system, and how they are likely to be labelled. For example, competency information records can be found under the label "*pedagogical objectives*" or "*learning goals*" in a digital certification transcript from an academic information management system, as well as under "*profile of skills and competences*" in the European supplement to a certificate (CEN, 2005) or under the label of "*Competency profile*" in the Alberta province (Ca) (Government of Alberta, 2005). This information coming from a specific *DSSC* context could be added to a CV compliant with the Europass directive (European Communities, 2009), and from there, matched to a "job profile" proposed by a *DSSC* service provided by a local Employment Agency.

Once these "*competency information records*" are identified and localized in the different databases, a first question appears: *how is this competency information structured in the record, and are the records structured in the same way*? Generally, the answer to this question is "*no*". This is why a DSSC Semantic Model could be useful.

A Multi-Layered Approach to Information Technology Standards

Level 0: The ITLET Conceptual Reference Model for Competency Information

The Conceptual Reference Model (CRM) is the most abstract level of the standardization process that we propose. A Conceptual Reference Model provides definitions and a formal structure for describing implicit and explicit concepts and relationships within a system. As noted in figure 2 below, the CRM for Competencies and Related Objects comprises classes of entities and relationships (called properties) between the entities. The Competency CRM includes classes of entities such as competency, actor, action, outcome, evaluation, and assessment process. For the CRM for Competencies and Related Objects, class properties are manifested as statements that refer to a common conceptualization of domain experts. The sum of these properties is called the intension of the class. A class that is identified as being present in a system can be the domain or range of one or more properties formally defined in a model.

The entity classes are categories of "entities" that are found in the real world. For the Competency CRM, instances of entities are present or involved in competency-related events. An entity plays the role of a noun either as a subject or object, in a competency model statement consisting of nouns (classes) and verbs (properties). The entity classes are hierarchical. Methods and attributes are inherited down the entity class hierarchies. It is important to note that the entity classes are optional and repeatable when used to describe real world instances that are being explored and examined using the Conceptual Reference Model. This provides flexibility and modularity to allow different systems to be represented and compared using the Conceptual Reference Model.

A property plays a role analogous to a verb in the sense that it needs to be defined with reference to both a domain and a range. Domain and range are analogous to the subject and object in a phrase (unlike classes, which can be defined independently). The relationships between entities are also class hierarchies that inherit methods and attributes. These relationships may be stated as triples that define the relationship class, the domain entity class and the range entity class.

The primary purpose of the CRM for Competencies and Related Objects is to support consistency and enhance understanding of various existing competency information models. Based on the CIDOC Conceptual Reference Model (CRM) (ISO, 2006), classes and properties have been identified that are common across multiple use cases. These classes and properties provide reference points for attributes and information structures included in the information models.

The CRM for Competencies and Related Objects, being developed by ISO/IEC JTC1 SC36 Information Technology for Learning, Education, and Training (ITLET), provides a common reference point to facilitate the exchange and management of competency information in IT

Figure 2. The Conceptual Reference Model for Competencies and Related Objects. ©ISO used with permission

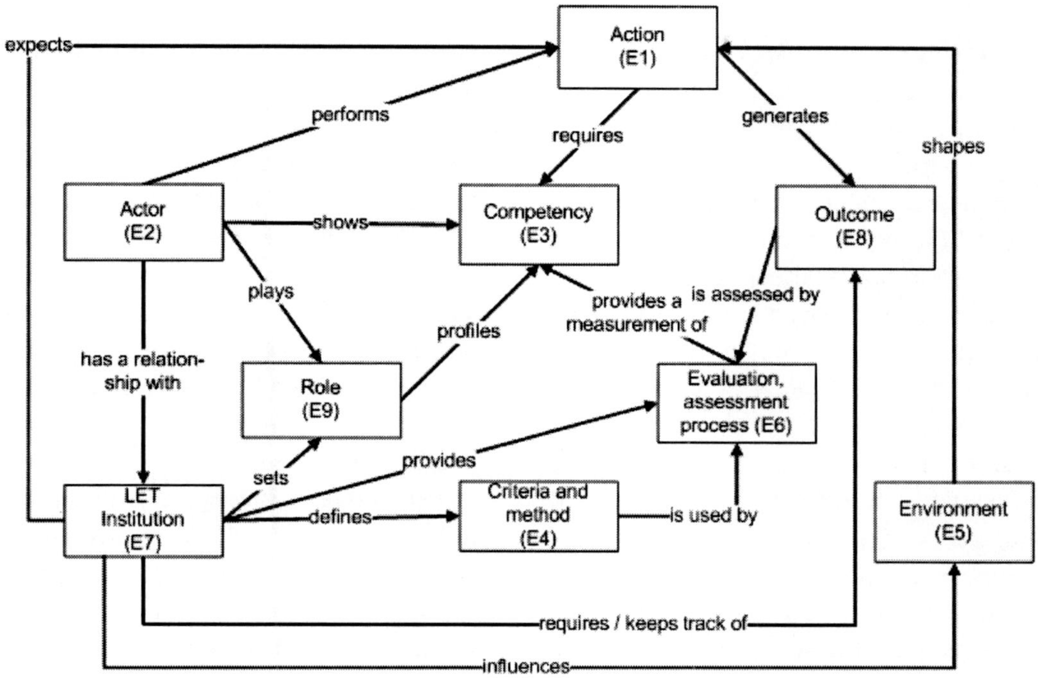

systems. In particular, the classes and properties identify roles and responsibilities for the creators and users of competency information. The properties of the Competency CRM link the roles to the competency information objects that they use or create. The links between competency information objects and their creators indicate requirements for labelling the information for tracking and auditing competency information. The CIDOC CRM provides guidance here because of its focus on tracking the provenance of objects in museums and libraries. Similarly, the links between users and the competency information objects that they require provides guidance for who should be allowed access to specific portions of these records. This is a critical aspect of competency information management in order to meet privacy requirements.

Level 1: The Meta Model

Competency information can be described in many ways such as:

- at different levels: for example at a very high level such as to be able to manage a department of 25 people in a medium-sized company, or at a very low level such as to be able to assess the performance of a subordinate using the methodology in use in the company;
- using different types of terms, such as a verb or a noun;
- employing different methodologies such as controlled vocabularies, taxonomies, and ontologies;
- including or omitting additional descriptive information such as metrics to be used, threshold, weight, etc.; and,

- providing additional contextual information.

If the structure is not equivalent in the systems being compared, then further information is needed to be able to identify the elements and the relationships between the elements that are present within the competency information records. This information may be considered at a semantic level to help determine if a described competency is equivalent to another one, if it is not equivalent at all, or if one description might be considered as included in the other. Here, a Semantic Model could be useful.

A first attempt has been made to explore these issues with the development of the Skill and Competency Meta Model developed by the Japanese national ETSS project. This Meta Model is mainly focusing on the content of competencies (Hirata, Ohara and Makiuchi, 2007, Hirata and Saito, 2009).

Though this part has not been developed so far in ISO/IEC JTC1 SC36, it is included in the programme of further work. In this chapter we make a suggestion regarding how to develop such a model, which could be considered as a complement to the Japanese approach. Since competency will never be described in exactly the same words across different organisations, the best way to facilitate interoperability of description is to provide something like "*competency thesauri*" which allow for the association of a language and a vocabulary to a competency information description, and can be used to define competency information descriptions as equivalent, or as belonging to a category of competency, etc. The basis for such "competency thesauri" could be a specification like the ZTHES specifications for thesaurus representation, access and navigation (http://zthes.z3950.org/). However, this needs further investigation.

Level 2: The Information Model

The information model defines requirements at an abstract level for the components of an information object. In general, the information model provides a "pseudo-code" representation of how queries to different databases could be used to produce a particular information object.

The information model derived from the Competency CRM is presented here in figure 3 as a first step to identify the relevant pieces of information related to competencies within the IT systems. It can be completed by more classical approaches specifying how to build an information model, but developing this is beyond the scope of this chapter. Figure 3 illustrates how the properties in the Competency CRM (shown as arrows) imply tables of information that are indexed by information associated with the entities. For example, the Actor information includes personal identification information about the people that are involved in the competency-related DSSC. Similarly, the environment information specifies the conditions under which the competency is either used or assessed. Also, work experience information usually includes information about the ITLET institution, the outcomes of use of the competency, and relevant environment information.

Once the detailed information has been gathered and modelled using the Competency CRM, the CRM diagram is used to derive an information model according to the structure noted in Figure 3 below. It should be noted that the information that is present in the information model will depend upon the classes that are present in the real world example that is being analyzed.

To derive this information model, it is assumed that:

1. Each entity of the real world composing the CRM can be represented or described in an Information System by a specific set of information, and

Figure 3. Information model derived from the CRM for Competencies and Related Objects. © ISO used with permission

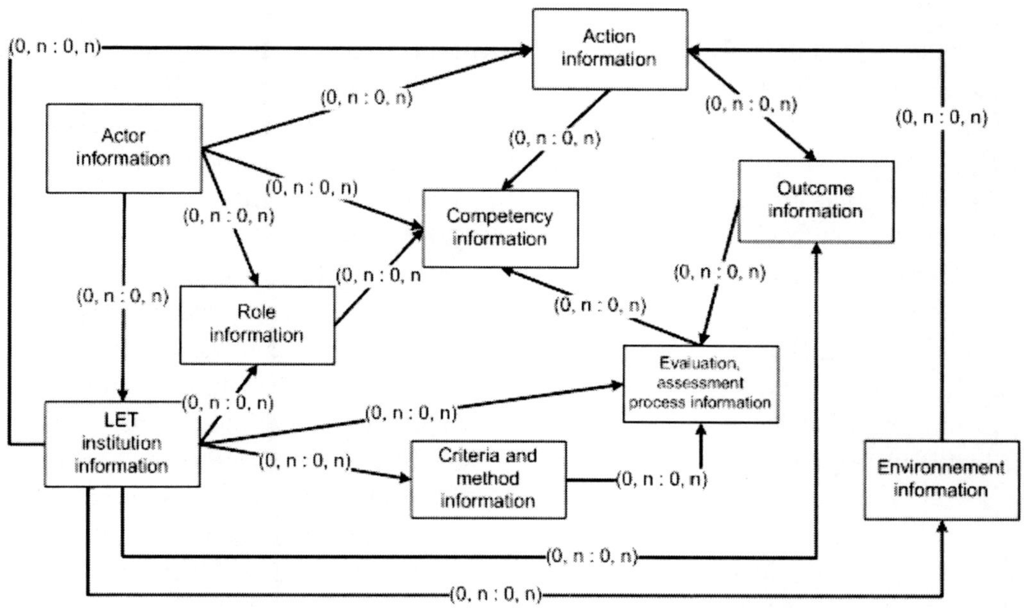

2. The properties of the CRM are preserved as relations between the different sets of information.

NOTE The quantifiers of the relations should be revised as appropriate according to the specific use-case(s) being analyzed.

A second notion that is important in this methodology is: "competency information object", which designates a set of recorded information that is collected to facilitate human exchanges about competency. The competency information object may include information from different parts of an IT system, gathered by queries. For example, a curriculum vitae generally comprises 4 parts, which might be stored independently in different parts of a system:

1. personal information
2. work experience information
3. education and training information
4. competency information

Commonly used competency information objects are: a resume (short CV), an e-portfolio, a job profile, a job advertisement, an academic transcript, a "diploma supplement"… All of these information objects comprise information about competencies, together with other information related to a person, an institution, etc. It is important to be able to identify these objects, in order to be able to process their competency information part: for example, to compare automatically a CV and a job advertisement, or to aggregate competency information provided within an academic transcript to a personal e-portfolio.

The use of the CRM to model the case helps to identify the competency information objects involved in the operation concerned.

Level 3: The Data Model and Representation Bindings

The data model defines required data fields needed to meet the requirements for an information object as specified in an information model.

At the data model level, sizing requirements and data formats are specified as a means of assuring interoperability between systems.

A representation binding is a mapping to a specific representation format, such as an XML data schema.

In general, data models corresponding to competency information records coming from disparate information objects represented in databases are different, and therefore not directly usable for data processing such as comparisons or aggregations. They need to be converted into an interoperable model before being processed. The use of a Semantic Model as described at level 1 will facilitate the creation of such an interoperable model.

A Narrative Use Case to Illustrate the Results of the DSSC Methodology

This case takes place in a near future, when standardized "*Competency Thesauri*" are provided in several geographical areas at regional, national or supra-national levels, and when *Digital Services Supply Chain providers* have set-up services to help their users to create and transfer complex information objects that are needed to perform actions related to the management of their career (completing a personal e-portfolio, searching for a new job, editing a CV…, etc).

Sonja is an *Actor* in the Competency CRM terminology. She has just finished a course providing a Social Science Master degree, and intends to apply for her first "real job" related to the competencies she acquired at the University (an *ITLET Institution* in the Competency CRM terminology). She has already had summer jobs, but they were not related to her primary field of study (according to the Competency CRM, the *Outcomes* of these jobs do not match the *Outcomes* required for the jobs she is considering). She nonetheless acquired competencies doing these jobs, which she has already put in her *e-portfolio provided by the Local Government (ITLET Institution)*. This e-portfolio is indexed by her personal identification information. Her e-portfolio job experiences describe the *Roles* that she undertook during summer jobs (e.g., camp counsellor), and the *Actions* she performed (supervising activities of children between 6 and12 years old) and the *Environments* (outdoor camps) in which those jobs were performed.

Her first task is to update her *e-portfolio*, in order to integrate the competencies acquired during her studies as described in the *diploma supplement* of her Master degree. So she asks her University to send her a copy of this document. The diploma supplement is evidence of the *Outcomes* of her studies and the *Assessments* conducted by the University. She sends her University her personal identification information and asks it to send her an electronic version of the *diploma supplement*, that describes the acquired competencies using the recently released *standardized Social Sciences Competency Thesaurus*. The University provides this electronic information and a hyperlink to the authenticated version of her records maintained in the University database.

Upon receiving this document, *she imports the list of competencies and associated assessment evidence included in the diploma supplement* into her e-portfolio. She then checks if all the competencies in her e-portfolio, including those listed for her summer jobs, are compliant with the new *standardized Social Sciences Competency Thesaurus,* since she used a previous version of the Thesaurus to enter competencies into her portfolio. *She exports the list of her competencies, and sends it for checking to the Social Sciences Competency Thesaurus Test Service*. The Test Service returns 12 competencies that are not compliant with the current version of the thesaurus. The thesaurus organizes the competencies into taxonomies associated with several views. For example, her experience as a camp counsellor may be abstracted according to a sports medicine taxonomy or a psychological counselling taxonomy. Since Sonja is interested in being a social worker, she selects the psychological counselling taxonomy and determines where in the taxonomy her acquired e-portfolio competencies relate to competencies for job descriptions that interest her. She also electronically forwards these changes to the Thesaurus maintenance team to help them prepare the next edition of the Thesaurus.

After completing this, 5 competencies appear not to be compliant. She decides to leave them as they were described, and to reorganize her *portfolio* in order to make explicit the competencies that are described in a standard way under the heading of "professional competencies" and put the others under the heading "other competencies".

Then, *she edits her CV* to integrate the newly added competencies sorted by categories, simply by ticking the relevant boxes. After a few minutes, *she sends the updated version of her CV to the EUROPASS web service*, which returns a completely formatted document she can edit using her favourite word processor.

She now can search for jobs in the field of Social Sciences. She goes to the most popular *Job Search website*, she registers, and then *completes a form simply by importing her CV information.* She selects criteria to match her job search by ticking the boxes (her diploma and her professional competencies) or by filling in a field for other criteria, (company location, wages…). Upon submitting, the Job Search website provides 15 job advertisements that match her competencies and supporting evidence and these are sorted by matching with the *Outcomes* and *Environments* identified in her job experience data. She filters the results with her personal preferences and decides to contact 3 companies, and *sends her CV and the matching results by clicking on the submit button.* She will be provided with an interview appointment in the following days.

Many parts of the DSSCs mentioned here (University Diploma Supplement delivery system, Local Government e-portfolio facility, Job search services, etc.) already exist and some are now widely used. However, they do not interoperate easily, mainly because of the lack of international standards related to the management and exchange of competency information!

A few initiatives, like the ETSS project in Japan, have made attempts to address these interoperability issues with the support of government. This type of initiative may provide interoperability on a national or a regional basis by offering a series of integrated systems and standardized competencies descriptions. However, such initiatives are not very common, and the same developments cannot easily integrate existing systems in an open employment market. Potential solutions have been explored, as mentioned in this chapter, but it is clear that further research is needed.

FUTURE RESEARCH DIRECTIONS

This section presents future research directions. The use case presented above illustrates a potential landscape of interoperable systems that require specific research directions in order to be implemented in the future. Those described here are probably not the only possible research directions. However, they are some of the ones that currently seem to be promising at an international level, emerging from discussions in several standardization bodies.

One direction is to continue research on systems competency ontologies (see the example of the US Navy above), which could improve interoperability between HRM and learning systems. A major emphasis of this work should be on techniques for using text mining technologies to process existing textual descriptions of competencies as a means of aligning existing competencies with new and evolving standards. A second emphasis of this research is on incorporating existing taxonomies (such as the SNOMED taxonomy of medical terms or equipment parts lists) into the competency descriptions. This approach allows competency definitions to take advantage of taxonomy definition efforts made by domain experts.

A second direction is to continue research on systems architecture (see the example of the C-March system above), where one of the primary goals is the construction of an integrated system. Such a system requires considerable research to develop a standardized description of competencies across all sectors. This perhaps could be implemented more easily at a national level, particularly if there is political consensus regarding a nation-wide competency framework.

A third direction, which has been adopted recently in Europe by the CEN-WSLT, aims at standardizing competency description, adding elements to the existing models such as the IMS – RDCEO. Elements added could be "the context", or a level conforming to the European Qualification Framework (EQF).

A fourth direction is based on the recognition that it is not possible to have a single worldwide competency framework, simply because of the existence of many languages, which will require the development of at least as many profiles of this competency framework as there are languages. Also, within a given language, the stakes and the stakeholders appear to be different for each type of DSSC, which makes interoperability a more complex issue.

From the perspectives outlined in this chapter, some of the main areas for future research directions are:

- definition of mechanisms to build "competency thesauri" that allow comparison, exchange and aggregation of competencies descriptions;
- delineation of the core specifications of the main "competency information objects" and standard mechanisms allowing for the extraction of all or component parts of the information contained in these objects, and related "competency information records"; and,
- provision of implementations of the complete process allowing for competency information exchange according to the 4 levels presented in this chapter.

CONCLUSION

In this chapter addressing interoperability issues for systems managing competency information, we have first described how this need has been addressed so far. It appeared that several standards describing competency definitions have been developed, but that, nonetheless, even basic interoperability problems were not solved, for different reasons, among which the description of the competency itself (impossible to differentiate a micro-competency from a macro-competency, no information available on the level of proficiency, etc.), and the absence of underlying supportive functionalities related to the use of competency information. Different attempts to overcome these problems have been tried in the past few years, which gave satisfaction when the projects were strongly supported by an organization or a government, but which appeared as limited to these projects.

In a second section, the issues related to the core of interoperability, i.e., sharing competency information across systems belonging to different DSSCs are described. Some of these issues are related to the use of the notion of DSSC itself, but the main ones relate to "organization and aggregation of competency information", knowing that "competency information" has several meanings. The way these issues are currently addressed is also described and analysed.

In a third section we present our view of the question, i.e., using what we have called the "Digital Services Supply Chain approach", which comprises 4 levels: a very general one, described by the "Conceptual Reference Model" developed in ISO/IEC JTC1 SC36; a semantic level, which is seen as facilitating the creation of "competency thesauri" that allow comparison and aggregation of competency definitions; an information level, with an abstract level that can be derived from the CRM in order to facilitate the mappings of different parts of real information models which are supposed to interoperate onto "competency information objects", which can be exchanged across systems. The Data model is the last level, which describes, in a machine readable format, the content of the "competency information objects". A narrative use case illustrates the potential results of such a methodology.

The final section presents the research directions currently proposed, together with the future research directions that our proposed approach requires to be implemented: building competency thesauri, providing a standard structure for the main "competency information objects" and exploring the ways to implement the competency information exchange, comparison and aggregation processes. This research programme could pave the way for future work in ISO/IEC JTC1 SC36.

REFERENCES

Al-Turki, U. M., Dufuaa, S., Ayar, T., & Demirel, O. (2008). Stakeholders integration in higher education: Supply chain approach. *European Journal of Engineering Education*, *33*(2), 211–219. doi:10.1080/03043790801980136

Beer, J., & Meethan, K. (2007). Marine and maritime sector skills shortages in the South West of England: Developing regional training provision. *Journal of Vocational Education and Training*, *59*(4), 467–484. doi:10.1080/13636820701650935

Bernstein, S., & Cashore, B. (2007). Can non-state global governance be legitimate? An analytical framework. *Regulation & Governance*, *1*, 347–371. doi:10.1111/j.1748-5991.2007.00021.x

Black, S. (2003). Scholarly journals should be treated as a public good. *The Serials Librarian*, *44*(1), 52–63. doi:10.1300/J123v44n01_07

CEN. (2005). CEN CWA 15455 (2005) *A European Model for Learner Competencies*. Retrieved 2009-04-09 from ftp://ftp.cenorm.be/PUBLIC/CWAs/e-Europe/WS-LT/CWA15455-00-2005-Nov.pdf

DCMI. (2005) Memorandum of Understanding between the Dublin Core Metadata Initiative and the IEEE Learning Technology Standards Committee. Retrieved 2009-07-18 from http://dublincore.org/documents/dcmi-ieee-mou/index.shtml

Deane, C. (2005). Transparency of qualifications: Are we there yet? *European Journal of Education*, *40*(3), 279–293. doi:10.1111/j.1465-3435.2005.00226.x

Ebert, C., & Jones, C. (2009). Embedded software: Facts, figures and future. *Computer*, *42*(4), 42–51. doi:10.1109/MC.2009.118

European Communities. (2009). The Europass curriculum vitae (CV). Retrieved 2009 April 9 from http://europass.cedefop.europa.eu/europass/home/vernav/Europasss+Documents/Europass+CV.csp.

European Communities (EC). (2009). Europass: Opening doors to working and learning in Europe. Retrieved 2009 July 27 from http://europass.cedefop.europa.eu/europass/home/hornav/Introduction.csp?loc=en_GB

Fleishmann, K. R. (2007). Standardization from below: Science and technology standards and educational software. *Journal of Educational Technology & Society*, *10*(4), 110–117.

Frank, G., Gemeinhardt, D., & Ostyn, C. (2005) Linking Reusable Competency Definitions to Learning Activities. Paper n°2056 *in Proceedings of the (I/ITSEC) 2005 Conference*.

Frank, G., Hubal, R., & O'Bea, M. (2007) Using Competency Definitions to Adapt Training for Mission Success. Paper n°7131 *in Proceedings of the (I/ITSEC) 2007 Conference*.

Government of Alberta. (2005). Records management competency profiles. Retrieved 2009-04-09 from http://www.im.gov.ab.ca/publications/pdf/RecordsMgmtCompetencyProfiles.pdf.

Harland, C. M., Lamming, R. C., Walker, H., Phillips, W. E., Caldwell, N. D., & Johnsen, T. E. (2006). Supply management: Is it a discipline? *International Journal of Operations & Production Management*, *26*(7), 730–753. doi:10.1108/01443570610672211

Hirata, K., & Brown, M. (2007). *Request for information on Skills Management Architecture*. Object Management Group.

Hirata, K., & Brown, M. (2008). Skill-Competency Management Architecture, *Workshop Proceedings of the 16th International Conference on Computers in Education, Taipei, Taiwan*. Downloaded 2009/07/14 from http://apsce.net/icce2008/Workshop_Proceedings/Workshop_Proceedings_0179-185.pdf

Hirata, K., Ohara, S., & Makiuchi, K. (2007). Meta Model for Skill and Competency Semantics. *Proceedings of the 8th International Conference on Information Technology Based Higher Education and Training. Kumamoto, Japan.*

Hirata, K., & Saito, M. (2009). Core Technology and Standardization of Skill Management System-In Case of ETSS. *SEC Journal*, *15*(2), 62–67.

Hirata, K., Seta, K., & Makiuchi, K. (2007). Skill and Competency Modelling Typology. *Workshop Proceedings of the 15th International Conference on Computers in Education, Hiroshima, Japan.*

IEEE 1484.12.1 (2002). Learning Object Metadata

IEEE 1484.20.1 (2008). Reusable Competency Definition

IMS GLC Inc. RDCEO (2002). *Reusable Definition of Competency or Educational Objective: Best Practice and Implementation Guide*. Retrieved 2009 October 13 from http://www.imsglobal.org/competencies/rdceov1p0/imsrdceo_bestv1p0.html

IMS GLC Inc. QTI 2.1 (2006). *Question and Test Interoperability Specification*. Retrieved 2009 October 1 from http://www.imsglobal.org/question/qtiv2p1pd2/imsqti_oviewv2p1pd2.html

ISO 21127. (2006). Information and Documentation – A reference ontology for the interchange of cultural heritage information.

ISO/IEC (2008) 19778 Part 1: Collaborative Workplace

ISO/IEC. (2009). *DTR 24763 project: Information Technologies for Learning*. Education and Training - A Conceptual Reference Model for Competencies and Related Objects.

Krain, B., & Gabel, L. (2007). Designing a Total Force Competencies Architecture for the Navy, *Proceedings of the Seventh Annual Navy Workforce Research and Analysis Conference. Arlington, VA, USA.*

Lau, A. K. W. (2007). Educational supply chain management: A case study. *Horizon*, *15*(1), 15–27. doi:10.1108/10748120710735239

LETSI Technical Roadmap Committee. (2009). *Assumptions document: SCORM 2.0 project report*. Retrieved 2009-04-09 from https://letsi.org/images/letsi_media/SCORM_2%200_Assumptions_2009Feb09.pdf

Lindgren, R., Henfridsson, O., & Schultze, U. (2004). Design principles for competence management systems: A synthesis of an action research study. *Management Information Systems Quarterly*, *28*(3), 435–472.

Lummus, R. R., Krumwiede, D. W., & Vokurka, R. J. (2001). The relationship of logistics to supply chain management: developing a common industry definition. *Industrial Management & Data Systems*, *101*(8), 426–431. doi:10.1108/02635570110406730

Mentzer, J. T., DeWitt, W., Keebler, J. S., Min, S., Nix, N. W., Smith, C. D., & Zacharia, Z. G. (2001). Defining supply chain management. *Journal of Business Logistics*, *22*(2), 1–25.

Morgan, A., Raidén, A., & Naylor, G. (2008). Unlocking the potential to influence government skills policy: A case study of the UK construction industry. *International Journal of Training and Development, 12*(4), 238–252. doi:10.1111/j.1468-2419.2008.00309.x

Najjar, J., & Klobučar, T. (Eds.). (2009). *iCOPER: ISURE: Report of study of learning needs building blocks and the standards to be used.* Retrieved 2009-06-22 from http://www.educanext.org/dotlrn/clubs/icoper/new-lors/Deliverables/Deliverables_-_Submitted/D2.1/D2.1_Final.pdf.

Namara, R. E., Hussain, I., Bossio, D., & Verma, S. (2007). Innovative land and water management approaches in Asia: Productivity impacts, adoption prospects and poverty outreach. *Irrigation and Drainage, 56*, 335–348. doi:10.1002/ird.308

Om, K., Lee, J., & Chang, J. (2007). Using supply chain management to enhance industry-university collaborations in IT higher education in Korea. *Scientometrics, 71*(3), 455–471. doi:10.1007/s11192-007-1690-3

O*Net (2009) *O*NET Online* U.S. Department of Labor Retrieved 2009-10-13 from http://online.onetcenter.org/.

Ostyn, C. (2005) *Competency Data for Training Automation.* Downloaded 2009 July 14 from http://www.ostyn.com/standardswork/competency/CompetencyDataForTrainingAutomation.htm

Pacquette, G., Marino, O., Hotte, R., & Moulet, L. Masmoudi, A., Cano, J., & Correal, D. (2007). *LORNET Project 2.3: Ontology and framework for knowledge and competency management (V. 3).* Retrieved 2009 July 14 from http://wiki.letsi.org/download/attachments/9076913/Additional+Competency+Presentations.zip

Sampson, D., Karampiperis, P., & Fytros, D. (2007). Developing a common metadata model for competencies description. *Interactive Learning Environments, 15*(2), 137–150. doi:10.1080/10494820701343645

Sauber, M. H., McSurely, H. B., & Rao Tummala, V. M. (2008). Developing supply chain management program: A competency model. *Quality Assurance in Education, 16*(4), 375–391. doi:10.1108/09684880810906517

Schubert, P., & Leimstoll, U. (2007). Importance and use of information technology in small and medium-sized companies. *Electronic Markets, 17*(1), 38–55. doi:10.1080/10196780601136799

SFIA Foundation. (2008). *Skills Framework for the Information Age: About SFIA.* Retrieved 2009 July 27 from http://www.sfia.org.uk/cgi-bin/wms.pl/296

Sgouropoulou, C., Grant, S., Wilson, S., & Vangen, G. (2009). *European learner mobility standardization: Sketching the landscape.* Retrieved 2009-07-03 from http://www.fs.usit.uio.no/presentasjoner/EUNIS2009/FS-09-092_Sgouropoulou-Grant-Wilson-Vangen-113.pdf.

Sherwood, A. L., & Covin, J. G. (2008). Knowledge acquisition in university-industry alliances: An empirical investigation from a learning theory perspective. *Journal of Product Innovation Management, 25*, 162–179. doi:10.1111/j.1540-5885.2008.00292.x

Standards Australia. (2007). *HB 256:2007 Metadata usage in Australian and New Zealand education and training.*

Thiriet, J.-M., Robert, M., Lapalainen, P., Hoffmann, M. H. W., Martins, M. J. M., & Seoane, A. (2002). Towards a pan-European virtual university in electrical and information engineering. *IEEE Transactions on Education, 45*(2), 152–160. doi:10.1109/TE.2002.1013880

U.S. Department of Education. (2004). *The elementary and secondary education act (The no child left behind act of 2001).* Retrieved 2009 July 29 from http://www.ed.gov/policy/elsec/leg/esea02/index.html.

Vervenne, L. (n.d.). *Competency Related Data Management (CRDM): A proposed reference model*. Retrieved 2009-06-23 from http://ieeeltsc.files.wordpress.com/2009/03/competency-related-data-management-prolix.pdf

Zouaq, A., Nkambou, R., & Frasson, C. (2007 July 18 - 20). Using a competence model to aggregate learning knowledge objects. In *Proceedings of the Seventh IEEE International Conference on Advanced Learning Technologies*, (pp. 836-840).

ZTHES specifications for thesaurus representation, access and navigation. (n.d.). Retrieved 2009/07/25 from http://zthes.z3950.org/

ADDITIONAL READING

Additional reading presents general documents related to e-learning standards, among which web sites of standardization committees dealing with competencies. Most of the documents which constitute the fundamentals on this topic for the reader are mentioned in the text of the chapter, and are referenced in the section above.

CEN TC353 - Information and Communication Technologies for learning education and training: http://www.cen.eu/CENORM/BusinessDomains/sectors/isss/cen+tc+353.asp

IEEE – LTSC (Learning Technology Standard Committee). http://ieeeltsc.wordpress.com/

ISO/IEC JTC1-SC36 (Public). http://sc36.org/

ISO/IEC JTC1-SC36 website: http://isotc.iso.org/livelink/livelink?func=ll&objId=806742&objAction=browse&sort=name/

Learning Technologies Standard Observatory. http://www.cen-ltso.net/Users/main.aspx

Workshop Learning TechnologiesC. E. N.http://www.cen.eu/cenorm/sectors/sectors/isss/activity/wslt.asp

KEY TERMS AND DEFINITIONS

Conceptual Reference Model (CRM): Provides definitions and a formal structure for describing the implicit and explicit concepts and relationships within a system.

Competency Information: Structured data about a competency that is communicated among individuals, organizations, and public administrations.

Competency Information Object: Set of competency information.

Interoperability: Ability of two or more IT Systems to exchange information and to make mutual use of the information that has been exchanged.

Section 2
Personalization, Interoperability and E-Learning Standards

Chapter 6
Do Current Standards Support Adaptive Sequencing Interoperability?

Sergio Gutiérrez-Santos
University of London, UK

ABSTRACT

In the complex world of e-learning, there are many aspects to consider: administrative issues (e.g. keeping track of the courses of a student), technical issues (e.g. packaging learning content in a platform-independent way), and academic issues. This chapter concentrates on one of the latter, namely the problem of adaptive sequencing. This problem can be stated like: given a student and a set of learning resources, find the optimum sequence for his or her special characteristics, goals, needs, and background. An appropriate sequencing, adapted to the student, has a positive impact on motivation and learning, hence its importance. However, this is a problem that has not been yet carefully considered in any standard or specification, hindering interoperability among platforms that adapt the sequencing of learning content to their users. This chapter reviews the two specifications most relevant for the standard expression of adapted sequencings: IMS Simple Sequencing and IMS Learning Design. The strong and weak points of each specification are highlighted, showing their implications on adaptive sequencing interoperability.

INTRODUCTION

The evolution and widespread presence of e-learning requires its material to be interoperable among different platforms. International specifications and standards define a common framework to make e-learning software adaptable, interoperable and reusable. E-learning is so wide and touches so many aspects that the task of defining such standards is being done gradually. This chapter concentrates on standards that are relevant for the sequencing of learning content.

One of the main advantages of Web Based Education is the large number of different resources that are provided to the user. There is the risk, however, of becoming lost in cyberspace (Edwards & Hardman, 1989). This problem becomes more important in those situations in which the amount

DOI: 10.4018/978-1-61692-789-9.ch006

of resources that a student uses is large. One possible approach to solve this problem is by filtering. Another approach is to adapt the sequencing of learning resources to the learners. Instead of creating courses with the same resources for every user, the resources can be authored so that an adapted environment is created for each learner (Cristea, 2004), i.e. every learner has its own sequence of learning activities, having into account their different backgrounds and different needs.

Having the possibility of providing each student with an adapted sequence of activities has a positive effect on their learning. The important effect that personalisation has on learning was first quantified by Benjamin Bloom, who called this ``the two-sigma problem' (Bloom, 1984). Bloom detected that learners that undergo a personalised learning experience get results that are two standard deviations above those of learners that get a one-size-fits-all experience (e.g. in a classroom of 30 students). Although Bloom's study was not framed in the context of technology-enhanced learning, its conclusions about the importance of adapting the material and improving the students' learning process are not invalidated by the use of technology.

Adapting the sequencing in the learning process properly is a problem that has drawn considerable attention from different fields like artificial intelligence in education, intelligent tutoring systems, and adaptive hypermedia. The earliest attempts to adapt the order in which some questions were presented to students date from the 70s (Barr, 1973). More modern systems continued the trend in the 80s (e.g. McArthur, 1988) and 90s (e.g. Rios et al., 1993), when the literature used to refer to this processes as 'task sequencing'. Based mostly on the grounds of instructional design, similar systems grew in complexity, being able to sequence sets of learning material (i.e. lessons), including questions and examples (Capell, 1993; Khuwaja, 1996). This process evolved naturally with the gradual expansion and mass-use of the WWW into the concept of course sequencing (Brusilovsky, 2000), where the goal is already to be able to generate an individualised course for each student. At this level, it is possible to sequence tasks, lessons, or even other teaching operations like examples and assessments (Brusilovsky and Vassileva, 2003). Different AI techniques can be used to generate an adapted course, including planning (Ulrich, 2005), ontology-based reasoning (Karampiperis & Sampson, 2004), and combination of semantic web techniques with SCORM (Baldoni et al., 2004).

In the days of the WWW, sequencing adaptation is more important than ever, especially in distance-learning scenarios. However, most modern Learning Content Management systems (LCMS) have little or no support at all for designing rich adaptive sequencings of learning material. The usual sequence is just a linear juxtaposition of elements, sometimes adding some hierarchy in the form of a tree. Part of the reason lies in the additional difficulty of creating an effectively adaptive sequencing strategy, compared to a typical linear sequence. Several authoring tools and frameworks have appeared to tackle this problem, but it is beyond the scope of this chapter to study them (interested readers can look at Hendrix et at., 2008; Cristea & Aroyo, 2002). Another important reason is the difficulty in reusing material from one LCMS into another: in other words, the additional constraints that sequencing adaptation puts on system interoperability.

This chapter focuses on the support of current standards to the reuse of adaptive sequencing strategies among e-learning platforms. Two are the main "standards" that relate to the problem of sequencing: IMS Simple Sequencing and IMS Learning Design. The first one is specifically designed for sequencing, but it is inherently limited. IMS Learning Design is more flexible than its counterpart, but it has not been specifically designed for sequencing, with several consequences. The chapter describes both specifications, analysing their strong points and their weaknesses, indicating possible solutions that have been proposed in the literature for some of them. But first, we need to understand the general landscape in which both specifications are framed.

BACKGROUND

The e-learning world has evolved at a fast pace during the last years. Current tools are able to integrate not only academic tasks, but also administrative tasks for educational institutions. Learning content management systems are able to cope with tasks that range from tuition fees management to personalised pedagogical approaches and collaborative learning tasks.

Such an extended presence of e-learning systems makes it desirable –if not necessary-- that learning material can be interchanged between different platforms. A course that can only be followed on a platform will only be used by a very small number of learners compared to its potential audience. On the other hand, this new scenario (with digital technologies that can be used by lecturers and learning designers) brings new learning materials, with a much greater variety of resources. In other words, the production process has increased its complexity. These two facts (proliferation of e-learning platforms, and complexity of learning material) lead to the necessity of interoperability of learning resources: the possibility of reusing resources (sometimes called learning objects[1]) from other courses increases the efficiency of the production process.

This need finds an answer in international standards, that define a common framework to make educational software adaptable, reusable and interoperable. For instance, institutions like IEEE or ISO have several work groups that create standards to guarantee that learning content management systems offer both a set of common features and a common data representation, so that learning material can be platform independent. Defining such standards requires a complex process, because e-learning involves several aspects from different fields. Available tools adopt these standards gradually, offering in some cases only partial compliance.

It is important to note that there are few real standards in e-learning. The process is long and complex before an official standardisation organisation ratifies a proposal that is accepted by the community. On the other hand, it is not uncommon to refer to specifications like those of IMS as "standards". Nowadays, there is some convergence in the e-learning community around the SCORM project. SCORM is putting together the work of organisations like AICC, IEEE LTSC and especially IMS.

This section provides a general overview of the SCORM project, the IEEE LOM standard, and some IMS specifications that are related to sequencing. The next two sections will describe in detail the two IMS proposals that are directly relevant for the sequencing problem.

Advanced Distributed Learning and SCORM

The Advanced Distributed Learning initiative (henceforth ADL) is an organisation, created by the Department of Defense of the USA. ADL works together with several specification and standardisation organisations (like ISO, IEEE, and IMS) to develop guidelines to make educational software accessible, adaptable, interoperable, and reusable. The most important contribution by ADL is the Shareable Content Object Reference Model, SCORM (Advanced Distributed Learning, 2004a). This model defines the way in which learning systems have to manage web-based content and deliver it to users. SCORM uses specifications and guidelines proposed by other institutions (especially IMS). The important contribution here is not in some specific aspect of e-learning, but rather on specifying how all of them have to be integrated.

The main idea in SCORM is considering a web based course as a collection of interconnected objects with content. There are several aspects to be considered here: content organisation, metadata, sequencing, etc. SCORM is divided in three sub-modules, each of them taking care of a different aspect of e-learning. The first sub-module is the Content Aggregation Model (CAM), that defines how the content has to be assembled, tagged, and packed. The SCORM model is based on objects (SCOs). The second module is the Runtime Environment (RTE), that describes the runtime process that a learning management system has to perform with a SCO, as well as the communication process between them. Finally, the third module is related to navigation and sequencing. It defines how sequencing interchanges with the rest of the RTE, but the description of the sequencing process is done using an external specification. In the case of SCORM 2004, this specification is IMS Simple Sequencing (analysed later in the chapter).

SCORM is the most widely accepted model today by current learning management systems. Many tools accept importing and exporting courses in SCORM, and this results in a certain level of sharing and reuse. However, the most important problem for real sharing of learning material is the level of compliance on the implementation. SCORM is a broad and complex model, and vendors usually export only a subset of its functionality. Due to the variety in these subsets, it is not uncommon that some SCORM-compliant material runs only in some platforms. This has motivated SCORM to publish a set of compatibility requirements with the critical aspects that need to be implemented to get a "SCORM-compliant" certification (Advanced Distributed Learning, 2004b); additionally, several companies have appeared that specialise on consultancy services with regard to SCORM certification.

IEEE Learning Object Metadata (LOM)

The Institute of Electric and Electronic Engineers (IEEE) is a non-profit organisation that offers technical and professional information, resources and services to the engineering community. One of the main services of IEEE is the certification of standards related to information and communication technologies. Inside IEEE, the Learning Technologies Standards Committee (LTSC) is focused on development and publication of technical standards related to educational technologies.

Their most relevant contribution is the Learning Object Metadata standard (LOM, described in IEEE 1484). LOM defines the structure of metadata that can be used to describe a learning object. The goal is to define the minimal set of attributes that have to be attached to a learning object for their management, including administrative aspects (e.g. author, title), pedagogical aspects (e.g. difficulty level), and legal aspects (e.g. copy restrictions). An important aspect of LOM is that it contemplates the possibility of extending the set of attributes for specific purposes. LOM attributes are divided in nine categories, as shown in Table 1.

As it was the case with SCORM, not all applications support LOM completely.

IMS Global Consortium (IMS)

IMS Global Consortium is a non-profit organisation oriented to facilitate the adoption of e-learning technologies in the world. Its members include content providers, software vendors, and academic institutions from more than fifty countries. IMS does not publish standards. Its work concentrates on promoting open technical specifications to achieve real interoperability between technologies. The impact of the consortium is beyond any doubt. Several of its specifications have become *de facto* standards for e-learning products and services.

IMS specifications deal with many different aspects of e-learning, and the number of specifications is huge. At the time of writing, there are twenty-seven different specifications[2], and the list continues to be updated. The two main specifications that are relevant to sequencing (Simple Sequencing and Learning Design) are analysed

Table 1. IEEE LOM categories

Category	Description
General	general information about the object, e.g. title, author, identifier, or keywords
Life cycle	describes the evolution of the object, e.g. version number, status (e.g. draft)
Meta-metadata	information about the metadata themselves, e.g. language, authors
Technical	information about how to manipulate the object, e.g. software needed, duration
Educational	with information about pedagogical aspects, e.g. interactivity level, difficulty level
Rights	legal information regarding intellectual property and copy restrictions
Relational	description of how this objects relates to others
Classification	to place this object in some taxonomy
Annotation	notes about how the object was actually used in an environment, with the purpose of sharing information and suggestions

in the next two sections. Four other specifications that are related to the other two are briefly presented here.

IMS Content Packaging (IMS-CP)

If learning content is to be shared and reused among different platforms, it is necessary to explain in detail how this content is organised. The problem is then how to produce and organise material in a platform-independent way. The IMS Content Packaging specification defines how learning material has to be organised to be imported, exported, aggregated and disaggregated. The main element of such description is a XML file called *imsmanisfest.xml*, which contains the collections of resources used in the package, as well as the information related to their organisation.

IMS Question and Test Interoperability (IMS-QTI)

Evaluation is a very important aspect when designing learning material. In general, evaluation involves a complex task with multiple variables. IMS-QTI defines a data model specifically oriented towards the design and reuse of questions. This kind of questions can be automatically graded to produce feedback for the student. The model defines the most common types of questions (e.g. true-false, fill the gaps, etc), and defines schemes for grading, organisation, random selection and automatic feedback generation.

IMS Learner Information Package (IMS-LIP)

This specification defines how to collect information about a learner, group of learners, or learning content producer. The goal is to facilitate the interchange of this type of data among different platforms. The specification is organised around several structures, including accessibility, skills and competencies, goals, interests, and others. Additionally, another crucial aspect that IMS-LIP takes care of is security, because of the sensitivity of personal data.

IMS Common Cartridge (IMS-CC)

This specification is relatively new, compared to the others. It comprises a combination of IMS-CP, IMS-QTI, IEEE LOM, and IMS Authorization Web Service (a specification that defines a standardized authorization scheme as an alternative for the proprietary authorization systems of the different LCMS). The goal is to facilitate interoperability between different platforms. To achieve

Figure 1. IMS Simple Sequencing scope

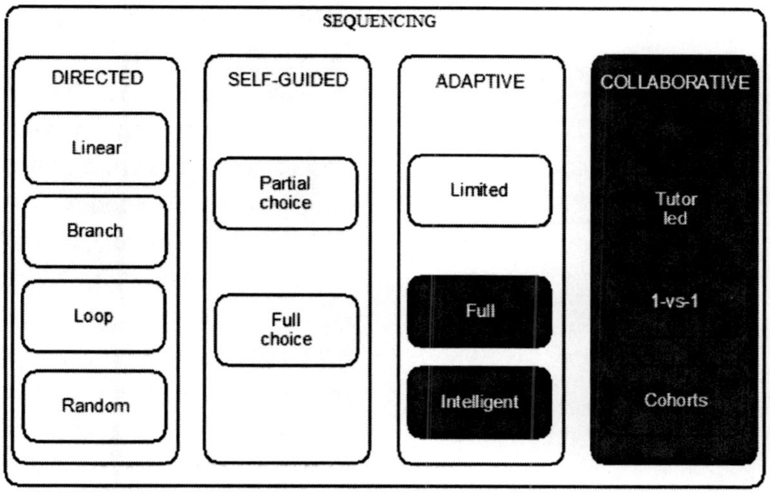

this, the constituting specifications have been profiled (i.e. limited), restricting their use to the more common features, eliminating options, and constraining permitted data in supported elements.

IMS Simple Sequencing

In the former section, we have presented several specifications published by IMS. There is another specification that IMS has produced aimed directly at the problem of sequencing: IMS Simple Sequencing (henceforth, IMS-SS). IMS-SS defines a method to define the sequence in which a group of learning activities is presented to the student. It incorporates rules that describe the flow or the branches of the activities according to the interaction between the learner and the activities.

The goal of IMS-SS is to be the meeting point between the different learning management systems in terms of sequencing of content. Therefore, IMS-SS intends to be totally neutral with respect to pedagogical models and the use of instructional methodologies.

The specification is called *simple sequencing*, but this does not mean that it is a short specification, or that it is relatively simple compared to other IMS specifications. On the contrary, the specification is relatively long, and many problems have been reported from several vendors that have tried to implement it (as reported by Bailey & Abel, 2009). The name *simple* comes from the fact that the specification is limited to some specific ways of defining sequences: direct sequences, self-guided sequences, and adapted sequences (only partially). This is illustrated on Figure 1.

IMS-SS has been designed to be integrated with IMS Content Packaging. In principle, it could be integrated with other equivalent specifications; IMS-CP is, however, the only mechanism that has been defined in IMS for the interchange of package instances. Information about the sequencing can be integrated with the IMS-CP manifest, or it can be defined on its own file.

IMS-SS defines a complete sequencing process with several stages, called behaviours: navigation, termination, roll-up, sequencing, and delivery. A detailed description of all behaviours would be excessively long for this chapter, plus it is not totally relevant for the present discussion. This chapter concentrates on those mechanisms provided by the specification to designers for defining different sequences that adapt to learners. Readers that are interested in the whole process are referred to (IMS Global Learning Consortium, 2003a).

Figure 2. Preorder traversal in IMS-SS

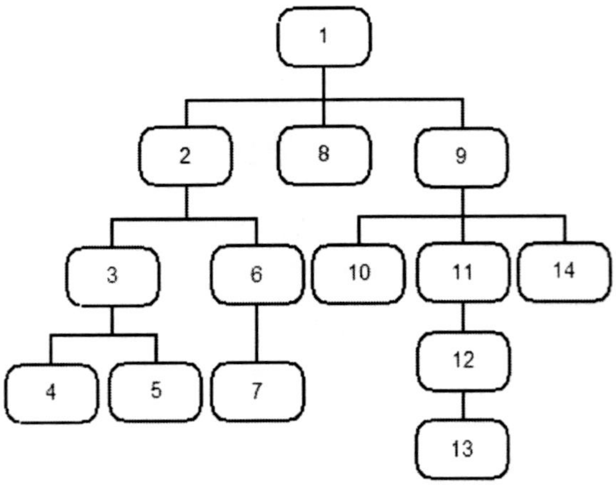

In the context of IMS-SS, a learning activity is defined as: "*a pedagogically neutral unit of instruction, knowledge, assessment, etc. It can have sub-activities and may be nested to an arbitrarily deep level. Each activity may have a tracking status associated for each learner that is assigned to experience the activity. Activities can be attempted any number of times, or the number can be specified. They can be suspended, abandoned, exited normally, etc. All activities are performed within the context of a parent activity*" (IMS Global Learning Consortium, 2003b). IMS-SS considers that learning activities are organised hierarchically. On the other hand, sub-activities are not considered to be part of the main (parent) activity. Learning activities are delivered one at a time; usually, the parent activity is delivered first, and then the children ones (see Figure 2). Learning activities can have auxiliary resources associated to them (e.g. a web page), and this is the expected behaviour by default; if this does not happen, the specification does not define any behaviour.

Learning activities are ordered in a tree structure. Every node and every leaf on the tree is a learning activity. Every node in the tree can have any number of nodes and/or leaves that depend on it; in other words, an IMS-SS tree needs not to be balanced. There is no relationship whatsoever between concepts like lessons, courses, etc; and the hierarchy of nodes in the tree. IMS-SS defines the canonical form in which the tree must be traversed as preorder traversal: parent nodes are traversed before children nodes, nodes on the same level are traversed from left to right, and all descendants from a node must be traversed before moving to the next node on the same level. Figure 2 shows an example.

IMS-SS allows the sequencing designer to select whether a group of children activities have to sequenced in a guided manner (i.e. with no intervention of the learner), or if the learner should be allowed to select the next activity. This is done using two properties on every node (not leaf): Sequencing Control Flow and Sequencing Control Choice. The status of these two properties determines the sequencing of those learning activities that are *children* of the current node. If those activities have children activities themselves, they must define their own policy giving different values to Sequencing Control Flow and/or Sequencing Control Choice. Additionally, it is possible to specify a certain level of randomness both to the flow and the choice policy, if the designer so wishes.

It is important to note that any sequencing policy defined by a node only affects that node and its direct descendants. This is called in IMS-SS a *cluster*: a set of sibling learning activities (nodes or leaves) and their parent node. The scope of IMS-SS policies is always a cluster: rules are defined at the parent activity, they affect the parent and/or the children activities, and they do not affect any other ancestor or descendants.

Of course, it is possible to modify the default preorder sequence by using rules. Rules are evaluated at running time. There are three types of rules: limit rules, roll-up rules, and sequencing rules.

Limit rules define restrictions to access a learning activity based on factors like day time, time used for the activity, or number of tries. Processes can reference limit conditions for any activity in the tree. This can influence the sequencing (see below).

Roll-up rules describe how success or failure on the children activities of a cluster influence the sequencing of the parent activity (and, indirectly, the siblings of the parent activity). Conditions that affect subordinate activities can have values like: satisfied, completed, tried, etc. There can be more than one condition for any subordinate activity, and they can all be combined by a global conjunction (logical AND: all conditions must be satisfied to execute the rule) or a global disjunction (logical OR: when any condition is satisfied, the rule is executed). Any condition can be negated (e.g. NOT tried, NOT satisfied). Additionally, any sub-activity can be considered optional, so it will be ignored and not influence the global sequencing strategy. A roll-up rule can be fired when all conditions of the subordinate activities are met, when none are met, or when some percentage of them is met. When the rule is applied, actions are executed that have an immediate effect on the parent activity of the cluster. Actions can change the state of the parent activity to: satisfied, completed, or their opposites. This has an effect on sequencing (see below).

There are three types of sequencing rules in IMS-SS: pre-conditions, post-conditions, and exit conditions. Any of them execute different actions with different effects on sequencing. Conditions evaluate several aspects of the activity (which can be modified with respect to limit or roll-up conditions in some cases). Examples of aspects considered by conditions are: some learning goal has been met or completed, some goal has been met or completed up to a threshold, the number of tries or the time used have exceeded some threshold, etc. Like in the former case, more than one condition can be selected for any activity, and conditions can be combined with a global logical conjunction or a global logical disjunction, and any condition can be negated (NOT tried, NOT satisfied, etc).

Actions in IMS-SS

Actions in pre-conditions are used when the activity tree is searched for an activity to deliver. Pre-conditions are evaluated before the activity is delivered. Possible actions are: *skip* (omit the current activity in a sequencing process flow; indirectly, this omits all subordinates of the current activity), *hidden from choice* (hide the current activity from the list of choices presented to the learner), *disable* (combines the former two), *stop forward traversal* (stops the forward traversal in the activity tree), and *ignore* (no action to be taken).

Actions in post-conditions are applied when the learner's attempt at the current activity finishes. Possible actions in this case are: *exit parent*, *exit all* (i.e. leave the system), *retry* (try again the current activity), *retry all* (try again all activities in the cluster), *continue* (try "next" activity), *previous* (try "former" activity), and *ignore* (no action). It is important to note that in the case of actions *continue* and *previous*, the next delivered activity will not always be the activity right after of before the current activity in the tree. Next activity to be delivered to the learner can vary depending on pre-conditions. Gutierrez et al. (2004a) offers an example, where pre- and post-conditions are combined to define a flexible sequencing strategy.

Actions in exit conditions are applied after an attempt in a subordinate activity finishes. They can be: exit (ends the activity unconditionally) or ignore (no action).

Limitations of IMS Simple Sequencing

IMS-SS is a step in the right direction. However, it suffers several important limitations:

Lack of flexibility

IMS-SS is based on a simple paradigm, that is useful to define quasi-linear sequences of information. In other words, the system of pre-conditions and post-conditions is very simple and allows a fair level of generality; but, on the other hand, it makes it very complex to define a sequencing that involves more complexity than a linear sequence with occasional hops. It is very difficult to define a sequencing that involves cycles, or one that involves jumping "backwards" to an activity that is behind the current one in the activity tree: the resulting XML files are huge, with a high number of pre-conditions and post-conditions (cf. Gutierrez et al., 2004a). Since the seminal work by Ausubel and Piaget, several authors have remarked the importance of cycles in the learning process (Marek & Cavallo, 1997), and these are difficult to define using IMS-SS semantics.

In principle, IMS-SS is designed to interchange low-level information between applications. Therefore, an author or designer should only worry about defining a sequencing for her material with any tool that used a convenient high-level metaphor. This sequencing would be later exported by the authoring tool to use the IMS-SS semantics. However, many tools are using the IMS-SS semantics directly, with its limitations from the authoring point of view (e.g. for defining cycles). Some authors have proposed ways in which this limitation can be improved in future versions of the specification (Gutierrez et al., 2004a; Wan et al., 2006)

Only Student Oriented

IMS-SS is designed to sequence learning activities only for students. It is not valid to define e.g. a course-guide for teachers, that helps the teacher to adapt the topics of the course to the needs of the class. This is a consequence of the implicit user model (see below).

Lack of General User Model

The IMS-SS specification states that it does not try to define completely adaptive sequencings. The self-defined scope of the specification is limited to: static sequences, semi-static sequences (guided only by the learner), and partially adaptive. Fully adapted sequences, intelligently adapted sequences, and collaborative sequencing are out of the scope of IMS-SS (see Figure 1). A future specification might cover those aspects.

The IMS SS Tracking Model (IMS Global Learning Consortium, 2003a) only accepts two data types: booleans and floats. A further constraint on the float type is that the value is normalized between 1.0 and -1.0. The tracking model defines three data models to record the state of an activity and its objectives: a first model to track the timing and completion progress of each attempt on an activity, a second model to track the timing and completion progress over all attempts on an activity, and a third one to track the result status of the objectives of an activity. There is nothing else to record or process information about the student.

This limitation has important consequences. It is not possible to complement the defined sequencing strategy using an external user model. There is no mechanism defined in IMS-SS to update an external user model, nor there is one to capture general data from learning activities. The only available information to drive the sequencing is the level of achievement in objectives, a consequence of the learner model used in the IMS Learner Information Package (IMS-LIP). In the scope of IMS-SS it is possible to store some specific information about the learner (e.g. time used for an activity, number of successful activities in a cluster, etc), but it is not possible to go beyond that and define or model abstract concepts with which to drive the sequencing of activities (e.g. whether the student prefers a top-down or a bottom-up approach to learning).

The lack of a generalised user model, or the possibility of combining with an external one, is maybe IMS-SS biggest limitation. This is one of the main reasons why many efforts in the community have moved towards IMS Learning Design. This specification is not focused on the sequencing problem, but offers some mechanisms to define sequences of activities, and its properties allow some modelling possibilities for the learners.

IMS LEARNING DESIGN

The goal of IMS Learning Design (henceforth IMS-LD) is to describe learning strategies and/or pedagogical approaches, as well as promoting the interchange of those among learning management systems. Therefore, its purpose is to document teaching strategies, establishing and using prescribed procedures to ensure a reliable documentation (IMS Global Consortium, 2003d).

The main task is to codify educational strategies in a consistent manner, that can be understood by computers and humans. Therefore, the context of a learning unit, course, or program, can be managed separately from the content itself. This information allows instructors to describe the approach they use in their work, connecting it to its contents. It makes it easier to share and reuse the content, because it has been designed for its own instructional strategy and discipline. On the other hand, this information can be used to adapt or interpret learning content under an instruction strategy that is different from the one the content was designed for. Additionally, having information about the pedagogical context of some learning content can facilitate its adaptation among different learning management systems.

IMS-LD allows to describe different types of learning strategies, but it keeps some distance with respect to them, and does not associate with any in particular. Thus, it offers a specific vocabulary to describe the different approaches to learning. IMS-LD uses its own metaphor to create a meta-language that can describe any approach. This metaphor is the script of a theatre play, film or game (Koper, 2005). It assumes that a script can model all types of behaviours and interactions between the actors that happen in the context of a complete environment and, therefore, it is able

Figure 3. Plays, acts and activities in IMS-LD

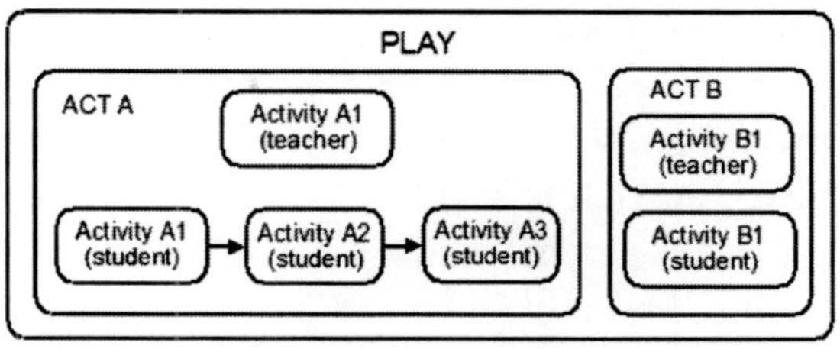

to express all types of situations. It can be very strict and detailed, or it can grant greater freedom to improvise. More important, the script is a *high-level description* of the play: it focuses on some aspects and abstracts from others; scripts are written in the same way independently of the theatre company that will play the piece, or whether it is a comedy or a drama. In other words, scripts need to be *interpreted.*

Therefore, IMS-LD uses a vocabulary based on plays, acts, roles, activities, and conditions. In principle, this vocabulary is adequate to represent any pedagogical strategy. *Plays* are composed of *acts*, and these are the means to synchronise different *activities* that happen concurrently (see Figure 3). Activities are performed by people who have a *role*. There are two families or types or roles: *student* roles and *teacher* roles. Finally, *conditions* allow some variability in the flow of the play (if something happens, then this happens; otherwise, this other thing will happen). A whole package comprising the definition of the pedagogical strategy or learning design, along with the resources and services needed for its development, is called a Unit of Learning (UoL). In IMS-LD, the process between the start and the end of a UoL is called a *run*.

Sequencing in IMS-LD

With regard to the problem of sequencing, conditions are the most important element of the specification. Conditions are the mechanism that allows to define different sequences of activities.

Without conditions, the default sequencing is a linear sequence of activities from the first one to the last one, like in IMS Content Packaging. The only difference with IMS Content Packaging is that it is possible to have several linear sequences running in parallel in IMS-LD (e.g. one with activities for the students and one with activities for the teacher). In this case, the points between acts are used as synchronisation points.

IMS-LD conditions are evaluated against *properties*. According to their behaviour through time, properties can be *local* or *global*; according to their scope, they can be *general*, *role-based*, or *personal*. Local properties do only exist during the current run; global properties, on the other hand, are maintained along different runs of the same UoL. General properties are associated to the whole UoL (e.g. maximum number of students allowed to take a role for the UoL); role-based properties are associated to a role (e.g. maximum time allowed to students to use at some activity); and personal properties describe or affect only one user (e.g. how much time some particular student has spent in the current act).These two classifications are independent: properties can be global and general, global and personal, local and role-based, etc.

They can be used for different purposes, but properties are the means to offer specific information about students. This makes it possible to adapt the UoL to the particular needs and/or capabilities of each student or group. The assignment (or change of value) of a property in a UoL involves the evaluation of conditions in IMS-LD. Properties have a name and an identifier, a type, and a value. In some cases, they can also bear some restrictions about the values that can store.

Conditions, as we have said, are evaluated against properties. When a condition is met, an action is performed. Conditions are evaluated every time the value of one of the relevant properties changes. There are three types of events in IMS-LD that can change the value of a property. First, there are events that are provided by a counter (e.g. the execution clock of the UoL). Second, there are events that are fired by the user (e.g. the user decides to complete an activity). Last, events are also generated when activities, acts, or plays are finished for any reason (e.g. user choice or time limit). These three types of events can be used indirectly to fire actions.

Conditions are boolean expressions, and can be combined with the logical operators of conjunction (AND), disjunction (OR), and negation (NOT). Conditions can evaluate situations like: whether a person does have a role; whether some activity, role part, act, or play has been completed; whether a property is defined; if a property is equal to, or different from, some constant value, as well as other mathematical operations; or questions about the time that has been used, to name but a few.

Every time one of the relevant properties of a condition changes its value, that condition has to be evaluated again. When the condition evaluates to *true*, an action is fired. There are four types of actions. First, the value of a property can be *changed*. It must be noted that this may produce another re-evaluation of the conditions. Some conditions that had not been met before might be met because of the change, which in turn can produce new changes in other properties, etc. Second, actions can *show* or *hide* an entity in the UoL, i.e. a learning object (e.g. a web page), a learning service (e.g. a forum), a learning environment, an activity, or even a full play. If an entity already hidden/showing is set to hide/show again, nothing happens. Finally, acts and activities can be *completed*. This may result in a change to the value of some properties, producing a re-evaluation of conditions as explained above.

The appropriate combination of hide and show actions can be used to perform some kind of adapting sequencing. For instance, two activities can be hidden for a student, which result in an effective jump to a third one. An example of such an approach can be found in Gutierrez-Santos et al. (2008).

There is a last set of elements in IMS-LD that is worth mentioning with respect to sequencing. *Global elements* are XML extensions designed to be used with learning resources written in XHTML. They allow to read and/or modify properties from within the learning activities. There are four types of global elements, that correspond to four different operations: view property, view property group, set property, and set property group.

There is no other way of modifying properties from the activities. Therefore, only XHTML resources that use global elements can influence the sequencing during the execution of a UoL. Any other decision related to sequencing adaptation must be made before the UoL is started, and they will have an effect during the whole run. It can be seen that the adaptation possibilities in the second case are much more limited.

Limitations of IMS-LD

This specification is not designed to deal with the problem of sequencing adaptation. Partially because of this, IMS-LD presents several limitations when it comes to expressing rich adaptive sequencing strategies.

Scalability

First, the condition model of IMS-LD follows a functional paradigm that does not scale well. When the number of conditions grows, it becomes increasingly difficult to keep track of all conditions and the possibility of side effects increases dramatically. Every condition must be checked for every possible case, leading to a debugging process that is both tedious and error-prone. Although this may be adequate for small control tasks, the creation of a big set of conditions and actions that control the sequencing of a large number of activities becomes infeasible unless some automatic tool is used to help. Additionally, conditions can only be embedded in a limited way: inside an *if* clause, the *then* branch cannot contain another *if*, while the *else* branch can (IMS Global Learning Consortium, 2003c).

Lack of Hierarchy

Second, the specification lacks a general-purpose mechanism to express hierarchy between elements, apart from the inherent "theatre play" hierarchy. There is a way to define a limited hierarchy between activities (with elements of type *activity-structure*), but this is not a real hierarchy from the point of view of sequencing: the sequence of activities cannot be defined in all levels of the hierarchy (cf. clusters in IMS-SS, where the children activities use the same types of rules than the father activity on its own cluster). Hierarchical grouping of activities is important to define sequencings for a large number of activities in a flexible and manageable manner.

Limited Flexibility

A related point is the difficulty to express cycles in a sequencing strategy contained in the UoL. Cycles are necessary in the learning process (Marek & Cavallo, 1997) because they are linked to reflection and also to memory, but it is difficult to express cycles using IMS Learning Design semantics. This is because activities in IMS-LD are expected to be completed only once. In the words of the specification: "*...a control must be available in the user-interface to set the activity status to 'completed'. A user can do this once (no undo). Once he/she indicated the activity to be completed, then this activity stays completed in the run*" (IMS Global Learning Consortium, 2003c, p83). In order to express activity cycles in the context of a UoL it is necessary to create a complicated combination of properties, conditions and show/hide operations. Although this complexity can be hidden from the learning designer by using appropriate high-level metaphors on the LMS authoring tool, it has been shown (Gutierrez-Santos et al., 2008) that there is a cost to pay in terms of limited expressiveness and huge sizes[3] of the resulting XML files, which might impose a heavy burden on the IMS-LD player.

Limited Communication with External Activities

Last, but not least, the communication mechanism between the learning activities and the learning design is limited. IMS-LD properties make it possible to define a flexible sequencing strategy, but the only way in which these properties can be modified by an external application is by using a global element *set-property* on an XHTML page. This has two consequences. First, learning activities that are not presented in XHTML format cannot influence the sequencing of activities. (However, XHTML is common enough to reduce the relevance of this limitation.) The second limitation has a tremendous impact in the way a sequence of learning units can be adapted. A *set-property* element means that only the user can modify the value of properties. A learning activity cannot modify these values by itself, so the sequencing decisions have to be carefully designed between the activity and the learning design, so that the change of a property by the user (e.g. the answer to an exercise) fires the calculation of other properties that are relevant for the sequencing (e.g. marks in the exercise, time employed, update of a level of knowledge in the *user model*, etc). This tight coupling between learning units and sequencing (i.e. in the learning design) is a negative outcome and it reduces the possibilities of sharing and reusing both the learning unit and the learning design.

DISCUSSION: SEQUENCING IN IMS-LD VS. SEQUENCING IN IMS-SS

Once we have described the two specifications, it is the moment to compare both. We have seen that both IMS-SS and IMS-LD can be used to grant interoperability between systems that have defined complex and adaptive sequencings of information. However, both specification have several limitations. The possible impact of these limitations on interoperability varies. The most relevant aspects are summarised in Table 2.

IMS Simple Sequencing is a specification aimed at describing paths through a collection of learning activities. It relies on the concept of learning units that are organized into a hierarchy tree. Sequencing rules are used to influence the order in which activities are presented to the learner. Limit rules, roll-up rules, and sequencing rules are used to influence which activity is sequenced next to a student.

IMS-SS lacks a student model in which to store the information that the system knows about the learner, apart from basic aspects like completion progress on an activity, timing on the attempts on an activity, etc. There is nothing else to record or process information about the student. In other words, it is not possible to express sequencings that depend on general, abstract concepts. For example, the sequencing cannot be influenced according to a ``skill level'' of the student, because there is no such concept in the specification and there are no means to implement it.

The second specification, IMS Learning Design, has general purpose properties that can be used to overcome this limitation. The specification is not designed specifically for adaptive sequencing definition (its goal is to describe pedagogical strategies in which collaborative learning and synchronization of different roles are important), and using it for that purpose means stretching the specification to its own limits, revealing clues about its current possibilities and conceivable extensions in the future.

Table 2. Comparison of IMS-SS and IMS-LD

Feature	IMS-SS	IMS-LD
Linear sequencing	Yes	Yes
Branched sequencing	Yes, using pre-conditions on the branches of the tree in a cluster	Yes, using different roles *a priori*, or using properties and conditions to show/hide activities
Repetition of activities	Yes	In principle, no
Cycles in the sequence	Limited, with heavy use of pre- and post-conditions	Limited, with heavy use or conditions and show/hide actions.
Mechanisms for sequence adaptation	Conditions	Properties and conditions
Style of adaptation language	Imperative, conditions are evaluated locally and in order	Declarative, conditions are evaluated globally
Synchronization for simultaneous users	No	Yes
Internal user modelling	Yes, using learning objectives	Yes, using properties
External user modelling	No	Yes, using properties
Interchange of information with external activities	No	Limited, using global-elements
Other goals apart from sequencing adaptation	No	Yes, sequencing adaptation is not even the main goal

The most relevant characteristic of IMS-LD with regard to adaptive sequencing expression is the use of properties. Properties allow learning designers to specify a low-level learner model based on pairs *<variable, value>*. This simple mechanism allows to build more flexible strategies for sequencing and other aspects of e-learning.

The functional paradigm of the condition model of IMS-LD makes it simpler to design units of learning with a small number of properties and conditions but, on the other hand, does not scale well. Complex and adaptive sequencings require a high number of conditions to take place, and these are difficult to maintain when every change in the value of a property can potentially fire a re-evaluation of all conditions. Every condition must be checked for every possible case, leading to a debugging process that is both tedious and error-prone. In this case, the use of a high-level authoring tool is mandatory.

Another important limitation of IMS-LD is the mechanism it proposes for the interaction with the learner. Interaction is only supported with the user through the so called *global-elements: set-property* and *get-property*. This behaviour is limiting, as it prevents applications (i.e. LCMS) to draw data from other resources apart from those XHTML documents especially prepared for IMS-LD. In other words, there is no mechanism to reuse some active activity like a web-based exercise (Brusilovsky & Sosnovsky, 2005; Tscherter, 2004; Azalov, 2005) and integrate it into a UoL, using the output parameters of the exercise (Gutierrez et al., 2008) to drive the sequencing of activities afterwards. All information interchange between the UoL and the activities must be mediated by the *global-elements*.

Most of these limitations can be seen as consequences of the same fact. Both the IMS-LD and the IMS-SS specifications assume that most sequencings will be linear or quasi-linear. Therefore, creating complex adapting sequences of learning material can prove to be difficult or even impossible. A future specification from IMS might take care of these considerations, taking into account different approaches that have been proposed (see next section). Meanwhile, e-learning systems that want to create rich sequencing strategies, while making these strategies shareable among platforms, will need to use sophisticated techniques and implement restricted sequencing functionalities. It is beyond of the scope of this chapter to analyse the details at the XML level, but the interested reader can look at (Gutierrez-Santos et al., 2008) and (Gutierrez-Santos, 2007, p.147).

In summary, IMS-LD is a broader specification, and embraces more aspects of educational practice than IMS-SS, which is focused only on sequencing. However, as we have already explained, the lack of a generalised learner model in IMS-SS (even in a simple form like the one provided by IMS-LD) imposes important constraints in the degree of sequencing adaptation that a system can provide for each student. In other words, an IMS-SS compliant system will find it hard to express an adaptive sequencing strategy (defined with its own authoring tool) in terms of IMS-SS so that it can be used by another system. This is the main limitation of IMS-SS, making IMS-LD a better choice to provide interoperability between systems with rich strategies integrated in their learning material.

FUTURE RESEARCH

There are currently two main lines of research related to adaptive sequencing and e-learning standards. The first one aims at finding better metaphors or tools to express flexible sequencings, while the latter tries to ascertain the level of adaptation that should be provided by the applications and not been expressed in terms of the standard.

Regarding the first strand of work, there are two main approaches. The first one is the use of general-purpose modelling languages like UML (Papasalouros et al., 2004; Dolog & Nejdl, 2003). The main advantage of using UML is that it is a well-known language for software engineers, so they do not need to learn any new tool. This is blessing and a curse, because UML can be too hard to use for teachers or designers without a technological background. UML is a complex language, and its use may be excessively demanding for many users interested in the design of adaptive sequencing strategies. Another possibility is the use of graph-based metaphors. The most successful initiative so far has been AHA! (de Bra et al., 2003), while Sequencing Graphs have already been used to test interoperability in terms of IMS-SS (Gutierrez et al., 2004a) and IMS-LD (Gutierrez-Santos et al., 2008), as referred earlier in the chapter.

Sometimes the sequencing of information cannot be stated at design time. It can be argued that in some scenarios the sequencing of learning material needs information that can only be accessed during execution time. This is the starting assumption for the work in (Zarraonandia et al., 2006). The paper presents an architecture for a IMS-LD player that provides a mechanism to add adaptation capabilities to UoL execution at runtime. The goal is to enhance reusability of the UoL introducing simple modifications into the original learning process. Another similar strategy is the integration of active components into the IMD-LD player, as proposed in (de la Fuente et al., 2009). The authors propose the integration of the player with active external components. They prove their point using Google Docs spreadsheets, but claim their architecture is general enough to integrate other plug-ins and services. This latter work is framed in a general tendency towards integration at the level of plug-ins (Wild et al., 2009), which has implication at many levels, and might prove as the better road to ensure interoperability for highly-flexible adaptive learning sequencing systems.

CONCLUSION

Digital technologies are having a clear impact on educational practice, and are pushing it to evolve. One of the most important changes that has been brought by technology is the new possibilities for sharing and reuse. In a digital world, where it is free to generate perfect duplicates, educational pieces of content can be shared with very little to lose and a lot to win. Teachers and lecturers all around the world have started to share educational content: presentation slides, on-line exercises and tutorials, or even whole courses (Vest, 2004). But as the possibilities of e-learning tools continue to increase, and the methods and tools necessary to create and maintain content and infrastructure applications become more complicated, there is an need for these tools to interoperate and exchange data in order to support the needs of learners, designers, and educators.

This chapter has concentrated on the problem of system interoperability from the point of view of adaptive sequencing. This problem has been the subject of an important amount of research efforts in several fields (e.g. AI in education, intelligent tutoring systems, adaptive hypermedia), and can be stated as this: given a student, and a set of learning resources, what is the best sequence of elements that can be provided to him or her. Although this problem has not been carefully considered yet in any standard or specification, there are two specifications by the IMS Global Learning Consortium that are especially relevant to it: IMS Simple Sequencing and IMS Learning Design. Both have been studied in this chapter, showing their strong points, their limitations, and the most promising lines of research that aim at overcoming the latter.

REFERENCES

Advanced Distributed Learning. (2004a). *SCORM 2004 Shareable Content Object Reference Model.*

Advanced Distributed Learning. (2004b). *SCORM conformance test suite*. Retrieved February 20, 2007 from http://www.adlnet.gov/scorm/20043ed/cts.cfm

Azalov, P. (2005). Synthetic exercises on the web. In *International Conference on Information Technology: Coding and Computing* (pp. 459-464).

Bailey, W., & Abel, R. (2009). *A Common Evolution for IMS Simple Sequencing?* Retrieved July 20, 2009 from http://www.imsglobal.org/evolutionforss.html

Baldoni, M., Baroglio, C., & Patti, V. & Torasso. L. (2004). Reasoning about learning object metadata for adapting SCORM courseware. In *Proceedings of the International Workshop on Engineering the Adaptive Web*, (pp.4-13).

Barr, A., Beard, M., & Atkinson, R. (1973). The computer as tutorial laboratory: the Stanford BIP project. *International Journal of Man-Machine Studies*, *8*, 567–596. doi:10.1016/S0020-7373(76)80021-1

Bloom, B. S. (1984). The 2 sigma problem: The search for methods of group instruction as effective as one-to-one tutoring. *Educational Research*, *13*, 3–15.

Brusilovsky, P. (2000). Course sequencing for static courses? applying its techniques in large-scale web-based education . In *Proceedings of Intelligent Tutoring Systems*. Berlin: Springer-Verlag. doi:10.1007/3-540-45108-0_66

Brusilovsky, P., & Sosnovsky, S. (2005). Individualized exercises for self-assessment of programming knowledge: An evaluation of Quizpack. *Journal of Educational Resources in Computing*, *5*(3). doi:10.1145/1163405.1163411

Brusilovsky, P., & Vassileva, J. (2003). Course sequencing techniques for large-scale web-based education. *International Journal of Continuing Engineering Education and Lifelong Learning*, *13*(1-2), 75–94.

Capell, P., & Dannenberg, R. (1993). Instructional design and intelligent tutoring: Theory and the precision of design. *Journal of Artificial Intelligence in Education*, *4*, 95–121.

Cristea, A. (2004). Authoring of adaptive and adaptable educational hypermedia: Where are we now and where are we going? In *International Conference in Web-Based Education*. New York: Acta Press.

Cristea, A., & Aroyo, L. (2002). Adaptive Authoring of Adaptive Educational Hypermedia. In *International Conference on Adaptive Hypermedia*, (pp. 122-132). Berlin: Springer-Verlag.

De Bra, P., Aerts, A., Berden, B., de Lange, B., Rousseau, B., Santic, T., et al. (2003). AHA! The adaptive hypermedia architecture. In *Proceedings of Conference on Hypertext and Hypermedia*, (pp.81-84). New York: ACM.

De la Fuente Valentín, L., Pardo, A., & Delgado Kloos, C. (2009). Using Third Party Services to Adapt Learning Material: A Case Study with Google Forms. In *Proceedings of European Conference on Technology-Enhanced Learning*, (pp.744-750). Berlin: Springer-Verlag.

Dolog, P., & Nejdl, W. (2003). Using UML and XMI for generating adaptive navigation sequences in web-based systems. In *Proceedings of UML 2003*.

Edwards, D., & Hardman, L. (1989). Lost in cyberspace: Cognitive mapping and navigation in a hypertext environment . In McAleese, R. (Ed.), *Hypertext: Theory into practice*. New York: Intellect Books.

Gutierrez, S., Losa, F. J., & Delgado Kloos, C. (2008). Towards a formalization of the automatic generation of exercises. In *International Workshop on Authoring of Adaptive and Adaptable Hypermedia, in International Conference on Adaptive Hypermedia*. Berlin: Springer-Verlag.

Gutierrez, S., Pardo, A., & Delgado Kloos, C. (2004a). Beyond simple sequencing: Sequencing of learning activities using hierarchical graphs. In *International Conference in Web-Based Education*. New York: Acta Press.

Gutierrez, S., Pardo, A., & Delgado Kloos, C. (2004b). An Adaptive Tutoring System Based on Hierarchical Graphs. In *International Conference on Adaptive Hypermedia*, (pp. 401-404). Berlin: Springer-Verlag.

Gutierrez-Santos, S. (2007). *Sequencing of learning activities oriented towards reuse and auto-organization for intelligent tutoring systems*, PhD. Thesis, University Carlos III of Madrid, Madrid, Spain.

Gutierrez-Santos, S., Pardo, A., & Delgado Kloos, C. (2008). Authoring Courses with Rich Adaptive Sequencing for IMS Learning Design. *Journal of Universal Computer Science*, *14*(17), 2819–2839.

Hendrix, M., de Bra, P., Pechenizkiy, M., Smits, D., & Cristea, A. (2008). Defining Adaptation in a Generic Multi Layer Model: CAM: The GRAPPLE Conceptual Adaptation Model. In *Proceedings of European conference on Technology Enhanced Learning*, (pp. 132 - 143). Berlin: Springer-Verlag.

IMS Global Learning Consortium. (2003a). *IMS Simple Sequencing Information and Behavior Model*. Retrieved July 20, 2009 from http://www.imsglobal.org/specifications.html

IMS Global Learning Consortium. (2003b). *IMS Simple Sequencing Best Practice and Implementation Guide*. Retrieved July 20, 2009 from http://www.imsglobal.org/specifications.html

IMS Global Learning Consortium. (2003c). *IMS Learning Design Information Model*. Retrieved July 20, 2009 from http://www.imsglobal.org/specifications.html

IMS Global Learning Consortium. (2003d). *IMS Learning Design Best Practice and Implementation Guide*. Retrieved July 20, 2009 from http://www.imsglobal.org/specifications.html

Karampiperis, P., & Sampson, D. (2004). Adaptive instructional planning using ontologies. In *Proceedings of the 4th IEEE International Conference on Advanced Learning Technologies*, (pp. 126–130).

Khuwaja, R., Desmarais, M., & Cheng, R. (1996). Intelligent guide: Combining user knowledge assesment with pedagogical guidance . In *Proceedings of Intelligent Tutoring Systems*. Berlin: Springer-Verlag.

Koper, R. (2005). Designing learning networks for lifelong learners . In Koper, R., & Tattersall, C. (Eds.), *Learning Design: A Handbook on Modelling and Delivering Networked Education and Training*. Berlin: Springer.

Marek, E., & Cavallo, A. M. (1997). *The Learning Cycle*. Berlin: Heinemann.

McArthur, D., Stasz, C., Hotta, J., Peter, O., & Burdof, C. (1988). Skill-oriented task sequencing in an intelligent tutor for basic algebra. In . *Proceedings of Instructional Science*, *17*, 281–307. doi:10.1007/BF00056218

Papasalouros, A., Retalis, S., & Papaspyrou, N. (2004). Semantic description of educational adaptive hypermedia based on a conceptual model. *Journal of Educational Technology & Society*, *7*(4), 129–142.

Rios, A. de la Cruz, J. L. P. & Conejo, R. (1993). SIETTE: Intelligent evaluation system using tests for basic algebra. In *Proceedings of workshop WWW-Based Tutoring, in Intelligent Tutoring Systems Conference*.

Tscherter, V. (2004). *Exorciser: Automatic Generation and Interactive Grading of Structured Exercises in the Theory of Computation*. PhD Thesis, Swiss Federal Institute of Technology, Switzerland.

Ullrich, C. (2005). Course generation based on HTN planning. In *Proceedings of 13th Annual Workshop of the SIG Adaptivity and User Modeling in Interactive Systems*, (pp.74-79).

Vest, C. (2004). Why MIT decided to give away all its course materials via the Internet. *The Chronicle of Higher Education*, 30.

Wan, L., Zhao, C., & Luo, Q. (2006). Navigation and sequencing strategy of learning process in distance learning context. In *Frontiers in Education*.

Wild, F., Kalz, M., Palmer, M., & Muller, D. (Eds.). (2009). Proceedings of the Second International Workshop on Mashup Personal Learning Environments, in *European Conference on Technology-Enhanced Learning*. *Available* at http://ceur-ws.org/Vol-506/ (retrieved Oct. 2009).

Wiley, D. A. (2002). Connecting learning objects to instructional design theory: A definition, a metaphor, and a taxonomy . In *The Instructional Use of Learning Objects*. Agency for Instructional Technology.

Zarraonandia, T., Dodero, J. M., & Fernández, C. (2006). Crosscutting Runtime Adaptations of LD Execution. *Journal of Educational Technology & Society*, *9*(1), 123–137.

ADDITIONAL READING

Boticario, J. G., & Santos, O. C. (2006). Issues in developing adaptive learning management systems for higher education institutions. In International Workshop on Adaptive Learning and Learning Design, in *International Conference on Adaptive Hypermedia*.

Brusilovsky, P. (2004). Adaptive Educational Hypermedia: From generation to generation. In Proceedings of *Hellenic Conference on ICT in Education*, pp.19-33.

Corbett, A. (2001). Cognitive Computer Tutors: Solving the Two-Sigma Problem. In Proceedings of *International Conference on User Modeling*, pp.137-147. Springer-Verlag.

De Bra, P., Smits, D., & Stash, N. (2006). The design of AHA! In Proceedings of Conference on Hypertext and Hypermedia, pp.133-134. ACM.

De la Fuente Valentin, L., Leony, D., Pardo, A., & Delgado Kloos, C. (2008). Mashups in Learning Design: pushing the flexibility envelope. In Proceedings of the First International Workshop on Mashup Personal Learning Environments, in *European Conference on Technology-Enhanced Learning*, pp. 18-27.

Gutierrez, S., Pardo, A., & Delgado Kloos, C. (2006). Some Ideas for a Collaborative Search of the Optimal Learning Path. In Proceedings of *International Conference of Adaptive Hypermedia*, pp. 430-434. Springer-Verlag.

Hernández, J., Baldiris, S., Santos, O. C., Fabregat, R., & Boticario, J. G. (2009). Conditional IMS Learning Design Generation Using User Modeling and Planning Techniques. In Proceedings of *International Conference on Advanced Learning Technologies*, pp.228-232. IEEE Computer Society.

Janssen, J., Berlanga, A., Vogten, H., & Koper, R. (2008). Towards a learning path specification. *International Journal of Continuing Engineering Education and Lifelong Learning*, *18*(1), 77–97. doi:10.1504/IJCEELL.2008.016077

Koper, R., & Tattersall, C. (Eds.). (2005). *Learning Design: A Handbook on Modelling and Delivering Networked Education and Training*. Springer.

Lazarinis, F., Green, S., & Pearson, E. (2009). Focusing on content reusability and interoperability in a personalized hypermedia assessment tool. In *Journal of Multimedia Tools and Applications*.

Murray, T. (2003). MetaLinks: Authoring and affordances for conceptual and narrative flow in adaptive hyperbooks. *International Journal of Artificial Intelligence in Education*, *13*(2-4), 199–233.

Zarraonandia, T., Dodero, J. M., Fernandez, C., Diaz, P., & Torres, J. (2006). Late Modelling: A Timing of Learning Activities Approach. In Proceedings of *International Conference on Advanced Learning Technologies*, pp. 656-658. IEEE Computer Society.

KEY TERMS AND DEFINITIONS

Adaptive Sequencing: The capacity of tailoring the order in which learning units are presented to learners to their specific characteristics.

Authoring Tool: A software tool that helps a designer, hiding most of the technical details with a friendly user interface.

IMS Learning Design: A specification by IMS to provide interoperability between systems that design learning situations.

IMS-LD Player: A software tool that shows a unit of learning containing the model of a learning process, as expressed by IMS Learning Design.

IMS Simple Sequencing: A specification by IMS to provide interoperability for limited adaptive sequencing systems.

Interoperability: The capacity of using the same material on different platforms or systems.

Learning Content Management System: A software application, usually web-based, that automates the administration, documentation, and delivery of learning material.

ENDNOTES

1. There is not a universally accepted definition of reusable learning object, but there are two that are usually referenced. David Wiley says

that a learning object is "*any digital resource that can be used to support learning*" (Wiley, 2002). The other definition is that of IEEE: "*Any entity, digital or otherwise, that can be used for learning, education, or training*". Furthermore, it is not uncommon to use the term to refer just to a SCORM package or a IMS Content Package.

[2] The complete list can be accessed at www.imsglobal.org/specifications.html.

[3] The size of the XML files grows like the cube of the number of activities (Gutierrez-Santos, 2007, p.100).

Chapter 7
A Standard-Based Framework to Support Personalisation, Adaptation, and Interoperability in Inclusive Learning Scenarios

O.C. Santos
The National Distance Education University of Spain (UNED), Spain

J.G. Boticario
The National Distance Education University of Spain (UNED), Spain

E. Raffenne
The National Distance Education University of Spain (UNED), Spain

J. Granado
The National Distance Education University of Spain (UNED), Spain

A. Rodriguez-Ascaso
The National Distance Education University of Spain (UNED), Spain

E. Gutierrez y Restrepo
The National Distance Education University of Spain (UNED), Spain

ABSTRACT

This chapter introduces a standards-based and adaptive framework whose main objective is to adapt user interfaces, content and learning environment to learners' needs, including their functional diversity issues (i.e., disabilities). The framework is intended to be general (e.g., two different learning management systems and two large pilot sites are being considered) and to that end it is implemented in terms of an open architecture, which aims at providing services for Accessible Lifelong Learning. The chapter focuses on accessibility and adaptation issues, and their interoperability requirements. The covered topics are the required standards, interoperability requirements of the architecture, user model, recommender

DOI: 10.4018/978-1-61692-789-9.ch007

system, and their application to the end-user services that are being implemented at UNED University, one of the large pilot sites of the EU4ALL European project. Some of the challenges and solutions provided are discussed as well as the future work of related research areas.

INTRODUCTION

Learning ideally should be a personalised and adaptive process for all, which from the beginning to the end must consider the learner's specific needs and preferences. Regretfully though, students with specific needs, such as those with functional diversity issues (i.e., the so-called disabilities), have problems in accessing learning because of the diverse barriers that may exist in the various stages they must go through to realise their learning or teaching goals. In fact, while many physical barriers have been removed in Higher Education (HE) Institutions, Information and Communications Technology (ICT) services are still not fully accessible to an increasing number of students whose main educational option is distance learning.

Actually, accessibility, adaptation and learning are three interrelated issues with a growing interest in our society (Iorio, Feliziani et al., 2006; Kelly et al., 2007, Lanzilotti, Ardito et al., 2006; Seale et al., 2008). For that reason, European level initiatives, especially the Lifelong Learning (LLL) Programme (LLL Programme, 2006), promote and regulate actions to enable the conditions for everyone to take part in the information society. The main goal is to bring about "services, procedures, and information in an accessible way for every person", assuming that "e-learning products and methods are able to take into account individual needs and learning-styles, and that they are not based on a 'one size fits all' philosophy, in which learners are seen as standardised 'units'" (eLearningPR, 2004). A wide range of international and national legislations support individual rights and attendance to functional diversity issues. To name but a few, in Europe the E-Government-Law in Austria; Equal Status Act in Ireland; BITV in Germany; LSSICE in Spain; SENDA in the UK, etc. (WAB Cluster, 2009), the well known ADA in the US, and needless to mention the relatively recent International Convention on the Rights of Persons with Disabilities, which remarks in its article 24.5 (Education) that "States Parties shall ensure that persons with disabilities are able to access general tertiary education, vocational training, adult education and lifelong learning without discrimination...".

Despite available legislation and expected benefits from student-centred approaches in HE, leveraged by the European Higher Education Area (EHEA, 2009), from enrolment to assessment, students have to negotiate pre-established general procedures. These procedures are nowadays mediated mainly by technology (EUNIS, 2009) and intended to fulfil a "standard" set of needs but are far from considering the students' individual needs and preferences. In fact, it is disturbing to note that the most basic requirements of people with disabilities are usually not attended in HE (Seale, 2006), and very often it is due to the unavailability of information before-hand, the lack of pre-established procedures to attend particular needs and the multiple and diverse barriers that have to be overcome to provide the required infrastructure (Cooper et al., 2006).

To mitigate the problems related to functional diversity issues in education and with a mainstream inclusive approach focused on attending the personal needs of the learner, the aDeNu (Adaptive Dynamic online Educational systems based oN User modelling) research and development group at UNED (Spanish National University for Distance Education) has developed standard based components designed to compose an open and adaptive framework. The main objective is to adapt user interfaces, content and learning environment to the needs of learners, including their functional diversity issues (i.e., disabilities), in a context where design for all concepts and user experience customisation are complementarily applied. To that end the framework, following the aDeNu approach (Boticario & Santos, 2008), draws on user modelling through a combination of dynamic adaptation techniques, and works in terms of a service oriented architecture in which different components are seamlessly combined.

Two key issues, personalisation (i.e., user-centred adaptation) and accessibility, must be addressed to cope with learners' personal needs while interacting with the learning management systems (LMS) provided by most HE Institutions. Firstly, it is well assumed that personalised learning is no longer a research issue faced in small-scale web-based education (Brusilovsky and Vassileva, 2003) and there have been several reviews that cover existing approaches (Cristea & Garzotto, 2004; Brusilovsky, 2004). Actually, personalised learning is a concrete challenge for current LMS (Boticario & Santos, 2007). However, personalisation, which covers adaptiveness and adaptability (Fink & Kobsa, 1998), is still an open issue and there is not currently any system that supports full adaptiveness.

Secondly, accessibility has implications all over the e-learning domain. Almost every step of any e-learning process has accessibility concerns, and almost every professional in an e-learning institution has a role on accessibility. In addition to this, e-learning is emergently relevant in different contexts of citizens' lives. As a consequence of all these facts and trends, standardisation in e-learning accessibility covers a wide range of science, technology and industry areas, currently with a number of open issues that will be discussed in this chapter.

Further, current LMSs do not properly cover personalisation and accessibility issues and they are still struggling to support the reusability requirements comming from the pervasive usage of standards. Furthermore, almost none of the existing LMS supports a wide range of educational standards (SCORM, IMS) (Santos et al., 2007b) and can guarantee that the functionality meets usability and accessibility requirements (Martin et al., 2007).

To illustrate some of the open issues involved in dealing with personalisation and accessibility in e-learning we present the current state of developments the aDeNu research group is leading within EU4ALL European project (IST-FP6-034778). The EU4ALL project aims at developing a general and flexible framework to support the needs of inclusive learning scenarios (Boticario et al., 2006). This framework defines and implements an open and extensible architecture of services for Accessible Lifelong Learning (ALL) in terms of standards, whose generality will be evaluated at the two largest distance learning universities in Europe, OU (Open University in the UK) and UNED (National University for Distance Education in Spain), which presents different institutional and developing needs and different types of users (students, faculty, specialised personnel and administrative people). From the technological viewpoint, these developments focus on personalisation issues and justify the various advantages of such general architecture. In particular, it supports interoperability requirements comming from the various needs in different educational contexts. Further, alternative LMS (such as dotLRN and Moodle) can be used at different institutions. On the other side, a wide variety of components are needed to support accessibility and personalisation, including user modelling subsystem, content personalisation module, tracker, ePortfolio, units of learning based on psycho-educational issues, recommender system, guidance for tutors and eServices Server. The latter is meant to facilitate, in terms of executable workflows (eServices), the definition and development of end-user services on top of the framework. The services that are being developed are open, secure, standard-based, accessible and interoperable, and prove the flexibility of the architecture to support assistive LLL for adult learners with disabilities.

In this context, we focus on the development of the user model and the recommender system components, the extension of the dotLRN LMS architecture to enable interoperability of the internal functionality of the LMS (such as the players for educational content) with the components developed in EU4ALL (i.e. user model, recommender system, content personalisation, device modelling, metadata repository, guidance for all, eServices server,...). With this technological support, it is possible to cover the needs of the learners in terms of end-user services. In this chapter we address the technological support provided to cover the existing needs of learners in inclusive learning scenarios at HE through personalisation/adaptation and interoperability.

There are related projects that are coping with some of the EU4ALL open issues. Adaptive and accessible learning is also addressed in GRAPPLE project (Grapple, 2009) and FLEXO (Flexo, 2009). Legal, political and socio-economic considerations are being considered at the HEAG (Higher Education Accessibility Guidelines) (Heag, 2009), the European Agency for the Development of Special Needs Education. There are other service oriented architectures, such as the e-Framework for Education and Research (e-Framework, 2009), the Open Knowledge Initiative (Oki, 2009), and the Fluid Project (Fluid, 2009). However, to the knowledge of authors, there are no similar implementations based on standards and service-oriented architectures to supporting students with disabilities in HE as is being proposed by the EU4ALL project.

This chapter presents a set of components designed to compose a flexible, standards based and adaptive framework, whose main objective is to adapt user interfaces, content and learning environment to the needs of learners, including their functional diversity issues (i.e., disabilities). These adaptations require an intensive data exchange in order to better support the needs of learners while accessing a wide variety of resources within different contexts. Moreover, different components are required to enrich the limited interoperability and adaptation capabilities of existing LMS so that these are able to deal with the increasing interoperability requirements coming from web-based educational tools. These needs make critical the research on interoperability of e-learning applications. Two approaches can be followed to meet the required LMS personalisation support: (1) a student-centred design approach, focused on modifying the functional logic of the system, and (2) a personalised interaction approach, by adding the required support when needed in the system. The former relates to issues such as content personalisation and personalised units of learning, which require modifications within the LMS. The focus is on the adaptation of the user interface and the content. The later refers to offering recommendations to extend the LMS with adaptive navigation support, and thus, modifying the learning environment to the needs of the learner. Both are supported by user modelling techniques which are managed with the appropriate standards.

In the following sections we introduce the background for our approach, which focuses on adaptability and accessibility based on standards in education. Afterwards, we present the EU4ALL framework and the scenarios are supported. Then, we comment on the main research areas where we are researching in the project: the modelling of learner preferences, the LMS support for content personalisation and personalised units of learning, and the recommendations support. Finally, we present some future trends in the research of standard-based frameworks to support personalisation/adaptation and interoperability in inclusive learning scenarios, including the limitations of current standards.

BACKGROUND ON ADAPTABILITY AND ACCESSIBILITY BASED ON STANDARDS IN EDUCATION

The accessibility of universities and colleges depends on the perspective adopted to assess student needs and deliver appropriate support. According to the *Selected Statistics on Higher Education - Background Report*, for the OECD Meeting of Ministers of Education in June 2006: "*Countries that have chosen needs-based approaches have a higher level of accessibility than countries having impairment-based perspectives that link the supports and the subsidies with a status of disability.* At the level of the HEIs, the needs perspective requires integrated strategies that enlarge their ability to deliver appropriate services and support to all students and to cope with diversity within the community" (OECD, 2006).

Many groups, institutions and associations are working to create standards in the field of education. This makes it difficult, to some extent, the development of a framework which is intended to be open and flexible, although there are an increasing number of alliances and agreements that lead to clarify the landscape of standardisation.

In this section, we review the most relevant standards for adaptability and accessibility in education. Next, we briefly describe the research projects carried out at aDeNu research group, highlighting the usage of standards done in them. Finally, we present a summary table of the different standards, specifications and recommendations that have been used in these projects.

Revision of Standards and Specification for Education

Some of the most important or that are taking the greatest impact are:

AICC - Aviation Industry CBT Committee

The recommendation of more widespread and greater impact, published by ADL is the recommendation for interoperability CMI (Computer-Managed Instruction) (AICC, 2005).

This specification was published in the mid-90s, and now the AICC seeks its implementation in the reference model of ADL SCORM, and publication as a standard from IEEE (IEEE, 2005). The purpose of this standard is to:

- Allow different lessons to work with different CMI systems
- Allow courses to move from one CMI system to another with minimal effort (Course interchange/interoperability)
- Allow modification/expansion of a course by any instructor with his/her preferred CMI tools
- Enable easier analysis of student data from different lessons.

The CMI runtime, incorporated in SCORM 1.2, facilitates intercommunication between content and the back end database of the LMS/LCMS. This allows simulations, and other more abstract tests built into content, to pass a score to the LMS/LCMS for processing/storage.

Institute for Electrical and Electronic Engineers Learning Technology Standards Committee (IEEE LTSC)

Most groups working in creating specifications in the education field are based on the standards working IEEE Learning Technology Standards Committee (LTSC) P1484 (LTSC, 2009). Their published standards included:

- 1484.20.1-2007 IEEE Standard for Learning Technology-Data Model for Reusable Competency Definitions

- 1484.4-2007 IEEE Trial-Use Recommended Practice for Digital Rights Expression Languages (DRELs) Suitable for eLearning Technologies
- 1484.11.3-2005 IEEE Standard for Learning Technology-Extensible Markup Language (XML) Schema Binding for Data Model for Content Object Communication
- 1484.12.3-2005 IEEE Standard for Learning Technology-Extensible Markup Language (XML) Schema Definition Language Binding for Learning Object Metadata
- 1484.11.1-2004 IEEE Standard for Learning Technology-Data Model for Content to Learning Management System Communication
- 1484.11.2-2003 IEEE Standard for Learning Technology-ECMAScript Application Programming Interface for Content to Runtime Services Communication
- 1484.1-2003 IEEE Standard for Learning Technology-Learning Technology Systems Architecture (LTSA)
- 1484.12.1-2002 IEEE Standard for Learning Object Metadata (LOM)

These standards cover topics as varied as computer managed instruction, student profiles, competency definitions, learning object metadata, course sequencing, localisation, and content packaging.

LOM (IEEE Learning Object Meta-Data) is the standard for e-learning that has been adopted in the IMS Learning Resource Metadata specification. LOM is based on previous developments for the description of educational resources carried out in projects ARIADNE, IMS and Dublin Core.

LOM aims at the creation of structured descriptions of educational resources. Its data model specifies which aspects of a learning object should be described and what vocabularies may be used in that description.

ISO International Organisation for Standardisation

For some time, the standardisation work on learning technologies has been shifted to the ISO standards body, and has established the ISO Joint Technical Committee 1 (JTC1) Sub Committee 36 (SC36) on Learning Technology (ISO, 2009). This subcommittee has 7 Working Groups and has now issued 12 standards, among which are:

- ISO/IEC 24751-1:2008: Information technology -- Individualised adaptability and accessibility in e-learning, education and training -- Part 1: Framework and reference model
- ISO/IEC 24751-2:2008: Information technology -- Individualised adaptability and accessibility in e-learning, education and training -- Part 2: “Access for all” personal needs and preferences for digital delivery. This part is also known as ISO PNP (Personal Needs and Preferences)
- ISO/IEC 24751-3:2008: Information technology -- Individualised adaptability and accessibility in e-learning, education and training -- Part 3: “Access for all” digital resource description.

ISO / IEC 24751 series has been developed taking into account the needs of older persons and persons with disabilities and any person in an environment that can be disabling. Describes and identifies the needs and preferences of the student and also provides a description of the relevant digital learning resources, so that individual learning preferences and requirements of the student can be met through user interface tools and appropriate digital learning resources. This part is also known as ISO DRD (Digital Resources Description).

This standard establishes a common framework for different additional parts, providing a description of the accessibility needs and preferences of the students, including a display and control of the digital resources, and secondly, a description of the characteristics of resources that affect the way in which the user can perceive, understand or interact with them. The latter takes into account what sensory modalities are used in the application, how to adapt the resource (i.e. if the text can be processed automatically), the input methods accepted by the resource, and the alternatives available.

Dublin Core

The Dublin Core Advisory Committee, DCAC created the working group on education, which aims to develop a proposal to simplify the use of Dublin Core metadata in the description of educational resources. The main outcome was the Dublin Core Metadata Element Set (DCMES) which contains 15 elements and can be refined to add greater richness to the description. The Dublin Core is well accepted when developing systems with metadata information.

Accessibility Term

The DC metadata term set did not provide adequate information for the matching of resources to users' needs in cases where those users had disabilities or are in disabling circumstances. So a comprehensive, stand-alone new term was proposed by the Accessibility Special Interest Group and it was to be known as an accessibility term. Recently, especially as a result of the increased mobility of information, it has become apparent that a number of communities have an interest in how content can be adapted and transformed for individual users or circumstances. The proposed term is suitable for a wider context and so its name was changed to adaptability for a while but it has proven more appropriate to the accessibility community to call it accessibility.

The term has been carefully re-modelled from the ISO/IEC version to be used in conjunction with existing DC terms.

It has been adopted in principle, awaiting DCMI recommendation, by the Australian Government as its standard, and has been recommended by the IMS Global Learning Consortium for IEEE/LOM metadata for learning resources. (Core, 2008).

The term is related to other documents, such as the aforementioned ISO/IEC N:24751 series, and with the IMS AccessForAll Metadata Specification (AccMD) Version 1.0: The requirements of the Adaptability Statement term proposal, specifically its ability to match resources to the accessibility preferences of a user, are highly influenced by the IMS AccMD specification.

IMS Global Learning Consortium

IMS Global Learning Consortium is the main promoter and developer of open specifications for e-learning. IMS GLC has approved and published some 20 standards that include meta-data, content packaging, common cartridge, enterprise services, question and test, sequencing, competencies, access for all, ePortfolio, learner information, tools interoperability, resource list, sharable state persistence, vocabulary definition, and learning design. Its aim is that from these specifications, to achieve interoperability of applications and services for e-learning that the authors of content and environments can work together

IMS Reusable Definition of Competency or Educational Objective Specification (RDCEO)

RDCEO is a specification, which provides a data model based on XML for the definition of competencies, although minimalist is extensible and adaptable to any standardisation system.

Provide unique references to descriptions of competencies or objectives for inclusion in other information models. The specification provides a means for creating a common understanding of the skills that are presented as part of a learning system or career plan, the requirements of an apprenticeship, or its results. The information model in this specification can be used to exchange these definitions between learning systems, human resource systems, learning content, repositories of competencies or skills, etc. The specification, at this time now to become an IEEE standard, and so far has been published in draft version.

Digital Repositories Specification

The IMS Digital Repositories v1.0 Final specification purpose is to provide recommendations for the interoperation of the most common repository functions. These recommendations should be implementable across services to enable them to present a common interface. On the broadest level, this specification defines digital repositories as being any collection of resources that are accessible via a network without prior knowledge of the structure of the collection. Repositories may hold actual assets or the meta-data that describe assets. The assets and their meta-data do not need to be held in the same repository. This specification is intended to utilise schemas already defined elsewhere (e.g., IMS Meta-Data and Content Packaging), rather than attempt to introduce any new schema.

Learning Design Specification (IMS-LD)

The main purpose of this specification is to provide a model to describe the structure of tasks and activities, assigning them to roles, and the flow of units of learning as "learning design". The IMS Learning Design specification was published in 2003 and supports the use of a wide range of pedagogies in online learning. Rather than attempting to capture the specifics of many different pedagogical approaches, it does this by providing a generic and flexible language. This language is designed to enable many different pedagogical strategies to be expressed. The approach has the advantage over alternatives in that only one set of learning design and runtime tools then need to be implemented in order to support the desired wide range of pedagogies. The language was originally developed at the Open University of the Netherlands (OUNL), after extensive examination and comparison of a wide range of educational approaches and their associated learning activities, and several iterations of the developing language to obtain a good balance between generality and pedagogic expressiveness.

IMS Question & Test Interoperability Specification (QTI)

There is currently a working draft of version 2.1 of this specification. The version 1.0 was published in 2000. The IMS Question & Test Interoperability Specification provides proposed standard XML language for describing questions and tests. The specification has been produced to allow the interoperability of content within assessment systems (Lesage, M. et al. 2008). This will be useful for publishers, certification authorities, teachers, trainers, publishers and creators of assessments, and the software vendors whose tools they use. Authoring tools, and publishers, publish XML and this data can be imported into other authoring tools and delivery systems (Martínez-Ortiz, I. et al, 2006). IMS Question and Test Interoperability v2.0 Final Specification has three key objectives:

1. To address relevant issues deferred from v1.0: a new information model has been defined with a new interaction model and a profile of XHTML to replace static material. Authors will now have more control over the behaviour and positioning of feedback and support for cloning using item templates has been added.
2. To define a method for putting QTI into content packages: a new document has also been created dedicated to meta-data and usage-data (item statistics)

3. To describe a method for using QTI with Learning Design, Simple Sequencing and the CMI data model.

IMS Learner Information Package (LIP)

The specification "Learner Information Package" (IMS LIP) is the first and most widely recognised specification on what was later called e-portfolio. It is a collection of information on students, individually or in groups, content creators, distributors or suppliers. Its main structures are based on: accessibility, accessibilities; activities; affiliations; competencies; goals; identifications; interests; qualifications, certifications and licences; relationship; security keys; and transcripts. Despite being widely known and mentioned, few people actually adopted it, and there was little sign of any practical and effective passing of information between systems using IMS LIP.

IMS ePortfolio Specification

The IMS ePortfolio specification was created in 2005 to make ePortfolios interoperable across different systems and institutions. The ePortfolio specification:

- Supports the advancement of lifelong learning important to many government initiatives.
- Makes exchanging portfolios from school to work transitions easier.
- Allows educators and institutions to better track competencies.
- Enhances the learning experience and improves employee development.

As we shall see later, the low implementation of the LIP and IMS ePortfolio specifications, have led to this year 2009 will create a new specification that aims to be simpler to implement, with a less hierarchical and more relational model.

IMS AccessForAll (AfA)

AccessForAll (AfA) is a framework designed to define and describe resource accessibility. Its goal is to provide a means whereby resources are matched to the individual accessibility needs and preferences of a particular person. The framework is divided into the following concepts, which, when used in conjunction, make possible the meeting of resources to needs and preferences and the description of resource accessibility:

- a statement of the needs and preferences of the individual user, at the time and in the context they are in (called the personal needs and preferences profile - PNP)
- a statement of the relevant characteristics of a resource to be matched to the PNP (called a digital resource description DRD)
- alternative resources that can be swapped into or appended to a given resource, when it is missing what the user needs

The main idea behind the AfA work is that while there are guidelines for making resources universally accessible, as the Web Content Accessibility Guidelines (WCAG) by the W3C, they are rarely used properly and they do not always solve all problems. AfA is about matching resources to an individual's requirements, even if it is not suitable for others. AfA anticipates the matching being done automatically but, if not, at least possible manually. (IMS, IMS Global Learning Consortium, 2004).

The Web Content Accessibility Guidelines (WCAG) are a set of principles and guidelines that define and explain the "requirements for making Web-based information and applications accessible to a wide range of people with disabilities." (W3C-WAI, 2008) The WCAG does not define new technologies, but rather techniques that can be applied to any type of content accessed through the Web. The AccessForAll framework defines a complementary approach to resource accessibility: The AccessForAll Framework describes (via metadata on resources) the accessibility properties that are recommended by the WCAG. This enables the AccessForAll Framework to provide a means whereby resources can be matched to the needs and preferences of persons.

There are two specifications involved in AfA: Accessibility for LIP (AccLIP) and Accessibility for Meta-data (AccMD). The specification "Accessibility for LIP (ACCLIP)" extends the 1.0 version of IMS LIP, adding descriptive material important to define the preferences for accessibility. The new features are entirely compatible with those in the LIP specification, especially with regard to privacy, access and integrity of information. The elements of ACCLIP provide a means to describe how the student wishes to access content and applications through a series of elements that indicate preferences. The elements are grouped and cover three categories: presentation of information, control information, and information on the contents. Therefore, offer students the possibility to create preferences for how content is presented in a particular context. These preferences go beyond support for disabled people to include kinds of accessibility needs such as mobile computing, noisy environments, etc.

The AccessForAll Meta-data specification is intended to make it possible to identify resources that match a user's stated preferences or needs. These preferences or needs would be declared using the IMS Learner Information Package Accessibility for LIP specification. The needs and preferences addressed include the need or preference for alternative presentations of resources, alternative methods of controlling resources, alternative equivalents to the resources themselves and enhancements or supports required by the user. The specification provides a common language for identifying and describing the primary or default resource and equivalent alternatives for that resource. This work represents open collaboration between working group members from IMS, Dublin Core, IEEE, CEN-ISSS, Eduspecs as well as other groups. The AccessForAll Metadata specification is a proposed unified approach to matching user needs and preferences with the resources that address those needs and preferences across the participating specifications bodies.

IMS Guidelines for Developing Accessible Learning Applications (GDALA)

The IMS has also published the "IMS Guidelines for Developing Accessible Learning Applications" (IMS, IMS Global Learning Consortium, 2004) offering, in addition to Principles for Accessibility in Online Distributed Learning, specific guidelines, including: Guidelines for accessible delivery of text, audio, images, and multimedia; guidelines for developing accessible asynchronous communication and collaboration tools; guidelines for developing accessible synchronous communication and collaboration tools; guidelines for developing accessible interfaces and interactive environments; guidelines for testing and assessment; guidelines for developing accessible authoring tools; and guidelines for topic specific accessibility.

W3C

Among the W3C specifications, two relevant sets can be commented: On the one hand, the Accessibility Guidelines specified by the W3C's Web Accessibility Initiative (WAI). On the other hand, the CC/PP specification to describe the device features.

WAI guidelines for Web content, user agents, and authoring tools are considered as the international standard for Web accessibility. Guidelines directly applicable to e-learning are dedicated to content and authoring tools, since they provide contents and most LMS include applications that allow users to create content and therefore these applications should be accessible in themselves, in addition they should support the generation of accessible content to all. Regretfully though, they do not provide such desired support.

In many countries version 1.0 of the Web Content Accessibility Guidelines (WCAG) are enforced by law. The current version, WCAG 2.0, has 12 guidelines that are organised under 4 principles: perceivable, operable, understandable, and robust. For each guideline, there are testable success criteria, which are at three levels: A, AA, and AAA.

The Authoring Tool Accessibility Guidelines (ATAG) documents define how authoring tools should help Web developers produce Web content that is accessible and conforms to WCAG. The ATAG documents also explain how to make authoring tools accessible so that people with disabilities can use the tools. The ATAG 1.0 was approved in February 2000 and is the stable and referring version. ATAG 2.0 is being developed to be compatible with WCAG 2.0.

These guidelines for web content and authoring tools, which are also referenced by IMS GDALA are applicable and should be applied to each of the resources or learning objects, to ensure accessibility by the broadest range of users.

CC/PP specification means Composite Capabilities/Preferences Profile and is a description of the capabilities of devices and user preferences. It is usually used to define the context of delivery of the final device and make a proper adaptation of content. The User Agent Profile (UaProf, 2009) vocabulary, proposed by Open Mobile Alliance and based on CC/PP, is the one currently used in practice.

Advanced Distributed Learning (ADL)

Applying some of the standards published by IEEE, the US Federal Government Advanced Distributed Learning Initiative (ADL, 2009) published the Shareable Courseware Object Reference Model (SCORM). SCORM is a compilation of technical specifications for e-learning

Among SCORM goals are to enable interoperability, accessibility and reusability of web-based learning content for industry, government, and academia. SCORM defines how to create "sharable content objects" or "SCOs" that can be reused in different systems and contexts. It is not really a standard in the formal sense. It is rather a reference model which has become a de facto standard. SCORM was not created from scratch, was created taking existing standards in the industry that solved part of the requirements, so that SCORM simply refers to existing standards and tells developers how to use them properly together. The last version is 1.3.3, called SCORM 2004, and allows more flexible persistence of data during sequencing experiences.

JISC CETIS: Centre for Educational Technology & Interoperability Standards

Both the standard British LeaP, published in 2004, as the IMS ePortfolio specification was based on IMS LIP, which may indicate why they were not widely implemented or used. The need for a simple specification and easy to implement, leading to the creation of LEAP2A.

LEAP2A Specification

The LEAP2A specification (CETIS, 2009) for portability and interoperability of e-portfolio information is intended to cover the representation of several kinds of information, centred around individuals, who collect, create and use their own information. Much of this plays a part in the individuals' learning, but rather than being learning materials authored by an educator, the information is typically authored, or collected, by the individuals themselves: what they have done, made, achieved, written, or are proud of; what or who helps or has helped them; what they aspire to; what they are good at; evidence for and reflections on any of these; and perhaps input from other people.

FOAF

Although closely related to the W3C, FOAF is a collaborative effort amongst Semantic Web developers on the FOAF Project. So this is not about a standard or specification endorsed by a given entity, but emerges, evolves and is maintained by the community and with the participation of people around the world. FOAF is the acronym of the popular expression "Friend of a friend". It is a machine-readable ontology describing persons, their activities and their relations to other people and objects (Brickley, 2007).

Application of Educational Standards and Specifications in E-Learning Projects

From this wide diversity of standards, specifications and recommendations the question is which is the appropriate selection to support personalisation/adaptation in inclusive learning scenarios. Some researchers have tried to find out an answer to this question through different projects. One of the most active groups in this sense has been the aDeNu research group (Adaptive Dynamic online Educational systems based oN User modelling). First, at aLFanet (IST-2001-33288) this group researched the most appropriate standards to support adaptation during the e-learning life cycle (Boticario & Santos, 2007). In aLFanet, the step-wise life cycle can be formulated as learner's driven tasks thanks to the combination of learning design and run time adaptations and a pervasive use of standards. In this way, a learning scenario adapted to the particularities of each learner along the learning process can be provided. The resulting approach focuses the adaptation process in the design created in IMS-LD, which contains the logic for the pre-designed adaptation and provides the hooks and the information upon which the runtime adaptation bases its reasoning. Relevant features to define users' profiles (such as learning style, knowledge, background, preferences, etc.) are managed with IMS-LIP. Learning materials are packaged in IMS-CP, which contain contents and activities described in terms of IMS-MD. The learning progress is evaluated using IMS-QTI. This intensive use of standards provided interoperability with the different components in the architecture. aLFanet approach was continued in the ADAPTAPlan project (Baldiris et al., 2008), where the emphasis is put in using a competence-based approach to build automatically IMS-LD UoL with planning techniques.

Next, in the ALPE project, aDeNu group researched how accessibility and reusability could be incorporated by taking into account content and accessibility standards (Santos et al., 2007a). For this, they defined a methodology to develop accessible standard-based courses which followed the W3C WAI, ADL SCORM and IMS QTI specifications. The courses developed here were also tested in the tele-centers network in Spain, as part of the ATODOS project. These two approaches are being combined in A2UN@ and EU4ALL projects. The idea is to support accessibility and adaptation along the e-learning life cycle by defining a framework for open, interoperable services to support personalisation/adaptation in inclusive learning scenarios. In the next sections we go into details regarding the EU4ALL approach. The A2UN@ project is still in the early stages, and thus, not results have been obtained yet.

Next, we summarised in Table 1 the different standards that the aDeNu group has applied in their projects.

THE EU4ALL FRAMEWORK

Introduction

Nowadays, in a knowledge based economy, education and work are integrated throughout people's lives. All citizens need ongoing access to learning to enable them to work. Technology is playing an increasing role in mediating this learning for an increasing number of people. However, students and professionals with functional diversity issues (disabilities) have problems in accessing Lifelong Learning (LLL) because of the diverse barriers

Table 1. Summary of standards and specifications used (or to be used) at aDeNu projects

Institution	Standard	Focus	Project implementation
AICC	CMI	Course interoperability	ALPE, ATODOS, EU4ALL
IEEE LTSC	RCD (Draft)	Competences	--
IEEE LTSC	LOM	Learning object metadata	aLFanet, ADAPTAPlan, ALPE, ATODOS, EU4ALL
ISO	ISO/IEC 24751	Adaptability and Accessibility	EU4ALL, A2UN@
Dublin Core	Accessibility Term	Adaptability and Accessibility	--
IMS	Digital Repository	Learning objects repositories	--
IMS	RDCEO	Competences	ADAPTAPlan, A2UN@
IMS	Digital Repository Specification	Learning objects repositories	--
IMS	Learning Design	Contents	aLFanet, ADAPTAPlan, EU4ALL, A2UN@
IMS	QTI	Assessments	aLFanet, ADAPTAPlan, ALPE, ATODOS EU4ALL, A2UN@
IMS	LIP	e-Portfolio	aLFanet, ADAPTAPlan, EU4ALL, A2UN@
IMS	AccLIP	Accessibility and Adaptability	EU4ALL, A2UN@
IMS	ePortfolio	e-Portfolio	EU4ALL
IMS	AfA	Accessibility	EU4ALL, A2UN@
IMS	GDALA	Accessibility and Adaptability	ALPE, ATODOS
W3C	WCAG 1.0	Accessibility and Adaptability	ALPE, ATODOS EU4ALL, A2UN@
W3C	CC/PP	User preferences and devices	EU4ALL, ADAPTAPlan, A2UN@
ADL	SCORM	Content packaging	ALPE, ATODOS, EU4ALL

that may exist in the various stages they must go through to realise their learning goals (Cooper et al., 2006; Seale et al., 2008). From enrolment, through engagement with the learning to assessment, students have to negotiate pre-established general procedures. Management issues are usually more focused on the institutions needs than the students and both management and learning issues generally consider a single standard set of student needs. These are far from attending the individual needs and preferences of their student. However learning ideally should be a personalised and adaptive process for all, which from the beginning till the end should consider the learner's specific needs. Students requiring "Accessible Lifelong Learning" (ALL), i.e. those with disabilities, suffer from a lack of information about pre-established procedures and practices that meet their needs. In addition, there are many difficulties in providing the appropriate infrastructure to support them.

As previously introduced, aDeNu is contributing to the development of a general framework to address the needs of ALL at HE, which is based on personalisation and accessibility. The approach supports interoperability requirements coming from the various needs in different educational contexts, including different LMS (dotLRN and Moodle). The different educational contexts consider not just the standard teaching and learning situations within a given course but a wide variety of needs, such as those of adult learners who enrol in university years after giving up on studying or those with functional diversity issues who are invited to take a personalised course to introduce them the university and the services provided to attend their needs. Some of these scenarios will be discussed later on.

To validate the generality of the approach two different LMS are being evaluated in two large pilot sites (so called large scale evaluations) supported by the two largest distance universities in Europe (OU and UNED). From the evaluation viewpoint the idea behind that is to address the accessibility, usability and adaptation issues of the services developed on top of the architecture while interacting with those LMS. From a technological perspective, if EU4ALL is successful in implementing the architecture into these two so different and well known LMS, it can be confirmed that the generality of the approach is sufficient. Moreover, the scenarios are running at two different institutions which have different services and require different needs. In the end, there will be two running systems, one on Moodle and the other one on dotLRN that integrate the individual components of the architecture and offer an integrated system where the end-user services defined according to user requirements will be provided.

EU4ALL Objectives

The EU IST eInclusion funded project called EU4ALL (European Unified Approach for Accessible Lifelong Learning, IST-2005-034778), which started in October 2006, seeks to define and construct an extensible "architecture" of European-wide services to support Lifelong Learning for ALL (Santos et al., 2007c). It is an integrated project composed of eight sub-projects.

The concrete objectives of EU4ALL are as follows:

1. From an in-depth research, achieve a unified, agreed, shared and usable vision of the standards work, users' requirements, service definition, technologies
2. Define practical specifications and implement in terms of standards an open and extensible architecture of services for ALL, which is prepared both to assist learners and to support service providers
3. Provide user-centred services that consider individual user's needs and preferences, pedagogical guidelines and adaptive behaviour based on users' interactions
4. Bring together major service providers, like mega-universities (e.g., Open University in the UK, UNED in Spain) and EADTU to foster the awareness of best practices in providing educational services for ALL
5. To impact on major standardisation bodies, identifying where the creation of new standards or extension of existing ones supports the establishment of the EU4ALL framework and pursue this into the relevant standard bodies
6. Create a channel for the diffusion and benchmarking of these research results in all major distance training universities in Europe by means of an European-wide ALL repository, which facilitates a common understanding of learning methodologies, access needs, cognitive requirements, assessment procedures and LLL issues for special needs population

The first objective cannot be reached without sharing the project goals and its users' requirement analysis with major stakeholders. The ultimate goal is to create a mechanism for leveraging the research on ICT application for people with functional diversity issues in LLL, while covering the research in the corresponding related fields. To achieve a unified view the scope in terms of users' requirements has focused on disabilities coverage: visual impairment, hearing impairment, physical impairment, categories of cognitive impairment (that do not hinder the access to higher education studies, e.g., dyslexia and dyscalculia). Users' requirements have covered adult learners with functional diversity needs and service providers (i.e., teaching, technical and administrative staff of educational institutions). Furthermore, the coverage of standards has included ongoing and planned work in the following bodies: IMS Global Learning Consortium; IEEE Learning Technologies Standards Committee; CEN-ISSS Workshop on Learning Technologies; ETSI activities on user profile management and emerging user interaction with new eservices; Dublin Core Metadata Initiative, ISO IEC JTC1 SC36, ISO IEC JTC1 Special Working Group on Accessibility; British Standards Institution; World Wide Web Consortium including but not exclusively the Web Accessibility Initiative (WAI).

The usage of educational (e.g. IMS, SCORM) and technological standards (e.g. WAI, WSDL) in objective 2, including those related to contents (WCAG), is intended to facilitate the integration of the services to be developed with current (e.g., Moodle, dotLRN) and future LMS and platforms. To this, a design framework for user service specification is provided with a twofold objective: to facilitate the development of non-dependent on technology services and to support the extensibility of the architecture and services initially provided.

One key issue in EU4ALL is to support the personalisation of services (see the services described below) to attend individual user's needs and their evolution over time. In this respect end-user services, following objective 3, are being integrated into the architecture according to an iterative process along different prototypes, which includes technology users and other relevant social actors throughout the entire process of design and redesign.

According to objective 4, the services and the standard-based framework are assessed and validated at a large scale and at European level via the involvement of potential users and other relevant stakeholders. Specifically, the architecture and services are evaluated in learning scenarios involving hundreds of users (adult learners with special needs and teachers) from the two large universities involved in the project.

To achieve objective 5, EU4ALL brings together partners with experience in managing metadata for accessibility. The developed system is supporting interaction between user profile data (part of the user model) that reflects the user's needs and preferences in their interaction with the computer and content metadata describing accessibility properties of a computer mediated resource. Both of these were initially defined according to the AccLIP (Norton & Treviranus, 2003) and AccMD (Jackl, 2003) specifications by IMS, and for the second prototype (expected September 2009) the framework has adopted the new standard ISO Individualised adaptability and accessibility in e-learning standard, also known as Personal Needs and Preferences, and Digital Resource Descriptions (DRD) (ISO/IEC 24751, 2009). Moreover, Learning Design (IMS-LD, 2003) is being used to describe services' work flows according to different pedagogical settings. EU4ALL standards approach is based on actual usage of available specifications to face real situations when providing accessible services for all in a personalised way.

Finally, project results are being disseminated (objective 6) to a network of Higher Education Institutions throughout Europe with more than 2 million students (EADTU, 2009). Through dissemination there have been regular discussions and exchange of information with an international group of institutions and individuals, from industrial, public and academic sectors. To this, the project's special interest group was set up as a dissemination channel and secondly provides the availability of a mechanism for inviting input from external stakeholders (EU4ALL, 2009). In terms of dissemination, the group acts as a dissemination channel to a group of people with declared interest in the activities of the project. An important theme within this group will be possible models that can be applied to Higher Education systems in order to offer training for all. Dissemination activities are considering peers and general public, and knowledge transfer between educational institutions and research institutes. The key issue here is to demonstrate to the public authorities and policy makers the benefits of implementing a unified, agreed, shared, and usable model of services to support equality of access to EHEA (European High-Education Area).

To guarantee users' involvement in an iterative development approach, EU4ALL architecture services are updated and evolved according to service validation cycles. To date (i.e., Summer 2009) the services of the first round have been developed and evaluated. The second round of services is under development and the large scale evaluation (third and last round of services) will take place during 2010. The services that are being implemented are selected after getting common agreements with the two large pilot sites so that they are meaningful, covering pending accessibility and adaptation issues and providing opportunities to prove the generality of the framework to cope with different needs and diverse technical and institutional requirements (see service descriptions below). The central idea here is to show the flexibility and applicability of the framework and services beyond project boundaries.

Once we have briefly described each of the six EU4ALL objectives, for the rest of the paper we focus on the way the second and third are covered through a standard-based framework to support personalisation/adaptation and interoperability in inclusive learning scenarios. In particular, we focus on the end-user services required at the UNED University and the aDeNu role in the project's developments to build this framework.

aDeNu Role in the Project

The aDeNu research group has a major role in defining and developing the EU4ALL framework. First, being Scientific Coordinators of the project, this group is in charge of ensuring effective scientific coordination and integration of technical work amongst the different sub-projects, improving the quality assurance of deliverables and technical developments. In particular, according to the current stage of the project, they support a clear development and product oriented research agenda, facilitating the integration of the user needs analysis and the technical specification and prototype realisation, improving the coordination among project partners, and the links between activities in terms of knowledge production, and providing justifications regarding deviations and explanations of choices that are made, which have an impact on the quality of deliverables and work-package implementation.

Second, UNED (with an average of 180.000 students enrolled per year) is one of the two large pilot sites of the project where users' needs have been identified and services are being evaluated. The project has considered user requirements for the various user groups of the EU4ALL Platform: including adult learners with disabilities, teachers and tutors who may have special needs themselves), technical and other support staff and administrators. A thorough analysis of different UNED users has been undertaken to ensure that all relevant user groups are represented. A variety of methods have been used to elicit the user requirements, like interviews, on-line surveys, observational and ethno-methodological techniques.

Actually, project activities at UNED are being managed in collaboration with the Disability Office, which supports the disabled users enrolled in this university, who are about half of the total of disabled students in the Spanish University as a whole (roughly 4.500 students). The students were contacted by the responsible to offer them the opportunity to participate in the project. Moreover, aDeNu is providing a virtual community to these students both 1) to manage their participation with aDeNu projects and 2) to provide a communication channel for the users interested in this area. This community, which currently supports over 400 students, is established itself on the LMS version used in the EU4ALL framework. Therefore, the improvements achieved from the project can be provided to the students from that community who are collaborating with the project. This increases both the motivation to participate and the sustainability of the community. The details of this collaboration are provided elsewhere (Rodríguez-Ascaso et al., 2008b). That situation has facilitated that 98 out of the 188 students that started the Spanish version of the project survey have fully completed it. Nearly half of these are male (48.41%) but there are a few more female students (51.59%) and practically all (except for 5 people) live in Spain. The age bracket expands from 18 to 79 years. Since the Spanish students are registered at a distance learning university a significant majority are older than 40, preponderantly concentrated in the 26 and 59 years range. 28% use assistive technologies to support their learning; out of these, 15% use software aids (i.e. screen readers such as JAWS, screen magnification, spoken Braille, Daisy book, head mouse & voice recognition), practically 6% use assistive hardware (i.e. loop induction system, scanner OCR, tape players, sound amplifiers & recorders) and more than 7% use enhancements such as audio and video descriptions through text captioning.

Third, aDeNu is the leader of the subproject focused on defining the Open and Accessible Service Architecture that structures the service provision to all kind of users. The architecture is prepared to provide ALL services to assist different types of users on the demand side (students with special needs) and different existing roles on the supply side (such as administrators, faculty staff or specialised support people involved in the provision of services, although we focus in this paper on the demand side). The architecture is open and extensible (based on a service oriented approach), both from the user point of view (new services can be added) and from the technological standpoint (built in terms of technological and educational standards). The user is central to the service provision and the architecture supports an adaptive behaviour based on users' interactions. To this, according to the "full lifecycle of adaptation" (Van Rosmalen et al., 2004), it is managing the user profile (in terms of standards) and applying an automatic adaptive approach to update user models based on user modelling techniques. Further, to facilitate interoperability with current services provided at HE, the architecture approach allows the integration of any kind of services following the open specifications defined in the service specification framework. These specifications are defined in terms of the Web Services Definition Languages (WSDL) and define the interfaces that the rest of the components of the framework have to comply to assure interoperability.

Fourth, aDeNu has developed several key components to support the architecture adaptive features, such as the User Model of the framework. The user is central to the service provision and follows a standard way, via ISO/IEC 24751 (2009), to define the "user with special needs" profile. The user model supports learner accessibility needs and preferences to be defined and managed in terms of standards. This component is involved in most framework adaptive features and is integrated with the LMS and most services focused on attending specific users' needs. Another key module to support adaptation is the recommender system, which delivers dynamic contextual recommendations to the user when coping with evolving psycho-educational scenarios. This innovative feature supports modelling at design time a wide variety of recommendations that take into account users' needs and their evolving context. It supports the course designer in describing recommendations in learning inclusive scenarios, presents additional information to the user to explain why the recommendation has been offered, and requests explicit feedback from the user when she has shown interest in the recommendation process to improve the recommender. The methodology followed to elicit the recommendations includes brainstorming sessions with psycho-educational experts and evaluation experiences with end-uses.

Fifth, aDeNu members have identified a taxonomy of psycho-educational strategies addressing needs of students with special needs in HE (Rodriguez-Ascaso et al., 2008b). These strategies were considered to develop adaptive learning flows via IMS-LD Units of Learning (UoL). The ultimate goal here is to improve the learner's psychological functioning and hence the learning performance, by using the active learner paradigm (i.e. the learner builds, modify and analyses) (Schank and Jona, 1991). Those standards-based UoLs are intended to support reusability features (i.e., they are meant to be applied in a wide range of learning scenarios) and they are included in end-user services focused on pedagogical adaptations that address learners' learning style and needs. Thus the learning activity is guided in runtime considering personalised workflows and with the aforementioned recommendations and user model the system is able to support adaptive interactions within the LMS.

In summary, the project considers user services coping with management issues that support the provision of accessible learning, such as those providing information on the accessibility features of courses and specific resources, and including looking up of adaptation services and accommodations offered within a given context (institution, external service providers) in order to estimate the severity of particular issues and whether or which adaptations exist to accommodate inaccessible course components. aDeNu group has been deeply involved in developing all these services, and especially those providing adaptive features. In order to understand how users can benefit from this approach, next we describe some scenarios and introduce the personalised support that can be provided in them.

END-USER SERVICES TO SUPPORT PERSONALISATION/ADAPTATION IN INCLUSIVE E-LEARNING

Adaptation in inclusive e-learning requires a holistic approach framed in a user centered design approach where personalisation techniques are used to meet users' needs. Standard ISO 13407 (1999) provides guidance on human centered design activities throughout the life cycle of computer-based interactive systems. According to the standard, human centred design consists of four different types of design activities:

- To understand and specify the context of use.
- To specify the user and organisational requirements.
- To produce draft (pilot) design solutions.
- To evaluate design against requirements.

This section includes a set of scenarios of inclusive e-learning where different roles make use of a set of services. In each of the services, inbuilt personalised support meets specific learning needs in a certain context. These scenarios complement other EU4ALL activities for collecting user requirements at UNED, such as interviews and on-line surveys. The use of scenarios for the collection of user requirements is described in Rosson & Carroll (2002). Furthermore, these scenarios may inspire the design of scenarios for the forthcoming evaluation of the EU4ALL framework.

Scenarios at UNED

We present below two scenarios, involving two students and one lecturer.

Student's Scenarios

Isa and Leo are UNED students with impairments. Provided they receive a personalised support according to their needs, they will be able to fully participate in the learning activities of their higher education studies.

Isa is a Law student with very low vision. During her primary and secondary educational stages, she has been receiving support from ONCE, the Spanish National Organisation for the Blind, in terms of adapted learning materials, assistive technologies and pedagogical orientation. She is skilled in using computers and internet.

Leo has an attention deficit disorder in addition to cerebral palsy. Because of a lack of support for his specific needs during high school, Leo did not follow the standard path to enrolling in university. Several years after giving up on studying, Leo has now decided to take a UNED course designed to facilitate the enrolment of adult learners (in this case considered people over 25) in university. His experience either with computers or with internet is rather poor.

One of students' first tasks after enrolment is updating their student profile through the preference settings functionality at aLF, UNED's personalised version of the dotLRN LMS.

Within the disability section there is a question about assistive technologies used and Isa selects Screen Reader and Screen Magnifier. Also, in the form she expresses her preference to access acoustic alternative formats to text.

Leo goes through questions about his learning style, the competencies he already has, his educational background his experience in using computers, and all these will reveal the psycho-educational curriculum to build on skills and abilities.

After fulfilling the questionnaire, Leo receives an email with an invitation to take a course that will introduce him to the university's virtual learning environment, as well as to support e-services available at the institution. The course has some in-built learning design, personalised to student's identified learning style and needs. The psycho-educational support embedded in the learning design consists of planning support, easy reading style, additional summaries, conceptual maps, and study registries at the end of each unit. In addition to this, the student receives dynamic guidance through recommendations based both on his preferences and performance while using the system (e.g. marks obtained in questionnaire based assessments, learning objects he has accessed, use of the forums to communicate with his peers, etc.).

As part of the activities of the Business Administration module Isa is registered in, she is participating in a group activity entitled 'Web entrepreneurs', together with other 4 students. As part of the group activity, the whole group communicates through the collaborative support provided by the LMS. Her assignment is to read the annual report of a successful spin-off web company, share her findings with her module peers, and elaborate a final report with the conclusions. She searches the report at the UNED electronic repository, e-spacio, and downloads it in DAISY version to her mobile phone, where she has a DAISY reader installed. She can read the report while on the train, as well as add personalised bookmarks to relevant sections, by using the voice recognition software which is also installed in her mobile phone. As an option available in the bookmark management application, she can decide whether each bookmark is shared with her peers through the collaborative tools.

Leo decides to leave UNED and register in a Spanish face to face university to follow some other undergraduate studies. He decides to make use of the export option available at the UNED eportfolio, and import it from the import option available at the new university's LMS. By doing that, he will take her personal information profile with him, including his accessibility preferences, competencies, etc.

Lecturer Scenario

Ana is a lecturer and tutor at UNED. She teaches Business Administration in the Faculty of Law.

Lecturer Ana is searching for new learning materials at the university electronic repository, in order to add them as complementary references for the nest year edition of the module she teaches. To do so, he requests the search service available at the VLE. She finds the last annual report of a small internet company, which she regards to be of interest as a complementary reference for the students of the module.

Before including this content as one of the module's materials, Ana selects the option 'Check accessibility' for this document. The enquiry reveals that this document is not available in any auditory alternative format, as required by some module's students. Then Ana decides to go for the 'Request accessibility transformation' option for this document. The system informs her that the audio format will be available in two weeks according to the estimation made by the transformation officers of ONCE. DAISY is the standardised format of audio materials which has been recently adopted in UNED, which is outsourcing ONCE for transformations to that format. After that period of time she will receive the transformed document in order to check its pedagogical validity, and then include it as one of the module's materials. The system also offers to her the training pill 'Introduction to DAISY'.

End-User Services

According to the user requirements and the subsequent specification of services, a set of end user services have been defined in EU4ALL for the UNED pilot site. The order in which the services are listed below corresponds to the order in which they are requested in the previous scenarios section. The interoperability is guaranteed thanks to the standards support, which is commented in each of them.

Need Assessment Service

This service allows users to complete and/or check the information stored by the system about their accessibility needs and preferences, as well as their psycho-educational style and needs. In this service, accessibility information is synchronised with the ePortfolio. This information is compliant with ISO/IEC 24751-2:2008 and with IMS Learner Information Package version 1.0.1. Generally speaking, this e-service should be complemented with a face to face assessment of user needs in order to ensure the applicability of the preferences identified.

Adaptive Psycho-Educational Support Service

In this service a student is invited to take a personalised course that will introduce her to the university's learning environment, as well as to support e-services available at the university. The course is based on an IMS-LD UoL, personalised to student's identified learning style and needs. The contents are characterised with ISO DRD and IMS MD. In addition to this, the student receives dynamic guidance through recommendations based both in their user model and in their interactions with the system.

Resource Accessibility Information Service

This service checks whether a learning media item would be accessible to a student based on their given user profile. It is invoked by a professional in order to retrieve the accessibility status of the media for a given student. ISO/IEC 24751 parts 2 and 3 are used to model correspondingly user preferences and electronic content in terms of accessibility.

Resource Adaptation Management Service

This service mediates the manual adaptation of an inaccessible resource through a management workflow tailored to conditions found at a respective institution. It allows a request to be made for the transformation of an inaccessible resource by either a professional or a student. The request for the resource transformation is sent to those departments within an organisation where the provision of the accessible resource is managed. The service ensures that the results of the transformation process are pedagogically valid by offering involved stakeholders the required communication channel and workflow support. The resources are characterised with ISO DRD and IMS MD.

User Model Management and Portability Service

This service synchronises the user's accessibility needs and preferences in ISO DRD, which are stored in ePortfolio, and those stored in the LMS. Furthermore, this service supports the portability of the user's preferences as well as the collection of information and digital artifacts that demonstrates development or evidences learning outcomes, skills or competencies of the user by supporting the portability of ePortfolio. This provides the opportunity to support users who wish to take their accessibility preferences and products, materials and records with them when moving to another LMS.

Adaptation Look Up Service

This service provides support resources to accommodate inaccessible course components. Resources range from training to adaptation of course contents, adapted to the context of the accessibility problem encountered. They are properly characterised with ISO DRD and IMS MD. This service would be triggered by the system after the Resource Accessibility Information is requested by a lecturer. Given the accessibility problem identified in the e-learning media, it would offer specific training as well as the service to request the needed adaptation (Resource Adaptation Management Service).

The resulting end user services are open, interoperable, and can be provided to the users thanks to the flexibility of the architecture.

Modelling of Learner Preferences and Matching Standards to Support the User Model

To provide user profiling and adaptation, two major tasks must be accomplished:

- to model both pedagogical user characteristics (such as learning environment, active communities and courses, competencies, goals...) and adaptation needs and preferences (e.g., display preferences such as screen reader, screen enhance, text reading highlight, Braille, tactile... defined in terms of ISO/IEC 24751-2), to support the LLL paradigm
- to store such models in a reliable repository, which must provide easy (and fast) access services to retrieve, manipulate and update such information as a whole, or by its parts (attributes)

EU4ALL initial prototypes allowed experimenting different techniques to accomplish such requirements, binding and combining modelling standards, and then testing if they fulfil the expectation. For the project first phase, and considering the availability of standards (ISO/IEC 24751 was under development) at that stage, modelling was finally done combining and integrating IMS-LIP (used for pedagogical data) and IMS-AccLIP (used for accessibility).

To support accessibility preferences, the "disability" node under "accessibility" was substitute

Figure 1. AccLIP main nodes

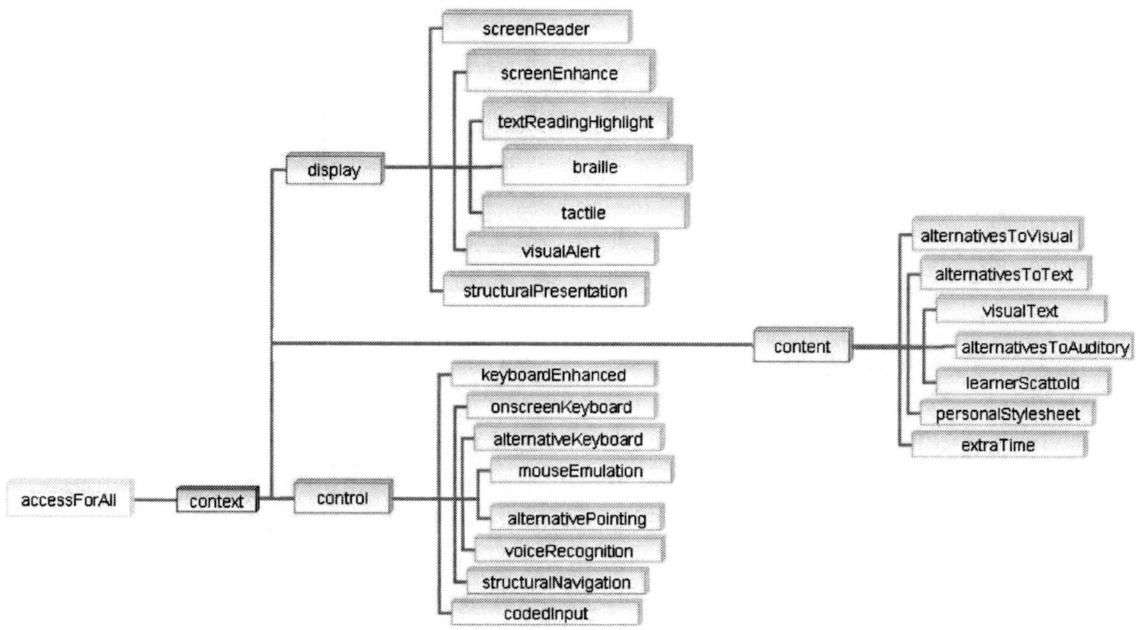

by the "AccessForAll" structure coming from AccLIP binding. The result is shown in Figure 1.

For the next project phase (at the time the paper was written), the LIP binding, which provides the support for pedagogical data, is kept, but a much more up-to-date accessibility standard (ISO PNP) is used instead of AccLIP. ISO PNP is also specially recommended to be a perfect match with Metadata Repository accessibility model (ISO DRD). Integration is performed at same binding point in LIP schema.

Model Repository

The repository for EU4ALL user models is a critical part of the system, performing a similar role as databases do in standard systems. Main requirements were:

- reliability: this is the first and more important one; system must be able to provide trustworthy services, as user data must be stored and provided congruently to other systems involved in the framework (i.e., within O-ASA)
- support for defined user model binding (schema)
- service for supporting full model operations: get/set/update/delete model
- services for supporting attribute model operations: get/set/update/delete model attribute
- services for specialised LMS operations: createUser, get/set PersonalUserData.
- confidentiality and security (see next section)

The first approach was to take advantage of Java Apache Axis framework (Axis2, 2009) to provide SOAP-based webservice access, so that communication was guaranteed for heterogeneous systems such as Moodle and dotLRN. Storage was supported by a standard relational database and attribute manipulation was provided by a proprietary syntax. The resulting system allows us to store, retrieve, modify or delete user models, or parts of them. Those models must followed,

Figure 2. UM architecture with XML databases

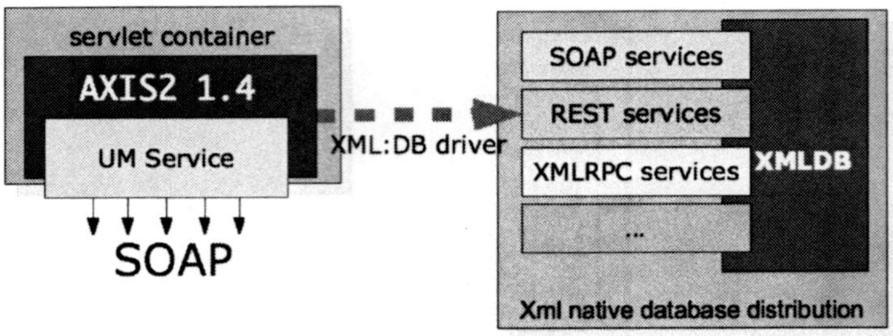

strictly, the schema defined through the combination of the standards (see previous section), so the only drawback was their manipulation through the services required a previous knowledge of those standards.

As those prototypes where evaluated, there was one main conclusion. For dealing with XML profiles, it is better to rely on native XML databases, and use standard XML syntax (xPath/xQuery) for attribute manipulation instead of a proprietary one. This syntax allows also testing the (easy) adoption of a new and much more recent standard for accessibility details, the ISO-123456-2, as stated before. Relying on open source frameworks, languages and standards, and constructing the service based on interoperable systems benefits the whole EU4ALL framework, as the interfaces exposed by the user model repository did not change from first prototypes (proven enough) to the actual ones. Architecture diagram is shown in Figure 2.

Security and Privacy Issues

Handling personal user information is a delicate issue, as private data such as identity, pedagogical progress or accessibility preferences require special treatment. Systems allowed to read this data, must be authenticated first, and only some special authorised services can access all that information at the same time (i.e. relating the identity with the accessibility data of a user). Also, some countries require special security measures when dealing with such delicate information. In the EU, for example, value-added (for example, personalised) services based on traffic or location data require the anonymisation of such data or the user's consent (Kobsa, 2007).

Being implemented using Java Apache Axis framework, user model repository allows us to start developing and testing without caring about any securisation. After integration, it is easy to involve all SOAP messages provided with desired level of security (HTTPS, tokens, digital signature, digital signed tokens...) using Rampart module (Rampart, 2009). This library provides ready-to-go implementations for WS-Security mechanisms defined by OASIS committee specifications (Oasis, 2009). It is also easy to connect the system with an LDAP server to store and retrieve authentication data, keys and/or digital signatures.

Experimental Services

The newly-introduced XML syntax allows experimenting a new way of exposing modelling services to other systems using abstract methods. Instead of sending instructions in xPath about which nodes must be modified (i.e. a new implementation of the services that do not require programmers to know about the underlying XML schemas, but about LLL concepts such as competencies, affiliations, identity details, etc.). This syntax is also allowing to create advanced services for making recommendations, such as comparing two users' competencies, goals and interests to recommend one of them to follow the other one.

Application to the UNED's Scenarios

Considering the scenarios introduced before, the user model components supports the following end user services:

- Need Assessment Service (managing the information)
- Adaptive Psycho-Educational Support Service (provides the user information)
- Resource Accessibility Information Service (provides the user information)
- User model management and portability service

In order to support scenarios, the user model needs to accommodate the selected preferences, test results or other values for each user. For the specific case of Felder test results (learning styles) (Felder and Silvermann, 2002), values are stored in accessibility/preference nodes. LMS first has to create the users through *sendRegistrationEvent()* service, then update preferences using *updateUserModelAttribute()*. For the accessibility preferences, accessibility values are stored in ISO schema. Once again, LMS creates the user and updates accessibility values using *updateUserModelAttribute()*. Figure 6 shows the nodes involved in the process.

LMS SUPPORT FOR CONTENT PERSONALISATION AND PERSONALISED UNITS OF LEARNING

This chapter introduces a standards-based and adaptive framework, whose main objective is to adapt user interfaces, content and learning environment to the needs of learners, including their functional diversity issues. These adaptations require an intensive data exchange in order to better support the needs of learners while accessing a wide variety of resources within different contexts. Different components are required to enrich the limited interoperability and adaptation capabilities of existing LMS so that these are able to deal with the increasing interoperability requirements coming from web-based educational tools. Example of these components are user model, recommender system, content personalisation, device modelling, metadata repository, guidance for all, eServices server, are required to support personalisation and adaptation. Following a student-centred design approach, focused on modifying the functional logic of the system, modifications in the LMS are required to support issues such as content personalisation and personalised units of learning. This requires the extension of the LMS architecture to enable interoperability of the internal functionality (such as the players for educational content) with the external components. With this technological support, it is possible to cover the needs of the users in terms of end-user services.

Open Standard-Based LMS (dotLRN)

dotLRN (one of the two Learning Management Systems –LMS- chosen for the EU4ALL project) provides learners with an integrated environment to access services, contents and learning and communication tools. To cope with the variety of users' needs, the LMS needs to serve adapted content and services. This can be done by extending the LMS in a monolithic way or by extending its architecture to enable interoperability with external frameworks such as EU4ALL.

To provide extensibility and openness, the Open and Accessible Services Architecture (O-ASA) is introduced in EU4ALL. O-ASA is based on Service Oriented Architecture (SOA) principles, using standards for its implementation to provide open and accessible services and to facilitate the extensibility with third-party service development. In this section, we introduce the different standards that are used in the EU4ALL framework and more particularly, those for which support has been implement in the LMS and how their implementation provides for interoperability with other services of the framework.

W3C Standards for Interoperability

EU4ALL framework interface is implemented as web services, using the W3C SOAP standard to exchange messages between each other and client systems such as the LMS. EU4ALL services contracts are described using WSDL allowing clients for services discovery over the network.

The web services infrastructure provides interoperability between the applications running on different nodes. Since web services use open standards and protocols, third parties services that implement the EU4ALL framework can be easily combined to provide an integrated service.

In turn, the LMS, acting as the user interface between the end user and the services framework, format the response to the user request using standard markup (HTML, XHTML, XML, etc.) according to the user agent and device being used.

W3C and ISO Standards for Accessibility and Personalisation

To guarantee that the system is accessible for ALL, it needs (1) to provide an accessible user interface and on the other hand, (2) to serve content that is adapted to the user needs. The former is achieved following the Web Content Accessibility Guidelines (WCAG) in the LMS, the latter by the Content Personalisation service provided by the EU4ALL framework.

Learning resources can be tagged using the ISO-DRD standard indicating the type of content and the existence of any alternative for it (e.g. a text alternative for an image). The metadata gathered is stored in the Metadata Repository (MR). On the other hand, the user can specify her needs and preferences for content (e.g. an alternative to visual preference). These preferences are stored using ISO-PNP standard in the User Model (UM) component of the framework. The Device Model (DM) captures the capabilities of the device used and passes that information in the request sent to the LMS. The LMS itself do not process this information, but forwards it to the adaptive modules

Figure 3. Interoperability of the LMS with the content personalisation service

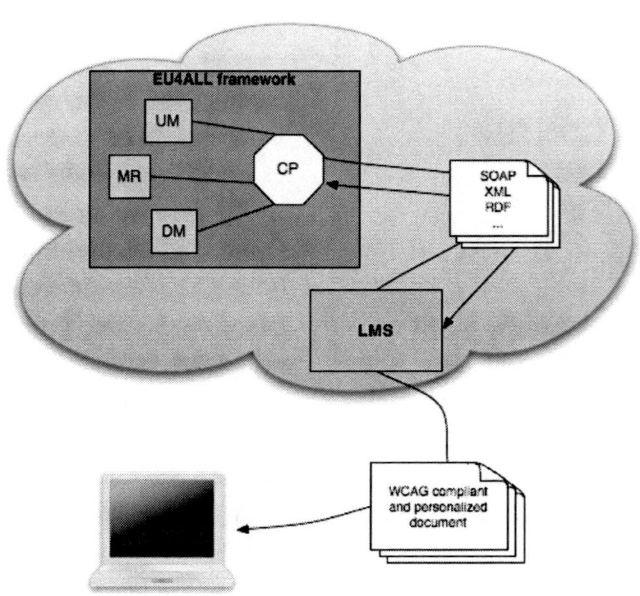

(i.e. the content personalisation and the recommender system).

When receiving a request, the LMS sends the headers of the HTTP request (using the HTTP-in-RDF specification) and the requested resource identifier to the Content Personalisation (CP) that in turn will consult the above-named components to get the specifics for each case and decide the best personalisation according to the user preferences and device and the availability of an appropriate alternative for the requested resource. Eventually the LMS will serve the WCAG compliant and personalised document to the user. The communication with the recommender system is explained in the next section.

Standards for Learner Profile, Content and Educational Tools

The dotLRN LMS implements IMS-LD, IMS-CP and IMS-QTI and provides an interface to an external service (e.g. EU4ALL framework) to store and retrieve learner information using the IMS-LIP specifications. This allow for requesting user properties stored in the User Model (IMS-LIP and IMS-accLIP/ISO PNP) from a unit of learning. Moreover, the units of learning and assessments are integrated to allow the exchange of the information obtained (Lazarinis, F. et al, 2009). For example, an assessment can be used by an unit of learning as an activity and its result used to decide the next activity for the user.

SCORM is also supported in dotLRN LMS. It specifies how to package course contents using a combination of existing standards (IMS-CP, IMS-MD) and how to realize the communication between the LMS and the content using the runtime environment API. A player is available in dotLRN to play compliant SCORM courses. The player is integrated into the EU4ALL framework and can make use of the Content Personalisation to adapt the learning resources at runtime according to the user preferences and needs.

Figure 4 presents graphically this relationship.

Application to the UNED's Scenarios

The LMS is involved in the following end-user services:

- Need Assessment Service (filling the information)
- Adaptive Psycho-Educational Support Service (plays the personalised contents)

Figure 4. Educational support and user modelling in the LMS

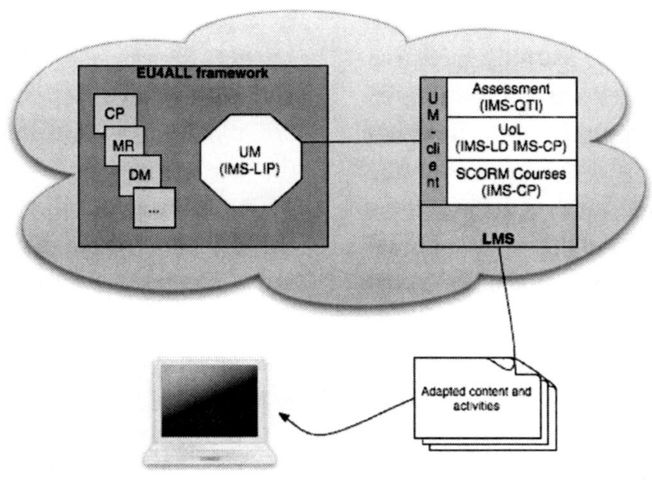

In particular, the learners use the LMS to fill in her accessibility preferences (e.g. assistive technologies used and preference to access acoustic alternative formats to text), learning style, competencies already achieved, experience in using computers. In turn, the LMS (i) offers support through a notifications service to invite them to the course, (ii) offers the contents via a _personalised learning design with dynamic guidance through recommendations and (iii) provides collaborative support.

SUPPORTING USERS WITH RECOMMENDATIONS

Regarding the support in terms of recommendations (personalised interaction approach), the objective of this chapter is to introduce the usage of a recommender system (RS) to support _personalisation/adaptation and interoperability in inclusive learning scenarios by delivering dynamic contextual recommendations to the learner when coping with pedagogical scenarios and contribute to enrich current LMS with adaptive navigation support. This innovative feature supports modelling at design time a wide variety of recommendations that take into account the learners' needs and their evolving context. These recommendations can be managed through a recommendations model that is built up following the appropriate standards. It supports the course designer in describing recommendations in learning inclusive scenarios, presents additional information to the user to explain why the recommendation has been offered, and requests explicit feedback from the learner when she has shown interest in the recommendation process to improve the recommender.

First, this section presents why and how recommender systems can be used within generic LMS. Next, it is introduced a recommendations model to support the interoperability of the RS with the different components of the architecture, including the different standards that can be involved in the process. As an example, we comment on the recommendations introduced in the UNED scenarios at the EU4ALL project, which were obtained from a brainstorming sessions with psycho-educational experts.

RS and LMS

Current LMS still provide little support for adaptation (Hauger & Kock, 2007). One of the research lines followed to support users in their learning has been to use RS for educational purposes. RS are the technical response to the fact that we frequently rely on other people's experience and recommendations when confronted with a new field of expertise, where we do not have a broad knowledge of all these facts or where such knowledge would exceed the amount of information humans can cognitively deal with (Deco et al., 2008). RS support users in finding their way through the possibilities offered in web-based environments by highlighting information a user might be interested in from the information already available in the system. RS can facilitate the teaching–learning interactions and improve online learning by supporting both learners and tutors (Zaine, 2002). In particular, their goal is to improve learning effectiveness and efficiency, as well as learners' satisfaction, while reducing the tutors' workload related to the follow-up and support of the learners. Generally speaking, RSs in e-learning deal with information about the learners (users) and learning activities (items) and would have to combine different levels of complexity for the different learning situations the learners may be involved in (Draschler et al., 2008). Moreover, according to the findings in the aLFanet project, this support should be provided along the e-learning life cycle and should be focused on the user and not on the LMS (Van Rosmalen et al., 2004). Regarding the recommendations approach, the key element for the user is that it provides a personalised support which is non-intrusive (Zaiane, 2002). The impact of this type of adaptation on the user can be analysed by data mining the interactions of the user in the LMS (i.e., if the user followed the recommendation or not). This information can be used by the system to modify its recommender behaviour based on its usefulness and not solely on users' learning styles and knowledge (Kravcik, Specht, 2005).

The Recommendations Model to Support Interoperability

Taking into account the previous issues, there is a need for a recommendations model that help to deal with the recommendations information along the different phases of the e-learning life cycle. In particular, it should support the modelling at design time of a wide variety of recommendations that take into account the learners' needs and their evolving context (Santos & Boticario, 2008).

This modelling of the recommendations has to describe (i) what should be recommended (different recommendation types have been identified and can be offered, which relate to the actions that can be done on the LMS objects, such as send a forum message, work on a particular objective or share some opinion), (ii) when a recommendation it is deemed appropriate (considering the user and course context, the conditions of application and the timeout restrictions), (iii) how a recommendation should be displayed (considering accessibility and usability criteria) and (iv) why a recommendation has been produced (in terms of what category the recommendation applies to, what technique has been used to generate it, and the source that originated the recommendation).

The model supports the course designer in describing recommendations in learning inclusive scenarios, presents additional information to the user to explain why the recommendation has been offered, and requests explicit feedback from the learner when she has shown interest in the recommendation process -to improve the recommender-.

Recommendations can be displayed to the user in the LMS by using the information of the model. The idea is to show the recommendations as a list of actions that the user can do in the system. Each element of the list (i.e. action) contains a link to the service of the LMS where the recommended action can be taken. The idea behind is to offer the recommendations in as less intrusive as possible. Thus, by having the recommended actions limited in a specific area of the LMS interface, the user can decided whether to read the recommendations or not (and of course, once read, she also has the freedom whether to follow them or not). An example of a recommendation is, recommend the user to comment a particular learning object. In this case a link points to the page where a comment can be done to that particular learning object. Next to the end of each element of the list, an icon links to additional information that explains why the recommendation was selected for the learner. To support the required interoperability between the RS and the LMS, there is an exchange of information provided by the recommender service to the LMS as a XML message, where the parameters are defined with WSDL. In this way, the RS can serve multiple LMS, such as dotLRN and Moodle.

In order to facilitate the understanding of what recommendations look like in an LMS and how they can be represented in terms of the model, we show next how recommendations have been integrated within dotLRN (Santos & Boticario, 2008).

The integration approach for the presentation has been to create a new portlet (i.e., from the user's viewpoint a portlet is information that is placed within a region on a page) to present the list of recommendations. The portlet is shown both at the user personal space (where general and course independent recommendations are offered) and at the entry page for each course (where course depended recommendations are provided). As it can be seen in the Figure 5, it is another portlet as the forums or learning materials. If we focus on the contents of this particular portlet, the first line corresponds to a greetings message that in-

Figure 5. The recommendations portlet within dotLRN LMS

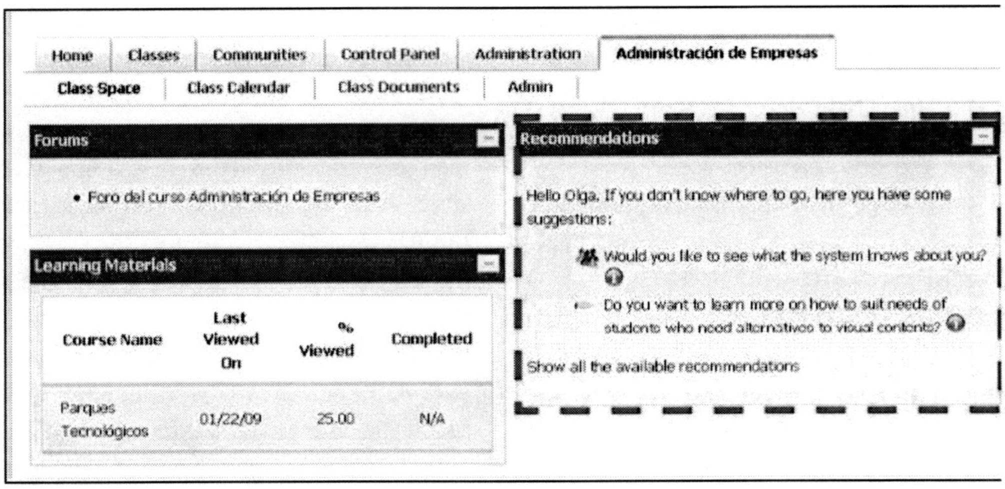

troduces the user to the list of recommendations. Each recommendation is preceded by an icon, which defines the origin of the recommendation. That is, if it is preferred by the user (as stated in her preferences), popular among similar users or suggested by the course design. The action is highlighted as a hyperlink. Finally, the blue icon on the left points to extra information, such as the category where the recommendation belongs to, the technique used to compute it and a detailed explanation of why the recommendation was provided. Since the focus of this chapter is not the recommending system, we do not provide a detailed description of the model. However, it can be consulted in (Santos & Boticario, 2008).

Interoperability in the Framework

The interoperability support is provided in the conditions clause of the recommendations model presented in the previous section. That is, at the time of describing when a recommendation should be provided. At this point, different kinds of information are required, and should be managed with the corresponding standard or specification:

- The learner profile: demographic information, competencies and learning styles can be managed with IMS-LIP. Information regarding accessibility can be managed with IMS-AccLIP or ISO PNP. Other emerging specifications that can be taken into account to describe the users are the vocabulary produced by the Friend of a Friend (FOAF) project or the LEAP2A eportfolio.
- The device capabilities: mobile manufactures use the UaProf Vocabulary (based on the CC/PP specification) to describe the capabilities of the devices produced
- The contents features: educational information can be provided with different standards, such as Dublin Core, IEEE LOM or IMS-MD. Moreover, accessibility information can be added with IMS-AccMD and ISO DRD.
- The evaluation progress can be computed with the IMS-QTI standard.
- The instructional design can be described with IMS-LD or SCORM 2004.

The above information is required by the RS to compute the recommendations. The process is as described in Figure 6. At design time, the recommendations are created by defining the required information in the model. In order to elicit recommendations that follow psycho-educational

Figure 6. Recommendation process

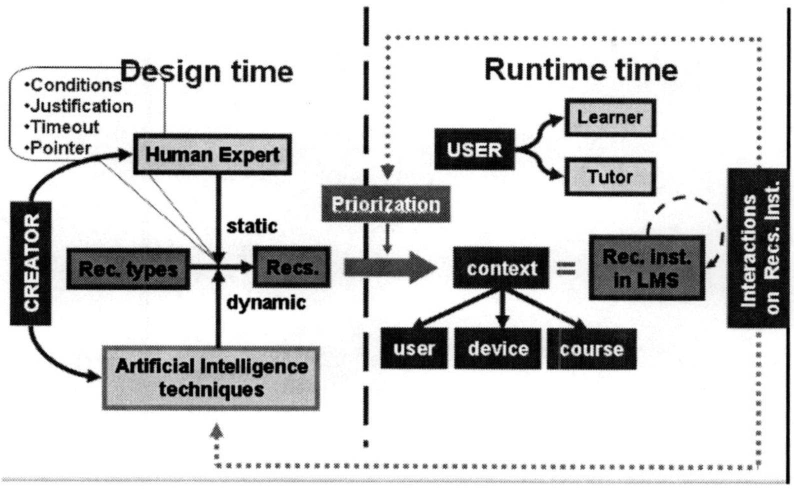

criteria, a user-centred methodology has been defined and followed (Santos et al., 2009). This methodology applies scenario-based methods (Rosson & Carroll, 2001) to involve psycho-educational experts in writing stories (i.e. scenarios) about the problems taking place in relevant situations that come to their mind during their teaching experience with LMS. The information obtained from the psycho-educational experts is used to transform the predefined recommendation types (i.e. any object that exist in the platform such a learning object or a forum message and can be potentially recommended to the learner) into recommendations that have associated the applicability conditions and restrictions. At runtime, that is, when the learner is in the LMS working in the course, the RS checks if the current context for this user matches the conditions defined for each of the recommendations. The context is described following the corresponding standards mentioned above for the user features, the device capabilities and the course description. The recommendations that match the conditions are instantiated and offered to the learner in the LMS interface, as shown in the previous snapshot in dotLRN (Figure 5). The recommendations are prioritised and the number of them presented is selected taking into account the screen size of the device.

Once the recommendations are offered to the user, the system tracks the user actions (Couchet et al, 2008) and infers if the recommendations were useful for the user in the context where they were provided. That is, it validates whether given conditions were properly defined. The results from this analysis are interpreted by the psycho-educational experts and may be used to modify the values in the model. Moreover, after a training period, the algorithms can suggest new values for the conditions.

This process requires an intensive exchange of the information among the different components of the framework. Figure 7 shows the different components of the framework and the information needed by the RS (in terms of the standards or specifications used in the context of the aDeNu approach). These components are the UM (user model), DM (device model), MR (metadata repository) and the UoL (units of learning), Eval (evaluation) and CR (content repository). The later three are part of the LMS.

In order to work, the RS requires information from the different components, and this information has to be provided via web services messages (i.e. SOAP) with the corresponding standard or specification. In more detail, the RS interoperates with four components: (1) the LMS, (2) the

Figure 7. Interoperability of the RS within the framework thanks to the standards support

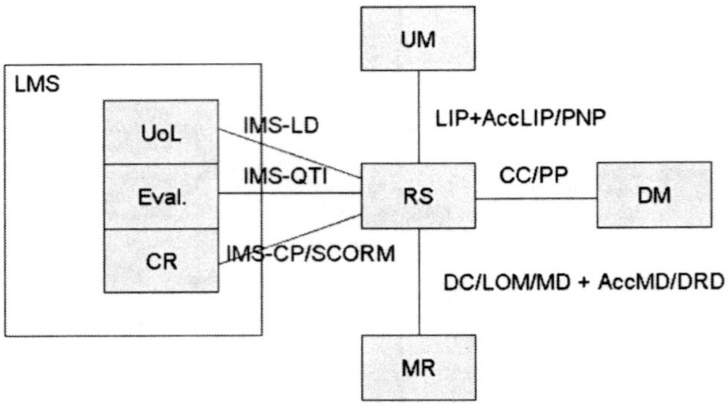

UM, (3) the DM and (4), the MR. The interoperability with the LMS is provided with educational standards. To exchange information about the users, it requires the user profiles information (e.g. IMS LIP, IMS AccLIP or ISO PNP). Contents have to be described with the associated metadata, such as DC, IEEE LOM, IMS MD, IMS AccMD and ISO DRD for the contents themselves, IMS-QTI for the assessments, IMS-CP for the packing of contents, and SCORM and IMS-LD for the instructional design. Finally, the device capabilities are obtained via the manufacture information, as UaProf vocabulary defined in terms of in CC/PP. In the EU4ALL project, the following standards are used: IMS-LIP combined with ISO PNP for the user modelling, IMS-MD and ISO DRD for the characterisation of the contents, IMS-CP for its packaging and IMS-LD for the Units of Learning.

Application to the UNED's Scenarios

The RS is involved in the adaptive psycho-educational support service (dynamic guidance). As an example, we comment on one of the recommendations introduced in the previous scenarios, which was obtained from a brainstorming sessions with psycho-educational experts as commented above. The following recommendations are identified:

1. Depending on the marks obtained in questionnaire, additional material is provided to the learner.
    - What is recommended: a learning object of the course
    - When: when the learner has submitted the responses to a questionnaire
    - How: a link to the learning object selected
    - Why: based on the previous knowledge of the learner
2. Foster collaboration by using the forums.
    - What is recommended: the forums service in the platform
    - When: when the learner has not communicated with her peers
    - How: a link to the forum tool
    - Why: promote collaboration among peers in the course

FUTURE RESEARCH DIRECTIONS

In this section we discuss future and emerging trends in the research of standard-based frameworks to support personalisation/adaptation and interoperability in inclusive learning scenarios. Fist, we comment on the potential and limitations of available standards. Next, we introduce an innovative research line which involves that application of the URC standard in e-learning scenarios. Another research direction involves getting more information from the user actions (though more physical means such as eye tracking or brainwaves analysis). Finally, we comment on the accessibility support for digital repositories and libraries from content generation to user access.

Potential and Limitations of Available Standards

Accessibility has implications all over the e-learning domain. Almost every step of any e-learning process has accessibility concerns, and almost every professional in an e-learning institution has a role on accessibility. In addition to this, e-learning is emergently relevant in different contexts of citizens' lives. As a consequence of all these facts and trends, standardisation in e-learning accessibility covers a wide range of science, technology and industry areas, currently with a number of open issues.

Accessible user interfaces help users with disabilities, as well as all potential users, operate computers and therefore to gain access to e-learning services and contents. More and more different ICT terminals and user agents are to be used in upcoming e-learning services, from mobile phones to digital television sets. Hence, standards about software and hardware accessibility to these new gadgets are needed to inform e-learning stakeholders: from managers to application developers, including users who have to decide which commercial gadget is closer to their accessibility needs and preferences. In close relation to this, interoperability between Assistive Technology (AT) and ICT systems is best facilitated via the use of standardised, public interfaces. ISO/IEC 13066-1 (currently under editing process) will provide a basis for designing and evaluating interoperability between IT and AT, by formalising a layered architecture of hardware to hardware, hardware to software, and software to software connections. This piece of work also identifies a variety of APIs that ISO plans to describe further in other parts of the 13066 series. These APIs can be used as frameworks to support IT-AT interoperability, which is crucial when using assistive technologies in e-learning. Furthermore, innovative user interface technologies and interaction concepts (like gesture recognition or multi-touch interaction) may turn out as powerful drivers towards more engaging and effective access to e-learning services. ETSI Specialist Task Force 377 'Inclusive eServices for all' currently investigates how current and future user interfaces and interaction concepts can be designed and deployed in ways that ensure that all users can benefit, regardless of their abilities or disabilities.

The purpose of on-going ISO 9241-129 'Ergonomics of human-system interaction — Part 129: Guidance on individualisation' is to provide guidance on the application of software individualisation in order to achieve as high levels of usability and accessibility as possible. This part of ISO 9241 addresses both user-initiated and system-initiated individualisation. It encompasses the concepts of configuration, adaptation, profiling, and internationalisation.

Providing users with their most suitable content is another relevant component in personalisation. It remains an open issue the standardised mapping of media types (video, images, sound, etc.) to accessibility functionalities (transcripts, audio descriptions, closed captions, etc.). This aspect is not addressed either in the series ISO/IEC 24751 'Individualised adaptability and accessibility in e-learning, education and training' or similar IMS approaches (Learner Information Package Accessibility or Accessibility Metadata). This mapping information would support training institutions to produce and deliver personalised content to their customers. Also, using metadata for describing the accessibility of simple pieces of electronic content has been already addressed in ISO/IEC 24751:3. However, describing accessibility features of more complex, multimedia aggregated objects often used in e-learning has not been specified in detail yet.

Modelling user's terminals ad agents constitutes another piece of the jigsaw. W3C's CC/PP specification led to the User Agent Profile (UaProf, 2009) vocabulary, proposed by Open Mobile Alliance. However, this is much focused on mobile phones, and does not include assistive technologies in the device modelling. Some effort was done in this direction in (Velasco, 2004), but no additional industry or research implementation has followed that inniative.

With regards to accessibility of contents, WCAG 1.0 and 2.0 define criteria against which web accessibility can be measured. Based on them, some countries have produced standardised certification schema. At the same time some criticism has raised, though. Some claim that what is in need of certification is the process, not the final, static picture of inherently live and dynamic web sites and services. This point of view seems to be perfectly transferrable to the e-learning domain. Production, provision and evaluation of accessible learning content through the web could be described theoretically in terms of generic processes with paired measurement criteria. Institutions could therefore assess their behaviour in this respect. However, defining generic processes to model complex and diverse e-learning institutions still poses a number of conceptual and practical problems.

Personalisation of systems has also to do with users' need to adjust accessibility settings of e-learning products prior to use. If this personalisation is not possible, some people will not be able to access these devices without help from another party. ISO is currently producing a standard (IEC 24786) that will contain specifies requirements and recommendations for making accessibility settings accessible.

ISO/IEC 24756 defines a framework for specifying a common access profile of needs and capabilities of users, systems, and their environments. This common access profile (CAP, according to the standard) introduces a model of accessibility as a basis for understanding access issues with the interactions between users and systems in various environments, where user and system must share capabilities of communicating. Evocation of e-learning scenarios looks rather straightforward in this framework, which also aims to support portability of information gathered regarding accessibility issues and solutions for individual users across systems and environments.

It also remains as an open issue the lack of support to accessibility in standards and specifications devoted to embed educational adaptation and responsiveness in e-learning systems. This is the case of IMS-LD and SCORM. It should be remarked here that ensuring an accessible interaction between humans and learning systems is only the beginning of the e-learning story. The real challenge is still managing to offer truly personalised educational approaches, aiming to optimise the outcomes of the learning process of everyone.

Abstract User Interfaces: The URC Standard

R&D activities around universal access to information services include works on languages that describe abstract user interfaces. These languages enable device-independent presentation by letting devices determine the most suitable presentation from a given universal description in terms of a predefined set of abstract user interface components (Lee, 2006). The idea is to offer an abstract description of every element of the user interface, which could be represented in the most suitable modality when the communication with the user takes place.

The Universal Remote Console (URC) framework is a set of ISO standards (ISO/IEC 24752) enabling remote and alternative interfaces for electronic products and services. These standards define a generic framework and an XML-based user interface language to use any device to act as a remote control in order to monitor or control electronic devices called "targets" (Zimmermann et al, 2004). The URC defines every target as a set of functional units called User Interface Sockets. The "UI Socket Description" document describes a Socket's functionality using variables, commands and notifications. At runtime, widgets or interactors can be instantiated on the URC and bound to these variables, commands and notifications, according to the specific user needs and the use context.

The "Universal Control Hub (UCH)" architecture is a specific configuration of the URC framework, using a gateway approach between controllers and targets. This architecture is of particular interest for web based learning services, since it supports controllers and targets that are not necessarily URC conformant. For e-learning platforms, a web server may include a "universal control hub" that instantiates concrete user interfaces based on a User Interface Socket. Thus the web server can provide the controller with a user interface that is adapted to the user's needs and preferences, by means of the URC framework.

Personalised user interfaces ("UI sockets") could be generated dynamically in the Universal Control Hub for access to learning "targets" according to user preferences and context. However, the URC framework has been initially designed for remote control of devices and services where the controller and the target are tightly synchronised. In contrast, e-learning services have been typically offered by web based information systems in an asynchronous way. Nevertheless, there are aspects of remote control inherent in e-learning systems, as the above example on the forum with message threads illustrates.

A successful application of URC ideas and paradigm to the learning application domain will require further research and analysis on available alternative configurations, for example the combination of the UCH and IMS ACCLIP. In addition, the URC paradigm could inspire future research about potential benefits of synchronised e-learning services. Ideas to apply this approach were introduced in Rodriguez-Ascaso et al. (2007).

New Ways of Input and Output Data to Support Adaptation in the RS

In this subsection, we discuss emerging trends on the application of recommender systems in the future, related to new ways of input data (eye tracking, sensors, etc.) and what implications exists in terms of interoperability. Some research efforts in the field are leading towards minimally invasive sensors technology, which can be put around each student' chair, mouse, monitor and wrist, to provide data about posture, movement, grip tension, arousal and facially expressed mental states. The goal is to capture student affective states (Cooper et al., 2009). Eye tracking techniques can also be used to obtain information about the users' affect and reasoning (Muldner et al., 2009). Other researchers are focused on predicting the learners' answers from their brainwaves (Heraz and Frasson, 2009).

If this information is proven useful to know about the user model, the existing standards should be extended to incorporate information such as the data gather from the sensors, the pupillary responses or the electrical brain metrics.

Accessibility Support in Digital Repositories and Libraries

In order to support accessibility in digital repositories and libraries from content generation to user access, several of the modules used to support accessibility and personalisation in e-learning scenarios can be reused (i.e. user modelling, content personalisation, metadata repositories and recommender systems). In this way, taking advantage of their interoperability, accessibility support could be provided to the full-cycle of digital content creation, storage and retrieval.

In order to introduce accessible tagging in a digital repository information cycle flow, the focus has to be put in its "actors", as shown in system diagram represented in Figure 8:

Figure 8. Accessibility support in digital repositories

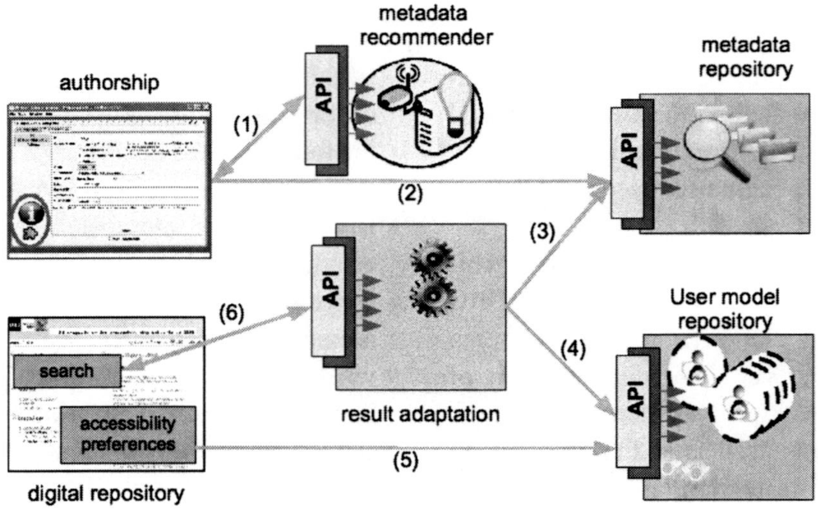

- The repository editor or administrator: when saving digital content, a personalised assistant (1) suggests the best metadata to distinguish the content accessibility of such content. This assistant is based on previous research with recommender systems, abstracted and personalised for this task. Once the metadata is accepted, it will be sent and stored accordingly into a metadata repository
- The repository end-user, which selects her accessibility preferences in the corresponding repository pages. Those preferences are sent and stored into the user model service (5). When the user makes a content search (6), the result is adapted (through a content personalisation system) combining the resource metadata (3) and the user model preferences (4). Results provid also invaluable feedback to adjust the metadata recommender suggestions (1).

The main objectives for this research direction are:

- To help authorship and digitalisation process, integrating artificial intelligence tools in content generation cycle, so metadata tagging process will be almost automatic for the repository authors and administrators, and not another burden to deal with.
- To help content storage and retrieval, integrating services for accessible metadata storage, information storage and accessible information retrieval. In this context, an abstract recommender module to be used by non-technical users, and easily modified to be applied in any environment can be developed. Rete algorithm-based software (BRMS) can provide such framework, and there are already open-source mature software (like Jboss Rules) which fit perfectly in these requirements. Previous experiences with recommender systems and other automatic technologies for rapid prototyping, like case-based reasoning systems based on templates, like Jcolibri (2009), can be taken into account.
- To help usage and evaluation, developing services for user modelling and content adaptation which will provide digital re-

positories and libraries with adapted services for their users' preferences, and tools to check the perfect fit of the adaptation served.

CONCLUSION

In this chapter we have presented a flexible, standards based and adaptive framework whose main objective is to adapt user interfaces, content and learning environment to the needs of learners, including their functional diversity issues (i.e., disabilities). Two approaches can be followed to meet the required LMS personalisation support: 1) a student-centred design approach, focused on modifying the functional logic of the system, and 2) a personalised interaction approach, by adding the required support when needed in the system. The former relates to issues such as content personalisation and personalised units of learning, which require modifications within the LMS. The focus is on the adaptation of the user interface and the content. The later refers to offering recommendations to extend the the LMS with adaptive navigation support, and thus, modifying the learning environment to the needs of the learner. We have followed both approaches supported by user modelling techniques which are managed with the appropriate standards.

The two key issues supporting the framework described in this chapter, namely accessibility and adaptation to the user needs (i.e., personalisation), have implications all over the e-learning domain. Almost every step of any e-learning process has accessibility concerns and should attend individual and evolving needs, and almost every professional in an e-learning institution has a role on accessibility and attending those needs. To make the interoperability requirements of this process manageable when dealing with the wide and increasing variety of context and devices, types of contents, and resources involved there is no alternative but standardisation at all levels. As previously discussed, the standardisation in e-learning accessibility covers a wide range of science, technology and industry areas, currently with a number of open issues. In that respect we have discussed the standards and specifications involved and the technological developments that the aDeNu group is providing within EU4ALL project, which is constructing a general and standards-based architecture of European-wide services to support LLL for ALL.

The Open Architecture of Services deals with interoperability requirements coming from the various needs in different educational contexts, including different LMS (dotLRN and Moodle). From the evaluation standpoint the generality of the approach is supported by the different educational contexts that are being considered at the two largest distance learning universities in Europe with the highest numbers of students with functional diversity issues. Further, the usage of the two different LMS within the architecture is being evaluated at large scale focusing on accessibility, usability and adaptation issues of the services developed. From a technological perspective, if we are successful in implementing the architecture into these two so different and well known LMS and covering a wide range of educational scenarios, we can confirm that the generality of the approach is sufficient.

To the knowledge of authors, there are no similar implementations based on standards and service-oriented architectures to supporting students with disabilities in higher education as is being proposed by the EU4ALL project. This situation is creating many challenges beyond those covered in this chapter, which have been the ones the aDeNu research group is involved in, namely required standards, interoperability requirements of the architecture, user model, recommending system, and their application to the services that are being implemented at UNED.

REFERENCES

W3C-WAI. (December 2008). W3C World Wide Web. Retrieved August 7, 2009, from W3C Web Accessibility Initiative: http://www.w3.org/WAI/intro/wcag.php

ADL. (2009, August 07). *Advanced Distributed Learning*. Retrieved August 07, 2009, from http://www.adlnet.gov/Technologies/scorm/default.aspx

AICC. (2005 June 28). *AICC - Aviation Industry CBT Committee*. Retrieved August 07, 2009, from: www.aicc.org/docs/AGRs/agr011v1.pdf

AICC. (2009 Feb. 03). *AICC - Aviation Industry CBT Committee*. Retrieved August 07, 2009, from: http://www.aicc.org/

Axis2 (2009). Retrieved from http://ws.apache.org/axis2/

Baldiris, S., Santos, O. C., Barrera, C., Boticario J. G., Velez, J., Fabregat, R. (2008). Integration of educational specifications and standards to support adaptive learning scenarios in ADAPTAPlan. *International Journal of Computer Science and Applications (IJCSA). Special Issue on New Trends on AI techniques for Educational Technologies, 5* (1).

Boticario, J. G., & Cooper, M. Montandon, L., van Dorp, K-J. (2006). Towards an Open, Standard-based, Reusable and Extensible Architecture of Services for Accessible Lifelong Learning: An Introduction to the EU4ALL Project. In *Proceedings of the EADTU 2006 Annual Conference: Widening participation and opportunities by e-learning in Higher Education*, Tallinn, Estonia, 22 – 24, November 2006.

Boticario, J. G., & Santos, O. C. (2007). An open IMS-based user modelling approach for developing adaptive learning management systems. *Journal of Interactive Media in Education. Adaptation and IMS Learning Design, 02*, 1–19.

Boticario, J. G., & Santos, O. C. (2008). A standards-based modelling approach for dynamic generation of adaptive learning scenarios. *Journal of Universal Computer Science, 14*(17), 2859–2876.

Brickley, D., & Miller, L. (November 2, 2007). *FOAF Vocabulary Specification 0.91*. Retrieved July 28, 2009, from http://xmlns.com/foaf/spec/

Brusilovsky, P. (2004). Adaptive Educational Hypermedia: From generation to generation. In *Proceedings of 4th Hellenic Conference on ICT in Education*, 19-33. New Technologies Pub.

Brusilovsky, P., & Vassileva, J. (2003). Course sequencing techniques for large-scale webbased education. *International Journal of Continuing Engineering Education and Lifelong Learning, 13*(1/2).

CETIS. J. (03 April, 2009). *JISC CETIS*. Retrieved August 07, 2009, from http://wiki.cetis.ac.uk/LEAP2A_specification

Cluster, W. A. B. (2009). The WAB Cluster is the European Web Accessibility Benchmarking Cluster. Retrieved June 26, 2009, from http://www.supporteam.org/Supporteam/Documentary/accessibility_policies.asp

Cooper, D. G., Arroyo, I., Woolf, B. P., Muldner, K., Burleson, W., & Christopherson, R. (2009). Sensors Model Student Self Concept in the Classroom. User Modeling, Adaptation, and Personalization Seventeenth International Conference, UMAP 2009, Trento, Italy, (LNCS 5535, pp. 30-41). Berlin: Springer-Verlag.

Cooper, M., Boticario, J. G., & Montandon, L. (2006). An introduction to Accessible Lifelong Learning (ALL) - a strategy for research and development uniting accessible technology, services, and e-learning infrastructure. *Fourth European Distance and E-Learning Network: Research into Online Distance Education and E-Learning*. Castellldefels, Spain, 25-28 October 2006.

Core, D. (October 10, 2008). *Dublin Core Metadata Initiative*. Retrieved August 07 2009, from Accessibility Term Proposal: http://dublincore.org/accessibilitywiki/NewElementProposal

Couchet, J., Santos, O. C., Raffenne, E., & Boticario, J. G. (2008). The Tracking and Auditing Module for the OpenACS Framework. *7th OPENACS /. LRN Conference,* Valencia, Spain.

Cristea, A. I., & Garzotto, F. (2004). ADAPT major design dimensions for educational adaptive hypermedia. In *ED-Media '04 conference on educational multimedia, hypermedia & telecommunications*. Association for the advancement of computing in education.

Deco, C., Bender, C., Casali, A., & Motz, R. (2008). Design of a Recommender Educational System. In *Proceedings of 3rd Latinamerican Conference of Learning Objects (LACLO 2008),* (pp. 63).

Drachsler, H., Hummel, H. G. K., Van den Berg, B., Eshuis, J., Waterink, W., Nadolski, R., et al. (2008). Effects of the ISIS Recommender System for Navigation Support in Self-Organized Learning Networks. In M. Kalz, R. Koper, V. Hornung-Prähauser & M. Luckmann (Eds.) *Proceedings of the 1st Workshop on Technology Support for Self-Organized Learners (TSSOL08) in conjunction with 4th Edumedia Conference 2008 Self-organised learning in the interactive Web – Changing learning culture?* (pp. 106-124). June, 2-3, 2008, Salzburg, Austria: CEUR Workshop Proceedings. Available at http://ceur-ws.org/Vol-349

E-Framework. (2009). Retrieved from http://www.e-framework.org/

EU4ALL. (2009). The European Unified Approach for Assisted Lifelong learning (EU4ALL) (IST-FP6-034778). Retrieved on July 10 from http://www.eu4all-project.eu

EADTU. (2009). *The European Association of Distance Teaching Universities*. Retrieved July 25, 2009, from: http://www.eadtu.nl

EHEA. (2009). *The European Higher Education Area in a global context. Report on overall developments at the European, national and institutional levels*. Approved by BFUG at its meeting in Prague, 12-13 February 2009. Retrieved on July 10 from http://www.ond.vlaanderen.be/hogeronderwijs/bologna/conference/documents/2009_EHEA_in_global_context.pdf

eLearningPR. Adopting a multi-annual programme (2004-2006) for the effective integration of Information and Communication Technologies (ICT) in education and training systems in Europe (eLearning Programme) (COM(2002) 751 - C5-0630/2002 - 2002/0303(COD)).

EUNIS. (2009). European University Information Systems. Retrieved July 25, 2009, from: http://www.eunis.org/

Felder, R. M., & Silverman, L. K. (2002). Learning and Teaching Styles In Engineering Education. *Engr. Education*, *78*(7), 674–681.

Fink, J., & Kobsa, A. Nill, A. (1998). *Adaptable and Adaptive Information Provision for All Users, Including Disabled and Elderly People.* Retrieved April 9, 2009, from: http://www.isr.uci.edu/~kobsa/papers/1998-NRHM-kobsa.pdf

FLEXO project. (2009). Retrieved from http://www.ines.org.es/flexo

Fluid. (2009). Retrieved from http://fluidproject.org/

GRAPPLE project. (2009). Retrieved from www.grapple-project.org

Hauger, D., & Kock, M. (2007). *State of the Art of Adaptivity in E-Learning Platforms. Workshop at Adaptivity and User Modeling in Interactive Systems ABIS 2007*. Germany: Halle/Salle.

HEAG. (2009). Retrieved from www.heagnet.org

Heraz, A., & Frasson, C. (2009). Detecting guessed and random learners' answers through their brainwaves. *User Modeling, Adaptation, and Personalization Seventeenth International Conference, UMAP 2009*, Trento, Italy, (LNCS 5535, pp. 367-372). Berlin: Springer-Verlag.

IEEE. (2005). *IEEE LTSC WG11: Computing Managed Instruction*. Retrieved August 9, 2009, from: http://ltsc.ieee.org/wg11/

IMS. (2004, August 23). *IMS Global Learning Consortium*. Retrieved August 07, 2009, from: IMS Guidelines for Developing Accessible Learning Applications http://www.imsglobal.org/accessibility/accessiblevers/index.html

IMS-LD. (2003). IMS Learning Design Specification. Retrieved January 21, 2009 from: http://www.imsglobal.org/learningdesign/

Iorio, A. D., Feliziani, A. A., Mirri, S., Salomoni, P., & Vitali, F. (2006). Automatically Producing Accessible Learning Objects. *Journal of Educational Technology & Society*, *9*(4), 3–16.

ISO. (August 07, 2009). ISO International Organization for Standardization. Retrieved August 07, 2009, from: JTC 1/SC 36: http://www.iso.org/iso/standards_development/technical_committees/list_of_iso_technical_committees/iso_technical_committee.htm?commid=45392

ISO 13407 (1999): "Human-centered design processes for interactive systems".

ISO/IEC 24751 (2009). Individualized adaptability and accessibility in e-learning, education and training.

ISO/IEC 24752 (2008) Information technology -- User interfaces -- Universal remote console

Jackl, A. (2004). IMS AccessForAll Meta-data XML Binding. Retrieved January 12, 2009 from http://www.imsproject.org accessed

Jcolibri (2009): http://gaia.fdi.ucm.es/grupo/projects/jcolibri

Kelly, B., Sloan, D., Brown, S., Seale, J., Petrie, H., & Lauke, P. Ball. S. (2007). Accessibility 2.0: people, policies and processes, In Proceedings of the 2007 international cross-disciplinary conference on Web accessibility (W4A), May 07-08, Banff, Canada.

Kobsa, A. (2007) Privacy Enhanced Personalization. Communications of the ACM, 50(8), pp.24-33, Aug.Proc. 2, Second International Conference on Mobile and Ubiquitous

Kravcik, M., & Specht, M. (2005). Experience with WINDS Virtual University In: P. Kommers, G. Richards (eds.) Proc. of the ED-MEDIA 2005 Conference, 642-649

Lanzilotti, R., Ardito, C., Costabile, M. F., & Angeli, A. D. (2006). eLSE Methodology: a Systematic Approach to the e-Learning Systems Evaluation. *Journal of Educational Technology & Society*, *9*(4), 42–53.

Lazarinis, F., Green, S., & Pearson, E. (2009) Focusing on content reusability and interoperability in a personalized hypermedia assessment tool, Multimedia Tools and Applications Journal, Springer, http://www.springerlink.com/content/u34211037737ur42/.

Lee, C., Helal, S., & Lee, W. (2006) Universal Interactions with Smart Spaces. Pervasive computing. January-March, 2006. pp 16-21.

Lesage, M., Riopel, M., Raiche, G., & Sodoke, K. (2008). IMS-QTI sub-standards in computerised adaptive testing and interfacing. *International Journal of Advanced Media and Communication*, *2*(2), 115–137. doi:10.1504/IJAMC.2008.018503

LTSC. I. (07 August, 2009). IEEE Learning Technology Standards Committee. Retrieved August 7, 2009, from: http://ieeeltsc.wordpress.com/

Martin, L., Gutiérrez y Restrepo, E., Barrera, C., Rodríguez Ascaso, A., Santos, O. C., & Boticario, J. G. (2007). Usability and Accessibility Evaluations along the eLearning Cycle. In Mathias Weske Mohand-Saïd Hacid and Claude Godart (Eds.), Web Information Systems Engineering (WISE 2007) (pp. 453- 458). Lecture Notes in Computer Science, 4832.

Martínez-Ortiz, I., Moreno-Ger, P., Sierra, J. L., & Fernández-Manjón, B. (2006) <e-QTI>: a Reusable Assessment Engine, 5th International Conference on Web-based Learning, Penang, Malaysia. LNCS 4181, pp. 134-145.

Muldner, K., Christopherson, R., Atkinson, R., & Burleson, W. (2009) Investigating the utility of eye-tracking information on affect and reasoning for user modeling. User Modeling, Adaptation, and Personalization Seventeenth International Conference, UMAP 2009, Trento, Italy, Volume LNCS 5535, Pages 138-149, Springer-Verlag, 2009.

Norton, M., & Treviranus, J. (2003). IMS Learner Information Package Accessibility for LIP XML Schema Binding. Retrieved January 21, 2009 from: http://www.imsproject.org

OASIS. (2009) http://www.oasis-open.org/committees/tc_home.php?wg_abbrev=ws-sx

OECD. (June 27, 2006). OECD. Retrieved August 07, 2009, from Selected Statistics on Higher Education - Background Report for Meeting of OECD Ministers of Education in June 2006: http://www.oecd.org/dataoecd/30/7/36960580.pdf

OKI. (2009) http://www.okiproject.org/

LLL Programme, (2006) Lifelong Learning Programme was published in the Official Journal of the European Union L327/45 on 24 November 2006.

Rampart (2009) http://ws.apache.org/axis2/modules/rampart/1_3/security-module.html

Rodriguez-Ascaso, A., Martin, L., Gutiérrez y Restrepo, E., Finat, C., Santos, O. C., & Boticario, J. G. (2008b) Design and Use of an Online Community for Students with Disabilities. The UNED Experience. Proceedings of the EADTU's 20th Annual Conference 2008

Rodriguez-Ascaso, A.; Santos, O.C.; Boticario, J.G.; Zimmermann, G. (2007) UM' 2007 Supplementary Proceedings: Towards user modelling and adaptive systems for all, Corfu, Greece, p.27-31 (2007)

Rodriguez-Ascaso, A., Santos, O. C., del Campo, E., Saneiro, M., & Boticario, J. G. (2008a). Personalised Support for Students with Disabilities Based on Psychoeducational Guidelines. *ICALT, 2008*, 1021–1022.

Rosson, M. B., & Carroll, J. M. (2001). *Usability engineering: scenario-based development of human computer interaction*. Morgan Kaufmann.

Santos, O. C., & Boticario, J. G. (2008). Users' experience with a recommender system in an open source standard-based learning management system. In proceedings of the 4th Symposium of the WG HCI&UE of the Austrian Computer Society on Usability & HCI for Education and Work (USAB 2008).

Santos, O. C., Boticario, J. G., Fernández del Viso, A., Pérez de la Cámara, S., Rebate Sánchez, C., & Gutiérrez y Restrepo, E. (2007a) "Basic skills training to disabled and adult learners through an accessible e-Learning platform", Proceedings of the 12th International Conference on Human-Computer Interaction: HCI applications and services: Julie Jacko (eds.), vol. 7, Springer Berlin / Heidelberg, Lecture notes in computer science (LNCS, 4556), pp. 796-805

Santos, O. C., Boticario, J. G., Raffenne, E., & Pastor, R. (2007b). Why using dotLRN? UNED use cases. In J.R. Rodriguez and M. Palomo (Eds.), FLOSS International Conference, (pp. 195-212), UCA Pub.

Santos, O. C., Martin, L., del Campo, E., Saneiro, M., Mazzone, E., Boticario, J. G., & Petrie, H. (2009). User-Centered Design Methods for Validating a Recommendations Model to Enrich Learning Management Systems with Adaptive Navigation Support. In: S. Weibelzahl, J. Masthoff, A. Paramythis, and L. van Velsen (Eds.) Proceedings of the Sixth Workshop on User-Centred Design and Evaluation of Adaptive Systems, held in conjunction with the International Conference on User Modeling, Adaptation, and Personalization (UMAP2009), Trento, Italy, June 26th, 2009 (pp. 64-67).

Santos, O. C., Rodriguez-Ascaso, A., Boticario, J. G., & Martin, L. (2007c) User modelling for attending functional diversity for ALL in Higher Education. International Workshop on Personalized Access to Web Information (PAWI). LNCS 4832.

Schank, R. C., & Jona, M. (1991). Empowering the Student: New Perspectives on the Design of Teaching Systems. *Journal of the Learning Sciences*, *1*, 7–35. doi:10.1207/s15327809jls0101_2

Seale, J. (2006). *E-learning and disability in higher education: accessibility research and practice*. Routledge London.

Seale, J. Draffan, E.A and Wald, Mike (2008) Exploring disabled learners' experiences of e-learning: LEXDIS Project Report. Southampton, UK, University of Southampton, 161pp.

UaProf. (2009). User Agent Profile is a standard defined and maintained by the Open Mobile Alliance (formerly the WAP Forum). Retrieved July 21, 2009, from http://www.openmobilealliance.org/tech/affiliates/wap/wap-248-uaprof-20011020-a.pdf

Van Rosmalen, P., Boticario, J. G., & Santos, O. C. (2004). The Full Life Cycle of Adaptation in aLFanet eLearning Environment. Learning Technology newsletter. Vol. 4, p. 59-61, 2004.

Velasco, C. A., Mohamad, Y., Gilman, A. S., Viorres, N., Vlachogiannis, E., Arnellos, A., & Darsenitas, J. S. (2004) Universal access to information services—the need for user information and its relationship to device profiles. Universal Access in the Information Society, Publisher Springer Berlin / Heidelberg, ISSN 1615-5297, Issue Volume 3, Number 1, pp 88-95.

Web, C. A. G. (WCAG) 2.0 - W3C Recommendation 11 December 2008. Retrieved January 15, 2009, from http://www.w3.org/TR/2008/REC-WCAG20-20081211/

Yang, S. J. H., Chen, I. Y. L., & Chen, R. (2007). Applying Content Adaptation to Mobile Learning, Second International Conference on Innovative Computing [IEEE Computer Society Press.]. *Information and Control, ICICIC*, 157.

Zaine, O. R. (2002). Building a Recommender Agent for e-Learning Systems", Proceedings of International. Conference on Computers in Education, Auckland, New Zealand, 3-6 December, pp. 55-59.

Zimmermann, G., Vanderheiden, G., Gandy, M., Laskowski, S., Ma, M., Trewin, S., & Walker, M. (2004). Universal remote console standard - toward natural user interaction in ambient intelligence. Extended Abstracts for the 2004 Conference on Human Factors in Computing Systems (pp. 1608-1609). New York: ACM Press.

ADDITIONAL READING

Adomavicius, G., & Tuzhilin, A. (2005). Toward the Next Generation of Recommender Systems: A Survey of the State-of-the-Art and Possible Extensions. *IEEE Transactions on Knowledge and Data Engineering*, *17*(6). doi:10.1109/TKDE.2005.99

Baldiris, S., Fabregat, R., & Santos, O. (2007). Modelling Competency upon dotLRN. In proceedings of the OpenACS international conference. Vienna.

Beshears. F.M. (2003). Open Standards and Open Source Development Strategies for e-Learning. Presentation for IS224 Strategic Computing and Communications Technology. Berkeley: Educational Technology Services.

Brooks, C., & Kettel, L. Hansen. C. (2005). Building a Learning Object Content Management System World Conference on E-Learning in Corx°porate, Healthcare, & Higher Education (E-Learn 2005).

Brusilovsky P., Millán E. User Models for Adaptive Hypermedia and Adaptive Educational Systems. (2007). The Adaptive Web, LNCS 4321, pp. 3 – 53. Springer-Verlag Berlin Heidelberg.

Burke, R. (2002). Hybrid recommender systems: survey and experiments. *User Modeling and User-Adapted Interaction*, *12*, 331–370. doi:10.1023/A:1021240730564

Cristea, A. I. (2004). What can the Semantic Web do for Adaptive Educational Hypermedia? *Journal of Educational Technology & Society*, *7*(4).

De Bra, P., Pechenizkiy, M., van der Sluijs, K., & Smits, D. (2008). GRAPPLE: Integrating Adaptive Learning into Learning Management Systems. In Proceedings of World Conference on Educational Multimedia, Hypermedia and Telecommunications 2008 (January 2008), pp. 5183-5188.

Dolog, P., & Nejdl, W. (2003). *2003*. Challenges and Benefits of the Semantic Web for User Modelling. In Adaptive Hypermedia.

Fedora (2008). Flexible Extensible Digital Object Repository Architecture. Version 3. http://www.fedora-commons.org/.

Ghali, F., & Cristea, A. (2008). Interoperability between MOT and Learning Management Systems: Converting CAF to IMS QTI and IMS CP, AH 2008: 5th Int. Conf. on Adaptive Hypermedia and Adaptive Web-Based Systems pp. 296–299. Berlin Heidelberg, Springer

Harrigan, M., Kravcik, M., Steiner, C., & Wade, V. (2009). What Do Academic Users Really Want from an Adaptive Learning System? The 17th International Conference on User Modeling, Adaptation, and Personalization (Trento, Italy), 2009, p. 455-460.

Hauger, D. (2009). *09: Adaptation and Personalization for Web 2.0.* Using Asynchronous Client-Side User Monitoring to Enhance User Modeling in Adaptive E-Learning Systems. In UMAP.

Heckmann, D. (2006). *Ubiquitous User Modeling*. Berlin, Germany: Akademische.

Heckmann, D., Schwartz, T., Brandherm, B., Schmitz, M., & von Wilamowitz-Moellendorff, M. (2005). Gumo – The General User Model Ontology. In: L. Ardissono, P. Brna & A. Mitrovic (eds.), Proceedings of the 10th International Conference on User Modeling (UM'2005) (pp. 428-432), Edinburgh, UK: Springer Verlag.

Henze, N., Dolog, P., & Nejdl, W. (2004). Reasoning and Ontologies for Personalized E-Learning. *Journal of Educational Technology & Society*, *7*(Issue 4).

Jameson, A. (2006). Adaptive user interfaces and agents. In Jacko, J. A., & Sears, A. (Eds.), *Human-Computer Interaction handbook* (2nd ed., pp. 433–458). Erlbaum.

Kareal, F., & Klema, J. (2006). Adaptivity in e-learning. In A. Méndez-Vilas, A. Solano, J. Mesa and J. A. Mesa: Current Developments in Technology-Assisted Education, Vol. 1, pp. 260-264.

Leshin, C. B., Pollock, J., & Reigeluth, C. M. (1992). *Instructional Design Strategies and Tactics*. Englewood Cliffs, NJ: Educational Technology Publications.

Longworth, N. (2003). Lifelong learning in action - Transforming education in the 21st century. Kogan page.

Martin, L., Roldán, D., Revilla, O., Aguilar, M.J., Santos, O. C., Boticario, J.G. (2008). Usability in e-Learning Platforms: heuristics comparison between Moodle, Sakai and dotLRN. OpenACS Conferences.

Mazzola, L., & Mazza, R. (2009) Supporting Learners in Adaptive Learning Environments through the Enhancement of the Student Model. Julie A. Jacko (Ed.): Human-Computer Interaction. Interacting in Various Application Domains, 13th International Conference, HCI International 2009.

Mejía, C., Baldiris, S., Gómez, S., & Fabregat, R. (2008). Adaptation process to deliver content based on user learning styles, International Conference of Education, Research and Innovation (IBSN: 978-84-612-5091-2), 2008, International Association of Technology, Education and Development, Madrid (Spain).

Morales, L., Castillo, L., Fernandez-Olivares, J., & Gonzalez-Ferrer, A. (2008). Automatic Generation of User Adapted Learning Designs: An AI-Planning Proposal. 5th Int. Conf. on Adaptive Hypermedia and Adaptive Web-Based Systems. Hannover.

Niederée, C., Stewart, A., Mehta, B., & Hemmje, M. (2004). A Multi-Dimensional, Unified User Model for Cross-System Personalization. In: Proceedings of the Workshop on Environments for Personalized Information Access at AVI'2004 (pp. 34-54), Gallipoli, Italy, from http://www.di.uniba.it/avi2004/e4pia/EPIA2004_proceedings.pdf

Recio-García, J., Díaz-Agudo, B., & González-Calero, P. (2008). Prototyping recommender systems in jcolibri, ACM Conference On Recommender Systems, pp.243-250, 2008 Proceedings of the 2008 ACM conference on Recommender systems

KEY TERMS AND DEFINITIONS

Accessibility: "The usability of a product, service, environment or facility by people with the widest range of capabilities" (ISO TS 16071).

Adaptable: Systems that allow the user to change certain system parameters, and thereby adapt the behaviour of these systems (Fink & Kobsa, 1998).

Adaptive: Systems that adapt to users automatically based on monitoring the users' interaction during runtime (Fink & Kobsa, 1998).

Adaptability and Adaptivity at the User Interface: This focuses on improving the overall access to the information system and includes special I/O devices (e.g., macro mouse, Braille display, and Speech synthesizer), visual and non-visual interface objects, and associated interaction techniques (Fink & Kobsa, 1998).

Adaptability and Adaptivity within Hypermedia Pages: This focuses on personalisation and includes the adaptation of the information content, information modality, information prominence, orientation and navigation aids, and links to other hypermedia pages (Fink & Kobsa, 1998).

Assistive Technology: Has been defined as "technology used by individuals with disabilities in order to perform functions that might otherwise be difficult or impossible" (National Center on Accessible Information Technology in Education, 2006), or, more formally in the Technology-Related Assistance for Individuals with Disabilities Act, as "any item, piece of equipment or product system, whether acquired commercially off the shelf, modified or customized, that is used to increase, maintain, or improve functional capabilities of individuals with disabilities". The term is used here to refer to products that interoperate with mainstream, "nonassistive" products to permit disabled users to perform the functions of the mainstream products.

Universal Design: or "**Design for All**": "the design of products and environments to be usable by all people, to the greatest extent possible, without the need for adaptation or specialized design" (Center for Universal Design, 1994).

Usability: "The effectiveness, efficiency and satisfaction with which specified users achieve specified goals in particular environments" (ISO IEC 9241)

Chapter 8
E-Learning Standards:
Beyond Technical Standards to Guides for Professional Practice

Stephen Marshall
Victoria University of Wellington, New Zealand

ABSTRACT

Over the past decade e-learning standards have attracted substantial and growing attention from practitioners, institutions and governments. Millions of dollars are being invested in a process of standardization that, while aimed at supporting e-learning, seems to have neglected pedagogy and the need to engage with practitioners who are not technology specialists. In parallel, a culture of quality assurance has developed internationally within higher education resulting in quality frameworks that are driven by external compliance agendas rather than directly influencing the quality of the student and teacher experience of education. The e-learning Maturity Model provides a standard that guides professionals and organizations in assessing their e-learning capability, but also complements this with quality enhancement and feasibility elements that support reflection, prioritization of resources and guide personal and organizational development of e-learning.

INTRODUCTION

Tanenbaum's wry observation on standards "The nice thing about standards is that there are so many to choose from" (Tanenbaum, 1981, p. 221) is an almost obligatory quote in papers that consider the role of standards in e-learning and higher education. However, when one assesses the standards available (Marshall, 2004) it is clear that if practitioners are seeking standards as guides for professional practice in e-learning they are not offered a wide selection of choices unless their interests run to interoperability or resource discovery.

Standards and standardization, rather than being seen positively as tools for simplifying and

DOI: 10.4018/978-1-61692-789-9.ch008

supporting professional work are widely regarded as irrelevant to most academics. The 'standard' approach to teaching implies a raft of negative connotations to those trying to improve the use of technology and the quality of the student e-learning experience. 'Quality' has similarly been transformed from a positive expectation to an idea tinged with negativity, the almost inevitable expectation that a quality agenda is one of auditing, compliance and expensive bureaucratic oversight.

It is easy to blame governments and consultants for the negative conceptions of standards and quality in higher education. However, some of the blame for these being 'secret standards business' (Mason, 2003) must lie with the lack of engagement by the wider academic community in setting their own professional standards. Part of the responsibility must lie with the culture of academic freedom, which many choose to interpret as a requirement for independence in all things and individual action without reference to the immediate institutional context or the needs of their programme or students. The reality is that collegiality is a strength of the university that requires collective action and responsibility, particularly as resources become ever more closely constrained and as universities take on a greater social role promoting equity and access to education for all groups.

This chapter explores the work on standards and quality that has been undertaken over the past decade. It takes a critical perspective on the extent to which this work has resulted in a greater sense of professional identity and participation amongst the e-learning community. The e-learning Maturity Model (eMM) is discussed as an example of how benchmarking and quality activities can be owned by the community and used as guides for professional practice, not just as a tool for management measurement and institutional accountability, but a positive force for growth and innovation.

E-LEARNING STANDARDS

The Technical Dominance of Standards

The term 'standard' is a both simple and complex in definition. In the formal sense (ISO/IEC, 1996, p8) it is "a document, established by consensus, that provides, for common and repeated use, rules, guidelines or characteristics for activities or their results, aimed at the achievement of the optimum degree of order in a given context." Standards in the strictest sense can only be created by specific organizations such as the International Standards Organization. In reality and common usage, as well as in the rest of this chapter, a standard can be an official document, but it also could be a de facto creation of a professional body or vendor, a specification, a reference model or framework, or a collection of guidelines. Guidelines or heuristics generated by expert practitioners and possessing strong face validity rather than empirical support constitute the predominant guides to good practice within e-learning evident in the literature.

The development of E-learning standards in all their myriad forms over the past decade has resulted in a complex ecology of organizations, working groups and documents that make engagement by non-specialists challenging (Friesen, 2005; Devedzic, Jovanovic & Gasevic, 2007). Key organizations include the IEEE Learning Technology Standardization Committee (LTSC; http://www.ieeeltsc.org), the ISO/IEC Joint Technical Committee I Standing Committee 36 (ISO/IEC JTCI SC36; http://www.jtclsc36.org), the IMS Global Learning Consortium (IMS; http://www.imsproject.org), and the Advanced Distributed Learning Initiative (ADL; http://www.adlnet.org), as well as a number of nationally or regionally focused organizations. The backgrounds of these groups provide an important context to their work. IMS arose from early work on meta-data standards undertaken by the EDUCAUSE organization; ADL is a US Defence Department initiative intended to reduce the costs of military training; while the IEEE and ISO/IEC are technical standards groups.

The e-learning standards activities undertaken by these groups consequently have a strong technical and economic focus, apparent in the benefits identified by those working in the field. The UK Centre for Educational Technology Interoperability Standards (CETIS 2004) claims these benefits for standards:

- ability to reuse e-learning resources despite rapid changes in technology;
- supporting the cataloging and discovery of learning resources;
- facilitating the transfer of student records and information between systems and institutions.

Olivier and Liber (2003) identify benefits in the interoperability, reuse and economics of e-learning:

- authors and publisher's learning products can work across multiple systems. They don't need to target a specific system or adapt them for different platforms;
- learning environment developers can ensure that a wide variety of content works on their systems. They don't have to persuade content authors and publishers to develop specifically for their platform;
- resource users can use a wider range of content for their chosen system. They don't have to worry about which resources work with which systems, or the consequences and costs if they want to change or add their content or system providers;
- standards remove some of the barriers to the development of the e-learning market and potentially provide the basis on which a learning object economy can be developed.

Varlamis and Apostolakis (2006) identify as benefits of increasing standardization:

- users able to move easily between learning applications due to standard interfaces;
- common content formats;
- reduction in development costs for tool vendors;
- component integration and reuse by application and platform designers.

The EU Learning Technology Standards Observatory (http://www.cen-ltso.net/) identifies standards and standard-like activities in nineteen areas, only three of which could be considered pedagogically focused (Assessment, Collaboration, and ePortfolios). However, there is currently no proposed specification or standard for Collaboration, and the work identified in the Assessment and ePortfolio areas is concerned with interoperability and data interchange between discrete systems (e.g. QTI, IMS ePortfolio).

The technical focus of standards researchers is apparent in papers such as that of Muñoz-Merino, Kloos and Naranjo (2009) where standards and specifications are categorized as either architectural, data or behavioural standards (the latter defining programming interfaces rather than staff or student activties). Pedagogy is not a factor in this classification. As well as illustrating the general lack of concern with pedagogy and teaching, the work of Muñoz-Merino *et al.* (2009) also demonstrates the problem of scope creep for technical standards. They propose specifications for activities such as assignment submission, chat and FAQs. The clear intent is that every particular use of technology be defined by a standard. This has the reasonable objective of facilitating interoperability, but also risks constraining the ways technology is used by teachers. Teachers need to understand how to make good educational use of different forms of information storage, presentation and communication. These pedagogical concerns are very different to the technical challenge of interoperability and maintaining a viable systems infrastructure.

The risk is that decisions made for technical expedience in managing different tools will constrain unnecessarily the ability of teachers to use these tools flexibly to discover new and innovative pedagogies. On the other hand, existing information on how to use the tools well from a pedagogical perspective can be hard to extract from the e-learning research literature, particularly if the teacher concerned is not an early adopter keen to tinker, but rather a busy practitioner concerned with efficacy and efficiency.

Pedagogical Constraints and Technical Standards

The risk of standards negatively impacting on pedagogical innovation and flexibility has been recognized by many in the field: "It is very difficult to define interchange standards that do not have some effect on functionality ... the priorities that different specifications make can represent a bias towards one educational approach amongst others" (CETIS 2004). Existing standard's conceptions of e-learning are limited and dominated by didactic and behavioural models rather than recognizing the rich diversity in pedagogical theory that is used to inform teaching in different disciplines (Blandin, 2004; Friesen, 2004a; Conole *et al.*, 2004; Ullrich, 2006), as well as the significant cultural differences and expectations held by disciplines (Littlejohn and Margaryan, 2006). Friesen (2004a) notes that "standards, specifications, and instances of content need to be conceptualized in terms of their pedagogical engagement and relevance, not in terms of their neutrality."

García-Barriocanal, Sicilia & Lytras (2007) discuss the challenge that when pedagogical classifications and recommendations are included in technical standards they provide limited information from single perspectives. Technical standards need to recognize the range of educational purposes particular technologies can support, depending on the intent of the teachers and the characteristics of the learners (Conole, Dyke, Oliver & Seale, 2004). A further complication is that existing standard's description of pedagogy is an end-point of a complex process. Standards need to describe the underlying theoretical and pedagogical objectives and the process that has been used to arrive at the current technology or activity (Sicilia, 2006). Attempts are being made to extend the richness of the metadata associated with technology use to encompass semantic information and ontologies (Al-Khalifa and Davis, 2006). However progress in semantic information use remains limited by the intent with which the metadata is used and the challenge of generating sufficient useful metadata for the majority of technology applications (Park, 2009).

A counter argument could be made that comment on standards by those engaged in teaching, supporting and developing e-learning is premature, and that a strong infrastructural framework is needed to support e-learning. Once we have such a framework, it is contended, we will then be able to add effective learning experiences as a form of "interior decoration" to the technological, organizational and economic framework provided (Welsch 2002). While this may have had some plausibility ten years ago, it must be noted that organizations such as IMS have only very recently started exploring more pedagogically founded aspects of e-learning. The work of the Student Induction to E-Learning project group (http://www.imsglobal.org/siel.cfm) and the Targeted Retention Systems project group (http://www.imsglobal.org/ia.html) has yet to result in public distribution of their proposed standards. There is also evidence to suggest that adding pedagogical concerns to existing standards is more complex than generally appreciated (Boyle, 2003).

Another risk arising from academic disengagement with the standards process is that established standards can be reified into an end in themselves. Compliance with the standard becomes the objective rather than a means to achieving wider outcomes, particularly those that the standard is only a limited abstraction of, rather than a complete description of the totality of the learning experience (Marshall, 2004). As Olivier and Liber (2003) ask "[The question is whether] eLearning standards will constrain Internet supported learning by freezing a sub-set of existing practices, or whether specifications can be provided that can support the development of new, enhanced, but yet to be developed approaches to learning which the Internet makes possible?"

In addition to being open to innovation and flexible enough to embrace new pedagogical approaches standards documents and the process used to create them needs to be able to evolve in a timeframe consistent with that of technology development. Technologies and pedagogies have complex relationships with each constantly redefining our perceptions of the other as experience and reflection generate new knowledge (Porter, 2005). The services approach to technical standards (Vossen and Westerkamp, 2008; Muñoz-Merino *et al.,* 2009) such as those described by the International e-Framework (http://www.e-framework.org/) may offer a more flexible approach to the technical aspects. Service design approaches may avoid the issue of technical inflexibility constraining pedagogical innovation and evolving good professional practice, but this activity still does not result in professional standards usable by teachers.

Professional and Pedagogical Standards for E-Learning Quality

" 'Professionalism' is commonly understood as an individual's adherence to a set of standards, code of conduct or collection of qualities that characterise accepted practice within a particular area of activity" (Universities UK *et al.,* 2004, p2). University teaching is increasingly seen as a professional activity distinct, but embracing, disciplinary research. The reconceptualisation of academic work by Boyer (2007) as well as the movements to professional qualifications in countries such as the UK (HEA, 2006) and Australia (Brew and Ginns, 2008) is supporting academics developing a stronger sense of their professional engagement in teaching.

Standards can have a significant positive benefit to university teachers as professional practitioners "Professional teaching standards can serve as an acknowledged reference point, defining expectations in a context reflecting aspirations, for staff, institutions, students and other stakeholders" (Universities UK *et al.,* 2004, p2). This depends on academic participation in the process rather than simply allowing the agenda to be defined by technologists (Mason, 2003). Ehlers (2007) argues that development of a quality culture in education requires the active participation of key stakeholders, including a development of professional conceptions of quality by teachers. The understandings of quality held by teachers (and the organizations within which they work) must be multidimensional constructs that recognize the myriad sources of student learning outcomes. Educational quality encompasses not just the teaching but also many of the organization's processes, infrastructure, disciplinary requirements as well as prior student experience and characteristics.

If academics are to take a more active role in developing professional standards informing pedagogy and university teaching then it is worth considering the form that the standards documents could usefully take. Technical standards are commonly specification documents describing how technology should behave in specific circumstances. The complexity of education, encompassing as it does the totality of human experience and knowledge, suggests that frameworks designed to be flexible rather than prescriptive are needed. The challenge is to avoid approaches dependent upon particular educational contexts or technologies.

In their simplest form these frameworks are guideline or heuristic documents that make statements about the student learning experience. Chickering and Gamson's (1987) Seven Principles is perhaps the most widely accepted heuristic or guideline used to guide practitioners seeking to ensure their work is high quality. They have been adapted to e-learning (Chickering and Ehrman, 1996; Graham, Cagiltay, Byung-Ro, Craner & Duffy, 2001) and few would argue that the principles are not important elements of a quality educational experience irrespective of the mode of delivery. The problem with the Seven Principles is that while the statements are clear, measuring whether they are being achieved and deciding how to improve individual or organizational performance of the items requires considerable additional work and experience.

This tension between generality and ease of application is also apparent in the technically based ISO/IEC 19796-1 quality standard for learning, education, and training (http://www.iso.org/iso/catalogue_detail?csnumber=33934). This standard provides a general framework for educational quality, but in its attempt to encompass the totality of educational work it is so general as to be essentially irrelevant to practitioners. Rather, it must instead be used by organizations as a guide for their own quality improvement processes (Pawlowski, 2007) diluting its wider role in defining professional approaches.

The need for standards as enablers for learning and teaching professionals was recognized in 2004 in the UK, along with the need for a framework that could be responsive to the range of demands placed on teachers in higher education: "[a standards framework] should also acknowledge that teaching takes place in a complex environment where staff have a multiplicity of roles. A standards framework would reflect appropriate expectations of the role in related academic areas, including disciplinary practice, and research and scholarship; and support areas, including specialist roles linked to innovative modes of delivery. The framework needs to recognise that teaching is one component of academic practice, and builds upon other activities and other expertise" (Universities UK *et al.* 2004, p6).

The HEA professional standards framework developed in the UK after a period of extensive consultation (HEA, 2006) aims to act as:

- an enabling mechanism to support the professional development of staff engaged in supporting learning;
- a means by which professional approaches to supporting student learning can be fostered through creativity, innovation and continuous development;
- a means of demonstrating to students and other stakeholders the professionalism that staff bring to the support of the student learning experience;
- a means to support consistency and quality of the student learning experience.

The HEA framework defines high-level descriptors for competencies in areas of teaching activity (e.g. "assessment and giving feedback to learners"), core knowledge of the subject and teaching (e.g. "how students learn, both generally and in the subject"), and professional values intrinsic to the teaching profession (e.g. "commitment to development of learning communities"). The framework does not specify how institutions must apply this framework or how staff can demonstrate their achievement of competence in the areas described. Institutions work with the HEA to become accredited in their use of the framework in a manner appropriate to their circumstances (Orr, 2008).

The HEA framework provides a strong encouragement for institutions to develop a culture valuing professional standards and supports an increasing professionalization of the education workforce, however identifying the elements that genuinely affect student learning outcomes remains challenging. Oliver (2005), in his review of issues facing those involved in promoting quality in e-learning, noted that the complexity and challenge of assessing the quality of learning and teaching prevents clear and unambiguous standards and criteria that can be widely adopted by practitioners and institutions. The use of technology and e-learning does, however, define a sufficiently limited scope consistent with a general framework. His framework describing quality e-learning (Oliver, Herrington, Stoney & Millar, 2006) encompasses input, process and output elements for students and institutions and attempts to cover the full range of activities needed for quality e-learning. The problem with such lists remains the lack of strong empirical evidence linking heuristics possessing strong face validity with specific outcomes for students (Mitchel, 2000; Conole, 2007). Consequently, practitioners and researchers have yet to agree on a common mechanism for validating standards and quality frameworks (Inglis, 2008).

Validation of standards will remain challenging until longitudinal studies demonstrating the impact of the standard on educational activities have been conducted. Inglis (2008) has identified the main validation techniques that have been used currently as:

- reviewing the research literature related to effectiveness in online learning;
- seeking input from an expert panel;
- undertaking empirical research;
- undertaking survey research;
- conducting pilot projects; and
- drawing on case studies.

Standards in the area of learning have another aspect beyond the technical and pedagogical concerns discussed above, which can prevent their use as supportive and developmental documents for professionals. Demers (2007, p34) identifies from the work of DiMaggio and Powell (1983) three mechanisms that drive institutional change:

- Coercive isomorphism which explains change as a consequence of formal informal pressures imposed on institutions externally, in the case of universities this includes the pressure to inform our teaching with research, and increasingly the need to produce graduates able to contribute to economic growth;
- Mimetic isomorphism which describes the tendency for institutions to adopt 'standard' or common approaches in uncertain times. This is seen in the adoption of popular management fads such as business process re-engineering or Total Quality Management, a trend that universities are not immune to;
- Normative isomorphism is change that is driven by professionalism and the emergence of 'legitimated professional practices' that result in pressure for institutions to conform because their staff are able to draw on organized professional networks and professional standards that guide their activities.

Coercive and mimetic isomorphism represent significant challenges to the identity of universities as collegial organizations owned by the academic faculty of the institution. Normative isomorphism can potentially ensure that staff retain the freedom to define their own agendas in e-learning, but only if we can agree on professional standards that are widely acceptable and compelling to institutional leaders as well as practitioners.

In taking ownership of the quality agenda there is also the need to be looking to the future, rather than repeating or improving what has gone before. Biggs (2001) distinguishes between retrospective quality assurance, essentially backward looking and associated with accountability and audit, and prospective quality assurance, being forward looking and supporting quality improvement and reflective practitioners. Biggs identifies the key components of quality assurance as being the *quality model*, or espoused theory underlying any decisions, the *quality enhancement* mechanism that enables improvement, and the *quality feasibility* mechanism that removes impediments that prevent improvement. In the next section, the eMM is presented as a quality improvement framework and standard that embodies these three aspects as well as encouraging a 'normative' model of reflection and improvement.

THE E-LEARNING MATURITY MODEL

The e-learning Maturity Model (eMM; Marshall and Mitchell, 2002) is a quality improvement framework developed to help guide organizations understanding their e-learning capabilities, which can also guide individual e-learning professionals in both the specifics of teaching with technology and also in their interactions with the work of others in their organization who provide essential infrastructure, support and an organizational direction to the use of technology. As a consequence of the desire for the eMM to support technological and organisational change, the meaning of e-learning implicit in the eMM is broadly defined. At the heart lies the impact of computers and related communication technologies on the range of activities traditionally undertaken by teachers and learners. However, as the eMM is institutionally focused, the model considers the wider implications of the use of digital technology, most particularly the systems and resources needed to ensure that the use of technology by students and teachers is efficient, effective, and can be sustained operationally and strategically.

The eMM does not rank institutions, but rather acknowledges the reality that all institutions will have aspects of strength and weakness that can be learnt from and improved. The rapid growth in the technologies being used, the ways that they are being applied across an ever widening group of academic disciplines and the evolving skills and experience of teachers and students means that e-learning is a moving target. Any benchmarking approach that presumes particular e-learning technologies or pedagogies is unlikely to meaningfully assess a range of institutions within a single country, let alone allow for useful international collaboration and comparison, particularly over an extended period of time.

The eMM uses as its quality model the capability maturity model originally developed to guide improvements in software development processes and now used in a wide variety of complex organizational contexts (Paulk, Curtis, Chrissis & Weber, 1993; El Emam, Drouin & Melo, 1998; SPICE, 2002). Capability maturity models propose that organizations need to develop a detailed self-awareness of complex activities they engage in if those activities are to be improved. Quality enhancement and quality feasibility are addressed within the eMM through the use of a defined set of processes and practices that enable the identification of areas of organizational strength and weakness in e-learning and which then form the basis of a guide to what areas could be addressed to improve the organization's e-learning capability.

As a capability maturity model, the eMM is designed to measure, analyse and improve e-learning capability. Capability in the eMM builds on the more general concept of organizational maturity and incorporates the ability of an institution to ensure that e-learning design, development and deployment is meeting the needs of the students, staff and institution. Critically, capability includes the ability of an institution to sustain e-learning delivery and the support of learning and teaching as demand grows and staff change. Capability is not an assessment of the skills or performance of individual staff or students, but rather a synergistic measure of the coherence and strength of the environment provided by the organization they work within.

The eMM assesses e-learning capability on five dimensions (Marshall and Mitchell, 2006). Rather than levels, which imply a hierarchical model of process improvement where capability is assessed and built in a layered and progressive manner, the concept underlying the eMM's use of dimensions is holistic capability. Each process is assessed from the synergistic perspectives of

Figure 1. eMM Process Dimensions

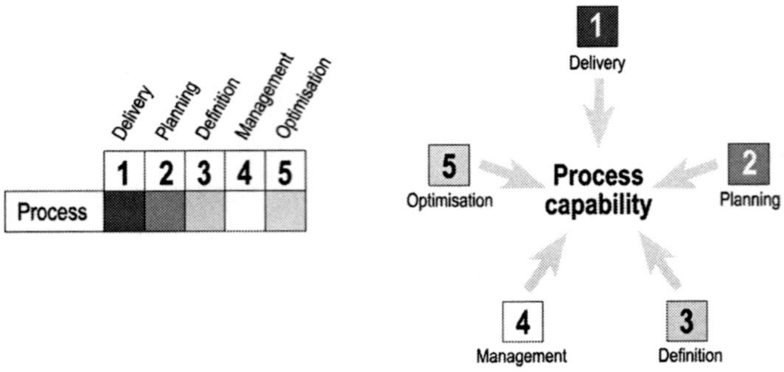

Delivery, Planning, Definition, Management and Optimisation (Figure 1).

The **Delivery** dimension is concerned with the creation and provision of process outcomes. Assessments of this dimension are aimed at determining the extent to which the process is seen to operate within the institution.

The **Planning** dimension assesses the use of predefined objectives and plans in conducting the work of the process. The use of predefined plans potentially makes processes more able to be managed effectively and reproduced if successful.

The **Definition** dimension covers the use of institutionally defined and documented standards, guidelines, templates and policies during the process implementation. An institution operating effectively within this dimension has clearly defined how a given process should be performed. This does not mean that the staff of the institution follows this guidance.

The **Management** dimension is concerned with how the institution manages the process implementation and ensures the quality of the outcomes. Capability within this dimension reflects the measurement and control of process outcomes.

The **Optimisation** dimension captures the extent an institution is using formal approaches to improve the activities of the process. Capability of this dimension reflects a culture of continuous improvement.

The eMM divides the capability of institutions to sustain and deliver e-learning into thirty five processes grouped into five major categories or process areas (Table 1) that indicate a shared concern. It should be noted however that all of the processes are interrelated to some degree, particularly through shared practices and the perspectives of the five dimensions. Each process in the eMM is broken down within each dimension into practices that define how the process outcomes might be achieved by institutions (Figure 2). The practice statements attempt to capture directly measurable activities for each process and dimension. The practices are derived from an extensive review of the literature, international workshops and experience from their application (Marshall, 2008).

Over the last eight years the eMM has been developed, refined and validated through a series of projects conducted in New Zealand (Marshall, 2005; Marshall, 2006a), Australia (Marshall, Mitchell & Beames, 2009), the United Kingdom (Sero, 2007; Bacsich, 2008; University of London, 2008) and the United States (Marshall, Udas & May, 2008). Using the Inglis (2008) framework discussed above it can be seen that the eMM is now a mature and well validated framework (Table 2).

An important component of the eMM is that it does not define the means by which an activity must be undertaken, just that it needs to be addressed. This allows for innovation, awareness of specific contextual aspects and a continuous development of professional understanding of what

Table 1. eMM Version 2.3 Processes (revised from Marshall 2006b)

Learning: Processes that directly impact on pedagogical aspects of e-learning	
L1.	Learning objectives guide the design and implementation of courses.
L2.	Students are provided with mechanisms for interaction with teaching staff and other students.
L3.	Students are provided with e-learning skill development.
L4.	Students are provided with expected staff response times to student communications.
L5.	Students receive feedback on their performance within courses.
L6.	Students are provided with support in developing research and information literacy skills.
L7.	Learning designs and activities actively engage students.
L8.	Assessment is designed to progressively build student competence.
L9.	Student work is subject to specified timetables and deadlines.
L10.	Courses are designed to support diverse learning styles and learner capabilities.
Development: Processes surrounding the creation and maintenance of e-learning resources	
D1.	Teaching staff are provided with design and development support when engaging in e-learning.
D2.	Course development, design and delivery are guided by e-learning procedures and standards.
D3.	An explicit plan links e-learning technology, pedagogy and content used in courses.
D4.	Courses are designed to support disabled students.
D5.	All elements of the physical e-learning infrastructure are reliable, robust and sufficient.
D6.	All elements of the physical e-learning infrastructure are integrated using defined standards.
D7.	E-learning resources are designed and managed to maximise reuse.
Support: Processes surrounding the support and operational management of e-learning	
S1.	Students are provided with technical assistance when engaging in e-learning.
S2.	Students are provided with library facilities when engaging in e-learning.
S3.	Student enquiries, questions and complaints are collected and managed formally.
S4.	Students are provided with personal and learning support services when engaging in e-learning.
S5.	Teaching staff are provided with e-learning pedagogical support and professional development.
S6.	Teaching staff are provided with technical support in using digital information created by students.
Evaluation: Processes surrounding the evaluation and quality control of e-learning through its entire lifecycle	
E1.	Students are able to provide regular feedback on the quality and effectiveness of their e-learning experience.
E2.	Teaching staff are able to provide regular feedback on quality and effectiveness of their e-learning experience.
E3.	Regular reviews of the e-learning aspects of courses are conducted.
Organisation: Processes associated with institutional planning and management	
O1.	Formal criteria guide the allocation of resources for e-learning design, development and delivery.
O2.	Institutional learning and teaching policy and strategy explicitly address e-learning.
O3.	E-learning technology decisions are guided by an explicit plan.
O4.	Digital information use is guided by an institutional information integrity plan.
O5.	E-learning initiatives are guided by explicit development plans.
O6.	Students are provided with information on e-learning technologies prior to starting courses.
O7.	Students are provided with information on e-learning pedagogies prior to starting courses.
O8.	Students are provided with administration information prior to starting courses.
O9.	E-learning initiatives are guided by institutional strategies and operational plans.

Figure 2. Relationships between processes, practices and dimensions

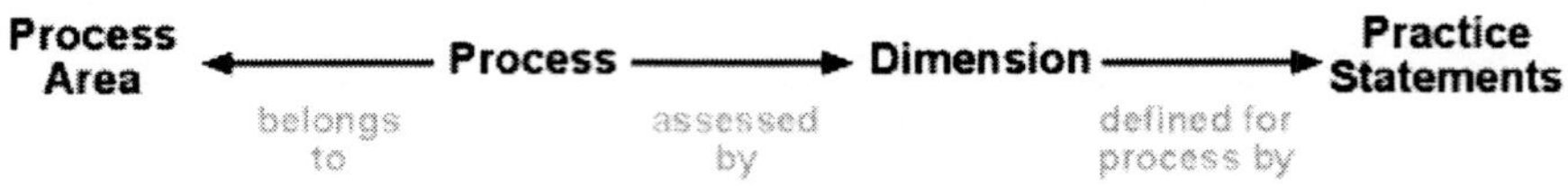

constitutes 'good practice' in any area of work. Observational models which describe the growth in complexity and use of technology such as those of Taylor (2001) and Monson (2005) describe historic techniques which may or may not be reliable guides for the future. Other models like CITSCAPE and MIT90 (Weedon, Jorna & Broumley, 2004; de Freitas, 2006) and many maturity models (e.g. Neuhauser, 2004) describe the increasing sophistication of technology use, but in merely describing what has happened in the past they fail to provide a mechanism for supporting and enhancing that change. Rigid definitions of quality are inconsistent with the pace of change in e-learning currently, both as a result of technology developments (Kurzweil, 2005) as well as research on pedagogy and the changing student demographics within higher education.

Figure 3 provides an example of the high level overview that the eMM provides organizations of their capability. The visual approach adopted is intended to make identification of patterns of capability more apparent when placed in a wider sector or international context. When an aspect of interest is identified, an organization can then examine the detail of the practice assessments that have resulted in that process assessment, and subsequently after consideration of all such areas, prioritise which practices will be addressed.

Comparing the institutional assessments in Figure 3 reveals a gradient of capability from left to right within each set of results, suggesting stronger capability in the Delivery dimension and weakest in the Optimisation dimension. This reflects the observation that many institutions are struggling to monitor and measure their own performance in e-learning (Management dimension) and that a culture of systematic and strategically-led continuous improvement of e-learning is lacking (Optimisation dimension).

Analyses such as those presented in Figure 3 can be used to identify areas of common weak-

Table 2. eMM validation activities

Validation Activity	eMM Activity
reviewing the research literature related to effectiveness in online learning	Creation of the original process set (Marshall and Mitchell, 2003), expansion to the current processes and practices (Marshall, 2006b)
seeking input from an expert panel	Expert consultation workshops conducted in New Zealand, Australia and the UK (Marshall, 2008)
undertaking empirical research	Correlation analysis with other factors potentially affecting quality (Neal and Marshall, 2008)
undertaking survey research	Surveys of practitioners (Marshall, 2008)
conducting pilot projects	Application in New Zealand (Marshall, 2005; Marshall, 2006a), Australia (Marshall *et al.*, 2009), the United Kingdom (Sero, 2007; Bacsich, 2008; University of London, 2008) and the United States (Marshall et al., 2008)
drawing on case studies	Sero (2007), University of London (2008)

Figure 3. eMM capability assessments of international universities

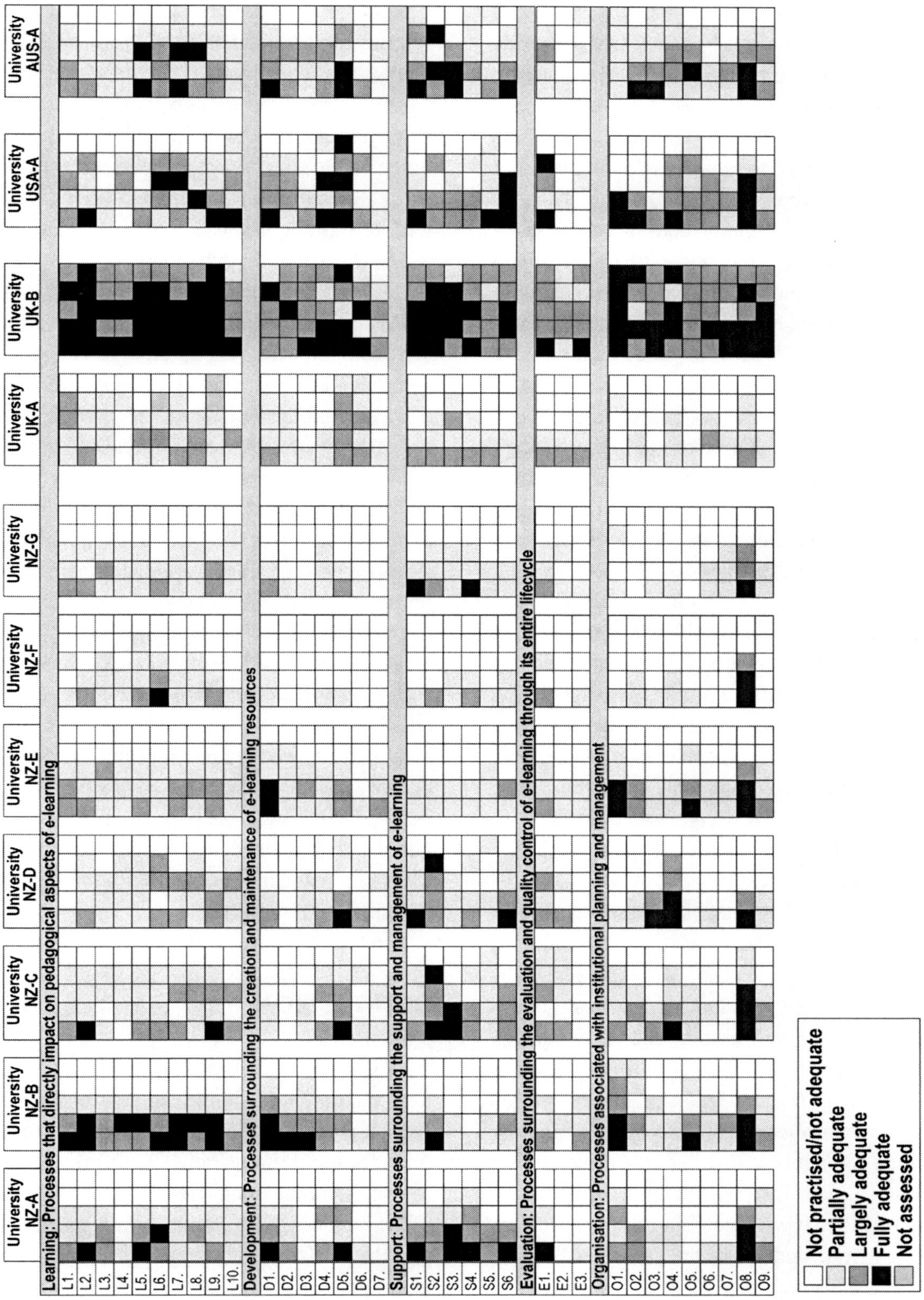

ness (process D7 and the E2 for example) or help place the individual institutional assessments in a regional or international context that can guide priority setting and planning. However, even in the absence of an institutional assessment an individual practitioner can use the model to reflect on their own work and improve those areas under their immediate control.

As a simple example, consider the use of learning objective statements. Learning objectives are a key component of modern e-learning course design and can be a valuable tool for communicating to students what a particular course or unit is intended to provide for them as part of an integrated programme of study (Allan, 1996; Laurillard, 2002). The importance of this concept means that the eMM recognizes the use of learning objectives as a major aspect of two processes L1 (Learning objectives guide the design and implementation of courses) and D3 (An explicit plan links e-learning technology, pedagogy and content used in courses). Table 3 summarises the practice statements relating to learning objectives for each. These statements provide a clear direction for practitioners and a guide to the specific ways they should use learning objectives, taking them from simply general statements about the course to specific guides for design and a mechanism for linking disparate course elements explicitly for students.

The individual processes themselves form a guide to addressing key aspects of learning an teaching. For example (Table 4) process L2 (Students are provided with mechanisms for interaction with teaching staff and other students) expands on the concept of interaction by describing the need to provide contact details, manage expectations of responsiveness, and explain the how the provided communication tools are expected to be used by students for their learning, as well as a range of other items, including the need to get feedback from students so the experience can be improved.

An important part of the use of the eMM in this way is that individual staff should not feel responsible for addressing all of these practices themselves. The practice statements can serve as a prompt for conversations with colleagues and managers as a way of taking collective responsibility and driving improvements from the bottom up as well as from institutional leaders, and as a tool for framing discussions setting priorities for action (Marshall, 2009b).

Beyond consideration of specific issues the eMM has been expressed as a tool for framing staff competencies and guiding professional development activities (Cappelli and Smithies, 2008) and a means of providing a wider context for staff researching their own teaching and understanding the student experience of their courses (Petrova and Sinclair, 2005). In the wider organizational context it can inform analysis of functional responsibilities and roles and the impact that is having on process capability and outcomes (Calverley, Cappelli, Dexter, Petch and Smithies, 2007).

As a proposed professional development framework it is worth considering the extent to which the eMM maps against the HEA's areas of activity for their professional standards framework (Table 5). Clearly, the eMM covers these areas in detail, and so could easily be used as the basis of either informal or formal professional development in a manner consistent with the objectives of the HEA framework.

CONCLUSION

"...a truly practical standard is one that will be used because it is simple enough to follow and flexible enough to allow for creativity... a tool that allows you to do more, rather than a grim necessity to which you must adhere" (Welsch 2002). The eMM provides a rich framework intended to support the work of professionals in e-learning. The underlying quality model has been proven in the many areas of information technology work and

Table 3. eMM processes L1 and D3 coverage of learning objectives

L1: Learning objectives guide the design and implementation of courses
Delivery
Course documentation includes a clear statement of learning objectives.
Learning objectives are linked explicitly throughout learning and assessment activities using consistent language.
Learning objectives are linked explicitly to wider programme or institutional objectives.
Learning objectives support student outcomes beyond the recall of information.
Course workload expectations and assessment tasks are consistent with course learning objectives.
Planning
Course documentation templates require the clear statement of learning objectives.
Learning objectives guide e–learning design and (re)development decisions regarding content and activities.
Learning objectives guide e–learning design and (re)development decisions regarding technology and pedagogy.
Institutional reviews monitor the linkages between course learning objectives and wider programme or institutional objectives.
Institutional reviews are guided by course learning objectives when assessing course structure, learning design and content.
E-Learning design and (re)development is guided by a researched evidence base of effective learning objectives and associated e-learning activities.
E–learning design and (re)development plans formally link learning objectives to institutional strategic and operational plans.
Staff are provided with assistance when engaged in e-learning design and (re)development.
Definition
Institutional policies require that a formal statement of learning objectives is part of all course documentation provided to students.
Teaching staff are provided with support resources (including training, guidelines and examples) on developing learning objectives that address the full range of cognitive outcomes appropriate to the discipline, pedagogical approach and students.
Teaching staff are provided with support resources (including training, guidelines and examples) on using learning objectives to guide e-learning design and (re)development.
Teaching staff are provided with support resources (including training, guidelines and examples) on assessing student achievement of learning objectives.
Institutional e-learning policies are guided by institutional learning objectives for all students.
Staff are provided with a researched evidence base of effective learning objectives and associated e-learning activities.
Management
Compliance with policies, standards and guidelines governing the incorporation of learning objectives in e-learning design and development activities is regularly monitored.
A variety of qualitative and quantitative metrics are used to assess student achievement of course learning objectives.
Course learning objectives are regularly monitored to ensure that they address the full range of cognitive outcomes.
Course learning objectives are regularly monitored to ensure that they are effective.
E-learning design and (re)development activities are subject to formal quality assurance reviews at key milestones.
Financial costs and benefits of delivering course learning objectives are regularly monitored.
Feedback collected regularly from students regarding the effectiveness of e-learning activities.
Feedback collected regularly from staff regarding the effectiveness of e-learning activities.
Optimisation
Information on student achievement of learning objectives guides e-learning design and (re)development.
Institutional learning objectives are guided by learning and teaching strategic plans.

Table 4. eMM process L2

L2: Students are provided with mechanisms for interaction with teaching staff and other students
Delivery
Courses provide a variety of mechanisms for interaction between staff and students.
Students are provided with teaching staff email addresses.
Students are provided with technical support for all of the communication channels in use.
Planning
Students are provided with course documentation describing all of the communication channels used.
Students are provided with course documentation describing how different communication channels will support their learning.
Course (re)development plans include a structured interaction design incorporating a variety of communication channels.
Course activities require the use of the communication channels.
Course documentation describes appropriate uses of different communication channels.
Course delivery plans include regular monitoring of communication channels.
E-Learning design and (re)development is guided by a researched evidence base of effective e-learning communication and interaction examples.
Institutional reviews monitor the effectiveness of the interaction designs and communication channels.
Definition
Institutional policies define requirements for staff responsiveness to student communication.
Institutional policies define requirements that staff support student engagement through a mix of different types of interaction.
Teaching staff are provided with support resources (including training, guidelines and examples) on effective ways of using communication channels to support student learning.
Standard communication channels are provided in all courses.
Institutional policies define requirements for appropriate use of communication channels.
Staff are provided with a researched evidence base of effective communication and interaction activities.
Management
Student and staff use of communication channels is regularly monitored.
Feedback collected regularly from students regarding the effectiveness of different communication channels.
Feedback collected regularly from staff regarding the effectiveness of the communication channels.
The impact of the use of communication channels on student learning is regularly monitored.
Financial costs and benefits of communication channels are regularly monitored.
Optimisation
Information on interaction between students and teaching staff guides resourcing of communication channels.
Information on interaction between students and teaching staff guides training and support resourcing.
Information on interaction between students and teaching staff guides the reuse of effective learning and teaching activities.
Information on interaction between students and teaching staff guides e-learning strategic planning.

shown in the series of international applications to be valid and useful to the individual institutions as well as the wider sectors and agencies supporting institutions. In this chapter the case has been made that it also provides a standard for individual e-learning professionals wishing to reflect on their role, the support they receive from their organization, and how the experience of e-learning for themselves and their students can be improved.

E-learning standards to date have been mechanisms for compliance, interoperability and

Table 5. eMM mapping to the HEA professional standards framework areas

HEA Areas of activity	eMM Process coverage
1. Design and planning of learning activities and/or programmes of study	Development process area processes D1-D4
2. Teaching and/or supporting student learning	Learning process area, with particular focus in L3, L5, L6, L8 and L10
3. Assessment and giving feedback to learners	Processes L5 and L8
4. Developing effective environments and student support and guidance	Support process area process S1-S4
5. Integration of scholarship, research and professional activities with teaching and supporting learning	Research on teaching and use of research to support teaching improvement is a specific aspect of the Planning and Definition dimensions of most processes
6. Evaluation of practice and continuing professional development	Evaluation process area.

specifications for technologists (Marshall 2004). To genuinely support professionalization of the e-learning experience they need to be much more:

- Standards must reflect the diversity of student learning capabilities and desired outcomes;
- Standards must evolve to meet the challenges of new forms of technology, and new types of pedagogy, and ideally they should stimulate the discussion, application and research that result in that evolution;
- Standards must be enablers of effective practice rather than constraints on the creativity and burdens to the passion of teachers;
- Standards must reflect an evidence base of effective teaching practice and research into ways of improving student learning;
- Standards must be expressed in a way that enables efficient determination of compliance and an ability to "benchmark" or document that compliance;
- Standards must support the management of institutions in identifying areas in need of development and strategic decisions about e-learning directions for the institution as a whole;
- Standards must support the development of e-learning capability across entire sectors of tertiary education, rather than encouraging piecemeal and isolated initiatives.

In conclusion, one more point should be made. The eMM is a complex model that asks challenging questions of an organization's e-learning activities and implies high expectations on individuals working in the field. No apology is made for this; e-learning represents a significant development in learning and teaching with the potential to reframe the experience of education for all participants. Our professional standards should similarly describe high aspirations for us and challenge individuals and organizations to do more than what has gone before: "We would also argue that the models themselves can act as a guide providing specific goals which educational institutions can aspire to and work towards" (Underwood and Dillon, 2005, p263).

REFERENCES

Al-Khalifa, H. S., & Davis, H. C. (2006). The evolution of metadata from standards to semantics in E-learning applications. In *Proceedings of the Seventeenth ACM Conference on Hypertext 2006* (pp. 69-72). New York: ACM Press.

Allan, J. (1996). Learning outcomes in higher education. *Studies in Higher Education, 21*(1), 93–108. doi:10.1080/03075079612331381487

Bacsich, P. (2008). *Higher Education Academy/ JISC E-learning Benchmarking Phase 2 Overview Report. Report to the Higher Education Academy 14pp.* Retrieved August 10, 2009, from http://elearning.heacademy.ac.uk/weblogs/benchmarking/wp-content/uploads/2008/04/BenchmarkingPhase2_BELAreport.pdf

Biggs, J. (2001). The reflective institution: assuring and enhancing the quality of teaching and Learning. *Higher Education, 41*, 221–238. doi:10.1023/A:1004181331049

Blandin, B. (2004). Are e-learning standards neutral? In *Proceedings CALIE 04: International Conference on Computer Aided Learning in Engineering Education*, Grenoble, France.

Boyer, E. L. (1997). *Scholarship reconsidered: Priorities of the professoriate.* San Francisco: Jossey-Bass.

Boyle, T. (2003). Design principles for authoring dynamic, reusable learning objects. *Australian Journal of Educational Technology, 19*(1), 46–58.

Brew, A., & Ginns, P. (2008). The relationship between engagement in the scholarship of teaching and learning and students' course experiences. *Assessment & Evaluation in Higher Education, 33*(5), 535–545. doi:10.1080/02602930701698959

Calverley, G., Cappelli, T., Dexter, H., Petch, J., & Smithies, A. (2007). Changing practices in the development of digital resources. In *Proceedings of SOLSTICE 2007 Researching E-Learning for Innovation and Development*, Edge Hill University, UK, 11 May 2007.

Cappelli, T., & Smithies, A. (2008). Learning Needs Analysis through Synthesis of Maturity Models and Competency Frameworks. In K. McFerrin et al. (Eds.), *Proceedings of Society for Information Technology and Teacher Education International Conference 2008* (pp. 2448-2455). Chesapeake, VA: AACE.

CETIS. (2004). *Learning technology standards: An overview.* Retrieved August 10, 2009, from http://zope.cetis.ac.uk/static/standards.html

Chickering, A., & Gamson, Z. (1987). Seven principles of good practice in undergraduate education. *AAHE Bulletin, 39*, 3–7.

Chickering, A. W., & Ehrmann, S. (1996). Implementing the seven principles: Technology as lever. *AAHE Bulletin, 49*(2), 3–6.

Conole, G. (2007). What constitutes good research in e-learning—are there lessons we can draw from the Research Assessment Exercise? *ALT-J, 15*(3), 183–188. doi:10.1080/09687760701673576

Conole, G., Dyke, M., Oliver, M., & Seale, J. (2004). Mapping pedagogy and tools for effective learning design. *Computers & Education, 43*(1–2), 17–33. doi:10.1016/j.compedu.2003.12.018

de Freitas, S. (2006). *Think piece for Becta On the 'e-mature learner.'* Retrieved 25 February, 2009, from http://tre.ngfl.gov.uk/uploads/materials/24877/Think_piece_for_BectaSdF.doc

Demers, C. (2007). *Organizational Change Theories: A Synthesis.* Los Angeles, CA: Sage Publications Incorporated.

Devedzic, V., Jovanovic, J., & Gasevic, D. (2007). The pragmatics of current e-learning standards. *IEEE Internet Computing*, (May-June): 19–27. doi:10.1109/MIC.2007.73

DiMaggio, P., & Powell, W. (1983). The iron cage revisited: Institutional isomorphism and collective rationality in organizational fields. *American Sociological Review*, *48*, 147–160. doi:10.2307/2095101

Duval, E., & Hodgins, W. (2003). A LOM Research Agenda. In *Proceedings of WWW2003 - Twelfth International World Wide Web Conference*, 20-24 May 2003, Budapest, Hungary (2003). Retrieved August 10, 2009, from http://www2003.org/cdrom/papers/alternate/P659/p659-duval.html.html

EduSpecs. (2004). *Benefits of specifications and standards*. Retrieved August 10, 2009, from http://www.eduspecs.ca/pub/specificationsandstandards/benefits_of_standards.html

Ehlers, U.-D. (2007). Quality Literacy - Competencies for Quality Development in Education and e-Learning. *Journal of Educational Technology & Society*, *10*(2), 96–108.

El Emam, K. Drouin, J-N. & Melo, W. (1998). *SPICE: The theory and practice of software process improvement and capability determination*. California: IEEE Computer Society.

Friesen, N. (2004a). Learning objects and standards: Pedagogical neutrality and engagement. In *Proceedings of the IEEE International Conference on Advanced Learning Technologies*. Joensuu, Finland. Retrieved August 10, 2009, from http://phenom.educ.ualberta.ca/n/papers/learning_objects_pedagogical_neutrality.pdf

Friesen, N. (2004b). Three Objections to Learning Objects. In McGreal, R. (Ed.). *Online Education Using Learning Objects*. London: Routledge/Falmer. Retrieved August 10, 2009, from http://phenom.educ.ualberta.ca/~nfriesen/

Friesen, N. (2005). Interoperability and learning objects: An overview of e-learning standardization. *Interdisciplinary Journal of Knowledge and Learning Objects*, *1*, 23–31.

Garcia, R., Blat, J., et al. (2004). Limitations of some eLearning standards for supporting learning. In *Proceedings of the International Conference of Interactive Computer-Aided Learning*, ICL 2004 (in cooperation with ACM-Austrian Chapter, and supported by IEEE Education Society), Villach, Austria, ICL. Retrieved August 10, 2009, from http://www.iua.upf.edu/~dgriffiths/papers/garcia-griffiths_villach.pdf

García-Barriocanal, E., Sicilia, M.-A., & Lytras, M. (2007). Evaluating pedagogical classification frameworks for learning objects: A case study. *Computers in Human Behavior*, *23*, 2641–2655. doi:10.1016/j.chb.2006.08.001

Graham, C., Cagiltay, K., Byung-Ro, L., Craner, J., & Duffy, T. (2001). Seven principles of effective teaching: A practical lens for evaluating online courses. *The Technology Source*, March/April 2001. Retrieved August 10, 2009, from http://technologysource.org/article/seven_principles_of_effective_teaching/

HEA. (2006). *The UK Professional Standards Framework for teaching and supporting learning in higher education*. New York: Higher Education Academy. Retrieved August 10, 2009, from http://www.heacademy.ac.uk/assets/York/documents/ourwork/professional/ProfessionalStandards-Framework.pdf.

IEEE. (2002). *IEEE 1484.12.1-2002 IEEE Standard for Learning Object Metadata*. Retrieved August 10, 2009, from http://ltsc.ieee.org/wg12/index.html

IMS. (2003). *IMS Content Packaging Specification Version 1.1.3*. Retrieved August 10, 2009, from http://www.imsglobal.org/content/packaging/

Inglis, A. (2008). Approaches to the validation of quality frameworks for e-learning. *Quality Assurance in Education*, *16*(4), 347–362. doi:10.1108/09684880810906490

ISO/IEC. (1996). *Guide 2: Standardization and related activities - General vocabulary*. Geneva: International Standards Organisation/International Electrotechnical Commission.

Kurzweil, R. (2005). *The singularity is near*. New York: Penguin.

Laurillard, D. (2002). *Rethinking University Teaching: A Conversational Framework for the Effective Use of Learning Technologies* (2nd ed.). London: Routledge. doi:10.4324/9780203304846

Littlejohn, A., & Margaryan, A. (2006). Cultural issues in the sharing and reuse of resources for learning. *Research and Practice in Technology Enhanced Learning*, *1*(3), 269–284. doi:10.1142/S1793206806000184

MacGregor, R. C. (1993). Are we recognising the organisational impact on educational software design? *Australian Journal of Educational Technology*, *9*(1), 59–68.

Marshall, S. (2004). E-learning standards: Open enablers of learning or compliance strait jackets? In R. Atkinson, C. McBeath, D. Jonas-Dwyer & R. Phillips (Eds), *Beyond the comfort zone: Proceedings of the 21st ASCILITE Conference* (pp. 596-605). Perth, 5-8 December.

Marshall, S. (2005). *Determination of New Zealand Tertiary Institution E-Learning Capability: An Application of an E-Learning Maturity Model: Report on the E-Learning Maturity Model Evaluation of the New Zealand Tertiary Sector*. Report to the New Zealand Ministry of Education. 132pp. Retrieved January 10, 2006, from http://www.utdc.vuw.ac.nz/research/emm/documents/SectorReport.pdf

Marshall, S. (2006a). *E-Learning Maturity Model Version Two: New Zealand Tertiary Institution E-Learning Capability: Informing and Guiding E-Learning Architectural Change and Development Project Report*. Report to the New Zealand Ministry of Education. 118pp. Retrieved August 10, 2009, from http://www.utdc.vuw.ac.nz/research/emm/documents/versiontwo/20060726TeLRFReport.pdf

Marshall, S. (2006b). *eMM Version Two Process Descriptions*. Wellington: Victoria University of Wellington. Report to the New Zealand Ministry of Education. 157pp. Retrieved August 10, 2009, from http://www.utdc.vuw.ac.nz/research/emm/documents/versiontwo/20060726ProcessDescriptions.pdf

Marshall, S. (2009a). (in press). A Quality Framework for Continuous Improvement of E-Learning: The E-Learning Maturity Model. *Journal of Distance Education*.

Marshall, S. (2009b). Benchmarking e-learning: Now what can we do when we have no money? *Online Educa Berlin 15th International Conference on Technology Supported Learning and Training*, 2-4 December, Berlin, Germany (abstract accepted).

Marshall, S., & Mitchell, G. (2002). An E-Learning Maturity Model?' In *Proceedings of the 19th Annual Conference of the Australian Society for Computers in Learning in Tertiary Education* (Auckland, 2002), Australian Society for Computers in Learning in Tertiary Education. Retrieved January 10, 2006, from http://www.unitec.ac.nz/ascilite/proceedings/papers/173.pdf

Marshall, S., & Mitchell, G. (2003). Potential Indicators of e-Learning Process Capability, In *Proceedings of EDUCAUSE in Australasia 2003* (Adelaide, May 6-9, 2003), EDUCAUSE. Retrieved January 10, 2006, from http://www.utdc.vuw.ac.nz/research/emm/documents/1009anav.pdf

Marshall, S., & Mitchell, G. (2004). Applying SPICE to e-Learning: An E-Learning Maturity Model? In *Proceedings of the Sixth Australasian Computing Education Conference* (Dunedin, January, 2004). Retrieved January 10, 2006, from http://portal.acm.org/ft_gateway.cfm?id=979993&type=pdf&coll=GUIDE&dl=GUIDE&CFID=62903527&CFTOKEN=3085292

Marshall, S., & Mitchell, G. (2005). *E-Learning Process Maturity in the New Zealand Tertiary Sector*. Paper presented at the EDUCAUSE in Australasia 2005 Conference, (Auckland, April 5-8, 2005). Retrieved January 10, 2006, from http://www.utdc.vuw.ac.nz/research/emm/documents/E-LearningProcessMaturity.pdf

Marshall, S., & Mitchell, G. (2006). Assessing sector e-learning capability with an e-learning maturity model. In *Proceedings of the Association for Learning Technologies Conference*, 2006, Edinburgh, UK.

Marshall, S., Mitchell, G., & Beames, S. (2009). *Report on the ACODE eMM Project*. Report to the Australasian Council on Open and Distance Education. 88pp. Retrieved August 10, 2009, from http://www.utdc.vuw.ac.nz/research/emm/acode/20090625ACODEReport.pdf

Marshall, S., Udas, K., & May, J. (2008). *Assessing Online Learning Process Maturity: the e-Learning Maturity Model*. Paper presented at the 14th Annual Sloan-C International Conference on Online Learning, Orlando Florida, 6-7 November, 2008.

Marshall, S. J. (2008). What are the key factors that lead to effective adoption and support of e-learning by institutions? In *Proceedings of HERDSA 2008* (Rotorua, New Zealand, HERDSA).

Marshall, S. J., & Mitchell, G. (2007). Benchmarking International E-learning Capability with the E-Learning Maturity Model. In *Proceedings of EDUCAUSE in Australasia 2007*, 29 April - 2 May 2007, Melbourne, Australia. Retrieved January 8, 2008, from http://www.caudit.edu.au/educause-australasia07/authors_papers/Marshall-103.pdf

Mason, J. (2003). Secret standards business? In *Proceedings EduCause in Australasia 2003*, Adelaide, Australia.

Mitchell, P. D. (2000). The impact of educational technology: a radical reappraisal of research methods. In Squires, D., Conole, G., & Jacobs, G. (Eds.), *The changing face of learning technology* (pp. 51–58). Cardiff: University Wales Press.

Monson, D. (2005). Blackboard Inc., An Educause platinum partner - the educational technology framework: charting a path toward a networked learning environment. Paper presented at the *Educause Western Regional Conference, April 26-28, 2005*, San Francisco, CA, USA. San Francisco: Educause. Retrieved February 25, 2009, from http://www.educause.edu/WRC05/Program/4954?PRODUCT_CODE=WRC05/CORP05

Muñoz-Merino, P. J., Kloos, C. D., & Naranjo, J. F. (2009). Enabling interoperability for LMS educational services. *Computer Standards & Interfaces*, *31*, 484–498. doi:10.1016/j.csi.2008.06.009

Neal, T., & Marshall, S. (2008). *Report on the Distance and Flexible Education Capability Assessment of the New Zealand ITP Sector*. Confidential Report to the New Zealand Tertiary Education Committee and Institutes of Technology and Polytechnics Distance and Flexible Education Steering Group.

Neuhauser, C. (2004). A maturity model: Does it provide a path for online course design? *The Journal of Interactive Online Learning, 3*(1). Retrieved February 25, 2009, from http://www.ncolr.org/jiol/issues/PDF/3.1.3.pdf

Oliver, R. (2005). Quality assurance and e-learning: Blue skies and pragmatism. *ALT-J, 13*(3), 173–187. doi:10.1080/09687760500376389

Oliver, R., Herrington, A., Stoney, S., & Millar, J. (2006). Authentic teaching and learning standards that assure quality higher education. In Herrington, A., & Herrington, J. (Eds.), *Authentic learning environments in higher education*. Hershey, PA: Idea Group.

Olivier, B., & Liber, O. (2003). Learning content interoperability standards. In Littlejohn, A. (Ed.), *Reusing online resources*. London, UK: Kogan Page.

Orr, K. (2008). Room for improvement? The impact of compulsory professional development for teachers in England's further education sector. *Professional Development in Education*, *34*(1), 97–108. doi:10.1080/13674580701832627

Park, J.-R. (2009). Metadata Quality in Digital Repositories: A Survey of the Current State of the Art. *Cataloging & Classification Quarterly*, *47*(3-4), 213–228. doi:10.1080/01639370902737240

Paulk, M. C., Curtis, B., Chrissis, M. B., & Weber, C. V. (1993). Capability Maturity Model, Version 1.1. *IEEE Software*, *10*(4), 18–27. doi:10.1109/52.219617

Pawlowski, J. M. (2007). The Quality Adaptation Model: Adaptation and Adoption of the Quality Standard ISO/IEC 19796-1 for Learning, Education, and Training. *Journal of Educational Technology & Society*, *10*(2), 3–16.

Petrova, K., & Sinclair, R. (2005). Business undergraduates learning online: A one semester snapshot. *International Journal of Education and Development using ICT, 1*(4). Retrieved August 10, 2009, from http://ijedict.dec.uwi.edu//viewarticle.php?id=100&layout=html

Porter, S. (2005). Issues in the relationship between technology and practice. *ALT-J*, *13*(3), 231–240. doi:10.1080/09687760500376496

Sero. (2007). *Baseline Study of e-Activity in Scotland's Colleges: Report to the Scottish Funding Council*, July 2007. Retrieved August 30, 2007, from http://www.sfc.ac.uk/information/information_learning/presentations_publications/sero_e_activity_study.pdf

Sicilia, M.-A. (2006). Semantic learning designs: recording assumptions and guidelines. *British Journal of Educational Technology*, *37*(3), 331–350. doi:10.1111/j.1467-8535.2006.00609.x

Tannenbaum, A. (1981). *Computer Networks* (2nd ed.). New York: Prentice-Hall.

Taylor, J. (2001). *Fifth generation distance education*. Keynote Address presented at the 20th ICDE World Conference, Düsseldorf, Germany, 1-5 April 2001.

Ullrich, C. (2006). The learning-resource-type is dead, long live the learning-resource-type! *Learning Objects and Learning Designs*, *1*(1), 7–15.

Underwood, J., & Dillon, G. (2005). Capturing complexity through maturity modelling. In Somekh, B., & Lewin, C. (Eds.), *Research Methods in the Social Sciences* (pp. 260–264). London: Sage.

Universities, U. K. The Standing Conference of Principals, The Higher Education Academy, The Higher Education Funding Council for England, The Scottish Higher Education Funding Council, The Higher Education Funding Council for Wales & the Department for Employment and Learning, Northern Ireland (2004). *Towards a framework of professional teaching standards*. Retrieved August 10, 2009, from http://www.scop.ac.uk/downloads/ProfStand.doc

University of London. (2008). *Benchmarking eLearning at the University of London: Report from the steering group*. London: University of London. Retrieved August 10, 2009, from http://www.londonexternal.ac.uk/quality/comte_zone/sys_tech_sub/stsc2/documents/stsc2_3.pdf

Varlamis, I., & Apostolakis, I. (2006). The present and future of standards for e-learning technologies. *Interdisciplinary Journal of Knowledge and Learning Objects*, *2*, 59–74.

Vossen, G., & Westerkamp, P. (2008). Why service-orientation could make e-learning standards obsolete. *International Journal of Technology Enhanced Learning*, *1*(1/2), 85–97. doi:10.1504/IJTEL.2008.020232

Weedon, E., Jorna, K., & Broumley, L. (2004). Closing the gaps in institutional development of networked learning: How do policy and strategy inform practice to sustain innovation? In *Proceedings of the Networked Learning Conference 2004*, 1-7 April, 2004 at Lancaster University, UK. Retrieved February 25, 2008, from http://www.networkedlearningconference.org.uk/past/nlc2004/proceedings/symposia/symposium8/weedon_et_al.htm

Welsch, E. (2002). SCORM: Clarity or calamity? *Online Learning Magazine*. Retrieved August 10, 2009, from http://www.onlinelearningmag.com/onlinelearning/magazine/article_display.jsp?vnu_content_id=1526769

KEY TERMS AND DEFINITIONS

Capability: Capability refers to the ability of an institution to ensure that e-learning design, development and deployment is meeting, and will continue to meet, the evolving needs of the students, staff and institution. Capability includes the ability of an institution to sustain e-learning support of teaching and learning as demand grows and staff change.

Coercive Isomorphism: Change as a consequence of formal informal pressures imposed on institutions externally, in the case of universities this includes the pressure to inform our teaching with research, and increasingly the need to produce graduates able to contribute to economic growth (Demers, 2007, p34).

Dimension: The eMM supplements the CMM concept of maturity levels, which describe the evolution of the organisation as a whole, with dimensions. The five dimensions of the eMM are: (1) Delivery; (2)Planning; (3)Definition; (4) Management; (5) Optimisation. The key idea underlying the dimension concept is holistic capability. Rather than the eMM measuring progressive levels, it describes the capability of a process from these five synergistic perspectives. An organization that has developed capability on all dimensions for all processes will be more capable than one that has not. Capability at the higher dimensions that is not supported by capability at the lower dimensions will not deliver the desired outcomes; capability at the lower dimensions that is not supported by capability in the higher dimensions will be ad-hoc, unsustainable and unresponsive to changing organizational and learner needs.

eMM: The eMM, or e-learning Maturity Model in full, is a benchmarking methodology designed to help organisations assess the sustainability and effectiveness of their e-learning activities. The eMM also attempts to identify and provide evidence of support for the key organisational processes and practices that determine sustainability and effectiveness of e-learning..

Maturity Model: Maturity models are models of organisational improvement that are built on the observation that organisations involved in complex endeavors move through levels of effectiveness. As organisations become more exerienced in those endeavors and develop effective systems supporting the activities, they become more "mature" in their approach. The maturity model approach was first applied with the very successful software engineering Capability Maturity Model which defined five maturity levels: (1) Initial; (2)Repeatable; (3) Defined; (4) Managed; (5) Optimizing. The eMM, while based on the CMM maturity paradigm, has been developed in a different direction and treats these as dimensions of capability which can be developed simultaneously, rather than sequentially.

Mimetic Isomorphism: The tendency for institutions to adopt 'standard' or common approaches in uncertain times. This is seen in the adoption of popular management fads such as business process re-engineering or Total Quality Management, a trend that universities are not immune to (Demers, 2007, p34).

Normative Isomorphism: Change that is driven by professionalism and the emergence of 'legitimated professional practices' that result in pressure for institutions to conform because their staff are able to draw on organized professional networks and professional standards that guide their activities (Demers, 2007, p34).

Practice: Practices are intended to capture the key essences of individual processes as specific items that can be assessed easily in a given institutional context. They specify the general concept defined by the process in detail so as to assist in the assessment of capability in that process. The practices are intended to be sufficiently generic that they can reflect the use of different pedagogies, technologies and organisational cultures. Each process is defined in this way by practices that address each of the five dimensions of the eMM.

Process: Processes define a key aspect of the overall ability of institutions to perform well in the delivery of e-learning. Each process is selected on the basis of its necessity in the development and maintenance of capability in e-learning. All of the processes have been created after a rigorous and extensive programme of research, testing and feedback conducted internationally.

Standard: "a document, established by consensus, that provides, for common and repeated use, rules, guidelines or characteristics for activities or their results, aimed at the achievement of the optimum degree of order in a given context" (ISO/IEC, 1996, p8). Standards in the strictest sense can only be created by specific organizations such as the International Standards Organization. In reality and common usage a standard can be an official document, but it also could be a de facto creation of a professional body or vendor, a specification, a reference model or framework, or a collection of guidelines. Guidelines or heuristics generated by expert practitioners and possessing strong face validity rather than empirical support constitute the predominant guides to good practice within e-learning evident in the literature..

Chapter 9
Interoperability, Learning Designs and Virtual Worlds:
Issues and Strategies

Helen Farley
University of Queensland, Australia

ABSTRACT

Given the relatively high costs associated with designing and implementing learning designs in virtual worlds, a strategy for the re-use of designs becomes imperative. IMS LD has emerged as the standard for the description and expression of learning designs. This chapter explores some of the issues associated with using the IMS LD specification for learning designs in virtual worlds such as Second Life and multi-player online role playing games such as World of Warcraft. The main issues relate to the inadequate description of collaborative activities and the inability to alter the design 'on-the-fly' in response to learner inputs. Some possible solutions to these problems are considered.

INTRODUCTION

Since 2003, the virtual world of Second Life has captured the imagination and ire of the general public, on the one hand concerned at the implications and complications for a first life, and on the other intrigued by the possibilities that such a flexible environment affords. Educators fall into this latter category. Higher education institutions have been quick to spot the possibilities for innovative teaching and learning in worlds such as Second Life, Twinity and Active Worlds. Given the escalating demands on educators' time and the increasing scrutiny given to the quality of education, it is prudent to consider the possibilities afforded by reusability of key components of educational designs, in turn leading to greater time efficiencies. Instructional Management System Learning Design (IMS LD) is a standard that has emerged as a way of describing learning activities while emphasizing the possibility of reuse, interoperability and adaptation.

This paper will briefly describe the IMS LD system and the nature of Massively Multiplayer Online Role Playing Games (MMORPGs) such as World of Warcraft, EVE Online and Ever-

DOI: 10.4018/978-1-61692-789-9.ch009

Quest II, and Multi-User Virtual Environments (MUVEs) such as Second Life, Active Worlds and Project Wonderland, before considering how these might interact. Two sets of issues relating to MMORPGs, MUVEs and IMS LD have been identified: (1) those issues not specific to MUVEs and MMORPGs but still significant to them, and (2) those issues more specifically relevant to them. Various strategies have been formulated to overcome these challenges and a discussion of these will constitute the latter part of this chapter.

What is 'Learning Design?'

Learning Design provides a vocabulary for describing teaching and learning processes, and is itself pedagogically neutral (Koper & Olivier, 2003: p. 2). The design becomes explicit and can be reflected upon by the designers themselves or by others who may further refine the design and share it within a community (Koper & Tattersall, 2005: p. 3, Koper & Manderveld, 2004: p. 538). Instructional Management System Learning Design (IMS LD) has emerged as the standard. It allows the expression of lesson plans as formally expressed Units of Learning (UOL). Learning designs with this specification are expressed in Extensible Markup Language (XML), making them machine-readable, i.e. learning designs can be run using IMS LD compatible software such as CopperCore or.LRN (which can be embedded within a learning management system), rendering the delivery and management of courses more economical (Koper & Tattersall, 2005: p. 3; Burgos, Tattersall & Koper, 2007: pp. 2661-2662).

IMS LD is based on Educational Modelling Language (EML) created by Rob Koper and his team at the Open University of the Netherlands (Koper & Tattersall, 2005: pp. 2-3). It is defined as 'a semantic information model and binding, describing the content and process within a "unit of learning" from a pedagogical perspective in order to support reuse and interoperability' (Koper, Rodrígues-Artacho, Lefrere, Rawlings, & Rosmalen, 2002: p. 7; Amorim, Lama, Sánchez, Riera, & Vila, 2006: p. 38). Building on this language, IMS LD was designed to 'to provide a containment framework of elements that describe any design of a teaching-learning process in a formal way' (Koper, Olivier and Anderson, 2003 cited in Caeiro-Rodriguez, Llamas-Nistal & Anido-Rifón, 2005: p. 4).

The IMS LD specification describes a set of activities (learning and support) to be performed by participants with either the roles of learner or staff, in environments consisting of resources and services (Caeiro-Rodriguez et al., 2005: p. 4; Amorim et al., 2006: pp. 39-40). These elements are organized according to a theatrical metaphor, i.e. role-parts are those roles assigned to activities; an act may consist of several role-parts which may be performed synchronously; acts performed in sequence constitute a play; and several plays may be considered sequentially in a method (Koper & Olivier, 2003: p. 6; Caeiro-Rodriguez et al., 2005: p. 4; Hernández Leo, Asensio Pérez & Dimitriadis, 2004: p. 351). There are three levels of LMS LD, designated A, B and C with A being the entry level. Levels B and C offer more flexibility with the introduction of notifications and conditions. Even so, IMS LD is a relatively new specification and the implementation of the standard is patchy and has not been implemented on a large scale (Koper & Tattersall, 2005: p. 4).

MULTI-USER VIRTUAL ENVIRONMENTS (MUVES) AND MASSIVELY MULTIPLAYER ONLINE ROLE-PLAYING GAMES (MMORPGS)

A Multi-User Virtual Environment (MUVE) is a computer-, server- or internet-based virtual environment that allows participants to move around and use various forms of communication (text chat, voice chat or instant messaging). It allows participants to create a virtual identity which persists beyond the initial session (Maher, 1999: p. 322; Ritzema & Harris, 2008: p. 110). The term was coined by Chip Morningstar and F. Randall Farmer in 1990 (see Morningstar & Farmer, 1991: p. 273) and is often used interchangeably with 'Virtual World' (VW) (see Castranova, 2001: pp. 4-5). Second Life is one of the most well-known MUVEs in part due to the intense media scrutiny it has attracted, but predominantly because the content is created almost exclusively by users. At the time of writing, it boasts nearly sixteen million user accounts; one and a quarter million residents having logged in during the previous sixty days (Linden Lab, 2009). Though Massively Multiplayer Online Role-Playing Games (MMORPGs) such as World of Warcraft resemble MUVEs in many ways, including users sharing the same virtual space and persistence of characters, they differ in important ways too. In MUVEs there are no 'levels' to be worked through or imbedded fiction that directs the activities of participants; instead the experiences are shaped by users (Ondrejka, 2008: p. 231).

MUVEs and MMORPGs are populated by motional 'avatars'; the term is derived from Sanskrit and used in Hindu mythology to denote the earthly form adopted by a deity, commonly Visnu (Leeming, 2001). In MUVEs and MMORPGs, this term denotes the representation of a character, controlled either by an individual or a software agent in the case of a 'bot', which acts somewhat like a virtual automaton (Duridanov & Simoff, 2007: p. 4). The choice of avatar can reflect a player's personality, gender or ethnicity. It is also possible for a participant to assume a completely different identity which in itself may constitute a significant learning experience, particularly important in role-playing scenarios. In addition, they are able to communicate with large groups of avatars (via voice- or text-chat or asynchronously with podcasting or inworld, text-based documents called notecards) or communicate more intimately with a single avatar (using instant messaging) (Tashner, Riedl & Bronack, 2005: p. 6). Avatars are able to interact with and modify the virtual environment and are even able to interact beyond the confines of the MUVE if objects are linked to web pages (called 'web on a prim' in Second Life) (Tashner, Riedl et al., 2005: p. 6).

The diversity of educational contexts enabled by MUVEs and MMORPGs provides an assortment of experiences that accommodate a range of learning styles. Fleming identified four types of learning styles: (a) visual; (b) auditory; (c) reading/writing; and (d) kinesthetic, tactile, or exploratory, resulting in the acronym VARK (Fleming & Baume, 2006: p, 6; Bonk & Zhang, 2006: p. 250). Beyond recognizing that these learning styles exist, learners born after the mid-1970s expect that learning will be responsive to their preferred style (Bonk & Zhang, 2006: p. 250). Given the diversity of students attending university, it seems prudent to seek out an environment where all learning styles can be accommodated. A MUVE such as Second Life could be such an environment, as long as careful consideration is given to the planning and implementation of learning strategies.

Such a design would ideally imbed more authentic learning through collaboration, teamwork, problem-based and adaptive learning, in alignment with those trends identified by Bonk, Kim, and Zeng (2006, pp. 550-568; Bonk & Zhang, 2006: p. 251). The increasing importance of hands-on learning in the next couple of years was similarly flagged; already glimpsed in the rising prevalence of realistic and complex, collaborative simulations, interactive scenarios and commutative news stories (Bonk & Zhang, 2006: p. 251). This in part could be achieved in MUVEs and MMORPGs through content creation in accordance with the learner's own ideas, learning goals and interests. This approach necessitates the acquisition of certain requisite skills which could be incorporated into educational designs favoring collaboration, peer-to-peer teaching and the creation of new types of 'learning communities' for both students and educators, underpinned by mediated immersion (Ondrejka, 2008: pp. 229-230; Clarke & Bede, 2005: p. 1; Tashner, Bronack, & Riedl, 2005: p. 2117).

Issues with IMS Learning Design and MUVEs and MMORPGs

Reusability of learning environments and their constituent parts has emerged as a significant agenda for learning design (Harper, 2003: p. 24). As Paramythis and Loidl-Reisinger indicate, one of the main reasons for striving for standardization for e-learning is cost. For example, the creation of Religion Bazaar, an educational build in Second Life used to facilitate student-centered learning for studies in religion students at the University of Queensland, included the purchase of virtual land, terraforming (virtual landscaping), the payment of tier fees (rent), employing a specialist builder to create a number of buildings, the creation of thirty avatars of various races and genders, equipping those avatars with a large variety of religious outfits and religious and cultural artifacts many of which had to be created *ex nihilo*, employing a specialist 'scripter' to animate objects and avatars such that they could interact meaningfully, and importantly, consultation with instructional designers to create an educationally meaningful and effective design. Once created, Religion Bazaar enabled students to role-play in religious rituals and create historical reenactments as part of their undergraduate studies. This design and its implementation cost in the vicinity of $USD25 000 without taking into account the extra time support and teaching staff spent on the project (see Robinson, 2008). This project is just one of hundreds – if not thousands – designed and built by higher education institutions in Second Life alone (see Kay, 2007). Many other institutions have invested heavily in other virtual worlds such as Active Worlds (for example, see (Dickey, 2005) or Croquet Project. As it stands today, the development of an adaptive learning environment (ALE), such as found in a MUVE or implicit in the deployment of a MMORPG, incurs high initial costs (in terms of time and other resources) and high ongoing maintenance costs (p. 181). The development of a mechanism for reuse and interoperability, as implied by the conformation to IMS LD standards, would protect the substantial investment necessary for the development of an ALE; should allow for interoperability in different environments; and the possibility for aggregation of content by subsequent users (Paramythis & Loidl-Reisinger, 2004: pp. 181-182).

At this time, there is no way to package a MUVE or MMORPG so that it can be embedded into a LD for ready use in another environment due largely to the fact that they usually exist on external servers which are able to be accessed by an unlimited number of users at any given time. Those environments created with OpenSim, an open source server platform for hosting virtual worlds, and Linden Labs' Nebraska are the exceptions, being able to be installed on local servers (Linden, 2009). In order for the MUVE or MMORPG to be used within a LD, it has to be provided as a learning object within an environment (see Rob Koper & Olivier, 2003: p. 7). The use of MMORPGs and MUVEs as educational settings, while not mainstream has existed in some form for in excess of a decade, yet there is scant literature that addresses the topic of using IMS LD with MUVEs or MMORPGs. Consequently, in order to approach this topic, it was necessary to survey the literature relating to the IMS LD specification with a view to identifying those problems not directly associated with but still relevant to MMORPGs and MUVEs because of the favored instructional methods in use in these environments. In addition, those challenges more especially associated with using IMS LD with MUVEs and MMORPGs were also identified.

PROBLEMS ASSOCIATED WITH IMS LD AND ACTIVITIES TAKING PLACE IN MMORPGS AND MUVES, BUT NOT SPECIFIC TO THEM

MMORPGs and MUVEs excel as collaborative workspaces facilitating the creation of learning opportunities anchored in real-world experiences (Childress & Braswell, 2006: p. 190). Role-playing, once only possible in a face-to-face context, can now be performed virtually while experimenting with gender and identity as well as adopting unfamiliar roles. In addition, learners can collaborate to create content in the form of buildings, artworks or vocational resources. They can work together to plan and implement a virtual enterprise, for instance a store selling virtual goods such as a clothing store, or services such as a music venue or instruction in a particular skill such as scripting or building. In an example amply demonstrating the collaborative possibilities afforded by virtual worlds, faculty from Johnson and Wales University formulated an experiential education activity in Second Life for students involved with Global Outreach Morocco. This interdisciplinary, community-based organization is concerned with promoting economic development in the country through increasing tourism and travel (Mason & Moutahir, 2006: p. 32). The students from disciplines including business, tourism and technology, worked collaboratively to create a 'virtual Morocco' by building popular landmarks, including the Hassan II Mosque, to be used as a marketing tool but also to raise funds through the sale of virtual goods (Mason & Moutahir, 2006: pp. 33-34). In large part, what makes MMORPGs and MUVEs so appealing to educators is this enormous potential for the design and implementation of a rich variety of collaborative learning activities.

Early e-learning standards only supported the use of a single learner (e.g. SCORM) which rendered them unsuitable for encoding the fertile collaborative activities afforded by MMORPGs and MUVEs. IMS LD offers a considerable advantage, allowing the integration of discussions and more complex collaborative approaches (Koper & Tattersall, 2005: pp. 4-5). Even so, there are a number of problems trying to describe the kinds of collaboration found in these environments using IMS LD. Obviously, there are often significant timing issues associated with collaboration. For example, one piece of a task to be undertaken by a learner may not be able to take place until another part of the task is completed by a different student; timing is crucial such as with a role-play with learners entering and leaving the activity at different times. Caeiro-Rodriguez, Llamas-Nistal and Anido-Rifón identified three types of timing issues associated with collaborative learning. These are:

1. Synchronization patterns, so that an activity undertaken by one learner occurs in temporal relation to another task undertaken by another learner according to the conditions of the collaboration (as in the previous example).
2. Scheduling patterns, for the determination of times when an event will occur or a product will become available, for example deadlines. And,
3. Allocation patterns, to determine how much time is spent on each task (pp. 11-12).

While some of the temporal elements are able to be defined (e.g. activity deadlines), most are not, significantly hindering the expression and subsequent management of collaborative activities (Caeiro-Rodriguez et al., 2005: p. 12). Additionally, it may be necessary for a group of students to come together to work through a 'treasure hunt' or to work together to build a model, event or role-play. Furthermore, in simulations – particularly in MUVEs but also in MMORPGs – there are often virtual actors ('bots') that may play the role of a patient in a medical simulation or act as virtual guides for example. It is possible for virtual actors to take the roles in IMS LD (Payr, 2005: pp. 211-212). Even though the distribution of learners or bots into groups is expressly supported, as is the ability for students to take on the same roles at different times (Koper & Tattersall, 2005: pp. 4-5; Hernández Leo et al., 2004: p. 350), it is still quite difficult to describe the formation of groups in IMS LD and this needs to be overcome before group work, whether in a MUVE, MMORPG or other environment, can be adequately described (Koper & Tattersall, 2005: p. 4). Given the nature of the sorts of activities taking place in MUVEs or MMORPGs, this is entirely restrictive (Hernández Leo et al., 2004: p. 350). In the current iteration of IMS LD, groups are defined via 'role concept' (Berggren et al., 2005: p. 6) but there is no specification to determine how members within those groups will interact (Santos, Boticario, & Barrera, 2004): p. 5). The only indication of interaction is via a service, only two of which are collaborative to any degree: discussion forum and email (Hernández Leo et al., 2004: p. 350). In order to overcome these difficulties, Hernández Leo, Asensio Pérez and Dimitriadis proposed an addition to the IMS LD service definition; that of 'group service'. This would accommodate those characteristics not currently allowed by IMS LD including the type of awareness information needed and provided by the service, the floor control policy that guides learners' actions, the communication skills required by these learners, and so on. However, even with these proposed amendments, deficiencies will still occur in some areas (p. 351). It was believed that some of these issues could be addressed in a further iteration of IMS LD, however, to date this has not been forthcoming.

Santos, Boticario and Barrera proposed another viable solution that would overcome some of the deficiencies of that proposed by Hernandez *et al.* Their solution was designed to 1) integrate the use of services within the context of the activity, 2) control any runtime adaptations from the design itself, and 3) facilitate feedback to the author (Santos, et al., 2004: p. 5). They used aLFanet (for Active Learning For Adaptive internet) that includes an authoring tool which facilitates the creation of courses utilizing the IMS LD standard by way of templates. Even so, the authors admitted this process was still quite difficult (Santos, et al., 2004: pp. 3-4). In order to deal with the deficiencies with regards to collaboration in IMS LD, two objectives were identified: 1) to identify the resources –both contents and services – to be used in the design of collaborative activities, and 2) to assign maximum and minimum values to various components within the activities, in order to regulate the runtime environment. This required a number of pieces of information to be supplied by the author of the particular LD including a list of learning objects including metadata specified by IEEE-LOM (a standard for learning object metadata), the name of the folder where learners are required to lodge their files, an activity description containing specific links to learning objects and service elements, and so on (Santos, et al., 2004: pp. 3-4). To facilitate the re-use of the design by adapting it to a novel context or purpose, the author is able to specify whether or not the design has been purposed for re-use, but also to designate which components are considered central to the design and need to remain unchanged. Conversely, the author is also able to identify which components are most suitable for adaptation. In addition, parameters for redesign can be supplied such that the runtimes for each activity can be refined. This in turn influences how the activity will be presented to the learner and how the services can be used, dependent on the characteristics of the individual user (Santos, et al., 2004: pp. 6-7). An Audit module also provides feedback to the author by comparing the initial learning design with the performance of the learners (Santos, et al., 2004): pp. 3-4).

Beyond the difficulties associated with collaboration and IMS LD in MUVEs and MMOR-

PGs, the inability of IMS LD to be altered while already running is a significant issue. It is sometimes crucial for students or instructors to edit the learning activities as situations challenge. This would be a common enough problem in a MUVE or MMORPG where constructionist learning is paramount and learners bring to the activity a wide variety of experiences and skill sets. Students are encouraged to use their prior experiences to contribute to the collective knowledge of the group and collaborate with peers, always adapting to emerging, and often unpredictable, circumstances. In the IMS LD, students are not able to edit the activities. Though staff can be assigned varying roles giving them a greater or lesser control over the running of the activities, the role of learner is inflexible in this regard. Learners need to be able to have some administrative rights so that they can lead groups, monitor activities and assess participation (Berggren et al., 2005: p. 6).

As an IMS LD is proscriptive, it is not possible to alter it 'on the fly' in response to changing circumstances using Reload (as an authoring tool) or with CopperCore (as a player) for example. Sometimes learning experiences are designed to be adaptive according to the characteristics of the individual learner or in response to learning outcomes. But in some cases, unpredictable characteristics of the learning environment itself may render an alteration of the learning design desirable. MUVEs and MMORPGs are generally not closed environments (though it may be possible to make them so under certain circumstances). Avatars not associated with the host institution are able to wander into a learning activity or online colleagues might drop by to see what is happening. Second Life, in particular, is much favored by educators and there is a strong sense of community. It is possible – and even likely – that if another educator heard about a novel assessment piece or learning activity, they might come by and observe. These chance meetings are excellent opportunities to enhance the learning experience and would be encouraged under normal circumstances, but are not compatible with the proscriptive nature of IMS LD. In a different scenario, another avatar from outside the original grouping may be a content expert and offer advice or valuable information or suggest an alternative method but again this transgression of the original activity could not be accommodated by IMS LD, even though the educational activity would be improved by that person's contribution via their avatar. In a less positive situation, participants may have difficulty with hardware, software or bandwidth. It is not uncommon for residents to lose the ability to use voice chat in Second Life for example. This could significantly impact on a role-play activity or in the production of a machinima (a misspelled amalgamation of 'machine' and 'cinema' which designates an animation crafted from a gaming or MUVE experience) as an assessment piece. Lack of bandwidth might preclude the use of builds that place a high load on the system. Similarly, someone learning in a MMORPG, such as World of Warcraft, might find their avatar killed by someone from a raiding guild, again derailing the original learning activity. Ideally, this would lead to a redesign or modification of the learning design.

At this time, it is not possible to alter or adapt an IMS LD while it is running (Berggren et al., 2005: p. 7). In contrast, a learning management system such as Moodle, which is based on socio-constructivist principles, enables activities to be adapted on the fly in response to this ideology. One possible way of overcoming the proscriptive nature of IMS LD would be to use an IMS LD-compliant authoring tool within Moodle. This could take the form of a 'template editor', supporting the creation of more course formats (a course is roughly equivalent to a UOL in IMS LD) that support roles and conditions. It would then be necessary to be able to export a later iteration of a LD while stripping user data, possibly through the development of an improved XML export system (Berggren et al., 2005: pp. 8, 12).

Problems with IMS LD Specific to MMORPGs and MUVEs

As previously flagged, very little has been done in regard to MUVEs and MMORPGs and IMS LD. There has been some work done on IMS LD and generic games and it is this literature that provides some insight into those challenges arising from the use of IMS LD with MUVEs and MMORPGs. Video games, MMORPGs and MUVEs have many characteristics in common: they provide short feedback cycles, they are immersive and highly interactive (see Moreno-Ger, Burgos, Sierra, & Fernández-Manjón, 2007: p. 247). In addition, like an activity in a MUVE or MMORPG, a video game can behave differently each time it is run. This becomes desirable when dealing with a learner cohort encompassing a large range of experience, skill levels and competencies. The adaptive nature of a game, MMORPG or activities within a MUVE, is an efficient way of providing appropriate learning experiences to such a diverse cohort (Moreno-Ger et al., 2007: p. 248).

Already these environments are being used within an educational context. But for the most part, the activities taking place within these environments run independently of the current e-learning systems as collateral activities, leading to a fundamental disconnect between the educational setting and the activity taking place within the MUVE or MMORPG (see Burgos, Tattersall et al., 2007: pp. 2658-2659; Burgos, Moreno-Ger, Sierra, Fernández-Manjón, & Koper, 2007: p. 256). It is desirable to forge a link between the activity and setting so that the activities that precede it contribute to its iteration and so that it in turn will add something to the system and hence, the activities that follow it. This is not possible when there is no communication between the activity in the MUVE or MMORPG and the e-learning system in use which provides the overarching structure to the UOL (Burgos, Tattersall et al., 2007: p. 2660).

A UOL running within a Learning Management System (such as Blackboard or Moodle), could involve a student or group of students formulating a detailed business plan (in the form of a wiki for example) in order to run a business making clothes for sale in the popular MUVE, Second Life. The activity would run for a specified amount of time and interim goals would be set. The student could be responsible for assembling the clothes or arranging for the clothes to be made, advertising the clothes and collecting fees. This activity could run for a specified period of time and comparisons could be made between the results of the actual activity and the proposed goals as defined in the business plan. The results would be collected in the LMS and feedback and support would be given along the way. Depending on the correlation between the actual results and the projected results, the activity could be run again with the parameters adjusted or the student may be able to move on to a more advanced activity with others who have achieved similar results. A student with prior experience in retail could be expected to excel in this kind of activity, and in order to continue to challenge that student so that he or she continues to learn in a meaningful way, the economic conditions or cost of materials could be increased or the student could be forced to move the business to another area with a different socioeconomic demographic.

Burgos, Tattersall and Koper writing about generic, educational games have suggested that a communication dispatcher be created which sits between the pedagogical modeler and the game. And this remains a possibility also between a MUVE or MMORPG and the pedagogical modeler. This would facilitate the transmission of variables in both directions, ensuring the most appropriate learning experience (Burgos, Tattersall et al., 2007: p. 2660; Burgos, Moreno-Ger et al., 2007: p. 257). This would have the advantage of being able to completely control the flow of the UOL and the MUVE/MMORPG activity within it instead of having the activity take place in parallel to the flow of the UOL. This was demonstrated by Burgos et al. with a generic game called *Caminatas*, developed by Burgos at the Open University of the Netherlands, using an IMS Learning Design editor such as CopperAuthor or Reload LD Editor (pp. 2664-2665). Even so, they acknowledged that the implementation of this solution was not yet possible, due to the complex nature of the task and the state of the available software, including IMS LD. In addition, there was not yet appropriate software to act as a communication dispatcher between the game (the example they used) and the educational wrapper (p. 2665).

Moreno-Ger, Burgos and Sierra came to a similar conclusion using a game created using the game authoring software <e-Adventure> (see Moreno-Ger et al., 2007). A UOL entitled *The Art and Craft of Chocolate* was created and deployed and consisted of three stages within an LMS:

1. Provision of traditional content and deployment of tests to determine the learner's level of knowledge about the topic.
2. Deployment of the game at a level commensurate with the learner's level of knowledge.
3. An in-game assessment is used to grade the learner or can be used to determine the rest of the learning flow (Moreno-Ger et al., 2007: p. 250).

They determined that the adaptation to IMS LD consisted of two stages (similar to those suggested above by Burgos et al.):

1. The game should infer adaptation properties from the UOL execution.
2. And that feedback from the game should be fed back into the UOL execution environment (Moreno-Ger et al., 2007: pp. 256-257).

The UOL was run on a SLeD (Service-based Learning Design) player which functioned as the front end for a CopperCore Runtime (CCRT) environment. The CopperCore Service Integration (CCSI) layer allowed the integration of different services, such as forums or assessments, in the CopperCore environment (Moreno-Ger et al., 2007: pp. 257-258). Neither the SLeD player nor IMS LD was set up to accommodate adaptive games so the CCSI layer had to be adapted to create a new service called 'Adaptive Game Service'. This was possible because the LD specification allows a certain flexibility when defining the services needed for the various activities and this is implemented by the CCSI which facilitates the definition, implementation and connection to these services (Moreno-Ger et al., 2007: p. 258). So again, there is a theoretical solution which would enable games, MMORPGs and activities in MUVEs to have some effect on the learning flow but the solution does not yet exist using LMS LD. If it did exist, the activity could run through an IMS LD compliant LMS. There has been some move in this direction by both Moodle (Berggren, 2006; Berggren et al., 2005) and Blackboard (Blackboard Inc., 2004). IMS Shareable State Persistence (IMS SSP) is a specification that allows passing state information from one learning object to another, so that for example, results of an assessment or game can be utilized to determine the further course of a learning sequence (Payr, 2005: pp. 210-211).

Re-Use

Given that the aforementioned difficulties can be overcome, three main tasks have been identified by Pernin and Lejeune (2006) in order for an IMS LD, including one incorporating the use of a MUVE or MMORPG, to be reused. The first task includes the analysis by way of comparison of the IMS LD as it was originally envisaged with its refinement or modification in the light of a more detailed examination of the context and content and finally, the actual iteration of the scenario. This enables an evaluation of the effectiveness of the design but also aids a determination of its suitability for re-use in a different context (Pernin

& Lejeune, 2006: pp. 9-10). This contextualization is the second step in the process. The variability of contexts in which the IMS LD will potentially be played out will to some extent determine the suitability for re-use of the scenario. If the IMS LD is to be re-used in a very similar context, then it could be expected that the LD will be highly suitable for re-use, with progressive improvement of the designs. If the context for re-use is markedly different, then the IMS LD may not be suitable for re-use without significant modification. A determination will need to be made as to whether it is more time and cost effective to use an existing IMS LD for iteration in the new context or whether it would be more efficient to create one from scratch. If the IMS LD is suitable for re-use then it will need to be catalogued, the final step in this process (Pernin & Lejeune, 2006: p. 10).

Alternative Solutions

In the meantime, there has been some move towards a solution not using IMS LD with the creation of Sloodle. Sloodle is an Open Source GNU-GPL project which integrates the MUVE Second Life with the learning-management system, Moodle. Sloodle comes as a Moodle module (Sloodle, 2008a). Students are registered to a Moodle site and then are required to log into Second Life and take their avatars to the 'Sloodle Access Checker' or in more recent versions of Sloodle, to an enrolment/registration booth (Sloodle, 2008b: p. 5). An object distributor allows content to be passed to Second Life avatars via Moodle so that students' avatars can be equipped with the materials they need to perform an activity in Second Life. The staff member is not required to be logged into Second Life to do this. Students can text chat next to a Sloodle Web Intercom in Second Life and the chat is logged and mirrored on a forum on the Moodle page (Sloodle, 2008b: p. 6). Other tools include a glossary tool, a blogging tool, voting and quiz tools and a 'prim' dropbox so that students can lodge objects created in Second Life with Sloodle. These tools link directly to the Moodle Gradebook (p. 7) and through some sort of adaptive release, can determine subsequent activities.

Developers of another prominent LMS, Blackboard, are similarly striving to create some interactivity between Second Life and their own LMS. A $US25 000 grant was awarded to Ball State University to develop a system to guide access to Second Life resources using the adaptive release features of Blackboard. Though Blackboard activities will determine the nature of the Second Life experience for students, it is unclear as to whether or not the Second Life experience impacts on the experience within Blackboard (Blackboard Inc., 2008). In addition, there are means of assessing in Second Life whereby quizzes and the results of quizzes or other activities can be collected and stored at a third party website (see www.deltalprinting.com) without the specific requirement for a LMS.

CONCLUSION

This chapter has attempted to introduce the topics of IMS LD and MUVEs/MMORPGs. Though there is not a literature dealing specifically with this topic, those issues that may be more often encountered in MUVEs and MMORPGs have been identified, specifically those associated with IMS LD and various aspects of collaboration and also the inability to adjust IMS LD on the fly in response to changing circumstances. Through identifying those issues common to gaming and multi-user environments and IMS LD, it becomes possible to formulate strategies to deal with these challenges. The possible resolution of these issues has been discussed, specifically through the addition of a service, specifically 'groupservice', even though it is unlikely to address all of the issues raised. Additionally, these issues may be addressed through the use of IMS LD templates to be used in aLFanet.

Further, those issues that relate more closely to MUVEs and MMORPGs were identified, specifically how the results of the activities that take place in these environments influence subsequent learning activities within the UOL and vice versa. The solution to this problem remains theoretical, with the creation of a communication dispatcher to sit between the game, MMORPG or MUVE and the LD being proposed. Looking outside of IMS LD, there are examples where MUVEs do interact with a LMS to influence subsequent activities. This is achieved using Sloodle, as a component of Moodle interacting with Second Life and is also being trialed with Blackboard (again with Second Life).

REFERENCES

Amorim, R. R., Lama, M., Sánchez, E., Riera, A., & Vila, X. A. (2006). A Learning Design Ontology based on the IMS Specification. *Journal of Educational Technology & Society, 9*(1), 38–57. Available from http://www.ifets.info/journals/9_1/5.pdf.

Annetta, L., Klesath, M., & Holmes, S. (2008). V-Learning: How Gaming and Avatars are Engaging Online Students. *Innovate: Journal of Online Education, 4*(3). Available from http://www.innovateonline.info/index.php?view=article&id=485.

Berggren, A. (2006). Current Status of IMS LD and Moodle. *Journal,* (October 2006). Retrieved from http://moodle.org/mod/forum/discuss.php?d=56713

Berggren, A., Burgos, D., Fontana, J. M., Hinkelman, D., Hung, V., & Hursh, A. (2005). Practical and Pedagogical Issues for Teacher Adoption of IMS Learning Design Standards in Moodle LMS. *Journal of Interactive Media in Education, 2005*(2), 1–24. Available from http://jime.open.ac.uk/2005/02/berggren-2005-02.pdf.

Blackboard_Inc. (2004). Blackboard Inc. and Open Universiteit Nederland Announce Strategic Alliance. *Journal,* (June 2004). Retrieved from http://www.blackboard.com/company/press/release.aspx?id=519762

Blackboard_Inc. (2008). Ball State Wins Greenhouse Grant for Virtual Worlds. *Journal,* (March). Retrieved from http://www.blackboard.com/company/newsletters/ASMarch2008d.htm

Bonk, C. J., & Zhang, K. (2006). Introducing the R2D2 Model: Online Learning for the Diverse Learners of the World. *Distance Education, 27*(2), 249–264. doi:10.1080/01587910600789670

Bovey, N. S., & Dunand, N. (2006). Seamless production of interoperable e-Learning units: stakes and pitfalls. *DSpace at Open Universiteit Nederland,* 1-6. Available from dspace.learningnetworks.org/bitstream/1820/759/1/Paper15.pdf.

Burgos, D., Moreno-Ger, P., Sierra, J. L., Fernández-Manjón, B., & Koper, R. (2007). Authoring game-based adaptive units of learning with IMS Learning Design and <e-Adventure>. *International Journal of Learning Technology, 3*(3), 252–268. doi:10.1504/IJLT.2007.015444

Burgos, D., Tattersall, C., & Koper, R. (2007). Repurposing existing generic games and simulations for e-learning. *Computers in Human Behavior, 23*(6), 2656–2667. doi:10.1016/j.chb.2006.08.002

Caeiro-Rodriguez, M., Llamas-Nistal, M., & Anido-Rifón, L. (2005). Towards a Benchmark for the Evaluation of LD Expressiveness and Suitability. *Journal of Interactive Media in Education, 4,* 1–14.

Castranova, E. (2001). *Virtual Worlds: A First-Hand Account of Market and Society on the Cyberian Frontier*. Munich, Germany: Center for Economic Studies & Ifo Institute for Economic Research.

Childress, M. D., & Braswell, R. (2006). Using Massively Multiplayer Online Role-Playing Games for Online Learning. *Distance Education, 27*(2), 187–196. doi:10.1080/01587910600789522

Clarke, J., & Bede, C. (2005). *Making Learning Meaningful: An Exploratory Study of Using Multi-User Environments (MUVEs) in Middle School Science.* Paper presented at the American Educational Research Association. Retrieved from http://muve.gse.harvard.edu/rivercityproject/documents/aera_2005_clarke_dede.pdf

Dickey, M. D. (2005). Three-dimensional virtual worlds and distance learning: two case studies of Active Worlds as a medium for distance education. *British Journal of Educational Technology, 36*(3), 439–451. doi:10.1111/j.1467-8535.2005.00477.x

Duridanov, L., & Simoff, S. (2007). 'Inner Listening' as a Basic Principle for Developing Immersive Virtual Worlds. *Online - Heidelberg Journal of Religions on the Internet, 2*(3).

/education/blog/2009 /05/08/a-big-first-case-western-reserve-is-first-edu-on-standalone-version-of-second-life

Fleming, N., & Baume, D. (2006). Learning Styles Again: VARKing up the Right Tree! *Educational Developments, 7*(4), 4–7.

Harper, B. (2003). Designing Learning Experiences: Supporting Teachers in the Process of Technology Change. In Dowling, C., & Lai, K.-W. (Eds.), *Information and Communication Technology and the Teacher of the Future* (pp. 15–28). Boston: Kluwer Academic.

Hernández Leo, D., Asensio Pérez, J. I., & Dimitriadis, Y. A. (2004, 30 August - 4 September 2004). *IMS Learning Design Support for the Formalization of Collaborative Learning Patterns.* Paper presented at the Fourth IEEE International Conference on Advanced Learning Technologies (ICALT'04), Joensuu, Finland.

Kay, J. (2007, 28 July). Educational Uses of Second Life. Wikispaces posted to http://sleducation.wikispaces.com/educationaluses.

Koper, R., & Manderveld, J. (2004). Educational modelling language: modelling reusable, interoperable, rich and personalised units of learning. *British Journal of Educational Technology, 35*(5), 537–551. doi:10.1111/j.0007-1013.2004.00412.x

Koper, R., & Olivier, B. (2003). Representing the learning design of units of learning. *Journal*, 1-18. Retrieved from http://dspace.ou.nl/bitstream/1820/19/2/IMSLD-article%20v1p07-final.pdf

Koper, R., Rodrígues-Artacho, M., Lefrere, P., Rawlings, A., & Rosmalen, P. (2002). Survey of Educational Modelling Languages (EMLs). *Journal,* (September 2002), 1-79. Retrieved from http://dspace.ou.nl/dspace/handle/1820/227

Koper, R., & Tattersall, C. (2005). Preface to Learning Design: A Handbook on Modelling and Delivering Networked Education and Training. *Journal of Interactive Media in Education, 18*, 1–7.

Leeming, D. (Ed.). (2001). *A Dictionary of Asian Mythology* (Oxford Reference Online ed.). London: Oxford University Press.

Linden, A. (2009, 29 July). *A Big First: Case Western Reserve is First EDU on Standalone Version of Second Life.* Retrieved from https://blogs.secondlife.com/community/community

LindenLabs. (2009, 28 July 2009). *Economic Statistics.* Retrieved Sunday 5 October, 2008, from http://secondlife.com/whatis/economy_stats.php

Maher, M. L. (1999). Designing the virtual campus. *Design Studies, 20*(4), 319–342. doi:10.1016/S0142-694X(98)00043-X

Mason, H., & Moutahir, M. (2006). *Multidisciplinary Experiential Education in Second Life: A Global Approach*. Paper presented at the Second Life Education Workshop at the Second Life Community Convention. from http://cleobekkers.files.wordpress.com/2008/03/slcc2006-proceedings.pdf#page=39

Moreno-Ger, P., Burgos, D., Sierra, J. L., & Fernández-Manjón, B. (2007). A Game-Based Adaptive Unit of Learning with IMS Learning Design and <e-Adventure. In Duval, E., Klamma, R., & Wolpers, M. (Eds.), *Creating New Learning Experiences on a Global Scale* (pp. 247–261). Berlin: Springer. doi:10.1007/978-3-540-75195-3_18

Morningstar, C., & Farmer, F. R. (1991). The Lessons of Lucasfilm's Habitat. In Benedikt, M. (Ed.), *Cyberspace: First Steps*. Cambridge, MA: MIT Press.

Ondrejka, C. (2008). Education Unleashed: Participatory Culture, Education, and Innovation in *Second Life*. In Salen, K. (Ed.), *The Ecology of Games: Connecting Youth, Games, and Learning* (pp. 229–252). Cambridge, MA: The MIT Press.

Paramythis, A., & Loidl-Reisinger, S. (2004). Adaptive Learning Environments and e-Learning Standards. *Electronic Journal on e-Learning, 2*(1), 181-194.

Payr, S. (2005). Not Quite an Editorial: Educational Agents and (e-)Learning. *Applied Artificial Intelligence, 19*(3), 199–213. doi:10.1080/08839510590910147

Pernin, J.-P., & Lejeune, A. (2006). Models for the re-use of learning scenarios. *DSpace*, 1-15. Retrieved from http://hdl.handle.net/1820/580

Rice, W. H. IV. (2006). *Moodle: E-Learning Course Development*. Birmingham, UK: Packt Publishing.

Ritzema, T., & Harris, B. (2008). The Use of Second Life for Distance Education. *Journal of Computing Sciences in Colleges, 23*(6), 110–116.

Robinson, P. (2008, 8 May 2008). UQ in Second Life. *UQ News*.

Santos, O. C., Boticario, J. G., & Barrera, C. (2004). *Authoring a Collaborative Task Extending the IMS-LD to be Performed in a Standard-based Adaptive Learning Management System Called Alfanet*. Paper presented at the International Conference on Web Engineering. Retrieved 29 July 2009, from http://arantxa.ii.uam.es/~rcarro/AHCW04/Santos.pdf

Sloodle. (2008a). *Sloodle: Learning System for Virtual Environments*. Retrieved 5 October, 2008, from http://www.sloodle.org

Sloodle (2008b). Using Sloodle: Dubai-Korea Virtual Cultural Exchange, Using Sloodle to Support Learning and Teaching. *Journal*, 1-8. Retrieved from http://www.sloodle.org/moodle/file.php/1/SLOODLEcasestudy1.pdf

Tashner, J. H., Bronack, S. C., & Riedl, R. E. (2005). *3D Web-Based Worlds for Instruction*. Paper presented at the Society for Information Technology and Teacher Education International Conference, Phoenix, AZ.

Tashner, J. H., Riedl, R. E., & Bronack, S. C. (2005, January 2005). *Virtual Worlds: Further Development of Web-Based Teaching*. Paper presented at the Hawaii International Conference on Education, Honolulu, Hawaii.

KEY TERMS AND DEFINITIONS

Avatar: The representation of a user in a virtual environment. In virtual worlds these representations are able to move and interact with the environment and each other.

Instructional Management System Learning Design (IMS LD): A standardized vocabulary for describing teaching and learning processes. It allows the expression of lesson plans as Units of Learning (UOL).

Learning Management System (LMS): A software program that facilitates the enrolment of students, administration, deployment of assessment and the aggregation of content in an elearning program or course. The term Virtual Learning Environment (VLE) is frequently used as an alternative in the European context. Examples of common LMS include Blackboard, Moodle, Sakai and WebCT.

Massively Multiplayer Online Role-playing Game (MMORPG): A virtual environment in which simultaneous users can log on and participate in role-playing activities. There is generally a narrative that drives the action in the game, with 'levels' or 'stages' to be worked through. The environment persists once users log off.

Multi-User Virtual Environment (MUVE): A Multi-User Virtual Environment (MUVE) is a computer, server- or internet-based virtual environment that can be accessed by multiple users simultaneously. The virtual environment persists after individual users have logged off.

Second Life: A MUVE commonly used by educators, created in 2003 by Linden Lab. It has around 16 million users. A separate Teen Grid for 13 to 17 year olds also exists.

Chapter 10
Specification of an Adaptable and Inclusive E-Learning Support System

Steve Green
Teesside University, UK

ABSTRACT

The chapter outlines the problems associated with inclusive e-learning and the role that user profiles and an adaptation service can have to support personalization. The chapter introduces the idea of an Adaptable Personal Learning Environment (APLE) and looks at how one component, the Transformation, Augmentation and Substitution Service (TASS), can be formally specified using Prolog. The compliance with a range of standards is identified: in particular the IMS ACCLIP and ACCMD standards for accessible learner profiles and learner object metadata and the AccessForAll proposals. The chapter also considers issues of IMS and SCORM content packaging, learner information profiles and the JISC definitions for a Personal Learning Environment, all within the context of inclusive e-Learning support.

INTRODUCTION

User-Centred Design, Learning Management Systems, Electronic Performance Support Systems and Formal Specification are all terms commonly applied within Computing, but they are not normally used together nor applied to the same context. Despite this these ideas are integral here within a chapter dealing with the definition of adaptable e-learning support based on accessibility standards.

DOI: 10.4018/978-1-61692-789-9.ch010

There are few educators, web designs or software developers these days totally ignorant of the need to make web-based content accessible to the widest possible audience. The majority are aware of the importance of ALT-tags for graphical images and the need to consider the possibility that someone with a sensory, motor or cognitive disability may be attempting to access the site. Typically web designers will claim to follow the W3C Web Content Accessibility Guidelines (W3C WCAG 1.0, 1999) and may even claim conformance level triple-A: that should mean conformance with all three priority levels. These levels relate to what a content developer *must*, *should* or *may* satisfy. However even if it were true that WCAG compliance was enough to ensure that content is accessible that would not guarantee that all instance of e-learning support are inclusive. Firstly there are real issues with the application of WCAG 1.0 in a variety of contexts. Typically conformance is subjective and difficult both to achieve and measure. Also it does not guarantee that content is fit for purpose or context or that it is presented in a way that makes appropriate use of the individual's environment or support tools. An often quoted criticism of WCAG is that it is based on a model of the world which assumes every browser conforms to the standards and the most common disability a person may have is visual impairment (Sloan et al., 2006). Clearly this is a gross misrepresentation of the contribution that WCAG 1.0 has made to the web and certainly WCAG 2.0 promises much more but the world of inclusive e-learning support goes well beyond the contribution of WCAG 1.0 or 2.0.

If we move beyond web accessibility guidelines when defining inclusive e-learning support there are a confusing range of standards, guidelines, models and frameworks. A number of these standards relate directly to e-learning content such as IEEE LOM (Learning Object Metadata), ASL SCORM (Schareable Content Object Model), IMS CP (Content Packaging), IMS LTI (Learning Tools Interoperability) and IMS QTI (Question Test Interoperability). Others relate specifically to accessible applications or content such as W3C/WAI ARIA (Accessible Rich Internet Applications), CEN-ISS APLR (Accessibility Properties for Learning Resources) and the W3C/WAI WCAG (Web Content Accessibility Guidelines) themselves. However this chapter will concentrate primarily on the IMS *AccessForAll* standards ACCMD (*AccessForAll* Metadata Information Model) and ACCLIP (Accessibility for IMS Learner Information Package). The aim of this chapter is to provide an overview of *AccessForAll* and the related standards and to indicate how a localized form of AccessForAll service can be embedded into an inclusive e-learning support environment, formally specified and defined using the logic-based programming language Prolog.

INCLUSIVE E-LEARNING SUPPORT

This section explores the issues of learning technologies, learning management systems, accessible e-learning content and accessibility guidelines and standards. The aim is to consider what current resources, thinking and standards can be incorporated into our e-learning support model.

Learning Technologies

Learning technologies refer to the range of hardware devices and software applications which are used in the learning context. These technologies might include personal computers, laptops, netbooks, mobile phones, PDAs, ipods, the web, wikis, blogs, learning object repositories, e-learning resources, e-learning activities, discussion tools, virtual learning environments, e-books, e-assessments and a whole range of electronic performance support systems.

In the context of inclusive e-learning support it is likely that the learner may also have access to assistive technology: this is '*any technology which can be used to help someone with an innate (or acquired) disability to overcome the limitations typically associated with that disability*'. Common examples are spectacles and hearing aids but they could also include mobility devices, interface devices and communication technologies (see Table 1). In the sense that assistive technologies are designed to allow individuals to overcome limitations or improve access, they can be seen as being an agent of fairness and equity - which is important from the perspective of education and employment.

Table 1. Device categories for assistive technologies

Device Category	Purpose	Examples
Mobility	To aid in physical movement and independent living	Electric wheelchair, mobility scooter, adapted car, robot arm, crutch, walking stick, prosthesis etc.
Input/Output and Control	To allow connections with computers and other intelligent or control devices	Adapted keyboards, button switches, suck-blow switch, head switch, tracker-ball, adapted mouse, eye-tracker, touch-screen, concept keyboard etc.
Display and Sensory	To display, read or show results. To provide augmented or alternative sensory experiences	Large screen displays, screen magnifiers, screen readers, Braille output, GPS position reader, echo-location, eye-glasses, hearing aid etc
Communications	To allow individuals to communicate via language and speech	Adapted speech boards, e-mail, SMS, mobile phones, symbol-systems, alternative or augmentative communication devices

Learning Management Systems

Almost all institutions use a learning object repository, learning portal or more commonly a learning management system to provide scaffolded support for e-learning provision. They can be broadly divided into four categories, learning portals, virtual learning environments (VLEs), managed learning environments (MLEs) and personal learning environments (PLEs) (see Table 2).

Almost as long as the internet has been available educators have placed learning material on-line often referenced directly from a personal or departmental web-page. Learning resources are made accessible in electronic form as a media elements linked directly from the web. This is essentially a learning portal, although many true learning portals may actually be much more sophisticated that this. If these resources are then linked with a set of educational tools for communication between students and tutors in a managed site, this is referred to as a Virtual Learning Environment (VLE) under the original JISC classification. A centralized VLE which also links to institutional administrative and management functions including course enrolment, course administration, finance and the library, would typically be called a Managed Learning Environment (or MLE). In fact the distinctions between a portal, a VLE and an MLE may be subtle, with a different term used for similar products and services in different contexts.

Table 2. classes of learning management systems

Category	Description	Examples	Accessible Learning Environments
Learning Portals	A set of links to on-line learning materials and resources organized as a set of references	*Various training and education sites*	
Virtual Learning Environments	A range of educations tools and content typically web-based but managed by a single application	Moodle	Boddington Common I Portland VLE
Managed Learning Environments	Centralised learning environment providing a range of tools similar to a VLE but linked to an institution administrative and management functions	Blackboard	
Personal Learning Environments	A collection of interoperable e-learning tools chosen and personalized by the individual learner rather than the learners institutions	PLEX	Boddington III An *APLE*

The big change in direction for learning management systems came with the idea of the Personal Learning Environment (PLE). The current view among researchers in education is that learning environments need to be supportive of learner preferences. The JISC (2005) in the UK consequently proposed the PLE as a learner management system that replaces some or all of the tools of a standard VLE with personal tools integrated with the student's own systems. The interface and tools are the personal choice of the learner not the institution, much the same way that the browser on a personal computer, or the widgets in iGoogle are the choice of the user. However for people with disabilities, personal preference may not go far enough. Added to this idea is the concept that content, tools and environment all need to be adaptable to the needs of the individual. Consequently a PLE which is also accessible Green, Pearson & Stockton (2006) refer to as an Adaptable Personal Learning Environment (APLE).

Accessibility Guidelines and Standards

IMS ACCMD and ACCLIP are the standards specifically extending the IMS learning standards to include accessibility issues. ACCMD is the standard for accessibility metadata definitions in learning resources, whereas ACCLIP extends the learner information package to include accessibility profiles – based on anonymous profiles of needs and preferences. Both these standards are considered in detail later. The other important IMS standards for our purposes are *Content Packaging* and *Learning Tools Interoperability*. The first of these (IMS CP) considers issues of learning content interoperability and interchange and in practice divides content into packages comprising a manifest (metadata, organizations, resources and submanifests) and the actual content (learning content, media, assessment, collaboration etc.). The same content packaging specification is also used by ADL (Advanced Distributed Learning) Initiative SCORM (Sharable Content Object Reference Model). The second (IMS LTI) is a new standard dealing with interoperability, re-use and interchange of learning tools as opposed to content.

In addition to these IEEE LOM (Learning Object Metadata) comprises a conceptual data schema for learning object metadata. This is a complex model but in brief it comprises nine main elements:

1. General (title, language, description ..)
2. Lifecycle (version, state)
3. Meta-metadata (metadataSchema)
4. Technical (format, size, location ..)
5. Educational (interactivityType, learningResource type, ..)
6. Rights (cost, copyright, ..)
7. Relation (kind)
8. Annotation (entity, date, description)
9. Classification (purpose, description, keywords)

Accessible E-Learning Content and Tools

While the IEEE LOM and IMS CP describe learning content their use is not specific to accessible learning objects or tools. However three further standards are - namely CEN-ISSS APLR and W3C/WAI ATAG and ARIA. The first of these APLR (or Accessibility Properties for Learning Resources) works directly with IEEE LOM to present an Accessibility Application Profile based on IMS ACCLIP. The second ATAG deals with accessible authoring tools. The third, ARIA (Accessible Rich Internet Applications) is designed to allow for improved accessibility and interoperability of web content and applications. ARIA covers a number of quite complex areas but in principle involves the concept of an accessibility API sitting between the user agent and assistive technologies. A similar but subtlety different model is given by Dodd et al. (2009). In principle

Table 3. Some important learning standards

Abbreviation	Standard	URL
ACCMD	IMS *AccessForAll Meta-data* Information Model	http://www.imsglobal.org/accessibility
ACCLIP	IMS Learner Information Package *Accessibility for LIP*	http://www.imsglobal.org/accessibility
APLR	CEN-ISSS Learning Technologies Workshop *Accessibility Properties for Learning Resources*	http://www.cen-ltso.net/Users/main.aspx?put=858
ARIA	W3C/WAI *Accessible Rich Internet Applications*	http://www.w3.org/TR/wai-aria
ATAG	W3C/WAI *Authoring Tools Accessibility Guidelines*	http://www.w3.org/TR/ATAG20
CP	IMS *Content Packaging*	http://www.imsglobal.org/content/packaging/
LOM	IEEE Standard for *Learning Object Metadata*	http://ltsc.ieee.org/wg12/
LTI	IMS *Learning Tools Interoperability*	http://www.imsglobal.org/ti/
WCAG	W3C/WAI *Web Content Accessibility Guidelines*	http://www.w3.org/TR/WCAG10

ARIA and Dodd's Carnforth model use a layered architecture in which one or more accessibility layers perform the task of converting display, control and content to be suitable to context and individual capability.

In principle adherence to a combination of these standards and guidelines will aid in the creation of accessible learning content and tools. However in practice a range of resources are needed to ensure that tutors and educators can understand what is required of them. These resources range from simple guidance, simulations or training materials (Papadopoulos et al., 2008) to full-blown authoring tools (Gkatzidou & Pearson, 2008). It is also believed that the new approach adopted by WCAG 2.0 and *AccessForAll* will ensure that the context and practical considerations will have a greater emphasis (Sloan et al., 2006).

Personalization and Adaptation

The terms *personalization* and *adaptation* are frequently applied to an e-learning context. The term *personalization* is specifically applied to educational and web content which is customized to the preferences or choices of an individual, profile or group. A PLE can be considered to be a learning environment which is both personal and capable of being personalized. *Adaptation* is a related but subtly different term. In a scientific context it was first used in biology for the ability of an organism to become better suited to its environment. In an educational context it was applied by the development psychologists, including Piaget to the processes of learning, which involves both *assimilation* and *accommodation.* Both are forms of adaptation, the first relating to our ability to change our environment, the second the ability for us to change ourselves to suit our environment. In the context of learning environments VLEs and MLEs typically require learners to adapt to them (accommodation), whereas PLEs and APLEs allow for a redress in the balance, in that the environment will also adapt to the learner (assimilation). In computer science (and by extension also in e-learning), adaptivity characterizes the behaviour of systems which can change automatically in response to user behaviour, the environment or implicit or explicit needs. Typically such systems are classified as semi-automated or automated control systems, intelligent environments or electronic performance support systems.

In the context of an APLE, many software systems try to personalize the environment to the preferences of the individual. An example of this is iGoogle (Google, 2009). In addition to the standard search box the user is presented with a range of tools on the page and is also allowed to customize the interface in a number of important ways:

1. by choosing or creating the window theme
2. by adding, editing, moving or deleting gadgets
3. by sharing and communicating themes, gadgets and content feeds with others.

Often web based applications are adapted or can be configured to handle small screen layouts. This might be to accommodate PDAs, mobile phones and other mobile devices or magnified displays. Most mobile phones offer user-selectable themes, widgets, gadgets or mini-applications for their customers. In the case of the Apple iPhone the number of applications offered through iTunes and the AppleStore is rapidly approaching six figures (Apple, 2009). It is accepted practice in product design to offer users choice in their interface, tools and software environment. This is a consequence of the Web 2.0 world in which users exercise choice and vote with their feet (or more commonly their fingers).

ADAPTABLE PERSONAL LEARNING

In this section we look at our perspective on the problems of providing an adaptable and inclusive e-learning support system. We believe that a framework for a truly adaptable PLE – an APLE can be the basis of a solution to this problem.

An Adaptable Personal Learning Environment

An Adaptable Personal Learning Environment merges the concepts of an Adaptable Virtual Learning Environment and a Personal Learning Environment. Alternatively it can also be viewed as the addition of the concepts of accessibility adaptations to the JISC concept of a PLE. Regardless of which perspective we take we might question why accessibility is not part of the PLE model in the first place. The reason may be as simple as the fact that many non-specialists (and a few specialists) believed that accessibility was primarily an issue of content presentation. Consequently many educational technologists were under the false impression that Web Content Accessibility Guidelines from the W3C WAI (1999) had already dealt with this: correctly defined web content, employing ALT-tags, correctly formed XHTML and CSS style sheets and meeting triple-A conformance to priority level 3 must, by its very definition, be accessible. This position is no longer tenable; not only does it fail to deal with issues such as context or user group, guidelines and standards have since moved on. WCAG 2.0 takes a fundamentally different approach to WCAG 1.0. In principle, however, the addition of concepts such as adaptation to the PLE produces a much more robust and sophisticated framework: hence the birth of the APLE (see Figure 1).

Figure 1. An APLE framework

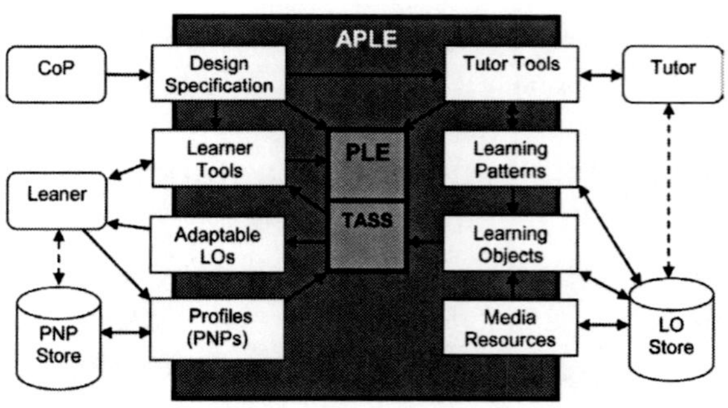

An APLE is defined in terms of a number of components and services conforming to a variety of e-learning and accessibility standards. The basic data components of the APLE are the user profiles and learning object store. Profiles will conform to IMS LIP and ACCLIP and the metadata for the learning objects to IEEE LOM and IMS ACCMD. In addition there will be a range of tools which would typically constitute a VLE but either chosen (as in the case of a PLE) or additionally adapted to meet the needs of the user, group and context as expressed in the profile. Other resources might also form part of the framework including, for example, an accessible and equivalent e-assessment repository. Tools might typically conform to IMS LTI (Learning Tools Interoperability) and assessments to IMS QTI (Question Test Interoperability).

In addition to the standard components found in a VLE, MLE or PLE an APLE is characterized by its transformation augmentation and substitution service (TASS). The TASS component is a localized *AccessForAll* service, in that although it handles adaptations to learning objects based on *AccessForAll* standards, it is designed to operate within the context of a local PLE. However it does rely on contributions from a wide ranging community of practice to provide the necessary primary and alternative learning resources, the learning patterns and learning profiles (IMS ACCMD and ACCMD). Given this information the TASS determines whether a learning object can be adapted to the needs and preferences of a given learner in a given context. If a learning object can be adapted then the TASS will apply the necessary adaptations to the learning object or environment to improve the accessibility of the learning experience. Before we specify the TASS in detail it is important that the reader understands the basic elements of IMS *AccessForAll*.

AccessForAll and Learner Profiles

The IMS *AccessForAll* metadata specification (IMS ACCMD) divides resources into primary and equivalent alternative resources. The primary resource is the default on which the learning object is based. An equivalent alternative resource behaves or functions in a similar way or addresses the same learning aims, objectives and outcomes. Basically it has the same semantic component but is expressed in an alternate medium. Equivalence is in practice difficult to define but generally relatively easy to recognize. Most people can understand that a large print or audio-book might be an equivalent to the original text or an audio-description an equivalent to a video sequence for someone with visual impairment. The IMS *AccessForAll* overview explains that metadata is held about a primary resource to describes its:

1. Access Modality
2. Adaptability
3. Equivalent alternatives

Access modality tells us whether the user requires the ability to see, hear, touch or understand text to access the resource. Adaptability is an indication of how amenable the resource is to transformation of display presentation or control. Finally known equivalent alternatives to the primary resource are identified. An equivalent alternative will have its own description of its access modality, adaptability and equivalent alternatives. Equivalent alternatives are divided into two types:

1. Supplementary equivalent alternatives
2. Non-supplementary equivalent alternatives

Throughout this chapter (and within our TASS) we refer to these forms of adaptations as augmentations and substitutions, but they are essentially the same. The first type of resource is designed to augment the primary resource to improve accessibility, such as captions for a video. The second type is substituted for the primary resource, such as an audio description for a video. This is frequently an arbitrary but functionally useful distinction when defining our adaptation service. *AccessForAll*

Figure 2. Overall Accessibility model

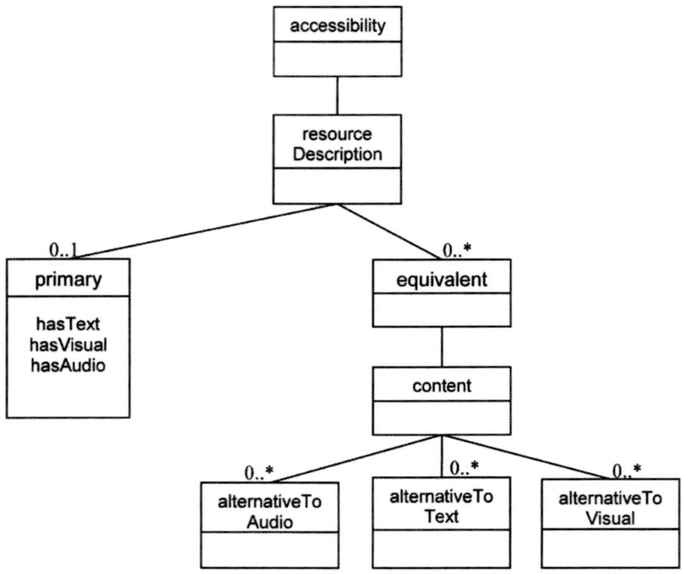

expresses its ACCMD and ACCLIP specification using UML (Unified Modelling Language) class notation. Instances and examples are expressed using XML (eXtensible Markup Language). The general accessibility class, the equivalence class and the *AccessForAll* profiles are of particular importance to the context of this chapter.

Accessibility Class

The overall accessibility data class defined by IMS ACCMD is presented above (Figure 2). The accessibility class has a resource description composed of an optional primary resource and any number of equivalent resources. An example instance in XML might be as shown in Box 1.

Box 1.

```
<accessibility xmlns="http://www.imsglobal.org/xsd/accmd">
  <resourceDescription>
   <primary hasText="false" hasVisual="true"
    hasAudio="true"/>
     <equivalentResource>
      urn:uuid:12345678-1234-1234-1234-123456789abc
     </equivalentResource>
    <equivalentResource>
     urn:uuid:12345678-1234-1234-1234-123456789123
    </equivalentResource>
   </primary>
  </resourceDescription>
</accessibility>
```

The example represents a primary audiovisual resource which has two equivalent resources each identified by a unique resource number (urn). The equivalent resources would then be identified by the equivalence class. This is presented in the next section.

Equivalence Class

The IMS equivalence class is presented above in Figure 2. An example equivalent supplementary resource or caption for the previous primary resource would look something like as shown in Box 2.

The supplementary resource (augmentation) described above is an alternative to audio in the form of enhanced captions in English with a reduced reading level but not reduced speed. These captions may or may not be needed; perhaps a different alternative such as an alternative to visual is required; that would depend on the context, needs and preferences of the individual. For that

Box 2.

```
<accessibility xmlns="http://www.imsglobal.org/xsd/accmd">
  <resourceDescription>
   <equivalent supplementary="true">
     <primaryResource>
     urn:uuid:12345678-1234-1234-1234-123456789000
     </primaryResource>
       <content>
     <alternativesToAuditory
       xmlns="http://www.imsglobal.org/xsd/acclip">
         <captionType xml:lang="en">
           <reducedReadingLevel value="true"/>
           <reducedSpeed value="false"/>
        <enhancedCaption value="true"/>
          </captionType>
       </alternativeToAuditory>
    </content>
   </equivalent>
  </resourceDescription>
</accessibility>
```

the *AccessForAll* profile of needs and preferences (drawn from the IMS ACCLIP specification) needs to be examined.

AccessForAll Profile

An *AccessForAll* Profile of Needs and Preferences typically takes the form of an XML description (See Box 3).

For a given context a profile is associated with an individual. An XML representation of an example profile is given above. This tells us that the user-context 'abc' relies on alternatives to visual resources with ALT and longDescription text in English. The user-context 'abc' might relate to a blind user or to someone who cannot rely on the visual modality in a given context. The reason for the need for an alternative to visual is not declared here and in fact that information is not required any way.

Box 3.

```
<accessForAll xmlns=http://www.imsglobal.org/xsd/acclip
  xmlns:xsi=http://www.w3.org/2001/XMLSchema-instance
  xsi:schemaLocation="http://www.imsglobal.org/xsd/acclip
  AccessForAllv1p0d27.xsd">
  <context identifier="abc" xml:lang="en">
  <content>
    <alternativesToVisual>
   <altTextLang xml:lang="en"/>
   <longDescriptionLang xml:lang="en"/>
       ..
  </content>
</accessForAll>
```

Transformation Augmentation and Substitution Service

The TASS described here is a localized form of *AccessForAll* service based on IMS ACCMD and ACCLIP. The TASS identifies and provides alternatives to learning resources which would otherwise result in a mismatch between the user's capabilities and the media components of the learning object. The TASS identifies three basic forms of adaptation, for which we use the terms:

1. Transformation
2. Augmentation
3. Substitution

The first of these relates to the IMS *AccessForAll* display transformation or control flexibility and usually requires an assistive technology or electronic performance support as part of the e-learning support environment. The latter two forms map directly to the IMS supplementary or non-supplementary equivalent alternative resources. All three forms refer to adaptations typically (but not exclusively) to a primary media component of a learning resource.

Transformation

A transformation occurs where an existing component can be replaced or supplemented by an alternative component using an automated process. Typically that would involve translating one media format into an alternate modality such as text to audio (speech), text or visual to tactile or audio (speech) to text. The process would typically be provided by the learning support environment and may involve the integration of specialist hardware or software with that environment either at the operating system level or within the APLE. An example of this is the use of a screen-reader such as JAWS. This provides an automated audio alternative to text and therefore text items can be translated into audio speech. Given this resource an individual needing an alternative to text will have an automated transformation available to them to render the content accessible. Similarly display can be rendered using alternative fonts, colours and colour contrasts, screen layouts and magnification based on style-sheets, magnification software or similar personalization software. Text could be translated into a tactile mode using a Braille reader or into an alternative language. Speech recognition software might transform an audio soundtrack into an automated transcript. Transformations have the advantage of relying on an automated process that does not need manual intervention to be applied for each media component. The results may be less than perfect although still usable: synthesized speech often sounds robotic, automatic speech recognition is extremely flawed, language translation software can produce incomprehensible results and alternative colours and layouts can leave the overall screen display cluttered or confusing. Despite this, transformation is an important form of adaptation rendering otherwise inaccessible content accessible.

Augmentation

An augmentation is an additional resource added to a primary resource to support the learner in accessing one or more modalities. An augmentation typically adds existing media forms to aid the learner in comprehending or perceiving the resource or replaces one or more of the modalities with the primary resource, although without replacing the whole primary resource. An example of this is the addition of captions to a video for a deaf learner. The captions are added to the video sequence so that the deaf student can comprehend the dialogue, although the video sequence is not replaced. Audio descriptions or foreign language subtitles might be used in a similar way or a transcript might be used to supplement a visual image, diagram or audiovisual sequence. Any additional resource might act as an augmentation. An augmentation might be applied to an existing primary resource or adaptation. Also the augmentation may be applied as a result of a declared need or preferences. However it supports the primary resource rather than totally replaces it. An augmentation need not reproduce all elements of the primary resource. It simply needs to deal with those elements or modalities which would otherwise limit the user's access in any given context. Typically an augmentation requires a manual intervention on an individual media component basis, in that the need would have to be predicted and the alternative provided before it is requested, possibly as part of the process of creating the learning object.

Substitution

A substitution occurs in those cases where the primary resource is totally replaced by one or more alternative resources. Typically this can be seen as a simple replacement of one inaccessible resource by an accessible alternative. For example a video sequence might be replaced by an audio description for a visually impaired user. The new resource fully describes the visual sequence and therefore it can be used as an alternative resource without further reference to the original. Alternative substitutions include video or audio substituted by a text description or transcript, text substituted by an alternative text either simplified or in an alternative language or text substituted by visual images, video sequences or animations. While in principle a substitution is the simplest form of adaptation, in practice it requires the most work to be done by the provider of the learning object: the substituted resource may have to do much more than an augmentation. Substitutions can also be applied to a previous adaptation, typically a previous augmentation: for example when captions are added to the video and stored as a single audiovisual stream, possibly also in a simplified or alternative language.

FORMAL SPECIFICATION OF AN ADAPTATION SERVICE

Having now defined in detail, the APLE and TASS, the following sections give an overview of the TASS specification using the logic-based programming language Prolog. The UML class notation and XML metadata models are used effectively to give the IMS *AccessForAll* specifications. However this research chooses to specify the TASS component in Prolog. The reason for this is simply that Prolog provides us with an opportunity to progressively define facts and rules, to build and gradually refine our model and to evaluate its effectiveness. Prolog is an executable language; consequently the specification can be animated and evaluated. The Prolog definition also has a close binding to the XML metadata model of IMS *AccessForAll*. It can act as an alternative description of the IMS standard and should also help us to critically evaluate our APLE, our TASS and indeed the standards themselves.

Prolog Specification of Learner Profiles

To identify how the TAS service might work an illustrative example was defined using the logic-based programming language Prolog (Clocksin & Mellish, 1984), a language which has the advantages of being simple and precise. Prolog is an AI language based on formal predicate logic. It has the ability to express both facts (explicit knowledge) and rules (mechanism to infer implicit knowledge based on patterns). For example consider a group of six disparate learners called (for the sake of argument) Anne, Ben, Cath, Dave, Edith and Franck, three of whom would traditionally be considered to have disabilities. In summary:

- Anne is able-bodied and has no declared disabilities. She has a learning style preference for kinaesthetic learning but this preference is not pronounced.
- Ben is blind and uses the JAWS screen-reader and a Braille device. He has no ability to see any visual media or text and relies on his screen reader and alternatives to visual elements.
- Cath has cognitive learning disabilities and uses symbols and switch input. She cannot read English unless it is at a very simple reading level presented alongside symbols or images.
- Dave is deaf and prefers British Sign Language (BSL) as his first language but he does understand written English albeit at a reduced reading level.
- Edith is elderly and she has reduced vision; she needs large text with high contrast. She has a good reading level but has reduced reaction time and cannot handle complex presentations.
- Franck is French. English is a second language to him. He prefers French transcripts or translations but can read English at a reduced level with aids including an on-line French-English dictionary.

In Prolog facts are always expressed in lowercase. Upper case is reserved for variables. Consequently a set of Prolog facts that lists our users could look like:

```
/* APLE and TASS users */
user(anne).
user(ben).
user(cath).
user(dave).
user(edith).
user(franck).
```

This would simply tell us that Anne, Ben, Cath, Dave, Edith and Franck are users. We know nothing else about them. However in Prolog the database of facts can be queried by posing questions:

```
?- user(andrew).
no
?- user(anne).
yes
```

This asks 'is Andrew a user?' to which the answer is 'no' and then is Anne a user to which the answer is 'yes'. An alternative question might be to ask who is a user. For that we replace our known element with a variable expressed in upper case such as 'X':

```
?- user(X).
X = anne
```

We have asked is there a match for 'X' who is a user. The first answer we get is Anne although the remaining names can also be listed by asking Prolog to look for another until there are no further options. This is typically done by using the 'or' operator which is represented by a semicolon:

```
?- user(X).
X = anne;
X = ben;
X = cath;
X = dave;
X = edith;
X = franck;
no
```

We could take this further and start to add other facts, including the declared disabilities of each of our users:

```
disability(ben, blind).
disability(cath, cognitive).
disability(dave, deaf).
```

This can be read as Ben's disability is he is blind, Cath's disability is cognitive, Dave is deaf etc. As Anne, Edith and Franck are not included we might infer that they have no declared disability. However this uses a disability model of learners. An alternative is to express a capability model of learners such as:

```
     /* user capabilities */
capability(anne, see).
capability(anne, hear).
capability(anne, read(english)).
capability(anne, touch).
     capability(ben, hear).
capability(ben, read(english)).
capability(ben, read(braile)).
capability(ben, touch).
     capability(cath, see).
capability(cath, hear).
capability(cath, touch).
/* .. etc. */
```

However this is a very verbose way of expressing the information needed. We could express capabilities based on Prolog rules such as:

```
capability(X, visual):-
not(disability(X, blind)).
```

This rule states that X has a visual capability if X is not blind. This is a very crude rule in that it implies that we can either see or not and it is still based on a disability rather than a capability model which many might find offensive. Consequently the approach is to adopt the model of explicit needs and preferences. These may be expressed as Prolog facts for example:

```
/* Needs media alternative */
needs(ben, alternativeToVisual).
needs(dave, alternativeToAudio).
needs(cath, alternativeToText).
/* Needs - transformations, scaffold-
ing or support */
needs(ben, screenReader).
needs(cath, symbols).
```

```
needs(edith, displayText(large-
font)).
needs(edith, displayColour(high-con-
trast)).
needs(franck, dictionary(english-
french)).
/* Preferences */
prefers(anne,
learningStyle(kinaesthetic)).
prefers(dave, signLanguage(bsl)).
prefers(franck, language(french)).
```

The first set of facts tells us whether a specific individual needs an alternative to visual, audio or text. This might be because they are blind, deaf or have a cognitive disability or maybe because of contextual reasons (such as driving). Another might need an alternative to audio because of a requirement to be quiet (such as in a library) or because the environment is noisy. Additionally the fact that Ben needs a screen reader, Claire symbols, Edith large-fonts and high-contrast are all explicit facts; as also are the fact that Dave prefers BSL, Franck French etc. In terms of IMS these facts relate closely to the ACCLIP Access-ForAll element type of the Learner Profile, which is defined in terms of context, language, display, control and content.

Prolog Specification of Adaptable Learning Objects

Given what we know about the learner and their context we need to consider how learning objects, media and resources can be adapted to meet learner needs and preferences. It is possible to define a set of facts and rules which determine what the system knows or can infer about a set of learning objects. Consider a simple object with three resources, namely a graphic (r1), some text (r2) and a video (r3). Defined equivalent alternatives are the ALT text (r4) for the graphic (r1), some captions (r5) for the video (r3) and an alternative to the graphic ALT text (r4) in French (r6). In Prolog this would be represented something like:

```
/* Learning object definitions ------
-------------------- */
lo(unit1,[visual(r1),text(r2),audiovi
sual(r3)]).
/* Learning resources and alterna-
tives ------------------ */
loResource(r1,primary,visual, 'g01.
jpg').
loResource(r2,primary, text, 't01.
html').
loResource(r3,primary,
audiovisual,'v01.mp3').
loResource(r4,r1,
alternativeToVisual(altText), 't02.
html').
loResource(r5,r3,
alternativeToAudio(caption), 't03.
txt').
loResource(r6,r4, alternativeToText(a
ltText(french)), 't04.txt').
```

Examining the Prolog, the first fact tells us that there exists an LO (learning object) called 'unit1' which uses three resources namely a visual (r1), text (r2) and audiovisual resource (r3). The square brackets are used to enclose a list of arbitrary length. This is a common Prolog structure which is typically decomposed recursively using a head (H) and tail (T) de-constructor [H|T] e.g.:

```
member(X, [X|_]).
member(X, [_,T]):- member(X,T).
```

This says if X is at the head of the list then X is a member, otherwise check for X recursively in the tail of the list. The loResource facts tells us a little more about the learning resources including their file names and whether they are a primary (r1, r2, r3) or alternative resource (r4, r5, r6). The primary resources are identified as 'primary' and have a range of modality identifiers, whereas alternatives indicate which primary or alternative resource they refer to and what type of alternative they are. The common primary and secondary modalities are given in the table (Table 4).

Given enough information on the learner and the learning objects, we can determine whether there is a mismatch. In the case of IMS this is described in terms of systems descriptions and behaviour examples expressed typically as a flow chart. However in Prolog these are simply more rules e.g.:

```
/* Check for mismatch in visual, au-
dio and text modalities -- */
mismatch(X, LO):-
lo(LO, Resources),
needs(X, alternativeToVisual),
member(visual(P), Resources),
not(loResource(Equivalent, P,
alternativeToVisual(Type)).
.. etc.
```

The first rule says that there is a mismatch between our learner X and a learning object LO if X needs an alternative to visual and the learning object LO contains a primary visual resource P which does not have an equivalent visual alternative. Further mismatch rules would do the same for auditory and text content. Other combinations such as audiovisual may also need a visual alternative. More sensibly our learning resource might be defined as having any combination of audio (A), visual (V), text (T) or haptic/tactile (H) as given above in Table 4. The set of rules to allow us to check media types would take the form:

```
/* check for audio, visual, text and
tactile content -- */
hasAudio(X):-
member(X,[audio(_),
audiovisual(_),audiotext(_), multime-
dia(_), richmedia(_)]).
hasVisual(X):-
     member(X,[visual(_),audiovisu
al(_), hypertext(_),multimedia(_),
richmedia(_)]).
hasText(X):-
     member(X,[text(_),hypertext(_),
audiotext(_),multimedia(_), richme-
dia(_)]).
hasTactile(X):-
     member(X, [tactile(_), richme-
dia(_)]).
```

The full set of mismatch rules then become:

```
mismatch(X, LO):-
lo(LO, Resources),
needs(X, alternativeToVisual),
member(P, Resources),
hasVisual(P),
not(loResource(Equivalent, P,
alternativeToVisual(Type)).
mismatch(X, LO):-
lo(LO, Resources),
needs(X, alternativeToAudio),
member(P, Resources),
hasAudio(P),
not(loResource(Equivalent, P,
alternativeToAudio(Type)).
mismatch(X, LO):-
lo(LO, Resources),
needs(X, alternativeToText),
member(P, Resources),
hasText(P),
not(loResource(Equivalent, P,
alternativeToText(Type)).
```

The Prolog Workflow and Process Model

Given a complete set of media and mismatch rules, we can then say (in IMS *AccessForAll* terms) that a learning object is accessible if there are no remaining mismatches between the learner (X) and the learning object's constituent primary or equivalent resources.

Table 4. Common media combinations and alternatives

Shorthand	A	V	T	H	Examples
Primary modalities					
audio	√				Sound, music, speech, podcast
visual		√			Graphic, animation, symbol etc
text			√		Description, plain text,
tactile				√	Haptic feedback, tactile, Braille
audiovisual	√	√			Video sequence or vodcast
hypertext		√	√		(X)HTML with image/links, text
audiotext	√		√		Text with audio commentary
multimedia	√	√	√		presentation, computer games
richmedia	√	√	√	√	interactive games
Alternatives To Audio / Visual / Text / tactile (Haptic)					
caption	x		√		Captions for the audiovisual
altText		x	√		An ALT text for an image
braille			x	√	Braille representation for text
altText(Languge)	x	x	√		An ALT text language alternative
audioDescription	√	x	x		Audio description for visuals or text
symbols(Set)		√	x		A symbols text equivalent
transcript	x		√		A text transcript of speech

```
accessibleLO(X, LO):-
     lo(LO, Resources),
not(mismatch(X, Resources)).
```

This is still a severely limited model, however, as it fails to take into account any real subtleties in the system such as whether the alternative really meets the needs of the individual or any of his/her preferences. For any given example, simply to say that there is an alternative to audio in the form of captions may not be enough. Perhaps the language, language level or speed needs to be reduced. Let us take the example of Franck: he prefers French which means where there is a French alternative text or transcript he will prefer to use this, if not then a reduced reading level of English and then failing that an on-line English-French dictionary. The system we propose here would not cater for this adequately, but then again neither would the IMS behaviour model. One advantage of Prolog is that a set of additional rules can be written to add sophistication to the system to deal with such concerns and find the best possible match. This could even be extended to handle preferred learning styles. Anne has stated a preference for kinaesthetic learning. It is a matter therefore of relating a learning object to a learning pattern (Green, Jones et al., 2006) and then identifying the learning styles which this pattern employs. An alternative learning pattern could then be adopted to reconstruct the learning object to work more closely to her preferences. This would therefore allow alternative but equivalent learning objects based on different learning styles, different languages, language levels, media components or resources.

Ultimately a range of intelligent agents working as part of the TASS could adapt our original learning object, tools and environment to get to a close match to the declared needs and preferences of the learner. Achieving this goal is difficult, requires some evolution to the current standards and a great deal of work from the community of practice, but it is possible in the longer term. Identifying the problem is half-way to achieving the solution.

Sample Prolog Program

This section presents a sample Prolog program fragment used for the purposes of this study. It is intended to be illustrative of the specification presented in this chapter (Box 4).

DISCUSSION

The current system as specified here is only a beginning. The Prolog specification helps us define and evaluate the APLE framework in general and the TASS in particular. There are a number of other components within the APLE which need further consideration and discussion, including the tutor tools which aid the production of adaptable learning objects and the learner tools which provide access to the learning environment. Given that a certain level of adaptation might be applied to these tools themselves, it becomes an interesting debate whether the TASS should also be the main component in a tool adaptation service. The issue here is that as it is based on *AccessForAll* the inevitable result is that the TASS concentrates on content, presentation and control rather than the selection or adaptation of tools. This is an area for future consideration, along with the integration and development of existing standards and guidelines.

The ability of the TASS to create new virtual learning objects based on alternative learning resources and ultimately learning patterns is the current focus of this research. The TASS has access to information on the learning object aggregations and the necessary replacements. This can be specified in a Prolog model. A number of augmentations, substitutions and transformations are identified and a new 'virtual' learning object created to meet the needs and requirements of the learner. In terms of Prolog this is represented by the assertion of new facts and the creation of a virtual learning object based on a new resource list. A Prolog fragment would look something like:

```
assertz(virtualLO(NewName, NewRe-
sourceList)).
```

Here we are dynamically asserting a new fact at run-time which in this case is our virtual learning object. This new learning object will be an adaptation of an existing learning object.

By using Prolog we can create a version of our specification which we can animate and evaluate. We can use it to say something about our proposed TASS and APLE and the standards themselves. In brief we might say that compliance with a wide range of e-learning and accessibility standards is difficult to achieve, but the *AccessForAll* working group, through IMS ACCMD and ACCLIP, have developed a working model, which offers an important starting point in the specification of adaptable and inclusive e-learning support. These standards can be applied, augmented and improved using a formally specified localized *AccessForAll* service as part of an APLE.

Currently example learning object metadata can be given to the system and a statement of whether the specified learning object is broadly 'accessible' can be determined. The system can then proceed to determine how a specific learning object should be adapted. Currently, it is a relatively simple process to add captions or augment a video with a script, at least in terms of our TASS specification and APLE framework. In reality though, this may require a great deal of time and effort from the tutor or some other member of our support community. In terms of our specification, however, our real difficulties begin when the learning object needs to be completely re-aggregated based on an alternative learning pattern or a range of alternative sensory modalities. At some point

Box 4.

```
/* learning objects --------------------- */
/* defines a specific learning object assessmbly */
learningObject(intro, [visual(introP1p1),text(introP1p2),text(introP2),audiovisual(introP3)]).
loAssembly(intro, intro, root_).
    loAssembly(introP1, intro, branch_).
        loAssembly(introP1p1, introP1, visual).
        loAssembly(introP1p2, introP1, text).
      loAssembly(introP2, intro, text).
      loAssembly(introP3, intro, audiovisual).
/* defines a set of learning resources */
loResource(introP1p1,primary,null,visual, 'introMod/graphic01.jpg').
loResource(introP1p2,primary,null,text, 'introMod/text01.html').
loResource(introP2,primary,null,text, 'introMod/text02.html').
loResource(introP3,primary,null,audiovisual, 'introMod/audioVisual01.mp3').
/* defines a set of explicit alternatives (augmentations or substitutions) */
loResource(introP1p1alt,augmentation, introP1p1,alternativeToVisual(altText), '<..alt text ..>').
loResource(introP3captions,substitution, introP3,alternativeToAudio(caption), 'introMod/audiovisualwithcaptions01.mp3').
loResource(introP3audio,substitution, introP3, alternativeToVisual(audioDescription), 'introMod/audioDescription01.mp3').
/* has media-type rules ----------------- */
hasAudio(X):-
    member(X,[audio(_),audiovisual(_), audiotext(_),multimedia(_), richmedia(_)]).
hasViual(X):-
    member(X,[visual(_),audiovisual(_), hypertext(_),multimedia(_), richmedia(_)]).
hasText(X):-
    member(X,[text(_),hypertext(_), audiotext(_),multimedia(_), richmedia(_)]).
hasTactile(X):-
    member(X, [tactile(_), richmedia(_)]).
/* mismatch rules ----------------------- */
mismatch(X, Y):-
    learningObject(Y, Z),
    needs(X, alternativeToVisual),
    (member(visual(_),Z); member(audiovisual(_), Z)),!.
mismatch(X, Y):-
    learningObject(Y, Z),
    needs(X, alternativeToAudio),
    (member(audio(_),Z); member(audiovisual(_), Z)), !.
mismatch(X, Y):-
    learningObject(Y, Z),
    needs(X, alternativeToText),
    member(text(_), Z), !.
/* mismatchReplace rules */
mismatchAfterReplace(X, Y):-
    learningObject(Y, Z),
    needs(X, alternativeToVisual),
    (member(visual(P),Z); member(audiovisual(P), Z)),
    not(loResource(_,_,P, alternativeToVisual(_), _)).
mismatchAfterReplace(X, Y):-
    learningObject(Y, Z),
    needs(X, alternativeToAudio),
    (member(audio(P),Z); member(audiovisual(P) Z)),
    not(loResource(_,_,P, alternativeToAudio(_), _)).
mismatchAfterReplace(X, Y):-
    learningObject(Y, Z),
    needs(X, alternativeToText),
    member(text(P), Z),
    not(loResource(_,_,P, alternativeToText(_), _)).

/* accessibility rules ------------------ */
```

continued on following page

Box 4. continued

```
accessibleLO(X, Y, Z):-
   learningObject(Y, Z),
   not(mismatch(X, Y)).
accessibleLO(X, Y, [tass_augmentations_substitutions|Z]):-
   learningObject(Y, Z),
   not(mismatchAfterReplace(X, Y)).

/* equivalency rules ---------------------*/
equivalent(X, Y, Type, augmentation):-
    loResource(X, augmentation(Y), Type).
equivalent(X, Y, Type, substitution):-
    loResource(X, substitution(Y), Type).
/* decomposition rules            ... */
/* re-aggregation & virtualLO rules  ... */
```

the learning object may begin to lose coherence or pedagogic value. Similar effects can occur with a display when style-sheet changes are applied at several levels. The ability of CSS to support cascading styles can lead to incoherence.

It has been suggested that a translation process from UML or XML to Prolog might be automated to aid in the process of animating the specification. This is certainly feasible (see Martinez-Otiz et al. 2009) but bindings to the AccessForAll workflow or behavioural model is not straightforward. In our opinion this part of the standards is simplistic and extremely flawed. Also the standards are in the process of evolution. Conversations with key members of the Accessibility standards working groups have indicated that *AccessForAll* version 2.0 (A4A 2.0) will take quite a different approach to the current model. Many of the perceived weaknesses are being addressed and the new standards are likely to be more amenable to manipulation by declarative or logic-based languages and language engineering approaches.

CONCLUSION

This chapter looks at the contribution of an APLE framework based on the IMS ACCLIP and ACCMD standards and *AccessForAll* to the evolution of an inclusive e-learning support environment.

The IMS ACCLIP and ACCMD and related standards have been referred to and discussed in only limited detail but we believe our APLE model and the Prolog specification itself can help researchers and educators understand the issues involved in defining inclusive e-learning support. It is our belief that the APLE framework can be specified and defined based on a community of practice, to encapsulate best practice in the provision of inclusive, personalized and adaptable e-learning. It has never been our intention to make a detailed critical evaluation of IMS ACCLIP and ACCMD. They clearly have their faults but until we have A4A 2.0, which will be soon, they are the best we have. However the fundamental principles are simple and sound and will go a long way towards achieving accessible, adaptable and personalized e-learning.

As for our APLE, the TASS is just one, albeit very important, component. In addition to the TASS, there are a range of tools for tutors, educators, designers, students, researchers and programmers that we need to specify design and develop. Many of these components exist but need to be integrated into our APLE or to be redesigned to take on board new thinking and changes to standards. However we believe our fundamental framework and principles and our use of a core of dedicated researchers coupled with a wider community of practice is represents an eminently sound approach. The goal is to provide a fully adaptable framework offering an inclusive personal support environment and adaptable e-learning content. This chapter presents some of the first steps in achieving that goal.

ACKNOWLEDGMENT

I acknowledge the significant contribution to this chapter and the work contained herein by Dr Elaine Pearson, Stavroula Gkatzidou and the others members of the Accessibility Research Centre (ARC) at Teesside University. In addition I wish to thank the editors, particularly Fotios Lazarinis, and the reviewers for their constructive comments. As always, the remaining errors are all my own.

REFERENCES

W3C. (1999). *Web Content Accessibility Guidelines (WCAG) 1.0*, W3C 5 May 1999, Retrieved 4th August 2009 from: http://www.w3.org/TR/WCAG10/

W3C. (2008). *Web Content Accessibility Guidelines (WCAG) 2.0*, W3C 11 December 2008, reformatted 3 March 2009, Retrieved 4th August 2009 from: http://beta.w3.org/TR/2009/REC-WCAG20-20090303/

W3C. (2009). Authoring Tool Accessibility Guidelines (ATAG) 2.0, W3C Working Draft 21th May 2009, Retrieved 4th August 2009 from: http://www.w3.org/TR/ATAG20/

W3C. (2009, February 24). *Accessible Rich Internet Applications (WAI-ARIA) 1.0*. W3C Working Draft. Retrieved 4th August 2009 from: http://www.w3.org/TR/wai-aria/

Apple (2009) *Browse web apps,* Retrieve on-line on 4th August, 2009 at: http://www.apple.com/webapps/

Clocksin, W., & Mellish, C. (1984). *Programming in Prolog*. Berlin: Springer-Verlag.

Dodd, R., Green, S., & Pearson, E. (2009). User Capabilities in an Adaptive World. In *Proceedings of ACM MSIADU09, 1st ACM Workshop on Media Studies and Implementations to Improve Access to Disabled Users, Beijing,* October 2009.

Gkatzidou, S., & Pearson, E. (2008). *A vision for truly adaptable and accessible learning objects. Australasian Society for Computers in Learning in Tertiary Education (ASCILITE)*. Melbourne, Australia: Conference.

Google. (n.d.). *Gadgets *API Developer's Guide*. Retrieved 4th August 2009 from: http://code.google.com/intl/en/apis/gadgets/docs/dev_guide.html

Green, S., Jones, R., Pearson, E., & Gkatzidou, S. (2006). Accessibility and adaptability of learning objects: responding to metadata, learning patterns and profiles of needs and preferences. *ALT-J. Research in Learning Technology*, *14*(1), 117–129.

Green, S., Pearson, E., & Gkatzidou, S. (2009). Formal Specification of an Adaptable Personal Learning Environment Using Prolog. In *Proceedings of ACM MSIADU09, 1st ACM Workshop on Media Studies and Implementations to Improve Access to Disabled Users, Beijing, October 2009.*

Green, S., Pearson, E., & Stockton, C. (2006). Personal Learning Environments: Accessibility and Adaptability in the Design of an Inclusive Learning Management System. *AACE World Conference on Educational Multimedia (EDMEDIA)*, Orlando, FL.

IEEE Standard for Learning Object Metadata IEEE Std 1484.12.1™ (2002). Retrieved November 1st 2005: http://www.ieeeltsc.org/wg12LOM

IMS. *AccessForAll*. (2004). IMS Global learning/Dublin Core AccessForAll project, Meta-data Specification Version 1.0 Final Specification: Overview, Information Model, XML Binding, Best Practice Guide 2004. Retrieved 4th August 2009 from: http://www.imsglobal.org/accessibility

IMS Global Learning Consortium. (n.d.). *Guidelines for Developing Accessible Learning Applications, version 1.0.* Retrieved 4th August 2009 from: http://ncam.wgbh.org/salt/guidelines/

IMS Global Learning Consortium Learner Information PackageAccessibility for LIP Version 1.0 Final Specification: Information Model, XML Binding. (2003). *Best Practice Guide, Conformance Specification, Use Cases, Examples, June 2003*. Retrieved 4th August 2009 from http://www.imsglobal.org/accessibility

ISO IEC JTC1 SC36 WG7 (2008). Individualized Adaptability and Accessibility in E-learning, Education and Training. *ISO/IEC 24751-1*.

Martinez-Ortiz, I., Sierra, J., Fernandez-Manjon, B., & Fernandez-Valmayor, A. (2009). Language Engineering Techniques for the Development of e-Learning Applications. *J. of Network and Computer Application*, *32*, 1092–1105. doi:10.1016/j.jnca.2009.02.005

Nevile, L., & Treviranus, J. (2006). Interoperability for Individual Learner Centred Accessibility for Web-based Educational. Systems. *Journal of Educational Technology & Society*, *9*(4), 215–227.

Papadopoulos, G., Pearson, E., & Green, S. (2008). Effective Simulations to Support Academics in Inclusive Online Learning Design. In *Proceedings of the 10th Inter-national ACM SIGACCESS Conference on Computers and Accessibility*, Halifax, Canada.

Personal Learning Environments. (2005). *JISC.* Retrieved 4th August 2009 from: http://www.jisc.ac.uk/index.cfm?name=cetis_ple

Piaget, J. (1928). *The Child's Conception of the World.* London: Routledge and Kegan Paul.

Sloan, D., Heath, A., Hamilton, F., Kelly, B., Petrie, H., & Phipps, L. (2006, May). Contextual web accessibility - maximizing the benefit of accessibility guidelines. In *ACM International Conference Proceeding, 134, W4A at WWW2006*, Edinburgh, UK.

Trafford, P. (n.d.). PLEs as Environments for Personal and Personalised Learning. *JISC PLE position paper.* Retrieved 4th August 2009 from: http://weblearn.ox.ac.uk/site/asuc/oucs/staff/pault/research/mobile/ramble/present/uploads/PaulT_Mini%20PLEPaper1.0.pdf

ADDITIONAL READING

Boni, M., Cenni, S., Mirri, S., Muratori, L. A., & Salomoni, P. 2006. Automatically producing IMS AccessForAll Metadata. In *Proceedings of the 2006 international Cross-Disciplinary Workshop on Web Accessibility (W4a): Building the Mobile Web: Rediscovering Accessibility?* (Edinburgh, U.K., May 22 - 22, 2006). W4A '06, vol. 134. ACM, New York, NY, 92-97. DOI= http://doi.acm.org/10.1145/1133219.1133237

Gay, G., Mirri, S., Roccetti, M., & Salomoni, P. 2009. Adapting learning environments with AccessForAll. In *Proceedings of the 2009 international Cross-Disciplinary Conference on Web Accessibililty (W4A)* (Madrid, Spain, April 20 - 21, 2009). W4A '09. ACM, New York, NY, 90-91. DOI= http://doi.acm.org/10.1145/1535654.1535676

Gkatzidou, S., Pearson, E. & Green, S. "The Use of Learning Object Patterns and Metadata Vocabularies to Design Reusable and Adaptable Learning Resources", *ED-MEDIA*, Orlando, Florida, USA, June 2006

Green, S., Jones, R., Pearson, E., & Gkatzidou, S. (2006, June). "Learning Patterns and Learner Profiles in Learning Object Design", *ALT-J. Research in Learning Technology*, *14*(2), 217–221.

Green, S., Nacheva-Skopalik, L., & Pearson, E. "An Adaptable Personal Learning Environment for e-Learning and e-Assessment", CompSysTech'08, International Conference on Computer Systems and Technologies, Gabrovo, June 2008.

Green, S., & Pearson, E. "Disability, Accessibility and Adaptive Electronic Support" to appear as a chapter in Barker, P. & VanSchaik, P. (eds) *Electronic Performance Support: Using Technology to Enhance Human Performance*, Gower Press, 2009 (in press)

Green, S., Pearson, E., & Gkatzidou, S. "Personalisation, Profiling and Adaptation For Inclusive E-Learning Support", *Proceedings of the International Conference on Information Technologies (InfoTech-2009) September2009, Bulgaria*

Green, S., Pearson, E. & Stockton, C. "Accessibility and Adaptability in the Design of an Inclusive Learning Management System", *ED-MEDIA*, Orlando, Florida, USA, June 2006

Harper, S., Yesilada, Y., & Goble, C. 2005. "Engineering accessible design": W4A -- international cross disciplinary workshop on web accessibility 2005 workshop report. *SIGACCESS Access. Computing.*, 83 (Sep. 2005), 64-72. DOI= http://doi.acm.org/10.1145/1102187.1102198

Kompen, T. R., Edirisingha, P., & Mobbs, R. "Building Web 2.0-based personal learning environments - a conceptual framework", EDEN conference, Pairs, October 2008, available on-line at: http://hdl.handle.net/2381/4398

Leadbetter, P., Thomas, P., & Weedon, R. (1991). *Prolog: From Formal Specification to Prototype*. Oxford: Blackwell Scientific Publications.

Pearson, E., Green, S., & Gkatzidou, S. "Widening Participation Through Adaptable Personal Learning Environments", *9th Annual Conference of the Subject Centre for Information and Computer Sciences*, HEA, Liverpool, August 2008, 147-151

Pearson, E., Green, S., & Gkatzidou, S. "Responding to the challenge of providing learner-centred, accessible, personalized and flexible learning". *IEEE Conference on Advanced Learning Technologies (ICALT)*. Riga, Latvia, 2009

Van Harmelen, M. "Personal Learning Environments", IEEE, Proceedings of the Sixth International Conference on Advanced Learning Technologies (ICALT'06), 815-816, 2006

KEY TERMS AND DEFINITIONS

AccessForAll: Working group and proposals culminating in the IMS ACCMD (Accessibility Metadata) and IMS ACCLIP (Accessible Learner Information Profile) standards.

Adaptable Personal Learning Environment (APLE): An 'Adaptable' PLE which combines the benefits of Adaptable and inclusive VLE (Virtual Learning Environment) with those of a PLE.

Adaptation: Any augmentation, substitution or transformation.

Augmentation: An additional alternative equivalent learning resource.

Substitution: A replacement alternative equivalent learning resource.

Transformation, Augmentation and Substitution Service (TASS): A localized AccessForAll service.

Transformation: An automated replacement learning resource or control.

Chapter 11
Building a Framework for an English Language Course in an LMS with SCORM Compliant Learning Objects and Activities

Francisco Arcos
University of Alicante, Spain

Pablo Ortega
University of Alicante, Spain

ABSTRACT

The human mind needs order to understand anything and, in this respect, standards are essential because they impose order on the world. More specifically, standards are bringing great new benefits to the e-learning realm. For instance, by adhering to standards, courseware builders can construct components completely independent of the management systems under which they are intended to run—that's interoperability. There is a tough struggle nowadays to find the most appropriate specification for learning content and to assure it is fully operative across the existing LMSs (Learning Management Systems) in the market. In that authors view, SCORM (Sharable Content Object Reference Model) is coming afloat, outplaying most —if not all— its competitors. For that reason, the authors have been using SCORM learning objects to manage their course in Moodle for their students of English at the University of Alicante, obtaining so far satisfactory results. The authors' purpose in this article is twofold: on the one hand, they give an account of the problems they have met using SCORM in Moodle and how they have solved them. On the other, they explain the guiding aims of their Language Blend, which broadly said are the following: to set up a standard in language learning by means of a framework, wherein e-learning and in-person lectures merge strategically so that the benefits of both are enhanced.

DOI: 10.4018/978-1-61692-789-9.ch011

INTRODUCTION

When we started building our course in Moodle, we had a wide range of goals in mind, high among which was our wish to make it last long and stand strong against the passing of time. It goes without saying there were other considerations along this process: for instance, we wanted to check whether our course fulfilled our expectancies in relation to learning; and, if so, to make it available to the rest of our colleagues, irrespective of their place of work or their preferred LMS. To that end, we had to put some order and logic into everything we were to do. The human mind needs order to understand anything; then, logic tells us what is feasible, what is superfluous and unnecessary, for the human mind to comprehend. (Arnheim, 1971).

In this light, turning to standards was the perfect solution to make our course available to anyone and to assure its functionality across any Course Management System. It is a fact that some people are against the use of standards (Friesen, 2003, p.70) claiming that in order to tackle the object of learning in a more proper way "it is necessary to look beyond systems, engineering techniques and standardization processes." But, in our opinion, their many benefits admit no denying; where would we be without standards like the metric system, international distress signals, and TCP/IP? World travellers know how to deal with the absence of uniform electrical standards, which very often translate into unexpected problems and discomfort. In any case, the lack of interoperability had been the norm up until the first LMSs started to upsurge and improve. A great advantage of the position we are endorsing is that, by adhering to standards, courseware builders can construct components completely independent of the management systems under which they are intended to run. The latter is often referred to as interoperability, thanks to which the life expectancy of a courseware component is greatly increased because we know that we can upgrade a management system and it still works, or because we reuse that component in a totally new course.

If we briefly stop now to consider the proprietary learning technologies of the past, we will soon realize that, while providing good service in their time, they did not provide the benefits available by adopting standards. In fact, some LMSs have had to build specific modules to import learning events built with authoring tools simply because there was no standard to export to. Thus, in our opinion, e-learning standards raise key questions about the future concerning interoperability, reusability, durability and accessibility. There is ample evidence in the literature that standards are transforming the latter from vague promises into reality. And the extraordinary advance we have seen in recent years is undoubtedly a collective achievement, the result of many small joined forces.

Let´s now focus our attention on the mechanisms that facilitate the reuse of learning content and which allow course authors to increase the life span of the content they develop. As these are often expensive and time consuming, to build up the potential for any reuse should be maximized to obtain the best possible return on investment. Reusability was our first concern and in order to endow our system with it we needed to make use of a standard that allowed for granularity of content, effective and descriptive metadata and effective cross-platform packaging. SCORM (Sharable Content Object Reference Model) was the standard to adhere to ever since it met all our needs.

The fact that large collections of e-learning content are often lost when learning management systems are changed requires no explanation. Anybody who has been working in this field will understand why our first learning objects are now practically useless: simply because we employed an authoring tool which had no ADL (Advanced Distributed Learning) compliant module to export or save our activities into SCORM. Many of these difficulties share a common origin, which is that most learning management systems, such as

Blackboard, WebCT and Moodle use proprietary database formats that make it very difficult or impossible to transfer learning content from one system to another or to reuse previously developed content in other courses. For that reason, moving a course between systems can be more costly than just redeveloping that course in the new system.

We used CLIC, now JCLIC, activities (http://clic.xtec.cat/es/jclic/index.htm) to build learning objects and later met with obvious difficulties when we migrated to Moodle and wanted to use them for our courses. Luckily this has now been solved packaging them as Java beans and building a resource especially suited to import these activities into Moodle. The problem will emerge if we need to use these packages in another system different from Moodle. And for the same reason, we cannot be too sure who will profit from these packages.

Today it is very difficult or impossible to transfer learning content from one LMS to another. There is a clear need for a common data exchange format for learning content. In the current environment, significant investments in developing e-learning content in any learning field make little sense if it is developed specifically for delivery on a specific LMS.

Similarly, this lack of uniformity slows down knowledge exchange as differences between learning management systems make it hard for authors to collaborate on projects which involve using common tools to build and deploy learning materials. This can not only increase the total cost of building e-courses, it can also lower the quality of the course. The better courses require a considerable investment in authoring and development time. Often the content expert, author, is not the person with the technical expertise to encapsulate this content into an online course. Without e-learning standards, authors collaborating on developing an e-course need to ensure that they either restrict their content development to standards-based technology, such as hypertext, or ensure that their learning management systems can share learning content.

Let´s now pay some attention to our own work milieu. All around the world, universities are recognizing the inherent value of high-quality online courses developed by their faculty. The University of Alicante, for example, is looking at the collaborative development of learning content for courses being taught at nearly every campus in and outside Spain. These are the core courses in translation, education, engineering, mathematics, sciences, English, etc. The syllabus for these courses is very similar from one campus to another, and each campus has content experts that can share on a team to develop high quality learning content for these courses. Until now this content has been developed independently at each campus. Fortunately, our university started, and still is, using a proprietary system alongside Moodle and both systems can import SCORM 1.2., although neither of them have tools to create SCORM compliant learning objects or activities. Collaboration in developing learning content for e-courses not only lowers development costs and shortens development time, it can also result in higher quality courses.

However, the collaborative development of courses is very difficult without a standard for sharing that content from one campus to another. The general lack of international standards for packaging e-courses adversely impacts the development of university e-courses in several ways:

1. Since content developed without standard is difficult to reuse in other courses, it contributes to increased development costs.
2. E-course copyrights for e-courses of core content are of little value since they are likely to be obsolete in a few years when learning management systems or Internet technology change.
3. Author collaboration on e-course development is difficult without e-course standards.

If, as it seems, the pivotal importance of standards is being recognized from all quarters, the next logical step is to establish how it will all be put into practice. Nowadays, there is a tough struggle to find the most appropriate specification for learning content and to assure it is fully operative across the existing LMSs in the market. SCORM is, in our view, coming afloat, outplaying most —if not all— its competitors. This superiority is attested to by the fact that both and new authoring tools incorporate SCORM compliant specifications to export activities to LMSs. We finally chose SCORM to export our learning objects to be compliant with it, and design our course framework in Moodle for our students of English at the University of Alicante. And although there have been some ups and down along the line, on the whole, the experience shows an upward trend of satisfaction. The efficiency and improvement in technology and communications worldwide as well as the semantic and syntactic interoperability between the systems and the learning standards has helped greatly.

Next, with regard to the question of building learning objects for our LMS (that is, the activities themselves), we were faced with a choice: either use the modules or programs provided by the LMS or turn to authoring tools.

Although Moodle (Modular Object-Oriented Dynamic Learning Environment) has lots of activities and resources that can be installed in the system to construct learning objects for the course, it may be necessary to emphasize here that they cannot be exported into any of the standards available. The most one can do is make backup copies of everything and store it for future use but only in a similar or upgraded version of this platform. Thus, if we were to build activities using these modules, we would fail to meet with one of the fundamentals we aimed at from the start: interoperability.

As it was useless to limit out learning activities to only one platform or system (Moodle in our case), we think it will be patent to all that we needed an alternative, and that was to use learning standards or authoring tools which made use of one of the learning standards available. Ideally SCORM was the one we preferred for the reasons we have already mentioned.

SCORM prescribes the development, packaging and delivery of education and training materials whenever and wherever they are needed. SCORM-compliant courses leverage course development investments by ensuring that compliant courses are "RAID", an acronym which stands for:

- **Re-usable:** easily modified and used by different development tools
- **Accessible:** can be searched and made available as needed by both learners and content developers.
- **Interoperable:** operates across a wide variety of hardware, operating systems and web browsers.
- **Durable:** does not require significant modifications with new versions of system software.

At this point, it may be useful to provide some details about SCORM, which is not a standard in itself, but rather a reference model that serves to test the effectiveness and real-life application of a collection of individual specifications and standards to create a "unified content model" to enable the re-use of learning materials across a range of products and platforms (Advanced Distributed Learning, 2003). It includes:

- specifications relating to the run-time environment,
- specifications for representing course structures or content aggregation and
- specifications for creating metadata records for courses, content, and raw media elements.

Then, most relevant for our purpose, is another SCORM feature: the use of runtime communications with the LMS. Not all courses require runtime communications with the learning management system (LMS).

However, many courses contain content that adapt to the learners actions in the course, including scores on assessments and reviewed content. This requires tracking of scores and progress of individual students, undoubtedly one of the major services provided by an LMS. Today, non-SCORM learning management systems use proprietary methods for obtaining and tracking runtime information. Our own view is that Moodle deals with this aspect satisfactorily, although some fine adjustments are required in its SCORM module so as to make it compatible with all the features included in the SCORM specification runtime communications.

Generally, this is restricted to assessment scores and simple indications of whether certain learning content has been reviewed. On the other hand, SCORM-compliant learning management systems are required to provide commands for reading and writing student information to its database, something which in Moodle is taken care of by an administrative module called "Grades".

Currently there are 8 commands available in SCORM (for both versions, 1.2. and 2004) for communicating 49 different student metadata elements. These student metadata include: 15 elements for capturing the learning state of the SCO, 8 elements for describing and tracking learning objectives associated with an individual SCO, 5 elements for student language, audio and video preferences, 4 elements for tracking a student's progress and time limits for individual SCOs, 13 elements for describing and tracking a student's responses and performance on quizzes and 4 elements for communicating data between SCOs and the LMS.

Besides, SCORM contains a rich dictionary of metadata terms that can be used for describing course content. These data are not needed if a course is never going to be archived in a learning repository or shared with other authors. However, there seems to be a common aim among researchers and instructors to create a learning economy in which authors and students will be able to search the Internet for learning resources. This type of searching and discovery requires that courses archived in a repository include not just its content, but also a readable description of that content. The University of Alicante runs a repository of Learning Objects and we are sure these data included in the metadata are extremely useful when looking for resources to be inserted in our course. It was for us when we made use this repository.

The SCORM metadata specification is essentially the IMS Learning Resource Metadata specification, which itself is based upon the IEEE Learning Technology Standards Committee and the Alliance of Remote Instructional Authoring and Distributions Networks for Europe (ARIADNE).

Considering all this, we naturally discarded Moodle embedded activity modules and opted for authoring programs such as Hot Potatoes, Textoys, eXe-learning, QuizCreator and Questionmark, all of which serve for building Sharable Content Objects (SCOs) and export them using SCORM compliant activities. Furthermore, by using authoring programs like the ones above, you don't have to be on line while building your activities. They can be built and tested locally and henceforth uploaded to the system; whereas if you had to use the programs inside the Moodle system you would always have to be logged in. This is quite a disadvantage if we take into account that communications are not always 100% stable and reliable. In consequence, a reasonable view would be to test everything beforehand and then, when everything is ready and consistent, upload it to the system, which in the end is what we did. Truly, one objection made to authoring tools of the past which were SCORM compliant, was that they were based on a single learner model. Let us try to spell this out in more detail: this model assumed that a learner interacted only with content objects and that the learning activities were content-based activities engaging the learner in the learning process. Thus, the support provided by SCORM-based courseware authoring tools in the authoring process was limited in supporting the creation and sequencing of single learner, content-based learning activities.

So, what changed this particular state of affairs? The answer is eXe-learning, whose appearance has brought about a radical change. The key design principle in this tool is the separation of the learning design process from the content packaging process. This separation enables the design of learning scenarios by defining the participating actors, the response of a learning system to their interaction with the learning content and the services provided by the learning system in such a way that it is independent from the learning content. Thus, it enables the same learning scenario to be used with different content, as well as, different learning scenarios to be used with the same content objects.

The way eXe-learning works will be best understood if we quickly review its main components, which are the following:

Learning Design subsystem. This part of the authoring system is based on the use of IMS Learning Design specification in order to provide the pedagogical designer with the environment for defining learning scenarios. The main scope is to enable the definition of generic, domain independent learning scenarios that can be used by the content packaging system in order to create learning activities based on the use of the learning objects stored in the content repository.

Content Packaging subsystem. This part of the authoring system enables the population and packaging of learning scenarios with the learning content. In our system implementation, the development of such packaging tool is based on the commonly used IMS Content Packaging, SCORM 1.2, or IMS Common Cartridge.

Learning Resources Metadata Authoring & Management subsystem. This part of the authoring system supports the metadata authoring and repository management. The main goal of this component is to provide an easy-to-use and ubiquitous platform capable of authoring, storing, managing and delivering the educational metadata produced for supporting searching and retrieval of learning resources. This is quite a pedagogical advantage since we can now store information relative to the subject, content, age of participants, etc. Furthermore, with the other tools (Hot Potatoes, Textoys, etc.) we have complemented eXe learning scenario with novel activities that are embedded inside the eXe learning interface, since these latter authoring tools do not have metadata authoring tab as eXe-learning has. That finished we export to SCORM 1.2 and thus profit from all the features of levels B and C of the IMS Learning Design Content Packaging Specification (LDCPS).

ADAPTIVE HYPERMEDIA FOR THEORY AND PRACTICE EXPLOITATION

Up to this point, we have argued for the basic need of common standards and we have also examined several authoring tools. However, the factors and tools depicted above do not directly improve the pedagogical quality of the content produced. Learners are known to respond well to content and education systems that adapt to their personal preferences and which find an echo in face-to-face lectures. The key to this process is an appropriate learner model constructed either explicitly through an online instrument or implicitly through the learner's interaction with the learning environment and in-person classes. As an example of how the different parts merge and interact in this functional model, it may be worthwhile to devote some attention to the one built by us. Our "Language Blend" is based on three fundamental lines:

1. Theory development and supportive resources.
2. Deployment of activity practice to assimilate theory.
3. In-person classes.

Initially, we need to establish the concept of Adaptive hypermedia (AH), which is an alternative to the traditional "one-size-fits-all" approach in the development of hypermedia systems. Adaptive hypermedia systems (AHS) build a model of the goals, preferences and knowledge of each individual user, and exploit this model throughout the interaction with the user, in order to adapt to the needs of that user (Brusilovsky, 1996, 2008). For example, a student in an adaptive educational hypermedia system will be given a presentation that is adapted specifically to his or her knowledge of the subject (De Bra, & Calvi, 1998), and a suggested set of most relevant links to proceed further (Brusilovsky, Eklund, & Schwarz, 1998b). AH systems can be useful in any application area where the system is expected to be used by people with different levels and knowledge, something quite often found in language learning, and where the hyperspace is reasonably big. Users with different levels and knowledge may be interested in different pieces of information presented on a hypermedia page and may use different links for navigation. AH tries to overcome this problem by using knowledge represented in the user model to adapt the information and links being presented to the given user. Adaptation can also assist the user in a navigational sense, which is particularly relevant for a large hyperspace. Knowing user goals and knowledge, AH systems can support users in their navigation by limiting browsing space, suggesting most relevant links to follow, or providing adaptive comments to visible links. In short, a Hypermedia System is an application which uses associative relationships amongst information contained within multiple media data for the purpose of facilitating access to, and manipulation of, the information encapsulated by the data, that is, the theory and activities we present.

The conclusion of the preceding paragraph is that any well-developed course should include AHS and provide its students with abundant help, either through links or in any other viable way. As we understand, AH has been a feature all throughout our course rather than an occasional digression at a certain point in time or occasion. Both in theory presentation and activity development, we have made numerous links providing explanation to the different relevant items students encounter as they work. Very much like the hyperlinks in "Wikipedia," where key words offer selective links which redirect learners to other web pages to help them out when doing their practice tasks. Naturally, our course is full of hyperlinks which clarify, expand and illustrate essential concepts if need be, or if the student feels he needs to learn more about certain aspects as he reads on. In this respect we have not make use of AH in its full sense but in so far as it served our purposes. Sometimes it was *adaptive navigation support* to locate the best links to clarify some points or for further research on the issues dealt with in theory presentation; and at other times it was extra practice or theory support when the learning object had been accomplished.

The same can be said of our theory presentations, in which we have structured different links for different levels of English. For instance, if you have a look at our theory units, you′ll see they contain abundant links which may lead you either to activities which practice what is being explained, or to profound exegesis into the nature of some grammatical concept or other. Something similar happens when using the authoring software mentioned above to build our practice activities. In such cases, we offer students important feedback related to the nature and cause of their mistakes as well as some links which focus on their deficiencies and help them solve their problem instantly. Every teacher knows that recurrent mistakes require immediacy of action: first with simple and clear instruction, and later with more practice. And, consequently, we have endeavored to build a resource-rich course: not only did we cater enough resources for the students to consult (on-line dictionaries, grammars, thesauri, etc.), but also we provided ample and specific information for anything they got wrong. These were either web pages built by ourselves or links to other on-line explanations. In this respect AH has saved us a lot of work when we diverted students to other web pages in search of a solution to their mistakes. We have adapted our links (those that can be configured as Google Books) "highlighting" what is important and "dimming" what is not relevant, so that what the students get is the gist of what we want them to learn. We do the skimming and the scanning and what they get is only the relevant information that would help them solve their problems they meet when interacting with the system. In this respect we reduce search time and effort and improve learning quality.

Right or wrong answers redirect students to different hypermedia links to provide enough feedback to resolve learning deficiencies. These *conditional activities* represent the scaffolding of a new standard feature in Moodle 2.0 onwards, which enables teachers to restrict the availability of any activity according to certain conditions such as dates, grade obtained, or activity completion. Each activity can also have conditions which need to be met before it is considered complete. In our course, we have only added links to account for learning deficiencies and further research; and very occasionally for further practice.

After what has been said above, we are now ready to claim that our Language Blend constitutes a framework for Adaptive Blended learning based on distributed, re-usable learning activities that we ourselves have developed using SCORM compliant learning objects and activities, built mainly by means of two authoring tools: Hot Potatoes and eXe-learning. The goal of The Language Blend is: first, to bridge the gap between the information power of modern educational material repositories, and the just-in-time delivery and personalization potential of LMSs and AH; and second: to fit it all together into a language course.

It is well known that most LMSs are web-based to facilitate access to learning content and administration. This holds for a learning management system (LMS) such as Moodle, software for delivering, tracking and managing training. In our case, we have used Moodle because of several other advantages, especially the fact that it is free; but also because it imports SCORM courses and learning objects based on SCORM. And since SCORM does not (currently) address instructional design issues, nor does it prescribe specific functionality for LMSs, we have provided one using the tools aforementioned so as to combine what we consider should be the a standard for (SLL) second language learning. It may also be interesting to explain why we have turned to authoring tools; simply put, because they are independent from the system we are working on, we do not depend on Internet for its building and they can be tested on and off line. But, probably, there is another reason which is even more important than the ones just given: they can be exported to SCORM specification, while activities which pertain to the Moodle environment, cannot. This feature is common to nearly all LMSs: they can all import SCORM compliant learning objects and even whole courses, but they cannot export them into any of the learning standards available.

Finally, we may gain some insight into the way our course works by having a look at its aspect.

This is how our course looks like in Moodle. The units are clearly separated from each other and, within each unit, first there is the classic box ( ) which indicates a SCORM compliant object, the theoretical grounding for each unit, and the hand with a potato ( ), synonymous with a Hot Potatoes or Textoys activity, which accounts for most of the practice in our language course. Moodle has a specific module to import and manage Hot Potatoes activities directly into the system; that is the reason why it is represented with a

Figure 1. Distribution of units in Moodle.

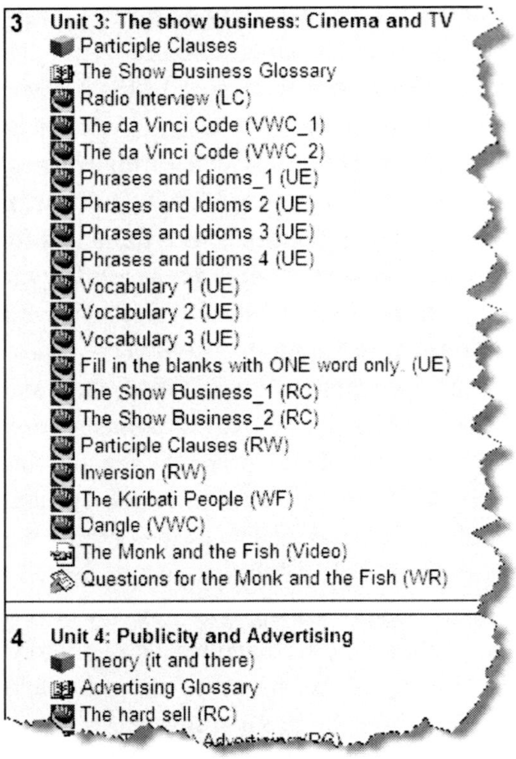

different icon, otherwise we would have exported it into a SCORM compliant object (SCO).

LANGUAGE ACQUISITION WITNIN THE FRAMEWORK OF BLENDED LEARNING

Computer-Based Instruction

If we pay now some attention to the evolution of blended learning in later years and make the effort of imagining that evolution plastically displayed along a time line, most people would agree that blended learning has greatly exceeded its initial promise. Among other things, it has become a building block for the new university thanks to two of its most remarkable features; flexibility and convenience. These features fit very well with the demands of ordinary students and working adults who decide to pursue postsecondary degrees. It is a hybrid of traditional face-to-face and online learning so that instruction occurs both in the classroom and online, and where the online component becomes a natural extension of traditional classroom learning. Blended learning is thus a flexible approach to course design that supports the blending of different times and places for learning, offering some of the conveniences of fully online courses without the complete loss of face-to-face contact. The result is potentially a more robust educational experience than either traditional or fully online learning can offer.

No doubt that the growth of blended learning has been favored by the changes higher education is experiencing. To begin with, structural changes of great significance in Europe are being carried out to implement the Bologna process; but then, on a wider scale, changes are also occurring in the traditional way of teaching and learning all around the world. And these changes are quite telling: from the de-emphasis on thinking about delivering instruction and the concurrent emphasis placed on producing learning, to using technology to expand distance education, to the recognition of the importance of sense of community. Having said that, only time will tell us how deep is the transformation of higher education we are witnessing.

One of the most vocal adherents of blended learning, Harvey Singh (2003, p.54) explains what for us has been the core of blending learning practice, and performance support:

Perhaps the finest form of blended learning is to supplement learning (organized prior to beginning a new job-task) with practice (using job-task (...) simulation models) and just-in-time performance support tools that facilitate the appropriate execution of job-tasks.

Cutting-edge productivity tools provide 'work-space' environments that package together the computer based work, collaboration, and performance support tools.

Indeed it is intuitively understood that to attain any kind of competence in any language one has to be able to master specific situations by means of linguistic skills and this is what we do with our practice activities and learning design. In a sense ours is a three-pronged instruction which takes into account theory, practice and real linguistic performance in real or unreal situations. This last part is accomplished within classroom proper.

Another common belief is that learning is the same as knowledge transfer (Koper et alter, 2001), a belief which brings another idea in its tail: that it is enough to make knowledge available to learners according to some pedagogical structure. However, providing adequate knowledge is not enough: it has to be *learned*. And, for that reason, our focus is fixed on this learning process when we discuss instructional design or learning design. Before we move on, we must grasp all the implications of the previous statement. So, let´s begin by asking yourself a somehow bewildering question: 'where is the *learning'* in eLearning? In answer to that, we guess many people will admit right away that a lot of learning does not come from knowledge resources at all, but clearly stems from the activities of learners solving problems, interacting with real devices, interacting in their social and work situation or in the classrooms. It could be considered a sort of metalearning.

Abundant research about learning processes support and clinch the theory that learning doesn't come from the provision of knowledge solely, but is also the result of all the learners' activities in the learning environment. This raises an issue of fundamental import, because we are not implying that knowledge objects are secondary or of no importance in learning situations; rather, we are highlighting the importance of the process itself in effective learning processes.

Once these general matters have been established, it's time to delve into some particulars of our course. Traditionally second language learning practice was performed along four main lines:

1. Comprehension (reading and listening).
2. Use of English (cloze tests, gap-filling exercises, rewriting, etc.).
3. Speaking.
4. Writing.

In a blended course such as ours, all the mechanical activities that involve "comprehension" and "use of English" have been shifted to the LMS, where they can be trained, with the great benefit of immediate feedback and remedial practice activities.

Now, if we compare this arrangement to traditional classroom practice, anyone with even the shortest teaching experience will know that the just referred areas (comprehension and use of English) were done in a painstaking, choral and in-turn manner with no attention to individual needs. And in this respect, "listening comprehension" was especially challenging for the teacher because it took for granted that all students in the group understood the spoken test at the same speed and with equal skill. But this is far from being true and, first the language laboratory, and now the computer, help us build exercises both for reading and listening comprehension that allow students to work at their own pace and go back and forward, stop, listen,/read again, check grammar appendixes, etc. whenever and as often as they need. In contrast to this scenario, picture yourself in the situation previously depicted: trying to respond to the many different demands that a listening comprehension exercise implies in a mixed-ability class. It's quite overwhelming, and for that reason we are convinced that some exercises are best done in isolation because their very nature calls for such diversity of action on the part of the learner. The difference in linguistic competence in most language classrooms is unquestionable, and from this point it is but a single step to the conclusion that most exercises done in a computer and in an LMS should adjust to meet the student's individual needs and his own rhythm of learning.

The same occurs with "Use of English" activities. *Hot Potatoes* is especially suited to work with cloze and multiple choice exercises to practice grammar and vocabulary. Practically all of the activities that pertain to what we usually call "Use of English" can be made with this authoring software with some variations and enhancements of traditional exercises. We can include video comprehension activities, phonetic transcription, etc.

Speaking and writing activities which require some sort of human intervention have been left for the face-to-face lectures or asynchronous review, correction, checking of delivered materials. These could either be written essays or audio feeds sent for evaluation. About these last two activities, a more profound feedback must be given in the classroom since they entail questions related tasks in connection with style, register, unity, cohesion, etc.; aspects which are not easily explained unless you are in front of the learner.

So far we have mentioned three types of activities which can be done in the LMS for second language acquisition:

1. Theory presentation and AH links to overcome the difference in students' knowledge and levels.
2. Self-check activities which were built by the lecturer beforehand and when they are done by the student they get immediate feedback and possible solutions to overcome weaknesses by means of AH links.
3. Activities which can be handed in using the LMS but that require a more personal feedback from the lecturer either to individual students or groups.

No need to say that there other management or communication tools within the LMS we have not mentioned, such as the "grading book", the "announcement board", "the forum", "chat", etc. All those are of great help both to lecturers and students as they keep everyone informed of what is going on in and outside the classroom and are constantly building a sense of community we are particularly fond of.

Finally, another important feature of our "Language Blend" deserves individual attention, and that is the use of collaborative tools within the LMS to promote group work and a feeling of belonging. The regular use of "wikis" and "workshops" in our learning devices fosters social constructivism. Collaborative groups are important because we can test our own understanding and examine the understanding of others as a mechanism for enriching, interweaving, and expanding our approach to particular issues or phenomena. More often than not we give students tasks which involve working in groups to develop written assignments or oral presentations.

This framework we have depicted hitherto, as far as the technological infrastructure is concerned, presents many great advantages, both from a pedagogic and technological viewpoint:

- Repositories offer large libraries of SCORM learning objects which can easily be reused to build our own courses thanks to built-in metadada inside the SCOs.
- SCOs integrate with most LMS.
- You are designing learning content that might be reused in other contexts.
- The interaction of students with the learning content tracks the learner's performance.
- Both AH and SCORM will monitor the learner and adapt according to the learner's needs

We have taken advantage of all this in our courses and the result is that while in the past there were only in-person lectures to communicate and interact with the students, always as a group; they were geared towards the average rather than the exceptional, now they have a feeling, so they say, that the attention span is greater than before and that more individual support and chances for participation is administered.

Face-To-Face Communication Tasks

Although it is obviously a platitude, it is important to point out for our line of reasoning that, in second language classrooms, the language, be it English or any other, is both the medium for teachers, and the goal for students, as the ultimate instructional aim of these lessons is acquiring that second language. Everything is mediated by the second language in classrooms where the latter is taught and acquired. Therefore, understanding the dynamics of classroom communication is essential for all those involved in second language education, even though we admit that is not a simple task. Classroom communication in general has been described as a "problematic medium" since differences in how, when, where, and to whom things are communicated can not only create slight misunderstandings, but can also seriously impair effective teaching and learning. Moreover, if that classroom is filled with students from a wide variety of linguistic and cultural backgrounds who possess a range of second language proficiency levels, then teachers cannot assume that their second language students will learn, talk, act, or interact in predictable ways. On the other hand, if teachers understand how the dynamics of classroom communication influence second language students' perceptions of and participation in classroom activities, they may be better able to monitor and adjust the patterns of classroom communication in order to create an environment that is conducive to both classroom teaming and second language acquisition.

It can be inferred from the ideas garnered above that the overall goal of face-to-face communication activities is to enable students to recognize how the patterns of communication are established and maintained in order to foster participation and thus shape the ways in which they use language for classroom learning and their opportunities for second language acquisition.

For example, it is often the case that university lecturers are often challenged by teaching communication skills. Their students have already spent most of their lives speaking and listening to a second language and, sometimes, they are overtly reluctant to being taught what they think they already know.

It may well be asked if this trend can be extrapolated to everyday life, and our own view is that it actually is. When natural and man-made disasters unfold on the news, horrified viewers seek out in-person opportunities to share their grief and gather information. It is easy to strike out a conversation about something everybody knows about and is of interest to him. Who could forget the sight of the pilgrimages to makeshift shrines following accidents such as Princess Diana's car crash or John F. Kennedy Jr.'s downed plane?

In the 21st century, men and women continually lurch between the impersonal nature of technology and the intimate reality of human relationships. There are many situations—often those involving learning a second language or real situations that could very well be exploited in the classrooms such as: escalating conflict, sensitive feelings, high priority, important authority, or a great deal of money—that demand people who are learning take the time and trouble to get into the same room to exchange information or practice by doing. Or at least they try to *simulate* face-to-face communication when individuals are in remote locations. Face-to-face communication skills remain one of the primary roads to learn to master a new language, achieve career success, or obtain many other personal assets, even in this computer age.

Everybody knows that most communication is carried out face-to-face with other individuals: asking for information, offering advice, your intervention in the classroom, or telling someone what you think of their performance—all tend to be done in a one-to-one situation. We strive to exploit and develop this general skill because we are convinced that this is one of the most critical areas of communication to get right and, for that reason, this is what we try to practice in our time with our students in the classroom.

Blended Learning combines face-to-face instruction with computer-mediated learning. We look for the synergy of these two different learning environments, taking the specific benefits that each environment provides, and merging them is such a way as to provide greater access to improved learning experiences in a cost-effective manner.

There are certain things that can be done better face-to-face than through computer-mediated instruction and vice versa; that´s why we have endeavored to identify the affordances that they both provide and strategically combine them. The most important consideration is to clarify the goals and learning objectives which will then determine the best mix or blend of these two environments. Above, we delineated what should be set aside to be done in the LMS, what should be left for face-to-face lectures and what aspects of the LMS should merge into the in-person classes.

As of today, computers are not witty enough to maintain a conversation with a person and to correct and assess students of a foreign language, they will be in a not-too-distant future, but until that time we will have to leave communication activities and creative writing for face-to-face lectures.

Two communication tasks are felt to be needed in our face-to-face sessions:

a. *Those connected with the writing activities.* Reading examples and eliciting from students the framework for our writing tasks. Whether they be paragraphs based on examples, contrast, definition (something which pertains to technical English), etc., or descriptions, narrative writing, discursive articles (general English), etc., the idea is to pull together a number of writing rubrics which will be the source for the writing activities. Using a Moodle tool called *workshop*, we set up a collaborative environment wherein, having explained and agreed upon the rubric for every specific writing task, students embark on this exhilarating, constructivist activity working in partnership to learn and monitor other fellow colleagues and help them improve their writing essays.

b. *Those connected with oral presentations and discussions.* Oral, aural activities are central in our lectures and take up most of the time of our face-to-face classes. These classes are well organized and prepared meticulously so as to avoid improvisation. Any loose ends in oral classes lead to a secure and downright failure, so we need to set up the adequate material and make sure it works well. Whether it be picture description, short presentations based on prompts, group discussion, exploitation of situational dialogues, function dialogue practice etc., we need something well prepared and leave nothing to chance. These activities prepare students for oral competence and are essential to practise the most common aspects of oral skills.

This distribution of machine-aided instruction together with in-person communication programs, constitute what for us should be the ideal framework for second language learning today. Our language Blend aims at setting up a standard to course builders and lecturers of foreign languages who seek to make the most of e-learning and face-to-face instruction. And we feel we're on the right path.

The Structure of the Language Blend

Let's now see with greater detail how our language blend is internally structured. We have elaborated a good number of learning objects and practical activities per unit, most of which are self-check, instantly-graded (with immediate feedback) and auto-regenerating (the exercise changes every time

Figure 2. The Language Blend

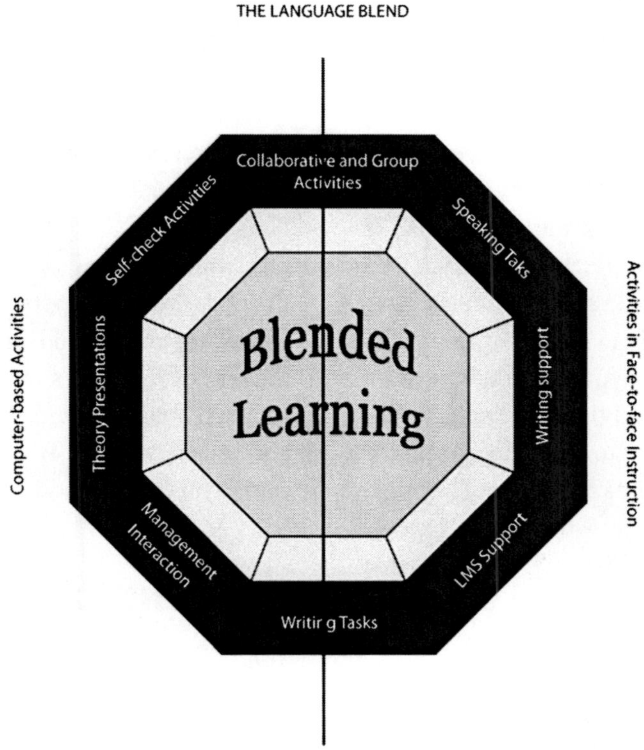

it opens), all of which offer self-monitoring paths to cater for all levels and knowledge. A few collaborative or individual assignments link on-line instruction with face-to-face classes, such as the writing tasks, workshops and speaking activities.

In this article we have laid the foundations of each half of the instruction: the computer-based activities and the face-to-face lectures. This diagram illustrates what we understand should be second-language, blended learning and the gravitational forces that have a bearing on each and every part of the instruction.

Each side of the octagon leads to the hub or centre where all the learning blends in one single nucleus that distinguishes no sections or subdivisions. The top and bottom sides share both halves of the instruction, viz, the writing and collaborative tasks. Management interaction and social communication with learners in the LMS is done by means of e-mails, chats and forums, all of them inside the LMS. Also, and especially at the beginning of each course, there is a lot of LMS support in the face-to-face classes to lay the groundwork we wish to apply for the rest of the course and make everything dovetail accurately.

CONCLUSION

All through this article we have highlighted the importance of standards to secure the future development of blended learning as well as to foster cooperation among professors based in different —and often faraway— locations. In our opinion, SCORM constitutes an important first step towards liberating learning content objects from local implementations. It represents currently a leading effort towards the reusability and interoperability of learning resources. Also SCORM's good compatibility with most of popular learning resource specifications ensures its widespread acceptance and bright application prospect in the near future. Our system, based on SCORM 1.2, is actually an early exploration to the great potential of SCORM. The new version of this specification (SCORM 2004) only shows the great demand it has worldwide. By using SCORM in combination with authoring tools which comply with SCORM standards, we liberate whatever materials we might be building from the systems where they are supposed to be running.

The World Wide Web hypertext/media system allows the user to freely navigate between nodes by following links in an extensive, decentralized network of information and knowledge. The open, free-browsing nature of the web affords exploratory and inquiry-based learning. At the same time however, given the extensive growth of the World Wide Web, the potential is great for user disorientation in such a large knowledge base. A further problem with hypermedia navigation is that it is not specifically designed to differentiate between and to accommodate users with different interests, goals and needs. Thus, traditional hypermedia systems present a disadvantage for educational use of the World Wide Web since without direct teacher or system support, students' learning experiences may not be very efficient or effective. While a discovery or inquiry-based type of online learning may be envisioned as an effective model, it nonetheless needs to be coupled with some type of system control or support. With Moodle and AH (Adaptive Hypermedia), we have tailored a system which caters for individual needs and knowledge focusing on specific tasks we wish to develop. At the same time we provide some system support and control to users which a free roaming of the web does not.

Our "language blend" clearly breaks up into small sections what should be taught / learnt with a computer (using a computer for practical purposes), in an LMS (as part of blended learning) and in the face-to-face classes. Essentially, the most common exercises which fall within the scope of "Use of English training" (rephrasing, listening, reading, word-formation, etc., exercises) can be done in the LMS, while direct communication activities are left for classroom instruction.

This three-pronged impact into ESL has brought great benefits into our teaching at the University of Alicante, and we have received numerous appraisals from university officials, but the ones we truly appreciate are those that come from our students and from the figures we get by the end of the year's term. Since its application, successful student figures have risen considerably and more importantly, the quality of instruction is also on the upgrade.

REFERENCES

Advanced Distributed Learning. (2003). *Sharable Content Object Reference Model (SCORM) Version 1.2*. Advanced Distributed Learning Inc. Available online at www.adlnet.org

Andrade, H., & Du, Y. (2005). Student perspectives on rubric-referenced assessment. *Practical Assessment Research & Evaluation, 10*(3), 1–11.

Arcos, F., Amilburu, A., & Ortega, P. (2008). The Language Blend. *INTED2008*. International Technology, Education and Development Conference.

Arnheim, R. (1971). *Entropy and Art*. Berkeley: University of California Press.

Bohl, O., Schellhase, J., Senler, R., & Winand, U. (2002). The sharable content object reference model (SCORM) - A critical review. *IEEE International Conference on Computers in Education (ICCE02),* (pp. 950-951).

Brusilovsky, P. (2008). *Adaptive Navigation Support for Open Corpus Hypermedia Systems, Adaptive Hypermedia and Adaptive Web-Based Systems* (pp. 6–8). Berlin: Springer.

Brusilovsky, P., Eklund, J., & Schwarz, E. (1998b). Web-based education for all: A tool for developing adaptive courseware. *Computer Networks and ISDN Systems, 30*(1-7), 291-300.

Brusilovsky, P., & Weber, G. (1996) Collaborative example selection in an intelligent example based programming environment. In *International Conference on Learning Sciences, ICLS-96*, Evanston, IL.

Chang, W., Hsu, H., Smith, T. K., & Wang, C. (2004). Enhancing SCORM metadata for assessment authoring in e-Learning. *Journal of Computer Assisted Learning, 20*(4), 305–316. doi:10.1111/j.1365-2729.2004.00091.x

De Bra, P., & Calvi, L. (1998). AHA! An open Adaptive Hypermedia Architecture. *New Review of Hypermedia and Multimedia, 4*, 115–139. doi:10.1080/13614569808914698

Friesen, N. (2003). Three Objections to Learning Objects and E-learning. In R. McGreal (Ed.), 2004. *Online Education Using Learning Objects,* (pp. 59-70). London: Routledge.

Jones, E. (2002). Implications of SCORM and Emerging E-learning Standards On Engineering Education. In *Proceedings of the 2002 ASEE Gulf-Southwest Annual Conference*, The University of Louisiana at Lafayette, March 20 – 22, 2002.

Karampiperis, P., & Sampson, D. (2004). A Flexible Authoring Tool supporting Adaptive Learning Activities. In *Proc. of IADIS International Conference on Cognition and Exploratory Learning in Digital Age (CELDA 2004)*, Lisbon, Portugal.

Koper, R. van Es, R. (2001). *Modeling units of learning from a pedagogical perspective.* Amsterdam: Open Universiteit Nederland.

Koper, R. (2006). Current Research in Learning Design. *Journal of Educational Technology & Society, 9*(1), 13–22.

Koper, R., & Olivier, B. (2004). Representing the learning design of units of learning. *Journal of Educational Technology & Society, 7*(3), 97–111.

Lazarinis, F. (2006) A hypermedia environment for managing online courseware based on adaptable templates. *International Conference on Virtual Learning,* (pp. 239-246).

Lazarinis, F., Green, S., & Pearson, E. (2009). Measuring the conformance of hypermedia assessment tools to QTI. *Int. J. of Innovation and Learning, 6*(2), 127–146. doi:10.1504/IJIL.2009.022809

Morimoto, Y., Ueno, M., Yokoyama, S., & Miyadera, Y. (2007) A SCORM-compliant Learning Management System that Enhances Learning By Managing the Learning Itself. In *Proceedings of the 7th IEEE International Conference on Advanced Learning Technologies (ICALT)*, (pp. 122-126).

Ortega, P., & Arcos, F. (2008). How e-homework can solve the homework debate in primary schools. *ENMA2008, International Conference on Engineering and Mathematics*, (pp. 5-10). Bilbao, Spain: Kopiak.

Ortega, P., & Arcos, F. (2008). Blended Learning: an efficient response to some of the problems raised by youths at risk. In *INTED2008, International Technology, Education and Development Conference.*

Ortega, P., & Arcos, F. (2009). CLIL Enhanced Through Digital Storytelling. *ENMA2009, International Conference on Engineering and Mathematics*, (pp. 350). Bilbao, Spain: Kopiak.

Simkins, M. (2000). *Developing and Implementing a Rubric for Assessing Student Multimedia Projects*. Presented at the Annual Meeting of the American Educational Research Association, Creating Knowledge in the 21st Century: Insights From Multiple Perspectives, April 2000. New Orleans, LA.

Singh, H. (2003, November - December). Building Effective Blended Learning Programs. *Educational Technology*, *43*(6), 51–54.

Singh, H., & Reed, C. (2001). *A White Paper: Achieving Success with Blended Learning*. Centra Software.

Smelser, L. M. (2002, March 20-23). *Making Connections in Our Classrooms: Online and Off.* Paper presented at the Annual Meeting of the Conference on College Composition and Communication, Chicago, IL.

Valiathan, P. (2002). Blended Learning Models. *Learning Circuits*. Retrieved from www.learningcircuits.org/2002/aug2002/valiathan.html

Young, J. R. (2002, March 22). 'Hybrid' teaching seeks to end the divide between traditional and online instruction. *The Chronicle of Higher Education*, A33.

KEY TERMS AND DEFINITIONS

Adaptive Hypermedia (AH): Links to diverse resources on the Net.

IMS LD: Specification for the design of learning objects.

Java Clic (JCLIC): An authoring tool for the creation of learning objects.

Leaning Management System (LMS): A system that allows teachers to run online courses.

Modular Object-Oriented Dynamic Learning Environment (MOODLE): One among the many possible LMSs.

Remote Instructional Authoring and Distributions Networks for Europe (ARIADNE): A project for the sharing and reuse of teaching material.

Sharable Content Object (SCO): It's the learning object itself.

Sharable Content Object Reference Model (SCORM): Standard specification for packaging learning objects.

Section 3

Metadata, Learning Objects, Ontologies and Semantic Web

Chapter 12
Enhancing Digital Repositories with Learning Object Metadata

Andreas D. Alexopoulos
University of Patras, Greece

Georgia D. Solomou
University of Patras, Greece

Dimitrios A. Koutsomitropoulos
University of Patras, Greece

Theodore S. Papatheodorou
University of Patras, Greece

ABSTRACT

In this chapter the authors present the basic characteristics about some existing educational metadata schemata and application profiles. They focus on the widely adopted IEEE LOM standard and give a brief analysis of its structure. Having in mind the utilization of educational metadata schemata by digital repositories preserving educational and research resources, they concentrate on a considerably popular system for this reason, DSpace. The authors want to show how the IEEE LOM metadata set can be incorporated in the default DSpace's qualified Dublin Core metadata schema, introducing enhancements to the existing University of Patras live installation. For this reason, they document a potential LOM to Dublin Core metadata mapping and reveal possible gains from such an attempt. Further, they propose an ontological model for the repository's metadata that takes also into account the educational characteristics of resources. In this way, they show how a semantic level of interoperability between educational applications can be achieved.

INTRODUCTION

The rapid growth of the World Wide Web in the past few years has led to a considerable increase of educational material that is available in electronic form. The increased amount of digital information renders the efficient search and retrieval of educational resources a more complex and difficult process. For this reason, it is of crucial importance the proper description and characterization of electronically available learning objects, using

DOI: 10.4018/978-1-61692-789-9.ch012

educational metadata. Such an effort would ensure the reusability and discoverability of learning objects whereas it would facilitate the interoperability of educational applications.

Having these in mind, our work is focused on one of the most popular existing metadata schemata, namely the IEEE LOM standard. LOM includes "the minimal set of attributes needed to allow learning objects to be managed, located, and evaluated" (Nair, & Jeevan, 2004) and has proved to be a widely adopted and internationally recognized open standard for the description of learning objects. But apart from IEEE LOM, other metadata schemata with similar characteristics have been deployed over time, aiming at fulfilling the same requisites in the race for the efficient management of educational resources. All of these standards, either directly related to LOM or not, make their own contribution to the characterization of learning objects and play an important role in the exchange of information in an interoperable way.

Nevertheless, the increasing number of applications that exploit educational metadata as well as the existence of many metadata specifications, sometimes poses the adoption of a sole metadata schema by an application a rather inefficient solution. As a better practice towards this direction, the use of application profiles is suggested. An application profile is defined as a combination of elements coming from different metadata schemata and is usually created in order to satisfy the needs of a particular application.

All these deployed metadata models are mainly utilized by digital repository systems that aim at preserving and managing educational material. A very popular system implemented for this reason is DSpace[1]. On top of DSpace many institutional repositories have been built worldwide. These systems exploit DSpace's inherent facilities and the fact that it uses the qualified Dublin Core element set as its base metadata schema. However, this schema is sometimes proven to be inadequate for the efficient characterization of the great amount of the educational and research assets that we imported in institutional or other repositories of related purpose. That's why the deployment of an application profile, extended with learning object metadata and specific to the needs of an educational repository, is attempted through this work.

This article is further organized as follows: We start by presenting the basic structure of the IEEE LOM schema. We then give a brief overview about other widely known learning object metadata standards and see how these standards may be related to the IEEE LOM. Some profiles specific to educational applications are also mentioned. In the next section we describe how we managed to incorporate the LOM metadata schema in the University of Patras institutional repository, which is built upon the DSpace system. Furthermore, we analyze the implemented enhancements to this particular digital repository system and explain how they can improve the end-user experience and interaction with the overall system. We proceed by referring some issues regarding interoperability and semantics in digital repository systems that manage educational resources. Finally, we talk about possible future implementations regarding the best possible utilization of learning objects through similar kind of repositories.

LEARNING OBJECT METADATA STANDARDS

Learning objects (Wiley, 2002), have been defined as "any entity, digital or non-digital, which can be used, re-used or referenced during technology supported learning". In (Danziel, 2002) learning objects are defined as "an aggregation of one or more digital assets, incorporating meta-data, which represent an educationally meaningful stand-alone unit" and according to (IEEE LTSC, 2002), a learning object is "any entity -digital or non-digital- that may be used for learning, education or training". Examples of reusable digital sources are images, video files, audio files or even a web page.

Learning Objects can be formally characterized by using metadata. Metadata can be defined as "data about data" or "information about information" (Berners-Lee, 1997). They are a set of attributes that try to best describe the content of a digital source. Hence, in a similar way, the content of a digital educational source can by described using the notion of educational metadata.

A widely adopted metadata element set, specifically applying to the field of education, is the IEEE LOM standard. IEEE LOM, which has been published by the Institute of Electrical and Electronics Engineers Standards Association, constitutes a standard designed for the description of learning objects. LOM has a wide range of elements for characterizing educational material that can be grouped into nine categories: *General, Lifecycle, Meta-Metadata, Technical, Educational, Rights, Relation, Annotation* and *Classification.*

The LOM data model is a hierarchy of elements, as shown in Figure 1. There are nine categories in the first level and each of them has some sub-elements that can be single ones or aggregations of other elements. Some of this data model's elements can be repeated either as single or as group elements.

When the LOM schema is deployed, it is not necessary to use all of the data model's elements. The creation of an application profile allows someone to define which of them will be used together with their permitted values. Some of them can be dropped out and some other can be added from another metadata schema.

Apart from LOM, other metadata sets have been implemented in order to be utilized in the characterization of educational resources. It seems, though, that these sets are somehow related to LOM as they have many characteristics in common. The most popular among these metadata element sets, are summarized below:

Figure 1.The elements of IEEE LOM standard

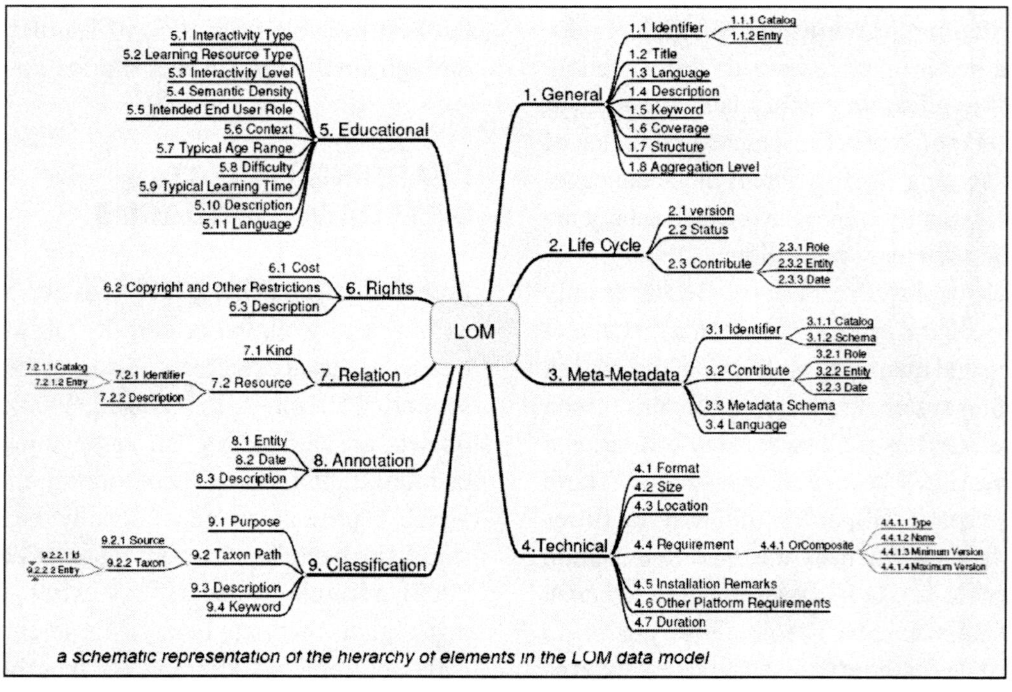

a schematic representation of the hierarchy of elements in the LOM data model

- The *Instructional Management Systems*[2] (IMS) Project started in 1997 as part of a non-profit organization in United Stated of America and constitutes an effort for the development of standards for online educational purposes. IMS is now a global organization and its main interests are the online access of educational objects. IMS develops and encourages open specifications that facilitate distributed online activities, like the locating and utilization of educational sources.
- The *ARIADNE* metadata standard[3] is the result of the work and the related experiments carried out till 1995 by various European and global organizations. The contents of this standard are described according to the XML schema. It is comprised of 47 elements, 27 of which can be directly mapped to the LOM elements. Similarly to LOM, the ARIADNE metadata schema can be organized into the following categories (Najjar, Duval, Ternier, & Neven, 2003) which are *General, Semantics, Pedagogical, Technical, Indexation* and *Annotations*.
- *Dublin Core* (DC) (DCMI, 2008) is a group of fifteen elements designed so as to provide a simple way to describe educational objects and to facilitate the latter's discovery and use. Optionally, additional attributes can be used. The DC metadata schema was one of the first that was adopted by plenty of metadata applications. Many organizations have adopted the DC schema, further augmenting them with more specific to their needs elements.

Application Profiles

A single metadata schema cannot always meet the needs of all kinds of applications. For this reason, the use of *Application Profiles* (Heery, & Patel, 2000) has been proposed. According to (Duval, Hodgins, Sutton, & Weibel, 2002), an application profile is an aggregation of metadata elements selected among one or more metadata schemata and combined in a new one. The latter's goal is to adequately fulfill the application's special needs and to retain interoperability with its base schema.

In particular, because the elements of the new profile usually come from more than one metadata schemata, this gives to the application the ability to cover its needs by exploiting the features of the existing schemata and to further augment them with new characteristics. As an example, one application can choose only a subset of the DC elements or create a totally new schema by combining the existing DC elements and by defining some new. Nevertheless, an application profile cannot be considered as being complete if it does not contain documentation that defines policies and practices about its proper usage.

In an application profile it is important to choose or define the correct vocabularies which will provide for the proper definition of the adopted elements. According to (Duval, & Hodgins, 2003), some techniques for producing complete definitions about application profiles are to give elements a mandatory status, to restrict the value space of data elements, to impose relationships between elements, not to include some elements and to identify taxonomies and classification.

Some known application profiles, aiming at providing a more effective description about learning objects, are the Canadian Core Learning Resource Metadata Application Profile[4] (CanCore), the SCORM[5] (Sharable Content Object Reference Model) model, the DC-Ed application profile, the UK Learning Object Metadata Core[6] and the GEM[7] (Gateway to Educational Materials) Metadata.

DIGITAL REPOSITORIES AND EDUCATIONAL METADATA

A digital repository is a mechanism responsible for storing, describing, preserving, managing and distributing any kind of digital material. Some widely known mechanisms upon which a digital repository can be built are DSpace, Eprints[8] and Fedora[9]. Most of them exploit a simple and more general in meaning metadata schema, like DC, in order to characterize their content. Embedding educational metadata, though, seems to provide a faster and easier way to access the learning objects stored in these systems. More precisely, the exploitation of educational-specific metadata in digital repositories particularly intended for educational purposes has the following benefits:

- Allows the characterization and categorization of learning resources based on widely accepted standards and specifications, thus further boosting interoperability between systems and applications
- Facilitates integration in more complex systems, where queries are not handled only by one repository
- Helps in preserving and disseminating learning objects of higher "quality", making them easily discoverable and reusable
- Contributes to the efficient management of the vast and continually increasing number of resources, which demand for a more precise and refined way for their characterization
- Allows the exploitation of educational metadata by learning specific tools and applications that are able to consume them after harvesting them through an appropriate metadata harvesting facility

In the past years though, a lot of institutions and organizations, mainly acting on research and education fields, have realized the necessity to exploit educational metadata for the proper characterization of their digital assets. Some of these organizations, that have built digital libraries either by using the aforementioned digital repository mechanisms or by deploying their own ones from scratch are CAREO[10], MERLOT[11], JA-SIC[12] and iLumina[13], included many others which are spread worldwide.

THE IEEE LOM STANDARD IN DIGITAL REPOSITORIES

One popular system particularly deployed for preserving and managing learning-specific resources is DSpace. DSpace is an open-source digital repository with one of the most rapidly growing user bases worldwide. It provides a way to manage research materials and scholarly publications in a professionally maintained repository, giving greater visibility and accessibility to its content over time. What is more, DSpace supports the Open Archives Initiative Protocol for Metadata Harvesting (OAI-PMH) (Lagoze, Van de Sompel, Nelson, & Warner, 2002) which offers a means to expose the repository's metadata. As a result, the repository's content is made available to service providers in an interoperable way.

On a default DSpace installation a qualified version of the Dublin Core schema is used which in turn based on the Dublin Core Libraries Working Group Application Profile (LAP) (DCMI Libraries Working Group, 2004). This schema can be extended with additional qualifications and elements. But apart from DC, other metadata schemata can also be imported in this system thus enhancing its capabilities and expanding its applicability to a more wide range of organizations and institutions.

Our work focuses on the University of Patras live DSpace installation[14], which has been developed as an institutional repository responsible for the preservation and dissemination of the University's research and educational material. Due to its intended role, we have extended the default metadata schema of this particular installation in order to incorporate the IEEE LOM data elements. The incorporation of this educational metadata standard finally enhances the repository's provided services and facilities in several ways, as described in the following section.

Why IEEE LOM

Among the various available metadata that were studied, we chose to adopt the IEEE LOM so as to characterize the learning objects stored in the University of Patras institutional repository. The LOM schema is designed specifically to describe educational objects. As already mentioned, this standard focuses on the minimal set of attributes, needed to allow learning objects to be easily managed, located, and evaluated. It became popular mostly because of its simplicity in use. Therefore, due to its popularity, it is considered as a means to obtain interoperability among repositories and digital libraries that also support this schema. Besides, as stated in (Neven, & Duval, 2002), where a survey among ten learning objects repositories was performed, nine of them seem to use IEEE LOM as their base metadata schema. Additionally, according to (Al-Khalifa, & Davis, 2006), one of the IEEE LOM main features is that it can be easily extended so that new elements can be added and thus better fulfill the needs of a specific application. This capability gives a great motivation to people creating their own application profiles to use IEEE LOM as their base educational metadata schema.

Educational Metadata in DSpace

In order to import the IEEE LOM schema in the institutional repository of the University of Patras, a number of changes had to be made to the underlying DSpace system. As a first step, we had to import the LOM metadata schema in the system's metadata registry. This process was accomplished through the system's administration interface. Actually, we needed to manually create the LOM schema in the registry, starting by assigning a name and a namespace to it. Afterwards, we supplied the name of the content elements of this schema, as well as their refinements. For each element, a small annotation indicating its usage was also possible. After the accomplishment of this step, we had to include the newly added fields in the submission process and to activate searching among those fields as well as their export through the OAI-PMH metadata harvesting facility.

In the University of Patras DSpace installation, though, not all elements of the LOM standard were incorporated. Some of them have a direct mapping to the DC metadata schema, as later explained in the section about interoperability issues and semantics. The rest are strictly provided for the characterization of educational resources and thus they have no correspondence to any of the existing terms of the provided DC metadata set. Therefore, we chose to adopt only a subset of LOM elements. This subset is comprised of elements that focus exclusively to the description of learning objects.

The import of the LOM metadata schema in the institutional repository had brought several enhancements in the system. These enhancements are reflected in the item submission and the advanced search process as well as in the item view and metadata harvesting facility, as described below and depicted in Figure 2.

Item Submission Process

When a new item is imported in the DSpace system, a standard submission process is followed which is normally comprised of three description steps followed by four general steps, necessary for completing the proper upload and storage of the item. During the description steps, users have to characterize the content they provide by filling its metadata values in the provided text fields. Each text field represents a specific DC element and the value assigned to it is the value supplied by the user in the corresponding textbox or list. For example, the content given by the user in the "Author" textbox becomes the value of the dc.contributor.author DC field whereas the "Title" corresponds to dc.title. Other kind of information

Figure 2.The incorporation of the LOM metadata schema in the DSpace system

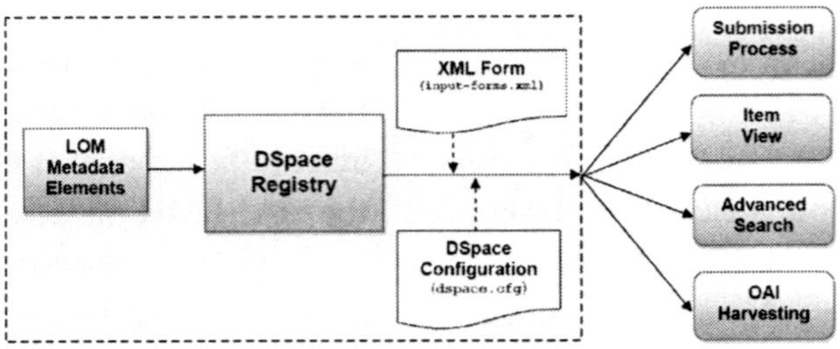

that users should supply about the submitted item concerns, for example, its type, its language and a set of subject keywords.

The metadata text fields are organized in pages and the process of filling a page's content fields is regarded as a distinct description step in the submission process. The structure of each page is defined in a fully parameterized XML file (input-forms.xml). Each page is represented by a form element in the XML file, where we have to declare the number of the page's fields and their correspondence to the DC elements.

In order for the proper utilization of the LOM metadata elements – apart from the initial process regarding their incorporation in the system's registry – we needed also to ensure their presence in the submission process. For this reason, we created a new form element inside the XML file that is responsible for the pages' structure. This form contains fields that correspond to the newly added LOM metadata fields and actually leads to the addition of a new page (description step) in the submission process, as shown in Figure 3. The new page is only activated and appears to users in case a "learning object" is submitted. The characterization of an object as being a "learning" one is provided in a preceding step, during the completion of the "Type" field. The LOM metadata fields that finally appear when submitting an item, together with their correspondent legal values, are presented in Table 1.

As shown in the Table 1, the incorporated LOM elements take values from a predefined value list. This simplifies the way a learning object is described during the submission process. What is more, it offers a uniform way in describing learning objects.

As a result of these enhancements, a more complete characterization of the institutional repository's content is provided. In case that educational material is submitted in the DSpace system, users can utilize the incorporated educational metadata elements. Finally, the organization of this subset of elements in a separate submission page, allows for their dynamic appearance to the users, according to their previous selections.

Advanced Search

An advanced search facility, performing search in DSpace content's metadata, is by default provided by DSpace. Users can select from a list the metadata fields among which the supplied keywords will be sought. In this list we also added the "Educational Metadata" option. In fact, in order to enable search among the LOM elements, the configuration file of the DSpace system had to be altered (dspace.cfg). We had also to include the name of the LOM metadata schema among the already used search indices, otherwise DSpace wouldn't be able to perform search in these fields. The additional search index corresponds to all educational metadata.

As a result of this modification, users can now request to obtain learning objects, just by providing their keyword in a search field which

Figure 3. The submission process in DSpace. The dashed-line rectangle in the upper part of the figure represents the additional description page. This page (shown in the lower part of the figure) contains the newly added educational metadata fields

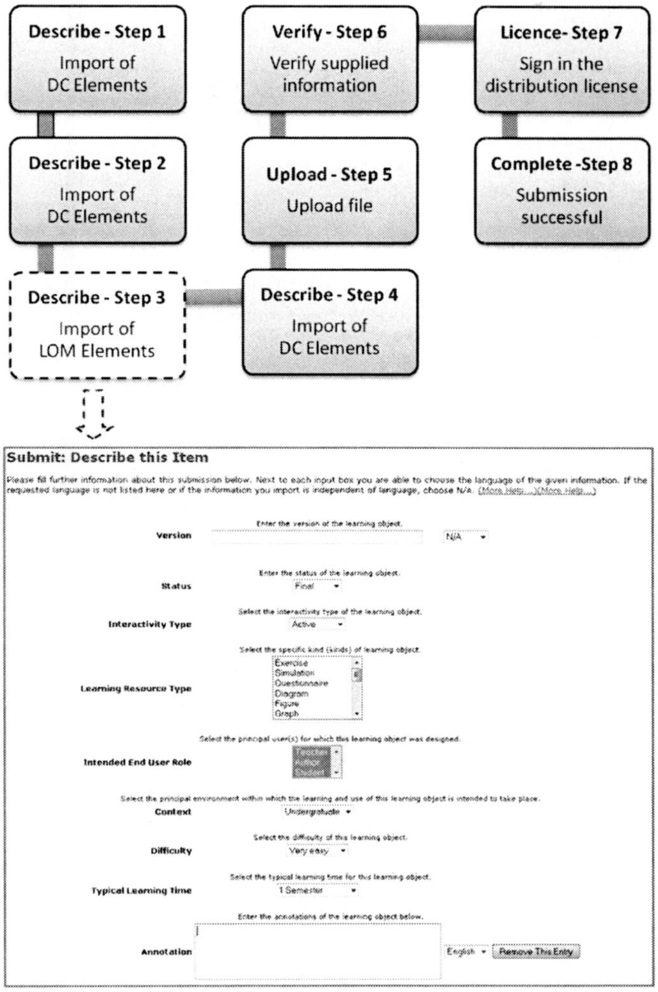

has the "Educational Metadata" option as a search type. Hence, the process of browsing educational resources becomes feasible though the standard – and familiar to the DSpace users – way.

Item View

After the successful submission of an item in a DSpace collection, the item can be retrieved through the simple or advanced search process. When the user selects to view a retrieved item, he is redirected to the "Item View" page. Here, the user can see the metadata describing the requested item either in short or long format. The item view page is a common and familiar to DSpace users interface as this is where the basic information about an object is exposed. What is now different is that the object's LOM metadata also appear, provided that this object has already been characterized as a learning one. The same holds for the full item record, where all the metadata information concerning the object appears. In Figure 4 we can see an example of the short item record of a learning object.

Table 1. The incorporated LOM elements in the University of Patras institutional repository.

LOM Element	Description	Value
2.1 Version	The current version of the submitted learning object	*free text*
2.2 Status	The status of the learning object, regarding its completion level	Draft, Final, Revised
5.1 Interactivity Type	The sort of interaction between the user and the learning object	Active, Expositive, Mixed
5.2 Learning Resource Type	The type of the learning object	Exercise, Simulation, Questionnaire, Diagram, Figure, Graph, Index, Slide, Table, Narrative text, Exam, Experiment, Problem Statement, Self Assessment, Lecture
5.5 Intended End User Role	The kind of user groups to which the learning object applies	Teacher, Author, Student
5.6 Context	The educational level of the audience to which the learning object applies	Undergraduate, 1st Year, 2nd Year, 3rd Year, 4th year, 5th year, 6th year, Postgraduate, PhD
5.8 Difficulty	The difficulty level of the learning object	Very Easy, Easy, Medium, Difficult, Very Difficult
5.9 Typical Learning Time	The typical type that the intended users should devote in order to fully understand the learning object	Less than 1 hour, 1 hour to 3 hours, 3 hours to 5 hours, 1 Day, 1 Week, 1 Semester, 1 Year
8 Annotation	Any kind of additional information that concerns the learning object and has not be included in previous fields	*free text*

Metadata Harvesting

DSpace supports OAI-PMH which is an HTTP based protocol for interoperable metadata harvesting. This means that the institutional repository, which is a DSpace installation, is able to export its content through the supported OAI-PMH interface. This harvesting facility is configurable as to what elements are to be exported, supporting by default the simple DC, as well as its qualifica-

Figure 4. LOM metadata through the "Item View" page. The newly added metadata can be viewed in the dotted rectangle

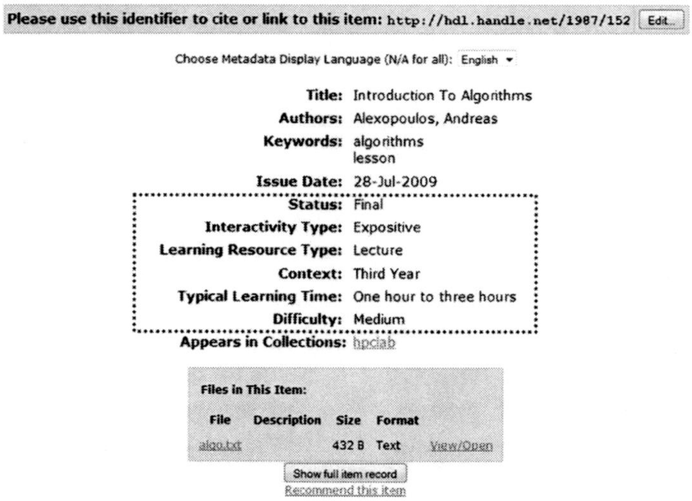

Figure 5. A DSpace metadata record in its LOM format, as exposed through the OAI harvesting facility


```xml
- <lom:lom xsi:schemaLocation="http://ltsc.ieee.org/xsd/lomv1.0 http://ltsc.ieee.org/xsd/lomv1.0/lom.xsd">
  - <Contribute type="LifeCycle">
      <Role>author</Role>
      <Entity xml:lang="en">Solomou, Georgia</Entity>
    </Contribute>
    <Language type="General" iso="iso639-2">en</Language>
    <Keyword type="General" xml:lang="en">algorithms</Keyword>
    <Keyword type="General" xml:lang="en">complexity</Keyword>
    <Title type="General">Introduction to Algorithms</Title>
  - <TaxonPath type="Classification">
      <Source>dspace</Source>
      <Entry type="Taxon" xml:lang="en">Learning Object</Entry>
    </TaxonPath>
  - <TaxonPath type="Classification">
      <Source>dspace</Source>
      <Entry type="Taxon" xml:lang="el">Μαθησιακό Αντικείμενο</Entry>
    </TaxonPath>
    <Annotation xml:lang="en">Exercises for revising chapters 5 & 6</Annotation>
    <Context type="Educational" xml:lang="en">Undergratuate</Context>
    <Context type="Educational" xml:lang="el">Προπτυχιακό</Context>
    <Difficulty type="Educational" xml:lang="en">Medium</Difficulty>
    <Difficulty type="Educational" xml:lang="el">Μέτριο</Difficulty>
    <IntendedEndUserRole type="Educational" xml:lang="en">Student</IntendedEndUserRole>
    <IntendedEndUserRole type="Educational" xml:lang="el">Φοιτητής</IntendedEndUserRole>
    <InteractivityType type="Educational" xml:lang="en">Active</InteractivityType>
    <InteractivityType type="Educational" xml:lang="el">Διαδραστικός</InteractivityType>
    <LearningResourceType type="Educational" xml:lang="en">Slide</LearningResourceType>
    <LearningResourceType type="Educational" xml:lang="el">Παρουσίαση</LearningResourceType>
    <Status type="LifeCycle" xml:lang="en">Draft</Status>
    <Status type="LifeCycle" xml:lang="el">Πρόχειρο</Status>
    <TypicalLearningTime type="Educational" xml:lang="en">One semester</TypicalLearningTime>
    <TypicalLearningTime type="Educational" xml:lang="el">Ένα Εξάμηνο</TypicalLearningTime>
    <Version type="LifeCycle">2</Version>
  </lom:lom>
```


tions. What we did was to extend this OAI service so that it can expose the LOM metadata as well (Figure 5). This extension could be beneficial in the case of LOM-conformant applications that are able to consume LOM directly.

In order to ensure interoperability of our implementation to a maximum possible level, we also activated the OAI-PMH interface so as to export the institutional repository's metadata in the qualified DC format. As we will explain in subsequent section, we provide a mapping from the LOM schema to the qualified DC element. Thanks to this mapping and to our selected parameterization to export the qualified DC metadata through the OAI-PMH interface, the export of LOM metadata becomes possible as well. Thus, our institutional repository becomes able to render "mapped" elements available to the data providers, among which the newly added educational metadata are also included.

INTEROPERABILITY ISSUES AND SEMANTICS

In this section we will study some issues regarding the interoperability and the semantics of digital repositories enhanced with educational metadata. Firstly, we describe a mapping from the LOM schema to the DC metadata element set. This mapping has as a primary goal to achieve interoperability between the various digital repository systems. Interoperability can be further enhanced by exploiting Semantic Web techniques, like ontologies that are expressed in the Web Ontology Language (OWL) (Bechhofer, et al, 2004). As an example an ontological model for the repository's metadata is proposed which takes also into account the educational characteristics of resources.

Choosing the Right LOM Elements

As already mentioned, the University of Patras DSpace installation uses by default a qualified version of the DC schema which can be further extended in order to enhance the system's capabilities. Our goal is to take advantage of the default DSpace schema's extension capability and enrich it with educational metadata. To achieve this we incorporate a subset of the LOM elements in the institutional repository. Among the LOM metadata elements that we chose to import in this system, there are some that appear to have a direct mapping to the inherent qualified DC metadata terms. So, we initially performed a mapping in order to investigate and find which exactly LOM elements correspond to the existing DC elements.

This mapping was considered necessary because it helped us to discover which of the LOM elements were already present in the repository's inherent schema through their DC correspondent. By this way we avoided repetition of elements in the repository's registry, namely we avoided the existence of multiple elements with the same semantic notions in our schema. The "missing" LOM elements were manually imported in the repository's metadata registry.

More specifically, the LOM metadata set comprises a hierarchy of elements, enumerating nine categories in the first level. Some of these elements have a direct mapping to DC terms, like for example *Title*, *Language* and *Contribute* which are mapped to dc.title, dc.language and dc.contributor respectively, as shown in Table 2. Consequently, the LOM elements with no explicit correspondence to DC that we finally chose to incorporate in DSpace were the following (nine in total): *Version*, *Status*, *Interactivity Type*, *Learning Resource Type*, *Intended End User Role*, *Context*, *Difficulty*, *Typical Learning Time* and *Annotation*.

Creation of a LOM Ontology

A process that took place right before the mapping of the newly added LOM elements to the DC terms was the creation of an ontology out of them. In particular, each LOM element that can accept values coming from a particular vocabulary list (controlled vocabulary) was considered as a separate class. The members of this element's value space were then considered as instances of this particular class. We thus managed to group LOM vocabulary values into classes and when it was semantically consistent, we also related them to dcterms classes. The correlation with the dcterms classes helped us in rendering the semantic interpretation between a LOM value and a DC-Term notion even more clear and precise.

As an example of the LOM ontology creation, let's consider the LOM element *Interactivity Type* which can accept one of the following values: {*Active*, *Expositive*, *Mixed*}. For this element we created the class lom:interactivitytype and we made the declaration that the instances *Active*, *Expositive*, and *Mixed* are members of this class. We have also asserted that the lom:interactivitytype is a subclass of the dcterms:MethodOfInstruction,

Table 2. Mapping of some LOM elements to the DC elements.

LOM Element	DC Element
General	dc.description
Identifier	dc.identifier.uri
Catalog	dc.identifier dc.identifier.govdoc dc.identifier.isbn dc.identifier.issn dc.identifier.sici dc.identifier.ismn dc.identifier.other
Title	dc.title
Language	dc.language
Description	dc.description.abstract
Keyword	dc.subject
Life Cycle	dc.description.provenance
Contribute	dc.contributor
Role	dc.contributor.advisor dc.contributor.author dc.contributor.editor dc.contributor.illustrator dc.contributor.other
Entity	dc.publisher
Date	dc.date.accessioned

thus creating a direct correlation between this particular LOM and dcterms class. A similar correlation is possible to be asserted for the LOM notions lom:typicallearningtime and lom:intendedenduserrole. We actually considered them as being subclasses of the dcterms classes dcterms:SizeOrDuration and dcterms:MethodOfInstruction respectively. The complete LOM ontology hierarchy can be viewed in more details in Figure 6.

The reason why we opted for such a semantic-aware approach was that it helped in better defining the meaning of the LOM elements. For example, when we mapped the LOM element *Learning Resource Type* (lom.learningresourcetype) to the DC-term property dcterms:type (as there was no other closer in meaning term) the result appeared to be rather incomplete. This is because the dcterms:type has a more general use than the more concrete *Learning Resource Type* which is used in order to state the exact type of a learning object. Furthermore, we wanted to utilize this work in a later implemented upgrade of the DC schema – together with the imported LOM metadata – to an OWL ontology (Koutsomitropoulos, Solomou, Alexopoulos, & Papatheodorou, 2009a).

Mapping LOM to DC

A remaining task was to map the nine LOM elements to the DC-Terms properties (DCMI Usage Board, 2008). We actually made an attempt to map these elements to those DC-Terms properties that seemed to better convey their meaning. The goal of such an attempt was to provide for semantic interoperability among repositories that serve educational purposes and that, like our institutional repository, utilize the qualified DC metadata. For this reason we took into consideration both the IEEE LOM specification (IEEE LTSC, 2002) and the work suggested in (IEEE LTSC, 2008) which proposes a potential LOM to DC Abstract Model (DCAM) (Powell, Nilsson, Naeve, Johnston, & Baker, 2007) mapping. According to that work a way to express LOM instances using the DCAM is proposed, arising from the necessity to have interoperable definitions of DC metadata terms

Figure 6. LOM ontology hierarchy

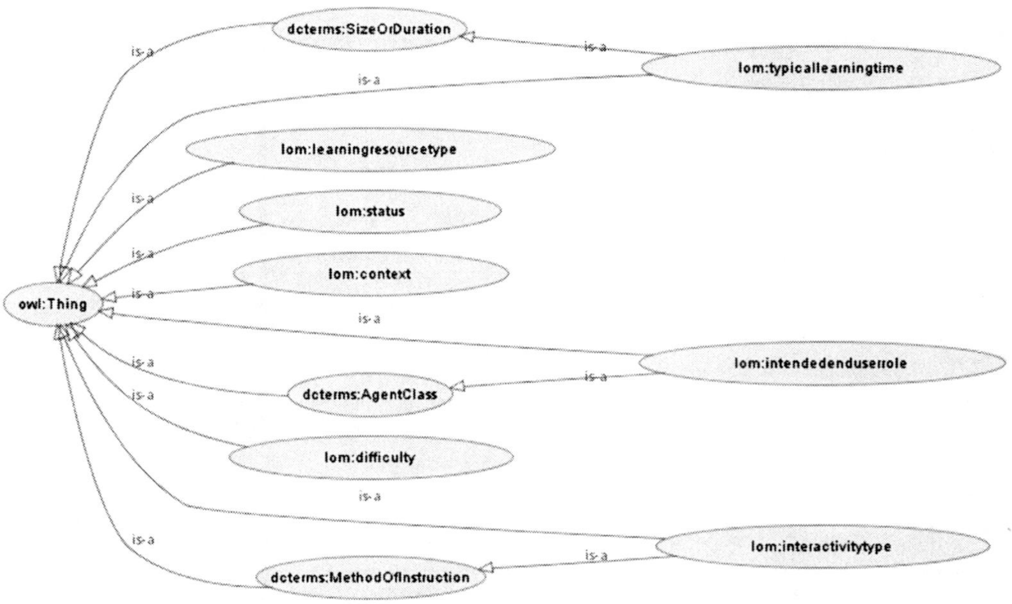

and learning object metadata elements that can co-operate. In addition, we studied some work regarding the provision of guidelines for the accommodation of additional metadata formats (like IMS-LOM) in DSpace, presented in (Prasad, 2006).

As a final step, we implemented the requested mapping from LOM to DC. We started by introducing and re-assigning namespaces. The dc: was replaced by dcterms: whereas LOM elements were prefixed with the lom: namespace. We then performed the requested mapping so that the LOM terms correspond to their closer in meaning DC-Terms. For example, we added in the DSpace metadata registry the elements lom.intendedEndUserRole and lom.interactivitytype which correspond to the LOM elements *Intended End User Role* and *Interactivity Type* respectively. We then mapped them to the most appropriate DC-Terms properties, namely the first one was mapped to dcterms:audience and the latter to dcterms:instructionalMethod. Finally, in order to better clarify these elements' actual value space, we have stated that dcterms:audience is of type lom:intendedenduserole and dcterms:instructionalMethod is of type lom:interactivitytype. Therefore, we explicitly define that whenever the DC-Terms properties dcterms:audience and dcterms:instructionalMethod are used, they are obliged to take values that come only from the lom:intendedenduserole and lom:interactivitytype classes respectively. For those LOM elements that no value space has to be defined, we just mapped them to the closest in meaning DC-Terms properties, without having to explicitly assign a value space (a type). The resulting mapping, concerning all the LOM elements, is presented in Table 3.

Exploiting a Learning Object Metadata Ontology

Because the use of ontologies leads to more interoperable applications and services, we exploit the upgraded DC metadata schema of the University of Patras institutional repository and we create an ontological model out of this schema. Having this ontology as a starting point, we further enhance the institutional repository with Semantic Web features. Besides, Semantic Web comes as a means to offer a new and challenging dimension in

Table 3. Mapping of LOM elements to the DC Terms properties

LOM Element		DC-Terms Property
2.1 Version	lom.version	dcterms:hasversion
2.2 Status	lom.status	dcterms:type type="lom:status"
5.1 Interactivity Type	lom.interactivitytype	dcterms:instructionalMethod type="lom:interactivitytype"
5.2 Learning Resource Type	lom.learningresourcetype	dcterms:type type="lom:learningresourcetype"
5.5 Intended End User Role	lom.intendedenduserrole	dcterms:audience type="lom:intendedenduserrole"
5.6 Context	lom.context	dcterms:educationLevel type="lom:context"
5.8 Difficulty	lom.difficulty	dcterms:type type="lom:difficulty"
5.9 Typical Learning Time	lom.typicallearningtime	dcterms:extent type="lom:typicallearningtime"
8 Annotation	lom.annotation	dcterms:description

the way information is managed and manipulated by traditional digital repositories.

In (Koutsomitropoulos, Solomou, Alexopoulos, & Papatheodorou, 2009a) we have proposed a method to create an ontological model for the institutional repository, by capturing the intended semantics of its DC metadata domain, taking into account the DC RDF(S) schema (Nilsson, Powell, Johnston, & Naeve, 2008). We actually created a semantic application profile of the qualified DC ontology, tailored for our repository's domain. We built upon the initial model and we didn't make any modifications in its original specification. In this process, we also took into account the LOM metadata, with which we have extended the original DSpace schema. Finally, we upgraded this ontology up to OWL and especially OWL 2 level (Hitzler, Krötzsch, Parsia, Patel-Schneider, & Rudolph, 2009), by incorporating new constructs and refinements, available only in these languages.

Therefore, through a series of syntax transformations, we have tried to better capture the semantic relations implied in these metadata as well as to construct the OWL specific instantiations, achieving a semantic level of compatibility with our ontology. The resulting ontology, including the new refinements, was afterwards populated in an automated way from metadata already existing within the live DSpace installation of our institutional repository, through its OAI-PMH interface.

The benefit of such an approach is that we are now able to utilize the original DC specification and to reuse it by providing a semantic application profile suitable for the particular domain's needs. We achieved this without interfering with the repository's internal data model and we have rather based upon the repository's inherent interoperability facilities, namely the OAI-PMH interface. As this approach is independent of the system architecture and relies mostly on interoperability interfaces, it can be likewise applied to enhance any modern digital repository system. Finally, looking back at the implemented mapping between DC-based information and LOM metadata, we see that the proposed improvements achieve semantic interoperability, even for the case that disparate schemata are used.

Moving a step forward, we have further extended our institutional repository by deploying some semantics-aware services on top of this ontology. These services provide for inference-based knowledge discovery, retrieval and navigation on top of the DSpace system, as we describe in (Koutsomitropoulos, Solomou, Alexopoulos, & Papatheodorou, 2009b). Because these services are possible to be implemented on top of other digital repository systems as well, a greater level of semantic interoperability can be gained.

FUTURE RESEARCH DIRECTIONS

As we saw in previous sections, the newly added LOM metadata can be exported through the OAI-PMH interface. This protocol enhances the interoperability of the system since it allows the metadata to be harvested in an automated machine-readable way. The OAI-PMH has been developed by the Open Archives Initiative which develops interoperability standards. A more recent protocol implemented by this organization is the Open Archives Initiative Object Reuse and Exchange (OAI-ORE) (Johnston, Nelson, Sanderson, & Warner, 2008). The OAI-ORE defines standards for the description and exchange of aggregations of Web resources. These aggregations are called compound digital objects, and may combine distributed digital resources with various types of objects like text, images, and video. An interesting aspect of the OAI-ORE protocol would be to be implemented for the DSpace system. Such an implementation could cause the supported compound digital objects to be created from resources stored in DSpace repository or even from resources stored in distributed DSpace repositories. Moreover, it would be interesting to see how educational metadata can smoothly cooperate with OAI-ORE so that we can create compound digital learning objects. By this way, namely by exploiting the OAI-ORE features, repository systems that manage educational resources could benefit as well.

Furthermore, our work has been concentrated on implementing the LOM schema in a live DSpace installation, leading to the enhancement of this particular system with the ability to store more information about learning objects. Apart from DSpace, many other repositories are in use for educational purposes worldwide, like Eprints and Fedora. So, it would be worth to try to incorporate the LOM schema in these repository systems as well. It might also be interesting to create an abstract model that would facilitate the incorporation of the LOM schema in various digital repositories. These educational metadata could then be exported through the OAI-PMH interface – if the latter is supported. Moreover, it would be challenging to try to integrate OAI-ORE in other repository systems – apart from DSpace – thus enhancing them with the ability to create aggregations of digital objects, coming from distributed repositories and digital library systems.

In addition, a deeper look into the Simple Web-service Offering Repository Deposit (SWORD) (Allinson, François, & Lewis, 2008) protocol could be beneficial. SWORD defines a standard and common mechanism for depositing into repositories and other systems. This functionality adds many features to digital repositories since more services can be built on top of it, like the ability to submit a file to multiple repositories at once or to submit files using desktop applications or even standard office applications. This protocol has already been implemented for various digital library systems like DSpace, Eprints and Fedora. A significant point would be to see this interoperability features offered by SWORD in practice and to further enhance this common mechanism with educational metadata.

As a final task, we focus on the deployment of the ontological model for digital repositories which seems to offer a significant means for further enhancing semantic interoperability in these systems. Although the proposed ontology has been enriched with LOM metadata, it could be interesting to see how other educational metadata schemata could be utilized in such an ontology, as long as their corresponding mapping to the DC-Terms properties is provided. What is more, a possible application of the populated ontology to other digital repository systems, apart from DSpace, would possibly reveal significant benefits from such a closer to Semantic Web approach.

CONCLUSION

In this work we have shown how the IEEE LOM standard can be utilized by digital repositories that manage educational resources. We presented several metadata schemata and applications profiles that have been constructed for the efficient characterization of learning objects. According to their characteristics, the one that seems to be more promising and has gained significant ground over the others is the IEEE LOM. The latter is a very popular standard has been adopted by many institutions and it has been implemented by many educational specific applications.

In order to exploit this schema's features, we incorporated it in the DSpace digital repository system, upon which the University of Patras institutional repository has been built. Actually, we have shown how we extended the repository's inherent DC metadata schema and enriched it with educational metadata. Therefore, we made this repository capable of characterizing its content in a more efficient way, rendering it easily accessible and utilizable. What is more, the result of this implementation became obvious in several DSpace facilities, like the item submission process, as well as in the advanced search and item view facility. This means that the imported LOM schema is now used in practice and can be exploited by the repository's users for the efficient description of the submitted material. What is more interesting, though, is that these facilities can be easily applied in other similar repository systems that use the DC element set for the characterization of their content.

In order for the LOM incorporation to be successfully accomplished, a mapping from the LOM to the qualified DC terms properties was preceded. Consequently, our repository is now consisted of educational and research material of higher "quality", where semantic relationships among items can also be implied. In addition, the system's metadata records can be fully exploited by the OAI harvesting service, through which a better level of interoperability can now be achieved. Besides, an extension to the OAI protocol so as to support LOM, along with the proposed mapping from LOM to DC, allowed us to easily expose these new metadata through the supported OAI-PMH interface (in their LOM or DC qualified format). This feature becomes true not only for the DSpace system, but also for any other OAI-compliant repository.

Finally, we implemented the LOM to DC mapping having in mind a later upgrade of this compound schema to an OWL ontology. We created LOM notions (classes), instead of mere LOM elements, whose members (instances) define the exact value space for the corresponding DC-Term. The creation of an ontological model out of these concepts and the use of Semantic Web features confirmed that new metadata concepts can be seamlessly integrated and further enhance the interoperability in this kind of applications.

REFERENCES

Al-Khalifa, H., & Davis, H. (2006). The evolution of metadata from standards to semantics in E-learning applications. In *17th ACM Conference on Hypertext and Hypermedia*.

Allinson, J., François, S., & Lewis, S. (2008). *SWORD: Simple Web-service Offering Repository Deposit*. Retrieved from http://www.ariadne.ac.uk/issue54/allinson-et-al/

Bechhofer, S., Harmelen, F., Hendler, J., Horrocks, I., McGuinness, D., Patel-Schneider, P., & Stein, L. A. (2004). *OWL Web Ontology Language Reference*. W3C Recommendation. Retrieved from http://www.w3.org/TR/owl-ref/

Berners-Lee, T. (1997). *Metadata Architecture*. Retrieved from http://www.w3.org/DesignIssues/Metadata.html

Dalziel, J. (2002). *Reflections on the COLIS (Collaborative Online Learning and Information Systems) Demonstrator Project and the "Learning Object Lifecycle"*. Retrieved from www.colis.mq.edu.au/projects/dalziel.doc

DCMI. (2008). *Dublin Core Metadata Element Set, Version 1.1*. DCMI Recommendation. Retrieved from http://dublincore.org/documents/dces/

DCMI Libraries Working Group. (2004). *Library Application Profile*. DCMI Working Draft. Retrieved from http://dublincore.org/documents/2004/09/10/library-application-profile/

DCMI Usage Board. (2008). *DCMI Metadata Terms. DCMI Recommendation*. Retrieved from http://dublincore.org/documents/dcmi-terms/

Duval, E., & Hodgins, W. (2003). *A LOM Research Agenda*. Retrieved from http://www2003.org/cdrom/papers/alternate/P659/p659-duval.html.html

Duval, E., Hodgins, W., Sutton, S., & Weibel, S. (2002). Metadata Principles and Practicalities. *D-Lib Magazine*, *8*(4). Retrieved from http://www.dlib.org/dlib/april02/weibel/04weibel.html. doi:10.1045/april2002-weibel

Heery, R., & Patel, M. (2000). *Application Profiles: Mixing and Matching Metadata Schemas*. Retrieved from http://www.ariadne.ac.uk/issue25/app-profiles/

Hitzler, P., Krötzsch, M., Parsia, B., Patel-Schneider, P., & Rudolph, S. (Eds.). (2009). *OWL 2 Web Ontology Language: Primer*. W3C Working Draft. Retrieved from http://www.w3.org/TR/owl2-primer/

IEEE LTSC. (2002). *Draft Standard for Learning Object Metadata (IEEE 1484.12.1-2002)*. Retrieved from http://ltsc.ieee.org/wg12/files/LOM_1484_12_1_v1_Final_Draft.pdf

IEEE LTSC. (2008). *Draft Recommended Practice for Expressing IEEE Learning Object Metadata Instances Using the Dublin Core Abstract Model (IEEE P1484.12.4/D1)*. Retrieved from http://dublincore.org/educationwiki/DCMIIEEELTSCTaskforce?action=AttachFile&do=get&target=LOM-DCAM-newdraft.pdf

Johnston, P., Nelson, M., Sanderson, R., & Warner, S. (Eds.). (2008). *ORE Specification - Abstract Data Model*. Retrieved from http://www.openarchives.org/ore/1.0/datamodel

Koutsomitropoulos, D., Solomou, G., Alexopoulos, A., & Papatheodorou, T. (2009a). Semantic Metadata Interoperability and Inference-Based Querying in Digital Repositories. *Journal of Information Technology Research*, *2*(4), 37–53.

Koutsomitropoulos, D., Solomou, G., Alexopoulos, A., & Papatheodorou, T. (2009b). Knowledge Management and Acquisition in Digital Repositories: A Semantic Web Perspective. In *international Conference on Knowledge Management and Information Discovery*.

Lagoze, C., Van de Sompel, H., Nelson, M., & Warner, S. (2002). *The Open Archive Initiative Protocol for Metadata Harvesting*. Retrieved from http://www.openarchives.org/OAI/openarchivesprotocol.html

Nair, S., & Jeevan, V. (2004). A Brief Overview of Metadata Formats. *DESIDOC Bulletin of Information Technology*, *24*(4), 3–11.

Najjar, J., Duval, E., Ternier, S., & Neven, F. (2003). Towards Interoperable Learning Object Repositories: the ARIADNE Experience. In *IADIS WWW/Internet 2003 Conference*, (pp. 219-226).

Neven, F., & Duval, E. (2002). *Reusable learning objects: a survey of LOM-based repositories. In 10th ACM international conference on Multimedia* (pp. 291–294).

Nilsson, M., Powell, A., Johnston, P., & Naeve, A. (2008). *Expressing Dublin Core metadata using the Resource Description Framework (RDF). DCMI Recommendation*. Retrieved from http://dublincore.org/documents/dc-rdf/

Powell, A., Nilsson, M., Naeve, A., Johnston, P., & Baker, T. (2007). *DCMI Abstract Model. DCMI Recommendation*. Retrieved from http://dublincore.org/documents/abstract-model/

Prasad, A. R. D. (2006). Implementing LOM Schema in DSpace. In *DRTC-ICT Conference on Digital Learning Environment*.

Wiley, D. (2002). *Connecting learning objects to instructional design theory: A definition, a metaphor, and a taxonomy*. Retrieved from http://reusability.org/read/chapters/wiley.doc

KEY TERMS AND DEFINITIONS

Digital Repositories: Mechanisms responsible for storing, describing, preserving, managing and distributing any kind of digital material.

Educational Metadata: Metadata about learning objects.

Application Profiles: Combinations of different metadata schemata.

IEEE LOM: A metadata standard about learning objects, published by the Institute of Electrical and Electronics Engineers Standards Association.

DSpace: A open source digital repository system that provides the tools for management of digital assets. It is mainly used for the deployment of institutional repositories.

Interoperability: The ability of diverse systems and applications to co-operate (inter-operate).

Mapping: Correspondence between two different data models.

ENDNOTES

1 http://www.dspace.org/

2 http://www.imsproject.org/

3 http://www.ariadne-eu.org/

4 http://www.cancore.ca/

5 http://www.adlnet.org/

6 http://zope.cetis.ac.uk/profiles/uklomcore/

7 http://www.thegateway.org/

8 http://www.eprints.org/

9 http://www.fedora-commons.org/

10 http://www.careo.org/

11 http://www.merlot.org/

12 http://www.mis2.udel.edu/ja-sig/

13 http://www.ilumina-dlib.org/

14 http://repository.upatras.gr/dspace/

Chapter 13
A Common Sense Approach to Interoperability

Kate Taylor
Newnham College, UK

ABSTRACT

E-learning promotes the use of structured learning materials which extend the book based metaphor of chapters, lists and diagrams using markup languages based on HyperText Markup Language (HTML). Educators working with eXtended Markup Language (XML) have a variety of XML based technologies to choose from: Moodle, Resource Definition Framework (RDF) and Web Ontology Language (OWL). Another option is to use XML to generate web resources from a relational database, such as MySQL, or with a knowledge database, such as Prolog. This chapter looks at how these three technologies can interchange information with the help of new intelligent resources such as the OpenMind project that are beginning to model the world around us. Advances in these areas pave the way for more automatic acquisition of knowledge from existing texts using tools such as MontyLingua to provide a basic semantic understanding of the material and promote interoperability. Examples of the technologies are used to illustrate the benefits of structuring new learning materials, and options for integrating heritage materials are examined.

INTRODUCTION

Learning materials are lovingly crafted to cover a syllabus and provide intellectual stimulus and entertainment during the learning process. From the earliest days of sticks and a flattish area of mud, through the abacus, paper and the invention of the printing press, it has been important to find a way of sharing learning materials as widely as possible. The advent of the personal computer in the 1980s finally made an electronic means of sharing a possibility, brought closer by the Internet's rise to prominence in the 1990s after decades of work to make computers and networks talk to each other without calling in a team of programmers. Now learning materials are shared across continents

DOI: 10.4018/978-1-61692-789-9.ch013

as well as counties, often for free, as electronic e-tutors. However, this sharing has happened largely at the level of the printed page, based on the idiom of the sharing of books. Only in the last few years has the markup language behind web sites developed enough to allow true sharing at the ideas level to become a possibility.

Systems like FIRE (2006) from the LIFE project funded by the European Commission (Education and Culture) provide a means of browsing learning objects from multiple sources and show great promise for systems being developed today for large organisations. However, as studies such as Mayes and de Frietas (2004) show, much of the material from currently available e-tutors is not in this form. The simplest web pages use Hyer Text Markup Language (HTML) tags such as *<font>* to indicate how to draw the page on the screen. More advanced pages structure the information in the page using eXtended Markup Language (XML). The Open Source Learning and Development Environment (LDE) Moodle, described in Cole and Foster (2007), is an example of tagged learning materials that provide a means for teachers themselves to develop learning resources. A strategy for interoperability must include tactics to deal with legacy systems and teacher-created materials to avoid valuable material being left behind.

All tag-based technologies can search the knowledge content for concepts. HTML and XML technologies achieve this through the tag metadata, whilst a relational database such as MySQL or a knowledge base such as Prolog can also use relationships between the metadata to process existing data and create new data derived from it. A knowledge base has the additional capacity to reason about the content from these relationships, often referred to as a semantic network. Both the relational model and the semantic network are built from the terms used as the metadata for database fields or tagged documents. In many current systems these are hand crafted, but in both fields there is a motivation for partially automating the process to provide a first draft that a human expert can then edit appropriately.

This chapter considers what is possible now when I write new learning materials for our reasoning e-tutor in an area where other e-tutors exist. The Interactive Verilog Compiler (IVC) system teaches how to programming the sequence of lights on a traffic light in the United Kingdom using the hardware definition language Verilog, a C-like language used in chip design. The tutor uses the network to generate answers to free text questions as well as for a framework for the learning materials. A real bottleneck in adapting IVC to work on other domains is the editing of new materials, which leads us to investigate interoperability.

In the following example, please imagine I have two colleagues, Alice and Bob. Bob is teaching young children about road safety using Moodle documents tagged in XML. The tags are referred to as *metadata.* Alice works with college students in town planning and associated industries and is using a MySQL database of road furniture to support and record metadata about each of her lessons, which are stored in XML documents. Ideally, I could use content and metadata that Alice and Bob have already created in their relational and XML systems. One approach would be for me to sit down and read the definitions and use my expertise to blend the three models together. This is time-consuming for more than the smallest subject area, but unfortunately I am not at the stage of interoperability that can directly translate from one format to another, especially as my materials are aimed at different age groups.

However, if some further manipulation is done on Alice and Bob's tags and the document content, then existing natural language processing tools can be used to reason more effectively about the relationship of concepts both within the tags and in the knowledge content itself to create a first draft for me to look over. The tools I have used are the lexical database WordNet described in Fellbaum (1998) and the commonsense knowledgebase and the natural-language-processing toolkit ConceptNet which was developed by Liu and Singh (2004). The advantages of even partially automating the process are that I do not have to re-type and re-format text. Anyone who has tried typing in HTML or XML documents will know that the task is error prone because the tags must match, and an error in one part of the document can make the rest display incorrectly, if at all. Instead, I use my human "common sense" to decide on my terminology and level of description based on my particular knowledge of my target audience, and get the computer to re-map the tags from one system to another, to merge systems together and to tell me where any inconsistencies appear to be. This can be thought of as an extension to the spell-checker and grammar checker in a word-processor, or text completion for sending text messages on a mobile phone.

First I introduce the technologies in more detail and then present a worked example showing the state of the art in moving from free text or tagged text to a semantic model that a reasoning web site could work from. I discuss developments in the Web Ontology Language OWL which undertakes this in the world of XML, and the issues and challenges still to be addressed in all interchange technologies. The various technologies have all evolved to meet a specific need for a specific group of users. The scale, budget and skill set of the author will always determine what can be done, but using the techniques described in this chapter ensures that the universities can reach back to schools and both look outwards to the world of vocational training to underpin true lifelong learning.

E-TUTOR TECHNOLOGIES

Reasoning Technologies

My family of e-tutors, Socrates, uses web-based materials with metadata stored in a knowledge base. Taylor and Moore (2005) describes how we hand crafted a semantic network for teaching the Verilog computer language and for teaching Operating Systems in Taylor (2006) such as Windows and Linux to first year Computer Science undergraduates at the Computer Laboratory at the University of Cambridge, United Kingdom. My first e-tutor is the Intelligent Verilog Compiler (IVC) with a free text question answering facility and multiple choice questions at the end of each chapter. Later chapters have a series of programming exercises. Figure 1 shows the programming of a traffic light in the United Kingdom as a series of state transitions that re then programmed into an emulation environment using Verilog.

The bottom panes show a conversation that the student has with the knowledge base, enabling the student to take control of the dialogue to refresh her memory of a previous point or to answer a question raised in her mind by the programming task set. The question answering uses the semantic network to reply in basic English. The better the network, the more often the student gets a helpful reply. For the IVC, the semantic network must provide *coverage* of the material, the ability to recognize *synonyms* and *taxonomy relations* and to understand *temporal relations* such sequences of events. At each chapter conclusion, a

diagrammatic representation of all the concepts taught is shown to the student as Figure 2. This *concept map* or *semantic network* is coloured to let the student know what they have covered, what is to be done and what they have answered questions or programming exercises on to encourage them to reflect on progress. It is a summary of the actual semantic network that the system uses to *understand* the relationships between the concepts in the subject material. This work was funded by the Cambridge MIT Institute (CMI) and the evaluation performed with the Centre for Applied Research in Educational Technology (CARET). My next step was to add more subject material to this core semantic network for the larger and more descriptive topic of operating systems. This

Figure 1. A screen from the IVC E-tutor on programming traffic lights showing the conversation with the student in the bottom pane

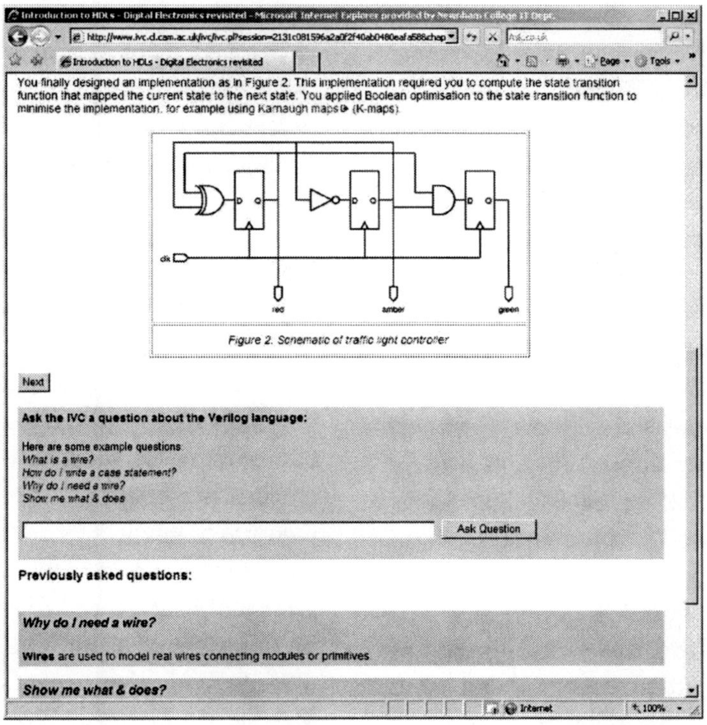

Figure 2. The summarised Verilog network shown to the student to promote self-reflection and appreciate the subject as a whole

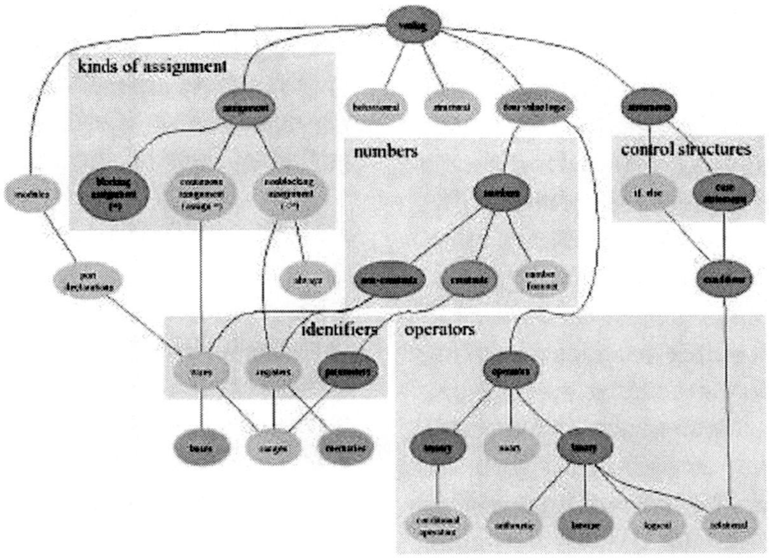

work is called the Socrates system because it aims to capture and store knowledge in a form that can be used for students to ask free text questions. Multiple choice questions can also be generated from the semantic network. The work with WEKA and MontyLingua described below was supported by Cambridge E-Science.

XML Technologies

Many teachers in the United Kingdom are working to create Moodle resources defined in eXtensible Markup Language (XML). There are two types of XML in Moodle, one used to import or export glossaries and one for question definition, usually called Moodle XML. When an educator backs up a course from Moodle, the compressed zip file created also contains an XML file containing the glossary and question definitions. The very flexibility of XML makes typographical and structural errors hard to detect without using some way of checking that what has been typed is the right "shape".

One approach to checking this is to use a Document Type Definition (DTD) which makes it possible to check what has been laboriously typed in, from missing angle brackets to spelling mistakes and missing fields, in the same way as you can spell check and grammar check your learning resources. Resources such as Yatskovsky (2009) capture the structure required for Moodle in a Microsoft Word document template (dot file) so the educator need only fill in fields rather than type tags.

This chapter is addressing what we need to do to make sure that shared materials are talking about the same concepts at a similar level of detail. For XML resources, this translates to making sure that the XML not only meets the rules about the shape of the data and whether a number or a piece of text is required, but also whether the values make any sense when used with other values in other tags. This cross-referencing is already done in relational databases to ensure that data is consistent, and so a logical step was to add this to the XML notation using Resource Definition Framework (RDF). RDF represents facts as well as displays them. It can be thought of as a set of three pieces of information *subject, predicate, object* known as an RDF-triple. For example, the following indicates that the traffic light is red:

http://mywebsite.net/traffic_lights/light.htm, http://mywebsite.net/traffic_lights/is_showing,"red"

The web reference for both the subject and the predicate are Uniform Resource Identifiers (URI) that point to the location of a precise definition of what is meant by both terms. An ontology is made up of many of these facts working together. RDF graphs are a visual representation of the groups of RDF facts. We based our concept map on this style of using XML to ensure a level or interoperability with other XML e-tutors such as Moodle. As Figure 1 shows, the URI is dropped to give a less cluttered visual picture.

The IVC is built in PERL, Prolog and XML. Prolog is a general purpose logic programming language used for artificial intelligence and linguistics. Like the relational technologies described next, Prolog represents the world via relations but has a more expressive language to be able to reason new information from existing data as well as find information already stored.

Relational Technologies

Large repositories of relational data evolved after the introduction of relational technologies in the 1980s from definitions of files created in the first wave of network-style databases. Relational data is grouped into *entities*, made up of related items of data, known as *attributes,* each of which has a name and a data type. The relationships between these entities are always one-to-many, a restriction which makes it easier to ensure the correctness of the data stored in the entities. For example,

Figure 3. An entity-relationship diagram showing that a traffic light contains lights with colour and position to represent the red, amber and green lights in a traffic light

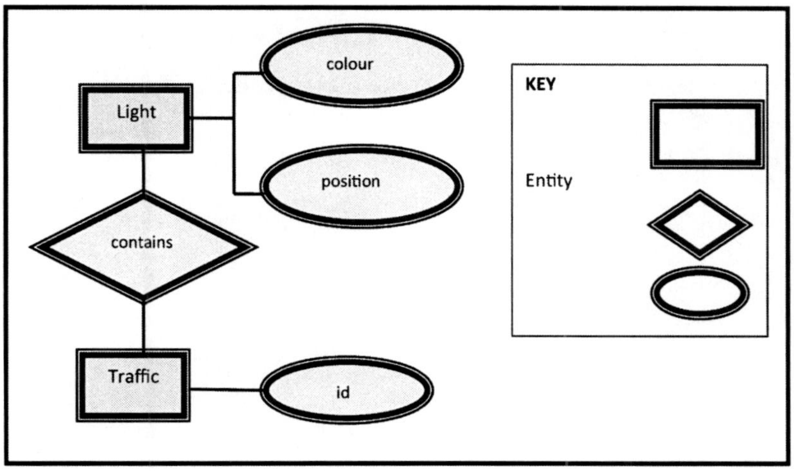

one traffic light contains three lights: one red, one amber and one green. The entities are shown graphically as a box and line diagram as shown in Figure 3. There is a strong resemblance to the RDF graphs and the concept network from the IVC, which can be derived from the entity-relationship diagram by omitting the attributes and using the relationship to name the verb.

Once a particular database has been chosen to store the entities in, they are usually known as *tables* and their attributes are known as *fields*. Structured Query Language (SQL) provides *insert, update* and *delete* operations to manipulate data. These operations are included in XML-based query languages developed twenty years later. Relational data can be exported in XML tagged format as well as in an SQL format. XML can also be used to present the contents of the database in a web format rather than through screens on a server.

Web Ontology Language (OWL)

XML processing technologies are being developed, with Web Ontology Language (OWL) being one of the most prominent at the time of writing. OWL is an XML markup built on top of RDF that allows processing and simple reasoning for the creation of an *ontology*. According to the Web Ontology Language (OWL 2003) Use Cases and Requirements document:

An ontology formally defines a common set of terms that are used to describe and represent a domain. Ontologies can be used by automated tools to power advanced services such as more accurate Web search, intelligent software agents and knowledge management

The process that an educator goes through to define the language and the scope of the material and setting the questions to test understanding of that material according to a syllabus is the human equivalent of defining an ontology. For Our purposes, the term *semantic network* and the data stored in an *ontology* can be used interchangeably. An ontology can be understood as a database with more advanced processing than just editing and more advanced data representation than just a list of facts. Powers (Powers 2003) describes the analogy between RDF and the relational technology modelled by techniques such as Unified Modelling Language (UML) used in Figure 4 as follows:

Figure 4. Open Mind's understanding of traffic lights

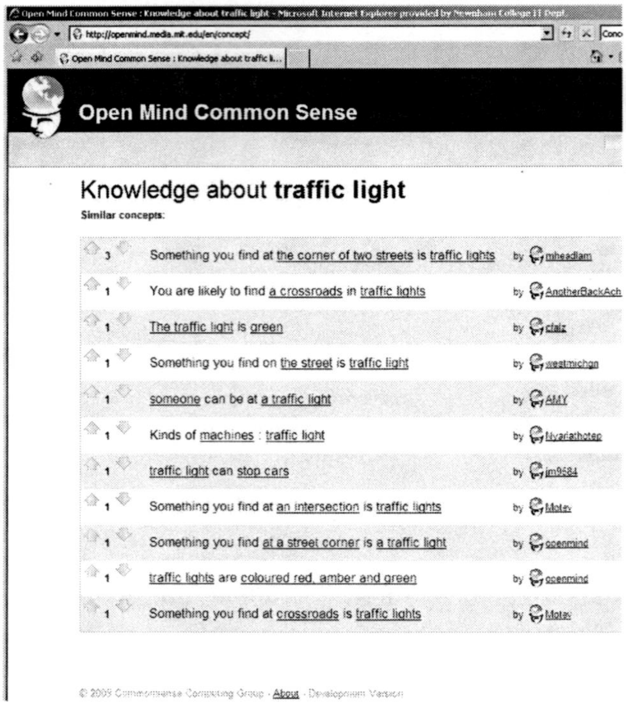

"If RDF and the relational data model were comparable, then RDF/XML is also comparable to the existing relational databases, and OWL would be comparable to the business domain applications such as PeopleSoft and SAP. Both PeopleSoft and SAP make use of existing data storage mechanisms to store the data and relational data model to ensure that the data is stored and managed consistently and validly; the products then add an extra level of business logic based on patterns that occur and reoccur within traditional business processes. This added business logic could be plugged in to a company's existing infrastructure without the company having to build its own functionality to implement the logic directly. OWL does something similar except that is builds in the ability to define commonly recurring inferential rules that facilitate how data is queried within an RDF/XML document or store".

OWL adds capabilities similar to the Prolog language to the XML scripting language to allow it to handle definition, display, processing and reasoning about data. We deliberately chose to model our data along the lines of RDF triples as described above to be able to utilise data from the Semantic Web project. The dream of the Semantic Web, often called Web 2.0, is to replace the existing Internet with pages tagged to promote interoperability. The problem of e-tutor interoperability is a case study in point. We consider that the issue of what to do with the existing HTML pages on the Internet and how to derive new learning materials are facets of the same problem. The next section looks at how computational linguistics and natural language processing can provide support for a level of understanding of the semantics of the text to help with automatic tagging.

Automatic Network Generation Technologies

I have been experimenting with generating first drafts of semantic networks like those in Figure 2 from our lecture notes. MIT's ConceptNet (Liu and Singh 2004) supports many practical textual-reasoning tasks over real-world documents, including *topic-jisting*. For example, a news article containing the concepts *butter, icing* and *flour* might suggest the topics *birthday* and *cake*. The knowledge base is a semantic network presently consisting of over 1.6 million assertions of commonsense knowledge encompassing the spatial, physical, social, temporal, and psychological aspects of everyday life. Whereas similar large-scale semantic knowledge bases like Cyc and WordNet are carefully handcrafted, ConceptNet is generated automatically from the 700,000 sentences of the Open Mind Common Sense Project – a World Wide Web based collaboration with over 14,000 authors.

The MontyLingua parser is used to read and tag the material for ConceptNet. One of the tools within MontyLingua is the Jister. This captures the intended meaning informally – the gist of the sentence – as a first approximation of a *subject-verb-object* or *subject-verb-object-object* relationship. An example of this is *traffic_light is_located_at Green Street*. Other work with MontyLingua has been undertaken by the Automated Learning Group at the National Center for Supercomputing Applications at the University of Illinois at Urbana-Champaign (Auvil et al. 2007). They use MontyLingua with their tools D2K and T2K to perform a lexical analysis of the documentation set, and compose the entity relation triples into a semantic network which is then viewed as a graph. Experimental results on sense discovery from Web documents (Miura, Tsuruko and Ysujii 2006) show that the obtained senses covered 71% of the senses described in WordNet.

THE TRAFFIC LIGHTS EXAMPLE

The following case study describes what I would have to do to be able to integrate material from my colleagues Alice and Bob into my knowledge base. I want to compare data they hold with my Verilog training tool which teaches how to program a traffic light in a simulation environment as part of an undergraduate computer science course and with text from Wikipedia. The detailed examples are there for the interested reader. I hope that looking at the emboldened text should be sufficient to see that the tags in the different formats are similar enough to allow some automatic translation by a computer.

Moodle XML

Bob is using Moodle to help him learn XML, and wants to use a Document Template Description (DTD) to be able to check the XML quickly for typographical errors as he does not have much spare time to build this resource in. His DTD states that each traffic light has a unique identifier and the current colour it is showing, and that any text can be written inside each tag. This means that the XML editor cannot help if Bob types *Geren* for *Green*, but can help if he misses out the tag altogether.

```
<?xml version="1.0"
encoding="UTF-8"?>
<!ELEMENT TrafficLight (Id) >
<!ELEMENT Position (#PCDATA)>
<!ELEMENT TrafficLight (Colour) >
<!ELEMENT Colour (#PCDATA)>
```

He writes some XML that defines an actual traffic light, with the red light, an amber light, and a green light, numbered 1 to 3, but not indicating which goes at the top of the lighting panel:

```
<?xml version="1.0"
encoding="UTF-8"?>
<TrafficLight>
        <Position>1</id>
        <Colour>Red</Colour>
</TrafficLight>
<TrafficLight>
        <Position>2</id>
```

```
        <Colour>Amber</Colour>
</TrafficLight>
<TrafficLight>
        <Position>3</id>
        <Colour>Green</Colour>
</TrafficLight>
```

He writes Moodle XML that defines a multiple choice question about a traffic light. If the questions is answered wrongly, a penalty of 0.1 out of 100 is deducted from the questionnaire score, to help avoid multiple guess tactics.

```
<question type>="multichoice">
<name><text>"question 3"</text>
<questiontext format="html">
<text>"In the United Kingdom, what
colour light(s) are shown after the
red light?"</text)
<penalty>0.1</penalty>
<single>true</single>
<answer fraction="100">
<feedback></feedback>
</answer>
<question>
```

Knowing the format of Bob's XML allows me to write a small PERL program that can glean some facts from the DTD. I can deduce that a *traffic light* has a *colour* and a *position*. However, Bob's data does not include the order of the traffic light, because that information is captured in the display of the question rather than in the data.

I store my data in a Prolog predicate rdf_triple(verb, subject, object. For example, rdf_triple(is_part_of, red_light, traffic_light) is read as *The red light is part of the traffic light.* These are definitions of generic traffic lights.

XML from a Relational Database

Alice has found a database of road furniture kept by the highway authority and believes that it will save her time to take the information from there rather than re-type it herself to give her web pages some real-life data. She has asked for the data to be exported from the MySQL database as an XML file to create the tables and the contents of the tables representing the actual items of road furniture owned by the highway authority. Here is part of that file, showing a traffic light on a road junction.

```
<?xml version="1.0"?>
<mysqldump xmlns:xsi="http:/www.
w3.org/2001/XMLSchema-instance">
<database name = "furniture">
<table_structure name="TrafficLight">
<field Field="ID" Type="int(11)"
Null="NO" Key="PRI"/>
<field Field="JunctionID"
Type="int(11)" Null="No" Key="FOR"/>
</table_structure>
<table_data name="TrafficLight">
<row>
<field name="ID">32891</field>
<field name="JunctionID">4523</field>
</row>
</table_data>
</database>
</mysqldump>
```

My rdf_triple statements need to be definitions about junctions, not instances of actual data like traffic light 32891 being at junction 4523 as in Alice's data above. I can get this information from the <table_structure> and <field Field> tags so I can automate this learning too.

```
rdf_triple(is_part_of, red_light,
traffic_light)
rdf_triple(located_at, traffic_light,
junction)
rdf_triple(connects_many, junction,
road)
```

Knowing the format of Alice's XML allows me to write a small PERL program that can glean some facts. Alice's XML allows me to derive automatically:

```
rdf_triple(related_to, traffic_light,
junction)
which I can then edit to the more
specific:
rdf_triple(located_at, traffic_light,
junction)
```

I am interested to see if WordNet and ConceptNet can help to do that translation automatically from their understanding of traffic lights, which is discussed below. I need to find a way to find the correct, more specific, verb, for example, converting *is_related_to* to *is_located_at.*

Passing Knowledge Back to Alice and Bob

I could use the text generation routines used to answer questions in the IVC to provide Alice and Bob with a paragraph of text summarising My knowledge. These work by reading off the *verb subject object object* and inserting punctuation and connectives to give a basic English style. Alternatively, I could generate XML to match their use of XML tags, disambiguating using the WordNet and ConceptNet resources. I would like to automatically work out the relationship between *street corner* and *intersection* and *crossroad*, or at least automatically show them as alternatives for the human editor to pick from to speed up the editing process. I want to use a controlled vocabulary for pedagogical reasons whilst keeping synonyms allows a richer language for my question answering.

Using WordNet and ConceptNet to Disambiguate and Refine

This section looks at the use of ConceptNet and WordNet to disambiguate the XML conversion and extends their use to undertake free text analysis for Wikipedia to provide more background knowledge. It recommends some ideas for best practice. Figure 5 shows an interactive use of WordNet

Figure 5. WordNet's understanding of junction

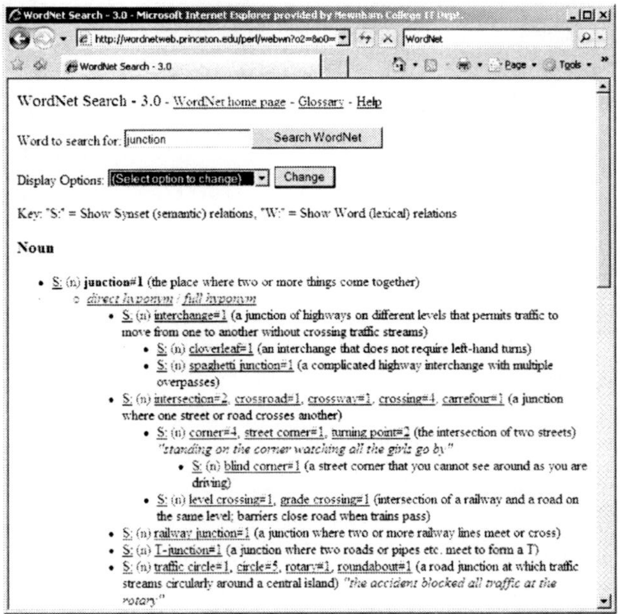

over the Internet, whereas I would use a query from my e-tutor directly to the WordNet database.

Here is another problem: I am now picking up information about railway junctions as well as road junctions. It is hard to give a computer a definitive list of items to ignore, whereas humans come ready programmed with knowledge of the difference between road and railways and an innate knowledge of the jargon associated with both. This is why our approach uses the computer to make a first draft, and the human to polish it to be appropriate and useful for the task in hand.

This problem of inappropriateness happens again when I look up the colours in WordNet. Several of the colours shown in Figure 6 are artist's pigments, so I would not want them in my database – few students are likely to refer to the colour of the second light on a traffic light as *gamboge* or *maize*! However, I decide I do want to retain *orange* or *yellow*, but that might be just my personal view on what an international group of students is likely to use.

There is no indication in WordNet of this higher level of semantic knowledge needed make my search for relevant concepts more directed because it is intended as a dictionary and thesaurus. If I use ConceptNet instead, then I get alternative meanings for *amber* such as *precious stone* as the syntactic information that *amber* is being used as an adjective here cannot rule out those alternative meanings either. We discuss various techniques to address multiple possible answers for a lookup later in this chapter, but note that for any piece of text, the possibilities have been shown to expand in a Catalan series, that is, worse than exponentially, for the worst case of concepts such as *traffic light* which are composed of several nouns with meanings in their own right.

If I use both systems together, it will help to reduce the possibilities, for example, search in WordNet and ConceptNet for traffic light and amber, and select only those entries that have both. There is an established way of searching for more than one concept, excluding certain combi-

Figure 6. WordNet's understanding of amber

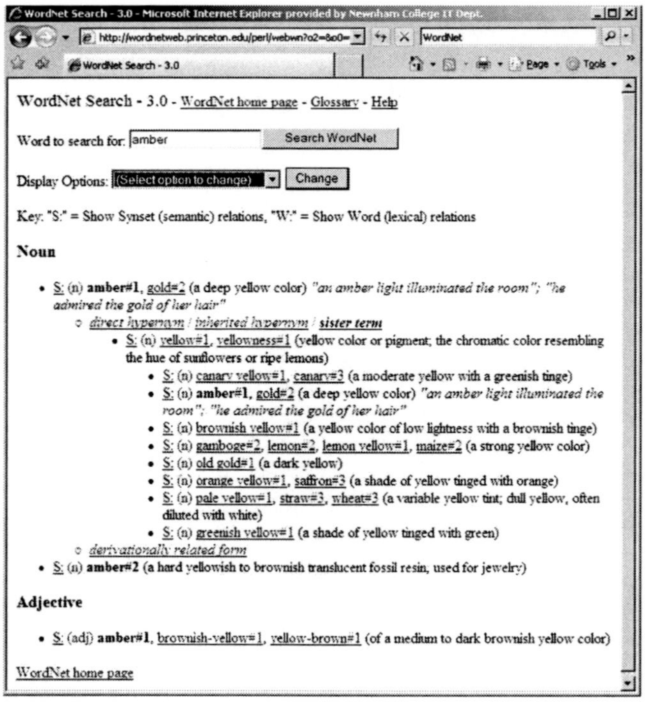

nations of other terms via Internet search engines such as Google, so if I can solve the problem of reducing English to definitions automatically or semi-automatically, I can enrich the information provided by WordNet and ConceptNet. Understanding concepts and their relationships comes from looking at examples and counter examples for both humans as they learn, and for machines. Whilst this is an anthropomorphic view which may make the reader slightly wary because of its resonance with science fiction, the development of large databases of knowledge which can be searched quickly make it a reasonable model for storing data.

Importing from Free Text

I use the MontyLingua tool used to populate ConceptNet and decide on Wikipedia as a source as it written in a reasonably structured English. Tools like MontyLingua have a model of English grammar, and whilst they can cope with basic inversions and references, using the most grammatical English available reduces their processing time.

I could also use Alice's and Bob's web page and question text, once I have removed the markup used to display the materials on the screen. If Alice and Bob have used italicisation or emboldening to define terms, it helps to focus on what the page is about and allows me to write a skeleton of RDF facts to start the database off.

I have looked up *traffic light* on Wikipedia (Wikipedia 2009) and immediately see that *traffic signal* is an alternative term.

This article is about a traffic control device. For the type of political coalition, see Traffic light coalition.

"Traffic Signal" redirects here.

I decide that *traffic light* is the normal usage in the United Kingdom, but use *traffic signal* as a synonym as I have an international audience of students. I have decided to use the following text to pass to MontyLingua:

Traffic lights, also known as traffic signals, stop lights, stoplight, traffic lamps, stop-and-go lights, robots or semaphore, are signaling devices positioned at road intersections, pedestrian crossings, and other locations to control competing flows of traffic. Traffic lights have been installed in most cities around the world to control the flow of traffic. They assign the right of way to road users by the use of lights in standard colors (Red - Amber - Green), using a universal color code (and a precise sequence, for those who are color blind). They are used at busy intersections to more evenly apportion delay to the various users. The most common traffic lights consist of a set of three lights: red, yellow (officially amber), and green. When illuminated, the red light indicates for vehicles facing the light to stop; the amber indicates caution, either because lights are about to turn green or because lights are about to turn red; and the green light to proceed, if it is safe to do so.

MontyLingua provides the following informal *jists* in {subject verb object object} format with a blank line showing the start of a new jist:

```
("know" "" "as traffic signal")
("stop" "" "light stoplight traffic
lamp stop-and-go light robot")
("semaphore" "")
("signal" "" "device")
("position" "device" "at road inter-
section pedestrian crossing and other
location")
("compete" "" "flow" "of traffic")
("install" "Traffic light" "in most
city" "around world")
("control" "" "flow" "of traffic")
("assign" "They" "right" "of way" "to
road user" "by use" "of light" "in
standard color")
("use" "" "universal color code")
```

```
("be" "who" "color" "blind")
("use" "They" "at busy intersection")
("more apportion" "" "delay" "to
various user")
("consist" "common traffic light")
("set" "" "of three light")
("When illuminate" "")
("indicate" "red light" "for vehi-
cle")
("face" "vehicle" "light")
("stop" "")
("indicate" "amber" "caution")
("be" "light")
("turn" "" "green")
("be" "light")
("turn" "" "red")
("proceed" "")
("be" "it" "safe")
("do" "")
```

Before I can convert this format into our RDF-like syntax or into facts for Bob and Alice's XML schema, I must sort out what They refers to in each case. In computational linguistics, this process is called resolving *anaphoric reference*, and is another area of current research on how to use semantic knowledge to reduce the number of possibilities to look at.

Lappin and Leass (1994) describe a procedure for using grammatical role, frequency of mention, proximity and sentence recency to model the human process of disambiguation which has been demonstrated to give the correct interpretation in 86% of cases and to rank alternatives. Proximity in this context refers to how many words and how much punctuation lies between the pronoun of the possible noun, whereas recency refers to whether the information is in the same sentence. This algorithm can be used to suggest the various possibilities for They and who in the following jists from MontyLingua. The previous jist is needed as there is no noun before They.

```
("install" "Traffic light" "in most
city" "around world")
("control" "" "flow" "of traffic")
("assign" "They" "right" "of way" "to
road user" "by use" "of light" "in
standard color")
("use" "" "universal color code")
("be" "who" "color" "blind")
```

Running Lappin & Leass' algorithm gives the possibilities for They as traffic, world, city, Traffic light. Adding in the knowledge from WordNet and ConceptNet increases the emphasis on *saliency* over the importance of *recency* in the previous sentence to help present the list of options for each pronoun in the best possible order for the human educator to select. This process prepares jists for the conversion to the format to store as RDF facts.

A Procedure to Integrate Sources

The previous sections have identified the issues in integrating XML and free text, and suggested some computer resources that can be used to help. We are not at a stage where the process is fully automated, but we do have a pipeline of searches, comparisons and conversions to assist the educator. The steps we follow are shown below, starting with either the XML data definition or web content, or both, to summarise the discussions in the previous sections.

Starting with XML

1. Identify structure of the XML from the DTD if available.
2. Write small PERL program to read out the data.
3. Construct rdf_triple skeleton from tag names.
4. Use the general term *related* to be refined below to a verb appropriate to the context.

Starting with Free Text

1. Identify source from Internet using a search engine or from web content in e-tutor.
2. Save in text format to remove the markup.
3. Use Lappin & Leass to turn pronouns in into list of noun possibilities for educator to select one.
4. Use MontyLingua to turn text into jists.

Display Draft RDF with Options

5. Create draft rdf_triple from each jist or tag set.
6. Pass noun or verb possibilities to WordNet and ConceptNet and display relevant matches.
7. Educator chooses correct noun or verb for each by hand.

Exporting Back to XML

1. If no DTD available, create one by examining the data held in Bob's system.
2. Use the DTD as a template to generate XML by writing a small PERL program to convert each Socrates rdf_triple fact into XML.
3. Relationships cannot be explicitly recorded in XML but are retained by putting them in XML comments:

```
<TrafficLight>
        <Position>3</id>
        <Colour>Green</Colour>
</TrafficLight>
-- green means safe to proceed --
```

Exporting to RDF

1. For each fact in the Socrates system stored in Socrates rdf_triple, generate an RDF format fact.

Advantages of the "First Draft" Approach

There are a number of steps that can be automated by using PERL or a similar language, but if these are not available, the educator can type in facts with the relevant resources open in other windows around the editor. Having tried this ourselves, we believe that it gives around a 40% gain in time over sitting down with a word processor and creating facts from expert knowledge.

The Socrates rdf_triple is a halfway house between tagged data and the full markup proposed as part of the Semantic Web. My knowledge base search facility has the advantages of Bob's approach in that queries are searching a semantic network rather than an entire repository to find relevant material. In addition, because I am using concepts that understand the relationship with parent concepts from ConceptNet and WordNet, I can provide an answer for a search where the term searched for does not directly appear, though a special case or a more general case does. Like a search engine, related terms can be handled to avoid the frustration of missing a good learning object because it has not used the phrase I have used. It is essential to provide a search facility for large learning object repositories with a wide subject field to help students find what they want quickly without the students or the system reading each document in turn. This provides the accessibility and the scalability that must go hand in hand with increased interoperability.

FUTURE RESEARCH DIRECTIONS

We chose to use Prolog in 2004 as RDF and OWL were young technologies at that time and we needed a reasoning engine for the work with the IVC electronic circuit simulation. Proponents of the Semantic Web talk of persuading everyone to use the same notation, RDF. However, this results in extra work for an educator working on a small project in Moodle or as a stand-alone system. Suggesting that small projects use a DTD to allow others to write code to make use of their work keeps the door open for interoperability, but is not essential as my approach could simply remove the tags of free format XML and treat it as free text without too much of an overhead. Performing a draft conversion to RDF automatically would make it a more attractive option to educators who have invested a lot of personal time and effort into creating electronic learning resources.

Use of RDF as a particular kind of XML to represent the learning resources and the processing for an e-tutor, such as defining multiple choice questions, is a step to ensuring that interoperability can happen. The decision by W3C to embed RDF in the OWL technologies future-proofs the investment of marking up resources in RDF today. We are all busy creating more detailed definitions ranging over all fields to support e-learning, so understanding the relationships between technologies is important. Once resources are defined, and as the technologies evolve and standardize, electronic translation will make the interoperability task more straightforward. Angle brackets are definitely for machines, not people! Some readers will remember writing documents with early word processors, which also required the user to type in tags. Nowadays, sorting out formatting in a word processor is done with menus and keyboard shortcuts. In ten years time, the markup tags that this chapter has described will also probably be something that the human user no longer has to deal with.

I have identified a number of linguistic tasks that are currently open problems. Effectively, we aim to automate simple techniques such as passing more than one term to WordNet and OpenMind to restrict the search, for example, *amber* in the sense of *colour*, and *junction* in the sense of *road* will do much to narrow down the search to make it more feasible and can utilise techniques developed by search engines such as Google. Promising lines of research to deal with vast domains to search for possible meaning is to use a probabilistic approach or to keep a history of what has been associated before.

Another Open Source system, WEKA from the University of Waitako (Witten & Frank 2005) provides a toolbox of machine learning techniques and data visualisation to correlate and cluster concepts. This concept mining approach is used in terrorism detection and in shopping basket analysis to hunt for associations in very large data repositories. If we succeed in solving the interoperability problem, the repositories we create could be equally as large. If a ranking of possible associations can be created using these data mining approaches, then probabilistic algorithms can produce a complete draft based on some assumptions. I have discussed examples which introduce choice of meaning in this chapter, and there is some way to go before these technologies would be mature enough to reliably interpret the correct meanings. For example, a probabilistic converter might find more references to precious stones than to traffic lights in its repository of knowledge, and redraft our knowledge base to a jewellery knowledge base. Whilst not useful to us, perhaps it would be just what someone else needs for their learning plan.

CONCLUSION

This chapter has demonstrated that the simple structures used by the IVC e-tutor to model the world around it are flexible enough to fit in with other tools such as Moodle. The data representation must be rich enough to represent the world around us whilst compact enough to allow searches to happen fast enough to satisfy web users. A taxonomical approach to classification with a second dimension of interpretation of synonyms captures this complexity whilst maintaining responsiveness and expressiveness. Finding additional text on the Internet enriches the experience of the educator and promotes critical thinking in learning resource development and presentation.

New learning materials written in this style are future proof as well as interoperable. My experiments are an indication that the technologies to translate different representations of learning resourced are becoming possible using ConceptNet to address the remaining challenges of disambiguation. Using ConceptNet as a backbone addresses the problem that just the tags that Alice or Bob set up at the time that the document was created are available, which restricts my use of their material. It also permits direct comparison and integration of all three learning materials. This approach helps to reduce the human effort in hand-crafting the tagging, improves the quality and the flexibility of the materials and ensures the pedagogical soundness of the materials by supporting access from many different points of view. These document analysis techniques are already in use in word processors as automatic summary generators. Effectively, I am using the MontyLingua parser to summarise text down to *noun-verb-noun* relationships. The relationships stored are taxonomy or classifications of objects (*what*) enhanced by further relationships that are causal (*why*), temporal (*when*) and actor (*who*).

I have presented a case study to demonstrate that my reasoning approach using linguistic resources provides a flexible aid to the educator's task of picking the scope, language and depth of the learning materials. Work proceeds in the field of computational linguistics to help with disambiguation so that it is not too unrealistic to envisage the percentage of translation that an automatic system could do will gradually increase. My example has emphasized that there will be many variants because of cultural differences, but what I am aiming for is a first draft generator for us to tailor to our own needs.

Future knowledge gathering programs, descendants of today's web bots, could be run over the entire Internet to produce Web 2.0 with such knowledge freely available. With the rate of change of human knowledge, such a web bot would be doomed to reading new material forever, like a latter day Sisyphus. Richard Mobbs at Leeds University (Mobbs 2006) defines the A4 of eLearning – Anytime, Anyplace, Any Pace, Any Subject. My approach adds a fifth dimension – Anything – by integrating information from tagged documents with the network of Common Sense understanding in ConceptNet. This is a step towards better drafts of learning objects generated by a computer from learning materials and the World Wide Web itself as well as addressing the integration of legacy systems.

REFERENCES

Auvil, L., Grois, E., Llòra, X., Pape, G., Goren, V., Sanders, B., & Acs, B. (2007). *A flexible system for text analysis with semantic networks.* Paper presented at Digital Humanities 2007, Univeristy of Illinois, Urbana-Champaign, Illinois.

Cole, J., & Foster, H. (2007) *Using Moodle - teaching with the popular open source course management system.* Sebastopol, CA: O'Reilly Community Press. Retrieved 22 July 2009 from http://download.moodle.org/download.php/docs/en/using_moodle_2e.zip

Fellbaum, C. (Ed.). (1998). *WordNet an electronic lexical database.* Cambridge, MA: MIT Press.

Lappin, S., & Leass, H. (1994). An algorithm for pronominal anaphora resolution. *Computational Linguistics, 20*(4), 535–562.

LIFE project. (2004). Retrieved 22 July 2009 from http://insight.eun.org/shared/data/insight/lre/LRE_Developments.ppt

Ling, M. (2006). An anthological review of research using MontyLingua: a python-based end-to-end text processor. *The Python Papers, 1*(1). Retrieved July 22, 2009, from http://repository.unimelb.edu.au/10187/1549

Liu, H., & Singh, P. (2004). Commonsense reasoning in and over natural language. In *Proceedings of the 8th International Conference on Knowledge-Based Intelligent Information & Engineering Systems (KES'2004)*. Wellington, New Zealand, September 22-24, (LNAI). Berlin: Springer.

Mayes, T., & de Freitas, S. (2004). Review of e-learning theories, frameworks and models. *JISC*. Retrieved July 22 2009 from http://www.jisc.ac.uk/uploaded_documents/Stage%202%20Learning%20Models%20(Version%201).pdf

Miura, K., Tsuruoka, Y., & Ysujii, J. (2004). *Automatic acquisition of concept relations from web documents with sense clustering*, (pp. 37-40). Paper presented at IJCNLP 2004 Interactive Poster/Demo.

Mobbs, R. (2006). *Advantages of e-learning*. Retrieved 22 July 2009 from http://www.le.ac.uk/cc/rjm1/etutor/elearning/advdofelearning.html accessed 20/04/2009

OWL. (2003). *Use Cases and Requirements*. Retrieved from http://www.w3.org/TR/webont-req

Powers, S. (2003). *Practical RDF*. Sebastopol, CA: O'Reilly. Retrieved 22 July 2009 from http://etutorials.org/Misc/Practical+resource+description+framework+rdf/Preface/

Taylor, K., & Moore, S. (2005) An intelligent interactive online tutor for computer languages. In *Proceedings of 25th Annual International Conference of the British Computer Society's Specialist Group on Artificial Intelligence (SGAI 2005)*, Cambridge, United Kingdom, December 10-12. Berlin: Springer-Verlag.

Taylor, K., & Moore, S. (June 2006) My *compiler really understands me*. Paper presented at Adaptive Hypermedia (AH 2006) Dublin.

Wikipedia. (2009). Retrieved 22 July 2009 from http://en.wikipedia.org/wiki/Traffic_light

Witten, I., & Frank, E. (2005). *Data mining: practical machine learning tools and techniques* (2nd ed., pp. 285–362). New York: Elsevier.

Yatskovsky. (2009). Retrieved 22 July 2009 from http://finemetronome.com/moodle

ADDITIONAL READING

Berners-Lee, T. Hendler, J. & O Lassilla, O. (2001) *The Semantic Web* Scientific American: The Semantic Web May 17, 2001 pp1-12

Budiu, R., & Anderson, R. (2002)*Comprehending anaphoric* metaphors in Memory & Cognition 2002. 30(1) pp158-165.

Butcher, C. (2004) http://www.leeds.ac.uk/sddu/online/bloom.html Bloom's Taxonomy. Retrieved 22 July 2009 from http://www.leeds.ac.uk/sddu/online/bloom.html

Carey, S. (1991). Knowledge acquisition: enrichment or conceptual change? In Carey, S., & Gelman, R. (Eds.), *The Epigenesis of Mind: Essays on Biology and Cognition*. Hillsdale, NJ: Lawrence Erlbaum Associates.

Davies, P. & Mangan, (2005) J. *Recognising threshold concepts: an exploration of different approaches*. Paper presented at European Association in Learning and Instruction Conference (EARLI) (August 23 – 27th 2005)

Dolog, P., Henze, N., Wolfgang Nejdl, W., & Michael Sintek, M. (2004). *Towards the adaptive semantic web in Lecture Notes in Computer Science* (*Vol. 2901*). Springer-Verlag Heidelberg.

Entwistle, N. (2003) *Concepts and conceptual change frameworks underpinning the ETL Project*. Edinburgh: ETL Project Occasional Report 3

Gruber, T., & Olsen, G. (1994) An ontology for engineering mathematics. In J Doyle, P Torasso, & E Sandewall (Eds). *FMyth International Conference on Principles of Knowledge Representation and Reasoning,* Gustav Stresemann Institut, Bonn, Germany, Morgan Kaufmann, 1994.

Guarino, N. (1998) *Formal ontology in information systems* in Proceedings of FOI'98, Trento, Italy IOS Press, pp. 3-15.

Hanson, N. (1958). *Patterns of discovery: an inquiry into the conceptual foundations of science.* Cambridge: Cambridge University Press.

Jean, S., Pierra, G., & Ait-Ameur, Y. (2006) *Domain ontologies: a database oriented analysis.* Paper presented at WEBIST 2006.

Kotis, K. (2005) *Using simple ontologies to build personal webs of knowledge.* Paper presented at 25th Annual International Conference of the BCS Specialist Group on Artificial Intelligence (SGAI 2005) Springer Verlag

Lee, M. (1994) *A model of story generation* MSc Thesis in System Design in the faculty of Science University of Birmingham, Retrieved 22 July from www.cs.bham.ac.uk/~mgl/research/papers/msc_thesis.ps

Li, L., & Kay, J. *Learner reflection in student self-assessment* Technical Report Number 568, University of Sydney NSW (2006)

Ling, M. (2006) An anthological review of research using MontyLingua: a python-based end-to-end text processor. *The Python Papers, 1(1).* Retrieved July 22, 2009, from http://repository.unimelb.edu.au/10187/1549

Liu, H. (2004). MontyLingua: *An end-to-end natural language processor with common sense.* Retrieved 22 July 2009 from http://web.media.mit.edu/~hugo/montylingua.

McDonald, P. (2004). *The nature of algorithm understanding: a phenomenographic investigation. School of Computer Science and Information Technology* (p. 3000). MelbMyne, Vic., Australia: RMIT University.

Meyer, E. & R. (2006) Threshold concepts and troublesome knowledge: an introduction. In Meyer E, Land R. (eds.) *Overcoming Barriers to Student Understanding: Threshold Concepts and Troublesome Knowledge* (Routledge, London)

Mitchell, T. (1997). Concept learning and the general to specific ordering. In *Machine Learning* (International edition, pp. 20–51). McGraw-Hill.

Moodle (2009) Retrieved 22 July 2009 from http://www.vlearn.org/moodle/

Pérez-Marín, D., Enrique Alfonseca, E., & Rodríguez, P. (2006) *On the dynamic adaptation of computer assisted assessment of free-text answers.* Paper presented at Adaptive Hypermedia 2006 Springer Verlag Semantic Web Tutorial Retrieved 22 July 2009 from http://www.w3schools.com/semweb/default.asp

Sparck-Jones, K. (2004) What's new about the Semantic Web? In *ACM SIGIR Forum, 38(2), pp18-23*

Taylor, K., & Moore, S. (December 2006) *Adding Question Answering to an e-tutor for programming.* Paper presented at 26th Annual International Conference of the BCS Specialist Group on Artificial Intelligence (SGAI 2006) Springer Verlag

Vosniadou, S. (1991) Designing curricula for conceptual restructuring: lessons from the study of knowledge acquisition. In *Astronomy JMynal of Curriculum Studies, 23(3), 219 – 237*

Watkins, C. (2003). *Learning: a sense-maker's guide.* London: Association of Teachers and Lecturers.

Wenger, E. (1998). *Communities of practice: learning, meaning and identity*. Cambridge: Cambridge University Press.

Witten, I., & Frank, E. (2005). *Data mining: practical machine learning tools and techniques* (2nd ed.). San Francisco: Morgan Kaufmann.

Wood, D. *How children think and learn: the social contexts of cognitive development* (2nd Edition). (Oxford: Blackwell) (1998) Vargus-Vera, A. & Motta, E. *(2004) AQUA- ontology based question answering system*. In Proceedings of MICAI 2004: pp 468-477, Mexico City

Wood, D., Bruner, J., & Ross, G. (1976) The role of tutoring in problem solving. In *JMynal of Child Psychology and Psychiatry, 17 89-100*

KEY TERMS AND DEFINITIONS

Anaphoric Reference techniques to establish which noun a pronoun refers to, or how a complex sentence structure indicates location and time ordering, for example, in the sentence *The man saw the boy in the park with his telescope.*

Attribute in data modelling a piece of information often part of a real world object or an abstract concept, for example, *colour* is an attribute of the entity *rainbow.*

Coverage is a quality measure of the percentage of the material that any automatic processing can recognize.

Database: A computer program which stores and retrieves information such as Microsoft Access or MySQL. Databases have been used since the 1950s for administrative tasks such as banking and for scientific data such as astronomy. A database organizes information in an electronic equivalent to an official form, and makes sure that this structure is used to keep the data valid.

Document Template Definition (DTD): A text document that defines what tags a piece of text must use and in what order to be valid. A DTD acts like a list of boxes to complete on an official form - if a piece of information is missing, then the form is not complete.

Entity: In data modeling a noun used to describe a real world object or an abstract concept, for example, a *rainbow.*

eXtended Markup Language (XML) extends HTML by giving text a particular structure that can be checked by a computer program if a DTD or XSD is provided.

Markup Language text annotated with directions to a computer on how to display or interpret the text. The name is thought to originate from the newspaper and book publishing term for the notations that book publishers use to direct human printers to get the required effect such as font size and indentation on the printed page.

HyperText Markup Language (HTML): The markup language used to tell web pages how to display themselves on the screen.

Lexical Analysis breaking words into their word stems in a human dictionary to allow processing against the electronic dictionary, for example, *running* becomes *run* and *children* becomes *child.*

Metadata: The information in a HTML or XML document held inside a tag: for example <name> Kate </name>.

Moodle: Open Source program used to construct XML resources.

Open Source refers to programs written and maintained by a user community who also contribute ideas on the future direction of the product.

Relationship: In data modeling a verb used to describe how two entities are related together, for example, a rainbow appears in rain and sunshine.

Resource Definition Framework (RDF) extends the capabilities of XML to model data to allow a web page to store and retrieve information rather than go to a database to find it.

Semantic Network a term used in computer language processing and in RF and OWL to refer to concepts linked by relationships. Memory maps are an informal example of a semantic network.

Synonym: Another word representing the same concept, for example, sunlight and sunshine, but not sheep and ewe, as an ewe is a particular female kind of sheep, hence a taxonomy relationship.

Tag: A pair of opening and closing markers to hold information inside an XML or HTML document, for example <name>Kate</name>

Web Ontology Language (OWL) extends the capabilities of RDF by defining a language to process and reason about the data rather than use a computer database or a knowledge base.

XML Schema Definition (XSD): A text document that defines what tags a piece of text must use and in what order to be valid. An XSD understands more about whether the information should be numeric or text based. It allows definitions such as (country code, district code, local code) to define an international telephone number to be defined once and then referred to in many text documents.

Chapter 14
Localising E-Learning Websites in the Semantic Web Era

Dimitris N. Kanellopoulos
University of Patras, Greece

ABSTRACT

Recently, ontologies have been applied for localisation of e-learning content in order to promote existing learning services to semantic-aware and intelligent localisation services. This chapter presents a localisation-aware semantic e-learning approach to integrate multilingual content provision, learning process and learner personality in an integrated semantic e-learning framework. The author proposes an architecture for supporting localisation of e-learning content and describes a basis for further development of automatic localisation services that will be able to reason on top of such an explicit infrastructure.

INTRODUCTION

Nowadays adaptive learning offers flexible solutions by dynamically adapting content to each individual's learning needs (Adler & Rae, 2002; Paule *et al*., 2008). Shang *et al.* (2001) argued the necessity of creating an intelligent learning environment, one that would be student centered, self-paced, highly interactive, and based on students' learning characteristics, including background knowledge and learning style. From another perspective, learners differ across regional, linguistic and country boundaries. They represent a multicultural community and their requirements are strongly influenced by their local cultural perspective. Learners are members of a culture, who share a common language and common cultural conventions. From one culture to another, many things differ such as measurement units, keyboard configurations, default paper sizes, character sets and notational standards for writing time, dates, addresses, numbers, currency, etc. Characteristically, De Troyer *et al.* (2005) state:

"Some jokes, symbols, icons, graphics or even colors may be completely acceptable in one country, but trigger negative reactions in another country. Sometimes the style or tone of the site's text might

DOI: 10.4018/978-1-61692-789-9.ch014

even be considered offensive by a particular cultural entity, as a result of which the text needs to be rewritten rather than merely translated."

Therefore, designers of learning management systems (LMS), such as Blackboard and WebCT, should address these issues. Many LMS provide for multiple languages but this does not necessarily include true localisation, which requires adaptation of the content and design to fit local cultures. *Localisation* is the process of adapting an e-learning product or service to a particular language, culture, and desired local "look-and-feel" (Clark, 2005). Localisation includes three types of adaptation (Harris & McCormack, 2000).

1. *Linguistic adaptation* affects course elements that include textual descriptions on screen and in graphics, user interface, browser window titles, text input fields and so on.
2. *Substantive adaptation* involves modifying the substance of the learning content for local audience. Examples of course elements that may be affected by substantive adaptation include: abbreviations, terminology, examples, cases, rules and regulations which are specific to the geographical area.
3. *Cultural adaptation* involves contextualizing the content for a specific culture. Examples of course elements affected by cultural adaptation include: symbols, icons, colour, graphic style/photographs, names, titles and forms of addressing people.

Authors of learning material have to address the needs of a culturally diverse user base. If e-learning content is not culturally sensitive, there is the potential for exclusion of local learners based on accessibility to information that is not culturally appropriate. The goal of localising e-learning material is to provide a technologically, linguistically and culturally neutral platform from which to launch global e-learning initiatives. Recently, there is a demand for improving e-learning solutions from pure web-based content provision to instructional and localised learner-centric learning and teaching environments. The success of the International Conference "*Open Education 2007: Localizing & Learning*" (held at Utah) is in line with the above trend (Open Education, 2007).

At the same time, the semantic Web is starting to be shaped up. *"The semantic Web is an extension of the current web in which information is given well-defined meaning, better enabling computers and people to work in cooperation"* (Berners Lee *et al.*, 2001). E-learning is estimated to be more intelligent in the new era of educational semantic web. Kanellopoulos *et al.* (2006) discuss how semantic web technologies, especially ontologies, could be used to present semantics of course's content and learner's information to the adaptive e-learning applications. Henze *et al.* (2004) present a logic-based approach for resource representation and reasoning based on RDF annotations. The RDF (*Resource Description Framework*) is a language for representing information about resources on the web (Lassila & Swick, 1999).

To facilitate the development process towards localisation of e-learning services, we present a localisation-aware semantic e-learning approach to integrate multilingual content provision, learning process and learner personality in an integrated semantic e-learning framework.

The remainder of the chapter is structured as follows. First, we discuss related work about learning objects, learning design, and localisation process in e-learning. Next, we present the proposed semantic framework for supporting localisation of e-learning content. Finally, we draw some conclusions and motivate our future work.

BACKGROUND

Learning Objects

A *learning object* (LO) is a reusable portion of instructional content. It represents the main key in the reuse process of instructional content, which is broken into small pieces that can be reused in different learning environments. The *IEEE Learning Technology Standards Committee* (LTSC) defines a LO as

"any digital entity that can be used, re-used or referenced during learning based on Information Technology".

The main characteristics of a LO are flexibility, easiness of update, customization and interoperability. The IEEE LTSC has proposed the *Learning Object Metadata* (LOM) specification that has become a de facto standard, which is supported by some means by all major learning object repositories and e-learning platforms. IEEE LOM (IEEE LTSC, 2002) describes a data structure that represents the metadata of a learning resource. It identifies 76 different aspects by which a LO can be annotated. In particular, it specifies the structure and semantic metadata of LOs, defining the attributes that are necessary to their description. IEEE LOM facilitates the search, evaluation, acquisition and use of LOs by learners, instructors or automatic software processes. It makes possible LOs sharing and interchange. Moreover, the LOM enables the development of catalogs and considers the diversity of language and cultural contexts in which LOs and their metadata could be used. Examples of LOs that can be described using the IEEE LOM are digital educational material, multimedia content, learning software and tools for supporting education.

Some LOM editors, that have been developed, are the *LOM Java Editor* from Darmstadt University ofTechnology, Germany (http://www.multibook.de/lom/), the *ImseVimse* from the Royal Institute of Technology (http://kmr.nada.kth.se/imsevimse/) Sweden, the *TreeLOM* from Cukurova University in Adana, Turkey (Cebeci & Erdogan, 2005) and the *LOM Metadata Editor* embedded in Authorware from Macromedia.

Learning Design

A *learning design* (LD) represents the learning activities and the support activities that are performed by different persons (learners, teachers) in the context of a learning unit (Koper, 2006). A '*learning unit*' can be any instructional or learning event (e.g. a course or a lesson) of any granularity. Learning activities are components performing specific learning functions and refer to different LOs and services used during the performance of the activities (Figure 1).

The combination of simple atomic learning activities could be regarded as a complex activity. Navigating, searching, reading, writing, communication, discussion, watching and listening to learning material, assessment, translating, and games on are typical activity types in self-directed learning. Learning contexts define the environment for the execution of related learning activities and are used for information exchange and activity execution coordination. In learning contexts, there are three categories of elements: (1) learning environment; (2) learning profile, and (3) curriculum information.

The *IMS Learning Design* (LD) specification (IMS, 2003) consists of a conceptual information model (ontology) that describes teaching-learning processes. The IMS-LD specification allows for the flexible definition of the relations between learning designs and learning objects such as enabling the reuse of the same learning design with different learning content. It provides the capability to reference external learning objects through URI (Uniform Resource Indicator) property elements and keeps a clear separation between LD and the content. It satisfies four specific requirements: *completeness, pedagogical expressiveness, personalization* and *comparability*. One component of this specification is called a "*binding*", viz. the technology used to represent the information model. Any teaching-learning process can be codified into an XML file with references to the LOs and services required to perform the

Figure 1. Learning design, activities, learning objects and SCOs

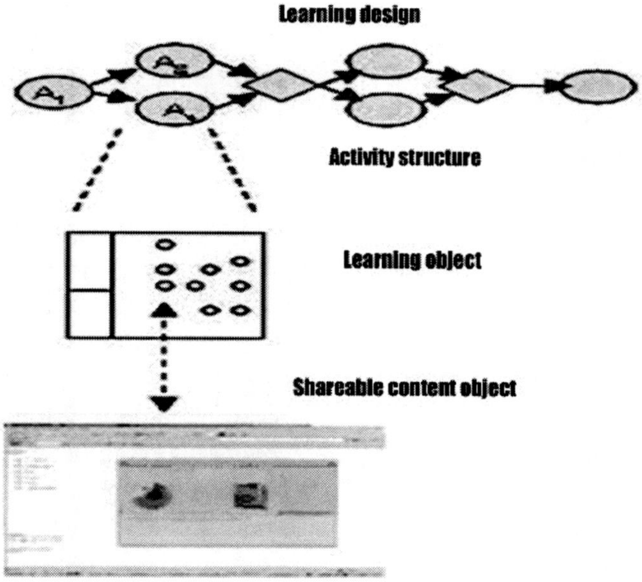

activities. Usually, the IMS LD specification is used to create a zip-file based on *IMS Content Packaging* specification (CP, 2004). A run-time engine, which is aware of learning design, can interpret this zip-file. Such engines manage the workflow ('activity management') by presenting all the actors with adequate activities and resources at any time in the teaching-learning process. Many authoring environments support the development of the learning design XML files. For example, we have *CopperAuthor* (2005), *Reload* (2005), and *Ask-LDT* (Karampiperis & Sampson, 2005). Amorim *et al.* (2006) and Knight *et al.* (2006) used OWL-schema instead of XML schema as a new 'binding'. In particular, Amorim *et al.* (2006) elaborated a precise definition of the learning design ontology. Knight *et al.* (2006) used a three part model: (1) an ontology for learning design (called LOCO), (2) an ontology for learning objects (ALOCoM), and (3) an ontology for the intermediate level between learning design and LOs (the learning object contextual model, LOCO-Cite). Baldoni *et al.* (2004) proposed the selection and composition of learning resources in the semantic web using the *Shareable Content Object Reference Model* (SCORM) (ADL, 2005). In contrast with IEEE LOM and IMS Learning Design, SCORM is not a different specification but a "*model that reference a set of interrelated technical specifications and guidelines, designed to meet high-level requirements for learning content and systems.*" SCORM provides a *Content Aggregation Model* (CAM) and a *RunTime Environment* (RTE) for learning objects in web-based learning. The SCORM model defines the assets in learning, shareable content objects (SCOs), content packaging and sequencing, and the common mechanism of learning resource communication. The *Sequencing and Navigation* (SN) model of SCORM provides comprehensive descriptions for the interoperability among learning objects and makes learning objects capable of being packed to SCOs for sharing and reusing among compatible LMS.

There are also many global repositories of instructional material on the Internet such as *TeleCampus*, *CAREO*, *ROSA* and *MERLOT*. These global repositories follow a centralized approach and keep links to web learning content. Not to forget to mention the multilingual academic exchanging portal *EducaNext* (http://www.educanext.org/) for sharing, retrieving and re-using didactic resources. De Moura *et al.* (2005) present the *LORIS* (Learning Objects Repositories' Integration System) architecture, which provides an integrated view of LOs throughout the PGL (*Partnership in Global Learning*) community. Buzza *et al.* (2004) report that the lack of a shared vocabulary is major obstacle in cataloguing and searching for learning designs in a repository.

Localisation Process in E-Learning

Localisation is the process of adapting the text and applications of a product or service such as to enable its acceptability for a particular cultural or linguistic market (Fry, 2001). Translation is the central activity of localisation. But, localisation goes beyond literal translation. In addition to idiomatic language translation, numerous locale details such as currency, national regulations, cultural sensitivities, product or service names, gender roles, and geographic examples among many other details must all be considered. A successfully localised e-learning service or product is one that seems to have been developed within the local culture. Localisation primarily includes:

1. Translating text content, software source code, websites, or database content (machine translation may be used in early stages).
2. Adjusting graphic and visual elements and examples to make them culturally appropriate.
3. Post-production quality control of content, systems and the integrated product.

There are three open XML-based standards for storage and exchange of data in the localisation process: (1) the *Translation Memory eXchange* (TMX) file format for exchanging translation memory; (2) the *TermBase eXchange* (TBX) format for terminology exchange; and (3) the *XML Localisation Interchange File Format* (XLIFF) for extracting and storing local-dependent resources in a common file format. Frimansson and Hogan (2005) evaluated the case of adopting XLIFF in localisation process and examined the usefulness of other standards (e.g. TMX, TBX) in this process. The *OASIS Translation Web Services* (OASIS TWS, 2005) Committee has considered localisation issues in relation to translation web services and is working on a specification for automating the communication between parties in the localisation process, retrieving and submitting localisation jobs, and querying the status of localisation jobs. Moreover, this specification covers querying language service provider and languages supported (Palas & Karasek, 2003). From another perspective, Sgouropoulou and Koutoumanos (2005) proposed extensions to the IEEE LOM standard to provide the necessary mechanisms for describing and relating alternative language versions of learning resources. Finally, in the *iClass* project, IEEE LOM is extended by adding contextual and pedagogical parameters. One of the contextual parameters is culture (Altuner & Turker, 2006).

Localisation Services

Text Localisation Service

For the majority of e-learning packages, the learning material is prepared in English. Consequently, the challenge is how to make the text understandable for learners who are not fluent in English. One solution is to use simplified English with a limited vocabulary and adhere to a set of writing rules that avoid complex sentences. But even in this case, a translation process/service is needed (from English to English). Consequently, one part of the localisation process is '*language localisation*'. This issue can be addressed by using ontologies, as the key-issue is the meaning behind the words and phrases (not the syntax of words and phrases). In particular ontologies can be used to capture the meaning of the words and to support the language translation (Mushtaha & De Troyer, 2005). The language localisation process can be applied to text, descriptions of images, user interface commands, menu items, instructions, help information, error messages and documentation.

Graphics and Design Elements Localisation Service

The interpretation of visual design depends on culture (Harris & McCormack, 2000). Different interpretations of colour abound throughout the world. Images, colours and text are combined to create a user interface and change to any of these things can have an impact on the entire visual design. Fonts, fashion, pictures, color, idioms, video, sound etc should be localised. This can be achieved if we describe, for each country, how every particular dimension affects the different graphic components. In addition, number, currency, date and time presentations are different in many countries or cultures. Besides, navigation within an e-learning website is affected by writing system direction. The most website navigation systems and even the layout of browser controls, assume a Latin writing system. A user of the Latin writing system will immediately look to the top left, because Latin script runs from left to write, top to bottom. On the other hand, a user of the Hebrew writing system will look to the top right because Hebrew script runs from right to left, top to bottom.

THE SEMANTIC E-LEARNING FRAMEWORK SUPPORTING LOCALISATION

Learning design provides great potential for content repurposing. However, it is expensive to develop various LDs to play content localised according to the needs of a learner because each LD should contain all possible content instances localised to a language or a culture. For this reason, we propose the use of an intelligent semantic e-learning framework, which addresses semantic information processing, localisation process support, and learning process support issues in an integrated environment. In our framework (Figure 2), a localisation model provides an integrated interface for all learning resources. Based on this model, multilingual knowledge retrieval is carried out in the learning process. We inspired our framework based on the work proposed by Huang *et al.* (2006) who presented a context-aware semantic e-learning approach to integrate content provision, learning process and learner personality in an integrated semantic e-learning framework. However, in their framework, Huang *et al.* do not consider localisation issues. In our framework, in the pre-learning process, instruc-

Figure 2. Architecture of a semantic e-learning framework supporting localisation

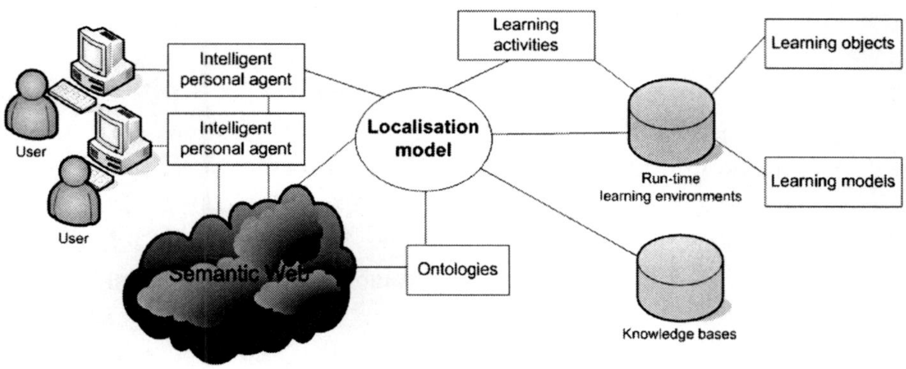

tors prepare online multimedia learning resources and provide localisation description of learning objects and contextual description of learning environments. Instructors design learning paths for learners of different cultures and they design learning activities and assessments for individual sessions and whole courses.

Hereafter, we describe the components of the proposed framework.

Intelligent Personal Agents

These software agents assist learner profiling, which involves identifying learner personality (... and culture) and learning style by doing a series of questionnaire tests, defining learning goals and learning preferences such as specific multimedia learning content that is represented in a language or culture. Throughout the learning process, an intelligent personal agent of the learner collects real-time localised learning data to monitor the learning progress. It uses learning signals to communicate with peer agents of other learners with similar cultures or with the system knowledge base against learning theories and paths in order to get adequate learning advice. After each learning session or at definite checkpoints, these software agents can generate a learning progress report against the predefined goals and outcomes.

Run-Time Learning Environment

A run-time learning environment is used usually by learners to access learning objects, which are directly linked to multimedia learning resources (e.g. lecture video, presentation slides). The most run-time learning environments are compatible with SCORM. By integrating dynamic and static learning related to semantic information in the same run-time learning environment, learning theories can be properly supported in practice (Huang *et al.*, 2006).

Learning Designs and Activities

LDs include learning activities and can choreograph the order in which the content will be presented, how it will be localised, how it will be sequenced, and how it will be assigned to multicultural learners. This presupposes that LOs are retrieved from a repository and LDs are used to integrate LOs to activities. The learning objects contain metadata that help a course's author to identify the most appropriate content for a specific purpose or language or culture. Nevertheless, this assumes that the LO will have a single LO localisation (LOL) for which it can be useful. It is beneficial for a LO to address many languages or cultures, so that expensive multimedia content elements could be reused in as many different LOs as possible. For example, a LO that contains pictures from '*Capitol of Rome*' could be used for both a History lesson in Italian language and a Sociology lesson in German language. In our framework, the LOs exist independently from any presupposed 'localisation'. That implies that they can be used in any situation in which a course's author finds them useful. In addition, a learning design does not "own" a LO since the learning object could be reusable in many other applications. LDs do not include the localisation information in order LD not to be tied to a particular language, which reduces learning design reusability. To facilitate the integration of LOs into a learning design without negotiating reusability we treat localisations of LOs (learning objects localisations-LOLs) as separate entities from the LOs themselves (Figure 3).

Equivalent Learning Objects

The process of localisation generates equivalent leaning objects. Course, module, lesson, or topic may have secondary, mirrored LOs in the database. These equivalent LOs are based on the same learning objective as their source (i.e. the initial LO), and appear at the same level in the

Figure 3. Learning Object Localisations (LOLs)

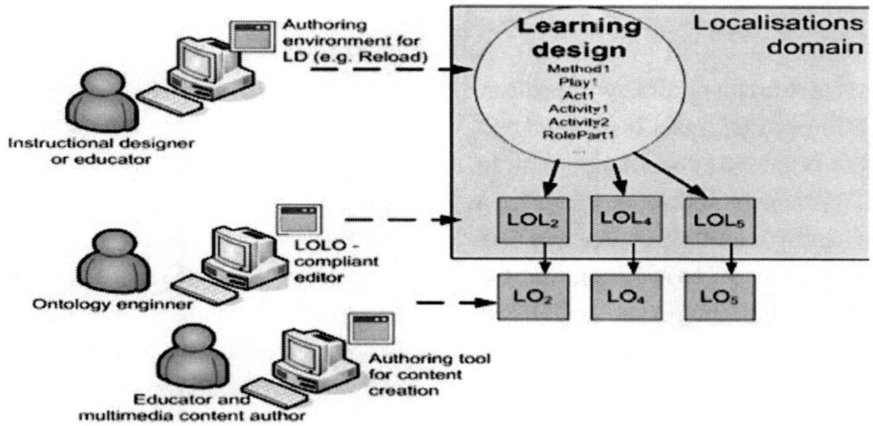

hierarchy, based on metadata. The difference is that they differ in media type, media quality, learning models, language, or "culture". For example, media type may include text, audio, video for a definition, example, or procedure. Media quality may include a high-resolution image for print and a low-resolution image for the Web. Different learning models may be applied to various situations. Finally, language and localised content for a specific example or a definition could be built to support the globalization of a course. There is always a logical link between the equivalent LOs and the learning objective. If source object is changed or retired, change modifications should go out to the authors and learners who rely on that object. Possibly, learners want to know where to locate the new version of the learning object, while authors want to know about a learning object change that may affect a course in which they use that learning object (Cisco Systems, 2003).

Ontologies

Practically, an ontology is a set of concepts from a specific domain. Ontologies can be used for representing knowledge to the e-learning domain. A learning ontology Ω can be defined as a 3-tuple: $\Omega = <CD, ID, RD>$ where *CD* is a set of classes, which defines the concepts used to the real object description; *ID* is a set of instances, which represents the instance of the concept defined in the set of classes; *RD* is a set of relations on the set of classes. The learning resources are represented in the knowledge level in terms of prerequisites (*P*) and objectives (*O*) in order to enable the use of automated reasoning techniques. Jovanović *et al.* (2005) designed the ALOCoM ontology for repurposing learning object content. Using ontologies, we can formalize our localisation model and automatically perform semantic operations such as searching and selecting. We can build conceptualizations on top of existing terminological bases like *OpenCyc* (http://www.opencyc.org). OpenCyc is the open source version of the Cyc knowledge base (Lenat, 1995), which contains over 100,000 atomic terms, and is provided with an associated efficient inference engine. OpenCyc 1.0 includes the entire Cyc ontology containing hundreds of thousands of terms, along with millions of assertions relating the terms to each other, however these are mainly taxonomic assertions, not the complex rules available in Cyc. The knowledge base contains 47,000 concepts and 306,000 facts and can be browsed on the OpenCyc website. Cyc uses its underlying definition language, a variant of predicate calculus called CycL, and it attempts to provide a comprehensive upper ontology of 'common sense' knowledge.

The Learning Object Localisation Ontology (LOLO)

Inside the extensive domain of different localisations, several different LOLs can be created and associated with LOs in a many-to-many relationship (Figure 3). If a course author chooses that a particular LO is useful in an Italian course, a new localisation object is created associating that LO with the Italian language. The reason of LOLs is not to have another group of learning objects. The IEEE LOM is not flexible enough to completely support alternative language versions of learning resources (Sgouropoulou & Koutoumanos, 2005). If we annotate the learning object with localisation information (e.g. writing style direction) applicable to the learning object in an Italian course, we establish an indirect ownership relation. In this case, the learning object can be owned by learning designs that target Italian courses. As an alternative, if we include the information in the learning design, the learning design will reduce its reusability. LOL can be used to track the usage of LOs and enable personalization/globalization of the learning process. A learning object localisation (LOL) contains data that is specific to a single learning object in a language (or culture). Learning objectives and evaluation are stored in this object, as opposed to the learning object, so that the learning object could be associated with multiple LOLs and different learning objectives and evaluation. The LOL could also contain localisation-specific subject domain ontology information, since the specification of subject domain annotations will be dependent of the localisation. A LOL is created by anyone who reuses a learning design with new learning objects. LOLs are created by future tools so as to abstract LOL's from the user. Associated information of LOL is source language, target language, source culture, target culture, writing system, textual description, user interface, terminology, abbreviations, rules, regulations, graphics style, symbols, icons, colors, titles of addressing people…

Relations

In our ontology-based framework, two types of relations have been used: "*Part-of*" and "*IS-A*". A "Part-of" relation means that one concept is a part of another one. For example, the "writing system" is a part of the "Linguistic adaptation", and the "target language" is a part of the "Localisation adaptation". The "IS-A" relation is the taxonomic one, used for creating categorical structures. For example, in this way, a "Linguistic adaptation" is a "Localisation adaptation". The terms provided by the "Localisation adaptation" ontology (LOLO) (depicted in Fig. 4) can be used to assert specific propositions about localisations or a situation in localisation. For example, we can represent a fact about a specific adaptation: "*For the learning object A, a substantive adaptation of terminology about "death" from English to Japanese should be achieved*". Once we have the basis for representing proposition, we can also represent knowledge involving propositional attitudes such as "*In cultural adaptation of learning object A, the target color should be white*" because the notion of death in Japanese is expressed using the white colour.

During the learning process, the repository of LOLs can be searched for LOL instances that 'match' the requirements of the current learning situation. These requirements can be expressed as a query using an ontology query language such as RDQL (Seaborne, 2004). Such a query should use the concepts/instances from relevant ontologies whenever it is possible. For example, if no LOL instance can be found that 'meets' the required situation, an instance with a 'similar' activity can be used instead.

SCOs Supporting Localisation

The localisation of LOs results to the generation of SCOs which support localisation. A SCO represent the most granular unit of content to be developed in our framework. Each SCO comprises a set of

Figure 4. The LOLO ontology

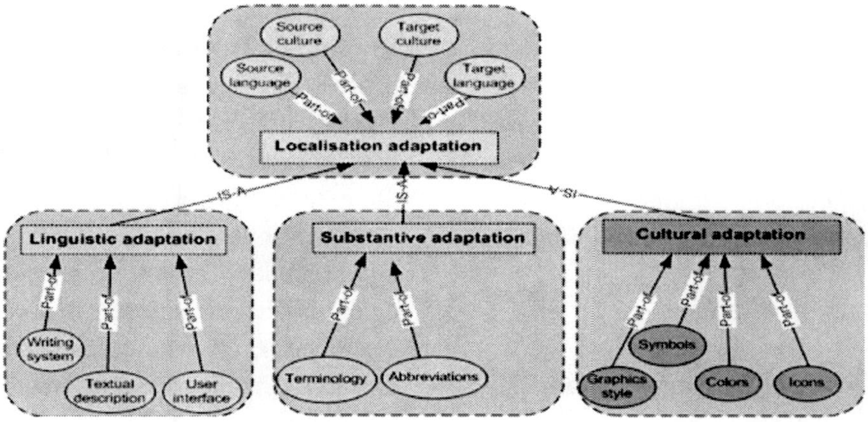

assets: *name, title, type, language, screen text, fonts, fashion, gestures, pictures, colour, idioms, humor, video (slider) and sound*. In our framework, practical localisation is supported in the SCO level, while SCOs are self-adaptive to user's language and culture. We adopted the structure of self adaptive SCOs, which was proposed by Rey-López *et al.* (2009) in order to permit the learning objects to adopt different behaviors according to the learner's language and culture.

This structure is composed of three elements (Figure 5):

1. The *JAVA template* contains the SCO functionality. For example, a Java class with some space for text, a video, a picture and some control buttons. The actual objects taking up these spaces are loaded in runtime.
2. *Configuration files*. Each configuration file (XML file) specifies the behavior of the SCO for a concrete localisation. It indicates which objects take up the spaces in the template and the properties (e.g. colour, position) of these objects. For each language or culture, there is a corresponding configuration file.
3. The *adaptation file* is an XML file, which contains the adaptation rules that indicate the SCO, which is the most appropriate behavior to adopt. These rules can be resolved according to the actual values of the localisation parameters, in order to know which is the configuration file it has to use for a concrete localisation.

Figure 5. Structure of a self adaptive SCO

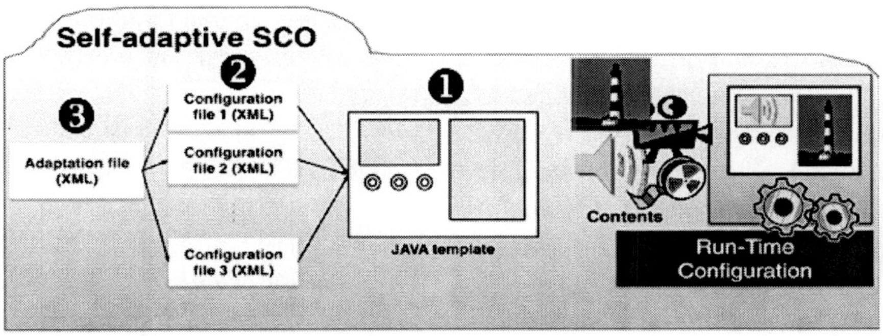

The above discussion let us to introduce the notion of semantic localisation as follows:

Definition: *Semantic localisation of an entity (i.e. an object) is a collection of semantic situational information that characterizes the entity's linguistic, substantive and cultural adaptations features and external relations under a specific situation.*

The Localisation Model

If localisation is supposed to happen automatically, all these requirements must be codified in some explicit manner. As we referred previously, the requirements for effective localisation include: (1) *linguistic adaptation;* (2) *substantive adaptation;* and (3) *cultural adaptation.* The first contribution of our framework is the semantic localisation-aware information service. The approach of semantic localisation can be used to structure an intermediate layer above existing syntax-oriented information presentation for semantic-oriented integration and interoperation in the future. The core component of the localisation-aware information service should be a localisation model for semantic representation of linguistic, substantive and cultural adaptations included in the localisation process. Kanellopoulos *et al.* (2009) propose such a localisation model and present an application example of it.

FUTURE RESEARCH DIRECTIONS

The localisation model should capture and represent various localisation features, including those that might already be in existing metadata formats, and those that are currently unstructured and to be structured in the meanwhile. This requires the localisation model to be generic and scalable enough to work across the semantic web and to interoperate with various learning content description specifications. By applying a new semantic localisation model, semantic information for static resources and dynamic process description will be easily encoded and retrieved across the semantic web, referring to ontologies or knowledge bases if necessary. The localisation model should enable process-oriented learning activity description. Future work on our framework includes further development of the semantic localisation service, interoperation with other learning specifications such as SCORM and LD. For this reason, ontology alignment (matching) should be applied to determine correspondences between the concepts, described in the ontologies related to SCORM and LD. Special semantic matching operators for lightweight ontologies must be proposed. We believe that the *S-Match* (Giunchiglia *et al.*, 2004) is a semantic matching operator which can be applied to this research initiative.

CONCLUSION

Learning is not only about content provision, it is also about localisation. Towards enabling intelligent semantic e-learning, this chapter presents a novel semantic e-learning framework that considers linguistic, substantive and cultural adaptation issues in an integrated environment such as to support localisation of content. The proposed framework features localisation-aware semantic information management, knowledge-enhanced learning model support and learner personality representation. We introduced the notion of semantic localisation and envisaged a scalable-layered localisation model for semantic representation of linguistic, substantive and cultural adaptations included in the localisation process. The localisation model constitutes the core component of the localisation-aware information service.

REFERENCES

ADL. (2005). *Advanced Distributed Learning – Shareable Content Object Reference Model (SCORM) Specification.* Retrieved October 10, 2007, from http://www.adlnet.gov/scorm

Adler, C., & Rae, S. (2002). Personalized learning: The future of e-learning is learner centric environment. *E-learning*, (January): 22–24.

Altuner, E. M., & Turker, M. (2006). Learning designs supporting localisation for personalised and adaptive e-learning. In *Proceedings of the ADALE Workshop at Adaptive Hypermedia 2006*.

Amorim, R., Lama, M., Sánchez, E., Riera, A., & Vila, X. A. (2005). A learning design ontology based on the IMS Specification. *Journal of Educational Technology & Society*, *9*(1), 38–57.

Baldoni, M., Baroglio, C., Patti, V., & Torasso, L. (2004). Reasoning about learning object metadata for adapting SCORM courseware. In *Proceedings of the International workshop on engineering the adaptive web, EAW'04: Methods and technologies for personalization and Adaptation in the Semantic Web*, Eindhoven, The Netherlands, (pp. 4-13).

Berners-Lee, T., Hendler, J., & Lassila, O. (2001). The Semantic Web. *Scientific American*, *284*(5), 34–43. doi:10.1038/scientificamerican0501-34

Buzza, D., Bean, D., Harrigan, K., & Carey, T. (2004). Learning design repositories: adapting learning design specifications for shared instructional knowledge. *Canadian Journal of Learning and Technology*, *30*(3), 79–101.

Cebeci, Z., & Erdogan, Y. (2005). Tree view editing learning object metadata. *Interdisciplinary Journal of Knowledge and Learning Objects*, *1*(1), 99–108.

Cisco Systems. (2003). *Reusable learning object strategy: designing and developing learning objects for multiple learning approaches* [White paper]. Retrieved September 13, 2005, from http://www.e-novalia.com/materiales/RLOW__07_03.pdf

Clark, D. (2005). *Localisation of e-learning,* [White paper]. EPIC Group. Retrieved October 13, 2009, from http://www.epic.co.uk/

CopperAuthor. (2005). *CopperAuthor Learning Design editor*. Retrieved May 1, 2006, from http://sourceforge.net/projects/copperauthor/

CP. (2004). *IMS Content Packaging v1.1.4 Final Specification*. Retrieved October 10, 2005, from http://www.imsglobal.org/content/packaging

De Moura, S., Coutinho, F., Siqueira, S., & Melo, R. (2005). Integrating repositories of learning objects using web services and ontologies. *International Journal of Web Services Practices*, *1*(1-2), 57–72.

De Troyer, O., Mushtaha, A., Stengers, H., Baetens, M., Boers, F., Casteleyn, S., & Plessers, P. (2005). On cultural differences in local web interfaces. *Journal of Web Engineering*, *5*(3), 246–264.

Frimansson, A., & Hogan, J. (2005). Adopting standards-based XML file formats in open source localisation. *Localisation Focus*, *4*(4), 9–23.

Fry, D. (2001). *Introducing the Localisation Industry Standards Association*. Retrieved May 23, 2003, http://www.lisa.org/press/Introducing_LISA_2001.pdf

Giunchiglia, F., Shvaiko, P., & Yatskevich, M. (2004). *S-Match: an algorithm and an implementation of semantic matching.* Technical Report # DIT-04-015, University of Trento, Department of Information and Communication Technology.

Harris, J., & McCormack, R. (2000). *Translation is not enough. Considerations for global Internet development*. Sapient Report. Retrieved June 13, 2009, from http://www.sapient.com

Henze, N., Dolog, P., & Neijdl, W. (2004). Reasoning and ontologies for personalized e-learning in the Semantic Web. *Journal of Educational Technology & Society*, *7*(4), 82–97.

Huang, W., Webster, D., Wood, D., & Ishaya, T. (2006). An intelligent semantic e-learning framework using context-aware Semantic Web technologies. *British Journal of Educational Technology, 37*(3), 351–373. doi:10.1111/j.1467-8535.2006.00610.x

IEEE Learning Technology Standards Committee (LTSC). (2002). *12.1Learning Object Metadata Final Draft Standard* (p. 1484). Piscataway, NJ: IEEE.

IMS Global Learning Consortium. (2003). *IMS Learning Design Information Model, Best Practice and Implementation Guide*. Version 1.0 Final Specification. Retrieved September 1, 2004, from http://www.imsglobal.org/learningdesign/

Jovanović, J., Gašević, D., Verbert, K., & Duval, E. (2005). Ontology of learning object content structure. In *12th International Conference on Artificial Intelligence in Education*, July 18-22, Amsterdam, The Netherlands.

Kanellopoulos, D., Kotsiantis, S., & Pintelas, P. (2006). Considering the educational Semantic Web. *Themes in Education, 7*(2), 145–164.

Kanellopoulos, D., Kotsiantis, S., & Pintelas, P. (2009). An ontology-based framework for supporting localisation of e-learning content. *Annals of Mathematics. Computing & Teleinformatics, 1*(6), 1–10.

Karampiperis, P., & Sampson, D. (2005). Designing learning services for open learning systems utilizing learning design. In V. Uskov, (Ed.), *Proceedings of the 4th IASTED International Conference on Web-based Education*, (pp. 279-284). Grindelwald, Switzerland: ACTA Press.

Knight, C., Gašević, D., & Richards, G. (2006). An ontology-based framework for bridging learning design and learning content. *Journal of Educational Technology & Society, 9*(1), 23–37.

Koper, R. (2006). Current research in learning design. *Journal of Educational Technology & Society, 9*(1), 13–22.

Lassila, O., & Swick, R. R. (1999). *Resource description framework (RDF) model and syntax specification.* Retrieved October 1, 2001, from http://www.w3.org/TR/1999/REC-rdf-syntax-19990222i

Lenat, D. (1995). CYC: a large-scale investment in knowledge infrastructure. *Communications of the ACM, 38*(11), 33–38. doi:10.1145/219717.219745

Mushtaha, A., & De Troyer, O. (2005). Towards localising e-learning websites. *Localisation Focus, 4*(4), 6–8.

OASIS TWS. (2005). *OASIS Translation Web Services TC.* Retrieved October 6, 2007, from http://www.oasis-open.org/committees/tc_home.php?wg_abbrev=trans-ws

Open Education. (2007). *Localizing & Learning.* Retrieved June 1, 2009, from http://www.51weeks.com/event_files/0000/0003/OpenEd-2007-Program-Updated.pdf

Palas, P., & Karasek, M. (2003). *Globalisation of Enterprise Data Using Web Services.* Retrieved May 9, 2006, from http://moravia-it.com/Download/Globalisation_of_Enterprise_Data_Using_Web_Services.pdf

Paule, M. P., Fernandez Diaz, M. J., Ortin Soler, F., & Perez, J. R. (2008). Adaptation in current e-learning systems. *Computer Standards & Interfaces, 30*, 62–70. doi:10.1016/j.csi.2007.07.006

Reload. (2005). *Reusable eLearning Object Authoring & Delivery Project.* Retrieved June 10, 2008, from http://www.reload.ac.uk/

Rey-López, M., Díaz-Redondo, R. P., Fernández-Vilas, A., Pazos-Arias, J., Garcia-Duque, J., Gil-Solla, A., & Ramos-Cabrer, M. (2009). An extension to the ADL SCORM standard to support adaptivity: The t-learning case-study'. *Computer Standards & Interfaces, 31*(2), 309–318. doi:10.1016/j.csi.2008.02.006

Seaborne, A. (2004). *RDQL- A Query Language for RDF*, W3C Member Submission. Retrieved May 13, 2005, from http://www.w3.org/Submission/RDQL

Sgouropoulou, C., & Koutoumanos, A. (2005). Applying metadata standards to multilingual learning objects. *International Journal of Learning Technology*, *1*(4), 425–442. doi:10.1504/IJLT.2005.007153

Shang, Y., Shi, H. C., & Chen, S. S. (2001). An intelligent distributed environment for active learning. *ACM Journal of Educational Resources in Computing*, *1*(2), 1–17.

ADDITIONAL READING

Bannerjee., et al. (2004). *Web Services Internationalization Usage Scenarios*. W3C Working Group Note, July 30, 2004. [Online:] http://www.w3.org/TR/2004/NOTE-ws-i18n-scenarios-20040730/

Bond, S., Ingram, C., & Ryan, S. (2008). Reuse, repurposing and learning design – Lessons from the DART project. *Computers & Education*, *50*(2), 601–612. doi:10.1016/j.compedu.2007.09.019

Budin, G. (2006) Localization. *Encyclopedia of Language & Linguistics*, 2006, pp.290-291.

Cyr, D., Head, M., & Larios, H. (2010). Colour appeal in website design within and across cultures: A multi-method evaluation. *International Journal of Human-Computer Studies*, *68*(1-2), 1–21. doi:10.1016/j.ijhcs.2009.08.005

DeCamp, J. (2004) Globalization. *Encyclopedia of Information Systems*, 459-474.

Dunn, P., & Marinetti, A. (2007). Beyond localization: Effective learning strategies for cross cultural e-learning. In Edmundson, A. (Ed.), *Globalized e-learning cultural challenges* (pp. 255–266). Information Science Publishing.

Edmundson, A. (2007). The cultural adaptation process (CAP) model: Designing e-learning for another culture. In Edmundson, A. (Ed.), *Globalized e-learning cultural challenges* (pp. 267–290). Information Science Publishing.

Esselink, B. (2000). *A Practical Guide to Localization*. Amsterdam, Philadelphia: John Benjamins Publishing Company.

Gonzalez-Barbone, V., & Anido-Rifon, L. (2008). Creating the first SCORM object. *Computers & Education*, *51*(4), 1634–1647. doi:10.1016/j.compedu.2008.04.004

Heyboer, G., & Sunnie, K. (2007). Localizing educational resources using WikiEducator: A case study. *Open Education 2007: Localizing & Learning*, September 26-28, 2007.

Hillier, M. (2003). The role of cultural context in multilingual website usability. *Electronic Commerce Research and Applications*, *2*(1), 2–14. doi:10.1016/S1567-4223(03)00005-X

Junuz, E. (2009). Preparation of the learning content for semantic e-learning environment. *Procedia - Social and Behavioral Sciences, 1*(1), 824-828.

Kanellopoulos, D., & Kotsiantis, S. (2007). Semantic Web: A state of the art survey. *International Review on Computers and Software*, *2*(4), 428–442.

Kanellopoulos, D., & Lazarinis, F. (2010). Developing a localization indicator for chain hotel websites: A Greek case study. *International Journal of Business Information Systems*, *5*(3), 309–327. doi:10.1504/IJBIS.2010.031932

Kerremans, R., & Temmerman, R. (2004). Towards multilingual, termontological support in ontology engineering. *Proceeding of Termino 2004, Workshop on Terminology*.

Lea, P. (2003). Understanding the culture of e-learning. *Industrial and Commercial Training*, *35*(4/5), 217–219. doi:10.1108/00197850310487377

Looi, C. K. (2002). Cultural issues and the design of e-learning. *Information and Systems in Education*, *1*(1), 32–37.

Marcus, A., & Gould, E. (2000). Crosscurrents: cultural dimensions and global web user-interface design. *Interactions (New York, N.Y.)*, *VII*(4), 32–46. doi:10.1145/345190.345238

Meng-Fen, G. L., & Lee, M. M. (2007). E-learning localized: The case of the OOPS project. In Edmundson, A. (Ed.), *Globalized e-learning cultural challenges* (pp. 168–186). Information Science Publishing.

Nantel, J., & Glaser, E. (2008). The impact of language and culture on perceived website usability. *Journal of Engineering and Technology Management*, *25*(1-2), 112–122. doi:10.1016/j.jengtecman.2008.01.005

Ngeow, K., & Kong, K. (2002). Designing culturally sensitive learning environments. *ASCILITE 2002* (pp.873-876). Retrieved June 20, 2008, from https://secure.ascilite.org.au/conferences/auckland02/proceedings/papers/055.pdf

Reinke, U. (2006) Translation Memories. *Encyclopedia of Language & Linguistics*, 61-65.

Sandrini, P. (2008). Localization and Translation. In Gerzymisch-Arbogast, (Eds.), *Translation Scenarios. muTra Journal* (*Vol. 2*, pp. 167–192).

Schell, M. (2007). How to globalize online course content. In Edmundson, A. (Ed.), *Globalized e-learning cultural challenges* (pp. 155–167). Information Science Publishing.

Shea, T., Ariguzo, G., & White, D. S. (2007). Putting the world in the world wide web: The globalisation of the internet'. *International Journal of Business Information Systems*, *2*(1), 75–98. doi:10.1504/IJBIS.2007.011417

Smith, A., Dunckley, L., French, T., Minocha, S., & Chang, Y. (2004). A process model for developing usable cross-cultural websites. *Interacting with Computers*, *16*(1), 63–91. doi:10.1016/j.intcom.2003.11.005

The Localisation Research Centre (LRC) is the educational and research centre for the localisation community. [Online:] http://www.localisation.ie/

KEY TERMS AND DEFINITIONS

Globalising Websites: Websites require careful internationalization, while graphics must be stored in source-file format and made available to localizers. Beyond design issues, effective web site globalization requires the use of technology to track and respond to changes in source content, as well as to manage the decisions as to what should and should not be translated.

Internationalisation: It is the process of designing a software application so that it can be adapted to various languages and regions without engineering changes.

Locale: It is a set of parameters that defines the user's language, country and any special variant preferences that the user wants to see in user interface. Usually a locale identifier consists of at least a language identifier and a region identifier.

Localisation Industry Standards Association (LISA): It is the leading international forum for organizations doing business globally. LISA has distilled the right ways and wrong ways of supporting international customers, products and services over the last 15 years from more than 500 corporate members, public and private institutions, government ministries, and trade organizations.

Localisation: It is the process of adapting internationalized software for a specific region or language by adding locale-specific components and translating text.

Translation Memory eXchange (TMX): It is an open XML standard for the exchange of translation memory data created by computer-aided translation and localisation tools. TMX is developed and maintained by OSCAR (Open Standards for Container/Content Allowing Re-use), a special interest group of Localisation Industry Standards Association.

XML Localisation Interchange File Format (XLIFF): It is an XML-based format created to standardize localisation. XLIFF was standardized by OASIS in 2002. XLIFF forms part of the Open Architecture for XML Authoring and Localisation (OAXAL) reference architecture.

Chapter 15
Interoperability:
Standards for Learning Objects in Science Education

Marta R. Ariza
University of Jaén, Spain

Antonio Quesada
University of Jaén, Spain

ABSTRACT

This chapter offers a brief overview of the main ideas underlying the learning object (LO) paradigm, with special emphasis placed on pedagogical aspects. Requirements for the interoperability and reusability of learning objects (LOs) are discussed, with attention drawn to the need of developing new metadata models to fully benefit from this approach. The authors also claim a wider utilization of LO principle design based on educational research, to improve the chances of promoting efficient learning. A literature review on technology and science education is also provided, revealing a gap between computer and learning science, in relation to the embracement of the LO paradigm. Reflections on this situation and implications for the science education community are also included. Finally, one project on computer-supported science education is analyzed from the perspective of interoperability and reusability.

INTRODUCTION

Learning Objects and Science Education

Information and Communication Technologies (ICT) are an increasingly ubiquitous component of everyday life, also having a significant impact on education. Literature shows how the learning of relevant science topics may be enhanced by introducing computer assisted teaching materials, and provides convincing evidence for the application of ICT into education (Butler, 2006; Edelson, 2003; Edelson and Reiser, 2006; Krajcik and Blumenfeld, 2006; Linn, 2003a, 2003b; Linn et al., 2003; Spitulnik et al., 2003; White, 2003; Venkataraman, 2009). In addition, an easier access to information is provided and new, more versatile and flexible ways of communication are possible, augmenting the opportunities for social construction of knowledge. As a consequence, computer-based resources are being increasingly

DOI: 10.4018/978-1-61692-789-9.ch015

introduced into instructional processes and some authors are drawing attention to both, making a critical used of technology (Butler, 2007; Hoyles and Noss, 2009; Linn, 2003a) and developing new approaches to evaluate the real impact of digital materials and tools on learning (Beers et al., 2006).

However, an advanced literature search through scopus (http://www.scopus.com/home.url), combining 'learning object' and 'science education' shows only a few results for the last nine years (1999-2009). This seems somewhat strange, when compared to the huge number of results displayed by the same search on just 'learning object' (over 1400 papers). These findings suggest that there is a gap between computer science and learning science in relation to the learning object approach, since most of the scientific works on LO are chiefly related to engineering and computer education.

On the contrary, research on technology-based science education reported a wide range of initiatives and projects, most of them, not explicitly embracing the LO paradigm (Butler, 2006, 2007; Edelson, 2003; Edelson and Reiser, 2006; Krajcik and Blumenfeld, 2006; Krange and Ludvigsen, 2009; Linn, 2003a, 2003b; Linn et al., 2003; Spitulnik et al., 2003; Su, 2008a, 2008b; White, 2003; Venkataraman, 2009).

Furthermore, many of the digital resources developed for science education are strictly designed for very specific teaching contexts or scenarios and therefore, the materials produced are not necessarily generic or exportable. Focussing on the development of versatile, shareable and reusable pedagogical materials will optimize creative efforts and allow the possibility of concentrating on improving resources, rather than duplicating efforts. Consequently, we argue that making the teaching science community aware of the potential benefits underlying the LO approach may enhance sharing and reusability of the technological resources developed for science learning.

The design of ICT-based resources may be carried out by those engaged in education, but this is not a guarantee that the materials produced will promote the desired effect. Frequently, these applications emerge from innovative teachers who act as designers and producers of their own pedagogical resources. Thus, the materials are created to suit their specific needs and classroom learning context. The development of effective electronic resources does not merely require intuition or the simple introduction of contents in specific formats using ready-made authoring tools. Teachers involved should look for answers on how to ensure efficient learning from ICT-based pedagogical materials, paying attention to any content types that may appear in e-learning approaches: facts, concepts, procedures, processes and strategic principles. Moreover, when approaching technological materials production, it would be convenient to take into account expert criteria based on available evidence. From this perspective, design-based research is focussed on connecting theory and educational research to orientate effective design of pedagogical resources (Design-based Research Collective, 2003). We develop this approach further in the next section.

In relation to design principles; one of the main concerns in the LO literature is the search of technical and pedagogical standards. These criteria are necessary to guide the production, search, delivery and sharing of reusable, high quality contents and tools for e-learning experiences. Furthermore, a review of LO literature reveals a main interest in concepts such as granularity and interoperability, as key aspects to facilitate the reuse of digital resources and tools. We discuss these issues in the next section, paying special attention to pedagogical aspects.

The main purpose of this chapter is to offer an analysis of technology impact on science learning, providing a literature review, which points out that, the LO perspective is not a common approach in the science education community. Furthermore, we intend to discuss key aspects of the LO paradigm to promote reflection on the convenience of making people aware of the potential benefits underlying this approach, especially, in these collectives where it is not so popular.

In order to do so, the background section starts offering an overview of the learning object paradigm. It provides several definitions and a wide range of approaches aimed at showing different perspectives. At the same time, we point out the essential features widely attributed to LOs. However, the main goal of this section is to focus on those aspects, critically associated with reusability and interoperability, both from the technical, and from the educational point of view. Due to the scarce literature on LOs for science instruction, and with the exception of a few specific instances of science education, all the issues discussed in this section are analysed from a general perspective, and could be readily applied to any discipline or field of knowledge.

The following section will initially analyse ICT impact on science instruction, with the emphasis on key contributions for enhancing science learning. Nevertheless, most of the initiatives and projects on computer-based resources developed in this field do not explicitly consider key LO features.

Finally a local innovative project where the authors are involved is briefly described, focussing on aspects coherent with the LO philosophy.

KEY FEATURES OF THE LEARNING OBJECT APPROACH

Learning objects (LOs) have been broadly understood as digital learning resources and are associated with a theoretical model that might be regarded as one of the most meaningful and effective ways to create contents for courses, lessons and instructional units at any of the e-learning modalities. LOs can be seen as "*pieces*" which, if set into an appropriate instructional design, have an extra-added value to enrich teaching practices. However, a wide range of definitions and approaches to this term are currently available in literature. We offer below a summarised overview of them.

Brief History of the Term Learning Object

A vast collection of terms and ways to designate LOs is found in literature. Among them, we may cite knowledge objects, educational objects, knowledge chunks, digital objects, digital educational computer programs, digital resources, electronic resources, multimedia resources and many others. Therefore, when looking for literature definitions of LOs, we may find a wide range of proposals; from the most general: "any pedagogical digital entity", to the most restrictive ones: "minimum and meaningful pedagogical unit required to achieve a learning goal objective".

Perhaps, the most cited definition of LO is "any entity, digital or non digital, that can be used, reused, or referenced during technology-supported learning". Wiley (2000) argued against this definition, and suggested an alternative one: "any digital resource that can be reused to support learning". Hence, Wiley's definition includes anything across the broad network, regardless of its size and format, provided it may be used to support learning; from an entire web page combining different kinds of multimedia, to a small picture. Although, as we will see later, a LO should have a minimal granularity to make it meaningful and also have a high instructional value.

Hodgins (2002) stated that "learning objects are fundamental elements of a new conceptual model for content creation and distribution. They are destined to change the shape and form of learning, ushering in unprecedented efficiency of content design, development, and delivery. Their most significant promise is to increase and improve the effectiveness of learning". Although these words arose in engineering e-learning contexts, they may be exportable to other knowledge disciplines. Therefore, although the LO paradigm was initially conceived in relation to object oriented programming practice in computer science, nowadays it is widespread, although not as much as is desired in some fields.

L´Allier (cited in Dumbraveanu 2006) defined LO as the "smallest independent structural experience that contains an objective, a learning activity and assessment". This definition restricts LO reusability because learning goals, activities and assessments might change depending on the situation (audience, context of application…), unless the LO allows customization and tailoring.

Many authors have failed in offering clear and generally accepted LO definitions. It may be attributed to their attempt to provide excessively broad definitions. In this sense, Boyle (2008) states that ambiguity in definitions might be due to co-existence of LO requirements, associated with desired technical characteristics, and those related to pedagogical features.

A more pedagogically focused definition of LO has been given by Kay and Knaack (2007). According to these authors, LOs are "interactive web-based tools that support the learning of specific concepts by enhancing, amplifying, and guiding the cognitive processes of learners". This view places the emphasis on specific pedagogical features rather than on technical requirements. However, by just referring to web-based resources, some other interesting computer-based materials are excluded as learning objects.

Schaalje (2007) states that "the most important goal of a learning object is to develop complex cognitive skills in any subject matter". This declaration should drive the design of any LO, if a minimal functionality for the cognitive domain is required. According to this author "a useful, valuable learning object is a digital presentation that can be reasonably discerned, which has an accompanying explanation, a minimum of one selected response question that addresses one of the levels of Bloom´s taxonomy of cognitive functioning to reinforce information in the presentation and explanation, and the overall structure of the object utilizes one or more sound theories of learning/instruction in its designs" (pg 48). This statement offers us an operational definition of what a LO is.

Learning Object Classifications

Many efforts have been made not only to define LOs but to establish a useful classification. An acceptable classification should allow LO to be "labelled, described, investigated and understood in ways that make the simplicity, compatibility and advantages claimed for them, readily apparent to teacher, trainers and other practitioners" (Friesen 2003). Shepherd (2000, cited in Lehman, 2007) presented a classification of LO attending to their main focus, or the principal purpose for what they had been designed. This author established three categories, each of them including different subcategories. The first category includes LO whose main goal is promoting knowledge integration (mini-tutorial, mini-cases, LO with supportive information…). The second group refers to LO focused on providing information *(*overviews, summaries, descriptions, definitions, demonstrations, models, examples, cases, stories, papers, articles, decision aids…). The third category includes LO providing different types of learning activities (problem-solving, case studies, games/simulations, drill-and-practice exercises, review exercises, tests/assessments…)

Redeker (2003) proposed a hierarchy of LO classified as course, partial course LO, learning units and knowledge units, according to their level of comprehensive structure. This approach is useful to facilitate basic generic sequencing strategies. Sequencing and adaptive sequencing is actually one of the current research issues associated with LO literature, but it is beyond the scope of this chapter,

Churchill (2006) offered a useful discussion on LOs and distinguished between six different types: presentation, practice, simulation, conceptual model, information and contextual representation objects. In the context of the proposed classification, a general definition was given as "a learning object is a representation designed to afford uses in different educational contexts", considering the term "representation" in a wide sense in order to include the six mentioned types of LOs.

Some authors have reflected on the convenience of making students participants of LO evaluation and classification. Kay and Knaack (2009) have recently proposed the LOES-S, a tool to assess learning, quality and student engagement in learning objects evaluation. LOES-S has showed an acceptable internal reliability, face, construct, convergent and predictive validity. It has been applied to a population of secondary school students of chemistry, biology and physics, among others. These research works have been carried out with students "trapped" within their concrete educational contexts and circumstances where their teachers decided to enhance their learning activities with new technologies. We must not forget that learners take part in the whole instructional process and might have their own conceptions about LO, which could differ, or not, from the teachers' view. It is not then surprising that when students express their preferences and views about how to improve digital pedagogical resources, they call for those which provide interaction and allow more control over the learning process. They also prefer game-like activities rather than conventional ones (Muspratt and Freeboy, 2007). As a consequence, learners use these criteria to classify LOs into good ones (interactive, controllable, enjoyable) and poor ones (those which lack the previously mentioned characteristics).

Reusability of Learning Objects

In relation to a recently published comprehensive review, Wiley (2007) confirmed that LOs literature has revealed a "largely disconnected group of research united by an interest in reusing educational materials but little else". However, in spite of the diverse terminology and the wide range of definitions provided for LO, reusability is an idea, ubiquitously present in all the different approaches. This concept may be understood as LO potential, to be reused or applied to different educational contexts and for various instructional purposes. On this line, Sicilia (2005) pointed out that all LO definitions, either tacitly or explicitly, include the concept of reusability.

The big promise of learning objects as reusable entities has gained attention among educational technology practitioners, teachers and students. A LO is pedagogically reusable if it may be successfully applied to different educational contexts and still promote effective learning, and this is clearly associated with one of its potential benefits. For a non well-informed teacher, the mere term "learning object" might not suggest any of its attributed features (simplicity, compatibility, reusability, interoperability) and does not clearly show any additional benefit with respect to other terms (digital resources, computer-based pedagogical materials…)

Reusability has also been defined as "the ability to take a LO as is and reuse it wholesale" (Wiley, cited in Murphy 2004). Nevertheless, it has been distinguished between the former term and repurposability, the latter referring to "the ability to extract portions of a learning objects and adapt them to new learning context". Thus, even when a LO could be considered as reusable, it might be not repurposable. However, since the term reusability is widely spread and generally loosely applied, from now on, by "Reusable Learning Object" (RLO) we will mean any LO which may be applied to different instructional contexts and for various educational goals, either wholesale, or customized.

Three types of reuse for LOs have been defined (Murphy, 2004):

- Sharing: "to use again, with little or no special treatment"
- Multipurpose "to use again, especially after special treatment or processing permitting reuse across medias"
- Repurpose: "to use again, especially after special treatment or processing permitting reuse across mediums and audiences"

Besides the previously mentioned works, a wide range of tools and approaches to assess LO usability and effectiveness is available in literature. Nesbit et al (2003) designed and applied the Learning Object Review Instrument (LORI). LORI evaluates the quality of LOs in relation to nine dimensions: content quality, learning goal alignment, feedback and adaptation, motivation, presentation design, interaction usability, accessibility, reusability, and standards compliance. These authors defined the reusability of a LO as "the ability to use it in varying learning contexts and with learners from differing backgrounds". Others authors (Kei and Mohan, 2004) proposed a model for evaluating LOs based on four major aspects: content design, back-end delivery, front-end presentation and the learning process and outcomes.

Mordago et al (2004) presented the evaluation tool HEODAR, which translated into English means Reusable Learning Objects Assessment Tools. It has been designed taking into account a broad variety of quality criteria for LOs, both from pedagogical and technical points of view. A different perspective is offered by Duval (2006). This author started his chapter by saying that the quality of a certain LO is not an intrinsic characteristic, but rather an aspect dependent on the particular instructional context (p. 457). If context dependency is assumed, the development of quality criteria for LOs becomes an even more complex task, and different approaches to quality are needed.

Pitkänen et all (2004) proposed three categories for pedagogical reusability of LOs as a basis for designing and facilitating the adaptation of LOs to a personalized learning process. These categories are based on the reusability models previously described, and include both, technical and pedagogical criteria. The quantitative analysis carried out by these authors shows that a given LO may be used in various contexts and pedagogical settings, even when the LO originally has been contextually designed to work in a particular learning situation (p. 4) Therefore, it is concluded that there are various educational contexts in which the object can have pedagogical value.

However, it is worthy to note that reusability is difficult to measure because it is learning content and learning context dependent, not to mention how to account for actual situations where the LO has already been applied.

Learning Objects Repositories and Reusability

Easy identification and access to the large amount of existing digital resources are also key issues in the LO approach. The phenomenon known as "information overload" is also applicable here, and reveals a serious need to provide mechanisms for proper localization and selection of information available through the internet. But the problem grows exponentially when no quality guarantee is ensured in learning object repositories (LOR). Variety in LOR also contributes to difficulties in the finding and proper selection of the target learning objects, hindering the concept of interoperability (Maarof and Yahya, 2008). Futhermore, highly irrelevant content, de-contextualized contents, high level of cognitive load in content or the lack of concern about the pedagogical principle design based on research evidence, hinder LO efficiency, even if they have been properly tagged with sufficient standardized metadata.

Interesting reflections may come from a survey conducted in 2006 (LIFE-project), where European teachers were asked if they thought that practitioners could easily search for instructional digital resources that fitted their needs and provided activities to match curricular requirements and target learning skills. The study concluded that, only one out of three educators gave positive answers and felt able to find the intended learning objects. This outcome is not very promising and suggests that it might be interesting to look for reasons about why, most teachers think that it is difficult to find reusable learning objects.

López (2007) developed an instrument to measure the reusability of LOs in free access LOR. The application of this instrument to a random sample of 70 computer science LO found in MERLOT (Multimedia of Educational Resources for Learning and On Line Teaching, 2009), showed general low reusability. It was attributed to the lack of explicit standard metadata and the inadequate levels of granularity associated with the LO studied. A low level of granularity makes it more difficult to reuse the LO in contexts differing from the one for which the LO was designed and/or conceived.

MERLOT is probably the largest repository for sharing educational resources, most of them, related to higher education. This site claims to have over 20949 materials, and more than 75,000 members (last visit 15 July). MERLOT includes links to approximately 9000 electronic teaching resources for Science and Technology education. Around 30% of the LO have been peer reviewed, and most have user comments or assignments attached. In addition to being a source of educational materials, the MERLOT project seeks to support the educational community by providing peer review on LO quality. Management, categorization and assessment of LOs in the repository is a time-consuming activity, facilitated partly, by the peer review process (Neven, 2002).

LOs in MERLOT are rated according to three general categories of assessment standards: Content quality, potential effectiveness as a teaching-learning tool and ease of use. This initiative is a step forward to tag LOs and contribute to the evaluation of their quality, increasing the chances for reusability. Guidelines are supplied to participants in order to advise the review process; nevertheless the subjective approach is still present. In any case, there is extra-metadata with content and context information, made by experts. Although peer-review may be considered as a process for quality guarantee, a survey on ten LOR showed that only four of them had it (Neven 2002).

Interoperability

The search for standards has been and will probably continue to be an issue of general interest, since the adoption of common patterns and criteria facilitates exchange, sharing, reusability and interoperability.

Solmedilla (2007) offered a review of some available definitions of technical interoperability and extracted various common key ideas related to this term. Among these, we find "the ability of working together to accomplish common task", "work in conjunction", "exchange and efficient use of information" and "the belief that interoperability must be provided at different levels'. In relation to the latter idea, it is worthy to note that the term interoperability may not only be associated with technical requirements, as it is discussed below.

Technical aspects related to the design and production of learning objects are essential to make interoperability feasible, and they have been widely discussed and reviewed in literature. As an instance, Prpitsch and Veith (2007) in a recent work, focus on the description of standards for e-learning, designed to provide technical interoperability of content packages (SCORM). However, according to Purves et al. (2005), "it is possible to take full advantage of technical aspects of interoperability only if notions of educational interoperability are properly addressed" (p. 191).

Van Assche (2007) defined interoperability as the ability of two systems to interoperate. Nevertheless, a remark is made in relation to the word "systems", claiming that it must be interpreted in a wider sense, referring not only to "technical systems" but also to "educational" systems. From this perspective, different aspects of interoperability may be analysed (physical, empirical, syntactical, semantic, pragmatic and social layers; the latter including interests, beliefs and commitments shared by potential users). The previously mentioned layers may be classified into two groups, the first one including technical considerations (physical, empirical and syntactical layers), and the second one addressing other different operability aspects (semantic, pragmatic and social).

As teachers and potential end-users or consumers of LOs, we are especially interested in the second domain. For example, concerning semantic interoperability, special attention has to be paid to the way information is given and interpreted. Pragmatic interoperability addresses among others, common pedagogical goals, relevant for affording reusability.

Learning Object Metadata

In spite of the numerous electronic resources currently developed, looking for specific ones on the world-wide-web may be an arduous, laborious and time-demanding task. It explains the general interest in the development of standards for metadata, which not only include information about technical aspects, but also key information to allow LO localization, retrieval and reusability. In this sense, the inclusion of metadata such as knowledge content (force, heat, climate change, water pollution, genetics…), target audience, context of application, learning activities, possibilities of feedback, previous experiences with the resource, etc, will facilitate their classification, and improve the possibilities of reuse. Several LO repositories have been developed but there is little real evidence about LO reusability dependent on appropriate metadata about knowledge contents (Neven and Duval, 2002).

IEEE Learning object metadata (IEEE LOM) was approved in 2002 as an international standard. The IEEE-LOM metadata describes LOs throughout a hierarchy of 76 elements and nine different categories: (1) *General*: description of the learning object as a whole (title, language, keywords, coverage, catalogue…); (2) *Lifecycle*: the history and current state of this learning object (author, publisher, version....); (3) *Meta-Metadata*: information about the metadata instance (scheme, language, author...) (4) *Technical*: technical requirements and technical characteristics (format, size, requirements...) (5) *Educational*: educational and pedagogic characteristics (learning time, difficulty level, interactivity level...) (6) *Rights*: intellectual property rights and conditions of use (price, copyright) (7) *Relation*: the relationship with other learning objects; (9) *Annotation*: comments on the educational use of the learning object; (10) *Classification*: relation to a particular classification system. Some of the metadata elements allow free text for value while others provide values from predefined vocabularies.

In relation to the possibility of introducing metadata as free text, a really interesting question was raised by Downes (2003): “What happens when different people have different points of view about what a learning object metadata might be?” For example, a certain LO author may tag an oak tree picture as “tree”, but other potential user may look for it as “hardwood”, while another one, would use the tag “flora and fauna of England”. Thus, it seems as if, the more subjective metadata are, the more varied terminology may be used to refer to the same thing, reducing the chances of reusability.

Several studies analyse the problems related to the generation of standards for metadata from the perspective of the educational practice, suggesting approaches including the analysis of the prospective users; others propose application profiles using descriptors that are selected according to the orientation and goals of specific communities of users. These studies show the complexity of devising a pedagogical metadata model which is able to be successfully employed by a variety of user communities; moreover, taking into account differences in language, background or motivations. The ideal pedagogical metadata model should combine generality with flexibility, so to be shareable and adaptable enough, to satisfy specific interests.

Another problem may arise when pedagogical metadata are insufficient (they are not compulsory in LOM model), incongruous or irrelevant. On this question, Buseti (2004) states that metadata are not in line with current didactical practice. Educational metadata include information which is of limited use from the didactical point of view, such as the "semantic density" and the "interactivity degree". Currently used metadata do not give enough explicit information on the educational model underlying the development of a LO (p. 3).

IEEE-LOM description of learning outcomes could be considered vaguely described by just using Keywords, Coverage and Purpose. It seems logical to think that, for example, different students with different backgrounds and knowledge level will eventually reach different learning outcomes, after the use of the same resource, and this is something which should, somehow, be taken into account.

Sampson et al (2008) have recently proposed a science education application profile based on the IEEE LOM for tagging science educational resources. An application profile is a simplified and interpreted version of standards and/or specifications, created by reducing the coverage of standards to adapt them to the needs of a particular community of users. These authors have proposed for the LOM sub-element 2.2.2 a controlled vocabulary. Waves, radioactivity, light, sound, energy, chemical reaction, and so on, in total 272 terms, recognized as key concepts in science and teaching science. To our understanding this profile is a step forward because it focuses on key science education concepts. Considering Farrow´s words (2006): My stance has always been that the Key Ideas of Science remain Key Ideas, no matter which "*pieces*" of science knowledge happen to be included in the current National Curriculum "*mosaic*" (pp. 3-4). However one of the criticisms against specific profiles is related to the fact that changing global standards would have a negative impact on interoperability based on specific patterns.

Other profiles, although not so specific, could be considered as a source of pedagogical metadata enrichments. The IMATI-ITD pedagogical metadata model (Alvino et al, 2008) integrates descriptors from main international metadata standards with others aimed at identifying the context of use, the educational features, the structure and the learning approach of the resource. Five categories of metadata are proposed: Pedagogical Model, General, Audience, Educational Features and Annotation. Combination of general and specific features makes this model appropriate to describe a wide variety of educational contexts.

Pedagogical Standards and Issues

A recent research work on learning object conceptualization shows divergent perspectives from the practitioners involved, not always consistent with commonly literature accepted definitions. One of the main findings is that participants pay more importance to how learning objects may be integrated into good pedagogical practices, than on technical attributes (Francis, 2008).

Boyle (2008) advocates the principles of cohesion and decoupling to create highly reusable LO designed to have pedagogical impact. To achieve high reusability, they cannot be meaningless pieces of content information, but have clearly defined learning goals and educational potential. In this sense Schaalje (2007) states that, a goal of a particular learning object is much more useful than an instructional objective. The goal is of great value and therefore should be included in metadata.

Boyle has summarized five pedagogical design principles to be considered when designing LO. These principles are focused on the promotion of effective learning experiences and are summarized as follows: to orient learners to the aim of the learning experience; to use visualization to engage learners in understanding; to offer interactive experiences; to provide learners with control on the learning experiences and to use "scaffolding" exercises. These principles are student-centred and it could be understood that their main purpose is to help individuals to achieve the goals for which the LO were designed.

Pedagogical content and context may be considered as inextricably linked; however there are split opinions among technology designers. Nurmi and Jaakkola (2006) state that ideally, in order to maximize reusability, LO should be independent of pedagogy. The design of LOs cannot be based on particular pedagogical decisions or methods that could restrict the way the materials are used (p. 272). We do not fully agree with these authors, since we believe that cognitive studies on how individuals learn, and research outcomes on effective pedagogical designs, should be considered when searching for learning processes enhancement. Neither do we think that pedagogical principle designs based on research evidence have to be a real limitation for the future reuse of LO. Lack of versatility, or serious limitations for reusability are more likely to be associated with LO granularity or other characteristics.

On this line Schaalje (2007) offers some guidelines to design LO with significant instructional value (and we understand here pedagogical value) considering the minimal functional-granularity which must be present. These strategies are summarized as follow:

- Select a well-researched theory of learning/instruction which assembles the specific needs of your subject matter.
- Presentation, explanations and response activities might be guided by that theory
- Develop response activities focusing on higher-order thinking skills.
- Allow LO objects stand-alones without being dependent on others when all elements, <Presentation><Explanation><Questionary><Theory> are present.

These guidelines place the emphasis on the promotion of deep processing and higher order cognitive skills, as the key or most valuable feature of a LO. This approach is especially relevant for science education.

Butler (2007), in her analysis of the differences between a digital resource and a cognitive tool, draws attention on the importance of providing information about the target audience for which the learning material has been designed. In this sense, the author suggests the inclusion of data about the intended audience (age, abilities, beliefs, prior knowledge…), as well as information about the learning goals pursued. In the case of science education, these learning goals include not only the science content which are going to be worked on with the resource, but also the scientific reasoning skills to develop in the students, or the target beliefs and attitudes about science. It is easy to assume that the provision of information about both, the pedagogical content associated with the learning object, but also the target audience and the conditions where it has been, or may be potentially applied, are essential to facilitate its reuse.

Teachers and educational researchers may be interested in identifying which characteristics of a learning resource contribute to its reusability. In our opinion, provided technical conditions to facilitate compatibility and adequate pedagogical metadata models, instructional reusability may be promoted by paying attention to the possibility of customization and tailoring.

Trying to develop reusable learning objects involves looking for a balance between specificity and generality. Learners object paradigm might suggest the tendency to develop resources general enough to be reusable, or able to catch the interest of a wide range of users. However, specificity is an increasingly pursued characteristic of pedagogical material, aimed at enhancing learning by adaptation to students' previous knowledge and capacities. Specificity is also related to the concern about promoting learners' engagement and motivation. Motivation is likely to appear when working contexts and learning goals are relevant to students, connected with their close environment, their interests and necessities (Ariza et al., 2008).

Therefore, how can educators design e-learning materials, content and context-specific, but at the same time, general enough to be reusable? One straightforward answer would be by making it possible and easy for new users to modify the resource in order to adapt it to different educational needs or contexts. Therefore, we draw attention on the importance of generating customizable learning objects. In this sense, Linn et al. (2003a) stated that "sustainable curricular innovations require extensive opportunities for customization and flexibly adaptive designs" (p. 517).

Finally, we would like to discuss design-based research (DBR) as a different approach for the establishment of LO design principles. DBR is an emerging paradigm for the study of learning in context through the systematic development and study of instructional strategies and tools (Design-Based Research Collective, 2003). The main purpose of this approach is to promote the connection between theory, instructional design and its implementation into authentic settings, in the search of effective learning design principles. This is fostered by systematic research through continuous cycles of design, enactment, analysis and re-designs. A group of faculty and researchers founded to examine, improve, and practice DBR methods in education have set up the DBR Collective (http://www.designbasedresearch.org).

Several authors have embraced this paradigm to guide and evaluate their educational innovations. (Hoadley, 2002; Sandoval and Reiser, 2004). The Design Principles Database (DPD) is being developed as an infrastructure for designers to publish, connect, discuss and review design ideas (http://www.edu-design-principles.org/dp/designHome.php). The main goal is to bridge research and design in a communicable and systematic manner. It also has the potential of enabling designers to build on the successes and failures of others, rather than reinventing solutions that others have struggled to develop. The potential of the Design Principles Database to support DBR through a process of peer-evaluation is described by Kali (in press).

TECHNOLOGY IMPACT ON SCIENCE EDUCATION

After having discussed the main issues associated with the LO approach, we would like to start this section by analysing ICT implementations in science instruction to end up reflecting on the influence of the LO paradigm on science education.

To understand the scope and significance of the impact of technology on science education, it would be necessary to draw attention to common troubles related to science teaching, as well as to analyse how these specific difficulties may be overcome by the use of computer-supported pedagogical resources and learning environments.

One of main problem with learning science is that students' previous knowledge about natural phenomena is often incompatible with normative scientific theories, making it difficult to integrate new scientific concepts into their existent personal explanatory frameworks. Some conflicting views come from everyday experience. These is the case of deeply rooted beliefs, such as motion always requires a force; heavy objects fall faster, metal feels colder than the wood in the same room, although the thermometer says they are the same temperature, etc. Others come from inaccurate language use or wrong attributed meaning in every day life settings (temperature and heat used indistinctively…).

As a consequence of this lack of coherence between students' prior ideas and scientific theories, research has repeatedly shown that students learn normative knowledge in a superficial way, just to face or deal with school activities and exams. However, they are unable to apply scientific theories to explain real world phenomena, and their preconceptions persist after years of instruction (Covián and Celemín, 2008; Franco and Taber, 2008; Taber, 2002). The analysis of this research evidence reveals the necessity to discover new approaches to science education.

Technology offers a wide range of applications to support students' conceptual change, conceptual development and knowledge integration of scientific theories. For example, data collection and representation devices, simulations and virtual laboratories may provide learners with significant evidence to question and review their prior conceptions. They also offer relevant experiences to make sense of scientific explanations and to apply them in a convincing and satisfactory way, promoting meaningful learning, and transferable knowledge (Krange and Ludvigsen, 2009; Su, 2008a, 2008b; Trindade et al., 2002; Venkataraman, 2009; Zucker and Hug, 2008).

Discussion has also been shown to be a useful strategy to promote students' reflection and revision of ideas. The potential of collaborative work for learning lies partly on the opportunity to raise debate and discussion between group members, promoting conceptual change or development. According to social constructivism view, individuals construct meaning through their interaction with others and through the use of language. On this line, team work has been widely recognised as a valuable instructional approach to facilitate meaningful and reflective learning (Gibbings and Brodie, 2008; Kearney, 2004; Moreno et al., 2007).

Besides time and space flexibility, computer based collaborative learning (CBCL) seems to have some additional advantages when compared to traditional class collaboration, such as increased participation and higher quality contributions (Linn, 2003a; Weinberger and Fischer, 2006). Electronic discussions provide time for reflection and learners seem to be more concerned about the quality of their contributions, since they become written evidence. However, class or electronic forum discussions do not necessary prompt reflection, conceptual development or learning. These outcomes are critically dependant on CBCL design and on teachers' capacity to monitor and orientate scientific debates, through scaffolding and inspiring prompts (Puntambekar, 2006).

Another significant contribution of technology is related to the possibility of providing students with meaningful learning contexts. Simulations, virtual laboratories or real data collection and representation devices are clear examples of technological tools which allow students to get in touch with authentic inquiry activities, facilitating scientific understanding and the development of useful skills and attitudes (Edelson, 2003; Erdosne et al., 2009; Floriano, 2008; Ko and Cheng, 2008).

Finally, we would like to mention other common students′ difficulties in learning science, related to the scientific use of abstract theories or models to explain natural phenomena. In this sense, technology provides a wide range of digital resources to promote students' understanding of scientific theories. Through the use of animations and simulations, it is possible to make individuals visualize abstract scientific models and to connect symbolic or micro-scale world with macro-scale properties and behaviours, promoting meaningful and enhanced learning (Hansen et al., 2004; Piburn et al., 2005; Venkataraman, 2009; Zucker and Hug, 2008).

A wide range of educational contexts, where technology has been successfully applied, are available in literature. Thus, enhanced learning has been demonstrated in different fields, such as measurement concepts and procedures (Kiboss, 2002), quantitative problem solving skills (Diederen et al., 2005), spatial abilities for geography and astronomy learning (Piburn et al., 2005; Hansen et al., 2004) or better understanding of chemical and physical concepts (Trindade et al., 2002; Venkataraman, 2009; Zucker and Hug, 2008).

Research has indicated that computer technology can support learning, and that it is especially useful in developing the higher-order skills of critical thinking, analysis, and scientific inquiry. However, the mere presence of computers in the classroom does not ensure their effective use. Some computer applications have been shown to be more successful than others and many factors influence how well, even the most promising applications, are implemented (Roschelle et al., 2000). In this sense, several works provide evidence for the effective use of simulations and other technology based resources (Blake and Scanlon, 2007; Hennessy et al., 2007; Krange and Ludvigsen, 2009; Wilensky, 2003). Research repeatedly indicates the importance of providing appropriate student guidance and scaffolding in order to avoid undesired effects, such as an individual's misconception reinforcement or performance orientation, rather that learning orientation.

Finally, in order to fully benefit from technology potential for educational purposes, several authors point out that institutional support and coherent curricular and assessment designs are required (Krange and Ludvigsen, 2009; Pedersen et al, 2009; Bostock, 1998); as well as ensuring that teachers' instructional perspectives agree with current insights into learning processes (Niederhauser and Stoddart 2001).

However, as it has been previously pointed out, the literature review on computer-supported pedagogical resources for science education reveals that most digital tools and learning environments have been designed without an emphasis on interoperability and reusability. These findings seem to suggest that the LO paradigm is widely embraced in computer sciences, but rarely explicitly addressed in learning sciences.

After discussing the impact of technology on science education, we would like to describe briefly one innovative project on computer supported science teaching. Design and development of this project will be analysed from the LO perspective.

Learning Objects in Laboratory Practical Work

We would like to describe here a local project based on the design and application of computer-based resources for chemistry learning. Designing and Applying Multimedia Repository for Experimental Sciences (DAMRES) was conceived as an innovative project involving a multidisciplinary team of teachers (Organic Chemistry; Physical-Chemistry and Didactics of Experimental Sciences) from different Departments at University of Jaén but with some common teaching concerns: application of ICT to science education. They are currently engaged in the design and implementation of multimedia resources for their laboratory-based learning and teaching activities in higher education. DAMRES is an example to illustrate a case study where design principles for pedagogical impact of LOs (Boyle, 2008), principles of multimedia learning theory (Mayer, 2003) and reusability issues have been explicitly addressed. This project was conceived bearing in mind a blended learning scenario (b-learning), emphasizing the integration of "computer-based self-study" and "traditional classroom teaching".

In higher education, practices in laboratories play an outstanding part in science courses since they are considered essential to understand the role of experimental work in the development of scientific knowledge. Moreover, they help students acquire important attitudes and skills related to problem solving, experimental design, manipulation, and application of lab techniques, systematic observation, data collection and processing, analysis and interpretation of results, etc.

The combination of "traditional practical work" and "the use of ICT" in laboratories offers to the end users (learners, teachers, and practitioners) new scenarios and teaching/learning opportunities. As in other previous related experiences in using LOs in teaching Science (Dumbraveanu, 2004), our pedagogical approach is based on a constructivist conception of learning, paying special attention to students´ involvement in the whole learning process.

With this project we have generated a compilation of LOs, ready to be used by a wide range of final users (novice learners), who have a common general instructional goal: "to learn about, and to know how to apply, laboratory techniques". As stated by Schaalje (2007), a concise and clearly defined instructional goal associated to a particular LO may be much more meaningful for students, than lengthy instructional objectives, which are not probably going to be retained by learners at the end of their instruction. We wanted to endow LOs with something more than simple information, which could be obtained by students from other alternatives sources.

When the design of the LO involved in the project was addressed, we assumed the importance of paying attention not only to the selection of key science contents, but also, to other features that may critically impact their effect on individuals' learning. Therefore, the multimedia resources developed were meant to be LO rather than just informational objects (Mills 2002). To accomplish this goal we decided that formative assessments should be an essential issue in our project. This is in agreement with the work by Schaalje (2007), where it is stated that a LO has a minimum of one selected response question. Thus, each of our LOs are provided with different pre-test and post-test tools, related to specific contents to be used before, during and after the presentations and explanations associated with the LO. Students may decide how to use assessment, allowing adaptation to personal learning rates. In this way, learners have also the opportunity to measure their initial knowledge about one of the selected "key topic" on study, for example "*weighting*", "*measuring volumes*", "*cooling*", "*mixing*", etc. In this stage, the LO incorporates questions only related with the low levels of Bloom´s cognitive aptitudes (knowledge and comprehension). Then, a sequence of questions is given to learners using an interactive flash presentation before the instruction starts. The use of pre-tests allows learners to focus later on those aspects in which they have initially failed (knowledge and comprehension are still present), but now the main focus of the questions are related to higher order skills (application, analysis and synthesis). Some of the quizzes are: short answer fill in the blank, short answer select from list, short answer ratings, short answer essay, multiple choice-single answer and multiple choice-multiple. Features such as rates per answer, scoring options, pass/fail percentages, numbers of attempts etc, depend on the kind of content to be assessed and its purpose (pre-test or post-test). Outcomes are saved into a report which is send to teachers if students wish so, providing an invaluable tool to give an individual adaptive feed-back.

The project has involved several stages: The purpose of the first one is to elaborate multimedia didactic material. The next step has consisted of integrating the new resources into proper teaching and learning sequences, acquiring different complexity levels, depending on the topic/subject requirements. The final stage is associated with the evaluation of the whole project, paying attention to: student self-learning assessment with LOs and the quality or appropriateness of LOs as pedagogical materials. All the phases of the project has been envisaged within the LO approach.

More details about technical features, design principles used, types of LOs included, specific contents, tailoring and resources interactivity may be found in Quesada et al (2009).

CONCLUSIONS AND FUTURE STEPS

This chapter offers a brief overview on the main ideas underlying the LO paradigm, showing various perspectives and different contributions associated with the search of common standards.

Requirement for LO interoperability and reusability are discussed, trying to draw attention on the need of developing new metadata models to fully benefit from this approach.

As educational researchers, we have placed special emphasis on pedagogical metadata aspects. By increasing and standardizing appropriate pedagogical metadata will facilitate LO location on the web, and help other potential users to decide whether a particular resource can satisfy their instructional needs or not. Under these conditions, LO designed for very specific purposes might be critically selected for similar or different ones. The possibility of customisation and tailoring will also promote reusability and allow specificity.

We also claim for a wider utilization of design-based research for the establishment of LO design principles. Design principles based on learning theories and educational research improve the chances of ensuring efficient instruction.

Defining and adopting quality and interoperability standards will help us avoid non-desirable features in the technology-based resources produced (invisibility, stereotyping, selectivity and imbalance, unreality, fragmentation and isolation, language inequality…). Being aware of the types of limitations and bias that can affect LOs is an essential step towards addressing quality, reusability and interoperability

Finally, the literature review carried out on technology and science education shows that most initiatives and research projects on computer-supported science education do not explicitly embrace the LO paradigm, suggesting that there is a significant gap between computer sciences and teaching sciences.

In the search of reasons to explain this situation some critical reflections appear:

The first straightforward answer could be that, the mentioned gap is due to an increasingly specialised scientific world, where any field of knowledge uses very specific and technical terminology. However, the term "learning object" suggests a direct connection with "learning", making it a paradox that this term is not widespread in the educational community. A reason for this might be found in the history of the LO paradigm, which is closely related to engineering and computer sciences. Differences in terminology account for a gap in specialised literature due to the use of different keywords to lead searches.

The generation of a proper set of technical, informational and pedagogical metadata to facilitate the interoperability of a LO is a hard and time-demanding activity. According to Purves et al. (2005), "developing materials that are suitable for adaptation to use in other contexts implies a significant overhead on the already hard-pressed academic's time in completing the necessary metadata and providing materials, which focus on concept-rich examples where contexts are interchangeable" (p.191).

Therefore, how can we persuade scholars and lectures to get involved in this task? Only a really good reason could motivate the investment of time and attention aimed at making the product of our own creativity and devotion, available and reusable by others. Another concern is related to ownership of the intellectual property rights (IPR) of LOs. In order to overcome teachers' fears about these issues, information about current mechanisms to address this problem should be provided.

A convincing argument to promote the adoption of the LO approach within the educational community could be the optimisation of pedagogical resources and creative efforts. Appreciation of the huge intellectual and cognitive load required for the design of innovative instructional materials could be a powerful motive, provided intellectual property rights. Focussing on the development of versatile, shareable and reusable pedagogical materials will optimize creative efforts and allow the possibility of concentrating on improving resources, rather than duplicating efforts. Consequently, we argue that making the teaching science community aware of the potential benefits underlying the LO approach may enhance sharing and reusability of the technological resources developed for science learning.

In the final section of this chapter, we briefly described an innovative project aimed at generating LO for laboratories practices in science education: Designing and Applying Multimedia Repository for Experimental Sciences (DAMRES). The reusability of the pedagogical resources developed for this project, is partly associated with the main focus underlying their design: The project LOs have been collaboratively produced by teachers at different university degrees, and they were conceived to be used by a wide population of students, who have a common instructional goals: to develop knowledge and skills related to laboratory experimental work. The resources allow different levels of prior knowledge and performance and are designed to be flexibly implemented into various university subjects, at different universities degrees.

The design of DAMRES LOs has been driven by design-based research, taking into account current insights into learning process and evidence from educational research (Mayer, 2003)

Pedagogical design principles discussed by Schaalje (2007), are also present in our project LOs, since they are also focussed on the promotion on higher order cognitive skills and they exhibit an adequate level of granularity, since they include presentation, explanation, question and theory sections. Special emphasis is placed on formative assessment, including pre and post-tests associated with any LO.

All these features are based on research and LO specific literature and are intended to ensure digital resources with high pedagogical value. However, the last stage of the DAMRES project will focus on the evaluation of these LOs, both from students' and from experts' point of view.

REFERENCES

Alvino, S., Forcheri, P., Ierardi, M. G., & Sarti, L. (2008). A general and flexible model for the pedagogical description of learning objects. In M. Kendall, & B. Samways (Eds.), *International Federation for Information Processing, Vol. 281, Learning to Live in the Knowledge Society* (pp. 55-62). Boston: Springer.

Ariza, M. R., Quesada, A., & Ocaña, M. T. (2008). An experience about promoting general and specific competences acquisition in Higher Education: autonomous work and collaborative skills in the development of a project aimed at eliciting motivation and contextualized learning. In L. Gómez, D. Belenguer, I. Candel (Eds.), *International Conference of Education, Research and Innovation* (pp. 1-7). Madrid: IATED.

Beers, P. J., Boshuizen, H. P. A., Kirschner, P. A., Gijselaers, W., & Westendorp, J. (2006). Cognitive load measurements and stimulated recall interviews for studying the effects of information and communications technology. *Educational Technology Research and Development, 56*(3), 309–328. doi:10.1007/s11423-006-9020-7

Blake, C., & Scanlon, E. (2007). Reconsidering simulations in science education at a distance: Features of effective use. *Journal of Computer Assisted Learning, 23*(6), 491–502. doi:10.1111/j.1365-2729.2007.00239.x

Bostock, S. J. (1998). Constructivism in mass higher education: A case study. *British Journal of Educational Technology, 29*(3), 225–240. doi:10.1111/1467-8535.00066

Boyle, T. (2008). The design of learning objects for pedagogical impact. In L. Lockyer, S. Bener, S. Agostinho, B. Harper (Eds.), *Handbook of research on learning design and learning objects: Issues, Applications and Technologies* (pp. 391-407). Hershey, PA: Information Science Reference (IGI Global).

Busetti, E., Dettori, G., Forcheri, P., & Ierardi, M. G. (2004). Guidelines towards the effective sharable LO. In Liy, W. (Ed.), *Advances in Web-based learning* (pp. 416–423). Heidelberg, Germany: Springer Berlin.

Butler, N. S. (2006). BioKIDS: An animated conversation of the development of curricular activity structures for inquiry science. In Sawyer, R. K. (Ed.), *The Cambridge Handbook of the Learning Sciences* (pp. 355–370). New York: Cambridge University Press.

Butler, N. S. (2007). Digital resources versus cognitive tools. In Abell, S. K., & Lederman, N. G. (Eds.), *Handbook of Research in Science Education* (pp. 471–492). Mahwah, NJ: Lawrence Erlbaum Associates Publishers.

Churchill, D. (2007). Towards a useful classification of learning objects. *Educational Technology Research and Development*, *55*(5), 479–497. doi:10.1007/s11423-006-9000-y

Covián, R. E., & Celemín, M. (2008). Diez años de evaluación de la enseñanza aprendizaje de la mecánica de newton en escuelas de ingeniería españolas. Rendimiento académico y presencia de preconceptos. *Ensenañza de las Ciencias*, *26*(1), 23–42.

Design-Based Research Collective. (2003). Design-Based Research: An emerging paradigm for educational inquiry. *Educational Researcher, 32*(1), 5-8. Retrieved July 20, 2009 from http://www.designbasedresearch.org/reppubs/DBRC2003.pdf

Diederen, J., Gruppen, H., Hartog, R., & Voragen, A. G. J. (2005). Design and evaluation of digital learning material to support acquisition of quantitative problem-solving skills within food chemistry. *Journal of Science Education and Technology*, *14*(5-6), 495–507. doi:10.1007/s10956-005-0224-0

Downes, S. (2003). Learning objects metadata. Retrieved May 1, 2009 from http://community.flexiblelearning.net.au/

Dumbraveanu, R., & Balmus, N. (2006). Using learning objects in teaching science. *International Journal of Emerging Technologies in Learning, 1*(1). Retrieved May 5, 2009, from www.i-jet.org

Duval, E. (2006). LearnRank: Towards a real quality measure for learning. In Ehlers, U., & Pawlowski, J. M. (Eds.), *Handbook on quality and standardization in e-learning* (pp. 457–500). Heidelberg, Germany: Springer Berlin. doi:10.1007/3-540-32788-6_30

Edelson, D. C. (2003). Realising authentic science learning through the adaptation of scientific practice. In Fraser, B. J., & Tobin, K. G. (Eds.), *International Handbook of Science Education* (pp. 317–331). London: Kluwer Academic Publishers.

Edelson, D. C., & Reiser, B. J. (2006). Making authentic practices accessible to learners: design, challenges and strategies. In Sawyer, R. K. (Ed.), *The Cambridge Handbook of the Learning Sciences* (pp. 335–354). New York: Cambridge University Press.

Erdosne, T. E., Morrow, B. L., & Ludvico, L. R. (2009). Designing blended inquiry learning in a laboratory context: A study of incorporating hands-on and virtual laboratories. *Innovative Higher Education*, *33*(5), 333–344. doi:10.1007/s10755-008-9087-7

Farrow, S. (2006). *The really useful Science book. A framework of knowldege for primary teachers*. London: Routledge.

Floriano, W. B. (2008). A portable bioinformatics course for upper-division undergraduate curriculum in sciences. *Biochemistry and Molecular Biology Education*, *36*(5), 325–335. doi:10.1002/bmb.20217

Francis, D. E., & Murphy, E. (2008). Instructional designers' conceptualisations of learning objects. *Australasian Journal of Educational Technology, 24*(5), 475-486. Retrieved July 1, 2008, from http://www.ascilite.org.au/ajet/ajet24/francis.html

Franco, A. G., & Taber, K. (2008). Secondary students' thinking about familiar phenomena: Learners' explanations from a curriculum context where 'particles' is a key idea for organising teaching and learning. *International Journal of Science Education*, *31*(14), 1917–1952. doi:10.1080/09500690802307730

Friesen, N. (2004). Three objections to learning objects and e-learning standards. In McGreal, R. (Ed.), *Online Education Using Learning Objects* (pp. 59–70). London: Routledge.

Gibbings, P., & Brodie, L. (2008). Team-based learning communities in virtual space. *International Journal of Engineering Education*, *24*(6), 1119–1129.

Hansen, J. A., & Barnett, M., MaKinster, J. G. & Keating, T. (2004). The impact of three-dimensional computational modelling on student understanding of astronomical concepts: A quantitative analysis. *International Journal of Science Education, 26*(11), 1365–1378. doi:10.1080/09500690420001673757

Hennessy, S., Wishart, J., Whitelock, D., Deaney, R., Brawn, R., & Velle, L. (2007). Pedagogical approaches for technology-integrated Science teaching. *Computers & Education, 48*(1), 137–152. doi:10.1016/j.compedu.2006.02.004

Hoadley, C. (2002). Creating context: Design-based research in creating and understanding CSCL. In Stahl, G. (Ed.), *Computer Support for Collaborative Learning* (pp. 453–462). Mahwah, NJ: Lawrence Erlbaum Associates.

Hodgins, H. W. (2002). The future of learning objects. In J.R. Lohmann & M.L. Corradini (Eds.), *ECI Conference on e-Technologies in Engineering Education Learning Outcomes Providing Future Possibilities: Vol. P11.* (pp. 1-8). Davos, Switzerland: ECI.

Hoyles, C., & Noss, R. (2009). The Technological Mediation of Mathematics and Its Learning. *Human Development, 52*, 129–147. doi:10.1159/000202730

Institute of Electrical and Electronics Engineers, Inc. (2002). [New York: Global Engineering Documents.]. *IEEE Computer Standard for Learning Objects Metadata, 1484*(12), 1.

Kali, Y. (in press). The design principles database as means for promoting design-based research. In Kelly, A. E., Lesh, R. A., & Baek, J. Y. (Eds.), *Handbook of Innovative Design Research in Science, Technology, Engineering, Mathematics (STEM) Education*. Mahwah, NJ: Lawrence Erlbaum Associates.

Kay, R. H., & Knaack, L. (2007). Evaluating the learning in learning objects. *Open Learning, 22*(2), 5–28. doi:10.1080/02680510601100135

Kay, R. H., & Knaack, L. (2009). Assessing learning, quality and engagement in learning objects: The learning object evaluation scale for students (LOES-S). *Educational Technology Research and Development, 57*(2), 147–168. doi:10.1007/s11423-008-9094-5

Kearney, M. (2004). Classroom use of multimedia-supported predict-observe-explain tasks in a social constructivist learning environment. *Research in Science Education, 34*(4), 427–453. doi:10.1007/s11165-004-8795-y

Kiboss, J. K. (2002). Impact of a computer-based physics instruction program on pupils' understanding of measurement concepts and methods associated with school science. *Journal of Science Education and Technology, 11*(2), 193–198. doi:10.1023/A:1014673615275

Ko, C. C., & Cheng, C. D. (2008). Web-based laboratories for internet remote Experimentation. *World Review of Science. Technology and Sustainable Development, 5*(3-4), 301–314. doi:10.1504/WRSTSD.2008.020285

Krajcik, J., & Blumenfeld, P. C. (2006). Project-based learning. In Sawyer, R. K. (Ed.), *The Cambridge Handbook of the Learning Sciences* (pp. 317–334). New York: Cambridge University Press.

Krange, I., & Ludvigsen, S. (2009). Original article: The historical and situated nature of design experiments - Implications for data analysis. *Journal of Computer Assisted Learning, 25*(3), 268–279. doi:10.1111/j.1365-2729.2008.00307.x

Lehman, R. (2007). Learning objects repositories. *New Directions for Adult and Continuing Education, 133*, 57–66. doi:10.1002/ace.247

Linn, M. (2003a). Technology and science education: starting points, research programs, and trends. *International Journal of Science Education, 25*(6), 727–758. doi:10.1080/09500690305017

Linn, M. (2003b). The impact of technology on science instruction: historical trends and current opportunities. In Fraser, B. J., & Tobin, K. G. (Eds.), *International Handbook of Science Education* (pp. 265–294). London: Kluwer Academic Publishers.

Linn, M. C., Clarck, D., & Slotta, J. D. (2003). WISE design for knowledge integration. *Science Education, 87*(4), 517–538. doi:10.1002/sce.10086

López, M. G., Maestre, A. J., & Sánchez-Alonso, S. (2007). *Reusabilidad de los objetos de aprendizaje almacenados en repositorios de libre Acceso.* Paper presented at the 4th Simposio Pluridisciplinar sobre Diseño, Evaluación y Desarrollo de Contenidos Educativos Reutilizables, Bilbao, SP. Retrieved July 12, 2009 from http://ftp.informatik.rwthaachen.de/Publications/CEUR-WS/Vol-318/Lopez.pdf

Maarof, M. H. S., & Yahya, Y. (2008). LORIuMET: Learning object repositories interoperability using metadata. In H. B. Zaman (Ed.), *International Symposium on Information Technology, 3*, (pp. 1-5). Kuala Lumpur: Malaysia.

Mayer, R. E., & Moreno, R. (2003). Nine ways to reduce cognitive load in multimedia learning. *Educational Psychologist, 32*, 43–52. doi:10.1207/S15326985EP3801_6

MERLOT. *Multimedia Educational Resource for Learning and Online Teaching.* (2009). Retrieved May 15, 2009, from http://www.merlot.org/merlot/index.htm

Mills, S. (2002). *Learning about learning objects with learning objects*. Paper presented at the SITE 2002 Conference, Nashville, TN. Retrieved May 20, 2009 from http://www.alivetek.com/learningobjects/site_paper.htm

Moreno, L., Gonzalez, C., Castilla, I., Gonzalez, E., & Sigut, J. (2007). Applying a constructivist and collaborative methodological approach in engineering education. *Computers & Education, 49*, 891–915. doi:10.1016/j.compedu.2005.12.004

Murphy, E. (2004). Moving from theory to practice in the design of web-based learning using a learning object approach. *E-journal of Instructional Science and Technology, 7*(1). Retrieved May 13, 2009 from http://www.ascilite.org.au/ajet/e-jist/

Muspratt, S., & Freeboy, P. (2007). *Students' perceptions of the characteristics of "good" and "poor" digital learning objects.* Paper presented at the International Educational Research Conference. Fremantle, AU.

Nesbit, J. C., Belfer, K., & Leacock, T. (2003). Learning Object Review Instrument (LORI). *E-Learning Research and Assessment Network.* Retrieved July 13, 2009 from http://www.elera.net/eLera/Home/Articles/

Neven, F., & Duval, E. (2002). Reusable learning objects: a survey of lom-based repositories. In *Proceedings of the 10th ACM international conference on Multimedia* (pp. 291-294). New York: ACM Press.

Niederhauser, D. S., & Stoddart, T. (2001). Teachers' instructional perspectives and use of educational software. *Teaching and Teacher Education, 17*, 15–31. doi:10.1016/S0742-051X(00)00036-6

Nurmi, S., & Jaakkola, T. (2006). Promises and pitfalls of learning objects. *Learning, Media and Technology, 31*(3), 269–285. doi:10.1080/17439880600893325

Pedersen, S., Arslanyilmaz, A., & Williams, D. (2009). Teachers' assessment-related local adaptations of a problem-based learning module. *Educational Technology Research and Development, 57*(2), 229–249. doi:10.1007/s11423-007-9044-7

Piburn, M. D., Reynolds, S. J., McAuliffe, C., Leedy, D. E., & Johnson, J. K. (2005). The role of visualization in learning from computer-based images. *International Journal of Science Education, 27*(5), 513–527. doi:10.1080/09500690412331314478

Pitkänen, S. H., & Silander, P. (2004). Criteria for pedagogical reusability of learning objects enabling adaptation and individualized learning processes. In C.K. Lui & E. Sutinen (Eds.), 4th IEEE *International Conference on Advanced Learning Technologies,* (pp. 246-250). Joensuu, Finland: IEEE Computer Society

Prpitsch, C., & Veith, P. (2006). Content and management standards: LOM, SCORM and content packaging. In Ehlers, U., & Pawlowski, J. M. (Eds.), *Handbook on quality and standardization in e-learning* (pp. 209–223). Heidelberg, Germany: Springer Berlin. doi:10.1007/3-540-32788-6_15

Puntambekar, S. (2006). Analyzing collaborative interactions: divergence, shared understanding and construction of knowledge. *Computers & Education, 47*(3), 332–351. doi:10.1016/j.compedu.2004.10.012

Purves, R. S., Medyckyj-Scott, D. J., & Mackaness, W. A. (2005). The e-MapScholar project: an example of interoperability in GIScience education. *Computers & Geosciences, 31*(2), 189–198. doi:10.1016/j.cageo.2004.08.007

Quesada, A., Ariza, M. R., Ortiz, A., & Bermejo, R. (2009). Designing and applying multimedia material for experimental sciences. Teacher and student assessment of its implementation. In L. Gómez, D. Martí, & I. Candel. *International Technology, Education and Development Conferences* (pp. 4911-4919). Valencia, Spain: IATED

Redeker, G. (2003). An educational taxonomy for learning objects. In *Proceedings of the IEEE Conference on Advanced Learning Technologies,* (pp. 250-251), Sapporo, Japan.

Roschelle, J. M., Pea, R. D., Hoadley, C. M., Gordin, D. N., & Means, B. M. (2000). Changing how and what children learn in school with computer-based technologies. *The Future of Children, 10*(2), 76–97. doi:10.2307/1602690

Sampson, D., & Zervas, P. (2008). Enhancing educational metadata with Science Education Information. In P. Díaz, I. Aedo, E. Mora. (Eds.), *8th IEEE International Conference on Advanced Learning Technologies,* (pp.1081-1082). Santander, Spain: IEEE Computer Society

Sandoval, W. A., & Reiser, B. J. (2004). Explanation-driven inquiry: Integrating conceptual and epistemic scaffolds for scientific inquiry. *Science Education, 88*(3), 345–372. doi:10.1002/sce.10130

Schaalje, J. (2007). Instructional design of learning objects for the cognitive domain. In Koohang, A., & Harman, K. (Eds.), *Learning Objects: Theory, Praxis, Issues, and Trends* (pp. 45–81). Santa Rosa, CA: Informing Science Press.

Sicilia, M. A. (2005). Reusability and reuse of learning objects: Myths, realities and possibilities. *Revista de educación a distancia, 2*, 1-12. Retrieved May 3, 2009, from http://www.um.es/ead/red/M2/

Spiltunik, M. W., Stratford, S., Krajcik, J., & Soloway, E. (2003). Using technology to support students' artefact construction in science. In Fraser, B. J., & Tobin, K. G. (Eds.), *International Handbook of Science Education* (pp. 317–331). London: Kluwer Academic Publishers.

Su, K. D. (2008a). An integrated science course designed with information communication technologies to enhance university students' learning performance. *Computers & Education, 51*(3), 1365–1374. doi:10.1016/j.compedu.2007.12.002

Su, K. D. (2008b). The effects of a chemistry course with integrated information communication technologies on university students' learning and attitudes. *International Journal of Science and Mathematics Education*, *6*(2), 225–249. doi:10.1007/s10763-006-9062-7

Taber, K. S. (2002). *Chemical misconceptions - prevention, diagnosis and cure*. London: Royal Society of Chemistry.

Trindade, J., Fiolhais, C., & Almeida, L. (2002). Science learning in virtual environments: A descriptive study. *British Journal of Educational Technology*, *33*(4), 471–488. doi:10.1111/1467-8535.00283

Van Assche, F. (2007). *Roadmap to interoperability for education in Europe*. Retrieved May 1, 2009, from http://insight.eun.org/shared/data/pdf/life_book.pdf

Venkataraman, B. (2009). Visualization and interactivity in the teaching of chemistry to science and non-science students. *Chemistry Education Research and Practice*, *10*(1), 62–69. doi:10.1039/b901462b

Weinberger, A., & Fischer, F. (2006). A framework to analyze argumentative knowledge construction in computer-supported collaborative learning. *Computers & Education*, *46*, 71–95. doi:10.1016/j.compedu.2005.04.003

White, B. Y. (2003). Computer Microworld and scientific inquiry: an alternative approach to science education. In Fraser, B. J., & Tobin, K. G. (Eds.), *International Handbook of Science Education* (pp. 295–316). London: Kluwer Academic Publishers.

Wilensky, U. (2003). Statistical mechanics for secondary school: The gaslab multi-agent modeling toolkit. *International Journal of Computers for Mathematical Learning*, *8*, 1–41. doi:10.1023/A:1025651502936

Wiley, D. A. (2000). Connecting learning objects to instructional design theory: a definition, a methapor and a taxonomy. In D.A. Wiley (Ed.), *The Instructional use of Learning Objects: Online version*. Retrieved July 15, 2009, from http://reusability.org/read/chapters/wiley.doc

Wiley, D. A. (2007). *The learning object literature*. Retrieved May 20, 2009 from http://opencontent.org/docs/wiley-lo-review-final.pdf

Zucker, A. A., & Hug, S. T. (2008). Teaching and learning physics in a 1:1 laptop school. *Journal of Science Education and Technology*, *17*(6), 586–594. doi:10.1007/s10956-008-9125-3

KEY TERMS AND DEFINITIONS

Granularity: LO feature related to its structural design, conceived to increase versatility and maximize the number of situations in which the resource may be applied. A minimum level of granularity is required in order to ensure the LO autonomy to acquired the target instructional goal.

Interoperability: LO ability to promote integration into different systems and to allow efficient exchange and use of information. It requires the adoption of appropriate standards and adequate metadata, both from the technical, and from the pedagogical or educational point of view.

Learning Object: Any digital resource designed to facilitate learning and to develop cognitive skills, with a minimum of granularity, which can be reused or applied to different instructional contexts and for different educational purposes.

Reusability: LO ability to be successfully applied to different audiences, educational contexts or for various instructional goals, either with no or with slight modifications.

Chapter 16
Semantic Mapping between LOM - SCORM Content Package and MPEG-7 Concepts

Varvara Vagiati
Ionian University, Greece

ABSTRACT

This chapter presents the current status of the efforts to harmonize MPEG-7 and SCORM Content Package (including the LOM description metadata, part of SCORM). In particular a model for the interoperability between these standards is developed. The MPEG-7 provides a standardized set of technologies for describing multimedia content, while SCORM is a collection of specifications for developing, organizing and delivering instructional content.The proposed model concerns the semantic mapping between the different elements of these standards, which are created to satisfy the specific needs of different communities. The followed approach is based on the main principles and procedures for metadata interoperability, such as on the crosswalking and mapping techniques. Moreover some empirical remarks conclude the mapping process.

INTRODUCTION

A content metadata standard is defined as an open specification that itemizes a set of elements and their meanings (Pierre, LaPlant, 1998); it is developed to support a specific community of interest. It is known that already a large number of metadata standards have been developed and many more are underway. Some examples of very familiar standards are Dublin Core, USMARC, Federal Geographical Committee (FGDC), Global/Government Information Locator Service (GILS), Multimedia Content Description Interface (MPEG-7), IEEE Learning Objects Metadata (LOM -representing the metadata part of SCORM). The developing of these standards according to the specific requirements of their communities may cause problems from the point of view of someone who wants to seek and retrieve information in different environments, because he has to face different metadata sets, and so, must

DOI: 10.4018/978-1-61692-789-9.ch016

have different tools in order to deal with them (Peig, Delgado, Pérez, 2001).

We understand then that information must be made available in accordance with a number of related metadata standards, so that it can reach the broadest community of users. As the number, size, and complexity of metadata standards continues to grow, supplying the metadata for each standard becomes more and more time consuming and tedious. With so many metadata schemes, how will chaos can be avoided? How can we ensure that systems that use different metadata schemes will be interoperable, in other words that information collected by one organization for a particular purpose can be exchanged, transferred or used by another organization for a different purpose (Hodge, 2005).

This chapter presents a model for the interoperability between MPEG-7 and SCORM Content Package and MPEG-7 and LOM (representing the metadata part of SCORM). The main objective is to solve an interoperability problem between digital library and eLearning metadata standards. These standards have been developed independently, although nowadays there is a need for the creation of educational repositories. More specific this study presents the first step of solving the interoperability problems between audiovisual digital libraries and eLearning applications, in order to support the modular development of personalized learning experiences. Library systems and e-learning systems actually need to interact in a variety of ways so that the eventual user begin to find new ways of developing learning activities which in turn influence the way he uses, or wishes to use, learning and information content.

The effort of harmonize a standard which describes multimedia content and a standard which develops, organizes and delivers instructional content has as a final aim the creation of a model which will allow users, that participate in eLearning activities, to browse and retrieve audiovisual objects, stored and managed by digital libraries, that match their interests, and use them as learning resources (Christodoulakis, Arapi, Moumoutzis, et al. 2006).

Some scenarios emphasizing the need of interoperability between information systems and e-learning systems are as follows (McLean & Lynch, 2004):

- A lecturer wishes to add a seamless link from the course management system to a specific library e-reserve article, then add another link to a broad-ranging search across various repositories for students to search for other similar articles with direct links to full-text versions of relevant articles, once discovered by student searches.
- A librarian wishes to ensure that digital rights, copyright and fair-use are properly managed within a collection of resources aggregated by a lecturer for use in the course management system, and then later to preserve any lecturer-created resources within the aggregation, as well as pointers to any external copyright materials.

An activity driven scenario can be depicted as follows:

- A student doing remedial mathematics has used a diagnostic test to identify key gaps in his/her basic mathematical concepts, at which point an automated search system seeks out the ideal mathematical remedial learning object to present to the student based on his/her weaknesses.

The first section of this chapter clarifies the main concepts and procedures, such as the notion of interoperability, of crosswalking, the procedure of element to element mapping, and a brief presentation of the involved standards MPEG-7 and SCORM Content Package. Then the mapping methodology of the mentioned standards is presented. The proposed methodology presents the mappings in different tables. The first table presents the mapping between MPEG-7 and LOM which is part of SCORM, while a second table is used for the mapping between MPEG-7 and SCORM Content Package. This separation is essential due to the great extensibility of the standards and the mapping, as well as the differences between the main objectives of SCORM Content Package and LOM is underlined. Nevertheless both of them constitute an integral tool for the management and delivery of learning objects: SCORM Content Package concerns the structural representation of the elements and their organization, whereas LOM deals with the description of the content of learning objects.

BACKGROUND

In the last years, many different metadata schemes have been proposed. Some of them have very specific focus and their usage is circumscribed to particular environments, but other ones are of general purpose and in some environments information providers that use different metadata schemes can be found together (Peig, Delgado, Pérez, 2001).

This situation forces applications to know all the schemes that may be found. Furthermore, it is also usual to find storage systems containing objects referred to following different metadata schemes at the same time. There is still another extra problem: we have to be aware of new metadata schemes that might appear. So, applications must be adapted to these new schemes.

Data sources can be heterogeneous in syntax, schema, or semantics, thus making data interoperation a difficult task. Syntactic heterogeneity is caused by the use of different models or languages. Schematic heterogeneity results from structural differences. Semantic heterogeneity is caused by different meanings or interpretations of data in various contexts. To achieve data interoperability, the issues posed by data heterogeneity need to be eliminated (Cruz, Xiao, 2005).

Consequently, there is a need to develop interoperability systems between metadata domains, with the purpose of simplifying the discovery and the access to the information, and to achieve a high level of automation in this access (Peig, Delgado, Pérez, 2001).We define interoperability very broadly as any form of inter-system communication, or the ability of a system to make use of data from a previously unforeseen source. Interoperability in general is concerned with the capability of differing information systems to communicate. This communication may take various forms such as the transfer, exchange, transformation, mediation, migration or integration of information (Patel, Koch, Doerr, & Tsinaraki 2005). Interoperability is an important issue in all information systems and services. Without syntactic interoperability, data and information cannot be handled properly with regard to its formats, encodings, properties, values, and data types etc., not merged nor exchanged. Without semantic interoperability, the meaning of the used language, terminology and metadata values cannot be negotiated or correctly understood.

For digital libraries, interoperability is becoming a major issue as the Internet unifies digital library systems of differing types, run by separate organizations which are geographically distributed all over the world. The researchers believe that modern information systems can be seen as a stack of layers where each one is built on top of the previous one. There are different data representations, objects, concepts, domains, contexts and metacontexts in the layer stack that should be efficiently managed in a standard way (Arapi, Moumoutzis, Mylonakis & Christodoulakis 2007).

METHODOLOGY

Crosswalking

A crosswalk is a specification for the mapping process from a source to a target metadata schema.

More specific, metadata crosswalks map the elements, semantics and syntax from one metadata scheme to those of another. A crosswalk allows metadata created by one community to be used by another community with a different metadata standard (Hodge, 2005).

The specification of a crosswalk requires a specialized knowledge of the associated metadata standards. The knowledge and the expertise in the metadata standards is also a difficult task because of their continuous and independent development. Therefore the maintenance of a crosswalk requires a continuous updating as the metadata standards change.

For harmonizing the MPEG-7 standard and SCORM (including also LOM) a metadata crosswalk is necessary. The degree to which crosswalks are successful depends on the similarity of the two schemes. The mapping of schemes with fewer elements (less granular or atomic) to those with more elements (more granular or atomic) is problematic. Despite similarity at the semantic level, the crosswalk becomes difficult if the syntactic rules differ from the original scheme to the target scheme. While these crosswalks are key to interoperability, they are also labor intensive to develop and maintain (Hodge, 2005). However, crosswalks are important for libraries and subject gateways that collect or search resources from a variety of sources and treat them as a whole collection.

Harmonization is the process of ensuring the consistency of the specification of related content metadata standards (Pierre, LaPlant, 1998) and therefore is essential to the development of crosswalks. Harmonization results in the ability to create and maintain only one set of metadata, and to map the metadata to any number of related metadata standards. The use of harmonization vastly simplifies the development, implementation and deployment of related metadata standards through the use of common terminology, methods and processes (Pierre, LaPlant, 1998). Some of these processes are:

- The extraction of common terminology,
- The extraction of common similar properties and the generalization of their concepts,
- A generic metadata document organization. That eases the ability to find information within given metadata standard, because a given section of one standard can be found in an analogous section of another standard.
- Unifying the selection process. Harmonization is achieved when the analogous processes of the standards are chosen to be the same.
- Determining the semantic mapping of elements between the source and target metadata standards.

As we can see metadata harmonization refers to a step further the level of system interoperability, and refers to interoperability *between metadata standards*. Harmonization thus refers to the ability to use several different metadata standards in combination in a single software system. The rest of the chapter will analyse the different groups of standards and try to find obstacles to harmonizations.

The current status of harmonization of MPEG-7 with SCORM Content Package is presented, whereas a different section presents the harmonization between MPEG-7 and LOM (which represents a part of SCORM). Mappings are provided between the Descriptions Schemes (DSs) & Descriptors (Ds) of MPEG-7 and the elements of SCORM Content Packaging & LOM. The mapping procedure inducts some thoughts which conclude to empirical remarks. Also there has been an effort to justify some correlations between the elements. But what we exactly mean with the term *metadata mapping* and in what ways this can be achieved?

Element to Element Mapping

One way for solving the incompatibilities between metadata standards is to produce mappings between them. All metadata standards specify a number of properties associated with the specification of the various metadata elements. For example, some of them qualify each element as repeatable or non-repeatable. Other standards, such as SCORM, indicate whether or not an element is mandatory or optional.

For crosswalk development these properties must be taken into consideration. The trivial case is mapping elements that have identical properties, e.g., mapping mandatory non-repeatable elements to mandatory non-repeatable elements of identical data content types (Pierre, LaPlant, 1998).

Another case is the one-to-many map. For example, the source standard may contain a non-repeatable "keywords" element. The element definition specifies that its element value is made up of or more keywords separated by a semicolon character. This element may map to a repeatable element in the target standard where each keyword must occur as a repeated element.

Another case is the mapping of one source element to two unique target elements or the mapping of many to one, or no corresponding mapping of some elements.

In our case there are several times that a LOM element can be mapped to more than one MPEG-7 paths.

Sharable Content Object Reference Model (SCORM)

Sharable Content Object Reference Model (SCORM, 2004a, 2004b) is probably the most important initiative currently occurring in the area of e-learning standards and specifications. SCORM is a collection of specifications and standards that have been bundled into a collection of "technical books." Each can be viewed as separate books gathered together into a growing library. These technical books are presently grouped under three main topics: the "Content Aggregation Model (CAM)", the "Run-time Environment (RTE)" and "Sequencing and Navigation (SN)."

The proposed mapping has as target schema SCORM Content Aggregation Model (SCORM, 2004b) which describes the components used in a learning experience, how to package those components for exchange from system to system, how to describe those components to enable search and discovery, and how to define the sequencing rules for the components. The CAM promotes consistent storage, labeling, packaging, exchange and discovery of content; it also provides guidelines and requirements for building content aggregations (e.g., course, lessons, modules, etc). It contains information on creating content packages, applying metadata to the components in the content package and applying sequencing and navigation details in the context of a content package. We can say that the SCORM Content Aggregation Model represents a learning taxonomy neutral means for designers and implementers of instruction to aggregate learning resources for the purpose of delivering a desired learning experience (SCORM, 2004b). A learning resource is any representation of information that is used in a learning experience. Learning experiences consist of activities that are supported by electronic or non-electronic learning resources.

One activity in the process of creating and delivering learning experiences involves the creation, discovery and gathering together, or aggregation, of simple assets into more complex learning resources and then organizing the resources into a predefined sequence of delivery.

The SCORM Content Model is made up of Assets, Sharable Content Objects (SCOs) and Content Organizations. Bellow these components are presented in more detail.

An Asset is the most basic form of a learning resource. Assets are an electronic representation of media, such as text, images, sound, assessment objects or any other piece of data that can be rendered by a Web client and presented to a learner. An Asset can be described with Asset Meta-data to allow for search and discovery within repositories, thereby enabling opportunities for reuse. The mechanism that provides this model is Content Package.

A SCO is a collection of assets that includes a specific launch-able asset that uses the SCORM run-time environment to communicate with an LMS. A SCO represents the lowest level of granularity of a learning resource and it can be used in different learning experiences to fulfil different learning objectives. A SCO should be independent of its learning context to improve its reusability. A SCO can be described with SCO Meta-data to allow for search and discovery within repositories, thereby enabling opportunities for reuse. The mechanism that provides this model is Content Package.

A Content Organization (Figure 1) is a map that represents the intended use of the content through structured units of instruction (Activities). This map shows how Activities relate to one another. The Activities may consist of other Activities and so we may have hierarchical levels of Activities, but this is not a requirement. Activities that do not consist of other Activities (leaf activities) will have an associated learning resource (SCO resource or Asset resource) that is used to perform the activity.

SCORM Content Packaging adheres strictly to the IMS Content Packaging Specification and provides additional explicit requirements and implementation guidance for packaging Assets, SCO and Content Organization.

To understand better the components of SCORM Content Packaging the standard provides the following conceptual diagram (Figure 2).

After describing the basic building blocks and how bundle them into content aggregations and packages, SCORM describes the components with metadata. SCORM recognizes that the IEEE LOM is the defacto standard for metadata within the learning community and strongly recommends that LOM should be used when describing SCORM Content Model Components. The IEEE LOM Information Model describes the set of data elements that are available to build metadata for a learning object. A learning object is any entity, digital or non-digital, which can be used, re-used or referenced during technology supported learning. Examples of technology supported learning include computer-based training systems, interac-

Figure 1. Content Organization. Adapted from SCORM

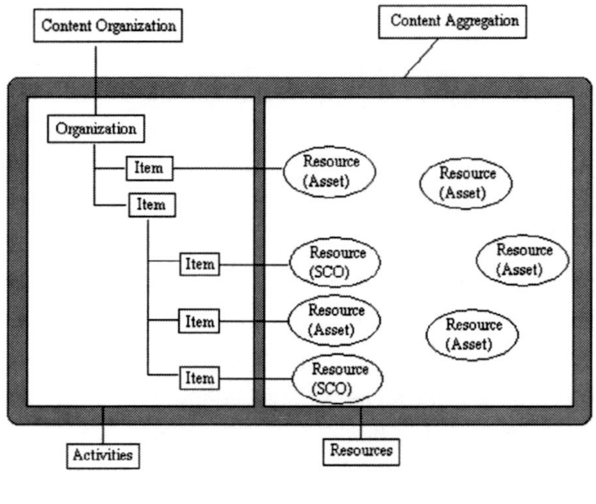

Figure 2. Content Package Conceptual Diagram. Adapted from SCORM

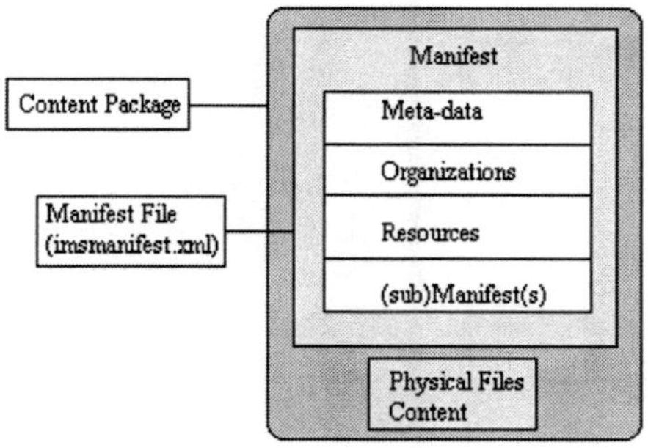

tive learning environments, intelligent computer-aided instruction systems, distance learning systems, and collaborative learning environments. Examples of learning objects include multimedia content, instructional content, learning objectives, instructional software and software tools, and persons, organizations, or events referenced during technology supported learning (Ogbuji, 2003).

The LOM Information Model is broken up into nine categories (IEEE LOM, 2002). These categories are based on the definitions found in the LOM Information Model. The nine categories of metadata elements are:

1. The General category
2. The Life Cycle category
3. The Meta-metadata category
4. The Technical category
5. The Educational category
6. The Rights category
7. The Relation category
8. The Annotation category
9. The Classification category

The table of mapping between the MPEG-7 concepts and LOM elements explains the use of these categories and specializes the relationships between parent elements and child elements of LOM metadata.

Multimedia Content Description Interface (MPEG-7)

The MPEG-7 provides a standardized set of technologies for describing multimedia content. The standard addresses a broad spectrum of multimedia applications and requirements by providing a metadata system for describing the features of multimedia content (MPEG-7, 2001). The goal of the MPEG-7 standard is to allow interoperable searching, indexing, filtering, and access of audio-visual (AV) content by enabling interoperability among devices and applications that deal with AV content description (Salembier & Smith, 2001).

The standard specifies four types of normative elements: Descriptors, Description Schemes (DSs), a Description Definition Language (DDL), and coding schemes (Salembier & Smith, 2001).

The MPEG-7 Descriptors are designed primarily to describe low-level audio or visual features such as color, texture, motion, audio energy, etc., as well as attributes of AV content such as location, time, quality, etc. On the other hand, the MPEG-7 DSs are designed to describe higher level AV features such as regions, segments, objects, events, and other immutable metadata related to creation and production, usage, and so forth.

The description tools of the Multimedia Description Schemes are organized on the basis of functionality as shown in Figure 3.

The basic elements form the building blocks for the higher-level description tools. The following basic elements are defined: schema tools (the root element, top-level types, description metadata, and packages), basic datatypes (integers, reals, vectors, matrices), linking and media localization tools (spatial and temporal localization), basic description tools (language, text, classification schemes).

The content description tools describe the features of the multimedia content and the immutable metadata related to the multimedia content. The following description tools for content description are defined: structure description tools (spatio-

Figure 3. Overview of the Multimedia Description Scheme (MDS) description tools

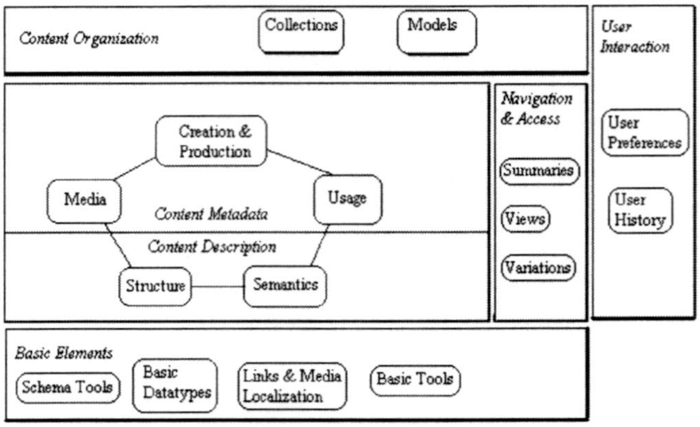

temporal segments of multimedia content) and semantic description tools (objects, events). The following description tools for content metadata are defined: media description (storage format, encoding), creation & production (title, creator, classification), and usage (access rights, publication). The content description and metadata tools are related in the sense that the content description tools use the content metadata tools. For example, a description of creation and production or media information can be attached to an individual video or video segment in order to describe the structure and creation and production of the multimedia content.

This brief theoritical presentation of the standards help us to understand the difference between their scopes. As it concerns SCORM it focuses on learning objects, while MPEG-7 focuses on audiovisual objects (AVO). An audio-visual object is the representation of a natural or synthetic object that has an audio and/or visual manifestation. Examples of audio-visual objects include a video sequence (perhaps with shape information), an audio track, an animated 3D face, speech synthesized from text, or a background consisting of a still image (MPEG-4, 2002).

This great difference can not forbid the complementarity of these two kinds of objects. For example, an audiovisual object after certain processes and the use of instructional ontologies (Arapi, Moumoutzis, Mylonakis & Christodoulakis, 2007) can be transformed to a SCORM learning object and finally be delivered to the student as an integrated learning experience.

A significant structural similarity is obvious between these standards. In SCORM, the Content Package provides a place for describing the structure (or organization) and the intended behavior of a collection of learning material. Similarly MPEG-7 Description Schemes describe entities or relationships pertaining to multimedia content and specify the structure and semantics of their components, which may be Description Schemes, Descriptors, or datatypes.

Implementation of Mapping between MPEG-7 and LOM

This part presents the table of semantic mapping between MPEG-7 concepts and LOM elements. In the table appear, apart from the mapping, the defintions of elements and the Description Schemes or Descriptors so that the correlations among them can be quite justifiable. Annotations and conclusions for the mappings are indicated at the end of the table, whereas some difficulties of the mapping procedure are analysed.

Structure of the mapping table: A critical concept which governs the mapping procedure is that of "path". We define an MPEG-7 path, a sequence of DSs with their own descriptors as the syntax of the standard defines. On the other hand a LOM path is a sequence of elements and their own subelements according to the standard's syntactic structure. The mapping table between MPEG-7 and LOM is based on a clustering effort of metadata elements from the different schemes with similar meaning. This effort has its origin in the attentive study and analysis of the element semantics of the specific metadata schemes.

The table icludes only the elements and concepts which can be contextually mapped, and is consisted of five columns. The first column presents the path of Description Schemes and Descriptors of MPEG-7 which find semantic coherence with LOM elements. The next column presents the definition of the last element of the MPEG-7 path which follows a "general to specific" sequence. In the next column the LOM element number is written, as it is revealed in the formal draft (IEEE, LOM, 2002) of the standard. Then the LOM path is appeared and in the next column its definition. The definitions of the elements are intentionally presented so that the mapping choises may have a primal justification.

Table analysis and mapping issues: The main objective of the mapping process was to choose the most semantically coherent MPEG-7 paths to each LOM path. It is remarkable that not only an one – to – one element mapping occurs but many MPEG-7 paths share the same meaning with one LOM path. The main reason for the multiple matching is the complexity and the great extensibility of MPEG-7 standard. Some remarks from the mapping are:

- It is possible to have a matching with many MPEG-7 paths because some of them derive from the Basic Elements and some others from the Content Metadata Tools, but all of them conclude to the same meaning, for example,
    - CreationInformation.Creation.Abstract (Content Metadata Tools) *or*
    - DescriptionMetadata.Comment.FreeTextAnnotation (Basic Elements) (see figure 3)
- In other cases several Content Metadata Tools conclude to the same meaning too, for example,
    - CreationInformation.RelatedMaterial.MediaLocator (Creation Description Tools) or
    - MediaInformation.MediaProfile.MediaInstance.MediaLocator (Media Description Tools)
- Sometimes we may conclude to an identical meaning by following a different path from the same Description Scheme, for example,
    - UsageInformation.Rights. or
    - UsageInformation.Availability.Rights

In general, most of the MPEG-7 equivalents can be found in the Content Description and Content Metadata tools.

A problem that was demostrated during the mapping process is the excessive complexity of MPEG-7 Description Schemes. Most of the MPEG-7 paths expand up to four hierarchical levels formulating a complex multilayered set of Description Schemes.

The duplication of metadata elements across multiple Descriptors and Description Schemes was also a problem. For instance the Identifier may appear in multiple locations. Furthermore in many cases the names can be duplicated but not their scope for functionality.

Implementation of Mapping between MPEG-7 and SCORM Content Package

This section presents the table of semantic mapping between MPEG-7 concepts and SCORM Content Package elements.

Table of mapping between MPEG-7 concepts and LOM elements

MPEG-7 Path	MPEG-7 Definition	LOM#	LOM Metadata Path	LOM Definition
MediaInformation.MediaIdentification.EntityIdentifier	Identifies uniquely the particular and unique multimedia and content entity (e.g. ISOs, ISAN).	1.1	general.identifier	Globally unique label for learning object.
MediaInformation.MediaIdentification. EntityIdentifier. UniqueID [@type]	Describes the type of the identifier (e.g., URI, ISAN, ISWC, UMID, UPID). If no value is specified, the identifier is assumed to be a URI.	1.1.1	general.identifier.catalog	Represents the name or designator of the identification or cataloging scheme for the entry. There are a variety of cataloging systems available (e.g. URI, URN, DOI etc.).
MediaInformation.MediaIdentification. EntityIdentifier. UniqueID	Describes the unique identification of a resource. An instance of this datatype contains a value (an identifier) that allows some resource to be identified. The identifying value can be either a textual or a binary value that is encoded in base16 or base 64 format.	1.1.2	general.identifier.entry	The value of the identifier within the identification or cataloguing scheme that designates or identifies this learning object. A namespace specific string.
CreationInformation.Creation.Title	Describes one textual title of the multimedia content. Multiple titles are allowed. They may correspond to different types (indicated by the type attribute) or to different languages (indicated by the xml:lang attribute).	1.2	general.title	Learning Object's name.
CreationInformation.Classification.Language	Describes the language of the spoken audio of the program.	1.3	general.language	Learning object's language.
CreationInformation.Creation.Abstract	Describes a textual abstract of the multimedia content (optional). It is a summary, assigned during the creation process, of what is conveyed in the multimedia content.	1.4	general. description	Describes learning object's content.
DescriptionMetadata.Comment.FreeTextAnnotation	Describes a free text annotation.			
CreationInformation.Classification.Genre.Name	Describes what the multimedia content is about (broad classification).	1.5	general.keyword	Keywords describing the resource.
DescritpionMetadata. Comment.TextAnnotation. KeywordAnnotation	Describes a keyword annotation.			
CreationInformation.Classification.Target	Describes the target of the multimedia content in terms of market classification, age and country or region.	1.6	general.coverage	Temporal / spatial characteristics of content. Specifically, used to describe the time, culture, geography or region to which the SCORM Content Model Component applies.
CreationInformation.Classification.Region	Describes one target country or region for the multimedia content.			
CreationInformation.Creation.CreationCoordinates. Location	Describes the place where the multimedia content was created (optional).			
CreationInformation.Creation.CreationCoordinates. Date	Describes the date or period when the multimedia content was created (optional).			
DescriptionMetadata.Comment.StructuredAnnotation (When, Where, Who)	The StructuredAnnotation datatype represents an annotation structured in terms of actions, animate object (people and animals), objects, action, places, time, purposes, and manner.			

continues on following page

Table continued

MPEG-7 Path	MPEG-7 Definition	LOM#	LOM Meta-data Path	LOM Definition
DescriptionMetadata.Version	Specifies the version of the description to which the description metadata is attached (optional). The format for the version information is application dependent.	2.1	lifeCycle. version	The edition of this learning object.
CreationInformation.Creation.Creator(role= "creator")	Describes one creator of the multimedia content (persons, organizations, groups…).	2.3.1	lifecycle.contribute.role	Kind of contribution.
DescriptionMetadata.Creator	Describes a creator of the description to which the description metadata is attached (optional).	2.3.2	lifecycle.contribute.entity	Entity or entities involved, most relevant first.
CreationInformation.Creation.Date	Describes the date or period when the multimedia content was created.	2.3.3	lifecycle.contribute.date	Date of contribution.
DescriptionMetadata.PublicIdentifier	Identifies the description to which the description metadata is attached using a public, globally unique identifier (optional).	3.1	meta-Metadata.identifier	A globally unique label that identifies this metadata record.
DescriptionMetadata. PrivateIdentifier	Identifies the description to which the description metadata is attached using a private, application dependent identifier (optional). The format of this identifier is application defined and need not be unique. Multiple private identifiers may be associated with a description.			
DescriptionMetadata.PublicIdentifier[@type]	Describes the type of the identifier (e.g., URI, ISAN, ISWC, UMID, UPID). If no value is specified, the identifier is assumed to be a URI.	3.1.1	meta-Metadata.identifier. catalog	The name or designator of the identification or cataloguing scheme for this entry. A namespace scheme.
DescriptionMetadata.PublicIdentifier	Describes the unique identification of a resource.	3.1.2	meta-Metadata.Identifier. entry	The value of the identifier within the identification.
DescriptionMetadata.Creator	Describes a creator of the description to which the description metadata is attached (optional). This can be a person, organization, or the software application that automatically generated the metadata. Multiple creators are allowed if the metadata was created as the result of several creators cooperating.	3.2.2	meta-Metadata.contribute. entity	The identification of and information about entities contributing to this metadata instance.
DescritpionMetadata.CreationTime.timePoint	Describes the time when the description to which the description metadata is attached was created (optional).	3.2.3	meta-Metadata.contribute. date.dateTime	The date of the contribution.
MediaInformation.MediaProfile.MediaFormat.FileFormat	Describes the file format of the media profile.	4.1	technical. format	Technical data type of the resource.
MediaInformation.MediaProfile.MediaFormat.FileSize	Indicates the size, in bytes, of the file where the media profile is stored.	4.2	techical.size	The size of the digital resource in bytes. Only the digits '0' — '9' should be used; the unit is bytes, not Mbytes, GB, etc.
MediaLocator.MediaURI	Describes the location of external media data (optional).	4.3	technical. location	A string that is used to access this learning object. It may be a location (URL), or a method that resolves to a location (URI).

continues on following page

Table continued

MPEG-7 Path	MPEG-7 Definition	LOM#	LOM Meta-data Path	LOM Definition
MediaInformation.MediaProfile.MediaFormat.System	Describes the broad media format of the media profile.	4.4	technical. requirement	The technology required to use this learning object, e.g. hardware, software, network, etc.
MediaInformation.MediaProfile.MediaFormat. System *(value taken from the corresponding Classification Scheme)*	Describes the broad media format of the media profile.	4.4.1.1	technical. requirement. orComposite. type.value	The technology required to use this learning object, e.g. hardware, software, network, etc.
MediaInformation.MediaProfile.MediaFormat. System *(value taken from the corresponding Classification Scheme)*	Describes the broad media format of the media profile.	4.4.1.2	technical. requirement. orComposite. name.value	Name of the required technology to use this learning object.
MediaTime.MediaDuration	Describes the duration of a media time period according to days and day time (optional).	4.7	technical. duration	Time a continuous learning object takes when played at intended speed.
CreationInformation.Classification.Purpose	Describes one purpose for which the multimedia content was created (optional). An example of CS is IntentionCS.	5.5	educational. intendedEndUserRole	Principal user(s) for which this learning object was designed, most dominant first.
CreationInformation.Classification.Age	Describes the targeted age range of the multimedia content (optional).	5.7	educational. typicalAgeRange	Age of the typical intended user.
UsageInformation.Rights	Describes information about the owners of the rights corresponding to the multimedia content, and how the multimedia content can be used (optional). Its appearance at this level precludes its appearance in the Availability DS instance of the same UsageInformation instance.	6	rights	This category describes the intellectual property rights and conditions of use for this learning object.
DescriptionMetadata.Rights	Describes the rights associated with the description to which the description metadata is attached and how the description to which this DS is attached can be used.			
UsageInformation.Availability.Rights	Describes information about the owners of the rights corresponding to the multimedia content, and how the multimedia content can be used (optional).			
UsageInformation.Availability.Financial	Describes the financial information related to the particular use described in the Availability description (optional).	6.1	rights.cost	Whether use of this learning object requires payment.
CreationInformation.Creation.CopyrightString	Describes one textual label indicating information that may be displayed or otherwise made known to the end user (optional). It is not a formal declaration of the usage rights of the multimedia content.	6.2	rights. copyrightAndOtherRestrictions	Whether copyright or other restrictions apply to the use of this learning object.
DescriptionMetadata.Rights. TextAnnotation.FreeTextAnnotation	Describes the rights associated with the description to which the description metadata is attached and how the description to which this DS is attached can be used. (These rights are described with free text annotation).	6.3	rights.description.string	Comments on the conditions of use of this learning object.

continues on following page

Table continued

MPEG-7 Path	MPEG-7 Definition	LOM#	LOM Metadata Path	LOM Definition
Segment.Relation	Describes a relation that the segment participates in (optional). The relations include structural relations defined in 11.10 and possibly other relations.	7	relation	This category defines the relationship between this learning object and other learning objects, if any.
DescriptionMetadata.Comment.TextAnnotation.FreeTextAnnotation	Describes a free text annotation.	8	annotation	Comments on the educational use of this learning object.
DescriptionMetadata.Creator.Agent.Person.Name	Describes an agent (abstract). The agent can be a person, a group of persons, or an organization. (This definition is for the AgentType).	8.1	annotation.entity	Entity that created this annotation (person, organization).
DesrciptionMetadata.Creator.Agent.Organization.Name	Describes an agent (abstract). The agent can be a person, a group of persons, or an organization. (This definition is for the AgentType).			
DescriptionMetadata.Comment.StructuredAnnotation.Who	Describes animate objects or beings (people and animals) or legal persons (organizations and person groups) using either free text or a term from a classification scheme.			
DescriptionMetadata.CreationTime.TimePoint	Describes the time when the description to which the description metadata is attached was created (optional).	8.2	annotation.date.dateTime	Date that this annotation was created.
DescriptionMetadata.Comment.StructuredAnnotation.When	Describes a time using either free text or a term from a classification scheme.			
DescriptioMetadata.Comment.TextAnnotation.FreeTextAnnotation	Describes a free text annotation.	8.3	annotation.description	The content of this annotation.
CreationInformation.Classification	Describes user oriented and service oriented classification of the multimedia content (optional).	9	classification	This category describes where this learning object falls within a particular classification system.
CreationInformation.Classification.Purpose	Describes one purpose for which the multimedia content was created (optional). An example of CS is IntentionCS.	9.1	classification.purpose	The purpose of classifying this learning object.
CreationInformation.Classification.Genre	Describes what the multimedia content is about (broad classification), such as sports, politics, economics, etc (optional). An example of CS is the GenreCS.	9.2.2	classification.taxon	A particular term within a taxonomy. A taxon is a node that has a defined label or term. A taxon may also have an alphanumeric designation or identifier for standardized reference. Either or both the label and the entry may be used to designate a particular taxon.
CreationInformation.Classification.Subject.TextAnnotation.FreeTextAnnotation	Describes the subject (specific classification) of the multimedia content (optional). The subject allows a textual annotation to classify the multimedia content.	9.3	classification.description	Description of the learning object relative to the stated 9.1:Classification.Purpose of this specific classification, such as discipline, idea, skill level, educational objective, etc.

continues on following page

Table continued

MPEG-7 Path	MPEG-7 Definition	LOM#	LOM Metadata Path	LOM Definition
CreationInformation.Classification.Subject.TextAnnotation.KeywordAnnotation.Keyword	Describes one keyword. A keyword can be a single word or an entire phrase made up of multiple words. For example, "President of the United States" can be treated as a keyword.	9.4	classification.keyword	Keywords and phrases descriptive of the learning object relative to the stated 9.1:Classification.Purpose of this specific classification, such as accessibility, security level, etc.

Structure of the mapping table: The mapping table between MPEG-7 and SCORM Content Package has the same logical construction as the previous table of mapping between MPEG-7 and LOM. It is consisted of five columns; the first column contains the Description Schemes of MPEG-7 and in the next column their definitions, whereas the third column presents the numeration of the elements of SCORM Content Package in accordance with IMS Content Packaging specifications. The fourth column apposes the SCORM Content Package paths and next to them their definitions.

Mapping of basic components: Before the presentation of the mapping table between the Description Schemes of MPEG-7 and SCORM Content Package elements, it is necessary to explain the matching procedure between the fundamental components of the standards. For the audiovisual standard we are talking about segments and for the eLearning model we are talking about SCOs and Assets.

A segment is a temporal and/or spatial unit of multimedia. For example, a video segment corresponds to a temporal unit or group of temporal units of video.

Assets are an electronic representation of media, such as text, images, sound, assessment objects or any other piece of data that can be rendered by a Web client and presented to a learner. The most basic form of a learning resource is an Asset.

A SCO is a collection of one or more Assets that represent a single launchable learning resource that utilizes the SCORM Run-Time Environment to communicate with a Learning Management System. A SCO represents the lowest level of granularity of a learning resource that is tracked by an LMS using the SCORM Run-Time Environment Data Model.

We may decide if a segment identifies a SCO or an Asset from the educational autonomy point of view. More specific, if a segment accomplishes a learning objective then it can be considered as a SCO. When a segment does not provide an educational perspective then it is considered as an Asset. For example, a single image can't be an integrated learning experience by itself. The mapping between segments to SCOs and Assets depends from the segmentation we have determined and whether the segment content reveals a learning autonomy.

The MPEG-7 standard has the Package Description Scheme which organizes and labels the description tools for ease of use and navigation of the description tools. The Package DS allows nesting of package descriptions within package descriptions. The following example presents a package which includes four different tools: ContentCollectionType, DescriptorCollectionType, ConceptCollectionType and MixedCollectionType.

```
Example
<Mpeg7>
<DescriptionMetadata>
<Version>1.0</Version>
<Package name=»Content Organization»>
<Package name=»Collections»>
<Scheme
name=»ContentCollectionType»/>
<Scheme name=»DescriptorCollectionTy
```

```
pe»/>
<Scheme
name=»ConceptCollectionType»/>
<Scheme name="MixedCollectionType"/>
        </Package>
      </DescriptionMetadata>
      <!—more elements here →
</Mpeg7>
```

On the other side SCORM has the Content Package which provides a standard way of learning content exchange among various information systems. Content Package is the place where we describe and organize the structure and the future comportment of a collection with learning content. SCORM define that the package represents a unit of learning (SCORM, 2004b). The unit of learning may be part of a course that has instructional relevance outside of a course organization and can be delivered independently, as a portion of a course, an entire course or as a collection of courses.

The packages of the involved standards may have a coherent matching because they concern the structure and the organization of their tools. These fundamental tools have a common function and role, which is clearly structural and organizational.

The following table reveals the effort of mapping MPEG-7 and SCORM Content Package with emphasis to the mandatory elements.

Table analysis and mapping issues: The Collection Description Scheme of MPEG-7 derives from the Content Organization Tools which describe the organization and modeling of multimedia content. More specific the Collection DS describes unordered collections. Examples include collections of multimedia content, segments, descriptors, concepts, or mixed collections (Figure 4).

The <manifest> element of SCORM Content Package represents a structured inventory of the content of an educational material package. If an educational package is intended for delivery to an end user, the <manifest> also contains information about how the content is organized (SCORM, 2004b). The organizational comportment of commonality between Collection DS and the <manifest> give the ignition for the mapping process.

Figure 4. Overview of the Collection tools. Adapted from MPEG-7

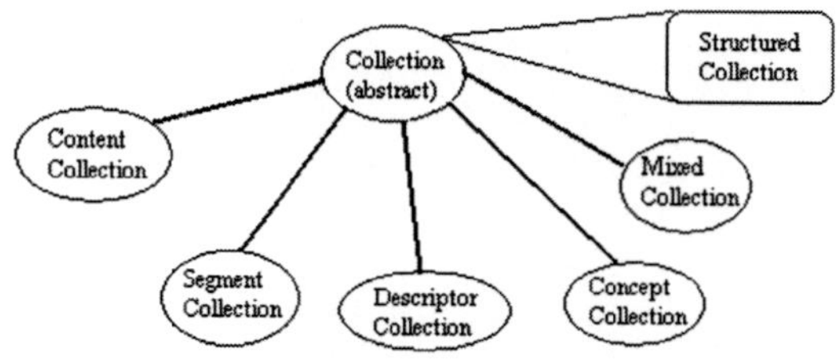

The mapping procedure begins with the Collection Description Scheme of MPEG-7 which is an abstract type that forms the base of the different specialized types of collection description tools, including ContentCollection, SegmentCollection, DescriptorCollection, ConceptCollection, and MixedCollection. The Collection DS allows the metadata production for the content description and authorizes the use of CreationInformation (for describing information related to the creation of the collection) and UsageInformation (for describing information related to the usage of the collection). The {metadata} of the <manifest> are placed in accordance with LOM metadata scheme respectively.

Afterwards the mapping of more specific types of Collection DS, such as ContentCollection DS, SegmentCollection DS and MixedCollection DS follows to the <organizations> element of the <manifest>. The above schemes of MPEG-7 may concerned as "organizations"which describe the structure of the collections and their content allowing a correlation with the <organizations> element of SCORM Content Package. The elements Content, ContentCollection (nested), Segment and SegmentCollection (nested) can be mapped to the <organization> element of the <manifest>

Table of mapping between MPEG-7 concepts and SCORM Content Package

MPEG-7	MPEG-7 Definition	IMS CP #	SCORM Content Package	SCORM CP Definition
Collection	Describes a collection related to multimedia content (abstract). Examples include collections of multimedia content, collections of descriptors, and collections of semantic concepts. CollectionType extends DSType.	1	Manifest	The <manifest> element represents a reusable unit of instruction that encapsulates meta-data, organizations and resource references.
(The metadata of the manifest obey to LOM, so it's going to be a matching only with those metadata which are determined from the mapping between MPEG-7 and LOM. The Collection Description Scheme give us the following schemes for the metadata description, so we have to consult the mapping table of MPEG-7 and LOM and choose the appropriate metadata.) Collection.CreationInformation Collection.UsageInformation	Describes information related to the creation of the collection. Describes information related to the usage of the collection.	1.4.3	Manifest. Metadata. schema.schemaversion. {Metadata}	Meta-data can be inserted into a manifest using an appropriate meta-data scheme. If using meta-data to describe SCORM Content Model Components, ADL highly recommends, at a minimum, the use of the IEEE LOM meta-data scheme.
Collection.ContentCollection	Describes a collection of multimedia content, which can include images, video, audio, sounds, graphics, and so forth. The ContentCollectionType may describe a mix of different types of multimedia content within a single content collection description.	1.5	Manifest.Organizations	The <organizations> element describes one or more structures or organizations for the content package.
Collection.SegmentCollection	Describes a collection of segments, such as video segments, audio segments, still regions, and so forth, which are possibly from different multimedia content. The described segment collection may contain a mix of different types of segments. SegmentCollectionType extends CollectionType.			
Collection.MixedCollection	Describes a mixed collection of content, segments, descriptors, and semantic concepts.			

continues on following page

because all of them concern the description and organization of the content.

Another interesting case is the mapping between the ContentCollection DS, the SegmentCollection DS and the MixedCollection DS with the <item> of the <organization> element of SCORM. The Description Scheme ContentCollection includes the Content element which describes the content of the collection. The syntax of the schema determines that the Content element is MultimediaContent such as Image, Video, Audio, etc. The elements StillRegion, ImageText, VideoSegment, etc. from the Segment Description Scheme and the elements of MixedCollection Description Scheme determine also the same Multimedia Content types. The <item> element of SCORM is a node that describes the hierarchical structure of the organization. The <item> element represents an

Table continued

MPEG-7	MPEG-7 Definition	IMS CP #	SCORM Content Package	SCORM CP Definition
Collection.ContentCollection. Content	Describes content that makes up the described content collection.	1.5.2	Manifest. Organizations. Organization	The <organization> element describes a particular hierarchical organization.
Collection.ContentCollection. ContentCollection(nested)	Describes a child content collection that is nested within the described content collection (optional).			
Collection.SegmentCollection. Segment	Describes a segment that makes up the described segment collection.			
Collection.SegmentCollection. SegmentCollection(nested)	Describes a child segment collection that is nested within the described segment collection (optional).			
Collection.SegmentCollection.Segment.SegmentDecomposition (SpatialSegmentDecomposition/ TemporalSegmentDecomposition/SpatioTemporalSegmentDecomposition/MediaSourceSegmentDecomposition)	Describes decompositions of segments.			
Collection.MixedCollection. Content	Describes content included in the described mixed collection.			
Collection.MixedCollection. Segment	Describes a segment included in the described mixed collection.			
Collection.MixedCollection. MixedCollection(nested)	Describes a child mixed collection that is nested within the described mixed collection.			
Collection.MixedCollection.Segment. SegmentDecomposition (SpatialSegmentDecomposition/ TemporalSegmentDecomposition/SpatioTemporalSegmentDecomposition/MediaSourceSegmentDecomposition)	Describes decompositions of segments.			
Collection.SegmentCollection. Segment.MediaInformation.MediaIdentification.EntityIdentifier	Identifies uniquely the particular and unique multimedia content entity. For example, ISO's ISAN.	1.5.2.1	Organization. identifier	An identifier for the organization that is unique within the manifest file. Typically this value is provided by an author or authoring tool.
Collection.ContentCollection. name	Identifies the name of the collection.	1.5.2.5	Organization. Title	The <title> element describes the title of the organization.
Collection.ContentCollection. CreationInformation.Creation. Title	Describes one textual title of the multimedia content.			
Collection.SegmentCollection. Segment.CreationInformation. Creation.Title	Describes one textual title of the multimedia content.			

continues on following page

Table continued

MPEG-7	MPEG-7 Definition	IMS CP #	SCORM Content Package	SCORM CP Definition
Collection.ContentCollection. Content.Image/Video/Audio/ Audiovisual/Multimedia/Ink-content/AnalyticEditedVideo	(Tools for describing different multimedia content entities. The different multimedia content entity tools correspond to the different types of multimedia content: images, video, audio, AV data, mixed multimedia content, signals, ink content, and edited video.)	1.5.2.6	Organization. Item	The <item> element is a node that describes the hierarchical structure of the organization
Collection.SegmentCollection. Segment /StillRegion/ImageText/Mosaic/StillRegion3D/ VideoSegment/MovingRegion/ VideoText/AudioSegment/ AudiovisualSegment/AudiovisualRegion/MultimediaSegment/InkSegment/Anal. Ed.VideoSegment/EditedVideo/ AnalyticClip/Shot/CompositionShot/IntraCompositionShot/ AnalyticTransition/GlobalTransition/CompositionTransition/ InternalTransition/EditedMovingRegion	Describes a segment that makes up the described segment collection.			
Collection.MixedCollection. Content. Image/Video/Audio/ Audiovisual/Multimedia/Ink-content/AnalyticEditedVideo	Describes content included in the described mixed collection.			
Collection.MixedCollection. Segment. /StillRegion/ImageText/Mosaic/StillRegion3D/ VideoSegment/MovingRegion/ VideoText/AudioSegment/ AudiovisualSegment/AudiovisualRegion/MultimediaSegment/InkSegment/Anal. Ed.VideoSegment/EditedVideo/ AnalyticClip/Shot/CompositionShot/IntraCompositionShot/ AnalyticTransition/GlobalTransition/CompositionTransition/ InternalTransition/EditedMovingRegion	Describes a segment included in the described mixed collection.			
Collection.ContentCollection. Content.Image.MediaInformation.MediaIdentification. EntityIdentifier (EntityIdentifier is an element for all content type).	Identifies uniquely the particular and unique multimedia content entity. For example, ISO's ISAN.	1.5.2.6.1	Organization. Item.identifier	An identifier attribute is an identifier, for the item, that is unique within the Manifest.
Collection.SegmentCollection. Segment.StillRegion.MediaInformation.MediaIdentification. EntityIdentifier (EntityIdentifier is an element for all segment type).	Identifies uniquely the particular and unique multimedia content entity. For example, ISO's ISAN.			

continues on following page

Table continued

MPEG-7	MPEG-7 Definition	IMS CP #	SCORM Content Package	SCORM CP Definition
Collection.SegmentCollection. Segment.CreationInformation. Creation.Title	Describes one textual title of the multimedia content.	1.5.2.6.3	Organization. Item.Title	The <title> element describes the title of the item.
Collection.SegmentCollection	The SegmentCollection DS describes collections of segments, such as video segments, audio segments, still regions, and so forth, possibly from different multimedia content.	1.6	Manifest. Resources	The <resources> element is a collection of references to resources.
Collection.ContentCollection	Describes a collection of multimedia content, which can include images, video, audio, sounds, graphics, and so forth. The ContentCollectionType may describe a mix of different types of multimedia content within a single content collection description.			
Collection.ContentCollection. Content.Image	Describes content that makes up the described content collection.	1.6.2	Manifest. Resources. Resource	The <resource> element is a reference to a resource (SCOs, Assets).
Collection.ContentCollection. Content.Video				
Collection.ContentCollection. Content.Audio				
Collection.ContentCollection. Content.Audiovisual				
Collection.ContentCollection. Content.Multimedia				
Collection.ContentCollection. Content.ImageSignal				
Collection.ContentCollection. Content.VideoSignal				
Collection.ContentCollection. Content.AudioSignal				
Collection.ContentCollection. Content.InkContent				
Collection.ContentCollection. Content.AnalyticEditedVideo				
Collection.ContentCollection. Content.Image/Video/Audio/ Audiovisual/Multimedia/Ink-Content/AnalyticEditedVideo/. UniqueID	Describes the unique identification of a resource. An instance of this datatype contains a value (an identifier) that allows some resource to be identified. The identifying value can be either a textual or a binary value that is encoded in base16 or base64 format.	1.6.2.1	Resource. identifier	The identifier attribute represents an identifier, of the resource, that is unique within the scope of its containing manifest file. This identifier is typically provided by an author or authoring tool.
Collection.ContentCollection. Content.Image/Video/Audio/ Audiovisual/Multimedia/Ink-Content/AnalyticEditedVideo/. MediaLocator.MediaURI	Describes the location of external media data.	1.6.2.3	Resource.href	The href attribute is a reference a Uniform Resource Locator (URL). The href attribute represents the "entry point" or "launching point" of this resource. External fully qualified URLs are also permitted.

continues on following page

Table continued

MPEG-7	MPEG-7 Definition	IMS CP #	SCORM Content Package	SCORM CP Definition
Collection.ContentCollection.Content.StillRegion.MediaLocator.MediaURI	Describes the location of media data in general.	1.6.2.7.1	Resource.File.href	The href attribute identifies the location of the file.
Collection.ContentCollection.Content.VideoSegment.TemporalSegmentLocator.MediaURI	Describes the location of temporal media data such as video and audio.			
Collection.ContentCollection.Content.AudioSegment.TemporalSegmentLocator.MediaURI				
Collection.ContentCollection.Content.AudiovisualSegment.TemporalSegmentLocator.MediaURI				
Collection.ContentCollection.Content.Image/Video/Audio/Audiovisual/Multimedia/ImageSignal/VideoSignal/AudioSignal/InkContent/ AnalyticEditedVideo.CreationInformation.RelatedMaterial	Describes material containing additional information about the multimedia content or related to it.	1.6.2.8	Resource.Dependency	The <dependency> element identifies a resource whose files this resource (the resource in which the dependency is declared in) depends on.
Collection.ContentCollection.Content.Image/Video/Audio/Audiovisual/Multimedia/ImageSignal/VideoSignal/AudioSignal/InkContent/ AnalyticEditedVideo.CreationInformation.RelatedMaterial.MediaLocator.MediaURI	Describes the media location of the related material.	1.6.2.8.1	Resource.Dependency.identifierref	The identifierref attribute references an identifier attribute of a <resource> (within the same package) or a (sub)manifest and is used to resolve the ultimate location of the dependent resource.

activity in the content organization. Taking into account this definition, which reveals the way that content is specialized and organized, the semantic mapping between an Image or a VideoSegment of MPEG-7 with the <item> element of SCORM is possible.

Additionally the scheme SegmentDecomposition describes the decomposition of specific types of multimedia content and their segments. Examples include spatial, temporal, spatio-temporal, and media source decompositions. The <item> element can be nested and repeated within other <item> elements to any number of levels (SCORM, 2004b). This structuring of <item> elements shapes the content organization and describes the relationships between parts of the learning content. Hence it is possible the semantic mapping between the various types of segments, which arise from the Decomposition tools, to a sequence of nested <item> elements.

SCORM Content Package specification states clearly that if an <item> is a leaf node, then the <item> shall reference a <resource> element. If the <item> refers to a <resource> then the <resource> constitutes an identifiable object for distribution and presentation to a learner. For example, an Image or any type of audiovisual content of the MPEG-7 has a UniqueID which can be mapped with the <identifier> of a <resource>.

A generic conclusion from the mapping table is that we may have many correlations between the elements of MPEG-7 and SCORM Content Package. These correlations are declared with multileveled description paths, which show the complexity of the MPEG-7 standard.

FUTURE RESEARCH DIRECTIONS

In general due to the great extensibility and variety of the Description Schemes of the audiovisual standard many MPEG-7 paths may be mapped to a path of the SCORM model. The MPEG-7 Summarization tools of the audiovisual model describe summaries that facilitate discovery, browsing, navigation, visualization and sonification of multimedia content. The Summarization tools enable fast and effective browsing and navigation of multimedia content by providing access to a set of multimedia summaries. A semantic correlation may occur between the specific Description Schemes of the Summarization tools and the components of the SCORM eLearning model.

After the creation of semantic mapping of the involved standards, it is possible the integration of the mapping through an upper ontology. Ontologies provide a shared understanding of a domain of interest to support communication among human and computer agents, typically being represented in a machine-processable representation language. Ontologies offer solutions to the semantic heterogeneity problem (Wache et al., 2001) and can be used in integration architectures as a global schema to which metadata from different sources can be mapped. An upper ontology may capture the meanings of the elements and the attributes of MPEG-7 and SCORM standards and their correlations.

CONCLUSION

Metadata semantic interoperability between the eLearning domain and the audiovisual domain is one of the main issues in the digital environment. This chapter presents an attempt to accomplish that goal, through the mapping procedure between MPEG-7 concepts and SCORM. The mapping process was complex enough because of the great extensibility of MPEG-7 and also because of the different scopes of the involved standards. Some remarks were underlined during the mapping procedure:

- Multileveled and sometimes complexed paths were created for representing the right description schema of MPEG-7. The goal of the proposed methodology was to provide a detailed mapping of the elements of MPEG-7 Description Schemes to the most similar SCORM elements.
- Many – to – one mappings occur. In particular many elements from the source standard MPEG-7 to one element from the target standard SCORM may be mapped. This is observed into both mapping tables.
- Some elements and concepts could not be mapped because of the different scope of the involved standards. The MPEG-7 provides a standardized set of technologies for describing multimedia content while SCORM is a collection of specifications for developing, organizing and delivering instructional content.

In general the proposed methodology reveals rich semantic correlations and can be considered an important tool for resolving interoperability issues among different digital environments. Future researchers must be aware of the importance of metadata for the short as well as the long-term efforts to contribute to the improvement of the world of electronic information resources. The completion of the interoperability puzzle would provide prolifically results to the peer communication.

REFERENCES

Arapi, P., Moumoutzis, N., Mylonakis, M., & Christodoulakis, S. (2007). A Framework and an Architecture for Supporting Interoperability Between Digital Libraries and eLearning Applications. In C. Thanos, F. Borri, & L. Candela (Eds.), *Digital Libraries: R&D*, (LNCS 4877, pp. 137-146). Berlin: Springer-Verlag.

Christodoulakis, S., Arapi, P., Moumoutzis, N., et al. (2006). *Interoperability of eLearning Applications with Digital Libraries*. Poster on the 10th European Conference on Research and Advanced Technology for Digital Libraries (ECDL 2006), September 2006, Alicante, Spain.

Cruz, I. F., & Xiao, H. (2005). The Role of Ontologies in Data Integration. *Journal of Engineering Intelligent Systems, 13*(4), 245–252.

Hodge, G. (2005). Metadata for electronic information resources: from variety to interoperability. *Information Services & Use, 25*(1), 35–45.

IEEE LOM. (2002). *IEEE 1484.12.1-2002 Learning Object Metadata Standard.* Retrieved June, 20, 2009, from http://ltsc.ieee.org/wg12/files/LOM_1484_12_1_v1_Final_Draft.pdf

McLean, N., & Lynch, C. (2004). Interoperability between Library Information Services and Learning Environments – Bridging the Gaps: A Joint White Paper on Behalf of the IMS Global Learning Consortium and the Coalition for Networked Information. *IMS Global Learning Consortium and CNI.* Retrieved June 20, 2009, from http://www.imsglobal.org/digitalrepositories/CNIandIMS_2004.pdf

MPEG-4. (2002). *Systems: Overview.* Retrieved June, 20, 2009, from http://www.chiariglione.org/mpeg/standards/MPEG-4/MPEG-4.htm

MPEG-7. (2001). *ISO/IEC JTC 1/SC 29/WG 11/N3966, Text of 15938-5 FCD Information Technology – Multimedia Content Description Interface – Part 5 Multimedia Description Schemes.* Singapore: MPEG Group.

Ogbuji, U. (2003). *Thinking XML: Learning Objects Metadata.* Retrieved June, 20, 2009, from http://www-128.ibm.com/developerworks/xml/library/x-think21.html

Overview). Retrieved June 20, 2009, from http://www.adlnet.org/scorm/index.cfm

Patel, M., Koch, T., Doerr, M., & Tsinaraki, C. (2005). Semantic Interoperability in Digital Library Systems. *Report of DELOS2 Network of Excellence in Digital Libraries.* Retrieved June 20, 2009, from http://delos-wp5.ukoln.ac.uk/project-outcomes/SI-in-DLs/SI-in-DLs.pdf

Peig, E., Delgado, J., & Pérez, I. (2001). Metadata Interoperability and Meta-search on the Web. *Proceedings of the Internationale Conference on Dublin Core and Metadata Applications.* Retrieved June 20, 2009, from http://www.nii.ac.jp/dc2001/proceedings/product/paper-37.pdf

Pierre, St. M., LaPlant, W. P. (1998). *Issues in Crosswalking Content Metadata Standards.* National Information Standards Organization (NISO). Retrieved June 20, 2009, from http://www.niso.org/publications/white_papers/crosswalk/

Salembier, P., & Smith, J. R. (2001). MPEG-7 Multimedia Description Schemes. *IEEE Transactions on Circuits and Systems for Video Technology, 11*(6), 748–759. doi:10.1109/76.927435

SCORM. (2004a). *Sharable Content Object Reference Model* (4th ed.). SCORM.

SCORM. (2004b). *Sharable Content Object Reference Model (SCORM), Content Aggregation Model, 4th edition, Version 1.0.* Retrieved June 20, 2009, from http://www.adlnet.org/scorm/index.cfm

Vagiati, V. (2006). *Semantic mapping between LOM – SCORM Content Package and MPEG-7 concepts (including the representation of the mapping through an ontology).* Unpublished master's thesis, Ionian University, Greece.

Wache, H., Voegele, T., Visser, U., Stuckenschmidt, H., Schuster, G., Neumann, H., & Huebner, S. (2001). Ontology-Based Integration of Information—A survey of existing approaches. *Proceedings of the IJCAI-01 Workshop on Ontologies and Information Sharing, Seattle, WA* (pp. 108-118).

ADDITIONAL READING

Anido, L. E., et al. (2002). Educational metadata and brokerage for learning resources. *Computers & Education, 38*, 351-374. Retrieved July, 21, 2009, from http://www.sciencedirect.com/

Arapi, P., Moumoutzis, N., & Christodoulakis, S. (2006). ASIDE: An Architecture for Supporting Interoperability between Digital Libraries and ELearning Applications. In *Proceedings of the 6th IEEE International Conference on Advanced Learning Technologies (ICALT 2006), Kerkrade (The Netherlands), 5-7 July 2006* (pp.257-261). Washington: IEEE Computer Society.

Baldoni, M., et al. (2004). Reasoning about learning object metadata for adapting SCORM courseware. In Proceedings of *International Workshop on Engineering the Adaptive Web, EAW'04: Methods and Technologies for personalization and Adaptation in the Semantic Web, EAW 2004*, Eindhoven, The Netherlands (2nd - 5th June 2004). Retrieved July, 21, 2009, from http://rewerse.net/publications/download/REWERSE-RP-2004-35.pdf

Breitman, K. K., Casanova, M. A., & Truszkowski, W. (2007). *Semantic Web: Concepts, Technologies and Applications*. Berlin, Heidelberg: Springer.

Christodoulakis, S., Arapi, P., Mylonakis, M., Moumoutzis, N., Patel, M., Kapidakis, S., Vagiati, V., Konsolaki, H. (2006). *Demonstrator of mapping between the eLearning and AV content description standards*, DELOS Deliverable 5.4.2, 25th July 2006.

Day, M. (2002). *Metadata: Mapping between metadata formats*. Retrieved July 21, 2009, from http://www.ukoln.ac.uk/metadata/interoperability/

Denaux, R., Dimitrova, V., & Aroyo, L. (2004). Interactive ontology-based user modeling for personalized learning content management. *Workshop on Applications of Semantic Web technologies for E-Learning (SW-EL)*. Retrieved July, 21, 2009, from http://wwwis.win.tue.nl/~swale/publications/Denaux-Dimitrova-Aroyo-SWEL-AH04.pdf

Devedžić, V. (2006). *Semantic Web and education*. Boston, MA: Springer Science+Business Media.

Duval, E., Klamma, R., & Wolpers, M. (Eds.). (2007). *Creating new learning experiences on a global scale: second European Conference on Technology Enhanced Learning, EC-TEL 2007, Crete, Greece, September 2007 proceedings*. New York: Springer.

Greenberg, J., & Wolfgang, K. (Eds.). (2008). *Metadata for Semantic and Social Applications: Proceedings of the International Conference on Dublin Core and Metadata Applications, Berlin, 22-26 September 2008: DC 2008: Berlin, Germany*. Göttingen: Univ.-Verl. Göttingen.

Hillmann, D. I., & Westbrooks, E. L. (Eds.). (2004). *Metadata in practice*. Chicago, IL: ALA Editions.

ISO. (2008). *Information technology – Semantic mapping procedure (SMMP)*. Retrieved July 21, 2009, from http://metadata-standards.org/metadata-stds/Document-library/Documents-by-number/WG2-N1201-N1250/WG2-N1217-WD_SMMP_20081119.pdf

Kakali, C., Lourdi, I., Stasinopoulou, T., Bountouri, L., Papatheodorou, C., Doerr, M., & Gergatsoulis, M. (2007). Integrating Dublin Core metadata for cultural heritage collections using ontologies. In *Proceedings of the International Conference on Dublin Core and Metadata Applications (DC 2007), Singapore, 27 - 31August* (pp.128-139).

Koohang, A., & Harman, K. (Eds.). (2007). *Learning Objects and Instructional Design*. Santa Rosa, California: Informing Science Press.

Lesk, M. (2004). *Understanding Digital Libraries*. Amsterdam: Elsevier.

Liu, X., & El Saddik, A. (2005). Multimedia learning object metadata management and mapping tool. In P. Kommers & G. Richards (Eds.), *Proceedings of World Conference on Educational Multimedia, Hypermedia and Telecommunications 2005* (pp. 1392-1400). Chesapeake, VA: AACE.

Miller, P. (2000). Interoperability, what is it and why should I want it? *Ariadne, 24*. Retrieved July, 21, 2009, from http://www.ariadne.ac.uk/issue24/interoperability/

Nilsson, M. (2008). Harmonization of Metadata Standards. *ProLEARN Deliverable D4.7 Final version, January 2008*. Retrieved July 21, 2009, from http://ariadne.cs.kuleuven.be/lomi/images/5/52/D4.7-prolearn.pdf

Nilsson, M., Johnston, P., Naeve, A., & Powell, A. (2007). The Future of Learning Object Metadata Interoperability . In Harman, K., & Koohang, A. (Eds.), *Learning Objects: Standards, Metadata, Repositories, and LCMS* (pp. 255–313). Santa Rosa, California: Informing Science Press.

NISO. (2004). *Understanding metadata*. Retrieved July 21, 2009, from http://www.niso.org/standards/resources/UnderstandingMetadata.pdf

Rowley, J., & Hartley, R. (2008). *Organizing knowledge: an introduction to managing access to information*. Hampshire, England: Ashgate Publishing Limited.

Srinivasan, U., & Nepal, S. (Eds.). (2005). *Managing multimedia semantics*. Hershey: IRM Press.

Stasinopoulou, T., Bountouri, L., Kakali, C., Lourdi, I., Papatheodorou, C., Doerr, M., & Gergatsoulis, M. (2007). Ontology-Based Metadata Integration in the Cultural Heritage Domain. In *Asian Digital Libraries. Looking Back 10 Years and Forging New Frontiers*, volume 4822 of *LNCS* (pp. 165-175). Berlin/Heidelberg: Springer.

Thanos, C., Borri, F., & Candela, L. (Eds.). (2007). *Digital Libraries: Research and Development: First International DELOS Conference, Pisa, Italy, February 2007: Revised selected papers*. Berlin/Heidelberg: Springer.

York, S., & Studer, R. (2005). *Semantic Web technologies for digital libraries*. Retrieved July 10, 2009, from http://www.aifb.uni-arlsruhe.de/WBS/ysu/publications/2005_sw_for_dl.pdf.

KEY TERMS AND DEFINITIONS

Digital Libraries: Libraries in which a significant proportion of the resources are available in machine-readable format, accessible by means of computers.

E-Learning: Any learning that utilizes a network for delivery, interaction or facilitation.

Interoperability: The ability to exchange and use information among computer systems of different types, designed and produced by a different vendor.

LOM: The IEEE LOM Information Model describes the set of data elements that are available to build metadata within the learning community.

MPEG-7: A standard for describing multimedia objects so that they can be accessed in a database.

Semantic Mapping: A method that extracts the semantic relations between each element of a given metadata standard and an element of another standard.

Sharable Content Object Reference Model (SCORM): A collection of standards and specifications for web-based e-learning.

Section 4
Approaches and Issues in Interoperable Applications

Chapter 17
Open Educational Resources in E-Learning:
Standards and Environment

Ricardo J. Rejas-Muslera
Universidad de Alcalá, Spain

Alvaro J. García-Tejedor
Universidad Francisco de Vitoria, Spain

Olga Peñalba Rodriguez
Universidad Francisco de Vitoria, Spain

ABSTRACT

According to Dr. B.R. Ambedkar's definition (Deshpande & Mugridge, 1994), Open Educational Resources (OER) are based on the philosophical view of knowledge as a collective, social product. In the last years the relevance of OER has been widely acknowledged and a high magnitude impact is to be expected for OER in the near future (Atkins et al, 2007), (Wiley & Gurrell, 2009), especially as a masterpiece in e-learning development. The aim of this chapter is to present an overview of OER in e-learning, focused on two fundamental aspects: (i) technical issues, mainly standards, and (ii) socio-economic and legal questions. This way the chapter deals with the most relevant issues in this matter: Which is the OER's role in education, especially for e-learning performance? Which are the technical resources and current standards needed for them? Which socio-economics and legal aspects influence the diffusion and use of OER?

INTRODUCTION

Terry Foote, one of the Wikipedia project's chair-person emphasizes this: "Imagine a world in which every single person is given free access to the sum of all human knowledge" (Wikimedia, n.d.). More and more educational resources, such as OER, are key contributors to the rise of distance learning and e-learning performance: OER includes both open contents (contents free of charge) for teaching and learning as well as tools and services allowing the development and diffusion of those contents. This expression "open educational resources" was first adopted at the UNESCO's 2002 Forum on the Impact of Open Courseware for Higher

DOI: 10.4018/978-1-61692-789-9.ch017

Education in Developing Countries, funded by the William and Flora Hewlett Foundation. Extending this set of concepts, OER reference not only the usual idea of digital resource (like an educative resource in a web format, including text, images or exercises). The OER definition includes other types of materials, such as guidelines on how to teach a determined subject, as well as datasets about the evaluation and performance of determined educative experiences.

OER represent a new approach, when compared to the current vision of the learning and teaching process in which a inherent mercantilism vision exists coming mainly from two sources: the teaching process and the contents development. In particular, OER enable both e-learning where the students do not need to pay tuition fees and in the third world countries without an advanced educational infrastructure.

The incredible possibilities that the diffusion of the OER could have for people in many countries have been noted by various international organizations, such as:

- The UNESCO, through its International Institute of Educational Planning (IIEP, n.d.) has developed an international community interested in OER with more than 600 member for 94 countries;
- The OCDE, across its Educational Research and Innovation Center (ERIC), which have develop an international study about OER; and
- Many private and public institutions like the World Bank or the Massachusetts Institute of Technology (MIT n.d.), which developed the MIT Open Courseware (MITopencourseware, n.d.), in which a lot of different courses are freely available.

In this way a critical reflection about some important aspects related to OER is quite important for the future of distance learning or e-learning. In this way, this chapter presents on overview of OER and their current usage. Following this introduction, the second section "Background. Socio-Economics And Legal Issues In OER" explores socioeconomic and legal issues as the Background in OER development in terms of distance education or e-learning. The socio-economic perspective of OER is focused in the knowledge economy postulates, and especially refers to two points: OER as a representative of the information economy and, in the other hand, the impact that for the third world countries could be the free access of their citizens to a high quality education and especially for their future economies. This socio-economic perspective of OER can be an important educational factor to change, in general terms, these societies and incorporating them to the set of developed countries (Vijay-Kumar, 2009). The section on the legal perspective tackles which legal aspects influence the diffusion and use of OER, especially the Creative Commons licenses as the main legal means for it. The third section analyzes the key factors for the success of the OER initiative from a technical point of view that are mainly accessibility features and standard compliance. Finally in "Conclusions" the more relevant points of the chapter are extracted.

BACKGROUND: SOCIO-ECONOMICS AND LEGAL ISSUES IN OER

The OER movement has his origin in the Open Source Software subjacent philosophy, and is supported in the communications advantages that offer the Information and Communication Technologies (ICTs) and specially the World Wide Web, that way and according with the Foundation Hewlett in the initiative Open Educational Resources: "The World Wide Web presents an extraordinary opportunity for people and institutions everywhere to create, share, and use valuable educational materials" (The William and Flora Hewlett Foundation, n.d.). In this new environment conformed by the ICTs OER and e-learning form a binomial with important socio-economic implications.

There are many definitions of OER. Hylén (Hylén, 2005) defines OER initiatives as a set of items: open courseware and content, open software tools, open material for e-learning capacity building of faculty staff, repositories of learning objects and free educational courses." In Wikipedia appear the most spread definition: OER are "resources offered freely and openly for anyone to use and under some licenses to re-mix, improve and redistribute", and included: Learning content (full courses, course materials, content modules, learning objects, collections, and journals), Tools, and Implementation resources in order to provide a legal framework (Wikipedia, 2009). In any case the subjacent philosophy in OER is not new, in the educational framework the teachers have shared commonly their materials with colleagues and, so much the scientific method, as the revisions for pairs are based on similar fundamentals (Schmidt, 2007). The new factors of this initiative are the IT facilities that allow massive distributions with an easy access and a legal system to organize the access, use and transformation. At a minimum OER are any resource (materials, tools, contents...) in the educational framework without cost to the consumer or user.

Such definitions evidence OER as a wide concept, with deep social and legal implications. In this environment the World Wide Web and specially e-learning techniques and tools, work as an important factor, amplifying the relevance of such implications, as OER can arrive by means of Internet and e-learning, easyly and fastly to any planet corner. In this way socio-economics conditions and legal framework conform the OER's environment, conditioning his creation, development and diffusion, with specific relevance if is e-learning the way of diffusion.

Socio-Economics Issues

There are two main subjects to discuss: OER as unquestionable representative of the knowledge economy postulates, and the OER impact, especially in the third world countries.

The OER, and the Knowledge Economy

OER could be considered as a reference example, in socioeconomic terms, of the knowledge economy wave. OER are (as the rest of educational resources) knowledge codification and therefore a product of primary information sector; in addition they possess a feature that distinguishes them of other economic goods; In education resources as Larsen and Vincent-Lancrin say, "The open sharing of one's educational resources implies that knowledge is made freely available on non-commercial terms", and, in the educational such fact implies that "the innovation impact is greater when it is shared: the users are freely revealing their knowledge and, thus work cooperatively." (Larsen & Vincent-Lancrin, 2006).

In short it seems that the Tragedy of the Commons (Hardin, 1968) postulates are not applicable to the educative resources field. In fact, and in according with the indicated by Larsen and Vincent-Lancrin (Larsen & Vincent-Lancrin, 2006), the effect is the opposite: the OER growth and diffusion is, in the last years, more and more increasing - in the following point some numbers on the subject are provided -. Three main issues support this fact:

The mass consumption of educational resources does not reduce its value: on the contrary, the worldwide diffusion tends to enrich its content through contributions of the educational community. For instance, the Wikipedia project is a successful example of collaborative efforts in this field. In this as well as it has indicated Eric S. Raymond in the Magic Cauldron OER also behave that Open Source Software: OER are an Inverse Commons (Raymond, 2001).

The second circumstance that moves away OER from the Tragedy of commons postulates is the OER author's non-profit aim. Generally will be facilitating the access education to the rundown social and regional areas, or looking for the notoriety in certain sphere of Knowledge. In this point OER are showing an important difference respect others economics goods, whose producers look for the obtaining of economics benefits.

Finally OER are a mind-facture, a knowledge codification product, and therefore an intangible asset. Such nature facilitates its reproduction, revision and improvement, since the different authors are able to act on the resource without physical barriers, circumstance that does not occur in the case of material assets.

Like in the rest of the intellectual property assets, the OER's diffusion depends, in great way, on the World Wide Web, in general, and specially on the e-learning, so allow a fast and economic spreading of OER, and in the specific case of e-learning provide an educational structure to a suitable OER´s use.

The OER Impact, Especially in the Third World Countries

To reaffirm the value of the education supposes to continue maintaining our culture and civilization then, as Guttman (Gutman, 1987) says, the education supposes the "conscious reproduction of the culture", and the persecution of those ideals bound to one more a righter society and human beings better equipped in its heads and more honestly formed in its hearts. As Forrester (Forrester, 2000) advise the investments in educations are indispensable; on them it depends the future and the survival of any civilization. Therefore in the Information Society, it is necessary to vindicate the idea of the education like a moral right and a social necessity, and not only like a mere instrument of creation of the abilities and competitions that demand the new times. All it in order to recover the Homo sapiens in all its fullness, and to stops its drift towards the homo Videns (Sartori, 1998). OER are a resolute bid in favor of it all.

In the first world countries the value of OER is evident in the light of the report Delors (Delors, 1997) who considers the continuous education, like key element in the access to 21st century supported its four basic pillars: Learn to know, learn to do, learn to live together, and learn to be. At the present time to learn constitutes a central process to be able to fulfill oneself in the knowledge society.

The OER production volume is not currently known in a precise manner, but there is evidence that the number of OER initiatives is increasing, in both small organizations and large ones:

- More than 150 universities in China are participating to the initiative 'China Open Resources for Education';
- 11 universities in France are participating to the project Paris Tech OCW, with more than 150 courses;
- 9 universities in Japan under the OCW Japanese alliance, with 250 courses in Japanese and 100 in English;
- 7 universities in the USA, including MIT and the Carnegie Mellon;
- Various university projects in Australia, Brazil, Canada, Hungary, India, Iran, Ireland, etc.

The second question is about the consumer. In this aspect could be easily seen that a wide spread in the OER use could have an extraordinary impact in the socioeconomic development in many countries around the world, especially in the third world countries. This is founded in the fact that the access of last knowledge developed would be more accessible for the people in these countries once the cost wall has been broken. A number of socioeconomic aspects could be improved, such as:

- Medical issues. Medical practitioners, teachers and students can have access to the most recent advances in medicine as well as to therapies in health care. Also for the people in general they could have access to lot more of health related techniques.
- Engineering issues. People related with the engineering and architecture could have access to new construction material and techniques, for instance to reduce costs

- Educational issues. Teachers and students for all degrees could have access to the same knowledge, making easy the mobility in looking for new opportunities.
- A key success factor for a wider use of OER is the diffusion of the knowledge of their existence: therefore, countries and supranational organizations must develop (and support) policies to develop and disseminate information about OER: the OER initiative in both the OCDE and UNESCO are good examples.

OER Legal Perspective

The first consideration, relative to the legal aspects of the open educative resources, must be centered in the type of rights related with the creation of such resources. The intellectual creations, including the literary and educative works, generate intellectual property that is copyrights for their authors. The preoccupation to protect such creations is old and goes back many centuries in history: for example, Marco Vitruvio, in year 25 b.c. in De Architectura, demanded a severe punishment for those who they used, like their own, the thought of other authors. The recognition, and consequently protection, of the Intellectual Property has been tied historically to the scientific, technological and really social progress.

Nevertheless the technological achievements in the field of the Information and Communications Technologies and, more recently, the appearance of electronic and digital media such as Internet, has caused a restructuring process in many economic and social sectors (Kalakota & Robinson, 2001). These changes are affecting in particular the form in which take place the interchanges, publicity and consumption of intellectual works and, among them, educative resources. Prior to the appearance of electronic and digital media and tools, the authors of educational, investigation or educative materials, edited and publish their works by means of physical supports, Internet has radically changed this situations (McCracken, 2006) with digital tools that allow to produce, to publish and to authorize the access to digital products. On the other hand, the Internet appearance favors the worldwide spread of this kind of works, allowing them to easily transcend the geographic and physical borders.

These circumstances, from the legal point of view, indicate the importance of the content of the licenses designed to regulate the digital transaction (conditions of use, distribution, publication, modification and commercialization) of the intellectual goods and, among them, the educational resources (Bissell, 2009). The content of the licenses on open educational resources is varied and heterogeneous: they typically respond to the particular preoccupations of each author on the protection that they want to grant to his work. The RoMEO project conducted in the United Kingdom in 2002 to 2003 a survey of 542 investigators on what type of rights wanted to maintain on their works (Gadd et al., 2003): it was found that more than 60% of the investigators surveyed would allow that third parties exposed, recorded, printed, mentioned or distributed their own articles, provided of course that the corresponding work was quote and as long as all the copies were literal. On the other hand, 55% wanted to limit the use of their works to educative and not commercial uses. The RoMEO report concludes that the protection granted to research articles by the intellectual property law is over which most of academic requests. This circumstance together with the fact that the education can be considered an essential and public good implies that the application, in this field, of the Intellectual Property laws must have certain particularities.

Indeed such particularities have been gathered in a new type of licenses that is having an ample diffusion in the publication and diffusion of opened educational resources. These denominated licenses of open content allow sharing, in controlled way, the copyrights of the author of the resources shown. In this sense, the author provides the equilibrium between his royalties and the right of the society to access to the knowledge (Lessig, 2004). The most extended licenses of this type are the Creative Commons license designed by the Creative Commons organization that was created in 2002 in the university of Stanford by professor Lawrence Lessing, and the GNU Free Documentation License, designed by the FSF (Free Software Foundation). This last one is more oriented to the software documentation, although it also presents certain diffusion in other documentary areas.

Particularly in the educative scope such type of licenses presents the advantage to provide certainty and clarity in the digital access and use of educational, educative or research contents generated by other authors, on the other hand, simplifies enormously the administrative proceedings relative to the transaction of author copyrights and, mainly and very specially, they grant to the author the possibility of designing a customized system of usage rights cession on the generated resources, allowing, for example, to establish a double system, in terms of economic rights:

Free use of the resource for educative or without intention of profit uses, and at the same time, payment for use rights if the work is used with commercial aims. The main goal of these kind of licenses is, within the educative perspective, to establish a legal framework, away from the traditional copyright system, that offer the necessary legal guarantees in the collective interchange of work educational, educating and scientific works, with the aim of spreading the culture, the training and the education.

Taking as example the Creative Commons license, perhaps the most spread at the present time, and centering the analysis in the educative field, the chosen system to carry out the task described in the previous paragraph, has been the development of an application Web that allows the design of six licenses by means of the combination of four variables. The different possible combinations allow the author to personalize the license content to regulate the use of its work. These variables are the following ones:

1. Attribution: You let others copy, distribute, display, and perform your copyrighted work — and derivative works based upon it — but only if they give credit the way you request.
2. Non-commercial: You let others copy, distribute, display, and perform your work — and derivative works based upon it — but for non-commercial purposes only
3. No Derivate Works: You let others copy, distribute, display, and perform only verbatim copies of your work, not derivative works based upon it.
4. Share alike: You allow others to distribute derivative works only under a license identical to the license that governs your work.

By means of the combination of such variables six different licenses can be obtained. They are the following ones:

1. Attribution Non-commercial No Derivatives (by-nc-nd). This license is the most restrictive one, allowing redistribution. This license is often called the "free advertising" license because it allows others to download your works and share them with others as long as they mention you and link back to you, but they can't change them in any way or use them commercially.
2. Attribution Non-commercial Share Alike (by-nc-sa). This license lets others remix, tweak, and build upon your work non-commercially, as long as they credit you and license their new creations under the identical terms. Others can download and redistribute your work just like the by-nc-nd license, but they can also translate, make remixes, and produce new stories based on your work. All new work based on yours will carry the same license, so any derivatives will also be non-commercial in nature.

3. Attribution Non-commercial (by-nc). This license lets others remix, tweak, and build upon your work non-commercially, and although their new works must also acknowledge you and be non-commercial, they don't have to license their derivative works on the same terms.
4. Attribution No Derivatives (by-nd). Choose by-nd license. This license allows for redistribution, commercial and non-commercial, as long as it is passed along unchanged and in whole, with credit to you.
5. Attribution Share Alike (by-sa). Choose by-sa license. This license lets others remix, tweak, and build upon your work even for commercial reasons, as long as they credit you and license their new creations under the identical terms. This license is often compared to open source software licenses. All new works based on yours will carry the same license, so any derivatives will also allow commercial use.
6. Attribution (by). Choose by license. This license lets others distribute, remix, tweak, and build upon your work, even commercially, as long as they credit you for the original creation.

This is the most accommodating of licenses offered, in terms of what others can do with your works licensed under Attribution. Once the author has selected the type of license that best meets his objectives, the system Creative Commons creates a license expressed in three different ways:

1. Commons Deed. A simple, plain-language summary of the license, complete with the relevant icons.
2. Legal Code. The fine print that you need to be sure the license will stand up in court.
3. Digital Code. A machine-readable translation of the license that helps search engines and other applications identify your work by its terms of use.

In order to use the license, the author must include in his Web site a Creative Commons "Some Rights Reserved" button near the work. This button will link back to the Commons Deed, so that the world can be notified of the license terms. Such preventive action allows the author to have legal grounds to sue under copyright breach. In such case, as for all other licenses, the author will be able to sue the violator by contractual breach and infringement of the intellectual property.

The Creative Commons licenses are settled down to perpetuity: that is, it grants protection to the work during all of its existence. Nevertheless such licenses are not of exclusive character: the author has the right to grant other licenses on the same work and to explode, at any time such work under anyone of the licenses that have chosen; also the author is totally free to remove the work or to modify it.

Finally it is necessary to indicate that the original Creative Commons licenses are based on the legislation on Intellectual Property of the United States, that although it is harmonized with the legislation of the rest of the world through treaties of the World Intellectual Property Organization (WIPO), it still presents, with the European legislation, certain differences, sometimes subtle, sometimes considerable. Therefore the licenses are adapted specifically by local lawyers to the regulations of each country.

After this outline of the terms and general characteristics of the Creative Commons license, it is time to analyze another type of license elaborated by this organization, that is the "Developing Nations" license. This specific type of creative commons licenses is that the configuration of its content offers almost limitless possibilities to universalize the education to nations whose citizens lack enough economic resources to access to educational resources under traditional licenses that demand the payment of economic rights. The fundamental aspect of such license is that it allows that the payments for author's copyrights by the use of their works are only demanded in the first world developed countries, whereas the same ones are offered open and free in the "developing nations". Such type of licenses is an important legal instrument for the diffusion of educational resources in opened form, because of its free character to allow the incorporation to the educative dynamics of sectors of the worldwide population that of another form would be excluded.

In addition to the "Developing Nations" license, the Creative Commons organization is looking into other types of licenses within the educational scope:

- The "Sampling License" that allows to unite fragments from different work to form a new work;
- The "Public Domain" License, a type of license specially designed for the United States that allows the author to decide if its work will be of public domain completely, thus resigning to the term of protection that the law grants to the authors, or finally
- The "Founders Copyright" License, similar to the previous license, nevertheless the work does not become immediately to public domain, but after 14 or 28 years from its publication.
- It can be observed that the open educational field is, in legal terms, supported by new types of licenses, generally called open license: they take as a starting point the benefits from the creative interactivity (Vercelli, 2004). Such licenses, on the one hand, are currently offering legal security in the digital interchange of such educative contents and, on the other, are allowing its universalization by means of its diffusion through electronic and digital media and tools such as the Internet.

OER TECHNICAL PERSPECTIVE

Internet and the World Wide Web provide the means for distributing information, in general, and educational contents, in particular, easily, quickly and at low cost, contributing in the last decades to the development of a different way of learning: e-learning.

In this context OER are intended to promote universal access and use of high-quality educational contents on a global scale, so OER should be accessible, reusable and sharable. To achieve this two are, in our opinion, the key factors: accessibility and standards compliance. The first one is crucial to "open" the educational resources to every individual around the world, that is, to break down the barriers that are excluding different groups of individuals from the information society. The second one is necessary to guarantee the reusability and sharability of any educational resource. Both aspects are analyzed in more detail in the next two subsections.

Accessibility and E-Inclusion

Accessibility is normally understood as the ability to access the functionality, and possible benefit, of an information system, and is often used to focus on people with disabilities. In this field, the most important advances come from the Web Accessibility Initiative (WAI, n.d) of the World Wide Web Consortium (W3C). One of the main contributions of the WAI is the *Web Contents Accessibility Guidelines* (WCAG, 2008), which covers a wide range of recommendations for making web content more accessible. Following these guidelines will make content accessible to a wider range of people with disabilities, including blindness and low vision, deafness and hearing loss, learning disabilities, cognitive limitations, limited movement, speech disabilities, photosensitivity and combinations of these. Web accessibility depends not only on accessible content but also on accessible Web browsers and other user agents. Authoring tools also have an important role in Web accessibility. For that reason, the WAI has also published the *User Agent Accessibility Guidelines* (UAAG, 2002) and the *Authoring Tool Accessibility Guidelines* (ATAG, 2000).

Apart from the general web accessibility features, the accessibility of educational contents has become the objective of some standardization initiatives and working groups within the e-learning community, such as those coming from the IMS Global Learning Consortium, described in the next section.

All these guidelines are focused on people with disabilities, as said before. In order to ensure a universal and global access to OER, it is important to take into account other population groups at risk of being excluded from information society developments, due to social, cultural, economical, geographical or other reasons. In this line, research activities and policy initiatives concerned with narrowing the digital divide, which is normally referred as e-Inclusion, should be promoted, especially by governments and other public institutions. As this problem is out of the technical scope, we are not going into more detail in this section.

Standards Compliance

The main goal of standard specifications is to facilitate the share and reuse of components and contents among different users, tools and systems. In the last ten years there has been a great effort in standardization within the e-learning community, with many organizations, consortiums and forums working in the definition of standard specifications that cover most of the aspects of the learning process and systems. The standards, initiatives and proposals can be classified in the following fields, according to the Learning Technologies Standards Observatory of the European Committee for Standardization (CEN-LTSC, n.d): accessibility, application profiles, architectures and interfaces, assessment, collaboration, competency definitions, content aggregation, digital repositories, educational modeling languages, ePortfolios, intellectual property and digital rights, learner information, localization and internationalization, metadata, platform and media, quality, runtime, user interfaces, vocabularies.

Below we present a summary of some of the most relevant standards for the definition, distribution and use of OER. For more information, we recommend to consult the Learning Technologies Standards Observatory of the European Committee for Standardization, where an exhaustive analysis of the current standards in e-learning can be found.

Accessibility

These initiatives are focused not only on people with disabilities. Individual learning styles, preferences and abilities are also considered in order to offer more options and greater flexibility in learning to every possible learner. The IMS Global Learning Consortium is carrying out the main efforts in this field (IMS Accessibility, n.d). The *IMS AccessForAll Meta-data* specification is intended to make it possible to identify resources that match a user's stated preferences or needs. These preferences or needs would be declared using the *IMS Learner Information Package Accessibility for LIP* specification. The *IMS Guidelines for Developing Accessible Learning Applications* provide a framework that will set the stage for what solutions currently exist, what the opportunities and possibilities are for implementing them, and the areas where more development and innovation are still needed to ensure accessibility in education.

More recent activities in relation to accessibility in education are carried out by the ISO/IEC ITLET-Culture, Language and Individual Needs working group (ISO/IEC JTC1 SC36 WG7, n.d), which is defining the standard *ISO/IEC 24751 Individualized Adaptability and Accessibility in e-Learning, Education and Training*, intended to meet the needs of learners with disabilities and anyone in context in which he/she is experiencing a mismatch in learner needs or preferences and education delivery. This is a multipart standard. Parts 1, 2 y 3 have already been published as standards: *ISO/IEC 24751-1:2008 Framework and Reference Model, ISO/IEC 24751-2:2008 "Access for all" personal needs and preferences for digital delivery, and ISO/IEC 24751-3:2008 "Access for all" digital resource description.*

Metadata and Application Profile

Metadata is the collection of data used to describe and catalogue an educational resource. It facilitates the management, search and retrieval of resources from digital repositories or other storage systems.

One of the most popular metadata specifications is LOM, the *IEEE 1484.12.1-2002 Learning Object Metadata* (IEEE LOM, 2002). It describes the structure of a metadata instance for a learning object, being a learning object any entity –digital or not digital– that may be used for learning, education or training. The metadata instance describes relevant characteristics of the learning object to which it applies, characteristics that are grouped into nine categories: general, lifecycle, meta-metadata, technical, educational, rights, relation, annotation and classification.

The *IMS Learning Resource Metadata specification* (IMS Learning Resource Metadata, n.d) has extended the IEEE LOM and provided some guidelines for its use and implementation. It is composed by three parts: the *IMS Learning Resource Meta-data Information Model*, that describes the names, definitions, organization and constraints of the IMS Meta-data elements, and uses the model defined by IEEE LOM; the *IMS Learning Resource Meta-data XML Binding*, that provides a XML implementation and XML control files to assist developers with the meta-data implementations, and uses the IEEE 1484.12.3 Standard for Extensible Markup Language (XML) Schema Definition Language Binding for Learning Object Metadata; and the *IMS Learning Resource Meta-data Best Practice and Implementation Guide*, that provides guidance about how an application may use LOM meta-data.

Another standard for metadata description has been proposed by the Dublin Core Metadata Initiative (Dublin Core, n.d), an open forum for the development of standard for interoperable online metadata. This initiative has been widely used in other fields, like information systems. The *Dublin Core Metadata Element Set* is a reduced and simplified application of the general model to the description of educational resources containing 15 metadata elements. It has been published as an international standard under the number ISO 15836.

When using a metadata standard in a particular application or educational environment, it is sometimes needed to adapt the standard for that particular use, in order, for example, to meet technical and other requirements specific to a project, domain or region, to address ambiguity and generality in the standard specification, or to facilitate testing for conformance and successful interoperability, etc. The adaptation, constraint and/or extension of a meta-data scheme to suit the needs of a particular community is referred as an application profile. The CanCore metadata, for instance, is an application profile of the IEEE LOM.

The IMS Global Learning Consortium has published *IMS Application Profile Guidelines* (IMS Application Profile, n.d) containing two parts: Management Overview, which defines what an application profile is in the context of the IMS specifications and its benefits, and Technical Manual, which describes, from a technical point of view, the profiling of specifications, primarily those developed by the IMS Global Learning Consortium.

Content Aggregation

Other important standard specifications are those related to the way in which educational resources are packaged or encapsulated for their sharing among different learning systems.

The most widely used specification is the *SCORM Content Aggregation Model* (SCORM, 2004). SCORM (*Sharable Content Object Reference Model*) is a set of standards specifications proposed by the ADL initiative. The process of creating and delivering learning experiences involves the creation, discovery and aggregation of simple electronic assets into more complex learning resources and then organizing those learning resources into a defined sequence for delivery. The SCORM Content Aggregation Model defines the technical methods for accomplishing these processes. It includes a Content Model, that describes how learning resources are aggregated into higher-level units of instruction, a Meta-data schema, Content Packaging, that provides the structure and intended behavior of a collection of learning content, and the Sequencing and Presentation, describing how to encode specific sequencing strategies in XML.

The *IMS Content Packaging Specification* (IMS Content Packaging, n.d) provides the functionality to describe and package learning materials, such as an individual course or a collection of courses, into interoperable, distributable packages. Content Packaging addresses the description, structure, and location of online learning materials and the definition of some particular content types. An IMS Package represents a unit of usable content. It includes a XML file called IMS Manifest that contains all the information about the packaged learning materials: metadata (optional), organizations, resources and sub-manifest (optional).

CONCLUSION

The main objective of the work has been to show how OER can change our vision of the educational contents, as we know them, especially in e-learning terms. More possibilities are opening for more people in many countries around the world. The first step was to introduce the concept of Open Educational Resources (OER), dealing with its socioeconomic and legal aspects that conform the OER's environment, conditioning its creation, development and diffusion.

Concerning socio-economic conditions, OER are special knowledge assets. They are "inverse commons". Its consumption does not reduce its value; on the contrary, worldwide diffusion tends to enrich its content through contributions of the educational community. It is a key factor, as OER are designed for massive distribution.

On the other hand OER are Intellectual Property assets. OER´s authors need a proper legal framework to design its access, use and transformation. Initiatives as Creative Commons are working in this sense.

From the technical point of view, the key factors for the success of OER initiatives are accessibility features and standards compliance. The first one is crucial to "open" the educational resources to every individual around the world, that is, to break down the barriers that are excluding different groups of individuals from the information society. The second one is necessary to ensure the reusability and sharability of any educational resource, especially for those standards related to learning contents description, classification and packaging. Both aspects have been briefly discussed in the OER Technical Perspective section.

REFERENCES

Accessibility, I. M. S. (n.d). *Specification*. Retrieved July 22, 2009, from http://www.imsglobal.org/accessibility/index.html

Application Profile, I. M. S. (n.d). *Guidelines*. Retrieved July 27, 2009, from http://www.imsglobal.org/ap/index.html

ATAG. (2000). *Authoring Tool Accessibility Guidelines*. Retrieved October 16, 2009, from http://www.w3.org/TR/WAI-AUTOOLS/

Atkins, D., Brow, J. S., & Hammond, A. L. (2007). *A Review of the Open Educational Resources (OER) Movement: Achievements, Challenges, and New Opportunities*. Report to The William and Flora Hewlett Foundation. Retrieved October 10, 2009, from http://www.oerderves.org/wp-content/uploads/2007/03/a-review-of-the-open-educational-resources-oer-movement_final.pdf

Bisell, A. N. (2009) Permission granted: open licensing for educational resources. *Open Learning: The Journal of Open and Distance Learning,* 97-106. Retrieved October 10, 2009, from http://pdf-serve.informaworld.com/442626__909092757.pdf

CEN-LTSO. (n.d). *Home page*. Retrieved July 19, 2009, from http://www.cen-ltso.net/

Content Packaging, I. M. S. (n.d). *Specification*. Retrieved July 27, 2009, from http://www.imsglobal.org/content/packaging/index.html

Delors, J. (1997). *Learning: The Treasure Within. UNESCO report for Education for the 21st Century*. Berlin, Germany: German UNESCO Commission.

Deshpande, P. M., & Mugridge, I. (1994). Preface. In P. M. Deshpande & I. Mugridge, (Eds.) *Quality Assurance in Higher Education*, (p. iii). Vancouver: The Commonwealth of learning. Dublin Core. (n.d). *Home page*. Retrieved July 22, 2009, from http://www.dublincore.org/

Forrester, V. (2000). *Une étrange dictature*. Paris, France: Librairie Arthème Fayard.

Gadd, E., Oppenheim, C., & Probets, S. (2003). How academics want to protect their open-access research papers. *Journal of Information Science, 29*(5), 333–356. doi:10.1177/01655515030295002

Guttmann, A. (1987). *Democratic Education*. Princeton, NJ: Princeton University Press.

Hardin, G. (1968). The Tragedy of the Commons. *Science, 162*(3859), 1243–1248. doi:10.1126/science.162.3859.1243

Hylén, J. (2005). *Open educational resources: Opportunities and challenges*. OECD-CERI. Retrieved June 22, 2009, from http://ihs.se/upload/3331/OpenEducationalResources%20-%20Opportunities%20and%20Challanges.pdf

IEEE LOM. (2002). *Draft standard*. Retrieved July 22, 2009, from http://ltsc.ieee.org/wg12/files/LOM_1484_12_1_v1_Final_Draft.pdf

IIEP, International Institute for Education Planning. (n.d.). *Home page*. Retrieved June 22, 2009, from http://www.iiep.unesco.org/

ISO/IEC JTC1 SC36 WG7. (n.d). *Home page*. Retrieved July 22, 2009, from http://isotc.iso.org/livelink/livelink?func=ll&objId=4920256&objAction=browse&sort=name.

Kalakota, R., & Robinson, M. (2001). *E-Business 2.0: Roadmap to Success*. Boston, MA: Addison-Wesley.

Larsen, K., & Vincent-Lancrin, S. (2006). The Impact of ICT on Tertiary Education: Advances and Promises . In Foray, D., & Kahin, B. (Eds.), *Advancing Knowledge and the Knowledge Economy*. Cambridge, MA: MIT Press.

Learning Resource Metadata, I. M. S. (n.d). *Specification*. Retrieved July 27, 2009, from http://www.imsglobal.org/metadata/index.html

Lessig l. (2004) *Free Culture* [On line]. New York: The Penguin Press. Retrieved Octobre 14, 2009, from http://www.free-culture.cc/freeculture.pdf

McCracken, R. (2006). *Cultural responses to open licences and the accessibility and usability of open educational resources*. Retrieved June 20, 2009, from http://www.oecd.org/dataoecd/48/38/36539322.pdf

MIT. (n.d.). *Home page*. Retrieved July 10, 2009, from http://web.mit.edu/

MIT OpenCourseware. (n.d.). *Home page*. Retrieved June 20, 2009, from http://ocw.mit.edu/OcwWeb/web/home/home/

Raymond, E. (2001). *The Cathedral & the Bazaar. Musings on Linux and Open Source by an Accidental Revolutionary*. Sebastopol, CA: O'Reilly Media, Inc.

Sartori, G. (1998). *Homo videns. La sociedad teledirigida*. Madrid: Taurus.

Schmidt, J. P. (2007). *Recursos educativos abiertos: estrategia para apertura y desarrollo social de la Educación Superior*. Global University Network for Innovation GUNI. Universia. Retrieved June 20, 2009, from http://www.universia.net.co/secciones-home/en-abierto-portada/los-recursos-educativos-abiertos-como-una-estrategia-para-la-apertura.html.

SCORM. (2004). *SCORM 2004* (4th Ed.). Retrieved October 16, 2009, from http://www.adlnet.gov/Technologies/scorm/default.aspx

The William and Flora Hewlett Foundation. (n.d.). *Education section*. Retrieved June 25, 2009, from http://www.hewlett.org/oer

UAAG. (2002). *User Agent Accessibility Guidelines*. Retrieved October 16, 2009, from http://www.w3.org/TR/WAI-USERAGENT/

Vercelli, A. (2004). *La conquista silenciosa del ciberespacio: Creative Commons y el diseño de entornos digitales como nuevo arte regulativo en Internet*. Retrieved June 02, 2009, from http://www.arielvercelli.org/lcsdc.pdf

Vijay-Kumar, M. S. (2009) Open Educational Resources in India's national development. *Open Learning: The Journal of Open and Distance Learning,* 77-84. Retrieved October 10, 2009, from http://pdfserve.informaworld.com/531234__909097030.pdf

WAI. (n.d). *Web Accessibility Initiative home page*. Retrieved July 16, 2009, from http://www.w3.org/WAI/

WCAG. (2008). *Web Contents Accessibility Guidelines*. Retrieved July 16, 2009, from http://www.w3.org/TR/WCAG20/

Wikimedia Foundation. (n.d.). *Home page*. Retrieved June 16, 2009, from http://wikimedia-foundation.org/wiki/Home

Wikipedia. (2009). *Open educational resources*. Retrieved July 12, 2009, from http://en.wikipedia.org/wiki/Open_educational_resources

Wiley, D., & Gurrell, S. (2009) A decade of development... *Open Learning: The Journal of Open and Distance Learning*. 11-21. Retrieved October 10, 2009, from http://pdfserve.informaworld.com/39175__909097159.pdf

KEY TERMS AND DEFINITIONS

Accessibility: The ability of a system or a piece of information to be accessible, that is, universally accessed by all kind of users. The term is normally focused on people with dissabilities. When refered to IT systems it is called e-Accesibility

e-Inclusion: Also called "*digital inclusion*". Term used to describe the research activities and policy initiatives concerned with narrowing the digital divide, helping the development of an inclusive information society

E-Learning: Distance learning using Information and CommunicationTechnology support

Knowledge Economy: Economic sector based on the production, transformation or consumption of immaterial goods

OER Licenses: Licenses to define and design copyrights on OER

OER: Any resource (materials, tools, contents...) in the educational framework without cost to the consumer or user

Standard Specifications: Guidelines and rules for designing and creating educational contents and tools so that they can be used and shared among different learning management systems and users.

Chapter 18
Interoperability of Web-Based Education Systems

Natalia I. Hughson
University of Advancing Technology, USA

ABSTRACT

The global society is becoming a reality. Inevitably this leads onto questions around the generation and exploitation of knowledge. Education systems grow to be more complex and interdependent. The Web makes a large number of learning resources within reach of anyone with Internet access. However, many valuable resources are difficult to use due to the lack of interoperability among various education systems. In this chapter, the fundamental principles of interoperability of complex and dynamic global education system are presented. The contemporary approaches to systems theory, entropy and autopoietic theory, social system theory, sociocybernetics, the strengths and limitations of these approaches, and their potential applications in education are examined. The nature of educational systems can be linked to biological concepts. When education principles and cybernetics are combined, the resulting theory turns on scientific principles instead of philosophical speculations. Proper utilization of such principles provides methodology that increases the effectiveness of web-based education systems.

INTRODUCTION

Education around the world is facing challenges that are an outgrowth of globalization, challenges that manifest themselves in ways that are increasingly common among different countries.

The speed at which the world is changing, the increasing complexity of life, and the complex nature of work are the defining characteristics of the modern time (IMF, 2000). The global society is becoming a reality. Inevitably this leads onto questions around the generation and exploitation of knowledge. An increasing group of scholars and lawmakers is arguing that the incoherency and fragmentation of the traditional education is a growing problem. What is needed is systemic reform that connects educational systems around the globe allowing the possibility of re-using

DOI: 10.4018/978-1-61692-789-9.ch018

instructional materials both within the same e-learning system and, even more, across different systems (Kuehn, 1999)

The assumption we start from is that an e-learning system (or a set of interoperating e-learning systems) can be interpreted and understood in the same way researches approach complex systems.

Modern systems theory provides a new paradigm for the analysis of society. While social system theory, entropy and autopoietic theory have been familiar approaches within general systems theory for years, they were, until recently, generally seen as applications within physical science or biology, with little or no application to education. According to systems theory, society is its communications: they are its empirical reality; the items that can be observed and studied. Systems theory identifies how communications operate within a physical world and how different sub-systems of communication operate alongside each other. Four fundamental systems approaches – Bertalanffy' General Systems Theory (1968) Miller's living systems theory (1978), Luhmann's Social Systems Theory (1995) and Bailey's (1994) social entropy theory are examined.

There are several important ideas linked to the emergence of education systems: first, that education systems evolve in response to the human need to survive in an environment where they are competing with many other systems for scarce resources; second, that humans survive and flourish by efficiently using their resources and energies; and third, that the evolution of education systems is a function of an ongoing cybernetic process involving all societal systems and their components.

The chapter is organized as follows. First, systems approach to education will be discussed with attempt to connect social system theory, entropy and autopoietic theory to modern view of the teaching/learning process. The nature of education systems can be linked to biological concepts. When education principles and cybernetics are combined, the resulting theory turns on scientific principles instead of philosophical speculations.

Second, several meanings of the concept of modularity in education systems are presented and discussed. "From molecules in a cell to organs in a body, from animals in a colony to ecosystems in the biosphere, patterns exist everywhere. But patterns are also the realm of art and human enterprise" (Callebaut, 2005, P. 181). There is a universality of patterns, which permeated education systems on various levels. Perhaps the concept of modularity would open the door to the elaboration of standards that promote higher functionality and interoperability of such systems.

The third section discusses the importance of interoperability. Interoperability is the ability of two or more networks, systems, devices, applications or components to exchange information between them and use the information so exchanged (OSJTF, 2009). In globalized society the increasing diversity of systems and applications, interoperability makes possible the development of a mass market and avoids the undesirable effects of fragmentation. There is desperate need at increasing the reuse of "learning objects", reducing their development effort and providing interoperability of content across delivery and management systems. Additionally, there exists a diverse collection of both public and private content repositories and digital libraries containing these learning and content objects (Miklos and Sobering, 2008).

IMPORTANCE OF SYSTEMS APPROACH TO EDUCATION

Human experiences are accumulated as a reservoir of knowledge, which influences positive changes in society known as a progress. The maximum adaptation in society depends on availability and proper utilization of knowledge by individuals as well as social groups. When members of a society or communities/institutions fail to acquire proper knowledge and skills, feedback arises that affects their lives in both subtle and obvious ways. Thus, the way in which people learn, apply and expand existing knowledge is linked to a cybernetic process that maximizes human survival.

Bailey (1994) points out many specific strengths of the systems approaches, that provide

- a framework for holistic analysis, macro-analysis, multidisciplinary analysis, and multidimensional analysis
- needed methodological rigor (e. g., critique of equilibrium, methodological analysis of the micro-macro link, the Q-R distinction, and three-level analysis), as well as an inventory of concepts and new vocabulary (e.g., autopoiesis, structural coupling, three-level model, etc.).
- a more methodological operationalization and theoretical specification of the problem of order; present an analysis of boundary theory; and link matter/energy and information.
- a new approach to see the relations between action/structure, process/structure, or agency/structure.
- a context for the analysis of conflict, interaction, networks, and a comprehensive specification of salient macro variables.
- an understanding of hierarchy and levels of analysis (eight system levels each with 20 critical subsystems), and space-time in social systems (diachronic analysis).
- an analyses of self-reproduction and self-regulation (autopoiesis), and action and order; dealing with complexity reduction through systems; and emphasizing change via entropy and non-equilibrium analysis.
- a relationship to ideational and empirical levels of analysis, and offer an analysis of systems philosophy and systems technology.
- a comprehensive framework (which does not preclude, exclude, or denigrate any line of inquiry) for diachronic comparison, both between and within groups.
- a foundation for cultural and normative analysis dealing with issues relating to the observer and the observed.

Scholars have extended the application of systems approaches to fields such as semiotics, knowledge and cognition, culture, music, language, and literature (Altmann and Koch, 1998).

Basic principles of systems theory can be applied to educational system in the following ways:

1. Educational systems arose and always existed within a special set of societal/environmental parameters to which it was originally adapted, and that subsequently influenced the course of evolutionary development of all kinds of educational institutions.
2. All such systems interact with their surroundings in complex ways, and the consequences of these interactions affect the outcomes for both the system and its surroundings.
3. Educational systems at all levels, and as a total system, always interacted with its societal/environmental surroundings in ways unique to the definition of education, and this constituted a form of non-linear control function that led to changes, both in the patterning of education and in the patterning of the societal environment that hosted education.
4. Social including educational systems have evolved towards more complex and elaborated patterns of organization at all levels of analysis.
5. Systems that co-evolve in any dimensions toward greater size or complexity, often expressed in terms of trait-complex hypertropism, find it more difficult than average to evolve back to simpler and smaller systems. Such systems reach what Bertalanffy called "an ecological cul-de-sac and an evolutionary precipice."

6. Systems development is historically irreversible. Systems tend towards increasing differentiation, and once differentiated, cannot as such return simply to more basic states. Increasing competition in the short run leads ultimately to either termination or modification with improvement.

A FUNCTIONAL PARADIGM OF EDUCATION SYSTEMS

Webster defines *education* as the process of educating or teaching. *Educate* is further defined as "to develop the knowledge, skill, or character of..." The word "education" derives from the Latin *educare*, meaning "to nouris'" or 'to raise."

The purpose of education is to develop the knowledge, skill, or character of students. It is commonly acknowledged that humans can neither perceive nor intuit perfect pictures of an absolute Truth. "With considerable more humility, we are satisfied with defining knowledge as the body of structured sets of the most reliable hypotheses of cause-effect relations yet constructed in that formal, public inquiry process by which we have learned to test human experience. It is the process of science" (Hutcheon, 2001, p.1).

All societal systems of a certain order and level of integration, including educational system, share certain basic principles of organization and functional interaction that demonstrate common patterns that raise fundamental questions:

1. Genesis: how education evolved, and what were the prerequisite conditions for such occurrence in the social history?
2. Dynamics: how do educational systems change evolutionarily with the function of time?
3. Sociocybernetics: how do educational systems transmit themselves through time in terms of their informational capacities?
4. Systematics: how do educational systems become integrated and increasingly diverse and complex over time?
5. Globalization: how does integration of educational systems of various nations constitute a single global educational system that interacts and actively reshapes the societal environment and forms its own contexts?
6. Network: how do different educational systems co-exist together in complex interactions and create mutual social environments that influence their development?

These six predicaments shape a general model of educational systems knowledge in a coordinated manner. Not only the answers to these questions are important, what is more significant is an understanding of how interconnections and interactions between each of the areas may help educators to analyze and improve functioning of such systems. Placed together, these fundamental perspectives constitute a kind of paradigm that forms educational system.

According to Bailey (1994), successful modeling of a complex social system requires special attention to the following problems:

1. An adequate definition of the system

Figure 1. Interaction of the Education System with the Society

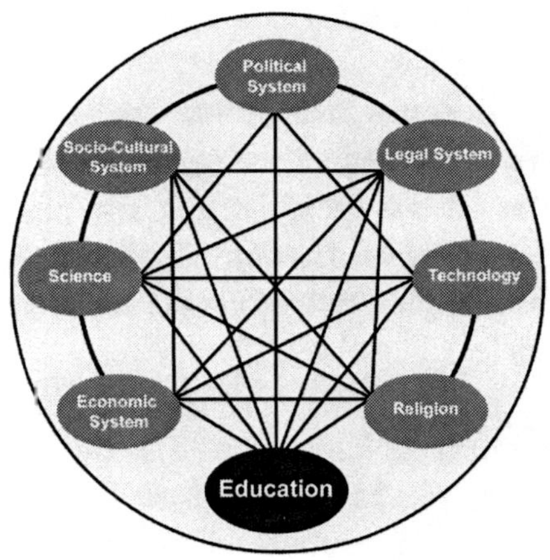

2. An adequate specification of the boundaries for the system as a whole, for systems components, and for subsystems (if any) and their components.
3. An adequate measure of system state and adequate operationalization of such a measure
4. The attainment of isomorphism between the theoretical systems model and the actual operating, empirical, complex system
5. The selection of a suitable set of explanatory variables out of almost infinite number that could be identified in a complex social system
6. An adequate understanding of the relationship among the components of the system and between each component, and the whole, to overcome the problem of unwitting displacement of scope
7. An adequate analysis of both micro and macro levels and their interrelationships to solve or avoid problems such as reductionism and emergence
8. A recognition of the needs of individuals and subgroups within the system and of the systems as a whole
9. An adequate defense against the critics that the systems analysis is an inappropriate organic or mechanical analogy
10. The recognition of individual, subgroup, and systems goals and an understanding of how they are attained
11. An understanding of the role of matter - energy and information in ongoing system functioning
12. An adequate diachronic analysis of the system, to understand change over time
13. The adequate explanation and prediction (including verification) of salient aspects of the complex system via the social systems model.

According to Banathy (1987), every educational enterprise has four subsystems regardless of context (e.g., public education, corporate

Figure 2. Banathy's Educational Enterprise

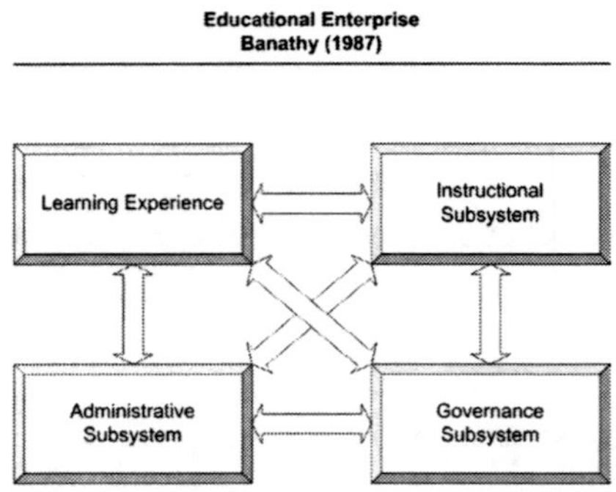

training, health education, military training, and higher education).

Learning experience - the learning experience subsystem. The learner processes information from the environment to construct knowledge or modify cognitive structures.

Administrative - Administrative subsystem. Administrators use information about instructional needs, as well as input from governance, to make decisions about resource allocation, including use of leadership

Instructional (ISD) - Instructional subsystem. Instructional designers and teachers use information about learning needs (determined from analysis activities), as well as administrative and governance input, to produce environments or opportunities for learners to learn

Governance - Governance subsystem. Owners (responsible/accountable people) use their goals and values to influence activities in the system, such as produce policies, leadership, provide resources, in order to meet the needs of stakeholders (learners, teachers, administrators).

Instructional subsystem as a basic unit of education system comprises multiple interdependent components.

Vanderstraeten (2006) examined the concept of 'socialization' that demonstrates the relationships between individual, education and society. He indicates that individuals have to interiorize the values, norms and knowledge forms upon

Figure 3. Instructional Systems Design

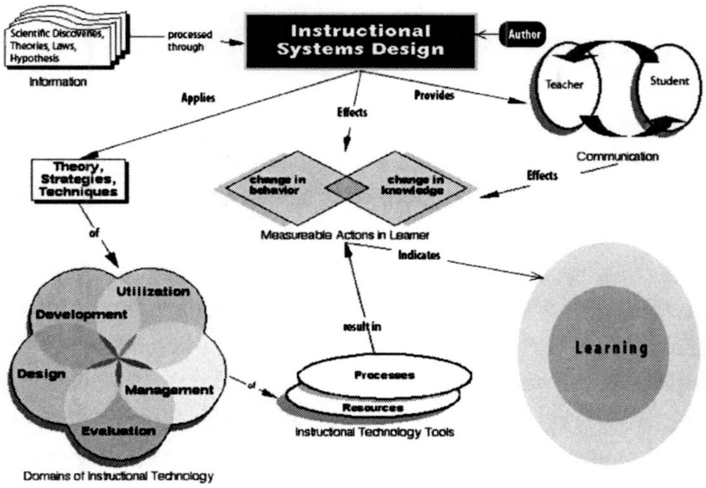

which the continuation of societal memes depends. Vanderstraeten questioned this typical meaning and analyzed the consequences of a hypothesis formulated by Heinz von Foerster (1961). Following this hypothesis, the more an element of a system acts 'trivially' (i.e. predictably), the weaker its influence on the global behavior of the system. Or - as von Foerster stated it metaphorically - individuals who act trivially will feel more 'alienated', because they will not 'recognize' themselves in their group's activities. Inversely, the more individual acts non-trivially, the greater his impact on the group, and the less his alienation is. Two conclusions of this hypothesis follow:

(1) The relations between the values which guide an individual's activities, and the social values which socialization/education are expected to transmit to assure individual and social well-being, do not have to be simple and rigid. Differences in this regard might account for processes of social evolution.
(2) The particular lay-out of classrooms (one teacher, several students) with their apparatus of tests seems to provoke almost inevitably a certain 'trivialization' of individuals. But one might also suspect that this constellation precisely invites deviant activities of pupils who oppose the processes of 'trivialization.' Intentional socialization creates its own side-effects.

EDUCATION AS AN OPEN, COMPLEX, ADAPTIVE, AND COGNITIVE SYSTEM

An open, complex, and adaptive system interacts with its environment, drawing certain inputs from the environment and converting it to outputs that are offered to the environment. The attainment of its preferred state is dependent on the efficiency with which it accomplishes its goals. It posses the following characteristics:

- A system is defined by its properties
- A system is a physical and/or conceptual entity composed of interrelated and interacting parts existing in the environment with which it may also interact
- The system has a preferred state
- The parts of the system may in turn be systems themselves
- A perfectly adaptive system can respond to any change or contingency in the environment

- All systems lie somewhere between non-adaptive and perfectly adaptive systems.
- In order to continue existing, any open system in a dynamic environment must adapt
- Cognitive systems have certain parts that are capable of thought. A single human being is a simple example of a cognitive system
- Cognitive systems are aware of their existence. More than this, they are to a greater or lesser extent aware of the relationship between the system and the environment
- Higher level cognitive systems will also attempt to change the environment to a state more suited to the system's preferred state.

Comparative Characteristics of Physical and Conceptual Systems

According to Luhmann (1995), autopoietic systems produce their own basic elements; they are self-organizing insofar as they create their own boundaries and internal structures; they are self-referential insofar as their elements refer to the system itself; and they are closed systems insofar as they do not deal directly with their environments, but rather with representations of their environments.

Table 1. Education system can be defined as an open, complex, adaptive, cognitive system.

Physical Systems	Conceptual Systems
Examples of Systems' Entities	
• an atom • a human being • the solar system • a factory • a machine	• a family • an economy • a religion • a government • a college
Components and Subsystems	
• atoms in a molecule • organs in a human body	• sectors of business • industries in an economy
Preferred State	
• atomic Hydrogen prefers to be molecular Hydrogen • Iron metallic prefers to be iron oxide (rust)	• firm prefers to be profitable • human being prefers to be physiologically and psychologically healthy

Society is an autopoietic system. Luhmann (1995) believes that the most basic element of society is communication, and anything that is not communication is part of a society's environment (e.g., biological and psychic systems). Both psychic and social systems — which are environments for each other — rely on meaning. In Luhmann's theory, meaning is comprehensible because of contingency. In other words, meaning emerges only because a specific action is different from other possible actions.

Double contingency refers to the fact that every communication must consider the way in which it will be received. In Luhmann's view, social structures (e.g., roles and norms) make it more likely that communications will be understood by both sender and receiver. Social structures also give communications some continuity over time. Double contingency thus provides much of the impetus for the evolution of social systems.

A complex adaptive system, Buckley (1998) said, must include four basic mechanisms.

1. Some degree of "plasticity" and "irritability" *vis-a-vis* its environment such that it carries on a constant interchange with environmental events, acting on and reacting to it.
2. Some source of variety, to act as a potential pool of adaptive variability to meet the problem of mapping new or more detailed variety and constraints in a changing environment.
3. A set of selective criteria or mechanisms against which the "variety pool" may be shifted into those variations in the organization or system that more closely map the environment and those that does not.
4. An arrangement for preserving and/or propagating these "successful" mappings.

An educational system as any social system must deal with the variety in its environment. In addition to its structure-maintaining features, it requires a structure elaborating and changing feature. As a result, in considering the term "steady-state", Buckley (1998, p. 47) said, it must "... not be identified with a particular structure of the system." In order to maintain a steady-state, the system must be capable of changing its structure. In describing these mechanisms Buckley uses the term "morphogenesis."

Evolution of Education Systems

Persistence in an adaptive complex system requires that essential variances in the system be held within certain limits. This maintenance may depend on pattern reorganization structuring, destructuring and restructuring, at widely varying rates and degrees as a function of the external social and non-social environment.

MODULAR VS. MONOLITHIC STRUCTURE OF COMPLEX ADAPTIVE EDUCATION SYSTEMS

Patterns infuse the universe at all levels of organization. Patterns are also the realm of education with common themes that recur over and over in fundamentally different systems and subsystems.

Modularity is defined through a process that starts by recognizing patterns or events that repeat at some scale of observation. "The way we partition an object in order to study it determines our perception of its modularity" (Callebaut, 2005, P. 181).

This section of the chapter is devoted to making sense of modularity as a recognizable, observable feature in complex education systems.

Simon's (1994) characterization of modularity in dynamical systems describes subsystems as having dynamics that are approximately independent

Table 2.

Historical Period	Pre-Literate Societies	Beginning of Civilization	Industrial Age	Information Age	Future (Speculation)
Means of Communication	Oral	Oral Written	Oral Written Printed	Oral Written Printed Radio Video Electronic	Oral Radio Video Electronic- Visual Instant
Educational Technology	Storytelling Imitation	Parchment Papyrus Paper	Printed Books Structured Curriculum Pedagogy	Variety of Instructions Flexibility of Curriculum Distance Education Androgogy	E-Books Distance Individual Specialized Flexible Simulation-Based Entertaining
Availability of Information	Person-to-Person	Highly Limited	Public		Globally Available
Educational Institutions	None	Schooling	Primary Secondary Higher Vocational	Primary Secondary Higher Vocational Training Adult/Continuing Alternative	Modularity High Variety Distance Individual Specialized No Teachers
Accessibility of Education	Do not apply	Available to Nobility Only	Available to Majority	Available to each Individual	Available to each Individual

of those of other subsystems (in the short term). This fits with the general intuition that modules must, by definition, be approximately independent. In the evolution of complex systems, such modularity may enable subsystems to be modified and adapted independently of other subsystems, whereas in a nonmodular system, modifications to one part of the system may result in deleterious side effects elsewhere in the system. But this notion of modularity and its effect on evolvability is not well quantified and is rather simplistic. In particular, modularity need not imply that intermodule dependences are weak or unimportant.

In dynamical systems this is acknowledged by Simon's suggestion that, in the long term, the dynamical behaviors of subsystems do interact with one another, albeit in an "aggregate" manner—but this kind of intermodule interaction is omitted in models of modularity for evolvability. In this brief discussion we seek to unify notions of modularity in dynamical systems with notions of how modularity affects evolvability. This leads to a quantifiable measure of modularity and a different understanding of its effect on evolvability.

In summary, basic properties of modules include:

1. There is informational overlap across modules, but on average each module is unique both in set of instructions and in the way these instructions are presented to learner.
2. Modules are often repeated and conserved in different and similar context.
3. There is strong connectivity within, and weak connectivity among modules. Different modules are semiautonomous during both development and evolution.
4. Modules vary and change over time.
5. Modules exist at a variety of levels.

A module is a set of some disassembly and/or non-disassembly components or parts. It usually is used not only in supporting or carrying out the same function, but also in decreasing the complexity of a system in maintenance. Traditionally, the module form of a system is created according to either the function requirements or the desing considerations. It is determined mainly depending on the individual condition of systems in designing, and has no concrete and scientific approach to progress system modularity. (TSAI, Y-T.; WANG, K-S.; LO S-P., 2003).

Modules are clusters of components that interact with their environment as a single unit. They provide the most widespread means of coping with complexity, in both natural and artificial systems.

Modularity can increase exponentially the number of possible task organization configurations achievable from a given set of requirements and capabilities, greatly increasing the flexibility of education systems. Modularity is a general systems concept: it is a continuum describing the degree to which a system can be separated and recombined, and it refers to both the tightness of coupling between elements and the degree to which the rules of the system enable (or prohibit) the mixing and matching of components' capabilities (Winther, 2005).

According to Rasmussen and Niles (2005), nature proved early on that in complex systems, modular designs are the ones that survive and thrive. An important contributor to this success is the critical reliability advantage of fault tolerance, in which a modular system can shift operation from failed modules to healthy ones while repairs are made.

Why the modular, multi-celled design in biological world prevails over the entrenched monolithic design? Borrowing idea of modular design from living systems and applying it to educational systems may increases their

- *Ability to scale and grow.* System growth, both in size and in addition of new capabilities, could be accomplished simply by adding new modules that could interact with existing ones using standard interfaces.

- *Simplification of the process of duplication.* Duplicating a number of smaller, less complex modules is easier, faster, and more reliable than duplicating a single complicated one.
- *Ability to specialize the function of modules.* Delegation and specialization of module tasks provides the same effectiveness and efficiencies inherent in teamwork. Drawing parallel with living systems, in the early multi-celled organisms, one kind of cell could be for locomotion, another kind for protection, another kind for sensing food, and so on.
- *Rapid adaptation to the constantly changing environment.* By adding, subtracting, or modifying modules, incremental design changes could be more quickly tried and either adopted or rejected.
- *Fault tolerance.* With modules redundancy, individual module could fail without degrading the system, allowing for concurrent module repair without system downtime (disintegration or degradation of educational system in this case).
- *Enhanced Performance.* Modularity enables the delivery of up-to-the-minute information and quick interactive response time for heavy user loads.
- *High Efficiency.* Less load and memory usage per server connection is required, resulting in higher performance and better efficiency of the server, which, in turn, translates into more users per server.
- *Uncomplicated Administration.* Installation and administration of the application is simple, saving the administrator time and effort, while giving end-users easy and secure access to the information they need.
- *Fully Customizable.* Modular education is fully customizable so as to cater to the different needs and requirements of various educational institutions.
- *Version Upgrades.* By providing regular version upgrades to introduce new technical and functional information, as well as latest statutory requirements that may arise from time to time, organizations can be assured that the application will never become obsolete, both technically and functionally.

Not surprisingly, modularity in education becomes fashionable. The reasons are well-rehearsed - new generation of students with new needs and mixed modes of study, credit frameworks, blurring boundaries between academic disciplines, new integrations between 'academic' and 'vocational' programs, claimed cost-effectiveness – require increasing flexibility and adaptability of education systems (Kalfoglou and Hu, 2007; Di Nitto and Tedesco, 2008).

The curricular case for well-designed modular programs is also well-rehearsed – student choice, learner autonomy, flexibility for individual student circumstances, adaptability to new modes of learning and assessment, speed of response to external pressures and agencies, openness to new kinds of knowledge and new connections. As with all things, however, its potential strengths are its possible weaknesses. Poorly designed modular programs are vulnerable to intellectual incoherence, to problems with continuity and progression of learning, to loss of student identity and to excessive bureaucracy. It may be that such charges can equally be leveled at some non-modular courses (coherence is not guaranteed by length of course and lack of student choice) but it seems true that modular programs are prone to fragmentation unless carefully designed and monitored.

Modularity can be approached from several angles.

I. Structural and functional modules

Callebaut (2005) suggested that it is useful to distinguish modularity of structure from modularity of process. Module is a unit that is a component part of a larger system and yet possessed of its own structural and/or functional identity (Moss, 2001, p. 91). Modules are internally integrated and relatively independent from other modules. They must persist as identifiable units for long enough time spans, and they must be more or less identical, repetitive, and reusable 'building blocks' of larger wholes and/or different systems (Muller and Newman, 2003).

Important characteristics of educational modules are congruence principles in order to incorporate them into large systems such as class, course, or program.

- Goal-directed modules. Goal-directed are characterized by plasticity and persistence. Such systems do not always achieve their goals, but they do show persistence when obstacles are put in their way, and they also exhibit plasticity in that they tend to have multi-le ways of achieving their end state (Brandon, 2005).

EDUCATION SYSTEMS INTEROPERABILITY

According to Merriam Webster dictionary, interoperability is the ability of a system to work with or use the parts or equipment of another system.

Technological advances in communication provide learners as well as educators with unique opportunity to expand teaching/learning environment far beyond traditional classroom. To take advantage of this situation, new services were developed, and the search, classification, organization, and peer-to-peer exchange of learning resources by learners, instructors, and course developers are becoming commonplace. Metadata helps to carry out these tasks, and several specifications for learning objects were produced. Related to them, specialized search engines and indexing tools for learning were also made available.

However, to find the appropriate learning resource is not enough. The learning objects developed for a particular system may not be reusable in others. Formats for animations, videos, simulations, educational games, and multimedia are standards or well-known specifications, but to offer them to learners, these elements should be organized in a structured way, because they usually need to be processed by software tools prior to delivery. Additionally, information related to the interaction of learners with these contents should also be generated. Content structure formats maintain the static and dynamic structure of learning object aggregations. There are also specifications available for course packaging, to facilitate the transfer of courses among systems. In a similar way, it is necessary to manage information about learners, and their interaction with courses. All these elements have been considered by several international projects and most relevant standardization bodies (Van Assche, et al, 2006).

Also, the increasing use of the Internet and its technological capabilities, in addition to the huge amount of learning resources, allowed a high number of technology-based learning platforms to show up. As they are usually developed *ad-hoc*, to meet the requirements of a particular institution, heterogeneous systems appear with no interoperability mechanism among them. When these systems are reviewed, our conclusion is that they provide very similar functionalities: content delivery, learner tracking, learner management and administration, questionnaires evaluation, communication and collaboration facilities, search tools, etc. Therefore, we can state that most online learning systems share some common functionality, usually implemented from the scratch by each one of them. In this sense, software reuse would be a must to reduce the *time-to-market* factor.

On the other side, there is a lack of interoperability mechanisms among heterogeneous platforms. Such mechanisms would allow, for instance, that a particular online learning system would provide its own content delivery module, which uses a common learner administration system provided by an external institution and, maybe, developed by a different vendor.

The identification of a common architecture, composed of basic software components that provide open interfaces, would contribute to both reuse and interoperability. Standardization would be reflected here through the definition of agreed interfaces for these components.

This convergence is becoming more apparent from a systemic perspective, particularly from a data needs viewpoint.

According to Saito and Simon (2008), interoperability - defined as the capability of different systems to share functionalities or data - has become a hot topic for educational technologists. From the educational point of view the increasing attention for interoperability research has been driven, for example, by

- the desire to collaborate on the development of content (maybe stored in multiple systems),
- the need for making content accessible in or via various systems (re-use),
- cross-organizational, collaborative learning and teaching,
- sharing of assessment data for the purpose of effective personalization of learning environments.

Economical motivations for interoperability include:

- securing investments in content development,
- making designs of learning environments exchangeable (good practices),
- increasing the user value of the systems provided by integrating components of other systems,
- allowing specialization in the field, so that vendors can focus on particular aspects of the educational
- value chain (e.g., content creation, assessment, skill management).

From the information systems (IS) design point of view interoperability is required in order to

- break up the technological isolation of learning management systems and alike by fully integrating them in a company's IT infrastructure,
- get access to crucial data stored in legacy systems,
- integrate business process-driven solutions with learning management,
- reduce time for and costs of system integration by providing reference specifications.

Park, J. and Sudha R. (2004) reviewed nine fundamental approaches to systems interoperability:

1. *Semantic interoperability.* Semantic interoperability is the ability for disparate systems to understand the semantics, or meanings, or each other despite incompatibilities in data formats, data meanings, etc. Semantic interoperability exists at the knowledge level and results from incompatibilities in implicit meanings, perspectives and assumptions. This is contract to syntactic interoperability which exists at the application level. Syntactic interoperability often happens in the form of software conflicts.
2. *Mapping-based approach to developing systems with semantic interoperability.* In this approach, it is necessary to develop or construct mappings between the information sources that are related semantically. This is accomplished by developing a federated or global schema, then constructing mappings between the federated schema and the local schemas for each information system. The problem with this approach is that it is not independent of the federated and local sche-

Figure 4. Interoperability of Education Systems

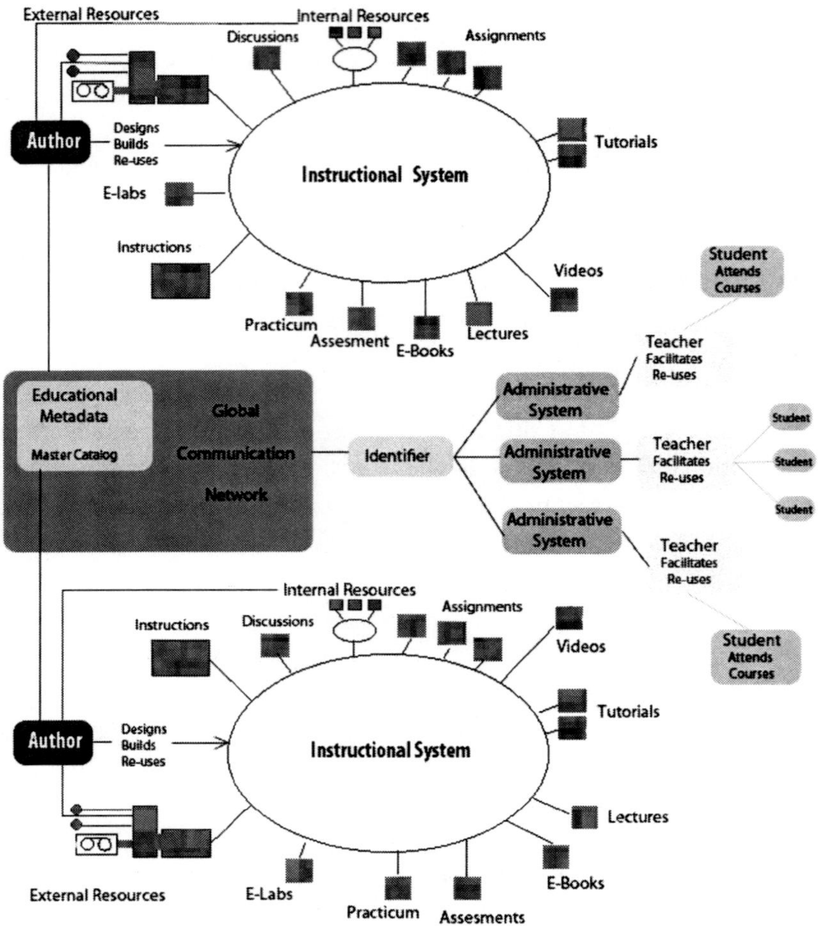

mas for which it is developed. This means the solution is not portable and does not adapt well to the addition of new systems.

3. *Intermediary-based approach.* This approach relies upon the development of intermediary mechanisms such as mediators, agents or ontologies in order to achieve interoperability. Most often, this approach relies upon created ontologies which allow the use of shared standardized vocabularies or protocols to allow systems or databases to communicate with each other. The ontology is domain specific, but is independent of local schemas and applications. As such, it is not feasible to maintain such ontologies due to the dynamic, autonomous and heterogeneous nature of local schemas.
4. *Query-oriented approach.* The query-oriented approach depends upon interoperable languages (usually logic-based languages or extended SQL). The important way that this approach stands out is in its ability to formulate queries to span several databases. The main drawback to this approach is that a heavy burden is placed upon the user to understand the differences in the different

databases and to resolve semantic conflicts themselves.

5. *Data level conflicts.* One level where semantic conflict can occur is at the data level. Generally, data level conflicts are differences in data which can be caused by multiple representations and interpretations of similar data. Examples of data level conflicts are data-value conflicts, data representation conflicts, data-unit conflicts, and data precision conflicts. Data-value conflicts are conflicts in data values. Data values may mean different things depending on their relationships to other factors. Data representation conflicts happen when the same data is represented in different ways (dates can be represented as 9/17/2006, 17-9-2006 and/or September 17, 2006). Data-unit conflicts are those where the same values are represented in different units – feet, yards, meters, etc. Data precision conflicts happen when the same type of data is represented in ways that differ conceptually. For example, different systems may rate the same item, but use different rating schemes.
6. *Schema level conflicts.* Schema level conflicts involve differences at the structural level of the systems. Examples of schema level conflicts are naming conflicts, entity-identifier conflicts, schema-isomorphism conflicts, generalization conflicts, aggregation conflicts, and schematic discrepancies. Naming conflicts happen when labels of the same schema elements are different from local schema to local schema. Entity-identifier conflicts arise when different primary keys are assigned to the same concepts in different databases.
7. *Schema-isomorphism conflicts* happen when the same concept is described by different, non-compatible attributes. Generalization conflicts occur when concepts or data values are modeled differently in various databases. As an example, the category of students can be classed in different ways – by year of graduation, school affiliation, etc. Aggregation conflicts happen when "aggregation is used in one database to identify a set of entities in another database" (Park and Ram, 2004). Schematic discrepancies arise when the data structure in one local schema has a different structure in another one.
8. *Schema mapping knowledge.* The schema mapping knowledge is created by establishing mappings between the disparate local schemas and then mapping the local schemas to the federated schema. It is essential that semantically similar concepts, ideas and data are identified. Park and Ram point out that human intervention is essential in this part of the system development process. This makes the schema mapping knowledge one of the most important parts of the CREAM model developed by Park and Ram.
9. *Ontology relationship knowledge.* This knowledge is the foundation of the reasoning process for semantic resolution. In this knowledge structure there are three different types of relationships: parenthood, sibling and domain-value relationships. The parenthood relationship is a vertical relationship (parent to child). The sibling relationship is a horizontal relationship between constructs or concepts. The domain-mapping relationship is used by the "semantic mediators to determine whether the actual data values that are mapped to instances can be transformed from one value to another and vice versa" (Park and Ram, 2004).

According to Miklos and Sobering (2008), effective interoperable model designers have to address the following questions:

- The standard requirements for learning content repositories that participate in a metadata

- The core policy and rules that repository must support
- The minimal constraints on system architecture and design
- The implications for consistent implementations that is needed for interoperability
- The relevant technologies
- The pertinent specifications, e.g., web, search, libraries, identifiers, learning technologies
- Connections of technologies and specifications into a consistent framework and model

The resulting model must support a set of core capabilities:

- "published" content wide availability
- content persistence outside of the context of a single course or other learning structure or delivery paradigm
- simple discovery of the content
- standard mechanisms for content access;
- content management (ownership, rights, access, provenance, persistence);
- the needs of the participating organizations and institutions satisfaction through customized operations
- employment of the open standards-based interoperability
- integration of and with current systems for repositories, management and content delivery.

Additionally, it is important to take into account some attributes of successful large infrastructure development. By observing the evolution of infrastructures in the past, it is possible to minimize current problems. History has shown that successful infrastructures

- evolved from local to global. They start with a local system for local uses and users, and then connect with other local systems to build the broader network
- grew in size and importance with demand and a cyclic feedback loop: more demand increased use and size, which increased demand, attracting more users
- used primarily core, scalable, reliable, existing technology.

Existing technology is refined, extended and adapted to build the infrastructure. No core technologies are created directly for the sole purpose of creating the infrastructure. Such infrastructures posses curtain qualities proved them being successful:

- have open connections and interfaces specified through minimal interoperability standards. Anyone who meets the stated interoperability requirements is permitted to join the network. Interconnection requirements are limited to only those essential for successful operations.
- seamlessly connect from source to sink. Provide a single model and approach for the user, eliminating technological impedance barriers between the interconnected elements and automating the flow of information or payload from its origin to its final destination.
- enable value-added services. Provide only core features in the common infrastructure, and support mechanisms for others to independently add their own services and features under their own business models.
- provide separate levels of functionality. Maintain independence, both in technology and management, of features such as generation, transport, delivery, and management.
- focus on the right users. Know who from the user community (developers, end-users, managers, individuals, businesses,

etc.) are key players and provide the functionality that they need.

- handle peak demand and fractional use. Know what the peak demands are, and build a system to support those, but understand that individual users have smaller demands. Users will need only a fraction of the power of the infrastructure at any time.
- enable local operations and policy. Allow the participants in the infrastructure to operate under their rules and policies.
- provide differentiated services. Identify when a single level of service or model will not suit all users and provide appropriate different models for different groups, possibly at different costs associated with the level of service.
- apply appropriate policies and governance. Both local and global management of the infrastructure are critical.
- make appropriate business decisions. Participants will all have different value propositions, and the solution must be attractive to both providers and consumers.
- move to ubiquitous or universal service. Provide a system that can provide a minimal level of service to all users.
- build systems, not components or payload. Focus on the infrastructure itself, both as technology and management.

CONCLUSION

Education is an open, complex, adaptive, cognitive system composed of multiple modules. Comparative analysis of systems theory, entropy and autopoietic theory, social system theory, and sociocybernetics demonstrates applicability of their principles to education systems. Proper utilization of such principles addresses a questions central to education theory: what are fundamental components of education as a system? How those components interact in the modern time globalized society? How to make such interaction more efficient?

Unlike conventional systems theory, this research seeks to provide an answer in terms of a general social theory: a methodology that answers these questions in a manner applicable not only to education, but also to all the other complex and highly differentiated systems within modern society, such as economy, politics, science, religion, the media, and technology. This truly sociological approach offers profound insights into the relationships amidst various components of the complex education system.

REFERENCES

Altmann, G. & Koch, W. (1998). *Systems: New Paradigms for the Human Sciences.*

Anido-Rifón, L., Santos-Gago, J., Ródríguez-Estévez, J., Caeiro-Rodríguez, M., Fernández-Iglesias, M., & Llamas-Nistal, M. (n.d.). *A Step ahead in E-learning Standardization: Building Learning Systems from Reusable and Interoperable Software Components*. Retrieved May, 2009 from http://images.google.com/imgres?imgurl=http://www2002.org/CDROM/alternate/136/p136-anido-fig04.gif&imgrefurl=http://www2002.org/CDROM/alternate/136/&usg=__n7yXle7JiYJJQgaH9CY9uVtPzGc=&h=524&w=565&sz=22&hl=en&start=10&tbnid=IUxNGh8krRHfYM:&tbnh=124&tbnw=134&prev=/images%3Fq%3Dinteroperability%2Bof%2Beducational%2Bsystems%26gbv%3D2%26hl%3Den%26sa%3DG Berlin/New York: Walter de Gruyter.

Bailey, K. (1994). *Sociology and the New Systems Theory*. Albany, NY: State University of New York Press.

Bailey, K. (2006). Living systems theory and social entropy theory. *Systems Research and Behavioral Science*, *23*, 291–300. doi:10.1002/sres.728

Baker, P. (1993). Chaos, order, and sociological theory. *Sociological Inquiry*, *63*, 12–22. doi:10.1111/j.1475-682X.1993.tb00300.x

Banathy, B. H. (1987). Instructional systems design. In Gagne, R. M. (Ed.), *Instructional technology: Foundations*. Hillsdale, NJ: Lawrence Erlbaum.

Bertalanffy, L. (1968). *General System Theory: Foundations, Development, Applications*. New York: George Braziller.

Brandon, R. (2005). Evolutionary Modules: Conceptual Analyses and Empirical Hypotheses. In *Modularity: Understanding the Development and Evolution of Natural Complex Systems* (pp. 51–61). Cambridge: MIT Press.

Buckley, W. (1967). *Sociology and Modern Systems Theory*. Upper Saddle River, NJ: Prentice Hall.

Buckley,W. (1968). *Modern Systems Research for the Behavioral Scientist*.

Buckley, W. (1998). *Society—A Complex Adaptive System: Essays in Social Theory*. New York: Routledge.

Callebaut, W. (2005). Evo-Patterns: Working toward a Grammar of Forms. In *Modularity: Understanding the Development and Evolution of Natural Complex Systems* (p. 181). Cambridge, MA: MIT Press.

Foerster, H., & Psk, G. (1961). A Predictive Model for Self-Organizing Systems. Part I: *Cybernetica,* 3, pp. 258–300; Part II. *Cybernetica*, *4*, 20–55.

Forrester, J. (1994). System Dynamics, System Thinking, and Soft OR. *System Dynamics Review*, *10*(2-3). doi:10.1002/sdr.4260100211

Heims, S. (1991). *The Cybernetics Group*. Cambridge, MA: MIT Press.

Heylighen, F. (1996). *Complex Adaptive Systems*. Retrieved November, 2007 from http://pespmc1.vub.ac.be/CAS.html

Hutcheon, P. (2001). *The Classroom as a Social System*. Retrieved November, 2007 from http://www.humanists.net/pdhutcheon/Books/classrm.htm

IEEE. (1990). *IEEE Standard Computer Dictionary: A Compilation of IEEE Standard Computer Glossaries*. New York: IEEE.

Kuehn, L. (1999, October). *Responding to Globalization of Education in the Americas— Strategies to Support Public Education*. Presentation to IDEA conference, Quito, Ecuador.

Kuhn, T. (1962). *The Structure of Scientific Revolutions*. Chicago: University of Chicago Press.

Luhmann, N. (1995). *Social systems*. Stanford, CA: Stanford University Press.

Merriam Webster On-Line Dictionary http://www.merriam-webster.com/dictionary/interoperability

Miller, J. G. (1978). *Living Systems*. New York: McGraw-Hill.

Miller, J. G., & Miller, J. L. (1992). Greater Than the Sum of its Parts I. Subsystems which Process Both Matter-Energy and Information. *Behavioral Science*, *37*, 1–38. doi:10.1002/bs.3830370102

Moss, L. (2001). Deconstructing the gene and reconstructing molecular developmental systems. In Oyama, S., Griffiths, P., & Gray, R. (Eds.), *Cycles of Contingency: Developmental Systems and Evolution* (pp. 85–97). Cambridge, MA: MIT Press.

Open Systems Joint Task Force (OSJTF). Retrieved May 2009 from http://www.acq.osd.mil/osjtf/termsdef.html

Park, J., & Ram, S. (2004). Information Systems Interoperability: What Lies Beneath. *ACM Transactions on Information Systems*, *22*(4), 595–632. http://scruffynerf.wordpress.com/2006/11/01/system-interoperability/. doi:10.1145/1028099.1028103

Provost, W. (2005). *Contingency and Complexity in the Social Theory of Niklas Luhmann*. Retrieved November, 2007 from http://www.geocities.com/~n4bz/lusoc/lusoc0.htm

Simon, H. (1995). Near decomposability and Complexity: How a Mind Resides in the Brain. In Morowitz, H. and Singer, J. (eds), *Mind, the Brain, and Complex Adaptive Systems*, (pp. 25-44). Santa Fe Institute Studies in the Sciences of Complexity, Proceedings vol. 22. Reading, MA: Addison-Wesley.

Tsai, Y., Wang, K., & Lo, S. (2003). A study of modularity operation of systems based on maintenance consideration. *Journal of Engineering Design, 14* (1), 41-56. Retrieved April, 2009 from http://www.ingentaconnect.com/content/tandf/cjen/2003/00000014/00000001/art00003;jsessionid=w7frr1f2c99s.alexandra

Van Assche, F., Duval, E., Massart, D., Olmedilla, D., Simon, B., & Sobernig, S. (2006). Spinning Interoperable Applications for Teaching & Learning using the Simple Query Interface. *Journal of Educational Technology & Society*, *9*(2), 51–67.

Vanderstraeten, R. (2006). *Sociocybernetics, socialization, education*. Retrieved November, 2007 from http://www.unizar.es/sociocybernetics/congresos/MONTREAL/absg1.html

Vanderstraeten, R. (2006). *Sociocybernetics, socialization, education*. Retrieved November, 2007 from http://www.unizar.es/sociocybernetics/congresos/MONTREAL/absg1.html

Walker, L. (2006). *The New Higher Education Systems, Modularity and Student Capability*. Retrieved from http://www.heacademy.ac.uk/assets/york/documents/resources/heca/heca_md02.pdf

Watson, R., & Pollack, J. (2006). *Modular Interdependency in Complex Dynamical Systems*. Retrieved May, 2009 from http://www.mitpressjournals.org/doi/abs/10.1162/106454605774270589?cookieSet=1&journalCode=artl

Werner, C. (2005). The Ubiquity of Modularity. In *Modularity: Understanding the Development and Evolution of Natural Complex Systems* (pp. 3–29). Cambridge, MA: MIT Press.

Winther, R. (2005). Evolutionary Developmental Biology Meets Levels of Selection: Modular Integration or Competition, or Both? In *Modularity: Understanding the Development and Evolution of Natural Complex Systems* (pp. 61–99). Cambridge: MIT Press.

World Economic Outlook. (2000, May). Asset Prices and the Business Cycle. Retrieved April 2009 from http://www.imf.org/external/pubs/ft/weo/2000/01/index.htm

KEY TERMS AND DEFINITIONS

System: is a combination of independent but interrelated elements comprising a unified whole.

Sociocybernetics: Is a theoretical framework based upon the General Systems Theory and cybernetics for responding to the basic challenges individuals, couples, families, groups, companies, organizations, countries, international affairs are facing today.

Autopoietic Theory: Explains fundamental relations between structure and function as well as their interactions and transformations.

Chapter 19
Diagnostic and Formative E-Assessment in Engineering on a Moodle-Based VLE

M. C. Mora-Aguilar
Universitat Jaume I, Spain

J. L. Sancho-Brú
Universitat Jaume I, Spain

ABSTRACT

Electronic learning is nowadays a reality that has been possible due to the recent advances in technology. Different new Web tools have been developed to be directly applied to the teaching/learning process at all levels, especially in higher education. In fact, e-learning tools are the key elements for carrying out educational innovation when dealing with overcrowded groups of students. This e-tools applied to assessment are analyzed in this chapter. In particular, diagnostic and formative e-assessment implemented on a Moodle-based VLE environment has been introduced in different basic Mechanics subjects, with similar contents but taught in different engineering degrees, in diverse years or with various group sizes. The benefits and underlying problems of this introduction are described here. This has been made in order to compare results of different subjects and to extract general conclusions, which could be extrapolated to any other engineering disciplines.

INTRODUCTION

In the last years, the development of the Information and Communication Technology (ICT) has allowed the creation of new Web tools which can be directly applied to the teaching/learning process. These tools allow the lecturer to experiment with new strategies impossible to carry out using classical teaching methodologies.

In addition, the new generation of students is very interested in information technologies,

DOI: 10.4018/978-1-61692-789-9.ch019

circumstance that allows accomplishing changes in the traditional education paradigm, as the introduction of e-learning tools.

Together with the development of e-learning, current trends in teaching methodologies are based on an individual support of the students to be performed by lecturers, turning their classical role of "transmitter of knowledge" into a new one of personal supervisor that guides the students in the construction of their own knowledge. The role of student gains significance in the learning process and his/her active participation is promoted, along with a formative and continuous learning assessment.

In spite of the fact that this motivating methodology introduces a lot of advantages for the students, sometimes the big number of students attending university classes prevents the lecturer from performing educational innovation in a direct manner. In this process, e-learning tools are the key elements able to compensate the lack of resources necessary to carry out the translation to the new educational paradigm when dealing with overcrowded groups of students. In fact, e-learning tools can substitute or complement traditional methods, giving more effective experience to the learner.

In this context, this chapter describes the introduction of e-learning tools in two Mechanics engineering subjects with the aim of performing educational innovation. These subjects have a big number of enrolled students, a factor that hinders the introduction of new teaching methodologies. The main goal of the chapter is to encourage the students to a continuous study of the subjects through the implementation of a contionuous assessment methodology, without increasing the academic workload. For this purpose, Moodle-based e-tools (Moodle, 2007) have been used in order to develop diagnostic and formative assessment within both subjects. The first one – diagnostic assessment – provides the instructor with information about students' prior knowledge and misconceptions before beginning the subject. The second one, the formative assessment, takes place during the learning activity and provides the instructor with information on how well the learning objectives of a given activity are being met. Similar e-tools have been used for both kind of assessment. The methodology explained here is based on previous work of the authors (Mora-Aguilar et al., 2008; Mora-Aguilar et al., 2009).

Remark that the same methodology has been applied in both subjects and the results obtained have been compared. Finally, general conclusions have been drawn that can be extrapolated to other engineering disciplines.

BACKGROUND

To begin with, it will be useful to define some of the terms included in the broad vocabulary that has recently appeared related to e-learning, closely related to the application of the ICTs to the teaching-learning process.

Nowadays, the electronic learning or e-learning (Streng et al., 2008) is experiencing a rapid development. This term includes the teaching-learning strategies that use Web technologies via the Internet as main support. Typically, this type of training involves a physical distance between the transmitter and the receiver, that is, between lecturer and student.

The increase in distance learning courses that have appeared during the last few years is closely related to the popularization of the Internet. In fact, emerging trends in ICT are in line to use web technology to stimulate social relationships with tools such as social networks, wikis, or blogs. For that reason, the concept of social network, also known as Web 2.0 (O'Reilly, 2005), has arisen. Similarly, the term e-learning 2.0 refers to the use of these "social" Web technologies in the field of education.

There are several specific technologies developed for educational purposes, with the two main systems being LMS (Learning Management

Systems) and LCMS (Learning Content Management Systems) (Rengarajan, 2001), whose main difference is that the former focuses on the management of the learning process while the second is more focused on the management of the learning content. There are various platforms that offer both types of approaches. Some of these platforms are privative software, such as webCT, eCollege and Desire2Learn, while others are open-source, such as Moodle, Sakai, Claroline, or ATutor.

In the present time, most universities have adopted one of these platforms to manage their e-learning courses. However, not every LMS/LCMS existing platform includes updated e-learning 2.0 tools, such as blogs or wikis. In particular, at the Universitat Jaume I, a Moodle-based free platform has been developed and is widely used. This platform is called "Aula Virtual" ("Virtual Classroom") (Aula Virtual, 2007) and it is an LMS-type system, although it can also be referred as CMS (Course Management System) or VLE (Virtual Learning Environment). Under the "Aula Virtual" different distance activities can be carried out and scored, content available to students can be managed, and tasks performed during the course can be supervised. Fortunately, Moodle is treating the challenge from Web 2.0 seriously and is gradually incorporating different "social" e-tools into the e-learning environment.

Teaching-learning methodologies that combine face-to-face and distance activities are framed on the concept of blended learning or b-learning (Ginns & Ellis, 2007), also referred to as hybrid learning or mixed mode learning. The new methods are involved in face-to-face courses in various degrees, ranging from an eventual help (leaving some documents accessible via the Internet) to an almost complete covering of the course (activities on the Web, streaming classes, etc.). The integration of e-learning and classical approaches depends on the particular features of the subject and the students, being currently a topic of educational research (Kelly et al., 2007; Barnard et al., 2009). Many institutions are adopting b-learning approaches maintaining consistency with their traditional values (Garrison & Kanuka, 2004).

In large groups these mixed methods can greatly facilitate the work of lecturers, reducing the time spent on correction tasks. In fact, the so-called e-assessment (electronic assessment) arises from the use of Web-specific tools for assessment. It can be used to assess theoretical knowledge (using e-testing software) as well as practical skills (using e-portfolios or simulation software). Most of the above-mentioned e-learning software platforms incorporate this kind of tools, such as multiple choice or short answers questionnaires. This type of testing allows the automatic marking, which saves lecturer time and provides an immediate feedback to students. Even some of them are able to customize the formative assessment to the particularities of the student (Lazarinis et al., 2009; Boticario & Santos, 2007).

An e-testing system basically includes an assessment engine and a question bank. The assessment engine includes the software to create and deliver a test. The software does not include the questions themselves, but these are provided by the question bank, created by the lecturer. The engine uses the question bank to generate a test that will be answered by the student.

E-assessment has many advantages over paper-based assessment. The advantages include economical and ecological savings (as no paper is used), instant feedback to students, flexibility in place and time, reliability (machine marking is much more reliable than human marking) and enhanced question styles incorporating interactivity and multimedia material. Unfortunately, there are also some drawbacks: e-assessment systems are difficult to introduce and maintain, as they require a lot of computational and human resources, as well as an important cost of lecturer training. Besides, e-assessment may not be suitable for every type of assessment, such as extended response questions.

SUBJECTS UNDER STUDY

Engineering University Degrees in Spain

Currently, Spanish universities are undergoing an adaptation process of their existing degrees with the aim to converge to the European Higher Education Area (EHEA). This process culminates in 2010-2011 with the final implementation of the new degrees that will hopefully fulfill the requirements of the Bologna directives.

Bologna directives focus on a more active role of students in the learning process, along with formative and continuous assessment. The proposed educational model is based on the student workload required to achieve the objectives of a program. These objectives are specified in terms of learning outcomes and competences to be acquired.

Nevertheless, the implementation of this new model implies a reorientation of most engineering studies in Spain, which is difficult to carry out in practice because of the particular features of Spanish higher education (Tovar & Cardeñosa, 2003).

The current Spanish higher education system is based on a centralized philosophy, where the government plays a major role in the definition of contents and subjects for a particular degree, leaving little autonomy to the universities. Instead, the new approach lies on a decentralized, self-governing model, where the university is free to decide the particular curricula, only restricted by a list of competences that must be reached by the student.

In the present system, public and private universities structure their degrees in two educational cycles, each one of them composed of subjects that can be classified as:

1. *Majors*: Compulsory subjects present in every curriculum leading to an official degree. This group represents 30% of the subject load during the first cycle and 25% in the second cycle.
2. *Compulsory Subjects*: These are designated by the university as compulsory for the student within the corresponding curriculum.
3. *Optional Subjects*: Each particular university establishes these subjects for students to choose from.
4. *Free-choice Credits*: Every curriculum devotes at least 10% of the subject load to free-choice activities, which might be standard subjects, seminars or other activities that can be freely chosen from those offered by the university or by another university, if permitted by the corresponding joint agreement.

The assessment unit is the credit, which corresponds to ten hours of theoretical or practical teaching. Credits are obtained by the appropriate verification of the acquired knowledge, usually through written, or occasionally oral, examinations.

Regarding to teaching methodologies, many Spanish universities still maintain the classical approach based on lectures and an evaluation through a single final exam. This methodology does not encourage the students to a continuous study of the subject.

Besides, it is very common to find large group sizes in the university, a fact that do not promote the academics to improve their teaching techniques, because the time spent in teaching tasks increases considerably. Large groups are common in most majors taught in the first years at Spanish universities.

It can be seen that the present higher educational system is quite a long way from the new model. As a preliminary step towards the implementation of the EHEA proposal, most Spanish universities have developed pilot experiences in order to modify their teaching methodologies.

A common feature of the new methodologies tested is that they are based on an individual guidance of the student. In this way, lecturers should turn their classical role of "transmitters of knowledge" into a new one of "personal supervisors", helping students in the construction of their own knowledge. The methodological changes needed are very difficult to carry out when dealing with large groups, where personalized monitoring of students is unfeasible. This is especially true in the most difficult disciplines that have a high failure rate and, as a consequence, have a large number of students enrolled every year. In these cases, changes demand a considerable effort from lecturers due to the student/lecturer ratio and the fact that the amount of work is directly related to the number of students. Many times, the large number of students attending university classes in Spain often prevents the lecturer from providing education in an innovative way. This is the current situation on most Spanish engineering degree courses.

Universitat Jaume I

Universitat Jaume I (UJI) came into being as a higher education and research centre on 27 February 1991 to meet the unanimous social demand in the East-Coast Spanish Castellón area. The main aim of the new institution was to extend its teaching and research activities to the northern part of the Spanish Valencian Community. From the moment it was set up, UJI has strived to become a modern, high quality university with a clearly European orientation, whose purpose is to attain a level of excellence in the teaching, research and services it offers to society.

Universitat Jaume I has consolidated itself as a dynamic and enterprising university. There are currently 28 degrees and diploma courses available to about 13,500 students. At UJI new, flexible, and competitive curricula and programs are taught, enabling students to satisfactorily cope with every challenge set by modern society. The interdisciplinary nature of Universitat Jaume I guarantee students' autonomy and increases the chances of getting a job in the future.

UJI has adopted a "group structure" within the university that is made up of the following centers:

- School of Technology and Experimental Sciences (ESTCE).
- Faculty of Humanities and Social Sciences (FCHS).
- Faculty of Law and Economics (FCJE).

Universitat Jaume I is a pioneer in the use of new information technologies. Indeed, UJI was the first academic institution in Spain to become part of the World Wide Web (WWW) and to develop a browser that could be used to search for information on the Internet. It is also the first university to have a Centre for Education and New Technologies (CENT), which is currently taken as a reference in Europe.

Finally, Universitat Jaume I has a wide network of international contacts made up of about 145 university-partners in Europe, the United States and Latin America, which has given rise to exchange programs between students and between members of the academic staff, as well as educational and research projects.

School of Technology and Experimental Sciences

Among the various centres within the overall structure of the Universitat Jaume I, the School of Technology and Experimental Sciences (ESTCE), already mentioned above, is the central goal of this study.

The ESTCE gathers degrees related to engineering and experimental sciences. At present, the degrees that are taught in the ESTCE are:

- Technical Architecture (3 years)
- Agricultural Engineering (3 years)
- Industrial Design Engineer (3 years)

- Systems Data Processing Engineer (3 years)
- Administrative Data Processing Engineer (3 years)
- Chemical Engineering (5 years)
- Chemistry (5 years)
- Industrial Engineering (5 years)
- Mechanical Engineering (3 years)

This chapter is focused on subjects taught in the last two engineering degrees, Industrial Engineering and Mechanical Engineering.

On the one hand, the degree of Industrial Engineering is one of the most traditional engineering degrees in Spain. The industrial engineer is a highly valued professional in the industry, because of its general background, which includes training on mechanics, electricity, hydraulics, thermodynamics, manufacturing processes, industrial construction, automation, management, etc. Thus, employment areas for the Industrial Engineer can be management, production supervising, maintenance, mechanical and electrical design, automation and control, project development, industrial construction, urban development and so on. After the common training, the student can specialize in *Planning and urban services*, *Electromechanics*, or *Processes and industrial management*. This degree is taught at the Universitat Jaume I since 1994.

On the other hand, the degree of Mechanical Engineer is a more specific one, as it provides special training in the field of mechanics applied to the industry. It focuses specially in the part of Industrial Engineering related to Mechanics. This degree enjoys great prestige in the industrial sector, and empowers to work, for example, developing industrial projects or new products, designing or maintaining machines, managing production, etc. The student can focus its training in *Industrial Maintenance* or *Facilities Maintenance*. This degree is taught at the Universitat Jaume I since 1998.

Mechanics Subjects: Main Characteristics

The subjects covered in this study are two:

- Mechanics for Engineers, belonging to the Industrial Engineering degree, and
- Mechanics, belonging to the Mechanical Engineering degree.

Mechanics for Engineers is a *compulsory subject* taught in first semester of the second year of the Industrial Engineering degree. At the Universitat Jaume I, it consists of 60 hours of classroom education, of which 30 are lectures, 20 are problem-solving sessions and 10 are laboratory sessions. It is preceded by core subjects of physics and mathematics, essential for tackling the subject successfully. In addition, Mechanics for Engineers is a fundamental discipline and is the basis of other majors taught in the following years of the degree

Mechanics is a *major* taught in the first year of the Mechanical Engineering degree. Its content is very similar to the previous one, with slight differences in the distribution of the activities. In this case, the 60 hours of classroom education are distributed in 30 lecture hours, 15 hours of problem-solving sessions and 15 hours of laboratory sessions. As in the Mechanics for Engineers case, it requires a previous training in physics and mathematics. Its importance in the rest of the degree is still greater than in the preceding subject.

Mechanics Subjects: Initial Situation

Traditionally, engineering disciplines at UJI have been taught using a methodology based on lectures and problem-solving sessions, in combination with laboratory sessions for assessing the practical skills of students. Subjects like Mechanics and Mechanics for Engineers have not been an exception to this.

A first step in the modernization of these subjects was to supplement the classic blackboard explanations with multimedia resources in order to make them more affordable and visual for students. These resources, particularly slide presentations, were introduced in lectures, but also were available for students to be used in their study as a supplement to the textbooks and notes taken in class.

Along with this material, a collection of suggested problems was designed with the aim to help the students in the self-assessment of their knowledge at the end of each content unit. These problems had the numerical solution included, but were the students who should reach the result by their own means. In this way, students could undertake a kind of continuous self-assessment using the support of the lecturer in the tutorial sessions.

To complete these materials a laboratory guide was annually produced as assistance for students in laboratory sessions. This document should be supplemented with the realization of a practical report including the experimental data obtained in each lab session and their relation to the theoretical concepts taught in class, as well as the relevant conclusions that the student had taken in its experiments. All these activities can be considered a prelude to what we call *formative assessment.*

This methodology conforms to a traditional evaluation scheme carried out mainly through a single examination at the end of the semester, also known as *summative evaluation*, supplemented by the delivery of the lab report described above. The percentages allocated to each of the activities within this approach are shown in Table 1.

Table 1. Traditional evaluation scheme previously used in Mechanics and Mechanics for Engineers

Assessment Type	Assessment Activity	%
Formative assessment	Suggested Problems (Self-evaluation)	**0%**
	Laboratory Sessions (reports)	**10%**
Summative assessment	Final Examination	**90%**
	Final mark	**100%**

Mechanics Subjects: Detected Problems and Objectives

The students regard both mechanics subjects as difficult disciplines. The reason is the complexity and variety of the matter taught, that requires constant effort and study from students. Both subjects are composed of two main blocks of content: Statics and Dynamics.

Nowadays, although students have good skills in information technologies, they usually lack autonomy and require personalized attention. Besides, many of them are not in the habit of studying every day and begin to study only when the final exam date approaches. Thus, they are not able to assimilate the subject properly in such a short time and, as a consequence, they either give up studying the subject or focus only on the first part – Statics, which is taught at the first half of the semester. In the latter case, and using an evaluation scheme as the one described above, the student can even pass the exam if he/she has studied properly the Statics part but lacks the skills and procedures taught in the Dynamics part, which are fundamental for subsequent years.

There is another important problem detected in these subjects. Given the practical methodology used in them, mainly based on a problem-solving strategy, most students do not review the theoretical concepts taught in class, and focus only in the practical aspects. Those students lack a proper conceptual basis to be applied to different problems that may arise throughout their careers.

Talking about group sizes, as few students pass the subjects, there is a large number of students enrolled every year, those enrolled for the first time plus the ones that failed in previous years. For instance, a total of 236 students enrolled Mechanics in the academic year 2006/2007. Only 90 of them were enrolling for the first time, but no more than 57 of the remaining 146 students had previously sat any examination of the major.

The particular numbers of each subject and each academic year are listed in Table 2.

Table 2. Number of enrolled students in Mechanics and Mechanics for Engineers in the last academic years

Academic Year	Mechanics	Mechanics For Engineers
2006/2007	235	96
2007/2008	196	83
2008/2009	2	80

This large number of students greatly hinders the development of educational innovation in the subject. In fact, lecturers usually employ the above-mentioned classical teaching methodology, as they are normally reticent about changes. Another factor that points out in the same direction is that lecturers feel their workload considerably increased whilst their retribution remains still. This means the lecturer is asked to apply methodologies that require few students per group, which are not feasible because it is not possible to increase the number of groups without an extra funding of the studies. Moreover, an increase of time spent in teaching tasks implies a considerable decrease in the time to be spent in research. This matter is especially troubling in academics that yet have not gotten a permanent position in the university and, consequently, need to obtain research results in order to improve their curricula.

Not only academics, but also students, show themselves reluctant to changes. Indeed, they often prefer the classical evaluation scheme rather than the continuous assessment one, because the latter requires a constant and continuous effort along the entire course, a fact that is not usually welcome.

Thus, the detected problems can be summed up in the following points:

- The classical teaching methodologies, based on lectures and an evaluation through a single final exam, do not encourage the students to a continuous study of the subject.
- An intermittent or sporadic study of the subject results in a high failure rate, mainly due to the amount of students that don't sit the examination. Students focus on what they perceive as the easier parts of the subjects, also avoiding the theoretical foundations, which leads to an incomplete training.
- Large group sizes do not encourage the academics to apply educational innovations due to the amount of work required.
- The new initiatives collide not only with the reservations of the teacher but also with the very attitude of the students who, in many cases, prefer to maintain the classical evaluation scheme rather than the continuous assessment.

Despite these problems, there is a great advantage of the students of today: its preparation and complete immersion in information and communication technologies. This fact has allowed exploring new lecturer-student ways of communication and interaction.

The overall objective of this work is to improve the performance of the teaching-learning process through the incorporation of ICT in the subjects. The aim is to motivate students and promote their autonomous learning by changing the pedagogy using the Virtual Classroom. In an indirect way, an increase in the percentage of students that pass the subjects is expected, compared to previous years.

These new initiatives, in the present case, are particularized in a proposal with a fourfold specific objective:

- First, to facilitate the change of methodologies in large groups without increasing the time spent by the lecturer in order to increment the amount of students that passes the subject. This means to implement a continuous assessment not only to verify the degree of fulfilment of the objectives established in each subject, but also to guide the students in their learning process. Moreover, if the students are able to continuously self-assess, they will also be able to correct their deficiencies in time. This requires giving not only their marks, but also a list of the concepts or techniques in which they do not reach the objectives established for each subject.
- Second, to adapt the assessment system with the aim of encouraging the students to study the subject every day and increasing their motivation.
- Third, to include the assessment of the theoretical foundation of the subject in the evaluation system. This will avoid the students to tackle problem-based activities without having properly studied the basics of the subject. In fact, if the assessment is problem-centred, a theoretical comprehension of the foundations of the subject is being assumed, and this may not be the case.
- Fourth, to achieve a balanced compensation between the student dedication to the different blocks that compose the subjects.

DIAGNOSTIC AND FORMATIVE MOODLE-BASED E-ASSESSMENT

Alternatives Considered

One of the most important factors involved in the teaching-learning process is the assessment method used in the subjects. It is the key element to be modified in order to fulfil the objectives drawn in the previous section.

Different alternatives for assessment were considered and their advantages and drawbacks are discussed here. On the one hand, the implementation of continuous assessment in overcrowded groups –i.e., with more than fifty students enrolled–, is difficult to carry out in practice because of the time spent in correction tasks. For that reason, although this is a good methodology in order to encourage the students to study the subject continuously, face-to-face continuous assessment was ruled out in the considered subjects.

On the other side, and taking into account that the Universitat Jaume I is a face-to-face university, the academics have to teach a minimum number of classes, and it made no sense to develop an entirely virtual subject.

These reasons lead inevitably to the development of a blended learning methodology. Nevertheless, it must be remembered that there are a wide variety of activities that fit into the framework of b-learning. Among them, e-assessment was considered as the most appropriate for the goals already established, i.e., to achieve the study of the theoretical foundations of the subject without a huge increase in the lecturers work.

Another essential consideration is that the evaluation system must maintain consistency between what is required and what is assessed. In addition, it is necessary to ensure that the assessment constitutes a motivating element for daily study rather than a discouragement one, as happens with the existence of a single final exam. In this sense, the introduction of the e-assessment has not been an easy-to-implement process, since it has required a major effort to thoroughly revise the contents of the subject, identifying those likely to be assessed using e-tools. Besides, as the implementation of e-assessment has an important component of technology, its proper development has required the full commitment of the lecturer relating to ICTs.

Methodology

First of all, it was necessary to determine what content can be evaluated through e-assessment tools and what other content must be evaluated using face-to-face activities. Once established this differentiation, the specific activities that could be done with the Virtual Classroom were determined, as well as the associated learning outcomes.

But prior to the design of the particular activities, it was necessary to determine the percentage of each content unit in the final mark. The percentages of time dedicated to each unit are directly related to the importance of the topic in the subject, and they are shown in Table 3.

Table 3. Percentages of importance of each content unit in Mechanics and Mechanics for Engineers

Content Unit	Percentage
1. Statics of Structures	30%
2. Friction	15%
3. Statics of cables	10%
4. Kinematics	20%
5. Kinetics	25%

As a result of what it is stated above, four kinds of activities were proposed:

1. Initial and compulsory assessment (e-test): This is a mandatory e-test for students to be aware of their prior knowledge on mathematics and physics required in order to tackle the subject properly.
2. Periodical tests (e-tests): These are electronic theoretical and practical tests carried out during the course for the various units of the subject. The aim of these tests was to ensure that the students learn or, at least, read and understand the theoretical foundations of each content unit before facing problems. These tests provide indirect guidance for students, because they allow them to check their knowledge in every unit of the subject and perform feedback.
3. Suggested problems (autonomous learning): A collection of problems was designed to help the students in the self-assessment of their knowledge at the end of each content unit. These problems are essentially the same as those used in the classical teaching methodology, and they were explained in a previous section.
4. Laboratory sessions (mixed learning): The laboratory sessions were optional, but contribute to the final mark. They were assessed through an e-report on the practical work done and with theoretical calculus verifying the measurements obtained in the laboratory. The handing in of these documents was performed electronically.
5. Partial Examinations (paper-based). During the course there were two partial exams allowing the students to assess their knowledge of the first part of the subject, Statics, and leaving the second part, Dynamics, for the final exam. Only if the mark in each partial examination was greater than or equal to 40% would the student be allowed to be assessed only on the second part of the program in the final examination.

To facilitate the adaptation of the students to the new assessment philosophy, they were allowed to choose between this alternative and a traditional one consisting of a single final examination supplemented with laboratory sessions, as explained above. The first option, the Continuous Assessment Methodology, was addressed to those students who regularly attend classes, who were able to test their knowledge throughout the course by means of the various activities described. The second option, the Classical Assessment Methodology, was kept thinking of those students who do not regularly attend classes for having attended in previous years or by personal preference.

The weights in the final mark of the activities that make up the evaluation are listed in Table 4, for each of the alternatives raised.

Moodle-Based Tools for E-Assessment

The e-assessment in the different subjects has been implemented using the Moodle platform. Moodle is the acronym for Modular Object-Oriented Dynamic Learning Environment. It is an open-source Virtual Learning Environment (VLE) for producing Internet-based courses and web sites. It is a modular system that offers considerable flexibility with the possibility of adding or removing functions at many levels.

Moodle was created by Martin Dougiamas, a WebCT administrator at Curtin University, Australia, who has graduate degrees in Computer Science and Education (Dougiamas & Taylor, 2002), (Dougiamas & Taylor, 2003). Moodle has been evolving since 1999 (since 2001 with the current architecture), being 1.9.5 its current version. It has been translated into 61 different languages.

As there are no license fees or limits to growth, an institution can add as many Moodle servers as needed. Indeed, the Open University of the UK is currently building a Moodle installation for their 200,000 users (Open University, 2005). The development of Moodle continues as a free software project supported by a large community continuously improving the software, based on documents and troubleshooting. It is based on constructivist pedagogical principles: learning is particularly effective when achieved through sharing with others (Moodle, 2007).

Moodle runs without modification on Unix, Linux, FreeBSD, Windows, Mac OS X, NetWare and any other systems that support PHP and a database, including most webhost providers. Also remark that data is stored in a single database.

Table 4.Assessment alternatives in Mechanics and Mechanics for Engineers

	Continuous Assessment Methodology		**Classical Assessment Methodology**	
Diagnostic assessment	Initial and compulsory assessment (e-test)	**0%**	Initial and optional assessment (e-test)	**0%**
Formative assessment	Periodical tests (e-tests)	**20%**	Suggested problems (autonomous learning)	**0%**
	Suggested problems (autonomous learning)	**0%**		
	Laboratory sessions (mixed learning)	**10%**	Laboratory sessions (mixed learning)	**10%**
Summative assessment	Partial Examinations (paper-based)	**38%**	Final Examination (paper-based)	**90%**
	Final Examination (paper-based)	**32%**		
	Final mark	**100%**	**Final mark**	**100%**

There are some free Moodle hosting providers, which allow educators to create Moodle-based online class without installation or server knowledge. There are some paid Moodle hosting providers which provide value added services like customization, content development.

Moodle platform is widely used in the Universitat Jaume I. One of its main advantages is that is easy to maintain and update. Except for the installation process, it requires virtually no maintenance by the administrator. Its interface allows the easy creation, management and usage of the course by the lecturer and also by the students. The registration and authentication of the participants is quite simple and secure.

We have implemented the e-assessment for the diagnostic and formative assessments while the summative assessment has remained the same (paper-based). On the Moodle platform there are very different tools, but we have mainly used the following:

- Quizzes
- Assignments
- Forums
- Dialogues
- Glossaries

Figure 1. Initial assessment: four questions of the designed quiz

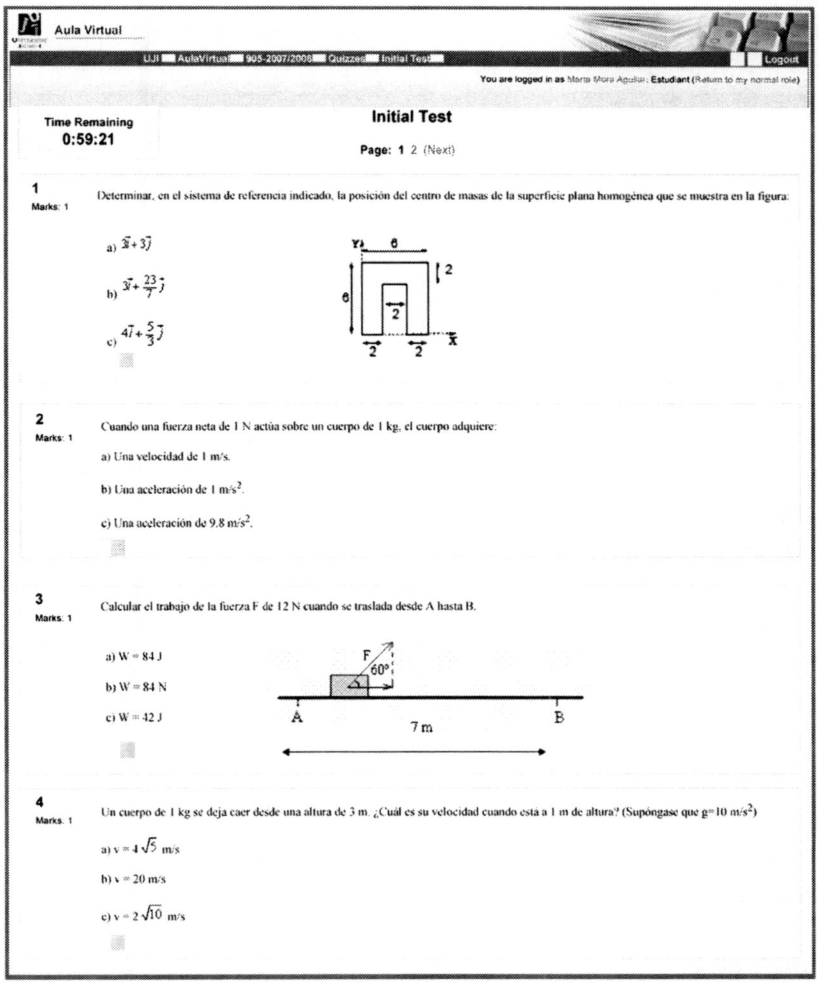

Diagnostic E-Assessment

Both mechanics subjects employ Quizzes for the initial diagnostic assessment.

The Quiz is a Moodle flexible tool that allows lecturers to design a variety of consistent tests and to establish assessment strategies that would be very difficult to carry out on paper. In fact, there is a wide diversity of questions (multiple choice, true/false, short answers, gap-filling, descriptions...) organized by categories within a Question Bank. The aim of this bank is to gather the various questions designed by the lecturer throughout the course for its re-use in other similar courses or in different years. Questions can be created directly in the Moodle HTML Editor, with multimedia elements if desired or can be imported from external text files. It is also possible to generate random quizzes from multiple choice questions stored in the bank. It has the great advantage that the time spent by the students in answering the e-test can be limited as well as the possible attempts to make it. It is important to remark that the correction and marking is immediate.

Figure 1 is an example of an e-test designed using the Quiz tool, consisting of multiple choice questions. The figure just shows the first four questions of the twenty composing the questionnaire. It can also be appreciated the above mentioned temporal limitation, which should be taken into account by the student. Indicate that some questions contain images, and it would also be possible to include multimedia animations.

Formative E-Assessment

Formative assessment is carried out through various types of tools available in Moodle. As a first tool, quizzes have been used for designing the e-test corresponding to the content units, in the fashion explained in the previous section. Each e-test has a homepage that allows access to the questionnaire only during the time provided. Students know in advance the date and time at which the test is activated, and can access it just once during that period. The homepage of an e-test, concretely, the one corresponding to the Kinematics unit, is shown in Figure 2.

Two examples of questions, also relating to kinematics, are displayed in Figure 3.

A second tool used in the formative assessment is the Assignment. Assignments are employed to manage the e-reports required in the evaluation of the laboratory tasks.

An Assignment is a Moodle tool that allows assigning work to students, which will be prepared in an electronic format and uploaded to the server. The documents are stored for later assessment, with the possibility of adding a review that will be sent to the student by e-mail.

For each e-report it is possible to specify the particular instructions for writing the document, the delivery period of time and the highest rating that can be given to the report. Deadlines of Assignments are displayed in the calendar of the course. This calendar is also a resource included in the Moodle platform.

Figure 2. Homepage of the e-test corresponding to the Kinematics unit

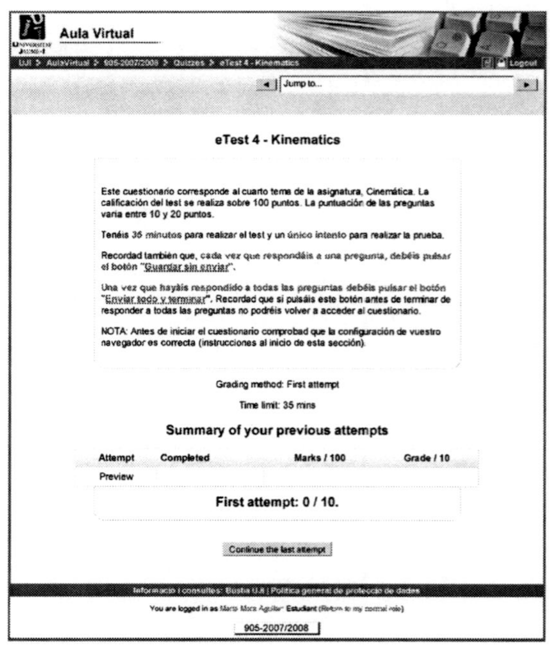

Figure 3. Two questions of the e-test corresponding to the Kinematics unit

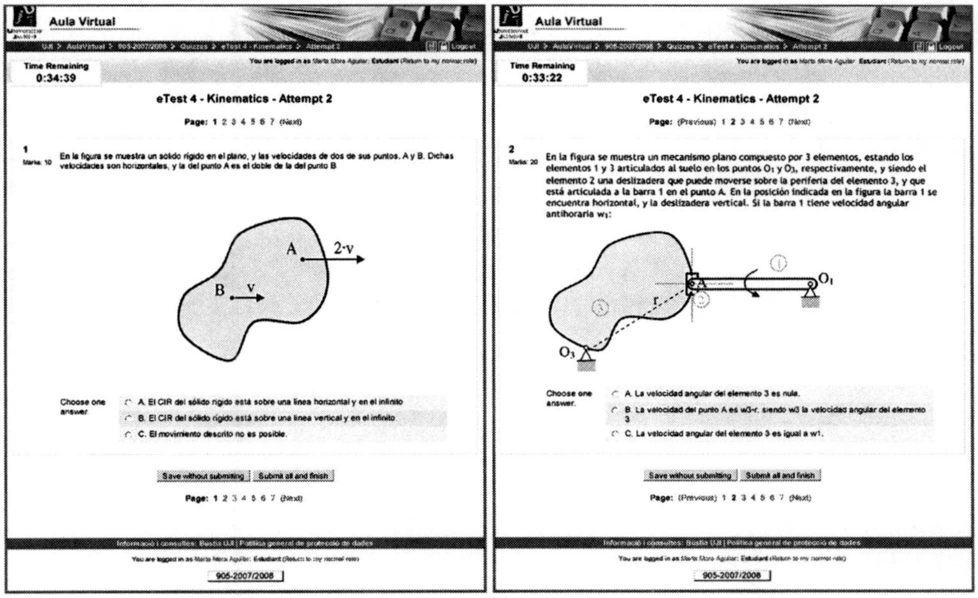

Figure 4. List of Assignments available in the Mechanics for Engineers subject

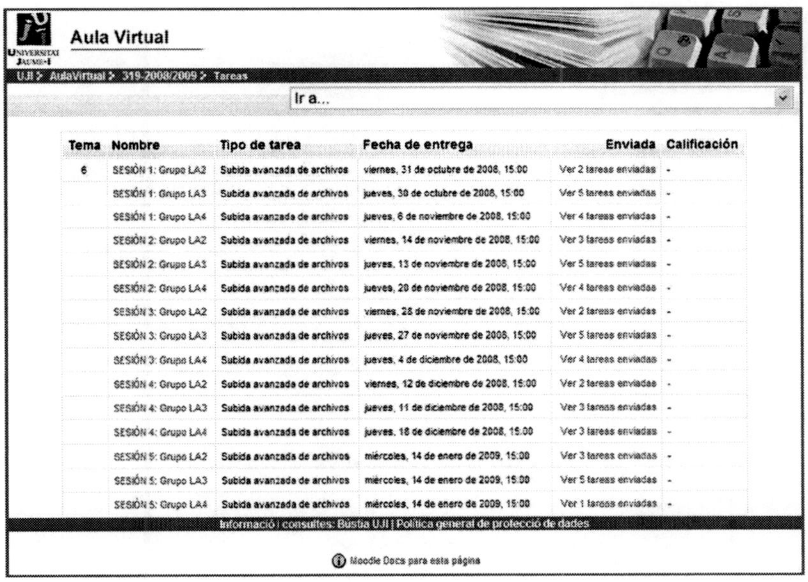

Tema	Nombre	Tipo de tarea	Fecha de entrega	Enviada	Calificación
6	SESIÓN 1: Grupo LA2	Subida avanzada de archivos	viernes, 31 de octubre de 2008, 15:00	Ver 2 tareas enviadas	-
	SESIÓN 1: Grupo LA3	Subida avanzada de archivos	jueves, 30 de octubre de 2008, 15:00	Ver 5 tareas enviadas	-
	SESIÓN 1: Grupo LA4	Subida avanzada de archivos	jueves, 6 de noviembre de 2008, 15:00	Ver 4 tareas enviadas	-
	SESIÓN 2: Grupo LA2	Subida avanzada de archivos	viernes, 14 de noviembre de 2008, 15:00	Ver 3 tareas enviadas	-
	SESIÓN 2: Grupo LA3	Subida avanzada de archivos	jueves, 13 de noviembre de 2008, 15:00	Ver 5 tareas enviadas	-
	SESIÓN 2: Grupo LA4	Subida avanzada de archivos	jueves, 20 de noviembre de 2008, 15:00	Ver 4 tareas enviadas	-
	SESIÓN 3: Grupo LA2	Subida avanzada de archivos	viernes, 28 de noviembre de 2008, 15:00	Ver 2 tareas enviadas	-
	SESIÓN 3: Grupo LA3	Subida avanzada de archivos	jueves, 27 de noviembre de 2008, 15:00	Ver 5 tareas enviadas	-
	SESIÓN 3: Grupo LA4	Subida avanzada de archivos	jueves, 4 de diciembre de 2008, 15:00	Ver 4 tareas enviadas	-
	SESIÓN 4: Grupo LA2	Subida avanzada de archivos	viernes, 12 de diciembre de 2008, 15:00	Ver 2 tareas enviadas	-
	SESIÓN 4: Grupo LA3	Subida avanzada de archivos	jueves, 11 de diciembre de 2008, 15:00	Ver 3 tareas enviadas	-
	SESIÓN 4: Grupo LA4	Subida avanzada de archivos	jueves, 18 de diciembre de 2008, 15:00	Ver 3 tareas enviadas	-
	SESIÓN 5: Grupo LA2	Subida avanzada de archivos	miércoles, 14 de enero de 2009, 15:00	Ver 3 tareas enviadas	-
	SESIÓN 5: Grupo LA3	Subida avanzada de archivos	miércoles, 14 de enero de 2009, 15:00	Ver 5 tareas enviadas	-
	SESIÓN 5: Grupo LA4	Subida avanzada de archivos	miércoles, 14 de enero de 2009, 15:00	Ver 1 tareas enviadas	-

Informació i consultes: Bústia UJI | Política general de protecció de dades

Moodle Docs para esta página

An example of the page with the list of Assignments is shown in Figure 4. The login page to a particular Assignment can be seen in Figure 5.

Another useful tool to promote communication between students and lecturers, and among students themselves, is the Forum. A Forum allows users to publish, read and find messages, so that they can maintain virtual discussions on specific topics. Its structure is organized by discussion threads and the student can join at any time. It is a fundamental tool to stimulate interaction and collaboration among participants in these courses.

Figure 5. Login page to a particular Assignment in the Mechanics subject

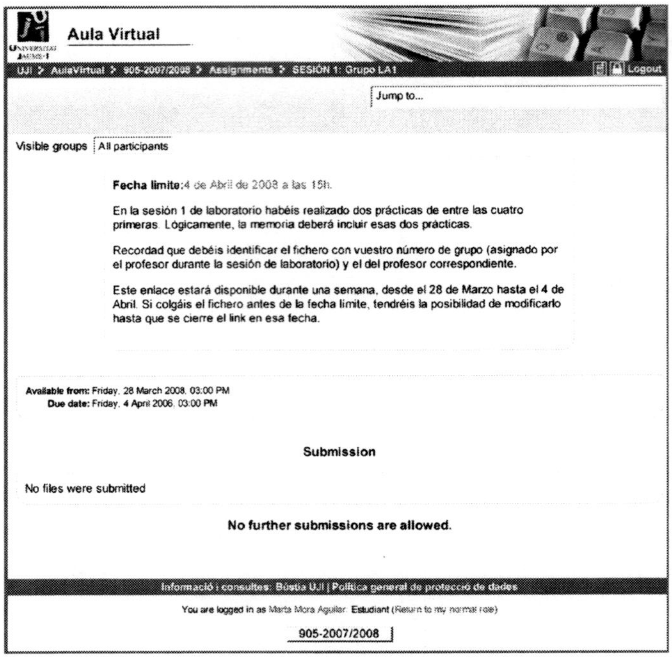

Figure 6. Public tutorial forum in the Mechanics for Engineers subject

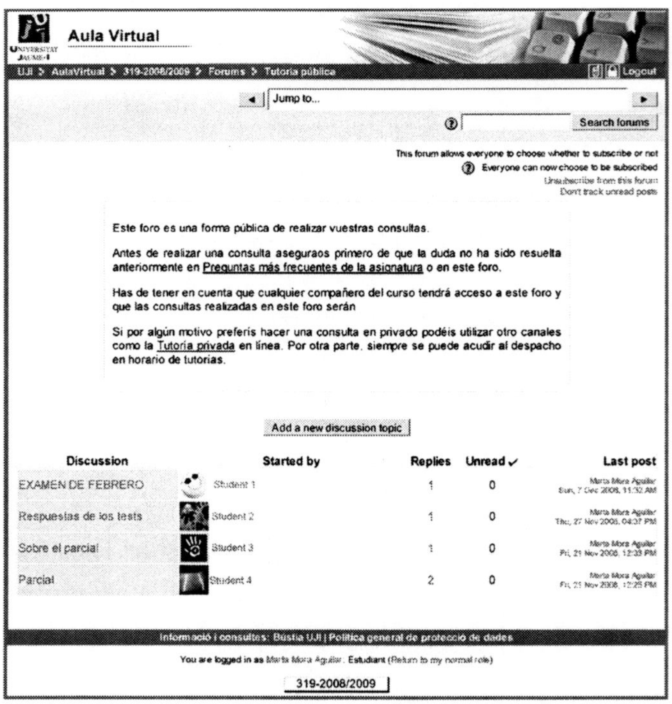

Figure 7. Examples of Dialogues in the Mechanics for Engineers subject

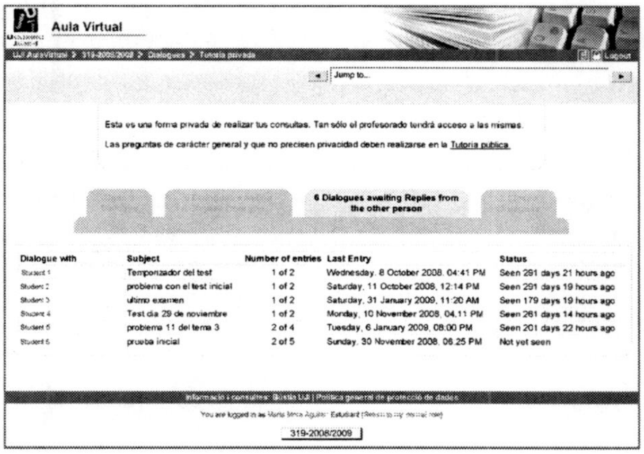

This particular tool is used to implement a kind of public tutorial sessions. Students can make questions that may interest the rest of the group, so the answer of the lecturer is available to everyone. An example of the forum is depicted in Figure 6.

There exists the possibility of a private bidirectional communication between a student and the lecturer, through the Dialogue tool, which has been called Private Tutoring. In this way, students can consult the teacher individually, without having to go to his office and without involving the rest of the group. Once the communication is started, the dialogue remains open until the receiver responds to the question. When the dialogue is finished, it is necessary that the receiver close it.

Some examples of Dialogues are shown in Figure 7.

Finally, the Glossary is a powerful learning tool able of helping the participants (lecturers and students) to build and maintain glossaries and include them within the courses. From a broader point of view, a glossary can be understood as a repository of structured information. This repository or database can store definitions of terms and concepts, like a dictionary, or group items, like an encyclopaedia. It is also possible to maintain a list of questions and answers. The latter is what has been implemented in both subjects. An example is shown in Figure 8.

Comparative Results

The changes made in both subjects have proved themselves to be quite effective in reaching the

Figure 8. An example of Glossary (Frequently Asked Questions) in the Mechanics for Engineers subject

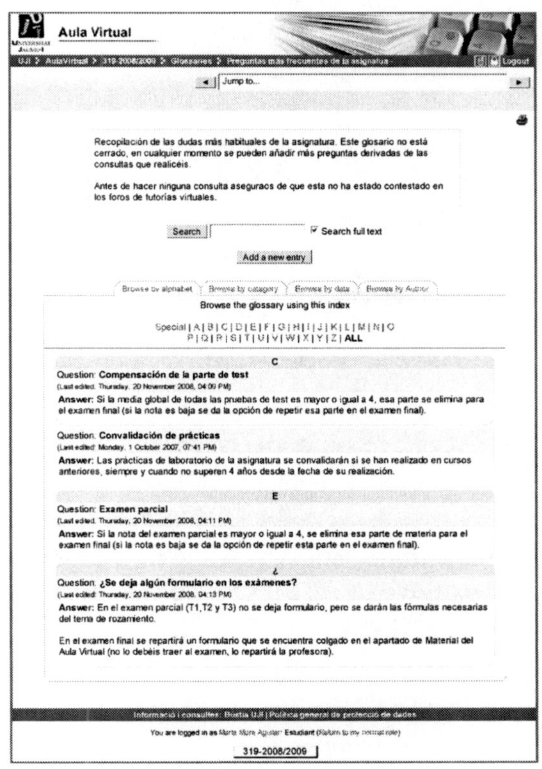

proposed goals, as it can be seen from the results outlined below.

In fact, and qualitatively speaking, there has been a notorious increase in the interest of students with regard to both subjects, a fact that has been observed mainly in the fairly continuous class attendance, tutorial sessions following, and virtual consulting using Forums, Dialogues and e-mail.

In addition, students have worked continuously during the course, and this fact was reflected in the number of students who completed the theoretical and practical e-tests and the partial examinations.

In particular, this methodology was introduced in the Mechanics subject during the academic year 2007/2008 and in the Mechanics for Engineers subject during the academic year 2008/2009. The following data reflect the changes operated in both subjects:

- *Percentage of students attending classes.* There is a 33.5% of students that regularly have attended classes in the Mechanics subject, and 45.8% for Mechanics for Engineers subject. Remark that in both subjects an important number of students have attended classes in previous year and do not attend them again. This situation is more frequent in the Mechanics subject, due to the specific features of the degree. With respect to students enrolled for the first time, the percentage is about 70% of attendance in both subjects.
- *Results of the continuous assessment methodology.* The continuous assessment activities have been carried out by a large percentage of students. In particular, the theoretical and practical e-tests in Mechanics have been conducted by the 68.2% of the enrolled students while the percentage is a little bit lower, 52.5%, when referring to the partial examinations. It is important to remark that the 89% of students who followed the continuous assessment option passed the subject. Participation in Mechanics for Engineers has been even greater, with the 80.8% of students following this option, a fact that denotes that the students have been motivated by the subject. Specifically, theoretical e-tests have been conducted by the 70.2% of students, and the 64.3% of students sat the partial examinations.
- *Percentage of students attending tutorial sessions.* An increase in attendance to tutorial sessions has been detected with respect to previous years, with an attendance average of 3 students per session in both subjects. However, this number is still quite small.
- *Percentage of students sitting the examinations.* The number of students who have followed the subject during the course, and conducted the exams has been increased. In particular, for the Mechanics for Engineers subject, a rate of 76.92% of students enrolled has been reached, whereas in the previous academic year the figure was 69%. In the Mechanics subject this percentage is 63% of students, even better when compared to the 36% obtained in previous academic years.
- *Percentage of students passing the subject.* This number has also been increased considerably. On the Mechanics for Engineers subject, it has risen from 22.4% in 2007/2008 to 56.67% during the 2008/2009 academic year. In the Mechanics subject, this percentage has reached 36%, whereas in previous courses had never exceeded 15%.
- *Average grade for the subject.* The average grade obtained by students in the Mechanics for Engineers subject has been 5, from a maximum value of 10, compared to 3.7 reached last academic year. This increase of more than one point on the average also appears in the Mechanics subject, and this fact indicates that students have followed the subject in a more continuous way, having improved their skills compared to students in previous courses. This increase in scores is particularly striking in the second part of the

subject, the Dynamics part, what confirms a higher dedication of students to the subject.

- *Student's appraisals and opinions.* Students in both subjects have considered the experience as positive, but they have complained about the amount of work that this type of methodology implies. However, the numbers of students that passed both subjects do not corroborate this perspective.

FUTURE RESEARCH DIRECTIONS

Although the obtained results are satisfactory, some limitations have been observed. On the one hand, the guiding task performed by the teacher is scarce and should be increased, taking into account the students profile. On the other hand, the lecturer's workload has increased, largely because of partial examinations, and also because of the e-tests. As no correlation between the marks in the e-tests and the marks in the partial examinations has been found, a more in-depth study should be done.

Some ideas that may be carried out for future improving are:

- Change the kind of partial examination, using other possibilities less time-consuming, such as multiple-choice questions tests. Maybe the partial examinations could be replaced by e-tests, with a smaller workload for the lecturer. But for performing this change it is necessary to ensure that e-tests can properly assess the skills and concepts that are currently being assessed using written examinations.
- The collaboration of the students may be promoted introducing other existing Moodle e-tools, as Wikis. The basic principle of a Wiki is to build a Web site for sharing and collaboration, which implies that every student is able to bring new content to the site, such as new documents or links. In short, it creates a community of users where each one creates materials for everybody. Pages contain links, images and any type of content that can be also edited by every user. This tool could be used for solving the suggested-problems in a collaborative way. The lecturer could also review the solution and give advice about the resolution procedures and the decisions taken by students.

CONCLUSION

This chapter analyzes the underlying problems may arise when introducing e-learning tools in different engineering subjects with the aim of performing educational innovation in large groups. Because of the particular features of this kind of groups, the improvement of the teaching-learning process is possible through the incorporation of ICT in the subjects.

In this case, a b-learning proposal has been made with the aim of motivating students and promoting their continuous and autonomous learning. In particular, a continuous assessment methodology has been implemented. It has been based in the introduction of diagnostic and formative e-assessments in order to assess cognitive and practical abilities in different basic Mechanics subjects, with similar contents but taught in different engineering degrees, in diverse years or with various group sizes. This has been made in order to compare their results and to extract general conclusions that can be extrapolated to any other engineering discipline.

The e-assessment in the different subjects has been implemented using the Moodle platform. It is an open-source Virtual Learning Environments for producing Internet-based courses and web sites that offers considerable flexibility.

It is important to remark that encouraging results have been obtained from the introduction of the e-assessment in the different subjects. In particular, a more continuous study has been achieved, according to the percentage of students that sat the e-tests. The e-tests have also helped ensure a proper and continuous study of the theoretical foundation of the subject. In this way, the students have been able to make a better use of their attendance in class. Besides, most of the students who followed the continuous assessment methodology did finally pass the subject. Also, the task of guidance carried out by the lecturer has indirectly increased, by means of the feedback given to the students in the e-test results.

Nevertheless, the lecturer's workload has increased because of the partial examinations and the e-tests. As no correlation between the marks in the e-tests and the marks in the partial examinations has been found, a more in-depth study should be carried out in order to ensure that the partial examinations could be replaced by e-tests, with a smaller workload for the lecturer.

Finally recall that the e-assessment methodology explained can be applied to any other engineering subject with large groups of students and similar problems.

REFERENCES

Barnard, L., Lan, W. Y., To, Y. M., Paton, V. O., & Lai, S. L. (2009). Measuring self-regulation in online and blended learning environments. The Internet and Higher Education, 12(1), 1–6. doi:10.1016/j.iheduc.2008.10.005

Boticario, J., & Santos, O. (2007). An open IMS-based user modelling approach for developing adaptive learning management systems. *Journal of Interactive Media in Education*, 2. Retrieved October 10, 2009 from http://www-jime.open.ac.uk/2007/02/

Dougiamas, M., & Taylor, P. C. (2002). Interpretive analysis of an internet-based course constructed using a new courseware tool called Moodle. In *Proceedings of the Higher Education Research and Development Society of Australasia (HERDSA) 2002 Conference*, Perth, Western Australia.

Dougiamas, M., & Taylor, P. C. (2003). Moodle: Using Learning Communities to Create an Open Source Course Management System. In *Proceedings of the EDMEDIA 2003 Conference*, Honolulu, HI.

Garrison, R., & Kanuka, H. (2004). Blended learning: Uncovering its transformative potential in higher education. The Internet and Higher Education, 7(2), 95–105. doi:10.1016/j.iheduc.2004.02.001

Ginns, P., & Ellis, R. (2007). Quality in blended learning: Exploring the relationships between on-line and face-to-face teaching and learning. The Internet and Higher Education, 10, 53–64. doi:10.1016/j.iheduc.2006.10.003

Kelly, H. F., Ponton, M. K., & Rovai, A. P. (2007). A comparison of student evaluations of teaching between online and face-to-face courses. The Internet and Higher Education, 10(1), 89–101. doi:10.1016/j.iheduc.2007.02.001

Lazarinis, F., Koutromanos, G., Green, S., & Pearson, E. (2009). Utilizing a multicriteria multimedia adaptive tool in formative assessments. In *Proceedings of the International Technology, Education and Development Conference* (pp. 1522-1528), Valencia, Spain.

Moodle, version 1.9. (2007). Retrieved July 10, 2009 from http://www.moodle.org

Mora-Aguilar, M. C., Sancho-Brú, J. L., & Iserte-Vilar, J. L. (2009). Alternatives for evaluation in overcrowded groups: the e-assessment. *Proceedings of the International Technology, Education and Development Conference*, Valencia, Spain, IATED eds.

Mora-Aguilar, M. C., Sancho-Brú, J. L., Rodríguez-Cervantes, P. J., & Iserte-Vilar, J. L. (2008). The challenge of improving teaching methodologies in overcrowded groups: experiences in basic mechanics. In *Proceedings of the International Technology, Education and Development Conference*, Valencia, Spain, IATED eds.

O'Reilly, T. (2005). *What Is Web 2.0 - Design Patterns and Business Models for the Next Generation of Software.* Retrieved July 2, 2009 from, http://www.oreillynet.com/pub/a/oreilly/tim/news/2005/09/30/ what-is-web-20.html

Open University. (2005). Open University going Moodle. *eGov monitor.* Retrieved July 1, 2009 from, http://www.egovmonitor.com/node/3460

Rengarajan, R. (2001). LCMS and LMS: Taking advantage of tight integration. *Click 2 Learn.* Retrieved May 6, 2009 from http://www.e-learn.cz/soubory/lcms_and_lms.pdf

Streng, S., Baur, D., Broll, G., De Luca, A., Wimmer, R., & Butz, A. (Eds.). (2008). Trends in E-Learning. Technical Report, University of Munich.

Tovar, E., & Cardeñosa, J. (2003). Convergence in higher education: effects and risks. In *The International Conference on the Convergence of Knowledge, Culture, Language and Information Technologies,* (pp. 1-5).

Virtual, A. University Jaume I. (2007). Web site: http://aulavirtual.uji.es

ADDITIONAL READING

Alexander, B. (2006). Web 2.0: A New Wave of Innovation for Teaching and Learning? EDUCAUSE Review, 41(2), 32–44.

Amelung, M., Piotrowski, M., & Dietmar, R. (2006). EduComponents: experiences in e-assessment in computer science education. *Proceedings of the 11th annual SIGCSE conference on Innovation and technology in computer science education* (pp. 88-92).

Angus, S. D., & Watson, J. (2009). Does regular online testing enhance student learning in the numerical sciences? Robust evidence from a large data set. British Journal of Educational Technology, 36, 255–272. doi:10.1111/j.1467-8535.2008.00916.x

Ball, S. (2009). Accessibility in e-assessment. Assessment & Evaluation in Higher Education, 34(3), 293–303. doi:10.1080/02602930801956000

Bersin, K. (2004). *The Blended Learning Book,* San Francisco: John Wiley and Sons Eds.

Bhattacharya, M., & Hartnett, M. (2007). E-portfolio Assessment in Higher Education. *Proceedings of the 37th ASEE/IEEE Frontiers in Education Conferenc,* (pp. 19-23).

Biggs, J. (2003). Teaching for quality learning at university (2nd ed.). Maidenhead: Open University Press.

Clausen, T. (2005). Undergraduate engineering education challenged by the Bologna declaration. IEEE Transactions on Education, 48(2), 213–215. doi:10.1109/TE.2005.846045

Davies, J., & Graff, M. (2005). Performance in e-Learning: On-line participation and student grades. British Journal of Educational Technology, 36, 657–663. doi:10.1111/j.1467-8535.2005.00542.x

Dermo, J. (2009). e-Assessment and the student learning experience: A survey of student perceptions of e-assessment. British Journal of Educational Technology, 203–214. doi:10.1111/j.1467-8535.2008.00915.x

Ebner, M. (2007). E-Learning 2.0 = e-Learning 1.0 + Web 2.0? *The Second International Conference on Availability, Reliability and Security* (pp. 1235-1239).

Govindasamy, T. (2002). Successful implementation of e-Learning: Pedagogical considerations. The Internet and Higher Education, 4, 287–299. doi:10.1016/S1096-7516(01)00071-9

Hernon, H., Dugan, R. E., & Schwartz, C. (Eds.). (2006). Revisiting Outcomes Assessment in Higher Education (pp. 151–164). Westport: Libraries Unlimited.

Higher Education Funding Council for England (HEFCE). (2007). *Effective Practice with e-Assessment. An overview of technologies, policies and practice in further and higher education* Report from HEFCE on behalf of JISC. Retrieved June 26 2009 from http://www.jisc.ac.uk.

Jochems, W., van Merriënboer, J., & Koper, R. (2004). An introduction to integrated e-Learning. In W. Jochems, J. vanMerriënboer, & R. Koper (Eds.), Integrated e-Learning: Implication for pedagogy, technology and organization. London: RoutledgeFalmer.

Jolliffe, A., Ritter, J., & Stevens, D. (2001). The online learning handbook. London: Kogan Page.

Laurillard, D. (2002). Rethinking university teaching: A framework for the effective use of educational technology. London: Routledge. doi:10.4324/9780203304846

Meyer, K. (2002). Quality in distance education. Focus on On-line learning. Hoboken: Jossey-Bass.

Oblinger, D. G., & Oblinger, J. L. (Eds.). (2005). *Educating the Net Generation*. Washington, D.C.: EDUCAUSE. Retrieved July 10, 2009, from, http://www.educause.edu/ir/library/pdf/pub7101.pdf

Pallof, R., & Pratt, K. (2003). The virtual student. San Francisco: Jossey Bass Wiley.

Whitelock, D. (2009). E-assessment: developing new dialogues for the digital age. British Journal of Educational Technology, 36, 199–202. doi:10.1111/j.1467-8535.2008.00932.x

KEY TERMS AND DEFINITIONS

Diagnostic Assessment: It is the initial assessment that provides the instructor with information about students' prior knowledge and misconceptions about any subject.

E-Assessment: Electronic assessment arises from the use of Web-specific tools for assessment. It can be used to assess theoretical knowledge (using e-testing software) as well as practical skills (using e-portfolios or simulation software).

E-Learning: Electronic learning includes the teaching-learning strategies that use Web technologies via the Internet as main support. Typically, this type of training involves a physical distance between the transmitter and the receiver, that is, between lecturer and student.

Formative Assessment: It is the assessment that takes place during the learning activity and provides the instructor with information on how well the learning objectives of a given subject are being met.

ICT: Information and communication technologies cover all advanced technologies in manipulating and communicating information. On the education community this term is preferred to the term Information Technology.

LCMS: Acronym for Learning Content Management Systems, which is a specific platform or system developed for educational purposes, being its main objective the management of the learning content.

LMS: Acronym for Learning Management Systems, which is a specific platform or system developed for educational purposes, being its main objective the management of the learning process.

Moodle: Acronym for Modular Object-Oriented Dynamic Learning Environment. It is an open-source Virtual Learning Environment for producing Internet-based courses and web sites.

Chapter 20
Interoperability Approach in E-Learning Standardization Processes

Carmen Bao
La Rioja University, Spain

José María Castresana
Basque Country University (UPV/EHU), Spain

ABSTRACT

Providing interoperability by using standards and specifications for E-learning resources is an important element of the virtual learning environments (VLEs). In this context, a large number of international organizations develop specifications that provide principles for reaching a common "language" to be used in exchanging resources among the virtual university. In this paper we turn your attention to an approach and reference for providing interoperability in different standards. The establishment of E-learning standards has promised to improve interoperability between E-learning systems, but can only be done through enforcement of these standards. Many existing E-learning systems are built on top of relational databases, and it is possible a framework which matches XML Schemas (from learning standards) and relational schemas semi-automatically. This type of framework can provide translation between learning objects and relational databases as well as an interface to manually refine existing schema mappings. The focus is E-learning standardization and synchronization in the international and national levels. The work presents a brief updated review and it presents some new challenges, concerning the E-learning standardization processes. This research is in the area of E-learning standardization and issue is one aspect of great interest for all organizations, authorities and experts working in the field of education. Moreover, the most recognized approaches are introduced in order to improve and optimize the management of the E-learning processes. While the establishment of E-learning standards has promised to improve interoperability between E-learning systems, and obviously, this can only be done through enforcement of E-learning standards and E-learning standardization processes. The aim of this work is to discover the useful E-learning technologies as technological tools for teaching. Therefore, teachers

DOI: 10.4018/978-1-61692-789-9.ch020

must keep in mind clearly that they must optimize teaching by means of them, such as an improvement of quality education for current society in terms of competences, as connections with the current reality that students spent long hours using them. It starts with a brief background to worldwide standardization activities in the field of educational technologies as means of enhancing the accessibility, interoperability, durability, reusability and efficiency of E-learning resources, but more important new demands and problems to be tackled are reviewed. Finally, experimental dates from studies have shown that it is useful a framework that also provides translation between learning objects and relational databases, as well as an interface to manually refine existing schema mappings.

INTRODUCTION

The advent of the Internet has reshaped 'Computer-Based Learning' permit that a widely available learning resources and commercial learning systems are now easily accessible with an Internet connection. The recent evolution of electronic learning (E-learning) systems has been greatly influenced by the emergence of various learning standards.

E-learning standards today influence various aspects of the E-learning process ranging from content packaging to integration with enterprise systems. Currently, most of the learning specifications are represented in XML format. The widespread availability of related tools and its self-describing nature have encouraged the use of XML in interoperation between information systems.

The development of courseware is an extremely time-consuming process. Hence, users want assurances that such courseware is 'exportable' to other platforms when they change or upgrade their learning systems. They expect interoperability through standards-compliance in the E-learning systems they adopt. In this work, a possible framework, which helps to reconcile different data models, by E-learning systems and learning standards and standardization process, has been analyses proposed.

BACKGROUND

Ongoing E-learning Developments

Over the past few years, numerous organizations such as IMS Global (Instruction Management System-www.imsglobal.org/) have been working on various aspects of E-learning standards, ranging from metadata to accessibility. More details of the current developments in E-learning standards can be found into the related literature. Today, many E-learning systems have been eagerly adopting the standards available. However, the compliance is often applicable to a certain version of the standard. Conformance to standards by E-learning software is, often, incomplete. It is strongly required to enforce these standards via implementation. First of all, we must provide support for managing standards-based XML data.

Database Support for XML-Based E-Learning Standards

While we cannot totally predict the future of storage management in enterprise information and learning systems, the current trend still points to one dominated by relational databases.

Other alternatives that could manage XML data include Object-Oriented Databases (OODBs) and Native XML Databases (NXDs). While Object-Oriented Databases (OODBs) technology is relatively mature, the use of such systems is relatively low. That is one of the reasons that most organizations systems are still unwilling to forsake their current relational databases for alternatives.

Moreover, Native XML Databases (NXDs) are designed to manipulate XML data directly in a proprietary manner. So that, in theory, Native XML Databases (NXDs) should provide better performances compared to manipulating XML data with Relational Databases Management Systems (RDBMSes).

However, Native XML Databases (NXDs) are still relatively young. In addition to standards-based XML data, E-learning systems are often required to store data that are relational in nature, and thus are more suitably supported by Relational Databases Management Systems (RDBMSes). The same reasons influencing the poor uptake of Object-Oriented Databases Management Systems (OODBs), may also affect the adoption of Native XML Databases (NXDs).

Review of the E-Learning Standardization Processes

It is generally accepted that the development of the Internet has growing influence on modern education. New information and communication technologies provide different methods for integration and creation of Virtual Learning Environments (VLEs) which are a fixed part of the new revolution in Education. Virtual Learning Environments provide management of the process of learning and the objects and subjects that participate in it, by creation, use and exploitation of various resources (information entities, tests, learning courses, etc.). In this context, together with the improving of the Virtual Learning Environments there must be developed specifications as a means of standardization of E-learning resources. By using standards, the developers can create coordinated information with which either E-learning standardization can work or other developers of this information which is formatted by the appropriate standards. So that, following an appropriate standard provides an opportunity to different Virtual Learning Environments (VLEs) to exchange learning resources and data. For this purpose it is necessary to take some resources from different sources in order to develop different E-learning strategies (by means of the use of uniform structures, to exchange dynamically data with them, to create/have access to integrated data, etc.).

Concerning E-learning in particular, the process of standardization for the purposes of ensuring interoperability, portability and reusability, includes architectures and reference models, educational metadata, course structures, student assessment, content packaging and encapsulation, student management, runtime environments, and other specifications. E-learning is a concept which comprises almost anything related to learning in combination with Information and Communication Technology (ICT) or Technology of information and Communications (TIC) strategies. In this way, the first treatment of the standards named "specification" consists of a combination of basic principles and rules. As a result of a large number of researches and experiments, accredited organizations recognize these specifications as international standards.

The application of standards and standardization process can be seen as driving factors in special for educational organizations. Moreover, the current importance of the World Wide Web (WWW), for example, is closely related to the usage of standardization and standards like: TCP (Transmission Control Protocol), IP (Internet Protocol), HTTP (Hyper Text Transfer Protocol) and HTML (Hyper Text Mark up Language). For another great example of standardization and standards as driving factor for the evolvement of an industry, we take a look at the video consumer market. Only after it had been decided that VHS-system would be the format for videotapes, the industry started to prosper and the consumer market started developing fast. In general, standards can help mitigate the risk of an investment in branches that are exposed to fast changing environments.

Although the E-learning industry is managed in some cases by economical factors and some arise from market environment and development of branches. However some additional factors have to be taken into account when designing E-learning standards and standardization processes.

It must be focus in some goals of standards and standardizations in E-learning such as:

- accessibility,
- interoperability,
- reusability,
- reuse of content,
- economical,
- flexibility,
- simplicity, and
- durability.

Related Works Review

A number of research efforts in the 'E-learning' and 'Schema Matching' fields can be considered as related work. While we have yet to see a similar framework within the E-learning domain, there are efforts which examine the interoperability of learning resources through the implementation of standards-based frameworks. However, the integration of the learning standards into the relational databases was manually performed in both cases.

The pervasiveness of relational databases discussed in the previous section is reinforced by the recent interests in the management of XML data with relational databases. Some research efforts have looked into algorithms and approaches towards the management of XML data within existing object-relational databases (e.g. Oracle).

In the area of Schema Matching, excellent surveys of generic schema matching applications can be found. In addition, we also examined three recent systems which are chosen for their diversity of approach in various stages of the matching process. The first employs machine-learning techniques to map between data sources semi-automatically. The main drawback is its need for quality training data. The second explores the use of Relational Databases Files as a common structure but the mapping rules are provided manually. The third, Cupid is a useful hybrid matcher but there was no evaluation available.

Teaching by means of E-learning involves working in standardization of the processes. It is a fact that a lot of organizations work on the development of specifications related to electronic education like metadata, information for students and courses, models of the learner, simplicity of contents, outlook of the learning resources, behaviour of the learning resources, operations with databases, etc.

In fact, nowadays, a huge number of organizations are competing E-learning market. Consequently, E-learning products developed by various educational companies encounter difficulties in resources sharing and systems interoperating due in part to the use of variant technology specifications. This situation creates a strong demand for the adoption of consistent E-learning standardization.

A fairly strong regimen of technical standards has been developed by these organizations to ensure good quality 'interoperability, reusability of resources and tools, durability, maintainability and adaptability' to meet the varied needs of international learning environments.

Taking into account this matter, some initiatives towards standardization of technical aspects have been undertaken at the international level by organizations and consortia among others, such as: the International Standards Organization (ISO), Advanced Distributed Learning (ADL), Aviation Industry CBT Committee (AICC), IMS Global Learning Consortium, Alliance of Remote Instructional Authoring and Distribution Networks for Europe (ARIADNE), World Wide Web Consortium (W3C), Australian Information and Communications Technology in Education Committee (AICTEC).

In this context, the presented E-learning project goal is to develop compatible Virtual Learning Environment. Although in the process of achieving the aims in the virtual context, we can see that unfortunately, in some cases, such compatibility cannot be fulfilled. This result is a consequence of the fact that some specifications are: quite general, others are based on early learning computer systems and need to be adapted to the Web applications, etc.

Technical Standards: International Initiatives

Some of the most important organizations and their actual participations in the development of the Virtual Learning Environments (VLE) are as follows:

- **ADL (Advanced Distributed Learning)**

ADL is a US government-sponsored organization that researches and develops specifications to encourage the adoption and advancement of Virtual Learning environments (VLEs). ADL is an initiative of the US government, which started originally in 1997 within the US Department of Defence, but now includes other Federal agencies. ADL includes ADL specification (SCORM 9 - Sharable Content Object Reference Model), a collection of standards and specifications for web-based E-learning. It defines communications between client side content and a host system called the run-time environment, commonly a function of a learning management system. SCORM also defines how content may be packaged into a transferable zip file.

The most widely accepted ADL publication is the ADL Shareable Content Object Reference Model (SCORM). SCORM specification combines elements of IEEE, AICC and IMS specifications into a consolidated document that is a specific model of agreement between disparate groups and interests.

The SCORM specification [SCORM (2004)] is developed in two levels:

- **SCORM Content Aggregation Model:** It provides technical methods for description of the learning contents that can be recognized, described, integrated into a course or a part of a course, or exchanged between Virtual Learning Environments (VLEs) or data storages. It consists of the following specifications:
    - **Content Model:** nomenclature defining the content components of learning experience;
    - **Meta-data**: a mechanism for describing specific instances of the components of the content model
- **Content Packaging**: This second level defines how to represent the intended behaviour of a learning experience (Content Structure) and how to package E-learning resources for movement between different environments. Content Packaging provides E-learning resources that can be reusable and interoperable across multiple Virtual Learning Environments.

There is a common way to start E-learning resources and a common mechanism for E-learning resources to communicate with a Virtual Learning Environment (VLE).

The SCORM Run Time Environment consists of:

- **Data Model:** a standard set of data elements used to define the information being communicated such as the status of the E-learning resource;
- **Launch:** a mechanism that defines a common way for Virtual Learning Environments to start Web-based learning resources. The communication protocols are standardized with the use of a common API;
- **Communication API:** the communication mechanism for informing the VLEs of the

state of the learning resource (e.g., initialized, finished or in an error condition).

- **Alliance of Remote Instructional Authoring & Distribution Networks for Europe (ARIADNE) Foundation**

ARIADNE is a foundation that provides projects for developing the higher education in Europe.

In fact, ARIADNE is a European foundation developing concepts and tools for computer-based and telematics-supported remote authoring, teaching, and learning, with a strong emphasis on the sharing and reuse of E-learning materials.

The foundation partners contribute to international standardization activities, notably for metadata, and have developed an operational infrastructure.

ARIADNE has been collaborating with the Learning Object Metadata (LOM) working group of the IEEE-LTSC.

In this context, the most famous project of this organization is the ARIADNE Standard. A completed XML text file can easily be used by Virtual Learning Environments (VLEs) to generate the actual online course, if the VLE is provided with operational access to the electronic pedagogical contents needed for the course and referenced in the XML text file.

ARIADNE defines elements that describe metadata for common E-learning resources but does not define the form of this metadata. ARIADNE submitted an early version of this specification in 1998 to the IEEE LTSC Learning Object Metadata (LOM). This version, together with a similar specification (contributed by the IMS Project, an early ARIADNE version) was the basis of the Learning Object Metadata (LOM) standard.

Nowadays, ARIADNE is being used as a profile of the Learning Object Metadata (LOM) standard.

The ARIADNE standard groups data elements in seven categories:

- General,
- Semantics of the resources,
- Pedagogical,
- Technical,
- Conditions for use, and
- Meta-data and Annotations,

However, other standards consist of nine categories for metadata description:

- General,
- Life cycle,
- Meta-metadata,
- Technical,
- Educational,
- Rights,
- Relation,
- Annotation, and
- Classification.

- **Aviation Industry CBT [Computer-Based Training] Committee (AICC)**

AICC is an international group of technology-based professional learning (AGR, 2004). It released specification for the interchange of the elements of the virtual course as text, graphics, motion (frame-based), audio and logic (Courseware Interchange). AICC develops guidelines for aviation industry in the development, delivery and evaluation of E-learning and related training technologies. The specifications developed by AICC e.g. CMI a learning management system have had the largest adoption in the marketplace.

However the AICC product certification comes with a disclaimer that proof of that product's quality or an indication of that product's robustness and a product may pass AICC certification tests but may not meet the needs. Hence care needs to be taken to thoroughly review and verify the functionality of the product before purchasing any training product.

The AICC currently offers certification testing. The types of products that can be certified are:

Assignable units, CBT courses, CMI systems, CMI Application Service Provider, Courseware Generation /Assessment Systems and Authoring Systems.

Moreover, the AICC certifies training products of the Computer Managed Instruction (file based), Web-based Computer Managed Instruction that comply with AICC Guidelines, and Recommendations (AGRs) via its independent test labs.

- **Institute of Electrical and Electronics Engineers (IEEE)**

IEEE is an international organization that develops technical standards and recommendations for electrical, electronic, computer and communication systems.

The most widely acknowledged IEEE-LTSC specification is the Learning Object Metadata (LOM) specification, which defines element groups and elements that describe learning resources. The IMS and ADL both use the LOM elements and structures in their specifications. The metadata instances that describe the E-learning resources can be used by various VLEs to create, to arrange, to assess or to exchange E-learning resources between different environments. However, specifications that define the way by which VLEs use a metadata instance for E-learning resources are not provided by the IEEE organization. In 2002 the LOM specification was turned into an IEEE approved standard.

- **Instructional Management System (IMS) Global Consortium**

IMS is a consortium of vendors and implementers which focuses on the development of XML-based specifications. These specifications describe the key characteristics of courses, lessons, assessments, learners and groups. In addition, the XML Specifications and Best Practices Guidelines provide a structure for representing E-learning metadata. As a matter of fact, IMS commands the largest number of specifications. IMS originated in 1997 in the US with its membership drawn from academic and commercial organizations. It has quickly grown to include international participation and its investment membership has broadened to include content developers and government agencies. IMS has over 200 "development network" members that review and use IMS-developed specifications. IMS specifications are aimed at delivering interoperability for systems that support online learning, education and training.

In this context, the most widely acknowledged IMS specifications are: IMS-QTI, IMS-Metadata and IMS-Content Packaging (IMS, 2006).

It is possible to describe the items as follows:

- IMS-QTI: Question and Test Interchange describes the structure of E-learning resources.
- IMS-Metadata provides description of these learning objects that can be integrated in larger structures, named packages, by using the mechanism of IMS-Content Packaging. The IMS-Metadata standard uses the same element as those in the LOM standard.
- IMS-Content Packaging: structures, named packages, by using of IMS-Content Packaging.

Database Support for XML-Based E-Learning Standards

Generally speaking, we cannot design the future of storage management in enterprise information and learning systems, but the current trend still points to one dominated by relational databases. Other alternatives that could manage XML data include object-oriented databases (OODBs) and native XML databases (NXDs). While Object-Oriented Databases technology is relatively mature, the use of such systems is relatively low. This is perhaps because most organization systems are still unwilling to forsake their current relational databases for alternatives. Native XML databases are designed to manipulate XML data directly in a proprietary manner. In theory, native XML databases should provide better performances compared to manipulating XML data with relational databases.

However, native XML databases are relatively new to compare enough real results with theory. In addition to standards-based XML data, E-learning systems are often required to store data that are relational in nature and thus are more suitably supported by Relational Databases Management Standards Systems (RDBMS). The same reasons perhaps are influencing the poor uptake of Object-Oriented Databases may also affect the adoption of Native XML Databases (NXDs).

Related Works

A number of research efforts in the 'E-learning' and 'Schema Matching' fields can be considered as related work. While we have yet to see a similar framework within the E-learning domain, there are efforts such as in several works (Miller, 1990; Papaioannou et. al., 2001) which examine the interoperability of learning resources through the implementation of standards-based frameworks.

However, the standardization management and the integration of E-learning standards into relational databases were manually performed in both cases. The pervasiveness of relational databases discussed in the previous section is reinforced by the recent interests in the management of XML data with relational databases. A great of research efforts (Kudrass & Conrad, 2002; Rahm & Bernstein, 2001) have looked into algorithms and approaches towards the management of XML data within existing Object-Relational Databases (e.g. Oracle).

In the area of Schema Matching, an excellent survey of generic schema matching applications can be found in the work by Qu & Nejdl (2002).

In addition, we can also exam three recent systems which are chosen for their diversity of approach in various stages of the matching process:

- The first one employs machine-learning techniques to map between data sources semi-automatically. The main drawback is its need for quality training data.
- The second one (Runapongsa & Patel, 2003) explores the use of Relational Databases Files as a common structure but the mapping rules are provided manually.
- The third one, Cupid is a useful hybrid matcher but there was no evaluation available.

MAIN FOCUS OF E-LEARNING MEDIATION FRAMEWORK

Issues, Controversies, Problems

Overview of E-Learning Mediation Framework

One of the most important aspects of E-learning systems, "search and retrieval of learning content", is usually through learning object metadata. To provide SQL based queries for metadata, it is need to map between the metadata XML documents and the relational databases as well as provide a platform and database independent framework to perform the import and export of metadata to and from storage.

A new proposed mapping mediation framework helps in order to improve the relationship between an existing relational database schema and an E-learning Metadata XML Schema is also necessary to assume that the relational database is an existing Learning Management System (LMS) and the metadata belongs to a learning object. It may operate with any Learning Management System (LMS) as it does not require any knowledge of the Learning Management System's internal functionalities.

Institutional Profile Considerations

In the context of optimizing E-learning management, it is need also to ascertain some aspects of the institution profile, such as:

- the background of the institution and it is necessary also to consider its edge (some parameters such as if it is a new organization or it has been in operation for a while).
- it is formal/non-formal/mixed mode/open and distance learning institution or entirely to E-learning.
- the institutional accreditation.
- the credibility of the organization in the academic world (kind of facilities, infrastructure and resources (human, technical and financial) that are available with the organization).

Moreover, the use of technology in E-learning requires significant investments in terms of software, hardware, delivery mechanism as well as operation of the equipment. Hence, political will of the organization to use technology on a sustained basis also needs to be assessed. Once the above questions have been addressed the specific need to use technology for E-learning needs to be established.

In this context it is also necessary to study the main reasons of E-learning, such as:

- if it is due to the fact that technology is available and needed to be used somehow, or because it is order of the day is considered fashionable and sells.
- if it has come in the form of a directive from a higher authority/agency/ministry asking an institution to adopt it.
- if there is a genuine need for using multimedia resources.

Keeping in mind the affirmative way, it is also necessary think about what is the broad aim:

- if they are used for teaching, training, technical or vocational training.
- if they are aimed at providing better job opportunities or they will be used for generating awareness, attitudinal changes or enrichment.

E-Learning Environment Study

It is recommended to ascertain the type of learning environment in which the materials will be used, whether in standalone format, or complementary or supplementary modes. Moreover, is also necessary to know if it is used in standalone format, then learning materials need to be exhaustive as learners will entirely depend on these materials. If used in complementary or supplementary modes such as in technology-enabled classrooms or Open and Distance Learning then E-learning component has to be properly integrated with the course materials (Lazarinis, Green & Koutromanos, 2009).

It is also necessary to consider the way of E-learning materials will be used (such as synchronous or in asynchronous modes):

- **Synchronous** communication, such as online chat session or a virtual classroom, will require the presence of learners in real time at different locations (whereas in asynchronous communication they can contribute at their own pace and convenient times).
- **Asynchronous** mode has been found pedagogically effective as it allows greater degree of freedom and flexibility to the learners who can carefully reflect over the material - edit, store and retrieve it at their own time and pace. It is also recommended to know whether the E-learning will be collaborative or individualized activity. And finally, it will be desirable to have certain

understanding of likely constraints learners may face during learning transaction (such as working in noisy surroundings, under or over illuminated rooms and so on).

Pedagogical Approaches

E-learning is purposive, positive and pragmatic in nature and its ultimate objective is pedagogy/andragogy. In sharp contrast to the direct teaching approach, E-learning makes use of experiential learning in which students 'act' rather than 'listen' hence, selection of appropriate teaching style for communicating with dispersed and heterogeneous groups is crucial.

In a traditional teaching situation, the teacher is in direct contact with learners. He/she presents the topic, explains the content, guides and encourages the students who in turn interpret (the messages, expressions, body language and variations of tone, etc.) of the teacher. However, since the teacher is not physically present in an E-learning transaction, he/she has to be built in the material to involve the learner. So that, E-learning transaction, can be done in various ways, such as, by incorporating inclusive expressions such as 'we', 'you', 'us' 'our' etc. to personalize the material.

Thinking that circular nature of information flow which 'talks with' learners also facilitates involvement of the learners. This approach, in contrast with the vertical top-down approach considers students as intelligent human beings who are equal partners in the learning process. Apart from the knowledge of content and preparing quality learning materials, an effective online teacher has to be a good facilitator, manager and motivator. He/she should have a sound understanding of human psychology to create positive learning environment. He/she needs to evince genuine interest in the problems and concerns of the learners through appropriate communication channels and also make efforts to address them. The teacher has to be a good manager or coordinating various activities related to assignments, examination and so on. The contribution of a teacher goes a long way in helping learners to apply the knowledge gained and develop critical thinking for making informed choices and in turn empowering them.

As knowledge-transmission alone does not constitute learning, it is now considered necessary to add activities that promote thinking and reflection. Hence, designing of appropriate activities which include completion of knowledge based assignments, finding solution to life-related problems and devising (and solving) self-tests is also an important contribution of an E-learning teacher (Poway, 2002). Computers have been found excellent for presenting and testing rule-based procedures, or areas of abstract knowledge in which answers are clearly correct.

Moreover, simple pedagogical approaches of creating content may lack flexibility and richness and downstream functionality whereas complex approaches can be difficult to set up and slow to develop. The share of various components such as online discussion forums, chatting, web conferencing between students, lecturers, professionals and other stakeholders for exchange of information needs to be thoroughly worked out and integrated. Whichever pedagogical approach is followed, the learning objectives need to be well defined, realistic and achievable. The concepts should be properly explained incorporating adequate examples, illustrations and supporting details. Individual differences of the learners having different learning styles also need to be taken into consideration. It also needs to be considered whether innovative approaches aimed at developing higher order skills such as thinking critically, analyzing, making inferences, synthesizing and solving problems have been used by optimally harnessing the potential of technology.

E-Learning Material Design Optimization

The use, optimization design and layout of E-learning materials are very important. Therefore, there is a variety of elements and the final results will be very different depending on how the different elements are interlinked. So that it is necessary to assess whether appropriate language and vocabulary both in terms of content and audience has been used. Moreover, clear and consistent navigation mechanism (which includes orientation information, navigation bars, site maps, tables of content etc.) has been provided for navigating within and between pages to increase accessibility and usability of materials. Moreover, it needs to be ascertained if the tools (visuals, pictures, diagrams, graphics, animation and flowcharts etc.) used in material design are optimized to facilitate clarity. And keeping on mind also whether the use of some parameters (such as colour, type and size of fonts) is appropriate to teach with efficiency (clarifying the electronic content, the movement of images, pacing, and speed of information facilitate readability, whether hyperlinks, tags, frames, titles and labels etc.) to help in signposting the E- learning materials.

In addition to hypertext, web also involves hypermedia, i.e., audio and video components which need to be properly audible/visible at the learning ends hence their reception quality merits assessment. The advance searching capabilities, proper links to reference material and knowledge repository, periodicity of storage of information in archives can also be examined.

The overall objective of all these optimized design elements should that the materials are user friendly which facilitate learning otherwise if technology is all presentation or simulation, then it may lead to passive assimilation of information rather than active construction of knowledge.

Keeping in mind that the different approaches of using new E-learning technologies offered around the world permit some different possibilities and ways of learning "along all the life" to the learners of the Society. In this context, Goods (2001) argued that online educators not only need expertise in traditional class room pedagogy and online communication and moderation, but also high levels of technical skills and awareness. Hence, it will be useful in this regard if subject specialists and content developers have good understanding of the design elements to use them sensibly.

Feedback Mechanism

While developing indicators for standardization, the feedback mechanism needs a thorough assessment. Moreover, interactivity being a two-way process, learners' ability to ask questions for clarifying doubts, seeking clarifications and guidance constitutes a prime condition for learning. Learners, therefore, need to be properly guided to raise relevant and appropriate questions. At the same time, teacher also needs to respond to the students' queries, guide and mentor them on a regular basis, hence the teacher's ability to respond to the learner queries also merits close assessment. So that is be useful to know what is the frequency and quality of response to the learner – if it show empathy to learner needs or it is cursory, mechanical and unhelpful and if teacher exude patience while responding to learner queries or displays irritation or impatience thus affecting learner's future participation.

Since E-learning requires greater discipline on the part of learners as compared to the conventional mode hence, learners need to be informed in advance about expectations from them such as completing the various components within specified time frame and so on. This would help learners to plan their agenda of study and achieve learning goals effectively.

In this context, lack of proper communication can impinge upon their involvement which may make them loose interest and focus midway. Moreover, it has been widely accepted that motivational factors such as appreciating the good work, ideas and suggestions infuse encouragement and motivate the learner. Thus, a mature handling of the learner queries and sensitivity towards their learning needs cannot be overstated. Apart from academic level, feedback mechanism needs to be assessed at the organizational level also. So that, it is useful know how receptive the organization is in responding to learner queries/problems and concerns, how soon their administrative matters are responded and addressed and how regularly information is communicated to learners, and so on.

Solutions and Recommendations

Overview of Framework

Perhaps, one of the most important aspects of E-learning systems, "search and retrieval of learning content", is usually through learning object metadata.

In order to provide System Quality Learning (SQL) based queries for metadata, we need to map between the metadata XML documents and the relational databases as well as provide a platform and database independent framework to perform the import and export of metadata to and from storage.

It had been assumed that the relational database is of an existing LMS (Learning Management System) and the metadata belongs to a learning object.

A proposed mapping mediation framework helps match between an existing Relational database schema and an E-learning Metadata XML Schema.

The proposed framework comprises of three main components:

- **Schema Matcher Module:** The Schema Matcher Module provides semi-automatic matching between a relational schema and an XML Schema. It may operate with any Learning Management Systems (LMS) as it does not require any knowledge of the Learning Management Systems (LMS's) internal functionalities. Moreover, developers may easily integrate an existing LMS with our framework as only a connection to the LMS's database is required for our operations.
    - First at all, the Schema Wrappers read the two schemas and convert both into abstract structures with a similar format (Schema Tree Instances).
    - Second, the lexical pre-processor reads the XML Schema tree instance and generates a list of lexically-equivalent terms for the leaf nodes with the aid of WordNet (Miller, 1990) and lexical matching is then performed. The lexical processor reads the XML Schema tree instance and generates a list of lexically-equivalent terms for the leaf nodes with the aid of WordNet and Lexical matching is then performed.
    - After, Mediation Framework matching both tree instances and the lexical-equivalent terms, scores are conferred depending on the degree of match. Substring, exact and lexically-equivalent matches are considered for both leaf and ancestor nodes.
    - Then the Structural Matcher examines the ancestry path information of both trees and compares the similarity between the locations of siblings and parents of both trees iteratively.
    - Based on a table of mappings between XML Schema and System Quality Learning (SQL) data types, the Datatype Matcher then determines varying degrees of matches between the two sets of data types.
    - Finally, the Schema Matcher displays the list of relational schema elements (relations and columns) as well as the corresponding 'best' XML Schema element match. The user may then choose to export the mappings into a Mapping Configuration XML document.

- **Translator Module:** While the previous module operate solely on the 'models' of both data sources, the Translator module acts as a bridge between the data.
    - By using the mappings created and refined from the previous two modules, the translator reads in the data from the XML learning objects metadata and with the help of the mappings, packages the data into a series of SQL 'insert' statements. These statements are thereafter executed to insert the learning object content into the E-learning system database.
    - Moreover, this translator formulates the statements while ensuring the correct order of 'inserts' with regards to the foreign key relationship constraints.
- **Mapper Tool Module:** The Mapper Tool is an intuitive interface which serves two main functions:
    - Firstly, it allows the developer to manually refine mappings to cope with inaccuracies from the Schema Matcher.
    - Secondly, it allows a developer the flexibility of manually creating the Schema mappings from scratch.

Monitoring and Evaluation

Monitoring and Evaluation of some developed prototypes has been completed and we performed initial evaluation on the Schema Matcher module while the performance and accuracy was acceptable. Currently, it is impossible for Schema Matching to achieve 100% accuracy, given the lack of semantic support. However, with WordNet, it is only possible to retrieve synonyms for single words. The evaluation showed that XML Schema Wrapper was also able to work with a number of XML Schemas (defined using different conventions) to produce Schema Tree Instances successfully. Moreover, with increasing interests in the integration of XML data and other sources, our XML Schema wrapper will be a useful component in many applications. The overall objective while identifying indicators for content design should be that material meets the learning objectives as well as prevalent educational standards and standardization process. In addition, words like 'cost-price' are foreign to lexical anthologies, like WordNet and semantics, are only available for 'single-word terms'. However, with present technology, it is impossible to obtain the semantics of such terms (Bao, López, Juárez & Castresana, 2009). So that, this makes lexical matching difficult. It is possible to adopt NLP (Natural Language Processing) techniques to aid in the process of matching and even with that, the matching is more structural than semantic-based (Bao, Juárez, López & Castresana, 2009; Boehm, 1981).

In order to make things clear, it is necessary to think about that many words have more than one meaning, depending on the context. So that, unless explicitly provided, machines will find it difficult to detect the context that a term is used in (Reigeluth, 1999; Weaver, 1993; Patching, 1990). Moreover, other than the lack of semantic support, it has been noticed that a number of 'real-world' schemas define attributes and relations using acronyms or other short forms. Examples include 'qty', and 'uom′' (Gagne, Briggs & Wager, 1992; Bloom, Hastings & Madaus, 1971). While human readers might be able to discern the actual meanings of these terms, the terms are not machine understandable and are difficult to perform matching on (Merrill, 1994). To cope with this, we are currently exploring the use of existing abbreviation libraries and user predefined localized libraries Authors have studied how to measure E-learning processes (Lazarinis, Green & Pearson, 2009; Clark, 1994; Lazarinis, 2004).

Keeping on mind that a proper examination system using appropriated testing tools and instruments (such as checking, monitoring, correcting mistakes and changing system if necessary), evokes confidence and credibility within and outside the system, and clarity to already acquired knowledge. Moreover, learners can get more involved in their studies by monitoring their progress through regular checking of their assignments and grades, hence the need for sound evaluation mechanism. It is also recommendable to consider if issues related to examination system could be conducted online or face to face or if can be conducted on demand. Additionally, it is necessary to think what will be the number, timing, format markers (number internal or contracted) for assignments and examination, how soon will grades be uploaded. So that, the access to question banks, flexibility and ease of usage, speed with which information can be accessed need to be thoroughly examined. Apart from the issues discussed above, it is also needed to know whether pricing of courseware is appropriate and proper cost analysis has been undertaken to arrive at the fee and what is the employability of courses offered through E-learning keeping in view the market trends and demands. It is also needed to ascertain whether the electronic content is peer reviewed or not and whether appropriate references have been cited. Additionally, whether the material has been reproduced elsewhere or it can be used for reference purpose, or there is any provision of reporting errors in the document and so on. It will be useful to evolve some mechanism to get the content validated and authenticated by an authoritative source to address some of these issues and also the growing menace of cut/copy-paste.

Possible Indicators

It is possible the above analysis points could be checked by some possible indicators for key areas which can be assessed for developing educational multimedia materials. These indicators are based on the following three assumptions: Target learner is the core or pivot of all E-learning activity; all indicators are geared towards meeting the E-learning objectives and Quality is an integral component and is subsumed in all the activities of E-learning.

Possible indicators (classified by relevance) could be as follows:

- **Availability** (Institutional)**:** Key Issues: Resources (human, technical, financial), Political will, Infrastructure, Facilities, Hardware, Software.
- **Accessibility** (Target Learner): Key Issues: resources, Hardware, Software, Internet connectivity
- **Interactivity:** Key Issues: Content, Material design, Teaching-Learning, Institutional, Administrative
- **Readability:** Key Issues: Content, Material design, Language
- **Reliability/Credibility:** Key Issues: Content, Pedagogy, Evaluation, Hardware, Software, Delivery mechanism, Learner support system, Pricing
- **User-friendliness:** Key Issues: Technology, Learning resources, Material design
- **Periodicity/Durability:** Key Issues: Content, Copyright, Software, IPR, Pricing, Security Mechanism
- **Flexibility/Adaptability:** Key Issues: Content, Material design, Pedagogy, Evaluation, Software, Hardware
- **Sensitivity:** Key Issues: Content, Material design, Pedagogy, Learner Needs, Inclusive groups

FUTURE RESEARCH DIRECTIONS

On the one hand, future emerging E-learning trends could be exploring ways to employ ontology to introduce machine-readable semantics into our lexical matching techniques and attempt some indicators for assessment leading to certification of materials must be checked. These indicators need to be thoroughly discussed; some of them may be merged together while others may be added to arrive at a holistic understanding of the issue. The viability and optimization of E-learning model (paradigm, model, implementation issues of proposed programs, etc.) that have been analyzed in our framework cater to the mapping between metadata specifications and learning systems. Moreover, framework is both database and platform-independent and is loosely-coupled with the underlying learning system. Hence, it is extremely extensible. So that it could be extended to other aspects of E-learning or learning domain.

On the other hand, currently, increasing numbers of standards and specifications are being defined in XML format. Hence, a framework that performs matching between XML and relational schemas is extremely useful. With rapid globalization, there is a greater need for the exchange of knowledge residing in heterogeneous information systems. Ontology may be the answer to this lack of semantic support and is a relatively new area of research because existing ontology is still incomplete.

At last but not at least, it is could suggest as future research opportunities within the E-learning to explore ways to employ ontology to introduce machine-readable semantics into our lexical matching techniques.

CONCLUSION

According with the quickly process of globalization, there is a greater need for the exchange of knowledge residing in heterogeneous information systems. Ontologies may be the answer to this lack of semantic support. Ontology engineering is a relatively new area of research and existing ontologies are still incomplete. While developing standards for E-learning we need to learn from our experiences and also from the best practices available and adapting them to our local needs. Though what constitutes 'best' always remains an elusive concept (Prasad, 2003). Whatever standards are developed, they should represent facts be achievable, reasonable and measurable. The standards need to be clearly specified, explicitly defined for key activities and should be consistent in different documents.

The E-learning systems are an important part during the development of the modern Virtual Learning Environments (VLEs). The use of the standards in the Virtual Learning Environments (VLEs) provides an excellent structure of the description of the learning resources, virtual courses and their participants. The basic purpose for future experiments is the description of other modules of the Virtual Learning Environments (VLEs) (like models of students, data for groups of students, design of the learning resources, etc.).

The development of these purposes will create an integrated environment for data exchange between Virtual Learning Environments (VLEs). At present, framework caters to the mapping between metadata specifications and learning systems. It can be easily extended to cater to other aspects of E-learning or even beyond the learning domain. Framework is both database and platform-independent and is loosely-coupled with the underlying learning system. Hence, it is extremely extensible. Currently, increasing numbers of standards and specifications are being defined in XML format. Hence, a framework that performs matching between XML and relational schemas is extremely useful.

Currently, it is impossible for Schema Matching to achieve 100% accuracy, given the lack of semantic support. With WorldNet, it is only possible to retrieve synonyms for single words. Words like 'cost-price' are foreign to lexical anthologies like WorldNet and semantics are only available for 'single-word terms'. With present technology, it is impossible to obtain the semantics of such terms. This makes it difficult for lexical matching. We may adopt NLP (Natural Language Processing) techniques to aid in the process of matching and even with that, the matching is more structural than semantic-based. In addition, many words have more than one meaning, depending on the context.

Unless explicitly provided, machines will find it difficult to detect the context that a term is used in. Other than the lack of semantic support, we notice that a number of 'real world' schemas define attributes and relations using acronyms or other short forms. Examples include 'qty', and 'uom'. While human readers might be able to discern the actual meanings of these terms, the terms are not machine understandable and are difficult to perform matching on. To cope with this, we are currently exploring the use of existing abbreviation libraries and user predefined localized libraries. The evaluation showed that our XML Schema Wrapper was also able to work with a number of XML Schemas (defined using different conventions) to produce Schema Tree Instances successfully. With increasing interests in the integration of XML data and other sources, our XML Schema wrapper will be a useful component in many applications.

As the main goal search in this paper, an attempt was made to identify some indicators for assessment leading to certification of materials. These indicators need to be thoroughly discussed. Some of them may be merged together while others may be added to arrive at a holistic understanding of the issue.

REFERENCES

Aviation Industry Committee. *AGR 010 – Web-based computer managed instruction AICC Guidelines and Recommendations (AGRs). AGR-010.* (2004). Retrieved July 29, 2009, from http://www.aicc.org

Bansal, K. (2002). *Educational Audio-Visual Media: Some Indicators for Evaluation.* Paper presented in Seminar organized by the Academic Staff College at Jamia Millia Islamia, December, 2,2002, New Delhi, India.

Bansal, K. (2003). *Educational Audio Programmes: Issues Related to Content.* Paper presented in National Seminar on Radio Broadcast as a Tool of Distance Learning, organised by Distance Education Programme (DEP), May 27-28, 2003, New Delhi, India.

Bao, C., Juárez, M., López, L., & Castresana, J. M. (2009). *A methodology of E-learning System Engineering.* Paper presented in ICERI, International Conference of Education, Research and Innovation, November 17-18, Madrid, Spain.

Bao, C., López, L., & Castresana, J. M. (2009). *Teaching in industrial Engineering: the traditional and the new EEES.* Paper presented in International Conference on Education and New learning Technologies, Edulearn-09, July 6-8, Barcelona, Spain.

Bao, C., López, L., Juárez, M., & Castresana, J. M. (2009). *Information technology optimization strategies in Science Higher Education.* Paper presented in International Conference on Education and New learning Technologies, Edulearn-09, July 6-8, 2009. Barcelona, Spain.

Bao, C., López, L., Juárez, M., & Castresana, J. M. (2009). Educating the engineer of 2020: adapting engineering education to the new century. In *International Technology, Education and Development conference INTED 2009*, March 9-11, Valencia, Spain.

Bloom, B. S. Hastings, J.T. & Madaus, G.F. (1971). *Handbook on Formative and Summative Evaluation of Student Learning.* New York: McGraw-Hill.

Boehm, B. W. (1981). *Software Engineering Economics.* Upper Saddle River, NJ: Prentice Hall.

Centre for Education Technology Interoperability Standards. CETIS. (2002). *Who's doing what?* Retrieved July 29, 2009, from http://www.cetis.ac.uk/static/who-does-what.html

Clark, R. (1994). Media will never influence learning. *Educational Technology Research and Development*, *42*(2), 21–29. doi:10.1007/BF02299088

Gagne, R. M., Briggs, L. J., & Wager, W. W. (1992). *Principles of Instructional Design*. Orlando, FL: Harcourt Brace Jovanovich publishers.

Green, S., Jones, R., Pearson, E., & Gkatzidou, S. (2006). Accessibility and adaptability of learning objects: responding to metadata, learning patterns and profiles of needs and preferences. *ALT-J. Research in Learning Technology*, *14*(1), 117–129.

IMS Meta-data Specification. *IMS Content Packaging*. (2006). Retrieved July 29, 2009, from http://imsproject.org

Lazarinis, F. (2004). A Template Based System for Automatic Construction of Online Courseware for Secondary Educational Schools. *Journal of Educational Technology & Society*, *7*(3), 112–123.

Lazarinis, F., Green, S., & Koutromanos, G. (2009). *Web-Based Learner Profile Management Using IMS IP. Paper presented in International Technology, Education and Development Conference (INTED 2009),* Valencia, Spain.

Lazarinis, F., Green, S., Pearson, E. (2009). Measuring the conformance of hypermedia assessment tools to QTI. *International Journal of Innovation and Learning*, *6*(2), 127–146. doi:10.1504/IJIL.2009.022809

Merrill, M. D. (1994). *Instructional Design Theory*. Upper Saddle River, NJ: Educational Technology Publications.

Miller, G. (1990). Wordnet: An on-line lexical database. *International Journal of Lexicography (special issue), Computational Linguistics*, *18*(1), 3(4), 235–312.

Panar, A. (2009). *SCORM-2004 Overview, Sharable Content Object Reference Model Run-Time Environment*. Retrieved July 29, 2009, from http://www.adlnet.org

Papaioannou, V., Karadimitriou, P., Papageorgiou, A., Karagiannidis, C., & Sampson, D. G. (2001). *From educational meta-data authoring to educational meta-data management*. Paper presented in IEEE International Conference on Advanced Learning Technologies-ICALT'01, August 6-8, Madison, USA.

Pillai, L. (2003). *Quality assurance and best practices, Best Practices in Open and Distance Education*. Hyderabad, India: B.R. Ambedkar Open University (BRAOU).

Prasad, V. S. (2003). *Problems and Concerns*. Hyderabad, India: Best Practices in Open and Distance Education. B.R. Ambedkar Open University (BRAOU).

Qu, C., & Nejdl, W. (2002). *Towards open standards: The evolution of an xml/jsp/webdav based collaborative courseware generating system*. Paper presented in International Conference on Web-based Learning-1, August 17-19, Hong-Kong, China.

Rahm, E., & Bernstein, P. A. (2001). A survey of approaches to automatic schema matching. *The Very Large Data Bases Journal*, *10*(4), 334–350. doi:10.1007/s007780100057

Reigeluth, C. M. (1999). *Instructional-Design Theories and Models: A New Paradigm of Instructional Theory*. Mawah, NJ: Lawrence Erlbaum Associates.

Runapongsa, K., & Patel, J. M. (2003). *Storing and querying xml data in object-relational dbmss*. Paper presented in EDBT 2002 Workshop on XML-Based Data Management, August 27-31, Cargese, France.

Smith, C., Shepherd, E., Brewer, L., & Lay, S. (2002). *IMS Question & Test Interoperability: An Overview*. Retrieved July 29, 2009, from http://www.imsglobal.org

Takwale, R. G. (2003), *Managing paradigm shift in parameters and benchmarks. Best Practices in Open and Distance Education*. Hyderabad, India: B.R. Ambedkar Open University (BRAOU).

Totkov, G. (2003). *Virtual Learning Environments: Towards New Generations*. Paper presented in International Conference on Computer Systems and Technologies, Compsystech-2003, June 19-20, Sofia, Bulgaria.

ADDITIONAL READING

Bao, C. (1991), *Selection of Industrial Materials*, Ph. D. Thesis dissertation, Industrial Engineering High School, Basque County University, Bilbao, Spain.

Kudrass, T., & Conrad, M. (2002), Management of xml documents in object-relational databases. In *EDBT 2002 Workshop on XML-Based Data Management (XMLDM'02)*, March 25-27, Prague, Czech Republic.

Madhavan, J., Bernstein, P. A., & Rahm, E. (2001), Generic schema matching with cupid. Paper presented in *27th International Conference on Very Large Data Bases, VLDB*, September 12-14, Roma, Italy

Miller, G, Wordnet (1990), An on-line lexical database. *International Journal of Lexicography (special issue), Computational Linguistics,* 18(1), 3(4): 235– 312.

Pillai, V. N. R. (2003). *Promotion of best practices in open and distance learning through participation in the NAAC's accreditation process, Best Practices in Open and Distance Education. B.R. Ambedkar Open University*. Hyderabad, India: BRAOU.

Qu, C., & Nejdl, W. (2002), Towards open standards: The evolution of an xml/jsp/webdav based collaborative courseware generating system. In *International Conference on Web-based Learning ICWL-2002*, Hong-Kong, China.

Somova, E. (2003). *Tools system for design, creation and support of virtual learning environments*, Ph. D. Thesis, University of Sofia, Bulgaria.

Tan, M. B. L. (2003). *A mediation framework to support schema matching in e-learning. Technical report, CAIS*. NTU Singapore.

Totkov, G., & Somova, E. (2003). A Planning Model with Resources in e-Learning. *International Journal Information Theories & Applications, 10*(2), 218–226.

Vdovjak, R. and Houben (2001), G-J. RDF-based architecture for semantic integration of heterogeneous information sources. Paper presented in *Workshop on Information Integration on the Web*, April 9-11, Rio de Janeiro, Brazil.

Weaver, P. L. (1993). *Practical SSADM.* London, UK: Pitman publishing.

KEY TERMS AND DEFINITIONS

E-Learning: It is the acquisition and use of knowledge distributed and facilitated primarily by electronic means. In particular, E-learning is the use of internet technology for the creation, management, making available, security, selection and use of educational content to store information about those who learn and to monitor those who learn, and to make communication and cooperation possible.

E-learningStandard: A published E-learning specification or documented agreements containing technical E-learning specifications or other precise criteria to be used consistently as rules, guidelines, or definitions of characteristics, to ensure that materials, products, processes and services are fit for their purpose, that establishes a common language, and contains a technical specification or other precise criteria and is designed to be used consistently, as a rule, a guideline, or a definition.

E-Learning Standardization: Process to manage E-learning by means of optimizing the international portage of E-learning materials in different environment of www.

Standard Accessibility: The ability to locate and access instructional components from one remote location and deliver them to many other locations.

Standard Durability: The ability to withstand technology changes without redesign, reconfiguration or recoding.

Standard Flexibility: The application of standards should not limit the teaching and learning processes.

Standard Interoperability: The ability to take instructional components developed in one location with one set of tools or platform and use them in another location with a different set of tools or platform and standards interoperability for learning technologies have to be independent from system environments and applications have to be independent from system environments and applications.

Standard Simplicity: The implementation of a standard should be effortless to increase the acceptance of developers and authors of learning applications.

Standard Reusability: The flexibility to incorporate instructional components in multiple applications and contexts of learning contents, teaching methods and specifications in different learning environments.

Section 5

Quality and Pedagogy in Learning Technology

Chapter 21
E-Learning:
Psycho-Pedagogical Utility, Usability and Accessibility Criteria from a Learner Centred Perspective

Marta Fuentes Agustí
Universitat Autònoma de Barcelona, Spain

Margarida Romero Velasco
Universitat Autònoma de Barcelona, Spain

María José Hernández Serrano
Universidad de Salamanca, Spain

ABSTRACT

Since the democratization of personal computers and Internet access formal and informal learning opportunities have multiplied, increasing the technological-supported contexts and contents. Despite the increasing opportunities for education, not all teachers have developed a satisfactory level of eCompetence (Schneckenberg, 2006), not being able to choose and implement a technology-supported learning solution efficiently. On the one hand we need to consider the phenomenon of digital emigrant teachers, which is linked to the avoidance of technologies; but on the other, we have a large number of technological-enthusiastic teachers that try to introduce tools and functionalities without assessing first: the cognitive load, the cost, the utility, the usability, the accessibility and the psycho-pedagogical criteria that must be considered before innovate with technologies. This chapter aims at both groups of teachers or instructional developers, by offering a review of the e-learning possibilities and criteria, based on several analyses carried out by the authors on higher educational settings. Based on the learner cantered perspective, this chapter purposes some criteria for assuring the quality in higher education e-learning contexts, mainly based on three categories: psycho-pedagogical utility, usability and accessibility. One of the principal goals of the chapter is to support -by means of the criteria- the selection of technologies and functionalities (collaborative tools, e-learning 2.0 solutions...), considering, above all, the learning objectives and the specific learning contexts. The chapter will introduce also some of the main technology-supported learning solutions and will provide a decision-framework to choose, implement and evaluate the integration of educational technology for e-learning.

DOI: 10.4018/978-1-61692-789-9.ch021

INTRODUCTION

The university has been democratized in most developed countries. Facing the wide and diverse students' targets, nowadays, university is coping with the challenge of quality assurance in learning within a context of complex social changes, basically two. One of these changes is the convergence towards the European Higher Education Area (EHEA), which aims the harmonization of university programs at a European level; the so-called Bologna process aims to improve the recognition of university degrees throughout Europe by facilitating student mobility and employability. The second major change is the introduction of Information and Communication Technologies (ICT) in the University for enhancing teaching and learning methodologies.

In some cases, European universities have seen both changes as a synergy. In this sense, e-learning have been considered as an opportunity to accomplish the Bologna objectives. Thus, the use of ICT in the university increases the learning contexts facilitating the student learning process, the continuous assessment and the eCompetence development (Schneckenberg, 2006). Nevertheless, in some cases, both changes have been considered as a top-down imposition that increases the workload of faculty staff and students. It is possible to observe how implementation of Bologna process means for some teachers incredulous feelings in their first approach to student-centred methodologies. Even worst, some of them feel overwhelmed confronted to the evolution of educational technologies along with the increasingly higher eCompetence of their learners. Worse yet, often these tools involve a high cognitive load (Sweller & Chandler, 1994; Amadieu, Tricot, & Marine, 2009) both by the students and the teachers. It is seems that the speed of technological change is more important than the speed of evolution in the teaching methodologies, or the time required for learning how to use these tools in educational settings. This is a one of the major stress for teachers, but also for some students, who sometimes prefer the traditional face-to-face context.

This chapter will consider the contribution of e-learning as a solution of these recent higher education challenges, and from the perspective of focusing on the educational criteria of usability, utility and acceptability that teachers should consider before using educational technologies. The benefit is for both teachers and students, as e-learning enhance the learner academic performances.

THE ROLE OF E-LEARNING IN THE STUDENT-CENTRED LEARNING PROCESS

The use of e-learning has a critical role for achieving the challenges of the convergence process in the EHEA. In 1998, the Declaration of the Sorbonne put into clear the objective to promote the Economy of Knowledge and Innovation in Europe. This declaration became the first step in the political process of a long-term change in higher education, it were promoted the convergence between national education systems within the different European states. A year later, the Bologna Declaration (1999) entailed a great deal of responsibility for the creation of the EHEA in accordance with principles of quality, mobility, diversity and competitiveness. The most important insight is that majority of the statements made for the implementation of the EHEA (Sorbonne Declaration, 1998 Bologna Declaration, 1999, Prague 2001, Berlin, 2003, Bergen 2005, London, 2007) highlight the need to change the teaching-learning process, for both the teacher and the students, through the use of ICT as a teaching resource, as an object of study, as a tool for educational management and an excellent tool for research (Bosco, 2005 ; De Pablos, 2007).

According to many statements and guidelines for the EHEA, it is required a shift towards a more complex pedagogical model. The pedagogical model that supports the EHEA promotes a learning process focused on student learning, or a learning centred on the student. Thus, in order to achieve the EHEA objectives, traditional teaching methods are not enough. Also, unidirectional teaching should be limited. It is necessary to promote more interactive process that enlarges the face-to-face processes and contexts. In all these challenges, educational technologies offer promising possibilities, supporting individual or collaborative learning activities, in and outside of the scenario of a traditional class.

E-Learning as a Mechanism of Flexibility for Higher Education

The use of educational technologies in higher education enables to create new learning contexts in formal and informal educational settings (Romero, 2009). Contrary to the main disadvantage for their use, in the process of introducing ICT in education, experts from the European Commission (2006) have corroborated that learning how to use the technological tool is a temporal phase that many countries have already passed; the improvement brings only when educational technologies provide innovative practices by supporting the educational processes of communication, evaluation and reflection, or by providing just-in-time feedback that enhance the learning process.

Studies on the evolution of e-learning in traditional universities (Coimbra Group, 2002; Lepori, Cantoni, & Succi, 2003) suggest that most of the higher education organizations have introduced some e-learning degrees in their undergraduate and graduate programs. Everyday it is more and more clear the assumption that e-learning can improve teaching quality in higher education, and specifically in the framework of EHEA. E-learning enables to access from remote locations, provides time flexibility for the development of virtual learning activities, anywhere and anytime learning (Cañellas, 2006). At the same time, educational technologies permit greater interaction with information among the members of the community of learning (Bos-Ciussi, Augier, & Rosner, 2008).

One of the most significant contributions of e-learning in teaching and learning activities is the overcoming of space-time barriers (Cañellas, 2006). From this perspective, it is assumed that some, or all, of the teaching and learning activities occur in a physical space that is not real (in a Virtual Learning Environment), which interaction, communication and access to information are processes developed 24 hours a day. Thus, academic institutions can offer the opportunity to follow a distance course, adapting their timetable to a variety of students that, temporary or permanent, are not able to attendant to class (job, hospitalisation, sport competition, etc).

Beside of this break in space-time coordinates can be combined with face-to-face activities, in some occasions technologies are replacing all classroom-learning times by distance learning activities. We are referring to the possibilities of Virtual Learning Environments (VLE) which allow fostering the openness, personalisation and flexibility of student-centred education. It is important to consider that in VLE the e-learning assumes the learner as a self regulated individual, capable of making right decisions to organize her own learning (Salinas, 1999), for this reasons e-learning operates better in higher education, or preferable with adult students.

VLE, such as higher education virtual campus, allow considering a wider range of levels, which are not just limited to the educational offer in traditional universities near the student location. At once, just-in-time learning could answer to specific individual training needs in a faster way by considering the contextual information (Romero & Wareham, 2009).

Finally, within the flexibility, technologies have facilitated a more personalized learning process. E-learning students can choose different materials and activities considering their knowledge background or, even, the specific needs of their learning process. The teachers could also make this personalisation (e.g. the teacher could suggest additional readings to the students who are facing more difficulties to achieve the learning objectives). E-learning technologies enable the possibility of adapting the information to the needs and characteristics of each user, both by the level of training, as well as for their preferences regarding the interacting channel. Therefore, in the learning design teachers can support the multiple intelligences approach (Gardner, 1983) considering preferences and aptitudes. By creating personalized learning sequences, accessible anywhere and anytime, educational technologies offer a real choice of when, how and where to learn.

E-Learning as a Mechanism for Improving Social Presence through Communication and Collaborative Work

E-learning can increase and improve communication between different actors in the process of teaching and learning. Enhancing communication not only allows the improvement of interactions, but also improves the social presence. In learning contexts with ICT, social presence has been defined by Garrison and Akyol (2009) as the ability of students to project themselves on the social and emotional development with other community members who are believed as true. According to Gunawardena and Zittle (1997), in distance education social presence is a key factor in the student satisfaction. More specifically, ICT can enhance social presence incorporating different forms of interaction between teachers and students, synchronous and asynchronously. Interaction promotes and increases the flow of information and collaboration between educational agents, beyond the physical and academic boundaries. Thus, for example, any student may pose questions, publish an assignment or contact a teacher at any time (Marques, 2001, p. 92).

Also, interaction is affected by social perception of others. As Bandura (2002) agrees, with many other authors, new electronic technologies provide opportunities for people to bring their influence to bear on collaborative actions. As well as Kavanaugh (2005) pointed, Bandura also warns, however, that ready access to technologies will not necessarily enlist active participation unless people believe that they can achieve desired results by this means. How the educational technologies change the face of social interaction will depend on perceived efficacy. Thus, it will be extremely important for teachers to assure the students perception of efficacy, by motivating them first, and offering quick feedback that engage students to participate again (Hernández-Serrano, González-Sánchez, & Muñoz-Rodríguez, 2009).

E-learning could improve communication among students too, by facilitating group activities designed for cooperative and collaborative learning (Cenich & Santos, 2005). Computer Supported Collaborative Learning (CSCL) encourages group discussion, shared knowledge construction, metacognition and other high order cognitive skills. For the teachers, e-learning can be a channel for improving communication, planning and managing tutoring sessions, collaboration an even co-teaching with colleagues from other universities and organizations. E-learning is in these cases a supplementary activity to face-to-face process; a support for the teaching activity allowing teachers to have more time of quality with the students.

E-Learning as a Mechanism of Motivation and Adaptation to Special Education Needs

From a student's perspective, e-learning versatility and interactivity enhances their attention (Fernández *et al.* 2006). In this sense, we can consider that high interest shown by students using e-learning tools becomes a motivational driving force for learning, collaborative learning and in depth thinking. Being so motivated, the students spend more time working on learning activities because when they interacting with computers they are permanently active.

Recent educational technologies allow the use of diverse multimedia resources (text, pictures, sounds, animations...) providing Rich Internet Applications (RIAs), which increase the user learning experience and strengthen the academic performance. It is also noteworthy that this information can be interactive, so the students abandon their role of "information receiver", becoming a "significant co-constructor" of the activity, who involves in it depending on their experience and prior knowledge, attitudes and beliefs, or higher-order thinking skills (Mayer, 2000). This means a new understanding where the learning process is not just a transmission of information, but an active construction of knowledge, which will require, first, gain competence on some informational complex processes such as searching, analyzing and (re)processing.

In addition, new technologies make possible enhance the cognitive and metacognitive support (Monereo & Romero, 2008) and the simulation of physical phenomena or recreation of environments through the use of microworlds. These simulated spaces help the students to experiment with and understand it better, intensifying their motivation for learning. Ultimately, these spaces facilitate learning from mistakes, by means of operating, recording or fixing the errors immediately, with the opportunity to try new responses or changing the course of an action to overcome difficulties (Ronteltap & Eurelings, 2002).

Additionally, self-assessment through the use of self-administered online questionnaires allows reinforcing general knowledge, or more specific methodologies (Coll *et al.* 2007). These tools improve the evaluation and monitoring of the student. Thus, e-learning solutions, by providing new tools for information processing and communication, with more interactive resources, could improve educational effectiveness in teaching methodologies.

Another of the challenges of e-learning is the inclusion of students to the extent that some educational special needs can be lessened; especially those related to physical, visual or auditory (Evans & Douglas, 2008) without limiting the possibilities of communication and access to information. In many cases the computer, with peripheral devices, may open alternative ways to solve limitations (Soto & Fernandez, 2003).

Technologies for Designing and Developing E-Learning

The proper use of ICT in higher education involves a range of benefits for teaching and learning and a progression of complexity in terms of its use (Fuentes, Feixas, Monereo, & Gairín, 2006).

Firstly, we can consider current *web technologies* (html pages, blogs...) as one of the simplest way to use ICT in education. Major uses are communicational and informational. Examples of the use of web technologies are the web of institutions, schools, departments or areas, the programs of the course, the teachers' blog…

Secondly, we consider the *learning portals* as the entry point where students find all the services or tools related to the course. The portals allow interaction, two-way communication and providing access to a range of information. Examples of this are most of the groupware solutions (Google Apps, Yahoogroups...).

Thirdly, the most common educational technologies today are the Learning Management Systems (LMS) or *learning platforms*. LMS are arranged in different settings and with resources and teaching tools that reinforce multidirectional communication, involving all educational stakeholders. LMS facilitate registration and monitoring of learning, organization by subjects or themes, individual and group planning, self and co-management of information, automatically generating learning activities, and reports for management, among others. Examples are: some of discussions forums, Virtual Learning Environments (VLE), Content

Figure 1. Capture of a Virtual Classroom in the Universidad Autónoma de Barcelona

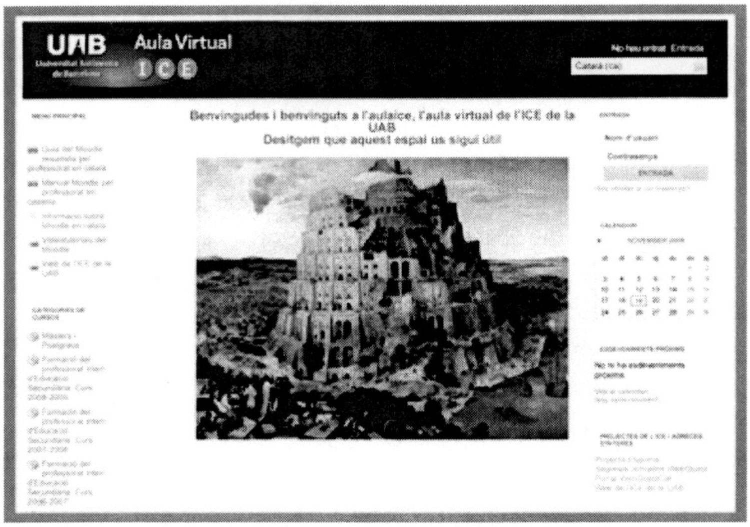

Management System (CMS), Learning Management System (LMS), the combination LCMS (Learning Content Management System). More specifically the virtual classrooms (VC) (Figure 1) are an excellent tool to help the teacher in the process of monitoring and assessment of learning.

With all this technologies, to define and design an e-learning environment needs also an analysis of the possibilities, according to the specific educational situation. The use of educational technologies must be considered before, and not after, the analysis of the psycho-educational objectives to achieve the teaching process. Considering an e-learning solution make a difference between face-to-face contexts and e-learning contexts (Sangrà, 2001). Educational technologies must add value to the e-learning context, and not just be and add-on tool in the learning situation. The same as to collaborative learning with technologies, due to innovation "is not only the interaction and information exchange among participants, but the nature and process of the activity" (Cabero-Almenara, 2000).

SELECTION, IMPLEMENTATION AND EVALUATION OF E-LEARNING TECHNOLOGIES

The use of each and every one of the e-learning technologies implies a clear way to understand and put into practice the teaching and learning processes. We highly recommend selecting educational technologies that can be useful for carrying out a desired learning outcome. It is not about resources, but about the use of these resources. To make a good choice, and therefore a successful learning design, we need to analyze educational technologies and resources considering their educational properties, but also taking into account the degree of eCompetence required.

We provide bellow a table considering four main criteria for selecting educational technologies (Table 1). It should be noted, however, that there are several ways to classify the tools and e-learning resources: time settings (synchrony / asynchrony), the unidirectional / bidirectional / multidirectional communication modalities, the degree of participation, the relationship between participants, etc.

Table 1. Typology of ICT tools for teaching and learning.

Informational resources	Communication tools	Course structure support	Teaching activity management
Calendar Announcement board or news Daily lessons Documentation Annotations Bibliography Links of Interest Social bookmarks Newsletter FAQ Audio and video conferences Grades Students and learning groups directory Teachers directory	Email Synchronous communication (chat) Forums Discussions Audio and video conferencing Virtual meeting room Teamwork space Shared files zone Collaborative writing editors (wikis) Tutoring tools Survey	Program website Course website Content activities Questionnaires and exercises E-portfolios Simulations Syllabus of the course Evaluation criteria Assignments	Teacher mailbox Student private folders Delivery activities Work delivery monitoring Log recording Grade book E-portfolio Recent activity online students Connection statistics

The most popular tools in e-learning, Learning Management Systems (LMS), include a wide diversity of functionalities to support the processes of learning. Among the most well known LMS we can consider Moodle, Sakai, Dokeos, Blackboard, ATutor, Claroline.net and the Knowledge Forum. Generally, the platform integrates a description of the options offered and gives the possibility to integrate 2.0 applications (iCal calendar, RSS, social bookmarking...). It is important that the teacher decides the functionality given to the platform, based on pedagogical reasons. For this choice various studies have analysed different platforms (Bremer & Bryant, 2005; Kljun *et al.* 2007). Based on these studies, and from our preliminary research results, in the next section we focus on the pedagogical contribution and usability criteria of educational technologies.

Usability, Utility and Acceptability In E-Learning

Once considered the educational potential of each ICT resource in accordance to our learning objectives and contents, the choice of a tool needs to take into account the teaching-learning context. This remains some usability criteria such acceptability, utility and usability (Table 2). We need to consider these criteria in computer-based learning environments, especially because of the role of the environment in the support of interactions and knowledge construction. The state of the art in the field of Human Computer Interaction applied to Education (HCI-Ed) could be of utmost interest for this purpose.

Relationship between the usability properties and the learning outcomes has been studied by several authors (Laurillard, 2002; Parlangeli, Marchigiani, & Bagnara, 1999). Well-designed computer-based learning environments contribute to the learning performance. On the contrary, poorly designed environments could have a terrible effect on learning. For Redish (2000) is necessary to design computer-based learning environments that allow the learners to find what they need, to understand what they find and to act appropriately within the time and effort needed for the task. We can mention to the work of Nielsen (1993) to take account of ergonomic

Table 2. Usability criteria in e-learning.

Usability criteria in educational technologies	**Acceptability**: Robustness, cost and reliability.
	Usability: Easy to learn and easy to use.
	Utility: Efficacy to enhance learning.

Figure 2. CLE ergonomic criteria based on Nielsen's Taxonomy of System Acceptability

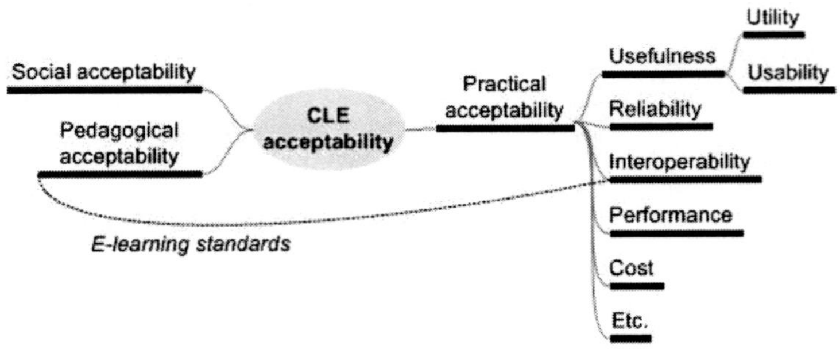

criteria applicable to Computer Learning Environments (CLE) and consider the commonalities between the pedagogicial acceptability criteria and Nielsen's practical acceptability criteria.

One of the key elements in learning with ICT is *usability*, which is defined by Preece *et al.* (1994) as a concept "concerned with making systems easy to learn and easy to use". In the context of educational technologies usability could be associated to efficiency, learnability, memorability, and even, learners' satisfaction (Tricot, 2007). For Allum (2001) teacher-designed spaces often fail in terms of usability. An environment must be easy to use and must support the learning activity in an efficient way. Usability is often associated with the functionalities of the Computer Learning Environments (CLE), specially the User Interface (UI).

Utility could be considered as synonymous of relevance or efficacy (Tricot, 2007) of the CLE considering the enhancement of learning process and outcomes when using the CLE. A computer-based solution that is very usable but has not utility for the learning process must be avoided. Utility could be dependant on the learning activity context.

A third item, that we can consider is the *practical acceptability*, which not only consider the usefulness and usability, but also robustness, cost and reliability of ICT applications.

Several studies have shown that user perceptions towards the UI of the computer environment are strongly related to apparent usability, and have an important impact on the overall system acceptability (Hassenzahl et al. 2000; Tractinsky, 1997; Schenkman & Jonsson, 2000 in Acton *et al* 2004). Acceptability emphasizes the idea that we need to adapt a user centred approach to Computer Learning Environments assessment. The ergonomic criteria have a responsibility in the learning process and could be implemented among different people as a qualitative or quantitative survey, focus groups, heuristic rules, critical incident approach or other methodologies. Heuristic rules that we could take into account are related to the optimal extension of the learning objects and other files, the learning times (allocated time, time on task...) and the readability.

Psycho-Pedagogical Criteria in E-Learning

Educational technologies could be very diverse, depending on the profile and role of the educational stakeholder. We can consider specific resources for teachers and other resources or options for students (e.g. the teacher's comments and annotations can be visible or not for students). The teacher needs to set the VLE in a way that permits to control the visibility and structure of the information and activities.

The selection of resources will be determined by the existing training needs, the socio-demographic characteristics of the students and the

Table 3. Psycho-pedagogical criteria in e-learning.

Psycho-pedagogical requirements in educational technologies	Learning objectives needs Characteristics of students Characteristics of teachers Contents requirements Collaborative exploitation of the learning sequence Commitment and flexibility Appropriate presentation of information Participation and interaction Monitoring and continuous assessment E-competence

contents of the course, but also, by the cost of technologies, about the return of investment from the integration of the e-learning solution. In addition to this dimensions, we need to consider some psycho-pedagogical criteria (Table 3).

These psycho-pedagogical criteria are totally related with the teacher methodology, and because of that need to be considered in relation to the teaching style and methodology (Coppola, Hiltz, & Rotter, 2001, Goodyear et al. 2001); also related with the role of virtual student (Peters, 2000).

In 1997, Reeves described 14 pedagogical dimensions for the analysis and evaluation of e-learning education (Figure 3). Reeves dimensions allow us to consider the links between the pedagogical model and its implementation during the instructional design and e-learning development phase.

Interoperability Criteria in E-Learning

The use of resources, tools, applications and contents in e-learning requires a balance between matching the e-learning solution to a given context, where it can be enhance the highest possible usability and, at the same time, the maximum reusability in both technology and pedagogy. In practice, these two properties, usability and reusability, are often in conflict. Generally the higher reusability leads to less usability and vice versa (Sicilia & Garcia, 2003).

To ensure that materials, products, processes and services are able to fit to users needs, there are rules, guidelines and definitions of features described by standards. E-learning standards seek to ensure the interoperability, portability and reusability of content, metadata and educational processes (Friesen, 2005). In addition to learning standards, we can consider some non-functional requirements (see Table 4) such as accessibility, interoperability, durability, affordability and reus-

Figure 3. Evaluating what really matters in computer-based education (adapted from Reeves, 1997)

Pedagogical Philosophy	*Instructivist*	⟷	*Constructivist*
Learning Theory	*Behavioural*	⟷	*Cognitive*
Goal Orientation	*Sharply Focused*	⟷	*General*
Kinaesthetic/Technical Skill	*Limited contexts*	⟷	*Multiple Contexts*
Material Application	*Theoretical*	⟷	*Authentic*
Martial Theory	*Simple*	⟷	*Complex*
Source of Motivation	*Extrinsic*	⟷	*Intrinsic*
Teacher role	*Instructional*	⟷	*Facilitative*
Metacognitive Support	*Unsupported*	⟷	*Integrated*
Collaborative Learning	*Individual*	⟷	*Collaborative*
Cultural Sensitivity	*Insensitive*	⟷	*Respectful*
Learning Delivery	*Fixed*	⟷	*Open*

Table 4. Non-functional criteria in e-learning.

Non-functional criteria in e-learning.	Accessibility: locating objects, access to them and get them easily from a remote location.
	Affordability: reduction in overall time and cost in teaching and learning.
	Durability: ability to withstand technological evolution without having to recode or develop again educational resources.
	Interoperability: learning contents compatibility within platforms
	Reusability (Pedagogical Reusability) flexibility to integrate and use the resources and tools contained in different educational contexts.

ability of learning objects (Advanced Distributed Learning, ADL, 2001). These non-functional requirements are of major interest in the e-learning economy because of the role they have in making an education technology acceptable, for both teachers and students, and efficient, for learning performances.

Concerning interoperability on different learning platforms, the exchange of e-learning content locally and globally could be achieved by introducing e-learning standards such SCORM. The Sharable Content Object Referent Model (SCORM) integrates the ideas from AICC, ARIADNE, and the IEEE LTSC groups, creating a standard that is widely recognised and used in the field of educational technologies. E-learning standards follow three principles: (a) separation of the Learning Management System and the learning contents, (b) labelling materials with metadata, i.e. data that describes other data, so that materials are classified according to certain criteria, (c) wherever possible, using specifications and open standards.

Non-functional criteria in e-learning are only suitable for certain types of educational contexts, specifically those that require just publishing documents capabilities. From our point of view, we need to enhance virtual learning environments with pedagogical neutrality, i.e. environments influenced by the context of learning (student-content-educational). In this regard, we must not relinquish for the reusability, interoperability, portability and durability necessary for communication and collaboration tools (groupware). These applications or tools such as workflow systems permit publish documents, send emails, share group calendars, writing collaboratively (i.e. wiki), communicate by audio and video conferencing, share whiteboards, or work on decision support systems (Gómez, Garcia, & Martinez, 2003)

Learning design specifications attempts to reach an upper stage, with no limitations in the interaction between the student and the materials, by using a formal language designed to describe the teaching and learning processes for fostering communication. According to this, we can apply four basic principles (Koper, 2006): (a) Completeness, should be able to fully describe the learning sequence, including references to learning materials, the necessary services to develop the activities of students and teachers, (b) The teacher should be able to make explicit the pedagogical meaning and functionality of the different elements of learning context, (c) Personalization, activities should include flexibility to adapt to the preferences, needs and circumstances of the students and the educational context in general, (d) Compatibility, use and effectively integrate other standards and specifications of existing e-learning. The latter principle requires the existence of interoperable, reusable and formal activities. Finally, in addition to psycho-pedagogical and non-functional criteria in e-learning it is possible to consider the technological quality criteria, for this matter we invite the reader to consider the technological perspective raised by Landon (2000).

CONCLUSION

The impact of e-learning in higher education is understood from the enhancement of the student-centred learning paradigm. Using educational technologies evoke a new relationship within the educational elements of the triangle of learning (teacher-student-content), which now are link with technologies as providers of synchronous and asynchronous communication and knowledge construction. In addition, educational technologies have the ability to transform the educational practices, not only by creating new spaces and educational contexts increasingly diverse, influential and critical, but also by combining e-learning practices with face-to-face contexts (blended-learning).

The greater or lesser quality of e-learning, and the process of knowledge construction itself, depends on many complex factors that we introduced as diverse criteria in this chapter. Beyond the interactivity and dynamism allowed by multimedia devices, it remains still necessary the figure of the teacher, mainly in the designing phase. The characteristics of resources and applications that encompass e-learning are not sufficient to guarantee effective learning, since it depends, primarily, on the quality of the interactions provided between the student and the content, and between the stakeholders (teachers and students).

E-learning involves the use of educational technologies (hardware and software) that must be socially accepted by teachers and students. One of the most popular educational technologies is the Virtual Learning Environment (VLE), which possibilities should be analyzed in order to design and use it according to the educational context; this led us to consider the psycho-pedagogical utility, usability and (social) accessibility criteria. Thus, VLE provide several tools and resources that teachers must select according to the expectations, objectives, contents, methods, interests and the learning objectives.

Another important issue in the selection of resources is that, contrary to what can be expected, the use of a great number of virtual resources does not relate to a higher quality of teaching and learning. The teacher should be aware of the role that ICT have, by putting them in the correct place for helping the process of teaching and learning - as supporters (Kettmer-Polley, 1999).

In the design is critical to start by defining the learning objectives, and then the resources and educational technologies needed for. Starting by thinking just on educational technologies, leads to a "technocentric" approximation that does not always work in terms of learning. For example, in "I want to use the forums on my course" the objective is to use the forum, but there are not educational objectives. If on the contrary, we say, "I want to encourage the exchange of ideas outside the classroom", which is a goal of teaching, this lead us to analyze various technological alternatives, and, among them, choose the best suitable for the pedagogical objective.

Considering the psycho-pedagogical utility, usability and accessibility criteria analysed in this chapter, we must prioritize the technologies that would enhance communication, collaboration, cooperation, coordination, solving problems, or negotiation, along with technologies that assure the reusability, interoperability, portability and durability. Notice that tools, even if they are learning technologies are not a guarantee of success in learning performance. Teacher must analyze to what extent the e-learning solution play a role on the achievement of the learning process. Hence, take into account some educational criteria is a priority for teachers; criteria which could guarantee the appropriateness of a tool to a specific learning situation, the quality of the practices and the effectiveness of results.

REFERENCES

Acton, T., Golden, W., Gudea, S. & Scott, M. (2004). *Usability and Acceptance in Small-Screen Information Systems*, CollECTeR (Europe), University of Surrey, Guildford, UK, 25 April.

Allum, P. (2001). Principles applicable to the production of CALL-ware: learning from the field of Human Computer Interaction (HCI). *ReCALL, 13*(2), 146–166. doi:10.1017/S0958344001000222a

Amadieu, F., Tricot, A., & Mariné, C. (2009). Prior knowledge in learning from a non-linear electronic document: Disorientation and coherence of the reading sequences. *Computers in Human Behavior, 25*, 381–388. doi:10.1016/j.chb.2008.12.017

Bandura, A. (2002). Growing primacy of human agency in adaptation and change in the electronic era . *European Psychologist, 7*(1), 2–16. doi:10.1027//1016-9040.7.1.2

Bos-Ciussi. M, Augier, M. & Rosner, G. (2008). Learning Communities Are Not Mushrooms - or - How to Cultivate Learning Communities. In C. Kimble, P. Hildreth and I. Bourdon (Eds), *Higher Education in Communities of Practice: Creating Learning Environments for Educators,* (pp. 2, 14, 287-308). Hershey, PA: Information Age Publishing.

Bosco, A. (2005). Las TIC en los procesos de convergencia europea y la innovación en la universidad: oportunidades y limitaciones. *Aula Abierta, 86*, 3–27.

Bremer, D., & Bryant, R. (2005). *A Comparison of Two Learning management Systems: Moodle vs Blackboard.* Paper presented at the 18th Annual Conference of the National Advisory Committee on Computing Qualifications, Tauranga, New Zealand.

Cabero Almenara, J. (2000). La formación virtual: principios, bases y preocupaciones. In R. Pérez Pérez, (Ed.), *Redes, multimedia y diseños virtuales,* (pp. 83-102). Oviedo, Italy: Departamento de Ciencias de la Educación de la Universidad de Oviedo. Retrieved July 23, 2009, from http://tecnologiaedu.us.es/bibliovir/pdf/87.pdf

Cañellas, A. (2006). Impacto de las TIC en la educación: un acercamiento desde el punto de vista de las funciones de la educación. *Quaderns Digitals: Revista de Nuevas Tecnologías y Sociedad*, 43.

Cenich, G., & Santos, G. (2005). Propuesta de aprendizaje basado en proyectos y trabajo colaborativo: experiencia de un curso en línea. *Revista Electrónica de Investigación Educativa, 7*(2). Retrieved July 23, 2009, from http://redie.uabc.mx/vol7no2/contenido cenich.html

Coimbra Group. (2002). *European Union Policies and Strategic Change for e-learning in Universities*. Brussels.

Coll, C., Rochera, M. J., Mayordomo, R. M., & Naranjo, M. (2007). Evaluación continuada y apoyo al aprendizaje. Una experiencia de innovación educativa con el apoyo de las TIC en educación superior. *Revista Electrónica de Investigación Psicoeducativa, 5*(13), 783–804.

Coppola, N. W., Hiltz, S. R., & Rotter, N. (2001). Recoming a virtual professor: pedagogical roles and ALN. In *Proceedings of the 34th Hawaii International Conference on System Sciences*.

De Pablos, J. (2007). El cambio metodológico en el Espacio Europeo de Educación Superior y el papel de las tecnologías de la información y la comunicación. *Revista Iberoamericana de Educación a Distancia, 10*(2), 5–44.

European Comisión – Information Society and Media Directorate General. (2006). *Benchmarking Access and Use of ICT in European Schools 2006*. Final Report from Head Teacher and Classroom Teacher Surveys in 27 European Countries. Report was elaborated by *Empirica*. Retrieved July 23, 2009, from http://ec.europa.eu/information_society/eeurope/i2010/docs/studies/final_report_3.pdf

Evans, S., & Douglas, G. (2008). E-Learning and Blindness: A comparative study of the quality of an E-Learning experience. *Journal of Visual Impairment & Blindness*, *102*(2), 77–88.

Fernández, B., Suárez, L., & Alvárez, E. (2006). El camino hacia el Espacio Europeo de Educación Superior: deficiencias metodológicas y propuestas de mejora desde la perspectiva del alumno. *Aula Abierta*, *88*, 85–105.

Friesen, N. (2005). Interoperatibility and Learning Objects: An Overview of E-learning Standardization. *Interdisciplinary Journal of Knowledge and Learning Objects, 1*.

Fuentes, M., Feixas, M., Monereo, C., & Gairín, J. (2006). *Guia didàctica pel disseny virtual de cursos de postgrau en modalitat e-learning. III Jornada de Campus d'Innovació Docent*. Barcelona, Spain: UAB.

Gardner, H. (1983). *Frames of Mind: The Theory of Multiple Intelligences*. New York: Basic Books.

Garrison, D. R., & Akyol, Z. (2009). Role of instructional technology in the transformation of higher education. *Journal of Computing in Higher Education*, *21*(1), 19–30. doi:10.1007/s12528-009-9014-7

Gómez, A. F., García, M. E., & Martínez, M. A. (2003). Nuevas tecnologías y herramientas en la teleformación . In Martínex, F. (Ed.), *Redes de formación en la enseñanza. Las nuevas perspectivas del trabajo coopertativo* (pp. 231–235). Barcelona, Spain: Paidós.

Goodyear, P., Salmon, G., Spector, M., & Tickner, S. (2001). Competences for Online Teching: A Special report. *Educational Techonology Research ¬ Development . ETR&D, 1*(49), 65–72. doi:10.1007/BF02504508

Gunawardena, C. N., & Zittle, F. J. (1997). Social presence as a predictor of satisfaction within a computer-mediated conferencing environment. *American Journal of Distance Education, 11*(3), 8–26. doi:10.1080/08923649709526970

Hassenzahl, M., & Wessler, R. (2000). Capturing Design Space From A User Perspective: The Repertory Grid Technique Revisited. *International Journal of Human-Computer Interaction, 12*(3-4), 441–459. doi:10.1207/S15327590IJHC1203&4_13

Hernández-Serrano, M. J., González-Sánchez, M. & Muñoz-Rodríguez, J. M. (2009). Designing learning environments improving social interactions: essential variables for a virtual training space. *Procedia - Social and Behavioral Sciences (ISSHP/ISI Proceedings-SSCI), 1*(1), 2411-2415.

IMS Global Learning Consortium Inc. (2003). *IMS Learning Design Standard Specification*. Retrieved July 23, 2009 from http://www.imsglobal.org/learningdesign/index.html

Kavanaugh, A., Carroll, J. M., Rosson, M. B., Reese, D. D., & Zin, T. T. (2005). Participating in civil society: the case of networked communities. *Interacting with Computers*, *17*(1), 9–33. doi:10.1016/j.intcom.2004.10.006

Kettner-Polley, R. B. (1999). The making of a virtual professor. *ALN Magazine*, (3)1.

Kljun, M., Vicic, J., Kavsek, B., & Kavcic, A. (2007). Evaluating Comparisons and Evaluations of Learning Management Systems. Information Technology Interfaces, 2007. In *29th International Conference on Information Technology Interface*, 25-28 June 2007, (pp. 363-368).

Koper, R. (2006). Current Research in Learning Design. *Educational Technology & Society, 9*(1), 13-22. Retrieved July 23, 2009 from http://ifets.info/journals/9_1/3.pdf

Landon, B. (2000). *On-line educational delivery applications: a web tool for comparative analysis*. A web site for the project supported by SCET, OLT and The Center for Learning Technologies at Mount Allison University. Retrieved July 23, 2009, from http://www.c2t2.ca/landonline/

Laurillard, D. (2002). *Rethinking University Teaching: A Conversational Framework for the Effective Use of Learning Technologies*. London: Routledge. doi:10.4324/9780203304846

Learning, A. D. (ADL) Initiative. (2001). Sharable Courseware Object Reference Model (SCORM). *The SCORM Overview*, October 1, 2001. Retrieved July 23, 2009, from http://www.adlnet.gov/Technologies/scorm

Lepori, B., Cantoni, L., & Succi, C. (2003). The introduction of e-learning in European universities: models and strategies . In Kerres, M., & Voss, B. (Eds.), *Digitaler Campus. Vom Medienprojekt zum nachhaltigen Medieneinsatz in der Hochschule* (pp. 74–83). Münster, Germany: Waxmann.

Marqués, P. (2001). Algunas notas sobre el impacto de las TIC en la universidad. *Educcar, 28*, 83–98.

Mayer, R. (2000). Diseño educativo para un aprendizaje constructivista . In Reigeluth, C. (Ed.), *Diseño de la Instrucción. Teorías y modelos* (pp. 154–171). Madrid, Spain: Aula XXI Santillana.

Monereo, C., & Romero, M. (2008). Los entornos virtuales de aprendizaje basados en sistemas de emulación cognitiva . In Coll, C., & Monereo, C. (Eds.), *Psicología de la educación virtual. Aprender y enseñar con las Tecnologías de la Información y la Comunicación*. Editorial Morata.

Nielsen, J. (1993). *Usability Engineering*. London: Academic Press.

Parlangeli, O., Marchigiani, E., & Bagnara, S. (1999). Multimedia systems in distance education: effects of usability on learning. *Interacting with Computers, 12*, 37–49. doi:10.1016/S0953-5438(98)00054-X

Peters, O. (2000). Digital learning environments:New possibilities and opportunities. *International Review of Research in Open and Distance Learning, 1*(1).

Preece, J., Rogers, Y., Sharp, H., Benyon, D., Holland, S., & Carey, T. (1994). *Human-Computer Interaction*. Harlow, UK: Addison-Wesley.

Redish, J. (2000). Readability formulas have even more limitations than Klare discusses. *Journal of Computer Documentation, 24*(3), 132–137. doi:10.1145/344599.344637

Reeves, T.C. (1997). *Evaluating what really matters in computer-based education.* Learning with Software-Pedagogies an practice.

Romero, M. (2009). Metacognition on the Educational Social Software, new challenges and opportunities . In Lambropoulos, N., & Romero, M. (Eds.), *Educational Social Software for Context-Aware Learning: Collaborative Methods and Human Interaction*. Hershey, PA: IGI Global.

Romero, M., & Wareham, J. (2009). Just-in-time mobile learning model based on context awareness information. *Learning Technology Newsletter*. Washington, DC: IEEE Computer Society Technical Committee on Learning Technology (TCLT).

Ronteltap, F., & Eurelings, A. (2002). Activity and interaction of students in anelectronic learning environment for problem based learning. *Distance Education, 23*(1), 11–22. doi:10.1080/01587910220123955

Salinas, J. (1999). Qué se entiende por una institución de educación superior flexible. *EDUTEC'99*, Universidad de Sevilla, Spain. Retrieved July 23, 2009, from http://www.uib.es/depart/gte/edutec99.html

Sangrà, A. (2001). La calidad en las experiencias virtuales de educación superior. *Cuadernos para la Educación Superior.* Barcelona, Spain: UOC. Retrieved July 23, 2009, from http://www.uoc.edu/web/esp/art/uoc/0106024/sangra.html

Santángelo, H. N. (2003). Modelos pedagógicos en los sistemas de enseñanza no presencial basados en nuevas tecnologías y redes de comunicación . In Martínez Sánchez, F. (Ed.), *Redes de Comunicación en la Enseñanza: Las Nuevas Perspectivas del Trabajo Corporativo* (pp. 63–91). Barcelona: Paidós Ibérica.

Schenkman, B. N., & Jonsson, F. U. (2000). Aesthetics and preferences of web pages. *Behaviour & Information Technology, 19*(5), 367–377. doi:10.1080/01449290075000063

Schneckenberg, D. (2006). Towards a Conceptualisation of eCompetence in Higher Education. In EDEN 2006 *Conference Proceedings 'E-Competences for Life, Employment and Innovation* (pp. 39-45). Vienna: European Distance and E- Learning Network.

Sicilia, M. A., & Garcia, E. (2003). On the Concepts of usability and Reusability of Learning Objects. *The Internacional of research in Open and Distance Learning, 4*(2). Retrieved July 23, 2009, from http://www.irrodl.org/index.php/irrodl/article/view/155/702

Soto, F. J., & Fernández, J. J. (2003). Realidades y retos de inclusión digital. *Comunicación y Pedagogía, 192*, 34–40.

Sweller, J., & Chandler, P. (1994). Why some material is difficult to learn. *Cognition and Instruction, 12*, 185–233. doi:10.1207/s1532690xci1203_1

Tractinsky, N. (1997) Aesthetics and apparent usability: empirically assessing cultural and methodological issues. In *Conference Proceedings on Human Factors in Computing Systems*, Atlanta, GA USA, March 22 - 27, (pp. 115-122).

Tricot, A. (2007). Utility, usability and acceptability: an ergonomic approach to the evaluation of external representations for learning. EARLI Symposium *«Understanding the role of external representations in supporting learning»*, Budapest, August 28 – September 1.

KEY TERMS AND DEFINITIONS

Accessibility: Locating objects, access to them and get them easily from a remote location.

Acceptability: Robustness, cost and reliability.

Affordability: Reduction in overall time and in cost on teaching and learning.

Collaborative Writing Tools: Allows a group of persons to write and comment a document in a shared workspace.

Digital Literacy: Competence on the use of digital technology for searching, organizing, understanding and creating information with digital devices.

Durability: Ability to withstand technological evolution without having to recode or develop again educational resources.

eCompetence: The ability to use ICT in teaching and learning in a meaningful way

e-Learning: Learning supported by computers. Most usual e-learning technologies are environment supported by continuously evolving, collaborative processes focused on increasing individual and organizational performance.

European Higher Education Area (EHEA): Is the objective of the Bologna process that is to create more comparable, compatible and coherent systems of higher education in Europe.

Gruopware: Software that integrates work on a shared workspace to enhance communication and collaboration among the members of a group or team.

Information and Communication Technologies (ICT): Is a set of synchronous and asynchronous digital technologies for manipulating information and communicating

Interactivity: Possibility that the user has to act on the elements of the digital interface.

Interoperability: Learning contents compatibility within platforms.

Learning Management Systems (LMS) and Virtual Learning Environment (VLE): LMS and VLE are systems designed to support e-learning. LMS allows the teacher to present to students, through a single, consistent, and intuitive interface, all the components required for training.

Reusability: Flexibility to integrate and use the resources and tools contained in different educational contexts.

Shared Workspace: Shared space where the team members can share documents and information, and keep notified each other of major changes.

Teacher Role: Set of functions, tasks and attitudes assigned to the teacher for dealing with the teaching situation.

Unidirectional, Bidirectional and Multidirectional Communication: Different types of communication that can be carried out in the process of learning, depending on the relationships between the sender and the recipients.

Usability: Easy to learn and easy to use. In the context of educational technologies usability could be associated to efficiency, learnability, memorability, and even, learners' satisfaction.

Utility: Efficacy to enhance learning.

Chapter 22
Satisfaction Measurement in Education

Lilyana Nacheva-Skopalik
Technical University of Gabrovo, Bulgaria

ABSTRACT

The chapter presents the importance of providing high quality e-learning and the need to apply the requirements of the standards from ISO 9000 series for continual improvement of the quality management systems in education. The work applies the main principles for multiple criteria decision making. An approach for satisfaction measurement is developed. It uses weighting coefficients as qualitative valuation of the importance of the quality characteristics and numerical valuation for the level of satisfaction with the quality characteristics. The suggested approach is suitable to apply for different purposes in education in order to achieve high quality e-learning. It is also suitable to apply to different areas within quality management systems.

INTRODUCTION

E-learning is becoming an education standard and the e-learning industry is gradually expanding. Providing e-learning courses is a complicated task and the various applications strongly need to interoperate and exchange data efficiently in order to better meet the needs and expectations of the students and the teaching team. E-learning standards aim to bring order in different aspects of the e-learning. Some organizations work to develop such standards. The Aviation Industry Computer-based training Committee (AICC) (http://www.aicc.org/) is the pioneer in creating e-learning standards. Though their standards are applicable mostly within government and aviation circles, they give a set of guidelines for interoperability. The IMS Global Learning Consortium (http://www.imsproject.org) works on the problems connected with the learning content in aspect of how to describe, discover and reuse that content, and to assure that it is fully interoperable within different administrative systems. IMS Meta-data Specification defines a method for describing learning

DOI: 10.4018/978-1-61692-789-9.ch022

content including a description of the content, the title, the author, location, cost and payment structure, prerequisites, and learning taxonomy. Institute of Electrical and Electronics Engineers (IEEE) Learning Technology Standards Committee (LTSC) (http://www.ieeeltsc.org:8080/Plone) develops technical standards guidelines and recommendations for e-learning components and systems. The Advanced Distributed Learning (ADL) Initiative (http://www.adlnet.org/Pages/Default.aspx), sponsored by the government, industry, and academic leaders, is directed to facilitate e-learning content development and delivery. They develop the Sharable Content Object Reference Model (SCORM). SCORM refers to design of an interoperable, durable learning system. It does not specify a programming language, authoring tool, or operating system and includes content meta-data.

The available standards cover different aspects such as learning management systems and learning environments, interoperability, learning objects standards, usability, security issues, metadata standards, reusability of learning data. The standards aim to provide preconditions for effective high quality e-learning; however they do not include tools for quality evaluation of the provided e-learning.

The educators have always worked towards the idea to achieve effective education. Modern e-learning systems still need further development to become effective learning environments for both student and teacher and it turned out to be a rather complicated task. A research study examines possibilities to achieve optimal learning. The research results in a PhD thesis entitled "An examination of an intelligent cybernetic learning model for formative assessment and diagnostics in open and distance learning" (Nacheva-Skopalik, 2007). The dissertation develops a cybernetic model of the learning process and suggests how the feedback channels can be used for optimal control of the learning process. During the investigation the author had to consider the standards for quality management. ISO 9000 series is the most established worldwide set of standards for quality management systems. The standards are suitable for any organization aiming to improve the way it operates toward increasing their market share, improving business performance, manages business risk, decreasing costs or improving customer satisfaction, regardless of the size and the sector of the company. Over 800 000 organizations in 170 countries currently use these standards and this is a basis to exchange and compare goods and collaboration on international market. Applying the ISO 9000 standards increases the company reputation clearly demonstrating to all interested parties its commitment to high standards and continual improvement. However, the companies that implement the standards throughout the whole organization rather than just at some departments are expected the best reward on their investment for using these standards. In order to achieve the best effect and to unlock the true potential of the company, applying ISO 9000 standards should be strategic approach of the company's top management (http://www.bsi-global.com/en/).

In practice the continual improvement of a quality management system is also an application of the cybernetic principles of control using a feedback channel. One of the practical realizations of the feedback channel here is the evaluation of customer satisfaction with a product. Therefore it is natural to apply the rich, well-grounded and powerful scientific theoretical basis from the theory of the area of automatic control for the purpose of optimal control of the quality of education.

The standards from the ISO 9000 series require customer satisfaction measurement however they do not specify any particular approach. There is a need to develop a suitable approach to fill this gap. This way the requirement of the standard will become an applicable methodology.

This chapter presents one approach for satisfaction measurement that is evaluated as reliable, sufficiently precise, universal and applicable, which gives good experimental results so far. Statistical methods are often used in quality control and in optimal control of technological processes. These methods require a lot of precisely measured data. These methods are not applicable for evaluation of customers' satisfaction for some important reasons. First of all, in most cases there is not sufficient data. Secondly, satisfaction is a very subjective perception. Therefore it is necessary to apply a suitable methodology from the area of subjective statistics in order to develop an approach for satisfaction measurement that gives reliable objective results. The importance of the quality characteristics, expressed by weighting coefficients, is an essential component of the approach for satisfaction measurement. At the same time the weighting coefficients can be used for other purposes in education such as making optimal control decisions and choosing the best offer.

Evaluation of students' satisfaction is an obligatory component for practical application of the continual improvement of the quality management system standards in e-learning and education to achieve high quality education.

IMPROVING QUALITY OF EDUCATION

The problem of improving quality of learning has always been high in the agenda of educational institutions at national and European level. It is still one of the main problems to solve in the demanding dynamic modern information society. The active use of the e-learning systems puts in the focus providing high quality e-learning. E-learning becomes educational standard and talking of the quality of education we often mean quality of e-learning.

Various institutions deal with the problems, concerning the quality in education. The European Association for Quality Assurance in Higher Education (ENQA) (http://www.enqa.eu/) is financed by the European Commission and currently includes 20 full members and 9 candidate members. The European Foundation for Quality in eLearning (EFQUEL) has the mission to enhance the quality of e-learning in Europe (http://www.qualityfoundation.org/). Institutions like Open & Distance Learning Quality Council (http://www.odlqc.org.uk/) and the Quality Assurance Agency for Higher Education (QAA) provide independent assessment and accreditation of higher education institutions in the UK concerning academic standards and quality (http://www.qaa.ac.uk/aboutus/default.asp). The main legislation document for the work of the universities in Bulgaria is the Higher Education Act (http://www.neaa.government.bg/ en/legal_base/laws). This document specifies the role of the quality management system to provide high quality of education through internal system of assessment and maintenance. Procedure of study of students' opinion at least once in an academic year is strongly required. The National Evaluation and Accreditation Agency at the Council of Ministers of Bulgaria (http://www.neaa.government.bg/en) is defined as a specialised state body for assessment, accreditation and control of the quality of education. The accreditation criteria include requirement to analyze and update periodically current educational documentation, while taking into consideration the opinions of students and other customers.

The global strategy of UNESCO for using Information and communication technologies (ICTs) in education is directed to ensure wider access to education, to provide equal opportunities for education, to ensure quality education for all at all levels (Patru, 2008). Quality Assurance and Accreditation in open distance e-learning is one of the main problems in the modern education (Jung, 2008). The quality assurance for the higher education, open distance e-learning and for lifelong learning organisations and continuing education (http://www.uniqm.net) have to be equally strong and at the same time to apply specific guidelines, criteria and methods for evaluation for the different modes of delivery.

A workshop is planned within the 2009 EDEN Annual Conference as a meeting point for decision makers in education. The stress is on the quality in the use of ICT for teaching and learning in the Higher Education Institutions as a tool for enhancing the quality of education (http://www.eden-online.org/eden.php?menuId=464). The main focus of the 4th European Quality Assurance Forum is to discuss the role of the current internal and external quality assurance approaches for institutional diversity and in supporting creativity in higher education (http://www.eua.be/quality-assurance/qa-forum-2009).

One of the resent projects of the Joint Information Systems Committee (JISC) is focused to investigate students' experience on ICT use and provision in Higher Education Institutions and to examine whether there is a mismatch between their expectations and the real conditions (http://www.jisc.ac.uk/publications/ documents/greatexpectations.aspx). E-Quality project (http://www.e-quality-eu.org/about.html) has the difficult task to overcome cultural and organisational diversity among European Higher Education Institutions and to achieve consensus on vocabulary and concepts concerning e-quality. The use of ICT in Higher Education institutions is increasing however at the same time the problems with the quality assurance of higher education is still highlighted more in the policy documents than in the daily practice. There is a need for a strategy to enhance the quality assurance aspects concerning structured integration of ICT in teaching and learning. The HEXTLEARN network and project (http://www.eden-online.org/eden.php?menuId=87) aim to involve directly the decision-makers in this process.

The acting standards in e-learning provide preconditions for quality e-learning; however they do not entirely guarantee that the developed courses are really high quality and meet the students need and expectations. To achieve educational service with guaranteed high quality it is necessary to apply the standards for quality management system, including evaluation of students' satisfaction.

The problem is high in the agenda for modernisation of European universities however, it is still necessary to increase the awareness of educational institutions world-wide of the importance of standardization activities in a more general sense and to apply the relevant standards in the in the everyday life of the institutions.

EDUCATION AS A SPECIFIC SERVICE

Learning is a very specific process; however the principles for quality management are applied to it. Education is seen as a service. As White (2008) states education is a service of great importance to the student; further more, it is also of great public importance and it is crucial to the success of society. That is why the quality of educational delivery matters. Quality assurance is about creating confidence, that it is constantly reviewing its own performance, in a continual effort to improve delivery. Quality assurance has much to contribute to both lifelong learning and student centered learning.

The philosophy of the system and process approach, the main principles and terminology from the ISO 9000 standards are applied to the education however it is necessary to consider the specific features of the educational service. The students are seen as main "customers" of the "service education". For some particular cases some other groups, involved in the education systems, can be also seen as customers.

QUALITY MANAGEMENT SYSTEM

The development of the ISO 9000 series standards is a milestone in the world strategy of production, management, trade and economical relationships. The standards from ISO 9000 series and EN

Figure 1. Continual improvement of the quality management system - ISO 9001:2000

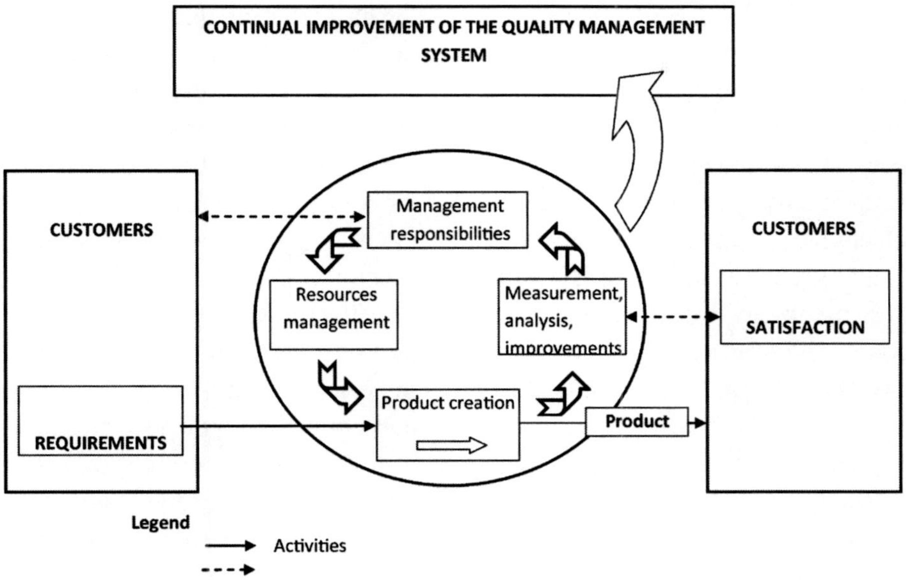

ISO 9001:2000 standard, "Quality management systems-Requirements" are particularly important for the European Union countries.

According to ISO 9000:2000 the term quality management means: "coordinated activities to direct and control an organization with regard to quality", i.e. the degree to which a set of inherent characteristics fulfills the requirements, i.e. the need or expectation that is usually implied or obligatory. Factors of great importance for a continual improvement of the quality management system are:

- Understanding and fulfillment of customer requirements;
- "Continual quality improvement based on objective measurements of the satisfaction with this quality" (ISO 9001:2000).

As seen in Figure 1, customers play an important role in defining the requirements. They influence both the product design and the product quality at two levels. Firstly, at the stage of designing a product, which has to satisfy their requirements and needs; secondly, after the product is manufactured, through their satisfaction with the product characteristics.

Customer Satisfaction

The term "customer satisfaction" is defined in ISO 9000:2000 standard: "customer satisfaction is the customer's perception of the degree to which the customer's requirements have been fulfilled", where requirement means: "need or expectation that is stated, generally implied or obligatory". The observation for customer satisfaction requires evaluation of the information concerning the customers' perception of the level at which the organization has fulfilled their requirements. The standard requires customer satisfaction measurement; however it does not specify particular method for it.

The approaches for satisfaction measurement are needed for different products. The standard EN ISO 9000:2000 specifies 4 categories of the term product: services (e.g. transport); software (e.g. computer program); hardware (e.g. engine mechanical part); processed materials (e.g. lubricant).

Satisfaction measurement is a real but not completely solved problem. Some teams of specialists deal with this problem, emphasized as a key factor of the continuing improvement of the product quality. Different approaches for satisfaction measurement are possible in practice because the standards do not include any particular method. This fact gives the author some freedom to develop a suitable approach. The satisfaction measurement methodology can be specific for particular products and services; however it is an advantage when the approach is more universal and applicable.

Objective methods are applied for evaluation of quality characteristics. Very often statistical methods are used, whereby data gathered by monitoring, observing and measurement is processed. The results are compared with the standard requirements and conclusions are drawn about the product quality level. Similar approach cannot be applied directly to define the customers' satisfaction with a particular product. Most of the quality characteristics in education are qualitative and the satisfaction is a strong individual and subjective perception; therefore it is necessary to find a reliable approach for defining the level of satisfaction for each individual customer. At the same time, if the producer wants to have the general evaluation for the level of satisfaction with the product for all potential customers, all individual opinions have to be generalized in a suitable and objective way.

The term "satisfaction measurement" is not correct from the point of view of the metrology science because there is no official physical standard for measuring like it is for other measurable quantities, for instance meter or kilogram. Nevertheless the term satisfaction measurement is accepted by the standard and the customer satisfaction can be "measured" in terms of "evaluated". The problem is how to evaluate something that has undetermined, individual, subjective and fuzzy characteristics. In such situation it is necessary to apply the theoretical knowledge and experience from the area of so called subjective statistics. Applying suitable approaches from this field the customer satisfaction can be measured using numbers, percentages, ranks or linguistically.

Customer satisfaction measurement can be seen as a complex management information system that has to continuously capture the "voice of the customer" concerning the fulfillment of his/her requirements connected with particular product. The information provided is a basis for strategic decision making directed to continual quality improvement and delivery of whatever is most important to customers. Customer satisfaction measurement helps also to: measure customer approval levels; improve customer retention; gauge interest in new products and service offerings; specify areas for improvement; make optimal decisions; change elements from the continual quality management system.

Quality, Quality Characteristics and their Importance

Quality of a product (service) is a complex characteristic that is in practice set of various characteristics. The quality is all specific characteristics of the product that are required by the customers and make the products differ from each other. According to ISO 9000:2000 the term quality means "3.1.1 degree to which a set of inherent characteristics (3.5.1) fulfills requirements (3.2.1)".

Each characteristic is distinguishing feature of the product (service). The term quality characteristic is defined in the standard as: " (3.5.2) inherent characteristic (3.5.1) of a product (3.4.2), process (3.4.1) or system (3.2.1) related to a requirement (3.1.2)".

Quality characteristics in education are indicators like: level of knowledge and skills, intensity of learning, students' performance trend, time for mastering, intermediate time for preparation, individual assignments, peer assessment, self-assessment, number of passed tests and self-study. Other possible learning characteristics are course content, learning resources, actuality of a specialty (teaching course), professional qualification of the teaching staff, curricula structure, learning technologies, learning methods, possibility for getting good theoretical training and practical skills, participation in research projects and international programs and obtaining additional qualification.

To achieve optimal quality of a product in practice means to optimize all quality characteristics of the product. In practice the quality characteristics are not equally important for the product quality. Therefore it is necessary to consider the importance of the quality characteristics in the quality optimization process.

OPTIMAL QUALITY CONTROL

The Multiple Criteria Decision Making Theory (MCDMT) is applicable to various areas in science and life. An example is that the Nobel Price for economics for 2002 was awarded to Daniel Kahneman of Princeton University "for having integrated insights from psychological research into economic science, especially concerning human judgment and decision-making under uncertainty" and to Vernon Smith of George Mason University "for having established laboratory experiments as a tool in empirical economic analysis, especially in the study of alternative market mechanisms" (http://nobelprize.org/nobel_prizes/lists/all/). With their investigation they both created conditions for the scientists when making decisions to rely less on the observation on the real economics and more on the controlled laboratory experiments.

Elements from MCDMT are applied to the learning process in this work. There is no information that the MCDMT or some elements from it have been used previously in the area of education and e-learning.

As soon as the quality of the product (service) is always characterised by multiple criteria it is necessary to apply the methods for multiple criteria optimisation in order to achieve optimal quality of the product (service).

Formulation and Specific Features of the Task for Multiple Criteria Optimization

The quality of a technological product, ecological advisability of production, operation of a system or the product (service) is a complex set of characteristics. In the optimization theory it is accepted to refer to these quality characteristics as a set of objective variables $\mathbf{y}=(y_1, y_2, ..., y_m)$. Each of these parameters has a certain importance however it is not sufficient to optimize a process or the quality of a product. Optimization by only one criterion is normally not the best solution. In practice, the real optimization tasks in technology and production as well as the tasks for quality optimization are always multiobjective. The optimal values for the different objective parameters are obtained for different values of the set of control variables $\mathbf{x}=(x_1, x_2, ..., x_n)$. The control variables vary according to the features of the product. They can be temperature, reagent consumption, time, and quantity of supplements or for education sector - teaching methods, learning technology, educational legislation, curricula, syllabuses, preliminary knowledge and skills, motivation, student personal characteristics. Normally control variables are within certain limits that define so called feasible region of control variables (constrained variables) and they can be unlimited or partially limited. Also they can be continuous such as time, pressure, and temperature and discrete, for example, number of workers, machines, fuel injections.

The objective variables $\mathbf{y}=(y_1, y_2, ..., y_m)$ are quality characteristics that can be various technical, economical, ecological or social requirements, which fulfill conditions asked by the customer, producer, society, standards, norms. The objective variables are presented mainly numerically (price, quantity of additives, physical-mechanical characteristics, quantity of emissions, weight, size), but they can also be expressed linguistically (smell, transparency, remoteness, color).

For some tasks for multiple criteria optimization it is possible to use one basic parameter (criterion) for optimization and the rest can play the role of region constraints. This division, however, is not always possible.

The main characteristic of the multiple criteria decision-making task is that it is incorrect because there is not only one single solution, but it has countless solutions within so called "region of compromises". There are a lot of different classifications of the compromise optimization methods available in the literature (Stoyanov, 1993). These methods can consider the priorities of the objective variables. For all optimization methods the choice of compromise optimal solution strongly depends on the importance of the objective variables (quality characteristics) expressed by the accepted weighting coefficients W_j for them. For this reason defining the importance by calculating of weighting coefficients is an essential stage in the multiple criteria decision making theory. The compromise solutions are different for the case of using and not using weighting coefficients of the quality characteristics. If the objective variables have different importance and for each of them is given a weighting coefficient W_j the compromise solution can be moved to direction to the more important variables. This principle is particularly suitable to apply for optimal quality control.

WEIGHTING COEFFICIENTS FOR QUALITY CHARACTERISTICS

The compromise optimal solution in multiple criteria optimization for quality management depends to a great extent on the adopted weighting coefficients W_j for the different quality characteristics. These weighting coefficients affect also the level of customer satisfaction with a product.

There are no strictly formalized methods to define the importance of the quality characteristics and their corresponding weighting coefficients. The opinion for the importance of the quality characteristics is subjective. Relatively reliable weighting coefficients are defined applying approaches from the subjective statistics to evaluate objectively the subjective customers' opinions. Customers' opinions are normally collected by enquiry. All people that take part in the enquiry will be referred to as customers; although in some particular cases concerning quality management or customer satisfaction measurement they can be experts, specialist or different category citizens (customers).

Calculation of Weighting Coefficients by Arranging the Objective Variables

One reliable method for defining weighting coefficients by customers' (experts') opinions (Nacheva-Skopalik, Stoyanov & Skopalik, 2004; Stoyanov, 2008) that uses rank correlation method (Kendal, 1957) is presented below.

A number of customers R are asked to give their opinion about the importance of quality characteristics y_j. The number of the quality characteristics is m. Customers fill an inquiry card arranging the quality characteristics with numbers from 1 to m. It is recommended that the objective variables be presented in a random sequence without numbering. The results obtained are presented in a rank matrix (Table 1). Each element $\alpha_{\lambda j}$ in the rank matrix is the weight (rank) which the customer λ gives for the quality characteristic j.

Customers are allowed to put the same rank for more that one characteristic. In this case there are related ranks. For the case of related ranks the methodology requires to normalize the rank matrix. The normalized matrix has to fulfill the requirement: the sum $\alpha_{\lambda j}$ for each row of the matrix equals S_p, where S_p is calculated by

$$S_p = \frac{m\ (m+1)}{2}, \qquad (1)$$

Table 1. Rank matrix

Objective variables → Customer ↓	y_1	y_2	...	y_j		y_m
1	a_{11}	a_{12}	...	a_{1j}	...	a_{1m}
2	a_{21}	a_{22}	...	a_{2j}	...	a_{2m}
3	a_{31}	a_{32}	...	a_{3j}	...	a_{3m}
...	...	...	...	...	...	...
λ	$a_{\lambda 1}$	$a_{\lambda 2}$	...	$a_{\lambda j}$	...	$a_{\lambda m}$
...	...	...	...	...	...	...
R	a_{R1}	a_{R2}	...	a_{Rj}	...	a_{Rm}
$\sum_{\lambda=1}^{R} a_{\lambda j}$						
Δj						
V_j						
W_j						

i.e.

$$\sum_{j=1}^{m} a_{\lambda j} = S_p. \quad (2)$$

For example, let us assume that customers λ, $(\lambda+1)$, $(\lambda+2)$ are given ranks for m=11 quality characteristics, as shown in Table 2. Customer $(\lambda+1)$ gives rank 6 for six characteristics (y_3, y_4, y_7, y_8, y_9 and y_{11}). Customer $(\lambda+2)$ gives rank 3 for two characteristics (y_3 and y_{10}), rank 7 for two characteristics (y_4 and y_6) and rank 8 for two characteristics (y_9 and y_{11}). There are no related ranks for customer λ. It is seen from Table 2 that the sum of $a_{\lambda j}$ for the three customers is different.

To be able to compare the related ranks with non-related ones it is necessary to normalize the matrix and to fulfill the requirement (2). Using the formula (1) for this case the sum is calculated by

$$\sum_{j=1}^{m} a_{\lambda j} = S_p = \frac{m(m+1)}{2} = \frac{7(7+1)}{2} = 28. \quad (3)$$

The rule for normalization of the matrix is: all quality characteristics, which are given the same rank, are assigned a rank that is the average value of the ranks they have to share. The requirement (2) is fulfilled for the normalized matrix. The normalized matrix for the example is presented in Table 3.

The values t_λ and the value T_λ are given also in Table 3. These values are used further in methodology for calculation of the weighing coefficients. The value t_λ is the number of separately related ranks for each customer. The value T_λ is calculated using the formula (9).

The weighting coefficients for the characteristics are calculated only if there is concordance in the customers' opinions.

The concordance in the customers' opinions is checked by calculating the concordance coefficient W_k using the rank correlation methods (Kendal, 1957). The calculations differ for the case without related ranks and for the case with related ranks.

Table 2. Part of a rank matrix

Objective variables → Customer ↓	y_1	y_2	y_3	y_4	y_5	y_6	y_7	y_8	y_9	y_{10}	y_{11}	$\sum_{j=1}^{11} a_{\lambda j}$
λ	1	5	6	2	9	10	8	7	4	3	11	66
$\lambda+1$	1	5	6	6	2	3	6	6	6	4	6	51
$\lambda+2$	1	2	3	7	6	7	5	4	8	3	8	54

Table 3. Part of a normalized matrix

Objective variables → Customer ↓	y_1	y_2	y_3	y_4	y_5	y_6	y_7	y_8	y_9	y_{10}	y_{11}	$\sum_{j=1}^{11} a_{\lambda j}$	t_λ	T_λ
λ	1	5	6	2	9	10	8	7	4	3	11	66	0	0
λ +*1*	1	5	8,5	8,5	2	3	8,5	8,5	8,5	4	8,5	66	6	17,5
λ +*2*	1	2	3,5	8,5	7	8,5	6	5	10,5	3,5	10,5	66	2+2+2	1,5

Concordance coefficient W_k in case when there are no related ranks is calculated by

$$w_k = \frac{S_\Delta}{R^2(m^3 - m)}, \tag{4}$$

where

$$S_\Delta = 12\sum_{j=1}^{m} \Delta_j^2; \tag{5}$$

$$\Delta_j = \sum_{\lambda=1}^{R} a_{\lambda j} - S_{cp}; \tag{6}$$

$$S_{cp} = \frac{R\ (m+1)}{2}, \tag{7}$$

S_{cp} is the average sum of all weights (ranks).

Δ_j is the deviation of the sum of the weights for each objective variable from the average sum.

The concordance coefficient in case of related ranks is calculated by

$$w_k = \frac{12\sum_{j=1}^{m} \Delta_j^2}{R^2(m^3 - m) - R\sum_\lambda T_\lambda}, \tag{8}$$

where

$$T_\lambda = \frac{1}{12}\sum_{t_\lambda}(t_\lambda^3 - t_\lambda). \tag{9}$$

t_λ is the number of separately related ranks for each customer.

It is obvious that in case without related ranks the second term in the denominator of formula (8) is missing and the formula (8) becomes identical with (4).

The concordance coefficient can change from 0 in case of full lack of concordance in the opinions to +1 in case of full concordance in the opinions. The significance of the calculated concordance coefficient W_k is evaluated using χ^2 criterion when $m \geq 7$, or using Z criterion when $m < 7$.

When $m < 7$ the value Z is calculated by

$$F = \frac{1}{2}\ln\frac{(R-1)w_k}{1 - w_k} \tag{10}$$

If $Z > Z_{tabl}(\alpha, v_1, v_2)$ the conclusion is that with probability $\beta = 1 - \alpha$, W_k is a significant concordance coefficient. Z_{tabl} is taken from a table (Kendal, 1957) at degrees of freedom v_1 and v_2 calculated by

$$\nu_1 = m - 1 - \frac{2}{R} \tag{11}$$

$$v_2 = (R-1)v_1. \tag{12}$$

The values v_1 and v_2 are rounded integer, α is level of significance that corresponds to probability $\beta=1-\alpha$.

When $m \geq 7$ the value χ^2_{calc} is calculated by

$$\chi^2_{calc} = R(m-1)W_k. \quad (13)$$

The concordance coefficient W_k is significant if

$$\chi^2_{calc} > \chi^2_{tabl}(\alpha, v). \quad (14)$$

χ^2_{tabl} is taken from a table (Kendal, 1957) for $v=m-1$ degrees of freedom and level of significance α that corresponds to level of probability $\beta=1-\alpha$.

It is obvious that the calculated weighting coefficients are more reliable for bigger value of probability β.

If the concordance coefficient W_k is significant i.e. there is concordance between the customers' subjective opinions the weighting coefficients are calculated by (Stoyanov, 1993)

$$W_j = \frac{V_j}{\sum_{j=1}^{m} V_j}; j=1, 2, \ldots, m, \quad (15)$$

where

$$V_j = \frac{\left(Rm - \sum_{\lambda=1}^{R} a_{\lambda j}\right)}{R(m-1)}. \quad (16)$$

For the calculated weighting coefficients is fulfilled

$$\sum_{j=1}^{m} W_j = 1.0. \quad (17)$$

Calculation of Weighting Coefficients by Customers' Opinion for the Priorities of the Objective Variables

Another approach to define weighting coefficients W_i is to use the specialists' or customers' knowledge, experience and intuition concerning the priorities of the quality characteristics. A heuristic approach, based on the customers' opinion about the mutual priorities of the objective variables (quality characteristics) uses an adopted three-degree membership function (Nacheva-Skopalik, Stoyanov & Skopalik, 2004). The approach is suitable to apply for a small number of the quality characteristics.

The suggested approaches for defining weighting coefficients can be successfully applied in the product quality management process, for customer satisfaction measurement as well as in various different areas such as sociology, technological processes, environment protection, health services, economics, and education.

Application of Weighting Coefficients of Quality Characteristics in Education and E-Learning

The approach for calculation of weighting coefficients by arranging the objective variables has been used in research studies to define the importance of the diagnostic test questions (Nacheva-Skopalik, 2007), the importance of the feedback channels in the cybernetic learning model (Nacheva-Skopalik, Skopalik & Stoyanov, 2007) and the component of a virtual learning environment.

An example for calculation of weighting coefficients for quality characteristics in e-learning is presented below (Nacheva-Skopalik, 2007).

Example 1: Weighting Coefficients of the Characteristics of the Learning Process

A research study investigates approaches to achieve optimal learning process suitable to apply for e-learning system and suggests applying the principles of cybernetic control. To develop a cybernetic model of learning it is necessary to create an adequate model of the object of control and its identification. For control purposes it is important to define the input and output parameters as well as the disturbances. There are strictly defined approaches for object identification in the theory of automatic control. The student is the object of control within the cybernetic learning model.

Examination of the student as an object of control shows that he/she is a complex biological object with pronounced individual features, classified as multidimensional dynamic object with fuzzy parameters that are difficult to measure, particularly in the contexts of e-learning. Traditional approaches for creating of a classic mathematical model of the object and defining its identification parameters, used in the technical systems, can not be directly applied for its identification. The approach to define the priorities and weighting coefficients of educational characteristics using an objective evaluation of subjective expert opinions by rank correlation methods and elements of the subjective statistics is a good solution for this specific task. There is no indication that this powerful approach from the multiple criteria decision making theory is used for educational purposes so far.

The chosen learning characteristics to explore are: individual time for learning (Y1), level of knowledge (Y2), level of skills (Y3), performance trend (Y4), deviation from the average level of knowledge (Y5), intensity of learning (Y6), uniformity in mastering (Y7).

The results from the enquiry among a group of experienced academic staff are shown in Table 4 and in Figure 2.

The coefficient of concordance W_k is significant for level of significance α=0,5 that means there is concordance in the subjective customers' opinions with probability not less than 95% and the weighting coefficients W_j for the identification parameters can be calculated.

The chart of the weighting coefficients is very useful for analysis because it gives very clear idea for the values and the differences between the weights of the characteristics, while the ranks only order them by their importance.

Level of knowledge (Y2) and level of skills (Y3) are the characteristics with biggest priority. Intensity of learning (Y6) has a priority 3. Priorities 4 and 5 are for uniformity in mastering (Y7) and performance trend (Y4). The less importance is given to individual time for learning (Y1) and deviation from the average level of knowledge (Y5). The deep analysis of these results shows that some of these characteristics are main ones and can be measured – these are level of knowledge (Y2) and level of skills (Y3). Others are result of calculations using the main ones. Intensity of learning is not directly measured. It is calculated using the quantity of mastered teaching material and the deviation from the time according to accepted schedule. The time deviation from the schedule(Y5) can be measured and for this reason the intermediate time for mastering each topic is defined as third output identification parameter of the student model (Nacheva-Skopalik L., 2007).

Considering the importance of the explored characteristics a model of student (student group) as an object of control for the cybernetic model of learning process is created and it is used for the structure scheme for automated learning process control, described in example 2 in this chapter.

AN APPROACH FOR SATISFACTION MEASUREMENT

Customer satisfaction with the quality of products and services is very subjective perception

Table 4. Weighting coefficients for the learning characteristics

Parameter → **Specialist ↓**	y_1	y_2	y_3	y_4	y_5	y_6	y_7	t_λ	T_λ
1.	1	4	5	6,5	6,5	3	2	2	0,5
2.	6	2	1	3	7	4	5	0	0
3.	4,5	1	2	3	6	7	4,5	2	0,5
4.	3,5	1,5	1,5	6	7	3,5	5	2+2	1
5.	5	3	4	6	7	1,5	1,5	2	0,5
6.	3	1,5	1,5	6	7	5	4	2	0,5
7.	1,5	3	4,5	4,5	6	1,5	7	2+2	1
8.	4	1,5	1,5	4	7	4	6	2+3	2,5
9.	5	1	2	6	7	4	3	0	0
10.	5	1	2	3	6	4	7	0	0
11.	7	1,5	1,5	4	3	6	5	2	0,5
12.	6	1,5	1,5	5	7	4	3	2	0,5
13.	6	2	2	2	7	5	4	3	2
14.	7	1,5	1,5	3	6	5	4	2	0,5
$\sum_{\lambda=1}^{14} \alpha_{\lambda j}$	64,5	26	31,5	62	89,5	57,5	61		$\sum T\lambda = 10$
$\Delta_j = \sum_{\lambda=1}^{R} \alpha_{\lambda j} - S_{sr}$	8,5	-30	-24,5	6	33,5	1,5	5		
Δ_j^2	72,25	900	600,25	36	1122,25	2,25	25	$\sum_{j=1}^{7} \Delta_j^2 = 2758$	
V_j	0,3988	0,8571	0,7917	0,4286	0,1012	0,4821	0,4405	$\sum_{j=1}^{7} V_j = 3,5$	
W_j	0,114	0,245	0,226	0,122	0,029	0,138	0,126	$\sum_{j=1}^{m} W_j = 1.$	
Rank	6	1	2	5	7	3	4		
$S_{sr} = \frac{R(m+1)}{2} = 56$									

Figure 2. Weighting coefficients for the learning characteristics

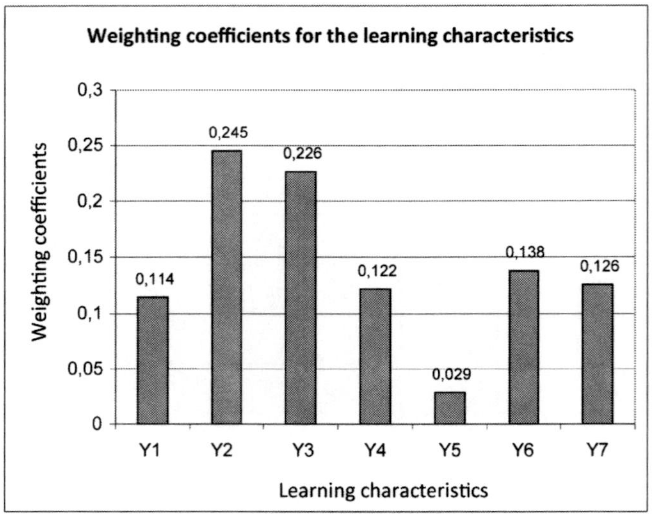

hence it is necessary to find a reliable approach to evaluate it for each individual customer. At the same time the process of continual quality improvement requires to have general evaluation for the level of satisfaction of all customers with particular product. In order to achieve this evaluation it is necessary to apply suitable and reliable approach to objectively evaluate subjective individual opinions and techniques used in the subjective statistics.

For the purpose of evaluation of customers' satisfaction each quality characteristic can be characterized by quantitative and qualitative valuations. The qualitative valuation defines the level of importance of the quality characteristic. The quantitative valuation gives the level of customer satisfaction with this quality characteristic. The combination of these two valuations gives a complex evaluation of the customer's satisfaction with the chosen quality characteristic (Nacheva-Skopalik, 2007).

The developed approach for satisfaction measurement applies the method for calculating weighting coefficients to define the importance of the characteristics (qualitative valuation).

The approach applies a numerical valuation of the level of customer's satisfaction with each characteristic as quantitative valuation. This quantitative valuation uses previously defined scale. A scale with values between 0 and 10 or values between 0 and 100 are often used. The value 0 means full no satisfaction, the value 10 (100) means full satisfaction. All customers' opinions, processed in a suitable way, give the general value for all customers.

Enquiry among Customers

The necessary data for satisfaction measurement are collected by an enquiry among customers. The interviewed customers are presented two enquiry cards.

The first enquiry card collects customers' opinions for the importance of the quality characteristics (qualitative value). A list with all quality characteristics for the product is presented to the customers. They have to range the suggested characteristics according to their importance (rank, priority). An example of such an enquiry card is given below.

Enquiry Card 1

Dear Madame/Sir,

The Company C1 is investigating customers' satisfaction with the product P.

Please, give your opinion by grading (arranging) the product quality characteristics by their importance. We will ask you to put ranks (priorities) to the 6 given characteristics in the table below using numbers.

The highest rank (priority) is 1.

The lowest rank (priority) is 6.

In your opinion, you can put in the table equal ranks for some of the characteristics.

Thank you in advance!

The enquiry is anonymous!

Quality characteristics for P	Rank
Y1*	
Y2	
Y3	
Y4	
Y5	
Y6	

Company manager

Date

*the quality characteristics are written

The second enquiry card collects customers' opinions for their level of satisfaction with each quality characteristic (quantitative value). The chosen scale is to use numbers between 0 and 10. The customers are asked to valuate with number between 0 and 10 the level of their satisfaction with each characteristic. An example of this enquiry card is given below.

Enquiry Card 2

Dear Madame/Sir,

The Company C1 is investigating the customers' satisfaction with the product P.

Please, give your opinion using a number between 0 and 10 in a column "Level of satisfaction with the characteristic (0-10)". This number will show the level of your satisfaction with each quality characteristic of P. The number 0 means full lack of satisfaction, number 10 means full satisfaction.

Thank you in advance!

The enquiry is anonymous!

Quality characteristics for P	Level of satisfaction with the characteristic (0-10)
Y1*	
Y2	
Y3	
Y4	
Y5	
Y6	

Company manager

Date

*the quality characteristics are written

Processing the Enquiry Data

The first step in processing the enquiry data is to calculate the weighting coefficients for the quality characteristics i.e. to define their importance. The weighting coefficients and the given quantitative valuations for the level of satisfaction of each customer with each characteristic are used for the following calculations. The different calculations

Table 5. Quantitative valuation of the quality characteristics

Characteristic → **Customer ↓**	y_1	y_2	...	y_j	...	y_m
1	k_{11}	k_{12}	...	k_{1j}	...	k_{1m}
2	k_{21}	k_{22}	...	k_{2j}	...	k_{2m}
...	...	...	...	...	...	
i	k_{i1}	k_{i2}	...	k_{ij}	...	k_{im}
...	....	...	...	...	...	
R	k_{R1}	k_{R2}	...	k_{Rj}	...	k_{Rm}

give information about the level of customers' satisfaction with a product from different point of view.

The data collected from the two enquiry cards are arranged in two separate tables. The number of asked customers is R and the number of quality characteristics for the product is m.

The first table is the rank matrix that contains the ranks for all characteristics given by the customers. This table is analogous to Table 1 that is used in the methodology for calculation of weighting coefficients. The weighting coefficients for the characteristics W_j, $j=1, 2, ..., m$ are calculated using the data from this table and the accepted methodology.

According to the methodology, weighting coefficients are calculated only if there is concordance in the customers' opinion (with defined probability). It is possible to have cases when there is no concordance in the customers' opinion. In such situation it is recommended to take actions to improve all quality characteristics and then to conduct new enquiry among the customers.

The second table (Table 5) contains the quantitative valuation k_{ij}, $j=1, 2,..., m$ for the level of satisfaction of the ith customer with the jth characteristic.

The combined table (Table 6) contains the calculated weighting coefficients for each characteristic W_j, $j=1,..., m$ and the level of satisfaction with these characteristics k_{ij}, $j=1,...,m$ for each customer $i=1, ..., R$.

The data from the combined Table 6 are processed in different ways to give information about the level of customers' satisfaction with the product from different points of view.

Table 6. Combined table

Characteristic → **Customer ↓**	y_1	y_2	...	y_j	...	y_m	Sc	Scr
1	k_{11}	k_{12}	...	k_{1j}	...	k_{1m}	Sc_1	Scr_1
2	k_{21}	k_{22}	...	k_{2j}	...	k_{2m}	Sc_2	Scr_2
..	...							
i	k_{i1}	k_{i2}	...	k_{ij}	...	k_{im}	Sc_i	Scr_i
...	....							
R	k_{R1}	k_{R2}	...	k_{Rj}	...	k_{Rm}	Sc_m	Scr_m
Weighting coefficients	W_1	W_2	...	W_j	...	W_m		
Sw	Sw_1	Sw_2		Sw_j		Sw_m		
Swr	Swr_1	Swr_2	...	Swr_j	...	Swr_m		Spr

Processing the data from one customer for all quality characteristics of the product defines the level of satisfaction of this particular customer with the product. In this case the data in the combined table are processed by rows.

Processing of the data from all customers for only one quality characteristic of the product gives general evaluation for the level of satisfaction for all customers with one particular quality characteristic of the product. In this case the data in the combined table are processed by columns.

Processing the data from all customers for all quality characteristics gives complex valuation for the satisfaction of all customers with all quality characteristics e.g. with the product as a whole.

Satisfaction of each Customer with the Product

The evaluation of satisfaction for the customer *i* is a sum from his/her satisfaction with each quality characteristic y_j, considering the weighting coefficient W_j (importance) for each characteristic. The maximum value of k_{ij} is 10 and it corresponds to the full satisfaction with each characteristic.

The satisfaction of the customer *i* with all characteristics Sc_i is calculated by

$$Sc_i = \sum_{j=1}^{m} k_{ij} W_j, \quad i = 1, 2, ..., R, \tag{18}$$

where

W_j – weighting coefficient for the characteristic *j;*

k_{ij} – degree/level of the satisfaction for customer *i* with the characteristic *j*;

R – number of the customers;

m – number of the characteristics.

The maximum satisfaction *Sc*max is calculated if for all characteristics is given level of satisfaction 10, e.g. $k_{ij}=10$ for *i*=1, 2, …, *R* and *j*=1, 2, …, *m*.

$$Sc\max = 10\sum_{j=1}^{m} W_j. \tag{19}$$

According to the methodology for defining the weighting coefficients the next equation is valid

$$\sum_{j=1}^{m} W_j = 1.0. \tag{20}$$

Consequently, *Sc*max=10.

The relative level of customer's satisfaction with the product Scr_i presented in % is calculated by

$$Scr_i = \frac{Sc_i}{SA\max} 100 \ \%, \tag{21}$$

or, for the case where a scale with maximal value 10 is used

$$Scr_i = \frac{Sc_i}{10} 100 \ \%. \tag{22}$$

Satisfaction of all Customers with One Quality Characteristic

The average value for all values given by all customers for the particular characteristic is calculated to define the all customers' satisfaction with this particular characteristic - Sw_j

$$Sw_j = \frac{\sum_{i=1}^{R} k_{ij}}{R}, j = 1, 2, ..., m, \tag{23}$$

The maximum value of the satisfaction with one particular characteristic *Sw*max is 10 when all customers are given the number 10 for their level of satisfaction.

$$Sw\max = 10. \tag{24}$$

Figure 3. Customer satisfaction with product quality characteristics

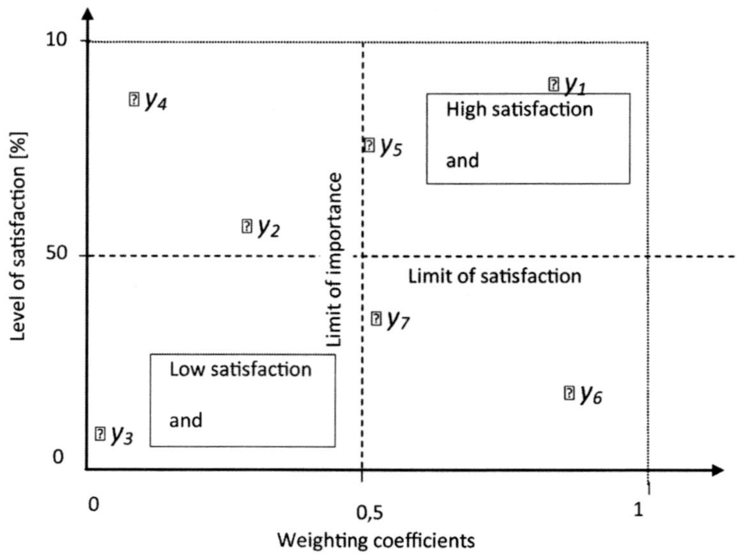

The relative value of the satisfaction for all customers with the chosen characteristic Swr_j is calculated by

$$Swr_j = \frac{Sw_j}{Sw\max} 100 \ \%, \tag{25}$$

or

$$Swr_j = \frac{Sw_j}{10} 100 \ \%. \tag{26}$$

Satisfaction of all Customers with the Product

The relative level of all customers' satisfaction with the product *Spr* is calculated as an average value for the relative level of satisfaction of all customers with the product

$$Spr = \frac{\sum_{i=1}^{R} Scr_i}{R} \ \%. \tag{27}$$

Graphical Presentation of Satisfaction Measurement Results

The graphical presentation of satisfaction measurement results is shown in Figure 3. The weighting coefficients are projected on the x-axis and the level of customers' satisfaction with each characteristic Swr_j (given in %) is projected on the y-axis.

For deeper analysis of the results it is recommended to accept limit of satisfaction. For the different cases this limit can be different. For the example from the figure the limit of satisfaction is accepted 50%. The accepted limit of satisfaction defines the areas with low and high satisfaction. The chosen limit for the areas of low and high importance depends on the number of the chosen quality characteristics and the values of the weighting coefficients. For bigger number of characteristics the weighting coefficients will be with closer values.

The graphical presentation clearly visualizes the results and facilitates the process of their analysis and decision making. It is easy to trace at the same time what is the importance of each characteristic and what is the level of satisfaction with this characteristic.

Four areas in the space of the weighting coefficients and the level of satisfaction are defined:

- Area of high satisfaction and high importance (y_1);
- Area of low satisfaction and low importance (y_3);
- Area of low satisfaction and high importance (y_6);
- Area of high satisfaction and low importance (y_4).

The satisfaction measurement results and the position of each characteristic in the chart area are important information in the process of making relevant decisions and actions for optimal quality management. In order to increase customers' satisfaction the aim is to achieve satisfaction above the accepted limit. This is particularly important for the quality characteristics with high importance. The evaluation of customers' satisfaction provides conditions to find optimal control of the product quality that improves the characteristics with low satisfaction without worsening the characteristics with high level of satisfaction. At the same time a deep analysis is necessary for characteristics with low importance and low level of satisfaction. Considering the satisfaction measurement results is essential contribution to the process of making decisions for improving quality of a product; however the particular decision depends also on the particular product (service) and the production and market strategy of the company.

So called "decision maker" has the key role and importance in the process of optimal quality control and his/her expertise is crucial for finding the best solution. Decision maker can be one person or a team of persons. First of all the decision maker have to have excellent knowledge for the product or process to explore. In addition to being expert at strategies and methods for multiple criteria optimization he/she has to fulfill various other requirements such as: to be able to make system, hierarchic, expert, and statistical and correlation analysis, analysis with fuzzy situations and under uncertainty. He has to recommend or make optimal decision based on the analysis of various different solutions. Normal practice is to make the optimal decision after intensive consultations and negotiations between producers, customers, managers, and people with knowledge and experience in methods for satisfaction measurement.

Choice of Quality Characteristics for Satisfaction Measurement

The choice of the quality characteristics that are used in the satisfaction measurement process is extremely essential factor for receiving reliable results. The choice of quality characteristics depends on different factors. The explored quality characteristics can be defined by legislation or norm requirements and regulations. They can depend on some specific features, for example: specific national and cultural features of the education system. The quality characteristics can be defined by the specialists' experience. One good approach is to explore experts' opinions for the importance of the quality indicators, using some of the methods described in this chapter. The chosen indicators have to describe all sides of the product in the best possible way. In order to receive realistic picture for the level of satisfaction that really contributes to improving the quality of the product, the characteristics that may cause conflict and "are expected" low level of customer satisfaction have to be also included in the enquiry.

The investigation can be made at two stages. The first stage can define the satisfaction with more general quality characteristics. For each of these quality characteristics or for those ones that need the special attention for decision making can be defined their own characteristics to characterize them in depth. The examination of satisfaction with these detailed characteristics (at a second level) gives better inside for the situation.

Information Providing in the Satisfaction Measurement

The developed approach for satisfaction measurement uses enquiry cards to collect customers' opinions. It is strongly recommended to present the quality characteristics in the enquiry form in a random sequence without numbering. The goal is not to influence people suggesting preliminary opinion. The enquiry card for the level of satisfaction with the quality characteristics is made so that the interviewed are able to give numerical dimension of his/her opinion for their satisfaction

The producer or the organization that require customer satisfaction measurement makes decision among which customer categories to do the investigation, depending on the particular aim and task. In some cases it is suitable, possible and/or recommendable to do general investigation among all customer categories. In other cases it is necessary to do investigation among specific or particular group of customers. When the product (service) is designed for a particular customer category, for example, teaching course in particular subject or specialty at a university, it is logical to do the investigation only among this customer category to define their satisfaction, i.e. the students from the course or specialty. When the product (service) is used by different customer categories, for instance, virtual learning environment (VLE) or administrative services, the investigation can be held among all customer categories regardless of their position, age, sex, social status etc. However, if the goal is to examine only the satisfaction for particular customer group, for instance age group, the investigation is held only among this customer category. In some cases it is worth to estimate the satisfaction for the biggest interested customer groups and it is always useful to compare the results from the different investigations.

It is normal and expected that the customer attitude to the product change with time. The reasons for this could be different: there are new products, fashion tendencies, materials and technologies on the market; political, social, economical changes. One good approach to get the up to date evaluation for the customers' satisfaction is to measure this satisfaction periodically. Essential conclusions concerning the level of customers' satisfaction and the tendencies in product quality improvement can be made when the results from the different investigations and measurements are compared.

The data collected by the described enquiry cards are used to numerical evaluation of customer satisfaction according to the suggested approach. Different techniques can be used to collect some additional information. Taking an interview from the customers by asking specific questions can contribute to better clarifying the level of customer satisfaction and can increase the reliability of its numerical valuation (Nacheva-Skopalik, Stoyanov & Skopalik, 2004). In all cases of collecting customers' opinion it is recommended the institution, which is investigating customers' satisfaction, to provide suitable conditions in order to receive honest customer opinions.

APPLICATIONS OF THE SATISFACTION MEASUREMENT APPROACH IN EDUCATION

The developed approach for satisfaction measurement is applicable for various products (services) such as economics, tourist services, and transport and health services. This approach can be successfully applied in education and e-learning for different purposes.

It is possible to evaluate students' satisfaction with university services (administrative, library), social conditions, attitude to students. Directly in the teaching process it is applicable to estimate the efficiency of a teaching course, learning environment, teaching methods, assessment methods, learning technologies. Estimation of satisfaction of academic and/or administrative staff is also possible.

Figure 4. Structure scheme for automated control of the learning process - main information channels

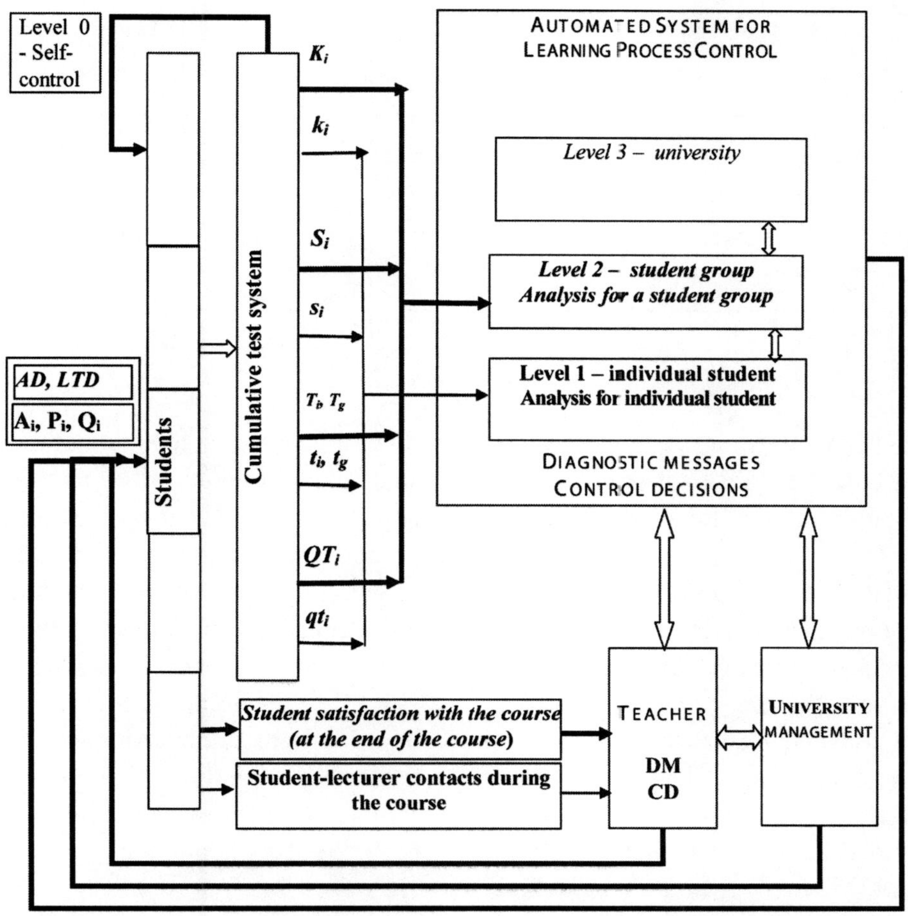

Example 2: Satisfaction Measurement within the Cybernetic Learning Model

The analysis and research investigation lead to the conclusion that it is necessary to include the main features of cybernetic control principles in order to develop an optimal and effective modern e-learning system (Nacheva-Skopalik, 2007).

The research investigation shows that the efficiency and optimization of the learning process depends also on the structure of education. Considering the hierarchic structure of the learning process, the object of control at first hierarchic level is the individual student and the object of control at second hierarchic level is the student group. The developed model of the student (student group) has the following output identification parameters: level of knowledge k_i (K_i); level of skill s_i (S_i); total time for learning t_g (T_g); intermediate time periods for mastering i[th] topic t_i, (T_i); type of the wrong/non answered questions qt_i (QT_i). The choice is based on the importance of the explored learning characteristics, discussed in example 1.

The input identification parameters for the student (student group) are: Q_i – quantity teaching material; A_i – administrative impacts; P_i – psychological impacts. The input control impacts for the student group are additionally grouped according the moment of their application – actual decisions (***AD***) for the current course and long term decisions (***LTD***) that will be applied to future courses (Figure 4).

Table 7. Satisfaction measurement for a VLE

Quality criteria for a VLE		W_i	Rank	Level of satisfaction[%]
Exercises/activities	Y1	0,06	6	49
Course content	Y2	0,06	6	64
Chat	Y3	0,12	5	31
Resources	Y4	0,26	1	61
E-mail	Y5	0,19	2	41
Assignments	Y6	0,13	4	62
Discussion	Y7	0,18	3	50

The chosen characteristics, using them separately or in combination, are estimated as sufficient for automated optimal control of the learning process.

"Cumulative" test system for formative and diagnostic assessment with its innovative features realizes the feedback channels for control of the learning process within the cybernetic learning model. The automated feedback to students is through diagnostic messages (DM) and control decisions (CD).

The structure scheme for automated learning process control (Figure 4) shows the hierarchic structure of control: self-control (level 0), control of the individual student (hierarchic level 1) and control of the student group (hierarchic level 2). It is based also on the accepted programmed learning.

Automated system for control of the learning process uses logical control algorithm for diagnostic analysis of all test results to generate relevant diagnostic messages and control decisions for most of the "typical cases". The teacher has highest priority and a key position in the automated system for control of the learning process. He makes control decisions for the specific cases and he can override the automated system at any moment. All information collected by the student-teacher contact is used by the teacher to improve the control of the student learning.

An essential contribution of the suggested system toward continual improvement the quality of e-learning is including of measurement of student's satisfaction with a teaching course as a part of the optimal control of learning for a student group. The results are used to improve quality of current and future teaching courses. What is more important, the students' satisfaction should be analyzed at the next hierarchic level – university - for making general relevant decisions for improvements at university level. In practice the students' satisfaction makes connection between the hierarchic levels in the education and it is part of the complex hierarchic control of learning.

Example 3: Evaluation of Satisfaction with a Virtual Learning Environment

The satisfaction measurement approach was presented at a research workshop of Accessibility Research Center (ARC), School of Computing, University of Teesside, UK.

The method was applied to examine the satisfaction with a virtual learning environment (VLE). Some general characteristics were chosen as exemplary quality characteristics. The enquired people were research students, academic lecturers, researchers. The results are shown in Table 7 and in Figure 5.

The biggest importance is given for resources for learning (Y4) and the satisfaction with this indicator is 61%. E-mail communication (Y5) and discussion forum (Y7) are also characteristics

Figure 5. Satisfaction measurement for a virtual learning environment

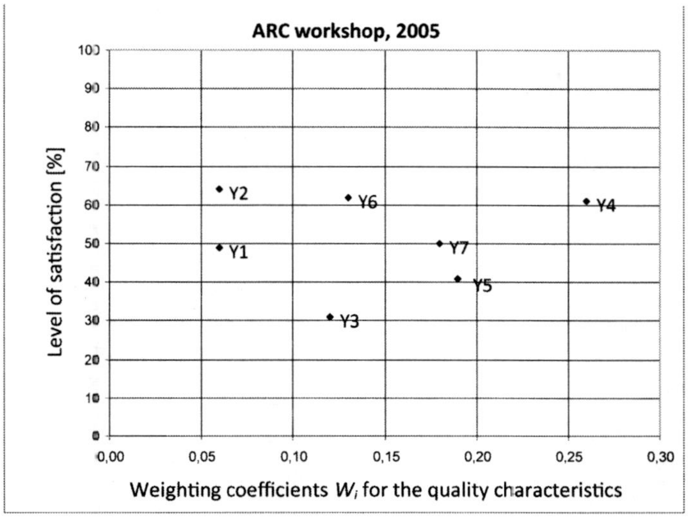

with high importance; however, the customers' level of satisfaction with them is 40% and 50%. These two features of the VLE definitely need improvement. Low level of importance is given for exercises/activities (Y1) and course content (Y2) and at the same time the level of satisfaction is 50% and 60%. It is necessary to analyze to what extent these characteristics need improvement. It is also suitable to explore detailed characteristics for some of the suggested quality indicators here, for example for exercises/activities, course content, and assignments, in order to make relevant decisions for improving the effectiveness of the VLE.

The number of the enquired people was small. To have a fuller picture for the situation it is necessary to collect the opinion of bigger number of users of the explored VLE.

Example 4: Evaluation of Student Satisfaction with a Specialty

Investigation to estimate the students' satisfaction with a specialty at TU - Gabrovo is presented. The quality characteristics are chosen based on the teaching experience gained and consultations with university lecturers.

Questioned students are from the third and fourth year of their bachelor study course and from the masters' course of the specialty. The total number of students is 64.

The quality characteristics, the results for the calculated weighting coefficients and the level of satisfaction are presented in Table 8 and in Figure 6.

Three of the characteristics - professional qualification of the teaching staff (Y2), actuality of the specialty (Y1), and possibility for getting good theoretical training (Y7) - are in the area with high satisfaction and high importance. Two of the characteristics are in the area with low satisfaction and low importance - possibilities for participating in international programs (Y11) and participation in research projects (Y10). Most of the characteristics are in the area with high importance and their satisfaction is around 50-54%. Two of the characteristics are in the area with relatively low importance and with satisfaction around 50% - obtaining additional qualification (Y12) and obtaining skills for unaided development of engineer projects (Y9). The evaluation of student's satisfaction with the specialty using the developed approach was the first one from this kind for the specialty. Analysis of the results and periodic evaluation of the student satisfaction

Table 8. Satisfaction measurement for a specialty

Quality criteria for a specialty		W_i	Rank	Level of satisfaction [%]
Actuality of the specialty	Y1	0,108	2	68,12
Professional qualification of the teaching staff	Y2	0,113	1	72,03
Well structured curricula and syllabus (suitable subjects)	Y3	0,106	4	54,37
Modern teaching conditions and technical equipment	Y4	0,099	5	48,75
Job opportunities after graduating	Y5	0,107	3	50,31
Modern learning methods (PC, Internet, library access etc.)	Y6	0,091	7	53,60
Possibility for getting good theoretical training	Y7	0,083	8	63,12
Possibilities for getting practical skills	Y8	0,093	6	49,53
Obtaining skills for unaided development of engineer projects	Y9	0,066	9	47,81
Participation in research projects	Y10	0,044	11	34,22
Possibilities for participating in international programs	Y11	0,039	12	35,47
Obtaining additional qualification	Y12	0,051	10	50,47
	Total satisfaction			54,80

would help in making relevant control decisions to improve the specialty characteristics and to make it more attractive for the students. The results are presented to the department management for analysis and further decisions however this is out of scope of this chapter.

Figure 6. Satisfaction measurement for a specialty

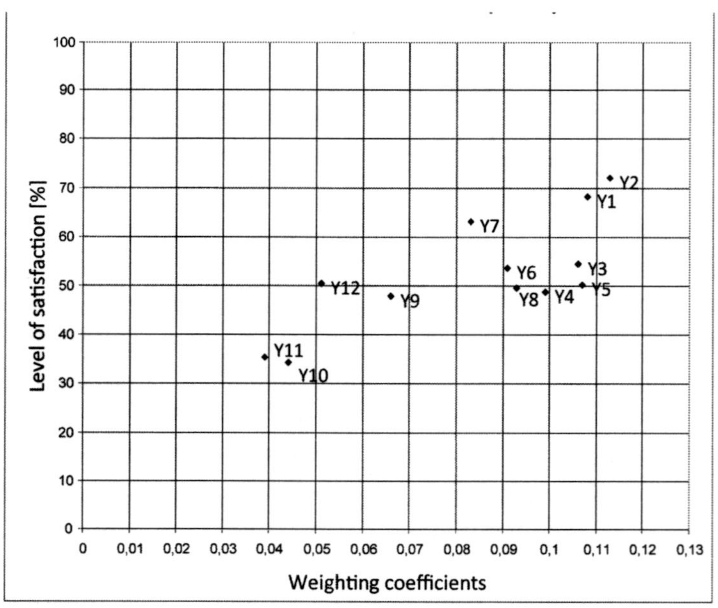

Table 9. Satisfaction measurement for a teaching course

Quality criteria for the teaching course		W_i	Rank	Level of satisfaction [%]
Quality of the teaching material for lectures	Y1	0,123	1	67,1
Quality of the teaching material and conducting of the practical sessions	Y2	0,099	2	57,9
Lecturers qualification	Y3	0,123	1	86,4
Topical teaching course and possibilities for its practical application	Y4	0,074	7	60,7
Level of practical knowledge and skill acquisition	Y5	0,097	3	52,1
Using modern technical tools and methods for teaching	Y6	0,071	8	35,0
Contribution of the assignments (task, project, casus etc) for improving your training	Y7	0,050	10	47,9
Access to additional resources of information for improving your training (literature, consultations, help, internet)	Y8	0,083	6	47,9
Conditions for conducting the course (equipment and comfort in the rooms and buildings, social conditions)	Y9	0,091	4	20,7
Objective and precise methods of knowledge and skill assessment	Y10	0,070	9	47,1
Level of theoretical knowledge and skill acquisition	Y11	0,087	5	55,7
Other	Y12	0,033	11	52,9
	Total satisfaction			54,7

Example 5: Evaluation of Student Satisfaction with a Teaching Course

An exemplary examination of students' satisfaction with a teaching course has been held among a group of bachelor degree students from the business faculty of Technical University of Gabrovo in June 2009. The number of the enquired students is 14. The quality characteristics to explore and the results are presented in Table 9 and in Figure 7.

The number of the quality characteristics is big and the values of the weighting coefficients is closer that require even more deep analysis.

The quality of the teaching material for lectures (Y1) and lecturers' qualification (Y3) are indicators with biggest importance and they are given high level of satisfaction – 67% and 86%. For most of the characteristics from the group with relatively high importance the level of satisfaction is around 50-60%. These are: quality of the teaching material and conducting of the practical sessions (Y2), level of practical knowledge and skill acquisition (Y5), level of theoretical knowledge and skill acquisition (Y11), access to additional resources of information for improving the training (Y8), topical teaching course and possibilities for its practical application (Y4), and objective and precise methods of knowledge and skill assessment (Y10). Improving of these characteristics would be essential contribution toward improving the course quality. It is necessary to pay special attention to the conditions for conducting the course (Y9) and using modern technical tools and methods for teaching (Y6) because they are relatively important and they are given low level of satisfaction. Contribution of the assignments for improving the training (Y7) has low importance for the students in this enquiry and level of satisfaction is around 50%; however the improvements here would increase the total level of satisfaction that is currently 54,7%. The students didn't specify particular characteristics as Y12.

The results are evaluated as significant contribution for the continual improvement of quality of learning and they will be considered from the

Figure 7. Satisfaction measurement for a teaching course

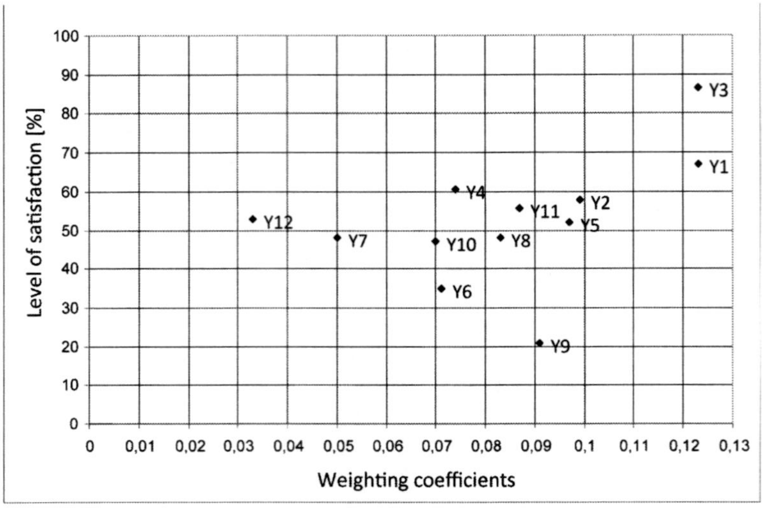

faculty management team applying quality assurance procedures.

Example 6: Evaluation of Student Satisfaction with Administrative Services

The satisfaction measurement approach is tested to evaluate of students' satisfaction with administrative services. The opinions of the students from only one student group at bachelor degree level from one of the faculties at Technical University of Gabrovo have been collected. 14 students took part in the enquiry in June 2009. The examined quality characteristics and the results are presented in Table 10 and in Figure 8.

The characteristics in the area of high importance are: staff competency (Y3), convenient working time and location of the offices (Y5), staff behaviour to the customers (Y6), speed of the service (Y4), and modern tools for communication with the administration offices (Y1). It

Table 10. Satisfaction measurement for administrative services

Quality characteristics of the administrative services		W_i	Rank	Level of satisfaction[%]
Modern tools for communication with the administration offices	Y1	0,116	5	53,8
Price of the administrative services	Y2	0,091	6	48,5
Staff competency	Y3	0,186	1	36,4
Speed of the service	Y4	0,117	4	37,1
Convenient working time and location of the offices	Y5	0,146	2	23,8
Staff behaviour to the customers	Y6	0,144	3	19,3
Possibilities of using of document templates	Y7	0,079	7	53,8
Time to issue official documents	Y8	0,076	8	55,7
Other	Y9	0,045	9	37,8
	Total satisfaction			38,1

Figure 8. Satisfaction measurement for administrative services

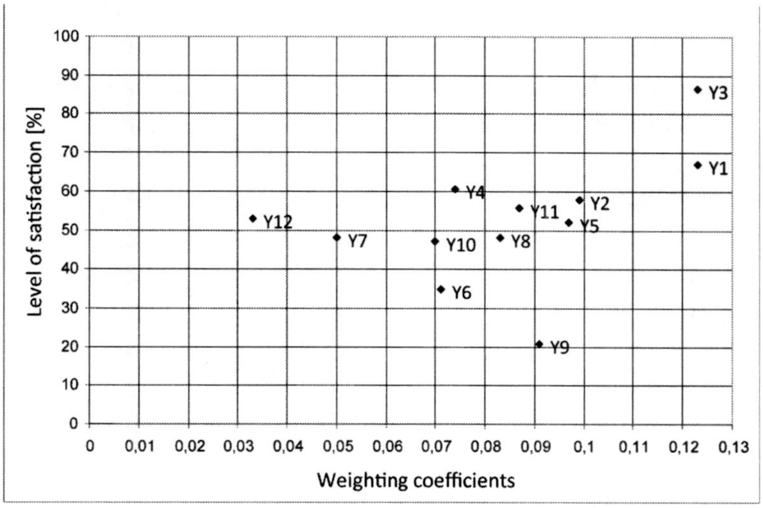

is seen that four of them - staff competency (Y3), convenient working time and location of the offices (Y5), staff behaviour to the customers (Y6), and speed of the service (Y4) are also in the area of low level of satisfaction. All these characteristics need improvement. It is also necessary to pay a special attention to the convenient working time and location of the offices (Y5) and staff behaviour to the customers (Y6).

All presented examples demonstrate that the suggested approach for satisfaction measurement is reliable, efficient and advisable. It combines the importance of the quality characteristics and the level of customers' satisfaction with them. The accepted methodology allows defining of weighting coefficients with chosen level of significance and based on the concordance of specialists' opinions. This is a precondition to obtain reliable results even when the opinions of smaller number of specialist are explored. However, investigation of the opinions of bigger number of students would give fuller picture for the level of satisfaction with the explored educational service.

The experimental application of the developed approach for satisfaction measurement gives promising results for the purpose of continual improvement of the educational quality management system.

FUTURE RESEARCH DIRECTIONS

The developed approach for satisfaction measurement has been accepted by the faculty management team as advisable for practical application within the quality assurance system. For some type of learning the quality characteristics to observe are specified by the educational legislation and course regulations. When such characteristics are not given they can be defined using evaluation of experts' opinions. There are not standards for most of the activities in e-learning and there are various different types of educational courses. It is of a great importance to take into account that the leaning is a process with very specific features. Therefore reliable objective evaluation of the specialists' opinions is the best way to define the quality characteristics in education. It is important to collect the opinion of different category specialist such as specialists in the subject domain, pedagogies, psychologists, administrative managers, university policy makers. It is also possible to compare the opinion of more that one expert group in order to choose the optimal set of criteria. For example: a team of specialists, working independently, suggested a list of quality criteria for satisfaction measurement with a teaching course. At the same time it turned out that there was a questionnaire used by the quality assurance system. Both working teams suggested very close number of the quality characteristics (10 and 11). The quality characteristics of the two variants were very similar and in practice they differed in the formulation. The quality characteristics used in the example 5 are in practice result of improving the formulation of the two suggested versions. The faculty management team plans to improve the formulation of the quality criteria using the expertise of psychologists and administrators and other specialists and to apply regularly investigation for the level of student satisfaction with all teaching courses at the end of the course as well as exploring the satisfaction with different university services. In practice this is a practical realization of the corresponding feedback channel from the cybernetic learning model (Figure 4) and a step toward making control decisions for optimal control of the university. It is necessary to collect the opinions of most students in order to prove the practical efficiency of the development.

E-learning is gradually increasing at the university and particular attention will be given to evaluation of students' satisfaction with different sides and components of the used e-learning platforms.

The basic cybernetic model is supplemented according to the specific features of the learning process (Nacheva-Skopalik, Skopalik & Stoyanov, 2007). The cybernetic model of learning specifies more than one feedback channels and they have different importance in the control process. To develop optimal automated e-learning environment it is needed to explore their importance. Further research in this direction in order to obtain fuller picture from different points of view will examine the opinions of a large number of specialists with experience in using e-learning platforms from different educational institutions and countries. The investigation will also consider the different requirements for the different type of teaching courses. It is also reasonable to repeat the investigation periodically and to update the solutions accordingly to the development and the changes of the used e-learning technologies.

Deeper investigation among specialists and all users of a VLE will contribute to achieving effective e-learning platform for providing of high quality e-learning. User' opinions for the importance of the components of a VLE and the level of their satisfaction will direct the improvements towards the more important characteristics.

The author's further research interest is in the area of adaptable e-assessment as integral part of an adaptable personal e-learning environment (APLE). APLE would facilitate participation by all students, including these with special needs or disability, considering also their learning preferences. Exploring the special needs and learning preferences of the students is essential stage in the process of development of a suitable structure and components for APLE. The evaluation of these components, using the suggested in this chapter approaches is applicable here. Evaluation of the users' satisfaction with a developed pilot version of an APLE will specify the directions for its improvement. There is still a considerable amount of research required in developing effective adaptive e-assessment tool that includes application of the suggested approaches for calculating of weighting coefficients and satisfaction measurement.

From the review in the area of quality in education it is seen that the educational institutions are required to apply quality assurance systems. The suggested approach is seen effective integral part of such a system. A software product facilitates the data processing. Improvement of the pilot version of the software for satisfaction measurement is envisaged. The developed approach and software for satisfaction measurement as well as the experience gained have to be disseminated as mush as possible among various educational institutions.

A kind of training of the academic staff concerning standards for quality management and the advantages of the suggested approach for satisfaction measurement will contribute to its successful practical application. It is especially important to involve the university management team and to persuade it for the advantages of evaluation of students' satisfaction.

CONCLUSION

E-learning standards are basis to achieve effective e-learning. They treat different aspects of e-learning such as learning management systems, learning environments, interoperability, learning objects, usability, security issues, meta-data and reusability of learning data. According to the ISO 9001 (Figure 1) these standards provide part of the customers requirements. To complete the scheme for continual improvement of the quality management system it is necessary to have a reliable tool to evaluate the effectiveness of the developed e-learning applications and to evaluate students' satisfaction with them.

One of the main indicators for high quality product is if it is sold well. However good sale is not always connected with a high quality, it can be caused by other reasons. Analogously, the fact that particular product is not on a mass sale or the sale does not increase it doesn't mean that the product is with poor quality. For decision makers that really want to achieve continual improvement and optimization of the quality investigation of customer satisfaction is of a great importance. This is particularly important for the strategic education sector where providing high quality education is valuable investment that multiplies in the society in the future. For example, increase or decrease the number of the students for particular university or a specialty is not sufficient indicator for quality learning. This number normally depends in a complex mechanism on the social, political, economical, demographical and other factors. Application of the ISO 9000 standards for continual improvement of a quality management system is a guarantee for providing high quality (e)learning. As far as the quality is to fulfill and satisfy requirements then exploring this satisfaction is motive force within the quality management system.

Except the direct activities connected with learning, teaching, assessment it is necessary to consider additional activities such as library services, administrative services, living standards and social conditions at the university, social climate and attitude to the students, and communication with students in order to cover in the best way the various factors that influence the education. Further more, all these components have to be revalued in the context of the modern education and to correspond to the conditions for providing high quality e-learning because increasingly when it is said education it includes or it is understood forms of e-learning.

The evaluation of students' satisfaction is an important factor in education used for: improving the quality of different educational activities and conditions; making decisions for optimal control of the learning process and/or administrative management of the university; making objective reports; updating teaching methodology; updating educational legislation and system. Evaluation of students' satisfaction is not the only factor to consider in the process of quality management in education; this is the new element to add to the existing approaches. However, it is part of the feedback channel for control within the developed cybernetic model of learning and it corresponds to the requirements of the standard for quality management and quality assurance system. The teaching course to examine is already designed with specified features such as learning material, teaching methods, learning technologies used and learning outcomes. Normally, it is also categorized concerning the difficulty level (for beginners, intermediate or advanced) and there are entry requirements. The student performance level and the final results achieved are essential for all courses. It is necessary to analyze and consider all this information, including the level of students' satisfaction, in order to have a fuller picture on the course. The relevant decisions for achieving successful course that meets the learning outcomes may suggest changes concerning either course design or students selection. The systems for quality assurance in education have to provide conditions to increase fulfilling the customers' requirements and expectations that is in practice increasing the level of customer's satisfaction. Evaluation of students' and/or staff satisfaction is necessary in order to apply the standards from the ISO 9000 series for continual improvment of the quality in e-learning and education.

The research study develops a reliable approach for satisfaction measurement, based on well-grounded theoretical knowledge from the area of optimal decision making and quality control. The subjective statistics approaches are applied to evaluate the priorities of characteristics and quality indicators of the learning process. Defining priorities of quality characteristics, expressed by the weighting coefficients, considered together with the level of satisfaction of the students (or teachers, or customers) are relatively new approaches in educational quality management. The reliability of the choice of the quality characteristics is essential for receiving reliable satisfaction measurement results and later on to make proper multicriteria decisions. The weighting coefficients for the characteristics have to be calculated only if there is concordance in the customers' opinions. The concordance in the customers' opinions for chosen level of significance is checked by calculating the concordance coefficient W_k using the rank correlation methods (Kendal, 1957). Essential advantage of the methodology used is that it gives reliable evaluation of the importance of the quality characteristics even if smaller number of specialists' (customers') opinions are possessed. To provide a comparison, it is necessary to collect and process a large number of e-learning data in order to obtain reliable results when using other statistical approaches. The time for collecting the enquiry data is commensurable with the time used to fill traditional questionnaire. The suggested approach for satisfaction measurement does not exclude the use of other approaches to collect customer's opinions, further more; the data collecting can be combined. At the same time the satisfaction measurement is more precise methodology, based on the well-grounded and proved in the science and practice approaches from the theory of multiple criteria decisions making. Sometimes, for research and practical purposes, it is recommendable to process separately the data collected by enquires among different groups and then to process all data together. Useful conclusions can be made comparing the results from these calculations.

Considering the importance of the quality characteristics is essential contribution for making optimal control decisions. The traditional questionnaire does not detect this information. It may turn out that students are satisfied with inessential characteristics and not satisfied with important ones. In this case the changes may not be directed to the right direction. The suggested satisfaction measurement approach allows us to improve the quality characteristics with low level of satisfaction (especially if they are with high importance) without worsening the characteristics with high level of satisfaction.

The satisfaction measurement fulfills the requirement to close the feedback loop for quality control and for control of the learning. Evaluation of customers' satisfaction is not the only factor in the decision making process; however its importance is significant and considerable. The approach is suitable to apply not only for optimal control of the learning process but also for optimal administrative control of the university. Education is a strategic area of society and students' satisfaction is an essential and obligatory factor for continual improvement of the educational quality management system and achieving optimal (e)learning. Sharing of the "good practice" of using the approach can contribute to multiplication of the effect of its application. In this sense, the publication of this chapter is valuable contribution presenting the suggested approaches to a wide audience of people with deeper and better understanding of the inside of the discussed topic which are able to work toward practical application of the developed methodology. Additionally, the satisfaction measurement approach can be successfully used in other areas as administrative services and control, transport, tourism and healthcare.

The educational institutions need to consider "the voice" of the students and other customers of the educational services in order to be flexible and able to respond to the requirements of the dynamic market. Continual quality improvement has to be a main priority and responsibility of the top management and decision makers of the universities. This is a key factor for the successful effective practical application of the discussed approaches for satisfaction measurement. The research work is done at high level however the practical application is out of the competences of the researchers. Our experience shows that often the practical applications of a lot of good research developments need time, funding, institutional support and sometimes changes in the normative requirements. European project in the area of the discussed topics providing funds and institutional support would be essential contribution for successful practical application of the ISO 9000 standards for continual improvment of the quality in e-learning and education.

REFERENCES

Jung, I. (2008). ICT and quality assurance to support ubiquitous access to distance education: Promises, realities, and recent breakthroughs. In *Fifth EDEN Research Workshop 20-22 OCTOBER, 2008* Paris, France. Retrieved July 26, 2009 from http://www.eden-online.org/eden.php?menuId=421

Nacheva-Skopalik, L. (2007). *An examination of an intelligent cybernetic learning model for formative assessment and diagnostics in open and distance learning*. PhD thesis, University of Teesside, UK.

Nacheva-Skopalik, L., Skopalik, E., & Stoyanov, S. (2007). Examination of feedbacks efficiency within automated system for distance education. *CEEPUS CZ – 103 International Summer School "Informatics systems in Automation", University of Maribor, FEECS, Maribor, Slovenia, 14-28.09.*2007. Retrieved July 26, 2009 from http://css07.feri-au.uni-mb.si/index.php?option=com_content&task=view&id=13&Itemid=29

Nacheva-Skopalik, L., Stoyanov, S., & Skopalik, E. (2004). *Satisfaction measurement. Leonardo da Vinci Project BG/02/B/F/PP-132088 Vocational Lifelong Training on Quality and Environmental Management for Staff Engaged in Small- and Medium-Sized Enterprises*. Gabrovo, Bulgaria: Vasil Aprilov University Publishing House of Gabrovo.

Patru, M. (2008). Attaining quality education for all: A UNESCO perspective. In *Fifth EDEN Research Workshop 20-22 OCTOBER, 2008* Paris, France. Retrieved July 26, 2009 from http://www.eden-online.org/eden.php?menuId=421

Stoyanov, S. (1993). *Process optimization*. Sofia, Bulgaria: Technika. (in Bulgarian). *ISO 9000:2000 Quality management systems – Fundamentals and vocabulary, CEN.* (n.d.). *ISO 9001:2000 Quality management systems – Requirements, CEN.* (n.d.). Kendall, M. (1957). *Rank correlation methods*. London, UK: Griffin.

Stoyanov, S. (2008). *Customer satisfaction and decision making in healthcare organizations*. Sofia, Bulgaria: Es Print.

White, D. (2008). Innovative Learning for Europe. In *EDEN Annual Conference, 11-14 June 2008, Lisbon, Portugal.* Retrieved July 26, 2009 from http://www.eden-online.org/contents/conferences/annual/Lisbon/Keynotes/White.pdf

KEY TERMS AND DEFINITIONS

Continual Improvement of a Quality Management System: Recurring activity to increase the ability to fulfill requirements.

Customer Satisfaction: Customer satisfaction is the customer's perception of the degree to which the customer's requirements have been fulfilled where requirement means: "need or expectation that is stated, generally implied or obligatory".

Decision Maker: Person (expert, specialist or manager) or a team of such persons, that is responsible for making decisions.

Quality Assurance: A set of planned and systematic activities directed to ensure that standards of quality are being met and the products (goods and/or services) satisfy customer requirements.

Quality Characteristics: Each characteristic is distinguishing feature of the product (service). The term quality characteristic is defined in the standard as inherent characteristic of a product, process or system related to a requirement.

Quality Management System: Management system to direct and control an organization with regard to quality.

Satisfaction Measurement: Evaluation of the information concerning the customers' perception of the level at which the organization has fulfilled their requirements concerning the quality of a product (service). Customer satisfaction can be "measured" in terms of "evaluated". It can be measured using numbers, percentages, ranks or linguistically.

Subjective Statistics: Part of the statistics, which interpret in statistical aspect the opinions, preferences, understanding, and requirements of the individual subject.

Weighting Coefficients: The weighting coefficients are quantitative expression of the importance of the quality characteristics.

Chapter 23
Quality E-Learning Guidelines and Their Implementation

John Milne
Massey University, New Zealand

Gordon Suddaby
Massey University, New Zealand

ABSTRACT

Quality e-learning guidelines have the potential to support staff and help provide e-learning that is learner centred, follows good practice, and is innovative, collaborative and sustainable. This chapter will introduce the e-Learning Guidelines for New Zealand and show how organisations have used them. It will present some of the benefits of the guidelines as well as the limitations and discuss how these limitations may be managed. The guidelines have been used in various ways in different organisations. Teaching staff have used the guidelines to search for information and ideas or to help in course design or redevelopment. Managers have used the guidelines to develop procedures to help staff in their use of e-learning. Staff developers have used them as a tool to inform debate about the quality of e-learning. The guidelines allow organisations to share their e-learning knowledge and experiences. Direction from the literature and experience from this project show that guidelines can enable organisations to improve their e-learning but that guidelines need careful implementation and staff support.

INTRODUCTION

The e-Learning Guidelines for New Zealand (e-learning guidelines) enable a community of practitioners to enhance learning and teaching enabled by technology, and to share good practice. The e-learning guidelines provide an overarching framework that an organisation can localise for its own situation and priorities. The e-learning guidelines inform staff of good practice, contribute to the design of effective learning, and offer a practical entry to discussions about quality in teaching through e-learning. People can contribute their expertise to them and so keep the guidelines relevant. The e-learning guidelines are a living concept and can be applied to diverse tertiary contexts.

DOI: 10.4018/978-1-61692-789-9.ch023

Quality guidelines provide the criteria organisations can use to identify good practice and point to improvements. In discussing quality guidelines for e-learning, the focus is on educational effectiveness and the support provided for teaching and learning. The philosophy underlying the pedagogical approach to the e-learning guidelines is that they promote reflection on teaching practice. For the organisation, Marshall (2004) suggests that guidelines identify areas that need strategic direction, development and support. This applies throughout the institution as the guidelines can operate at the management level as well as the teaching and learning level. As Ehlers (2009) in citing Wolff (2004) notes (p343):

We are entering a new era in quality management for higher education. While it is difficult to mark its exact beginning, it is clear that it is moving away from a mechanistic to a holistic and cultural view of quality in education.

And continues:

...the focus is more and more on mastering change, allowing ownership for individual development, promoting champions in organisations and enabling professionals in higher education contexts.

With the rapid increase of technology in education, there is a real danger that the technology will drive the learning. The e-learning guidelines provide a clear focus on the pedagogy and see the technology as an aid. This is further emphasised by Ellis, Jarkey, Mahaoney, Peat and Sheely (2007) when they comment (p.10): "A separation of the responsibilities for resource allocation and for quality learning outcomes can be problematic when teachers want to integrate e-learning into course design. This is because decisions based on learning and teaching imperatives often have implications for the resourcing base of the information and communication technologies (ICT)".

Guidelines provide information on techniques to help perform certain tasks. They help to streamline processes and allow the processes to be more predictable, with the aim of improving the quality of the outcome. A key point of a guideline should be its flexibility. From this perspective a guideline should be a suggestion, not a rule that must be slavishly followed.

The e-learning guidelines help teaching and support staff, policy makers and managers. In our view the guidelines are a road map to effective practice, flexible so they can be adapted to different contexts, and evolving as technology and pedagogy change. They are a vital tool to enable teachers and administrators to ensure quality of teaching and learning remains their goal.

There are a many of sets of quality guidelines supporting and informing tertiary organisations and their staff in the e-learning context. Some are specific to distance education (AFT, 2002; ADEC, 2003; ODLQC, 2005) while others are specific to e-learning (IHEP, 2000; Barker, 2002; Barker, 2007; JISC, 2004; Butterfield *et al.* 1999; Garrison & Vaughan, 2008). Many similarities have been reported in the guidelines (IHEP,2000; Twigg, 2001; Frydenberg, 2002; Bates & Poole, 2002). This is reassuring as it reflects general agreement on what is good practice. However the guidelines do have differences in their focus and scope. They also differ in the ways they are implemented. Some are designed for the regional or organisational level while others operate at the level of degree or course. The number of different sets of guidelines reflects the differing contexts for the guidelines and shows their potential to support staff and organisations to provide effective learning environments.

The New Zealand Tertiary Education Commission through the Innovation and Development Fund funded a year-long project on implementing a set of e-learning guidelines which had previously been developed in another Tertiary Education Commission-funded project led by the authors. The project started in July 2007 and involved

Figure 1. A diagram showing how users can navigate the e-learning guidelines. Users go from the cube to the guidelines and from there to more information

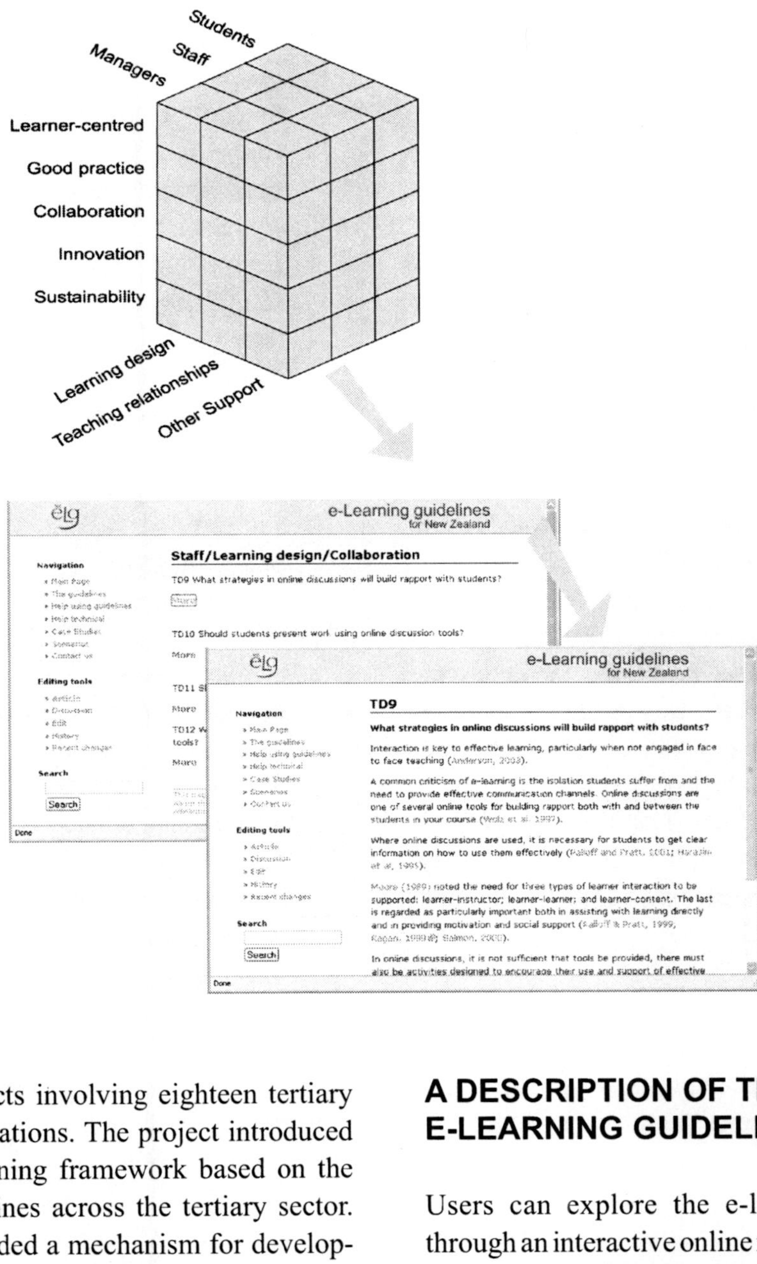

twenty-one projects involving eighteen tertiary education organisations. The project introduced a common e-learning framework based on the e-learning guidelines across the tertiary sector. The project provided a mechanism for developing, introducing, trialling, evaluating and sharing the e-learning guidelines. This chapter will report on the experience gained in this project. We will describe the e-learning guidelines, their benefits and limitations and outline how they have been used. The e-learning guidelines are available at http://elg.massey.ac.nz.

A DESCRIPTION OF THE E-LEARNING GUIDELINES

Users can explore the e-learning guidelines through an interactive online representation in the form of a cube (Figure 1). The three dimensions are (1) the intended audience of the e-learning guidelines (teaching staff, managers or students) (2) the e-learning principle (see below) and (3) the teaching activity (learning design, teaching relationships or other support).

Principles

There are five e-learning principles that aim to ensure effective e-learning drawn from a related review of the literature.

- Learner-centred guidelines: these are about the diversity of students and their needs. They include guidelines related to enhancing student learning and the benefit of implementing e-learning technology.
- Best practice guidelines: these encourage the use and sharing of good practice.
- Collaboration guidelines: these are about sharing of information and the use of collaborative approaches such as sharing courses and resources. Support staff and teachers need to collaborate for e-learning to be successful. This needs to be within a supportive management structure.
- Innovation guidelines: these facilitate the exploration of new ways of implementing and delivering e-learning and outline the support that is needed.
- Sustainability guidelines: these aim to ensure that e-learning is affordable and sustainable from a teaching and an institutional perspective.

The e-learning guidelines are presented in a 'question' and 'answer' format, aimed at encouraging thought and reflection. A yes or no answer is not intended; instead the question stimulates ideas on how to improve practice. Each guideline is illustrated by a short exemplar which outlines some relevant research, highlights potential issues for consideration, and provides suggestions to consider. Users can search the e-learning guidelines site where there are also case studies and scenarios incorporating the guidelines.

The areas covered within the guidelines framework were broad. The focus was on e-learning however a number of the guidelines are relevant to all learning. They cover areas from student recruitment to learning design, student-teacher interaction, assessment, student and staff support, and institutional commitment. These areas are outlined in more detail below:

- Student recruitment involves ensuring course information and enrolment admission procedures result in a good student-course fit.
- Learning design includes the process of identifying the diversity of students and their needs in order to ensure high quality outcomes. It also includes setting of learning outcomes, planning teaching strategies, choosing resources and planning evaluations that identify the impact of the teaching.
- Student-teacher interaction ensures effective course delivery and management. It includes sections on expectations and communication.
- Student assessment covers feedback provided to students during the learning and fair and relevant moderation against stated learning outcomes.
- Student support includes guidance on learning and technical issues to ensure students are able to make best use of e-learning opportunities and achieve positive learning outcomes.
- Staff support covers staff development and support in content, technical and instructional aspects of e-learning to assist staff to provide quality learning environments.
- Institutional commitment covers policies and having funding in place to encourage sustainable development and delivery of e-learning. It also includes legal aspects.

Characteristics of E-Learning Guidelines

The e-learning literature provided direction on the philosophical approach to use in the development of guidelines. Guidelines should be presented as suggestions for good practice, rather than a document demanding compliance (QAA, 2004; Meyer, 2003; Marshall, 2004). One way to show that guidelines are suggestions is to frame the guidelines as questions. The approach is to ask staff to use the questions to reflect on their practice and identify areas that could be improved. Notably, Meyer (2003) used the term 'guidelines' when discussing criteria for quality in online courses. Meyer's implication was that guidelines are like a road map that supports staff in unfamiliar territory: something that guides rather than directs. The term 'e-learning quality guidelines' may also be better than 'standards' as it avoids the confusion with accredited standards.

Guidelines should be seen as enabling rather than restricting (Meyer, 2003; Inglis, 2005). They can enable by being easily understood, with a minimum of complexity and jargon (Jackson & D'Alessandro, 2003). Ambiguity in interpretation and overlapping of standards are common problems when standards are applied as discussed by Sundar (2002) when writing about an academic audit in the New Zealand polytechnic sector. This needs to be avoided.

It is also important to realise that the implementation of quality processes may involve a cultural change in an organisation. A key to this is to make professional development an important part of organisational planning (Avdjieva and Wilson, 2002) and the framing of the guidelines as questions is a critical factor in guiding such a change.

Davies (2007), in a study that investigated how academic culture affected quality processes, determined that to facilitate effective implementation an ideal mix was to emphasise teamwork rather than individualism, appeal to the self improvement aspect of academic staff and to provide a supportive environment for staff.

A general criticism that has been levelled at quality processes is that the process is seen as more important than the outcome. One of the key aims of quality processes in higher education is the improvement of the student experience (Carr & Jennings 2009). Such an improvement can be achieved through internal methods such as reviews and monitoring focusing on student feedback, internal improvement audits, re -evaluation of programmes and staff reflection. These processes have a more positive effect on the student experience than an occasional external quality process (Harvey, 2005) and drawing on the guidelines provides a framework for such improvement.

BENEFITS OF E-LEARNING GUIDELINES

Quality guidelines have a number of benefits. They can help define the quality of the teaching, build consensus about the process for developing a course, and help staff learn new aspects of their job more quickly (Schulz-Novak, 2002). They are also important in informing staff of good practice, helping them in the design of learning, and offering (in staff development) a useful practical entry to the discussion of quality in online teaching. They can also serve as a checklist to evaluate online learning materials (Oliver & Herrington, 2003).

The e-learning guidelines provide the critical framework unifying the organisation with an approach to quality enhancement. This is further reinforced by Jackson and D'Alessandro (2003) who noted an Australian university context where guidelines were used as standards to help to provide consistency in the presentation of courses, guide online developers and were also an evaluation checklist for schools and faculties.

Potential Problems with E-Learning Guidelines

Quality guidelines potentially have some drawbacks that those implementing the guidelines will need to manage. Reports identify that teaching staff feel pressured by the increasing administrative demands on their time, and that the quality assurance process can be seen as burdensome (Jackson and D'Alessandro, 2003). In an online course review of teaching staff Chao, Sat and Tessier (2006) cite time as an issue, raising questions about how often such a review should be carried out to obtain the most accurate and effective results.

Also, people may rigidly follow guidelines even when they are not working (Schulz-Novak, 2002). This can occur if the guidelines are interpreted as rules, resulting in staff seeing the process as more important than the outcomes. This results in a reduction in the flexibility and creativity of those staff. Meyer (2003) reiterates this point and suggests that guidelines 'should not be a bible of inviolable rules' (p98). Chao, Sat and Tessier (2006) suggest that another limitation of the quality review process is that it can only check the static design and presentation, not the actual operational processes.

Realising the Benefits of the E-Learning Guidelines

The potential problems associated with the use of guidelines need to be identified and managed so the benefits can be realised. These benefits will be discussed in the areas of support for staff and management of the implementation process. Insight is provided into how to successfully implement quality processes informed by the guidelines in the tertiary sector as well as exploring the factors that ensure successful quality processes.

Support for Staff

The effectiveness of the implementation of quality processes increases with the perceived level of support in the organisation. A key component of successful implementation and support is the development of feedback mechanisms based on continual assessment and reflective evaluation (Avdjieva and Wilson, 2002).

Lomas (2007) stated that it is clear that without sufficient support, academics will ignore or resist quality process initiatives. Lomas went on to suggest that there are a number of factors that assist academics and organisations in achieving the successful implementation of quality processes. These include ensuring that academics have sufficient support and input into the indicators of quality chosen for the quality initiatives. This enhances staff confidence in the implementation process and with compliance.

Jackson and D'Alessandro (2003) note that for administrative improvement staff needed to be kept continually aware of the quality process, the steps involved, and key dates, to ensure online materials are available in time for students.

Adjusting terminology associated with quality processes so it is more relevant to university organisations has been shown to increase success (Davies, 2007). Another important factor in terms of academic support is the recognition and support for the scholarship of learning. Avdjieva and Wilson (2002) noted that higher education organisations needed to foster linkages between teaching, learning and research. Successful implementation using the workshop approach to self assessment supports team building, familiarises teams with the model, can provide motivation towards improvement, and has been found to facilitate successful implementation (Davies, 2007). Generally organisations that have successfully implemented quality frameworks have their quest for excellence within the organisational effort rather than as a separate quality issue (Avdjieva and Wilson, 2002).

The quality process needs to be as time efficient as possible with straightforward procedures otherwise there will be significant resistance from amongst staff. Teaching staff need support and guidance for improvement and encouragement in the form of readily available and user-friendly support. When the support is not available, teaching staff tend to think e-learning is not feasible and not worth investing their time in (Mayes 2001).

Management of the Implementation Process

One of the key elements to success with quality assurance systems is to have effective management of the process. Flexibility and adaptive techniques are critically important to continue to achieve an improvement in the quality assurance process (McNaught, 2001). McNaught also reports that it is possible to overcome potential disadvantages of quality systems and implement the systems successfully. Staff initially seem to regard the review of all online courses with a great deal of suspicion, but through collaboration this problem can be ironed out. The process discussed by McNaught based on a checklist and used for evaluation and feedback involved all course owners and provided successful outcomes.

Quality assurance processes are critically important in ensuring new technology is incorporated, is of a high standard and in line with educational aims. The quality processes help to align changes with the organisational goals and objectives, inform how the impact of these outcomes can be investigated and measured, as well as identify criteria for the significance and reliability of the data (Higgins, 2004).

The sort of problems facing the successful implementation of the quality processes can include resistance to quality processes within the academic community and a feeling amongst academic staff that the quality evaluation process is more about compliance than effective dialogue or results (Lomas, 2007). Srikanthan and Dalrymple (2003) voiced concerns which reflected issues of academic freedom and the potential mismatch between quality management and educational processes. Teachers also are concerned that quality assurance may encourage conformity in teaching (Lomas, 2007) and thus constrain variety and innovation.

McNaught (2001) stated that quality issues will be more widely accepted, taken more seriously and are more rigorous, if staff who are influenced by the changes are involved in the development and implementation of the quality measures. For example peer review sessions have been found to be an extremely valuable staff development exercise with the process involving staff working through partially developed online courses then providing comments leading to an open discussion (McNaught, 2001). This is reinforced by Hodgkinson and Kelly (2007) who note (p.89);

It is argued that introducing one particular way forward will not be successful without an awareness of the existing organisational culture and that introducing any model, process or approach will not, in itself, create or sustain a quality enhancement culture. To achieve this, appropriate structures, communication channels, the involvement of all individuals at all levels and from all aspects of a school's work need to be included.

Avdjieva and Wilson (2002) argue that if quality processes are to be taken seriously, managers need to lead by example and do more consultation with academic staff resulting in a bottom up influence which has significantly greater ownership and relevance for the individual academic staff member. Moreover, to create and support a quality culture, managers need to be involved in the process with all staff members as participants and not just 'drivers'.

It is clear that too much emphasis put on external quality monitoring will only contribute to resentment and place added stress on academic staff, meaning a balance must be reached between quality monitoring and academic autonomy. Harvey (2005) argues that having a reflective self-critical academic community is the best safeguard of academic standards and ultimately staff development, innovation and scholarship will be far more beneficial to the improvement of quality in universities if the academic staff feel part of the process, engaged with it and essentially 'owning' it.

Figure 2. The approach to implementing the guidelines

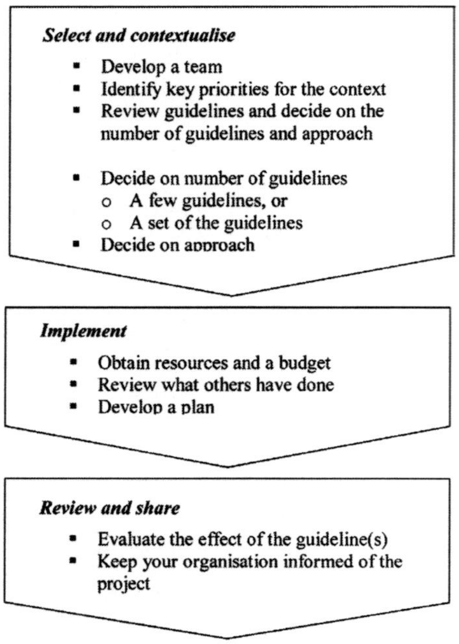

FRAMEWORK FOR USING THE E-LEARNING GUIDELINES

Eighteen tertiary education organisations implemented the New Zealand e-learning guidelines as part of an Innovation and Development Fund project that was funded by the New Zealand Tertiary Education Commission. These organisations all implemented the e-learning guidelines differently, but their practice could be described by the framework of 'select and contextualise, implement, review and share' (Figure 2).

The select and contextualise phase is about planning. At this stage, the organisations considered the local context and how the guidelines would help to improve the quality of e-learning. All of the organisations had a team that included teaching staff, support staff, and senior managers (who sponsored and signed-off on the project). This team considered the organisation, its context, and key issues of e-learning quality with respect to their specific institutional context.

In their initial review of the guidelines, the organisations decided whether they would implement a set of guidelines or just one or a few guidelines. Those that used a set of guidelines used them to review practices and/or processes. Those that selected one or a few guidelines targeted a defined area and worked on enhancing quality within a specific area. In both cases, the guidelines were a used as a tool to guide improvements and development. An important feature of the guidelines is that staff take ownership of the process when they localise them for a particular context.

The organisations focused either at the course level or the organisation level. Those that worked at course level had direct contact with students. Data was collected from students, which showed the effect of the changes that resulted from implementing the guidelines. Those that worked at an organisational level put in processes to help staff provide high-quality e-learning and brought about institutional level changes.

In the implementation phase, teams formalised a plan and then implemented it. Because all organisations had external funding through the evaluation of the overall project, they had plans with milestones. This was critical to the project's progress and in fact essential to the completion of the process: without these milestones, which were also key funding points, it is highly likely the project would have been far less successful.

The review and share phase was when the team examined the process of quality improvement and shared their findings at the e-learning guidelines website through case studies and in exemplars associated with the guidelines. The teams also shared findings within their organisations and at an international higher education conference.

USING THE E-LEARNING GUIDELINES IN PRACTICE

There were four broad categories that reflected how the organisations used the e-learning guide-

Table 1. How organisations used the e-learning guidelines

		Number of guidelines	
		Set	Few
Level that the guidelines are used	Course	Use a set of guidelines to improve courses	Use a few guidelines to improve courses
	Organisation	Use a set of guidelines to improve organisational processes	Use a few guidelines to improve organisational processes

lines (Table 1), encompassing two dimensions. The first dimension is the number of guidelines that have been used. This is either a few or a set. The second dimension is the level at which the guidelines are being used, either in a course or at an organisational level.

A Few E-Learning Guidelines to Improve Courses

Some organisations used a few guidelines to improve courses. The focus was on teaching staff who were designing or reviewing an e-learning course or programme. Key factors seen as essential for e-learning to thrive include designing activities that facilitate students to reach their intended learning outcomes, relevant resources, and providing effective delivery strategies and support structures. The guidelines focus on these areas. The approach was to consider the guidelines against existing practice to identify improvements and then provide a pathway for that improvement. The process (see Figure 2) was to localise the guidelines, apply the guidelines to a course/programme, and then review the impact of the guidelines.

Step 1 – Select and Contextualise

Each organisation formed a team. Generally the team had teaching staff with expertise in e-learning, and support staff. Their first step was to select the guidelines relevant to a particular course/programme. To do this, they identified key issues including the organisational goals and context, and then reviewed the guidelines to identify those that covered that particular area. This step used the guidelines as a tool to help consider aspects of e-learning. The outcome of this process was the identification of guidelines relevant to the course/programme and the staff training and support that was needed to help frame the implementation of the guidelines. Some teams used feedback from students, others used discussion or questionnaires that provided a snapshot of the initial status.

The teams worked on projects that used guidelines on student persistence and on student choice. Other organisations implemented guidelines related to using technology in the courses – examples included guidelines to support language social networking sites, for virtual guest speakers, and for using mobile technology.

Step 2 – Implement: Apply the E-Learning Guidelines to Courses

The second step involved applying the guidelines to identify gaps between current practice and the guidelines. This involved using the guidelines to assess potential improvements by revealing what aspects of the guidelines needed to be considered in relation to the course. From this analysis came the need to implement changes within the course. The teams would review the changes and then apply them in the course/programme.

Summary: how to compare current practice to the guidelines:

- Consider whether and how the course achieves the guidelines; list possible changes.
- Evaluate the feasibility of implementing these changes.
- Evaluate the material and personnel costs involved in bringing the course in line with guidelines.
- Determine administrative changes required to support the teaching staff.
- Initiate the changes to the course.

Step 3 – Review the Impact of the E-Learning Guidelines

The third step was to review the impact of the changes. Feedback from students was essential to determine ongoing quality enhancement outcomes. Data from students informed the process, highlighted successful instances of using technology, and indicated areas for further change and development. Changes were then made to the course based on this information.

The teams shared their experiences through their case studies and updated the exemplar information on the guideline at the website. This allowed the projects to contribute to a larger resource. The e-learning guidelines website was used for guidance and information on implementation and improvement processes. Users could explore the guidelines, find guidelines relating to specific topics, and search a wide range of information relating to the guidelines.

A Set of E-Learning Guidelines to Improve Courses

Some of the organisations selected a set of guidelines focused on refining a particular course or programme. The first step was to review the guidelines to identify those which were relevant to the course. This required discussion with teaching and support staff, and the adaptation of the guidelines in light of the discussions. Typically, discussions included the identification of guidelines relevant to the course/programme and justification of criteria to determine the forms of evidence needed to indicate that the guidelines would be met. The second step was to apply the guidelines to identify gaps between them and apparent current practice. The third step was to review and evaluate the effect of the changes. This included locating the localised guidelines where staff could easily access them; obtain information on how to use them; and learn who was available to provide support in their use. The guidelines were often built into the process of course development and review. Finally, staff shared the information with the tertiary community at the e-learning guidelines website.

A Few E-Learning Guidelines to Improve Organisational Processes

Some organisations focused on organisational level improvements by implementing a few context and/or process-specific guidelines. Examples of issues they worked on included staff development, and the realm of copyright and intellectual property policy. The planning phase included a review of the current practices of the organisation to identify key issues and then a review the e-learning guidelines to consider other relevant key areas. This resulted in establishing e-learning guidelines that were applicable to the particular organisation and practice. The implementation phase included a literature review, and development of a resource or initiating research into the most effective ways of implementing the guidelines. The final stages were reviews of the processes and the development of material to share on the e-learning guidelines website in addition to changes in the institution's policy and practices.

Table 2. Example of a way to link e-learning guidelines to action

Guideline	Advice	Current situation at organisation	Action	Person responsible
Guideline 1 here	Advice here	Current situation here	Action listed	Name here
Guideline 2 here	Advice here	Current situation here	Action listed	Name here

A Set of E-Learning Guidelines to Improve Organisational Process

The challenge of quality in e-learning is clearly identified by Jara and Mellar (2009, p.221) when they say;

The internal QA/QE procedures in place in HEIs were designed to assure and enhance the quality of campus-based courses and it is not clear to what extent they remain useful for e-learning courses.

In making decisions about using the guidelines, organisations worked on improving their processes and quality by using the guidelines. This work was often integrated into the organisations' policies. These include examples from the projects such as those using the guidelines as a basis for developing tools for the course design process and implementing a selection of guidelines in order to improve staff development practices.

An example of the way one organisation implemented the complete set of e-learning guidelines across their organisation has been described in Fox (2006), also in Donohue, Fox and Torrence (2007), and Whittaker (2007). A key factor for successful implementation of the guidelines was that all departments within an institution considered and acted on the guidelines. This required that staff understood the rationale for the guidelines and their role in implementation. Part of the process was that staff were able to contribute their expertise to the process and discuss the guidelines rationale and what they could achieve. This was a significant and successful staff and organisational development initiative driven by the guidelines process.

The organisation used the tool shown in Table 2 to link the guidelines to people who took action to implement the guidelines. This allowed the organisation to organise staff and enabled the person responsible for affecting the change to take the actions that were necessary to support and implement the process. The guidelines and advice were made available in a wiki and an Excel spreadsheet accessible by all staff.

This organisation identified an administrator to oversee the process of implementation and to embed the guidelines in institutional culture and practice. The chief executive officer played a critical role in the process, had a deep understanding of guidelines and their potential and provided the institutional buy-in for the process.

CONCLUSION

Bates and Poole (2002) stated that it is one thing to know what a set of e-learning guidelines are but another to know what to do to achieve them. It takes consideration and effort to know how to achieve the standards they describe. Implementing guidelines is complex and needs careful management and support for staff. The organisations who implemented the e-learning guidelines showed that the e-learning guidelines can inform people and enable them to provide effective e-learning practice. The organisations used the guidelines in different ways, but all ultimately supported staff to help them make good decisions about e-learning.

The aims of the e-learning guidelines are to inform and enable effective practice rather than constrain it. To achieve these aims, the guidelines have been designed to be flexible so they can be adapted to different contexts and evolve as technology and pedagogy develop. The focus of the guidelines is on student outcomes rather than management compliance and control. The overarching approach to the guidelines has been to focus on students and their learning.

Bates and Poole (2002) suggest guidelines should focus on the students or more importantly that guidelines need to inform the learning processes. It is critical that the educational focus is clarified, and then to identify what is difficult for the students, what are the critical aspects of their learning, and how technology can help with this. To ensure a focus on learning quality, the e-learning guidelines are based on pedagogical principles and not technology. By applying these guidelines the expected results are staff who are actively involved, and learners who are attracted to the course, engage fully with the subject and process, and are successful in achieving the learning outcomes.

As Jara and Mellar note (2009, p.229):

The enhancement function of the quality mechanisms largely relies upon the capacity of the teams to take ownership of them and to use them as tools for improvements.

The e-learning guidelines are a tool that staff can take ownership of and use to enhance the quality of teaching and learning.

ACKNOWLEDGMENT

Thanks to the New Zealand Tertiary Education Commission who funded this work through the Innovation and Development Fund.

REFERENCES

ADEC. (2003). *ADEC Guiding Principles for Distance Teaching and Learning*. Retrieved 29 November, 2009, from http://www.adec.edu/admin/papers/distance-teaching_principles.html

AFT. (2002). *Distance education. Guidelines for Good Practice*. Retrieved 29 November, 2009, from http://www.aft.org/pubs-reports/higher_ed/distance.pdf

Avdjieva, M., & Wilson, M. (2002). Exploring the development of quality in higher education. *Managing Service Quality*, *12*(6), 372–383. doi:10.1108/09604520210451858

Barker, K. (2002). *Canadian recommended e-learning guidelines (CanRegs)*. Retrieved 29 November, 2009, from http://www.futured.com/pdf/CanREGs%20Eng.pdf

Barker, K. C. (2007). E-learning Quality Standards for Consumer Protection and Consumer Confidence: A Canadian Case Study in E-learning Quality Assurance. *Journal of Educational Technology & Society*, *10*(2), 109–119.

Bates, A. W., & Poole, G. (2002). *Effective teaching with technology in higher education: foundations for success*. San Francisco, CA: Jossey-Bass, Wiley.

Butterfield, S., Chambers, M., Moseley, B., Prebble, T., Uys, P., & Woodhouse, D. (1999). *External quality assurance for the virtual institution*. New Zealand Universities Academic Audit Unit.

Carr, S., & Jennings, J. M. (2009). External and Internal Quality Assurance – Towards a Model for Integration. In *Proceedings of AUQF2009 Internal & External Quality Assurance: Tensions & Synergies*. Alice Springs, Australia 1–3 July 2009.

Chao, T., Saj, T., & Tessier, F. (2006). Establishing a Quality Review for Online Courses. *EDUCAUSE Quarterly*, *29*(3).

Davies, J. (2007). The effect of academic culture on the implementation of the EFQM Excellence Model in UK universities. *Quality Assurance in Education*, *15*(4), 382–401. doi:10.1108/09684880710829965

Donohue, C., Fox, S. & Torrence, D. (2007). Early Childhood Educators as eLearners. Engaging Approaches to Teaching and Learning Online. *Beyond the Journal,* July 2007.

Ehlers, D. (2009). Understanding quality culture. *Quality Assurance in Education*, *17*(4), 343–363. doi:10.1108/09684880910992322

Ellis, R. A., Jarkey, N., Mahony, M. J., Peat, M., & Sheely, S. (2007). Managing quality improvement of eLearning in a large, campus-based university. *Quality Assurance in Education*, *15*(1), 9–23. doi:10.1108/09684880710723007

Fox, S. (2006). *A Pilot Case Study – New Zealand Tertiary College*. Retrieved 29 November, 2009 from http://elg.massey.ac.nz/index.php?title=Implementing_guidelines

Frydenberg, J. (2002). Quality Standards in eLearning: A Matrix of Analysis. *International Review of Research in Open and Distance Learning*, *3*(2).

Garrison, D. R., & Vaughan, N. D. (2008). *Blended learning in higher education: framework, principles, and guidelines* (1st ed.). San Francisco: Jossey-Bass.

Harvey, L. (2005). A history and critique of quality evaluation in the UK. *Quality Assurance in Education*, *13*(4), 263–276. doi:10.1108/09684880510700608

Higgins, A. (2004). *Distance Education in Australia and New Zealand: Challenges and Successes*.

Hodgkinson, M., & Kelly, M. (2007). Quality management and Enhancement processes in UK Business schools: a review. *Quality Assurance in Education*, *15*(1), 77–91. doi:10.1108/09684880710723043

IHEP. (2000). *Quality on the line: Benchmarks for success in Internet-based education*. Retrieved 29 November, 2009, from http://www.ihep.org/Publications/publications-detail.cfm?id=69

Inglis, A. (2005). Quality improvement, quality assurance, and benchmarking: comparing two frameworks for managing quality processes in open and distance learning. *International Review of Research in Open and Distance Learning*, *6*(1).

Jackson, K., & D'Alessandro, N. (2003). *Implementation of a quality assurance system for online units at the University of Tasmania*. Paper presented at the Interact, Integrate, Impact: Proceedings of the 20th Annual Conference of the Australasian Society for Computers in Learning in Tertiary Education. Adelaide.

Jara, M., & Mellar, H. (2009). Factors affecting quality enhancement procedures for e-learning courses . *Qulatiy Assurance in Education*, *17*(3), 220–232. doi:10.1108/09684880910970632

JISC. (2004). *Effective Practice with e-Learning. A good practice guide in designing for learning*. Retrieved 29 November, 2009, from http://www.jisc.ac.uk/uploaded_documents/jisc%20effective%20practice3.pdf

Lomas, L. (2007). Zen, motorcycle maintenance and quality in higher education. *Quality Assurance in Education*, *15*(4), 402–412. doi:10.1108/09684880710829974

Marshall, S. (2004). *E-learning standards: Open enablers of learning or compliance straitjackets?* Paper presented at the Beyond the comfort zone: Proceedings of the 21st ASCILITE Conference, Perth.

Mayes, T. (2001). Learning technology and learning relationships . In Stephenson, J. (Ed.), *Teaching & learning online: new pedagogies for new technologies* (pp. 16–26). London: Kogan Page.

McNaught, C. (2001). *Quality assurance for online courses: from policy to process to improvement?* Paper presented at the Meeting at the Cross-roads, Proceedings of the 18th Annual Australian Society for Computers in Learning in Tertiary Education 2001 Conference, University of Melbourne.

Meyer, K. A. (2003). *Quality in Distance Education: Focus on On-Line Learning* (*Vol. 29*). Hoboken, NJ: Jossey-Bass.

ODLQC. (2006). *ODL QC Standards*. Retrieved 29 November, 2009, from http://www.odlqc.org.uk/odlqc/gpgindex.htm

Oliver, R., & Herrington, J. (2003). Factors influencing quality online learning experiences . In Davies, G., & Stacey, E. (Eds.), *Quality Education @ a Distance*. London: Kluwer Academic Publishers.

QAA. (2004). *Code of practice for the assurance of academic quality and standards in higher education*. Section 2: Collaborative provision and flexible and distributed learning (including e-learning). Retrieved 29 November, 2009, from http://www.qaa.ac.uk/academicinfrastructure/codeOfPractice/section2/default.asp

Schulz-Novak, D. K. (2002). *Building Quality into Distance Education: Establishing Standards*. Paper presented at the Pan-Commonwealth Forum on Open Learning, Durban, South Africa.

Srikanthan, G., & Dalrymple, J. (2003). Developing alternative perspectives for quality in higher education. *International Journal of Educational Management*, *17*(3), 126–136. doi:10.1108/09513540310467804

Sundar, A. (2002). *Evaluation of compliance and effectiveness of academic quality management in the tertiary institution: The case of Eastern Institute of Technology*. Paper presented at the HERDSA.

Twigg, C. A. (2001). *Quality Assurance for Whom? Providers and Consumers in Today's Distributed Learning Environment*. Retrieved 29 November, 2009, from http://www.thencat.org/Monographs/Mono3.pdf

Whittaker, J. (2007). Quality Online Teaching? Who's asking? *He Kupu*, *1*, 18–27.

ADDITIONAL READING

Benson, A. D. (2003). Dimensions of Quality in Online Degree Programs. *American Journal of Distance Education*, *17*(3), 145–159. doi:10.1207/S15389286AJDE1703_2

Biggs, J. B. (1999). *Teaching for quality learning at university: what the student does*. Philadelphia: Society for Research into Higher Education: Open University Press.

Ehlers, U.-D., & Pawlowski, J. M. (2006). *Handbook on quality and standardisation in e-learning*. Berlin: Springer.

Hay, D. B., Kehoe, C., Miquel, M. E., Hatzipanagos, S., Kinchin, I. M., & Keevil, S. F. (2007). Measuring the quality of e-learning. *British Journal of Educational Technology*, *39*(6), 1037–1056. doi:10.1111/j.1467-8535.2007.00777.x

Herrington, A., Herrington, J., Oliver, R., Stoney, S., & Willis, J. (2001). *Quality guidelines for online courses: The development of an instrument to audit online units*. Paper presented at the ASCILITE 2001: Meeting at the crossroads, The University of Melbourne, Melbourne. Retrieved 28 November, 2009, from http://elrond.scam.ecu.edu.au/oliver/2001/qowg.pdf

Higgins, A. (2002). *Creating a National E-Learning Strategy in the Open Learning Environment: A New Zealand Case Study*. Paper presented at the Pan-Commonwealth Forum on Open Learning Theme: Open Learning: Transforming Education for Development, Durban, South Africa. Retrieved 29 November, 2009, from www.col.org/pcf2/papers/higgins_1.pdf

Hosie, P., Schibeci, R., & Backhaus, A. (2005). A framework and checklists for evaluating online learning in higher education. *Assessment & Evaluation in Higher Education, 30*(5), 539–553. doi:10.1080/02602930500187097

Inglis, A., Ling, P., & Joosten, V. (2002). Improving the quality of online learning programmes . In *Delivering digitally: managing the transition to the knowledge media* (2nd ed.). London: Kogan Page.

Kirkpatrick, D. (2005). Quality assurance in open and distance learning. Retrieved 3 August 2009, from http://www.col.org/SiteCollectionDocuments/KS2005_QA.pdf

Marshall, S. (2004). *Literature Review: Determination of New Zealand Tertiary Institution E-Learning Capability: An Application of an E-Learning Maturity Model*. Retrieved 29 November, 2009, from http://www.utdc.vuw.ac.nz/research/emm/documents/literature.pdf

Marshall, S. J., & Mitchell, G. (2007). Benchmarking International E-learning Capability with the ELearning Maturity Model. In Proceedings of EDUCAUSE in Australasia 2007, 29 April – 2 May 2007, Melbourne, Australia. Retrieved 29 November, 2009, from http://www.caudit.edu.au/educauseaustralasia07/authors_papers/Marshall-103.pdf

New Zealand Council for Educational Research. (2004). *Critical Success Factors and Effective Pedagogy for e-learning in Tertiary Education*. Retrieved 29 November, 2009, from http://www.minedu.govt.nz/NZEducation/EducationPolicies/TertiaryEducation/PublicationsAndResources/~/media/MinEdu/Files/EducationSectors/TertiaryEducation/NZCERFinalReport.pdf

Oliver, R. (2003). *Exploring benchmarks and standards for assuring quality online teaching and learning in higher education*. Paper presented at the Proceedings of 16th Open and Distance Learning Association of Australia Biennial Forum, Canberra. Retrieved 29 November, 2009, from http://elrond.scam.ecu.edu.au/oliver/2003/odlaa.pdf

Oliver, R. (2005). Quality assurance and elearning: blue skies and pragmatism. *ALT-J, 13*, 173–187. doi:10.1080/09687760500376389

Parker, N. K. (2008). The Quality Dilemma in Online Education. In T. D. Anderson & F. Elloumi (Eds.), *Theory and Practice of Online Learning, 2nd edition*: Athabasca University. Retrieved on 29 November, 2009 from http://cde.athabascau.ca/online_book/ch16.html

Pawlowski, J. M. (2007). Quality mark e-learning: developing process- and product-oriented quality for learning, education and training. *International Journal of Learning Technology, 3*(1), 51. doi:10.1504/IJLT.2007.012367

Quality Matters. (2004). *Quality Matters: Peer Course Review of Online Courses: Matrix of Review Standards*. Retrieved 29 November, 2009, from http://www.qualitymatters.org/Documents/Matrix%20of%20Research%20Standards%20FY0506.pdf

Suddaby, G., & Milne, J. (2008). Coordinated, Collaborative And Coherent: Developing And Implementing E-Learning Guidelines Within A National Tertiary Education System. *Campus-Wide Information Systems, 25*(2), 114–122. doi:10.1108/10650740810866602

Van Melle, E., Cimellaro, L., & Shulha, L. (2003). A Dynamic Framework to Guide the Implementation and Evaluation of Educational Technologies. *Education and Information Technologies, 8*(3), 267–285. doi:10.1023/A:1026312110143

Wang, Q. (2006). Quality assurance - best practices for assessing online programs. *International Journal on E-Learning, 5*(2), 265(210).

Chapter 24
Online Delivery of Deaf Studies Curricula in Ireland at Third Level

Brian Nolan
Institute of Technology, Ireland

Lorraine Leeson
Trinity College Dublin, Ireland

ABSTRACT

Irish Sign Language (ISL), an indigenous language of Ireland, is recognized by the European Union as a natural language. It is a language separate from the other languages used in Ireland, including English, Irish, and, in Northern Ireland, British Sign Language. Some 5,000 Deaf people use ISL. Given the history of suppression of signed languages across what is now the European Union, the average Deaf person leaves school with a reading age of 8.5 to 9 years. It is no surprise, therefore, that Deaf people are the most under-represented of all disadvantaged groups at third level. This poses two challenges: (1) getting Deaf people into third level and (2) presenting education in an accessible form. In the authors' work, they address directly these challenges in an Irish context, and this chapter reports on this work. In Ireland, two Dublin based institutions, Trinity College Dublin (TCD) and the Institute for Technology Blanchardstown, Dublin (ITB) have partnered to create a unique elearning environment based on MOODLE as the learning management system, in the delivery of Deaf Studies programmes at TCD. This partnership delivers third level programmes to students in a way that resolves problems of time, geography and access, maximizing multi-functional uses of digital assets across our programmes. Students can take courseware synchronously and asynchronously. The authors have built a considerable digital asset and have created a re-architected framework to avail of current best practice in rich digital media over Moodle with learning objects for ISL. Their digital assets include a corpus of ISL, the 'Signs of Ireland Corpus' which is one of the largest, most richly annotated in the world. They have operated online delivery since 2005, hosted by ITB. The hallmark of this project is the delivery of blended learning, maximizing ICT in the teaching and learning of ISL. It is important to note that there are currently no other universities delivering Deaf Studies programmes with this degree of online content internationally. Thus, this programme and its associated research is cutting edge innovation in its philosophy,

DOI: 10.4018/978-1-61692-789-9.ch024

its rich content and its utilization of rich media. Signed languages, by their nature, are visual-gestural languages, which (unlike spoken languages) do not have a written form. Given this, the online content is required to be multi-modal in nature and the authors utilize rich-media learning objects in their delivery. Within ITB and TCD, the authors have a number of doctoral level studies linked to this project. These focus, at one end of the continuum, on focusing on Deaf culture and is linked to the perspectives on Deaf Studies teaching modules, and at the opposite end of the continuum on describing, for ISL, the phonological-morphological interface in ISL ad which will enrich the digital corpus of ISL. These feed into the online programme.

BACKGROUND

Irish Sign Language (ISL), an indigenous language of Ireland, is recognized by the European Union as a natural language. It is a language separate from the other languages used in Ireland, including English, Irish, and, in Northern Ireland, British Sign Language. Some 5,000 Deaf people use ISL. Given the history of suppression of signed languages across the EU, the average Deaf person leaves school with a reading age of 8.5 to 9 years. Given this, it is no surprise that Deaf people are the most under-represented of all disadvantaged groups at third level. This poses two challenges: (1) getting Deaf people into third level and (2) presenting education in an accessible form.

Two institutions, Trinity College Dublin (TCD) and the Institute for Technology, Blanchardstown, Dublin (ITB) have partnered to create a unique elearning environment based on MOODLE as the learning management system, in the delivery of Deaf Studies programmes at TCD. This partnership delivers third level programmes to students in a way that resolves problems of time, geography and access, maximizing multi-functional uses of digital assets across our programmes. Students can take courseware synchronously and asynchronously. We have built a considerable digital asset and plan to re-architect our framework to avail of current best practice in digital repositories with learning objects vis-à-vis ISL. Our digital assets include a corpus of ISL, the 'Signs of Ireland Corpus' which is one of the largest, most richly annotated in the world. We have operated online delivery since 2005, hosted by ITB, and in early 2008 were successful in attracting significant Irish government funding to expand delivery of a series of undergraduate diplomas to degree level nationwide under the Strategic Innovation Fund, Cycle II.

The hallmark of this project is the delivery of blended learning, maximizing ICT in the teaching and learning of ISL. It is important to note that there are currently no other universities delivering Deaf Studies programmes with this degree of online content internationally. Thus, this programme and its associated research is cutting edge innovation in its philosophy, its rich content and its utilization of rich media. Signed languages, by their nature, are visual-gestural languages, which (unlike spoken languages) do not have a written form. Given this, the online content is required to be multi-modal in nature and we utilize rich-media learning objects in our delivery. This presents a number of serious and important challenges. Specific challenges include:

- Universal design in an online curriculum for Deaf students
- Identifying what aspects of ISL learning can best be supported & assessed online
- Assessing signed language interpreting skill in an online context
- Decisions regarding ISL annotation & mark-up standards
- Using the Signs of Ireland corpus in blended learning contexts

- Leveraging a corpus within digital learning objects in a MOODLE environment
- Architecture of a digital learning environment to support ISL learning
- Issues of assessment in an elearning context

We are instigating a range of doctoral level studies linked to this project, focusing on the deployment of rich digital media as learning objects to support online delivery of Deaf Studies, the online assessment of ISL, and the phonological-morphological interface in ISL.

This paper outlines the establishment and annotation of the Signs of Ireland corpus, currently the largest digital annotated corpus in Europe insofar as we are aware, and the success of the corpus to date in supporting curricula and research. We focus on moving the corpus forward as an asset to develop in elearning and blended learning. This paper also outlines the challenges inherent in this process, and outlines our plans and our progress to date in meeting these objectives. Our two institutions, Trinity College Dublin (TCD) and the Institute for Technology Blanchardstown Dublin (ITB) have partnered to create a Moodle-based elearning environment for the delivery of Deaf Studies programmes at TCD. This partnership delivers third level programmes to students such that students can take courseware synchronously and asynchronously.

IRISH SIGN LANGUAGE

Irish Sign Language is an indigenous language of Ireland. It is used by some 5,000 Irish Deaf people as their preferred language (Matthews 1996) while it is estimated that some 50,000 non-Deaf people also know and use the language to a greater or lesser extent (Leeson 2001). The Signs of Ireland corpus is part of the Languages of Ireland programme at the School of Linguistic, Speech and Communication Sciences, TCD. It comprises data from Deaf Irish Sign Language (ISL) users across Ireland in digital form, and has been annotated using ELAN, a software programme developed by the Max Planx Institute, Nijmegan. The corpus is housed at the Centre for Deaf Studies, a constituent member of the School.

While technology has opened the way for the development of digital corpora for signed languages, we need to bear in mind that signed languages are articulated in three dimensional space, using not only the hands and arms, but also the head, shoulders, torso, eyes, eye-brows, nose, mouth and chin to express meaning (e.g. Klima and Bellugi 1979 for American Sign Language (ASL); Kyle and Woll 1985, and Sutton-Spence and Woll 1999 for British Sign Language (BSL); and McDonnell 1996; Leeson 1996, 1997, 2001; O'Baoill and Matthews 2000 for Irish Sign Language (ISL)) leads to highly complex, multi-linear, potentially dependent tiers that need to be coded and time-aligned. As with spoken languages, the influence of gesture on signed languages has begun to be explored (Armstrong, Stokoe and Wilcox 1995, Stokoe 2001; Vermeerbergen and Demey (2007)), while discussion about what is linguistic and what is extra-linguistic in the grammars of various signed languages continues (e.g. Engberg-Pedersen 1993, Liddell 2003, Schembri 2003). While these remain theoretical notions at a certain level, decisions regarding how one views such elements and their role as linguistic or extra-linguistic constituents plays an important role when determining what will be included or excluded in an annotated corpus. Such decisions also determine how items are notated, particularly in the absence of a written form for the language being described.

EUDICO LINGUISTIC ANNOTATOR (ELAN)

Originally developed for gesture research, ELAN (EUDICO Linguistic Annotator) has become the standard tool for establishing and maintaining signed language corpora. It is an annotation tool that allows one to create, edit, visualize and search annotations for video and audio data. ELAN was developed with the aim of providing a sound technological basis for the annotation and exploitation of multi-media recordings. *(ECHO Project:*

http://www.let.ru.nl/sign-lang/echo/index.html?http&&&www.let.ru.nl/sign-lang/echo/data.html)

The Corpus

The corpus currently consists of data from 40 signers aged between 18 and 65 from 5 locations across the Republic of Ireland. It includes male and female signers, all of whom had been educated in a school for the Deaf in Dublin (St. Mary's School for Deaf Girls or St. Joseph's School for Deaf Boys). None were sign language teachers, as we wished to avoid the collection of data from signers who had a highly conceptualized notion of 'correct' or 'pure' ISL. All use ISL as their preferred language and acquired it before they were 6 years. While some of the signers are native signers insofar as they come from Deaf families, the majority are not – and this reflects the reality for Deaf signed language users. Several contributors have Deaf siblings. The distribution of locations was from Dublin, Wexford, Waterford and Cork, in the Republic of Ireland.

Data was collected by a female Deaf research assistant, Deirdre Byrne-Dunne. This allowed for consistency in terms of data elicitation and also meant that (due to the demographics of the Irish Deaf Community) Ms. Byrne was a known entity to all participants. This is evident in some of the on-screen interaction between informants and data collector, allowing for some interesting sociolinguistic insights. The fact that Ms. Byrne-Dunne is herself Deaf, and an established member of the Irish Deaf community, meant that the potential for 'Observer's Paradox' (Labov 1969) while not reduced, took on a positive spin: knowing who the interviewer/ recorder of data was, and knowing their status as a community member, lent itself to the informants opening up and using their 'natural' signs rather than a variety that they might have assumed a university researcher would 'expect' or 'prefer'.

It also meant that the informants who knew Deirdre, either as a former class-mate or from within the Deaf community, code-switched to use lexical items that would not typically be chosen if the interlocutor was unknown. For example, some 'school' signs were used (e.g. BROWN). And in other instances, informants, telling stories that they had self-selected, referred to Deirdre during the recounting of their personal stories. We also asked participants to tell 'The Frog' story, which is a picture sequence format telling the story of a young boy who, with his dog, searches for his frog, which has escaped from a jar. Informants were also asked to sign the content of the Volterra picture elicitation task, a series of 18 sets of paired pictures showing a series of situations that aim to elicit transitive utterances. Both the 'frog' story and the Volterra picture elicitation task have been used widely in signed language specific descriptions and in cross-linguistic comparisons, including ISL (e.g. Leeson 2001; Johnston, Vermeerbergen Schembri and Leeson (2007); Volterra et al. 1984; Coerts 1994).

Annotating the Corpus

One of the myths of annotating data is that the annotators are neutral with respect to the data and that they simply 'write down what they see'. ISL does not have a written form, so there is no standard code for recording it. While some established transcription keys exist (HamNoSys, Sign Writing, Stokoe Notation), none of these are compatible with ELAN and none are fully developed for ISL. Another issue is that these transcription systems are not shared 'languages' – that is, in the international sign linguistic communities,

Figure 1. WHAT (1)

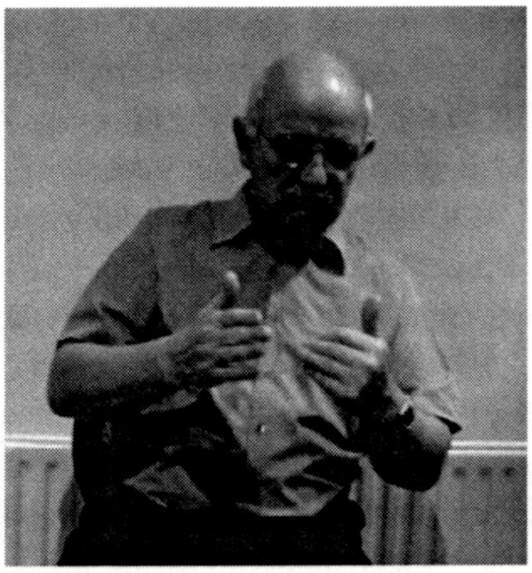

Figure 2. WHAT (2)

these transcription codes are not conventionally used, and to use one in place of a gloss means limiting the sharing of data to an extremely small group of linguists. However, glossing data with English 'tags' is also problematic. Pizzutto and Pietrandrea (2001) point out the dangers inherent in assuming that a gloss can stand in for an original piece of signed language data. They note that "It is often implicitly or explicitly assumed that the use of glosses in research on signed [languages] is more or less comparable to the use of glosses in research on spoken languages ... this assumption does not take into account, in our view, that there is a crucial difference in the way glosses are used in spoken as compared to signed language description. In descriptions of spoken (or also written) languages, glosses typically fulfil an ancillary role and necessarily require an independent written representation of the sound sequence being glossed. In contrast, in description of signed languages, glosses are the primary and only means of representing in writing the sequence of articulatory movements being glossed" (2001: 37). Later, they add that: " ... glosses impose upon the data a wealth of unwarranted and highly variable lexical and grammatical information (depending upon the spoken/written language used for glossing)." (ibid: 42). Thus, the glossing of signed data is problematic, even with a highly trained team who cross-check annotations as ours did. The Signs of Ireland project appears to be unique in that *all* annotated data was verified by a Deaf research assistant who holds a masters degree in applied linguistics.

ELAN allows for the stream of signed language data to run in a time-aligned fashion with the annotations, but a key challenge is that any search function is restrained by the consistency and accuracy of the annotations that have been inputted. For example, several ISL signs may be informally glossed in the same way, but the signs themselves are different, for example, WHAT (1), which is articulated using two hands, both taking an 'L' handshape, and having contact at c. locus. This is considered the 'citation form' of the sign:

In contrast, WHAT (2) is articulated on one hand, with the palm facing the signer. The middle finger wriggles a little in articulation. This is considered to be an informal variant - for example, it would not usually be taught in a formal ISL class. The fact that both of these signs are glossed in the same way demonstrates that any frequency count that would subsequently be carried out using ELAN would not distinguish between the two on the basis of the gloss, WHAT, alone. Instead a global count for WHAT (incorporating both variants) would result.

Figure 3. A screenshot from the Signs of Ireland corpus

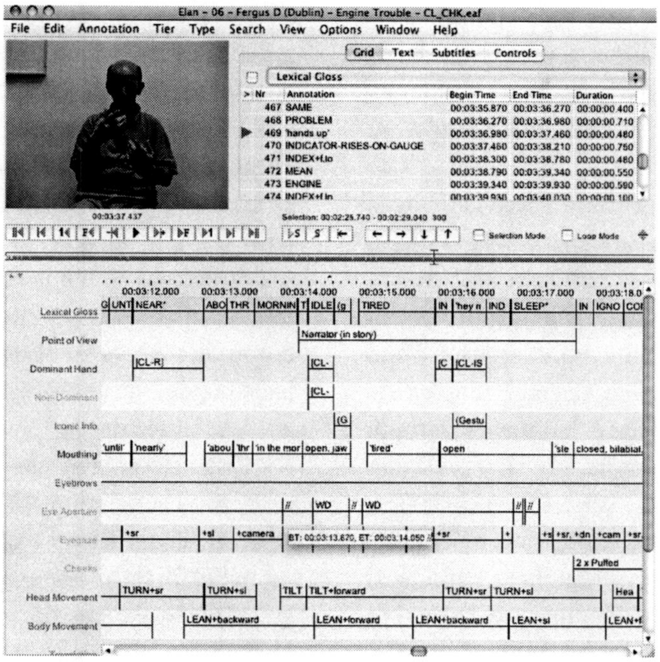

The tagging of items for grammatical function poses another challenge: we have not tagged the SOI data for linguistic function because we do not yet know enough about ISL to accurately code to that level. Despite this, our annotations do reflect assumptions about the nature and structure of certain items. We have also taken seriously concerns arising from early codification of signed languages (Van Herreweghe and Vermeerbergen 2004).

Despite the fact that we wanted to avoid making assumptions about word class and morpho-syntax, the act of annotating a text means that certain decisions have to be made about how to treat specific items. For example, we know that non-manual signals, articulated on the face of the signer, provides information that assists in parsing a message as for example, a question or a statement, or in providing adverbial like information about a verbal predicate (e.g. Leeson 1997; O'Baoill and Matthews 2000, Sutton-Spence and Woll 1999, Brennan 1992, Deuchar 1984; Liddell 1980). When annotating such features, we had to make decisions about whether we would treat non-manual features as dependent tiers, relative to the manual signs that they co-occur with, or as independent tiers containing information that may be supra-segmental in nature. We decided to treat all levels as independent of each other until we could ascertain a relationship that held consistently across levels.

At the lexical level, we had to decide on what constitutes a word in ISL. While established lexical items with citation forms in dictionaries or glossaries of ISL were 'easy' to decide on, there was the issue of how to determine if a sign was a 'word' or a 'gesture' or part of a more complex predicate form, often described as classifier predicates. The fact that some signers used signs related to their gender or age group challenged us: we had to decide if a sign that was 'new' to us was a gendered variant (Le Master 1990, 1999-2000, Leeson and Grehan 2004), a gendered generational variant (Le Master ibid, Leonard 2005), a mis-articulation of an established sign (i.e. a 'slip of the hand' (Klima and Bellugi 1979), an idiosyncratic sign, a borrowing from another signed language (e.g.

BSL), or a gesture. Our team's expertise helped the decision making process here and all decisions were recorded in order to provide a stable reference point for further items that challenged that shared characteristics with items that were discussed previously.

The use of mouth patterns in signed languages provide another challenge for annotators working with signed languages. Mouthings and mouth gestures have been recognized as significant in signed languages, and while mouthings are often indicative of the language contact that exists between spoken and signed languages, mouth gestures are not (for example, see Boyes Braem and Sutton-Spence 2001, Sutton-Spence 2007). Given that the Signs of Ireland corpus will, in the first instance, be used by researchers looking at the morpho-syntax of the language, we opted to not annotate the mouth in a very detailed manner. Instead, we have provided fairly general annotations following from those listed in the ECHO project annotations list.

Using the Corpus in Elearning/ Blended Learning

The Signs of Ireland corpus has been piloted in elearning and blended learning at the Centre for Deaf Studies in the academic years 2006-7 and 2007-8 across a range of courses, but specifically, Irish Sign Language courses, an introductory course focusing on the linguistics and sociolinguistics of Irish Sign Language, and a final year course that focuses on aspects of translation theory and interpreting research (TIPP). At present the corpus exists on each client-side computer (Nolan & Leeson 2009a, 2009b). Students are provided with training in how to use ELAN in order to maximize use of the corpus. The implications of this are that students must be able to access the corpus in a lab, presenting a challenge for blended learning delivery where students require Internet access to the corpus.

This also creates challenges in terms of data protection legislation, distribution, copyright and general access issues that need to be resolved as we move forward. For example, subsets of the data are already used as digital learning objects, but no decision has yet been made regarding optimal management and deployment of the corpus. We have developed assessments to Council of Europe Common European Framework of Reference level B1 (productive/ expressive skill) and B2 (receptive/ comprehension skill) level for ISL. This includes a receptive skills test which includes multiple choice questions linked to data taken from the Signs of Ireland corpus.

The corpus data sits amid other test items, which are outlined in Table (1). We also use the corpus as part of the continuous assessment of

Table 1. Sample ISL Receptive Test Using Digital Objects

Test Item	Domain	Duration	Test Format
Multiple Statements	Life Experience	1 1/2 minutes video (10 minutes)	1. Visual images (10 items)
The Deaf Summer Camp (SOI)	Life Experience Travel Deaf Current Affairs	1 minute video (10 minutes total)	1. MCQ 2. Paraphrase 3. True/False Qs 4. Pen & paper (10 items)
"My Goals"	Ambitions Professional Focus	1 minute video (10 minutes total)	1. MCQ 2. Paraphrase 3. True/False Qs 4. Pen & paper (10 items)

Figure 4. Our Model of Horizontally Integrated Teaching

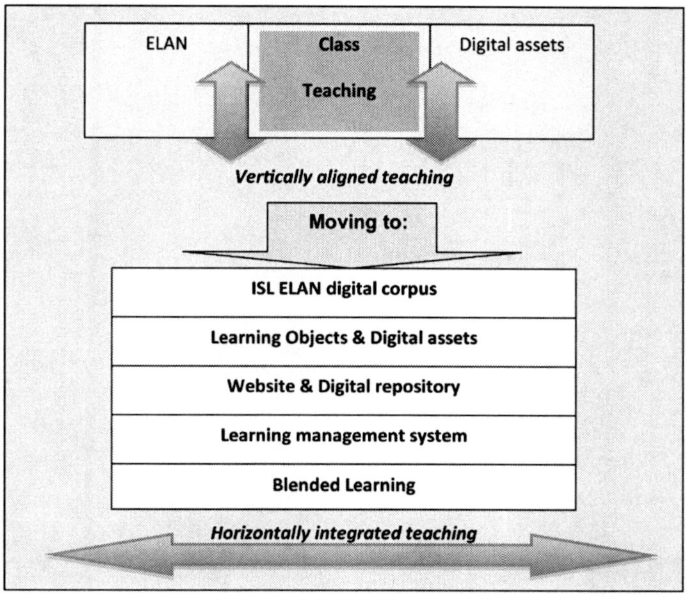

students in our Introduction to the Linguistics and Sociolinguists of Signed Languages course. For example, students are required to engage with the corpus to identify frequency patterns, distribution of specific grammatical or sociolinguistic features (e.g. lexical variation) and to draw on the corpus in preparing end of year essays.

In the Translation and Interpreting: Philosophy and Practice course, students engage with the corpus to explore issues of collocational norms for ISL, look at the distribution of discourse features and features such as metaphor and idiomatic expression (See Leeson 2008 for further discussion).

LEVERAGING THE CORPUS WITH DIGITAL LEARNING OBJECTS

To optimally leverage the Signs of Ireland corpus within a learning environment, we will initially begin by determining what the actual functional requirements are with respect to how the application will be used by both students and academics in the blended learning context. At the moment, Moodle is populated with a wide variety of modules delivered within the suite of CDS undergraduate programmes. The Signs of Ireland digital corpus is tagged in ELAN. We have traditional classroom and blended delivery of content. The present programme architecture is very vertical in orientation (Figure 4). The challenge is to achieve horizontal integration through the use of information technology, the Internet and a blended learning approach.

ONLINE ARCHITECTURE FOR SIGNED LANGUAGE LEARNING

Planning is also required with respect to the overall architecture and framework (Nolan & Leeson 2009c). We are in the process of determining what profiling and other user related information we require to capture and tag data regarding the user environment and their interaction with the digital classroom and curriculum.

Additionally, we have started the analysis that will indicate (i) types of learning objects required for each lecture for each of the programme's modules and (ii) number and type of items, with

Figure 5. A MOODLE Screenshot from the ITB hosted site

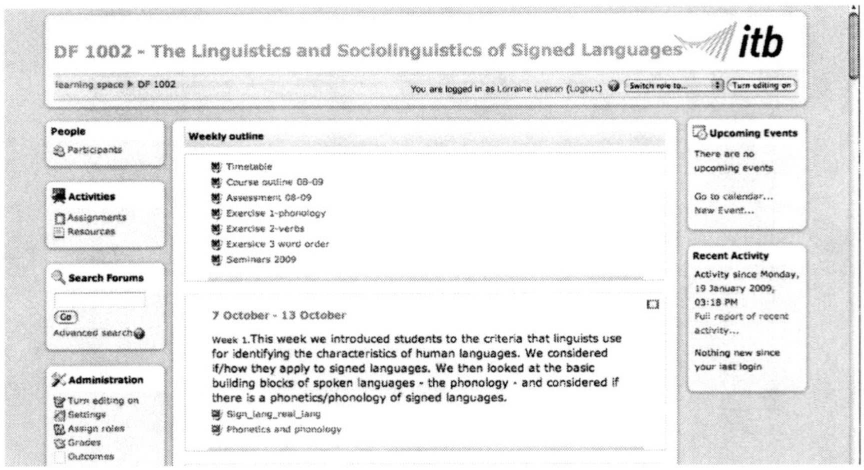

the intention of making our blended learning Diplomas and Degrees available online from September 2009. Our initial base assumption is that target client devices are browsers on Internet aware laptops and desktops. This assumption can be expected to evolve, over time, into mobile devices such as the Apple iPhone, iPod Touch and similar computing appliances. This will deliver to us a plan for the capture and creation of the respective digital rich media that we intend to deploy within our learning objects.

Issues of Assessment in an Elearning Context

We are also developing an assessment model, based on best pedagogical practice as appropriate to our online blended learning environment. From there, as an integral part of our design phase, we will determine how to implement this online. We will need to link, in a principled and structured way, the assessments to the learning outcomes of individual modules, for example, An Introduction to the Linguistics and Sociolinguistics of Signed Languages, and to a particular lecture's thematic learning outcomes as appropriate. We also consider the effectiveness of the assessment with students in a blended learning situation.

Moving Forward to Student Success

Our Strategic Innovation Fund (SIF II) Deaf Studies project is scoped for a three-year window commencing in 2009. A challenging year one plan has been created that will yield infrastructure changes, achievements and digital assets as well as the approval of a four year degree in Deaf Studies; ISL Teaching, and ISL/English Interpreting. We are presently completing an analysis phase to identify the learning objectives of a particular lecture and its themes on a week-by-week basis for each of the modules taught in year one. For example, week 1, lecture 1 has learning objectives LO1, LO2 and LO3, etc.

Typically, this will broadly equate with a lecture plan that is rolled out over a semester. For example, the module 'An Introduction to the Linguistics and Sociolinguistics of Signed Languages' is delivered over two semesters totalling 24 weeks with 24 2-hour lectures over the academic year. We will need to make explicit the learning objectives of each of these lectures such that each objective may be supported by up to, say, four learning objects (figure 6) initially.

These learning objects are expected to form a composite unit, but will be made up of different media types. A composite unit, therefore, will be

Figure 6. Learning object components as a unit within a module

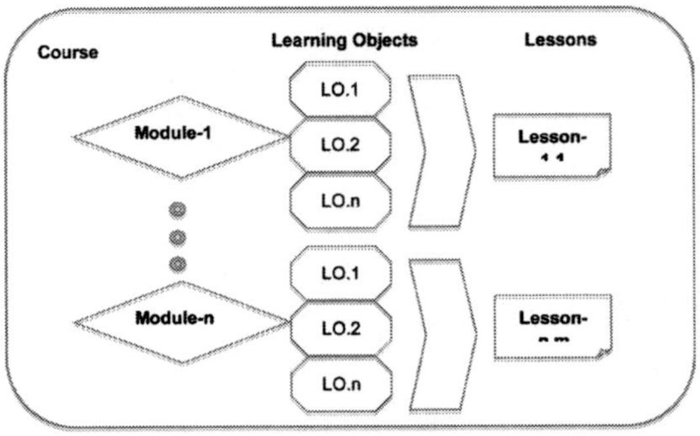

expected to include the lecture notes (.pdf or . ppt), Moodle quizzes and exercises, video data of signing interactions (in Macromedia Breeze, Apple QuickTime and/or other formats), and ELAN digital corpora. To make a composite unit, each learning object needs to be wrapped with proper tagging. This tagging will facilitate searches for these learning objects within a digital repository. We plan that this will be done for all modules across all weeks.

We will identify and implement appropriate assessment models for a blended learning delivery of signed language programmes. This will be aided by our participation in the Leonardo da Vinci funded D-Signs Programme, led by Bristol University (see www.bris.ac.uk/deaf/english/research/active/active02.html). In addition to an assessment model, we will need to devise a model for determining the overall effectiveness of the programme within the blended learning approach that will take a more holistic and pedagogical perspective to the programme objectives. We intend to deploy this programme nationally following from initial Dublin based trials. When this national deployment occurs these effectiveness key performance indicators will assume a greater importance that will enable us to determine the answer to the question: Are we successful with this programme and how can we tell?

Following from our initial trial period, and with a sufficiency of initial data, we will compare and contrast assessments with anonymous (but marked for age and social background, gender, hearing status, etc.) and start to compare longitudinal figures with the initial first year outputs for this blended programme. As this programme is to be modelled for a blended learning environment, we will need to build in a model of student support to include in an appropriate way, online college tutors, peer-learning and mentoring, in order to address any retention issues that may arise and provide the students with the ingredients of their learning success within a productive and engaging community of practice.

We intend to create a website for this SIF II Deaf Studies Project with links to the learning management system/Moodle, other technology platforms including, for example, Macromedia Breeze, and the rich digital media assets as we determine to be useful in support of the teaching of Irish Sign Language within 3rd level education. We will also use this website to disseminate programmatic and research outcomes and other relevant information. We will address the technology related issues pertinent to the design and implementation of the framework for digital learning objects in a repository to facilitate access-retrieval, update, and search. We will determine the tagging standards that will operate across this. While we will deploy the blended learning approach initially in the Dublin area, we will also start planning for national deployment. We will therefore pilot data in the Centre for Deaf Studies in Dublin from September 2008 as supplementary to traditional modes. We will capture feedback from students and analyse this critically. Following this, we will rollout in selected region/s across the country via local 3rd level institutes of higher education in 2009-10. We have agreements with many of these secured at this time.

In terms of the human resources required to build the framework and create the digital assets for the full programme, and the appropriate skill-levels required, we will shortly be seeking to recruit a number of individuals with postgraduate qualifications with a specific research focus. These individuals will be required to determine the appropriate assessment models and how this can be implemented for elearning, backed up by a digital repository of learning objects that leverage the Signs of Ireland digital corpus. We have recruited a Deaf co-coordinating project manager with relevant post-graduate qualifications. He has excellent people-influencing skills and is a bilingual/bi-cultural ISL/English user. He has good organizational and financial management skills and can leverage key community insights with empathy and diplomacy – an essential requirement for the project at hand. In time, we will recruit academic staff for local delivery of ISL in the regions, interpreting lecturer/s and also general Deaf Studies academic/s. We will recruit an elearning/ digital repository/ digital media specialist as well as ISL/English interpreters. Additionally, to contribute to the research of the programme, we intend to recruit at Ph.D level to investigate the following research areas: (1) Assessment models appropriate to ISL in an elearning and blended learning context; (2) Developing and maturing the Signs of Ireland corpus, including meta-tagging and enriching the data; (3) Signed language/spoken language interpreting; (4) Design and build of rich digital media for Irish Sign Language. There are considerations regarding the cultural and work practice implications for academic staff delivering curricula in this manner. There are also corresponding implications for students receiving education in a blended learning approach via elearning technology. What will assume a greater importance immediately for academics and students is the minimum level of computer literacy skills and access to modern computing equipment and a fast broadband network required to engage in this kind of learning environment. We also plan, therefore, to devise a training programme for academic staff to induct them into the new teaching and learning environment and plan for a similar induction for students enrolled on the programme.

ASSESSMENT OF DEAF STUDENTS – PRINCIPLES AND PRACTICE

Assessment is an important consideration in any educational context and is an important metric of quality within the educational process. Typically, many different types of assessment are discussed within the blended learning environment from the tradition and frequently used pop quiz to multi choice question. In our environment however, we prefer to take a more philosophical, and hopefully, innovative approach that takes due cognisance of the Deaf modality used by our students in their communications, and support Deaf culture as best we can. This approach provides challenges and difficulties, especially within an online environment, for the delivery of modules to our Deaf students. For us, within this context, three principal factors (1) are of importance in motivating the relationship between learning and assessment:

1. The relationship between learning and assessment – important factors
    a. The nature and structure of the assessment tasks for ISL that appropriately direct students' effort within the language.
    b. The characteristics of feedback that make it helpful in promoting ISL language learning.
    c. The kinds of involvement by students in the assessment process itself that can lead students developing the capacity to evaluate the quality of their own work. This is a capacity that will become essential in their later professional lives.

Formative assessment is generally used to aid learning. In our educational setting, it is used to provide feedback to a student on their work. It is not generally used for grading purposes. Summative assessment / evaluation, in contrast, refers to the assessment of the learning and additionally summarizes the development of learners at a particular time. Formative assessment is intended to inform students how to improve their learning. A formative assessment can be any task that provides feedback to students on their learning achievements. The emphasis in formative assessment is in encouraging more understanding in the students in relation to their strengths, weaknesses, and gaps in knowledge.

We recognise that formative assessment, especially with larger groups of students, can be time consuming for the lecturer/tutor, and, as they do not lead to credits for 'passing a module', they are used less often than summative assessments. Additional considerations apply when one considers that the modality with Deaf students is different. By default, one thinks of spoken and written texts and tasks. However, with our students learning about Deaf culture and Irish Sign language, the majority are from Deaf backgrounds and many have ISL as their native L1 language. English for many is a second language. When Deaf students have English as an L2, it is employed via a written modality and not in a spoken one.

The purpose of assessment in our environment is therefore to

1. To assist student learning
2. To identify students strengths and weaknesses
3. To assess the effectiveness of a particular instructional strategy
4. To assess and improve the effectiveness of curriculum programs
5. To assess and improve teaching effectiveness
6. To provide data that assist in decision making
7. To communicate with our student community

The challenge then is to incorporate appropriate assessment, both formative and summative, into the blended learning environment for our Deaf and hearing ISL students. We are guided by best practice and are influenced by considerations (2) of Blooms taxonomy (Bloom 1956). In reality this is a huge challenge and, at present we have not completely solved it yet. We use, at the moment, traditional assessment methods that are based on face to face approached for to test, for example both the competence and performance of an ISL language user in the use of their of the productive lexicon of ISL. Within the Moodle environment we do make use of 'pop quizzes' as appropriate within a set of learning objects.

To do signed ISL assessment in real-time via the blended learning environment would require significant financial, people and technological resources. It would require us, for example, to use webcams in real-time, possibly with recorded footage of the assessment so that feedback can be delivered. Often in the face-to-face environment video cameras are employed, especially for final examinations where a permanent record of the examinations is needed so that it can be examined and scored by the examining lecturer at a later time. Additionally, on occasion, external examiners will require a view of the same footage. It may also need to be viewed in the event of a student appeal. The difficulties in delivering such functionality in a blended learning environment are not inconsiderable, at both the client end, where users will need a good webcam, and at the server end, where each video session will need the potential to be recorded, stored and tagged for later use.

2. The levels of Blooms taxonomy (based on Bloom 1956)
    a. **Knowledge**: Recalling the material one has learned (including facts, principles, steps in a sequence).
    b. **Comprehension**: Understanding the material and being able to explain what one knows.
    c. **Application**: Be able to use the material in new situations and apply concepts, principles, rules, theories and laws to find solutions to new problems that have not been seen before.
    d. **Analysis**: Be able to disassemble information and identify relationships between constituent parts

e. **Synthesis**: Be able to compositionally and creatively assemble information.
f. **Evaluation**: Be able to use what one knows about a subject area to make critical judgments.

We employ best practice to our approach to assessment of language skills in our classes with respect to ISL. In particular, we implement Blooms taxonomy in our assessment strategies of the various modules for ISL learning, ISL production and comprehension, and language interpreting.

EVOLVING THE FRAMEWORK

Linked to the assessment plan is our plan for collaboration with students within an online collaborative model within our framework. While we have discussed the difficulties of assessment in real-time within the Deaf modality for ISL language learning, another goal is to evolve the learning framework to communicate with the ISL user as interactively as possible using ISL online. When a Deaf user sees a traditional webpage it is in a written language such as English. It is very rare that a user will encounter a signed language.

Our goal is to evolve to a point where we can present information in signed form, that is, natively in Irish Sign language. This may, in the fullness of time, be achieved via an avatar using machine translation and sign language generation strategies but, in the near term, we envisage that video movies with particular messages (perhaps also used as learning objects) will at least be provided. We need to evolve towards this and, again, significant technical issues need to be resolved to do with the provision and hosting of a server, backup of materials on the site, creation and editing of the signed language movies with an appropriate video resolution to ensure playback quality for comprehension. Significant finances are required to achieve this too.

At the present time, we are evaluating an extension to Moodle, developed by ourselves, to provide a technical solution to facilitate these in-screen sign language movies as learning objects, and we expect these to go live in a controlled way for our first cohort of students by the end of 2009 at the latest. We will determine network bandwidth requirements for different resolutions and file sizes of these learning object movies. We will progress this outwards towards our students on a larger scale once we have gained an understanding of the student experience of these within the learning environment.

SUMMARY

In this paper we have discussed decisions we have made regarding annotation of the Signs of Ireland corpus. We discussed ongoing work to place Irish Sign Language learning online through the application of MOODLE as the platform of choice as we move forward. We outlined the range of applications currently made with respect to the Signs of Ireland corpus in elearning/ blended learning contexts. We indicated how we will leverage the corpus within a framework for elearning and blended learning, situated in an online architecture to support signed language learning. Issues of assessment in an elearning context were also addressed.

REFERENCES

Bloom, B. S. E. (1956). *Taxonomy of educational objectives: The classification of educational goals: Handbook I, cognitive domain*. New York: Longman.

Boyes Braem, P., & Sutton-Spence, R. (Eds.). (2001). The Hands are the Head of the Mouth: The Mouth as Articulator in Sign Languages. *International Studies on Sign Language and Communication of the Deaf, 39*.

Coerts, J. (1994). Constituent order in Sign Language of the Netherlands. In M. Brennan & G.H. Turner (eds.), *Word-order Issues in Sign Languages – Working Papers*, (pp 47-71). The International Sign Linguistics Association (ISLA),Durham.

Emmorey, K. (Ed.). (2003). *Perspectives on Classifier Constructions in Sign Languages*. Upper Saddle River, NJ: Lawrence Erlbaum and Associates.

Engberg-Pedersen, E. (1993). *Space in Danish Sign Language*. Hamburg, Germany: Signum Verlag.

Johnston, T., Vermeerbergen, M., Schembri, A., & Leeson, L. (2007). 'Real data are messy': Considering cross-linguistic analysis of constituent ordering in Australian Sign Language (Auslan), Vlaamse Gebarentaal (VGT), and Irish Sign Language (ISL). In Perniss, P., Pfau, R., & Steinbach, M. (Eds.), *Visible Variation: Comparative Studies on Sign Language Structure*. Berlin: Mouton de Gruyter.

Klima, E., & Bellugi, U. (1979). *The Signs of Language*. Cambridge, MA: Harvard University Press.

Kyle, J. G., & Woll, B. (1985). *Sign Language: The Study of Deaf People and their Language*. Cambridge, UK: Cambridge University Press.

Labov, W. (1969). The Logic of Nonstandard English. In *Georgetown Univeristy 20th Annual Round Table, Monograph Series on Languages and Linguistics*, No. 22.

Le Master, B. (1990). *The Maintenance and Loss of Female and Male Signs in the Dublin Deaf Community*, PhD. Dissertation, Los Angeles, University of California, Los Angeles, CA.

Le Master, B. (1999-2000). Reappropriation of Gendered Irish Sign Language in One Family, *Visual. Anthropological Review*, *15*(2), 1–15.

Le Master, B. (2002). What Difference Does Difference Make? Negotiating Gender and Generation in Irish Sign Language. In Benor, S., Rose, M., Sharma, D., & Shang, Q. (Eds.), *Gendered Practices in Language*. Stanford: Centre for the Study of Languages and Information Publication.

Leeson, L. (1996). *The Marking of Time in Signed Languages with Specific Reference to Irish Sign Language*. Unpublished M. Phil Dissertation, Centre for Language and Communication Studies, University of Dublin, Trinity College.

Leeson, L. (1997). *The ABC of ISL. Booklet to accompany the TV series*. Dublin: RTE/Irish Deaf Society.

Leeson, L. (2001). *Aspects of Verb Valency in Irish Sign Language*. Unpublished Doctoral Dissertation, Centre for Language and Communication Studies, TCD, Dublin.

Leeson, L. (2008). Quantum Leap. Leveraging the Signs of Ireland Digital Corpus in Irish Sign Language/English Interpreter Training. *The Sign Language Translator and Interpreter*, *2*(2), 231–258.

Leeson, L., & Grehan, C. (2004). To the Lexicon and Beyond: The Effect of Gender on Variation in Irish Sign Language. In Van Herreweghe, M., & Vermeerbergen, M. (Eds.), *To The Lexicon and Beyond: The Sociolinguistics of European Sign Languages* (pp. 39–73). Washington, DC: Gallaudet University Press.

Leeson, L., & Nolan, B. (2008). *Digital Deployment of the Signs of Ireland Corpus in Elearning*. LREC2008 – 3rd Workshop on the Representation and Processing of Sign Languages: Construction and Exploitation of Sign Language Corpora. Marrakech, Morocco.

Leeson, L., Saeed, J., Leonard, C., Macduff, A., & Byrne-Dunne, D. (2006). *Moving Heads and Moving Hands: Developing a Digital Corpus of Irish Sign Language: The 'Signs of Ireland' Corpus Development Project*. Paper presented at the IT&T conference, Carlow.

Leeson, L., & Saeed, J. I. (2003). *Exploring the Cognitive Underpinning in the Construal of Passive Events in Irish Sign Language (ISL).* Paper presented at the 8th International Cognitive Linguistics Association Conference, Spain, July 2003.

Leeson, L., & Saeed, J. I. (2004). The Windowing of Attention in Simultaneous Constructions in Irish Sign Language. In T. Cameron, C. Shank & K. Holley (eds.), *Proceedings of the Fifth High Desert Linguistics Conference*, 1-2 November 2002, Albuquerque, University of New Mexico.

Leeson, L., & Saeed, J. I. (2005). *Conceptual Blending and the Windowing of Attention in Simultaneous Constructions in Irish Sign Language (ISL).* Paper Presented at the 8th International Cognitive Linguistics Association Conference, Seoul. *Korea & World Affairs*, (July): 2005.

Leeson, L., & Saeed, J. I. (2007). Conceptual Blending Blending and the Windowing of Attention in Simultaneous Constructions in Irish Sign Language (ISL). In Vermeerbergen, M., Leeson, L., & Crasborn, O. (Eds.), *Simultaneous Constructions in Signed Languages – Form and Function.* Amsterdam: John Benjamins.

Leonard, C. (2005). Signs of Diversity: Use and Recognition of Gendered Signs among Young Irish Deaf People. *Deaf Worlds, 21*(2), 62–77.

Liddell, S. K. (2003). *Grammar, Gesture, and Meaning in American Sign Language.* Cambridge, UK: Cambridge University Press. doi:10.1017/CBO9780511615054

Matthews, P. A. (1996). *The Irish Deaf Community* (*Vol. 1*). Dublin: ITE.

McDonnell, P. (1996). *Verb Categories in Irish Sign Language.* Unpublished Doctoral Dissertation, Centre for Language and Communication Studies, University of Dublin, Trinity College.

McDonnell, P. (Ed.). (2004). *Deaf Studies in Ireland: An Introduction.* Doug McLean, Glouc.

McGreal, R. (Ed.). (2004). *Online education using learning objects. Open and flexible learning series.* London: Routledge Falmer.

Meir, I. (1998). *Thematic Structure and Verb Agreement in Israeli Sign Language*, PhD Dissertation, Hebrew University of Jerusalem, Israel.

Mosel, U. (2006). Fieldwork and Community Language Work. In Gippert, J., Himmelmann, N. P., & Mosel, U. (Eds.), *Essentials of Language Documentation* (pp. 67–86). Berlin: Mouton de Gruyter. doi:10.1515/9783110197730.67

Nolan, B., & Leeson, L. (2009a). Signs of access in a digital world. In *Conference Proceedings of INTED2009: International Technology, Education and Development Conference*, Valencia, Spain.

Nolan, B., & Leeson, L. (2009b). Working towards blended learning. In *Conference Proceedings of Multilingualism, Regional & Minority Languages: Paradigms for Languages of the Wider World Conference. School of Oriental and African Studies (SOAS),* London.

Nolan, B., & Leeson, L. (2009c). Creating access to education with progression Pathways via blended learning of deaf studies at Third level in Ireland: open innovation with Digital assets. In *Conference Proceedings of the 9th Information Technology and Telecommunications Conference 2009.* Dublin: Dublin Institute of technology, Ireland.

O'Baoill, D., & Matthews, P. A. (2000). The Irish Deaf Community: *Vol. 2. The Linguistics of ISL.* Dublin: ITE.

Pizzutto, E. & Pietrandrea, P. (in press). The Notation of Signed Texts. *Sign Language and Linguistics, 4* (1/2), 29-45.

Reflective learning, future thinking: digital repositories, e-portfolios, informal learning and ubiquitous computing. ALT/SURF/ILTA Spring Conference Research Seminar. Retrieved from http://www.alt.ac.uk/docs/ALT_SURF_ILTA_white_paper_2005.pdf. Accessed March 2008.

Roberts, G., W. A., Feijen, M., Harvey, J., Lee, S., & Wade, V. P. (2005).

Sallandre, M. (2008). Simultaneity in French Sign Language Discourse. In Vermeerbergen, M., Leeson, L., & Crasborn, O. (Eds.), *Simultaneous Constructions in Signed Languages – Form and Function*. Amsterdam: John Benjamins.

Sandler, W., & Lillo-Martin, D. (2006). *Sign Language and Linguistic Universals*. Cambridge, UK: Cambridge University Press.

Schembri, A. (2003). Rethinking 'Classifiers' in Signed Languages. In Emmorey, K. (Ed.), *Perspectives on Classifier Constructions in Sign Languages* (pp. 3–34). Mahwah, NJ: Lawrence Erlbaum and Associates.

Seifart, F. (2006). Orthography Development. In Gippert, J., Himmelmann, N. P., & Mosel, U. (Eds.), *Essentials of Language Documentation* (pp. 275–299). New York: Mouton de Gruyter. doi:10.1515/9783110197730.275

Stokoe, W. C. (2001). *Language in Hand: Why Sign Came Before Speech*. Washington, DC: Gallaudet University Press.

Sutton-Spence, R. (forthcoming). Mouthings and Simultaneity in British Sign Language. In Vermeerbergen, M., Leeson, L., & Crasborn, O. (Eds.), *Simultaneous Constructions in Signed Languages – Form and Function*. Amsterdam: John Benjamins.

Sutton-Spence, R., & Woll, B. (1999). *The Linguistics of British Sign Language*. Cambridge, UK: Cambridge University Press.

Talmy, L. (1997). The Windowing of Attention in Language. In Shibitani, M., & Thompson, S. A. (Eds.), *Grammatical Constructions- Their Form and Meaning* (pp. 235–287). Oxford, UK: Clarendon Press.

Tsunoda, T. (2005). *Language Endangerment and Language Revitalisation – An Introduction*. Berlin: Mouton de Gruyter.

Van Herreweghe & Vermeerbergen. (2004). Flemish Sign Language: Some Risks of Codification. In Van Herreweghe, M. & M. Vermeerbergen, *To the Lexicon and Beyond: The Sociolinguistics of European Sign Languages*, (pp. 111-140). Washington, DC: Gallaudet University Press.

Van Valin, R. D., & La Polla, R. J. (1997). *Syntax-Structure, Meaning and Function*. Cambridge, UK: Cambridge University Press.

Vermeerbergen, M., & Demey, E. (2007). Sign + Gesture = Speech + Gesture? Comparing Aspects of Simultaneity in Flemish Sign Language to Instances of Concurrent Speech and Gesture. In Vermeerbergen, M., Leeson, L., & Crasborn, O. (Eds.), *Simultaneous Constructions in Signed Languages – Form and Function*. Amsterdam: John Benjamins.

Vermeerbergen, M., Leeson, L., & Crasborn, O. (in press). Simultaneous Structures in Signed Languages: An Introduction. In Vermeerbergen, M., Leeson, L., & Crasborn, O. (Eds.), *Simultaneous Constructions in Signed Languages – Form and Function*. Amsterdam: John Benjamins.

Volterra, V., Laudanna, S., Corazza, E., & Natale, F. (1984). Italian Sign Language: The Order of Elements in the Declarative Sentence. In Lonke, F. (Ed.), *Recent Research on European Sign Languages* (pp. 19–48). Lisse, The Netherlands: Svets and Zeitlinger.

Wilbur, R. (1994). Eyeblinks and ASL phrase structure. *Sign Language Studies*, *84*, 221–240.

Wilbur, R. B. (1994). Eyeblinks and ASL Phrase Structure. *Sign Language Studies*, *84*, 221–240.

Wilcox, S. (2004a). Gesture and Language: Cross-linguistic and Historical Data from Signed Languages. *Gesture*, *43*, 43–73. doi:10.1075/gest.4.1.04wil

Wilcox, S. (2004b). Cognitive Iconicity: Conceptual Spaces, Meaning and Gesture in Signed Languages. *Cognitive Linguistics*, *15*(2), 119–147. doi:10.1515/cogl.2004.005

KEY TERMS AND DEFINITIONS

Blended Learning: Blended learning is an innovative teaching approach that aims to foster learner autonomy by using a combination of learning methods: such as e-Learning, face-to-face instruction, group and individual study, and coaching.

Irish Sign Language (ISL): Irish Sign Language (ISL), an indigenous language of Ireland, is recognized by the European Union as a natural language. It is a language separate from the other languages used in Ireland, including English, Irish, and, in Northern Ireland, British Sign Language. Some 5,000 Deaf people use ISL.

Visual-Gestural Languages: Human sign languages, in contrast to oral spoken languages are visual gestural languages. The signer typically makes natural use of the two hands and the upper body including the head, eyes, mouth and shoulders in a communicative dialogue. The sign shapes constitute the visual element in a two-way discourse.

Signs of Ireland Corpus: The 'Signs of Ireland Corpus' is one of the largest, most richly annotated in the world of sign language in natural use by male and female adult signers across a range of ages. It contains annotated signed data of Irish Sign Language.

Chapter 25
Learner Management Systems and Environments, Implications for Pedagogy and Applications to Resource Poor Environments

Olúgbémiga T. Ekúndayò
Jackson State University, USA

Francis Tuluri
Jackson State University, USA

ABSTRACT

Knowledge management is essential for realizing that knowledge is power, and power is explored by the learner for meeting existing demands and challenges. Advances in technology, education and learning are therefore linked to using technology. Education is the pathway to productivity, thus the learner is the agent and technology the medium. Among others, e-Learning will play a dominant role in shaping learner management systems and associated learning environments. This chapter addresses the learner and learning management describing some of its implications for pedagogy. It then describes and proposes some implications of the application of these systems for development in resource poor environments. It is divided into three main sections. The first section describes contemporary definitions of LMS and its concepts. It proposes a comprehensive definition of LMS and describes possible future directions of these definitions as a concept in change. The second section describes various tools and classifies them according to current applications in the industry. It describes in principle, the current cutting edge technologies that are being used in the area and how these were developed. It then proposes a Model Structure for Learner Management Systems. It describes and compares classical, e-based and blended learning pedagogy, A third section discusses some current concepts and methodologies in research, pedagogy and LMS, proposing some defining questions for the three areas as a group. The third section first defines and describes resource poor environments. It then highlights and discusses some need areas in resource poor settings. Further, it describes and discusses some of the implications of LMS technology and applications to resource poor settings, with a focus on it's relevance and validity for specific resource poor environments. Following this discussion, the section describes some applications and limitations

DOI: 10.4018/978-1-61692-789-9.ch025

of LMS approaches and blended learning in resource poor environments. Finally, it describes some applications and limitations of LMS and blended learning technology in resource poor environments.

INTRODUCTION

This chapter describes trends in learner management systems and learning environments, and their impact on student learning and preparation. Knowledge management is essential for imparting the power of knowledge, skills and competence. That power is explored and applied by the learner for meeting past, current and future challenges and demands. Advances in education and learning are linked to the use of technology. Since education is the pathway to productivity, the learner is the agent and technology the medium. Among others, e-Learning will play an increasingly dominant role in shaping learner management systems and associated environments for knowledge, skill and competency transfer and acquisition.

Educational institutions and corporate bodies are turning to e-Learning primarily because it has capabilities to effectively impact a larger community for the least amount of investment and expense. Secondarily, it is contributing to an increase in retention and recruitment. To fully apprehend the results of e-Learning, it is important to examine the systems of learning available, how to manage them, and how they can be integrated with other learning environments.

Available e-Learning systems and tools must be managed to address effective translation. For example during initial learning, the organization determines how to present new skills and concepts to the new learner. Management will monitor the process to assure that learning tools are providing the learner with a foundation of the knowledge delivered in a particular area of interest. The tools applied are also assessed for learner progress from entry-level competence required to the end of learning. Application of tools also requires managing the transfer of skills for learning the tools in a particular area from one person to another.

This chapter addresses the learner and learner management, and describes/discusses some of its implications for pedagogy (teaching approaches). It then describes and proposes some implications of applying these systems for development in resource poor environments.

LEARNING AND LEARNER MANAGEMENT SYSTEMS

Definitions of LMS

We begin by looking at various users and researchers, and their definitions of **LMS**. We identify formal and informal systems and elaborate in short on each. We then explore and review practical definition groups, and theory-driven definitions. Finally, we present amore encompassing definition that accommodates all the different classes, both practical and theoretical

Formal and Informal Systems Definitions and Applications

Various definitions have been appended to learner management systems (LMS) and their corollaries, depending on who makes the definition and their environments. There are currently three main environments: formal and informal. The formal systems have two main sectors: corporate and academic. The informal system is much more ubiquitous and seems to contain more content, with no specific evaluation systems except to see changes in common usage as the system grows. This system is growing with few controls for proprietary content. The system also provides a major social learning medium today, especially for young people. It ranges from simple one-on-one interactions in synchronous space, to much more complex parallel interactions in asynchronous and synchronous space. The most common one-on-one synchronous state and tool is the instant mail while the most common asynchronous one on one space is the e-mail. However, the more complex randomly synchronous spaces include the newly emerging chat rooms, with multiple discussions going on in the same space at the same time. They are akin to the real-space market environments with multiple transactions taking place at the same time. A less randomly complex and dynamic asynchronous space environment is the u-tube, facebook, and dating systems that allow for both one-on-one and complex interactions. They include the dating systems. These social learning environments are being increasingly adopted by the academic systems with the corporate sector closely following. Overall, the definitions range from the purely practical to the deeply theoretical. The various definitions are grouped into these two extreme points, using a few key examples.

Practical Definition of LMS

In the practical area, the definitions focus on utility and utilization approaches to imparting knowledge, skills and competence in educational and technical areas.

According to Wikipedia (2009), LMS is defined as software for delivering, tracking and managing training/education. According to Avgeriou et al (2003) LMS can also be defined as specialized Learning Technology Systems (IEEE LTSC, (2001a)), based on the state-of-the-art Internet and WWW technologies in order to provide education and training following the open and distance learning paradigm. In addition, a corporate definition is provided by adobe systems, where they define LMS as the term used to describe a server-based system that is designed to manage learning content and learner interactions. These definitions` thus add the dimensions of the medium for delivery and manipulation of knowledge through the Internet (as a key technology delivery vehicle), with geographical distance as a key component. This highlights the use of technology to bridge distance and impart knowledge far beyond the confines of geographical location.

Theoretical or Theory Driven Definitions

On the more theoretical level, LMS may be defined as a class of information systems, referred to as knowledge management systems promoted by IS researchers whose purpose is to support creation, transfer, and application of knowledge in organizations (Alavi and Leidner (1999, 2001)). The use of the word knowledge is more encompassing and expands the area of LMS applications to deeper theoretical concepts.

Basic Definition Emerging

Generally, these definitions firmly place LMS within the realm of technology. Summarizing therefore, we define LMS as the aapplication of technology to learning and teaching, or the use of various techniques to impart information and skill or competence through a learning environment. However, since learning itself is essentially an information acquisition, manipulation and decision making process for behavior, it is safe to define LMS as a medium for information, knowledge and skills transfer. In other words we transfer knowledge from one person to another and then determine whether the knowledge has been appropriately and adequately transferred to impact skills and competence for specific functions and usages. Recently, several researchers (Boticario and Santos (2007), Greenhow (2008), Heo (2009), Lee et al (2006), Papastergiou (2006), Thieman (2008)) implied that LMS is a form of technologically driven environment that can be used for more than just knowledge transfer. It can also be argued that LMS should be part of a holistic learning environment that gives the end user flexibility and control to move in various paths. (Siemens (2004)) Thus learner management includes not only technology, but also psychosocial, behavioral and ecological dimensions for knowledge, skill and competence transference. This definition allows for a more robust consideration of elements needed for actual, in-life function.

LMS Tools

In order to determine the range of LMS tools, it is important to identify the areas of applications and the class of content being used in this highly interactive environment. We therefore explore the various services and functions expected in an LMS; we then review the various environments and content to be delivered. We then assign various tools to these classes of function and material.

Services Provided by LMS

McCormack and Jones (1997) wrote on the services that should be provided by an LMS. They included information distribution, management of learning material, multiple communication facilities and class management. Siemens (2004) advocated a set of tools that will have certain characteristics. These characteristics include modularity, social interaction, connected specialization and a learning ecology. He mentioned such tools as those that offer simple content management, social interaction, collaboration and emerging connection-making protocols. According to Avgeriou et al (2003), current LMS working on learning environments is a complex process of four interrelated steps: 1. Design of the learning experience based on objectives, learning activities, resources and services; 2. Administration involving management of all data including users' roles, access rights and services configuration; 3. Usage entailing actual use of designed activities on the learning environment within the class context; and 4. Auditing, in which authors get reports on how users have performed on learning activities, in order to adjust course design. In addition to these functions, teaching increasingly involves competence transmission that includes research competence. Thus data management and research activities can also be taught using LMS if the appropriate tools are embedded. These include data management, analyses and reporting environments that involve multiple users and functions. In addition, work groups management assists the learner to access and utilize data from wide sources and configurations. These usages therefore necessitate a wide range of communication tools including discussion forums, asynchronous and synchronous chat, assignment file drop-boxes, data management and analyses systems, self-scoring quizzes and grade books.

Classes of Materials Delivered

Within each tool, there are five classes of materials delivered: 1. Text, 2.Graphic, 3. Data, 4. Audio and 5. Visual. The text ranges from one or more key words to whole textbooks and sets of books. The graphic range from simple still shapes in simple formats to complex design models in various formats including portable, text, scanned and directly uploaded formats. The data materials delivered include two, three and even multi-dimensional databases, simple and complex analytic software, from simple data summarization to complex artificial intelligence based analytic tools and routines in appropriate software. The audio classes range from simple spoken words to music, radio streaming and voice-over and web cast formats. The visual classes can include whole programs delivered in a streaming fashion to stored, timed broadcast modules for teaching and learning to complex graphics for interactive in-depth critical assessment and development in a web cast environment delivering content over wide distance to multiple locations or providing multiple simultaneous accesses for both non gated and gated (secured) access.

Areas of LMS Application Tools

As earlier stated, a review of the areas of application so far indicates that there are two main areas in which the tools have been applied: the formal and informal. In the formal, there are two main environments: these are the academic and corporate; in which though the needs appear to be different, the overall goals have remained similar, which is to impart knowledge and develop skills to provide human capital for specific uses or needs. Thus, merging the two areas, functions in LMS will include:

- Managing facilities, users, courses, instructors, roles, and generating reports,
- A Course calendar outlining the timelines for course or assignment,
- A Learning Path or the means of identifying how the student and faculty will complete the knowledge and other competencies,
- Student messaging and notifications,
- Assessment/testing capable of handling student pre/post testing,
- Display scores and transcripts,
- Grading of coursework and roster processing, including wait listing,
- Web-based or blended course delivery.

Characteristics more specific to corporate learning, which sometimes includes franchisees or other business partners, includes:

- Autoenrollment (enrolling Students in courses by predefined criteria),
- Administrator/Manager enrollment and approval,
- Definitions for prerequisites or equivalencies (generally boolean),
- Integration with performance tracking and management systems,
- Planning tools to identify skill gaps at departmental and individual level,
- Curriculum, required and elective training requirements at an individual and organizational level,
- Grouping students according to demographic units (geographic region, product line, business size, etc.),
- Assign corporate and partner employees to more than one job title at more than one demographic unit.

These areas of application imply the use of various tools and techniques for materials and content. With these, a myriad of tools have been developed, and are being developed to preclude naming them. However, the reader should learn to select appropriate and relevant tools use them.

Model Structure for Learner Management Systems and their Implications for Pedagogy

Model Structure for Learner Management Systems

With the foregoing, a model structure begins to emerge factoring five main areas and levels: These are 1. Strategic Objective, 2. Learning Content, 3. Learning Tools and Technology, 4. Delivery tools, 5. Learning and Research Environment.

As shown in Figure 1 below, these five areas interact in a way designed to optimally transfer knowledge and translate it both intellectually and in practice, during and after the transference process. A thematic domain chart is proposed that illustrates these interactions and the complex dynamics of players in the system. This thematic structure involves the various tasks of developing, organizing and delivering information, skills and competence.

These tasks are performed in an ecological milieu with technology forming the enabling environment for implementing all the specific

Figure 1. Model of human, technology, research and pedagogical systems interactions in the delivery of information, knowledge, skills and competence

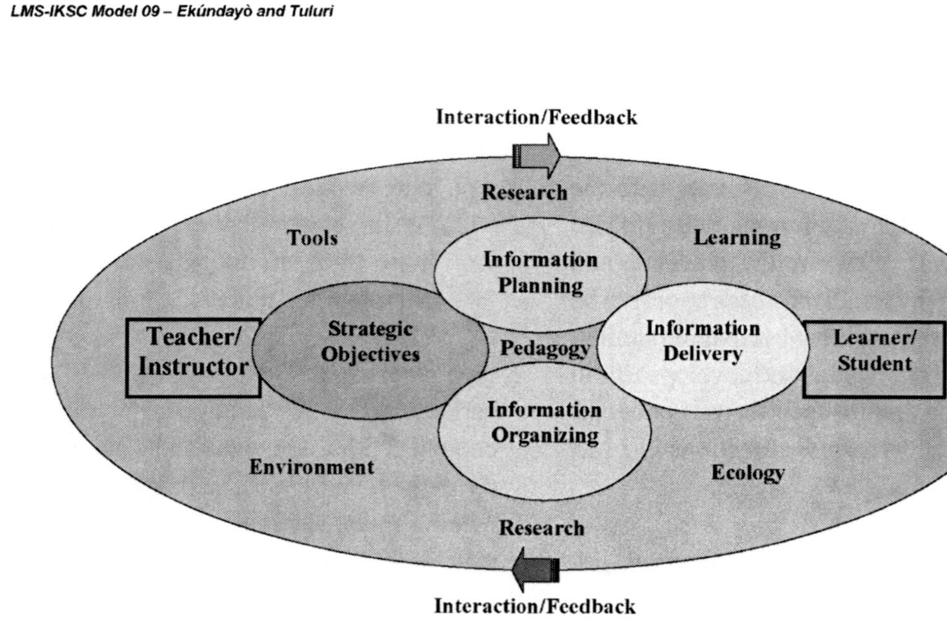

stages. Each of the stages contains mixtures of activities, theoretical models and technological applications.

The strategic planning phase entails identifying the need and developing a strategic plan factoring all the different elements for knowledge, skill and competence transfer. Information planning entails curriculum design and development, resource development, technology readiness and systems configuration for implementation. The information organizing entails designing and developing the class syllabus, configuring all elements for interaction and preparing the technological environment for knowledge, skills and competence transfer. The delivery phase entails activities for delivery, interactions and embedding. Many of the technological tools are focused on this last phase with delivery vehicles for knowledge content and knowledge management. Also, within this stage, many of the elements of planning and organizing are implemented, including knowledge content. The technology for many of the activities of LMS is focused on this phase. However, more recently, practice environments are being included for real life, real time and product oriented competency measurement, especially in the service professions including the health field where clinical competence is largely measured by practice through rotations. Much of this is being driven by e-based commerce and other practice based transactions that allow for product and service delivery without much physical contact. The Trainer/Teacher and Learner/Student interact in a complex of past and developing experience as well as feedbacks that provide the basis for continuous quality improvement, validity and reliability. Thus, apart from the information delivery and transmission vehicles, LMS systems have begun to include product delivery and assessment approaches that enhance pedagogical effectiveness in transmitting competence, especially in many practice based education systems, including for example, medicine, engineering, public health, security and others. The continuous quality improvement aspect is propelled by research

This schematic can be used to identify need areas, assess competency within the program, measure student needs, and assess teacher gaps and guide teacher focus and emphasis. In addition, it can be used to collect data for research in developing more robust internal models for competence transference.

Overview of Traditional, Non E-Based Pedagogy

Principles of teaching have been traditionally established in methods of instruction for a while and extensively researched. According to Meyen et al (2002), pedagogy includes teaching methods related to the following

a. presentation of experiences,
b. engagement of learners,
c. reinforcement,
d. motivation,
e. organization of teaching tasks,
f. feedback,
g. evaluation, and
h. curriculum integration

In most theoretical models of pedagogy, many of these elements have been researched to determine the most significant factors with what, who, when, where and how. However, certain common themes have emerged over time including:

1. learner
2. teacher
3. learning environment
4. learning content
5. learning support systems/tools

The learner receives the information, skill and/or competence planned or desired. Roles can change or be simultaneous between the teacher and student. All of these combine to eventuate the movement of information through embedded sources to another needing the information. In addition, they have combined to transfer skills and competence and increase the dissemination of activity into distances far removed from the place of transmitted activity, transmission and transformation. In the process, transformation occurs in all five thematic areas. It is important to recognize that changes in any one will generate response, modifications and changes in all the others.

Effectiveness in Pedagogy

Measuring effectiveness in pedagogy therefore depends on outcome objective. In other words, what is the end product desired or planned? Thus evaluating competence requires tools and approaches that may not necessarily be the same as those required for evaluating skills or knowledge. However, because many established fields and emerging ones are now more product driven, the outcome will depend on what product is planned or desired. For example, when an institution trains teachers, is the institution's effectiveness evaluated on the basis of the following?

i. number of teachers produced,
ii. practices and approaches to teaching and producing the teachers and evaluating them?
iii. failure, passing, college admission or attendance rates of the students produced by the teacher or the institutions in which they teach?
iv. how many students go on from the school to be classified as successful professionals
v. e.t.c.?

On the other hand, when an institution trains medical practitioners, how is the effectiveness of the institution measured?

In measuring effectiveness therefore, it is important to identify which level of effectiveness is the target, in the planning, implementation and evaluation phases. However, the impact of education must also be a measure of the success of the teacher producing institution.

Overview of E-Based Pedagogy

According to Meyen et al (2002), e-Learning is a form of pedagogy, and the effectiveness of pedagogical practices can be measured. A knowledge base of pedagogical practices has evolved over time and is currently still a work in progress. Examples include practices related to communication, assessment, instructional design and mediation. Many different pedagogical models have been proposed from content-based pedagogy to software standards to psychopedagogical issues (Alonso et al (2005)). Although the learning environment may be virtual, e-based pedagogy may also be based in real space and time and competency can be measured by examples of real outputs produced by the learner. For example in music, Lewis (2003) wrote in her pedagogical guidelines that just as students may be characterized on the basis of age, they also may be described by their level of proficiency. The continuum in general use is beginner-intermediate-advanced. The foundation for each level should be independence and control. The key in e-based pedagogy is to find the best ways to develop and measure skills, proficiency and competence. Also, Friesen (2003) raises objections to learning objects in the interests of fostering an open discussion that would bring the concepts and thinking associated with them to more fruitful relationship with the practices of learning and education. He further stated that e-Learning standards and specifications are expected to be able to support multiple forms learning and learning practices. Terms used to describe these capabilities were "pedagogical neutrality" or "pedagogically agnostic" (Conole (2002); IMS (2003a)). Thus e-Learning, must be increasingly able to support pedagogy that transfers not only knowledge, but must also transfer competence. In addition to this, due to the increasingly social environment of the e-World, e-Learning must also increasingly accommodate social learning pedagogy so that the learning and competence experiences become more complete. For these needs to be filled, such features as flexibility, collaboration, sharing, inclusiveness, authenticity, relevance and extended institutional boundaries (geographical, social, operational and financial) must increasingly dominate institutional pedagogical and administrative practices. Of these seven features, only the last has yet to begin realization in e-Learning.

Traditional/Classical and E-Learning Systems

In both systems, the themes are the same and the players have been stable. What has changed is that the traditional environment more strongly emphasizes a hierarchical structure for learning with the teacher controlling the environment, and a more limited social environmental learning. However, because classical learning also includes limited space (in distance and time) for physical contact, it also has some social learning environments. This is in contrast to the virtual environment where several learning processes may be simultaneously engaged in several private spaces that may include two or more people. Thus the "hubbub" of the communication environment can be "controlled" for more private interactions without the other learning "relationships" being aware of the exchanges in the virtual spaces. However, the virtual environment lacks the physical interactions of the real environment, thus the avenues for information transmission to all the senses is currently limited. For example, the senses of smell, taste or touch are not yet transmitted; while the emphasis has been on the two senses of hearing and sight). In order for the full range of learning experiences to be transmitted for full competence therefore, the pedagogical practices of both environments have now begun to merge in the form of Blended Learning.

Blended Learning Pedagogy

Areas of Coincidence and Implications for Future Learning

The need to begin combining e-Learning pedagogy with classical pedagogy has necessitated the development of techniques that put a person in the picture to direct the learning, skill and competence building process. Pedagogy in this area has yet to be comprehensively researched and theoretical patterns developed. However, areas of coincidence for both e-Learning and classical pedagogies include those of objectives and goals, common operational outlines and common needs. Coming from this position, especially in resource poor environments, the need to have a body in the learning space necessitates the deployment of blended learning to provide for this need. However, current accounts and reports of blended learning utilizing different approaches and pedagogies have produced varying results (McCalla 2004, Singh 2003, Kiser 2002, Bonk & Graham 2004, Alonso et al 2005, Rovai & Jordan, 2004, Rovai & Jordan, 2004, Heinze & Procter 2004, Johnson & Walker 2007, Lee, Yeh, Kung & Hsu 2007, Tracy, Vyortkina and Belgrove 2008, deFreitas & Nuemann 2008, Hwang & Arbaugh 2009). For example, Andrews and Crowther (2003) in their *Three Dimensional Pedagogy* models, described the learning environment of the 21st century as one that will require a mixture of three components: 1. Research-based Framework for Enhancing School Outcomes; 2. A five-phase implementation strategy labeled *initiating, discovering, envisioning, actioning* and *sustaining*. with four key theoretical concepts: metastrategy (Limerick et al. 1998); appreciative inquiry (Cooperrider and Whitney 1996); action learning (Argyris and Schon 1996; Kolb 1984; Zuber-Skerrit 1990) and organizational capacity building (Newmann, King and Youngs (2001)); 3. Pedagogy (personal, school wide and authoritative). Mays and DiFreitas proposed the theoretical space for learning in the future in four main areas: 1. Associationist, 2. Cognitive Constructivist, 3. Socially mediated constructivist and 4. Communities of practice. Alonso et al (2005) added psychopedagogy. In 2007, the TESEP pedagogy (Mays 2007) was outlined by five main principles: 1. Raising the level of engagement by giving learners more responsibility over their choice of learning tasks, 2. Peers learning together (building a learning community), 3. Giving the learner gradually-increasing control over the learning activities: project-based, resource-based, enquiry-based, discussion based learning, 4. Learning tasks, discussion and frequent feedback, and 5. Formative and self-assessment. In addition to these, Vrasidas wrote in 2004, quoting Mara (2002), that the vision for an "ideal online learning environment" is one that scaffold's and supports maximal intellectual development in learners. An example of future developments is the use of constraint-based conversation tools. During an online discussion, messages are usually threaded and the teacher or moderators choose the topic's heading and title. Also, with blended learning pedagogy, the need for scaffolding can become more included. This area is still a work in progress as the demands of student types, environment (social, working and technology), the needs of individual teachers, students and institutions and not the least, the market place determine new areas of pedagogy and practice yet to be discovered. The implications for all of these is that effective learning, knowledge, skills and competencies transference still hold potentials for development and modifications to reach a level of maturity that produces competent practitioners in all professions and walks of life. In all these, the changing e-Learning environment represents a challenge to address and reach harmony with. However, it is acknowledged that all learning environments require resources (including the human, technological and educational) in order to be effective. Not all geopolitical situations are resource rich. Thus pedagogy must adapt itself to different resource environments and still transmit the same knowledge, skills and competencies regardless of the resource base.

With the foregoing, it is apparent that pedagogy has been undergoing significant transitions because of the vast possibilities opened by technology. However, technology itself is being shaped by pedagogy in order to provide even more effective learning environments while keeping an eye on affordability for most people. This apparently symbiotic relationship promises to open new thought processes and products for shaping a new world.

Research, Pedagogy and LMS

LMS as an environment for learning is a natural environment for research since research is essentially a way of learning. However, there are challenge areas that can be addressed by LMS and there are those that may not be readily accessible to utility in LMS. The effectiveness of using LMS for research and for teaching research will necessarily depend on how well the adaptation process is engineered and applied in both real and virtual spaces.

Applications of LMS to Pedagogy in Research

In pedagogy, perhaps the most popular area of application in research is in using LMS to teach explorations of informational material in schools. However, more specific areas involve using LMS to teach research methodology, application and other areas of research training at higher education levels with specific focus on the production of research outputs. Another area of increasing application of LMS is dissemination of research findings. The fastest growing area of dissemination expansion today is in e-journals. A further application of LMS to research is in the area of research survey, where the e-environment can be used to interview, support activities and provide real time feedbacks for data collection. With regard to data, LMS has been used for data collection, data storage and analyses as well as dissemination while playing the now more "normative" role of providing easily accessible communication through technology.

In addition to this, research in LMS provides the base for high level training and improvement in outcome. For example, Moodle (an open source course management system) was developed using a doctoral dissertation that borrowed significantly from social theories and constructs in a participatory action research context (Dougiamas, M. & Taylor, P. 2003). Also, LMS currently supports a wide array of research approaches in the classical pedagogical tradition. However, with more interactivity, research will need to adapt to and/or adopt new or more appropriate approaches to research that may expand beyond the classical pedagogical paradigms. An example of this is in animation where current applications and approaches are still rudimentary compared to advances in, for example, video games, which increasingly simulate life. This implies that, as for example in Public Health where risk factor teaching, research and policy lag far behind commercial enterprise in changing and modifying behavior, research and pedagogy in the LMS medium still must effectively address real life environments. Thus we come to the contributions of field research to pedagogy and research within the LMS environment. According to Snow and Thomas (1994), field research can contribute to the development of theory and models. However, certain conditions will need to be met to make this effective. They include a balanced research agenda, multifaceted research approaches, innovative data gathering techniques, and an applied futuristic orientation. LMS as an applied futuristic environment does positively impact these and can even expand knowledge in this context. This was pointed out by Checkland in 1999, who indicated that the area of interaction between practice and theory have the potential to grow knowledge, especially in action research. With simulations and some adaptations of classical pedagogy, research in basic science, some aspects of medical training and research, and some research in technology and engineering have made some inroads. However, many systems still must rely on a blend of simulations and historical data for their estimations. Although field and outcome research have gained some important foothold in the use of LMS for research, field impact and outcome research in social and mental systems, are yet to gain strong inroads into the use of LMS. A further area of application for LMS is in collaborative research, where multi-field, trans-disciplinary approaches may provide the background for discovering entirely new paradigms, theories and practice models. LMS can make the process faster, through much more efficient synchronous and asynchronous communication as is currently being done using virtual workspaces, streaming technology and webcasts. This can help save resources to more effectively facilitate research and research practice.

Research Methodology and LMS

An additional area of research application for LMS is in the research of research methodologies. For example, Baskerville and Wood-Harper (1998) described the different frameworks, assumptions and goals that characterise the diverse forms of action research. They advocated for a more inclusive action research paradigm that offers basis for validating a wider range of IS research. This is partly because, due to the differences between virtual and real environments, classical pedagogical approaches to research methodology may need significant modification or entirely new paradigms and definitions for 1. What is research, 2. What are the acceptable standards of scientific research, and 3. What research methodologies are scientific. These may necessitate even deeper enquiry and perhaps fundamental modification of the definition of science and scientific inquiry. We propose that these questions can be answered in the context of viewing LMS solely as a facilitating environment for the implementation of a vast array of activities, which include research.

IMPLICATIONS FOR PEDAGOGY, AND APPLICATIONS TO THE RESOURCE-POOR ENVIRONMENT (RPE)

The Resource-Poor Environment

The quality of education depends on educational and technological resources (including trained and prepared personnel) available for instruction and learning. That the prevailing environment is poor or rich in resources depends not only on socio-economic conditions, but also on the attitudes for implementing and utilizing available resources efficiently and effectively. On one end, signs of a resource-poor environment include: lack of knowledge repositories, including libraries, archives and access to the internet or access to people with, and access to knowledge. It also includes low infrastrutural facilities and limited instructional supplies, high student-teacher ratios, unqualified or poorly prepared teachers, and lack of learning activities. Since e-Learning is a blend of learning through internet, the threshold for resource poor environment would be tools related to web technology. At the other end of the spectrum, is the resource rich environment with appropriately adequate schools, knowledge repositories, including libraries, archives and access to the internet or access to people with access knowledge, text books availability, teaching and learning tools and activities enhanced by the use of contemporary technologies (Arnold, Admiraal, Ristimaki &Uggeri 2007).

Usually, a resource poor environment may not necessarily be an excuse for the teacher or the student to withdraw or recede, but a challenge to advance and effectively utilize the prevailing limited resources. In contrast, the resource rich environment may not provide higher quality education if the resources are not effectively applied. In a resource rich environment, the learner has the advantage of access to the exploration and utilization of pedagogical and learning resources and thus discovers learning faster and more effectively. However, in a resource poor environment, effective use of moderate technologies coupled with learning activities developed with the instructor can help raise student imagination and comprehension skills.

Technology in the Resource Poor Environment

Technology and creativity in e-Learning can help compensate for and overcome levels of resource poverty. Recent advances in computer technology have made e-Learning a major component of the learning environment. Teachers and students are challenged to upgrade their skills for appropriate use of the technology to meet pedagogical and didactic needs. The virtual environment allows and encourages students to initiate their learning. The instructor/teacher's role becomes more supportive, flexible and responsive, to meet and address the student's requirements while the instructor also expands his/her repertoire of tools and competencies. The continuous quality improvement approach will eventually evolve an efficient and effective teaching and learning process between instructor and student.

Arnold et al (2007) studied the use of e-Learning for higher education teachers. Major changes in the traditional academic model of university professors (as the "the source of knowledge" and transmission through lectures and publications) are taking place through adopting new pedagogical tools suitable to the e-Learning environment and student. By learning and implementing new skills, teachers can introduce new approaches such as multimedia course design, tutoring, managing collaborative work groups, problem-based learning, product development or any emerging technologies to encompass new teaching and learning in contrast to traditional teaching methods. This high quality, effective and efficient learning process for both students and teachers can be brought about by improved teacher training (Arnold et al 2007, Ramboll 2004, Attwell et al 2003).

To make pedagogy effective, teachers can design and develop courses (FGCU 2006, Athabascau 2004, Illinois Online Network 2007) of interest and make them available on-line for communicating with the student remotely. The design must incorporate necessary skills for understanding – conceptual, cognitive, psychometric, and attitudinal, among others – knowledge, skills and competence transfer. Such measures do not require much resources for the teacher; rather, it utilizes available technologies to gain interaction with the student. The web technologies may include using videos/streaming technology, podcasts, and videoconferencing (University Library, University of Illinois at Urbana-Champaign 2008) through distance learning platforms like WebCT. Use of e-Learning is not an end by itself; imparting learning to the student also comes with the teacher using technology to foster continued teacher-student relationship (TLT Group). Using technology to advance contact, cooperation, and communication can overcome barriers between the teacher and learner. In addition, using technology to advance collaborations can help to strengthen professional relationships. This becomes even more so as the face of the learner changes and increasingly includes leaders in the field and positions of authority who seek to expand or deepen their competence in order to be provide improved services. These kinds of relationships can help foster more effective leadership as academia, with its knowledge resources, works with the leadership community through close professional relationships.

On-Line Resources

A number of resources (Teach Online 2005, Nash & Smith 2005) are available for the teacher to stay current and informed on trends, tools and new e-

Learning skills. These resources help the teacher to make the course available on-line and incorporate implementing lecture presentations – audio/video, class discussions, enlivening techniques, and assessment. Alternatively, teachers may also periodically take professional development training in web-based instruction. The training would encourage and help the teacher to promote effective pedagogical instruction that is more student centered and not instructor centered (Carlson, Tidiane & Gadio 2002). On-line resources and professional development training make teachers add other communication tools such as video, sound, graphics, interactive responses to the traditional text and verbal instruction.

The Teaching, Learning and Technology Cycle: Using Technology to fill Resource Gaps

Zhu and Kaplan (2002) proposed that teaching and learning form a circular pathway through technology. In using technology to implement pedagogy, the teacher applies technological tools to deliver the course. The student then makes use of technological tools to learn the course. The cycle revolves, repeating until the student receives the planned or expected learning. Utilizing available technological tools, the teacher can make an impact on student learning if the tools fit into the student's life style. It is not only the content that matters, but transforming the content through technological tools for didactics is also important. Bottino and Robotti (2007) studied the effectiveness of ARI@ITALES tools for enhancing the mathematical skills of fourth grade students. They found that the tools helped students to visualize difficult concepts, and proved to be effective in understanding difficult methods in arithmetic problem solving. Teachers were also satisfied with the use of technology.

An enthusiastic teacher would think of the student as a target in the process of knowledge transfer. By taking basic measures, the teacher can integrate technologies into the instruction and help increase student learning through creating a learning environment that is more accessible and economical for the student (Koszalka & Wang 2002). Using course websites, the teacher can address a wide variety of learning environments such as discussion groups, social support, and information database related to the course content. Ranasinghe and Leisher (2009) pointed out that the use of technologies gives a visual representation to higher order concepts and meet students learning style. Technological tools provide the student with a means to find a needed knowledge source and learn its contents in a way suitable to their level of comprehension (Siemens & George 2004). Hindrances to implementing e-Learning in the resource poor environment may be ameliorated or eliminated by how available technologies are utilized to create an appropriate learning environment for the student (Maeers 2002, Maeers & Friesen 2001, Maeers 2001, Maeers 2000).

Identifying Areas of Resource Needs

To cope in the resource poor environment, it is necessary to assess the resource needs that can alleviate gaps in the learning environment. These gaps are then filled appropriately to produce a more effective teaching and learning environment for both teacher and student. Due to developments in computer and web technologies, a critical area of resource need may be access, in the form of basic hardware and software tools such as personal computer, internet connectivity, and related software for teaching, learning, skill building and competency development (elearnspace, everything learning 2002). Educational institutions and organizations must incline themselves to create the desired environment with a view to focus on providing quality education. Teachers, with organizational support, can explore the environment and provide necessary guidance and opportunities to ensure learners are well prepared for their career and that they can succeed.

Transforming the Resource Poor into a Resource Rich Environment

Relevance:

Education has in the last two decades, become increasingly contextual and product oriented. This means that learning and the learning environment must adapt to provide knowledge, skills and competence for the needs identified or expressed in a specific environment. For example, in an area where food production is needed, an e-Learning environment that provides relevant and appropriate knowledge, skills and competence will be better than one that is only generic and does not provide the specific wherewithal for the learner to utilize in addressing the needs in their environment. Thus the LMS must adapt or be adaptable, especially in resource poor environments for which they were not initially conceived or designed, to provide the environment for appropriate and relevant learning. The same goes for the teacher/instructor, who must ideally develop the appropriate relevance for the self and the course in order to be effective. Education and knowledge management are thus currently targets of a new internet revolution. To exploit e-Learning potentials therefore, the teacher needs to first orient themselves to the specific needs of the learner's need environment. The instructor must then help the learner meet their specific requirements for the use of web technology. Thus for example, e-Learning technologies form a wide range of techniques that encompass the learning needs of a high school student in a village, struggling with math skills, or a management graduate doing distance learning education in a sales/administrative setting.

Accessibility and Pedagogy

Information technology has made the world become smaller, and globalization has significantly impacted education. (Peterson, Robert & Jaffray 2000). The resource needs of teaching and learning revolve around how much web or other technology access can be acquired within the limits of financial investment. Thus a resource poor environment can be transformed into a rich one through internet access because the internet is inherently high network technology (a continuous variable with no apparent set boundaries). In e-Learning the instructor uses the internet to design a course and make it available (Masie 2009, Malisuwan, Colonel, Settapong Sivaraks & Jesada 2008) for learning by as many students as can have access to it even in remote locations. Thus, a fundamental resource need is access to the internet and its associated accessories. Thus with recent advances in computer and networking technology, the internet can, with appropriate pedagogy, transform a resource poor environment through a one-or-two-step transition or a giant leap to exploring almost limitless resources and potential tools for e-Learning. In addition, blended learning approaches can help to smoothen or facilitate the learning process, reduce training time, increase understanding, improve skills and strengthen competence.

Cost

Initially, it would appear that e-Learning involves large expenditure, however with the appropriate relevance and pedagogy, return-on-investment (roi) is exponential with regard to reach, quality education and learning. Effective wireless communication technologies open access for, and to rural and remote areas (Masie & Elliott 2009, Malisuwan, Colonel, Settapong, Sivaraks & Jesada 2008). The basic resources may be classified as infrastructure, connectivity, IT facilities, training, software, and compatibility or ubiquity of technologies for wide ranging learning tools and contexts.

Affordability, Adaptability and Sustainability

With recent improvements in computer memory and other functions technology, prices have been falling for almost all forms of hardware, especially personal electronic hardware. Thus the cost of hardware increasingly takes only a shrinking fraction of the individual's technology budget. What have been less accessible are the specialized learning environments of software systems with gated networking for multiple, synchronous and asynchronous access and functions, including monitoring, evaluation, management and financial control. These have tended to cater to large systems and have been accessible only to government agencies or relatively large private establishments, requiring numerous highly specialized components that may be prohibitive or too complex for resource poor environments. The costs of these do limit access to them and make them available only to the relatively few institutions that can afford these features which include, aside from financial requirements, time, personnel outlay, overhead and sustainability challenges. In a resource poor environment therefore, these large systems become less accessible, responsive or relevant to most of the population. What may be more accessible are simple internet and wireless personal hardware that they can purchase and use without having to go into economic depression. In order to address this challenge, multi-jurisdictional, multi-field collaborations and cooperation may be necessary in addition to development of LMS that are adaptive to these specific contexts.

The Individual Learner

Thus for the individual learner, the resources needed are a lap-top/desktop personal computer (PC), software and internet connectivity for accessing the course remotely. With recent improvements in personal communication systems and added utility, even hand held systems may contribute to the development of highly mobile learning environments. The student thus has more options for selection, depending on their personal style, pace and affordability.

Educational Institutions

Educational institutions provide infrastrutural facilities such as computer laboratories, wireless internet connectivity through servers, and electronic learning software including virtual environment platforms like WebCT or Blackboard. The institution's information technology outfit organizes the infrastructure developed. Internet technology comes with a wide variety of tools that can be explored depending on their importance (relevance, applicability and utility) and cost. For example content tools are useful for delivering and accessing text, documents, videos, e-labs, simulators, etc; while communication tools like forums, e-mail, virtual classroom, etc are useful for communication, interaction or both. For greater interactivity, interactive resources like internet phone, net meeting, live meeting, videoconference media, email, chat, and discussion boards may be added (Perrin 2005, Becta 2009, Vicent et al 2006). Various media assist the instructor to deliver course contents with technological flavor consisting of html tutorials, interactive videos, and lively presentations combined with flash animations.

Policy and Technology Access

Critical to e-Learning resource needs are economic and policy issues that determine how the needs are met as well as how technology is utilized. Budget to provide resources may come from educational institutions alone, or by collaborating with community, local or governmental administration as well as the private sector for funding. Further, policies regarding acquiring efficient internet connectivity such as the availability of broad bandwidth, servers and basic energy infrastructure such as electricity in rural areas (Hare 2009), can be pivotal in providing or impeding technology access for resource poor environments. The financial and political commitment for providing infrastrutural facilities for blended/e-Learning may also be a barrier, but it can be overcome through committed collaborations between all segments of society, including – educational, community, government and private sectors. In addition to this, policy can be driven by demand such that, for example to acquire wider bands may be a function of current utilization level(s). Thus a critical level of utilization may need to be attained in order to open up the community for even greater bandwidth. This is usually attained through education that helps to increase knowledge, skills, desires and demands that drive these policy changes.

Implications of LMS Technology for Training in Resource Poor Environments, and the Use of LMS and its Technology to Address Specific Resource Needs

Use of LMS for Training

Learner management systems (LMS) have tools that can be used to monitor progress and performance of learner groups – instructors, students, employees, employers, learning materials and technology - in their training and applications. Also, LMS facilitate managing and evaluating the learning process while storing the user activity/performance for future research, planning and development. LMS are critical especially when dealing with training learners in resource poor environments where people may lack skills for using e-Learning tools. e-Learning, in the blended learning format, can help facilitate remote/distance learning and begin to provide experience for the learner. Implementing LMS adds additional load to organizational budget, but a suitable unit can be selected from the variety of available systems (Trivantis' 2007, Rully et al 2007, Bahati 2008, Facer at al 2004, Uden 2007, Lalos, Lazarinis and Kanellopoulos 2009). LMS is not used to create course content, but is software basically used to deliver course contents online for distance education. However, future capability for developing content from within LMS cannot be ruled out especially with the advent of increasingly functional Artificial Intelligence (AI). LMS are also known by other terms such as virtual learning environment, managed learning environment, course management system or learning support system. In their prime function, LMS are used to manage learning activities, track and evaluate learner progress and instructor performance. LMS contain such features as content tools, communication tools and assessment tools applied through the web or internet for online instruction and learning. When switching to e-Learning in resource poor environments, the transitional process must prepare the user - instructor/student - for the new environment, providing training in basic skills for using the tools of new technology (e-Learn space, everything learning 2002). Instructors additionally require training and skills in the use of LMS. The role of the organization's information technology (IT) department must be included right from the beginning in implementing e-Learning. The IT unit can initiate e-Learning related software installation, using the internet, networking connectivity, online learning habits, and course management. They may also work with, and train instructors in virtual learning platforms such as WebCT or Blackboard, using software and communication tools – word processor, spread sheet, power point presentation, email and chat etc (Pervenanze 2003, Becta 2009). Instructors can also be provided training in how to use LMS. The scope of functions desired in LMS depends on the number of learning activities versus cost of the managing system. Some of the basic learning activities are resources, forums, quizzes, assignments, glossaries, surveys, and email; they may also include such advanced features as live chats and videoconferences (Andreatos 2007).

Monitoring Training Effectiveness

LMS can be used to monitor and evaluate learning effectiveness based on quality of the online learning environment. Index parameters may be designed to reflect users' performance, training needs, and adequacy of infrastructural facilities. LMS may include management functions for monitoring and evaluating learning through feedback from issues such as learning relevance, pedagogical versus content delivery, level of learner interactiveness, adequacy of instructor support, skills deficiencies, how to provide good training, and adequacy of resources for effective usage of technologies.

Upgrading LMS

In e-Learning, the internet is the medium for distance education, and LMS are an integral part of the delivery mechanisms. An upgrade or a new LMS not only demands budgetary considerations for institutions buying the product, but also requires an overall training for users during the transitional period (Petherbridge & Chapman 2007). In a resource poor environment, it is a difficult for the institutions to make decisions for upgrading of LMS, while they are in the process of providing basic technological resources for e-Learning. In view of the growth in new technologies, new and advanced LMS products become available (within short periods, especially just as the one installed begins to "take") making it difficult for resource poor environments to keep pace with costs, installation, training and often systems reallignment. However, the institutions can come-up with an economical campus edition product with reasonably good features. On the upper side, quality education can be imparted by the use of LMS which can promote student learning and management sufficiently and efficiently and promote student enrollment indirectly for pursuing higher education using a "pipeline" model to generate appropriate manpower in the resource poor environment.

LMS Benefits for the Resource Poor Environment

The benefits of LMS are multifarious – managing and delivering e-Learning, management of training administration, tracking training information, monitoring performance efficiency and efficacy, managing effective learning programs, generating ideas and engaging in research and development, etc. Institutions have greater load of responsibility for using LMS in providing training and technical support to the users. They also have obligations in supporting LMS maintenance staff, and upgrading depending on the demand of technological challenges encountered initially, in the short and long term.

Alternative Resources

Alternatively in resource poor environments, suitable open source LMS can be developed (Ganjalizadeh 2006) that have basic features – course content, forums, journals, quizzes, surveys, assignments, chats, workshops, email and the like, that are available in proprietary softwares. Two of the currently popular open source LMS are Moodle and Sakai (Moodle 2009, Sakai 2009). Educational institutions with budget constraints can utilize the open source LMS and cut costs on purchasing commercial softwares, and at the same time give e-Learning to the students in resource poor environments.

Open source LMS may provide cost savings, but there are many technicalities to take into account in the decision to implement (COL LMS 2003, Beer & Jones 2008, IEEE Software 2007, Aberdour 2007b, Kineo open source 2008, Bersin Associates 2009). Some of the technicalities include: costs for licensing and custom developments, level of expertise required to operate, speed, reliability, compatibility, content and communication tools, documentation, and training etc. If needs and expectations for use are minimal – smaller size organization, limited administration and tracking tools, - open source LMS may be the right choice (Boehle 2007, Aberdour 2007b). On the negative side, how long the open source software is usable based on the technical support and services available by the provider, is an important consideration. This, among other factors, ultimately determines sustainability of technology engagement. However, the availability of the source code, makes open source suitable to many resource poor environments if the open source LMSs are correspondingly customized (Kalinga et al 2007).

The Use of Blended Learning Approaches to Address Specific Resource Needs

In e-Learning, the terms blended learning and hybrid courses are synonymously used to refer to a combination or integration of face-to-face class room instruction with online instruction (Graham 2005). Blended learning incorporates the best features of the two learning approaches. Regardless of whether the environment is resource rich or resource poor, the blended learning helps to bridge gaps in learning. Learners will have face-to-face instruction, a wealth of learning activities available online for independent learning, and reduce drawbacks in resources for class instruction and time.

In resource poor environments, it is necessary to assess the level of blending required based on the resource needs available for class room and online instruction. If the quality of instructors, buildings, or space is a limitation, then online instruction makes a greater contribution and has greater weight; but a balance is more critical to the learner's needs. Blending is an ongoing process and evolves with time, until effective delivery of instruction is attained for both instructor and learner. The reduction of class room time will also help retain students who are limited by other constraints such as transportation, family responsibilities, occupation, and/or being otherwise engaged. Blended learning allows students to make up for class hours with online instruction available for them to study at their own pace and style.

Blended learning also provides more options for the teacher to manage and organize course curriculum. Online instruction can be used to deliver a major portion of course contents, while class room instruction can be utilized for discussing difficult aspects of learning or for problem solving (Doo & Seung 2008). The blended learning environment puts greater responsibility on the instructor to design the course to address the needs of the learner based on the best pedagogy applicable to the student. LMS may help to monitor and track student performance, and throw light on blended instruction effectiveness. Initially, instructors begin with small blending steps in order to initiate adoption of e-Learning along with classroom instruction. The literature suggests several ways of creating blending environments (Driscoll 2002, Frattini 2006, Garisson & Kanuka 2004, Koohang 2009). Instructors may consider their peer experiences in determining their implementation approaches. Examples include introducing assignments or quizzes, emailing and messaging, delivering web resources for additional learning materials, or delivering learning activities. By monitoring the performance, and with the availability of better internet technology resources, the instructor can add multimedia tools and communications tools and allow a more dynamic blending mix.

The blending environment is continually changing, affected by many factors including resources, demand, technology, finance, and policies. However it does have tremendous impact on the quality of education (Fong et al 2005, Beniest et al 2008, Dennis et al 2006, Ally 2004, Andreatos 2007). The drawbacks and advantages of each of the component must be weighed for a viable and efficient system with a view to address the needs of learners in resource poor environments.

Applications of LMS to Professional Training

Professional training requires building knowledge, skills and competence in individuals, a group or team. LMS can be applied to train teams and at the same time emphasize individual tasks and goals for team members. Team building training makes the team a stronger unit than each of the individual members taken separately. The high end of LMS training is to impart teamwork skills training to individuals. In an educational institutional environment, the team can, for example, be school officials, teachers, staff, and students. LMS training can help managers and staff develops better understanding and communication among members, while they reach their learning goals and objectives. Trainees in the e-Learning environment can be students, teachers, staff, school or organizational administrators, IT staff, managers, or parents.

The primary goal of using LMS is to deliver course material and tests, and evaluate the students' learning performance. LMS provides the tools for organizing instructional material, and e-Learning makes available, technology to teach or receive instructional material locally or remotely. Online capabilities of LMS, make learning material accessible remotely at the learner's place, time, style and pace. LMS can also be used as a tool for offering instructional material for training team members, while evaluating individual and team performance.

In an educational environment, LMS is used for course instruction, communication, testing, evaluation, class management and more. In using LMS for training, the course material is replaced by training material and the purpose is similar. Whatever gains the LMS has in educational environment the same can be achieved for training environment: ability to manage larger numbers of participants, track training progress, communicate between the trainer and trainee, access the instructional material, learning activities and more. Similar to delivering course materials, LMS is also a tool for delivering training courses or training material to employees so that they may attain higher performance in the workplace.

With recent, accelerating advances in computer and networking technology, it is essential that teachers/instructors/trainers obtain LMS training on a regular basis to help them acquire required skills to perform efficiently, meet the demands institutional goals, and upgrade their skills and competence (Bhattacharya 2006). LMS are also used to deliver and manage training to health care organizations and providers in clinical care and public health (Walter 2006). Training sessions can be designed to create group learning environments in order to impart a sense of community in members. For this purpose, LMS course design is ideal for establishing a collaborative environment through its synchronous and asynchronous multiple activity tools such as chat boards, chat rooms group discussions, instant messaging, blogs, videoconferences, wikis, etc. LMS provide necessary media for learners to actively engage in the learning process contributing individual skills to the group. LMS training gives learners skills required to achieve the expected quality of competence.

Applications of LMS to Research in Resource Poor Environments

Currently, especially in resource rich and pedagogical environments, LMS increasingly plays pivotal roles in research, assessment, learning and management. This necessitates exploring and outlining areas of LMS relevance for pedagogy and research in resource poor environments

LMS can play a significant role in transforming resource poor to resource rich environments for research. With the advent of the internet, development of learning structures, and improvements in the packaging process, it is possible to have very low cost access to populations and materials for research. Another area that is still in infancy with regard to exploration for research is the application of current "entertainment" approaches, with video games and such interactive media forming a strong base for data collection based on the "play" system interactions with real life humans or other materials to research. The space for innovation and development in this area is exponential since the potential for new theories, methodologies and paradigms show so much promise. Areas of research that may currently be most adaptable to this environment include health, humanities, engineering and management especially because they readily accommodate "field" level research. However, processes for data collection currently may need extensive re-thinking, redesign, and reapplication. Currently, applications have been limited to some very specific and highly circumscribed areas.

In a resource poor environment, mobile learning allows learners acquire easier access to learning materials offline. The limitations of bandwidth and slow connecting speeds are obstacles to the delivery of e-Learning. For example, SyberWorks Mobile Learning Module allows the learners to download their courseware, and work offline, and then connect to upload their results (http://www.syberworks.com/product_mobile.htm). Mobile learning facilitates online training features for learners in remote places where web infrastructure is lacking.

SyberWorks Mobile Learning allows users to take their tests at their own pace. Mobile Learning gives learners flexibility because they can do their coursework on the road, at home, in their office, or on a laptop at their child's soccer game with all the features available in the web-based SyberWorks Training Center Learning Management System/Learning Content Management System.

http://www.syberworks.com/product_mobile.htm

CONCLUSION

Trends in learner management systems and learning environments, and their impact on student learning and preparation have been presented. A variety of definitions of LMS are presented for clarification, and the tools and areas of applications are discussed. A model structure for LMS is provided with regard to effectiveness in pedagogy. Also, a description of the various applications of LMS to research in pedagogical contexts has been made with emphasis on future potentials for application, in resource rich and resource poor environments.

The implications of e-learning pedagogy in LMS are described and discussed with regard to resource poor environments. The descriptions include an exploration of the effects of technology on the ease and efficacy of training in resource poor environments; with technology filling resource gaps that would otherwise remain obstacles and challenges to the availability of knowledge and knowledge management. The ability of technology to transform resource poor to resource rich environments was discussed within the ambit of relevance, accessibility and pedagogy, cost affordability, adaptability, sustainability, the individual learner, educational institutions and their roles as well as policy and technology access. The implications of LMS for training were outlined with regard to use, monitoring of training effectiveness, upgrading, benefits and alternative resources. Blended learning approaches to addressing specific resource needs in resource poor environments was also briefly discussed along with applications of LMS to professional training. The overall goal of LMS was to deliver course materials and health.

REFERENCES

Aberdour M. (2007). Achieving Quality in Open Source Software. *IEEE Software, 24* (1, Jan./Feb.), 58-64.

Aberdour, M. (2007b). *Epic; Open Source Learning Management Systems Emerging open source LMS markets Recommended LMS for each market Getting off on the right foot.* Retrieved from http://content.tibs.at/pix_db/documents/whitepaper_os_lms.pdf

Adobe Systems Incorporated. (2008). *Adobe solutions for Learning Management Systems* (p. 95010771). USA: LMS.

Alavi, M., & Leidner, D. E. (2001). Review: Knowledge Management and Knowledge Management Systems: Conceptual Foundations and Research Issues. *Management Information Systems Quarterly, 25*(1), 107–136. doi:10.2307/3250961

Ally, M. (2004). Foundations of Educational Theory for Online Learning. In Anderson, T., & Elloumi, F. (Eds.), *Theory and Practice of Online Learning* (pp. 3–31). Alberta, Canada: Creative Commons.

Alonso, F., López, G., Manrique, D., & Viñes, J. M. (2005). An instructional model for web-based e-learning education with a blended learning process approach. *British Journal of Educational Technology, 36*(2), 217–235. doi:10.1111/j.1467-8535.2005.00454.x

Andreatos, A. (2007). Virtual Communities and their Importance for Informal Learning. *International Journal of Computers, Communications & Control, 2*(1), 39–47.

Andrews, D., & Crowther, F. (2003). *3-dimensional pedagogy-the image of 21st century teacher professionalism.* In Crowther, F. (ed.), *Teachers as leaders in a knowledge society. College Year Book/Deakin ACT 2003*, (pp. 95-111). Deakin West, Australia: Australian College of Educators. Retrieved from http://eprints.usq.edu.au/3341/

Argyris, C., & Schon, D. (1996). *Organisational learning II: Theory, method and practice.* Reading, MA: Addison-Wesley Publishing.

Arnold, D., Admiraal, W., Ristimaki, E., & Uggeri, M. (2007, November 19th). Developing Effective Learning Materials for a Resource-Poor Environment: eLene-TT: e-learning network for teacher training teachers are lifelong learners too. Retrieved from http://blog.olenepal.org/index.php/archives/95

Athabascau. (2004). Retrieved from http://www.athabascau.ca/frontpage/articles/online_15Apr04.ht

Attwell, G., Dirckinck-Holmfeld, L., Fabian, P., Karpati, A., & Littig, P. (2003). *E-learning in Europe - Results and Recommendations, Thematic Monitoring under the Leonardo da Vinci Programme*, (pp. 32). Retrieved from http://www3.socleoyouth.be/static/Bots/docbots/LEONARDO/impuls_10.pdf

Avgeriou, P., Papasalouros, A., Retalis, S., & Skordalakis, M. (2003). Towards a Pattern Language for Learning Management Systems. *Journal of Educational Technology & Society, 6*(2), 11–24.

Bahati. (2008). *IT infrastructure and eLearning Opportunities.* Retrieved from ESWSTANFORD http://Www.Stanford.Edu/Group/Esw/Wiki/Bahati_It_Infrastructure_And_Elearning_Opportunities

Baskerville, R., Wood-Harper, A. T. (1998, June 1). Diversity in information systems action research methods. *European Journal of Information Systems, 7*(2), 90-107(18).

Becta leading next generation learning. (2009). *Harnessing Technology schools survey 2008.* Retrieved from http://partners.becta.org.uk/index.php?section=rh&&catcode=&rid=15952

Beer, C., & Jones, D. (2008). Learning networks: harnessing the power of online communities for discipline and lifelong learning. Lifelong Learning: reflecting on successes and framing futures. In *Keynote and refereed papers from the 5th International Lifelong Learning Conference*. Rockhampton, Australia: Central Queensland University Press.

Beniest, J., Coe, R., Poole, J., Ochieng, H., Vandenbosch, T., Clark, C. & Janssens-Bevernage, A. (2008). *Lessons Learned from a Blended Learning*.

Bersin Associates. (2009). *Learning Management Systems: Facts, Practical Analysis, Trends, and Vendor Profiles; The industry's most comprehensive review and buyer's guide of learning management systems, designed for corporate buyers, vendors, and consultants*. Retrieved from http://store.bersinassociates.com/lms.html

Bhattacharya, I. (2006). *DOEACC Society Premier Institution for Quality Education and Training in the areas of Information, Electronics & Communication Technology (IECT)*, Aug 24, Government of India. Retrieved from http://www.digitallearning.in/dlindia/presentation/day24/Indrajeet.pdf

Boehle, S. (2007). Is Open Source Right for You? *ManageSmarter, August 01*. Retrieved from http://www.trainingmag.com/msg/content_display/publications/e3i5adce9be1b1efb206c-4d540a4194c9d3

Bonk, C. J., & Graham, C. R. (Eds.). (2004). *Handbook of blended learning: Global Perspectives, local designs*. San Francisco, CA: Pfeiffer Publishing.

Bottino, R. M., & Robotti, E. (2007). Transforming classroom teaching & learning through technology: Analysis of a case study. *Journal of Educational Technology & Society*, *10*(4), 174–186.

Carlson, S., & Tidiane, C. Gadio. (2002). Teacher Professional Development in the Use of Technology. *aed.org: Technologies for Education*. Available: http://www.aed.org/publications/TechnologiesForEducation/TechEdChapters/08.pdf

Checkland, P. (1999). *Soft Systems Methodology: a 30-year retrospective*. Chichester, UK: J. Wiley.
Col, L.M.S. (2003). *Open Source; Commonwealth of Learning*. Retrieved from http://www.col.org/SiteCollectionDocuments/03LMSOpenSource.pdf

Conole, G. (2002). Systematising learning and research information. *Journal of Interactive Media in Education*, (7). Retrieved 08/06/2009 from http://www-jime.open.ac.uk/2002/7

Cooperrider, D. L., & Whitney, D. (1996). *Appreciative inquiry consultation workbook*. Taos, NM: Taos Institute.

de Freitas, S., Neumann, T. (2009, February). The use of 'exploratory learning' for supporting immersive learning in virtual environments. *Computers & Education, V 52* (2), 343-352. Retrieved 08-14-09 from http://www.sciencedirect.com/science?_ob=ArticleURL&_udi=B6VCJ-4TVY5BD&_user=10&_rdoc=1&_fmt=&_orig=search&_sort=d&_docanchor=&view=c&_searchStrId=980888894&_rerunOrigin=scholar.google&_acct=C000050221&_version=1&_urlVersion=0&_userid=10&md5=6fd6acded17944000361237dc924d9e1_noRerunResults=1

Dennis, A., Bichelmeyer, B., Henry, D., Cakir, H., Korkmaz, A., Watson, C., & Bunnage, J. (2006). The CISCO Networking Academy: A Model for the Study of Student Success in a Blended Learning Environment. In Bonk, C. J., & Graham, C. R. (Eds.), *The Handbook of Blended Learning: Global Perspectives, Local Designs* (pp. 120–135). San Francisco: Pfeiffer.

Derntl, M., & Motschnig-Pitrik, R. (2005). The role of structure, patterns, and people in blended learning. *The Internet and Higher Education*, *8*(2), 111–130. doi:10.1016/j.iheduc.2005.03.002

Doo, H. L., & Seung, W. Y. (2008). Team learning and collaboration between online and blended learner groups. *Performance Improvement Quarterly*, *21*(3), 59–72. doi:10.1002/piq.20031

Dougiamas, M., & Taylor, P. (2003). Moodle: Using Learning Communities to Create an Open Source Course Management System. In D. Lassner & C. McNaught (Eds.), *Proceedings of World Conference on Educational Multimedia, Hypermedia and Telecommunications 2003,* (pp. 171-178). Chesapeake, VA: AACE. Retrieved from http://www.editlib.org/p/13739

Driscoll, M. (2002). Blended Learning. *E-learning*, *3*(3), 26–29.

elearnspace, everything learning. (2002). *Preparing Students for Elearning.* Retrieved fromhttp://www.elearnspace.org/Articles/Preparingstudents.htm

Facer, K., Joiner, R., Stanton, D., Reid, J., Hull, R., & Kirk, D. (2004). Savannah: mobile gaming and learning? *Journal of Computer Assisted Learning*, *20*, 399–409. doi:10.1111/j.1365-2729.2004.00105.x

FGCU. (2006). Retrieved from http://www.fgcu.edu/onlinedesign/designDev.html

Fong, S. F., Ng, W. K., Ong, S. L., Hanafi, A., & Rozhan, I. (2005). Research in E-Learning in a Hybrid Environment - A Case for Blended Instruction. *Malaysian Online Journal of Instructional Technology*, *2*(2), 124–136.

Frattini, R. (2006). IMARK: A Partnership for Training. *INASP Newsletter*, *33*, 3–4.

Ganjalizadeh S. (2006). Overview of open source learning. *Management Systems, Educause Evolving Technologies committee*, 2006.

Garisson, D. R., & Kanuka, H. (2004). Blended Learning: Uncovering its Transformative Potential in Higher Education. *The Internet and Higher Education*, *7*(2), 95–105. doi:10.1016/j.iheduc.2004.02.001

Graham, C. R. (2005). Blended Learning Systems: Definition, Current Trends, and Future Directions. *Handbook of blended learning: Global Perspectives, local designs.* San Francisco, CA: Pfeiffer Publishing.Retrieved from http://media.wiley.com/product_data/excerpt/86/07879775/0787977586.pdf

Group, T. L. T. (n.d.). *Seven Principles.* Retrieved from http://www.tltgroup.org/Seven/Library_TOC.htm

Hare, H. (2009). *E-learning experts in Tanzania call for cheaper bandwidth: iicd.* Retrieved from http://www.iicd.org/articles/IICDnews.import2302/

Heinze, A., & Procter, C. T. (2004). *Reflections on the use of blended learning, in*: *Education in a Changing Environment,* September 13-14, 2004. Retrieved from http://www.ece.salford.ac.uk/proceedings/papers/ah

Hewett, E. C. (1884). *A Treatise on Pedagogy for Young Teachers.* New York: Van Antwerp, Bragg & Co.; American Book Company. Digitized by Google and Retrieved 7/23/09 from Google Books at http://books.google.com/books?id=ERhKAAAAIAAJ&dq=pedagogy&printsec=frontcover&source=bl&ots=XaSQiCGsrY&sig=3jLq4dY082zzzO6ubumQWy2ebLQ&hl=en&ei=RR9qSu-jGMawtge5i-C7Cw&sa=X&oi=book_result&ct=result&resnum=1

http://www.educause.edu/EDUCAUSE+Quarterly/EDUCAUSEQuarterlyMagazineVolum/OpenSourceSoftwareinEducation/162873

Hwang, A., & Arbaugh, J. B. (2009). Seeking feedback in blended learning: competitive versus cooperative student attitudes and their links to learning outcome. *Journal of Computer Assisted Learning, 25*(3), 280 – 293. Retrieved 08-14-09 from http://www3.interscience.wiley.com/journal/122294318/abstract?CRETRY=1&SRETRY=0

IEEE Software. (2007). Achieving Quality in Open Source Software. *Aberdour*, (Jan/Feb). *Illinois Online Network.* (2007). Retrieved from http://www.ion.uillinois.edu/resources/tutorials/id/index.asp

IMS. (2003a). *IMS Learning Design Information Model: Version 1.0 Final Specification.* Retrieved from http://www.imsproject.org/learningdesign/ldv1p0/imsld_infov1p0.html

Johnson, E. M., & Walker, R. (2007). The Promise and Practice of E-Learning within Complex Tertiary Environments. In *Seventh IEEE International Conference on Advanced Learning Technologies*, (ICALT 2007), (pp: 753-757). Retrieved from http://ieeexplore.ieee.org/xpl/freeabs_all.jsp?arnumber=4281149

Kalinga, E. A., & Burchard, R. B., Bagile, Trojer, L. (2007). Strategies for Developing e-LMS for Tanzania Secondary Schools. *International Journal of Social Sciences, 2*(3), 145–149.

Kineo open source. (2008). *Open source learning management systems: a primer.* Retrieved from http://www.kineoopensource.com/index.php/free-resources/insights/Open-source-learning-management-systems.html

Kiser, K. (2002). Is Blended Best? [Electronic Version]. *E-learning Magazine.* Retrieved from http://www.elearningmag.com/elearning/article/article Detail.jsp?id=21259

Kolb, D. (1984). *Experiential Learning: Experience as the source of learning and development.* Englewood Cliffs, NJ: Prentice-Hall.

Koohang, A. (2009). A learner-centred model for blended learning design. *International Journal of Innovation and Learning, 6*, 76–91. doi:10.1504/IJIL.2009.021685

Koszalka, T. A., & Wang, X. (2002). Integrating technology into learning: A summary view of promises and problems. *Journal of Educational Technology & Society, 5*(1).

Lakhan, S. E., & Jhunjhunwala, K. (2008). *EDUCAUSE Quarterly, 31(2, April–June).* Retrieved from.

Lalos, P., Lazarinis, F., & Kanellopoulos, D. (2009). E-snakes and ladders: a hypermedia educational environment for portable devices. *Int. J. Mobile Learning and Organisation, 3*(2), 107–127. doi:10.1504/IJMLO.2009.024421

Lee, C., Yeh, D., Kung, R. J., & Hsu, C. (2007). The influences of learning portfolios and attitudes on learning effects in blended e-learning for mathematics. *Journal of Educational Computing Research, 37*(4), 331. doi:10.2190/EC.37.4.a

Lewis, M. B. (2003). *Pedagogical Guidelines.* Retrieved from http://www.marthabeth.com/pedagogical_guidelines.html

Limerick, D., Cunnington, B., & Crowther, F. (1998). *Managing the new organisation: Collaboration and sustainability in the post-corporate world* (2nd ed.). Sydney, Australia: Business and Professional Publishing.

Maeers, M. (2000). *Using Technology in Teaching: Challenges and Opportunities for Higher Education.* A presentation made at Teaching Development Days and Faculty Orientation, Teaching Development Centre, University of Regina, SK, September, 2000.

Maeers, M. (2001). Integrating Technology into Mathematics teaching and Learning. In Rogerson, A. (Ed.), *The Mathematics Education into the 21st Century Project Proceedings* (pp. 152–155). Palm Cove, Queensland, Australia.

Maeers, M. (2002). *Integration of the Internet (and Other Resources) into Mathematics*. A presentation made at the National Council of Teachers of Mathematics Regional Conference, October 2002, Regina, SK.

Maeers, M., & Friesen, D. (2001). *What Difference Can Networked Classrooms Make?* A presentation made to the Technology Summit on Education 2001, SIAST Campus, Regina, November 21, 2001.

Malisuwan, S., & Sivaraks, J. (2008). *eLearning through Wireless Communication for Rural and Remote Areas in Thailand.* Retrieved from http://www.elearningap.com/eLAP2008/Online/35_fullpaper_Settapong%20Malisuwan_eLearning%20through%20Wireles%85.pdf

Marra, R. M. (2002). The ideal online learning environment for supporting epistemic development: Putting the puzzle together. *Quarterly Review of Distance Education*, *3*(1), 15–31.

Masie, E. (2009). *The Masie Center and learning consortium.* Retrieved from http://www.masie.com/

Mayes, J. T., & De Freita, S. (2004) Review of e-learning theories, frameworks and models. *Report for JISC.* Retrieved from http://www.jisc.ac.uk/uploaded_documents/Stage%202%20Learning%20Models% 20(Version%201).pdf

Mayes, T. (2007). TESEP: *The Pedagogical Principles*. Transform website: www.napier.ac.uk/transform. Retrieved 07/23/09 from http://www2.napier.ac.uk/transform/TESEP_Pedagogical_Principles.pdf

McCalla, G. (2004). The Ecological Approach to the Design of E-Learning Environments: Purpose-based Capture and Use of Information About Learners. *Journal of Interactive Media in Education*, *2004*(7).

Meyen, E. L., Aust, R., Gauch, J. M., Hinton, H. S., & Isaacson, R. E. (2002). e-Learning: A programmatic research construct for the future. *Journal of Special Education Technology*. Retrieved August 4, 2009, from http://citeseerx.ist.psu.edu/viewdoc/download?doi=10.1.1.99.6062&rep=rep1&type=pdf

Moodle. (2009). *an Open Source Course Management System (CMS)*. Retrieved from http://moodle.org/

Nash, Smith and Susan. (2005). Learning objects, learning repositories, and learning theory: preliminary best practices for online courses. *Interdisciplinary Journal of Knowledge and Learning Objects, 1*. Retrieved from http://66.102.1.104/scholar?num=50&hl=en&lr=&newwindow=1&client=firefox-a&q=cache:yAPq2jHovxwJ:ijklo.org/Volume1/v1p217-228Nash.pdf+

Newmann, F. (1996). Authentic achievement: Restructuring schools for intellectual quality. In Newmann, F., King, B., & Youngs, P. (Eds.), *Professional development to build organizational capacity in low achieving schools: Promising strategies and future challenges*. Madison, WI: Center on Organization and Restructuring of Schools, University of Wisconsin–Madison.

Perrin, D. G. (2005). *A Tutorial Paper, Creative Online Learning Environments.* Retrieved from http://www.itdl.org/Journal/Apr_05/article04.htm

Peterson, R. & Jaffray. (2000). *Piper Facts, figures, and forces behind e-learning, compiled and prepared of eLearnFrame.* Retrieved from http://www.learnframe.com/aboutelearning/elearningfacts.pdf

Petherbridge, D., & Chapman, D. (2007). Upgrading or Replacing Your Learning Management System: Implications for Student Support. *Online Journal of Distance Learning Administration, 10*(1, Spring). Retrieved from http://www.westga.edu/~distance/ojdla/spring101/petherbridge101.htm

Ramboll, P. L. S. (2004). Studies in the context of the e-learning initiative: Virtual Models of European Universities (Lot 1). *executive summary*, p.ii. Retrieved from http://www.elearningeuropa.info/extras/pdf/virtual_models.pdf

Ranasinghe, A. I., & Leisher, D. (2009). The Benefit of Integrating Technology into the Classroom. *International Mathematical Forum*, *4*(40), 1955–1961.

Retrieved from http://www.crlt.umich.edu/publinks/CRLT_no18.pdfAsdf

Rovai, A. P., & Jordan, H. M. (2004). Blended Learning and Sense of Community: A comparative analysis with traditional and fully online graduate courses. *International Review of Research in Open and Distance Learning*, *5*(2).

Rully, A., Untoro, A., Fujisaki, T., Kanemitsu, H., & Thu, Y. K. (2007). Wireless LAN and Power Line Communication platform for e-Learning multimedia system in underdeveloped area in Lombok Island]. In *Proceedings of the 6th WSEAS Int. Conf. on Electronics, Hardware, Wireless and Optical Communications*, Corfu Island, Greece, February 1, (pp. 6-19).

Sakai. (2009). open-source *Sakai CLE*. Retrieved from http://www.sakaiproject.org

Schiering, M. & Honigsfeld, A. (2002). Pedagogy: a matter of sharing one's experiential past for today's learning. *Academic Exchange Quarterly*, (Spring).

Siemens, G. (2004). *Connectivism: A Learning Theory for the Digital Age*. [updated: May, 26 2009]. Retrieved from http://www.elearnspace.org/Articles/connectivism.htm

Singh, H. (2003). Building Effective Blended Learning Programs. *Educational Technology*, *43*(6), 51–54.

Smart, K. L., & Cappel, J. J. (2006). Students' Perceptions of Online Learning: A Comparative Study. *Journal of Information Technology Education*, *5*, 201–219.

Snow, C., & Thomas, J. B. (1994). Field research methods in strategic management: contributions to theory building and testing. *Journal of Management Studies*, *31*(4), 457–480. doi:10.1111/j.1467-6486.1994.tb00626.x

Ssemugabi, S., & de Villiers, R. (2007). In *Proceedings of the 2007 annual research conference of the South African institute of computer scientists and information technologists on IT research in developing countries. ACM International Conference Proceeding Series;* (Vol. 226, pp. 132 - 142), Port Elizabeth, South Africa.

Teach Online. (2005). East Lansing, MI: Michigan State University. Retrieved from http://teachvu.vu.msu.edu/public/

Tracy, H., Vyortkina, D., & Belgrove, M. (2008). Nurturing Excellence in E-learning Practice Through an Academic Programme (MA Online and Blended Learning). In *Proceedings of World Conference on Educational Multimedia, Hypermedia and Telecommunications 2008* (pp. 3549-3556). Chesapeake, VA: AACE. Retrieved from http://www.editlib.org/p/28876

Trivantis'. (2007). *CourseMill—The Affordable Learning Management System Course*. Retrieved from http://www.trivantis.com/products/coursemill.html

Tucker, J. S., McGilvray, D. H., Leibrecht, B. C., Strauss, C. B., Perrault, A., Gesselman, A. N., & Northrop Grumman Corp Columbus, G. A. (2009). Training Digital Skills In *Distributed Classroom Environments: A Blended Learning Approach. Storming Media: Pentagon Reports*. Retrieved 08-14-09 from http://www.stormingmedia.us/13/1375/A137594.html

Uden, L. (2007). Activity theory for designing mobile learning'. *Int. J. Mobile Learning and Organisation*, *1*, 81–102. doi:10.1504/IJMLO.2007.011190

University Library, University of Illinois at Urbana-Champaign. (2008). *Instructional strategies and pedagogy.* Illinois Online Network. Retrieved from http://www.library.illinois.edu/diglit/faculty/teaching/pedagogy.html

Uschi, F. (2005). E-learning pedagogy in the third millennium: the need for combining social and cognitive constructivist approaches. *ReCALL*, *17*(1), 85–100. doi:.doi:10.1017/S0958344005000716

Vicent, L., Avila, X., Riera, J., Badia, D., Anguera, J., & Montero, J. A. (2006). Appropriateness of e-learning resources for the development of transversal skills in the new European Higher Education Area. *Frontiers in Education Conference, 36th Annual*, (pp. 27-31). doi: 10.1109/FIE.2006.322671

Vrasidas, C. (2004). Issues of Pedagogy and Design in e-learning Systems. *Symposium on Applied Computing: Proceedings of the 2004 ACM symposium on Applied computing* Nicosia, Cyprus. Session: Engineering e-learning systems (ELS). (pp. 911– 915).

Vrasidas, C., & McIsaac, M. S. (1999). *Principles of Pedagogy and Evaluation for Web-Based Learning.* In *ICEM*, Slovenia. Retrieved 07-23-09 from http://seamonkey.ed.asu.edu/~mcisaac/ICEM99/pedagogymss.html

Walter, J. (2006). LMS in health care, online education. *Latitude consulting group*. Retrieved from http://www.latitudecg.com/Portals/0/pdf/Articles/LMS%20in%20Healthcare.pdf

Wikipedia, the free encyclopedia. (2008). Learning management system. Retrieved July 22, 2009, from http://en.wikipedia.org/wiki/Learning_management_system

Zhu, E., & Kaplan, M. (2002). An introduction to teaching online. In Coryell, P. (Ed.), *Technology and teaching; McKeachie's Teaching Tips: Strategies, Research and Theory for College and University.*

Zuber-Skerrit, O. (1990). *Action learning for change and development.* Aldershot, UK: Gower-Avebury.

KEY TERMS AND DEFINITIONS

Learner Management Systems: Electronic and other environments that include technology, psychosocial, behavioral and ecological dimensions for knowledge, skill and competence transference

E-Learning: The use of distant learning technologies for imparting the power of knowledge, skills and competence.

E-Learning Systems and Tools: Technological tools used in e-learning systems

Resource Poor Environments: Learning environments that are poor in learning tools and their supporting infrastructures

Affordability, Adaptability and Sustainability: Limitations to meeting, financial, time, personnel outlay, and overhead requirements, of large learning systems that make them less accessible, adaptable and sustainable.

Blended Learning: The combination of e-Learning pedagogy with classical pedagogy

Professional Training: Building knowledge, skills and competence in individuals, a group or team

Mobile Learning: Alternative processes for learners to acquire easier access to learning materials offline

Compilation of References

A QTI White Paper from IMS. (2000). IMS Global Learning Consortium, Inc. Retrieved July 4, 2009, from http://www.imsglobal.org/question/whitepaper.pdf

Aberdour M. (2007). Achieving Quality in Open Source Software. *IEEE Software, 24* (1, Jan./Feb.), 58-64.

Aberdour, M. (2007b). *Epic; Open Source Learning Management Systems Emerging open source LMS markets Recommended LMS for each market Getting off on the right foot.* Retrieved from http://content.tibs.at/pix_db/documents/whitepaper_os_lms.pdf

Accessibility, I. M. S. (n.d). *Specification.* Retrieved July 22, 2009, from http://www.imsglobal.org/accessibility/index.html

Acton, T., Golden, W., Gudea, S. & Scott, M. (2004). *Usability and Acceptance in Small-Screen Information Systems*, CollECTeR (Europe), University of Surrey, Guildford, UK, 25 April.

ADEC. (2003). *ADEC Guiding Principles for Distance Teaching and Learning.* Retrieved 29 November, 2009, from http://www.adec.edu/admin/papers/distance-teaching_principles.html

ADL. (2005). *Advanced Distributed Learning – Shareable Content Object Reference Model (SCORM) Specification.* Retrieved October 10, 2007, from http://www.adlnet.gov/scorm

ADL. (2009). *Sharable Content Object Reference (SCORM) 2004.* Advanced Distributed Learning, 4th, version 1.0 edition. Retrieved 2009-08-06, from http://adlnet.gov/.

ADL. (2009, August 07). *Advanced Distributed Learning.* Retrieved August 07, 2009, from http://www.adlnet.gov/Technologies/scorm/default.aspx

Adler, C., & Rae, S. (2002). Personalized learning: The future of e-learning is learner centric environment. *E-learning*, (January): 22–24.

Adobe Systems Incorporated. (2008). *Adobe solutions for Learning Management Systems* (p. 95010771). USA: LMS.

Advanced Distributed Learning. (2003). *Sharable Content Object Reference Model (SCORM) Version 1.2.* Advanced Distributed Learning Inc. Available online at www.adlnet.org

Advanced Distributed Learning. (2004a). *SCORM 2004 Shareable Content Object Reference Model.*

Advanced Distributed Learning. (2004b). *SCORM conformance test suite.* Retrieved February 20, 2007 from http://www.adlnet.gov/scorm/20043ed/cts.cfm

AFT. (2002). *Distance education. Guidelines for Good Practice.* Retrieved 29 November, 2009, from http://www.aft.org/pubs-reports/higher_ed/distance.pdf

AICC. (2009 Feb. 03). *AICC - Aviation Industry CBT Committee.* Retrieved August 07, 2009, from: http://www.aicc.org/

Alavi, M., & Leidner, D. E. (2001). Review: Knowledge Management and Knowledge Management Systems: Conceptual Foundations and Research Issues. *Management Information Systems Quarterly, 25*(1), 107–136. doi:10.2307/3250961

Al-Khalifa, H. S., & Davis, H. C. (2006). The evolution of metadata from standards to semantics in E-learning applications. In *Proceedings of the Seventeenth ACM Conference on Hypertext 2006* (pp. 69-72). New York: ACM Press.

Allan, J. (1996). Learning outcomes in higher education. *Studies in Higher Education, 21*(1), 93–108. doi:10.1080/03075079612331381487

Allinson, J., François, S., & Lewis, S. (2008). *SWORD: Simple Web-service Offering Repository Deposit.* Retrieved from http://www.ariadne.ac.uk/issue54/allinson-et-al/

Allum, P. (2001). Principles applicable to the production of CALL-ware: learning from the field of Human Computer Interaction (HCI). *ReCALL, 13*(2), 146–166. doi:10.1017/S0958344001000222a

Ally, M. (2004). Foundations of Educational Theory for Online Learning. In Anderson, T., & Elloumi, F. (Eds.), *Theory and Practice of Online Learning* (pp. 3–31). Alberta, Canada: Creative Commons.

Almond, R. G. Steinberg, l., et al. (2001). A sample assessment using the four process framework. *CSE Report 543. Center for study of evaluation.* Los Angeles: University of California.

Alonso, F., López, G., Manrique, D., & Viñes, J. M. (2005). An instructional model for web-based e-learning education with a blended learning process approach. *British Journal of Educational Technology, 36*(2), 217–235. doi:10.1111/j.1467-8535.2005.00454.x

Altmann, G. & Koch, W. (1998). *Systems: New Paradigms for the Human Sciences.*

Altuner, E. M., & Turker, M. (2006). Learning designs supporting localisation for personalised and adaptive e-learning. In *Proceedings of the ADALE Workshop at Adaptive Hypermedia 2006.*

Al-Turki, U. M., Dufuaa, S., Ayar, T., & Demirel, O. (2008). Stakeholders integration in higher education: Supply chain approach. *European Journal of Engineering Education, 33*(2), 211–219. doi:10.1080/03043790801980136

Alvino, S., Forcheri, P., Ierardi, M. G., & Sarti, L. (2008). A general and flexible model for the pedagogical description of learning objects. In M. Kendall, & B. Samways (Eds.), *International Federation for Information Processing, Vol. 281, Learning to Live in the Knowledge Society* (pp. 55-62). Boston: Springer.

Amadieu, F., Tricot, A., & Mariné, C. (2009). Prior knowledge in learning from a non-linear electronic document: Disorientation and coherence of the reading sequences. *Computers in Human Behavior, 25*, 381–388. doi:10.1016/j.chb.2008.12.017

Amorim, R. R., Lama, M., Sánchez, E., Riera, A., & Vila, X. A. (2006). A Learning Design Ontology based on the IMS Specification. *Journal of Educational Technology & Society, 9*(1), 38–57. Available from http://www.ifets.info/journals/9_1/5.pdf.

Anderson, T., & Whitelock, D. (2004). The Educational Semantic Web: Visioning and Practicing the Future of Education. *Journal of Interactive Media in Education, 1*(9).

Andrade, H., & Du, Y. (2005). Student perspectives on rubric-referenced assessment. *Practical Assessment Research & Evaluation, 10*(3), 1–11.

Andreatos, A. (2007). Virtual Communities and their Importance for Informal Learning. *International Journal of Computers, Communications & Control, 2*(1), 39–47.

Andrews, D., & Crowther, F. (2003). *3-dimensional pedagogy-the image of 21st century teacher professionalism.* In Crowther, F. (ed.), *Teachers as leaders in a knowledge society. College Year Book/Deakin ACT 2003*, (pp. 95-111). Deakin West, Australia: Australian College of Educators. Retrieved from http://eprints.usq.edu.au/3341/

Anido-Rifón, L., Santos-Gago, J., Ródríguez-Estévez, J., Caeiro-Rodríguez, M., Fernández-Iglesias, M., & Llamas-Nistal, M. (n.d.). *A Step ahead in E-learning Standardization: Building Learning Systems from Reusable and Interoperable Software Components*. Retrieved May, 2009 from http://images.google.com/imgres?imgurl=http://www2002.org/CDROM/alternate/136/p136-anido-fig04.gif&imgrefurl=http://www2002.org/CDROM/alternate/136/&usg=__n7yXle7JiYJJQgaH9CY9uVtPzGc=&h=524&w=565&sz=22&hl=en&start=10&tbnid=IUxNGh8krRHfYM:&tbnh=124&tbnw=134&prev=/images%3Fq%3Dinteroperability%2Bof%2Beducational%2Bsystems%26gbv%3D2%26hl%3Den%26sa%3DG Berlin/New York: Walter de Gruyter.

Annetta, L., Klesath, M., & Holmes, S. (2008). V-Learning: How Gaming and Avatars are Engaging Online Students. *Innovate: Journal of Online Education, 4*(3). Available from http://www.innovateonline.info/index.php?view=article&id=485.

Antoniou, G., & Harmelen, F. v. (2004). *A Semantic Web Primer*. Cambridge, MA: The MIT Press.

APIS home page, Assessment Provision through Interoperable Segments. (n.d.). Retrieved Oct. 10, 2009, from http://www.jisc.ac.uk/whatwedo/projects/apis.aspx

Apple (2009) *Browse web apps,* Retrieve on-line on 4th August, 2009 at: http://www.apple.com/webapps/

Application Profile, I. M. S. (n.d). *Guidelines*. Retrieved July 27, 2009, from http://www.imsglobal.org/ap/index.html

Appraisal360 home page. (n.d.). Retrieved July 12, 2009, from http://www.appraisal360.co.uk/home

AQuRate homepage. (n.d.). Retrieved Oct. 10, 2009, from http://aqurate.kingston.ac.uk/indexold.htm

AQuRate. *A QTI-2.x Authoring Tool*. (n.d.). Retrieved July 29, 2009, from http://aqurate.kingston.ac.uk/index.htm.

Arapi, P., Moumoutzis, N., Mylonakis, M., & Christodoulakis, S. (2007). A Framework and an Architecture for Supporting Interoperability Between Digital Libraries and eLearning Applications. In C. Thanos, F. Borri, & L. Candela (Eds.), *Digital Libraries: R&D,* (LNCS 4877, pp. 137-146). Berlin: Springer-Verlag.

Arcos, F., Amilburu, A., & Ortega, P. (2008). The Language Blend. *INTED2008*. International Technology, Education and Development Conference.

Argyris, C., & Schon, D. (1996). *Organisational learning II: Theory, method and practice*. Reading, MA: Addison-Wesley Publishing.

Ariza, M. R., Quesada, A., & Ocaña, M. T. (2008). An experience about promoting general and specific competences acquisition in Higher Education: autonomous work and collaborative skills in the development of a project aimed at eliciting motivation and contextualized learning. In L. Gómez, D. Belenguer, I. Candel (Eds.), *International Conference of Education, Research and Innovation* (pp. 1-7). Madrid: IATED.

Arnheim, R. (1971). *Entropy and Art*. Berkeley: University of California Press.

Arnold, D., Admiraal, W., Ristimaki, E., & Uggeri, M. (2007, November 19th). Developing Effective Learning Materials for a Resource-Poor Environment: eLene-TT: e-learning network for teacher training teachers are life-long learners too. Retrieved from http://blog.olenepal.org/index.php/archives/95

Aroyo, L., & Dicheva, D. (2001). AIMS: Learning and Teching Support for WWW-based Education. *International Journal of Continuing Engineering Education and Lifelong Learning, 1*(1/2), 152–164. doi:10.1504/IJCEELL.2001.000390

Aroyo, L., & Dicheva, D. (2004). The New Challenges for E-learning: The Educational Semantic Web. *Education Technology and Society, 7*(4), 59–69.

ASDEL. *Assessment Delivery Engine for QTIv2 Questions*. (n.d.). Retrieved July 29, 2009, from http://www.asdel.ecs.soton.ac.uk/.

Assessment: JISC. (n.d.). Retrieved July 29, 2009, from http://www.jisc.ac.uk/whatwedo/topics/assessment.aspx.

ASSIS. home page, (n.d.). Retrieved July 12, 2009, from http://www.hull.ac.uk/esig/assis.html

Astin, A. W. (1991). *Assessment For Excellence: The Philosophy And Practice Of Assessment And Evaluation In Higher Education*. American Council on Education Oryx Press Series on Higher Education. Phoenix, AZ: Oryx Press. doi: 10.1336/1573565512.

ATAG. (2000). *Authoring Tool Accessibility Guidelines*. Retrieved October 16, 2009, from http://www.w3.org/TR/WAI-AUTOOLS/

Athabascau. (2004). Retrieved from http://www.athabascau.ca/frontpage/articles/online_15Apr04.ht

Atkins, D., Brow, J. S., & Hammond, A. L. (2007). *A Review of the Open Educational Resources (OER) Movement: Achievements, Challenges, and New Opportunities*. Report to The William and Flora Hewlett Foundation. Retrieved October 10, 2009, from http://www.oerderves.org/wp-content/uploads/2007/03/a-review-of-the-open-educational-resources-oer-movement_final.pdf

Attwell, G. (2007, January). Personal Learning Environments - the future of eLearning? *eLearning Papers, 2*(1). Retrieved from http://www.elearningpapers.eu/

Attwell, G., Dirckinck-Holmfeld, L., Fabian, P., Karpati, A., & Littig, P. (2003). *E-learning in Europe - Results and Recommendations, Thematic Monitoring under the Leonardo da Vinci Programme*, (pp. 32). Retrieved from http://www3.socleoyouth.be/static/Bots/docbots/LEONARDO/impuls_10.pdf

Auvil, L., Grois, E., Llòra, X., Pape, G., Goren, V., Sanders, B., & Acs, B. (2007). *A flexible system for text analysis with semantic networks*. Paper presented at Digital Humanities 2007, Univeristy of Illinois, Urbana-Champaign, Illinois.

Avdjieva, M., & Wilson, M. (2002). Exploring the development of quality in higher education. *Managing Service Quality, 12*(6), 372–383. doi:10.1108/09604520210451858

Avgeriou, P., Papasalouros, A., Retalis, S., & Skordalakis, M. (2003). Towards a Pattern Language for Learning Management Systems. *Journal of Educational Technology & Society, 6*(2), 11–24.

Aviation Industry Committee. *AGR 010 – Web-based computer managed instruction AICC Guidelines and Recommendations (AGRs). AGR-010*. (2004). Retrieved July 29, 2009, from http://www.aicc.org

Axis2 (2009). Retrieved from http://ws.apache.org/axis2/

Azalov, P. (2005). Synthetic exercises on the web. In *International Conference on Information Technology: Coding and Computing* (pp. 459-464).

Backs, R. W., da Silva, S. P., & Han, K. (2005). A comparison of younger and older adults, self-assessment manikin ratings of affective pictures. *Experimental Aging Research, 31*, 421–440. doi:10.1080/03610730500206808

Bacon, R. A. (2003). Assessing the use of a new QTI assessment tool within Physics. In *the 7th CAA Conference*, Loughborough University, Loughborough, UK.

Bacsich, P. (2008). *Higher Education Academy/JISC E-learning Benchmarking Phase 2 Overview Report. Report to the Higher Education Academy 14pp*. Retrieved August 10, 2009, from http://elearning.heacademy.ac.uk/weblogs/benchmarking/wp-content/uploads/2008/04/BenchmarkingPhase2_BELAreport.pdf

Bahati. (2008). *IT infrastructure and eLearning Opportunities*. Retrieved from ESWSTANFORD http://Www.Stanford.Edu/Group/Esw/Wiki/Bahati_It_Infrastructure_And_Elearning_Opportunities

Bailey, K. (1994). *Sociology and the New Systems Theory*. Albany, NY: State University of New York Press.

Bailey, K. (2006). Living systems theory and social entropy theory. *Systems Research and Behavioral Science, 23*, 291–300. doi:10.1002/sres.728

Bailey, W., & Abel, R. (2009). *A Common Evolution for IMS Simple Sequencing?* Retrieved July 20, 2009 from http://www.imsglobal.org/evolutionforss.html

Baker, P. (1993). Chaos, order, and sociological theory. *Sociological Inquiry*, *63*, 12–22. doi:10.1111/j.1475-682X.1993.tb00300.x

Baldiris, S., Santos, O. C., Barrera, C., Boticario J. G., Velez, J., Fabregat, R. (2008). Integration of educational specifications and standards to support adaptive learning scenarios in ADAPTAPlan. *International Journal of Computer Science and Applications (IJCSA). Special Issue on New Trends on AI techniques for Educational Technologies, 5* (1).

Baldoni, M., Baroglio, C., Patti, V., & Torasso, L. (2004). Reasoning about learning object metadata for adapting SCORM courseware. In *Proceedings of the International workshop on engineering the adaptive web, EAW'04: Methods and technologies for personalization and Adaptation in the Semantic Web*, Eindhoven, The Netherlands, (pp. 4-13).

Banathy, B. H. (1987). Instructional systems design. In Gagne, R. M. (Ed.), *Instructional technology: Foundations*. Hillsdale, NJ: Lawrence Erlbaum.

Bandura, A. (2002). Growing primacy of human agency in adaptation and change in the electronic era. *European Psychologist*, *7*(1), 2–16. doi:10.1027//1016-9040.7.1.2

Bansal, K. (2002). *Educational Audio-Visual Media: Some Indicators for Evaluation*. Paper presented in Seminar organized by the Academic Staff College at Jamia Millia Islamia, December, 2,2002, New Delhi, India.

Bansal, K. (2003). *Educational Audio Programmes: Issues Related to Content*. Paper presented in National Seminar on Radio Broadcast as a Tool of Distance Learning, organised by Distance Education Programme (DEP), May 27-28, 2003, New Delhi, India.

Bao, C., Juárez, M., López, L., & Castresana, J. M. (2009). *A methodology of E-learning System Engineering*. Paper presented in ICERI, International Conference of Education, Research and Innovation, November 17-18, Madrid, Spain.

Bao, C., López, L., & Castresana, J. M. (2009). *Teaching in industrial Engineering: the traditional and the new EEES*. Paper presented in International Conference on Education and New learning Technologies, Edulearn-09, July 6-8, Barcelona, Spain.

Bao, C., López, L., Juárez, M., & Castresana, J. M. (2009). Educating the engineer of 2020: adapting engineering education to the new century. In *International Technology, Education and Development conference INTED 2009*, March 9-11, Valencia, Spain.

Bao, C., López, L., Juárez, M., & Castresana, J. M. (2009). *Information technology optimization strategies in Science Higher Education*. Paper presented in International Conference on Education and New learning Technologies, Edulearn-09, July 6-8, 2009. Barcelona, Spain.

Barker, K. C. (2007). E-learning Quality Standards for Consumer Protection and Consumer Confidence: A Canadian Case Study in E-learning Quality Assurance. *Journal of Educational Technology & Society*, *10*(2), 109–119.

Barker, K. (2002). *Canadian recommended e-learning guidelines (CanRegs)*. Retrieved 29 November, 2009, from http://www.futured.com/pdf/CanREGs%20Eng.pdf

Barnard, L., Lan, W. Y., To, Y. M., Paton, V. O., & Lai, S. L. (2009). Measuring self-regulation in online and blended learning environments. *The Internet and Higher Education*, *12*(1), 1–6. doi:10.1016/j.iheduc.2008.10.005

Barr, A., Beard, M., & Atkinson, R. (1973). The computer as tutorial laboratory: the Stanford BIP project. *International Journal of Man-Machine Studies*, *8*, 567–596. doi:10.1016/S0020-7373(76)80021-1

Bartram, D. (2005). Testing on the Internet: Issues, Challenges and Opportunities in the Field of Occupational Assessment. In Bartram, D., & Hambleton, R. (Eds.), *Computer-Based Testing and the Internet: Issues and Advances*. Chichester, UK: John Wiley and Sons. doi:10.1002/9780470712993.ch1

Baskerville, R., Wood-Harper, A. T. (1998, June 1). Diversity in information systems action research methods. *European Journal of Information Systems, 7*(2), 90-107(18).

Bates, A. W., & Poole, G. (2002). *Effective teaching with technology in higher education: foundations for success*. San Francisco, CA: Jossey-Bass, Wiley.

Bechhofer, S., Harmelen, F., Hendler, J., Horrocks, I., McGuinness, D., Patel-Schneider, P., & Stein, L. A. (2004). *OWL Web Ontology Language Reference*. W3C Recommendation. Retrieved from http://www.w3.org/TR/owl-ref/

Becta leading next generation learning. (2009). *Harnessing Technology schools survey 2008*. Retrieved from http://partners.becta.org.uk/index.php?section=rh&&catcode=&rid=15952

Beer, J., & Meethan, K. (2007). Marine and maritime sector skills shortages in the South West of England: Developing regional training provision. *Journal of Vocational Education and Training*, *59*(4), 467–484. doi:10.1080/13636820701650935

Beer, C., & Jones, D. (2008). Learning networks: harnessing the power of online communities for discipline and lifelong learning. Lifelong Learning: reflecting on successes and framing futures. In *Keynote and refereed papers from the 5th International Lifelong Learning Conference*. Rockhampton, Australia: Central Queensland University Press.

Beers, P. J., Boshuizen, H. P. A., Kirschner, P. A., Gijselaers, W., & Westendorp, J. (2006). Cognitive load measurements and stimulated recall interviews for studying the effects of information and communications technology. *Educational Technology Research and Development*, *56*(3), 309–328. doi:10.1007/s11423-006-9020-7

Beniest, J., Coe, R., Poole, J., Ochieng, H., Vandenbosch, T., Clark, C. & Janssens-Bevernage, A. (2008). *Lessons Learned from a Blended Learning*.

Berggren, A., Burgos, D., Fontana, J. M., Hinkelman, D., Hung, V., & Hursh, A. (2005). Practical and Pedagogical Issues for Teacher Adoption of IMS Learning Design Standards in Moodle LMS. *Journal of Interactive Media in Education*, *2005*(2), 1–24. Available from http://jime.open.ac.uk/2005/02/berggren-2005-02.pdf.

Berggren, A. (2006). Current Status of IMS LD and Moodle. *Journal,* (October 2006). Retrieved from http://moodle.org/mod/forum/discuss.php?d=56713

Berners-Lee, T., Hendler, J., & Lassila, O. (2001). The Semantic Web. *Scientific American*, *284*(5), 34–43. doi:10.1038/scientificamerican0501-34

Berners-Lee, T. (1997). *Metadata Architecture*. Retrieved from http://www.w3.org/DesignIssues/Metadata.html

Bernstein, S., & Cashore, B. (2007). Can non-state global governance be legitimate? An analytical framework. *Regulation & Governance*, *1*, 347–371. doi:10.1111/j.1748-5991.2007.00021.x

Bersin Associates. (2009). *Learning Management Systems: Facts, Practical Analysis, Trends, and Vendor Profiles; The industry's most comprehensive review and buyer's guide of learning management systems, designed for corporate buyers, vendors, and consultants*. Retrieved from http://store.bersinassociates.com/lms.html

Bertalanffy, L. (1968). *General System Theory: Foundations, Development, Applications*. New York: George Braziller.

Bhattacharya, I. (2006). *DOEACC Society Premier Institution for Quality Education and Training in the areas of Information, Electronics & Communication Technology (IECT),* Aug 24, Government of India. Retrieved from http://www.digitallearning.in/dlindia/presentation/day24/Indrajeet.pdf

Biggs, J. (2001). The reflective institution: assuring and enhancing the quality of teaching and Learning. *Higher Education*, *41*, 221–238. doi:10.1023/A:1004181331049

Bisell, A. N. (2009) Permission granted: open licensing for educational resources. *Open Learning: The Journal of Open and Distance Learning,* 97-106. Retrieved October 10, 2009, from http://pdfserve.informaworld.com/442626__909092757.pdf

Black, S. (2003). Scholarly journals should be treated as a public good. *The Serials Librarian*, *44*(1), 52–63. doi:10.1300/J123v44n01_07

Blackboard_Inc. (2004). Blackboard Inc. and Open Universiteit Nederland Announce Strategic Alliance. *Journal,* (June 2004). Retrieved from http://www.blackboard.com/company/press/release.aspx?id=519762

Blackboard_Inc. (2008). Ball State Wins Greenhouse Grant for Virtual Worlds. *Journal,* (March). Retrieved from http://www.blackboard.com/company/newsletters/ASMarch2008d.htm

Blake, C., & Scanlon, E. (2007). Reconsidering simulations in science education at a distance: Features of effective use. *Journal of Computer Assisted Learning, 23*(6), 491–502. doi:10.1111/j.1365-2729.2007.00239.x

Blandin, B. (2004). Are e-learning standards neutral? In *Proceedings CALIE 04: International Conference on Computer Aided Learning in Engineering Education*, Grenoble, France.

Bloom, B. S., & Krathwohl, D. R. (1956). *Taxonomy of educational objectives: The classification of educational goals by a committee of college and university examiners.* New York: Longman.

Bloom, B. S. (Ed.). (1956). *Taxonomy of Educational Objectives, Handbook 1: Cognitive Domain.* White Plains, NY: Longman.

Bloom, B. S. (1984). The 2 sigma problem: The search for methods of group instruction as effective as one-to-one tutoring. *Educational Research, 13*, 3–15.

Bloom, B. S. Hastings, J.T. & Madaus, G.F. (1971). *Handbook on Formative and Summative Evaluation of Student Learning.* New York: McGraw-Hill.

Boehle, S. (2007). Is Open Source Right for You? *ManageSmarter, August 01.* Retrieved from http://www.trainingmag.com/msg/content_display/publications/e3i5adce9be1b1efb206c4d540a4194c9d3

Boehm, B. W. (1981). *Software Engineering Economics.* Upper Saddle River, NJ: Prentice Hall.

Bohl, O., Schellhase, J., Senler, R., & Winand, U. (2002). The sharable content object reference model (SCORM) - A critical review. *IEEE International Conference on Computers in Education (ICCE02),* (pp. 950-951).

Bonk, C. J., & Zhang, K. (2006). Introducing the R2D2 Model: Online Learning for the Diverse Learners of the World. *Distance Education, 27*(2), 249–264. doi:10.1080/01587910600789670

Bonk, C. J., & Graham, C. R. (Eds.). (2004). *Handbook of blended learning: Global Perspectives, local designs.* San Francisco, CA: Pfeiffer Publishing.

Bos-Ciussi. M, Augier, M. & Rosner, G. (2008). Learning Communities Are Not Mushrooms - or - How to Cultivate Learning Communities. In C. Kimble, P. Hildreth and I. Bourdon (Eds), *Higher Education in Communities of Practice: Creating Learning Environments for Educators,* (pp. 2, 14, 287-308). Hershey, PA: Information Age Publishing.

Bosco, A. (2005). Las TIC en los procesos de convergencia europea y la innovación en la universidad: oportunidades y limitaciones. *Aula Abierta, 86*, 3–27.

Bostock, S. J. (1998). Constructivism in mass higher education: A case study. *British Journal of Educational Technology, 29*(3), 225–240. doi:10.1111/1467-8535.00066

Boticario, J. G., & Santos, O. C. (2007). An open IMS-based user modelling approach for developing adaptive learning management systems. *Journal of Interactive Media in Education. Adaptation and IMS Learning Design, 02*, 1–19.

Boticario, J. G., & Santos, O. C. (2008). A standards-based modelling approach for dynamic generation of adaptive learning scenarios. *Journal of Universal Computer Science, 14*(17), 2859–2876.

Boticario, J. G., & Cooper, M. Montandon, L., van Dorp, K-J. (2006). Towards an Open, Standard-based, Reusable and Extensible Architecture of Services for Accessible Lifelong Learning: An Introduction to the EU4ALL Project. In *Proceedings of the EADTU 2006 Annual Conference: Widening participation and opportunities by e-learning in Higher Education*, Tallinn, Estonia, 22 – 24, November 2006.

Bottino, R. M., & Robotti, E. (2007). Transforming classroom teaching & learning through technology: Analysis of a case study. *Journal of Educational Technology & Society*, *10*(4), 174–186.

Boud, D., & Cohen, R. (1999). Peer Learning and Assessment. *Assessment & Evaluation in Higher Education*, *24*(4), 413–426. doi:10.1080/0260293990240405

Boud, D. (2000). Sustainable assessment: rethinking assessment for the learning society. *Studies in Continuing Education*, *22*(2), 151–167..doi:10.1080/713695728

Bouzo, J., Batlle, H., & Blat, J. (2007) *Enhancing IMS QTI assessment with web maps*, TENCompetence Open Workshop on Current Research on IMS Learning Design and Lifelong Competence Development Infrastructures. Retrieved July 04, 2009, http://dspace.ou.nl/handle/1820/1114

Bovey, N. S., & Dunand, N. (2006). Seamless production of interoperable e-Learning units: stakes and pitfalls. *DSpace at Open Universiteit Nederland*, 1-6. Available from dspace.learningnetworks.org/bitstream/1820/759/1/Paper15.pdf.

Boyer, E. L. (1997). *Scholarship reconsidered: Priorities of the professoriate*. San Francisco: Jossey-Bass.

Boyes Braem, P., & Sutton-Spence, R. (Eds.). (2001). The Hands are the Head of the Mouth: The Mouth as Articulator in Sign Languages. *International Studies on Sign Language and Communication of the Deaf, 39*.

Boyle, T. (2003). Design principles for authoring dynamic, reusable learning objects. *Australian Journal of Educational Technology*, *19*(1), 46–58.

Boyle, T. (2008). The design of learning objects for pedagogical impact. In L. Lockyer, S. Bener, S. Agostinho, B. Harper (Eds.), *Handbook of research on learning design and learning objects: Issues, Applications and Technologies* (pp. 391-407). Hershey, PA: Information Science Reference (IGI Global).

Bradner, S. (1996). *The Internet standards process – revision 3. RFC 2026 (BCP 9), Internet Engineering Task Force*. Retrieved 2008-10-17, from http://ietf.org/html/rfc2026.

Brandon, R. (2005). Evolutionary Modules: Conceptual Analyses and Empirical Hypotheses. In *Modularity: Understanding the Development and Evolution of Natural Complex Systems* (pp. 51–61). Cambridge: MIT Press.

Bremer, D., & Bryant, R. (2005). *A Comparison of Two Learning management Systems: Moodle vs Blackboard.* Paper presented at the 18th Annual Conference of the National Advisory Committee on Computing Qualifications, Tauranga, New Zealand.

Brew, A., & Ginns, P. (2008). The relationship between engagement in the scholarship of teaching and learning and students' course experiences. *Assessment & Evaluation in Higher Education*, *33*(5), 535–545. doi:10.1080/02602930701698959

Brickley, D., & Miller, L. (November 2, 2007). *FOAF Vocabulary Specification 0.91*. Retrieved July 28, 2009, from http://xmlns.com/foaf/spec/

Brooks, F. P. Jr. (1995). *The Mythical Man-Month* (2nd ed.). Harlow, UK: Addison-Wesley.

Brusilovsky, P. (2000). Course sequencing for static courses? applying its techniques in large-scale web-based education. In *Proceedings of Intelligent Tutoring Systems*. Berlin: Springer-Verlag. doi:10.1007/3-540-45108-0_66

Brusilovsky, P., & Sosnovsky, S. (2005). Individualized exercises for self-assessment of programming knowledge: An evaluation of Quizpack. *Journal of Educational Resources in Computing*, *5*(3). doi:10.1145/1163405.1163411

Brusilovsky, P., & Vassileva, J. (2003). Course sequencing techniques for large-scale web-based education. *International Journal of Continuing Engineering Education and Lifelong Learning*, *13*(1-2), 75–94.

Brusilovsky, P. (2008). *Adaptive Navigation Support for Open Corpus Hypermedia Systems, Adaptive Hypermedia and Adaptive Web-Based Systems* (pp. 6–8). Berlin: Springer.

Brusilovsky, P. (2004). Adaptive Educational Hypermedia: From generation to generation. In *Proceedings of 4th Hellenic Conference on ICT in Education*, 19-33. New Technologies Pub.

Brusilovsky, P., & Weber, G. (1996) Collaborative example selection in an intelligent example based programming environment. In *International Conference on Learning Sciences, ICLS-96*, Evanston, IL.

Brusilovsky, P., Eklund, J., & Schwarz, E. (1998b). Web-based education for all: A tool for developing adaptive courseware. *Computer Networks and ISDN Systems, 30*(1-7), 291-300.

Buckley, W. (1967). *Sociology and Modern Systems Theory*. Upper Saddle River, NJ: Prentice Hall.

Buckley, W. (1998). *Society—A Complex Adaptive System: Essays in Social Theory*. New York: Routledge.

Buckley,W. (1968). *Modern Systems Research for the Behavioral Scientist.*

Burgos, D., Moreno-Ger, P., Sierra, J. L., Fernández-Manjón, B., & Koper, R. (2007). Authoring game-based adaptive units of learning with IMS Learning Design and <e-Adventure>. *International Journal of Learning Technology, 3*(3), 252–268. doi:10.1504/IJLT.2007.015444

Burgos, D., Tattersall, C., & Koper, R. (2007). Re-purposing existing generic games and simulations for e-learning. *Computers in Human Behavior, 23*(6), 2656–2667. doi:10.1016/j.chb.2006.08.002

Busetti, E., Dettori, G., Forcheri, P., & Ierardi, M. G. (2004). Guidelines towards the effective sharable LO. In Liy, W. (Ed.), *Advances in Web-based learning* (pp. 416–423). Heidelberg, Germany: Springer Berlin.

Butler, N. S. (2007). Digital resources versus cognitive tools. In Abell, S. K., & Lederman, N. G. (Eds.), *Handbook of Research in Science Education* (pp. 471–492). Mahwah, NJ: Lawrence Erlbaum Associates Publishers.

Butler, N. S. (2006). BioKIDS: An animated conversation of the development of curricular activity structures for inquiry science. In Sawyer, R. K. (Ed.), *The Cambridge Handbook of the Learning Sciences* (pp. 355–370). New York: Cambridge University Press.

Butterfield, S., Chambers, M., Moseley, B., Prebble, T., Uys, P., & Woodhouse, D. (1999). *External quality assurance for the virtual institution*. New Zealand Universities Academic Audit Unit.

Buzza, D., Bean, D., Harrigan, K., & Carey, T. (2004). Learning design repositories: adapting learning design specifications for shared instructional knowledge. *Canadian Journal of Learning and Technology, 30*(3), 79–101.

Cabero Almenara, J. (2000). La formación virtual: principios, bases y preocupaciones. In R. Pérez Pérez, (Ed.), *Redes, multimedia y diseños virtuales,* (pp. 83-102). Oviedo, Italy: Departamento de Ciencias de la Educación de la Universidad de Oviedo. Retrieved July 23, 2009, from http://tecnologiaedu.us.es/bibliovir/pdf/87.pdf

Caeiro-Rodriguez, M., Llamas-Nistal, M., & Anido-Rifón, L. (2005). Towards a Benchmark for the Evaluation of LD Expressiveness and Suitability. *Journal of Interactive Media in Education, 4*, 1–14.

Callebaut, W. (2005). Evo-Patterns: Working toward a Grammar of Forms. In *Modularity: Understanding the Development and Evolution of Natural Complex Systems* (p. 181). Cambridge, MA: MIT Press.

Calverley, G., Cappelli, T., Dexter, H., Petch, J., & Smithies, A. (2007). Changing practices in the development of digital resources. In *Proceedings of SOLSTICE 2007 Researching E-Learning for Innovation and Development*, Edge Hill University, UK, 11 May 2007.

Cañellas, A. (2006). Impacto de las TIC en la educación: un acercamiento desde el punto de vista de las funciones de la educación. *Quaderns Digitals: Revista de Nuevas Tecnologías y Sociedad*, 43.

Capell, P., & Dannenberg, R. (1993). Instructional design and intelligent tutoring: Theory and the precision of design. *Journal of Artificial Intelligence in Education, 4*, 95–121.

Cappelli, T., & Smithies, A. (2008). Learning Needs Analysis through Synthesis of Maturity Models and Competency Frameworks. In K. McFerrin et al. (Eds.), *Proceedings of Society for Information Technology and Teacher Education International Conference 2008* (pp. 2448-2455). Chesapeake, VA: AACE.

Carlson, S., & Tidiane, C. Gadio. (2002). Teacher Professional Development in the Use of Technology. *aed.org: Technologies for Education.* Available: http://www.aed.org/publications/TechnologiesForEducation/TechEdChapters/08.pdf

Carr, S., & Jennings, J. M. (2009). External and Internal Quality Assurance – Towards a Model for Integration. In *Proceedings of AUQF2009 Internal & External Quality Assurance: Tensions & Synergies.* Alice Springs, Australia 1–3 July 2009.

Case, S. M., & Swanson, D. B. (2002). *Constructing Written Test Questions For the Basic and Clinical Sciences,* (3rd ed.). National Board of Medical Examiners, Philadelphia, PA. Retrieved 2008-10-17, from http://www.nbme.org/PDF/ItemWriting2003/2003IWGwhole.pdf

Castranova, E. (2001). *Virtual Worlds: A First-Hand Account of Market and Society on the Cyberian Frontier.* Munich, Germany: Center for Economic Studies & Ifo Institute for Economic Research.

Cebeci, Z., & Erdogan, Y. (2005). Tree view editing learning object metadata. *Interdisciplinary Journal of Knowledge and Learning Objects, 1*(1), 99–108.

CEN. (2005). CEN CWA 15455 (2005) *A European Model for Learner Competencies.* Retrieved 2009-04-09 from ftp://ftp.cenorm.be/PUBLIC/CWAs/e-Europe/WS-LT/CWA15455-00-2005-Nov.pdf

Cenich, G., & Santos, G. (2005). Propuesta de aprendizaje basado en proyectos y trabajo colaborativo: experiencia de un curso en línea. *Revista Electrónica de Investigación Educativa, 7*(2). Retrieved July 23, 2009, from http://redie.uabc.mx/vol7no2/contenido cenich.html

CEN-LTSO. (n.d). *Home page.* Retrieved July 19, 2009, from http://www.cen-ltso.net/

Centre for Education Technology Interoperability Standards. CETIS. (2002). *Who's doing what?* Retrieved July 29, 2009, from http://www.cetis.ac.uk/static/who-does-what.html

CETIS. (2004). *Learning technology standards: An overview.* Retrieved August 10, 2009, from http://zope.cetis.ac.uk/static/standards.html

CETIS. J. (03 April, 2009). *JISC CETIS.* Retrieved August 07, 2009, from http://wiki.cetis.ac.uk/LEAP2A_specification

Chang, W., Hsu, H., Smith, T. K., & Wang, C. (2004). Enhancing SCORM metadata for assessment authoring in e-Learning. *Journal of Computer Assisted Learning, 20*(4), 305–316. doi:10.1111/j.1365-2729.2004.00091.x

Chao, T., Saj, T., & Tessier, F. (2006). Establishing a Quality Review for Online Courses. *EDUCAUSE Quarterly, 29*(3).

Checkland, P. (1999). *Soft Systems Methodology: a 30-year retrospective.* Chichester, UK: J. Wiley. Col, L.M.S. (2003). *Open Source; Commonwealth of Learning.* Retrieved from http://www.col.org/SiteCollectionDocuments/03LMSOpenSource.pdf

Cheetham, G., & Chivers, G. (2005). *Professions, Competence and Informal Learning.* Cheltenham, UK: Edward Elgar Publishing.

Chickering, A., & Gamson, Z. (1987). Seven principles of good practice in undergraduate education. *AAHE Bulletin, 39,* 3–7.

Chickering, A. W., & Ehrmann, S. (1996). Implementing the seven principles: Technology as lever. *AAHE Bulletin, 49*(2), 3–6.

Childress, M. D., & Braswell, R. (2006). Using Massively Multiplayer Online Role-Playing Games for Online Learning. *Distance Education, 27*(2), 187–196. doi:10.1080/01587910600789522

Christodoulakis, S., Arapi, P., Moumoutzis, N., et al. (2006). *Interoperability of eLearning Applications with Digital Libraries.* Poster on the 10th European Conference on Research and Advanced Technology for Digital Libraries (ECDL 2006), September 2006, Alicante, Spain.

Churchill, D. (2007). Towards a useful classification of learning objects. *Educational Technology Research and Development, 55*(5), 479–497. doi:10.1007/s11423-006-9000-y

Cisco Systems. (2003). *Reusable learning object strategy: designing and developing learning objects for multiple learning approaches* [White paper]. Retrieved September 13, 2005, from http://www.e-novalia.com/materiales/RLOW__07_03.pdf

Clark, R. (1994). Media will never influence learning. *Educational Technology Research and Development, 42*(2), 21–29. doi:10.1007/BF02299088

Clark, D. (2005). *Localisation of e-learning,* [White paper]. EPIC Group. Retrieved October 13, 2009, from http://www.epic.co.uk/

Clarke, J., & Bede, C. (2005). *Making Learning Meaningful: An Exploratory Study of Using Multi-User Environments (MUVEs) in Middle School Science.* Paper presented at the American Educational Research Association. Retrieved from http://muve.gse.harvard.edu/rivercityproject/documents/aera_2005_clarke_dede.pdf

Clocksin, W., & Mellish, C. (1984). *Programming in Prolog.* Berlin: Springer-Verlag.

Cluster, W. A. B. (2009). The WAB Cluster is the European Web Accessibility Benchmarking Cluster. Retrieved June 26, 2009, from http://www.supporteam.org/Supporteam/Documentary/accessibility_policies.asp

Coerts, J. (1994). Constituent order in Sign Language of the Netherlands. In M. Brennan & G.H. Turner (eds.), *Word-order Issues in Sign Languages – Working Papers,* (pp 47-71). The International Sign Linguistics Association (ISLA), Durham.

Coimbra Group. (2002). *European Union Policies and Strategic Change for e-learning in Universities.* Brussels.

Cole, J., & Foster, H. (2007) *Using Moodle - teaching with the popular open source course management system.* Sebastopol, CA: O'Reilly Community Press. Retrieved 22 July 2009 from http://download.moodle.org/download.php/docs/en/using_moodle_2e.zip

Coll, C., Rochera, M. J., Mayordomo, R. M., & Naranjo, M. (2007). Evaluación continuada y apoyo al aprendizaje. Una experiencia de innovación educativa con el apoyo de las TIC en educación superior. *Revista Electrónica de Investigación Psicoeducativa, 5*(13), 783–804.

Conole, G. (2007). What constitutes good research in e-learning—are there lessons we can draw from the Research Assessment Exercise? *ALT-J, 15*(3), 183–188. doi:10.1080/09687760701673576

Conole, G., Dyke, M., Oliver, M., & Seale, J. (2004). Mapping pedagogy and tools for effective learning design. *Computers & Education, 43*(1–2), 17–33. doi:10.1016/j.compedu.2003.12.018

Conole, G. (2002). Systematising learning and research information. *Journal of Interactive Media in Education,* (7). Retrieved 08/06/2009 from http://www-jime.open.ac.uk/2002/7

Content Packaging, I. M. S. (n.d). *Specification.* Retrieved July 27, 2009, from http://www.imsglobal.org/content/packaging/index.html

Cooper, D. G., Arroyo, I., Woolf, B. P., Muldner, K., Burleson, W., & Christopherson, R. (2009). Sensors Model Student Self Concept in the Classroom. User Modeling, Adaptation, and Personalization Seventeenth International Conference, UMAP 2009, Trento, Italy, (LNCS 5535, pp. 30-41). Berlin: Springer-Verlag.

Cooper, M., Boticario, J. G., & Montandon, L. (2006). An introduction to Accessible Lifelong Learning (ALL) - a strategy for research and development uniting accessible technology, services, and e-learning infrastructure. *Fourth European Distance and E-Learning Network: Research into Online Distance Education and E-Learning.* Castellldefels, Spain, 25-28 October 2006.

Cooperrider, D. L., & Whitney, D. (1996). *Appreciative inquiry consultation workbook.* Taos, NM: Taos Institute.

CopperAuthor. (2005). *CopperAuthor Learning Design editor.* Retrieved May 1, 2006, from http://sourceforge.net/projects/copperauthor/

CopperCore, home page. (n.d.). Retrieved Oct. 12, 2009, from http://coppercore.sourceforge.net/

Coppola, N. W., Hiltz, S. R., & Rotter, N. (2001). Recoming a virtual professor: pedagogical roles and ALN. In *Proceedings of the 34th Hawaii International Conference on System Sciences*.

Core, D. (October 10, 2008). *Dublin Core Metadata Initiative*. Retrieved August 07 2009, from Accessibility Term Proposal: http://dublincore.org/accessibilitywiki/NewElementProposal

Couchet, J., Santos, O. C., Raffenne, E., & Boticario, J. G. (2008). The Tracking and Auditing Module for the OpenACS Framework. *7th OPENACS /. LRN Conference,* Valencia, Spain.

Covián, R. E., & Celemín, M. (2008). Diez años de evaluación de la enseñanza aprendizaje de la mecánica de newton en escuelas de ingeniería españolas. Rendimiento académico y presencia de preconceptos. *Ensenañza de las Ciencias*, *26*(1), 23–42.

CP. (2004). *IMS Content Packaging v1.1.4 Final Specification*. Retrieved October 10, 2005, from http://www.imsglobal.org/content/packaging

Craigh, S., & Hannum, K. (2006). Research update: 306 degree assessment. *Consulting Psychology Journal: Practice and Research*, *58*(2), 117–122. doi:10.1037/1065-9293.58.2.117

Cristea, A. (2004). Authoring of adaptive and adaptable educational hypermedia: Where are we now and where are we going? In *International Conference in Web-Based Education.* New York: Acta Press.

Cristea, A. I., & Garzotto, F. (2004). ADAPT major design dimensions for educational adaptive hypermedia. In *ED-Media '04 conference on educational multimedia, hypermedia & telecommunications*. Association for the advancement of computing in education.

Cristea, A., & Aroyo, L. (2002). Adaptive Authoring of Adaptive Educational Hypermedia. In *International Conference on Adaptive Hypermedia*, (pp. 122-132). Berlin: Springer-Verlag.

Cristea, P., & Tuduce, R. (2005). Automatic Generation of Exercises for Self-testing in Adaptive E-learning Systems: Exercises on AC Circuits. In *3rd Workshop on Adaptive and Adaptable Educational Hypermedia at the AIED'05 conference, (A3EH)*.

Cruz, I. F., & Xiao, H. (2005). The Role of Ontologies in Data Integration. *Journal of Engineering Intelligent Systems*, *13*(4), 245–252.

Dalziel, J. (2002). *Reflections on the COLIS (Collaborative Online Learning and Information Systems) Demonstrator Project and the "Learning Object Lifecycle"*. Retrieved from www.colis.mq.edu.au/projects/dalziel.doc

Dancik, G., & Kumar, A. (2003). A Tutor for Counter-Controlled Loop Concepts and Its Evaluation. *Frontiers in Education Conference*, USA.

Danver, D., & Kanvounias, P. (2005). Student involvement in assessment: a project designed to assess class participation fairly and reliable. *Assessment & Evaluation in Higher Education*, *30*(4), 445–454. doi:10.1080/02602930500099235

Davies, H., & Archer, J. (2005). Multi-source feedback: development and practical aspects. *The Clinical Teacher*, *2*(2), 77–81. doi:10.1111/j.1743-498X.2005.00064.x

Davies, J. (2007). The effect of academic culture on the implementation of the EFQM Excellence Model in UK universities. *Quality Assurance in Education*, *15*(4), 382–401. doi:10.1108/09684880710829965

DCMI Libraries Working Group. (2004). *Library Application Profile*. DCMI Working Draft. Retrieved from http://dublincore.org/documents/2004/09/10/library-application-profile/

DCMI Usage Board. (2008). *DCMI Metadata Terms. DCMI Recommendation*. Retrieved from http://dublincore.org/documents/dcmi-terms/

DCMI. (2005) Memorandum of Understanding between the Dublin Core Metadata Initiative and the IEEE Learning Technology Standards Committee. Retrieved 2009-07-18 from http://dublincore.org/documents/dcmi-ieee-mou/index.shtml

DCMI. (2008). *Dublin Core Metadata Element Set, Version 1.1*. DCMI Recommendation. Retrieved from http://dublincore.org/documents/dces/

De Bra, P., & Calvi, L. (1998). AHA! An open Adaptive Hypermedia Architecture. *New Review of Hypermedia and Multimedia*, *4*, 115–139. doi:10.1080/13614569808914698

De Bra, P., Aerts, A., Berden, B., de Lange, B., Rousseau, B., Santic, T., et al. (2003). AHA! The adaptive hypermedia architecture. In *Proceedings of Conference on Hypertext and Hypermedia*, (pp.81-84). New York: ACM.

de Freitas, S. (2006). *Think piece for Becta On the 'e-mature learner.'* Retrieved 25 February, 2009, from http://tre.ngfl.gov.uk/uploads/materials/24877/Think_piece_for_BectaSdF.doc

de Freitas, S. Neumann, T. (2009, February). The use of 'exploratory learning' for supporting immersive learning in virtual environments. *Computers & Education, V 52* (2), 343-352. Retrieved 08-14-09 from http://www.sciencedirect.com/science?_ob=ArticleURL&_udi=B6VCJ-4TVY5BD&_user=10&_rdoc=1&_fmt=&_orig=search&_sort=d&_docanchor=&view=c&_searchStrId=980888894&_rerunOrigin=scholar.google&_acct=C000050221&_version=1&_urlVersion=0&_userid=10&md5=6fd6acded1794400036123 7dc924d9e1_noRerunResults=1

De la Fuente Valentín, L., Pardo, A., & Delgado Kloos, C. (2009). Using Third Party Services to Adapt Learning Material: A Case Study with Google Forms. In *Proceedings of European Conference on Technology-Enhanced Learning*, (pp.744-750). Berlin: Springer-Verlag.

De Moura, S., Coutinho, F., Siqueira, S., & Melo, R. (2005). Integrating repositories of learning objects using web services and ontologies. *International Journal of Web Services Practices*, *1*(1-2), 57–72.

De Pablos, J. (2007). El cambio metodológico en el Espacio Europeo de Educación Superior y el papel de las tecnologías de la información y la comunicación. *Revista Iberoamericana de Educación a Distancia*, *10*(2), 5–44.

De Troyer, O., Mushtaha, A., Stengers, H., Baetens, M., Boers, F., Casteleyn, S., & Plessers, P. (2005). On cultural differences in local web interfaces. *Journal of Web Engineering*, *5*(3), 246–264.

Deane, C. (2005). Transparency of qualifications: Are we there yet? *European Journal of Education*, *40*(3), 279–293. doi:10.1111/j.1465-3435.2005.00226.x

Deco, C., Bender, C., Casali, A., & Motz, R. (2008). Design of a Recommender Educational System. In *Proceedings of 3rd Latinamerican Conference of Learning Objects (LACLO 2008)*, (pp. 63).

Delors, J. (1997). *Learning: The Treasure Within. UNESCO report for Education for the 21st Century*. Berlin, Germany: German UNESCO Commission.

Demers, C. (2007). *Organizational Change Theories: A Synthesis*. Los Angeles, CA: Sage Publications Incorporated.

Dennis, A., Bichelmeyer, B., Henry, D., Cakir, H., Korkmaz, A., Watson, C., & Bunnage, J. (2006). The CISCO Networking Academy: A Model for the Study of Student Success in a Blended Learning Environment. In Bonk, C. J., & Graham, C. R. (Eds.), *The Handbook of Blended Learning: Global Perspectives, Local Designs* (pp. 120–135). San Francisco: Pfeiffer.

Derntl, M., & Motschnig-Pitrik, R. (2005). The role of structure, patterns, and people in blended learning. *The Internet and Higher Education*, *8*(2), 111–130. doi:10.1016/j.iheduc.2005.03.002

Deshpande, P. M., & Mugridge, I. (1994). Preface. In P. M. Deshpande & I. Mugridge, (Eds.) *Quality Assurance in Higher Education*, (p. iii). Vancouver: The Commonwealth of learning. Dublin Core. (n.d). *Home page*. Retrieved July 22, 2009, from http://www.dublincore.org/

Design-Based Research Collective. (2003). Design-Based Research: An emerging paradigm for educational inquiry. *Educational Researcher, 32*(1), 5-8. Retrieved July 20, 2009 from http://www.designbasedresearch.org/reppubs/DBRC2003.pdf

Devedzic, V., Jovanovic, J., & Gasevic, D. (2007). The pragmatics of current e-learning standards. *IEEE Internet Computing*, (May-June): 19–27. doi:10.1109/MIC.2007.73

Dicheva, D., Dichev, C., & Wang, D. (2005). Visualizing Topic Maps for e-Learning. In *Proceedings of IEEE International Conference on Advanced Learning Technologies*, Kaohsiung, Taiwan.

Dicheva, D., Sosnovsky, S., Gavrilova, T., & Brusilovsky, P. (2005). Ontological Web Portal for Educational Ontologies. In *Proceedings of Artificial Intelligence in Education*, Amsterdam, Netherlands.

Dickey, M. D. (2005). Three-dimensional virtual worlds and distance learning: two case studies of Active Worlds as a medium for distance education. *British Journal of Educational Technology*, *36*(3), 439–451. doi:10.1111/j.1467-8535.2005.00477.x

Diederen, J., Gruppen, H., Hartog, R., & Voragen, A. G. J. (2005). Design and evaluation of digital learning material to support acquisition of quantitative problem-solving skills within food chemistry. *Journal of Science Education and Technology*, *14*(5-6), 495–507. doi:10.1007/s10956-005-0224-0

DiMaggio, P., & Powell, W. (1983). The iron cage revisited: Institutional isomorphism and collective rationality in organizational fields. *American Sociological Review*, *48*, 147–160. doi:10.2307/2095101

Dodd, R., Green, S., & Pearson, E. (2009). User Capabilities in an Adaptive World. In *Proceedings of ACM MSIADU09, 1st ACM Workshop on Media Studies and Implementations to Improve Access to Disabled Users, Beijing,* October 2009.

Dolog, P., & Nejdl, W. (2003). Using UML and XMI for generating adaptive navigation sequences in web-based systems. In *Proceedings of UML 2003*.

Donohue, C., Fox, S. & Torrence, D. (2007). Early Childhood Educators as eLearners. Engaging Approaches to Teaching and Learning Online. *Beyond the Journal,* July 2007.

Doo, H. L., & Seung, W. Y. (2008). Team learning and collaboration between online and blended learner groups. *Performance Improvement Quarterly*, *21*(3), 59–72. doi:10.1002/piq.20031

Dougiamas, M., & Taylor, P. (2003). Moodle: Using Learning Communities to Create an Open Source Course Management System. In D. Lassner & C. McNaught (Eds.), *Proceedings of World Conference on Educational Multimedia, Hypermedia and Telecommunications 2003,* (pp. 171-178). Chesapeake, VA: AACE. Retrieved from http://www.editlib.org/p/13739

Dougiamas, M., & Taylor, P. C. (2002). Interpretive analysis of an internet-based course constructed using a new courseware tool called Moodle. In *Proceedings of the Higher Education Research and Development Society of Australasia (HERDSA) 2002 Conference*, Perth, Western Australia.

Downes, S. (2003). Learning objects metadata. Retrieved May 1, 2009 from http://community.flexiblelearning.net.au/

Drachsler, H., Hummel, H. G. K., Van den Berg, B., Eshuis, J., Waterink, W., Nadolski, R., et al. (2008). Effects of the ISIS Recommender System for Navigation Support in Self-Organized Learning Networks. In M. Kalz, R. Koper, V. Hornung-Prähauser & M. Luckmann (Eds.). In *Proceedings of the 1st Workshop on Technology Support for Self-Organized Learners (TSSOL08) in conjunction with 4th Edumedia Conference 2008 Self-organised learning in the interactive Web – Changing learning culture?* (pp. 106-124). June, 2-3, 2008, Salzburg, Austria: CEUR Workshop Proceedings. Available at http://ceur-ws.org/Vol-349

Draganidis, F., & Mentzas, G. (2006). Competency based management: a review of systems and approaches. *Information Management & Computer Security*, *14*(1), 51–64. doi:10.1108/09685220610648373

Driscoll, M. (2002). Blended Learning. *E-learning*, *3*(3), 26–29.

Duffy, F. D., & Holmboe, E. S. (2006). Self-assessment in Lifelong Learning and Improving Performance in Practice. *Journal of the American Medical Association, 296*(9), 1137–1139. doi:10.1001/jama.296.9.1137

Dumbraveanu, R., & Balmus, N. (2006). Using learning objects in teaching science. *International Journal of Emerging Technologies in Learning, 1*(1). Retrieved May 5, 2009, from www.i-jet.org

Duridanov, L., & Simoff, S. (2007). 'Inner Listening' as a Basic Principle for Developing Immersive Virtual Worlds. *Online - Heidelberg Journal of Religions on the Internet, 2*(3).

Duval, E., Hodgins, W., Sutton, S., & Weibel, S. (2002). Metadata Principles and Practicalities. *D-Lib Magazine, 8*(4). Retrieved from http://www.dlib.org/dlib/april02/weibel/04weibel.html. doi:10.1045/april2002-weibel

Duval, E. (2006). LearnRank: Towards a real quality measure for learning. In Ehlers, U., & Pawlowski, J. M. (Eds.), *Handbook on quality and standardization in e-learning* (pp. 457–500). Heidelberg, Germany: Springer Berlin. doi:10.1007/3-540-32788-6_30

Duval, E., & Hodgins, W. (2003). A LOM Research Agenda. In *Proceedings of WWW2003 - Twelfth International World Wide Web Conference*, 20-24 May 2003, Budapest, Hungary (2003). Retrieved August 10, 2009, from http://www2003.org/cdrom/papers/alternate/P659/p659-duval.html.html

Duvekot, R. (2002). The dynamics of non-formal learning and the opening-up of national learning systems. In D. Collardyn (Ed.), *Lifelong Learning: which ways forward,* 89-104. Utrecht, The Netherlands: Lemma.

Dysthe, O., & Engelsen, K. T. (2004). Portfolios and assessment in teacher education in Norway: a theory based discussion of different models in two sites. *Assessment & Evaluation in Higher Education, 29*(2), 239–257. doi:10.1080/0260293042000188500

EADTU. (2009). *The European Association of Distance Teaching Universities*. Retrieved July 25, 2009, from: http://www.eadtu.nl

Ebert, C., & Jones, C. (2009). Embedded software: Facts, figures and future. *Computer, 42*(4), 42–51. doi:10.1109/MC.2009.118

Edelson, D. C. (2003). Realising authentic science learning through the adaptation of scientific practice. In Fraser, B. J., & Tobin, K. G. (Eds.), *International Handbook of Science Education* (pp. 317–331). London: Kluwer Academic Publishers.

Edelson, D. C., & Reiser, B. J. (2006). Making authentic practices accessible to learners: design, challenges and strategies. In Sawyer, R. K. (Ed.), *The Cambridge Handbook of the Learning Sciences* (pp. 335–354). New York: Cambridge University Press.

EduSpecs. (2004). *Benefits of specifications and standards*. Retrieved August 10, 2009, from http://www.eduspecs.ca/pub/specificationsandstandards/benefits_of_standards.html

Edwards, D., & Hardman, L. (1989). Lost in cyberspace: Cognitive mapping and navigation in a hypertext environment. In McAleese, R. (Ed.), *Hypertext: Theory into practice*. New York: Intellect Books.

Effective Practice with e-Learning. (2004). JISC. Retrieved June 24, 2009 from www.jisc.ac.uk/elearning

E-Framework. (2009). Retrieved from http://www.e-framework.org/

EHEA. (2009). *The European Higher Education Area in a global context. Report on overall developments at the European, national and institutional levels*. Approved by BFUG at its meeting in Prague, 12-13 February 2009. Retrieved on July 10 from http://www.ond.vlaanderen.be/hogeronderwijs/bologna/conference/documents/2009_EHEA_in_global_context.pdf

Ehlers, U.-D. (2007). Quality Literacy - Competencies for Quality Development in Education and e-Learning. *Journal of Educational Technology & Society, 10*(2), 96–108.

Ehlers, D. (2009). Understanding quality culture. *Quality Assurance in Education, 17*(4), 343–363. doi:10.1108/09684880910992322

El Emam, K. Drouin, J-N. & Melo, W. (1998). *SPICE: The theory and practice of software process improvement and capability determination*. California: IEEE Computer Society.

eLearningPR. Adopting a multi-annual programme (2004-2006) for the effective integration of Information and Communication Technologies (ICT) in education and training systems in Europe (eLearning Programme) (COM(2002) 751 - C5-0630/2002 - 2002/0303(COD)).

elearnspace, everything learning. (2002). *Preparing Students for Elearning*. Retrieved fromhttp://www.elearnspace.org/Articles/Preparingstudents.htm

Elliott, B. (2008). *Assessment 2.0: modernising assessment in the age of Web 2.0*. Retrieved July 9, 2009, from http://www.scribd.com/doc/461041/Assessment-20

Ellis, R. A., Jarkey, N., Mahony, M. J., Peat, M., & Sheely, S. (2007). Managing quality improvement of eLearning in a large, campus-based university. *Quality Assurance in Education, 15*(1), 9–23. doi:10.1108/09684880710723007

Emmorey, K. (Ed.). (2003). *Perspectives on Classifier Constructions in Sign Languages*. Upper Saddle River, NJ: Lawrence Erlbaum and Associates.

Engberg-Pedersen, E. (1993). *Space in Danish Sign Language*. Hamburg, Germany: Signum Verlag.

Erdosne, T. E., Morrow, B. L., & Ludvico, L. R. (2009). Designing blended inquiry learning in a laboratory context: A study of incorporating hands-on and virtual laboratories. *Innovative Higher Education, 33*(5), 333–344. doi:10.1007/s10755-008-9087-7

EU4ALL. (2009). The European Unified Approach for Assisted Lifelong learning (EU4ALL) (IST-FP6-034778). Retrieved on July 10 from http://www.eu4all-project.eu

EUNIS. (2009). European University Information Systems. Retrieved July 25, 2009, from: http://www.eunis.org/

European Comisión – Information Society and Media Directorate General. (2006). *Benchmarking Access and Use of ICT in European Schools 2006*. Final Report from Head Teacher and Classroom Teacher Surveys in 27 European Countries. Report was elaborated by *Empirica*. Retrieved July 23, 2009, from http://ec.europa.eu/information_society/eeurope/i2010/docs/studies/final_report_3.pdf

European Communities (EC). (2009). Europass: Opening doors to working and learning in Europe. Retrieved 2009 July 27 from http://europass.cedefop.europa.eu/europass/home/hornav/Introduction.csp?loc=en_GB

European Communities. (2009). The Europass curriculum vitae (CV). Retrieved 2009 April 9 from http://europass.cedefop.europa.eu/europass/home/vernav/Europasss+Documents/Europass+CV.csp.

Evans, S., & Douglas, G. (2008). E-Learning and Blindness: A comparative study of the quality of an E-Learning experience. *Journal of Visual Impairment & Blindness, 102*(2), 77–88.

Evansa, A. W., & McKennaa, C. (2005). Trainees' perspectives on the assessment and self-assessment of surgical skills. *Assessment & Evaluation in Higher Education, 30*(2), 163–174. doi:10.1080/0260293042000264253

Facer, K., Joiner, R., Stanton, D., Reid, J., Hull, R., & Kirk, D. (2004). Savannah: mobile gaming and learning? *Journal of Computer Assisted Learning, 20*, 399–409. doi:10.1111/j.1365-2729.2004.00105.x

Farrow, S. (2006). *The really useful Science book. A framework of knowldege for primary teachers*. London: Routledge.

Felder, R. M., & Silverman, L. K. (2002). Learning and Teaching Styles In Engineering Education. *Engr. Education, 78*(7), 674–681.

Fellbaum, C. (Ed.). (1998). *WordNet an electronic lexical database*. Cambridge, MA: MIT Press.

Fernández, B., Suárez, L., & Alvárez, E. (2006). El camino hacia el Espacio Europeo de Educación Superior: deficiencias metodológicas y propuestas de mejora desde la perspectiva del alumno. *Aula Abierta*, *88*, 85–105.

FGCU. (2006). Retrieved from http://www.fgcu.edu/onlinedesign/designDev.html

Field, A. (2005). *Discovering Statistics Using SPSS* (p. 779). London: SAGE Publications Ltd.

Fink, J., & Kobsa, A. Nill, A. (1998). *Adaptable and Adaptive Information Provision for All Users, Including Disabled and Elderly People*. Retrieved April 9, 2009, from: http://www.isr.uci.edu/~kobsa/papers/1998-NRHM-kobsa.pdf

Fleishmann, K. R. (2007). Standardization from below: Science and technology standards and educational software. *Journal of Educational Technology & Society*, *10*(4), 110–117.

Fleming, N., & Baume, D. (2006). Learning Styles Again: VARKing up the Right Tree! *Educational Developments*, *7*(4), 4–7.

FLEXO project. (2009). Retrieved from http://www.ines.org.es/flexo

Floriano, W. B. (2008). A portable bioinformatics course for upper-division undergraduate curriculum in sciences. *Biochemistry and Molecular Biology Education*, *36*(5), 325–335. doi:10.1002/bmb.20217

Fluid. (2009). Retrieved from http://fluidproject.org/

Foerster, H., & Psk, G. (1961). A Predictive Model for Self-Organizing Systems. Part I: *Cybernetica,* 3, pp. 258–300; Part II. *Cybernetica*, *4*, 20–55.

Fong, S. F., Ng, W. K., Ong, S. L., Hanafi, A., & Rozhan, I. (2005). Research in E-Learning in a Hybrid Environment - A Case for Blended Instruction. *Malaysian Online Journal of Instructional Technology*, *2*(2), 124–136.

Forrester, V. (2000). *Une étrange dictature*. Paris, France: Librairie Arthème Fayard.

Forrester, J. (1994). System Dynamics, System Thinking, and Soft OR. *System Dynamics Review*, *10*(2-3). doi:10.1002/sdr.4260100211

Fox, S. (2006). *A Pilot Case Study – New Zealand Tertiary College*. Retrieved 29 November, 2009 from http://elg.massey.ac.nz/index.php?title=Implementing_guidelines

Francis, D. E., & Murphy, E. (2008). Instructional designers' conceptualisations of learning objects. *Australasian Journal of Educational Technology, 24*(5), 475-486. Retrieved July 1, 2008, from http://www.ascilite.org.au/ajet/ajet24/francis.html

Franco, A. G., & Taber, K. (2008). Secondary students' thinking about familiar phenomena: Learners' explanations from a curriculum context where 'particles' is a key idea for organising teaching and learning. *International Journal of Science Education*, *31*(14), 1917–1952. doi:10.1080/09500690802307730

Frank, G., Gemeinhardt, D., & Ostyn, C. (2005) Linking Reusable Competency Definitions to Learning Activities. Paper n°2056 *in Proceedings of the (I/ITSEC) 2005 Conference*.

Frank, G., Hubal, R., & O'Bea, M. (2007) Using Competency Definitions to Adapt Training for Mission Success. Paper n°7131 *in Proceedings of the (I/ITSEC) 2007 Conference*.

Frattini, R. (2006). IMARK: A Partnership for Training. *INASP Newsletter*, *33*, 3–4.

Freeman, M., & McKenzie, J. (2002). Implementing and evaluating SPARK, a confidential web-based template for self and peer assessment of student teamwork: benefits of evaluating across different subjects. *British Journal of Educational Technology*, *33*(5), 553–572. doi:10.1111/1467-8535.00291

FREMA. *e-learning framework reference model for assessment.* (n.d.). Retrieved July 29, 2009, from http://www.frema.ecs.soton.ac.uk/.

Friedl, J. (2002). *Mastering Regular Expressions* (2nd ed.). Sebastopol, CA: O'Reilly.

Friesen, N. (2004). Three objections to learning objects and e-learning standards. In McGreal, R. (Ed.), *Online Education Using Learning Objects* (pp. 59–70). London: Routledge.

Friesen, N. (2004a). Learning objects and standards: Pedagogical neutrality and engagement. In *Proceedings of the IEEE International Conference on Advanced Learning Technologies*. Joensuu, Finland. Retrieved August 10, 2009, from http://phenom.educ.ualberta.ca/n/papers/learning_objects_pedagogical_neutrality.pdf

Friesen, N. (2005). Interoperatibility and Learning Objects: An Overview of E-learning Standardization. *Interdisciplinary Journal of Knowledge and Learning Objects, 1*.

Frimansson, A., & Hogan, J. (2005). Adopting standards-based XML file formats in open source localisation. *Localisation Focus*, *4*(4), 9–23.

Fry, D. (2001). *Introducing the Localisation Industry Standards Association*. Retrieved May 23, 2003, http://www.lisa.org/press/Introducing_LISA_2001.pdf

Frydenberg, J. (2002). Quality Standards in eLearning: A Matrix of Analysis. *International Review of Research in Open and Distance Learning*, *3*(2).

Fuentes, M., Feixas, M., Monereo, C., & Gairín, J. (2006). *Guia didàctica pel disseny virtual de cursos de postgrau en modalitat e-learning. III Jornada de Campus d'Innovació Docent*. Barcelona, Spain: UAB.

Gadd, E., Oppenheim, C., & Probets, S. (2003). How academics want to protect their open-access research papers. *Journal of Information Science*, *29*(5), 333–356. doi:10.1177/01655515030295002

Gagne, R. (1970). November 4, 2000. "Robert Gagne's Nine Steps of Instruction." Retrieved January 3, 2006, 2006, from http://www.nwlink.com/~donclark/hrd/learning/development.html

Gagne, R. M., Briggs, L. J., & Wager, W. W. (1992). *Principles of Instructional Design*. Orlando, FL: Harcourt Brace Jovanovich publishers.

Ganjalizadeh S. (2006). Overview of open source learning. *Management Systems, Educause Evolving Technologies committee*, 2006.

Garbett, R., Hardy, S., Manley, K., Titchen, A., & McCormack, B. (2007). Developing a qualitative approach to 360-degree feedback to aid understanding and development of clinical expertise. *Journal of Nursing Management*, *15*(3), 342–347. doi:10.1111/j.1365-2834.2007.00692.x

Garcia, R., Blat, J., et al. (2004). Limitations of some eLearning standards for supporting learning. In *Proceedings of the International Conference of Interactive Computer-Aided Learning*, ICL 2004 (in cooperation with ACM-Austrian Chapter, and supported by IEEE Education Society), Villach, Austria, ICL. Retrieved August 10, 2009, from http://www.iua.upf.edu/~dgriffiths/papers/garcia-griffiths_villach.pdf

García-Barriocanal, E., Sicilia, M.-A., & Lytras, M. (2007). Evaluating pedagogical classification frameworks for learning objects: A case study. *Computers in Human Behavior*, *23*, 2641–2655. doi:10.1016/j.chb.2006.08.001

García-Robles, R., Blat, J., Sayago, S., Griffiths, D., Casado, F., & Martinez, J. (2004). Limitations of some eLearning standards for supporting learning. In M. Auer & U. Auer, (Ed.), *Proceedings of the International Conference of Interactive Computer-Aided Learning, ICL 2004, Villach (Austria)*. In cooperation with ACM-Austrian Chapter, and supported by IEEE Education Society. Retrieved 2008-10-17, from http://www.iua.upf.es/ dgriffit/papers/garcia-griffiths_villach.pdf

Gardner, H. (1983). *Frames of Mind: The Theory of Multiple Intelligences*. New York: Basic Books.

Garisson, D. R., & Kanuka, H. (2004). Blended Learning: Uncovering its Transformative Potential in Higher Education. *The Internet and Higher Education*, *7*(2), 95–105. doi:10.1016/j.iheduc.2004.02.001

Garrison, D. R., & Akyol, Z. (2009). Role of instructional technology in the transformation of higher education. *Journal of Computing in Higher Education*, *21*(1), 19–30. doi:10.1007/s12528-009-9014-7

Garrison, D. R., & Vaughan, N. D. (2008). *Blended learning in higher education: framework, principles, and guidelines* (1st ed.). San Francisco: Jossey-Bass.

Gehringer, E. F. (2001). Electronic peer review and peer grading in computer-science courses. In *Proceedings of the 32nd SIGCSE Technical Symposium on Computer Science Education, Charlotte, North Carolina.*

Gennari, J. H., Musen, M. A., Fergerson, R. W., Grosso, W. E., Crubézy, M., & Eriksson, H. (2003). The Evolution of Protégé: An Environment for Knowledge-Based Systems Development. *International Journal of Human-Computer Studies*, *58*(1), 89–123. doi:10.1016/S1071-5819(02)00127-1

Gibbings, P., & Brodie, L. (2008). Team-based learning communities in virtual space. *International Journal of Engineering Education*, *24*(6), 1119–1129.

Gibbs, G., & Simpson, C. (2004). Conditions under which assessment supports students' learning. *Learning and Teaching in Higher Education, 5*(1), 3–31. Retrieved 2008-10-17, from http://www.glos.ac.uk/shareddata/dms /2B70988BBCD42A03949CB4F3CB78A516.pdf

Ginns, P., & Ellis, R. (2007). Quality in blended learning: Exploring the relationships between on-line and face-to-face teaching and learning. *The Internet and Higher Education*, *10*, 53–64. doi:10.1016/j.iheduc.2006.10.003

Gipps, C. (1999). Socio-cultural perspective on assessment. *Review of Research in Education*, *24*, 355–392.

Giunchiglia, F., Shvaiko, P., & Yatskevich, M. (2004). *S-Match: an algorithm and an implementation of semantic matching.* Technical Report # DIT-04-015, University of Trento, Department of Information and Communication Technology.

Gkatzidou, S., & Pearson, E. (2008). *A vision for truly adaptable and accessible learning objects. Australasian Society for Computers in Learning in Tertiary Education (ASCILITE)*. Melbourne, Australia: Conference.

Gómez, A. F., García, M. E., & Martínez, M. A. (2003). Nuevas tecnologías y herramientas en la teleformación. In Martínex, F. (Ed.), *Redes de formación en la enseñanza. Las nuevas perspectivas del trabajo coopertativo* (pp. 231–235). Barcelona, Spain: Paidós.

Goodyear, P., Salmon, G., Spector, M., & Tickner, S. (2001). Competences for Online Teching: A Special report. *Educational Techonology Research ¬ Development. ETR&D*, *1*(49), 65–72. doi:10.1007/BF02504508

Google. (n.d.). *Gadgets *API Developer's Guide*. Retrieved 4th August 2009 from: http://code.google.com/intl/en/apis/gadgets/docs/dev_guide.html

Gorissen, P. (2003). *Quickscan QTI: Usability study of QTI for De Digitale Universiteit.* Retrieved 2008-10-17, from http://www.gorissen.info/Pierre/qti/Quickscan_QTI_UK.pdf

Gorissen, P. (2006). *Quickscan QTI – 2006: Usability study of QTI for De Digitale Universiteit.* Retrieved 2008-10-17, from http://www.gorissen.info/Pierre/qti/Quickscan_QTI_2006.pdf

Government of Alberta. (2005). Records management competency profiles. Retrieved 2009-04-09 from http://www.im.gov.ab.ca/publications/pdf/RecordsMgmtCompetencyProfiles.pdf.

Graham, C. R. (2005). Blended Learning Systems: Definition, Current Trends, and Future Directions. *Handbook of blended learning: Global Perspectives, local designs.* San Francisco, CA: Pfeiffer Publishing. Retrieved from http://media.wiley.com/product_data/excerpt/86/07879775/0787977586.pdf

Graham, C., Cagiltay, K., Byung-Ro, L., Craner, J., & Duffy, T. (2001). Seven principles of effective teaching: A practical lens for evaluating online courses. *The Technology Source*, March/April 2001. Retrieved August 10, 2009, from http://technologysource.org/article/seven_principles_of_effective_teaching/

GRAPPLE project. (2009). Retrieved from www.grapple-project.org

Green, S., Jones, R., Pearson, E., & Gkatzidou, S. (2006). Accessibility and adaptability of learning objects: responding to metadata, learning patterns and profiles of needs and preferences. *ALT-J. Research in Learning Technology*, *14*(1), 117–129.

Green, S., Pearson, E., & Gkatzidou, S. (2009). Formal Specification of an Adaptable Personal Learning Environment Using Prolog. In *Proceedings of ACM MSIADU09, 1st ACM Workshop on Media Studies and Implementations to Improve Access to Disabled Users, Beijing, October 2009.*

Green, S., Pearson, E., & Stockton, C. (2006). Personal Learning Environments: Accessibility and Adaptability in the Design of an Inclusive Learning Management System. *AACE World Conference on Educational Multimedia (EDMEDIA)*, Orlando, FL.

Group, T. L. T. (n.d.). *Seven Principles.* Retrieved from http://www.tltgroup.org/Seven/Library_TOC.htm

Gulikers, J., Sluijsmans, D., Baartman, L., & Bartolo, P. (2009). The power of assessment in teacher education. In Swennen, A., & van der Klink, M. (Eds.), *Becoming a teacher educator. Theory and practice for teacher educators* (pp. 173–188). Dordrecht: Springer.

Gunawardena, C. N., & Zittle, F. J. (1997). Social presence as a predictor of satisfaction within a computer-mediated conferencing environment. *American Journal of Distance Education*, *11*(3), 8–26. doi:10.1080/08923649709526970

Gutierrez, S., Losa, F. J., & Delgado Kloos, C. (2008). Towards a formalization of the automatic generation of exercises. In *International Workshop on Authoring of Adaptive and Adaptable Hypermedia, in International Conference on Adaptive Hypermedia*. Berlin: Springer-Verlag.

Gutierrez, S., Pardo, A., & Delgado Kloos, C. (2004a). Beyond simple sequencing: Sequencing of learning activities using hierarchical graphs. In *International Conference in Web-Based Education*. New York: Acta Press.

Gutierrez, S., Pardo, A., & Delgado Kloos, C. (2004b). An Adaptive Tutoring System Based on Hierarchical Graphs. In *International Conference on Adaptive Hypermedia*, (pp. 401-404). Berlin: Springer-Verlag.

Gutierrez-Santos, S., Pardo, A., & Delgado Kloos, C. (2008). Authoring Courses with Rich Adaptive Sequencing for IMS Learning Design. *Journal of Universal Computer Science*, *14*(17), 2819–2839.

Gutierrez-Santos, S. (2007). *Sequencing of learning activities oriented towards reuse and auto-organization for intelligent tutoring systems,* PhD. Thesis, University Carlos III of Madrid, Madrid, Spain.

Guttmann, A. (1987). *Democratic Education*. Princeton, NJ: Princeton University Press.

Hansen, J. A., & Barnett, M., MaKinster, J. G. & Keating, T. (2004). The impact of three-dimensional computational modelling on student understanding of astronomical concepts: A quantitative analysis. *International Journal of Science Education*, *26*(11), 1365–1378. doi:10.1080/09500690420001673757

Hanson, P., Tomecka, A., & Wawrzaszek, S. (2007). *LTS statement on course management systems at Brandeis University*. Technical report, Brandeis University, Library & Technology Services, Waltham, MA, USA. Retrieved 2007-04-19, from http://latte.brandeis.edu/project/LTS-statement-on-CMS-at-Brandeis.pdf

Hardin, G. (1968). The Tragedy of the Commons. *Science*, *162*(3859), 1243–1248. doi:10.1126/science.162.3859.1243

Hare, H. (2009). *E-learning experts in Tanzania call for cheaper bandwidth: iicd.* Retrieved from http://www.iicd.org/articles/IICDnews.import2302/

Harland, C. M., Lamming, R. C., Walker, H., Phillips, W. E., Caldwell, N. D., & Johnsen, T. E. (2006). Supply management: Is it a discipline? *International Journal of Operations & Production Management*, *26*(7), 730–753. doi:10.1108/01443570610672211

Harper, B. (2003). Designing Learning Experiences: Supporting Teachers in the Process of Technology Change. In Dowling, C., & Lai, K.-W. (Eds.), *Information and Communication Technology and the Teacher of the Future* (pp. 15–28). Boston: Kluwer Academic.

Harris, J., & McCormack, R. (2000). *Translation is not enough. Considerations for global Internet development.* Sapient Report. Retrieved June 13, 2009, from http://www.sapient.com

Harvey, L. (2005). A history and critique of quality evaluation in the UK. *Quality Assurance in Education, 13*(4), 263–276. doi:10.1108/09684880510700608

Harzallah, M., Berio, G. & Vernadat, F. (2006). Analysis and Modeling of Individual Competencies: Toward Better Management of Human Resources. *IEEE Transactions on Systems, Man and Cybernetics: Part A: System and Humans, 36*(1).

Hassenzahl, M., & Wessler, R. (2000). Capturing Design Space From A User Perspective: The Repertory Grid Technique Revisited. *International Journal of Human-Computer Interaction, 12*(3-4), 441–459. doi:10.1207/S15327590IJHC1203&4_13

Hauger, D., & Kock, M. (2007). *State of the Art of Adaptivity in E-Learning Platforms. Workshop at Adaptivity and User Modeling in Interactive Systems ABIS 2007.* Germany: Halle/Salle.

HEA. (2006). *The UK Professional Standards Framework for teaching and supporting learning in higher education.* New York: Higher Education Academy. Retrieved August 10, 2009, from http://www.heacademy.ac.uk/assets/York/documents/ourwork/professional/ProfessionalStandards-Framework.pdf.

Heery, R., & Patel, M. (2000). *Application Profiles: Mixing and Matching Metadata Schemas.* Retrieved from http://www.ariadne.ac.uk/issue25/app-profiles/

Heims, S. (1991). *The Cybernetics Group.* Cambridge, MA: MIT Press.

Heinze, A., & Procter, C. T. (2004). *Reflections on the use of blended learning, in: Education in a Changing Environment,* September 13-14, 2004. Retrieved from http://www.ece.salford.ac.uk/proceedings/papers/ah

Hendrix, M., de Bra, P., Pechenizkiy, M., Smits, D., & Cristea, A. (2008). Defining Adaptation in a Generic Multi Layer Model: CAM: The GRAPPLE Conceptual Adaptation Model. In *Proceedings of European conference on Technology Enhanced Learning,* (pp. 132 - 143). Berlin: Springer-Verlag.

Hennessy, S., Wishart, J., Whitelock, D., Deaney, R., Brawn, R., & Velle, L. (2007). Pedagogical approaches for technology-integrated Science teaching. *Computers & Education, 48*(1), 137–152. doi:10.1016/j.compedu.2006.02.004

Henze, N., Dolog, P., & Neijdl, W. (2004). Reasoning and ontologies for personalized e-learning in the Semantic Web. *Journal of Educational Technology & Society, 7*(4), 82–97.

Heraz, A., & Frasson, C. (2009). Detecting guessed and random learners' answers through their brainwaves. *User Modeling, Adaptation, and Personalization Seventeenth International Conference, UMAP 2009,* Trento, Italy, (LNCS 5535, pp. 367-372). Berlin: Springer-Verlag.

Hernández Leo, D., Asensio Pérez, J. I., & Dimitriadis, Y. A. (2004, 30 August - 4 September 2004). *IMS Learning Design Support for the Formalization of Collaborative Learning Patterns.* Paper presented at the Fourth IEEE International Conference on Advanced Learning Technologies (ICALT'04), Joensuu, Finland.

Hernandez-Leo, D., Moghnieh, A., Navarrete, T., Blat, J., Gilabert, S., Santos, P., & Perez-Sanagustin, M. (2008). From planning learning paths to assessment: Innovations to the practical benefits of Learning Design. In *European LAMS Conference 2008* (pp. 139-140). June, 25-27, 2008, Cádiz, Spain.

Hernández-Serrano, M. J., González-Sánchez, M. & Muñoz-Rodríguez, J. M. (2009). Designing learning environments improving social interactions: essential variables for a virtual training space. *Procedia - Social and Behavioral Sciences (ISSHP/ISI Proceedings-SSCI), 1*(1), 2411-2415.

Hersh, W. R., Bhupatiraju, R. T., Greene, P. S., Smothers, V., & Cohen, C. (2006). Adopting e-learning standards in health care: competency-based learning in the medical informatics domain. *AMIA... Annual Symposium Proceedings / AMIA Symposium. AMIA Symposium, 2006*, 334–338.

Hewett, E. C. (1884). *A Treatise on Pedagogy for Young Teachers*. New York: Van Antwerp, Bragg & Co.; American Book Company. Digitized by Google and Retrieved 7/23/09 from Google Books at http://books.google.com/books?id=ERhKAAAAIAAJ&dq=pedagogy&printsec=frontcover&source=bl&ots=XaSQiCGsrY&sig=3jLq4dY082zzzO6ubumQWy2ebLQ&hl=en&ei=RR9qSu-jGMawtge5i-C7Cw&sa=X&oi=book_result&ct=result&resnum=1

Heylighen, F. (1996). *Complex Adaptive Systems*. Retrieved November, 2007 from http://pespmc1.vub.ac.be/CAS.html

Higgins, A. (2004). *Distance Education in Australia and New Zealand: Challenges and Successes.*

Hirata, K., & Brown, M. (2007). *Request for information on Skills Management Architecture*. Object Management Group.

Hirata, K., & Saito, M. (2009). Core Technology and Standardization of Skill Management System-In Case of ETSS. *SEC Journal, 15*(2), 62–67.

Hirata, K., & Brown, M. (2008). Skill-Competency Management Architecture, *Workshop Proceedings of the 16th International Conference on Computers in Education, Taipei, Taiwan*. Downloaded 2009/07/14 from http://apsce.net/icce2008/Workshop_Proceedings/Workshop_Proceedings_0179-185.pdf

Hirata, K., Ohara, S., & Makiuchi, K. (2007). Meta Model for Skill and Competency Semantics. *Proceedings of the 8th International Conference on Information Technology Based Higher Education and Training. Kumamoto, Japan.*

Hirata, K., Seta, K., & Makiuchi, K. (2007). Skill and Competency Modelling Typology. *Workshop Proceedings of the 15th International Conference on Computers in Education, Hiroshima, Japan.*

Hitzler, P., Krötzsch, M., Parsia, B., Patel-Schneider, P., & Rudolph, S. (Eds.). (2009). *OWL 2 Web Ontology Language: Primer*. W3C Working Draft. Retrieved from http://www.w3.org/TR/owl2-primer/

Hoadley, C. (2002). Creating context: Design-based research in creating and understanding CSCL. In Stahl, G. (Ed.), *Computer Support for Collaborative Learning* (pp. 453–462). Mahwah, NJ: Lawrence Erlbaum Associates.

Hodge, G. (2005). Metadata for electronic information resources: from variety to interoperability. *Information Services & Use, 25*(1), 35–45.

Hodgins, H. W. (2002). The future of learning objects. In J.R. Lohmann & M.L. Corradini (Eds.), *ECI Conference on e-Technologies in Engineering Education Learning Outcomes Providing Future Possibilities: Vol. P11.* (pp. 1-8). Davos, Switzerland: ECI.

Hodgkinson, M., & Kelly, M. (2007). Quality management and Enhancement processes in UK Business schools: a review. *Quality Assurance in Education, 15*(1), 77–91. doi:10.1108/09684880710723043

Hoyles, C., & Noss, R. (2009). The Technological Mediation of Mathematics and Its Learning. *Human Development, 52*, 129–147. doi:10.1159/000202730

Huang, W., Webster, D., Wood, D., & Ishaya, T. (2006). An intelligent semantic e-learning framework using context-aware Semantic Web technologies. *British Journal of Educational Technology, 37*(3), 351–373. doi:10.1111/j.1467-8535.2006.00610.x

Hutcheon, P. (2001). *The Classroom as a Social System.* Retrieved November, 2007 from http://www.humanists.net/pdhutcheon/Books/classrm.htm

Hwang, A., & Arbaugh, J. B. (2009). Seeking feedback in blended learning: competitive versus cooperative student attitudes and their links to learning outcome. *Journal of Computer Assisted Learning, 25*(3), 280 – 293. Retrieved 08-14-09 from http://www3.interscience.wiley.com/journal/122294318/abstract?CRETRY=1&SRETRY=0

Hylén, J. (2005). *Open educational resources: Opportunities and challenges.* OECD-CERI. Retrieved June 22, 2009, from http://ihs.se/upload/3331/OpenEducationalResources%20-%20Opportunities%20and%20Challanges.pdf

IEEE. (1990). *IEEE Standard Computer Dictionary: A Compilation of IEEE Standard Computer Glossaries.* New York: IEEE.

IEEE Learning Technology Standards Committee (LTSC). (2002). *12.1Learning Object Metadata Final Draft Standard* (p. 1484). Piscataway, NJ: IEEE.

IEEE LOM. (2002). *Draft standard.* Retrieved July 22, 2009, from http://ltsc.ieee.org/wg12/files/LOM_1484_12_1_v1_Final_Draft.pdf

IEEE LTSC. (2008). *Draft Recommended Practice for Expressing IEEE Learning Object Metadata Instances Using the Dublin Core Abstract Model (IEEE P1484.12.4/D1).* Retrieved from http://dublincore.org/educationwiki/DCMIIEEELTSCTaskforce?action=AttachFile&do=get&target=LOM-DCAM-newdraft.pdf

IEEE Software. (2007). Achieving Quality in Open Source Software. *Aberdour,* (Jan/Feb). *Illinois Online Network.* (2007). Retrieved from http://www.ion.uillinois.edu/resources/tutorials/id/index.asp

IEEE Standard for Learning Object Metadata IEEE Std 1484.12.1™(2002). Retrieved November 1st2005:http://www.ieeeltsc.org/wg12LOM

IEEE. (2002). *IEEE 1484.12.1-2002 IEEE Standard for Learning Object Metadata.* Retrieved August 10, 2009, from http://ltsc.ieee.org/wg12/index.html

IEEE. (2005). *IEEE LTSC WG11: Computing Managed Instruction.* Retrieved August 9, 2009, from: http://ltsc.ieee.org/wg11/

IHEP. (2000). *Quality on the line: Benchmarks for success in Internet-based education.* Retrieved 29 November, 2009, from http://www.ihep.org/Publications/publications-detail.cfm?id=69

IIEP, International Institute for Education Planning. (n.d.). *Home page.* Retrieved June 22, 2009, from http://www.iiep.unesco.org/

IMS GLC. (2003). *IMS Simple Sequencing Specification.* IMS Global Learning Consortium. Retrieved 2008-10-17, from http://imsglobal.org/simplesequencing/. Version 1.0

IMS GLC. (2004). *IMS Content Packaging Specification.* IMS Global Learning Consortium. Retrieved 2008-10-17, from http://imsglobal.org/content/packaging/. Version 1.1.4

IMS GLC. (2005). *IMS Question & Test Interoperability Specification.* IMS Global Learning Consortium. Retrieved 2008-10-17, from http://imsglobal.org/question/. Version 2.0 Final Specification.

IMS GLC. (2008). *IMS Common Cartridge Profile.* IMS Global Learning Consortium. Retrieved 2009-08-06, from http://www.imsglobal.org/cc/. Version 1.0 Final Specification.

IMS Global Learning Consortium Inc. (2003). *IMS Learning Design Standard Specification.* Retrieved July 23, 2009 from http://www.imsglobal.org/learningdesign/index.html

IMS Global Learning Consortium Learner Information PackageAccessibility for LIP Version 1.0 Final Specification: Information Model, XML Binding. (2003). *Best Practice Guide, Conformance Specification, Use Cases, Examples, June 2003.* Retrieved 4th August 2009 from http://www.imsglobal.org/accessibility

IMS Global Learning Consortium, Inc. (2006) *IMS Question and Test Interoperability Version 2.1 Public Draft Specification.* Retrieved July 01, 2009, from http://www.imsglobal.org/question/qtiv2p1pd2/imsqti_oviewv2p1pd2.html

IMS Global Learning Consortium. (2003a). *IMS Simple Sequencing Information and Behavior Model*. Retrieved July 20, 2009 from http://www.imsglobal.org/specifications.html

IMS Global Learning Consortium. (2003b). *IMS Simple Sequencing Best Practice and Implementation Guide*. Retrieved July 20, 2009 from http://www.imsglobal.org/specifications.html

IMS Global Learning Consortium. (n.d.). *Guidelines for Developing Accessible Learning Applications, version 1.0*. Retrieved 4th August 2009 from: http://ncam.wgbh.org/salt/guidelines/

IMS Global Learning Consortium. *IMS Common Cartridge Profile Date: 1 October 2008. Version 1.0 Final Specification*. (2008). Retrieved July 10, 2009, from http://www.imsglobal.org/cc/ccv1p0/imscc_profilev1p0.html#0_pgfId-1754146

IMS Global Learning Consortium. *IMS Question & Test Interoperability Specification*. (n.d.). Retrieved July 29, 2009, from http://www.imsglobal.org/question/.

IMS LD. (2003). *IMS Learning Design Specification*. Retrieved July 12, 2009, from http://www.imsglobal.org/learningdesign/index.cfm

IMS Meta-data Specification. *IMS Content Packaging*. (2006). Retrieved July 29, 2009, from http://imsproject.org

IMS QTI. (2003). *IMS Question and Test Interoperability Specification*. Retrieved July 12, 2009, from http://www.imsglobal.org/question/index.html

IMS QTI. (2006). *IMS Question and Test Interoperability Overview*. Retrieved November 4, 2008, from http://www.imsglobal.org/question/qtiv2p1pd2/imsqti_oviewv2p1pd2.html

IMS SS. (2003). *IMS Simple Sequencing Specification*. Retrieved July 12, 2009, from http://www.imsglobal.org/simplesequencing/index.html

IMS. (2003). *IMS Content Packaging Specification Version 1.1.3*. Retrieved August 10, 2009, from http://www.imsglobal.org/content/packaging/

IMS. (2003a). *IMS Learning Design Information Model: Version 1.0 Final Specification*. Retrieved from http://www.imsproject.org/learningdesign/ldv1p0/imsld_infov1p0.html

IMS. (2004, August 23). *IMS Global Learning Consortium*. Retrieved August 07, 2009, from: IMS Guidelines for Developing Accessible Learning Applications http://www.imsglobal.org/accessibility/accessiblevers/index.html

IMS. *AccessForAll*. (2004). IMS Global learning/Dublin Core AccessForAll project, Meta-data Specification Version 1.0 Final Specification: Overview, Information Model, XML Binding, Best Practice Guide 2004. Retrieved 4th August 2009 from: http://www.imsglobal.org/accessibility

IMS-LD. (2003). IMS Learning Design Specification. Retrieved January 21, 2009 from: http://www.imsglobal.org/learningdesign/

Inglis, A. (2008). Approaches to the validation of quality frameworks for e-learning. *Quality Assurance in Education*, *16*(4), 347–362. doi:10.1108/09684880810906490

Inglis, A. (2005). Quality improvement, quality assurance, and benchmarking: comparing two frameworks for managing quality processes in open and distance learning. *International Review of Research in Open and Distance Learning*, *6*(1).

Institute of Electrical and Electronics Engineers, Inc. (2002). [New York: Global Engineering Documents.]. *IEEE Computer Standard for Learning Objects Metadata*, *1484*(12), 1.

Instructional Technology Resource Center. (2007). *Final evaluation and recommendation report*. Technical report, Idaho State University, Pocatello, Idaho, USA. Retrieved 2008-12-11, from http://www.isu.edu/itrc/resources/LMS_FINAL_REPORT_MOODLE.pdf.

Interoperability: JISC. (n.d.). Retrieved July 29, 2009, from http://www.jisc.ac.uk/whatwedo/topics/interoperability.aspx.

Iorio, A. D., Feliziani, A. A., Mirri, S., Salomoni, P., & Vitali, F. (2006). Automatically Producing Accessible Learning Objects. *Journal of Educational Technology & Society*, *9*(4), 3–16.

ISO (International Organization for Standardization) (1996). ISO/IEC 14977:1996. Information technology – Syntactic metalanguage – Extended BNF.

ISO (International Organization for Standardization) (2003). ISO/IEC 19757-2:2003. *Information technology – Document Schema Definition Language (DSDL) – Part 2: Regular-grammar-based validation – RELAX NG.*

ISO (International Organization for Standardization). (1986). [E] [. Information processing — Text and office systems — Standard Generalized Markup Language] [SGML]. *ISO*, *8879*, 1986.

ISO 13407 (1999): "Human-centered design processes for interactive systems".

ISO 21127. (2006). Information and Documentation – A reference ontology for the interchange of cultural heritage information.

ISO IEC JTC1 SC36 WG7 (2008). Individualized Adaptability and Accessibility in E-learning, Education and Training. *ISO/IEC 24751-1.*

ISO. (August 07, 2009). ISO International Organization for Standardization. Retrieved August 07, 2009, from: JTC 1/SC 36: http://www.iso.org/iso/standards_development/technical_committees/list_of_iso_technical_committees/iso_technical_committee.htm?commid=45392

ISO/IEC. (1996). *Guide 2: Standardization and related activities - General vocabulary*. Geneva: International Standards Organisation/International Electrotechnical Commission.

ISO/IEC. (2009). *DTR 24763 project: Information Technologies for Learning*. Education and Training - A Conceptual Reference Model for Competencies and Related Objects.

ISO/IEC 24751 (2009). Individualized adaptability and accessibility in e-learning, education and training.

ISO/IEC 24752 (2008) Information technology -- User interfaces -- Universal remote console

ISO/IEC JTC1 SC36 WG7. (n.d). *Home page*. Retrieved July 22, 2009, from http://isotc.iso.org/livelink/livelink?func=ll&objId=4920256&objAction=browse&sort=name.

Jackl, A. (2004). IMS AccessForAll Meta-data XML Binding. Retrieved January 12, 2009 from http://www.imsproject.org accessed

Jackson, K., & D'Alessandro, N. (2003). *Implementation of a quality assurance system for online units at the University of Tasmania.* Paper presented at the Interact, Integrate, Impact: Proceedings of the 20th Annual Conference of the Australasian Society for Computers in Learning in Tertiary Education. Adelaide.

Jara, M., & Mellar, H. (2009). Factors affecting quality enhancement procedures for e-learning courses. *Qulatiy Assurance in Education*, *17*(3), 220–232. doi:10.1108/09684880910970632

Jellema, F., Visscher, A., & Scheerens, J. (2006). Measuring change in work behavior by means of multisource feedback. *International Journal of Training and Development*, *10*(2), 121–139. doi:10.1111/j.1468-2419.2006.00248.x

JISC. (2004). *Effective Practice with e-Learning. A good practice guide in designing for learning.* Retrieved 29 November, 2009, from http://www.jisc.ac.uk/uploaded_documents/jisc%20effective%20practice3.pdf

Johnson, E. M., & Walker, R. (2007). The Promise and Practice of E-Learning within Complex Tertiary Environments. In *Seventh IEEE International Conference on Advanced Learning Technologies*, (ICALT 2007), (pp: 753-757). Retrieved from http://ieeexplore.ieee.org/xpl/freeabs_all.jsp?arnumber=4281149

Johnston, L., & Miles, L. (2004). Assessing contributions to group assignments. *Assessment & Evaluation in Higher Education*, *29*(4), 751–768. doi:10.1080/0260293042000227272

Johnston, T., Vermeerbergen, M., Schembri, A., & Leeson, L. (2007). 'Real data are messy': Considering cross-linguistic analysis of constituent ordering in Australian Sign Language (Auslan), Vlaamse Gebarentaal (VGT), and Irish Sign Language (ISL). In Perniss, P., Pfau, R., & Steinbach, M. (Eds.), *Visible Variation: Comparative Studies on Sign Language Structure*. Berlin: Mouton de Gruyter.

Johnston, P., Nelson, M., Sanderson, R., & Warner, S. (Eds.). (2008). *ORE Specification - Abstract Data Model*. Retrieved from http://www.openarchives.org/ore/1.0/datamodel

Jones, E. (2002). Implications of SCORM and Emerging E-learning Standards On Engineering Education. In *Proceedings of the 2002 ASEE Gulf-Southwest Annual Conference*, The University of Louisiana at Lafayette, March 20 – 22, 2002.

Joosten - ten Brinke, D., Van Bruggen, J., Hermans, H., Latour, I., Burgers, J., Giesbers, B., & Koper, R. (2007). Modeling Assessment for Re-use of Traditional and New Types of Assessment. *Computers in Human Behavior, 23*(6), 2721-2741.

Joosten-ten Brinke, D. (2008). *Assessment of prior learning*. Heerlen, The Netherlands: Open Universiteit Nederland.

Jovanovic, J., Gasevic, D., & Devedzic, V. (2006). Ontology-Based Automatic Annotation of Learning Content. *Semantic Web and Information Systems*, *2*(2), 91–119.

Jovanović, J., Gašević, D., Verbert, K., & Duval, E. (2005). Ontology of learning object content structure. In *12th International Conference on Artificial Intelligence in Education*, July 18-22, Amsterdam, The Netherlands.

Jung, I. (2008). ICT and quality assurance to support ubiquitous access to distance education: Promises, realities, and recent breakthroughs. In *Fifth EDEN Research Workshop 20-22 OCTOBER, 2008* Paris, France. Retrieved July 26, 2009 from http://www.eden-online.org/eden.php?menuId=421

Kalakota, R., & Robinson, M. (2001). *E-Business 2.0: Roadmap to Success*. Boston, MA: Addison-Wesley.

Kalfoglou, Y. (2001). *Exploring Ontologies 1: Fundamentals* (pp. 863–887). Washington, DC: World Scientific Publishing.

Kali, Y. (in press). The design principles database as means for promoting design-based research. In Kelly, A. E., Lesh, R. A., & Baek, J. Y. (Eds.), *Handbook of Innovative Design Research in Science, Technology, Engineering, Mathematics (STEM) Education*. Mahwah, NJ: Lawrence Erlbaum Associates.

Kalinga, E. A., & Burchard, R. B., Bagile, Trojer, L. (2007). Strategies for Developing e-LMS for Tanzania Secondary Schools. *International Journal of Social Sciences*, *2*(3), 145–149.

Kanellopoulos, D., Kotsiantis, S., & Pintelas, P. (2006). Considering the educational Semantic Web. *Themes in Education*, *7*(2), 145–164.

Kanellopoulos, D., Kotsiantis, S., & Pintelas, P. (2009). An ontology-based framework for supporting localisation of e-learning content. *Annals of Mathematics. Computing & Teleinformatics*, *1*(6), 1–10.

Karampiperis, P., & Sampson, D. (2004). A Flexible Authoring Tool supporting Adaptive Learning Activities. In *Proc. of IADIS International Conference on Cognition and Exploratory Learning in Digital Age (CELDA 2004)*, Lisbon, Portugal.

Karampiperis, P., & Sampson, D. (2004). Adaptive instructional planning using ontologies. In *Proceedings of the 4th IEEE International Conference on Advanced Learning Technologies*, (pp. 126–130).

Karampiperis, P., & Sampson, D. (2005). Designing learning services for open learning systems utilizing learning design. In V. Uskov, (Ed.), *Proceedings of the 4th IASTED International Conference on Web-based Education*, (pp. 279-284). Grindelwald, Switzerland: ACTA Press.

Karampiperis, P., Sampson, D., & Fytros, D. (2006). Lifelong Competence Development: Towards a Common Metadata Model for Competencies Description - The Case Study of Europass Language Passport. In *Proceedings of the 6th IEEE International Conference on Advanced Learning Technologies*, Kerkrade, The Netherlands.

Kavanaugh, A., Carroll, J. M., Rosson, M. B., Reese, D. D., & Zin, T. T. (2005). Participating in civil society: the case of networked communities. *Interacting with Computers*, *17*(1), 9–33. doi:10.1016/j.intcom.2004.10.006

Kay, R. H., & Knaack, L. (2007). Evaluating the learning in learning objects. *Open Learning*, *22*(2), 5–28. doi:10.1080/02680510601100135

Kay, R. H., & Knaack, L. (2009). Assessing learning, quality and engagement in learning objects: The learning object evaluation scale for students (LOES-S). *Educational Technology Research and Development*, *57*(2), 147–168. doi:10.1007/s11423-008-9094-5

Kay, J. (2007, 28 July). Educational Uses of Second Life. Wikispaces posted to http://sleducation.wikispaces.com/educationaluses.

Kearney, M. (2004). Classroom use of multimedia-supported predict-observe-explain tasks in a social constructivist learning environment. *Research in Science Education*, *34*(4), 427–453. doi:10.1007/s11165-004-8795-y

Kelly, H. F., Ponton, M. K., & Rovai, A. P. (2007). A comparison of student evaluations of teaching between online and face-to-face courses. *The Internet and Higher Education*, *10*(1), 89–101. doi:10.1016/j.iheduc.2007.02.001

Kelly, B., Sloan, D., Brown, S., Seale, J., Petrie, H., & Lauke, P. Ball. S. (2007). Accessibility 2.0: people, policies and processes, In Proceedings of the 2007 international cross-disciplinary conference on Web accessibility (W4A), May 07-08, Banff, Canada.

Keppel, M., Ada, E. A., & Chan, C. (2006). Peer learning and learning-oriented assessment in technology enhanced environments. *Assessment & Evaluation in Higher Education*, *31*(4), 453–464.

Kettner-Polley, R. B. (1999). The making of a virtual professor. *ALN Magazine*, (3)1.

Khuwaja, R., Desmarais, M., & Cheng, R. (1996). Intelligent guide: Combining user knowledge assesment with pedagogical guidance. In *Proceedings of Intelligent Tutoring Systems*. Berlin: Springer-Verlag.

Kiboss, J. K. (2002). Impact of a computer-based physics instruction program on pupils' understanding of measurement concepts and methods associated with school science. *Journal of Science Education and Technology*, *11*(2), 193–198. doi:10.1023/A:1014673615275

Kineo open source. (2008). *Open source learning management systems: a primer*. Retrieved from http://www.kineoopensource.com/index.php/free-resources/insights/Open-source-learning-management-systems.html

Kirby, N. F., & Downs, C. T. (2007). Self-assessment and the disadvantaged student: potential for encouraging self-regulated learning? *Assessment & Evaluation in Higher Education*, *32*(4), 475–494. doi:10.1080/02602930600896464

Kiser, K. (2002). Is Blended Best? [Electronic Version]. *E-learning Magazine*. Retrieved from http://www.elearningmag.com/elearning/article/ articleDetail.jsp?id=21259

Klima, E., & Bellugi, U. (1979). *The Signs of Language*. Cambridge, MA: Harvard University Press.

Kljun, M., Vicic, J., Kavsek, B., & Kavcic, A. (2007). Evaluating Comparisons and Evaluations of Learning Management Systems. Information Technology Interfaces, 2007. In *29th International Conference on Information Technology Interface*, 25-28 June 2007, (pp. 363-368).

Knight, C., Gašević, D., & Richards, G. (2006). An ontology-based framework for bridging learning design and learning content. *Journal of Educational Technology & Society*, *9*(1), 23–37.

Ko, C. C., & Cheng, C. D. (2008). Web-based laboratories for internet remote Experimentation. *World Review of Science. Technology and Sustainable Development*, *5*(3-4), 301–314. doi:10.1504/WRSTSD.2008.020285

Kobsa, A. (2007) Privacy Enhanced Personalization. Communications of the ACM, 50(8), pp.24-33, Aug. Proc. 2, Second International Conference on Mobile and Ubiquitous

Kolb, D. (1984). *Experiential Learning: Experience as the source of learning and development*. Englewood Cliffs, NJ: Prentice-Hall.

Koohang, A. (2009). A learner-centred model for blended learning design. *International Journal of Innovation and Learning*, *6*, 76–91. doi:10.1504/IJIL.2009.021685

Koper, R., & Burgos, D. (2005). Developing advanced units of learning using IMS Learning Design level B. *International Journal on Advanced Technology for Learning*, *2*(4), 252–259.

Koper, R., & Olivier, B. (2004). Representing the Learning Design of Units of Learning. *Journal of Educational Technology & Society*, *7*(3), 97–111.

Koper, R., & Manderveld, J. (2004). Educational modelling language: modelling reusable, interoperable, rich and personalised units of learning. *British Journal of Educational Technology*, *35*(5), 537–551. doi:10.1111/j.0007-1013.2004.00412.x

Koper, R., & Tattersall, C. (2005). Preface to Learning Design: A Handbook on Modelling and Delivering Networked Education and Training. *Journal of Interactive Media in Education*, *18*, 1–7.

Koper, R., & Olivier, B. (2004). Representing the learning design of units of learning. *Journal of Educational Technology & Society*, *7*(3), 97–111.

Koper, R. (2005). Designing learning networks for lifelong learners. In Koper, R., & Tattersall, C. (Eds.), *Learning Design: A Handbook on Modelling and Delivering Networked Education and Training*. Berlin: Springer.

Koper, R. (2006). Current Research in Learning Design. *Educational Technology & Society, 9*(1), 13-22. Retrieved July 23, 2009 from http://ifets.info/journals/9_1/3.pdf

Koper, R. van Es, R. (2001). *Modeling units of learning from a pedagogical perspective.* Amsterdam: Open Universiteit Nederland.

Koper, R., & Olivier, B. (2003). Representing the learning design of units of learning. *Journal*, 1-18. Retrieved from http://dspace.ou.nl/bitstream/1820/19/2/IMSLD-article%20v1p07-final.pdf

Koper, R., Rodrígues-Artacho, M., Lefrere, P., Rawlings, A., & Rosmalen, P. (2002). Survey of Educational Modelling Languages (EMLs). *Journal,* (September 2002), 1-79. Retrieved from http://dspace.ou.nl/dspace/handle/1820/227

Koszalka, T. A., & Wang, X. (2002). Integrating technology into learning: A summary view of promises and problems. *Journal of Educational Technology & Society*, *5*(1).

Koutsomitropoulos, D., Solomou, G., Alexopoulos, A., & Papatheodorou, T. (2009a). Semantic Metadata Interoperability and Inference-Based Querying in Digital Repositories. *Journal of Information Technology Research*, *2*(4), 37–53.

Koutsomitropoulos, D., Solomou, G., Alexopoulos, A., & Papatheodorou, T. (2009b). Knowledge Management and Acquisition in Digital Repositories: A Semantic Web Perspective. In *international Conference on Knowledge Management and Information Discovery*.

Krain, B., & Gabel, L. (2007). Designing a Total Force Competencies Architecture for the Navy, *Proceedings of the Seventh Annual Navy Workforce Research and Analysis Conference. Arlington, VA, USA.*

Krajcik, J., & Blumenfeld, P. C. (2006). Project-based learning. In Sawyer, R. K. (Ed.), *The Cambridge Handbook of the Learning Sciences* (pp. 317–334). New York: Cambridge University Press.

Krange, I., & Ludvigsen, S. (2009). Original article: The historical and situated nature of design experiments - Implications for data analysis. *Journal of Computer Assisted Learning*, *25*(3), 268–279. doi:10.1111/j.1365-2729.2008.00307.x

Kravcik, M., & Specht, M. (2005). Experience with WINDS Virtual University In: P. Kommers, G. Richards (eds.) Proc. of the ED-MEDIA 2005 Conference, 642-649

Kuehn, L. (1999, October). *Responding to Globalization of Education in the Americas— Strategies to Support Public Education*. Presentation to IDEA conference, Quito, Ecuador.

Kuhn, T. (1962). *The Structure of Scientific Revolutions*. Chicago: University of Chicago Press.

Kurzweil, R. (2005). *The singularity is near*. New York: Penguin.

Kyle, J. G., & Woll, B. (1985). *Sign Language: The Study of Deaf People and their Language*. Cambridge, UK: Cambridge University Press.

Labov, W. (1969). The Logic of Nonstandard English. In *Georgetown Univeristy 20th Annual Round Table, Monograph Series on Languages and Linguistics*, No. 22.

Lagoze, C., Van de Sompel, H., Nelson, M., & Warner, S. (2002). *The Open Archive Initiative Protocol for Metadata Harvesting*. Retrieved from http://www.openarchives.org/OAI/openarchivesprotocol.html

Lakhan, S. E., & Jhunjhunwala, K. (2008). *EDUCAUSE Quarterly, 31(2, April–June)*. Retrieved from.

Lalos, P., Lazarinis, F., & Kanellopoulos, D. (2009). E-snakes and ladders: a hypermedia educational environment for portable devices. *Int. J. Mobile Learning and Organisation*, *3*(2), 107–127. doi:10.1504/IJMLO.2009.024421

Landon, B. (2000). *On-line educational delivery applications: a web tool for comparative analysis*. A web site for the project supported by SCET, OLT and The Center for Learning Technologies at Mount Allison University. Retrieved July 23, 2009, from http://www.c2t2.ca/landonline/

Lanzilotti, R., Ardito, C., Costabile, M. F., & Angeli, A. D. (2006). eLSE Methodology: a Systematic Approach to the e-Learning Systems Evaluation. *Journal of Educational Technology & Society*, *9*(4), 42–53.

Lappin, S., & Leass, H. (1994). An algorithm for pronominal anaphora resolution. *Computational Linguistics*, *20*(4), 535–562.

Larsen, K., & Vincent-Lancrin, S. (2006). The Impact of ICT on Tertiary Education: Advances and Promises. In Foray, D., & Kahin, B. (Eds.), *Advancing Knowledge and the Knowledge Economy*. Cambridge, MA: MIT Press.

Lassila, O., & Swick, R. R. (1999). *Resource description framework (RDF) model and syntax specification.* Retrieved October 1, 2001, from http://www.w3.org/TR/1999/REC-rdf-syntax-19990222i

Lau, A. K. W. (2007). Educational supply chain management: A case study. *Horizon*, *15*(1), 15–27. doi:10.1108/10748120710735239

Laurillard, D. (2002). *Rethinking University Teaching: A Conversational Framework for the Effective Use of Learning Technologies* (2nd ed.). London: Routledge. doi:10.4324/9780203304846

Lazarinis, F., Green, S., & Pearson, E. (2009). Measuring the conformance of hypermedia assessment tools to QTI. *International Journal of Innovation and Learning*, *6*(2), 127–146. doi:10.1504/IJIL.2009.022809

Lazarinis, F. (2004). A Template Based System for Automatic Construction of Online Courseware for Secondary Educational Schools. *Journal of Educational Technology & Society*, *7*(3), 112–123.

Lazarinis, F., Green, S., & Koutromanos, G. (2009). *Web-Based Learner Profile Management Using IMS IP. Paper presented in International Technology, Education and Development Conference (INTED 2009),* Valencia, Spain.

Lazarinis, F., Green, S., Pearson, E. (2009). Measuring the conformance of hypermedia assessment tools to QTI. *International Journal of Innovation and Learning*, *6*(2), 127–146. doi:10.1504/IJIL.2009.022809

Lazarinis, F. (2006) A hypermedia environment for managing online courseware based on adaptable templates. *International Conference on Virtual Learning,* (pp. 239-246).

Lazarinis, F., Green, S., & Pearson, E. (2009) Focusing on content reusability and interoperability in a personalized hypermedia assessment tool, Multimedia Tools and Applications Journal, Springer, http://www.springerlink.com/content/u34211037737ur42/.

Lazarinis, F., Green, S., & Pearson, E. (n.d.). *Engineering an interoperable multimedia assessment authoring and run-time environment conforming to IMS QTI.*

Lazarinis, F., Koutromanos, G., Green, S., & Pearson, E. (2009). Utilizing a multicriteria multimedia adaptive tool in formative assessments. In *Proceedings of the International Technology, Education and Development Conference* (pp. 1522-1528), Valencia, Spain.

Le Master, B. (1999-2000). Reappropriation of Gendered Irish Sign Language in One Family, *Visual. Anthropological Review, 15*(2), 1–15.

Le Master, B. (2002). What Difference Does Difference Make? Negotiating Gender and Generation in Irish Sign Language. In Benor, S., Rose, M., Sharma, D., & Shang, Q. (Eds.), *Gendered Practices in Language*. Stanford: Centre for the Study of Languages and Information Publication.

Le Master, B. (1990). *The Maintenance and Loss of Female and Male Signs in the Dublin Deaf Community*, PhD. Dissertation, Los Angeles, University of California, Los Angeles, CA.

Learning Resource Metadata, I. M. S. (n.d). *Specification*. Retrieved July 27, 2009, from http://www.imsglobal.org/metadata/index.html

Learning, A. D. (ADL) Initiative. (2001). Sharable Courseware Object Reference Model (SCORM). *The SCORM Overview*, October 1, 2001. Retrieved July 23, 2009, from http://www.adlnet.gov/Technologies/scorm

Lee, C., Yeh, D., Kung, R. J., & Hsu, C. (2007). The influences of learning portfolios and attitudes on learning effects in blended e-learning for mathematics. *Journal of Educational Computing Research, 37*(4), 331. doi:10.2190/EC.37.4.a

Lee, C., Helal, S., & Lee, W. (2006) Universal Interactions with Smart Spaces. Pervasive computing. January-March, 2006. pp 16-21.

Leeming, D. (Ed.). (2001). *A Dictionary of Asian Mythology* (Oxford Reference Online ed.). London: Oxford University Press.

Leeson, L. (1997). *The ABC of ISL. Booklet to accompany the TV series*. Dublin: RTE/Irish Deaf Society.

Leeson, L. (2008). Quantum Leap. Leveraging the Signs of Ireland Digital Corpus in Irish Sign Language/English Interpreter Training. *The Sign Language Translator and Interpreter, 2*(2), 231–258.

Leeson, L., & Saeed, J. I. (2005). *Conceptual Blending and the Windowing of Attention in Simultaneous Constructions in Irish Sign Language (ISL)*. Paper Presented at the 8th International Cognitive Linguistics Association Conference, Seoul. *Korea & World Affairs*, (July): 2005.

Leeson, L., & Grehan, C. (2004). To the Lexicon and Beyond: The Effect of Gender on Variation in Irish Sign Language. In Van Herreweghe, M., & Vermeerbergen, M. (Eds.), *To The Lexicon and Beyond: The Sociolinguistics of European Sign Languages* (pp. 39–73). Washington, DC: Gallaudet University Press.

Leeson, L. (1996). *The Marking of Time in Signed Languages with Specific Reference to Irish Sign Language.* Unpublished M. Phil Dissertation, Centre for Language and Communication Studies, University of Dublin, Trinity College.

Leeson, L. (2001). *Aspects of Verb Valency in Irish Sign Language*. Unpublished Doctoral Dissertation, Centre for Language and Communication Studies, TCD, Dublin.

Leeson, L., & Nolan, B. (2008). *Digital Deployment of the Signs of Ireland Corpus in Elearning.* LREC2008 – 3rd Workshop on the Representation and Processing of Sign Languages: Construction and Exploitation of Sign Language Corpora. Marrakech, Morocco.

Leeson, L., & Saeed, J. I. (2003). *Exploring the Cognitive Underpinning in the Construal of Passive Events in Irish Sign Language (ISL).* Paper presented at the 8th International Cognitive Linguistics Association Conference, Spain, July 2003.

Leeson, L., Saeed, J., Leonard, C., Macduff, A., & Byrne-Dunne, D. (2006). *Moving Heads and Moving Hands: Developing a Digital Corpus of Irish Sign Language: The 'Signs of Ireland' Corpus Development Project.* Paper presented at the IT&T conference, Carlow.

Lehman, R. (2007). Learning objects repositories. *New Directions for Adult and Continuing Education, 133,* 57–66. doi:10.1002/ace.247

Lenat, D. (1995). CYC: a large-scale investment in knowledge infrastructure. *Communications of the ACM, 38*(11), 33–38. doi:10.1145/219717.219745

Leonard, C. (2005). Signs of Diversity: Use and Recognition of Gendered Signs among Young Irish Deaf People. *Deaf Worlds, 21*(2), 62–77.

Lepori, B., Cantoni, L., & Succi, C. (2003). The introduction of e-learning in European universities: models and strategies. In Kerres, M., & Voss, B. (Eds.), *Digitaler Campus. Vom Medienprojekt zum nachhaltigen Medieneinsatz in der Hochschule* (pp. 74–83). Münster, Germany: Waxmann.

Lesage, M., Riopel, M., Raiche, G., & Sodoke, K. (2008). IMS-QTI sub-standards in computerised adaptive testing and interfacing. *International Journal of Advanced Media and Communication, 2*(2), 115–137. doi:10.1504/IJAMC.2008.018503

Lessig l. (2004) *Free Culture* [On line]. New York: The Penguin Press. Retrieved Octobre 14, 2009, from http://www.free-culture.cc/freeculture.pdf

LETSI Technical Roadmap Committee. (2009). *Assumptions document: SCORM 2.0 project report.* Retrieved 2009-04-09 from https://letsi.org/images/letsi_media/SCORM_2%200_Assumptions_2009Feb09.pdf

Leuf, B., & Cunningham, W. (2001). *The Wiki Way: Quick Collaboration on the Web.* Harlow, UK: Addison-Wesley.

Lewis, M. B. (2003). *Pedagogical Guidelines.* Retrieved from http://www.marthabeth.com/pedagogical_guidelines.html

Liddell, S. K. (2003). *Grammar, Gesture, and Meaning in American Sign Language.* Cambridge, UK: Cambridge University Press. doi:10.1017/CBO9780511615054

LIFE project. (2004). Retrieved 22 July 2009 from http://insight.eun.org/shared/data/insight/lre/LRE_Developments.ppt

Limerick, D., Cunnington, B., & Crowther, F. (1998). *Managing the new organisation: Collaboration and sustainability in the post-corporate world* (2nd ed.). Sydney, Australia: Business and Professional Publishing.

Linden, A. (2009, 29 July). *A Big First: Case Western Reserve is First EDU on Standalone Version of Second Life.* Retrieved from https://blogs.secondlife.com/community/community

LindenLabs. (2009, 28 July 2009). *Economic Statistics.* Retrieved Sunday 5 October, 2008, from http://secondlife.com/whatis/economy_stats.php

Lindgren, R., Henfridsson, O., & Schultze, U. (2004). Design principles for competence management systems: A synthesis of an action research study. *Management Information Systems Quarterly, 28*(3), 435–472.

Ling, M. (2006). An anthological review of research using MontyLingua: a python-based end-to-end text processor. *The Python Papers, 1*(1). Retrieved July 22, 2009, from http://repository.unimelb.edu.au/10187/1549

Linn, M. (2003a). Technology and science education: starting points, research programs, and trends. *International Journal of Science Education, 25*(6), 727–758. doi:10.1080/09500690305017

Linn, M. C., Clarck, D., & Slotta, J. D. (2003). WISE design for knowledge integration. *Science Education, 87*(4), 517–538. doi:10.1002/sce.10086

Linn, M. (2003b). The impact of technology on science instruction: historical trends and current opportunities. In Fraser, B. J., & Tobin, K. G. (Eds.), *International Handbook of Science Education* (pp. 265–294). London: Kluwer Academic Publishers.

Littlejohn, A., & Margaryan, A. (2006). Cultural issues in the sharing and reuse of resources for learning. *Research and Practice in Technology Enhanced Learning, 1*(3), 269–284. doi:10.1142/S1793206806000184

Liu, H., & Singh, P. (2004). Commonsense reasoning in and over natural language. In *Proceedings of the 8th International Conference on Knowledge-Based Intelligent Information & Engineering Systems (KES'2004).* Wellington, New Zealand, September 22-24, (LNAI). Berlin: Springer.

LLL Programme, (2006) Lifelong Learning Programme was published in the Official Journal of the European Union L327/45 on 24 November 2006.

LMIS Committee. (2008). *Learning management system recommendation.* Technical report, University of Puget Sound, Tacoma, WA, USA. Retrieved 2008-10-17, from http://projects.ups.edu/rwthornton/LMS_Moodle_final-draft.pdf

Lockyer, J. (2003). Multisource feedback in the assessment of physician competencies. *The Journal of Continuing Education in the Health Professions, 23*(1), 4–12. doi:10.1002/chp.1340230103

Lomas, L. (2007). Zen, motorcycle maintenance and quality in higher education. *Quality Assurance in Education, 15*(4), 402–412. doi:10.1108/09684880710829974

López, M. G., Maestre, A. J., & Sánchez-Alonso, S. (2007). *Reusabilidad de los objetos de aprendizaje almacenados en repositorios de libre Acceso.* Paper presented at the 4th Simposio Pluridisciplinar sobre Diseño, Evaluación y Desarrollo de Contenidos Educativos Reutilizables, Bilbao, SP. Retrieved July 12, 2009 from http://ftp.informatik.rwthaachen.de/Publications/CEUR-WS/Vol-318/Lopez.pdf

Lorenz, A. (2009). Elchtest in Austria – Umstände eines LMS-Wechsels und seine Folgen – ein Prüfbericht. In Apostolopoulos, N., & Schwill, A. (Eds.), *Lernen im digitalen Zeitalter. GMW09 – 4. Europäische Jahrestagung Gesellschaft für Medien in der Wissenschaft (GMW).* GMW.

LTSC. I. (07 August, 2009). IEEE Learning Technology Standards Committee. Retrieved August 7, 2009, from: http://ieeeltsc.wordpress.com/

Luhmann, N. (1995). *Social systems.* Stanford, CA: Stanford University Press.

Lummus, R. R., Krumwiede, D. W., & Vokurka, R. J. (2001). The relationship of logistics to supply chain management: developing a common industry definition. *Industrial Management & Data Systems, 101*(8), 426–431. doi:10.1108/02635570110406730

Maarof, M. H. S., & Yahya, Y. (2008). LORIuMET: Learning object repositories interoperability using metadata. In H. B. Zaman (Ed.), *International Symposium on Information Technology, 3*, (pp. 1-5). Kuala Lumpur: Malaysia.

MacGregor, R. C. (1993). Are we recognising the organisational impact on educational software design? *Australian Journal of Educational Technology, 9*(1), 59–68.

Maeers, M. (2001). Integrating Technology into Mathematics teaching and Learning. In Rogerson, A. (Ed.), *The Mathematics Education into the 21st Century Project Proceedings* (pp. 152–155). Palm Cove, Queensland, Australia.

Maeers, M. (2000). *Using Technology in Teaching: Challenges and Opportunities for Higher Education.* A presentation made at Teaching Development Days and Faculty Orientation, Teaching Development Centre, University of Regina, SK, September, 2000.

Maeers, M. (2002). *Integration of the Internet (and Other Resources) into Mathematics.* A presentation made at the National Council of Teachers of Mathematics Regional Conference, October 2002, Regina, SK.

Maeers, M., & Friesen, D. (2001). *What Difference Can Networked Classrooms Make?* A presentation made to the Technology Summit on Education 2001, SIAST Campus, Regina, November 21, 2001.

Maher, M. L. (1999). Designing the virtual campus. *Design Studies, 20*(4), 319–342. doi:10.1016/S0142-694X(98)00043-X

Mahlow, C. (2010). Choosing the appropriate e-learning system for a university. In Kats, Y. (Ed.), *Learning Management Systems Technologies and Software Solutions for Online Teaching: Tools and Applications*. Hershey, PA: IGI Global. doi:10.4018/978-1-61520-853-1.ch004

Malisuwan, S., & Sivaraks, J. (2008). *eLearning through Wireless Communication for Rural and Remote Areas in Thailand.* Retrieved from http://www.elearningap.com/eLAP2008/Online/35_fullpaper_Settapong%20 Malisuwan_eLearning%20through%20Wireles%85.pdf

Marek, E., & Cavallo, A. M. (1997). *The Learning Cycle.* Berlin: Heinemann.

Marqués, P. (2001). Algunas notas sobre el impacto de las TIC en la universidad. *Educcar, 28*, 83–98.

Marra, R. M. (2002). The ideal online learning environment for supporting epistemic development: Putting the puzzle together. *Quarterly Review of Distance Education, 3*(1), 15–31.

Marshall, S. (2009a). (in press). A Quality Framework for Continuous Improvement of E-Learning: The E-Learning Maturity Model. *Journal of Distance Education.*

Marshall, S. (2004). E-learning standards: Open enablers of learning or compliance strait jackets? In R. Atkinson, C. McBeath, D. Jonas-Dwyer & R. Phillips (Eds), *Beyond the comfort zone: Proceedings of the 21st ASCILITE Conference* (pp. 596-605). Perth, 5-8 December.

Marshall, S. (2005). *Determination of New Zealand Tertiary Institution E-Learning Capability: An Application of an E-Learning Maturity Model: Report on the E-Learning Maturity Model Evaluation of the New Zealand Tertiary Sector.* Report to the New Zealand Ministry of Education. 132pp. Retrieved January 10, 2006, from http://www.utdc.vuw.ac.nz/research/emm/documents/SectorReport.pdf

Marshall, S. (2006a). *E-Learning Maturity Model Version Two: New Zealand Tertiary Institution E-Learning Capability: Informing and Guiding E-Learning Architectural Change and Development Project Report.* Report to the New Zealand Ministry of Education. 118pp. Retrieved August 10, 2009, from http://www.utdc.vuw.ac.nz/research/emm/documents/versiontwo/20060726TeLRFReport.pdf

Marshall, S. (2006b). *eMM Version Two Process Descriptions.* Wellington: Victoria University of Wellington. Report to the New Zealand Ministry of Education. 157pp. Retrieved August 10, 2009, from http://www.utdc.vuw.ac.nz/research/emm/documents/versiontwo/20060726ProcessDescriptions.pdf

Marshall, S. (2009b). Benchmarking e-learning: Now what can we do when we have no money? *Online Educa Berlin 15th International Conference on Technology Supported Learning and Training,* 2-4 December, Berlin, Germany (abstract accepted).

Marshall, S. J. (2008). What are the key factors that lead to effective adoption and support of e-learning by institutions? In *Proceedings of HERDSA 2008* (Rotorua, New Zealand, HERDSA).

Marshall, S. J., & Mitchell, G. (2007). Benchmarking International E-learning Capability with the E-Learning Maturity Model. In *Proceedings of EDUCAUSE in Australasia 2007*, 29 April - 2 May 2007, Melbourne, Australia. Retrieved January 8, 2008, from http://www.caudit.edu.au/educauseaustralasia07/authors_papers/Marshall-103.pdf

Marshall, S., & Mitchell, G. (2002). An E-Learning Maturity Model?' In *Proceedings of the 19th Annual Conference of the Australian Society for Computers in Learning in Tertiary Education* (Auckland, 2002), Australian Society for Computers in Learning in Tertiary Education. Retrieved January 10, 2006, from http://www.unitec.ac.nz/ascilite/proceedings/papers/173.pdf

Marshall, S., & Mitchell, G. (2003). Potential Indicators of e-Learning Process Capability, In *Proceedings of EDUCAUSE in Australasia 2003* (Adelaide, May 6-9, 2003), EDUCAUSE. Retrieved January 10, 2006, from http://www.utdc.vuw.ac.nz/research/emm/documents/1009anav.pdf

Marshall, S., & Mitchell, G. (2004). Applying SPICE to e-Learning: An E-Learning Maturity Model? In *Proceedings of the Sixth Australasian Computing Education Conference* (Dunedin, January, 2004). Retrieved January 10, 2006, from http://portal.acm.org/ft_gateway.cfm?id=979993&type=pdf&coll=GUIDE&dl=GUIDE&CFID=62903527&CFTOKEN=3085292

Marshall, S., & Mitchell, G. (2005). *E-Learning Process Maturity in the New Zealand Tertiary Sector*. Paper presented at the EDUCAUSE in Australasia 2005 Conference, (Auckland, April 5-8, 2005). Retrieved January 10, 2006, from http://www.utdc.vuw.ac.nz/research/emm/documents/E-LearningProcessMaturity.pdf

Marshall, S., & Mitchell, G. (2006). Assessing sector e-learning capability with an e-learning maturity model. In *Proceedings of the Association for Learning Technologies Conference*, 2006, Edinburgh, UK.

Marshall, S., Mitchell, G., & Beames, S. (2009). *Report on the ACODE eMM Project*. Report to the Australasian Council on Open and Distance Education. 88pp. Retrieved August 10, 2009, from http://www.utdc.vuw.ac.nz/research/emm/acode/20090625ACODEReport.pdf

Marshall, S., Udas, K., & May, J. (2008). *Assessing Online Learning Process Maturity: the e-Learning Maturity Model*. Paper presented at the 14th Annual Sloan-C International Conference on Online Learning, Orlando Florida, 6-7 November, 2008.

Martin, L., Gutiérrez y Restrepo, E., Barrera, C., Rodríguez Ascaso, A., Santos, O. C., & Boticario, J. G. (2007). Usability and Accessibility Evaluations along the eLearning Cycle. In Mathias Weske Mohand-Saïd Hacid and Claude Godart (Eds.), Web Information Systems Engineering (WISE 2007) (pp. 453- 458). Lecture Notes in Computer Science, 4832.

Martinez-Ortiz, I., Sierra, J., Fernandez-Manjon, B., & Fernandez-Valmayor, A. (2009). Language Engineering Techniques for the Development of e-Learning Applications. *J. of Network and Computer Application*, *32*, 1092–1105. doi:10.1016/j.jnca.2009.02.005

Martínez-Ortiz, I., Moreno-Ger, P., Sierra, J. L., & Fernández-Manjón, B. (2006) <e-QTI>: a Reusable Assessment Engine, 5th International Conference on Web-based Learning, Penang, Malaysia. LNCS 4181, pp. 134-145.

Masie, E. (2009). *The Masie Center and learning consortium.* Retrieved from http://www.masie.com/

Mason, H., & Moutahir, M. (2006). *Multidisciplinary Experiential Education in Second Life: A Global Approach.* Paper presented at the Second Life Education Workshop at the Second Life Community Convention. from http://cleobekkers.files.wordpress.com/2008/03/slcc2006-proceedings.pdf#page=39

Mason, J. (2003). Secret standards business? In *Proceedings EduCause in Australasia 2003*, Adelaide, Australia.

Matthews, P. A. (1996). *The Irish Deaf Community* (*Vol. 1*). Dublin: ITE.

Mayer, R. E., & Moreno, R. (2003). Nine ways to reduce cognitive load in multimedia learning. *Educational Psychologist*, *32*, 43–52. doi:10.1207/S15326985EP3801_6

Mayer, R. (2000). Diseño educativo para un aprendizaje constructivista. In Reigeluth, C. (Ed.), *Diseño de la Instrucción. Teorías y modelos* (pp. 154–171). Madrid, Spain: Aula XXI Santillana.

Mayes, T. (2001). Learning technology and learning relationships. In Stephenson, J. (Ed.), *Teaching & learning online: new pedagogies for new technologies* (pp. 16–26). London: Kogan Page.

Mayes, J. T., & De Freita, S. (2004) Review of e-learning theories, frameworks and models. *Report for JISC*. Retrieved from http://www.jisc.ac.uk/uploaded_documents/Stage%202%20Learning%20Models% 20(Version%201).pdf

Mayes, T. (2007). TESEP: *The Pedagogical Principles*. Transform website: www.napier.ac.uk/transform. Retrieved 07/23/09 from http://www2.napier.ac.uk/transform/TESEP_Pedagogical_Principles.pdf

Mayes, T., & de Freitas, S. (2004). Review of e-learning theories, frameworks and models. *JISC*. Retrieved July 22 2009 from http://www.jisc.ac.uk/uploaded_documents/Stage%202%20Learning%20Models%20(Version%20 1).pdf

McArthur, D., Stasz, C., Hotta, J., Peter, O., & Burdof, C. (1988). Skill-oriented task sequencing in an intelligent tutor for basic algebra. In. *Proceedings of Instructional Science*, *17*, 281–307. doi:10.1007/BF00056218

McCalla, G. (2004). The Ecological Approach to the Design of E-Learning Environments: Purpose-based Capture and Use of Information About Learners. *Journal of Interactive Media in Education*, *2004*(7).

McCracken, R. (2006). *Cultural responses to open licences and the accessibility and usability of open educational resources*. Retrieved June 20, 2009, from http://www.oecd.org/dataoecd/48/38/36539322.pdf

McDonnell, P. (Ed.). (2004). *Deaf Studies in Ireland: An Introduction*. Doug McLean, Glouc.

McDonnell, P. (1996). *Verb Categories in Irish Sign Language*. Unpublished Doctoral Dissertation, Centre for Language and Communication Studies, University of Dublin, Trinity College.

McGreal, R. (Ed.). (2004). *Online education using learning objects. Open and flexible learning series*. London: Routledge Falmer.

McLean, N., & Lynch, C. (2004). Interoperability between Library Information Services and Learning Environments – Bridging the Gaps: A Joint White Paper on Behalf of the IMS Global Learning Consortium and the Coalition for Networked Information. *IMS Global Learning Consortium and CNI*. Retrieved June 20, 2009, from http://www.imsglobal.org/digitalrepositories/CNIandIMS_2004.pdf

McNaught, C. (2001). *Quality assurance for online courses: from policy to process to improvement?* Paper presented at the Meeting at the Cross-roads, Proceedings of the 18th Annual Australian Society for Computers in Learning in Tertiary Education 2001 Conference, University of Melbourne.

Meir, I. (1998). *Thematic Structure and Verb Agreement in Israeli Sign Language*, PhD Dissertation, Hebrew University of Jerusalem, Israel.

Mentzer, J. T., DeWitt, W., Keebler, J. S., Min, S., Nix, N. W., Smith, C. D., & Zacharia, Z. G. (2001). Defining supply chain management. *Journal of Business Logistics*, *22*(2), 1–25.

MERLOT. *Multimedia Educational Resource for Learning and Online Teaching*. (2009). Retrieved May 15, 2009, from http://www.merlot.org/merlot/index.htm

Merriam Webster On-Line Dictionary http://www.merriam-webster.com/dictionary/interoperability

Merrill, M. D. (1994). *Instructional Design Theory*. Upper Saddle River, NJ: Educational Technology Publications.

Merrill, M. D. (1999). *Instructional Transaction Theory (ITT): Instructional Design Based on Knowledge Objects*. Retrieved January 3, 2009, from http://www.indiana.edu/~idtheory/chapter_17_summary.html

Meyen, E. L., Aust, R., Gauch, J. M., Hinton, H. S., & Isaacson, R. E. (2002). e-Learning: A programmatic research construct for the future. *Journal of Special Education Technology*. Retrieved August 4, 2009, from http://citeseerx.ist.psu.edu/viewdoc/download?doi=10.1.1.99.6062&rep=rep1&type=pdf

Meyer, K. A. (2003). *Quality in Distance Education: Focus on On-Line Learning* (*Vol. 29*). Hoboken, NJ: Jossey-Bass.

Miao, Y., van der Klink, M., Boon, J., Sloep, P. B., & Koper, R. (2009). Enabling Teachers to Develop Pedagogically Sound and Technically Executable Learning Designs [special issue: Learning Design]. *Distance Education*, *30*(2), 259–276. doi:10.1080/01587910903023223

Miao, Y., & Koper, R. (2007b). An Efficient and Flexible Technical Approach to Develop and Deliver Online Peer Assessment. In A. Clark Chinn, Erkens, G., Puntambekar, S. (Ed.), *Mice, Minds, and Society, Proceedings of the 7th Computer Supported Collaborative Learning (CSCL 2007) conference*, (pp. 502-511), July 16-21, 2007, New Jersey, USA.

Miao, Y., Sloep, P., & Koper, R. (2008) Modeling Units of Assessment for Sharing Assessment Process Information: towards an Assessment Process Specification. In *Proceedings of the 7th International Conference on Web-based Learning (ICWL 2008)*, (LNCS 5145, pp. 132-144), Jinhua, China. Berlin: Springer.

Miao, Y., Vogten, H., Martens, H., & Koper, R. (2007a). The Complementary Roles of LD and QTI in Supporting Effective Web-based Formative assessment. In V. Uskov (Ed.), *Proceedings of the 10th IASTED International Conference on Advanced Technologies in Education (CATE 2007)*, 212-218. October, 8-10, 2007, Beijing, China.

Miller, J. G. (1978). *Living Systems*. New York: McGraw-Hill.

Miller, J. G., & Miller, J. L. (1992). Greater Than the Sum of its Parts I. Subsystems which Process Both Matter-Energy and Information. *Behavioral Science*, *37*, 1–38. doi:10.1002/bs.3830370102

Miller, G. (1990). Wordnet: An on-line lexical database. *International Journal of Lexicography (special issue), Computational Linguistics, 18*(1), 3(4), 235–312.

Mills, S. (2002). *Learning about learning objects with learning objects*. Paper presented at the SITE 2002 Conference, Nashville, TN. Retrieved May 20, 2009 from http://www.alivetek.com/learningobjects/site_paper.htm

MIT OpenCourseware. (n.d.). *Home page*. Retrieved June 20, 2009, from http://ocw.mit.edu/OcwWeb/web/home/home/

Mitchell, P. D. (2000). The impact of educational technology: a radical reappraisal of research methods. In Squires, D., Conole, G., & Jacobs, G. (Eds.), *The changing face of learning technology* (pp. 51–58). Cardiff: University Wales Press.

Miura, K., Tsuruoka, Y., & Ysujii, J. (2004). *Automatic acquisition of concept relations from web documents with sense clustering,* (pp. 37-40). Paper presented at IJCNLP 2004 Interactive Poster/Demo.

Mobbs, R. (2006). *Advantages of e-learning*. Retrieved 22 July 2009 from http://www.le ac.uk/cc/rjm1/etutor/elearning/advdofelearning.html accessed 20/04/2009

Monereo, C., & Romero, M. (2008). Los entornos virtuales de aprendizaje basados en sistemas de emulación cognitiva. In Coll, C., & Monereo, C. (Eds.), *Psicología de la educación virtual. Aprender y enseñar con las Tecnologías de la Información y la Comunicación*. Editorial Morata.

Monson, D. (2005). Blackboard Inc., An Educause platinum partner - the educational technology framework: charting a path toward a networked learning environment. Paper presented at the *Educause Western Regional Conference, April 26-28, 2005*, San Francisco, CA, USA. San Francisco: Educause. Retrieved February 25, 2009, from http://www.educause.edu/WRC05/Program/4954?PRODUCT_CODE=WRC05/CORP05

Moodle. (2009). *an Open Source Course Management System (CMS)*. Retrieved from http://moodle.org/

Mora-Aguilar, M. C., Sancho-Brú, J. L., & Iserte-Vilar, J. L. (2009). Alternatives for evaluation in overcrowded groups: the e-assessment. *Proceedings of the International Technology, Education and Development Conference*, Valencia, Spain, IATED eds.

Mora-Aguilar, M. C., Sancho-Brú, J. L., Rodríguez-Cervantes, P. J., & Iserte-Vilar, J. L. (2008). The challenge of improving teaching methodologies in overcrowded groups: experiences in basic mechanics. In *Proceedings of the International Technology, Education and Development Conference*, Valencia, Spain, IATED eds.

Moreno, L., Gonzalez, C., Castilla, I., Gonzalez, E., & Sigut, J. (2007). Applying a constructivist and collaborative methodological approach in engineering education. *Computers & Education*, *49*, 891–915. doi:10.1016/j.compedu.2005.12.004

Moreno-Ger, P., Burgos, D., Sierra, J. L., & Fernández-Manjón, B. (2007). A Game-Based Adaptive Unit of Learning with IMS Learning Design and <e-Adventure. In Duval, E., Klamma, R., & Wolpers, M. (Eds.), *Creating New Learning Experiences on a Global Scale* (pp. 247–261). Berlin: Springer. doi:10.1007/978-3-540-75195-3_18

Morgan, A., Raidén, A., & Naylor, G. (2008). Unlocking the potential to influence government skills policy: A case study of the UK construction industry. *International Journal of Training and Development, 12*(4), 238–252. doi:10.1111/j.1468-2419.2008.00309.x

Morimoto, Y., Ueno, M., Yokoyama, S., & Miyadera, Y. (2007) A SCORM-compliant Learning Management System that Enhances Learning By Managing the Learning Itself. In *Proceedings of the 7th IEEE International Conference on Advanced Learning Technologies (ICALT)*, (pp. 122-126).

Morningstar, C., & Farmer, F. R. (1991). The Lessons of Lucasfilm's Habitat. In Benedikt, M. (Ed.), *Cyberspace: First Steps*. Cambridge, MA: MIT Press.

Mosel, U. (2006). Fieldwork and Community Language Work. In Gippert, J., Himmelmann, N. P., & Mosel, U. (Eds.), *Essentials of Language Documentation* (pp. 67–86). Berlin: Mouton de Gruyter. doi:10.1515/9783110197730.67

Moss, L. (2001). Deconstructing the gene and reconstructing molecular developmental systems. In Oyama, S., Griffiths, P., & Gray, R. (Eds.), *Cycles of Contingency: Developmental Systems and Evolution* (pp. 85–97). Cambridge, MA: MIT Press.

MPEG-4. (2002*). Systems: Overview*. Retrieved June, 20, 2009, from http://www.chiariglione.org/mpeg/standards/MPEG-4/MPEG-4.htm

MPEG-7. (2001). *ISO/IEC JTC 1/SC 29/WG 11/N3966, Text of 15938-5 FCD Information Technology – Multimedia Content Description Interface – Part 5 Multimedia Description Schemes*. Singapore: MPEG Group.

Muldner, K., Christopherson, R., Atkinson, R., & Burleson, W. (2009) Investigating the utility of eye-tracking information on affect and reasoning for user modeling. User Modeling, Adaptation, and Personalization Seventeenth International Conference, UMAP 2009, Trento, Italy, Volume LNCS 5535, Pages 138-149, Springer-Verlag, 2009.

Muñoz-Merino, P. J., Kloos, C. D., & Naranjo, J. F. (2009). Enabling interoperability for LMS educational services. *Computer Standards & Interfaces, 31*, 484–498. doi:10.1016/j.csi.2008.06.009

Murphy, E. (2004). Moving from theory to practice in the design of web-based learning using a learning object approach. *E-journal of Instructional Science and Technology, 7*(1). Retrieved May 13, 2009 from http://www.ascilite.org.au/ajet/e-jist/

Mushtaha, A., & De Troyer, O. (2005). Towards localising e-learning websites. *Localisation Focus, 4*(4), 6–8.

Muspratt, S., & Freeboy, P. (2007). *Students' perceptions of the characteristics of "good" and "poor" digital learning objects.* Paper presented at the International Educational Research Conference. Fremantle, AU.

Myller, N. (2007). Automatic Generation of Prediction Questions during Program Visualization. [ENTCS]. *Electronic Notes in Theoretical Computer Science, 178*, 43–49. doi:10.1016/j.entcs.2007.01.034

Nacheva-Skopalik, L. (2007). *An examination of an intelligent cybernetic learning model for formative assessment and diagnostics in open and distance learning*. PhD thesis, University of Teesside, UK.

Nacheva-Skopalik, L., Skopalik, E., & Stoyanov, S. (2007). Examination of feedbacks efficiency within automated system for distance education. *CEEPUS CZ – 103 International Summer School "Informatics systems in Automation", University of Maribor, FEECS, Maribor, Slovenia, 14-28.09.*2007. Retrieved July 26, 2009 from http://css07.feri-au.uni-mb.si/index.php?option=com_content&task=view&id=13&Itemid=29

Nacheva-Skopalik, L., Stoyanov, S., & Skopalik, E. (2004). *Satisfaction measurement. Leonardo da Vinci Project BG/02/B/F/PP-132088 Vocational Lifelong Training on Quality and Environmental Management for Staff Engaged in Small- and Medium-Sized Enterprises*. Gabrovo, Bulgaria: Vasil Aprilov University Publishing House of Gabrovo.

Nagel, D. (2007). Louisiana State moves to Moodle. *Campus Technology*. Retrieved 2008-10-17, from http://www.campustechnology.com/article.aspx? aid=52667

Nair, S., & Jeevan, V. (2004). A Brief Overview of Metadata Formats. *DESIDOC Bulletin of Information Technology*, *24*(4), 3–11.

Najjar, J., & Klobučar, T. (Eds.). (2009). *iCOPER: ISURE: Report of study of learning needs building blocks and the standards to be used.* Retrieved 2009-06-22 from http://www.educanext.org/dotlrn/clubs/icoper/new-lors/Deliverables/Deliverables_-_Submitted/D2.1/D2.1_Final.pdf.

Najjar, J., Duval, E., Ternier, S., & Neven, F. (2003). Towards Interoperable Learning Object Repositories: the ARIADNE Experience. In *IADIS WWW/Internet 2003 Conference*, (pp. 219-226).

Namara, R. E., Hussain, I., Bossio, D., & Verma, S. (2007). Innovative land and water management approaches in Asia: Productivity impacts, adoption prospects and poverty outreach. *Irrigation and Drainage*, *56*, 335–348. doi:10.1002/ird.308

Nash, Smith and Susan. (2005). Learning objects, learning repositories, and learning theory: preliminary best practices for online courses. *Interdisciplinary Journal of Knowledge and Learning Objects, 1*. Retrieved from http://66.102.1.104/scholar?num=50&hl=en&lr=&newwindow=1&client=firefox-a&q=cache:yAPq2jHovxwJ:ijklo.org/Volume1/v1p217-228Nash.pdf+

Neal, T., & Marshall, S. (2008). *Report on the Distance and Flexible Education Capability Assessment of the New Zealand ITP Sector*. Confidential Report to the New Zealand Tertiary Education Committee and Institutes of Technology and Polytechnics Distance and Flexible Education Steering Group.

Nesbit, J. C., Belfer, K., & Leacock, T. (2003). Learning Object Review Instrument (LORI). *E-Learning Research and Assessment Network.* Retrieved July 13, 2009 from http://www.elera.net/eLera/Home/Articles/

Neuhauser, C. (2004). A maturity model: Does it provide a path for online course design? *The Journal of Interactive Online Learning, 3*(1). Retrieved February 25, 2009, from http://www.ncolr.org/jiol/issues/PDF/3.1.3.pdf

Neven, F., & Duval, E. (2002). Reusable learning objects: a survey of lom-based repositories. In *Proceedings of the 10th ACM international conference on Multimedia* (pp. 291-294). New York: ACM Press.

Nevile, L., & Treviranus, J. (2006). Interoperability for Individual Learner Centred Accessibility for Web-based Educational. Systems. *Journal of Educational Technology & Society*, *9*(4), 215–227.

Newmann, F. (1996). Authentic achievement: Restructuring schools for intellectual quality. In Newmann, F., King, B., & Youngs, P. (Eds.), *Professional development to build organizational capacity in low achieving schools: Promising strategies and future challenges*. Madison, WI: Center on Organization and Restructuring of Schools, University of Wisconsin–Madison.

Ngu, A. H. H., Shepherd, J., & Magin, D. (1995). Engineering Peers: Computer-Assisted Approach to the development of Peer Assessment System. *Research and Development in Higher Education, 18*, 582-587. *Blending Tradition and technologies, HERDSA 95*, Rockhampton, Queensland.

Niederhauser, D. S., & Stoddart, T. (2001). Teachers' instructional perspectives and use of educational software. *Teaching and Teacher Education*, *17*, 15–31. doi:10.1016/S0742-051X(00)00036-6

Nielsen, J. (1993). *Usability Engineering*. London: Academic Press.

Nilsson, M., Powell, A., Johnston, P., & Naeve, A. (2008). *Expressing Dublin Core metadata using the Resource Description Framework (RDF). DCMI Recommendation*. Retrieved from http://dublincore.org/documents/dc-rdf/

Nolan, B., & Leeson, L. (2009a). Signs of access in a digital world. In *Conference Proceedings of INTED2009: International Technology, Education and Development Conference*, Valencia, Spain.

Nolan, B., & Leeson, L. (2009b). Working towards blended learning. In *Conference Proceedings of Multilingualism, Regional & Minority Languages: Paradigms for Languages of the Wider World Conference. School of Oriental and African Studies (SOAS),* London.

Nolan, B., & Leeson, L. (2009c). Creating access to education with progression Pathways via blended learning of deaf studies at Third level in Ireland: open innovation with Digital assets. In *Conference Proceedings of the 9th Information Technology and Telecommunications Conference 2009*. Dublin: Dublin Institute of technology, Ireland.

Norton, M., & Treviranus, J. (2003). IMS Learner Information Package Accessibility for LIP XML Schema Binding. Retrieved January 21, 2009 from: http://www.imsproject.org

Nurmi, S., & Jaakkola, T. (2006). Promises and pitfalls of learning objects. *Learning, Media and Technology*, *31*(3), 269–285. doi:10.1080/17439880600893325

O*Net (2009) *O*NET Online* U.S. Department of Labor Retrieved 2009-10-13 from http://online.onetcenter.org/.

O'Baoill, D., & Matthews, P. A. (2000). The Irish Deaf Community: *Vol. 2. The Linguistics of ISL*. Dublin: ITE.

OASIS. (2009) http://www.oasis-open.org/committees/tc_home.php?wg_abbrev=ws-sx

OASIS TWS. (2005). *OASIS Translation Web Services TC*. Retrieved October 6, 2007, from http://www.oasis-open.org/committees/tc_home.php?wg_abbrev=trans-ws

ODLQC. (2006). *ODL QC Standards*. Retrieved 29 November, 2009, from http://www.odlqc.org.uk/odlqc/gpgindex.htm

OECD. (June 27, 2006). OECD. Retrieved August 07, 2009, from Selected Statistics on Higher Education - Background Report for Meeting of OECD Ministers of Education in June 2006: http://www.oecd.org/dataoecd/30/7/36960580.pdf

Ogbuji, U. (2003). *Thinking XML: Learning Objects Metadata*. Retrieved June, 20, 2009, from http://www-128.ibm.com/developerworks/xml/library/x-think21.html

Oliver, R. (2005). Quality assurance and e-learning: Blue skies and pragmatism. *ALT-J*, *13*(3), 173–187. doi:10.1080/09687760500376389

Oliver, R., & Herrington, J. (2003). Factors influencing quality online learning experiences. In Davies, G., & Stacey, E. (Eds.), *Quality Education @ a Distance*. London: Kluwer Academic Publishers.

Oliver, R., Herrington, A., Stoney, S., & Millar, J. (2006). Authentic teaching and learning standards that assure quality higher education. In Herrington, A., & Herrington, J. (Eds.), *Authentic learning environments in higher education*. Hershey, PA: Idea Group.

Olivier, B., & Liber, O. (2003). Learning content interoperability standards. In Littlejohn, A. (Ed.), *Reusing online resources*. London, UK: Kogan Page.

Om, K., Lee, J., & Chang, J. (2007). Using supply chain management to enhance industry-university collaborations in IT higher education in Korea. *Scientometrics*, *71*(3), 455–471. doi:10.1007/s11192-007-1690-3

Ondrejka, C. (2008). Education Unleashed: Participatory Culture, Education, and Innovation in *Second Life*. In Salen, K. (Ed.), *The Ecology of Games: Connecting Youth, Games, and Learning* (pp. 229–252). Cambridge, MA: The MIT Press.

Open Education. (2007). *Localizing & Learning*. Retrieved June 1, 2009, from http://www.51weeks.com/event_files/0000/0003/OpenEd-2007-Program-Updated.pdf

Open Systems Joint Task Force (OSJTF). Retrieved May 2009 from http://www.acq.osd.mil/osjtf/termsdef.html

Open University. (2005). Open University going Moodle. *eGov monitor*. Retrieved July 1, 2009 from, http://www.egovmonitor.com/node/3460

O'Reilly, T. (2005). *What Is Web 2.0 - Design Patterns and Business Models for the Next Generation of Software*. Retrieved July 2, 2009 from, http://www.oreillynet.com/pub/a/oreilly/tim/news/2005/09/30/ what-is-web-20.html

Orr, K. (2008). Room for improvement? The impact of compulsory professional development for teachers in England's further education sector. *Professional Development in Education*, *34*(1), 97–108. doi:10.1080/13674580701832627

Ortega, P., & Arcos, F. (2008). Blended Learning: an efficient response to some of the problems raised by youths at risk. In *INTED2008, International Technology, Education and Development Conference*.

Ortega, P., & Arcos, F. (2008). How e-homework can solve the homework debate in primary schools. *ENMA2008, International Conference on Engineering and Mathematics*, (pp. 5-10). Bilbao, Spain: Kopiak.

Ortega, P., & Arcos, F. (2009). CLIL Enhanced Through Digital Storytelling. *ENMA2009, International Conference on Engineering and Mathematics*, (pp. 350). Bilbao, Spain: Kopiak.

Ostyn, C. (2005) *Competency Data for Training Automation*. Downloaded 2009 July 14 from http://www.ostyn.com/standardswork/competency/CompetencyDataForTrainingAutomation.htm

OWL. (2003). *Use Cases and Requirements*. Retrieved from http://www.w3.org/TR/webont-req

Pacquette, G., Marino, O., Hotte, R., & Moulet, L. Masmoudi, A., Cano, J., & Correal, D. (2007). *LORNET Project 2.3: Ontology and framework for knowledge and competency management (V. 3)*. Retrieved 2009 July 14 from http://wiki.letsi.org/download/attachments/9076913/Additional+Competency+Presentations.zip

Pacurar, G., Trigang, P., & Alupoaie, S. (2005). A QTI editor integrated into the netUniversite web portal using IMS LD. *Journal of Interactive Media in Education*, 9.

Palas, P., & Karasek, M. (2003). *Globalisation of Enterprise Data Using Web Services*. Retrieved May 9, 2006, from http://moravia-it.com/Download/Globalisation_of_Enterprise_Data_Using_Web_Services.pdf

Panar, A. (2009). *SCORM-2004 Overview, Sharable Content Object Reference Model Run-Time Environment*. Retrieved July 29, 2009, from http://www.adlnet.org

Papadopoulos, G., Pearson, E., & Green, S. (2008). Effective Simulations to Support Academics in Inclusive Online Learning Design. In *Proceedings of the 10th International ACM SIGACCESS Conference on Computers and Accessibility*, Halifax, Canada.

Papaioannou, V., Karadimitriou, P., Papageorgiou, A., Karagiannidis, C., & Sampson, D. G. (2001). *From educational meta-data authoring to educational meta-data management*. Paper presented in IEEE International Conference on Advanced Learning Technologies-ICALT'01, August 6-8, Madison, USA.

Papasalouros, A., Retalis, S., & Papaspyrou, N. (2004). Semantic description of educational adaptive hypermedia based on a conceptual model. *Journal of Educational Technology & Society*, *7*(4), 129–142.

Paramythis, A., & Loidl-Reisinger, S. (2004). Adaptive Learning Environments and e-Learning Standards. *Electronic Journal on e-Learning, 2*(1), 181-194.

Park, J.-R. (2009). Metadata Quality in Digital Repositories: A Survey of the Current State of the Art. *Cataloging & Classification Quarterly*, *47*(3-4), 213–228. doi:10.1080/01639370902737240

Park, J., & Ram, S. (2004). Information Systems Interoperability: What Lies Beneath. *ACM Transactions on Information Systems*, *22*(4), 595–632. http://scruffynerf.wordpress.com/2006/11/01/system-interoperability/. doi:10.1145/1028099.1028103

Parlangeli, O., Marchigiani, E., & Bagnara, S. (1999). Multimedia systems in distance education: effects of usability on learning. *Interacting with Computers*, *12*, 37–49. doi:10.1016/S0953-5438(98)00054-X

Patel, M., Koch, T., Doerr, M., & Tsinaraki, C. (2005). Semantic Interoperability in Digital Library Systems. *Report of DELOS2 Network of Excellence in Digital Libraries*. Retrieved June 20, 2009, from http://delos-wp5.ukoln.ac.uk/project-outcomes/SI-in-DLs/SI-in-DLs.pdf

Patru, M. (2008). Attaining quality education for all: A UNESCO perspective. In *Fifth EDEN Research Workshop 20-22 OCTOBER, 2008* Paris, France. Retrieved July 26, 2009 from http://www.eden-online.org/eden.php?menuld=421

Paule, M. P., Fernandez Diaz, M. J., Ortin Soler, F., & Perez, J. R. (2008). Adaptation in current e-learning systems. *Computer Standards & Interfaces*, *30*, 62–70. doi:10.1016/j.csi.2007.07.006

Paulk, M. C., Curtis, B., Chrissis, M. B., & Weber, C. V. (1993). Capability Maturity Model, Version 1.1. *IEEE Software*, *10*(4), 18–27. doi:10.1109/52.219617

Pawlowski, J. M. (2007). The Quality Adaptation Model: Adaptation and Adoption of the Quality Standard ISO/IEC 19796-1 for Learning, Education, and Training. *Journal of Educational Technology & Society*, *10*(2), 3–16.

Payr, S. (2005). Not Quite an Editorial: Educational Agents and (e-)Learning. *Applied Artificial Intelligence*, *19*(3), 199–213. doi:10.1080/08839510590910147

Pedersen, S., Arslanyilmaz, A., & Williams, D. (2009). Teachers' assessment-related local adaptations of a problem-based learning module. *Educational Technology Research and Development*, *57*(2), 229–249. doi:10.1007/s11423-007-9044-7

Peig, E., Delgado, J., & Pérez, I. (2001). Metadata Interoperability and Meta-search on the Web. *Proceedings of the Internationale Conference on Dublin Core and Metadata Applications*. Retrieved June 20, 2009, from http://www.nii.ac.jp/dc2001/proceedings/product/paper-37.pdf

Pernin, J.-P., & Lejeune, A. (2006). Models for the re-use of learning scenarios. *DSpace*, 1-15. Retrieved from http://hdl.handle.net/1820/580

Perrin, D. G. (2005). *A Tutorial Paper, Creative Online Learning Environments*. Retrieved from http://www.itdl.org/Journal/Apr_05/article04.htm

Personal Learning Environments. (2005). *JISC*. Retrieved 4th August 2009 from: http://www.jisc.ac.uk/index.cfm?name=cetis_ple

Peters, O. (2000). Digital learning environments:New possibilities and opportunities. *International Review of Research in Open and Distance Learning*, *1*(1).

Peterson, R. & Jaffray. (2000). *Piper Facts, figures, and forces behind e-learning, compiled and prepared of eLearnFrame*. Retrieved from http://www.learnframe.com/aboutelearning/elearningfacts.pdf

Petherbridge, D., & Chapman, D. (2007). Upgrading or Replacing Your Learning Management System: Implications for Student Support. *Online Journal of Distance Learning Administration*, *10*(1, Spring). Retrieved from http://www.westga.edu/~distance/ojdla/spring101/petherbridge101.htm

Petrova, K., & Sinclair, R. (2005). Business undergraduates learning online: A one semester snapshot. *International Journal of Education and Development using ICT*, *1*(4). Retrieved August 10, 2009, from http://ijedict.dec.uwi.edu//viewarticle.php?id=100&layout=html

Piaget, J. (1928). *The Child's Conception of the World*. London: Routledge and Kegan Paul.

Piburn, M. D., Reynolds, S. J., McAuliffe, C., Leedy, D. E., & Johnson, J. K. (2005). The role of visualization in learning from computer-based images. *International Journal of Science Education*, *27*(5), 513–527. doi:10.1080/09500690412331314478

Pierre, St. M., LaPlant, W. P. (1998). *Issues in Crosswalking Content Metadata Standards*. National Information Standards Organization (NISO). Retrieved June 20, 2009, from http://www.niso.org/publications/white_papers/crosswalk/

Pillai, L. (2003). *Quality assurance and best practices, Best Practices in Open and Distance Education*. Hyderabad, India: B.R. Ambedkar Open University (BRAOU).

Piotrowski, M. (2009). *Document-Oriented E-Learning Components*. PhD thesis, Otto-von-Guericke-Universität, Magdeburg, Germany. Retrieved 2009-10-25, from http://edoc.bibliothek.uni-halle.de/servlets/DocumentServlet?id=7205

Pitkänen, S. H., & Silander, P. (2004). Criteria for pedagogical reusability of learning objects enabling adaptation and individualized learning processes. In C.K. Lui & E. Sutinen (Eds.), 4th IEEE *International Conference on Advanced Learning Technologies,* (pp. 246-250). Joensuu, Finland: IEEE Computer Society

Pizzutto, E. & Pietrandrea, P. (in press). The Notation of Signed Texts. *Sign Language and Linguistics, 4* (1/2), 29-45.

PmWiki - Main - QTItalk (new version, under development). (n.d.). Retrieved July 29, 2009, from http://qtitalk-dev.nbwebsites.com/pmwiki.php?n=Main.HomePage.

Porter, S. (2005). Issues in the relationship between technology and practice. *ALT-J, 13*(3), 231–240. doi:10.1080/09687760500376496

Powell, A., Nilsson, M., Naeve, A., Johnston, P., & Baker, T. (2007). *DCMI Abstract Model. DCMI Recommendation.* Retrieved from http://dublincore.org/documents/abstract-model/

Powers, S. (2003). *Practical RDF.* Sebastopol, CA: O'Reilly. Retrieved 22 July 2009 from http://etutorials.org/Misc/Practical+resource+description+framework+rdf/Preface/

Prasad, A. R. D. (2006). Implementing LOM Schema in DSpace. In *DRTC-ICT Conference on Digital Learning Environment.*

Prasad, V. S. (2003). *Problems and Concerns.* Hyderabad, India: Best Practices in Open and Distance Education. B.R. Ambedkar Open University (BRAOU).

Preece, J., Rogers, Y., Sharp, H., Benyon, D., Holland, S., & Carey, T. (1994). *Human-Computer Interaction.* Harlow, UK: Addison-Wesley.

Provost, W. (2005). *Contingency and Complexity in the Social Theory of Niklas Luhmann.* Retrieved November, 2007 from http://www.geocities.com/~n4bz/lusoc/lusoc0.htm

Prpitsch, C., & Veith, P. (2006). Content and management standards: LOM, SCORM and content packaging. In Ehlers, U., & Pawlowski, J. M. (Eds.), *Handbook on quality and standardization in e-learning* (pp. 209–223). Heidelberg, Germany: Springer Berlin. doi:10.1007/3-540-32788-6_15

Puntambekar, S. (2006). Analyzing collaborative interactions: divergence, shared understanding and construction of knowledge. *Computers & Education, 47*(3), 332–351. doi:10.1016/j.compedu.2004.10.012

Purves, R. S., Medyckyj-Scott, D. J., & Mackaness, W. A. (2005). The e-MapScholar project: an example of interoperability in GIScience education. *Computers & Geosciences, 31*(2), 189–198. doi:10.1016/j.cageo.2004.08.007

QAA. (2004). *Code of practice for the assurance of academic quality and standards in higher education.* Section 2: Collaborative provision and flexible and distributed learning (including e-learning). Retrieved 29 November, 2009, from http://www.qaa.ac.uk/academicinfrastructure/codeOfPractice/section2/default.asp

QTI related files. (n.d.). Retrieved July 29, 2009, from http://www.gorissen.info/Pierre/QTI/.

QTI Training Guide - CETISwiki. (n.d.). Retrieved July 29, 2009, from http://wiki.cetis.ac.uk/QTI_Training_Guide.

QTItools. (n.d.). Retrieved July 29, 2009, from http://qtitools.org/.

Qu, C., & Nejdl, W. (2002). *Towards open standards: The evolution of an xml/jsp/webdav based collaborative courseware generating system.* Paper presented in International Conference on Web-based Learning-1, August 17-19, Hong-Kong, China.

Quesada, A., Ariza, M. R., Ortiz, A., & Bermejo, R. (2009). Designing and applying multimedia material for experimental sciences. Teacher and student assessment of its implementation. In L. Gómez, D. Martí, & I. Candel. *International Technology, Education and Development Conferences* (pp. 4911-4919*).* Valencia, Spain: IATED

R2Q2: Rendering and Response processing services for QTIv2 questions. (n.d.). Retrieved July 29, 2009, from http://www.r2q2.ecs.soton.ac.uk/.

Rada, R., Acquah, S., & Ramsey, R. (1993). Collaborative learning and the MUCH System. *Computers & Education*, *20*(3), 225–233. doi:10.1016/0360-1315(93)90022-B

Rahm, E., & Bernstein, P. A. (2001). A survey of approaches to automatic schema matching. *The Very Large Data Bases Journal*, *10*(4), 334–350. doi:10.1007/s007780100057

Ramboll, P. L. S. (2004). Studies in the context of the e-learning initiative: Virtual Models of European Universities (Lot 1). *executive summary*, p.ii. Retrieved from http://www.elearningeuropa.info/extras/pdf/virtual_models.pdf

Rampart (2009) http://ws.apache.org/axis2/modules/rampart/1_3/security-module.html

Ranasinghe, A. I., & Leisher, D. (2009). The Benefit of Integrating Technology into the Classroom. *International Mathematical Forum*, *4*(40), 1955–1961.

Raymond, E. (2001). *The Cathedral & the Bazaar. Musings on Linux and Open Source by an Accidental Revolutionary*. Sebastopol, CA: O'Reilly Media, Inc.

Redeker, G. (2003). An educational taxonomy for learning objects. In *Proceedings of the IEEE Conference on Advanced Learning Technologies,* (pp. 250-251), Sapporo, Japan.

Redish, J. (2000). Readability formulas have even more limitations than Klare discusses. *Journal of Computer Documentation*, *24*(3), 132–137. doi:10.1145/344599.344637

Rees, C., & Shepherd, M. (2005). The acceptability of 360-degree judgements as a method of assessing undergraduate medical students' personal and professional behaviours. *Medical Education*, *39*(1), 49–57. doi:10.1111/j.1365-2929.2004.02032.x

Reeves, T.C. (1997). *Evaluating what really matters in computer-based education.* Learning with Software-Pedagogies an practice.

Reflective learning, future thinking: digital repositories, e-portfolios, informal learning and ubiquitous computing. ALT/SURF/ILTA Spring Conference Research Seminar. Retrieved from http://www.alt.ac.uk/docs/ALT_SURF_ILTA_white_paper_2005.pdf. Accessed March 2008.

Reigeluth, C. M. (1999). *Instructional-Design Theories and Models: A New Paradigm of Instructional Theory*. Mawah, NJ: Lawrence Erlbaum Associates.

Reload. (2005). *Reusable eLearning Object Authoring & Delivery Project*. Retrieved June 10, 2008, from http://www.reload.ac.uk/

Rengarajan, R. (2001). LCMS and LMS: Taking advantage of tight integration. *Click 2 Learn*. Retrieved May 6, 2009 from http://www.e-learn.cz/soubory/lcms_and_lms.pdf

Respondus (2008). *Respondus User Guide*. Respondus, Inc., Redmond, WA, USA. Retrieved 2008-10-17, from http://www.respondus.com/downloads/Respondus35UserGuidePN.doc

Respondus: Assessment Tools for Learning Systems. (n.d.). Retrieved July 29, 2009, from http://www.respondus.com/.

Rey-López, M., Díaz-Redondo, R. P., Fernández-Vilas, A., Pazos-Arias, J., Garcia-Duque, J., Gil-Solla, A., & Ramos-Cabrer, M. (2009). An extension to the ADL SCORM standard to support adaptivity: The t-learning case-study'. *Computer Standards & Interfaces*, *31*(2), 309–318. doi:10.1016/j.csi.2008.02.006

Rice, W. H. IV. (2006). *Moodle: E-Learning Course Development*. Birmingham, UK: Packt Publishing.

Rios, A. de la Cruz, J. L. P. & Conejo, R. (1993). SIETTE: Intelligent evaluation system using tests for basic algebra. In *Proceedings of workshop WWW-Based Tutoring, in Intelligent Tutoring Systems Conference.*

Ritzema, T., & Harris, B. (2008). The Use of Second Life for Distance Education. *Journal of Computing Sciences in Colleges*, *23*(6), 110–116.

Roberts, G., W. A., Feijen, M., Harvey, J., Lee, S., & Wade, V. P. (2005).

Robinson, P. (2008, 8 May 2008). UQ in Second Life. *UQ News*.

Rodriguez-Ascaso, A., Santos, O. C., del Campo, E., Saneiro, M., & Boticario, J. G. (2008a). Personalised Support for Students with Disabilities Based on Psychoeducational Guidelines. *ICALT, 2008*, 1021–1022.

Rodriguez-Ascaso, A., Martin, L., Gutiérrez y Restrepo, E., Finat, C., Santos, O. C., & Boticario, J. G. (2008b) Design and Use of an Online Community for Students with Disabilities. The UNED Experience. Proceedings of the EADTU's 20th Annual Conference 2008

Rodriguez-Ascaso, A.; Santos, O.C.; Boticario, J.G.; Zimmermann, G. (2007) UM' 2007 Supplementary Proceedings: Towards user modelling and adaptive systems for all, Corfu, Greece, p.27-31 (2007)

Romero, M. (2009). Metacognition on the Educational Social Software, new challenges and opportunities. In Lambropoulos, N., & Romero, M. (Eds.), *Educational Social Software for Context-Aware Learning: Collaborative Methods and Human Interaction*. Hershey, PA: IGI Global.

Romero, M., & Wareham, J. (2009). Just-in-time mobile learning model based on context awareness information. *Learning Technology Newsletter*. Washington, DC: IEEE Computer Society Technical Committee on Learning Technology (TCLT).

Ronteltap, F., & Eurelings, A. (2002). Activity and interaction of students in anelectronic learning environment for problem based learning. *Distance Education, 23*(1), 11–22. doi:10.1080/01587910220123955

Rosbottom, J. (1994, September). *Software Tools for Peer Assessment*. Paper presented at the 2nd All Ireland Conference on the Teaching of Computing, Dublin, Ireland.

Roschelle, J. M., Pea, R. D., Hoadley, C. M., Gordin, D. N., & Means, B. M. (2000). Changing how and what children learn in school with computer-based technologies. *The Future of Children, 10*(2), 76–97. doi:10.2307/1602690

Rosson, M. B., & Carroll, J. M. (2001). *Usability engineering: scenario-based development of human computer interaction*. Morgan Kaufmann.

Rovai, A. P., & Jordan, H. M. (2004). Blended Learning and Sense of Community: A comparative analysis with traditional and fully online graduate courses. *International Review of Research in Open and Distance Learning, 5*(2).

Rully, A., Untoro, A., Fujisaki, T., Kanemitsu, H., & Thu, Y. K. (2007). Wireless LAN and Power Line Communication platform for e-Learning multimedia system in underdeveloped area in Lombok Island]. In *Proceedings of the 6th WSEAS Int. Conf. on Electronics, Hardware, Wireless and Optical Communications*, Corfu Island, Greece, February 1, (pp. 6-19).

Runapongsa, K., & Patel, J. M. (2003). *Storing and querying xml data in object-relational dbmss*. Paper presented in EDBT 2002 Workshop on XML-Based Data Management, August 27-31, Cargese, France.

Rushton, C., & Ramsey, P. (1993). Peer assessment in a collaborative hypermedia environment: A case-study. *Journal of Computer-Based Instruction, 20*(3), 75–80.

Sakai. (2009). open-source *Sakai CLE*. Retrieved from http://www.sakaiproject.org

Salembier, P., & Smith, J. R. (2001). MPEG-7 Multimedia Description Schemes. *IEEE Transactions on Circuits and Systems for Video Technology, 11*(6), 748–759. doi:10.1109/76.927435

Salinas, J. (1999). Qué se entiende por una institución de educación superior flexible. *EDUTEC'99*, Universidad de Sevilla, Spain. Retrieved July 23, 2009, from http://www.uib.es/depart/gte/edutec99.html

Sallandre, M. (2008). Simultaneity in French Sign Language Discourse. In Vermeerbergen, M., Leeson, L., & Crasborn, O. (Eds.), *Simultaneous Constructions in Signed Languages – Form and Function*. Amsterdam: John Benjamins.

Sampson, D., Karampiperis, P., & Fytros, D. (2007). Developing a common metadata model for competencies description. *Interactive Learning Environments, 15*(2), 137–150. doi:10.1080/10494820701343645

Sampson, D., & Zervas, P. (2008). Enhancing educational metadata with Science Education Information. In P. Díaz, I. Aedo, E. Mora. (Eds.), *8th IEEE International Conference on Advanced Learning Technologies,* (pp.1081-1082). Santander, Spain: IEEE Computer Society

Sandler, W., & Lillo-Martin, D. (2006). *Sign Language and Linguistic Universals*. Cambridge, UK: Cambridge University Press.

Sandoval, W. A., & Reiser, B. J. (2004). Explanation-driven inquiry: Integrating conceptual and epistemic scaffolds for scientific inquiry. *Science Education, 88*(3), 345–372. doi:10.1002/sce.10130

Sangrà, A. (2001). La calidad en las experiencias virtuales de educación superior. *Cuadernos para la Educación Superior.* Barcelona, Spain: UOC. Retrieved July 23, 2009, from http://www.uoc.edu/web/esp/art/uoc/0106024/sangra.html

Santángelo, H. N. (2003). Modelos pedagógicos en los sistemas de enseñanza no presencial basados en nuevas tecnologías y redes de comunicación. In Martínez Sánchez, F. (Ed.), *Redes de Comunicación en la Enseñanza: Las Nuevas Perspectivas del Trabajo Corporativo* (pp. 63–91). Barcelona: Paidós Ibérica.

Santos, O. C., & Boticario, J. G. (2008). Users' experience with a recommender system in an open source standard-based learning management system. In proceedings of the 4th Symposium of the WG HCI&UE of the Austrian Computer Society on Usability & HCI for Education and Work (USAB 2008).

Santos, O. C., Boticario, J. G., & Barrera, C. (2004). *Authoring a Collaborative Task Extending the IMS-LD to be Performed in a Standard-based Adaptive Learning Management System Called Alfanet.* Paper presented at the International Conference on Web Engineering. Retrieved 29 July 2009, from http://arantxa.ii.uam.es/~rcarro/AHCW04/Santos.pdf

Santos, O. C., Boticario, J. G., Fernández del Viso, A., Pérez de la Cámara, S., Rebate Sánchez, C., & Gutiérrez y Restrepo, E. (2007a) "Basic skills training to disabled and adult learners through an accessible e-Learning platform", Proceedings of the 12th International Conference on Human-Computer Interaction: HCI applications and services: Julie Jacko (eds.), vol. 7, Springer Berlin / Heidelberg, Lecture notes in computer science (LNCS, 4556), pp. 796-805

Santos, O. C., Boticario, J. G., Raffenne, E., & Pastor, R. (2007b). Why using dotLRN? UNED use cases. In J.R. Rodriguez and M. Palomo (Eds.), FLOSS International Conference, (pp. 195-212), UCA Pub.

Santos, O. C., Martin, L., del Campo, E., Saneiro, M., Mazzone, E., Boticario, J. G., & Petrie, H. (2009). User-Centered Design Methods for Validating a Recommendations Model to Enrich Learning Management Systems with Adaptive Navigation Support. In: S. Weibelzahl, J. Masthoff, A. Paramythis, and L. van Velsen (Eds.) Proceedings of the Sixth Workshop on User-Centred Design and Evaluation of Adaptive Systems, held in conjunction with the International Conference on User Modeling, Adaptation, and Personalization (UMAP2009), Trento, Italy, June 26th, 2009 (pp. 64-67).

Santos, O. C., Rodriguez-Ascaso, A., Boticario, J. G., & Martin, L. (2007c) User modelling for attending functional diversity for ALL in Higher Education. International Workshop on Personalized Access to Web Information (PAWI). LNCS 4832.

Sartori, G. (1998). *Homo videns. La sociedad teledirigida.* Madrid: Taurus.

Sauber, M. H., McSurely, H. B., & Rao Tummala, V. M. (2008). Developing supply chain management program: A competency model. *Quality Assurance in Education, 16*(4), 375–391. doi:10.1108/09684880810906517

Schaalje, J. (2007). Instructional design of learning objects for the cognitive domain. In Koohang, A., & Harman, K. (Eds.), *Learning Objects: Theory, Praxis, Issues, and Trends* (pp. 45–81). Santa Rosa, CA: Informing Science Press.

Schank, R. C., & Jona, M. (1991). Empowering the Student: New Perspectives on the Design of Teaching Systems. *Journal of the Learning Sciences*, *1*, 7–35. doi:10.1207/s15327809jls0101_2

Schelfhout, W., & Dochy, F. (2004). The use of self, peer and teacher assessment as a feedback system in a learning environment aimed at fostering skills of cooperation in an entrepreneurial context. *Assessment & Evaluation in Higher Education*, *29*(2), 177–201. doi:10.1080/0260293042000188465

Schembri, A. (2003). Rethinking 'Classifiers' in Signed Languages. In Emmorey, K. (Ed.), *Perspectives on Classifier Constructions in Sign Languages* (pp. 3–34). Mahwah, NJ: Lawrence Erlbaum and Associates.

Schenkman, B. N., & Jonsson, F. U. (2000). Aesthetics and preferences of web pages. *Behaviour & Information Technology*, *19*(5), 367–377. doi:10.1080/014492900750000063

Schiering, M. & Honigsfeld, A. (2002). Pedagogy: a matter of sharing one's experiential past for today's learning. *Academic Exchange Quarterly,* (Spring).

Schmidt, A., & Kunzmann, C. (2006). []. Berlin: Springer.]. *Lecture Notes in Computer Science*, *4278*, 1078–1087. doi:10.1007/11915072_10

Schmidt, J. P. (2007). *Recursos educativos abiertos: estrategia para apertura y desarrollo social de la Educación Superior*. Global University Network for Innovation GUNI. Universia. Retrieved June 20, 2009, from http://www.universia.net.co/secciones-home/en-abierto-portada/los-recursos-educativos-abiertos-como-una-estrategia-para-la-apertura.html.

Schneckenberg, D. (2006). Towards a Conceptualisation of eCompetence in Higher Education. In EDEN 2006 *Conference Proceedings 'E-Competences for Life, Employment and Innovation* (pp. 39-45). Vienna: European Distance and E- Learning Network.

Schubert, P., & Leimstoll, U. (2007). Importance and use of information technology in small and medium-sized companies. *Electronic Markets*, *17*(1), 38–55. doi:10.1080/10196780601136799

Schulz-Novak, D. K. (2002). *Building Quality into Distance Education: Establishing Standards*. Paper presented at the Pan-Commonwealth Forum on Open Learning, Durban, South Africa.

Sclater, N. (2007). The demise of eAssessment interoperability? In Davis, H., Duval, E., Muramatsu, B., White, S., and Van Assche, F., editors, *Proceedings of the Workshop on Exchanging Experiences in Technology Enhanced Learning – What Went Wrong? What Went Right? (WW-Wrong'07)*, volume 317 of *CEUR Workshop Proceedings*, pages 70–74, Sissi, Greece. CEUR-WS.org. Retrieved 2008-10-17, from http://ceur-ws.org/Vol-317/paper07.pdf

Sclater, N., Low, B., & Barr, N. (2002). Interoperability with CAA: does it work in practice? In M. Danson, (Ed.), *Proceedings of the 6th International Conference on Computer-Assisted Assessment*, (pp. 317–326). Loughborough University. doi: 2134/1890

SCORM. (2004). *SCORM 2004* (4th Ed.). Retrieved October 16, 2009, from http://www.adlnet.gov/Technologies/scorm/default.aspx

SCORM. (2004b). *Sharable Content Object Reference Model (SCORM), Content Aggregation Model, 4th edition, Version 1.0.* Retrieved June 20, 2009, from http://www.adlnet.org/scorm/index.cfm

Seaborne, A. (2004). *RDQL-A Query Language for RDF*, W3C Member Submission. Retrieved May 13, 2005, from http://www.w3.org/Submission/RDQL

Seale, J. (2006). *E-learning and disability in higher education: accessibility research and practice*. Routledge London.

Seale, J. Draffan, E.A and Wald, Mike (2008) Exploring disabled learners' experiences of e-learning: LEXDIS Project Report. Southampton, UK, University of Southampton, 161pp.

Seifart, F. (2006). Orthography Development. In Gippert, J., Himmelmann, N. P., & Mosel, U. (Eds.), *Essentials of Language Documentation* (pp. 275–299). New York: Mouton de Gruyter. doi:10.1515/9783110197730.275

Sero. (2007). *Baseline Study of e-Activity in Scotland's Colleges: Report to the Scottish Funding Council*, July 2007. Retrieved August 30, 2007, from http://www.sfc.ac.uk/information/information_learning/presentations_publications/sero_e_activity_study.pdf

SFIA Foundation. (2008). *Skills Framework for the Information Age: About SFIA*. Retrieved 2009 July 27 from http://www.sfia.org.uk/cgi-bin/wms.pl/296

Sgouropoulou, C., & Koutoumanos, A. (2005). Applying metadata standards to multilingual learning objects. *International Journal of Learning Technology, 1*(4), 425–442. doi:10.1504/IJLT.2005.007153

Sgouropoulou, C., Grant, S., Wilson, S., & Vangen, G. (2009). *European learner mobility standardization: Sketching the landscape*. Retrieved 2009-07-03 from http://www.fs.usit.uio.no/presentasjoner/EUNIS2009/FS-09-092_Sgouropoulou-Grant-Wilson-Vangen-113.pdf.

Shang, Y., Shi, H. C., & Chen, S. S. (2001). An intelligent distributed environment for active learning. *ACM Journal of Educational Resources in Computing, 1*(2), 1–17.

Sherwood, A. L., & Covin, J. G. (2008). Knowledge acquisition in university-industry alliances: An empirical investigation from a learning theory perspective. *Journal of Product Innovation Management, 25*, 162–179. doi:10.1111/j.1540-5885.2008.00292.x

Sicilia, M.-A. (2006). Semantic learning designs: recording assumptions and guidelines. *British Journal of Educational Technology, 37*(3), 331–350. doi:10.1111/j.1467-8535.2006.00609.x

Sicilia, M. A. (2005). Reusability and reuse of learning objects: Myths, realities and possibilities. *Revista de educación a distancia, 2*, 1-12. Retrieved May 3, 2009, from http://www.um.es/ead/red/M2/

Sicilia, M. A., & Garcia, E. (2003). On the Concepts of usability and Reusability of Learning Objects. *The Internacional of research in Open and Distance Learning, 4*(2). Retrieved July 23, 2009, from http://www.irrodl.org/index.php/irrodl/article/view/155/702

Siemens, G. (2004). *Connectivism: A Learning Theory for the Digital Age*. [updated: May, 26 2009]. Retrieved from http://www.elearnspace.org/Articles/connectivism.htm

Simkins, M. (2000). *Developing and Implementing a Rubric for Assessing Student Multimedia Projects*. Presented at the Annual Meeting of the American Educational Research Association, Creating Knowledge in the 21st Century: Insights From Multiple Perspectives, April 2000. New Orleans, LA.

Simon, H. (1995). Near decomposability and Complexity: How a Mind Resides in the Brain. In Morowitz, H. and Singer, J. (eds), *Mind, the Brain, and Complex Adaptive Systems*, (pp. 25-44). Santa Fe Institute Studies in the Sciences of Complexity, Proceedings vol. 22. Reading, MA: Addison-Wesley.

Singh, H. (2003). Building Effective Blended Learning Programs. *Educational Technology, 43*(6), 51–54.

Singh, H., & Reed, C. (2001). *A White Paper: Achieving Success with Blended Learning*. Centra Software.

Sitthisak, O., Gilbert, L., & Davis, H. C. (2008). An evaluation of pedagogically informed parameterised questions for self assessment. *Learning, Media and Technology, 33*(3), 235–248. doi:10.1080/17439880802324210

Sitthisak, O., Gilbert, L., Davis, H. C., & Gobbi, M. (2007). Adapting health care competencies to a formal competency model. In *the ICALT*, Niigata, Japan.

Sloan, D., Heath, A., Hamilton, F., Kelly, B., Petrie, H., & Phipps, L. (2006, May). Contextual web accessibility - maximizing the benefit of accessibility guidelines. In *ACM International Conference Proceeding, 134, W4A at WWW2006*, Edinburgh, UK.

Sloodle (2008b). Using Sloodle: Dubai-Korea Virtual Cultural Exchange, Using Sloodle to Support Learning and Teaching. *Journal*, 1-8. Retrieved from http://www.sloodle.org/moodle/file.php/1/SLOODLEcasestudy1.pdf

Sloodle. (2008a). *Sloodle: Learning System for Virtual Environments*. Retrieved 5 October, 2008, from http://www.sloodle.org

Sluijsmans, D., Brand-Gruwel, S., van Merriënboer, J., & Martens, R. (2004). Training teachers in peer assessment skills: effects on performance and perceptions. *Innovations in Education and Teaching International*, *41*(1), 60–79. doi:10.1080/1470329032000172720

Smart, K. L., & Cappel, J. J. (2006). Students' Perceptions of Online Learning: A Comparative Study. *Journal of Information Technology Education*, *5*, 201–219.

Smelser, L. M. (2002, March 20-23). *Making Connections in Our Classrooms: Online and Off.* Paper presented at the Annual Meeting of the Conference on College Composition and Communication, Chicago, IL.

Smith, C., Shepherd, E., Brewer, L., & Lay, S. (2002). *IMS Question & Test Interoperability: An Overview.* Retrieved July 29, 2009, from http://www.imsglobal.org

Smythe, C., & Roberts, P. (2000). An overview of the IMS Question & Test Interoperability specification. In *Proceedings of the 4th CAA Conference*, Loughborough, England. Loughborough University. Retrieved 2008-10-17, from http://hdl.handle.net/2134/1784.

Snow, C., & Thomas, J. B. (1994). Field research methods in strategic management: contributions to theory building and testing. *Journal of Management Studies*, *31*(4), 457–480. doi:10.1111/j.1467-6486.1994.tb00626.x

Soto, F. J., & Fernández, J. J. (2003). Realidades y retos de inclusión digital. *Comunicación y Pedagogía*, *192*, 34–40.

Spiltunik, M. W., Stratford, S., Krajcik, J., & Soloway, E. (2003). Using technology to support students' artefact construction in science. In Fraser, B. J., & Tobin, K. G. (Eds.), *International Handbook of Science Education* (pp. 317–331). London: Kluwer Academic Publishers.

Srikanthan, G., & Dalrymple, J. (2003). Developing alternative perspectives for quality in higher education. *International Journal of Educational Management*, *17*(3), 126–136. doi:10.1108/09513540310467804

Ssemugabi, S., & de Villiers, R. (2007). In *Proceedings of the 2007 annual research conference of the South African institute of computer scientists and information technologists on IT research in developing countries. ACM International Conference Proceeding Series;* (Vol. 226, pp. 132 - 142), Port Elizabeth, South Africa.

Standards Australia. (2007). *HB 256:2007 Metadata usage in Australian and New Zealand education and training.*

Stojanovic, L., Staab, S., & Studer, R. (2001). eLearning based on the Semantic Web. In *World Conference on the WWW and Internet*, Orlando, Florida, USA, (pp. 23-27).

Stokoe, W. C. (2001). *Language in Hand: Why Sign Came Before Speech.* Washington, DC: Gallaudet University Press.

Stoyanov, S. (2008). *Customer satisfaction and decision making in healthcare organizations.* Sofia, Bulgaria: Es Print.

Stoyanov, S. (1993). *Process optimization.* Sofia, Bulgaria: Technika. (in Bulgarian). *ISO 9000:2000 Quality management systems – Fundamentals and vocabulary, CEN.* (n.d.). *ISO 9001:2000 Quality management systems – Requirements, CEN.* (n.d.). Kendall, M. (1957). *Rank correlation methods.* London, UK: Griffin.

Streng, S., Baur, D., Broll, G., De Luca, A., Wimmer, R., & Butz, A. (Eds.). (2008). *Trends in E-Learning.* Technical Report, University of Munich.

Strobbe, C. (2006). Accessibility issues in two specifications for e-learning tests: IMS QTI 1.2 and IMS QTI 2.0. In *Computers Helping People with Special Needs, 10th International Conference, ICCHP 2006, Linz, Austria, July 11–13, 2006* (LNCS 4061, pp. 544–551). Berlin: Springer. doi: 10.1007/11788713_81.

Stuart, E. (2008). University to implement Moodle by end of year. *Daily Reveille, 112*(127). Retrieved 2008-10-17, from http://www.lsureveille.com/news/1.762154.

Su, K. D. (2008a). An integrated science course designed with information communication technologies to enhance university students' learning performance. *Computers & Education*, *51*(3), 1365–1374. doi:10.1016/j.compedu.2007.12.002

Su, K. D. (2008b). The effects of a chemistry course with integrated information communication technologies on university students' learning and attitudes. *International Journal of Science and Mathematics Education*, *6*(2), 225–249. doi:10.1007/s10763-006-9062-7

Sundar, A. (2002). *Evaluation of compliance and effectiveness of academic quality management in the tertiary institution: The case of Eastern Institute of Technology.* Paper presented at the HERDSA.

Sutton-Spence, R., & Woll, B. (1999). *The Linguistics of British Sign Language*. Cambridge, UK: Cambridge University Press.

Sutton-Spence, R. (forthcoming). Mouthings and Simultaneity in British Sign Language. In Vermeerbergen, M., Leeson, L., & Crasborn, O. (Eds.), *Simultaneous Constructions in Signed Languages – Form and Function.* Amsterdam: John Benjamins.

Sweller, J., & Chandler, P. (1994). Why some material is difficult to learn. *Cognition and Instruction*, *12*, 185–233. doi:10.1207/s1532690xci1203_1

Taber, K. S. (2002). *Chemical misconceptions - prevention, diagnosis and cure*. London: Royal Society of Chemistry.

Takwale, R. G. (2003), *Managing paradigm shift in parameters and benchmarks. Best Practices in Open and Distance Education*. Hyderabad, India: B.R. Ambedkar Open University (BRAOU).

Talmy, L. (1997). The Windowing of Attention in Language. In Shibitani, M., & Thompson, S. A. (Eds.), *Grammatical Constructions- Their Form and Meaning* (pp. 235–287). Oxford, UK: Clarendon Press.

Tannenbaum, A. (1981). *Computer Networks* (2nd ed.). New York: Prentice-Hall.

Tashner, J. H., Bronack, S. C., & Riedl, R. E. (2005). *3D Web-Based Worlds for Instruction.* Paper presented at the Society for Information Technology and Teacher Education International Conference, Phoenix, AZ.

Tashner, J. H., Riedl, R. E., & Bronack, S. C. (2005, January 2005). *Virtual Worlds: Further Development of Web-Based Teaching.* Paper presented at the Hawaii International Conference on Education, Honolulu, Hawaii.

Taylor, J. (2001). *Fifth generation distance education.* Keynote Address presented at the 20th ICDE World Conference, Düsseldorf, Germany, 1-5 April 2001.

Taylor, K., & Moore, S. (2005) An intelligent interactive online tutor for computer languages. In *Proceedings of 25th Annual International Conference of the British Computer Society's Specialist Group on Artificial Intelligence (SGAI 2005),* Cambridge, United Kingdom, December 10-12. Berlin: Springer-Verlag.

Taylor, K., & Moore, S. (June 2006) My *compiler really understands me.* Paper presented at Adaptive Hypermedia (AH 2006) Dublin.

Teach Online. (2005). East Lansing, MI: Michigan State University. Retrieved from http://teachvu.vu.msu.edu/public/

The William and Flora Hewlett Foundation. (n.d.). *Education section.* Retrieved June 25, 2009, from http://www.hewlett.org/oer

Thiriet, J.-M., Robert, M., Lapalainen, P., Hoffmann, M. H. W., Martins, M. J. M., & Seoane, A. (2002). Towards a pan-European virtual university in electrical and information engineering. *IEEE Transactions on Education*, *45*(2), 152–160. doi:10.1109/TE.2002.1013880

Topping, K. J. (1998). Peer assessment between students in colleges and universities. *Review of Educational Research*, *68*(3), 249–276.

Totkov, G. (2003). *Virtual Learning Environments: Towards New Generations.* Paper presented in International Conference on Computer Systems and Technologies, Compsystech-2003, June 19-20, Sofia, Bulgaria.

Tovar, E., & Cardeñosa, J. (2003). Convergence in higher education: effects and risks. In *The International Conference on the Convergence of Knowledge, Culture, Language and Information Technologies,* (pp. 1-5).

Tractinsky, N. (1997) Aesthetics and apparent usability: empirically assessing cultural and methodological issues. In *Conference Proceedings on Human Factors in Computing Systems*, Atlanta, GA USA, March 22 - 27, (pp. 115-122).

Tracy, H., Vyortkina, D., & Belgrove, M. (2008). Nurturing Excellence in E-learning Practice Through an Academic Programme (MA Online and Blended Learning). In *Proceedings of World Conference on Educational Multimedia, Hypermedia and Telecommunications 2008* (pp. 3549-3556). Chesapeake, VA: AACE. Retrieved from http://www.editlib.org/p/28876

Trafford, P. (n.d.). PLEs as Environments for Personal and Personalised Learning. *JISC PLE position paper.* Retrieved 4th August 2009 from: http://weblearn.ox.ac.uk/site/asuc/oucs/staff/pault/research/mobile/ramble/present/uploads/PaulT_Mini%20PLEPaper1.0.pdf

Trichet, F., & Leclère, M. (2003). *A Framework for Building Competency-Based Systems Dedicated to Human Resource Management (LNCS 2871).* Berlin: Springer.

Tricot, A. (2007). Utility, usability and acceptability: an ergonomic approach to the evaluation of external representations for learning. EARLI Symposium *« Understanding the role of external representations in supporting learning»*, Budapest, August 28 – September 1.

Trindade, J., Fiolhais, C., & Almeida, L. (2002). Science learning in virtual environments: A descriptive study. *British Journal of Educational Technology*, *33*(4), 471–488. doi:10.1111/1467-8535.00283

Trivantis'. (2007). *CourseMill—The Affordable Learning Management System Course.* Retrieved from http://www.trivantis.com/products/coursemill.html

Trotter, A. (2008). Blackboard vs. Moodle: Competition in course-management market grows. *Digital Directions, 2*(Spring/Summer), 21. Retrieved 2008-10-17, from http://edweek.org/dd/articles/2008/06/09/01moodle.h02.html

Tsai, Y., Wang, K., & Lo, S. (2003). A study of modularity operation of systems based on maintenance consideration. *Journal of Engineering Design, 14* (1), 41-56. Retrieved April, 2009 from http://www.ingentaconnect.com/content/tandf/cjen/2003/00000014/00000001/art00003;jsessionid=w7frr1f2c99s.alexandra

Tscherter, V. (2004). *Exorciser: Automatic Generation and Interactive Grading of Structured Exercises in the Theory of Computation.* PhD Thesis, Swiss Federal Institute of Technology, Switzerland.

Tsunoda, T. (2005). *Language Endangerment and Language Revitalisation – An Introduction.* Berlin: Mouton de Gruyter.

Tucker, J. S., McGilvray, D. H., Leibrecht, B. C., Strauss, C. B., Perrault, A., Gesselman, A. N., & Northrop Grumman Corp Columbus, G. A. (2009). Training Digital Skills In *Distributed Classroom Environments: A Blended Learning Approach. Storming Media: Pentagon Reports.* Retrieved 08-14-09 from http://www.stormingmedia.us/13/1375/A137594.html

Twigg, C. A. (2001). *Quality Assurance for Whom? Providers and Consumers in Today's Distributed Learning Environment.* Retrieved 29 November, 2009, from http://www.thencat.org/Monographs/Mono3.pdf

U.S. Department of Education. (2004). *The elementary and secondary education act (The no child left behind act of 2001).* Retrieved 2009 July 29 from http://www.ed.gov/policy/elsec/leg/esea02/index.html.

UAAG. (2002). *User Agent Accessibility Guidelines.* Retrieved October 16, 2009, from http://www.w3.org/TR/WAI-USERAGENT/

UaProf. (2009). User Agent Profile is a standard defined and maintained by the Open Mobile Alliance (formerly the WAP Forum). Retrieved July 21, 2009, from http://www.openmobilealliance.org/tech/affiliates/wap/wap-248-uaprof-20011020-a.pdf

Uden, L. (2007). Activity theory for designing mobile learning'. *Int. J. Mobile Learning and Organisation, 1*, 81–102. doi:10.1504/IJMLO.2007.011190

Ullrich, C. (2006). The learning-resource-type is dead, long live the learning-resource-type! *Learning Objects and Learning Designs*, *1*(1), 7–15.

Ullrich, C. (2005). Course generation based on HTN planning. In *Proceedings of 13th Annual Workshop of the SIG Adaptivity and User Modeling in Interactive Systems*, (pp.74-79).

Underwood, J., & Dillon, G. (2005). Capturing complexity through maturity modelling. In Somekh, B., & Lewin, C. (Eds.), *Research Methods in the Social Sciences* (pp. 260–264). London: Sage.

Universität Hamburg. (2009). OLAT – eine neue eLearning-Plattform an der Universität Hamburg. *UHH Newsletter*, (3). Retrieved 2009-08-05, from http://www.uni-hamburg.de/newsletter/OLAT-ndash-eine-neue-eLearning-Plattform-an-der-Universitaet-Hamburg.html

Universities, U. K. The Standing Conference of Principals, The Higher Education Academy, The Higher Education Funding Council for England, The Scottish Higher Education Funding Council, The Higher Education Funding Council for Wales & the Department for Employment and Learning, Northern Ireland (2004). *Towards a framework of professional teaching standards*. Retrieved August 10, 2009, from http://www.scop.ac.uk/downloads/ProfStand.doc

University Library, University of Illinois at Urbana-Champaign. (2008). *Instructional strategies and pedagogy.* Illinois Online Network. Retrieved from http://www.library.illinois.edu/diglit/faculty/teaching/pedagogy.html

University of London. (2008). *Benchmarking eLearning at the University of London: Report from the steering group*. London: University of London. Retrieved August 10, 2009, from http://www.londonexternal.ac.uk/quality/comte_zone/sys_tech_sub/stsc2/documents/stsc2_3.pdf

Uschi, F. (2005). E-learning pedagogy in the third millennium: the need for combining social and cognitive constructivist approaches. *ReCALL*, *17*(1), 85–100. doi:. doi:10.1017/S0958344005000716

Vagiati, V. (2006). *Semantic mapping between LOM – SCORM Content Package and MPEG-7 concepts (including the representation of the mapping through an ontology)*. Unpublished master's thesis, Ionian University, Greece.

Valiathan, P. (2002). Blended Learning Models. *Learning Circuits*. Retrieved from www.learningcircuits.org/2002/aug2002/valiathan.html

Valk, A. (2009). Recognition of prior and experiential learning in European universities. *Assessment in education, principles, policies & practice, 16*(1), 83-95.

Van Assche, F., Duval, E., Massart, D., Olmedilla, D., Simon, B., & Sobernig, S. (2006). Spinning Interoperable Applications for Teaching & Learning using the Simple Query Interface. *Journal of Educational Technology & Society*, *9*(2), 51–67.

Van Assche, F. (2007). *Roadmap to interoperability for education in Europe*. Retrieved May 1, 2009, from http://insight.eun.org/shared/data/pdf/life_book.pdf

Van der Heijden, B., & Nijhof, A. (2004). The value of subjectivity: problems and prospects for 360-degree appraisal systems. *International Journal of Human Resource Management*, *15*(3), 493–511. doi:10.1080/0958519042000181223

Van Herreweghe & Vermeerbergen. (2004). Flemish Sign Language: Some Risks of Codification. In Van Herreweghe, M. & M. Vermeerbergen, *To the Lexicon and Beyond: The Sociolinguistics of European Sign Languages*, (pp. 111-140). Washington, DC: Gallaudet University Press.

Van Rosmalen, P., Boticario, J. G., & Santos, O. C. (2004). The Full Life Cycle of Adaptation in aLFanet eLearning Environment. Learning Technology newsletter. Vol. 4, p. 59-61, 2004.

Van Valin, R. D., & La Polla, R. J. (1997). *Syntax- Structure, Meaning and Function*. Cambridge, UK: Cambridge University Press.

Vanderstraeten, R. (2006). *Sociocybernetics, socialization, education.* Retrieved November, 2007 from http://www.unizar.es/sociocybernetics/congresos/MONTREAL/absg1.html

Varlamis, I., & Apostolakis, I. (2006). The present and future of standards for e-learning technologies. *Interdisciplinary Journal of Knowledge and Learning Objects, 2*, 59–74.

Velasco, C. A., Mohamad, Y., Gilman, A. S., Viorres, N., Vlachogiannis, E., Arnellos, A., & Darsenitas, J. S. (2004) Universal access to information services—the need for user information and its relationship to device profiles. Universal Access in the Information Society, Publisher Springer Berlin / Heidelberg, ISSN 1615-5297, Issue Volume 3, Number 1, pp 88-95.

Venkataraman, B. (2009). Visualization and interactivity in the teaching of chemistry to science and non-science students. *Chemistry Education Research and Practice, 10*(1), 62–69. doi:10.1039/b901462b

Vercelli, A. (2004). *La conquista silenciosa del ciberespacio: Creative Commons y el diseño de entornos digitales como nuevo arte regulativo en Internet*. Retrieved June 02, 2009, from http://www.arielvercelli.org/lcsdc.pdf

Vermeerbergen, M., & Demey, E. (2007). Sign + Gesture = Speech + Gesture? Comparing Aspects of Simultaneity in Flemish Sign Language to Instances of Concurrent Speech and Gesture. In Vermeerbergen, M., Leeson, L., & Crasborn, O. (Eds.), *Simultaneous Constructions in Signed Languages – Form and Function*. Amsterdam: John Benjamins.

Vermeerbergen, M., Leeson, L., & Crasborn, O. (in press). Simultaneous Structures in Signed Languages: An Introduction. In Vermeerbergen, M., Leeson, L., & Crasborn, O. (Eds.), *Simultaneous Constructions in Signed Languages – Form and Function*. Amsterdam: John Benjamins.

Vervenne, L. (n.d.). *Competency Related Data Management (CRDM): A proposed reference model*. Retrieved 2009-06-23 from http://ieeeltsc.files.wordpress.com/2009/03/competency-related-data-management-prolix.pdf

Vest, C. (2004). Why MIT decided to give away all its course materials via the Internet. *The Chronicle of Higher Education*, 30.

Vicent, L., Avila, X., Riera, J., Badia, D., Anguera, J., & Montero, J. A. (2006). Appropriateness of e-learning resources for the development of transversal skills in the new European Higher Education Area. *Frontiers in Education Conference, 36th Annual*, (pp. 27-31). doi: 10.1109/FIE.2006.322671

Vijay-Kumar, M. S. (2009) Open Educational Resources in India's national development. *Open Learning: The Journal of Open and Distance Learning*, 77-84. Retrieved October 10, 2009, from http://pdfserve.informaworld.com/531234__909097030.pdf

Virtual, A. University Jaume I. (2007). Web site: http://aulavirtual.uji.es

Vleuten, C. P. M. d., & Schuwirth, L. W. T. (2005). Assessing professional competence: from methods to programmes. *Medical Education, 39*(3), 309–317. doi:10.1111/j.1365-2929.2005.02094.x

Vogten, H., Martens, H., Nadolski, R., Tattersall, C., Rosmalen, P., & Koper, R. (2006). CopperCore Service Integration - Integrating IMS Learning Design and IMS Question and Test Interoperability. In *Proceedings of The 6th IEEE International Conference on Advanced Learning Technologies*, (pp. 378-382), Kerkrade, The Netherlands. Washington, DC: IEEE Computer Society.

Volder, M. D., Rutjens, M., Slootmaker, A., Kurvers, H., Bitter, M., Kappe, R., et al. (2007). *Espace: A New Web-Tool for Peer Assessment with In-Built Feedback Quality System*. Paper presented at ABR & TLC Conference, 2007, Hawaii, USA.

Volterra, V., Laudanna, S., Corazza, E., & Natale, F. (1984). Italian Sign Language: The Order of Elements in the Declarative Sentence. In Lonke, F. (Ed.), *Recent Research on European Sign Languages* (pp. 19–48). Lisse, The Netherlands: Svets and Zeitlinger.

Vossen, G., & Westerkamp, P. (2008). Why service-orientation could make e-learning standards obsolete. *International Journal of Technology Enhanced Learning, 1*(1/2), 85–97. doi:10.1504/IJTEL.2008.020232

Vrasidas, C. (2004). Issues of Pedagogy and Design in e-learning Systems. *Symposium on Applied Computing: Proceedings of the 2004 ACM symposium on Applied computing* Nicosia, Cyprus. Session: Engineering e-learning systems (ELS). (pp. 911– 915).

Vrasidas, C., & McIsaac, M. S. (1999). *Principles of Pedagogy and Evaluation for Web-Based Learning.* In *ICEM*, Slovenia. Retrieved 07-23-09 from http://seamonkey.ed.asu.edu/~mcisaac/ICEM99/pedagogymss.html

W3C. (1999). *Web Content Accessibility Guidelines (WCAG) 1.0*, W3C 5 May 1999, Retrieved 4th August 2009 from: http://www.w3.org/TR/WCAG10/

W3C. (2004). *OWL Web Ontology Language (OWL).* Retrieved October 27, 2007, from http://www.w3.org/TR/owl-ref/

W3C. (2005). *SKOS Core Guide.* Retrieved November 4, 2008, from http://www.w3.org/TR/swbp-skos-core-guide/

W3C. (2008). *Web Content Accessibility Guidelines (WCAG) 2.0*, W3C 11 December 2008, reformatted 3 March 2009, Retrieved 4th August 2009 from: http://beta.w3.org/TR/2009/REC-WCAG20-20090303/

W3C. (2009). Authoring Tool Accessibility Guidelines (ATAG) 2.0, W3C Working Draft 21th May 2009, Retrieved 4th August 2009 from: http://www.w3.org/TR/ATAG20/

W3C. (2009, February 24). *Accessible Rich Internet Applications (WAI-ARIA) 1.0.* W3C Working Draft. Retrieved 4th August 2009 from: http://www.w3.org/TR/wai-aria/

W3C-WAI. (December 2008). W3C World Wide Web. Retrieved August 7, 2009, from W3C Web Accessibility Initiative: http://www.w3.org/WAI/intro/wcag.php

Wache, H., Voegele, T., Visser, U., Stuckenschmidt, H., Schuster, G., Neumann, H., & Huebner, S. (2001). Ontology-Based Integration of Information—A survey of existing approaches. *Proceedings of the IJCAI-01 Workshop on Ontologies and Information Sharing, Seattle, WA* (pp. 108-118).

WAI. (n.d). *Web Accessibility Initiative home page.* Retrieved July 16, 2009, from http://www.w3.org/WAI/

Walker, L. (2006). *The New Higher Education Systems, Modularity and Student Capability.* Retrieved from http://www.heacademy.ac.uk/assets/york/documents/resources/heca/heca_md02.pdf

Walter, J. (2006). LMS in health care, online education. *Latitude consulting group.* Retrieved from http://www.latitudecg.com/Portals/0/pdf/Articles/LMS%20in%20 Healthcare.pdf

Wan, L., Zhao, C., & Luo, Q. (2006). Navigation and sequencing strategy of learning process in distance learning context. In *Frontiers in Education.*

Watson, R., & Pollack, J. (2006). *Modular Interdependency in Complex Dynamical Systems.* Retrieved May, 2009 from http://www.mitpressjournals.org/doi/abs/10.1162/106454605774270589?cookieSet=1&journalCode=artl

WCAG. (2008). *Web Contents Accessibility Guidelines.* Retrieved July 16, 2009, from http://www.w3.org/TR/WCAG20/

Web, C. A. G. (WCAG) 2.0 - W3C Recommendation 11 December 2008. Retrieved January 15, 2009, from http://www.w3.org/TR/2008/REC-WCAG20-20081211/

Weedon, E., Jorna, K., & Broumley, L. (2004). Closing the gaps in institutional development of networked learning: How do policy and strategy inform practice to sustain innovation? In *Proceedings of the Networked Learning Conference 2004*, 1-7 April, 2004 at Lancaster University, UK. Retrieved February 25, 2008, from http://www.networkedlearningconference.org.uk/past/nlc2004/proceedings/symposia/symposium8/weedon_et_al.htm

Weinberger, A., & Fischer, F. (2006). A framework to analyze argumentative knowledge construction in computer-supported collaborative learning. *Computers & Education, 46*, 71–95. doi:10.1016/j.compedu.2005.04.003

Welsch, E. (2002). SCORM: Clarity or calamity? *Online Learning Magazine*. Retrieved August 10, 2009, from http://www.onlinelearningmag.com/onlinelearning/magazine/article_display.jsp?vnu_content_id=1526769

Werner, C. (2005). The Ubiquity of Modularity. In *Modularity: Understanding the Development and Evolution of Natural Complex Systems* (pp. 3–29). Cambridge, MA: MIT Press.

White, B. Y. (2003). Computer Microworld and scientific inquiry: an alternative approach to science education. In Fraser, B. J., & Tobin, K. G. (Eds.), *International Handbook of Science Education* (pp. 295–316). London: Kluwer Academic Publishers.

White, D. (2008). Innovative Learning for Europe. In *EDEN Annual Conference, 11-14 June 2008, Lisbon, Portugal.* Retrieved July 26, 2009 from http://www.eden-online.org/contents/conferences /annual/Lisbon/Keynotes/White.pdf

Whitehouse, A., Hassel, A., Bullock, A., Wood, L., & Wall, D. (2007). 360 degree assessment (multisource feedback) of UK trainee doctors: Field testing of team assessment of behaviors (TAB). *Medical Teacher*, *29*, 171–176. doi:10.1080/01421590701302951

Whittaker, J. (2007). Quality Online Teaching? Who's asking? *He Kupu*, *1*, 18–27.

Whittington, D. (2001). *Testing IMS in real context implementing IMS specifications implications and best practice*. University of Glasgow. Retrieved April 26, 2009, from http://www.gla.ac.uk/rcc/projects/tircs/tircs-full.pdf

Wikimedia Foundation. (n.d.). *Home page*. Retrieved June 16, 2009, from http://wikimediafoundation.org/wiki/Home

Wikipedia, the free encyclopedia. (2008). Learning management system. Retrieved July 22, 2009, from http://en.wikipedia.org/wiki/Learning_management_system

Wikipedia. (2009). *Open educational resources*. Retrieved July 12, 2009, from http://en.wikipedia.org/wiki/Open_educational_resources

Wilbur, R. (1994). Eyeblinks and ASL phrase structure. *Sign Language Studies*, *84*, 221–240.

Wilcox, S. (2004a). Gesture and Language: Cross-linguistic and Historical Data from Signed Languages. *Gesture*, *43*, 43–73. doi:10.1075/gest.4.1.04wil

Wilcox, S. (2004b). Cognitive Iconicity: Conceptual Spaces, Meaning and Gesture in Signed Languages. *Cognitive Linguistics*, *15*(2), 119–147. doi:10.1515/cogl.2004.005

Wild, F., Kalz, M., Palmer, M., & Muller, D. (Eds.). (2009). Proceedings of the Second International Workshop on Mashup Personal Learning Environments, in *European Conference on Technology-Enhanced Learning. Available* at http://ceur-ws.org/Vol-506/ (retrieved Oct. 2009).

Wild, F., Mödritscher, F., & Sigurdarson, S. (2008). Designing for change: Mash-up personal learning environments. *eLearning Papers, 9*. Retrieved July 29, 2009 from http://www.elearningeuropa.info/files/media/media15972.pdf

Wilensky, U. (2003). Statistical mechanics for secondary school: The gaslab multi-agent modeling toolkit. *International Journal of Computers for Mathematical Learning*, *8*, 1–41. doi:10.1023/A:1025651502936

Wiley, D. A. (2002). Connecting learning objects to instructional design theory: A definition, a metaphor, and a taxonomy. In *The Instructional Use of Learning Objects*. Agency for Instructional Technology.

Wiley, D. A. (2007). *The learning object literature*. Retrieved May 20, 2009 from http://opencontent.org/docs/wiley-lo-review-final.pdf

Wiley, D., & Gurrell, S. (2009) A decade of development... *Open Learning: The Journal of Open and Distance Learning*. 11-21. Retrieved October 10, 2009, from http://pdfserve.informaworld.com/39175__909097159.pdf

Williams, W. M. (2004). Blissfully incompetent. *Psychological Science in the Public Interest*, *5*(3), i–ii. doi:10.1111/j.1529-1006.2004.00017.x

Wills, G., Davis, H., Gilbert, L., Hare, J., Howard, Y., & Jeyes, S. (2009). Delivery of QTIv2 question types. *Assessment & Evaluation in Higher Education, 34*(3), 353–366. doi:10.1080/02602930802071106

Wills, G., Davis, H., Gilbert, L., Hare, J., Howard, Y., & Jeyes, S. (2009). Delivery of QTIv2 question types. *Assessment & Evaluation in Higher Education, 34*(3), 353–366. doi:10.1080/02602930802071106

Wills, G., Davis, H., Chennupati, S., Gilbert, L., Howard, Y., Jam, E. R., et al. (2006). R2Q2: Rendering and Reponses Processing for QTIv2 Question Types. In M. Danson (ed.), *Proceedings of the 10th International Computer Assisted Assessment Conference*, (pp. 515-522). Loughborough University, UK.

Wilson, S. (2005, January 21). *In Praise of Simpler Standards?* Scott's Workblog, Retrieved April 22, 2009, from http://zope.cetis.ac.uk/members/scott/entries/20050121223821

Winther, R. (2005). Evolutionary Developmental Biology Meets Levels of Selection: Modular Integration or Competition, or Both? In *Modularity: Understanding the Development and Evolution of Natural Complex Systems* (pp. 61–99). Cambridge: MIT Press.

Witten, I., & Frank, E. (2005). *Data mining: practical machine learning tools and techniques* (2nd ed., pp. 285–362). New York: Elsevier.

World Economic Outlook. (2000, May). Asset Prices and the Business Cycle. Retrieved April 2009 from http://www.imf.org/external/pubs/ft/weo/2000/01/index.htm

World Wide Web Consortium. (2002). *XHTML 1.0 The Extensible HyperText Markup Language*. Retrieved 2008-10-17, from http://www.w3.org/TR/html

World Wide Web Consortium. (2006). *Extensible Markup Language (XML) 1.0*. Retrieved 2008-10-17, from http://www.w3.org/TR/xml.

Woukeu, A., Wills, G., Conole, G., Carr, L., Kampa, S., & Hall, W. (2003). Ontological Hypermedia in Education: A framework for building web-based educational portals. *World Conference on Educational Multimedia, Hypermedia & Telecommunications*, Honolulu, Hawaii, USA.

XQuestion - Surveys. *Assessment, Tests from XML.* (n.d.). Retrieved July 29, 2009, from http://www.xquestion.com/.

Yang, S. J. H., Chen, I. Y. L., & Chen, R. (2007). Applying Content Adaptation to Mobile Learning, Second International Conference on Innovative Computing [IEEE Computer Society Press.]. *Information and Control, ICICIC*, 157.

Yatskovsky. (2009). Retrieved 22 July 2009 from http://finemetronome.com/moodle

Young, J. R. (2002, March 22). 'Hybrid' teaching seeks to end the divide between traditional and online instruction. *The Chronicle of Higher Education*, A33.

Zaine, O. R. (2002). Building a Recommender Agent for e-Learning Systems", Proceedings of International. Conference on Computers in Education, Auckland, New Zealand, 3-6 December, pp. 55-59.

Zarraonandia, T., Dodero, J. M., & Fernández, C. (2006). Crosscutting Runtime Adaptations of LD Execution. *Journal of Educational Technology & Society, 9*(1), 123–137.

Zhu, E., & Kaplan, M. (2002). An introduction to teaching online. In Coryell, P. (Ed.), *Technology and teaching; McKeachie's Teaching Tips: Strategies, Research and Theory for College and University.*

Zimmermann, G., Vanderheiden, G., Gandy, M., Laskowski, S., Ma, M., Trewin, S., & Walker, M. (2004). Universal remote console standard - toward natural user interaction in ambient intelligence. Extended Abstracts for the 2004 Conference on Human Factors in Computing Systems (pp. 1608-1609). New York: ACM Press.

Zouaq, A., Nkambou, R., & Frasson, C. (2007 July 18 - 20). Using a competence model to aggregate learning knowledge objects. In *Proceedings of the Seventh IEEE International Conference on Advanced Learning Technologies*, (pp. 836-840).

ZTHES specifications for thesaurus representation, access and navigation. (n.d.). Retrieved 2009/07/25 from http://zthes.z3950.org/

Zuber-Skerrit, O. (1990). *Action learning for change and development*. Aldershot, UK: Gower-Avebury.

Zucker, A. A., & Hug, S. T. (2008). Teaching and learning physics in a 1:1 laptop school. *Journal of Science Education and Technology*, *17*(6), 586–594. doi:10.1007/s10956-008-9125-3

About the Contributors

Fotis Lazarinis holds a PhD in Educational Technology with an emphasis on adaptive testing tools and on the use of e-learning standards for representing and managing testing data. He is a visiting lecturer in the Department of Cultural Heritage and New Technologies at the University of Western Greece. He has authored over 50 refereed papers in international or national conferences, journals and research handbooks. He has also published several Computer Science educational books in Greek and served as a review member for conferences and workshops

Steve Green is Director of Undergraduate Programmes in the School of Computing, Teesside University, UK. He is also a founder member of the Accessibility Research Centre and Digital Futures Institute at Teesside. Dr Green has been among the academic staff at Teesside University for over twenty years during which time he has published extensively in the areas of accessibility and educational technology. His research interests include accessible and adaptable systems, e-learning, mobile technologies, web technologies and learning environments. Over the years he has supervised a number of doctoral and masters students and is part of a very active community of researchers looking at accessible and adaptable personal learning environments, tools and learning content.

Elaine Pearson is Director of the Accessibility Research Centre and a member of the Digital Futures Institute at Teesside University, UK. Her research and consultancy expertise lies in the use of digital media design and technology to support the needs and preferences of disabled people. This research has been supported by grants from British and European funding bodies including the Leverhulme Trust, Higher Education Funding Council (HEFCE), and European Social Fund (ESF) EQUAL initiative. She has published extensively on accessibility and adaptability issues and been invited to present in the UK, Ireland, Spain and Australia. Dr Pearson is also Director of Post Graduate Programmes in the School of Computing. Her teaching interests as a Principal Lecturer lie in aspects of web and mobile design for accessibility and adaptaibility.

* * *

Philip Barker is a distinguished emeritus professor within the school of computing at Teesside University in the United Kingdom. He is a founder member of and a principal researcher in the interactive systems research group - a multidisciplinary team of computer scientists and psychologists involved in studying various aspects of human-computer interaction and the effects of electronic technology on people's mental and physical behaviour. Professor Barker is a national teaching fellow of the UK's higher education academy and acts as co-editor of the journal 'innovations in education and teaching international'. He has published numerous books and research papers. His latest book entitled 'Electronic Performance Support: Using Digital Technology to Enhance Human Ability' was published in February 2010 by Gower. He is currently working with Springer on a major reference work entitled the 'Encyclopaedia of the Sciences of Learning' for which he is the associate editor for the section that deals with cognitive psychology and cognitive science. Further details are available at http://refworks.springer.com/.

Yongwu Miao received a master degree in computer science and technologies from the Wuhan University, P.R. China. He received a PhD in information technologies from the Technical University of Darmstadt, Germany, while he worked at German national Research Center for Information Technologies - IPSI. Currently he works as assistant professor at the Centre for Learning Sciences and Technologies (CELSTEC) in the Open University of the Netherlands (OUNL). His current research interests include educational process modelling and execution environment, CSCL, computer-assisted assessment, competence information systems.

Jo Boon is an educational sociologist and educational technologist. She is working as associate professor and as human resource manager at CELSTEC. Different aspects of the relation between learning and work are her points of interest in research. Hence her publications cover themes as employability, lifelong learning, assessment and development of professional competencies.

Marcel van der Klink started his academic career after receiving a master degree in andragogy. During his years at the University of Twente, the Netherlands, he received a PhD degree in educational technology. Until 1998 he works at the Open University of the Netherlands. His recent publications focus on workplace learning, professional development throughout the life-span, design and implementation of new assessment forms, and e-learning. Besides research activities his job as associate professor includes supervision of PhD students and master students and consultancy activities for various organizations. He is a member of several editorial boards of scholarly journals in the domain of human resource development and education.

Peter B. Sloep is the Programme Director of the Research and Technology Development Programme on Learning Networks of CELSTEC. His current research interest include distributed learning systems, particularly the technical – including specifications for interoperability - and the social affordances of learning networks that are conducive to the emergence of a viable learning and working environment for lifelong learning.

Rob Koper is the dean of the CELSTEC in the OUNL. His personal research concentrates on professional development in self-organized distributed learning networks. In the past he developed the Educational Modeling Language (the predecessor of IMS Learning Design) and led the OUNL's contribution to the IMS LD specification activities. He is furthermore coordinating the European Integrated Project TENCompetence that aims to develop an infrastructure for lifelong competence development.

Sergio Gutierrez-Santos obtained his Engineering degree and his PhD from University Carlos III of Madrid. His PhD thesis combined adaptive sequencing and standards-based reutilisation. He has worked in several projects with Spanish, British and European funding. Among other topics, he has published several papers related to sequencing of learning material, adaptive hypermedia, and the use of learning standards to achieve interoperability (especially IMS-CP, IMS-QTI, IMS-SS, and IMS-LD). His other research interests include artificial intelligence techniques, from Bayesian inference to genetic algorithms and swarm intelligence; and their application to engineering education, exploratory learning environments, and user modelling. Since 2007 he works as a Research Officer at the London Knowledge Lab (Birkbeck College).

Vladimir Tomberg is a research associate of the Centre for Educational Technology in Tallinn University, Estonia. Vladimir holds a Bachelors degree in Information Technology from Audentes University and a Master of Science in Multimedia and Learning Systems from Tallinn University. His MSc study was devoted to adaptation of IMS QTI specifications for Learning Management Systems. Currently his research interests are wider extended with questions of interoperability between LMS and especially for Personal Learning Environment. Also Vladimir does research in field of software design for e-learning; particularly he is working with Learning Flow and Course metadata issues.

Mart Laanpere, is head of the Centre for Educational Technology in Tallinn University, Estonia. He received MSc in Educational & Training Systems Design from University of Twente, the Netherlands in 1997. His main focus in research is conceptual design and analysis of affordances of technology-enhanced learning systems and tools, also implementing ePortfolios for competency management in teachers' professional development. Recently he has been working as a pedagogical and technical policy expert for the national technology enhanced learning development programmes in the Republic of Georgia and the Republic of Moldova. He is a member of Program Committees for European Conference of Educational Research (ECER), workshop on Mash-up Personal Learning Environments (MUPPLE), International Conference on Web-based Learning.

Olga C. Santos, R&D Technical Manager of aDeNu group. Her research interests focuses on taking into account adaptation and accessibility requirements, both at design and runtime, to provide open educational user-centred services to ubiquitously and dynamically adapt to the evolving needs in the e-learning context. For this, user-centred design methods are being applied. The focus is put on applying recommendation strategies to provide adaptive navigation support in existing learning management systems. She has participated in 12 international and national research projects, published over 80 research articles in conferences and journals, been member of the program committee of several conferences and journals and co-chaired workshops on user modelling and accessibility. For details, see aDeNu group website.

Jesús G. Boticario, Ph.D. in Physical Sciences (PS) at UNED (prize awarded as the most outstanding PhD, 1994). B.Sc. in Computer Science, School of Computer Science at Madrid Polytechnic University. Associate Professor at UNED's CSS. Invited speaker at National and International conferences. He has published over 200 research articles. Participation in 18 R&D funded projects (Spain, USA, EU). Head of aDeNu research group (https://adenu.ia.uned.es). Current scientific coordinator in a European and National funded projects. Program Committee member of National and International Conferences. He has co-chaired International Workshops in the areas of User Modeling and Accessibility. He is reviewer of research projects and international journals. Hold several positions at UNED in the ICT area (e.g. Innovation and Technological Development Vice-principal). dotLRN Board of Directors member. He is an expert counsellor at the UNED's Center for Supporting Students with Disabilities. He is the coordinator of an educational innovation network "Accessibility and Functional Diversity" (UNED).

Emmanuelle Raffenne is a computer engineer with more than 10 years experience in e-Learning system, collaborative platforms, service oriented architectures and web applications. Her actual research focuses on adaptive learning systems, accessibility and usability. She is a member of the aDeNu group (department of Artificial Intelligence at UNED) since 2006 and she participates in several national and international projects as an expert in Learning Management Systems. She is currently coordinating the EU4ALL project (IST-2006-034778). She has been coordinating the Innova team at UNED, in charge of the development and exploitation of aLF (LMS based on dotLRN), from 2001 to 2006.

Jorge Granado, M.Sc. in Telecommunications Engineering specialized in Telematics, at Madrid Polytechnic University (UPM). He started working in 1991 for the first Spanish ISP (Goya Servicios Telematicos), developing web platform systems for different companies. After working as a technical director for an arts & entertainment web portal, he joined the Major Events division in SchlumbergerSema to develop the INFO system for the Olympic Winter Games in 2002, and then in AtosOrigin Utilities department he managed the software development for several European Energy Companies. He has been working also as Key expert for EU Phare programs in Romania and Bulgaria. Since April 2007, he is a researcher at the aDeNu Group at the Artificial Intelligence Department (UNED) and working on the following funded projects: Adaptation based on machine learning, user modelling and planning for complex user-oriented tasks – ADAPTAPlan (MEC: TIN2005-08945-C06-01), EU4ALL (IST-2006-034778): European Unified Approach for Assisted Lifelong Learning.

Alejandro Rodríguez-Ascaso has a PhD. in Telecommunication Engineering. He is a lecturer and a researcher at the aDeNu (Adaptive Dynamic online Educational Systems based on User Modelling) group at the National Distance Learning University of Spain (UNED). He has participated as a researcher in more than fifteen National and International research projects in the field of electronic accessibility and IT mediated support to independent living of people with disabilities. Alejandro Rodríguez-Ascaso has published more than fifteen related works in relevant Books, Journals and Proceedings of International Scientific Conferences. He is also member of the ICT Advisory Board of Fundacion ONCE. He is the convener of the Accessibility Group of the Telecommunications Technical Committee of the Spanish Association for Standardisation and Certification (AENOR). He has also participated in STFs 377, 299 and 264 of the European Telecommunications Standards Institute (ETSI), within its Human Factors Technical Committee.

Emmanuelle Gutiérrez y Restrepo, Accessibility Expert of aDeNu Group, graduated in Communication Science, Master of Communication in Society and Social Problems, Expert on Corporate Image and Communication, by the Complutense University of Madrid.Patron of the Foundation Sidar - Universal Access, is computer accessibility evangelist since 1995. She has developed, along with collaborators, applications for Web accessibility of international concern as HERA, and materials and simulations for teaching web accessibility. Invited speaker at national and international conferences. Participated in the Working Group for drafting the W3C-WAI's WCAG 1.0 in "Good standing", as well as for the version 2.0 drafting, and currently is Invited Expert in the W3C Web Accessibility Initiative (WAI) Education and Outreach Working Group (EOWG). Head of working group that focuses on Internet Accessibility for the Elderly and Disabled of the Spanish Association for Standardisation and Certification AENOR (GT3-SC8-CTN139), also participates as a member of the CTN 133/GT 3.

Andreas Alexopoulos has received his BSc in Computer Science from the Computer Science Department of University of Crete in Greece. He is currently a postgraduate student in the Department of Computer Engineering & Informatics of the University of Patras. His master thesis and his research interests are about educational metadata and interoperability in digital repositories.

Georgia Solomou is currently pursuing a doctoral degree in Semantic Web technologies at the University of Patras in Greece. She holds a master's degree in computer science from the same University. She is a member of the High Performance Information Systems Laboratory (HPCLab) where she has taken part in many European research projects. Georgia's research interests are related to the Semantic Web standards and technologies, mainly focusing in the field of Digital Libraries.

Dimitrios Koutsomitropoulos is an Adjunct Assistant Professor at the Department of Computer Engineering and Informatics and a researcher at the High Performance Information Systems Laboratory (HPCLab), University of Patras. He has received a Ph.D., an M.Sc. and a Computer and Informatics Engineer diploma from the same department. His research interests include knowledge discovery, automated reasoning, ontological engineering, metadata integration, semantic interoperability and the semantic web.

Theodore Papatheodorou is a Professor at the Department of Computer Engineering and Informatics, University of Patras, since 1984. Since 2005 he is the Department's Chairman. He is the head of the High Performance Information Systems Laboratory (HPCLab). He has received a Ph.D. in Computer Science in 1973 and a M.Sc. in Mathematics in 1971 from Purdue University as well as a B.Sc. in Mathematics from University of Athens in 1968. He has authored hundreds of scientific publications in several areas of Computer Engineering and Computer Science.

Lester Gilbert received his MSc in Psychology (cum laude) and his BSc (Hons) (First Class) from the University of Cape Town. After a number of years in commerce and industry as a programmer, consultant, and technical director in the field of what would now be called technology-enhanced learning, Lester returned to academia with a text, Principles of e-Learning Systems Engineering, integrating his business-oriented practical experience of technical systems development with instructional engineering. His current research interests focus upon competency modelling. Lester is the author of over 60 academic papers.

Onjira Sitthisak was born in Thailand. She received her B.Sc. in Computer Science (First Class honors) from Prince of Songkla University, Thailand, in 1999, and her M.Sc. in Applied Statistics (Information Systems Management) from National Institute of Development Administration, Thailand, in 2002. She undertook her Ph.D. between 2005-2009 at the University of Southampton, UK, with research on adaptive assessment and competency, funded by the Royal Thai Government. She has worked as a lecturer since 1999 at the Department of Mathematics, Computer Science group, Thaksin University, Thailand. She is currently the Head of the Information Technology group. She has published more than 10 papers, 2 book chapters, and 1 journal in the past 4 years.

Michael Piotrowski is a senior research associate at ZHAW Zurich University of Applied Sciences in Winterthur, Switzerland and a lecturer at the University of Zurich. He holds a doctorate in computer science from Otto von Guericke University, Magdeburg, Germany, and a master's degree in computational linguistics from Friedrich-Alexander-University Erlangen Nuremberg, Germany. He is one of the designers of the eduComponents, an open-source component-based e-learning platform based on the free content management system Plone. His research interests are in the areas of e-learning and computational linguistics, and he is the author of numerous peer-reviewed articles in both fields.

Bernard Blandin has a PhD in Sociology and an Accreditation to Supervise Research in Educational Sciences. He is Research Director of CESI Group and Research Fellow at the Research Centre in Education and Training of Paris Ouest University (France). His research work aims at understanding the effects of Learning Environments on the learning processes, how the learners' dispositions interact with the learning environment, and what are the conditions for the configuration learner / environment to be efficient for learning. A particular focus is put in his work on how technical objects, and in particular computers, affect the learning process. His involvement in e-learning standards development is a result of this interest. He is currently Convener of ISO/IEC JTC1 SC36 - WG3, and co-editor of the ISO/IEC 24763 Conceptual Reference Model for Competencies and Related Objects.

Simone Laughton is an Instructional Technology Liaison Librarian at the University of Toronto Mississauga Library. In her current work, she explores the use of different technologies to assist with online information literacy competency assessments and the effective use of technology to support teaching and learning. Prior to becoming a Librarian, she worked with community-based non-profit organizations, private for-profit businesses, and with federal, provincial, and municipal governments on diverse topics such as economic development (industrial sector), health and social planning, multiculturalism, and long-term care. In September 2005, she began volunteering with the Canadian Advisory Committee of the JTC1 SC36. She is Project Co-Editor for ISO/IEC 24763 Conceptual Reference Model for Competencies and Related Objects, and participates in several SC36 Working Groups. Some of the SC36 issues she focuses on include: competencies, eAssessment, and quality.

Geoffrey Frank is a Principal Scientist at RTI International. He holds a PhD in Computer Science from the University of North Carolina at Chapel Hill. Dr. Frank is a co-editor of the ISO/IEC JTC1 Subcommittee 36 technical report on a conceptual reference model for competency information. He is also a member of the IEEE Learning Technology Standards Committee, and has contributed to the development of use cases for the IEEE Reusable Competency Definition Standard, P1484.20.1. He is a co-author of an IEEE technical report on the interoperability of simulations and learning management systems. His research interests include student performance assessment using simulations, Semantic Web technologies, and the modeling of human behavior.

Kenji Hirata, Ph.D., is associate professor in Department of Social Psychology, Toyo University, Japan. He received a bachelor in Education from Waseda University, and a Ph.D. from Tokyo Institute of Technology. His main research interest is "expert science", i.e. acquisition, assessment and management of knowledge, ability, skill and competency from the viewpoints of psychometrics and informatics. He has worked in a management-consulting firm for 17 years as training and e-Learning developer, and as consultant on OD and HRM. He is also consultant in workplace learning. He contributes to standardization activities as: Project editor of ISO/IEC 19796; vice president of Society for HRML; committee member of Embedded Technology Skills Standard; IT Skills Standards, Bio-Tech Industry Skills Standard, and other skills standards; Chair of Skills Management in OMG; Japan delegate to ISO/IEC JTC1 SC36 and to ISO/TC 236; Chair of quality management WG in Asian e-Learning Network. He received several awards: outstanding contribution award from HR-XML consortium, and ISO standard development award from Japan Industrial Standards Committee.

Michael Piotrowski is a senior research associate at ZHAW Zurich University of Applied Sciences in Winterthur, Switzerland and a lecturer at the University of Zurich. He holds a doctorate in computer science from Otto von Guericke University, Magdeburg, Germany, and a master's degree in computational linguistics from Friedrich-Alexander-University Erlangen Nuremberg, Germany. He is one of the designers of the eduComponents, an open-source component-based e-learning platform based on the free content management system Plone. His research interests are in the areas of e-learning and computational linguistics, and he is the author of numerous peer-reviewed articles in both fields.

Stephen Marshall is Acting Director and Senior Lecturer in Educational Technology at the Victoria University of Wellington University Teaching Development Centre. Stephen is a member of the New Zealand Ministry of Education Tertiary E-Learning Reference Group and an executive member of the Australasian Council on Open and Distance Education. He is an auditor for the Australian Universities Quality Forum and also a member of the funding panel for the Ministry of Education Tertiary E-Learning Research Fund. Stephen researches in the areas of e-learning benchmarking, plagiarism and academic integrity, intellectual property and the of development of policy and strategy to support and encourage the effective use of technology. His e-learning maturity model (eMM) work has been adopted internationally and is used to guide e-learning improvement initiatives in New Zealand, Australia, the UK and the USA.

Antonio Quesada studied Chemical Sciences at the University of Jaen (Spain), where he obtained his Ph.D. in June 2003. He worked at this University from 1998 to 2005 in the Organic Chemistry Department. During this time, his scientific production was related to synthetic products with antitumor activity, pheromones and structural studies by x-ray diffraction. He joined the Department of Didactics of Sciences as a lecturer in April 2005. Currently, his research interests focus on the application of information and communication technologies for the teaching and learning science at primary and secondary school, and at higher education. For the last two years, he has been involved in some innovative local projects about design, application and evaluation of multimedia resources for b-learning, to complement laboratory work and enhance thinking and learning in science.

Marta R. Ariza studied Chemistry at the University of Granada and carried out her Ph.D. work and thesis in Organic Chemistry, at this University. She spent several years researching on the chemical properties of natural products with biological activity, but in 2005 changed her interests, focussing on science education. Currently, she is a lecturer at the Department of Didactics of Sciences in the University of Jaén, in the South of Spain. She has worked on the development of innovative strategies and resources to facilitate science understanding and meaningful knowledge in students. Her main research interests at the moment, are related to technology potential to enhance science learning through the use of simulations, modelling tools, virtual laboratories and computer supported collaborative learning.

Helen Farley is a Research Fellow at the Centre for Educational Innovation and Technology (CEIT) at the University of Queensland, Brisbane, Australia. He research focuses on the use of Multi-user Virtual Environments (MUVEs), particularly Second Life, in tertiary education. She is particularly concerned with issues surrounding reusability and interoperability in these environments. She is the project leader of the highly acclaimed UQ Religion Bazaar project. A second stream in her research relates to the haptic feedback and 3D movement in virtual environments. Helen is also a lecturer in higher education at the Teaching and Educational Development Institute (TEDI) also at the University of Queensland where she is involved in staff development relating to the implementation of technology into the curriculum.

Dimitris N. Kanellopoulos holds a PhD in multimedia communications from the Department of Electrical and Computer Engineering of the University of Patras, Greece. Currently, he is a member of the Educational Software Development Laboratory in the Department of Mathematics at the University of Patras. His research interests include multimedia communications, intelligent information systems, knowledge representation, web engineering and web-based education. He has authored many papers in international journals and conferences at these areas. He serves as a member of the editorial boards in several academic journals.

Marta C. Mora Aguilar received her PhD in Industrial Engineering in 2009 at the Universidad Politécnica de Valencia. She is Assistant Professor at the Universitat Jaume I since 2006, within the Area of Mechanical Engineering. She has taught some of the main subjects of the Mechanical Engineering discipline (mechanics and machine theory) in various engineering degrees. She has also taught subjects related to Simulation and Control Engineering at Universidad Politécnica de Valencia, within the Computer Science Engineering degree and the postgraduate CAD/CAM/CIM master. Her research currently focuses on various fields: e-learning in Mechanical Engineering , mobile and manipulator robots and the biomechanics and control of the human hand.

Joaquín L. Sancho-Bru is the head of the Mechanical Engineering Degree at the Universitat Jaume I (Castellón, Spain). He obtained his PhD in Industrial Engineering with a doctoral thesis related with a biomechanical model of the hand to assist hand-held tools design. He began his teaching work at the Universitat Jaume I in 1995, within the Area of Mechanical Engineering. He holds a permanent position as Associate Professor since 2002. He has taught most of the main subjects of Mechanical Engineering discipline (mechanics, machine theory and design, vibrations, etc…) in various engineering degrees. He has also participated teaching in the PhD program of Advanced Design of Industrial Products and in the postgraduate masters of Occupational Hazard Prevention and Design and Manufacturing. His research currently focuses on the field of e-learning in Mechanical Engineering and in the field of biomechanics, primarily hand modelling, but also dental and knee biomechanics.

Ricardo J. Rejas-Muslera is Ph.D in Computer Science from the University of Alcalá and Master in Information Systems (University Juan Carlos I of Madrid), also he is B.S. degree in Law from the Carlos III University of Madrid, and Master in Law (Complutense University of Madrid). He worked at American Telecom as legal advisor from 1999, in 2002. In the fall of 2005 he moved at the University of Francisco de Vitoria of Madrid where he was full Professor, and since 2007, assistant director at the Engineering Department until 2008.In addition since 2005 he has been coordinator and professor in

Master Program at the Alcalá University of Madrid. Dr. Rejas-Muslera research interests include different aspects of Information Technology management and educational issues. Since 2006 he is the head of the 6SPIN, an integrant part of the Software Process Improvement Network (Software Engineering Institute, University of Carnegie Mellon).

Álvaro J. García Tejedor has a Ph.D. in Chemistry and has been connected for the last ten years to the university both teaching and as a researcher. He is now full-time Professor at the Computer ScienceDepartment of Universidad Francisco de Vitoria as well as Head of CEIEC, a University's Research Institute for social applications of IC Technologies. He previously worked for 15 years in Consulting and Software Development companies, involved in R&D (European and National) and customer's projects within the Artificial Intelligence, Communications and IP Services areas. His main research interest is Technology Enhanced Learning, specially applying Artificial Intelligence to cognitive and educational processes. He has also been using videogames and competitive techniques to improve students' motivation and learning capabilities

Olga Peñalba, Ph.D in Computer Science, is an Associate Professor at the Universidad Francisco de Vitoria and Head of the Research Group on Computer Supported Education. She has 10 years of teaching experience in Higher Education, in the field of computer science and technology, and more than 10 years of research activity in the fields of digital systems and computer architecture and, more recently, e-learning and b-learning. She is really concerned about the challenges of the European Space for Higher Education, and has promoted several research projects in relation to new teaching methods and techniques, being in charged of several projects funded by the Universidad Francisco de Vitoria as well as two national projects funded by the the Spanish Ministry of Industry, Tourism and Trade. Professor of University of Advancing Technology (Tempe, Arizona) teaching Psychology of Creativity and behavior related courses in the general studies department. After the social and economic upheaval following the breakup of the former Soviet Union, she tried first immigrate to Argentina and finally to the United States. She left the Ukraine where she had taught Psychology and Psychiatry at Ukrainian Medical School in the City of Poltava for 13 years. She also had an established psychiatric practice plus she worked in a mental institution providing biological treatment as well as various kinds of therapies and forensic expertise. While there she conducted research and published 58 articles on Psychiatry and Clinical Psychology topics, she became one of the three leading art therapists in the former Soviet Union, which led to her interest in the relationship between mental health and creativity. It was during this work that she began to understand that tapping into creativity is not only good therapy for people who are out of balance, but extremely good maintenance for healthy people. She presented her research in psychology and creativity on the World Congress of the World Federation for Mental Health in Lahty, Finland, in 12th International Conference on Creativity in Colleges and Universities, Michigan, and 5th Annual Conference of American Association of Behavioral and Social Sciences, Las Vegas, 13th, 17th, and 19th International Conferences on Teaching and Learning, Florida where she get reward for her outstanding achievements in the field of creativity. She is a co-author of the following textbooks: *Psychology of Creativity, Creativity Step by Step, Therapy through Creativity, as well as Psychology of Conflict and Violence.* In 2002 UAT students selected her as the most influential instructor and she became a member of *Alpha Beta Kappa* National Honor Society. Her course *Psychology of Creativity* became one of the most popular at UAT.

Kate Taylor read Computer Science at Imperial College, London, focusing on artificial intelligence techniques in large data sets before working on large database development at Logica and the University of Cambridge. She worked on the IVC under Dr Simon Moore at the Computer Laboratory and with Massachusetts Institute of Technology (MIT) and helped a Bioinformatics course at the Computer Labroatory. This work led use of emerging XML technologies as a means of data interchange for e-tutors at the Centre for Applied Educational Technologies (CARET) at the University of Cambridge and work with the Knowledge Management Institute (KMi) at the Open University on applying these e-tutor techniques to a corporate setting. She now works at the Sanger Institute in Cambridge using XML for interchange between very large sequencing databases, and continues as subject tutor at Pembroke College, Cambridge and Newnham College, Cambridge where her students are keen guinea pigs for e-tutors.

Varvara Vagiati is a librarian born in Athens. She obtained her BSs from the Department of Library Science and Information Systems, Faculty of Management and Economics of the Technical Educational Institution of Athens in 2002. In 2006 she graduated succesfully her MSc in Information Science from the Department of Archives and Library Science of Ionian University in Corfu. Her research interests concern of processing and management of metadata standards, knowledge management, ontologies, ontology languages, digital libraries and information retrieval. She participated in european and greek research initiatives, such as DELOS II, WP5 – Task 5.4 for the Interoperability of eLearning Applications with Digital Libraries and the research for the development, management and documentation of the educational material of National Centre for Public Administration and Local Government of Greece (E.K.D.D.A.). Currently she continues her research activity in information science and widens her knowledge field with an additional master degree in the domain of cultural management and administration.

Francisco Arcos García is a part-time professor at the University of Alicante and full-time Teacher Consultant / Trainer at the Teacher's Centre in Alicante. Currently he is in charge of setting up courses for teachers which require the use of a Learning Management Systems. His main areas of interest are in the fields of pedagogy, translation and computer mediated instruction. Now, he is mainly interested in the pedagogic design and pedagogic strategies to carry out blended learning. He graduated in English Philology – from the University of Valencia in 1982 and read his doctoral thesis in 1993. He started working in the field of distance learning and blended learning some 8 years ago when Moodle appeared. He has published a score of articles related with e-learning and blended learning for the teaching of English. For 5 years running he has been implementing blended learning in his university classes.

Pablo Ortega worked as a teacher of English for some years before becoming a principal, a post he held at several secondary schools. Presently, he works full time as an inspector of education, giving initial training to future teachers and supervising the teaching practice of tenured teachers. He wrote a doctoral dissertation on Discourse Analysis, and has published several articles on that field. Later on, he shifted his focus of attention to the teaching of languages, especially through ICT means. He has presented communications at many ICT conferences. He has been working as an assistant professor at the University of Alicante for the last ten years.

Marta Fuentes Agustí, Ph.D. in educational behavior by the Autonomous University of Barcelona and a degree in Educational Psychology. Specialized teacher on educational sciences, e-learning, teaching and learning strategies. Over the past few years she has been working on issues of training, assessment and educational quality through the use of Information and Communication Technologies at all levels of education, as well as on the evaluation and improvement of university teaching quality, the creation and management knowledge and networking. She is a member of SINTE an Excellence Research and Innovation Group recognized by the AGAUR of Catalunya (renewed under file 2013SGR2009-134).

Margarida Romero is a researcher on learning innovation and educational psychology. For the last 10 years she has collaborated with international academic and professional organizations in educational projects (ITIN University in Paris, IUFM French Guyana, Educational Ministry of Algeria, IQPC Brazil…). She has developed her passion for teaching during her experience as lecturer at Universitat Ramon Llull (Blanquerna), Université de Limoges, Institut Universitaire Professionnalisé de Nîmes and Centre National des Arts et Métiers (CNAM). She's currently managing the elearning area in Esade and associate professor in Universitat Autònoma de Barcelona. Active member of the most representative European educational associations, she leads Euro-CAT-CSCL, a research project within the FP7 Marie Curie IAPP actions. In 2007, she won the 3rd price on Technology Transfer from the EU Network of Excellence Kaleidoscope. In 2006, she won ex-aequo the Artificial Intelligence French Association Award for a communication claiming the need to introduce a metacognitive support into elearning systems.

Maria Jose Hernandez-Serrano, European Ph.D. from the University of Salamanca (Spain), working as an Assistant Professor in the University of Salamanca at the Department of Theory and History of Education. She works on the field of informational and learning competences with technologies. She attended to different international conferences as a lecturer, and has been publish some scientific papers on the topic of e-learning and e-lifelong learning. She is member of an Excellence Research and Innovation Group in the University of Salamanca named "Educational Processes, Spaces and Practices" from which has been developed several national and international projects. She also teaches courses and workshops on searching and researching on the Internet, as well as sociability and interactivity on virtual spaces.

Lilyana Nacheva-Skopalik is a principal lecturer at the Department of Applied Informatics, Technical University of Gabrovo, Bulgaria. She has been working as a lecturer at the same university since 1988, teaching Informatics, Information technologies, Programming and Using Computer Systems in undergraduate and postgraduate courses. Her research in the area of e-learning, particularly in formative and diagnostic assessment resulted in getting her PhD at School of Computing, University of Teesside, UK in 2007. Dr Nacheva-Skopalik has experience working within national and international teams that includes teacher mobility between Technical University of Gabrovo and University of Teesside, School of Computing within the European Program Socrates/Erasmus; work within Central European Exchange Programme for University Studies (CEEPUS); participation in National Research Fund projects, and research within Leonardo da Vinci program. She has various research publications at national and international conferences. Her current research interests are in the area of accessible e-assessment.

Carmen Bao is a Professor in Mechanical Department of Engineering Higher School from La Rioja University of Spain. She has also been teaching during years in the Basque Country University of Spain. At the same time, during more than twenty years, she has developed her professional carrier in several multinational industries, EU technological and management centres. She has also been working for international consulting and training companies. In 1991, she obtained her Ph. D. at Engineering High

School of Basque country University. She has obtained five technical Masters (Business Administration, Environmental Management, International Commerce and Marketing, Quality and Excellence Management and Human Resources). Dr. Carmen Bao has a great experience in teaching virtual and on-line e-learning's environments and she has participated into numerous International Congress and publications relative to teaching innovations, engineering technology and management. Moreover, she has been active member of technical international Standardization Committees, and she belongs to referees board of several journal and she takes part of some professional Associations.

Jose Mª Castresana-Pelayo is Environmental Manager in a chemical global company. His main duties are overseeing technical standards concerning environmental, safety aspects, and developing improvements in eco-efficiency. He audits the implementation of environmental standards both in Spain and other industrial sites in European Union. Since 2004, he is also Associate Professor in Chemical Engineering Department, Basque Country University of Spain, where he obtained a M. Sc. degree in 1982 and Ph.D. doctorate in 1987. He received a Master in Innovation Management from Basque Government in 1991. Prior to joining chemical sector, he was formerly with a steelmaking company, working mainly in the fields of process optimisation, safety procedures and waste management. Dr. Castresana-Pelayo has been active with the Spanish Standardisation Association (AENOR) CTN-150 Working Group from 1995 till 2000. From 1996, he is active member of "Responsible Care Committee" of the Spanish Chemical Industry Federation (FEIQUE) dealing with internal standardization for best industrial practices.

John Milne is an e-learning specialist in the Centre of Academic Development and e-Learning at Massey University. He was the project manager for the implementation of e-learning guidelines project and was part of the team that developed the guidelines in 2005. For much of his career John has supported staff to effectively use technology in their teaching. He can be contacted at j.d.milne@massey.ac.nz.

Gordon Suddaby is Director of the Centre for Academic Development and e-Learning at Massey University. His Centre has responsibility for leading the implementation of the open source LMS platform Moodle across the University in a 3-year project which will result in the vast majority of Massey's more than 6000 paper offerings being delivered in blended mode. He led Massey University's successful bid to host New Zealand's National Centre for Tertiary Teaching Excellence, Ako Aotearoa, in addition to leading a number of other national e-learning projects. He is in his second term as President of the Australasian Council on Open Distance and E-learning, the Australasian peak body in this area and is an auditor for both the Australasian University Quality Agency and New Zealand's Institute and Polytechnics Quality organization.

Brian Nolan is Head of Department of Informatics at the Institute of Technology Blanchardstown, Dublin in Ireland. His research interests include computational approaches to speech and language processing; computational linguistics; linguistic theory at the morphosyntactic-semantic interface, argument structure, valence and event structure in language, and the architecture of the lexicon. His educational research interests range over elearning, digital content creation and learning object design. His linguistic work has been in the functional linguistic model of Role and Reference Grammar and he has published extensively internationally. Recent computing/computational linguistic research has concentrated on: 1) The development of a framework with supporting application suite for mobile and distributed command and control of robotic devices using speech recognition as the core enabling technology; 2) The development of a rule –based Arabic to English machine translation engine that uses Role and Reference Grammar as the linguistic model supporting an interlingua bridge. Dr. Brian Nolan is currently authoring a book, for publication in 2010 by Equinox in London, on the linguistic structure of Irish entitled: 'The structure of Irish: A functional account'.

Lorraine Leeson has been the Director of the Centre for Deaf Studies at the School of Linguistic, Speech and Communication Studies at Trinity College Dublin (TCD) since its establishment in 2001. Her research interests are concerned with the linguistics and sociolinguistics of signed languages, with special reference to the morpho-syntax and semantics of Irish Sign Language (ISL). She is interested in language planning issues vis-a-vis Deaf education and the use of Irish Sign Language, as well as gendered issues in the Irish Deaf community, particularly in terms of language use. Dr. Lorraine Leeson is also concerned with, and involved in, the training of signed language interpreters. Cognitive linguistics interests include the role of metaphor and metonymy in ISL, the impact of iconicity on the language, simultaneity in signed languages and point of view predication. She is editor of the Centre for Deaf Studies monograph series, and the journal, 'The Sign Language Translator and Interpreter', and an Associate Editor of Deaf Worlds.

Olúgbémiga T. Ekúndayò is Associate Professor, Department of Epidemiology and Biostatistics, School of Health Sciences, College of Public Service, Jackson State University. He graduated from Medical School at the University of Ibadan, Nigeria and went on to obtain a Master of Public Health and Doctor of Public Health from Morgan State University in Baltimore Maryland, U.S.A. He is currently Coordinator of the Doctor of Public Health Program at Jackson State University, Jackson, Mississippi, United States and Principal Investigator on several research projects in Public Health. His area of teaching interest is in the use of learning techniques to assure the development and measurement of competence using practice in environments of trans-disciplinary pedagogy. His research areas of interest include underserved populations: community engaged participatory action research, health and policy effects of disasters, STI/HIV, Tobacco and Cancer.

Francis Tuluri has over two decades of experience in teaching and research. He has taught multiple areas to students at undergraduate and graduate level, and has excellent experience in using current technology in teaching. His areas of interest in knowledge management are e-Learning, distance learning, learner management systems, pedagogical implications of interoperable educational tools. His research areas of interest also include imaging and data integration, computer modeling and visualization by GIS environments. He leads many research projects that involve interns, pre- and post doctoral fellows. He has written on research development and the thought processes that go into research. His research focus is in the area of community engagement research with a concentration on community empowerment and action research especially with regard to disaster, men's health and reproductive health.

Index

B

C

D

J

K

L

M

T

U

V

W

X

Breinigsville, PA USA
12 October 2010
247154BV00001B/1/P